MAGNA CARTA, imposed on King John by his barons in 1215, and its two most famous clauses (in black). Still valid in statute law, they are often regarded as the very foundations of civil and political liberty in England.

Reproduced by permission of the British Library. (Cotton MS. Aug. II. 106.)

Translation overleaf →

¶ No free man shall be seized or imprisoned, or stripped of his rights or possessions, or outlawed or exiled, or deprived of his standing in any other way, nor will we proceed with force against him, or send others to do so, except by the lawful judgment of his equals or by the law of the land.

¶ To no one will we sell, to no one deny or delay right of justice.

Translation by Dr G. R. C. Davis. (Reproduced by permission of the British Library.)

YOU
AND YOUR
RIGHTS

Reader's Digest

YOU AND YOUR RIGHTS

An A to Z Guide to the Law

PUBLISHED BY THE READER'S DIGEST ASSOCIATION LIMITED
London · New York · Montreal · Sydney · Cape Town

YOU AND YOUR RIGHTS
was edited and designed by
The Reader's Digest Association Limited,
London

Third Edition
Copyright © 1981
The Reader's Digest Association Limited,
25 Berkeley Square, London W1X 6AB

All rights reserved.
No part of this book may be reproduced,
stored in a retrieval system, or transmitted
in any form or by any means,
electronic, electrostatic, magnetic tape, mechanical,
photocopying, recording or otherwise,
without permission in writing
from the publishers

® Reader's Digest is
a registered trademark of
The Reader's Digest Association, Inc.
of Pleasantville, New York, U.S.A.

Typesetting: Vantage Photosetting Co. Ltd.,
Southampton and London
Separations: City Engraving Co. Ltd., Hull
Cover marble design: Mitchell and Malik Ltd., Salisbury
Paper: Bowater Paper Co. Ltd., Sittingbourne
Printing and Binding:
Waterlow (Dunstable) Ltd.,
Hazell Watson & Viney Ltd., Aylesbury
Sir Joseph Causton & Son Ltd., Eastleigh

The main text of YOU AND YOUR RIGHTS
is typeset in 9 on 10 point Times New Roman

Printed in Great Britain

CONSULTANT EDITOR

Harry Street CBE, LLM, PhD, LLD, FBA
Professor of English Law, Manchester University

CONTRIBUTORS

J. E. Adams LLB, *Solicitor, Professor of Law, Queen Mary College, University of London*

Geoffrey Bindman, *Solicitor*

C. D. Brandreth MA *(Oxon), Solicitor*

Margaret Brazier LLB, *Lecturer in Law, Manchester University*

A. L. Diamond, *Professor of Law in the University of London*

Frank Eaglestone LLB, FCII, FCIArb, *Barrister-at-Law*

Terence Flanagan LLM, *Solicitor, Lecturer in Law, Manchester University*

J. F. Garner LLD, *Solicitor. Professor of Public Law, University of Nottingham*

E. R. Hardy Ivamy LLB, PhD, LLD, *Barrister-at-Law. Professor of Law in the University of London*

Diana M. Kloss LLM, *Senior Lecturer in Law, Manchester University*

Sarah Leigh, *Solicitor*

Tony Lynes

Andrew J. Martin MA, *Barrister-at-Law*

Dr Vincent Powell-Smith LLB (Hons), LLM, D Litt, FCIArb, FRSA, FSA *Scotland*

John Pritchard, *Solicitor*

W. E. Pritchard BA, FTII, *Lecturer and consultant in taxation*

Margaret Puxon MD, FRCOG, *Barrister-at-Law*

Paul Puxon, *Barrister-at-Law*

Bert Raisbeck TD, LLB, ACIS, *Principal Lecturer in Law, Lanchester Polytechnic, Coventry*

Alec Samuels, JP, *Barrister-at-Law, Reader in Law in the University of Southampton*

Michael F. Saunders FCII

Felicity Taylor

Bobbie Vincent-Emery

Mary Vitoria PhD, *Barrister-at-Law*

David W. Williams LLM, PhD, ATII, *Solicitor, Senior Lecturer in Law, Manchester University*

Carol Wilson PSW, CQSW, *Assistant area officer, Social Services Department, London Borough of Hammersmith*

David Yates MA, *Professor of Law, University of Essex*

Cartoons by David Langdon

Picture sequences drawn by Barbara Walker (Saxon Artists)

Other artwork by Hayward and Martin Limited

The laws described in this book are those of
England and Wales at the time of printing.

There are substantial differences in the laws of
Scotland, Northern Ireland, the Republic of Ireland,
the Isle of Man and the Channel Islands.

Inevitably some of the figures used in this book change
from year to year, especially tax rates and social security levels.
To obtain up-to-date tax figures, ask at a local tax office.
For up-to-date social security figures, ask at a
social security office for any of these free leaflets:
NI 196 (social security benefit rates)
NI 208 (national insurance contribution
rates) MPL 151 (war pensions).

Foreword

by

The Rt Hon. THE LORD HAILSHAM OF ST MARYLEBONE CH, FRS, DCL
LORD CHANCELLOR

HOUSE OF LORDS,
SW1A 0PW

They say that if a man acts as his own lawyer, he has a fool for his client. This is a theory to which I heartily subscribe, perhaps most of all when the client in question is himself a member of the legal profession. Not only can a lawyer not be a judge in his own cause, but in all the traumatic incidents of life – birth, marriage, divorce, illness, accident, death (whether in anticipation of one's own, or facing the consequence of bereavement) – the presence of an independent, detached, dedicated, but emotionally uninvolved adviser or advocate is an essential condition of a satisfactory outcome.

But this is not the whole of the story. Many of the specialised professions require some general knowledge of the law, particularly in their own field, in order to perform their own specialised functions. Often they even have to consult specialised legal textbooks, ordinarily used by only solicitors, barristers or law students. The law of a subject can be as much part of a modern profession as the technical expertise required for its exercise. Obvious examples are accountants, bankers, architects and surveyors, and even doctors and engineers.

But what of the ordinary householder, that is, each one of us in our private capacity, whether or not in our position in society we have acquired some specialised acquaintance either with the law in general, or of some particular branches of it? The answer, I am afraid, is that more and more a handbook giving some general guidance is as much a necessity for the average householder as a book on first aid, household hints, cookery, or elementary medicine. Such a reference book enables us to avoid pitfalls, identify problems, carry out simple procedures, recognise dangers and generally conduct our lives in a more practical efficient manner.

Most of us own motor cars, and the problems of credit, hire purchase, insurance, product liability and the constantly changing requirements of highway regulation press heavily upon us. Obviously no book of reference will substitute for a solicitor or barrister when one is needed. But there are many situations which fall short of this where some elementary knowledge of these matters is a necessity either for the conduct of correspondence, or, at worst, to identify the occasions on which it is necessary to call in professional assistance. Again, most of us have children, and their education, clothing, care, health and sometimes their behaviour are all regulated or give rise to questions which require attention from time to time. So also, we all need housing accommodation, bought, mortgaged, rented, furnished, or unfurnished, and it must be insured for it may be burgled or, worse still, burnt to the ground. The more acute cases can, of course, be dealt with by advice, but even here, some elementary understanding of necessary immediate steps in legal framework is necessary.

Neighbours, landlords, tenants, local authorities, public utilities such as water, gas and electricity, all have their impact on the householder. We cannot turn for guidance on every occasion to the solicitor or barrister who knows the law. We have to deal with day to day situations as they arise. Ought we to consult an architect? Do we need planning permission for our DIY alterations? Can we keep a caravan in our garden? What about our pets? Or may we keep bees in a suburban garden, and what happens if they swarm or sting our neighbour's grandchildren? Some of us, of course, can take advantage of the legal advice and assistance scheme. Many of us know full well that in certain dire circumstances we must get the advice of a solicitor, or have someone to represent us in court. But on plenty of occasions we have to find out in a hurry the elementary facts we need to know in order to deal with an everyday situation. Well here, if you need it in a hurry, is the very thing you require to assist you in your time of stress.

I hesitate to suggest that such a serious book can even provide entertaining reading. But some of the examples given, all I believe from real life, are positively hilarious. I especially commend to the law reformer, or even the casual student of the ridiculous, the paradoxical results obtained in the course of developing the disreputable jurisprudence of the breathalyser.

All in all I wish this volume all its deserved success, and commend it to the readers alike for instruction and entertainment.

Hailsham

PS.

I did not know, of course, when I undertook with the publishers to write this foreword that, by the time it came out, I should again be Lord Chancellor. I hope that that proves a bonus for them and not an undue embarrassment to my colleagues, or a quarry of quotations for critics of the Government.

Crown copyright forms are reproduced in this book
by permission of The Controller of Her Majesty's Stationery Office.
All names and details in the forms are fictitious.

ABANDONED VEHICLE

When the local council is responsible

If you believe that a vehicle has been abandoned on a public road or in the open air on your property, complain to the environmental health or borough engineer's department of the local council which has a duty as well as the power to remove such vehicles.

After inspecting the vehicle, a council official, if he is satisfied that the vehicle has been abandoned, will decide whether it should be destroyed. If so he must fix a notice on the vehicle to warn the owner that, unless the vehicle is removed by the date stated, it will be removed and destroyed.

If the official decides the vehicle is worth selling, he can arrange to have it removed at once, without notifying the owner. If it is on private property, however, the landowner must be given an opportunity to object before the vehicle is removed.

The local authority is released from its duty to clear an abandoned vehicle from private property if the cost is out of all proportion to the nuisance it causes.

The money raised by selling an abandoned vehicle belongs to the owner, but the council is entitled to deduct any expenses it has had in removing and selling the vehicle. If the proceeds do not cover the expenses, the owner is liable to pay the balance.

Anyone who abandons a vehicle or part of a vehicle on someone else's property is committing an offence, but he is likely to be prosecuted only if he abandoned the vehicle personally or authorised someone else specifically to do so.

Maximum penalties For a first offence, a £100 fine; for a subsequent offence, £200 and 3 months' imprisonment.

The fact that a vehicle has been abandoned does not exempt the owner from needing MOTOR INSURANCE and a VEHICLE EXCISE LICENCE, unless it is in such a state that it would be impossible to get it going again.

ABDUCTION

Laws that protect women and girls

Abduction is the taking away of a girl under 18 without her parents' or guardian's consent, or the seizing of a woman of any age against her will.

The three major offences are:
1. Taking away a girl under 14.
2. Taking away a girl under 16.
3. Taking away an unmarried girl under 18 with whom the abductor or someone else is to have sexual intercourse.

'Taken away,' in this context, means at least being kept away from the parental home overnight. A young man who takes his girl for a walk against her father's wishes is not committing an offence.

The law is designed to protect girls from ill-advised affairs and to make elopement with young girls illegal. In any of those cases, the abductor, who can be a man or woman, is guilty even if the girl suggests or agrees to being taken.

Maximum penalties Girl under 14, 7 years' imprisonment; girl under 16, 2 years' imprisonment; unmarried girl under 18, 2 years' imprisonment.

The maximum penalty for the forcible taking away of a woman of any age against her will or the seizing of an heiress is 14 years' imprisonment. *See:* KIDNAPPING

ABORTION

When a woman wishes to end her pregnancy

A woman does not have an automatic right to an abortion, but she can usually get one if she is determined not to have a child. It is not always possible, however, to arrange one free under the National Health Service.

If a woman wants her pregnancy to be terminated, she should see her own doctor as soon as possible. In early pregnancy the operation is usually quite simple; it becomes more difficult as the pregnancy advances, and cannot be performed after the 28th week unless the woman's life is in danger.

The 1967 Abortion Act says a woman may have an abortion on any one of four grounds:
1. That continuation of the pregnancy would involve risk to the mother's life.
2. That the pregnancy is a risk to her physical or mental health. The woman's social circumstances can be taken into account.
3. That it is a risk to the physical or mental health of her existing children.
4. That there is a risk that the child would be born with a physical or mental abnormality.

The consent of the father of the unborn child is not necessary, and while doctors usually want to know his attitude, he has no power to prevent his wife having an abortion.

If a doctor considers an abortion is appropriate he refers the woman for a second opinion, usually to the gynaecologist who will perform the operation. Both doctors have to certify the grounds for the abortion.

If a place is not available under the National Health Service, one can usually be arranged at a registered clinic or nursing home approved by the Secretary of State for Social Services to provide private treatment. Any such establishment admitting a high proportion of abortion patients must satisfy the Department of Health and Social Security that its scale of charges is fair.

If the doctor refuses

A doctor may be opposed to an abortion either because he or she thinks there are no medical grounds for it or because of a personal conviction that all abortions are wrong. No doctor or nurse can be compelled to be a party to an abortion if it is against his or her moral principles, unless there is an emergency and the woman's life is in danger.

If a woman does not accept her own doctor's decision, she can try to find another general practitioner who takes a different view.

That can be difficult, however, and can cause dangerous delay. She is more likely to find immediate help and advice through one of the many Pregnancy Advice Bureaux that can be found in most cities and many large towns throughout Britain.

Although a charge will normally be made if the patient has to be referred to a private clinic, fees can be reduced or waived in hardship cases.

ABSENTEEISM

Persistent absence from work may be grounds for dismissal

An employee who is frequently away from work or absent for a prolonged period without good reason and without informing his employer is breaking his EMPLOYMENT CONTRACT and may be liable for DISMISSAL. *See:* DISCIPLINE AT WORK; UNFAIR DISMISSAL

Absenteeism is also a kind of misconduct and so disqualifies the employee from receiving UNEMPLOYMENT BENEFIT for up to 6 weeks.

ABSOLUTE DISCHARGE

Not all convictions carry a punishment

If a court does not think that it would be appropriate to punish an accused

person who has been found guilty of an offence – for example, if he was convicted on a technicality and was not blameworthy in any way – it may decide to impose an absolute discharge. The conviction is nevertheless recorded.

An absolute discharge cannot be granted in cases where the penalty is fixed by law as, for example, with the crimes of murder or treason. *See:* SENTENCE

ABUSIVE WORDS OR BEHAVIOUR

When even speaking can be an offence

Using abusive, insulting or threatening words or behaviour in public can be a criminal offence, if the words used are considered by the court to be 'very strong'.

In addition, it must be proved that the words or behaviour caused, or were intended to cause, a BREACH OF THE PEACE – or that they were likely to do so.

THE PENALTY FOR BEING OUTSPOKEN

Using abusive, insulting or threatening words in public can be a criminal offence, although normally a first offender who had not also threatened violence would simply be bound over to keep the peace. The court must always be convinced that the words used were likely to cause a breach of the peace.

THE ANTI-APARTHEID DEMONSTRATORS

A charge of using abusive or insulting words, or of behaving in an abusive or insulting way, is unlikely to be proved unless the accused's actions can be shown to have been 'very strong'.

Mr Brutus and 10 colleagues ran on to a court at the Wimbledon tennis championships, blowing whistles and scattering leaflets, in protest against the inclusion of white South African players in the tournament. They were charged with 'insulting behaviour'.

DECISION

Not guilty. Their behaviour had affronted the spectators but had not been sufficiently strong to be 'insulting'.

Maximum penalties The charge can be tried only in a magistrates' court where, on conviction, an accused person can be fined £1,000 and gaoled for 6 months.

A first offender who did not threaten violence will usually simply be bound over to keep the peace, and will be fined only if he fails to do so. *See:* BINDING OVER

ACCESS, Public right of

Using someone else's land

A person who uses land or water – for example a lake or reservoir – that is not his or her own is trespassing unless the owner has given permission or unless there is an established public right of way across, or access to use, the area.

That rule applies to public and private property and covers land beside a public right of way. *See:* TRESPASS

ACCESS TO CHILDREN

When separated parents cannot agree

When two separated or unmarried parents cannot agree on the conditions under which one of them may see or visit their child or children, the parent with whom the child is not living can apply to the High Court, county court or magistrates' court for an access order.

The courts, however, are less concerned with the parents' rights than with the right of the child to enjoy and benefit from contact with both its parents. Generally they refuse access only when they think it could cause real harm.

They would also be unlikely to grant access when the child had never known the parent applying because the parents had never lived together during the child's lifetime.

The arrangements can cover either regular visits and outings or quite long stays, for instance for part of the school holidays.

The courts listen to both parents or their lawyers and decide what seems to be the most reasonable arrangement in the interest of the child. If it seems appropriate, they may ask a social worker to see both parents and the child and make recommendations.

ACCIDENT

When collecting evidence is the first priority – if you are able

Whenever you are involved in an accident, try to make sure that someone collects evidence on your behalf. Make sure, particularly, that you find out the names of any witnesses and make a drawing of the scene.
See: ACCIDENT AT WORK
AIR ACCIDENT
ROAD TRAFFIC ACCIDENT

ACCIDENT AT SCHOOL

A teacher's duty to look after the children

A school is responsible for the safety and well-being of its pupils during the time they are in its charge. If some harm befalls a child and the parents can show that it happened because a teacher or some other school employee did not take reasonable care, the child can take legal action to recover damages for its suffering and for any disablement that results.

The parents can claim separately on their own behalf for any medical or other expenses, such as travel, that resulted from the injury.

If an accident involves a private school, the action must be taken against the proprietor or governing body; in a state school, it is taken against the local education authority.

The basic question always to be answered is whether the school took the sort of care of the child that a 'reasonable' parent would have taken in the same circumstances.

When the teacher is responsible

Usually it is a question of supervision. If a child is burned in a chemistry experiment or in cookery class, the parents would need to find out if the teacher had the form under proper control and had taken commonsense precautions to try to stop such an accident happening. If the teacher can show that he or she gave proper instruction and warnings but one

> ### THE SCHOOLGIRL WHO LOST AN EYE
>
> *Although in principle the law does not expect a child to behave as responsibly as an adult, there have been instances where the courts have decided that a teacher was not to blame for an accident involving injury to a pupil.*
>
> In July 1964, a teacher taking a class of 37 nine-year-old and ten-year-old girls gave out pointed scissors so that the girls could cut out pictures.
> While the teacher was looking after one girl, another waved her scissors about and injured a classmate. Eventually the classmate lost the sight of one eye.
> Damages of £3,500 were awarded against the education authority by a lower court, which held that the waving about of scissors should have been prevented by proper supervision.
>
> #### DECISION
> The Court of Appeal reversed that finding. The teacher had run the class in a good and efficient way, and there was no justification in finding either the teacher or the education authority at fault.

member of the class behaved quite unpredictably, the court would probably dismiss a claim.

In some circumstances, a teacher is held to have an added responsibility because of his or her specialist training. The chemistry teacher is expected to be aware of the potential danger of various substances in the laboratory, and a physical education teacher to have a special understanding of safety problems in a gymnasium.

When an accident is caused by another child in the school – for example, when one child throws a dart that hits another in the eye – the injured child could sue him, but there would be little to gain.

The culprit would be unlikely to have money to meet even a successful claim, and its parents would have no liability since they were not present and the child was in the charge of the school.
See: PARENTAL OBLIGATIONS

If it could be shown, however, that the children were not properly supervised at the time of the accident, the injured child would succeed in a claim against the school.

Outside school hours

A school's responsibilities are not limited to school hours. If, for example, children are allowed to leave school before their parents are due to collect them and one is run over, the school could be held responsible for the accident. Similarly, children travelling to and from school on a school bus must be properly supervised – although not necessarily by a teacher. One court held that two senior pupils were sufficient.

When the premises are dangerous

In some cases it is not the staff of the school that is at fault but the premises. For instance, in one case when a schoolgirl had put her hand through the glass of a swing-door, it was found that the glass was not thick enough to conform to the standards laid down by the Department of Education and Science. Because of that breach of regulations, judgment was given against the school.

When the school is not to blame

On other occasions, however, it has been established that the child was itself at fault in some way and helped to bring about its own misfortune. Yet the law does not expect the same standard of conduct from a child as it would from an adult. Usually the contributory negligence of the child does not entirely invalidate its claim for damages, although the amount awarded would be reduced.

A school is not responsible for the conduct and actions of its employees when they are acting outside the terms of their employment. *See:* EMPLOYER'S LIABILITY

If, for example, a teacher sends a child on a personal errand outside the school and the child is injured as a result, any claim has to be made against the teacher personally rather than the school. That can be unsatisfactory as the teacher may have neither the means nor the insurance to pay any award that a court may make.

ACCIDENT AT WORK

*How to get compensation
if you are injured*

More than 700,000 people are injured at work in Britain every year. In a great many cases, the employer (or his insurers) has to pay compensation.

If you have an accident at work, you may be entitled to compensation on one of three grounds:
1. Your employer's negligence.
2. Your employer's failure (or that of someone for whom he is responsible) to carry out safety measures ordered by Parliament.
3. A colleague's negligence.

When the employer is to blame

An employer has a legal duty to take reasonable care for the safety of all his workers. That duty may be neglected in three ways:
1. The employer may have engaged an unqualified or incompetent person, with the result that another worker, whose safety depends on that person's skill and competence, is injured.
2. The employer may have failed to provide safe premises and plant – by not installing necessary equipment, such as a safety guard on a machine; by installing defective equipment or by failing to maintain the premises or plant properly.
3. The employer may have failed to do enough to make a job safe.

For example, if the job involves a risk of skin disease, it is not enough for the employer to provide a protective cream. He must also make sure that his em-

ployees know when and how to use the cream – and he must put up notices warning of the health risk involved.

If you make a claim against your employer, alleging that he was negligent, he cannot evade liability by showing that unsafe equipment was the fault of the manufacturer who supplied it or the contractor who installed it.

When another employee is to blame

If you are injured as a result of some wrongdoing by someone who is carrying out his job, you are entitled to claim against his employer. The employer's indirect responsibility is known as vicarious liability.

Many injury claims arise from accidents at work caused by the carelessness of the victims' fellow-employees.

For example, a fork-lift truck driver may have stacked a load so carelessly that part of it falls and injures an employee. The accident is not the employer's personal fault – but he is still liable for the negligence of the person who stacked the load.

When safety laws are broken

Regulations laid down by Parliament set out in great detail safety precautions

THE MAN WHO TRIPPED PEOPLE UP

Many injury claims arise from accidents at work that are caused by the carelessness, foolishness or negligence of the victim's fellow employees.

Harold Chadwick had indulged himself for years in horseplay at the expense of workmates – tripping them up and other 'jokes'. This went on for 4 years, despite a reprimand from his employers.

Then one of the workmates he tripped broke a wrist.

DECISION
A court decided that the employers were not liable indirectly for Harold Chadwick's negligence, because tripping people up was not in the course of his employment. However, the firm was ordered to pay compensation for its own direct negligence – failing to make sure that Chadwick stopped his horseplay.

THE TRAIN DRIVER WHO LEANED OUT OF HIS CAB

When an employer's instructions on how a job should be done are the direct cause of an accident, the victim or his dependants can claim damages for his injury or death.

An engine driver, Thomas Henry McArthur, who had been told to drive his locomotive with the coal tender in front

had to lean out of his cab to see a signal near an unusually low bridge. His head struck the bridge as the train passed.

DECISION
The driver's employers, British Railways, were held liable to pay his widow damages.

THE SEAMAN WHO FELL DOWN A HATCH

Even where there is no specific legislation stating that certain safety precautions are necessary, the courts are likely to award damages to any employee who is injured through no direct fault of his own, if he can show that the environment in which he was expected to work was inherently unsafe and likely to cause an accident.

Robert Morris, a young seaman, fell down a 40 ft deep hatch on his ship. The

accident happened as he was making his way along a 12 ft wide way beside the open hatch. There was no guard rail.

The shipowners claimed it was common practice to have such unfenced hatches when ships were at sea.

DECISION
The seaman's claim for damages, because of negligence, was upheld by the House of Lords.

WHAT TO DO AFTER AN ACCIDENT

Many working accidents seem trivial at the time, but produce more serious effects later on – perhaps even making it impossible for the employee to go on earning a living.

1 As soon as you have an accident at work, take steps to protect your right to compensation: report the incident immediately to someone in authority.

2 If you work for a company that employs 10 or more people on the premises, or in a factory, mine or quarry, your employer must by law keep a special 'accident book'.

Make sure that your accident is recorded in the book – and unless you are too badly injured, make sure that you see the entry for yourself. If you eventually have to claim compensation, it may be crucial evidence in your favour.

3 If you have to rely on a workmate, union steward or supervisor to check the accident entry, you must write as soon as possible to your employer (or ask someone to do so on your behalf) setting out details of your accident. Do not just telephone the company: you will have no proof that the message was received.

4 Even if your injury has been treated by your employer's first-aid staff, and you feel fit to carry on working, see your own doctor as soon as possible.

5 The doctor may think that there is a risk of later complications from the injury. If so, safeguard your right to claim the state INDUSTRIAL INJURY BENEFIT by immediately applying to have your mishap declared an industrial accident. To apply, you need form B1 95, obtainable from any social security office.

6 Then – whether you are actually claiming benefit, considering suing your employer or just taking precautions in case your injury leads to complications – you should collect evidence about the accident.

7 If possible, get signed statements from people who saw the accident, while the details are still fresh in their minds. Make sure that you have their home addresses, in case they have left the company by the time you need your witnesses again.

that an employer must take. These include fencing and guarding machinery, making sure that ladders are securely fixed and ensuring that roofs – in coalmines, for example – are properly supported.

Any employer who is found breaking a safety law is liable to criminal prosecution as well as to pay compensation to anyone injured because of his neglect.

If you are injured at work, check whether the safety regulations were being broken at the time of your accident. Many injured employees have won compensation from their employers, even though they could not prove that anyone had been negligent, simply by showing that at the time of the accident, safety regulations were being broken on the premises. *See:* HEALTH AND SAFETY AT WORK

Claiming benefit

When an accident forces you to stay away from work, and it has been accepted as an industrial accident, claim INDUSTRIAL INJURY BENEFIT as quickly as possible. Thousands of people lose part of their claims every year because they have not claimed within the time allowed – 6 days if you have made a claim for injury benefit, sickness benefit or non-contributory invalidity pension before, 21 days if it is your first claim.

Deciding whether to sue your employer

Your employer is legally bound to insure against the risk of an unlawful accident to an employee. This makes it possible for him to pay compensation if you make a successful claim for accidental injury at work.

If you are injured, do not just seek social security benefit. Take advice about the possibility of suing the employer for direct or indirect negligence or breach of his duty under the safety laws. If your injuries are serious enough to consider suing, consult a solicitor. If you are a member of a trade union which handles such claims, you may ask the union to take up the matter through its own legal advisers.

If your legal claim succeeds, the damages awarded are likely to be much more than the amount of your industrial injury benefit – although you should still claim that.

When damages are assessed, the court will deduct half the value of any benefit for injury, disablement, sickness or invalidity which you receive in the first 5 years after your accident.

ACCIDENT INSURANCE

Protecting yourself against the risk of personal injury

Most insurance companies offer policies giving cover against the possibility that you could be injured in an accident. *See:* PERSONAL ACCIDENT INSURANCE

ACCOMMODATION AGENCY

When you should pay by results

One means of finding a rented flat or house is through an accommodation agency or bureau. If you consult such a service, pay it a fee only when you agree to rent one of the properties on its lists.

It is illegal for the agency to demand a fee simply for registering your name and requirements or for providing you with a list of addresses, with or without particulars of the properties on it. Refuse to pay if such a fee is requested. The agency is committing an offence for which its proprietors can be fined up to £100 or be imprisoned for 3 months or both.

If you have already paid an agency a fee which they had no right to ask, you can attempt to recover your money by reporting the matter to the police. In a successful prosecution, the magistrates can order the agency to return your payment.

ACT OF PARLIAMENT

When a proposal becomes the law of the land

The legislation that governs us becomes law through an Act of Parliament binding on all individuals and all courts. The validity of laws cannot be challenged as Parliament is supreme; only Parliament has the power to change its laws.

The process of creating an Act of

Parliament or 'statute' involves the House of Commons, the House of Lords and the Queen. It begins with a draft of the legislation required – known as a Bill. *See:* PARLIAMENTARY BILL

ACUPUNCTURE

Medical treatment with needles

Acupuncture, the ancient Chinese science of inserting needles at various points in the body to relieve pain and heal ailments, is readily available in Britain. About 150 registered doctors practise it, and there are about 200 lay acupuncturists, who have no medical qualifications.

Anyone can practise acupuncture, or any other kind of alternative medicine, with or without qualifications, provided that he does not commit an offence – for example, misrepresenting himself as a qualified doctor or injuring or killing a patient.

When treatment can be free

Your National Health Service doctor can, if he feels it may help your condition, send you to a doctor who specialises in acupuncture therapy, but if he himself is trained in acupuncture, he can treat you himself. If your doctor refuses, you cannot insist on acupuncture treatment, but you can arrange to transfer to another doctor who approves of acupuncture. *See:* DOCTOR AND PATIENT

Obtaining private treatment

If you want acupuncture treatment and your doctor does not agree to prescribe it under the Health Service, ask him for the name of a local doctor who gives private acupuncture treatment. As doctors are not allowed to advertise, only another doctor can obtain for you the name of a medical acupuncturist. If your doctor refuses to give you the information, ask another or contact the area health executive who keep a list of all doctors and their special interests and qualifications.

The cost of private acupuncture by a doctor is generally about the same as for orthodox PRIVATE MEDICINE. If you belong to a private health insurance scheme, it will cover the cost of treatment only if the treatment was pre-scribed by a doctor and is practised by a specialist of consultant status. Otherwise, you may have to pay as much as £50 for each private treatment.

When you receive acupuncture treatment from a doctor, whether privately or under the Health Service, you have the same legal protection as you would for any conventional treatment. If you have been injured, maltreated or neglected, or if you have any other complaint, you can report the doctor to the General Medical Council and sue him for damages. *See:* MEDICAL NEGLIGENCE

Treatment by a lay acupuncturist

Acupuncture administered by a lay expert is generally cheaper than that given by a medical practitioner. However, do not accept treatment from a non-medical acupuncturist unless you are sure he is competent. Ask the British Acupuncture Association for its list of registered members.

The association sets the professional standards for its members and insures them against any claims for negligence. That means that you would, if you decided to sue, have some chance of receiving compensation for bad or negligent treatment.

ADOPTION

The legal process by which a child gains new parents

If you are looking for a child to adopt contact an adoption society or a local authority social services department (or its adoption agency).

Because of widespread birth control and abortion, fewer and fewer unwanted babies – or babies needing bet-

WHO MAY BE ADOPTED

A child can be adopted once it is at least 18 weeks old. No one over 18 years old can be adopted. Nor can anyone who has been married, even if still under the age of 18.

If a child has been adopted once, it can nevertheless be adopted again.

WHO IS ENTITLED TO ADOPT A CHILD

Anyone over 21 years old is legally eligible to adopt a child, but in practice there are restrictions.

Single people are rarely allowed to adopt. A single man is unlikely to be allowed to adopt a girl. Two people who are living together but not married cannot jointly adopt a child.

Most adoption agencies and local authorities also insist that applicants must be under 35 (for a woman) or 40 (for a man), to ensure that they will still be active and vigorous when the child is growing up.

A married person cannot adopt without his or her spouse's being a party to the adoption, unless the court is satisfied that the spouse:
1. Cannot be found, by the usual processes involved in attempting to serve notice of legal proceedings.
2. Is too ill to join in the application (that must be certified by a doctor: it can be done by the applicant's family doctor).
3. Lives permanently apart from the applicant.

ter care than a natural mother feels she can ever provide – are available for adoption in Britain.

You may have to wait for some time, and make the rounds of several adoption agencies more than once, before a suitable child is found. Some agencies may have temporarily closed their lists of applicants when you contact them. If so, try again, from time to time.

Some types of children are more likely to be available for adoption – for example, older children, those of mixed race, slow learners or the physically or mentally handicapped.

The applicants most likely to be successful are young married couples, living in reasonably good circumstances with a secure home.

Getting on the waiting list

Once you have contacted a society or local authority, it begins extensive inquiries into your background and motives for adopting. A social worker meets each partner several times, together and separately.

Both partners must have full medical examinations and provide character references for themselves.

Choosing a child Children available for adoption are not usually put on show to the would-be adopters, although an exception may be made with a very young baby. Prospective parents are normally given only photographs and descriptions of the child available.

Taking the child home

Once chosen, the child is put into the provisional care of the adoption applicants.

Unless the child is over 16, you or the agency must notify the council social services department (or its adoption agency) of the proposed adoption.

Once the council has been notified, the child becomes protected, which means that the child is visited regularly by council social workers to make sure that the home is suitable.

If the parent (or guardian) has agreed to adoption, he or she is not entitled to remove the child without a court's permission. Protected status does not apply to a child who is to be adopted by a natural parent, or who is over 16. An adoption order cannot be made for at least 3 months after the council has been notified. During the 3 months, the child is protected.

Private adoptions If the child to be adopted has not been found through an agency or local council, the applicants must notify the council social services department and the child will have protected status for at least 3 months before an adoption order can be made.

Adopting a child who is a relative

In many cases, the child to be adopted is a relative of one of the adopting parents. For example, a parent who is divorced and has remarried may wish to adopt his or her own child, with the new step-parent.

Adoption in such circumstances excludes the other natural parent from any right to see the child, and a court must therefore make a custody order unless it can be shown that adoption is in the child's best interests.

A natural father or mother, acting alone, can adopt his or her own child if the court is satisfied that the other parent is dead, or cannot be found – or that there is some other good reason for excluding that parent (if, for example,

WHEN FOSTER PARENTS WANT TO ADOPT

If a child has been living with the adoption applicants – for example, with foster parents or relatives – for 5 years or more, it cannot legally be taken away from them before the adoption hearing, unless the child is a ward of court and the court has ordered its removal.

Anyone who does take away a child without a court order in such circumstances – for example, a natural parent who opposes adoption – commits a criminal offence. The maximum penalty is 3 months' imprisonment or a £400 fine, or both.

If a child is illegally taken away, the courts can order premises to be searched and the child returned to the adoption applicants.

If the child has been living with the applicants for less than 5 years, it can be removed, unless it has acquired protected status with a view to adoption.

he or she has been convicted of a serious criminal offence against the child or the adopting parent).

Preparing an application

If an adoption is arranged by an agency or local authority, the agency or authority attends to all the formalities. A council makes no charge, but an agency may ask for expenses.

However, even if you decide to arrange the adoption privately, the procedure is generally straightforward:

1. Notify the local authority social services department, in writing, at least 3 months before you intend to seek an adoption order in the magistrates' court or county court.

2. Obtain two adoption forms – one to be completed by you, the other by the child's natural parent or guardian – from the court office.

3. Complete your own application form, naming anyone or any organisation with a possible right to be heard in court when your application is heard.

People who should be named include:

● The child's natural parent or guardian.

● The local authority (unless one spouse is the natural parent).

● The natural father, if the child is illegitimate and he has been granted cus-

tody, or if an affiliation order has been made against him or if he has agreed to maintain the child.

4. Ask the child's parent or guardian to complete the second form, giving consent to the adoption.

5. Ask your family doctor to issue medical certificates for you, your spouse and the child. The certificates must show that both adopting parents are physically and mentally fit. The child's certificate should indicate any handicap or illness, although that will not affect the application to adopt.

6. Send both completed forms and the medical certificates to the court office.

What the court does next

As soon as your application is received, the court fixes a date for a hearing, and appoints a guardian ad litem (guardian in the case), usually a social worker or probation officer.

The guardian's job is to investigate, on the court's behalf, all the circumstances surrounding the proposed adoption – the applicant's suitability, personality, marriage, home, religion and health, and whether he or she fully understands what is involved.

HAVING A BABY ADOPTED

An expectant mother who wants to discuss having her baby adopted can contact the adoptions officer in the social services department of her local authority, or any of the adoption societies or agencies.

The mother can discuss whether to go ahead with the adoption and what other choices may be open to her.

If she decides to proceed, she will be able to discuss – and sometimes choose – the type of family she would like her child to go to.

The father of an illegitimate child will have a right to be heard only if he has a custody order – in which case his consent is needed for an adoption – or if there is an affiliation order against him, or if he wishes to be heard, in which case he can put his views to the court.

As soon as a baby is 6 weeks old, the prospective adopters can apply for a court hearing. Once the adoption order is signed, neither natural parent has any further right or obligation concerning the baby.

Inquiries about the child will include finding out whether it has been baptised and (if old enough to understand the meaning of adoption) what its own wishes are.

Anyone who has taken part in the adoption arrangements will be interviewed for the report by the guardian ad litem.

What happens at the hearing

Everyone whose consent is needed will be told by the court when and where the adoption hearing is to be. However, it is not usually necessary for those giving consent to attend the hearing: written agreement is enough.

Consent or not Normally, a child cannot be adopted unless both natural parents have given their written consent. However, if the parents are not mar-

ADVANTAGES AND DISADVANTAGES OF ADOPTION

For the adopting parents, an adoption order has the advantage that once granted, it cannot be withdrawn unless there is a successful appeal to the High Court or Court of Appeal.

A custody order, on the other hand, can be changed by court order, on the application of the other natural parent if circumstances alter – if, for example, the person given custody becomes unable, through illness, to look after the child properly.

If the other natural parent has been

paying MAINTENANCE for the child, an adoption order automatically ends the obligation to do so. It also cancels an AFFILIATION ORDER. A custody order does not bring maintenance payments to an end, or affect an affiliation order.

Adoption enables the adopting parents to exclude a natural parent or parents from contact with the child. A custody order will usually allow the parent who has not custody to have access to the child, at times agreed or fixed by court order.

ried, the father is not legally regarded as a parent, so his consent is not needed unless he has legal custody of the child.

That does not mean that the father is prevented from putting his views to the

court. If he can be found, the guardian ad litem will notify him of the proposed adoption, and the court can hear him.

A father who is paying maintenance under a court order must be notified.

WHEN A MOTHER DECIDES SHE CANNOT GIVE HER CHILD A PROPER HOME
The legal process from first counselling to a court hearing behind closed doors

1 A woman expecting an unwanted baby tells a social worker she is thinking of having the baby adopted. She is put in touch with an adoption agency, which interviews her at length.

2 The baby is born. A social worker from the agency takes the child to a foster family to be cared for until suitable adoptive parents can be chosen and inquiries can be made into their suitability.

3 Six weeks after the birth, the mother gives her consent to the adoption in the presence of a court officer. Later a special guardian appointed by a court checks that her consent is genuine.

4 The baby must live with its proposed future parents for at least 13 weeks. The couple are visited frequently by a social worker from the local authority who makes sure that all is well with the child.

5 The court sits in private, without the Press present, for adoption hearings. Usually the only other people present are the special guardian and the couple seeking adoption, with the child and their solicitor. The natural mother is informed of the hearing and can oppose the order if she has changed her mind since signing the consent. If the child is illegitimate, the father has no rights but the court can hear what he has to say.

If the child has a legally appointed GUARDIAN – whether or not it is living with the guardian – the guardian's consent is necessary.

A parent or guardian is not allowed to make conditions for the adoption – for example, about the child's religious upbringing – but the court may do so.

APPLICANTS WHOSE HOME IS ABROAD

If an adoption is sought by people who do not normally live in England, Wales or Scotland, only a provisional adoption order can be granted – either by a county court or by the High Court.

The child must have been in the continuous care of the applicant for at least 3 consecutive months, and the local authority must have been given at least 3 months' notice of the application.

Applicants from abroad must provide sworn evidence about the adoption law in the country where they normally live. They must also satisfy the court that they intend to adopt the child fully, under their own country's law, when they return to that country.

A provisional order made in these circumstances can never become a full order in Britain: it merely enables the applicant to take the child overseas legally, with a view to adopting him fully, abroad.

English and Welsh courts are soon to recognise adoptions made in some foreign countries – including most of the Commonwealth, and countries that are members of the EEC.

The court may decide that a parent's consent is not necessary if that parent:
● Cannot be found.
● Is incapable of giving consent – for example, because of mental disorder.
● Has abandoned the child.
● Has been guilty of persistent neglect or ill treatment.
● Has been guilty of serious ill treatment of the child or other children.
● Has failed to show proper affection, care and interest.
● Is withholding consent unreasonably.

In one case, a court granted an adoption order without the mother's consent, after she had given and withdrawn it several times.

However, withholding consent is not unreasonable merely because the child's welfare would be improved by adoption. The court must be convinced that a reasonable parent would have consented to adoption.

When the case comes to court

If the adoption hearing is at a magistrates' court or county court, the child must normally be present. If the hearing is in the High Court, its presence is not required.

The person applying to adopt the child must always attend the hearing, although if the application has been made jointly by a married couple, the court may allow one of them to be absent – for example, because of work or other commitments.

At the hearing, the report by the guardian ad litem is read by the magistrates or judge. The proposed adopters, who do not see the report, may be asked further questions.

Adoption opposed The application must be introduced by the applicants (or their lawyer) with a brief outline of facts and dates.

The applicants then give evidence and may be cross-examined by the respondent who opposes the adoption, or by the opposing lawyer. Other witnesses may give evidence.

The respondent must then give his or her reasons for opposing the adoption and may also be cross-examined. The respondent (or lawyer) is allowed to sum up the case against the adoption; and the final speech to the court is made by the applicants (or their lawyer).

The court then decides whether to grant the adoption order.

When the order has been granted

If the application succeeds, the adopters can normally collect their copy of the order, free of charge, before leaving the court building.

The order, which gives the child his new parents' surname and records the date of the adoption, has to be produced to the registrar of births, marriages and deaths so that an adoption and birth certificate can be issued.

Appealing against an order

Once an adoption order has been made (or refused), a respondent or applicant who wishes to appeal against the decision must go to a High Court judge (from a magistrates' court) within 28 days, or to the Court of Appeal (from a county court or the High Court) within 6 weeks.

After the adoption

Once adopted, a child has the same legal rights as any natural child born to the adopting parents, except that it cannot inherit a title. There is no restriction on the right to inherit the adopting parents' money or property. *See:* INHERITANCE

If, after an adoption, the parents have a child of their own, and eventually die without leaving a will, the adopted child and his younger step-brother or step-sister inherit the parents' estate equally. Any title, however, can be inherited only by the parents' natural, legitimate offspring.

Marriage restrictions An adopted child cannot marry its natural parent or its adoptive parent. Prohibitions on marriage with other members of the natural family also still apply. *See:* INCEST; MARRIAGE

Even if a child is adopted for a second time, by a different couple, the bar against marrying the first adoptive parent remains. However, an adopted child can legally marry the adoptive parents' son or daughter and any other adoptive brother or sister.

Tracing natural parents

At the age of 18 – or under 18, if about to marry – an adopted child is legally entitled to information about the natural parents.

However, in the past, natural parents were led to believe that their child would never have official access to such information, so anyone who was adopted earlier than November 12, 1975, must see a counsellor nominated by the Registrar General, before being allowed information from his records.

Anyone adopted after that date is entitled but not obliged to seek a counsellor's advice.

In both cases, the counsellor has no power to deny the applicant access to the records. His role is to discuss the implications of obtaining the information – including the possible effect on a natural parent.

The information to which an adopted person is entitled includes:
1. His or her original name before the

REGISTERING THE ADOPTION OF A CHILD

The certificate that confirms the new parents' status and provides the child with his proof of identity

Only the new name of the child is given on the short adoption certificate and on the birth certificate. The place and date of birth remain unchanged, however. The short form of birth certificate does not give the names of either the child's natural parents or its new ones The adopting couple are named in the full one

Only the names and occupations of the new parents are given on the adoption certificate. The natural parents are not mentioned. The court order, containing details of the natural parents and the child's original name, is kept by the General Register Office in Titchfield. Information can be obtained from it only by order of a court, or by the child itself at the age of 18

Copies of fictitious register entries supplied by and reproduced with the approval of the Registrar-General

Application No. 728

QHA 007502

CAUTION:—Any person who (1) falsifies any of the particulars on this certificate, or (2) uses a falsified certificate as true, knowing it to be false, is liable to prosecution.

CERTIFIED COPY OF AN ENTRY

1. No. of entry 849

2. Date	Sixth January 1974
and country of birth of child	England

Registration District Bromley

Sub-district Beckenham

3. Name and surname of child Emma Mary Lacey

4. Sex of child Female

5. Name and surname
address
and
occupation of
adopter or adopters

James Edward Lacey, 4 Sunnington Road, Upper Edmonton, N.18 Member of Parliament and his wife Pamela Winifred Lacey of the same address.

6. Date of adoption order
and description of court by which made

Twenty-sixth November 1974
Edmonton County Court

7. Date of entry Third December 1974

8. Signature of officer deputed by Registrar General to attest the entry K. V. Jones

---

XC 586001

728/74

1 & 2 ELIZ. 2 CH. 20

CERTIFICATE   OF BIRTH

Name and Surname	Emma Mary Lacey
Sex	Female
Date of Birth	Sixth January 1974
Place of Birth { Registration District	Bromley
{ Sub-district	Beckenham

Certified to have been compiled from records in the custody of the Registrar General. Given at the General Register Office, London, under the Seal of the said Office, the ....4th.... day of ...December... 1974.

CAUTION:—Any person who (1) falsifies any of the particulars on this certificate, or (2) uses a falsified certificate as true, knowing it to be false, is liable to prosecution.

849/82

...try in the Adopted Children Register maintained at the ...field, Fareham, Hants., England. Given at the General ...Office.

on Fourth December 19 74.

...58 Section 20. This Act provides that the particulars in spaces 2, 3, 4, 5 and 6 ...e Adoption Order.

...he Adopted Children Register, if purporting to be sealed or stamped with the ...rther or other proof of the entry, be received as evidence of the adoption to

When a court finally approves the adoption of a child, it sends an adoption order to the General Register Office at Titchfield, in Hampshire, where it is entered in the Adopted Children Register. The order from the court names the child's adoptive parents. A new birth certificate, which does not mention that the child is adopted, is sent at once to the adoptive parents. A full version of the birth register entry can be obtained from the General Register Office at Titchfield. In even that complete form, however, the natural parents are not identified.

adoption order was made by the court.

2. The name of the natural mother and possibly the natural father.

3. The name of the court where the adoption order was made.

To apply for access to your birth records write for an application form to the General Register Office in London.

ADULTERY

When a husband or wife is unfaithful

Voluntary sexual intercourse between someone who is married and a member of the opposite sex other than the marriage partner is called adultery. A married man who commits rape is an adulterer; a married woman who is raped is not. Sexual activity short of intercourse is not adultery.

Artificial insemination by a donor other than the husband is not adultery, nor is it adultery for a husband to act as an insemination donor for a woman other than his wife.

Adultery and divorce

Adultery is one of the facts that can be given as a reason for seeking a DIVORCE. However, a person seeking a divorce, the petitioner, must prove in addition that he or she finds it intolerable to live with his or her partner – not necessarily because of the adultery. If the other partner, the respondent, denies the adultery it may be necessary to prove in court that it took place.

Circumstantial evidence is usually enough. For instance, if the respondent is living with the person with whom adultery is alleged, called the CO-RESPONDENT, or if a man and woman shared a hotel room, the court will normally infer that adultery took place.

When adultery is proved, the court may order the co-respondent to pay the petitioner's divorce costs, especially when the co-respondent is a man.

A co-respondent can defend a charge of adultery even if the respondent decides not to do so. It is possible for a court to find adultery by the respondent proved but to dismiss the case against the co-respondent for lack of evidence.

A respondent who admits adultery can sign a written admission, giving details of when and where it took place, and may have the signature witnessed

by an independent person. A respondent may choose not to name the other person. A co-respondent who admits the adultery can also sign an admission.

If the petitioner has continued married life under the same roof (but not necessarily resuming sexual intercourse) for a total of more than 6 months after finding out about the adultery and the adultery has ceased, the court will not regard the adultery as a reason for a divorce. That total of 6 months may have been interrupted by periods of living separately.

Sometimes a petitioner seeking a divorce on any ground admits to – or is proved to have committed – adultery. If known, the person with whom the adultery is alleged is 'the party cited'. The court can give a divorce decree to either the petitioner or the respondent, or can give 'cross-decrees' to both.

ADVERTISING

Protection against misleading claims

Whether an advertisement appears in a newspaper or magazine, on television or radio, on a poster or packet or simply in a shop window, it must state the truth. If it does not, or if it is illegal or offensive, there are several courses of action open to the public.

Code of advertising practice

The standards of newspaper, magazine and cinema advertising and of promotional leaflets delivered door-to-door are governed by the British Code of Advertising Practice. Strict standards are applied to advertisements concerning credit, drugs and alcohol.

If you believe that an advertisement is misleading, illegal or offensive, you should write to the Advertising Standards Authority, 15 Ridgmount Street, London WC1E 7AW, providing full details of your complaint. The advertiser will then have to satisfy the authority that your complaint is unjustified. If he cannot, the authority will recommend that the advertisement no longer be displayed or delivered and will publish a report of the matter.

If a complainant has suffered some loss because of false claims made in the advertisement, the advertiser may decide to offer compensation. The Au-

thority has no power to demand such a payment, however.

Standards for television and radio

The Independent Broadcasting Authority's Code of Advertising Practice is basically the same as the British Code of Advertising Practice, but it also bans entirely the advertising of certain products, such as cigarettes, and does not allow subliminal advertising – where the 'message' is flashed on the screen for fractions of a second so that the viewer is not aware of seeing it, yet his brain absorbs the message.

If you have a complaint, write to the Authority's advertising control department, 70 Brompton Road, London.

Poster advertising

Besides being governed by the British Code of Advertising Practice, many posters are also covered by a voluntary code established by the British Poster Advertisers Association.

If you have a complaint about a poster, write to either the association or the Advertising Standards Authority.

Local posters and handbills – advertising, for example, a sale of carpets or a Scout concert, are not subject to the strict standards of the major codes governing commercial posters. But they are still governed by the general laws on advertising and must not contain false statements or be offensive.

When an advertiser can be prosecuted

If an advertisement contains a false or misleading description of the goods it advertises, there is another channel of complaint open to a member of the public: the local council's trading standards department which can bring a criminal prosecution against the person or company responsible for the advertisement. *See:* TRADE DESCRIPTIONS

For a criminal offence to have been committed, the description in the advertisement must have been false 'to a material degree'. Some legal authorities maintain that people are sensible enough not to believe everything they read in advertisements.

If the court finds the advertiser guilty, it may order the payment of compensation to the person who complained to the council if he suffered some loss, damage or personal injury as a result of believing the claims of the advertisement.

> ### THE 'CURE' FOR GREY HAIR
>
> *If a court finds an advertiser guilty of breaking a definite promise in his advertisement it can at the hearing award compensation to the complainant.*
>
> Mr Wood read the following advertisement for a comb which contained a small battery: *Great news for hair sufferers. What is your trouble? Is it grey hair? In 10 days not a grey hair left. £500 guarantee.*
>
> Mr Wood bought the comb and used it for 10 days. His greying hair remained grey. He sued for the £500.
>
> The defence argued that the claim in the advertisement was obviously impossible and could deceive no one.
>
> DECISION
> The court ordered payment of the £500.

It is also possible to bring a civil action against an advertiser, but the complainant then has to prove misrepresentation or breach of contract and show what loss or injury he has actually suffered.

ADVISORY, CONCILIATION AND ARBITRATION SERVICE (ACAS)

The government-backed way to settle disputes at work

ACAS is a free service – set up by the Government to help to prevent or to settle industrial strife and individual employer/employee disagreements. It is not a government agency, however; trade unions and employers are represented equally on its council.

It offers codes of general practice to improve industrial relations and also specific advice to employers and employees, collectively or individually, on such matters as union recognition, redundancy, equal pay for women or race discrimination.

If an employee thinks he has been dismissed unfairly, he can ask ACAS to discuss his case with his employer and, perhaps, reach a satisfactory solution without having to wait to go to an INDUSTRIAL TRIBUNAL. However, if you do not make a claim to an industrial tribunal within 3 months of being dismissed, your claim will not be heard, even if you have been dealing with ACAS in the meantime.

But if you make a complaint to an industrial tribunal it will automatically notify ACAS. If a settlement is reached through ACAS you can then withdraw your complaint. The service can be contacted through the local job centre or office of the Department of Employment.

ACAS conciliation officers have no official powers, and seeking their help does not prevent an employee or employer from pursuing other courses of action later.

The conciliation officers try to find common ground between the two sides and to get them talking. In major disputes, they can, if both sides agree, arrange to have the case heard by the government-backed CENTRAL ARBITRATION COMMITTEE.

AFFIDAVIT

When it is necessary to put legal evidence down in writing

An affidavit is a written statement of evidence used in a civil legal action. For instance, a householder who wants to prevent his neighbour from making excessive noise or a businessman who wants to stop a competitor infringing his patents, for example, both have to swear affidavits to support their claims.

Affidavit evidence is used also in divorces when the parties provide statements of their finances (affidavit of means) or in support of claims for custody of the children.

Those applying to adopt a child must also swear an affidavit setting out their personal circumstances and their relationship to the child.

In a debt case, the creditor will usually swear an affidavit confirming that requests for payment were sent to the debtor.

The author of an affidavit swears that it is true and signs it before an independent witness – a solicitor who is not otherwise acting on his behalf, a Justice of the Peace or a court official.

A solicitor charges a fee of £2 for acting as witness, and 50p for signing each of any attached documents, such as a court order, that are to be used as exhibits in the case.

A person who swears the truth of a false affidavit commits PERJURY.

AFFILIATION ORDER

A single woman's claims on the father of her child

When a single woman is pregnant or has given birth to an illegitimate child she may enter into an agreement with the child's father that he is to pay her a

WHEN MOTHER AND FATHER AGREE

The father and mother of an illegitimate child may agree to the father's maintaining the child by paying the mother a regular sum of money.

Ideally, the agreement should be in writing and be drafted by a solicitor. The National Council for One Parent Families produces a standard agreement form. Its address is 255 Kentish Town Road, London NW5 2LX.

If the father later refuses payment, the mother will more easily be able to get the agreement enforced by a court.

When an agreement is not written, the mother has to give the same evidence in court as she would in proceedings for an affiliation order.

Whether the mother takes action to enforce the agreement in a county court or the High Court depends on the amount of payment. If it is more than £2,000, apply to the High Court.

An agreement does not prevent the mother from applying to a magistrates' court later for an affiliation order – even if the agreement specifically releases the father from any other payment. But the court would take into account the amount that the father was already paying.

regular amount of money to maintain the child.

If the father will not agree, the mother may apply to a magistrates' court for an affiliation order – an order that affiliates or associates the father with the child and makes him responsible for maintaining it.

The application is usually made by the mother; or by the Supplementary Benefits Commission, if the mother receives social security benefits for the child; or by the local authority, if it is caring for the child.

How to apply for an affiliation order

Go to the local magistrates' court and issue a 'complaint' against the alleged father as soon as possible, either before the child is born or within 3 years of its birth. The application must be made within this time unless the alleged father maintains the child for any time within 3 years of its birth, when there is no time limit for making the complaint.

If he leaves England and Wales within 3 years of the birth, the complaint must be issued within 12 months of his return. The court can make an order against an alleged father living in Scotland or Northern Ireland only if conception is claimed to have taken place in England or Wales.

If the child was born abroad, an application can still be made to an English or Welsh magistrates' court, provided that the mother, child and alleged father are in England or Wales when proceedings are started.

The hearing of the application

The hearing is in private before a court of no more than three magistrates of both sexes. The press can be present, but reporting is restricted. *See:* MATRIMONIAL ORDER

Proceedings may take place without the attendance of the defendant, if the magistrates are satisfied that he has been properly notified of the place and date of the hearing. If the defendant admits he is the father of the child, and the amount to be paid by him has been agreed, the mother does not have to appear and the order is made without difficulty.

But in contested cases where the defendant denies that he is the father, the mother will probably have to give evidence about her first meeting with the defendant and about the occasions when they had sexual intercourse – in particular those that took place around the probable time of conception.

THE LAWYER'S CHILD

When affiliation proceedings are contested and the man denies that he is the father, the court may make a decision based on the balance of probabilities.

In a case in London in 1976 a lawyer was accused by an assistant with whom he had been having an affair of being the father of her child. The issue was complicated by the fact that on the night when, according to medical evidence, the woman was in the period of maximum fertility, another colleague said that he had spent the night with her, though she denied that intercourse had taken place.

DECISION

The magistrates found the lawyer to be the father, even though he had not had intercourse with the woman for 2 weeks before, and never after, the date of maximum fertility. He was ordered to maintain the child fully.

After giving evidence, the mother may be cross-examined by the defendant or his legal representative. She will then call any witnesses who can support her case – anyone to whom the defendant has admitted he is the father of the child, for example.

Before the court can make an affiliation order, some material part of the mother's evidence, for example that she has been on intimate terms with the defendant, must be corroborated. This may be done by the defendant's own admission that he had sexual intercourse with the mother about the probable date of conception; or there may be evidence such as affectionate letters written by the defendant to the mother or admissions of intimacy made by the defendant to third parties.

The defendant then gives evidence and calls his witnesses. If it is shown that the mother has had intercourse with another man during the probable period of conception, she will not usually obtain an affiliation order unless she can convince the court that contraceptives were used with the other man but not with the defendant or that there is some other reason why the other man could not be the father.

In contested proceedings evidence obtained from BLOOD TESTS may also be given. They cannot prove that the defendant is the father, although they can prove that he is not. The court may order blood samples to be taken from the defendant and the mother and child, but it cannot enforce this order. However, if either party refuses to take the test, the court may draw the inference that he or she fears the result of the test.

What the order says

If the mother proves her case, the court will make a finding that the defendant is the 'putative father' (meaning the supposed father) of the child and may make an affiliation order under which he will have to pay for the expenses of the child's birth and a weekly sum for the maintenance and education of the child.

If the application is made within 2 months of the birth of the child, maintenance money is payable from the date of birth. If it is made later than 2 months after the birth, it is payable from the date of the hearing.

Maintenance must usually be paid until the child reaches the age of 16, but can be extended to 18 or beyond if the child is receiving full-time education or training.

How much? In theory a court can make an affiliation order for any amount. In practice it takes account of the income and capital of both the mother and the defendant and tries to make an order sufficient to maintain the child at the parents' standard of living.

The money must be paid regularly to the clerk of the magistrates' court, who will normally send the money on to the mother. If the father fails to pay, the mother or the clerk can bring him before the court, and an attachment of EARNINGS order can be made.

However, if the mother is already receiving supplementary benefits for the child she can ask for the affiliation order payments to be made direct to the Supplementary Benefits Commission.

The advantage of this is that if the man defaults on his payments it is up to the commission to recover the arrears and the mother will continue to receive the same amount each week. If a local authority is caring for the child the payments must be made to the authority.

Getting an order changed If the father's or mother's means change substantially after the order has been made, either can apply to the original court to have the amount altered.

If the child is adopted, the affiliation order ceases, although the father is still liable to pay up any arrears. However, even if the mother marries a man able to support her and her child, the father must nevertheless maintain his payments though they may be reduced.

Appealing against the court's decision

The mother or putative father may appeal to the crown court against the magistrates' decision but not against the amount of the order. If the mother obtains fresh evidence after her application for an affiliation order has been dismissed, she may make a second application. Either party can also appeal against an order varying the amount.

AFFRAY
An ancient offence

If two or more people are fighting or preparing to fight, they may be committing what has been an offence for centuries: causing an affray. They commit the offence if they are likely to frighten or intimidate reasonable people.

An affray can take place in public, as on the streets, or in private, as at a party.

Prosecutions for affray are few. The police usually prefer to deal with minor disturbances by prosecuting the offenders for ASSAULT AND BATTERY or ABUSIVE WORDS OR BEHAVIOUR, because these charges are usually easier to prove.

Maximum penalty An unlimited fine and/or imprisonment.

AGE OF CONSENT
When a girl can say 'yes' to a man

It is a criminal offence to have sexual intercourse with a girl under 16, or to fondle her in a sexual manner, even if she raises no objections. A girl must be 16 before her consent can be a defence

to a man charged with a sexual offence. *Maximum penalty* For full intercourse with a girl under 13, life imprisonment; with a girl over 13 but under 16, 2 years' imprisonment. For indecent assault on a girl under 13, 5 years' imprisonment; on a girl over 13 but under 16, 2 years' imprisonment.

AGE OF MAJORITY
When a child takes on the rights and duties of an adult

Boys and girls come of age on their 18th birthdays. Until then a young person is regarded as a MINOR, without all the rights and obligations of an adult and with special legal protection.

In general, once people are 18 the law considers them capable of making decisions in all civil matters and of accepting liability for the consequences. They can vote in general elections, enter into binding contracts, sue and be sued and buy and sell property in their own name, for example.

Parents are no longer bound to maintain their children once they are 18 unless they are in full-time education and there is a court order in force. Nor

---

THE SIGNIFICANT AGES OF MAN AND WOMAN
From the moment of birth until the age of 80 there are several legal milestones

Age	Rights and responsibilities	Age	Rights and responsibilities
From birth	Can have a deposit or current account with a bank or with a building society and hold Premium Bonds	10–14 years	Can be found guilty of a crime only if it is proved that he was capable of discerning between right and wrong. Can be convicted of a criminal offence although the mode of trial and sentence are different from that of an adult
12 hours	Mother of twins or more can claim an extra maternity grant for each child who survives for that period		
48 hours	Can sue person responsible for being born deformed or disabled	12 years	Can buy a pet
0–3 years	Parent can claim £9 death grant on child's death	13 years	Can do light work as permitted under bye-laws – not before 7 a.m. or after 7 p.m., not during school hours or for more than 2 hours on a school day or Sunday, and not involving any heavy lifting or carrying
3–5 years	Parent can claim £15 death grant on child's death		
5 years	Must start full-time education. Can drink intoxicating liquor with a meal on licensed premises, but cannot buy it or be served. Can enter cinema. Can receive mobility allowance	14 years	Can be fingerprinted if he or a magistrate agrees. A boy can be convicted of rape or assault with intent to commit rape. Can see an AA film if escorted by an adult, or an A film unescorted. Can own a shotgun or airgun and have ammunition. But if under 15 he can have the assembled shotgun only under the supervision of someone over 20. Under 14 he must be under the supervision of someone over
6–17 years	Parent can claim £22.50 death grant on child's death		
7 years	Can have a deposit account in National Savings and Trustee Savings Banks and draw money on his own signature		

Age	Rights and responsibilities
14 years *Continued*	21 or be at a rifle club or shooting gallery Can be taken into a bar but he must not consume any alcoholic drink Can pawn goods
15 years	Parent loses right to child benefit unless child is receiving full-time education
15–21 years	Can be sent to borstal Can join the armed forces with his parents' consent. If sent on active service, can make a will
16 years	Can marry with the consent of either his parents or of a magistrate. Marriage without this consent is valid but it is a criminal offence to give false particulars A girl can legally consent to sexual intercourse Can nominate a person to take over, in the event of his death, money deposited in a National or Trustee Savings Bank Can fly solo in a glider Can buy beer, cider or perry in a restaurant or pub restaurant, but cannot buy it in a bar, off-licence or supermarket Can apply for a passport if married or in the armed forces Can refuse or consent to medical treatment and choose his own doctor. It would be a breach of confidence for the doctor to tell the parents Can join a trade union Can sell scrap metal Can buy tobacco Can be used for begging Boys can work underground in mines Can ride a moped of up to 50 cc and drive an invalid carriage Can leave school and take a full-time job but only after the Easter following his 16th birthday, or at Whitsun or at the end of the summer term If employed must pay national insurance contributions Can apply for supplementary, sickness and unemployment benefits Can buy fireworks Must pay National Health Service prescription charges Must pay National Health Service dental charges if no longer at school Can buy horror comics
17 years	Can drive a car and fly an aircraft solo Can be licensed to buy ammunition Can trade in the streets Can have an airgun and ammunition in public Cannot be committed to the care of a local authority Can be sent to prison for a criminal offence
18 years	Can donate blood or a body organ or tissue Can apply for a passport Can go abroad as a performer without a licence Can leave home without parents' consent Can change his name Can vote Can make a will

Age	Rights and responsibilities
18 years *Continued*	Can serve on a jury Can sign contracts, can sue, and can be sued Can own land in his own name Can hold shares in his own name Can marry without parental consent Can buy alcoholic drinks Can give a receipt in satisfaction of a legal claim Can act as the administrator or executor of a will Can bet in a betting shop Is released from any custody order Can be granted a mortgage Can obtain credit Can be tattooed Can be hanged for treason Local authority care orders generally cease Parent loses right to child benefit If child above that age, you can make effective tax saving by covenant in his favour Can submit a football pool coupon Can see an X film and an AA film unescorted
21 years	Can adopt a child Can stand for a council or Parliament Can drive a lorry or bus Can hold a licence to sell liquor Males can consent to homosexual acts Can be a bookmaker
24 years	A male charged with unlawful sexual intercourse with a girl under 16 can no longer rely on the defence that he did not know the girl's age
40 years	Widow over that age when her husband dies can claim age-related widow's pension on her late husband's contributions Widow over 40 when she ceases to draw an allowance for her child is entitled to higher rate of industrial death benefit
50 years	Widow over that age when her husband dies can claim standard widow's pension on her late husband's contributions, or where appropriate the higher rate of industrial death benefit.
60 years	Women no longer have to pay national insurance contributions, or National Health Service prescription charges A woman is entitled to the old-age pension if she has paid sufficient national insurance contributions
65 years	Men no longer have to pay national insurance contributions, or National Health Service prescription charge Retirement pension for man who has paid sufficient contributions, and for his wife. No earnings limit for woman receiving retirement pension on her own contributions No longer eligible for jury service
70 years	No earnings limit for man receiving retirement pension
80 years	Entitled to non-contributory retirement pension if resident in UK during 10 of preceding 20 years

can people over 18 be made wards of court.

If, however, in a will or some other legal document drawn up before January 1, 1970, when the legal age was lowered from 21, the age of majority is mentioned, it still means 21.

AIDING AND ABETTING

The offence of helping somebody to commit a crime

Someone who encourages or helps someone else to commit a crime can be charged with aiding and abetting him but only if he was close enough to the scene of the crime to help the criminal.

WHEN IGNORANCE WAS INNOCENCE

Someone charged with aiding and abetting an offence can be acquitted if able to prove ignorance of the fact that the offence was being committed.

Mrs Weaving was a publican and the police found customers drinking in her pub after the 10 minutes' 'drinking-up time'. They charged her with aiding and abetting a breach of the licensing laws, and the case went to the magistrates' court.

There Mrs Weaving pleaded not guilty. She said she had told her staff to collect customers' glasses on time, but they had failed to do so. She had not been in the bar at closing time.

DECISION

Mrs Weaving was found guilty, but she appealed. The High Court held that although her staff might have been guilty of aiding and abetting, she could not have been guilty as she had not known the offence was being committed.

For example, if a man keeps watch while others break into a house, he is guilty of aiding and abetting. But if he is only a bystander he cannot be prosecuted, even if he does nothing to prevent the housebreaking.

Maximum penalty Can be the same as for committing the offence, although in practice it is usually less heavy than that imposed on the principal criminals.

AIR ACCIDENT

When you can claim compensation for an injury

If you are injured on board an airliner, or while boarding or disembarking, you are entitled to some compensation without having to prove that the airline or its staff were at fault.

Compensation for injuries suffered in an air accident is governed by international agreements or conventions which set out what maximum payments can be made. These limits depend on the nationality of the airline involved, whether the flight was international or domestic and whether the journey began or ended in the United States.

However, the maximum agreed compensation is low, compared with what might be obtained in an ordinary legal action for NEGLIGENCE.

An airline can avoid paying compensation even within these agreed limits, if it can prove that all necessary measures were taken to avoid your injury, or that it was not possible to take such measures.

On the other hand, you can get compensation above the agreed limits if you can prove that your injury resulted from something that the airline or its staff did (or failed to do) recklessly, or with intent to cause damage, or knowing that damage would probably result. Successful claims on such grounds have been rare, however.

If there is evidence that the accident was caused by careless design or manufacture of the aircraft, you can overcome the compensation limits by suing the manufacturers, who are not covered by the airline agreements.

Where an accident is caused by the negligence of a third party – for example, the pilot of another aircraft, or air-traffic control staff, or perhaps both – the international limits do not apply, and you can sue the culprit or his employers for negligence.

However, there are serious practical difficulties in pursuing claims outside the agreements.

It will be expensive to assemble the expert evidence needed to prove negligence. Your claim may have to be fought in a foreign court and according to foreign law, and you get no legal aid for actions abroad.

Should you wish to pursue such a claim, consult a specialist aviation lawyer. An ordinary solicitor can refer you to one.

If you are one of many victims of an accident, try to get publicity for your claim: others may join you in making similar claims through the same lawyer, and so share the heavy legal costs.

The most practical way to make sure of getting adequate compensation after an air accident is to take out insurance, before the flight, against personal injury or death. Any money paid out on an insurance policy is in addition to compensation from the airline.

Hovercraft are covered by similar rules. The maximum compensation payable on a death is £30,000. The maximum for lost or damaged luggage is £216.

If an aircraft crashes or crash-lands on your property, or if something falls on to it from an aircraft, you can sue for damages even though the pilot may not be to blame.

AIR POLLUTION

Regulations that keep the air fit to breathe

The emission of any kind of smoke from a chimney other than one on a private dwelling is prohibited through-

KEEPING THE AIR FREE FROM POLLUTION

It is an offence to have a bonfire in the garden, even on Guy Fawkes' day, if it causes a nuisance to other people.

out Britain if it causes a NUISANCE. Causing 'dark smoke' by burning old motor tyres, for example, is not allowed anywhere, even if nuisance is not proved. Many local councils have declared smoke-control areas where it is an offence to use any fuel other than those authorised in government regulations – for example, oil, gas, electricity and smokeless solid fuels. Most coal merchants can give advice on what can be used in an area. If you are in doubt, consult your nearest Solid Fuel Advisory Centre (usually listed in the telephone directory).

It is illegal for a trader to offer unauthorised fuel – for example wood – in a smoke-control area, but the responsibility for burning it is nevertheless the householder's, and he can be fined up to £100 for breaking the law.

The law does not apply only to chimneys. It can be an offence to have a bonfire even on Guy Fawkes' day.

If a council decides to impose smoke-control regulations it must advertise its intention in the *London Gazette* and in local newspapers for at least 2 weeks. If you want to object, write at once to the council's chief executive who is legally obliged to consider your objection before confirming the order. But you have no right to appeal against an order.

The order will come into effect on a date fixed by the council.

If your house is in an area covered by an order, apply to the council for a grant to help with the cost of adapting heating equipment – up to 70 per cent of the total cost is allowable if the council approves your proposed changes. If the equipment is movable, however, you may be asked to repay the grant within 2 years. This grant is not available in the London area

Councils are obliged to make such grants only for private property, but they may also decide to help to convert the heating systems in churches and halls used by voluntary bodies.

AIR SPACE

A householder's limited protection against intrusion

Every householder has control of the air space immediately above his land, even if he is only a tenant.

If a neighbour puts a sign on the side of his house so that the sign projects over your boundary, for example, you can apply to a court for an order requiring him to take it down. *See also:* NEIGHBOUR

THE PEER WHO SUED

Although you have complete control over the air space immediately above your property, you cannot claim that your rights have been infringed if someone flies over at a reasonable height – even if he does so to photograph your property.

When an aerial photography company offered to sell Lord Bernstein photographs of his Kent farm, he demanded all negatives and prints be destroyed. In reply, the company, which had been taking and selling aerial photographs of private property for 17 years, offered him the negatives for £15. Lord Bernstein sued.

DECISION

Since the aircraft had flown several hundred feet above Lord Bernstein's property, the company had not interfered with any air space that was necessary for his enjoyment of his property. He was not entitled to compensation or damages.

You cannot, however, legally stop aircraft flying over your land at a reasonable height. For passenger airliners, the reasonable height is generally 2,000 ft or more, and for private light aircraft, 1,000 ft.

AIR TRAVEL

Compensation for hitches and delays

If you travel by air and your flight is delayed, you may be entitled to claim compensation for any loss that you suffer. But that loss must be something an airline could foresee arising from a delay – for example, the cost of staying overnight at a hotel.

Compensation cannot be claimed for 'unforeseeable' damage, such as loss of profit through missing a valuable business contract because of the delay.

The airline is not liable if it can show that all necessary measures were taken to avoid your loss, or that such measures could not be taken. If your flight is delayed by bad weather or by a strike outside the airline's control, for example, the airline would not be liable. However, if the delay is caused by repairs to an aircraft that had not been properly maintained, the airline could not claim that it had taken all necessary measures, and so would be liable to pay compensation.

In practice, delayed passengers are often accommodated in hotels at the airline's expense.

When a flight is overbooked

To allow for the non-appearance of passengers who have reservations, most airlines book more passengers for a flight than the aircraft can carry. If everyone does check in, some would-be passengers have to be turned away – normally on a first come first served basis.

Some airlines, including British Airways, now offer compensation agreements for passengers turned away because of overbooking. They generally undertake to get the passenger to his destination within 2 hours (on a domestic flight) or 4 hours (overseas flights) of the arrival time of the original flight. If that cannot be done the passenger is entitled to:

1. Reasonable expenses for accommodation, meals, telephone calls and so on while awaiting alternative transport.
2. A refund of half the fare for the leg of the flight that was overbooked, with a minimum of £10 and a maximum of £100.

The passenger has to sign a receipt giving up any other rights he may have to compensation for the delay, but the uncertainties of legal action make it worthwhile to accept the offer.

Luggage difficulties

Compensation can also be claimed for luggage that is delayed, although an airline's liability is limited to a maximum of about £10 for each kilogram (2.2 lb.).

If your suitcase is flown to the wrong place, the airline will probably be liable for the cost of spare nightclothes and toilet articles such as toothbrush and razor – and also the cost of any extra

PURSUING A COMPLAINT

If you are not satisfied with an airline's response to a complaint, you can appeal to the Airline Users' Committee, set up by the Civil Aviation Authority, to investigate any complaints by air travellers.

The committee will try to help you with any complaint about airlines or airport facilities, including problems of overbooking, wrong booking and lost luggage. It cannot deal with complaints about hotels or claims for compensation.

journey you have to make to the airport to collect the case when it is available.

When luggage is lost If luggage is lost while it is in the airline's care, you can claim compensation to a maximum of about £10 per kilogram. The airline, however, has a defence if it can show that all necessary measures were taken to avoid the loss.

When luggage is damaged If your luggage is damaged when it is in the care of the airline, complain at once. If you accept it without complaint, it is assumed in law to have been delivered back to you in good condition.

There may, however, be damage that is not obvious from the outside. If so, you should claim compensation, in writing, as soon as the damage is discovered – and not later than seven days after you have collected the luggage. If you do not, the airline is no longer liable.

AIRCRAFT NOISE

When you may be able to have something done about it

If you live near an airport and are disturbed by aircraft noise, find out whether the airport is governed by legally enforceable regulations. These generally control the amount of noise permitted during taxiing, take-off and landing; they may also state the hours during which jet aircraft can operate and the rules about noise which they must then observe.

It is an offence to disregard these regulations, and airlines that do so can be prevented from using that airport.

To find out what regulations do apply

to your local airport, contact the nearest office of the Civil Aviation Authority, listed in the telephone directory.

In addition, the Government can require specified airports to make grants towards the cost of soundproofing homes and other buildings. For instance, Heathrow, Gatwick and Manchester have been required to make grants available to neighbouring property owners for this purpose.

If an aircraft while taking off, landing or in flight causes damage to your property, you can sue the owner for compensation. If, therefore, the noise or vibration broke windows in your house, you have a claim. If there is no physical damage, and the flying regulations are being complied with and the aircraft is flying at a reasonable height, you have no claim for NUISANCE merely on the ground that the enjoyment of your home is being interfered with.

AIRPORT INSURANCE

Short-term insurance cover for a single flight

Insurance against death or injury while travelling by air can be taken out at most airports.

There is usually a maximum amount (often £100,000) for which you can insure yourself and the cover is usually available from the time you board the aircraft to the time you disembark after your journey – and again for the return flight.

By paying an extra premium, you can insure against the risk of hi-jacking or terrorist attacks.

To take out insurance, go to the airport desk marked 'Flight Insurance'. You will be given a form to complete on the spot and you will need to show your flight ticket.

ALIBI

When an accused person claims he was elsewhere

Anyone accused of a crime who claims that he was not at the scene when it was committed can plead an alibi – the Latin word for 'elsewhere' – as his defence. But he must prove where he was

at the time of the crime.

For example, if a man is charged with committing a burglary in London, but claims to have been staying at a hotel in Birmingham on the day of the crime, he can plead that alibi as his defence.

He must, however, prove not only that he was in Birmingham on the day in question, but also that he could not have been in London at or near the time of the burglary. If he cannot prove that conclusively, with witnesses to support his claim, it is for the jury or magistrates to decide whether he is likely to be telling the truth.

If the case is to be tried in a magistrates' court, the accused person can produce his alibi without notice. The court, however, can adjourn the case so that the prosecution have an opportunity to check the alibi.

In COMMITTAL PROCEEDINGS, in a magistrates' court, the accused is told that if he intends to produce an alibi at his trial, he must give notice to the prosecution, either at the committal proceedings or not more than 7 days after they finish.

The notice of alibi must include names and addresses of any witnesses who are to be called to support his claim. If the accused person does not have those details, he must give the police all possible help in tracing the witnesses.

If notice of an alibi is given during the magistrates' court hearing, it can be given orally. Notice given after the hearing must be in writing, to the magistrates' clerk for the prosecution's attention.

Unless due notice is given, the trial judge at the crown court may refuse to allow the accused to call evidence in support of an alibi.

ALIEN

Visitor whose rights in Britain are limited

Aliens are citizens of any country, apart from Eire, that does not belong to the Commonwealth.

The rules governing IMMIGRATION divide aliens into three groups:
1. Citizens of any of the other seven countries of the EEC. They have many of the same rights as United Kingdom

citizens in the UK. *See:* EUROPEAN COMMUNITIES

2. Citizens of certain countries – for example, the USSR – who need a VISA to travel to the UK for any purpose.

3. Other aliens – for example, US citizens who have no special privileges within the UK, but who do not need visas. They can apply for admission to the immigration officer on arrival, but they would be well advised to apply for entry clearance before leaving their own country, particularly if they are coming from certain areas – for example, North Africa.

ALLOTMENT

Council land for local gardeners

Most district councils provide allotments, small portions of land which can be rented cheaply for cultivation. If the allotments are statutory, or permanent, the council has a duty, if it takes over the land for other purposes, to provide the allotment tenants with other land of roughly the same size. That does not apply to temporary allotments – including many that were established between 1939 and 1945 and which still remain 'temporary'.

The tenant's duties and rights The tenant of an allotment should always obtain a written agreement from the council stating the terms of his tenancy. They

---

ALLOTMENT LAND FOR
LOCAL RESIDENTS

To end the lease of a council-owned allotment the council must give the tenant 12 months' notice, or the tenant must give the council 6 months' notice.

'Sorry – Eviction Order'

---

may include conditions about keeping the allotment tidy, what can be grown and what animals kept. The council normally reserves the right to inspect the allotment at any time.

To end a lease, the tenant must normally give the council 6 months' written notice, and the council must give the tenant 12 months' notice. The council must make sure that its notice period ends on or before April 6, or on or after September 29, to ensure that the tenant does not lose his allotment in the middle of the growing season. If a council failed to observe that rule, the tenant could claim compensation for crops lost and fertiliser wasted.

When there is a waiting list for allotments, priority is given to residents of the district. If you have to wait an unusually long time, complain to your local councillor; if you suspect you have been treated unfairly ask him to refer your complaint to the local OMBUDSMAN.

Private allotments

In some parts of the country, another way of obtaining an allotment is through an allotments association, a private organisation whose members rent or buy a tract of land for parcelling up into allotments.

ALL-RISKS INSURANCE

Protection for valuables and goods in transit

All-risks insurance policies are widely used to cover goods in transit and personal possessions and valuables – for example, paintings and jewellery.

Such policies protect the items covered against risks of every kind except those arising from inherent defects in the articles themselves, and those commonly excluded from all policies – for example, civil commotion, riot and war. *See:* INSURANCE

The exclusion of inherent defects means that the insurance company would not be liable if the colours in a painting faded with the passage of time, or if a clock spring broke because of a mechanical fault. There is no liability if goods in transit are damaged because they were not properly packed.

In making a claim, the insured person

WHEN THE WOOL WAS WET

When an insured person makes a claim for loss of or damage to goods in transit, he has to show that the loss or damage occurred by accident, and that it could not normally have been expected.

Mr Gaunt, a Bradford mill owner, bought a consignment of wool from Patagonia, in the south of Argentina. He insured it 'from the sheep's back' to Bradford 'with all risks'. On arrival, it was found the wool had been damaged by water.

Mr Gaunt lodged a claim against the insurers. The insurance company resisted the claim.

In the ensuing court action, it was not established satisfactorily at what point between the sheep's being sheared and the wool's being delivered it had been damaged by water.

DECISION

The court found in favour of Mr Gaunt. He had, it said, proved all that he had to prove: that the damage 'did not occur, and could not be expected to occur, during the course of a normal transit'.

---

has to show that the goods concerned were damaged or lost by accident. But he does not have to prove the exact cause of the loss.

AMBULANCE

Sometimes a doctor's authority is needed

Victims of accidents, wherever they occur, and women going into labour have a right to an ambulance to take them to hospital. So have those who fall ill in an office or in any other public place. In such circumstances, anyone can call an ambulance by dialling 999.

In all other cases, a doctor must normally decide whether an ambulance should be summoned.

If someone falls ill at home, the ambulance services will usually insist that the family doctor is called first. They will help to trace him or his deputy if he is difficult to locate. Where the doctor cannot be found and the patient seems to need urgent help, most services will agree to send an ambulance.

People attending hospital as out-patients may require transport.

If the GP in charge of the case considers an ambulance is necessary, he will tell the local health authority. Where the patient has been discharged from hospital, but is returning as an out-patient, the hospital doctor will arrange the ambulance if he feels one is needed.

There is generally no right of appeal against a doctor's decision not to recommend the provision of an ambulance – although he could be sued if it could be established that he had been negligent.

In London, the ambulance service is the responsibility of the South-west Thames Regional Health Authority; elsewhere area health authorities are responsible. If a patient died or suffered greater injuries as a result of delay in providing an ambulance, and that appeared to be due to negligence on the part of either the ambulance crew or controller, an action for damages could be brought against the authority.

If a service is disrupted or withdrawn because of industrial action it is unlikely that there would be any legal redress available to anyone harmed as a result.

ANCIENT MONUMENT

Protecting the nation's heritage

Any structure or site that the Secretary of State for the Environment considers to be of national historical importance can be scheduled as an ancient monument. The Department of the Environment is then responsible for its upkeep, usually through a local authority.

If a site is on private land, the owner has no legal right to object to scheduling. If the Department insists on public access against his will, it can compulsorily acquire the land or take it into guardianship.

Where possible the public must have access – subject to local regulations on hours and admission charges – to monuments that are owned by the Department or a local authority, or in their guardianship.

It is an offence to carry out demo-lition, removal or repair work on a scheduled monument without permission. Maximum penalty: £1,000 fine. Vandalism and other breaches of local regulations carry a £50 fine.

When history is unearthed

If remains of historical importance are believed to be underground, the Secretary of State can designate the land an archaeological area.

That means anyone who plans flooding or tipping operations, or other work that could disturb the ground, must give the local authority at least 6 weeks' notice. Failure to give notice is punishable by a fine of up to £1,000.

Metal detectors It is an offence to use a metal detector on a scheduled monument site, or in a designated archaeological area, without the Secretary of State's consent. Maximum penalty: £200 fine.

ANIMAL

How the citizen is protected against another's pets

If you own an animal, look after one for someone or use one for work or recreation, the law imposes obligations on you. It also provides redress for any-

PROTECTING THE CITIZEN AGAINST ANOTHER'S PETS

Anyone who owns, or is in charge of, an animal has a legal duty to take reasonable care that the animal does not cause injury or damage. The law provides redress for anyone who suffers injury or damage through someone else's animal.

'HEEL!'

one who suffers injury or damage because of someone else's animal.

The law gives animals certain 'rights' also. Game and endangered species are safeguarded by law, and cruelty to animals is a criminal offence.

Responsibility for domestic pets

Most household pets, except dogs and dangerous animals (those listed in the Dangerous Wild Animals Act), can be kept in Britain without a licence. However, tenancy agreements for council and privately rented property often prohibit tenants from keeping certain pets. *See:* LANDLORD AND TENANT

Anyone who owns an animal, or who is left in charge of one, has a legal duty to take reasonable care that the animal does not cause injury or damage. If he fails to fulfil that duty, he may be sued. (Where the owner or keeper of an animal is under 16, the head of the household is liable.)

But keepers of domestic pets other than those classed as dangerous are generally held to be responsible only when it can be proved that their negligence resulted in the injury, accident or damage caused by the animal.

Owners of cats are seldom held to be liable for any damage caused by them, not because cats enjoy any special status under the law, but because it is difficult to prove the owner's negligence if, for example, the cat ruins a neighbour's lettuces.

Keeping pets that are 'dangerous'

Any pet that attacks people or has a disease that could affect humans is dangerous in law. So is any pet or domestic animal likely to cause severe harm because it has characteristics not normally found in others of the same species.

If the keeper of such an animal – the owner or the person in possession of it – is aware of the abnormality, he is liable for the harm the animal does, even though he may not be to blame for it. If the keeper is under 16, the head of the household is responsible.

When the victim is to blame

The victim may also have been partly to blame for the incident – perhaps be-

> ## THE HORSES THAT BOLTED
>
> *Anyone who takes an animal on to a public highway can be made to pay for any damage it causes if he did not take every possible precaution to prevent it.*
>
> One afternoon, a delivery man left his van, drawn by two horses, in a street in Rotherhithe, London, while he went to obtain a receipt for goods he had delivered.
>
> Two boys, just coming out of school, threw stones at the horses, which bolted, endangering the passers-by. A policeman saw what was happening and, at great personal risk, seized one horse. He was dragged 15 yds and was seriously injured, but he managed to stop the runaways.
>
> ### DECISION
>
> The Court of Appeal awarded PC Haynes damages against the owners of the horses because the van driver had been negligent in leaving them unattended in a busy street which he knew well, and in which he could have expected there to be mischievous boys.

cause he was trespassing – and any damages he won would be reduced. If the injury is entirely his fault he will recover nothing.

Keeping wild animals

Any wild animal that is not commonly domesticated in Britain and which, unless restrained, is capable of causing severe damage is, in law, dangerous.

Its keeper is liable for any harm it may do, whether or not the animal had previously shown itself to be dangerous and whether or not the keeper was at fault.

The law applies not only to obviously dangerous beasts such as lions and tigers, but also to some animals native to Britain, for example, foxes.

Under the Dangerous Wild Animals Act 1976, anyone (other than zoos, circuses and licensed pet shops) who keeps certain species of wild animals – for example alligators, poisonous snakes and some monkeys – must have a licence from the local authority. If you are in doubt about whether you may need a licence, contact the environmental health department of the local council.

Before a licence is granted, the council has to be satisfied that the keeper is a responsible adult and that the granting of the licence would not be contrary to the public interest. An official will inspect the premises where the animal will be kept and the licence covers only those premises. As a keeper, you ought to insure yourself against liability for any damage the animal may cause.

If a licence is refused, or if you object to the conditions attached, you can appeal to the local magistrates' court.

The council can charge a fee for a licence – perhaps as much as £50.

Keeping livestock

Anyone who owns livestock – that is cattle, horses, sheep, pigs, goats and poultry – is responsible for any injury or damage the animal does if it strays on to a road, only if he was negligent in allowing it to escape there.

On the road Whether negligence can be proved depends on the circumstances. If a rambler left a gate open immediately before the animal escaped on to the road, the owner would not be liable, although the rambler might be. But if the animal escaped because the fence around the owner's field was defective, he would be liable.

Anyone who takes an animal on to a highway may be held responsible for damage caused because he did not take reasonable care. A parent who lets an inexperienced child ride a pony on a busy road, for example, may be liable to pay damages to any motorist whose car collides with the pony.

On someone's land If livestock stray on to someone else's land, the owner of the livestock is liable for damage to property, even though he may not have been to blame.

The livestock owner has the following legal defences:
● The victim was wholly to blame. If he is partly to blame, the damages would be apportioned. *See:* CONTRIBUTORY NEGLIGENCE
● The livestock were making lawful use of the public highway and strayed from there.
● The victim was responsible under a covenant or condition in the deeds of his property to maintain a fence around his own land.

Holding the strays A landowner is entitled to hold stray livestock until he gets compensation for any damage they have done. He must feed and water the animals and must inform the police, and if possible the owner, within 48 hours.

If the cost of the damage has not been paid within 21 days and if proceedings to secure the return of the strays have not started, the person holding the animals can sell them at a market or a public auction. But he must give the proceeds, less his expenses and the cost of repairing the damage, to the animal's owner. He may also later sue the animal's owner for damages.

If the owner of strays is not found, the person on whose land they were found is entitled in law to keep them.

How the law protects animals

Cruelty to animals, whether they belong to someone or are wild, is a criminal offence for which the penalty is a fine of up to £50, or 3 months' imprisonment, or both. Courts can also ban anyone convicted of cruelty from keeping specified types of animals.

Forms of cruelty which can be punished by the law include: striking or torturing an animal; neglect through, for example, inadequate feeding; and improper killing, such as drowning kittens or puppies. If an animal has to be killed, go to the RSPCA.

It is an offence to abandon an animal, for example when going on holiday.

Pests, including foxes, rats and coypu, may usually be killed on sight, but many species of wild animals are protected by special laws. *See:* PEST CONTROL

Protected species Animals protected because they are in danger of extinction include otter, most species of bats, sand lizard, great crested newt, smooth snake, natterjack toad, and most species of dolphin and porpoise.

Other species may be added to the protected list by Act of Parliament or by government order. If you feel a species is endangered, you could raise the matter with your local Member of Parliament, or try to persuade the Nature Conservancy Council to make a recommendation to the Government.

It is an offence to kill, injure or take possession of these animals except to prevent serious damage to property, or for purposes permitted by the Ministry of Agriculture or the Nature Conservancy Council. It is also an offence to sell protected animals alive or dead.

Under the Badgers Act 1973, the killing or attempted killing of badgers is illegal, and it is an offence to injure, dig or set a trap for or cruelly ill-treat a badger or to be in possession of a recently killed one. Badgers may be killed or caught only to prevent serious damage to land.

It is also an offence to snare, trap, drug or poison any wild mammal, or to use any automatic weapon, bow, gas or explosive or light to help to kill or catch a wild mammal, unless it is done under licence. The maximum penalty is a £500 fine.

Many kinds of wild BIRDS, their eggs and nests are also protected, as are some INSECTS.

Game animals and birds – for example hares, rabbits and pheasants – are also specially protected. *See:* GAME

Protecting deer Deer do not come into the category of game, but are covered by the law in much the same way. It is an offence to kill deer between 1 hour after sunset and 1 hour before sunrise or in the close season – unless you are protecting your land or have a special Ministry of Agriculture licence. *See also:* DOG CONTROL

The close seasons for deer are:

Fallow and roe deer

Bucks	May 1–July 31
Does	March 1–October 31

Red and Sika deer

Stags	May 1–July 31
Hinds	March 1–October 31

APPRENTICESHIP

An ancient way to start a new career

Apprenticeship is a special kind of practical training that gives young people the skills of a trade or craft.

An apprenticeship is usually regarded as the best qualification for a craft, and those who have completed one generally command top wages. But

---

STARTING WORK AS
AN APPRENTICE

An apprentice's training is governed by a contract in which an employer promises to teach the apprentice his craft and the apprentice agrees to learn it and to obey the 'master's' instructions.

'Good lad'

the pay during apprenticeship is low and the training period – usually 4 years – is long compared with other methods of job entry.

A person entering an apprenticeship must usually be over 16 years old, but theoretically there is no upper age limit. In practice there often is, and older women seeking training who have problems should contact the Equal Opportunities Commission.

Training is governed by a written contract, often called indentures, in which the apprentice's 'master' – an individual, a partnership or a company – promises to teach him his craft, and the apprentice agrees to learn it and to obey the master's instructions.

The wage offered under an apprenticeship contract is usually low, but the trainee has no legal right even to that, for the master, in theory and occasionally in practice, can demand a premium or fee for giving instruction.

If the apprentice-to-be is under 18, a parent or guardian must sign the contract on his or her behalf. If the apprentice were to fail to finish his indentures satisfactorily, the parent who had signed the contract could be sued for any loss or damage the master had been caused.

When an apprentice is dismissed

Employers have stronger powers to discipline apprentices than other em-

ployees, but it is more difficult to dismiss them. An apprentice dismissed before the end of indentures could probably sue for damages in the county court or the High Court to compensate for lost earnings and training during the rest of the contract period, and for lost opportunity and reduced status in the future.

An apprentice can also claim UNFAIR DISMISSAL before an industrial tribunal if he or she has been in the job for at least 52 weeks. That qualification does not need to be satisfied if he has been dismissed for trade union activity. In this case, the apprentice can apply for a speedy hearing and for the contract to continue until the hearing takes place.

Some grounds for dismissing an apprentice – for example, stubborn refusal to learn, habitual neglect of studies, persistent illness or behaviour which interferes with instruction – are not unfair in law, provided the employer had given previous warnings.

But employers are traditionally expected to suspend and discipline apprentices who misbehave, rather than

> ### THE APPRENTICE WHOSE MANNER CHANGED
>
> *An employer has greater powers to discipline apprentices than he has over other workers; but his rights to dismiss an apprentice are more restricted. He must be able to show that he gave the apprentice several warnings and chances to mend his ways.*
>
> When Mr Smedley was first apprenticed to his horticultural firm, he proved a very capable worker – the best apprentice to date, according to his employers. He passed proficiency exams, and after a while was paid a craftsman's wage.
>
> But then his behaviour changed. He challenged instructions, would not work in a group and declined to do overtime.
>
> He was given warning after warning verbally, and finally a warning in writing. Eventually, he was dismissed.
>
> DECISION
> The dismissal was fair, the Employment Appeal Tribunal ruled.

dismiss them, particularly if the contract is nearing its end. If an employer suspends an apprentice, the apprenticeship must be extended for an equivalent period.

When an apprentice is redundant

Apprentices made redundant during their contract term can claim redundancy payment only if they have reached the age of 20 and have completed at least 2 years' service. They might win a claim for unfair REDUNDANCY if their employer did not find a new master for them, or did not give enough warning.

If an apprentice who has lost his job sues for breach of contract, the employer cannot plead that it was due to redundancy unless the company has actually gone out of business.

When an apprenticeship is over, no redundancy payment is due if the employer refuses to take on the newly qualified journeyman under a fresh contract, nor can the apprentice claim UNFAIR DISMISSAL, unless the employer had previously promised him a job, or unless, as in some sections of engineering, it is a strong custom of the trade to offer continued employment.

National insurance contributions

From the age of 16, apprentices must pay national insurance contributions if they earn more than the qualifying weekly wage – £27 in 1981–2.

APPROVAL, Goods on

When goods can be sent back without payment

Goods are sometimes advertised for sale 'on approval', which means that after sending for them you need keep and pay for them only if you like them; if not, you can return them.

The goods are usually on approval for a limited period – 10 days, for example. If you do not want them and fail to tell the seller this within the time limit, you will have to keep and pay for them.

If no time limit is mentioned, the law states that you must decide to keep or return them within a reasonable time.

In fact, if you do not want the goods it is best not to delay returning them by even a day or two. You could find yourself liable to pay for them.

If you use the goods as though you owned them, before the stipulated or reasonable time expires, you are likely to be regarded in law as having 'adopted the transaction' – that is, agreed to buy the goods.

A person who pawned jewellery which he had received on approval was held to have adopted the transaction. Even if you simply lend someone a book sent to you on approval, this could be interpreted in the same light.

APPROVED SCHOOL

When children are taken into the care of the local authority

The term approved school is no longer used officially, but local authorities still run residential homes for children who have – for one of a number of reasons – been taken into council care. They are now generally known as Community Homes with Education (CHEs). *See:* CHILDREN IN CARE

ARBITRATION

The informal way to settle a legal dispute

The usual way of settling a civil dispute – for example, a claim over faulty goods or an unpaid debt – is to start court proceedings which will be dealt with by a judge.

A more informal, faster and cheaper way is to refer it to an independent arbitrator – but there is a major disadvantage: the arbitrator's decision is final. If either side later obtains fresh evidence, the case cannot be reopened: there is generally no right of appeal.

The Arbitration Act 1979 allows appeals only on points of law, and even then court permission must be obtained.

Going to an arbitrator may be voluntary – by agreement between the two parties in the dispute – or in some cases compulsory. If the sum involved in a dispute is not more than £200, either side can apply to the county court office,

WHEN THE SMALL PRINT WAS BINDING

When a contract specifies that any dispute must be settled by arbitration it usually allows some flexibility in the choice of an arbitrator; but there is generally no way in which a complainant can otherwise seek damages.

Mr and Mrs Bill Ford were dissatisfied with the service they received on a holiday cruise in the Adriatic and on their return home they tried to sue the travel company involved. They found, however, that the booking form which they had signed included a clause:

'In the event of any dispute . . . the decision of a mutually acceptable independent arbitrator shall be accepted by all parties as final.'

DECISION
The Appeal Court ruled that Mr and Mrs Ford could not sue, but must accept arbitration.

asking for arbitration. Over £200 both sides must agree to arbitration. There are also arbitration schemes run by trade organisations, to deal with complaints by customers.

A customer who claims to have been sold a faulty refrigerator, for example, can seek arbitration if the retailer belongs to the Radio, Electrical and Television Retailers' Association, which has its own arbitration scheme. Most British manufacturers of domestic electric appliances are covered by a special arbitration scheme that deals with complaints about servicing.

Disputes involving electricity boards may be covered by the retail scheme, but the boards generally encourage dissatisfied customers to take complaints to the local consultative council.

When you must accept arbitration

Apart from cases involving no more than £200, where the other party may insist on arbitration, you must accept an arbitrator if you have signed an agreement that includes a clause saying that any dispute will be settled by an independent arbitrator.

For example, if you own the leasehold of a flat, the lease may state that any dispute between you and a tenant is to be settled by arbitration and not by court proceedings. Most insurance policies, too, have a clause making arbitration compulsory if there is a dispute about the amount to be paid.

Where arbitration is compulsory, a claim cannot be dealt with by a court. If you were dissatisfied with an arbitration award, it would be possible technically to appeal against it to a court, but only on the grounds that the arbitrator had applied the law wrongly, or had misused his powers. Any appeal against an arbitrator's decision would be unlikely to succeed, and would generally only increase a claimant's legal costs.

If, when you enter an agreement or buy something, you want to reserve your right to go to court, you can ask to have the arbitration clause struck out before you sign any form or document. That, however, can be done only if the other party agrees, and such consent is unlikely – especially with an insurance policy.

Seeking arbitration through the county court

For anyone with a relatively small claim (over a faulty washing-machine,

for example, or minor damage to a car), arbitration through a county court is particularly useful.

If the claim does not involve more than £200, even the loser in a county court arbitration will not be ordered to pay any part of the costs. That means that someone with a small claim, able therefore to insist on arbitration, can start an action in the county court without fear of having to pay heavy legal costs. Costs may be ordered by the court, however, if the claim was for more than £200.

Before you can ask for arbitration, the normal pre-trial procedures have to be followed. If you are suing someone, you must prepare a detailed claim; if you are being sued you must file your answer to the other person's claim. *See:* HOW TO MAKE A COMPLAINT, p.731.

When these steps have been taken, the county court registrar holds an informal, private, pre-trial meeting in a room at the courthouse and it is then that either side can ask for arbitration instead of trial.

The registrar will normally make an order setting out the rules for the conduct of the arbitration hearing, usually in the form of a 'round the table' discussion, rather than a formal court hearing. Arbitration hearings need not follow the strict rules of what evidence can be

allowed. For example, second-hand EVIDENCE – what a witness was told by someone else – and documents that might not be admitted in a formal court case, may be taken into account.

Choosing the arbitrator

An arbitrator appointed to settle a dispute need not be a qualified lawyer, although he will have qualifications in some relevant profession.

Most contracts that call for arbitration do not name any particular person as arbitrator. Usually they state that if the parties in the dispute cannot agree on a suitable person, the arbitrator will be chosen by the head of a named professional body.

In a county court arbitration, the arbitrator will often be the court registrar whose services are available free. If the parties involved choose someone else, they must pay for any fee involved.

Advice on finding an arbitrator, and on procedures and likely costs, can be obtained from the Institute of Arbitrators.

If the parties still cannot agree, they can apply to the High Court for a nomination, but that is an expensive step, and will probably cancel out the cheapness that is a main advantage of arbitration.

BINDING RULE IN AN AGREEMENT
When you are obliged to settle a dispute without going to law

Arbitration
(6) If any difference shall arise as to the amount to be paid under this Policy (liability being otherwise admitted) such difference shall be referred to an arbitrator to be appointed by the parties in accordance with the statutory provisions in that behalf for the time being in force. Where any difference is by this condition to be referred to arbitration the making of an award shall be a condition precedent to any right of action against the Company

Choice of arbitrator
The Arbitration Acts 1950 and 1970 set out a procedure for deciding who will be the arbitrator. This provision binds both parties

Limiting legal action
The person signing the agreement has no right to press court action against the company until after any claim has been considered.

Limiting the scope
Arbitration may apply only to a dispute about the amount involved. If the company refuses to pay anything the case should go to court

Look in the small print when signing an agreement. If it includes an arbitration clause, similar to the one above, you will not be able to take your case to court in any subsequent dispute – and that may be to your disadvantage, for there is no means of appeal.

ARMED FORCES

The rights of servicemen often differ from those of civilians

Members of the armed forces – including reservists in training and, in some cases, members of Service families – are subject not only to ordinary law but also to military law. Its purpose is to maintain discipline, and the officers who administer it – in all three Services – do so by the authority of Parliament.

How military law works

Most serious offences – whether they would be crimes in civilian life, such as theft, or are purely military offences, such as desertion – can be tried by a COURT MARTIAL. Someone who committed a crime during his service can be tried by court martial even after he has returned to civilian life.

However, if a civilian court has tried a

WHO MAY BE SUBJECT TO MILITARY LAW

In some circumstances, civilians are subject to military law, just as if they were members of the armed forces.

Civilian workers who accompany a forces unit on active service are subject to military law. So are certain civilians on official duty outside the United Kingdom even if not on active service.

Those affected include some civil servants, NAAFI staff, members of their families living abroad with them, and members of any Service family living abroad with the serviceman.

A serviceman's employee – for example, a nanny – is also subject to military law and so are any members of the employee's family who are living abroad with the serviceman if they are British subjects. But if the employee is a national of the country where she is living, she will then be subject to the local civil law.

A visiting relative who does not reside with the serviceman – someone who for example stays with him overnight or merely visits him from time to time – is not subject to military law.

serviceman, he cannot be tried again by his Service for 'substantially' the same offence. For example, a serviceman who steals from a shop while on leave and is dealt with by a civilian court, cannot be tried again for the theft by a court martial.

Usually a serviceman who has committed a crime will be prosecuted by whoever finds him first – the civil police or the military. The two co-operate closely and sometimes the military police will hand over the case to the civilian police even if the military authority made the arrest.

If the serviceman who stole was a deserter or absent without leave, however, he could still be prosecuted by the Service for desertion or his absence.

Serious crimes The most serious offences – murder, treason, manslaughter or rape – cannot be tried by military courts if they are committed in the United Kingdom.

Outside the United Kingdom the Services have power to try all cases against anyone who is subject to military law. But this right is often waived, especially if the local police have made the arrest.

How families are affected

A serviceman's wife and children normally live with him in married quarters, for which he pays rent even if he is sent elsewhere for a while. He can choose to arrange his own accommodation and many servicemen are home-owners.

Medical treatment A serviceman's family in married quarters can have treatment from the unit medical officer, but they are still entitled to register with a National Health Service family doc-

tor. They can, in fact, do both while in the United Kingdom.

Abroad, medical treatment is arranged by the Service, but a Service family can go to a local doctor and pay for private treatment if they want.

Education In the United Kingdom, servicemen's children go to civilian schools. If the family go abroad, the children can attend a school provided by the British Forces Education Service and, if the father's base is not near enough to such a school for the children to go there every day, they can become boarders.

When the children reach secondary-school age, their father is entitled to a special allowance to enable him to send them to boarding school in the United Kingdom. Even if the father is moved back to the United Kingdom from time to time, he is still entitled to the allowance to ensure that the children's education is not disrupted.

Reserve forces

Members of the reserve forces are subject to military law like full-time servicemen when:
● They are in training.
● Have been called out on permanent service.
● Are helping the civil power – for example, the police.

If a serviceman is injured

If a serviceman is injured on duty and is discharged as a result, he is entitled to a disability pension.

Where a superior officer or authority causes damage or injury by abusing or exceeding his powers, the serviceman can obtain damages in the civil courts –

but only if the court is satisfied that the officer or authority was motivated by malice, cruelty or oppression. That restriction means that a serviceman has fewer rights than a civilian in such circumstances.

A serviceman who is injured through the negligence of a fellow-serviceman while on duty cannot sue his comrade or his employer, the Ministry of Defence. Nor can he sue if he is injured by an enemy at a time when the United Kingdom is formally at war. But he can sue a civilian who injures him by an act of terrorism. He cannot sue the Ministry for injuries caused by defects in premises, ship, aircraft, vehicle, equipment or supplies.

The only right he can rely on, in such circumstances, is his right to a disability pension.

Criminal injury A serviceman either on or off duty who is injured by a criminal act – such as by a terrorist bomb – is entitled to seek criminal injuries compensation.

If a serviceman dies

When a member of the forces dies as a result of being injured on duty or from an illness contracted because of his service, his dependants are entitled to a pension.

Dependants are normally a wife and children, not a girl-friend. More than one pension can be paid – for example, to a wife and to a widowed-mother who had been partly supported from a serviceman's pay. The amount depends on the applicant's degree of dependency.

SOCIAL SECURITY FOR THE FORCES

Members of the armed forces pay a reduced rate for Class 1 NATIONAL INSURANCE CONTRIBUTIONS, but they are not eligible for unemployment, sickness or invalidity benefit or non-contributory invalidity pension.

Servicemen are normally entitled to full social security benefits immediately they leave the forces.

If someone is dismissed after a court martial or civilian court case, however, he cannot claim unemployment benefit for the first 6 weeks. But if he is discharged at his own request or if he is invited to resign, he is eligible at once.

Leaving the Service

Full-time servicemen cannot usually leave the forces before they have served the period for which they signed on. However, if they are serving for the first time they can claim a discharge in the early months of service, by paying a £20 fee – or without fee in the case of boys recruited under the age of 17½. Female recruits have a right to free discharge in the first 3 weeks.

SERVICEMEN AND POLITICS

A full-time serviceman is not allowed to become a Member of the House of Commons or the House of Lords. Nor can he campaign for a politician – in or out of uniform.

If a serviceman wants to stand for Parliament, he must apply for a discharge. He is not allowed to run a campaign until the application is approved by a special Home Office committee which has to be satisfied that he is a genuine candidate.

Any serviceman is allowed to vote in parliamentary or local elections by post or by proxy.

Arranging early retirement

Early retirement may be allowed, but only with the consent of the Service. A serviceman who tried to walk out of his job would face trial by his commanding officer, or by court martial. If found guilty a soldier could be imprisoned. An officer could also be imprisoned and would be cashiered, or dismissed.

ARREST

The right of every citizen – but one that must be exercised with care

Every citizen has the right under certain circumstances to make a CITIZEN'S ARREST of another, but if he does so he runs the risk of being sued later for FALSE IMPRISONMENT. Even the POLICE have to have good grounds for detaining someone.

They may obtain a warrant from a magistrate authorising the arrest or in certain circumstances, arrest a person without a warrant.

RESISTING POLICE ARREST

Even someone who knows that he is innocent, and really believes that the POLICE have no grounds for arresting him, should go quietly – until he can be given an opportunity to contact a lawyer.

If he does not, he can be charged with resisting arrest or obstructing a police officer in the execution of his duty and with assaulting a police officer – all of which could result in imprisonment.

The proper place for disputing the correctness of an arrest is at the police station or in court – not at the scene of the arrest. In the rare cases where a victim proves that an arrest was illegal he may be able to sue for FALSE IMPRISONMENT.

When a warrant for arrest is not required

The police do not require a warrant to arrest a person they suspect of committing an offence that carries a penalty of 5 years' imprisonment or more for a first offence.

There are also certain Acts of Parliament which give power to the police to arrest without a warrant – for example, those dealing with PUBLIC ORDER offences such as BREACH OF THE PEACE, OBSTRUCTION or possessing an OFFENSIVE WEAPON.

What happens when a warrant is issued

To obtain a warrant, the police must apply to a magistrate, giving a written statement containing the details of the case and why a warrant is required. The magistrate decides if a warrant will be issued.

If it is issued, the police are entitled to arrest the person named in the warrant at any time of the day or night.

A policeman does not have to have the warrant in his possession when he makes the arrest, but it is usual for him to do so. However, the person being arrested is entitled to see the warrant on request.

If a person believes that the warrant is incorrect or does not refer to him, he may refuse to be arrested. If the warrant does not refer to him but he is arrested, he can sue the police for false imprisonment.

If the person arrested on a warrant is subsequently released without being charged, he has no means of obtaining damages from the police, provided that they have kept him in custody legally and that they did not keep him for an unreasonable time after finding that he was not to be charged.

When the police make an arrest

When a person is arrested he must be told by a policeman the reason why the arrest is being made. If he is not, and is later acquitted, he may sue the police for false imprisonment.

In certain cases – for example, where a person being arrested is struggling violently – it may not be possible for a policeman to tell him why he is being arrested. He must, however, tell the arrested person as soon as possible.

The explanation need be only in general terms and no specific charge need be made. For example, a policeman may say 'I am arresting you for unlawfully killing Mary Smith', but he need not say whether the charge will be murder or manslaughter.

The police are entitled to use reasonable force to arrest a person. They may use handcuffs if they believe a person might escape without them, or if they think the arrested person might try to harm himself or someone else.

If the police use excessive force or use handcuffs for any other reason, they may later be sued for ASSAULT AND BATTERY.

A person who refuses to be arrested or struggles with a policeman may be charged with resisting arrest.

'Helping the police with their inquiries'

A person who has not been arrested may also be asked to go to a police station – usually called in the Press, helping the police with their inquiries. He is entitled to refuse to do so, but if he agrees to go with the policeman, he may leave the police station at any time, provided that he has not been subsequently arrested.

If the police try to stop a person from

leaving or use physical force to stop him from leaving when he has not been arrested, they may be sued for assault and battery or false imprisonment.

What happens at the station

If a person is lawfully arrested, he is taken to a police station where the police may want to put further questions to him. Anyone being questioned is entitled to remain silent. *See:* JUDGES' RULES

The police may search anyone who has been arrested for evidence connected with the suspected crime. They will remove anything with which the

> ### THE LADY WHO LOST HER BRA
>
> *The police have no right or power to take away an arrested person's property unless there is good reason for doing so.*
>
> Janet Lindley, arrested in 1978 in Exeter for disorderly behaviour while drunk, was taken to a police station. She refused to be searched by a policewoman. Despite her violent resistance, the policewoman did search her and remove her brassière. Janet Lindley was charged with assaulting a policewoman in the execution of her duty.
>
> VERDICT
> She was found not guilty. It was irrelevant that the policewoman was under instructions from her superior to remove brassières from women in custody for their own protection.
> The High Court ruled that the removal of the brassière was unlawful because there was no ground for believing that it was necessary to protect Janet Lindley from suffering accidental injury.

suspect can injure himself or others or with which he can cause damage in the police station.

They may also take away any item that may be used to escape or as a weapon. If they think a person may try to take his own life, they may remove items such as his tie, belt and shoelaces.

If the police take away a person's belongings, they:
● List all the items they take.

● Ask the person to check the list.
● Package and seal the property.

The police are entitled to keep any article for use as evidence in court. When a person is released or after his trial, even if he has been convicted, the police must usually return all the items they have taken. If they fail to do so, he can apply to a magistrate to have the items returned.

If a convicted person is committed by the court to prison, all his belongings are transferred there, and he will have them returned only when he is eventually released from prison at the end of his sentence.

Bringing the accused to court

If a person has been arrested, he must be charged with the offence and brought before a magistrate as soon as practicable.

Usually, a suspect is brought before a court within 24 hours of his arrest – or 48 hours if he is arrested at a weekend.

However, under the Prevention of Terrorism Act, the police can detain suspected terrorists for up to 72 hours without taking them before a magistrate.

Anyone who is detained unlawfully or for too long by the police, can ask his solicitor to obtain an order from a High Court judge for HABEAS CORPUS against the police. If the judge is satisfied that the detention is lawful, he will allow it to continue. Otherwise, a person must be released.

If the police have refused to allow someone to see a solicitor, his wife or other relative may approach a solicitor and ask him to obtain a habeas corpus writ.

When the suspect must be charged

Judges' Rules state that as soon as a police officer has evidence that someone has committed an offence, he must warn or caution him in a formal way that the person need not answer any more questions if he does not wish to do so.

If a person is charged with an offence, the duty officer at the police station enters it on the charge sheet or charges book. The charge details the person's name, the offence with which he has been charged and the law that has been broken.

The accused is always given a copy of the charge.

He does not have to say anything, but if he does speak the police note what he says and may use the statement in court.

After a person is charged he should not be questioned further unless:
● His previous answers need to be clarified.
● He is accused of another separate offence.
● The police consider that another person might be harmed or suffer loss if he is not questioned further.

If further questions are put, the accused must be cautioned again – and in the same formal way – that he need not say anything. Again, if he does, it may be taken down in writing.

When an accused can be freed

Once someone has been charged, the police decide whether he will be released on BAIL or kept in custody in the police station until he appears before a magistrate.

Once a person has been charged and either granted or refused bail, he is ready to appear before the local magistrates' court. *See:* CRIMINAL PROCEEDINGS

If he is cleared of the charge by the court, he may be able to claim damages. *See:* MALICIOUS PROSECUTION

ARSON

When treatment may be more necessary than punishment

Arson, which means deliberately setting fire to property, is now treated in law as CRIMINAL DAMAGE.

Fire-raising can lead to a prosecution in either the magistrates' court (maximum penalty, 6 months' imprisonment and £1,000 fine) or in the crown court (maximum penalty, life imprisonment and unlimited fine).

A more serious charge of aggravated arson is brought if the fire endangered someone's life. Aggravated arson can only be tried in the crown court (maximum penalty, life imprisonment and unlimited fine).

In deciding sentence, the courts usually call for medical reports to establish whether the arsonist needs psychiatric treatment.

ARTIFICIAL INSEMINATION

When nature is helped to take its course

A woman can be made pregnant artificially by the injection of a man's semen or by the implanting of a fertilised ovum (egg).

When the husband's semen is used (artificial insemination by husband or AIH) there is no legal problem.

The child has exactly the same status in law as one conceived normally.

If the semen comes from a man other than the woman's husband, however (artificial insemination by donor or AID), the child is illegitimate, although the woman is not held to have committed ADULTERY.

If the husband were to leave the mother before the child was born and then refused to accept it as his own, he could not legally be made to maintain the child.

When the donor can be made to pay

The donor of the semen, on the other hand, could be made responsible for it, but his identity is usually known only to the doctor who carried out the insemination. The mother is rarely, if ever, told his identity because the code of medical ethics dictates that the doctor should not disclose any names.

In practice, doctors make sure that the husband approves the use of AID. They may be reluctant to approve AID for single women.

The child has no normal, family inheritance rights unless it is adopted by the husband.

But as a 'child of the family' – that is a child who has been accepted in a household, like a step-son or step-daughter – it could claim maintenance.

Sometimes a court may be prepared to make an order giving financial provision for such a child out of a dead person's estate.

Registering the birth of an AID child

It is a criminal offence when registering an AID birth to show the mother's husband as the father of the child, although a prosecution would be extremely unlikely.

ASSAULT AND BATTERY

The difference between threats and force

Assault is a threat to use force, and battery is the actual use of force. Brandishing a weapon or a fist at someone is assault without battery, whereas stealing up behind him and striking him without giving any warning is battery without assault. In practice, this distinction is usually not made and the accused is charged with common assault, which covers both crimes.

If someone accused of battery proves that he was acting in self-defence he will be acquitted, but only if he used what is considered to be reasonable force in the circumstances.

He will also be acquitted if he can show that the victim in some way consented. For instance, a man is not guilty of battery if he injures someone who has voluntarily engaged in a boxing match with him.

> *MOTORIST PARKED ON POLICEMAN'S FOOT*
>
> *It is rarely possible for someone to be acquitted of an assault charge simply by claiming that the injury or damage was caused by something he did not do, rather than something he did.*
>
> A police constable asked Mr Fagan to pull his car into the kerb so that he could examine his driving documents. In doing so, Fagan drove a front wheel on to the constable's left foot. The constable repeatedly told Fagan to get off his foot, but Fagan merely turned off the ignition. Fagan was charged with common assault.
>
> Fagan's defence was that his omission to drive off the constable's foot was not the commission of an assault.
>
> DECISION
>
> On appeal, it was held Fagan's conduct after he knew the wheel was on the policeman's foot constituted more than omission.

However, someone who consents to enter hospital to have his left leg amputated and then has the other cut off in error can sue the surgeon for battery – as well as for negligence.

Both assault and battery are also TORTS, which means that a victim can sue for compensation in a civil action if he thinks his assailant has enough money to pay damages or can ask the police to prosecute. The victim cannot, however, instigate a prosecution then sue later.

ASSESSMENT CENTRE

Temporary home for children

Assessment centres are run by local authorities to examine the problems of children who, because of difficulties at home or because they have committed offences or failed to attend school regularly, have been placed in care. *See:* CHILDREN IN CARE

The staff of an assessment centre includes social workers, teachers, psychologists and psychiatrists who study the child and recommend to the court or local authority what should be done for its educational, social and emotional welfare.

Usually the assessment centres are residential, and the child may have to live in one for a short time in the care of the local authority while the case is being examined. In some circumstances – for example, when it is thought better for the child to be with its parents – the child may be required instead to attend the centre daily during assessment.

Certain specialist centres provide facilities for very difficult children and those facing major criminal charges who have been remanded in care by a court. *See:* REMAND

ATTEMPTED CRIME

Failure carries the same penalties as success

The law makes no difference between a person who sets out to commit a crime but fails and one who succeeds. In practice, however, it is often more difficult for the prosecution to prove an attempted crime than a successful one. It has to prove that the accused intended to commit a crime and had a serious try at doing so.

The court normally needs to be satisfied that there is no other reasonable explanation of the accused person's behaviour.

ATTENDANCE ALLOWANCE

Financial help for the severely disabled

An attendance allowance is a weekly tax-free payment to people who have been severely disabled, physically or mentally, for at least 6 months and who need a lot of looking after, at home or in private institutions. It is paid by the Department of Health and Social Security.

HOW A DISABLED PERSON QUALIFIES

To qualify for the weekly tax-free attendance allowance paid by the Department of Health and Social Security, an invalid must have been so severely disabled, physically or mentally for at least 6 months, as to need:
● Continual supervision by day or by night to avoid danger to himself or herself or to others.
● Frequent attention by day to help with bodily functions.
● Prolonged or repeated attention by night to help with bodily functions.
● Must have been suffering from the disability for at least 6 months.
Spells of treatment for the disability as a hospital in-patient count towards the 6 month qualifying period, but payment of the allowance will stop after the first 4 weeks if the disabled person enters a hospital under the National Health Service or a local authority home.
● Must be over the age of 2.
● Must live in the United Kingdom, be present here and must have been for at least 26 weeks out of the previous 12 months.
● Must, if under 16, require considerably more attention than that normally given to a child of the same age and sex.

Qualifications for the benefit are assessed by the Attendance Allowance Board, comprising mainly doctors, and every applicant must be examined –

usually at home – by a doctor nominated by the board. The claimant does not need to have paid national insurance contributions, nor does he or she have to prove that attendance is actually being provided. To show that it is required is enough to qualify.

There are two rates of allowance. The lower one (£14.45 a week in 1981) is paid to those who need attention or supervision only by day or only by night. There are higher rates (£21.65 a week in 1981) for those requiring round-the-clock attention.

If both a daytime and a night-time condition are met, the higher allowance is given.

How to claim

To claim the benefit, complete form NI205 'Attendance Allowance', obtainable from any office of the Department of Health and Social Security.

A disabled adult should complete the form if he or she is able. Otherwise, someone else can do it. The mother should generally make the claim for a child who is still under 16.

If the disabled person has met the medical requirements for 6 months or more, the claim should be made immediately. The allowance cannot be backdated.

If the disabled person meets the medical requirements, but has not done so for 6 months, the claim should be submitted after 4 months of disability. That allows time for the medical report to be made and a decision reached before the end of the qualifying period.

A claim for a child should not be made before he or she is 22 months old.

The examining doctor will submit his report to another Board doctor, who takes the final decision.

How to appeal

If an applicant is dissatisfied, either because he has been rejected for the allowance or because only the lower rate has been granted, he is allowed 3 months in which to ask for a review. An applicant can ask his doctor to submit a report, and written evidence from relatives can also be sent.

If that is unsuccessful, an appeal can sometimes be made to the National Insurance Commissioner on a form obtainable from offices of the Department of Health and Social Security.

How payment is made

The allowance is normally made payable to the claimant unless he or she cannot manage his or her own affairs, when it is paid to the person legally responsible for administering them. In the case of a child, the benefit is paid to the mother, father or the person with whom the child is living.

Payment is by books of orders which can be cashed at a named post office.

AU PAIR

When a foreign girl joins a British family

A girl from abroad who wants to come to Britain for a limited period can stay for up to 2 years, living with a family as an 'au pair'. She does not need a work permit, provided that the immigration officer at her port of arrival or the Home Office approves the arrangement. Since November 1979 this arrangement has been available only for girls who come from Western European countries, Malta, Cyprus and Turkey.

If she is from an EEC country, she is not subject to the 2 year limit, as EEC nationals are guaranteed the complete right to live and work in Britain. *See:* EUROPEAN COMMUNITIES

An au pair must be between 17 and 27 years old and must be unmarried. The Home Office has sometimes objected even to an au pair who has been married in the past. There is no official au pair arrangement for boys.

She is not a domestic servant, but a temporary member of the host family (which must be English-speaking). A domestic servant would have to have a work permit (unless she was an EEC national).

The au pair is expected to do some of the housework and/or help with the children in return for her keep and pocket money. The Home Office recommends that she should not be asked to do more than 5 hours' work a day. She should be able to enter into family life, have a room of her own and have time for her own recreation, study and any religious observance.

To find an au pair, contact a specialist agency, listed in the Yellow Pages section of local telephone directories.

It is advisable to settle in writing details of duties, pocket money, time off and travel expenses to and from her own country before she arrives.

Immigration formalities An au pair should not need a VISA or other entry clearance to enter the UK, unless she is a national of a country whose citizens need visas to enter the UK for any purpose. Normally an immigration officer will want to see only a letter from the host family inviting her.

If she is coming to the United Kingdom from Turkey or Cyprus, however, it might be wise for her to apply for an entry clearance before travelling, and for the host family to meet her at the airport.

The immigration officer should admit the au pair for 12 months, and he will stamp the time limit on her passport, together with a notice forbidding her to take employment within the UK.

An au pair has no claim to remain here when her 2 years expire and she will not be allowed to transfer to another job, unless she is a citizen of an EEC country.

An au pair who has been here before on an au pair basis will have the earlier period taken into account in calculating the 2 years she is allowed here. Someone who is already in Britain – for example – as a student – and who wants to stay on as an au pair, must apply to the Home Office, either in person or by writing. The same procedure applies when the first 12 months' leave expires.

The application must be made and received by the Home Office before the leave stamped in her passport runs out, otherwise she commits a criminal offence by remaining, and has no right of appeal if the Home Office refuses her application.

In that case the notice refusing her application is served on her by the local police, who notify her that she will be prosecuted for over-staying her leave if she does not go within 14 days.

Otherwise, if the application was made in time, and they do refuse, she does have a right of appeal to an adjudicator. *See:* IMMIGRATION

National insurance contributions

An au pair is not required to pay national insurance contributions, provided that her income in Britain is not above the lower earnings limit for such contributions – £27 a week in 1981–2. The value of an au pair's keep is not taken into account.

However, girls from countries which have social security agreements with Britain and who are paying contributions in their own countries may benefit by continuing to pay while in Britain.

When the arrangements breaks down

If an au pair falls out with her host family, the Home Office will allow her to be an au pair with another family, but not to take a regular job.

AUCTION

Practices and pitfalls of the salerooms

Sales at an auction are binding only when the auctioneer brings his hammer down. Until that point the bidder can withdraw his bid and the auctioneer can withdraw the lot.

Goods up for auction are usually subject to a reserve price, below which the owner will not sell, but it is not revealed to the public. If the reserve price is not reached, the seller has the right to withdraw the goods from sale – even if the auctioneer has mistakenly brought down the hammer on a bid below the reserve price. Some auctions are advertised as being without reserve, which means that the bidders are assured of being able to buy everything on offer, however low the highest bid.

It is theoretically possible for a seller to bid for his own goods (perhaps through an agent) and so force up the price. But if he intends to do so, any notice advertising the auction must state that this is being done. Such a notice would usually drive away potential buyers and the tactic would therefore be self-defeating.

When auctions are illegal

If a seller does bid at an auction without informing the genuine buyers, any sales that are made are not legally binding. The buyers are entitled to return the goods and to have their money refunded in full.

Auction rings One fraudulent practice, which affects the seller, not the buyer, is that operated by a ring or group of dealers who agree that only one of their number will bid. By eliminating any competitive bidding, they can buy the goods for less than their worth and auction them privately among themselves later.

Rings are illegal, but prosecutions are rare because it is difficult to obtain proof of their operations.

Mock auctions Auctions that attract customers by pretending falsely that all the goods are on offer at extremely low prices or are even being given away were made illegal by the Mock Auctions Act 1961. The maximum fine is £1,000.

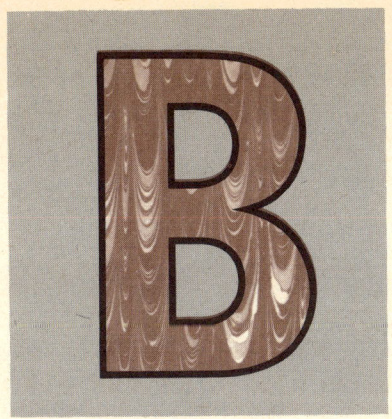

BAIL

Freedom between arrest and trial

When someone has been arrested and charged with an offence, he may be allowed by the police or magistrates to go free on condition that he reports to court or the police station at a fixed date and time. If he fails to do so, he can be arrested without warrant for the separate offence of absconding. The maximum penalties are 3 months' imprisonment and a £400 fine in the magistrates' court, and 12 months' imprisonment and an unlimited fine in the crown court.

If a person has been arrested on a warrant, the police cannot grant bail unless the warrant specifically allows them to do so.

The police are entitled, however, to grant bail at their own discretion if a person has been arrested without a warrant. They are unlikely to do so if a person is charged with a serious offence or has a history of breaking bail.

The decision to grant bail must be taken by the officer in charge of the station to which the arrested person has been taken.

A child under 14 must be granted bail unless he is suspected of murder or manslaughter. A person aged between 14 and 17, arrested for anything other than murder or manslaughter, must also be granted bail unless the senior police officer considers it would be in the young person's interest to remain in custody or a serious crime is involved.

If the police do not grant bail, the accused should ask for it when he appears before the magistrates for the first time – unless he is acquitted on that first hearing.

If the offence is not imprisonable, the magistrates must grant the accused bail unless he has previously absconded and in their view is likely to do so again.

If the offence is imprisonable the accused person is always granted bail unless the magistrates have reason to believe that he will abscond, commit an offence or interfere with witnesses.

Magistrates sometimes grant bail on certain special conditions: for example, that the accused reports to the police station at stated intervals or surrenders his passport or deposits cash or other assets as security.

When bail is refused

When magistrates reject a bail application, they must give the accused their reasons. He can then choose from three courses of action:
● To wait 8 days for his next appearance before the magistrates and reapply – by that time he may have secured, for example, sureties who are more acceptable to the court;
● To apply for bail to the crown court, if his case has been committed there for trial by jury;
● To appeal against the magistrates refusal of bail to a High Court judge.

Appealing against refusal

If a defendant intends to appeal against a magistrates' decision, or against the conditions imposed on his bail, he must obtain an appeal form from the magistrates immediately.

He cannot submit the appeal himself – or even attend the hearing – but must engage a solicitor to argue the case before a judge 'in chambers', in his private rooms. A decision is obtained quickly, often on the day the appeal is lodged.

No legal aid, however, is available for such appeals and the defendant or his family will have to meet the legal costs – perhaps as much as £200. If he does not want – or cannot afford – a solicitor, he can ask the Official Solicitor, an official of the High Court, to present the appeal.

The Official Solicitor, however, cannot argue the case in person. He is allowed only to submit documents to the judge, and the application procedure takes a long time.

Applying for bail after conviction

After being convicted in a magistrates' court, a defendant can apply for bail if there is to be a delay before sentence is passed – for example, when the magistrates ask for a medical report, or when they commit the case to a crown court for a heavier sentence. He can also apply if he is lodging an appeal against sentence.

The grounds on which magistrates grant bail after conviction are the same as those that apply before trial.

WHEN AN ACCUSED PERSON
ASKS FOR BAIL

If you are asked to stand surety for an accused person seeking bail, do not do so lightly. Bear in mind that the accused could abscond and you may have to forfeit the surety money.

WHEN THE MAGISTRATES REFUSE BAIL ON A FIRST APPEARANCE

How an accused may regain his freedom – pending trial – by engaging a solicitor to apply to a judge in chambers

Magistrate Chairman Magistrate

Prosecuting solicitor

Accused's solicitor

Accused making bail application

Clerks

Press box

Probation officers

1 When an accused person first appears – within 48 hours of his arrest – before the local magistrates, he is entitled to ask for bail if the case is not to be heard immediately. If the offence is not imprisonable, the magistrates must grant bail unless the accused has previously absconded and is considered likely to do so again. If he breaks any conditions of his bail, or if he does not present himself for trial, he and any other people who have stood surety for him must forfeit their money.

2 If the magistrates refuse bail, because they think the accused is likely to abscond, commit further offences or interfere with witnesses, he can be held for 8 days in a prison or remand centre before he has to be brought again before a court. In that time he can ask the prison authorities to allow him to consult a solicitor to decide whether to reapply for bail or try to find new sureties who may be more acceptable to the magistrates. If he is to reapply for bail, the solicitor will be able to tell him whether legal aid is available to pay his costs.

3 If the solicitor feels that the accused has a good case, he may advise him to appeal to a High Court judge against the magistrates' original refusal of bail – without waiting 8 days. Legal aid is not available for an appeal, which is made by the solicitor to whichever judge is on duty in the privacy of his chambers.

4 If the accused is freed, he must observe all the bail conditions – or face a £400 fine and 3 months' imprisonment, as well as forfeiting any surety offered.

Magistrates usually grant bail only on condition that the accused provides sureties – people who undertake to pay a certain sum if the accused fails to turn up for trial. The magistrates decide whether the sureties have the financial resources and character to be acceptable. If they are found unacceptable, the accused can try to find others who are acceptable and is detained until he does so.

When the accused intends to apply for bail which he knows will be dependent on sureties, he should arrange to have the sureties present in court so that the magistrates are more likely to decide on bail there and then.

Anyone asked to act as a surety should not do so lightly but should bear in mind the possibility of the accused absconding and of the surety money being forfeited as a result. If you have stood as surety and fear that the accused will abscond, you can cancel your surety by informing the court.

BAILIFF

How county courts can enforce their orders

County courts employ bailiffs to enforce their judgments and deliver notices, summonses and other documents. Most bailiffs are officers of the courts, but private companies of certificated bailiffs, who have more limited powers, are also used to seize goods or collect arrears of rent, rates or taxes.

A bailiff's powers vary in different circumstances but, in general, he or she must be careful not to exceed the order of the court and must execute the order in a way that is reasonable in the circumstances. For example, it might be considered reasonable to evict a troublesome male squatter at 3 a.m., but the court would probably think that its bailiff was unreasonable in throwing a family with children into the streets at such an hour.

When a bailiff calls

If a bailiff calls at your home, first ask for proof of identity, noting particularly whether he or she is a court officer or a certificated bailiff. Then ask to see the court order and read the terms carefully.

BAILIFFS' POWERS OF ENTRY INTO A PRIVATE HOME
When a court allows outsiders to enter your property to seize your possessions or evict you

	Grounds	Time	Document required	If you refuse permission
County court officers (bailiffs)	1. To carry out court orders to seize goods that may be sold to raise money to pay creditors	Day or night, but not on Sunday	Judgment summons, court order or warrant of execution against goods, otherwise known as a distress warrant	Officers cannot break in, but they may enter through unlocked doors or windows which are partly open
	2. To carry out court orders to seize particular goods – hire-purchase property, papers needed in a trial, for example	Day or night, but not on Sunday	Warrant for delivery	Officers can use any force necessary to enter premises and carry off goods or documents
	3. To evict a tenant	Reasonable hours	Warrant for possession	Officers can use any force necessary to secure an eviction
	4. To seize anyone charged with contempt of court	Day or night	Court order	Officers may use any force necessary
	5. To take possession of premises – from, say, squatters	Day or night	Court order	Officers may use any force necessary. The maximum penalty for resisting is 6 months' imprisonment and a £1,000 fine
Certificated bailiffs	To carry out court orders to seize goods and subsequently sell them to pay rent or taxes	Between sunrise and sunset, but not on Sunday	Distress warrant issued for arrears of rent, rates or tax	Certificated bailiffs can enter an open building without permission, but can force entry only if the occupier has allowed them to enter on a previous occasion. They can lawfully, however, push open a closed, but unfastened, door; climb through an open window or skylight. Once inside the building, force can be used on an inner door or on the lock of a lodger's apartment.

If you know nothing of the court proceedings that led to the order being made, ask the bailiff to postpone execution for 48 hours so that you can instruct a solicitor to apply to the court to have the order revoked. The bailiff does not have to agree to the delay, but usually will.

If everything seems to be in order, however, co-operate with the bailiff within the terms of the order and offer no resistance. If a householder does resist, or threaten resistance, the bailiff can ask the police to help to execute the order, and help will normally be given on the ground that a breach of the peace is likely to occur. Moreover, a court can commit anyone who does resist its bailiff to prison for CONTEMPT OF COURT. A trespasser, for example a squatter, who resists or obstructs a bailiff in the execution of a court order commits an offence under the Criminal Law Act 1977. *See:* SQUATTER

If the order is for the removal of goods, take an inventory of the goods removed and try to arrange for an independent witness to see what is taken. Make a note of any damage caused during the removal.

Goods that cannot be removed

There are certain goods that the bailiff cannot remove: essential clothing for the debtor or his family; their beds; the debtor's tools of trade, up to a value of about £100; and goods belonging to someone else.

If the bailiff is told that things in the house belong to the debtor's wife or to some other member of the family, or that goods are still subject to a hire-purchase agreement and are therefore the property of the finance company he or she will not usually risk seizing them. If he makes a mistake and takes the wrong goods, the owner can bring an action against him for their return and for damages. *See:* DISTRESS WARRANT

BANK ACCOUNT, Joint

Sharing the management of money

Any two people can open a joint bank account, on which each may draw cheques. It is commonly used by married couples as a simple way of pooling their income and allowing either to pay household bills. But neither husband nor wife can insist on such an arrangement. Each is entitled by law to sole ownership of his or her property.

WHEN MORE THAN ONE SIGNATORY IS NOT NEEDED

A joint bank account, which depends on mutual trust, is commonly used by married couples so that either can easily write cheques to pay the bills.

A joint account depends on mutual trust. In the case of business partners, for example, one could draw out large sums without the other's knowledge, and both would be equally liable to pay off any overdraft. Either party in any joint bank account can sue the other for any loss.

If a husband or wife dies or becomes bankrupt, or if the marriage ends in divorce or separation, a court will usually regard the balance of any joint account as held in equal shares, whatever the individual contributions might have been. However there may be evidence of a contrary intention – letters between the two people, or specific instructions to the bank – indicating how the account is to be shared.

BANK LOAN

Borrowing money in the High Street

Ordinary High Street banks lend money to individual customers in three main ways: by overdraft, personal loan or bridging loan (for a property transaction).

Arranging an overdraft

A bank overdraft is an arrangement by which the customer is allowed to draw more money than he has in his current account – up to an agreed limit.

The bank manager may set a date by which the overdraft is to be cleared. But the bank is also entitled to call in the overdraft at any time, without notice.

If the overdraft is large, the bank may require some type of security – for example, the deposit of share certificates, or national savings or unit trust certificates.

Interest charged will be higher than for a personal loan, and an individual cannot normally claim overdraft interest as an expense against income tax. *See:* INCOME TAX ALLOWANCES

An overdraft, under the Consumer Credit Act, is running-account credit. Even when the loan limit has been reached, the customer by reducing his debt – for example, by paying in a salary cheque – can restore the state of his account and resume borrowing, up to the agreed limit.

A bank overdraft is normally arranged by word of mouth and does not require the special documents called for in other types of CONSUMER CREDIT agreement.

Since it is a debtor-creditor agreement, in which the lender has no business arrangement with any supplier, the bank is not liable for the quality of goods or services bought with the money borrowed.

However, an overdraft is still subject to some of the Consumer Credit Act rules for making and ending a credit agreement.

Going over the limit

If an overdraft limit set by the bank manager exceeds £5,000, the overdraft will not normally be covered by the Consumer Credit Act. However, if the overdraft was not expected to exceed £5,000 – or if it goes over that figure only temporarily – the arrangement is covered by the Act.

That situation could arise, for example, if you draw a cheque that takes you over the limit and the bank – to protect your reputation of being credit-worthy – decides to honour the cheque on condition that you take prompt steps to reduce your debt.

If you exceed the limit of an overdraft without permission, the bank is entitled to refuse to honour the cheque and also to suspend your overdraft without notice – although normally the bank manager will write or telephone, telling you of his action.

The bank is also entitled to demand full repayment of an overdraft loan, without notice, so long as the demand complies with the terms of the agreement – for example, if the time limit has run out.

As a last resort, the bank can sue for the money, but will be subject to the controls of the Consumer Credit Act.

Arranging a personal loan

Another way of borrowing from the bank is by personal loan – a fixed sum, borrowed over a fixed period and usually cleared by regular payments from a current account to cover the amount borrowed plus a proportion of the interest.

A personal loan is arranged with more formality than an overdraft: you are normally required to sign an agreement. The loan, unlike an overdraft, cannot be suddenly called in at any time.

If the loan is taken out for certain purposes, the interest is tax-deductible. **When you can save tax** Interest on a loan to an individual is tax-deductible if the loan is to be used to buy or improve property or land that is or will be your main residence, or occupied by a dependent relative (or separated spouse), or let to someone else.

Tax relief can also be claimed if the loan is to buy a life annuity, pay capital transfer tax, acquire an interest in a partnership or buy plant or machinery to be used in a partnership or employment.

Provided that your personal loan does not exceed £5,000 you are protected by the Consumer Credit Act. *See:* CREDIT AGREEMENT

Arranging a bridging loan

If you are buying a house or other property and need to raise most of the price by a MORTGAGE, you may need to complete the deal before the mortgage lender is ready to hand over the money. In that case, you may raise a bridging loan, to avoid the risk of losing the property to a rival bidder.

A bridging loan is usually provided by a bank – probably for 3 to 6 months – to tide you over the delay.

You may also need a bridging loan if you are buying a house and selling another and need to pay for the new house before the other one is sold.

Provided that a bridging loan does not exceed £5,000, it is covered by the protection of the Consumer Credit Act. For example, the county court can be asked to grant relief if you are in difficulty in repaying.

Because of the need to avoid delay in many property transactions, however, there is no need for an unsigned advance copy of the loan agreement to be sent to you – as normally required for loans not exceeding £5,000 secured on property for purposes other than house purchase or improvement.

With a bridging loan, there is also no cooling-off period in which you may cancel the agreement. But the bank cannot suddenly call in a bridging loan, unless the borrower defaults. *See also:* INTEREST CHARGE

BANK REFERENCE

When a bank may give information about clients

Banks are generally obliged to keep details of their customers' accounts secret, but when a customer gives the name of his bank as a reference, he voluntarily lifts that condition of secrecy.

In giving a reference, the bank will not reveal the details of a customer's financial affairs, but it will make general comments – 'without responsibility'. That means that a customer who is unhappy over a reference or someone who thinks he has been misled by a reference has little chance of redress.

It may now be possible to persuade a court that the condition 'without responsibility' is not permissible under the Unfair Contract Terms Act 1977, but until a definitive ruling is given, it has to be assumed that the pre-1977 law stands.

If you are seeking a bank reference about someone, ask first for written permission to obtain it and for the name and address of the bank concerned. Then ask your own bank to secure the reference on your behalf: most banks will not provide references to individual inquirers.

The bank's reply may be informative, such as: 'respectable, and considered good for your figures'. It may be non-committal: 'we believe he would not undertake any commitment he was unable to fulfil'. If the reply is: 'the sum quoted is larger than we are accustomed to see', or 'we cannot speak for your figures', be warned. *See also:* REFERENCE

BANKRUPTCY

What happens if someone cannot meet his debts

If someone cannot or will not pay his debts, the people to whom he owes money – provided his debts total more than £200 – can ask the courts to declare him bankrupt, so that any assets he possesses can be used to pay some or all of what he owes.

The debtor can ask for his own bankruptcy: that course may sometimes be advisable for someone whose debts exceed the total value of his property, and who has no hope of paying.

Only an individual or a partnership can be made bankrupt. For a limited company, the equivalent is winding up.

How proceedings begin

To start bankruptcy proceedings, the creditor or debtor must present a bankruptcy petition to the county court (in London, the High Court). Whoever petitions must put down a £90 deposit against legal costs.

A debtor cannot be made bankrupt unless he commits an 'act of bankruptcy'.

Acts of bankruptcy are regarded as warning signs that the debtor cannot pay. It is an act of bankruptcy, for example, for someone to petition for himself to be made bankrupt. Other such acts include:
● Failing to comply with a bankruptcy notice issued by the courts.
● Giving away or transferring property to someone else, to thwart creditors, or putting it into the hands of a trustee who will then deal with the debts.
● Telling creditors that a debt will not be met.
● Leaving Britain, or leaving home, to delay payment.
Bankruptcy notice issued A majority of bankruptcy petitions are presented because the debtor fails to comply with

a bankruptcy notice issued by a county court or the High Court.

Such a notice can be issued only at the request of a creditor who has already obtained a court order for payment of a debt, and has not been paid.

The notice, which must be served on the debtor in person, within a month of being issued, warns him that unless he settles the debt within 10 days of being served with the notice, the creditor may start bankruptcy proceedings.

Presenting the petition

A bankruptcy petition must be presented to the county court or High Court office within 3 months of the act of bankruptcy.

The court registrar can appoint an Official Receiver – a government official – to take temporary charge of the debtor's property so that it cannot be sold, and may also put a temporary bar on any legal proceedings which have been started against the debtor or his property.

The petition is heard by the registrar not less than 8 days after it has been personally served on the debtor – unless in the meantime the debtor has declared that he cannot pay, or has absconded.

The debtor can oppose a petition either on the ground that he has a counter-claim big enough to offset the debt or on the ground that the petition contains wrong statements.

If he has a counter-claim, he must apply to the court within 3 days of being served with the petition, to have the petition set aside. The application is made on a form obtainable from the court office, and must be accompanied by a sworn statement giving details of the counter-claim.

If the debtor disputes statements in the petition, he must give the registrar written notice, setting out the statements to which he objects. Copies must be sent to the petitioning creditor or creditors not less than 3 days before the petition is due to be heard.

At the hearing

The petition is heard by the registrar, in private. Only the debtor, creditors, legal advisers and witnesses can attend.

The creditor presenting the petition must produce his own sworn statement that he is still owed the money. He must also prove that the debtor lives or works in the area covered by that court, that the sum owed is not less than £200, after allowing for the value of any security that he holds; that the petition has been served and that the act of bankruptcy mentioned in it has been committed.

If the registrar decides that the petition is in order, he will make a receiving order, putting the Official Receiver in charge of the debtor's property.

A receiving order does not make the debtor a bankrupt, but it prevents him from dealing in his own property. He must also give the Official Receiver a statement of his financial affairs, listing all debts and assets. If he fails to do so, he is guilty of CONTEMPT OF COURT.

Meeting of creditors

A 'first meeting of creditors' must be held within 14 days after the receiving order is made. The Official Receiver advertises the time and place in the official London Gazette and a local paper, giving 6 clear days' notice.

Creditors named in the statement of affairs are also informed direct and supplied with a summary of the statement of affairs.

The debtor must attend the meeting, and must be given 3 days' notice.

At the meeting, the Official Receiver, or his nominee, acts as chairman. The purpose of the meeting is to decide whether the debtor should be made bankrupt, or whether any scheme he has for meeting his debts should be accepted.

If the creditors insist on bankruptcy, the petition goes to the court, to be dealt with by the registrar. He may simply adjudge the debtor bankrupt, or may instead order a public examination in bankruptcy.

Public examination

If a public examination is ordered, the debtor must give evidence on oath about his finances. He can be questioned by the Official Receiver, the creditors and the registrar.

A debtor undergoing public examination, unlike a defendant or witness in any other type of court proceedings, cannot refuse to answer questions even if the replies may show that he has committed a criminal offence.

If a debtor fails to appear for his public examination, without reasonable excuse, the court can issue a warrant for his arrest.

At the end of the public examination, the registrar can adjudge the debtor bankrupt.

If he does so, he will appoint a trustee – normally the Official Receiver – to investigate and settle creditors' claims.

The trustee seizes all the bankrupt's property (except for tools of his trade, clothes and bedding worth a maximum of £250) and sells it.

Priority is given to claims for income tax, rates, national insurance contributions and – if the bankrupt was an employer – unpaid wages of employees.

The remaining creditors share what is left, in proportion to the size of their claims. The payment is called a dividend and is expressed as a number of pence in the pound. If the dividend is 10p in the pound, a creditor owed £1,000 will get £100.

What it means to be bankrupt

Once someone is adjudged bankrupt, any financial claims against him come to

---

WHAT HAPPENS TO DEPOSITS

When a company or individual goes into liquidation, or is adjudicated bankrupt, after a payment has been made in advance for goods or services, the general rule is that the customer is merely an unsecured creditor. He may lose the whole of his deposit or receive only a small amount back.

That general rule does not apply, however, where the deposit is held in TRUST by the trader. The trust may be created by the trader – for example, if all deposits are held in a separate bank account – or the trust may be imposed by the customer if he stipulates at the time of paying his deposit that it is to be held in trust until his order is completed.

Where a trust can be proved, the customer has his deposit returned in full – provided only that the deposit is still held by the trader at the date of liquidation or bankruptcy and has not been spent.

The Newspaper Publishers' Association operates a voluntary scheme to reimburse readers' deposits lost through answering mail order advertisements carried in its newspapers, where the mail order advertiser is made bankrupt.

HOW THE STATE COMPENSATES EMPLOYEES

Even if an employee is a preferential creditor, there is no guarantee that his debt will be paid in full. Winding-up or liquidation take several months, so in any case he will have to wait for his money.

In many cases, however, the Department of Employment takes over the employer's debt and then tries to recoup it from the bankrupt firm's assets. Any money not paid by the Department of Employment can be claimed from the employer through the liquidator or receiver.

Not all employees are eligible for the scheme. Part-timers and outworkers, for example, are excluded. *See:* EMPLOYMENT PROTECTION

The debts that can be claimed from the state by eligible employees are:

1. Back wages for up to 8 weeks at a maximum of £120 a week. 'Wages' include: guarantee payments; payments during medical suspension; pay for time off on union duties or while seeking work under redundancy notice; and protective awards.

2. Wages in lieu of notice up to a maximum of £120 a week for 12 weeks. The Department calculates the notice entitlement on the statutory minimum. If the employment contract provided for more than the statutory notice period, it is ignored. *See:* NOTICE

If the employee received some pay during the notice period, or claimed unemployment benefit, the amount is deducted from his entitlement.

3. Holiday pay earned but not paid, up to a maximum of 6 weeks' money and £120 a week.

4. Any basic award for unfair dismissal ordered against the employer by an industrial tribunal and not paid. *See:* UNFAIR DISMISSAL

5. Any payment due for redundancy as a result of the firm's bankruptcy.

6. Pension contributions unpaid by the employer.

How to apply

Any employee who wants to claim under the Department of Employment scheme should ask the liquidator or receiver for an application form – form IT1.

Once the form has been completed, the employer's representative calculates the entitlement and prepares a claim. The employee must agree and sign it. The employer's representative then forwards it to the Department.

If the claim includes wages in lieu of notice, a supplementary application form – form IT2 – must be completed. That, too, can be obtained from the receiver or equivalent, and is processed and forwarded by him. A claim for payment in lieu of notice cannot be submitted until the notice period has expired.

If there is no receiver or liquidator

If no employer's representative has been appointed to look after the affairs of the bankruptcy or liquidation, an employee should claim direct to his local Department of Employment.

How payment is made

Once a claim has been submitted to the Department of Employment, it is reviewed and, if it is approved, the money is sent direct to the employee.

The process normally does not take longer than 6 months. If no payment or notification has been received after 6 months, the employee should write to the Department of Employment.

When a claim is reduced or refused

The Department of Employment may reject a claim or reduce the amount – for example, by refusing to take overtime into account when calculating payment in lieu of notice. If the employee disagrees with the Department's action, he can appeal to an industrial tribunal. The appeal must be lodged within 3 months of receiving notification from the Department of its decision on the claim. *See:* INDUSTRIAL TRIBUNAL

---

an end. Anyone with a claim must present it to the Official Receiver.

The disadvantages for a bankrupt are that he is forbidden to obtain credit of more than £50 – or trade under a different name from the one in which he was bankrupted – without disclosing that he is an undischarged bankrupt.

He is also forbidden to act as a company director without the court's consent, or to be a practising solicitor, Member of Parliament or magistrate.

At the end of a public examination (or if no examination is ordered) the court can make an order discharging a bankruptcy automatically after 5 years.

A bankrupt can apply to the court for a discharge at any time, whether or not such an order has been made. If such an order has not been made, the Official Receiver must apply for a discharge, on the bankrupt's behalf, after 5 years.

When an employer goes bankrupt

If an employer goes bankrupt – or, in the case of a limited company, into liquidation – some of his debts to employees are treated as preferential claims, to be paid in full from his assets before claims by ordinary creditors are met.

The bankruptcy laws recognise three types of preferential claims from employees:

1. Back wages. Unpaid wages for up to 4 months before the winding-up started, or the receiving order was made, are preferential debts, up to a limit of £800. Any amount above that figure becomes an ordinary debt.

'Wages' include: guarantee payments if the worker is laid off or on short time; payments during suspension for medical reasons; pay due for time off while carrying out trade union duties, or while looking for work when under REDUNDANCY notice; and protective awards – for example, for redundancy.

2. Unpaid holiday pay – for example, if 5 weeks' holiday is owed, 5 weeks' wages can be claimed.

3. Pension contributions due to have been paid by the employer during the 4 months before the winding-up started or the receiving order was made.

How to get the money The official receiver or liquidator administering the bankruptcy draws up the lists of preferential and ordinary debts, and determines what is due to whom. An employee with a claim against a bankrupt employer should contact the liquidator or receiver and give details of his claim. Alternatively, he could apply direct to the Department of Employment – a possibly more profitable procedure.

BARRISTER

A specialist in pleading cases in any court

Barristers form the senior branch of the legal profession. Solicitors make up the other main branch; they spend much of their time in day-to-day legal business and can represent clients only in the lower courts. Barristers give specialist opinion and advice on complicated issues and can plead cases in any court.

Unlike a solicitor, a barrister wears a wig (except in a magistrates' court) and is referred to as counsel. There are 4,000 practising barristers in Britain, and together they make up what is known as the Bar.

How to obtain the services of a barrister

If you know that you will be requiring counsel in a court case, you must first approach a solicitor, because only a solicitor can engage a barrister. Even if you have a particular barrister in mind, you cannot contact him directly. And, later, if you want to discuss a matter with him – which always means going to his chambers – you can do so only if accompanied by your solicitor.

When you have presented your case to the solicitor, he will decide whether to instruct the barrister to accept your case or to ask him for his professional advice about it first. In either case, after you have paid him the barrister's fee on account, the solicitor will send the barrister a typewritten summary of the case and copies of any relevant documents – all of which is known as a 'brief'.

Any barrister instructed by the solicitor to take the case is almost bound to

SPECIALISTS OF THE
LEGAL PROFESSION

When a solicitor presents a barrister with a brief that falls within his specialisation, Bar etiquette requires the barrister to accept it if he is available and the fee is reasonable.

accept, because the Bar's etiquette requires him to take on any brief that falls within his field of specialisation, subject to agreement on a reasonable fee and, of course, the barrister's availability.

Queen's Counsel If the barrister is a Queen's Counsel (a senior barrister who has 'taken silk' – that is, who wears a silk gown instead of the ordinary, cotton type), he charges higher fees and normally appears in court only if a junior (an ordinary barrister) assists him. The client has to pay the junior's as well as the Q.C.'s fees.

Paying a barrister

A barrister becomes entitled to his fee as soon as he receives the brief from the solicitor. Neither the solicitor nor his client can discuss the barrister's fee with him personally; all negotiations must be conducted through the barrister's clerk, who receives a percentage, often 10 per cent, of the fee.

Once the solicitor has negotiated the fee and the brief has been delivered to the barrister, the solicitor is professionally obliged to pay the barrister.

The barrister's fee covers only his first 5 hours in court – basically, one day's work. If the case lasts more than a day, the barrister will claim a further daily fee, known as a refresher.

In practice, many civil cases are settled before the hearing at the door of the court, when the parties and their witnesses assemble. If that happens, the barrister retains the full day's fee. If the case is settled long before the date of the hearing, and the barrister has had the brief delivered to his chambers, but has not yet looked at it, he is still entitled to charge his full fee.

A barrister can be sued only for any negligent or bad advice he gives before a hearing. He cannot be sued for a bad performance in court.

BATTERED WIFE

Getting protection against violence at home

A woman who has been assaulted by her husband or by a man with whom she is living can ask the police to prosecute him. She may also apply to a COUNTY COURT or to the High Court for an INJUNCTION, restraining him from

further violence, and, in cases of repeated or serious attacks, ordering him to leave the joint home. If he ignores the injunction he may be sent to prison.

A battered wife may seek an injunction against her husband through a magistrates' court, but that right does not apply to a woman living with a man to whom she is not married.

Seeking refuge

The local authorities have a duty under the Housing Act 1977 to provide accommodation for wives and children made homeless because of domestic violence. They may offer temporary bed and breakfast accommodation in a hotel or space in a refuge run by the National Women's Aid Federation.

Women generally stay in refuges for short periods. Housing authorities try to provide permanent accommodation for a woman with children as quickly as possible if it is clear that she is not likely to return to her husband. Some authorities insist that the woman should first have a court order giving her CUSTODY of the children. *See also:* CRIMINAL COMPENSATION ORDER; MATRIMONIAL ORDER

BEACHCOMBING

Who owns the pebbles on the beach

Your right to keep anything you find at the seaside – even an attractive pebble – is limited. Objects such as pebbles, forming part of the beach, belong to the landowner. Above high-water mark that may be a private individual or a body such as the National Trust; below high-water mark it is usually the Crown.

Sometimes local rights to take sand or other material from a beach have been established by custom, but there is no general right of removal.

You can take live fish and shellfish from the sea and foreshore, but dead fish and seaweed belong to the landowner. Things found under the beach, such as TREASURE TROVE, also belong to the landowner.

Any objects from a wreck must be handed to the local Receiver of Wrecks to await claims from the owner. Unclaimed wrecks belong to the Crown, as do lost or abandoned fishing boats and gear. Beachcombers may keep abandoned or unidentifiable objects found loose on the beach. Even then if something appears to be valuable you should report your find to the police or take some steps to find the owner. If you do not, keeping what you find could amount to theft. If you do report the find, you may receive it eventually as LOST PROPERTY if the owner does not come forward. *See also:* FORESHORE

BEES

Restrictions on keeping a hive in your garden

You do not need a licence to keep a bee-hive in your garden. Bees in a hive are your property and if your neighbour removed your hive, you could claim compensation for his interference.

A neighbour can complain that your keeping an excessive number of bees is a nuisance. If he can show that from time to time they interfere with his enjoyment of his land, he can obtain an injunction whereby the court will order you to cease your bee-keeping.

If you keep an excessive number of bees without taking care to prevent their escape, you are liable for the consequences of their escape. For example, if the bees stung a passing motorist so that he lost control of his car and was injured in a resulting accident, you would be liable for your negligence. *See also:* NUISANCE

BETTING

How the law controls the lucrative business of betting and gambling

All public betting is strictly controlled by law. Although there are no restrictions on wagers laid privately, the law does not allow commercial gambling unless certain safeguards are provided to protect the public, especially children. *See:* GAMBLING

BETTING TAX

When the Government takes part of your winnings

Customs and Excise levies duty on all forms of commercially operated GAMBLING, except a LOTTERY.

The tax is payable by the people or organisations taking the bets – that is, bookmakers, casinos, bingo clubs or pools companies. They may or may not deduct it from an individual gambler's winnings.

Bookmakers and the tote

The duty payable on bets laid at the racecourse is 4 per cent – 4p in the £. Off-course, bets are taxed at the rate of 7.5p in the £. Both bookmakers and the Tote deduct the whole amount from the client's winnings.

In addition, off-course bookmakers deduct the horserace betting levy of about 0.5p to 1p in the £, plus a small charge for running costs. The off-course customer, therefore, loses a total of 9p in the £ on his winnings.

Betting-shop and off-course gamblers have the choice of paying the tax only on their stake before the race is run. If they win, they pay no further tax.

This is called betting 'tax-on' and can make a substantial difference to winnings. For example, a winning bet of £1 at odds of 10 to 1 would normally make the gambler liable for tax of 7.5 per cent of £11 – 82.5p. If he bets 'tax-on', he is liable only for 7.5 per cent of £1 – 7.5p.

This system improves the gambler's odds if he wins, but increases his losses if he is unsuccessful.

Gaming clubs

Individual gamblers in a gaming club pay no betting tax.

Any club or casino that has a licence to run games of unequal chance must pay duty based on the rateable value of the property and the number of tables in use.

Private members' clubs, bridge and whist clubs and clubs running equal chance games, without a banker, are exempt.

Bingo clubs

Betting tax is not payable on prize games – where the winnings are not in money: nor on games played as a club activity, provided that:
● The annual subscription is not more than £2.
● The admission charge is not more than 5p.
● No other payment is required.

Bingo is otherwise taxed at a rate of 7½ per cent – more if the promoter subsidises the prize money. He passes the tax directly to the players by deducting it from the total stake before the prizes are paid. *See:* BINGO CLUB

Pool betting

The duty on pool bets – for example a football pool – is normally 40 per cent, deducted by the promoters from the stake money before it is redistributed as winnings. The client pays nothing directly.

In the case of charity pools, the amount that actually goes to the charity – usually less than 10 per cent of the total stake – is exempt from betting tax. Seven charity pools, registered before the 1971 Pools Competitions Act, pay tax of only 33⅓ per cent. *See:* POOL BETTING

Gaming machines

The operators of gaming machines pay betting tax at three different rates, depending upon the amount of money needed to play the machine and whether a local authority permit or 'holiday season' licence has been granted. The players pay nothing directly.

BIGAMY

When the law forbids multiple marriages

A person who marries while knowingly married to someone else commits the crime of bigamy, and that bigamous second marriage is void.

The children of such a marriage are illegitimate only if both parties knew it was bigamous.

Even if only one of the partners believed the marriage was valid, the children are legitimate and that person can claim financial provision after the other's death.

If the unmarried partner in a bigamous 'marriage' knew of the bigamy, he or she can be prosecuted as well as the bigamist, on a charge of counselling the bigamy.

The legal wife or husband can be called to give prosecution evidence in a bigamy case, even without the consent of the other spouse.

Possible defences It is a defence to a bigamy charge to show an honest belief, at the time of the second 'marriage', that the legal spouse was dead. It is also a defence that the first marriage had been dissolved.

It is likewise a defence if the legal spouse was absent for 7 years continuously before the second 'marriage', and if the prosecution cannot prove that the accused person knew he or she was still alive.

Multiple marriages legally contracted abroad – for example, by Moslems or certain Hindus – are not considered bigamous if the people concerned come to live in Britain later.

Any further marriage contracted in this country would be bigamous, however.

Maximum penalty In practice, bigamy prosecutions are rare – brought mainly when there has been some attempt to obtain financial benefit.

The maximum penalty is 7 years' imprisonment.

BILL-POSTING

When permission is needed to advertise

Advertisements cannot be displayed on the outside of a building anywhere without the consent of the local district council. Anyone who does put up bills or posters can be ordered to take them down at his own expense. Local authorities are entitled to charge a fee for consent to display an advertisement.

There are, however, certain exceptions: election notices; notices advertising the house for sale or to let; notices of religious, educational or social events that are not commercial; advertisements appropriate to business premises on which they are posted; advertisements on hoardings that have existed since 1949, or for which consent has been granted.

It is a criminal offence to post an advertisement without permission on someone else's property. This applies to posters stuck on fences, walls and even lamp-posts. The maximum penalty is a fine of £100.

A local council can refuse an application to display an advertisement only on the grounds that it injures the amenities of the district or is a hazard to public safety. It could, for example, decide that a swimsuit advertisement showing a girl in a bikini could be a danger to motorists at a major road junction.

An applicant can appeal against refusal to the Secretary of State for the Environment. He will usually decide the issue from letters sent between the applicant and the local authority, but he has the power to call an inquiry.

BINDING OVER

Penalty for future misbehaviour

When someone is bound over by a court, he agrees to pay a sum of money if he commits a breach of the peace, or certain other offences, during some specified time in the future. That predetermined sum is in addition to the penalty that will be imposed on him for the subsequent offence. There is no maximum period for which a person can be bound over, but it is not normally for more than 12 months.

The person bound over may also have to provide sureties – people who guarantee to pay the court a sum of money if he commits one of the specified offences.

Normally a court binds someone over only if he has already committed a breach of the peace, but the court can also bind someone over if it merely believes that he is likely to break the peace in the future. No one can be bound over without his agreement, but refusal will eventually lead to imprisonment for up to 6 months.

Anyone bound over can appeal against the decision to the crown court.

BINGO CLUB

Playing the modern version of housey-housey

Bingo is a form of POOL BETTING, played for money or – in the case of prize bingo – for goods. It is generally played for money in the commercial clubs, where the total stake from the participants is redistributed as winnings and the players have an enforceable legal contract with the promoter. That means either side can sue in a dispute.

Unlike with other pool systems, however, the proprietor of a commercial bingo club cannot deduct his profits or running costs from the stake money. All he can deduct is the BETTING TAX that he has to pass on to Customs and Excise.

A bingo club derives its income in two ways: from an admission fee – usually about 20p per session – and a participation fee – from 5p a game to about £1 for a two-hour session.

The players pay these amounts in addition to their stake money for each game.

Games of bingo must not start before 2 p.m. on weekdays or Sundays and must be ended by 11 p.m. On Saturdays, or on New Year's Eve, games are allowed to continue until midnight.

Players' rights

No one can play bingo in a commercial club until he has been a member of it, or one of its branches, for at least 24 hours. People under 18 can watch but not play.

The club needs the consent of the Gaming Board and a licence from the local magistrates before it can start operating. Anyone with good reason to object to the club or the activities of its staff can write to the board or oppose the granting or renewal of the licence. An application for renewal must be made annually and it must be advertised in the local press.

Limits on winnings

There is no limit on the prize money in normal bingo, except that the club itself cannot donate more than £500 towards it in any one week.

In 'linked' bingo – when a game is played simultaneously by landline in several clubs in the same area – there is a weekly limit of £1,000 in the total prize money.

Prize bingo

Because the winnings are in the form of household goods, for example, or food and drinks, prize bingo is regarded as an amusement rather than serious gaming.

It may be operated on premises open to the public, like a fairground, with a permit from the local authority, and the promoter can keep as much of the stake money as he wants.

BIRDS

*Wild birds are stringently
protected by law*

With a few exceptions, it is an offence to kill, injure or take any wild bird, to damage its nest or to take or destroy even one of its eggs. The maximum penalty is usually a £50 fine for each bird, nest or egg.

However, at certain times of the year or under certain conditions, some species are not protected in this way.

How birds are classified The following species, which are regarded as pests, may be killed, their nests destroyed and their eggs taken by someone acting for the landowner (if the birds are on private property) or by someone authorised by a local council, a water board or the Nature Conservancy Council (if the birds are on publicly owned land).

Collared dove	House sparrow
Crow	Jackdaw
Domestic pigeon	Jay
turned wild	Magpie
Gulls, lesser	Rook
black-backed	Starling
and herring	Wood-pigeon

All other wild birds, except GAME birds, are protected throughout the year, and it is a particularly serious offence to kill any of the following species or to take them, their eggs or their nests.

The maximum penalty is a £500 fine and 3 months' imprisonment for each bird, egg or nest.

Avocet	Merlin	Goldeneye duck	Scaup duck
Bee-eater	Osprey	Greylag goose	Pintail duck
Bittern and little	Owl, barn and	(in some areas)	
bittern	snowy		
Black redstart	Peregrine		
Black-tailed godwit	Plover, Kentish and		
Black-winged stilt	little-ringed		
Bluethroat	Purple heron		
Brambling	Red kite		
Bunting, cirl,	Red-backed shrike		
Lapland and snow	Red-necked		
Chough	phalarope		
Common quail	Redwing		
Corncrake	Ruff		
Crossbill (all	Sandpiper, green,		
species)	purple and wood		
Diver (all species)	Scarlet rosefinch		
Dotterel	Scoter, common		
Eagle (all species)	and velvet		
Fieldfare	Serin		
Firecrest	Shorelark		
Gargeney	Short-toed		
Golden oriole	treecreeper		
Goshawk	Spoonbill		
Grebe, black-necked	Spotted crake		
and Slavonian	Stone curlew		
Greenshank	Temminck's stint		
Gull, little and	Tern, black, little		
Mediterranean	and roseate		
Gyr falcon	Tit, bearded		
Harrier (all	and crested		
species)	Warbler, Cetti's,		
Hobby	Dartford, marsh		
Honey buzzard	and Savi's		
Hoopoe	Whimbrel		
Kingfisher	Whooper swan		
Leach's petrel	Woodlark		
Long-tailed duck	Wryneck		

In addition, the following are specially protected from February 1 to August 31 inland, and from February 21 to August 31 at sea or on the foreshore.

There are few exceptions to these restrictions. But, a landowner, for example, may kill any birds except those specially protected in order to prevent damage to his crops or property. And someone who finds a seriously injured bird may kill it for humane reasons.

Wild birds' eggs

The only wild birds' eggs that can be sold without authority are those of the black-headed gull or the common gull for eating, or those of the lapwing if they are taken between January 1 and April 15. Authority to sell any other eggs can be granted only by the Department of the Environment (Countryside and Recreation Division), the Nature Conservancy Council or the Ministry of Agriculture.

Disturbing protected birds while they are nesting can be as harmful as destroying their eggs or nest; it is particularly an offence to do so in a sanctuary. The maximum penalty is a fine of £500 and 3 months' imprisonment.

BIRTH CERTIFICATE

*Proof of identity that is
always needed*

A birth certificate has to be produced whenever you are required to prove your age or place of birth – for example, to get a passport or claim a pension.

There are two kinds: short and standard. The short one records only the name of the child, the date of birth, the sex and the district where the birth took place. The standard certificate also includes details of the father and mother of the child – which means that if a child is illegitimate this may be evident because the father's name is likely to be omitted altogether.

If you have lost your birth certificate, you can get a replacement from the Superintendent Registrar of the district where you were born. When applying, give your full name (maiden surname if you are a married woman), date and place of birth and your mother's maiden surname.

WHEN PROTECTED BIRDS MAY LEGALLY BE KILLED

Rules that afford the sportsman a shooting chance without endangering species

Aug 12 – Jan 31	Sept 1 – Jan 31	Sept 1 – Jan 31 (inland) Sept 1 – Feb 20 (at sea or on the foreshore)	Oct 1 – Jan 31
Common snipe	Common redshank	Common pochard	Capercaillie
Jack snipe	Coot	Gadwall	Woodcock
	Curlew (other	Goldeneye	
	than stone	Goose, Canada,	
	curlew)	greylag, pink-footed,	
	Godwit, bar-	white-fronted	
	tailed	Mallard	
	Golden plover	Pintail	
	Moorhen	Scaup	
	Wigeon	Shoveler	
		Teal	
		Tufted duck	

From a Superintendent Registrar, the fee for a short certificate is £2; for a standard one, £3.50. If the register is still in the custody of the registrar of births and deaths, both short and standard certificates can be obtained for £1.25 each. Special certificates, required under various Acts of Parliament for certain purposes, cost £1.25.

Alternatively, you can get the certificate from the General Register Office in London.

If you apply there in person, the fees are the same as those charged by a Superintendent Registrar. By post, a short certificate costs £6.50 and a standard one is £8. *See also:* BIRTH REGISTRATION

BIRTH REGISTRATION

Your duty to record the birth of a child

Every child born in Britain must be registered by the father or mother with the registrar of births and deaths for the sub-district in which the child was born.

The registrar records the place and date of birth, name and sex of the child, the full names, occupation and place of birth of the father and the full name, maiden name and place of birth of the mother. He gives the parents, free of charge, a short certificate of the registration, omitting details about the parents. Full certificates can be obtained for a fee. *See:* BIRTH CERTIFICATE

Still-births Any child born after the 28th week of pregnancy must be registered, even if there is no sign of life after birth. A still-birth is recorded in a separate register, and no certificate is given.

Illegitimate children Only the mother

TWO KINDS OF BIRTH CERTIFICATE

The circumstances in which the names of a child's parents need not be shown

The short birth certificate, which is supplied free when a baby's birth is registered, gives no details about the parents. The fuller standard certificate always gives the mother's name and usually the father's, unless the child is illegitimate

Either the mother or father of a legitimate child can register the birth. If they are unable to do so the occupier of the house or hospital where the child was born – or a person present at the birth or whoever is in charge of the child – must register it

If after registration parents change their minds about the names in which they want their child baptised, they should produce a baptismal certificate to the registrar within a year of registration

The shortened form of birth certificate, which does not disclose whether a child is illegitimate or adopted, is sufficient for virtually all his later purposes, like obtaining a passport or joining a pension fund – any instance where he has to submit proof of identity. Either sort can be obtained from the register office where the birth was originally recorded or from the General Register Office in London.

Copies of fictitious register entries supplied by and reproduced with the approval of the Registrar-General

has an obligation to register the birth of an illegitimate child. The registrar can record the name of the father only if:

● The mother produces an AFFILIATION ORDER, naming him.
● The father as well as the mother signs the register.
● The father signs a statutory declaration form, which can be obtained from the registrar.

If the father's name is not recorded in the original registration, he can make a statutory declaration later and the child can be re-registered with the father's name.

Time limit All the details about the child and the parents must be given to the registrar, by the father or the mother in person, within 42 days of the child's birth. In the case of a live birth, parents can give the details in the form of a declaration to the registrar of another district if it is more convenient. Still-births, however, can be registered locally only.

If the parents are both dead, or unable to register the child for some other reason, the occupier of the house in which the child was born, or anyone who was present at the birth of the child, for instance a relative, doctor, nurse or midwife, or the person in charge of the child, can register the birth. The registrar is empowered to summon them to his office, if necessary, to provide relevant information.

Quite apart from the information that has to be given to the registrar, details of the child's birth must be sent within 36 hours to the district community physician of the Area Health Authority. That is normally done by the doctor or midwife, but if the child was born at home, it is the father's duty.

Penalty Failure to provide particulars of birth within the required time is punishable by a fine of up to £20.

Inspection If you wish to inquire into someone's birth and parentage, all records are kept at the General Register Office. The records are indexed and the index can be searched, free of charge, in the public search rooms, which are open from 8.30 a.m. to 4.30 p.m. from Monday to Friday. The indexes of registrations in all local superintendent registrars' offices are also open to inspection free of charge, but if the search is to cover a period of more than 5 years a fee of £10 is charged.

BLACKMAIL
When persuasion can be a crime

A blackmailer is someone who makes menaces or improper threats to obtain a benefit for himself or another or a loss to someone else.

A person who is owed money can write to the debtor: 'Pay me by next week or I will sue you.' He cannot write: 'Pay me next week, or I will beat you up.'

Anything that would influence a normal person into agreeing unwillingly to do something may be a menace. The court's decision will be based on a commonsense view of all the surrounding circumstances.

Maximum penalty 14 years' imprisonment.

BLASPHEMY
How the law protects the Christian faith

It is a criminal offence in Britain to attack the Christian religion with writ-

THE COLLEGE RAG THAT CAME TO COURT

Anyone trying to make money by offering 'protection' could certainly be guilty of blackmail – unless it could be shown that there were good grounds for believing that the so-called 'menaces' were not meant seriously.

The treasurer of a college Rag Committee sent letters to 115 local shopkeepers, asking each to buy a poster for between £1 and £5 in support of charity, to 'protect you from any rag activity which could in any way cause you inconvenience'.

A few shopkeepers complained, and none of those who did so paid.

Was this blackmail by the Rag Committee?

DECISION
No. On a commonsense test, the letter had not amounted to a menace.

THE CUSTOMER WHO WAS TOLD 'STEP OUTSIDE'

A person who is owed money can make reasonable demands for settlement, but he cannot back these up with threats of force.

Pomroy repaired roofs. He did some work for a Mr Thorn, having previously agreed a price of £195, but Mr Thorn was unhappy with what was done. He paid Pomroy £125 and promised the other £70 when the job was properly completed.

Pomroy told his customer that unless the rest of the money was paid, Thorn would have to 'look over his shoulder' – a threat of physical violence. Four days later, Pomroy called on Thorn again, bringing a muscular 'friend' with him. Thorn was told: 'Step outside . . . and we will sort this matter out.'

DECISION
Pomroy and his companion were charged with blackmail and found guilty in view of the menaces they had made.

THE BLACKMAIL VICTIM WHO WAS NAMED

The victim of a blackmailer may well have committed some indiscretion which might harm his reputation. For that reason the courts often protect the identity of witnesses in blackmail cases.

A blackmail case involving a singer, Miss Janie Jones, aroused great public interest in 1974 because of the revelations of sexual misbehaviour by several well-known people. To protect the good name of one witness the judge ordered him to be referred to as Mr Y.

Despite the judge's ruling the *Socialist Worker* newspaper printed an article disclosing Mr Y's true identity. The publishers and editor of the paper were prosecuted for contempt of court.

DECISION
The publishers and editor were found guilty. The judge said it was essential for the identity of blackmail victims to be protected, otherwise they would not be prepared to come forward and give evidence.

> ## THE BLASPHEMOUS POEM
>
> *Charges of blasphemy are comparatively rare in modern times, but the offence remains on the statute book, and even a private citizen can decide to make use of it.*
>
> In 1977 Mrs Mary Whitehouse privately prosecuted Mr Denis Lemon, editor of the magazine *Gay News*, for publishing a poem by Professor James Kirkup which she regarded as blasphemous. The poet described imaginary sexual acts performed with Christ's body after the Crucifixion.
>
> ### DECISION
>
> The jury found Lemon guilty of criminal blasphemy, and Judge King-Hamilton sentenced him to 12 months' imprisonment, suspended.
>
> Lemon appealed unsuccessfully to the Court of Appeal and then to the House of Lords. The Law Lords declared that the guilt of the offence of publishing a blasphemous libel did not depend on the accused's having an intent to blaspheme. It was enough for the prosecution to prove that the publication had been intentional and that the matter published was blasphemous.

ten or spoken words that are violent, scurrilous or ribald, that are beyond the limits of decent controversy and are calculated to outrage the feelings of Christians. Only Christianity has that protection under the law.

BLINDNESS

Help that is available for people with defective sight

Someone who is wholly or partly blind may be entitled to a wide range of benefits and services. To qualify for them, he must register as blind or partially sighted.

The first step is to ask the family doctor to arrange an outpatient appointment with an ophthalmologist under the National Health Service or contact the director of social services at the local council office (in London, the borough council) and arrange an appointment for a medical examination. That examination can be carried out by an ophthalmic surgeon in the applicant's home or at a hospital or clinic.

If the doctor is satisfied that the person is technically blind – so blind as to be unable to do work for which eyesight is essential – or seriously and permanently handicapped by defective vision, he completes a confidential document recommending registration (form BD 8), and sends it to the council's social services department.

Once the doctor's recommendation arrives, the council arranges for a social worker to visit the blind person and explain the benefits of registration – from direct financial help to opportunities for training in new skills.

What financial help is available

Direct financial help is provided for people registered as technically blind but not for the partially sighted. The assistance includes:

Income tax An extra personal allowance can be claimed.

Supplementary benefit A blind person already eligible for SUPPLEMENTARY BENEFIT because of low income is entitled to a slightly higher rate of benefit than other people.

Attendance allowance A blind person who is also deaf may be entitled to an ATTENDANCE ALLOWANCE to pay for a helper's services. If an application for the allowance is rejected, the Royal National Institute for the Blind may help an applicant with an appeal against the decision.

Cash help Local and national voluntary organisations may also provide small weekly pensions or make grants for specific purposes.

Applications to such organisations are normally made on behalf of blind people by local council social workers, but a voluntary worker or a relative can apply.

What other help is available

Blind and partially sighted people are eligible for special services and facilities provided by local authorities and by state and voluntary organisations.

Travel Registered blind people are generally entitled to free bus travel, although the concession may apply only outside peak hours.

Blind people can also get fare concessions for business travel on the railways and on a number of domestic airline routes.

Many local authorities allow free parking for vehicles in which registered blind people are regular passengers.

White sticks Local authorities issue white walking sticks to the technically blind and to partially sighted people whose sight is likely to get worse. The stick has no legal significance but it is universally recognised as a warning symbol.

Sticks – for which the recipient may have to pay a small charge – can also be obtained from the Royal National Institute for the Blind or from the Metropolitan Society for the Blind in London.

Holidays Most local authorities arrange holidays – free of charge or partly subsidised – for blind and partially sighted people. Voluntary societies also make such arrangements.

Housing Both councils and voluntary organisations provide housing for many blind people who are also elderly and/or infirm. In many cases, special facilities are needed for the blind residents. Inquiries about special housing arrangements should be made to the council housing authority.

Postage Articles for the blind are carried post free in the mail. Special labels are sometimes supplied by blind people's organisations but it is enough to mark a package or letter 'Blind Material'.

Radio VHF radio sets are issued – and maintained – free to registered blind people by the British Wireless for the Blind Fund.

Television Any registered blind person is entitled to a slight reduction in the price of the broadcasting licence. The concession is obtained by producing evidence of registration when renewing the licence.

Guide dogs A small number of blind people – mainly young and active – are supplied with guide dogs, for a nominal 50p charge. Most such dogs are provided by the Guide Dogs for the Blind Society, which trains the dogs. Their owners may contribute to feeding and veterinary expenses. No licence is needed for a dog supplied by the society.

The dog becomes the property of the

PEOPLE BLINDED IN WAR

People whose sight was damaged or destroyed on war service can get special help from St Dunstan's.

That help covers not only members of the armed forces and merchant seamen but also civil defence workers such as air raid wardens and auxiliary firemen. Troops and civilian workers – for example, policemen and firemen – serving in the Northern Ireland emergency are similarly covered.

St Dunstan's provides rehabilitation and training and advises on possible pension claims. For example, a man receiving a small pension for war-service damage to one eye can apply for full pension if the sight of his other eye deteriorates later in life, even though that deterioration is not caused by war service.

blind person, but the society reserves the right to buy it back if it ceases to work properly or if there is maltreatment.

Aftercare visits to the blind person's home are made about once a year so that the dog's abilities can be assessed. When a guide dog is nearing the end of its working life, probably at about 8 years of age, the blind person may be given a new young dog. The old dog is not generally taken away.

A guide dog with its owner is usually allowed in public places even where an ordinary dog is not. However, it may be prohibited in – for example – a food shop or restaurant, or where there is an escalator on which dogs must be carried to avoid risk of being injured.

Education and training

Local authorities have the same duty to educate children with defective sight as they have for other children. They provide specially trained teachers and special teaching facilities for registered blind children – starting before the normal school age of 5 and continuing beyond the minimum leaving age of 16.

Some partially sighted children do better if they can attend an ordinary school, helped by special facilities. Others benefit more at a special school among other children who have sight problems. Parents have the right to be consulted as to which sort of school they

think is best for their child's future.

School leavers For children who do not seek higher education, special guidance and assessment centres can advise on choice of skills in which they can be trained.

Courses are available, for example, in light engineering, shorthand and typing, telephone work, physiotherapy and piano-tuning.

Adults Someone who is born with normal sight, but who loses it through accident or illness, can be helped by a social worker to choose the right training for a new livelihood. Courses can be taken at home or in residential units.

It may be possible to train the person to continue in his previous job – particularly with office or professional work. If that is not possible, contact the disablement resettlement officer at the local Department of Employment to arrange employment or training.

Books and tape recordings for the blind

Books printed in the Braille and Moon blind-reading systems are provided by most councils, which also arrange to teach blind people to read by those systems.

Local councils also normally arrange for blind people in their area to become a member of the National Library for the Blind – based in London and Manchester – which has a wide range of books, fiction and non-fiction.

Tape-recorded books and playback machines can be obtained from the British Talking Book Service, with the rental fee paid for by the local authority.

Weekly papers, monthly magazines and sheet music in Braille are available from the Royal National Institute for the Blind.

All Braille publications are carried free of charge in the post.

For partially sighted people, books in specially large print are on loan from local libraries.

BLOOD TEST

Medical evidence in parental and other disputes

Study of a man's blood can show whether he might be the father of a child

whose paternity is in dispute, if it is considered in conjunction with samples of the mother's and the child's blood. Such a blood test can never establish that he is actually the father, but it can prove that it is impossible that he is.

Courts sometimes call for blood tests before making an AFFILIATION ORDER and in actions involving ADULTERY, rights of inheritance and claims to titles. The parties do not have to supply blood samples if they do not want to. The courts, however, are entitled to infer from a refusal by any party that he or she has doubts about the claim being made. *See also:* DRINK AND DRIVING

BOATING

Regulations governing the use of waterways

You have a right under common law to use your boat at sea or in the tidal stretches of rivers, but you need permission to sail it on lakes, canals or non-tidal rivers.

If the water is owned privately, permission must come from the owner. Where the water belongs to a public body, for example, a local council or a waterways board, the conditions of use will be laid down in regulations or bye-laws. These are generally displayed on noticeboards at the waterside. The local council offices will advise in cases of doubt.

Canals Most canals are administered by the British Waterways Board, which lays down terms and conditions for their use. Pleasure craft sailing on the board's canals need a licence, the cost of which depends on the length of the boat.

Off-shore boating Boating rights at seaside resorts may be restricted by local bye-laws which, for example, may lay down maximum speeds for motorboats near the shore. Such rules are usually displayed by the waterside, or can be obtained from the council offices.

Council bye-laws apply to the foreshore, which is the area between high and low-water marks and to an area 1,000 m. seaward.

Mooring a boat

Mooring a boat without permission is a TRESPASS. In harbours, rivers and canals, mooring is controlled by detailed local regulations displayed on noticeboards, or which can be obtained from local council offices. However, you are normally entitled to anchor for a limited time to await favourable weather or while repairs are carried out. **Houseboats** If a residential boat is permanently moored by agreement between its owner and the owner of water rights, either party has the right to sue for breach of contract. If someone else interferes with the mooring, he can be restrained by court injunction and sued for damages.

Insuring a boat

It is not compulsory to insure a boat, even against third-party claims for personal injury. But insurance is advisable because the law of NEGLIGENCE applies to boat-owners as much as it does to motorists. Anyone who carelessly allows his boat to collide with another is liable for negligence. Breaking local navigation rules at the time of an accident may be evidence of negligence.

Hiring a boat

If you hire a boat, you are liable for your own negligence, just as if you owned it. Check with the person you hire from that there is insurance cover for damage to the boat, and to third parties and their boats.

BODILY HARM

Broken bones and black eyes

Distinguishing between causing grievous bodily harm – g.b.h. – and the lesser charge of actual bodily harm – a.b.h. – is usually a matter of degree. A black eye can be a.b.h.; a broken bone may be g.b.h. When the seriousness of an injury is in doubt, the police generally prosecute for both a.b.h. and g.b.h., leaving the court to decide.

Maliciously causing g.b.h., with intent to do so, is a more serious charge than maliciously inflicting g.b.h., when the injury was not deliberately intended. The more serious charge has a maximum penalty of life imprisonment; the lesser has a maximum of 5 years' imprisonment and an unlimited fine. Both are usually heard in the crown court.

WIFE WHO JUMPED OUT OF THE WINDOW

The offence of maliciously causing grievous bodily harm carries a maximum penalty of life imprisonment. The lesser charge of maliciously inflicting grievous bodily harm is generally used when an injury is not deliberately intended.

Mr Lewis was a wife-beater. On one occasion when his wife locked him out of their 3rd-floor flat he became so enraged that he started to break in. The terrified Mrs Lewis was so alarmed at the sound of the breaking glass that she jumped from the window and broke both her legs. Her husband was charged with maliciously inflicting grievous bodily harm.

VERDICT

Mr Lewis was found guilty. Although he did not push his wife and was not in the same room, her injuries were held to be a reasonably foreseeable consequence of his behaviour.

However, if the magistrates and defendant agree, the lesser charge can be heard in the magistrates' court where it carries a maximum of 6 months and £1,000 fine.

Actual bodily harm

The charge of occasioning actual bodily harm relates to any injury that interferes with anyone's comfort or health – not only a bruise or graze, but also perhaps a state of distress that leaves the victim hysterical or nervous. The maximum penalty in a magistrates' court is 6 months' imprisonment and £1,000 fine. In a crown court 5 years and an unlimited fine.

BOMB HOAX

The penalties for raising a false alarm

Charges involving hoax bomb alarms, like hoax fire alarms, will be heard in a magistrates' court unless the defendant decides to opt for trial by jury – or unless the magistrates feel it should be tried in the crown court.

Maximum penalty Magistrates' court: 3 months' imprisonment *and* a £1,000 fine. Crown court: 5 years' imprisonment. *See:* HOAX CALL

BORROWING

Neighbourly rights and obligations

Borrowing and lending, even on the most friendly basis, involves legal rights and obligations. If, for example, someone borrows a lawnmower and it breaks down because he does not take proper care while using it, he is obliged to have it repaired. And if he is asked to return the machine and fails to do so, he is held liable if anything happens to it later. For example, if it is lost or damaged, even through no fault of his own, he must pay for its replacement or repairs.

The lender can sue If someone lends his property and it is not returned he can sue the borrower. However, if his action is successful, the court cannot enforce the return of the property, only its worth in cash instead. The exception is if the object is unique and cannot be replaced. A borrower would be compelled to return an original painting, for example.

If the lender goes on to the borrower's land to recover his property, he is subject to the laws of TRESPASS.

BORROWING FROM A FRIENDLY NEIGHBOUR

If a person borrows his neighbour's property and does not return it when asked to do so, the borrower is liable to pay for its repair or replacement if it is lost or damaged.

'May I borrow my mower back?'

ESTABLISHING THE LEGAL BOUNDARIES BETWEEN HOUSES

Who owns what when there is a borderline dispute over the garden fence

WHOSE FENCE?

A person whose property is on the same side as the fence posts is almost always regarded as the owner of the fence.

When there are no posts, you may get some clue to ownership by comparing the fence with others in neighbouring gardens.

HEDGE AND DITCH RULE

When there is a dispute over a boundary formed by a hedge and a ditch a legal argument sometimes applied is that the person whose land adjoins the hedge also owns the ditch. That is not an invariable rule, however, and the eventual outcome of such a dispute greatly depends on tradition and practice in the area.

Grass verges

The county or district council is normally responsible for most roadside verges. When a house owner can prove from his title deeds that he owns a strip of grass between the pavement and his front fence, it is his responsibility to maintain it. It is also his responsibility if someone meets with an accident there through his negligence.

READING THE PLANS

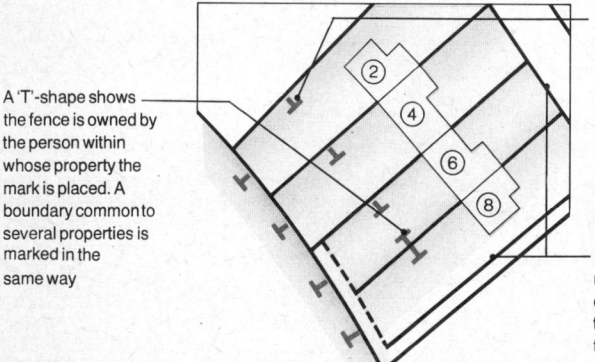

A 'T'-shape shows the fence is owned by the person within whose property the mark is placed. A boundary common to several properties is marked in the same way

When a fence is shared between two properties the boundary is marked by a double 'T'. Neither owner must do anything that could cause his neighbour's half to collapse

If neither the deeds nor an examination of the fence help, there is no other way to establish ownership

The title deeds and plans of a property can often help to settle a dispute over boundaries. You may already have your house deeds. If you have a mortgage, however, the deeds will be held by your building society which will, on request, let you inspect them.

BOUNDARIES, WALLS AND FENCES

Settling disputes with your neighbours

Boundaries can be the source of various disputes. Neighbours may quarrel over which of them owns the hedge separating their properties, over whose duty it is to repair a wall, or whether a new fence erected by one of them encroaches on the other's land.

In many cases there is simply no way of arriving at a clear solution.

The title deeds of a property often – but not always – settle the question of who owns its enclosing walls, fences, hedges or other boundaries. If you have a mortgage, the deeds will be held by your building society. Ask the society to make them available for inspection at the office of any local solicitor who is on the society's panel.

If the deeds, which often include a plan of the property, do not make the position clear, there are two legal rules on boundary ownership that may do so. One is that where a hedge and ditch forms the boundary between two pieces of land, the person whose land adjoins the hedge also owns the ditch.

The other rule is that a fence is owned by the person whose property is on the same side as the fence posts.

If neither the deeds nor these two rules help, an examination of the construction and materials of the wall or fence may show that it is more likely to belong to one property than the other.

There is a common belief that each owner in a row of houses owns only one of the fences or walls enclosing his property and that this fence or wall is on the same side of the garden for each house. But this belief is more often wrong than right. It is probably based on the fact that, where all the houses in a row are sold at the same time, the deeds of each property sometimes specify the ownership of the boundaries in this way.

When boundaries need repair

In the London area, and a few other places, house owners are obliged by local Acts or regulations to keep their walls and fences in good repair. (If you want to know the position in your own area, ask at your local council offices.)

Some title deeds also contain a condition that the owner must maintain his walls or fences in good condition.

Apart from those special cases, you

are not legally obliged to repair boundary walls or fences.

Even if part of your wall collapses and your neighbour successfully sues you for damages for injuries he has sustained, you still have no legal obligation to repair the wall. If the wall is a party structure, legally shared by you and a neighbour, your only duty is not to dismantle or do anything else to your half that could cause your neighbour's half to collapse.

When the boundary is in dispute

When a property owner replaces an old boundary wall or fence, his neighbour may accuse him of erecting it in the wrong position so depriving that neighbour of part of his land.

In such cases, the disputing neighbours may consult their solicitors. But often the argument cannot be legally resolved: all signs of the position of the original wall or fence may have been obliterated, and the plans of the properties on the title deeds may be indistinct, not drawn to scale or too small in scale. (If the title is not registered, there may be no plans in the deeds at all.)

It is better to avoid such disputes in the first place by keeping the boundaries that enclose your property in good repair so that they do not need to be replaced.

BREACH OF PROMISE

New laws on engagements to marry

Until 1970, when the law was changed, anyone who got engaged to marry entered into a contract that could be legally binding. If one partner broke off the engagement without the agreement of the other – that is, committed what was known as a breach of promise – he or she could be sued for damages. Usually it was the woman who brought the action, to recover the expenses she or her father had incurred in preparing for the marriage.

Since the change in the law, a promise to marry is no longer a legal contract.

However, anyone whose engagement is broken off has a right to recover whatever he or she has contributed to property acquired for the marriage. This contribution can be tangible, such as a washing machine, or it can be the

value of any work done: for example, if a woman decorates some rooms of the house her fiancé has bought for the future matrimonial home and the engagement is then broken off, she can claim for the proportion of the property's value represented by her work. *See also:* ENGAGEMENT

BREACH OF THE PEACE

When someone's behaviour could cause danger

There is no precise definition of what constitutes a breach of the peace, but it is generally taken to mean the use, or the threat, of force against someone, or behaviour 'which causes someone reasonably to apprehend danger'.

The police have the power to arrest not only someone who is actually causing a breach of the peace but also anyone whose behaviour they consider is likely to result in such a breach. For example, it is an offence to use threatening, abusive or insulting words or behaviour if these are considered likely to lead to a breach of the peace. *See:* ABUSIVE WORDS OR BEHAVIOUR

The charge is regularly used against demonstrators who may have had no intention of causing a breach of the peace.

GUARDIANS OF THE PEACE

The police have the power to arrest anyone who is causing a breach of the peace or whose behaviour they consider is likely to result in such a breach.

The courts generally use great discretion in deciding whether to convict. *See also:* PUBLIC ORDER

BREAKDOWN OF MARRIAGE

The basic condition for obtaining a divorce

Since 1971, irretrievable breakdown of marriage has been the only ground on which the courts in England and Wales may grant a decree of DIVORCE or a judicial SEPARATION.

For the breakdown to qualify as irretrievable, the person asking for the decree must prove one of five facts: ADULTERY; behaviour which makes it unreasonable to expect the other spouse to go on with the marriage; DESERTION by the other spouse for at least 2 years; a separation of at least 2 years if both parties agree to the divorce; or a separation of at least 5 years if the other spouse does not agree.

BREATH TEST

Police powers to arrest a motorist who refuses to co-operate

When the police stop a driver because they believe he has committed some moving driving offence, or when he has been involved in an accident or when they have stopped him for some other reason and believe that he has alcohol in his body, they have the right to ask him to take a breath test.

If the crystals turn green over the line – that is, if the result is positive – or if the driver fails to blow up the bag sufficiently, he will be arrested and taken to the police station for a further breath test and, if that is positive, for a blood or urine sample.

A motorist who refuses the initial breath test can be arrested and may be prosecuted for refusing – an offence in itself. *See:* DRINK AND DRIVING

BRIBERY

When a kindness can be corrupt

Bribery is offering a gift or favour to a public employee in an attempt to influence him in the carrying out of his public duties. The person receiving the bribe is also guilty of the offence. *See:* CORRUPT GIFT

BRIDGING LOAN

When you need a substantial sum to 'tide you over' for a few weeks

Not all loans are long term. You may need a substantial sum of money for only a short period – say, between having to pay for a new house and actually getting the money from the person who is buying your old one.

The rules about such a loan, called a bridging loan, are similar to those governing any other BANK LOAN, except that the need to avoid delay in many property transactions results in a relaxation in the rules over the supply of copies.

There is no need for the bank to send you an unsigned advance copy of the loan agreement for your consideration, as would normally be the case if you were borrowing less than £5,000 on the security of property for purposes other than specifically for house purchase or improvement. *See:* CONSUMER CREDIT

BRITISH EMBASSY

Guardians of the interests of United Kingdom citizens abroad

An embassy represents its country abroad. Its headquarters are invariably situated in the capital of the host country, with local representation, known as consulates, in other major towns.

The British Government maintains an embassy or its equivalent (in Commonwealth countries it is known as a high commission) in almost every foreign country. The exceptions are Britain's dependent territories and colonies, such as Gibraltar, and those countries with which we have broken off diplomatic relations.

The dependencies are ruled by a British governor or commissioner and have no need of an embassy; and in the countries where embassies have been withdrawn, British interests are handled by the embassy of a friendly foreign state.

How to obtain advice or assistance abroad

The consular department of the British embassy in a foreign capital and the individual British consulates in the country's major towns are there to advise, help and protect the rights of British citizens living in or visiting that country. They also have a duty to assist the master of any British ship who seeks their help.

The consular department is generally run by consuls and vice-consuls, but in less-important towns, British interests may be represented by a single, honorary consul – often a British businessman. An honorary consul has the same powers as a full-time official.

Sickness and death The consul will provide 'help in cases of illness and death'. Consuls may also act as guardian for any British citizen suffering mental illness and as executor of the local ESTATE of any British person who dies abroad.

Lack of money If a British citizen runs out of money the consul may agree to obtain tickets for him to take the cheapest convenient form of transport back to Britain. The money for this passage home is provided as a loan, and to ensure that the debt is repaid to the Foreign Office, the consul endorses the visitor's passport, which is then held by immigration officials at the British port of entry. It will not be released, nor will a new passport be issued, until the loan has been repaid.

After an arrest When a British citizen is arrested abroad, the foreign police have a duty to inform the British consul without delay. By international agreement, the consul then has the right to visit the arrested person within a reasonable time of his arrest and to obtain legal help for him.

If there is a trial, the consul may attend as an observer, though this is not a right in all countries. And if the penalty for the offence is imprisonment, the consul will visit the prisoner from time to time to ensure that he is being treated properly.

If a consul's rights are denied, the Foreign Office in London can use high-level diplomatic pressure to influence events.

Property seized When a British citizen's property is seized by a foreign government or authority, the local British embassy will make representations to have it returned, but in most cases where official policy is involved the Foreign Office in London will have to pursue any claim for compensation.

If you need help in those circumstances contact your MP.

Marriage Some consuls are authorised to conduct marriage ceremonies between British subjects.

Children born abroad When a child is born to British subjects overseas, they should register the birth with the local British consul as soon as possible to ensure that the child claims its right to British CITIZENSHIP. But a woman who is a citizen of the United Kingdom and is unmarried, or married to a man who is not a citizen of the United Kingdom, cannot register her child.

Help for businesses The commercial department of the embassies provides information, facilities and contacts for British exporters doing business in the host country. To make use of these, contact the Export Services and Promotions Division of the Department of Trade.

BRITISH SUBJECT

British subject or subject of the UK and colonies

The terms 'British subject' and 'British National' mean anyone who is a citizen of almost any Commonwealth country, including the United Kingdom itself.

You must normally be a British subject to get a job in the Civil Service; and a ship is not regarded as a British ship unless it is owned by a British citizen or company.

You must be either a British subject or a citizen of Eire to vote in a parliamentary or local ELECTION or to serve on a JURY, to be an MP or to be a privy councillor. Whether you are a British subject may in some circumstances determine whether you have been guilty of TREASON.

The expression 'British subject' no longer has any relevance in immigration applications and appeals (although British subjects as citizens of the UK and Commonwealth countries do have certain rights).

People who are born in the United Kingdom and in territories that are still British colonies, or who acquire citizenship there, are citizens of the United Kingdom and colonies as well as being British subjects. *See:* CITIZENSHIP

BROADCASTING

Legal checks on television and radio programmes

If you have a complaint about a television or radio programme, the way you go about making it must depend on the nature of the complaint and whether the programme was broadcast by the BBC, one of the Independent Broadcasting Authority companies or the Fourth Channel.

BBC programmes

The British Broadcasting Corporation transmits its programmes under government licence. But the Government does not control or supervise broadcasts – although the licence gives it the right to forbid or order a particular broadcast.

Apart from a general duty not to express a BBC opinion in any broadcast, there are few specific rules. Instead, the BBC has its own voluntary set of guidelines on decency, quality and accuracy.

General complaints If you feel that a BBC programme has offended against a general principle, write to the Director-General, Broadcasting House, London W1A 4AA.

Alternatively, write to the producer whose name appears on the screen or Radio Times – or telephone the duty officer (in London) or information department (in other regions).

Unfair treatment Complaints about unfair broadcasts or infringements of your privacy may be made to the Broadcasting Complaints Commission.

IBA programmes

The rules that are self-imposed by the BBC are imposed by law on independent broadcasting.

Programmes transmitted by the independent television and radio companies, under the Independent Broadcasting Authority, must not offend against good taste or decency or be likely to lead to crime or disorder or be offensive to public feeling.

In addition, all news bulletins and current affairs programmes must be accurate and impartial.

Programmes must also comply with the IBA Code on Violence, which limits the portrayal of violence on the screen, and the Family Viewing Policy, which ensures that all programmes shown before 9 p.m. must be suitable for viewers of any age.

The IBA has power to prevent the showing of any programme that does not meet any of the requirements.

Similar rules apply to ADVERTISING on television.

Making a complaint If you have a complaint about a particular programme, write to the Programme Controller of your regional independent television company.

If your complaint involves some aspect of IBA supervision – for example, if you feel that a particular programme was of a kind that should not have been shown before 9 p.m. – complain direct to the IBA, 70 Brompton Road, London SW3 1EY.

If you feel the broadcast is unfair to you, or infringes your privacy, you may complain to the Broadcasting Complaints Commission.

Complaints about ADVERTISING are dealt with separately.

The Fourth Channel

In most of the country, the Fourth Channel is being run by the Independent Television companies under the control of the IBA, but in Wales a Welsh Fourth Channel Authority, separate from both BBC and IBA, has control over programme schedules. Programmes from 6.30 p.m. to 10 p.m. must be mainly in Welsh.

Teletext services

The Ceefax service (run by the BBC) and Oracle (run by the IBA) are subject to the same general controls as other programmes. You need no special licence to receive them. But Prestel (run by British Telecom through your telephone) is the responsibility of each person who provides a 'page'. You may be charged a small fee (on your telephone bill) for each page viewed.

Controls over use of equipment

It is a criminal offence to transmit a radio or television signal, or to receive a television signal, without a licence or Home Office consent.

Licences to broadcast are issued by the Home Office to the BBC, independent broadcasting companies, and amateur radio operators. To apply for a licence write to the Home Office Radio Regulatory Department.

Amateur applicants must pass an examination controlled by British Telecommunications to make sure they are proficient in the use of a transmitter.

You need both a Home Office and a British Telecommunications licence to run a programme distribution system – that is, any cable relaying service either for your own programmes or for broadcasts.

However, a licence is not required for a programme distribution system if it is contained entirely within one building, if it is a hospital programme, if it carries

---

AN INDEPENDENT COMPLAINTS BODY

The Broadcasting Act 1980 set up the Broadcasting Complaints Commission to deal with complaints about any television or radio broadcast.

The commission will investigate any complaint that a programme actually transmitted was unjust or unfair to any participant, to anyone who has died in the previous 5 years or anyone else directly interested in the topic covered. It will also look into any complaint that a programme actually broadcast involved an unwarranted infringement of the privacy of a person, or that privacy was infringed in obtaining material for the broadcast.

Complaints must be made in writing by those subjected to the unfairness or invasion of privacy, or someone authorised by them (such as a neighbour). They must be made within a reasonable time of the broadcast.

The commission will ask the broadcasters to provide a repeat of the broadcast and for comments. If the complaint is upheld, the broadcasting company may be required to broadcast or publish details of the complaint and the commission's decision. But the commission need not deal with a complaint if it could be dealt with in the courts or is frivolous.

education programmes for education institutions only, if it carries business information within one business, or if it is a news agency service, such as Reuters.

Anyone making unauthorised broadcasts can be imprisoned for 3 months, fined £400 and ordered to surrender his equipment.

Citizens' Band Radio The Government intends to introduce Citizens' Band radio into Britain, to be called Open Channel. Anyone using approved equipment will be able to broadcast and receive messages on the set frequencies of this channel without any licence or fee. In 1980, it was still an offence to use Citizens' Band equipment in Britain without permission.

A radio receiver does not need a licence, but it is an offence to listen to certain broadcasts, such as police or fire service messages, which are not intended for public reception.

Pirate broadcasting It is a criminal offence to broadcast unauthorised 'pirate' programmes either from a land-based station or from a ship or aircraft.

Anyone who takes part in such a broadcast, or buys advertising time on it or supplies the station with goods or services, also commits a crime.

The maximum penalties are 2 years' imprisonment and an unlimited fine plus seizure of equipment.

Improving reception If your television or radio is being interfered with from some outside source, ask the Post Office to investigate. There is no charge.

The Home Office has power to prevent the sale or use of any machine or apparatus likely to cause accidental interference with reception of broadcasts.

Deliberate interference with broadcasts – 'jamming' – is illegal.

BUDGET ACCOUNT

Buying by easy instalments

A budget account is an arrangement by which a customer can have permanent credit with a retailer. The customer will buy, say, clothes on credit and pay monthly instalments off the debt but he is not required to clear the debt altogether. As long as the customer pays the agreed instalments, he can continue to have goods, up to an agreed limit.

That arrangement, like a bank overdraft, is running account credit and the agreement will be covered by the CONSUMER CREDIT Act.

If you have a budget account you are entitled to a statement of account whenever any movement is recorded in it – an instalment paid, or a charge made for goods or interest. However much or little you use a budget account, you are entitled to a statement at least once a year.

If a lender fails to supply the required statements, he cannot sue you, repossess goods, suspend the account or demand repayment of the entire sum owed, instead of instalments. If he is more than a month late with a statement, he commits a crime for which he can be fined up to £200.

The lender is bound by any figures supplied in a statement of account. If a mistake is made, and the statement shows that the borrower owes less than he really does, the lender must stand by the mistaken figure.

The reverse does not apply: a borrower is not bound by what the statement shows if it is wrong.

However, a county court can waive that rule if a lender has made a genuine, honest and excusable mistake which is being taken advantage of by an unscrupulous borrower.

If you have a credit account with a shop, but are required to settle it in full each month, the arrangement is exempt from the Consumer Credit Act and the

shopkeeper does not have to supply statements. *See also:* INTEREST CHARGE

BUILDING PRESERVATION

The protection of historic architecture

Buildings of special architectural or historic interest (such as Longleat, Chatsworth House and many Georgian or Victorian buildings) may be 'listed' – that is, designated as being worth preserving – by the Secretary of State for the Environment.

The owner of a building cannot object to its being listed, but if he obtains planning permission to alter or demolish a building that has not yet been listed, he may apply to the Secretary of State for a certificate to the effect that there is no present intention to list the building. This will then prevent the building (if a certificate is issued) from being listed for a period of five years.

The owner is forbidden by law to demolish, extend or alter such a building without the consent of the district council (in London the borough council is the responsible authority). The applicant for consent may have to pay a fee to the local authority. If a council withholds consent, the owner can appeal to the Secretary of State for the Environment.

When consent is given to demolish or

HOW TO HAVE A BUILDING LISTED

If you know of a building that you think should be preserved because it is of special architectural or historic interest, ask your local council's planning department to serve a 'building preservation notice' on both the owner and the occupier of the building.

If you can, enclose an up-to-date photograph and any relevant information about the building – for example, its date, historical associations, the architect, and details of any interior features of interest.

The preservation notice, which is effective immediately it has been served, protects the building, as if it were listed, for 6 months. The notice ceases to be effective if, during the 6 months, the Secretary of State for the Environment lists the build-

ing or informs the local authority that he does not intend to do so.

If the Secretary of State decides against listing the building, the owner and occupier will be notified, and the local authority will be debarred from serving another preservation notice on the building within 12 months.

If the Secretary of State refuses to confirm a preservation notice the owner of the building can claim compensation from the council for any loss or damage he may have suffered.

Ancient monuments – for example, Hadrian's Wall or the castles of North Wales – are usually the property of the Crown and are protected under the Ancient Monuments Acts.

alter a listed building, the owner must allow the Royal Commission on Historic Monuments an opportunity to photograph and make records of the building.

Similar rules apply to buildings within a CONSERVATION AREA.

The owner of a listed building may be able to obtain a grant towards its maintenance from the district council or the Secretary of State for the Environment. Voluntary bodies such as the Georgian Group or the Society for the Protection of Ancient Buildings also have money available.

BUILDING REGULATIONS

Legal duties as you improve your home

Planning is concerned with the way land is developed and the effect that buildings have on their surroundings. Building regulations, on the other hand, deal with precise standards of construction, detailed choice of materials and safe design.

To construct a new building or an extension to an existing one – for example a new garage or extra room – you must have building regulations approval from your local district council.

In most areas, you have to complete two copies of a special council application form.

You will also be required to pay a fee varying according to the estimated cost of the building work when you apply for consent, and again when the local authority's official comes to inspect the foundations.

In inner London, which is covered by the London Building Acts and Greater London Council bye-laws, the procedure is different.

If PLANNING PERMISSION is required in addition to building regulation approval, a further two copies must be submitted to the council.

Approval under the regulations is needed for: alterations to existing structural work; new or altered staircases; new or extended habitable rooms; new or altered internal or external drainage; new, altered or replaced flue pipes; fitting new heating appliances, except as explained below; new lavatory accommodation.

BUILDING REGULATIONS IN INNER LONDON

Building in inner London, the area covered by the former London County Council, is controlled by the London Building Acts of 1930–9 and bye-laws.

The main difference between these and the regulations in force elsewhere is that control is not based on formal approval or rejection of a proposed scheme, but on the continual supervision by a district surveyor over the execution of the work.

Another important difference in inner London is that in London there is no control over acoustic and thermal insulation, but the storage of oil for oil-burning appliances is controlled.

A builder must give the district surveyor at least 48 hours' notice of his detailed plans before starting work. In practice, discussions start at a much earlier stage – probably even before a firm price has been agreed between the builder and the householder – to ensure that the plans are not completely beyond acceptability.

The Greater London Council charges the builder for the surveyor's services – based on the value of the work – which ranges from £5 for a £100 job to about £5,000 for a £2 million construction. Naturally the builder will pass this charge on to his client.

Approval is not needed for: general repairs; fitting electric heating appliances; fitting new gas appliances, provided the work is done by the area gas board and complies with the relevant building regulations; replacing heating or sanitary appliances, provided the work complies with the regulations and the local authority is given notice before an existing underground drain is renewed; fitted furniture; fences and garden walls (but you may need planning permission for these); construction of certain small buildings.

Procedure and requirements

Your first step should be to buy copies of the building regulations from a local bookshop or from Her Majesty's Stationery Office. These give details of, for example, the type of materials and sizes of timber required for any given job.

Along with the application form you have to submit to the council a full set of working drawings, plans and elevations. Your scheme may be approved as it stands or, if it is only a little short of satisfactory, the building inspector may contact you to suggest improvements before the council considers the scheme.

Professional advice from a builder or architect may improve your chances of having a scheme approved.

You must give periodic notices to the local authority during the course of the building and after its completion, so that they may check that the work is being carried out according to the specifications. For example, at least 24

hours' notice must be given before covering up any excavation, foundation or damp-proof course and before laying concrete or other material over a site or covering up a drain. Notice must also be given not more than 7 days after a drain trench has been filled in.

Failure to give any of these notices may mean that the building inspector orders the work to be opened up.

If your application is accepted

By law, you are entitled to a decision from the council within 5 weeks of the date of your application. The council's approval is valid for 3 years. If you hear nothing from the council within 5 weeks, you can assume approval and go ahead with the proposed work. However, the building inspector can still call a halt or demand alterations to the work if it fails to comply with any of the regulations.

If your plans are complicated, the council has the right, before the 5 weeks are up, to ask you for up to 2 months more to consider your application. If you do not agree, and the plans are faulty, it can immediately refuse approval and ask you to re-apply.

If your application is rejected

You can appeal against a rejection to the local magistrates' court, but there is no chance of success if your proposals do not match the requirements of the regulations or if your plans have not been adequately prepared.

Sometimes – for example, if you plan

to use unusual, but nonetheless reasonable constructional methods or materials – you may persuade the council to relax the regulations. If you fail, you have the right of appeal to the Department of the Environment. The local authority will tell you how to submit the appeal, but the advice of an architect or building expert will certainly be desirable.

In other cases, if the council is unsure of its grounds for rejection, it may join with you in submitting the case to the Department of the Environment.

Whatever the reasons for the rejection, you can discuss them with the council's building inspectors with a view to sending in a revised application.

If work not complying with the building regulations is done – without approval – the owner of the building may be prosecuted.

Maximum penalty £100, plus a maximum of £10 for each day on which the offence continues after conviction.

The council may order the offending work to be pulled down and rebuilt at the owner's expense. In such a case, the owner has the right of appeal only to the local magistrates.

BUILDING SOCIETY

Investing in other people's homes

Building societies are a major source of loans for people buying their own homes. The loans are secured on the property being bought.

A building society has two classes of member: borrowing and investing. Borrowers pay a higher interest charge than is paid to investors, to cover the society's running costs and to create more funds that can be lent to other home-buyers..

Investing members receive interest on their investments.

If you take a building society loan, and are not already an investor with the society, you become a member by the technicality of buying one nominal share. The cost of the share, usually 50p, will probably be deducted from your loan.

If you are already an investor, you may be given priority over non-investors when seeking a mortgage from your society if funds are scarce

or if government controls restrict the society's lending.

When you seek a building society loan, you will normally be expected to find part of the price of the property – often 10 per cent to 20 per cent – from your own resources. *See:* MORTGAGE

For investors, interest is paid after deduction of income tax at the basic rate. Anyone who does not already pay basic-rate tax cannot claim back any tax automatically paid on building society interest. Someone who pays tax at more than the basic rate will have to pay the difference between what is automatically deducted and what he would be charged on the entire amount of interest at his highest tax rate.

Example: Mr A, whose highest tax rate is 40 per cent, receives £140 interest from his building society (£200 less £60 tax already deducted).

Mr A's liability on full £200 at 40%	£80
minus	
Tax already deducted at 30%	£60
Net tax liability is therefore	£20

In the rare event that a building society could not meet its obligations, it would be wound up. Although there is always a clause allowing any society to call in the whole debt on, usually, 6 months' notice, that is normally only used in these extreme cases. In practice most borrowers would be offered new mortgages by other societies.

An investor in the same society will be entitled to a share of any remaining assets in proportion to the investment he had at the time of the society's collapse. His only obligation will be to complete any agreed regular payments into his share account, up to the date when the society is wound up.

BURGLARY

When trespassing does become a crime

A burglar is anyone who enters a building, or a part of it in which he is not entitled to go, as a trespasser – that is, without permission – intending to commit THEFT, CRIMINAL DAMAGE, grievous BODILY HARM or RAPE.

It makes no difference whether the

offence takes place during the day or at night, but a night-time burglar is usually given a stiffer sentence.

Maximum penalty Magistrates' court: 6 months' imprisonment and a £1,000 fine. Crown court: 14 years' imprisonment and an unlimited fine. (In deciding the sentence the court takes into account such factors as whether an old or infirm person was alone on the premises, the value of any property involved and the burglar's previous record.)

The courts can also seize anything used in the burglary, such as a vehicle in which stolen goods were driven.

Aggravation A burglar who carries a gun, an imitation gun or any OFFENSIVE WEAPON can be charged with aggravated burglary, which carries a maximum sentence of life imprisonment.

Carrying burglary tools

If police find someone outside his own home in possession of housebreaking tools, or other equipment they believe could be intended to aid him in burglary, theft or cheating, he may be prosecuted for the offence of 'going equipped for stealing'.

If an article is clearly made for such a purpose – for example, a set of lock-picks – a court will accept that its illegal use was intended. However, when articles are found that might have innocent uses – for example, crowbars or gloves – the police have to bring other evidence to show that the accused was on his way to commit a crime.

Maximum penalty Magistrates' court: 6 months' imprisonment and £1,000 fine. Crown court: 3 years' imprisonment and unlimited fine. A court can order confiscation of the equipment. If it was intended for use in stealing a car, the motoring penalties of endorsement, driving disqualification and totting-up also apply.

BURIAL

The choice between churchyard or public cemetery

Everyone is entitled to be buried in the churchyard of the parish in which he lived, provided that there is still space left for burial. Otherwise his relatives or administrators must seek burial at the

nearest local authority cemetery. Any undertaker in the area should be able to advise on whether a churchyard burial is possible.
See: CEMETERY
FUNERAL

BUSES AND COACHES

Your rights as a passenger

Your rights when you travel by bus or coach are usually governed, at least in part, by the operator's conditions of carriage. In some cases, however, those conditions may not be binding on you, since they do not have the force of law and take effect as terms in a contract only if the operator has taken reasonable steps to draw them to your attention. Even then, if they are not fair and reasonable they may be invalid under the UNFAIR CONTRACT Terms Act.

Tickets and seats

If you make a firm booking for a seat on a coach, you have a contract with the operator even before you pay for the ticket. That means that you have certain rights. If by mistake the same seat is allocated to two people and one passenger has to travel on a later coach, he

---

BOOKING A SEAT ON A BUS
OR COACH

If you make a firm booking for a seat on a bus or coach, even if you have not paid for the ticket at the time, you have a contract with the operator which gives you certain rights to that seat.

'I'll get 'em for Breach of Contract'

'

THE BURST TYRE THAT KILLED FOUR

When a driver is found to have been even partly responsible for an accident that led to injury, his company will be held liable to pay damages to the victims.

Mr Barkway was on his way to work in a double-decker bus when a front tyre burst. The bus veered across the road, went through iron railings and fell over an embankment on to a railway line, Mr Barkway and three other passengers were killed.

Mr Barkway's widow sued the bus company for damages. The company denied negligence. It said the tyres were inspected twice a week and the impact fracture which caused the blow-out could not have been detected by visual examination.

DECISION

The House of Lords thought the fracture had probably been caused by a heavy blow against a kerb. The driver should have reported any such blow. His failure to do so was negligence and the bus company was liable. So Mrs Barkway was awarded £2,000 damages.

'

would in most cases be able to claim that there had been a breach of contract and demand compensation – for example, the cost of overnight accommodation.

The ticket conditions may say that no liability is accepted in such cases, but under the Unfair Contract Terms Act 1977 such a condition would be valid in law only if it could be proved in court to be fair and reasonable.

Cancellations and delays

Timetables usually say that there is no guarantee or undertaking on the part of the operators that buses or coaches will run on time – or at all. Under the Unfair Contract Terms Act it may be possible to win an action for damages on the grounds that such a stipulation is unreasonable. In the first years of the Act's operation, no cases on this issue had been reported.

When there is an accident

If there is an accident, the operator of the bus or coach is not necessarily

bound to pay compensation for injuries. His liability will depend on whether there has been a failure on his own part or that of his staff to take reasonable care.

For example, if the accident was caused by a failure to maintain the vehicle properly, the operator will be liable.

If the driver negligently tries to drive the bus under a bridge that is too low, there will be liability on the operator. Similarly, if there is a collision caused in part by the driver's negligence, the operator will have to pay compensation if a passenger sues.

No conditions on tickets can exclude or limit liability in such cases.

But if the accident is caused solely by the negligence of another driver or of a pedestrian, the bus or coach operator is not liable to the passengers. They will have the right only to sue the person whose negligence caused the accident. If that person was driving a motor vehicle, insurance is compulsory and a claim should be worth making; but a claim against a pedestrian would be worth making only if he or she had the financial resources to meet it. In rare cases accidents happen without anyone being to blame. In such cases there is no one against whom to claim.

Hiring a coach

If you hire a coach, the hiring company is obliged to take reasonable care to see that the vehicle is fit for the journey. If the coach broke down, for example, on an outing, the company would be liable for breach of contract unless the fault was one that inspection would not have revealed and proper maintenance would not have prevented.

Any clause or term in the hire agreement stating that the company is not liable for breakdowns can be challenged under the Unfair Contract Terms Act.

Complaining about the service

If you have a complaint about local, excursion or express bus services take it up first with the operating company.

However, if the operator seems unable or unwilling to do anything, send the complaint to the Traffic Commissioners for your area, and ask them to look into it.

The Traffic Commissioners supervise all bus services on behalf of the Department of Transport. They issue licences for every route, service, vehicle, driver and conductor in their area. In the last resort the local Commissioners have the power to refuse or revoke licences, which could stop a service.

The Commissioners will consider any serious complaint about a service – such as fare staging, routes, frequency, unsafe driving or rudeness of staff.

The complaint, particularly if it is not an isolated one, will be pursued and may result in a reprimand or even suspension or termination of a service.

Any new bus route or fare increase also needs approval by the Commissioners: so does alteration of an existing service. Licences for each service must be renewed every 3 years. If you have grounds for objecting to the service (for instance, that the route used is not safe or that a proposed alteration is against the public interest), write to the Commissioners. At the Commission chairman's discretion you will probably be able to put your objection in person at the licence hearing.

BUSINESS, Starting a

How different kinds of firms have different legal responsibilities

Anyone setting up a business has a choice of three ways of conducting it: as a sole trader, in a partnership or through a company. Each form has its advantages and disadvantages.

Trading on your own

You can carry on a business under your own name without any legal formalities whatsoever. You simply start trading and retain sole ownership of the assets and goodwill of the business. You can employ staff and buy or lease property and equipment in connection with the business. You must, however, keep books recording all financial transactions so that you can be assessed for income tax and value added tax. For income tax you will be assessed under Schedule D as a self-employed person; similarly, you will have to pay class 2 NATIONAL INSURANCE CONTRIBUTIONS.

If you want to trade under a name other than your own, you must register that BUSINESS NAME.

The main advantages of being a sole trader are the freedom and independence it gives and the fact that all profits accrue to the trader. The main disadvantage is that the trader also has unlimited personal responsibility for any losses. If your business fails you may lose not only all your business assets but also your home, your car, your personal savings and anything else you own. *See:* BANKRUPTCY

Creating a partnership

Two or more people can start a business in just the same way as a sole trader. No legal formalities are necessary unless they wish to register a business name.

The business relationship between the partners is regulated by the Partnership Act 1890, unless the partners agree otherwise. Under the Act, each is entitled to an equal share of the profits and has an equal responsibility for any losses. If the partnership is dissolved, each partner is entitled to take out the amount of capital he has put in. The rest of the assets are then divided equally.

In most businesses, 20 is the maximum number of partners allowed. Professional men, like lawyers, doctors and accountants, however, can form partnerships with as many partners as they like.

Partners usually have a partnership agreement or deed drawn up by a solicitor to define their relationship and prevent possible disagreement if only the general terms of the Partnership Act were relied on.

The partnership deed should cover such points as the aims and scope of the partnership, how decisions are to be made, how financial matters are to be arranged, and how a partner can withdraw without causing the dissolution of the partnership.

Whatever arrangements are made, however, each partner remains personally responsible to any outside creditors for the whole of the partnership's liabilities, even if these were incurred by another partner without him knowing.

Forming a company

The only way to limit the personal responsibility that sole traders and partners have for business liabilities is to form a company.

A company is a legal entity quite

separate from its owners with many of the same rights as an individual. It is entitled to all the assets of the business and it is responsible for any liabilities. The people who formed and run it are not personally liable.

In order to form a company it is necessary to submit various documents to the Registrar of Companies, the most important of which are:

Memorandum of association The memorandum is the 'constitution' of the company and must state the name of the company, whether its registered office will be in England, Scotland or Wales, the business purpose for which it is formed and the maximum amount of capital which may be put into the company (the authorised capital). The authorised capital must be divided into fixed portions called shares.

Each share has a nominal value and may be sold by the company for that value – or more. It is not necessary for all shares in the company to be sold. The nominal value of shares sold is the issued capital.

Articles of association The articles lay down the rules that are to govern the day-to-day running of the company – such as the appointment and powers of directors, and the rights and responsibilities of shareholders.

If you do not register your own set of articles, the law assumes that a model laid down in the Companies Act applies. But it is better to use your own.

The price of limited liability

Having formed a company, a businessman has achieved the major advantage of limited liability. However, there are also disadvantages. Besides the cost of forming the company (more than £100), there is annual expenditure on having the accounts audited and filing these and other documents with the Registrar of Companies. Accounts and other documents filed with the Registrar are open to public inspection. Privacy is therefore lost; competitors and employees are able to see how well or how badly the business is doing.

Buying a company 'off the peg'

The process of forming a company from scratch usually takes several weeks. If you urgently require a company, it is possible to buy one that has already been registered. The disadvan-

THE PARTNER WHO WAS FROZEN OUT

Although changing a partnership into a company substantially alters its status in law, the courts recognise that behind the company there are still 'partners' who must act fairly towards each other.

Mr Ebrahimi and Mr Nazar were partners in a carpet business. They shared the work and the profits. In 1945 they formed a company. Each partner became a director, with 250 £1 shares.

Later, Mr Nazar's son became a director. Mr Nazar and Mr Ebrahimi each transferred 100 shares to Mr Nazar junior.

The company flourished, but no dividends were paid on the shares: profits were divided up as directors' fees.

In 1969, after a dispute, Mr Nazar and his son voted Mr Ebrahimi off the board. They were entitled to do so, under the Companies Act, and the result was that Mr Ebrahimi not only received no dividends – because of the way the company was run – but also ceased to get a director's fee.

Mr Ebrahimi went to court. He asked that either Mr Nazar and Mr Nazar junior should be ordered to buy his shares from him, or that the company should be compulsorily wound up, so that as a shareholder he could get his share of the assets.

DECISION

The House of Lords eventually ordered the company to be wound up, under a section of the Companies Act that allows such an order when it is 'just and equitable'. Giving judgment, Lord Wilberforce said there was room in company law to recognise that behind a company there were 'individuals with rights, expectations and obligations'.

There had not been sufficient 'misconduct or oppression' against Mr Ebrahimi for the court to order the purchase of his shares. But Mr Ebrahimi had been treated unfairly, and the company should be wound up, so that Mr Ebrahimi could at least get his share of the assets.

THE SHAREHOLDER WHO DID NOT HAVE TO PAY

That rule of separate entities means that a sole founder of a company can quite legally enter into binding contracts with it.

Mr Salomon was a sole trader in the leather and bootmaking business. Then he formed a company.

The company's share capital was 40,000 £1 shares. Mr Salomon, his wife, daughter and four sons each bought one share.

The company then issued Mr Salomon with debentures – a form of security giving first claim to the company's assets – to the value of £10,000, in part payment for the business.

Mr Salomon in turn used the debentures as security to get a £5,000 loan from Mr Broderip. The interest rate was 8 per cent. Mr Salomon failed to pay. So Mr Broderip obtained a liquidator's order to wind up the company and recover his money.

When that had been done, there were still assets totalling £1,055. Other creditors claimed those assets. But Mr Salomon also laid claim to them – and asserted that he had priority over the other creditors because he was a debenture holder.

The rival creditors claimed that the formation of the company was a fraud, that the company was a mere 'alias' for Mr Salomon – and that he should pay in some money, to be shared among them.

DECISION

The court held that the company had been properly formed and that Mr Salomon's liability was therefore limited – so he need not pay money in for the benefit of other creditors. Furthermore, since he and the company were separate legal 'persons', with a legitimate contract, he was entitled to preferential treatment with his debentures and so had a prior claim to the assets.

THE BOSS WHO WAS ALSO AN EMPLOYEE

One of the most fundamental rules of company law is that every company is a legal unit, an individual quite distinct from its owners or shareholders.

Mr Lee, a New Zealand businessman, had a limited company whose trade was aerial crop-spraying. The nominal capital was 3,000 £1 shares. Mr Lee held 2,999 of them and was governing director.

He was also employed on a salary as chief pilot. In 1956, while flying for the company, he was killed in a crash. His widow claimed compensation from the company, for herself and her children, under the New Zealand Workers' Compensation Act.

The company, which had insured Mr Lee, resisted the claim on the ground that he was not really a 'worker' since he was the controlling shareholder, governing director and employer with sole control of his work.

The case eventually came before the Privy Council in London.

DECISION

Mr Lee and the company were separate legal entities, even though he owned and ran the company. Mr Lee had a valid contract with the company as its chief pilot and in that capacity was an employed worker. Therefore his estate was entitled to compensation.

---

tages are that the business purposes stated in the memorandum may not be appropriate, and the name of the company will almost certainly not be. Such matters can be altered subsequently, but that involves further expense and inconvenience.

Private and public companies

A private company cannot offer to sell its shares to the public. A public company may do so, but must have an authorised capital of at least £50,000.

Before it starts to carry on business, a public company must also have an *issued* capital of at least £50,000.

In future, the names of all public companies will have to end with the words 'public limited company' or 'p.l.c.'. Existing companies have a period of 18 months from December 22, 1980 in which to comply with the new law.

Every company – private and public – must have at least two shareholders, one director and one secretary. There

need be no limit on the number of members, although private companies do usually limit their numbers to 50.

Most public companies raise money by issuing shares which are quoted on the Stock Exchange. It is a criminal offence for a director of a public company or someone with similar access to 'inside information' to deal on the Stock Exchange in the shares of any company with which he is connected if he is making use of such information. If an 'insider' gives a tip to someone else, knowing that the other will deal in the shares, both commit an offence. The maximum penalty in each case is 2 years' imprisonment and an unlimited fine.

BUSINESS NAME

Restrictions on the names that businesses can use

A business can trade under any name it chooses provided that:
1. It does not use the name of another business in the same field.
2. If its trading name is not that of the owner or partners, it is registered with the Registrar of Business Names.

Duplicate names

The owner of a business is prohibited from using a trading name that is likely to confuse the public into believing that his business is the same as another. That applies even if the name is the trader's own. It is a civil, not a criminal matter, however, and the responsibility for seeking redress lies with the person or

> ### THE TWO WINE MERCHANTS
>
> *A new company cannot use a name so similar to a competitor that it is likely to confuse people.*
>
> Short's Ltd had been a noted wine and spirit merchants in the Strand, London, for nearly 200 years when, during the First World War, Ernest Short began business in the same trade at Woolwich, a London suburb.
>
> At first Ernest Short traded under the name of Short's Wine House, but eventually he abbreviated this to Short's.
>
> Short's Ltd sought an injunction against his using the name Short's or any other name that would lead the public to believe the two businesses were the same.
>
> DECISION
> The injunction was granted.

company whose name has been copied. He has to take civil action, by seeking an INJUNCTION against the offender in the county court.

Registering a business name

Any business that wants to trade under a name other than that of its owner or owners must apply to the Registrar of Business Names. Application forms are obtainable from most banks. Failure to apply is a criminal offence.

The Registrar can refuse to register the name if he considers it misleading or undesirable. For example, he will not accept any name which suggests that a company is a bank or investment trust or that it is connected with the Royal Family, the Co-operative Society or a building society – unless, of course, these claims are true.

The Registrar may also reject any name that resembles that of an existing business – even if it is not exactly the same.

BUSKING

The risky trade of the itinerant musician

Buskers – actors, showmen or musicians who perform in streets and public places in London and other large cities – are almost certain to be breaking the law wherever they stop to play.

About the only time a busker is within the law is when he plays on private property with the permission of the owner. Perhaps a cinema manager may have one in his foyer to attract custom.

But even then, the busker may break a local BYE-LAW on NOISE OFFENCES.

Without the owner's permission, the busker is trespassing and can be ejected, using reasonable force, if necessary. TRESPASS is not usually a criminal offence in itself, but can lead to an arrest for BREACH OF THE PEACE.

All railway property is private, and both British Rail and London Transport have bye-laws against singing or performing 'to the annoyance of any other person'. The maximum penalty is a fine of £50.

Street busking is almost always illegal, whether the busker is in the road or on the pavement. A common charge is obstructing the public highway, but there may also be local bye-laws forbidding music near houses, churches or hospitals. Some councils prohibit busking entirely.

BYE-LAWS

Local regulations that safeguard the well-being of a community

Local authorities and public bodies make bye-laws under powers given them by Parliament, and it is as much a criminal offence to break a bye-law as to break any other law.

The most common bye-laws are those made by district councils (in London, borough councils) to prohibit specific nuisances. Other public bodies – for example, British Railways Board, the Atomic Energy Authority and the National Trust – make bye-laws to control the behaviour of the public while they are on their property.

How to oppose a new bye-law

Before submitting a bye-law to the government for confirmation, a local authority must give the public 1 month's notice of its intention to do so by advertising in a local newspaper that a copy of the draft bye-law can be inspected at the council offices.

If, after having seen such a proposed bye-law, you wish to oppose it, write to the government minister to whom it is being submitted. His address will be in the advertisement.

If the minister thinks you have reasonable grounds for opposing the law, he may order a local inquiry. You will be given notice of this and be allowed to attend and put your case.

Even after a bye-law has been confirmed by the minister, it can be challenged at any time in the courts. A bye-law that prohibited singing in the street was abolished as unreasonable in the courts, because it did not restrict the offence to cases where the singing definitely annoyed members of the public.

CAPITAL GAINS TAX

When you need not pay for making a profit

When any property (including goods which have been damaged) is disposed of, capital gains tax may have to be paid.

The tax, which applies to personal as well as business assets, is levied on any increase in the value of an item between when it was acquired and when it was disposed of. No allowance is made for the fact that the increase may be purely the result of inflation.

There are, however, many types of assets and circumstances when tax is not payable or can be postponed, or when the gross liability can be reduced.

Gains that are always exempt

Capital gains tax is never payable on the disposal of:

1. Any motor vehicle suitable for private use, including vintage and veteran cars.

2. Small gifts whose combined total is not more than £100 in any one tax year. A gift that does not rise in value while you own it is exempt when you give it away, even if it is worth more than £100.

3. Cash acquired for your own use – although other forms of tax, such as capital transfer tax, may apply.

4. Betting, gambling and lottery winnings.

5. Compensation for personal injuries or wrongs – although compensation for damage to property or goods can be taxable, unless the whole of the money is spent on restoring or replacing the asset, when the tax can be partly or wholly postponed.

6. Chattels – that is, movable objects – including coins, old furniture and paintings, if no individual item is sold for more than £2,000 and if you are not buying and selling so frequently as to be considered a trader.

7. 'Wasting assets' which are also tangible, movable objects with a useful life of not more than 50 years – except for business plant and machinery.

8. Life assurance policies when they mature or are cashed in.

9. A private house which has been your family's main or only home throughout the time you have owned it.

10. Medals and other decorations for valour, as long as you did not buy them, but won or inherited them.

11. Government securities – such as short-term stocks – provided that you inherited them, or if you bought them but do not sell for at least 12 months.

Assets partly exempt Other assets may be partly exempt. For example, assets acquired before April 6, 1965, will be taxed only on any gain made after that date.

There are two ways in which you can choose to have the taxable gain worked out, but special rules apply to quoted shares.

One is to divide the overall gain in proportion to the periods for which the assets were held before and after April 6, 1965. If they were held for 5 years before that date and sold 2 years after it, the taxable gain would be two-sevenths of the total profit.

The other is to take the value as at April 6, 1965 and deduct it from the value at the time of disposal.

The second method would be an advantage if, for example, the assets made a big gain before April 6, 1965, and grew more slowly thereafter.

For example, if the total gain was £700, of which £500 was made before April 6, 1965, the taxable amount would be £200 as with the first method. However, if the gain before the relevant date was £650, it would benefit you to adopt the second method, because that would leave only £50 on which to pay tax.

If the greatest gain was made after April 6, 1965, under the second method of assessment you would have to pay more tax.

If you wish the second method to apply, you must tell the Inland Revenue in writing within 2 clear tax years after the date of disposal. However, if a large sum is involved, take specialist advice from an accountant.

Gains on which some tax relief is given

If the total gains made by an individual or married couple in a year do not exceed a certain amount – £3,000 a year from 1980–1 – they are entirely free of capital gains tax. There are also special reliefs for those selling a business on retirement.

Unit Trusts If you sell unit trusts, you are liable to pay capital gains tax on any profit you make.

Until April 5, 1980, there was given a 'tax credit' of 10 per cent which could be offset against your tax liability on the units, but that was abolished for sales on or after April 6, 1980.

Shares There may be special relief on the sale of quoted shares if they have been the subject of a takeover bid and if no cash was received on the takeover. New shares issued in exchange for old, at the same cost, are not liable for tax until they are sold.

Shares in a private, unquoted company are subject to the same general rules, but valuing them is a matter for a specialist.

If you invested in the shares of an unquoted trading company on its formation and you eventually dispose of them at a loss, you may be able to offset that loss against your taxable income. However, the conditions are complicated, and an accountant's advice is needed.

The 'roll-over' facility

From April 6, 1980, when an individual makes a gift to someone else, including a company or a trustee, the gain can be 'rolled over' if the donor and the recipient make a joint claim. That means that the recipient receives the asset at the value the donor originally acquired it. Thus, the donor pays no tax on any increase in its value during his ownership. Tax is paid by the recipient when he disposes of the gift.

If any CAPITAL TRANSFER TAX is paid on the gift, it is added to the original cost of the asset and therefore reduces the taxable profit on any subsequent sale.

For example, Mr George Forrest acquired a holiday home for £15,000 in 1972. In 1981, he gives it to his son, David Forrest, when it is worth £60 000, and £2,000 of capital transfer tax is paid on the gift. David sells it in 1985 for £80,000. The taxable gain is:

Sale price		80,000
Father's original cost	15,000	
Capital transfer tax paid on gift	2,000	17,000
		———
David's taxable profit		63,000

RATES AT WHICH CAPITAL GAINS ARE TAXED

For individuals – not businesses – there is a special exemption from capital gains on the first £3,000 of net gains in each tax year. This exemption first applied in 1980–1.

For example, if a man made net gains of £4,000 in a year, he would pay tax of £300 (£1,000×30 per cent). A husband and wife qualify for only one £3,000 exemption per year between them.

Capital gains tax is payable 9 months after the end of the tax year (on or before December 1).

When you make a loss

If an asset is sold at a loss – or otherwise disposed of when the value has dropped – the loss can be set off against gains in the same tax year or carried forward to another tax year.

The loss cannot be used to offset gains in a previous tax year or to reduce liability for income tax as opposed to capital gains tax.

A self-employed person cannot set off a business trading loss against a capital gain, but someone who lends or guarantees money to a trader and does not get repaid can claim a loss.

The relationship between losses and the £3,000 exemption limit is difficult. Losses of the current year must be offset against capital gains of the same year, even if that reduces the net gains to less than £3,000 (thus exempt from tax), but losses brought forward need be used only to the extent that they reduce the gains to the £3,000 exemption level.

For example, a man has unused losses of £2,000 from a previous year, and in the current year losses of £600 and gains of £4,100.

Gains of year		4,100
Losses of current year fully offset		600
		———
		3,500
Losses brought forward	2,000	
Partly used	500	500
	———	———
Carry forward	1,500	
	———	
Net gains (exempt)		3,000
		———

Special rules for husbands and wives

In assessing capital gains tax, a husband and wife are treated as one person. Any transfer of property between them is not taxable. Losses made by one can be set against gains made by the other.

If a couple get divorced, capital gains tax can be charged on property transferred after the decree is made absolute. But the matrimonial home is exempt, if it is transferred as part of a divorce settlement.

Selling the family home

Normally the profit on selling your home is exempt from capital gains tax. However, in certain circumstances you should take steps to avoid becoming liable.

Business use If you use part of your home for business and intend to claim part of the running costs against your income tax liability, try to assess what the effect would be if you later sold your home for a good profit.

It is possible for capital gains tax on a house that greatly increases in value to outweigh the benefit of expenses claimed against income tax.

Capital gains tax is charged on part of the profit, in proportion to the amount of it used for business purposes.

For example, if the owner of a 5-roomed house has claimed the use of a room as a study, he may face capital gains tax on one-fifth of any profit, when he eventually sells. However, if someone buys another home and again uses a room in it for business he can postpone paying capital gains until he eventually sells the second home.

If you sell a house that you use partly for business and re-invest in another property, you will not be liable for capital gains tax on any profit relating to the business part – provided that you spend it all on the business part of the new property.

You can 'roll over' on every such sale and purchase: tax is not payable even on death.

When only part is used If you use part of your home for business only occasionally and that part is also sometimes used for private purposes, you are not liable for capital gains tax, even though you can claim for its business use against income tax.

When part of your home is let

If part of the home is exclusively let – say, as a bedsitter – you may when you sell it get some exemption from capital gains tax on the let part (up to a maximum of £10,000, or equal to the gain you have made in proportion to the whole house) – provided that you live in. The house and the proportionate gain is less than £10,000.

For example, a widow lets off the top floor of her house as a self-contained flat. She bought it in 1975 for £20,000 and sells it for £50,000 in 1981. Assuming her flat and the flat that is let are of equal value, she will pay tax on:

Sale price		50,000
Cost		20,000
Total gain		30,000
Exempt:		
Gain on her own flat	15,000	
Gain on let flat	10,000	25,000
Pay tax on		5,000

When you have a lodger If part of the house is used by a lodger or paying guest, make sure that he has no exclusive use of it – by reserving your right to enter and inspect it, for example, and by allowing your own family to use it when there is no guest.

If the garden is very large Tax may be levied if the garden of your home is more than 1 acre – unless you can show that its size is reasonable for the size and character of the house, or that it is required for the reasonable enjoyment of the house as a private home.

If you have to pay tax, it will be charged on the excess area of garden as a proportion of the value of the entire property.

If you sell part of your garden to be built on, but keep the house, it may be against your interests to apply for planning permission for the proposed buildings yourself. If you do so, you may have to pay capital gains tax on any profit from the sale. It is often advisable to leave the planning application to the purchaser.

When you are away from home for long periods

If you leave your house unoccupied for long periods, you may be liable for capital gains tax on part of the profit when you sell.

The taxable gain is worked out according to the proportion of absence to occupation during your period of ownership.

There are, however, exemptions. You can be absent from the house throughout the last 2 years before selling. That allows a period of grace in which to dispose of the property after moving elsewhere.

You also escape tax if your periods of absence do not total more than 3 years during ownership. But you must have lived in the house before and after those absences, unless that is impracticable –

for example, if you have emigrated.

If you work away from home, elsewhere in the United Kingdom, you are entitled to a total of 4 years' absence. If you are employed overseas, you are entitled to be absent as much as you like without becoming liable to capital gains tax.

If you buy a plot of land on which to build a private home for yourself, any absence does not begin to be calculated until you have built the house and moved in.

If you own two homes

Only one home at a time can normally be exempt from capital gains tax. If you own two homes, the one that you choose as your main residence is exempt.

To establish which home you wish to be considered tax exempt, notify the Inland Revenue in writing within 2 years of buying the second home.

Otherwise the question will be decided according to which home is in fact your main residence, at the time when you sell one or other of the properties. If that question cannot be agreed between you and the tax inspector, it will be decided by the Inland Revenue Appeal Commissioners.

When a second home is exempt A second home is exempt from capital gains tax if it is occupied, rent-free, throughout your ownership, by a dependent relative – a widowed mother or mother-in-law, or by a relative who is over 65 or unable to look after himself or herself because of mental or physical disability.

But if the dependent relative pays rent at any time the property will be immediately liable to capital gains tax.

Selling a business

Profit on the sale of land, buildings and goodwill in a business are all liable to capital gains tax.

Profit on stock-in-trade, cash and debts owed to the business are exempt.

If machinery or fixtures sell at a profit, capital gains tax may be charged.

Putting off the tax When a business asset is sold, the capital gains tax on any profit can be postponed if the entire sale price is reinvested in another business asset. That is known as 'rollover relief'.

The replacement asset need not be of the same type as the old one. You can

use the profit from the sale of a shop to buy machinery for an entirely different kind of business.

However, rollover relief is restricted to land, buildings, goodwill, fixed plant and machinery, ships, aircraft and Hovercraft.

The replacement asset must be bought not more than 1 year before and not more than 3 years after the sale of the other asset.

If only part of the sale money is spent on the new asset, tax will be assessed on the amount retained.

Retirement relief Someone over retiring age who is in business can sometimes claim retirement relief on profits made by disposing of business assets or shares in a family trading company.

To qualify for the full relief you have to be over 60 and to have worked continuously in the business for at least 10 years before disposing of it. If you worked for less than 10 years the relief to which you are entitled is reduced. You need only dispose of assets to qualify for relief: you are not obliged to retire.

Relief begins at £10,000 one year after the 60th birthday and increases by £10,000 each year – with proportionate increases for parts of a year – to a maximum of £50,000.

If the relief is being claimed on the sale of shares in a family company, the person claiming must have been a full-time working director for the previous 10 years, with restricted relief for shorter periods.

Furthermore he must own no fewer than 25 per cent of the voting shares himself, or his immediate family must have more than 51 per cent of which he must have 5 per cent.

Relief on such shares may be due only on a proportion of the profit.

When someone dies

In assessing capital gains liability, the value of inherited property is taken to be whatever it was worth at the time of the owner's death. Tax is chargeable only on any increase in value from that date onwards.

For example, if a man buys a painting for £4,000 and when he dies it is valued at £7,000, if his son inherits it and later sells it for £10,500, capital gains tax is chargeable only on the £3,500 by which the value rose during his ownership.

CAPITAL TRANSFER TAX

When giving generously has its penalties

Capital transfer tax is two related taxes in one:

1. A tax on gifts of money or property made by someone in his or her lifetime, charged according to a 'lifetime' scale.

2. Duty on the estate of a dead person, or on gifts made less than 3 years before the donor's death, charged according to a 'death' scale.

On taxable sums of less than £310,000, the lifetime rate of tax is lower than that on the death scale. Above that figure, both rates are the same. There may also be a CAPITAL GAINS TAX liability on a lifetime gift of certain assets.

Capital transfer tax, like income tax, is progressive; the amount to be taxed is treated in slices and the more it is, the higher the proportion of tax on the upper slice.

When tax need not be paid

Not all gifts are liable to tax. Some escape because they are specifically exempt – for example, gifts worth a total of less than £250 made to any one person in a tax year. Others which in principle should be taxed escape because their value is below the threshold at which the tax begins to operate.

Even if you are entitled to no other exemptions from capital transfer tax, you can make gifts worth a total of at least £2,000 in any tax year without having to pay capital transfer tax. In the case of a married couple each could make a £2,000 gift.

Gifts that fall into the second of these categories are said to be 'chargeable', and although they escape tax, their value is taken into account in establishing liability for tax on other gifts.

Everyone is entitled during his lifetime to make gifts that would normally attract capital transfer tax up to a total of £50,000 without having to pay.

In addition, there is a tax-free allowance on chargeable gifts of £2,000 in any one tax year. If the annual total includes gifts on which relief or exemption has been given, the allowance may be higher than £2,000.

The effect of those two rules is that no capital transfer tax is payable by anyone until he or she has given away a total of £50,000 in chargeable gifts over the years, plus £2,000 in any one tax year. The figures of £50,000 and £2,000 applied in the tax year 1980–1.

Capital transfer tax is chargeable only on gifts that are intended to benefit the recipient. If there is no such intention, tax is not charged.

So, for example, if you give an old book to a jumble sale believing it to be worthless, and if it is found later to be a valuable first edition, you would escape tax.

Even when benefit is intended it is not taxable if the cost is an allowable expense of your business for income tax purposes.

Gambling losses and loans that have to be written off because the borrower has gone bankrupt are similarly exempt, because they were not in the first place intended as gifts.

Even where the transfer was intended to benefit the recipient, there are two

TAX ON TRANSFERS OF SHARES

Gifts or bequests of shares in companies quoted on the Stock Exchange and of unit trust holdings are subject to the same rules as other transfers of property.

The tax is calculated on the quoted value of the shares on the day the transfer took place or the day the donor died.

If you inherit shares in a public company and sell them within 1 year of the donor's death, you can ask to have the tax computed on the price you got for them, rather than on the probate value, if the sale price was lower. However, if you reinvest the proceeds in quoted shares or in unit trusts within 2 months of the sale, you may lose the relief.

Capital transfer tax on shares in unquoted companies is harder to compute. When deciding their value the tax authorities will take into account the number of shares held by the transferer and spouse, the assets held by the company and its business prospects. If together the husband and wife have a controlling interest, the value of their shares will be higher than if they do not.

Transfers of unquoted shares may qualify for relief at up to 50 per cent of their value.

If you are making or have received a gift or bequest of unquoted shares, ask an accountant to prepare an assessment of their value.

RATES OF CAPITAL TRANSFER TAX

How transfers of capital or property are taxed at an increasingly higher rate

The rates apply to transfers made on or after March 26, 1980. The lifetime rates are half those on death up to £110,000, begin to catch up between £110,000 and £310,000 and are the same above £310,000.

Gross cumulative total	Lifetime rate of tax (%)	Rates applicable on death and on gifts within 3 years of death (%)
£0 to 50,000	0	0
50,001 to 60,000	15	30
60,001 to 70,000	17½	35
70,001 to 90,000	20	40
90,001 to 110,000	22½	45
110,001 to 130,000	27½	50
130,001 to 160,000	35	55
160,001 to 210,000	42½	60
210,001 to 260,000	50	60
260,001 to 310,000	55	60
310,001 to 510,000	60	60
510,001 to 1,010,000	65	65
1,010,001 to 2,010,000	70	70
Over £2,010,000	75	75

HOW TO PAY THE TAX

Transfers of cash or property which may be liable to capital transfer tax must be reported to the Inland Revenue – in London, the Capital Taxes Office – within 12 months from the end of the month in which it took place. The tax falls due within 6 months of the end of the month of transfer, unless the gift was made between April 6 and September 30, in which case payment does not fall due until April 30 of the following year.

To do so, you must complete form CTT 1, available from any Inland Revenue tax office. There is space on the form to state who will be responsible for paying the tax – the person making the gift or the one receiving it. If the form is not completed, or if no arrangement has been made about who should pay, the donor is legally responsible.

You have no need to work out the tax due. The Inland Revenue will compute the amount that you are due to pay, and send you a demand.

The tax authorities may charge interest on overdue tax at the rate of 9 per cent a year on lifetime gifts and 6 per cent on transfers after death.

In some circumstances, the person owing the tax can ask for time to pay, in 8 annual instalments or in 16 half-yearly ones. But this is allowed only if:
1. The transfer is on death or, if made during the donor's lifetime, the recipient agrees to pay the tax.
2. The property is land or buildings worth £250,000 or less held as business assets; or is a controlling holding in company shares; or is certain other types of unquoted shares; or is other types of business asset.

forms of exemption – property exemption and transfer exemption.

Exempt property

Certain property is never taxable:
1. Any interest in property that reverts to the original settler on the death of an original beneficiary. For example, if you give a home to your mother for her lifetime and it reverts to you on her death, the estate is not liable to tax when you inherit.
2. Property outside the United Kingdom if the owner is not domiciled here. Your place of DOMICILE is the country in which you are officially regarded as living, even if you do not actually live there. Someone domiciled outside Britain can come here frequently or actually live here without losing his or her original place of domicile and without attracting tax on overseas property.
3. Some UK government securities, such as War Loan, if the owner is domiciled abroad.
4. Survivor's pensions paid under approved retirement annuity schemes for the self-employed.
5. Pensions, including death payments, and returns of contributions from some former employers, such as foreign governments.
6. Property owned by members of visiting armed forces and NATO personnel, and diplomats.
7. National Savings Certificates, Premium Bonds and similar forms of savings held by people domiciled in the Channel Islands or the Isle of Man.

Exempt transfers

Many transfers of property are exempt or partly exempt from capital transfer tax:
1. Those between husband and wife are wholly exempt if they were living together when the transfer took place or at the time of the death of one of them. But if the partner receiving the property has his or her domicile outside the United Kingdom, only the first £50,000 (1980–1) of gifts received from the other spouse during his or her lifetime, or on death, is exempt.
2. Transfers from one spouse to the other after the breakdown of a marriage are wholly exempt if ordered by a court. Otherwise, they are taxed. If the former partners agree a division of property, they should get the court to approve it to escape the tax. *See:* MAINTENANCE
3. Lifetime gifts or bequests to maintain or educate the donor's child, whether legitimate or not, or any child in his long-term care, or to maintain a former spouse or to make reasonable provision for a dependent relative are wholly exempt.
4. Lifetime gifts to a couple getting married are exempt up to limits that vary according to the relationship between donor and recipient.

Each parent of the partners can give up to £5,000 without attracting tax.

Each grandparent or great-grandparent may give £2,500, and each partner may give the other £2,500 prior to the marriage – afterwards there is no limit (1980–1).

The tax-free limit on wedding gifts from all other sources is £1,000 per donor (1980–1).
5. 'Normal' lifetime expenditure out of income – for example, on life assurance is exempt.

To qualify as 'normal', the payment must be made from after-tax income, must not lower the usual standard of living of the person making it and must be made regularly.

In practice, two payments of a fixed sum, made on the same date a year apart, are accepted by the tax authorities as regular.
6. Outright lifetime gifts up to the first £250 of value made to any one person in one tax year are wholly exempt.
7. The first £2,000 worth of lifetime gifts made during any one tax year is exempt. If the whole exemption is not used in one year, the balance can be carried forward to the next one.

If you made no transfers at all in the tax year 1980–1, you could transfer £4,000 worth of chargeable property in

HOW THE GROSS TAX METHOD WORKS

A agrees to pay the tax due on his gift to B of a picture worth £1,000. There are no exemptions to be taken into account. The rate of tax applicable to the gift is 5 per cent.

The tax authorities consider that the value of the picture lost to A is only 100 per cent less the 5 per cent rate of tax – that is, 95 per cent – of the total value of the transaction.

The total value of the transfer is therefore:

Value of picture £1,000.00
plus
The grossed-up proportion of the 5% rate of tax:

$$£1,000 \times \frac{5}{95} = \text{.......................... } £52.63$$

The total value of the transaction is therefore £1,052.63

The tax payable at 5% is therefore £52.63

HOW RELATED PROPERTY IS TAXED

Property where the whole is worth more than the parts is called related property and is subject to special capital transfer tax calculations.

A owns a piece of land suitable for a small housing development. A development company is prepared to pay £12,000 for it.

However, A does not want to sell. Instead, he gives part of the land – by itself too small for housing and worth £2,000 – to a cousin to grow vegetables.

The rest he keeps for himself. It, too, is now too small for development, and is worth £3,000.

The tax calculation on A's gift to his cousin is:

Value of entire plot £12,000
minus
Value of plot retained by A £3,000

The loss of value to A
is therefore
£12,000 – £3,000 = ... £9,000

Tax is charged on £9,000, and not on the £2,000 value of the plot given by A to his cousin.

1981–2. If you transferred nothing in 1979–80, the exemption for 1982–3 would still be £4,000.

8. Gifts to charities are exempt without limit, unless they were made within 1 year of death, when the ceiling is £2,000.

The same rule applies to gifts to political parties which have at least two members sitting in Parliament, or which captured at least one seat and 150,000 votes at the general election before the gift was made.

9. Gifts and bequests made for the public benefit to artistic or scientific bodies, such as universities or public art galleries are wholly exempt.

10. In the case of mutual transfers – for example, when A makes a gift to B and B later returns it – the original capital transfer charge on A, or a proportion of it, can be reclaimed.

Lifetime gifts on which tax has to be paid

Three types of gift are taxable:
1. Gifts whose value to any one reci-

pient in one tax year is more than £250. Only the amount over £250 is taxable.

2. Sales of property or other commercial arrangements at less than the full commercial price, so that they contain an element of a gift.

If you sell a painting that could fetch £2,500 to a friend for £1,000 you will be liable for tax on the difference between the price actually charged and the full commercial price – in the case of the picture £2,500 less £1,000.

3. A loan or lease of property for a fixed period at less than the rent or interest rate that would have been charged commercially.

If you rent a house to your son for £5 a week over 3 years, and similar property in the area is being rented at £10 a week, you may be liable for tax on the difference – that is, £5 per week.

How tax is charged on lifetime gifts

The amount of tax charged on lifetime gifts is calculated upon the loss of value to the donor as the result of making the gift, less the value of any exemptions to which he is entitled.

The tax may be charged net if the person receiving the gift agrees to pay it, or gross if the donor pays. The tax authorities calculate the amount due, and eventually demand it.

The net method of taxation is straightforward. If A gives B a picture worth £1,000, on which the full amount of capital transfer tax is due because A has used up all his exemptions, the appropriate percentage rate of tax is simply applied to the value. If the appropriate rate is 30 per cent, B has to pay

that proportion of £1,000 in tax – £300.

The gross method is more complicated. The tax authorities consider that, because the donor is paying the tax, the loss of value to him is not only the value of the gift, but the tax as well. They then gross the two up, and tax the total, so the amount of tax levied under the gross method is more than it would be on the same gift if the tax were paid net.

When a complete property is divided

Sometimes the value of an entire property is greater than the sum of its individual parts. When that happens, and part of the property is given away, the tax charges are based, not on the value of the portion transferred but on the loss of value to the donor.

The situation arises most commonly when shares in private companies are transferred, and husband and wife hold more than 51 per cent and thus have a controlling interest. In this case their shares will have a higher value attributed to them by the tax authorities than those of other parties. A gift of shares which left them with less than 50 per cent, for example, would be a loss far greater than the face value of the shares because they would have lost their controlling interest.

Collections of coins, stamps or works of art may be more valuable in their entirety than the sum value of each item treated individually.

Tax payable after death

Capital transfer tax is charged on the net value of a dead person's estate – that is, the value of all assets less any out-

HOW TAX IS ASSESSED AFTER DEATH

B, a widower, makes chargeable gifts during his lifetime worth £65,000. He would have been liable to tax on the last £15,000 of these gifts.

When he dies, B leaves a net estate of £28,000. The tax applied to his estate is based upon the total of chargeable lifetime gifts, £65,000, plus the net value of the estate, £28,000 – that is, £93,000.

The estate is therefore taxed as follows:

£5,000 (65,000 to 70,000) × 35%	£1,750
£20,000 (70,000 to 90,000) × 40%	£8,000
£3,000 (90,000 to 93,000) × 45%	£1,350
£28,000	**Total tax due** £11,100

standing debts and funeral expenses and any exempt transfers. The charge is on the 'death' scale – which means a higher rate of charge than that applied to lifetime gifts, at least at the lower end of the scale.

To find what rate of tax is payable, the value of all the deceased's chargeable gifts (after applying other exemptions) made during his or her lifetime is added to the net value of the estate. If the total is less than £50,000, no tax is payable.

If it is more than £50,000, capital transfer tax is charged on the estate on a sliding scale.

Gifts within 3 years of death

If someone makes a lifetime gift on which tax is charged and dies within 3 years of doing so, the gift becomes taxable – on the 'death' scale. It will be reassessed by the tax authorities when they compute duty on the dead person's estate, and the person who received it will get a demand for any difference between the tax paid on the 'lifetime' scale and that chargeable at 'on death' rates.

If you receive a chargeable gift from someone and fear that you may have to pay more tax because they could die within 3 years, you can take out an insurance policy against such a risk. Seek the advice of an insurance broker.

CAR DEALER

When a code of practice may protect you

If you buy a new or used car, or if you have to have repairs made to your own car, and then have cause to complain, you may choose to exercise your rights under the law. *See:* DEFECTIVE GOODS; REPAIRER

But if the car dealer belongs to a trade association you can also pursue your complaint through it. Such a course of action is simpler, quicker and generally cheaper than starting court proceedings. It does not, however, jeopardise your legal rights. If you are dissatisfied with the trade association's response to your complaint, you can still take legal action later.

Dealers who belong to an association generally exhibit the symbol at the en-

CODE OF PRACTICE

The motor trade association code of practice lays down the following rules:

Buying a new car
● Every customer should be given a maker's handbook for the car and should be shown a copy of the dealer's pre-delivery inspection check-list.

Buying a secondhand car
● Used cars should be inspected by the dealer before sale and the customer should be shown the check-list. If the customer has reason to complain about the condition of the car after the sale, the list could be produced as evidence although it would not be conclusive.
● All documents provided by previous owners – for example, service records, repair invoices and inspection reports – should be passed to the customer.
● The dealer should take reasonable steps to verify the mileage shown on the car. *See:* TRADE DESCRIPTIONS

trance to the garage or showroom and may reproduce it on letter headings and invoices.

Voluntary codes of practice

The four main motor trade associations – the Motor Agents' Association Ltd (MAA), the Society of Motor Man-

WHEN YOUR NEWLY BOUGHT
CAR BREAKS DOWN

A customer with a complaint about his car should first approach the dealer, then the dealer's trade association and finally, if all else fails, should consider taking legal action.

ufacturers and Traders Ltd (SMMT), the Scottish Motor Trade Association Ltd (SMTA) and the Vehicle Builders and Repairers Association Ltd – have produced voluntary codes of practice after negotiations with the Office of Fair Trading.

These codes cover the sale of new cars, the sale of used cars and repairs and servicing. Although their provisions are not usually binding in law, the associations try to see that their members observe the rules. The codes also provide an ARBITRATION scheme for disputes which reach deadlock. Arbitration is not, however, compulsory.

Making a complaint

Under the basic code agreed by the four main associations, a customer must first ensure that the dealer has been made aware of his complaint. It should be addressed to a senior executive or to the person appointed by the dealer to handle complaints.

If the customer is still dissatisfied he should find out to which trade association the dealer belongs and refer the complaint to it in writing. Each association promises to use its 'best endeavours' to try to resolve the complaint. If those efforts fail, the dealer will agree to go to arbitration, unless his trade association advises him that would be unreasonable. If there is an arbitration clause in the contract between the dealer and the customer, the dealer would be bound to go to arbitration.

Main agents and manufacturers

Some car dealers call themselves agents or main agents for a particular manufacturer. That does not mean that they are agents in the legal sense that they act on a manufacturer's behalf. It is a business term to describe an outlet for a particular manufacturer's goods.

The distinction is important, for if you decide to make a claim under the

SETTING UP AS A DEALER

Car dealers do not need any special licence. However, they must make special insurance arrangements. Ordinary motor policies usually exclude cover if a vehicle is used in connection with the motor trade.

Sale of Goods Act, it is the dealer not the manufacturer you must sue.

In addition, however, you may have rights under the manufacturer's warranty.

See: GUARANTEE
MANUFACTURERS' LIABILITY

CAR HIRE

Your right to be hired a car in good condition

If you hire a car, the company or person who hires it to you is legally responsible for making sure that it is roadworthy.

That responsibility cannot be passed on to you, whatever the terms of your hire agreement, unless you hire the car for business use.

Nevertheless, if you drive the vehicle when it is in an unroadworthy condition or when there are other illegal faults – from a dirty windscreen to a bald tyre – you could be in breach of the Motor Vehicle (Construction and Use) Regulations.

That could mean that both you and the owner were liable to prosecution under the Road Traffic Act 1972, which says that it is an offence to drive a car that does not comply with those regulations.

See: GOODS RENTAL
MOTOR VEHICLE

CAR INSURANCE

The duty imposed on every motorist to insure against accidents

It is a criminal offence to drive a motor vehicle on a public road or in a public place without being insured.

Driving while disqualified means that any insurance a driver might have had is invalid. If he is involved in an accident, and negligently causes injury or damage, he is possibly liable to pay the damages.

The insurance companies operate a scheme, known as the Motor Insurers' Bureau (MIB), which pays compensation to the victim and then sues the driver to recover the money. *See:* MOTOR INSURANCE

CAR PARK

The risks you run when you leave your car

The operators of a car park do not necessarily agree to look after your car or to keep it safe. Usually they simply permit you to leave the car on their property. You are not entitled to expect the car park to be supervised even if a charge is made for leaving your car.

When a car has been damaged or stolen in a car park you can claim against the operators only if they were negligent. Where the car park is un-supervised and no charge is made, negligence is difficult to prove. Even if a ticket was issued it would not be easy to prove negligence unless there was something to indicate that the car park employees had been somehow involved in the loss or damage.

That might be possible in a case where cars were parked unlocked and the keys left so that vehicles could be moved by the staff. If an employee negligently moved a car so that it – or another – was damaged, the operators of the car park would be liable.

However, there might be a valid exclusion clause in the contract.

THE JEWELS THAT VANISHED FROM A ROLLS-ROYCE

Written conditions – on the car park ticket, for example – do not always free the operators from liability for loss or damage.

Mr Mendelssohn parked his friend's Rolls-Royce on the 1st floor of a car park. When the attendant told him he could not lock the car, Mr Mendelssohn explained that there was a suitcase of jewellery on the back seat under a rug. The attendant agreed to lock the car as soon as he had moved it.

An hour later Mr Mendelssohn came back and paid his fee. The car door was unlocked and the key was in the ignition. The rug was still on the back seat.

Mr Mendelssohn drove away and only later moved the rug. He found the suitcase was missing. He returned to the car park and made inquiries, but the suitcase was never found. He sued the car park proprietors.

DECISION

The court found that the suitcase had been stolen from the car park. Although the printed ticket contained a condition that the proprietors were not responsible for loss of vehicle contents, the judge ruled that the attendant's promise to lock the car took priority over this. The proprietors were held responsible.

THE BOGUS FRIEND WHO DROVE AWAY A CAR

To use a car park is merely to pay for or borrow space on someone else's premises. You cannot expect the car to be supervised or looked after continuously.

Mr Ashby parked his car in a seaside car park at Southend. He paid the fee, and the attendant handed him a ticket.

When he came back a few hours later the car had gone. Mr Ashby asked the attendant why he had let someone without the ticket drive away. The attendant said he had been told that the person who took the car was the owner's friend. Mr Ashby sued the operators of the car park.

DECISION

The court said the operators were under no obligation to take care of the car. Mr Ashby's fee simply allowed him to leave the car on their premises.

AN ACCIDENT ON THE CAR LIFT

Although car park operators can be held responsible for injuries on their premises, the onus is also on the individual to exercise care.

Mr Thornton left his car at a multi-storey car park where large lifts took cars to the upper floors.

But when he went to collect his car there was an accident as the lift machinery moved. Mr Thornton was badly injured.

DECISION

The court found that the car park proprietors and Mr Thornton were equally to blame for the accident, as Mr Thornton had stood in the way of the machinery. His damages were reduced by 50 per cent because his own negligence had contributed to the accident.

WHEN CONDITIONS ARE BINDING

Conditions set out on notices in car parks or on tickets protect the operators from liability for loss or damage only if reasonable steps are taken to draw customers' attention to them.

Display of conditions

In one case, for example, a ticket issued by machine at a car park entrance said: 'This ticket is issued subject to the conditions of issue as displayed on the premises.'

In the car park there was a long printed list of conditions which would have taken a considerable time to read. The notice to customers was therefore held by a court to be inadequate.

Timing of notice

In the same case, the judge pointed out that the first attempt to draw the attention of customers to these conditions was after they had collected a ticket. It was then practically impossible for them to withdraw from the premises.

The judge commented: 'It does not take much imagination to picture the indignation of the proprietors if their potential customers, having taken their tickets, were one after the other to get out of their cars, leaving the cars blocking the entrance, in order to search for, find and peruse the notices. Yet unless the proprietors genuinely intended the potential customers should do just that, it would be fiction, if not farce, to treat those customers as persons who have been given a fair opportunity, before the contracts are made, of discovering the conditions by which they are to be bound.'

Fairness

Even if the conditions are properly drawn to the attention of customers they can protect the operators from liability only if they are fair and reasonable as defined by the Unfair Contract Terms Act 1977. *See:* UNFAIR CONTRACT

But if an employee borrowed a parked car to go joyriding and caused an accident, the car park owners might say that he had been acting outside the course of his employment. The car owner would succeed in his claim if he could prove that the car park staff had not been adequately supervised.

Insurance taken out by the car park operators covers them only against their own liability. It does not help the owner of a damaged or missing car unless he can first prove that the operators were liable for his loss.

When someone is injured

Car park operators are liable to pay compensation for any injury caused by unsafe premises or the negligence of an employee.

In such cases no conditions on tickets or notices, however prominently displayed, and even if they are signed by customers, can exclude or limit the operators' liability.

CAR REPAIR

Your right to satisfactory workmanship

When you have your car repaired or serviced, you are entitled to expect the repairer to use reasonable care in the work, and to ensure that any spare parts supplied are reasonably fit for their purpose.

A code of practice, drawn up by the Motor Agents' Association Ltd, the Society of Motor Manufacturers and Traders Ltd, and the Scottish Motor Trade Association Ltd, although not legally binding, recommends:

Cost Wherever possible, a garage should give a firm quotation for the cost of major repairs, and state whether the amount shown includes VAT. When the customer accepts a quotation, both sides are bound by it.

If the garage has to dismantle parts before giving an estimate, the customer should be warned about the dismantling costs in advance, and there should be a clear understanding on whether he has to pay these costs if he rejects the estimate.

Guarantees Repair work and servicing must always be guaranteed against failure due to faulty workmanship, for a specified mileage or length of time after the work is done.

The repairer should be adequately insured against any claim for loss arising out of bad workmanship – for example, damage to the customer's vehicle, or other vehicles, in an accident caused by the faulty repair or servicing.

Parts Spare parts should be readily available from the time a new model is offered for sale. When a model is going out of production, the manufacturer should indicate the minimum time during which parts will remain generally available to the trade.

When new parts are fitted, the old ones should be made available for the customer to collect, if he wishes, for a 'reasonable period'. Dealers should display notices showing how long they will keep such parts available.

Damage or loss Dealers should take adequate care to protect customers' cars and possessions and should be insured against loss or damage. They are legally responsible (unless the loss or damage was not through their negligence) and should not try to avoid that responsibility by posting notices disclaiming liability.

If your repairer is a member of one of the trade associations mentioned, and does not follow the code of practice or deal satisfactorily with your complaint, complain to the association.

CARAVANS

When you may need permission to park

You do not need permission to keep a holiday caravan in your garden, but you must take care not to block the light your neighbour gets through his windows. *See:* LIGHT, Right to

If, however, you or someone else lives in the caravan, using it as another room of the house, you must have PLANNING PERMISSION.

Similarly, if you own a piece of land not connected with your home and you want to park any caravan, including your own, on it for more than 28 days in the year, you must have not only planning permission but also a site licence from the planning office of your local district council.

If you use a caravan as your main home, your right to remain on a site you have rented is protected to some extent. *See:* MOBILE HOME

On holiday Be careful where you park your caravan while touring. If you park on private land without the owner's consent, you are guilty of TRESPASS. *See also:* TRAILERS.

CARE

Circumstances in which children may be looked after by the council

In many circumstances – for example, when children are beyond the control of their parents, when the parents die or disappear or when the children are being neglected or hurt – the local authority has the right and sometimes the duty to assume responsibility for their upbringing and safety. *See:* CHILDREN IN CARE

CARELESS DRIVING

A motorist must be alert and considerate

The term careless driving covers two offences: driving without due care and attention and driving without reasonable consideration for other users of the road, including pedestrians. The offences are equally serious and are treated in law as the same, with the same maximum penalty.

Driving without due care and attention

Every driver is legally obliged to be constantly alert to the situation on the road, including traffic and weather conditions, speed limits and road signs. When a court considers a charge of

KEEPING YOUR EYES AND
MIND ON THE ROAD

Drivers must constantly be alert, prudent, careful, attentive and considerate to other road users. Shaving or kissing in the car may lead to a conviction.

driving without due care it compares the evidence of the accused motorist's behaviour with how a prudent driver would have driven. The standard is the same for everyone, including a learner driver.

An error of judgment or momentary inattention can amount to driving without due care and attention. A court does not, however, expect a driver to react perfectly in all situations.

A motorist who makes a mistake in a hazardous situation may not be guilty of an offence unless it was his own driving that caused the hazard.

Accident or not Most cases arise because of accidents, but there need not be an accident for the police to prosecute. They must, however, warn that proceedings will be considered or serve a NOTICE OF INTENDED PROSECUTION before starting proceedings, if there has not been an accident.

It can be a defence for the motorist to show that an accident was caused by a mechanical defect of which he or she had no knowledge. In such a case it is usual for the police to inspect the vehicle to see if it had been maintained properly and whether a prudent motorist could reasonably have suspected the defect.

It may also be a defence to show that the driver was suddenly overcome by illness – for example a blackout or a fit of sneezing. The defence could succeed, however, only if the indisposition was not to be expected and was not connected with any deliberate act by the driver. Even then the driver must stop immediately and not swerve about.

If the driver had blackouts regularly or if sneezing was caused by the driver's taking a pinch of snuff, neither occurrence would help his or her case. Falling asleep through exhaustion is also no defence.

Driving without reasonable consideration

The alternative charge under the general heading careless driving is less a matter of inattention than of deliberate bad manners – for example, driving at night with undipped headlights; cutting in after overtaking; blocking traffic by turning right from the inside lane; or splashing pedestrians by driving through a visible puddle at speed.

Maximum penalties The maximum fine for either offence is £500. Endorsement of the licence is automatic unless there are special reasons. Disqualification can also be imposed and the court has power to order anyone convicted to take a driving test. *See:* DRIVING DISQUALIFICATION

CARRIAGE OF GOODS

The significance of the small print

A carrier who transports goods, including house removals, by road or rail can avoid his basic legal liability to make good any loss or damage suffered by his customers by the way in which he words his conditions of carriage.

You are not bound by such conditions, however, if you did not know of them and did not sign them when you sent the goods. If the carrier can show that he took reasonable steps to draw your attention to the conditions before the contract is made, you will be bound.

On the other hand, under the Unfair Contract Terms Act 1977, the carrier cannot be immune against a claim for negligence if his conditions are unfair or unreasonable.

If you have to make a claim, it is important to do so within any time limit laid down in your agreement – probably 7 or 14 days after loss or damage is discovered. *See:* UNFAIR CONTRACT

Care of the goods The basic legal rule for carriers is that they must take reasonable care of goods in their possession. A carrier is not liable for loss or damage if it is not his fault, but he must prove that he did take reasonable care.

If goods carried in a van are damaged in an accident with another vehicle, and the carrier can prove that it was entirely the fault of the other driver, the carrier will not be liable. However, if his own driver was even slightly to blame, the carrier will be fully liable.

If goods are stolen while a lorry is left unattended, the carrier's liability will depend on the circumstances. A driver on a long journey is not expected to stay with the vehicle every moment of the day and night, so he may not necessarily be negligent in leaving it. In that case, the only way to get compensation for loss of goods if the carrier is not liable, would be through insurance.

> ### THE SPARE PART THAT ARRIVED TOO LATE
>
> *When prompt delivery is required, tell the carriers so, and tell them also the reason for the urgency. Otherwise, they cannot be held responsible for any delay.*
>
> A firm of carriers agreed to deliver a broken piece of machinery to repairers. They delivered it several days late. As a result, the machine was out of action for several days longer than it should have been.
>
> The owners of the machine claimed damages for loss of profits which would have been made if the machinery had been working earlier.
>
> #### DECISION
>
> The carrier was not liable for the customer's loss of profits because it did not know that the machinery was going to be out of action and so could not have foreseen the loss of profits.

However, if the driver leaves the vehicle unattended and unlocked for an unreasonably long time – for example, all night in a lorry park – he may be held negligent and the carrier held liable for any loss.

Insuring against loss

To avoid uncertainty about the carrier's liability for your goods, it is advisable to insure them yourself independently. The carrier may arrange the insurance for you.

Railway risk One carrier, British Rail, carries goods either at 'owner's risk' or at 'carrier's risk'.

Conditions for 'owner's risk' exempt the railway from most responsibility. 'Carrier's risk' conditions mean that British Rail accepts responsibility.

It is usually advisable to choose owner's risk – and insure the goods yourself, separately, because any claim against the railway is likely to be more restricted than one against your own insurers.

If goods are delayed

You are entitled to have goods delivered within a reasonable time, even if no fixed delivery date is specially agreed.

However, you cannot get compensation from the carriers for loss caused by delay if they did not know (and could not reasonably foresee) that delay would cause you loss. So you should always specify fast delivery when promptness is necessary, and also explain to a senior official of the company why it is necessary.

Sending goods abroad

Carriers handling international traffic are governed by special rules. The rules for international carriers apply even while a vehicle is in the United Kingdom, so long as it is engaged in international carriage.

Road transport When goods are sent abroad by road, the carrier is liable, under international agreement, for loss of goods or damage from the time he takes charge of the goods until they are delivered. He is also liable for any delay in delivery.

However, the carrier can avoid these liabilities if he can show that the loss, damage or delay was caused by circumstances he could not foresee or avoid – for example, if weather conditions stop a ferry, or if a ship sinks.

A carrier's liability is generally limited, under the agreement, to about £4 per kg. (£1.50 per lb.) for loss or damage, and to the total of the carriage charges in case of delay. Those limits do

....

WHEN GOODS GET DAMAGED OR LOST IN TRANSIT

A commercial carrier or transporter must take reasonable care of the goods in his possession if he wants to avoid a claim against him for loss or damage.

....

not apply when you have declared the value of the goods or stated your special interest in delivery by a fixed date.

Sea transport When goods go by sea, there is usually a limit to the carrier's liability – about £400 for each package or £1.15 per kg. (50p per lb.), whichever is the higher.

Air transport When goods go by air, the airline will be liable for loss, damage or delay unless it can prove that it and its servants took all necessary measures to avoid loss or damages or that such measures were impossible.

Airline liability is limited to a maximum of about £10 per kg. (£4.50 per lb.) of goods, regardless of their value.

CARRIAGE OF PASSENGERS

Damages for passenger injury

If you are injured while being carried by inland public transport – including taxis or hired cars – you are entitled to sue the carriers for any negligence by their employees.

Any conditions printed on your ticket cannot take away or limit this right.

See also: AIR TRAVEL
BUSES AND COACHES
RAIL TRAVEL
SEA TRAVEL

CASINO

Controlling the growth of gambling houses in Britain

There are strict laws governing the setting up and running of any club that allows gaming on its premises. People who want to operate such clubs, called casinos, must have a licence from the local magistrates, and they are liable to have their premises inspected at any time by officials of the Gaming Board.
See: GAMBLING

CASUAL WORKER

The rights of those whose work is irregular

Although the term 'casual worker' is widely used, it has never been legally defined and it may describe several types of worker whose hours are short or irregular.

Most commonly, casual workers are those who are employed for fewer than 16 hours a week and who do not qualify, through length of service or other circumstances, to be classified as part-timers. *See:* PART-TIME WORKER

Someone who undertakes several short jobs for different people during a week – for example, a window-cleaner or jobbing gardener – may be regarded by his various employers as casual labour, but if that work is his main source of income he is SELF-EMPLOYED.

A third type of casual worker may work long hours during a short period – for example, as a fruit-picker. *See:* SEASONAL WORKER

Casual employees, like all other employed people, have an EMPLOYMENT CONTRACT, though often it is not in writing and its terms may be so vague as to be meaningless. Self-employed people who do casual work have a contract for services which also may not be in writing.

Rights and obligations

A casual worker is liable for INCOME TAX and also NATIONAL INSURANCE CONTRIBUTIONS on his earnings.

His employer is obliged to pay national insurance contributions on his behalf if his wages from the employment are more than the lower-earnings limit and he is not paying stamps as a self-employed person.

A casual worker has the same right as permanent staff to compensation for industrial injury and, if he is an employee, he can also claim industrial injury benefit.

His holiday entitlement is restricted, however. He cannot be made to work on usual bank holidays, but he will not be paid for them unless his contract specifically says so. Any other paid holiday must be written into the contract.

Casual workers are not entitled to paid sick leave unless that is provided for in a contract. They are unlikely to be able to claim statutory EMPLOYMENT PROTECTION rights – for example, notice of dismissal, redundancy payment and maternity pay – because their work is by nature irregular or for short periods and they therefore do not meet the qualifying conditions.

CAVEAT EMPTOR

Advice to the buyer that may still be necessary

'Let the buyer beware' – in Latin *caveat emptor* – is still sound advice if you are buying from anyone who does not have an established business. There is, for example, little legal redress against a doorstep salesman who never reappears after taking your money. Nor can the law greatly help if you buy defective goods at a one-day sale from a seller who moves on.

Otherwise, the buyer is well protected in modern law. If he buys goods from someone who sells in the course of business, and those goods prove to be unfit for their purpose, he can demand his money back or, if necessary, sue the seller for its return. That is a right that cannot be taken away by small print in the seller's literature or by a notice saying 'No money returned'. *See:* DEFECTIVE GOODS

CEMETERY

Buying a grave space or fighting the closure of a burial ground

There are two kinds of burial grounds: cemeteries owned by a local council (or, more rarely, by a private company) and churchyards. Anyone may buy the exclusive right to a particular grave space in a cemetery or a churchyard. In the case of a churchyard it is up to the incumbent to decide whether a person of another religion should be buried there.

Where grave space has been bought, the owner, or some other person with his written consent, may be buried in that space within a stated period of up to 100 years. This right in both cemetery or churchyard may be transferred and, in the absence of a specific bequest, passes to the next of kin after the death of the buyer.

A burial right can be taken over by a local authority by COMPULSORY PURCHASE. But the owner is entitled to compensation.

Closure orders Only when a burial ground is full, can it be closed and then only by an order of the Privy Council. The local authority can then give permission for it to be used as an open space or even for development so long as decent arrangements are made for the human remains in the ground.

Before a closure order is confirmed it must be published in *The London Gazette* and posted on the doors of churches in the parish or in some other conspicuous public place in the area.

Anyone may object to the local authority about a closure order, and if there is strong opposition the Privy Council may be persuaded to change its mind.

To prevent any change in use of a burial ground it is always better to object to the closure at the time instead of trying to influence the local authority over possible later use.

Closure orders by the Privy Council override the rights of people who have bought a grave space. However, the council may grant special exemptions. For instance, in the case of a deep family vault, they may allow it to be used after the site has been closed or developed.

Epitaphs are not subject to any general censorship rules and there are no general rules about the kind of memorial that may be erected. Local church authorities will decide if any are unacceptable and local authorities often make their own regulations.

CENSUS

Rules for survey of the nation

The Government has power, under the Census Act 1920, to carry out a census (the word comes from the Latin *censere*, to rate) not more than once every 5 years. Parliament must give its approval before each census is taken, normally once every 10 years.

The Census Act also empowers the Government to hold a selective census in a certain area, subject to Parliament's approval.

When a census is conducted, a questionnaire has to be completed for every household. Normally one member of the household is required to complete the questionnaire to the best of his or her ability with details of all the people in the household. Traditionally the head of the household is responsible. For 1981, that means the head, joint heads or adult members depending on the type of household. It is an offence not to answer all the questions asked or to give false information.

If you do not wish the person completing the questionnaire for your household to know the personal details asked about you, obtain a separate form and complete it yourself.

If you do not answer

Anyone who refuses to give information required in the census can be fined up to £50.

Everyone involved in taking a census is bound to secrecy. For census officials, including the collector to whom the forms are given, the maximum penalty for disclosing census information to an unauthorised person is an unlimited fine and 2 years' imprisonment. The person who completes the questionnaire for the household can be fined up to £50 for divulging information which the other members of the household have given to complete the form.

When you need not answer

The word 'census' is sometimes used by local authorities and private market research organisations when they conduct their own surveys. Such surveys are voluntary, and no one is obliged to answer the questions.

CENTRAL ARBITRATION COMMITTEE

Union complaints against individual companies

The role of the Central Arbitration Committee includes hearing complaints by unions – not individual members – against companies which refuse to give a union the information needed for effective wage bargaining. *See:* COLLECTIVE BARGAINING

Committee members are usually union leaders appointed by the ADVISORY, CONCILIATION AND ARBITRATION SERVICE as well as independent members and representatives of employers. In general, cases are referred to the committee only if they have not been satisfactorily settled by ACAS.

The committee can change agreements, pay structures and wages orders to remove unfair differences in treat-

ment between men and women. *See:* SEX DISCRIMINATION

If an employer refuses to act on the committee's award, the committee can seek a High Court order that would make it legally enforceable. An employer who wants to challenge an award must ask the High Court for an order to quash it.

CESSPIT

The basic form of sewerage that is provided in some areas

In some parts of England and Wales – particularly in rural areas – there is no public system of pipeline sewerage. Instead, each home or sets of homes is responsible for maintaining an adequate cesspit or septic tank. *See:* DRAIN

CHARITIES

Rules for collecting from the public

If you want to run a charity collection you need written permission from the Home Office, the police or the local authority – depending on where you live and the type of collection you want to make.

House-to-house collections

For a national house-to-house collection, you need the Home Secretary's permission: a London-only collection has to be approved by the Chief Commissioner of the Metropolitan Police.

In each case there is an official application form that can be obtained from any local police station.

For other large-scale collections, outside London, you must get permission from your local authority. However, if you plan a purely local collection which will be over quickly, you need only a certificate from your local police station.

Before issuing a certificate, the police will want to establish that you are a fit and proper person to hold a collection. Someone who has a criminal record will not be considered suitable.

The certificate may also be refused if the organiser proposes to pass on too small a percentage of the collection to

the charity, after expenses, or if collecting agents are to receive 'excessive' payments.

In making your application, you will be asked to state the scale of any such proposed payments.

Rules for collectors

Every charity collector should wear a badge – obtainable from HM Stationery Office – and carry a certificate of authority from the organisers. Failure to do so is an offence carrying a maximum fine of £5.

If a collector calls at your home, you are entitled to ask to see both badge and certificate. If you do not wish to give to his or her particular charity, the collector is not entitled to annoy you, or to stay on your doorstep after being asked to leave. A collector who does either of those things can be punished by a small fine.

Collections in the street

If you want to organise a street collection for charity, you must get permission from the local authority and all collectors should wear badges and carry certificates of authority.

The authority may set conditions about when and where collectors can operate, and you are obliged to conform to those conditions. Anyone who does not do so can be fined up to £5.

Setting up a charity

A group raising funds or collecting materials for a worthy cause is more likely to attract support from the public if it is an officially registered charity. In addition, if it is registered, donations made to it may qualify for relief from INCOME TAX and CAPITAL GAINS TAX, increasing their value, and, if it has its own premises, it is entitled to a reduction of at least 50 per cent in the RATES.

To obtain registration by the Charity Commission, the group must show that its aims fall into one of four categories: relief of poverty; advancement of education; the spreading of Christianity or another religion; or 'other purposes beneficial to the community' – for example, disaster relief or the rehabilitation of former prisoners.

If the aim is poverty relief, the charity can restrict its scope to one single, small section of society – for example, the former employees of one company. But those whose intentions come into one of the other three categories must show that they will benefit a 'substantial proportion' of the community. A sports club with restricted membership formed purely for entertainment and recreation would therefore not normally qualify, but an organisation to provide recreational facilities for the handicapped or other deprived people probably would.

Projects to protect animals qualify only if they benefit humans as well. That condition may be met by declaring that the aim is 'to safeguard public morality' by preventing cruelty to animals.

Registering a charity

To register a charity, you must submit a draft of its constitution and a statement of its proposed activities to the Charity Commission, the publicly financed body in charge of charities.

If the Commission approves in principle, the group applying for registration must formally adopt the constitution and statement, and resubmit them to the Commission with form REI, obtainable from the Commission.

In preparing the draft constitution and aims, consult a solicitor with experience in that field. Another local charity may be able to suggest one. The solicitor can also advise you on the legal format – for example, a TRUST – that is best suited to the aims of your charity.

A registered charity must comply strictly with regulations about the keeping of accounts and the duties of trustees who must be appointed by the chairman to run its affairs.

Even if you decide not to try to register your charitable activities – for example, if they are limited to occasional fund raising for the local Scouts association – it is desirable to appoint trustees and to have clearly written rules for the project.

CHECK TRADING

Credit for consumers on a low income

Trading checks, paid for by instalments, allow the customer to buy goods on credit at shops that have agreed to deal in the checks.

They are a comparatively easy way for someone on a low income to get credit. Because the sums borrowed are not large, the check company is not bearing a big risk on any one transaction.

A check trading or finance company which issues checks is just as liable as a retailer for DEFECTIVE GOODS or MISREPRESENTATION if the goods or services bought with the checks are faulty in some way. If you agree to buy checks, you must be given a copy of the written agreement, signed on behalf of the company issuing the checks, before or when you receive them.

Legally, you accept trading checks when you sign them on the front, sign a receipt for them, use them at a shop – or merely tell the trader who issues the checks that you accept them.

Checks are usually sold by a doorstep salesman.

If he does not have a canvassing licence, he is committing a criminal offence for which he can be imprisoned for up to two years and be fined up to £1,000. *See:* DOORSTEP CREDIT

If you receive trading checks that you have not asked for and do not want, complain to your local trading standards department. It is an offence to give anyone trading checks which have not been ordered unless an existing agreement is being renewed. *See also:* INTEREST CHARGE

CHEQUE

Telling your bank to hand over your money

A cheque is simply an instruction to a bank to pay money out of your account and pass it to someone else. Legally you do not need to use the bank's printed cheque form: a bank has been known to pay out on all sorts of 'cheques', from those written on plain paper to one written on the side of a cow. However, it is as well to keep to the prescribed form, except in an emergency.

If you have more than one account, do not mix your cheques. A cheque normally has the branch and account numbers printed in magnetic computer characters: the cheque you use is likely still to find its way to the account for which it was issued even although you alter the details in ink.

For the same reason, it is unwise to use someone else's cheque form, or let him have one of yours.

Most cheques have the customer's name printed on them. That does not, by itself, enable someone else to steal from you by forging your signature. It is up to your bank to recognise your signature and not to pay out on a forged one.

If money is lost as a result of your carelessness, however, the bank may try to make you bear the loss.

You have a duty to make it difficult for someone to alter a cheque. You should make sure there is no room for a word or a figure to be added to what you write (for example, by altering 'twenty pounds' to 'one hundred and twenty pounds' and changing £20 to £120).

If what you write does not take up all the space, draw lines to fill the rest.

Crossed or uncrossed There are two types of cheque form – 'crossed' and 'open'. A crossed cheque has two parallel lines across the face – up and down, or diagonally – or in some cases a broad tinted band which serves the same purpose.

It cannot be exchanged for cash, even at the bank named on the cheque: a crossed cheque can only be paid into a bank account and it is therefore difficult for a thief to avoid detection.

Banks supply whichever type you ask for, but it is generally safer to use the crossed type.

An open cheque has no crossing lines and can be cashed at the bank branch named on it. The open cheque carries a greater risk of theft and fraud, but can be turned into a crossed cheque simply by drawing in the two parallel lines. Even if someone gives you an open cheque, you can cross it yourself as a security measure until you can pay it into your bank.

If you lose your cheque book

When a cheque book is lost or stolen, and someone manages to obtain money from the bank by using it, the bank must bear the loss – as long as the customer has not been negligent.

For example, if you discover that your cheque book is missing, you should warn the bank immediately – especially if you lose your cheque guarantee card at the same time. *See:* CHEQUE GUARANTEE CARD

You should also warn the bank at

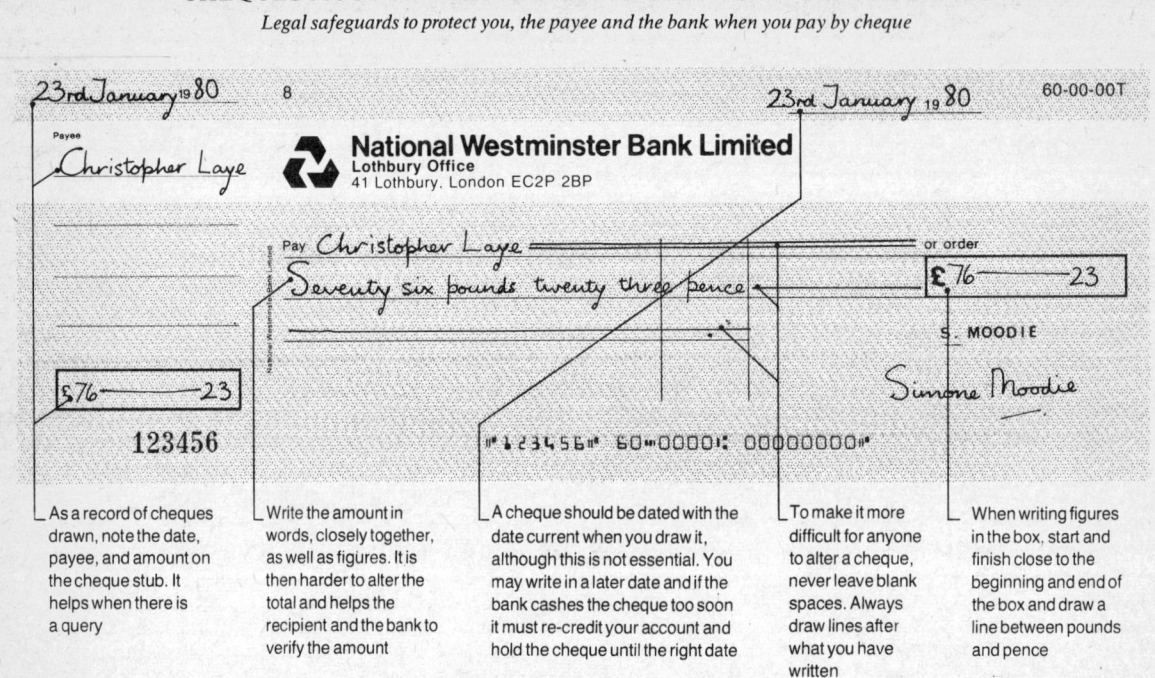

CHEQUES MUST BE WRITTEN CORRECTLY TO AVOID PROBLEMS
Legal safeguards to protect you, the payee and the bank when you pay by cheque

23rd January 19 80   8

Payee
Christopher Laye

National Westminster Bank Limited
Lothbury Office
41 Lothbury. London EC2P 2BP

23rd January 19 80   60-00-00T

Pay Christopher Laye ————————— or order

Seventy six pounds twenty three pence ————

£76 ———— 23

S. MOODIE

Simone Moodie

£76 ———— 23

123456

⑈123456⑈ 60⑈0000⑈ 00000000⑈

- As a record of cheques drawn, note the date, payee, and amount on the cheque stub. It helps when there is a query

- Write the amount in words, closely together, as well as figures. It is then harder to alter the total and helps the recipient and the bank to verify the amount

- A cheque should be dated with the date current when you draw it, although this is not essential. You may write in a later date and if the bank cashes the cheque too soon it must re-credit your account and hold the cheque until the right date

- To make it more difficult for anyone to alter a cheque, never leave blank spaces. Always draw lines after what you have written

- When writing figures in the box, start and finish close to the beginning and end of the box and draw a line between pounds and pence

A cheque must be signed on the back – that is, endorsed – by the person to whom it is made payable, unless it is being paid into that person's bank account. When you do endorse a cheque, make sure that you use exactly the name on the front, even if that is not your normal signature. In the example, Christopher Laye, who normally signs himself C. Laye, should sign himself Christopher Laye.

once if you ever suspect that someone may have forged your signature on a cheque, or tampered with it in any way. The bank will 'stop' the cheque on your instructions, if it has not already paid it.

If you lose a signed cheque

Warn your bank as soon as you discover that any cheque has gone astray, and ask it to stop payment.

A crossed cheque which has been properly made out to someone and signed should be of no value to anyone else who finds or steals it – although if the cheque is not crossed, he may be able to cash it at the branch on which it is drawn.

The only risk with a crossed cheque is that a thief may persuade someone to exchange it for cash, in the belief that he is the person to whom it is made out.

Anyone who accepts the cheque cannot pay it into his bank account unless it is endorsed – signed on the back by the person to whom it is made out. Therefore he must get the thief to endorse it.

When a theft or forgery comes to

light, the person likely to lose money is whoever gave the thief cash for the stolen cheque. His own bank will not be liable because they are not expected to recognise the signatures of people who are not their customers. (If a branch on which a cheque was drawn paid out cash for a crossed cheque, it would lose its protection, but that is unlikely to happen.)

If you find that someone has cashed a stolen cheque belonging to you, you are entitled to claim the money from him: he has no legal right to it.

A cheque may be lost or stolen on its way to you. If that happens, there is no question of your having been paid. You still have a legal right to the payment if it is a debt, but not if it is a gift: you do not lose that right simply because a cheque has been put in the post.

Even if you receive the cheque but then lose it, you will not lose your money if you have not endorsed it on the back. However, if for some reason you have endorsed it, you are likely to lose your money.

In any case you should immediately warn the person who wrote the cheque to stop payment on it.

If the cheque is paid into a bank, you should be able to trace the person who paid it in. All banks keep records of cheques that are banked or paid out. After that, your right to claim the money from him will depend on whether or not you endorsed the cheque.

If it was not endorsed when you lost it, you are entitled to claim from him. If it was endorsed, you cannot claim unless you can prove that he knew the cheque had been stolen (or possibly that he obtained it without giving full cash value for it).

Blank cheques

If you want to make a payment but are not sure what the exact amount will be, do not simply sign a blank cheque, leaving details to be filled in by the other person once the figure is known. Your bank might make you stand any loss if the cheque is stolen.

Instead, fill in everything but the amount and write across the face of the cheque the largest amount you want the other person to draw. If the sum is £15, write 'Not exceeding £15'.

If a stranger asks you to cash a cheque for him, you run no risk as long as the cheque is made out by him and made payable to you, and he has a CHEQUE GUARANTEE CARD.

The cheque should be signed in your presence and should have the same code number as appears on the card. Check that the card has not expired and that the signatures compare. Write the

THE WIFE WHO FORGED HER HUSBAND'S CHEQUES

A bank normally has to stand the loss of any money paid out on a forged cheque – but not if the account holder has been negligent by failing to warn the bank.

Mr Greenwood, a dairyman, discovered that his wife had been drawing money from his bank account by forging his signature. When challenged, she said she did it to raise money for her sister, who was having legal problems.

Mrs Greenwood implored her husband not to tell the bank about her forgeries, and he agreed. Later, he found out that the story about the sister was a lie.

After Mrs Greenwood died, Mr Greenwood tried to get the bank to repay him the money his wife had obtained with forged cheques. Eventually, he sued.

DECISION
Mr Greenwood lost his claim, because he had failed to tell the bank as soon as he discovered what his wife had been doing.

THE COMPUTER THAT PAID A 'STOPPED' CHEQUE

Having more than one account with the same bank can lead to confusion, mistakes and even costly litigation – unless both the bank and the holder of the accounts take extra care not to mix the cheques.

Mr Burnett had two accounts at different branches of the same bank. He used a cheque form from one branch to pay £2,300 out of his account at the other. He altered the branch and account details in ink.

After handing over the cheque, Mr Burnett decided to stop payment. He gave instructions to that effect to the branch which was to have paid out the money.

However, the bank computer read the original branch and account details as printed in magnetic characters, and the cheque was paid – out of that account.

DECISION
The bank was ordered to give Mr Burnett back the £2,300 wrongly paid out.

THE DECORATORS WHOSE PAY CHEQUE 'BOUNCED'

It is a criminal offence, punishable by up to 5 years' imprisonment, to present a cheque knowing that the bank is unlikely to meet it.

Mr Turner hired two decorators to do some work. When they had finished and asked to be paid, he said he had no cash. They accepted his cheque for £38.

Two days later, the cheque was returned by the bank, unpaid.

Mr Turner was prosecuted for obtaining a financial advantage by deception.

VERDICT
Mr Turner was guilty, because he knew there was no money in his bank account to meet the cheque.

THE GAMBLER WHO MISUSED HIS CHEQUE CARD

If two or more cheques are presented in any one transaction, and collectively they amount to more than the limit on the cheque guarantee card, the bank can refuse to honour the guarantee if there is not enough money in the account.

Derek Charles had an account with the National Westminster Bank, a £100 overdraft limit and a cheque card, which guaranteed cheques up to £30 each.

One evening, while gambling at the Golden Nugget club, he used all the 25

cheques in his cheque book, backed by his cheque card, to buy £750 worth of gambling chips.

The bank refused to pay because of the excess overdraft and the number of cheques issued. Mr Charles was prosecuted by the police for obtaining a financial advantage by deception – pretending that he had a bank account that would meet his £750 worth of cheques.

VERDICT
Derek Charles was found guilty.

THE MAN WHO TOOK A CHANCE

Anyone who 'bounces' a cheque, without deliberately intending to be dishonest, may still be prosecuted if he carelessly made no effort to check the state of his account.

Joseph Lewis, a Canadian, arrived in England with no money and cashed two cheques. There were no funds in his bank account to meet the cheques and he was prosecuted for obtaining a financial advantage by deception.

He explained that he had been expecting a relative to pay money into his account, but had not checked whether that had been done.

VERDICT
Joseph Lewis was guilty because he behaved recklessly in issuing the cheques. He was sentenced to 21 months to run concurrently on two counts.

THE BUSINESSMAN WHO WAS CARELESS

Do not sign a blank cheque, a cheque that has been only partly completed or one that can be altered easily – otherwise the bank may be able to absolve itself from any responsibility for loss or theft.

A clerk in a City firm had the job of writing out cheques to be signed by a partner.

He wrote out a cheque for £2, but left a space on each side of the figure '2' – and did not write out the amount in words. Nevertheless the partner signed.

Afterwards, the clerk added figures and words so that the signed cheque became worth £120. Because the alterations were in the same handwriting as the original details, they could not be detected.

The firm's bank paid out the £120 and the firm sued the bank.

DECISION
The firm's partner had been negligent in signing a cheque that could so easily be altered, and the bank was therefore not ordered to refund the £120.

card number on the back of the cheque yourself.

Do not take more than one cheque for any one transaction: if there are no funds, the bank may refuse to honour the guarantee if the card's cash limit has been exceeded.

The cheque card is useless as a guarantee for a cheque written by a third party. If you cash such a cheque for someone who says he is the person to whom the cheque is payable, the bank can refuse to pay it.

If you know the other person, you may be willing to cash the cheque. If so, get him to endorse it on the back, signing exactly as he is named on the front. Then get him to write, above the endorsement, an instruction: 'Pay ...' (with your name).

When you pay the cheque into your bank, you will have to endorse it yourself – and may have to explain how you come to have it.

Stopping a cheque when there is a dispute

If you decide to stop payment on a cheque that you have written, the bank must obey your instruction, unless the cheque was backed by a cheque guarantee card – in which case it must be paid.

Otherwise, once you have given the instruction, if the bank mistakenly pays, it must bear the loss.

However, when payment has been stopped, you can be sued by the person to whom you originally made out the cheque. *See:* DEBT

In a dispute The most common reason for stopping a cheque is dissatisfaction with something you have bought.

If you stop a cheque because goods you have bought are faulty and the shopkeeper will not replace them (perhaps insisting on repair, instead), give him your reason in writing – and keep a copy of the letter. You should see that the goods are returned or collected by the seller.

The shopkeeper can sue you for the money, but you can claim against him for the value of the goods.

When issuing a cheque may be an offence

Anyone who writes a cheque knowing that his bank is unlikely to meet it

commits a criminal offence – obtaining a financial advantage by deception, for which the maximum penalty is 5 years' imprisonment.

The deception is that by writing the cheque, he falsely implies that the bank will pay out on the cheque.

It is also illegal to pay someone by cheque, with the intention of stopping payment on it.

Anyone who obtains an unauthorised overdraft by using his cheque card to draw cash when there is no credit in his bank, also commits a criminal offence.

Even someone who writes a cheque without meaning to be dishonest, but who is merely reckless by not checking his account or advising his bank, could face a criminal charge. The maximum penalty in a magistrates' court would be 6 months' gaol and a £400 fine; in a crown court 10 years and an unlimited fine.

CHEQUE GUARANTEE CARD

The token that says the bank will meet your cheque

A cheque guarantee card is a token by which your bank promises to meet any of your cheques, up to a limit shown on the card.

The limit must not be exceeded for any one transaction, otherwise the bank's guarantee does not apply. For example, if the limit is £50 and you buy something costing £60, the shopkeeper must not accept two cheques – one for £50, say, and one for £10. You will have to pay the excess in cash.

If someone exceeds his limit by writing two cheques and has not enough money in his account to meet either of them, the bank is entitled to refuse to honour both.

Some cheque cards, such as Barclaycard, are also a CREDIT CARD and can be used to obtain goods or cash without a cheque, as well as to guarantee a cheque.

Even a straightforward cheque card, however, is covered by the Consumer Credit Act. That is because the card represents potential credit: even if you do not expect ever to write a cheque that could not be met from your own funds at the bank, in theory you could withdraw all your money and then write

a cheque which someone accepts on the strength of the card. If you did so, the bank would have to honour the cheque and try to recover the money from you.

An agreement covering the issue of a cheque guarantee card has to comply with most of the Consumer Credit Act rules protecting borrowers. If a customer overdraws by using his cheque card, and cannot refund the money as quickly as the bank demands, he asks a county court to decide how he should repay. *See:* CREDIT AGREEMENT

However, the protection generally applies only to agreements made after the Act came into force. If you have a cheque card issued under an agreement made before 1981, it may be advisable to make sure of your protection under the Act by handing the card back to the bank and a few days later asking for a new one.

If you lose your cheque card

You should tell the bank at once if your cheque card is lost or stolen. The bank will cancel the old card, issue a new one and circularise all banks with the number of the cancelled card, so that it cannot be used to draw cash.

Provided that you are not negligent, reporting the loss as soon as it is realised, you will not be liable for unauthorised use of the lost card – for example, if someone finds or steals your cheque book as well as your card. *See:* CHEQUE

Sign your cheque guarantee card on the front as soon as you get it. Note the card number in your diary, with the telephone number of your bank.

CHERISHED NUMBER

If you are a motorist and want a special ('cherished') number-plate for your car, you may be able to make the change. *See:* NUMBER-PLATE

CHILD ABUSE

Protection against neglect and ill-treatment

Children under the age of 16 have complete legal protection against assault, ill-treatment or neglect, all of which are criminal offences.

A child can be smacked as a punishment, but a court would consider it ill-treatment to strike a child so violently as to cause broken bones, or to cause it to suffer repeated injury such as bruising over a long period. It is also an offence to cause a child mental suffering, to abandon it or to fail to provide food and clothing.

Anyone – parent, guardian or child minder – who is convicted of causing a child unnecessary suffering can be sentenced to 2 years' gaol and an unlimited fine.

When ill-treatment is suspected

Cases of suspected child ill-treatment may be reported to the local council's social services department, the NSPCC or the police, by a neighbour, school, social worker, day nursery, family doctor or hospital where the child has been treated for injury.

Once a report has been made it will be investigated. If the suspicions are confirmed a case conference will be called at which the social workers, doctors, health visitor and sometimes the police will decide whether to recommend the local authority to take action. Parents are not invited to the conference, but they are normally told by the social services that a meeting is being held, though there is no legal obligation to do so.

When a child is considered to be 'at risk' an application may be made to the local magistrates for a place of safety order. That entitles the council to remove the child immediately to a foster home, children's home or hospital for up to 28 days while decisions are made about its future, such as whether an application should be made for it to be placed in care. *See:* CHILDREN IN CARE

Parents can appeal against a place of safety order at any time. While a child is held in a safe place the parents are allowed to visit, but must not take the child away, even for a short period.

CHILD ALLOWANCE

Tax allowances if you have children

For most parents tax allowances for children were abolished as from April 6, 1979 when the old taxable family allowance was replaced by the non-taxable child benefit. *See:* INCOME TAX ALLOWANCE

CHILD BENEFIT

The state's weekly handout to every young family

If you have a child under 16 you are entitled to child benefit – a non-taxable weekly cash payment, which in 1981 amounted to £4.75 per child. It is normally paid to the mother but can be claimed by anyone who is responsible for maintaining a child.

Someone with whom the child is living has a prior claim to child benefit over someone who merely contributes towards the child's upkeep – and who therefore is not responsible for the child's immediate needs.

If your child is over 16

Benefit is paid for any child over 16, but under 19, who is receiving full-time education at a school or other officially recognised educational establishment.

It is not paid if the child is taking an advanced course for a degree, diploma of higher education, higher national diploma or teaching qualifications – or any other course higher than ordinary national diploma or GCE A level.

The benefit continues during school holidays or if your child is away ill, up to a maximum absence of 6 months.

Awaiting exam results If your child is awaiting examination results before deciding whether to continue full-time education, you can still draw benefit for the time being. But you must write to the social security office, explaining the circumstances – and also notify it as soon as you have decided whether the child is to continue his education.

If you do not keep in touch, the social security department may ask you to repay any benefit received since the end of the child's last term at school.

When a child is in hospital

You are entitled to child benefit for up to 12 weeks if your child is admitted to hospital or a home for the handicapped or mentally ill.

After that time, a parent may draw child benefit only if he is spending money on the child – for example, paying fares to visit him.

Someone who has been drawing benefit because he contributes to the support of a child who was not living with him is entitled to continue to draw it while the child is in hospital, for however long, providing he continues to support the child.

Children 'in care'

When a child is in the care of a local authority – in a council home, boarded out with foster parents or placed with a voluntary organisation by the council – the parents may still receive benefit for up to 8 weeks. After that time, benefit may be drawn only if the local authority has agreed to allow the child regularly to spend at least two nights a week at home. *See also:* CHILDREN IN CARE

Going abroad temporarily

If you and your child go abroad for a time, you can continue to claim for 26 weeks.

If you go abroad by yourself, you are absolutely entitled to benefit for 8 weeks, but for the remaining 18 weeks only if you intend to return and you contribute to the child's support – at least the amount of benefit – while you are away.

Special arrangements allow benefit for more than 26 weeks if you are visiting the Isle of Man, Northern Ireland, the Channel Islands, any Common Market country, Australia, New Zealand, Denmark or Finland.

If your child goes abroad by himself, you can draw the benefit for 26 weeks, again depending on your own contribution to his support. Benefit can be paid

CLAIMING CHILD BENEFIT

You should claim child benefit as soon as you realise you are entitled to it: it cannot be back-dated more than a year from the day you apply.

Go to the nearest social security office and ask for the necessary forms. You will also receive a prepaid addressed envelope in which to send off the claim. Make sure that you enclose the child's birth or adoption certificate.

If for some reason your claim is not accepted, you will receive a letter setting out the reasons and telling you how to appeal to an independent tribunal, if you wish to.

If your claim is accepted, you will be notified that a book of payment orders in your name is being sent to whichever post office you nominated in your application.

Collecting the money

Benefit is paid once a week – on the day stated on the front of the order book.

You need not call at the post office every week, but you are not allowed to cash any order more than 3 months after the date on it.

If you cannot collect

Normally, child benefit orders can be cashed only by the person named on the book. But if for some reason you cannot go to the post office, you are entitled to send someone else.

To do so, complete the front of the order as usual and then complete the back, authorising the other person to collect your benefit. The person you send will also have to sign a receipt at the post office.

---

beyond the 26 weeks if the child is going abroad for full-time education or for his health.

If you and/or your child move abroad permanently, benefit stops on the day you leave Britain.

Returning from abroad

Parents who have just returned to Britain from abroad, and intend to stay for at least 6 months, are eligible for child benefit at once, if either husband or wife received it at any time in the previous 3 years.

Anyone who has not drawn the benefit within that time, or who has not lived in Britain before, becomes entitled to the payments only after one or other spouse starts a job. In those circumstances, benefit is paid from the first week after the job is started.

Other people arriving from abroad can normally claim benefit only after spending 26 out of 52 weeks in Britain.

There are, however, special arrangements allowing benefit although the usual requirements have not been met, for people arriving from Common Market countries, Australia, Austria, Canada, the Channel Islands, Northern Ireland, the Isle of Man, New Zealand, Spain or Switzerland.

Child benefit increase

A single parent – a widow, if she is not receiving a WIDOW'S PENSION, widower, divorcee or unmarried or separated person – may be entitled to

child benefit increase, provided that he or she is not living with someone as husband or wife. *See:* COHABITATION

The increase is paid for the first child only and is not taxable. In 1981, child benefit increase was £3 a week.

In the case of separation, the claim can be made once husband and wife have lived apart for 13 weeks. In all other circumstances the increase can be claimed immediately.

If the spouse is absent only for a time, or is in hospital but not otherwise living apart, child benefit increases cannot be claimed.

From February 1, 1980, certain other people, such as single or lone grandparents, who are bringing up children, have also been able to claim child benefit increase.

How to claim To claim child benefit increase, get form CH11A from your social security office, then claim as you would for child benefit.

Retirement pension protection

As long as you receive child benefit for a child under 16, you can have the number of qualifying years you need for a retirement pension reduced accordingly. This is called 'home responsibilities protection'.

To qualify, a mother must be eligible to pay full-rate national insurance contributions when at work (the married women's lower rate does not qualify). A father who does not work can get protection if the child benefit, with his

wife's written agreement, is paid to him. *See:* RETIREMENT PENSION

The scheme ensures that when your pension is being calculated, the number of years for which you get home responsibilities protection is taken away from the number of qualifying years of contributions needed. You can get a full pension if the reduced number of years does not fall below 20.

You do not need to apply for home responsibilities protection – it is given automatically until child benefit stops or your youngest child reaches 16, whichever is the earlier.

When a child's special allowance can be claimed

A mother whose marriage has been dissolved or annulled and whose former husband dies may be entitled to a child's special allowance. The allowance is not paid to a father whose ex-wife dies. Certain conditions must be satisfied.

● The child must be under 16 (or under 19 if in full-time education) and living with the mother.

● The mother must not have remarried nor be living with a man as his wife.

● She must have been eligible both when her ex-husband died and when she claimed the special allowance.

● Her ex-husband must have been paying a minimum weekly amount towards the child's support, or have been obliged to do so under a court order or maintenance agreement which she tried to enforce.

● Her ex-husband must have paid a minimum number of national insurance contributions amounting to at least 50 times the weekly LOWER EARNINGS LEVEL in any income tax year after 1975. For example, in 1980–1 the lower limit was £23, so he would have to have paid contributions on earnings of at least £1,150.

Child's special allowance, £7.50 a week in 1981, can be drawn in addition to child benefit, but if the mother or anyone receives child benefit increase or national insurance sickness benefit for the child, the rule of OVERLAPPING BENEFITS applies: the total payment cannot come to more than the biggest of those benefits.

How to claim To claim child's special allowance, get form CS1 from the social security office. You will need to produce your marriage certificate, evidence of divorce or annulment, or a death certificate, and details of your ex-husband's payments towards the child's support.

Even if all the documents are not immediately available, it is advisable to claim at once. The allowance will not be back-dated more than 3 months unless you can show good cause for delay in claiming – and it will never be back-dated more than 12 months.

CHILD GUIDANCE

Help for children with problems

Children who have special emotional or social problems can be helped at child-guidance clinics. The clinics, which are non-residential, are available in most areas – either linked to a psychiatric hospital or run by the local authority or local education authority. They are staffed by social, educational and medical workers.

They deal with children up to 16 years of age who suffer from such difficulties as excessive shyness, withdrawn behaviour, over-activity, stealing, aggression, truancy or other delinquency, disturbed sleep or bedwetting.

Getting help

Parents worried about a child's emotional or social problems can make an appointment at their local child-guidance clinic through the head of the child's school, their doctor, education welfare service or a hospital – or may be able to make one direct.

Parents cannot insist on their child having clinic treatment, and an education authority cannot insist on treatment against the parents' wishes. However, when a child shows disturbed behaviour which can be brought before a court – for example, failure to attend school regularly – the education authority can ask a juvenile court to order child-guidance treatment under a SUPERVISION ORDER, but the parents would have to agree in court.

Treatment in hospital

A child-guidance clinic aims at helping a child without removing him from his home. But sometimes the clinic team may recommend that a child should go into hospital, or a special boarding school.

The child cannot be sent away against his parents' wishes unless the child is under a care order. *See:* CHILDREN IN CARE

CHILD MINDER

Looking after other people's children

Anyone who is paid – in cash or kind – to mind children under 5 years of age for more than 2 hours a day for other people is legally obliged to register with the local authority's social services department, so that it can make sure that the children are properly cared for in safe, stimulating conditions.

When an application is received, the authority sends a social worker to inspect the applicant's home and it can refuse registration if the applicant or the premises seem unfit for children.

Electrical wiring must be up-to-date and sound, there must be a satisfactory fire exit and other safety precautions.

The premises may be inspected at any time, without notice.

The applicant herself (or himself, for men may also apply to be registered child minders) must be in good health and may be asked to have a chest X-ray. This will be done free of charge at a clinic or hospital. References may also be required: if any member of the household has ever been convicted of any offence against a child, the application will be refused. Permission of the applicant must be given before the police can be asked about criminal records.

A child minder may be held liable in NEGLIGENCE and have to pay compensation if any child in her care is injured through her careless supervision. She should insure against that liability.

Limit on numbers

The local authority will decide how many children a child minder can register for. The law does not fix a limit but in practice the child minder will not be allowed to look after more than three children under 5 years of age, including any children of her own.

Once registered, the child minder must keep a written record of the chil-dren left in her care including names, addresses and ways of contacting parents in an emergency. She must also allow a social worker to make regular visits, to make sure that the children are well looked after and are being given a substantial cooked meal every day.

Benefits for child minders

A registered child minder is entitled to a milk allowance for children in her care at the rate of one-third of a pint per child per day. The benefit comes as a cash allowance, which can be claimed on a form available from the council's social services department or social security office. Many local authorities also provide equipment or an equipment grant.

Minders on supplementary benefit

A child minder who draws SUPPLEMENTARY BENEFIT, or whose husband does, should report any child-minding payments to the social security office, as benefit may be affected.

Only one-third of the child-minding payments is treated as earnings. Any reasonable expenses incurred in looking after the children can be deducted from that one-third.

For example, if a woman is paid £24 a week as a child minder and has no other earnings, and her child-minding expenses amount to £2 a week, her earnings will be £8 (one-third of £24) less £2 expenses, leaving £6 a week.

Of that amount, the first £4 is ignored (or £5 if she is a single parent). The balance of £2 a week (£1 for a single parent) is deducted from supplementary benefit.

If the expenses of child minding come to more than the amount allowed, the minder should tell the social security office. If the local office does not accept the level of expenses, the minder is entitled to appeal.

CHILDREN IN CARE

How a local authority can take the place of parents

A child may be taken into the care of a local authority for one of several reasons. The local authority may ask a court to put a child in its care because he is neglected, ill-treated, in moral or physical danger or in need of care and control. If a child is lost or abandoned, or if its parents or guardians cannot properly provide for it, the local authority must take it into care.

If a child over the age of 10 and under 17 commits a criminal offence, he can be put into care by a juvenile court instead of being punished.

A child under 10 is legally considered

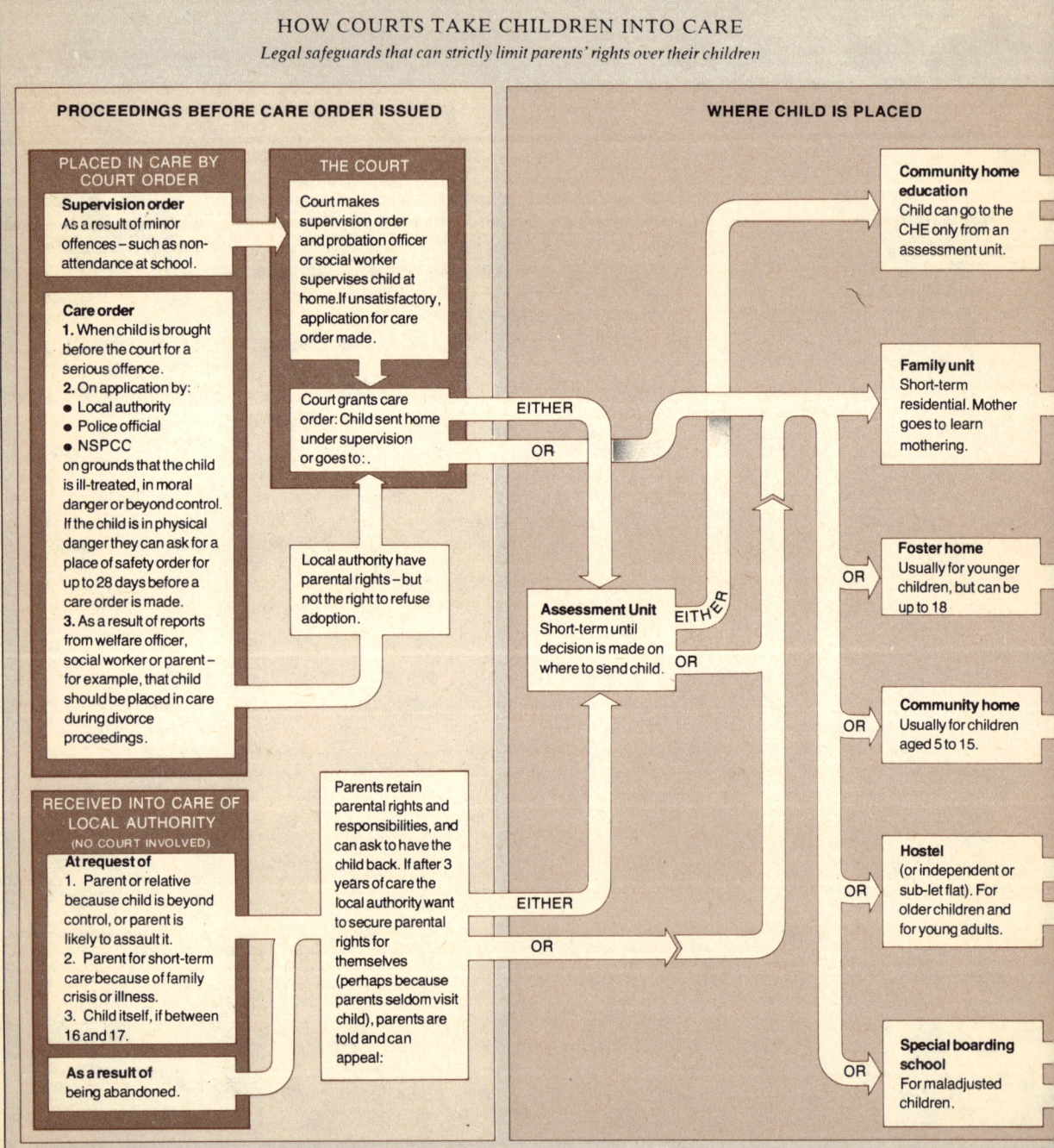

HOW COURTS TAKE CHILDREN INTO CARE
Legal safeguards that can strictly limit parents' rights over their children

PROCEEDINGS BEFORE CARE ORDER ISSUED

PLACED IN CARE BY COURT ORDER

Supervision order
As a result of minor offences – such as non-attendance at school.

Care order
1. When child is brought before the court for a serious offence.
2. On application by:
• Local authority
• Police official
• NSPCC
on grounds that the child is ill-treated, in moral danger or beyond control. If the child is in physical danger they can ask for a place of safety order for up to 28 days before a care order is made.
3. As a result of reports from welfare officer, social worker or parent – for example, that child should be placed in care during divorce proceedings.

RECEIVED INTO CARE OF LOCAL AUTHORITY
(NO COURT INVOLVED)

At request of
1. Parent or relative because child is beyond control, or parent is likely to assault it.
2. Parent for short-term care because of family crisis or illness.
3. Child itself, if between 16 and 17.

As a result of
being abandoned.

THE COURT

Court makes supervision order and probation officer or social worker supervises child at home. If unsatisfactory, application for care order made.

Court grants care order: Child sent home under supervision or goes to:.

Local authority have parental rights – but not the right to refuse adoption.

Parents retain parental rights and responsibilities, and can ask to have the child back. If after 3 years of care the local authority want to secure parental rights for themselves (perhaps because parents seldom visit child), parents are told and can appeal:

EITHER

OR

Assessment Unit
Short-term until decision is made on where to send child.

EITHER

OR

EITHER

OR

WHERE CHILD IS PLACED

Community home education
Child can go to the CHE only from an assessment unit.

Family unit
Short-term residential. Mother goes to learn mothering.

OR

Foster home
Usually for younger children, but can be up to 18

OR

Community home
Usually for children aged 5 to 15.

OR

Hostel
(or independent or sub-let flat). For older children and for young adults.

OR

Special boarding school
For maladjusted children.

Laws relating to juveniles are concerned more with protecting them than with punishing them. In some cases, courts take the grave decision that a child's parents are not the best people to guide and care for it.

Such a decision is taken less in response to the specific matter that has brought the child to the notice of the court than as a result of an extensive study of the child's whole background and circumstances.

incapable of committing a criminal offence. But if he does something that would be a crime if he were over 10, he can be brought before a juvenile court in care proceedings and may be put in care.

The right to start care proceedings is limited to local authorities, police officers, and any officer of the National Society for the Prevention of Cruelty to Children.

Whoever brings the proceedings

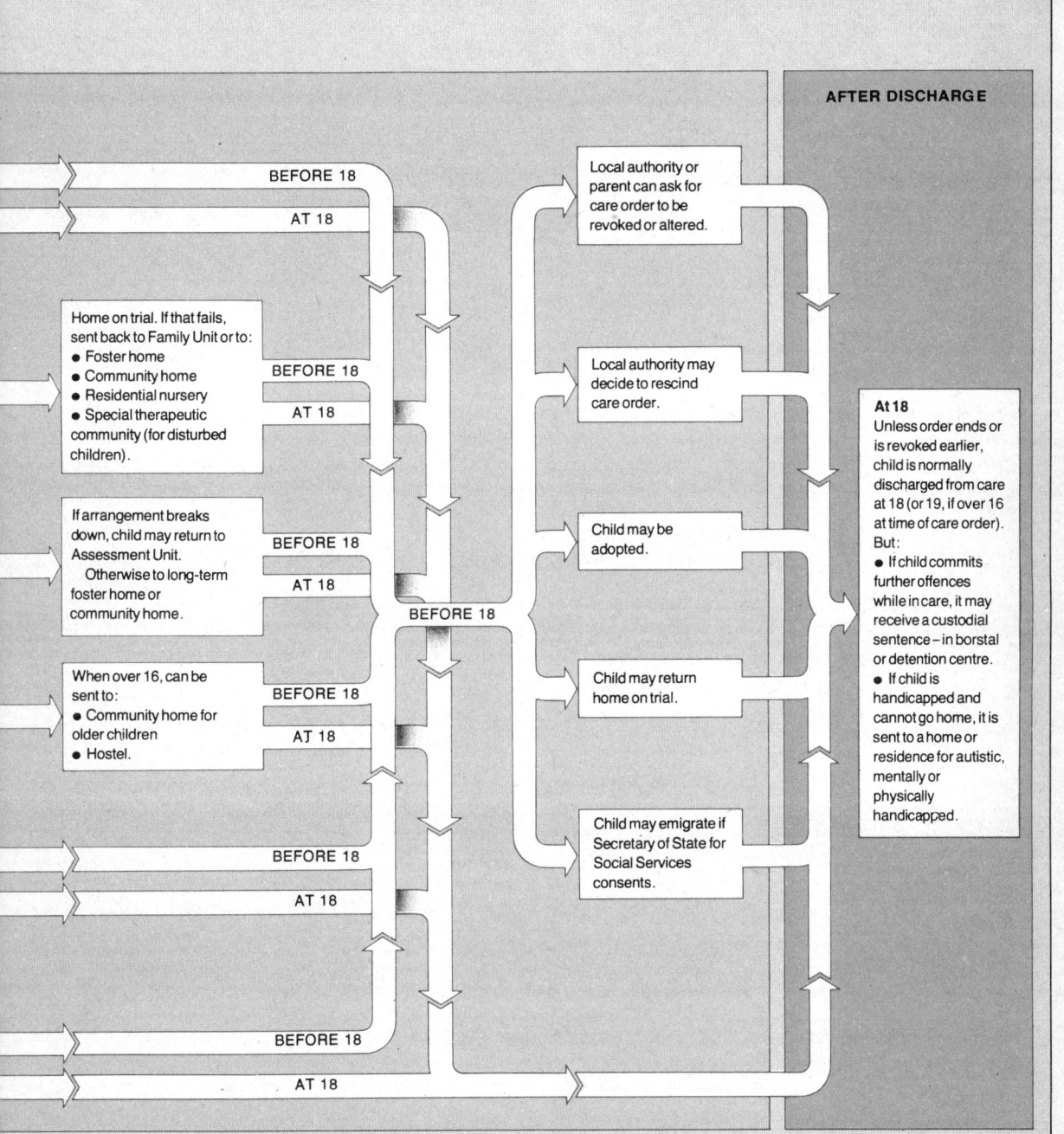

AFTER DISCHARGE

BEFORE 18

AT 18

Home on trial. If that fails, sent back to Family Unit or to:
● Foster home
● Community home
● Residential nursery
● Special therapeutic community (for disturbed children).

BEFORE 18

AT 18

If arrangement breaks down, child may return to Assessment Unit.
Otherwise to long-term foster home or community home.

BEFORE 18

AT 18

When over 16, can be sent to:
● Community home for older children
● Hostel.

BEFORE 18

AT 18

BEFORE 18

AT 18

BEFORE 18

BEFORE 18

AT 18

Local authority or parent can ask for care order to be revoked or altered.

Local authority may decide to rescind care order.

Child may be adopted.

Child may return home on trial.

Child may emigrate if Secretary of State for Social Services consents.

At 18
Unless order ends or is revoked earlier, child is normally discharged from care at 18 (or 19, if over 16 at time of care order). But:
● If child commits further offences while in care, it may receive a custodial sentence – in borstal or detention centre.
● If child is handicapped and cannot go home, it is sent to a home or residence for autistic, mentally or physically handicapped.

The parents do not necessarily have to accept that the court is right. They can appeal to a higher court which will, in effect, re-hear the case. Alternatively, if the parents accept that the court was right at the time, *they can later ask it to cancel or alter the order if they can show that home conditions have improved. In general, the local authority will itself keep any case involving the care of a child under continual review.*

must notify the local authority in advance. If the child is over 13, the local probation office must also be told.

Parents or guardians cannot themselves start care proceedings. However, if the child is under 17, they can ask the local authority to do so – if, for example, the child is so unruly that he cannot be controlled at home.

If the request is refused, the parent or guardian can apply to the juvenile court for an order directing the authority to start care proceedings.

Bringing a child to court

If care proceedings are being brought by the local authority, it issues a summons requiring the child and its parents or guardians to attend a juvenile court. *See:* CRIMINAL PROCEEDINGS

If the child is under 5 years of age, the court can direct that he need not attend. In all other cases, the child must be present.

To obtain a care order, the local authority must show that the child is beyond the control of its parents or guardian and/or that one of six conditions exists:
1. The child's health or development is being hindered or neglected or it is being ill-treated.
2. There has been a previous case in the same household and it is probable that the same conditions still exist.
3. The child's welfare is likely to be harmed by the presence in the household of a person who has been convicted of offences against children.
4. The child is exposed to moral danger.
5. It is not receiving suitable education.
6. It is guilty of a criminal offence.

The court must also be satisfied that the child needs care and control that he is unlikely to receive unless a care order is made.

If there is an accusation against the child, his parent, guardian or a lawyer can represent him at the hearing.

If there is an accusation against the parents – for example, an allegation of ill-treatment or neglect – they are entitled to answer those allegations and be represented by a lawyer. The court can allow LEGAL AID for the child. The parent or guardian may apply for aid, but only on behalf of the child. No legal aid is available for the adult.

The court may order that the child be represented separately from the parents, because it feels that the parent or guardian should not represent the child – for example, when it is alleged that the child has been ill-treated.

If such a decision is made, and the child is not old enough to understand what is going on, the court will appoint a guardian ad litem to look after his interests.

Before making a care order, the court asks the local authority to provide a social inquiry report – information about the child's home, school record, health and character.

The report is usually shown to the parents and also to the child if he is old enough to understand it.

When an order has been made

An order putting a child into the care of a local authority can last until the child is 18 – or 19 if the child was over 16 when made. Once it has been made, the court has no further say in the child's upbringing.

However, the parent or guardian – or the authority – can apply to the court to alter or end the order.

Assessing the needs A child placed in the council's care is often sent first to an assessment centre, a children's home where his needs can be examined over a short period. He may live in or attend day by day.

Residential staff, including a psychologist, psychiatrist, teacher and social worker talk to the child and his parents, and make plans for his future educational and emotional needs.

The child can be put in a council home or placed with foster parents or – as is often done – returned to the care of his own parents, under the supervision of local authority social workers.

Arranging visits If a child is sent to foster parents or a council home, his own parents will be encouraged to visit him regularly. The local authority has power to help with the cost of fares and overnight accommodation, if the visits are likely to help to get the child home again. But if the council refuses financial assistance, the parents have no right of appeal.

Supplementary benefit is not normally paid for the cost of visiting a child in care.

When a child over 5 years old has no parents, or when they fail to keep in touch, the local authority appoints a visitor to befriend him and advise him as a parent might do.

Supervision instead of care

Instead of putting a child into care, the court may decide to make a SUPERVISION ORDER, placing him under the supervision of the local authority or a probation officer. The order will run for up to 3 years or until the child's 18th birthday.

The order may include special provisions – for example, that the child must live with a person named by the court, or have treatment for a mental condition.

The supervisor's duty is to befriend, advise and help the child. A probation officer cannot be appointed supervisor unless the child is over 13, the probation service has already been involved in his household and the local authority has asked for that appointment to be made.

At any time while the order is in force, the child or his supervisor can ask the court to end it. If supervision has not been effective, a care order can then be substituted.

Appealing against an order

An appeal against the magistrates' care order – or refusal to make one – can be made to the crown court. The crown court must be notified within 28 days of the magistrates' decision.

The appeal takes the form of a re-hearing of the application.

Children 'received into care'

A local authority is required by law to receive into care any child under 18 who seems in need of such care, if it has no parent or guardian, is abandoned or lost or if the parent or guardian is incapable of providing for it.

Being received into care is different from being put into care, although the child may stay in the same accommodation as those dealt with through the courts.

An authority receiving a child into care does not assume the rights of the parents – and the parents may remove the child at any time, but if a child remains in care for more than 6 months, the parents are required to give 28 days' notice, in writing, of their intention to remove him.

Whenever a local authority is asked

to receive a child into care, it first explores other means of helping – for example, by providing the family with a home help or DAY NURSERY place or arranging for the child to be cared for by relatives, friends or neighbours – giving financial assistance if necessary.

If a child is received into care, the council must do everything possible to enable him to keep in touch with his parents.

Parents usually have to supply information about the child's background and medical and school history and to give a signed statement about their own financial situation. The parents of a child who is under 16 are required to contribute to his upkeep. A child over 16 who is working will usually be required to make some contribution to his own upkeep.

Taking away the parents' rights

When a child has been received into care, the local authority has power to go further and pass a resolution to take over all the rights and duties of the parents.

Parents who lose their rights to the local authority under such a resolution are still liable to contribute to the child's maintenance.

The council's power, however, is strictly limited. Such a resolution can be passed only if the child has been in its care for more than 3 years, or if he has no parent or guardian or his parents have abandoned him or are incapable of caring for him.

A parent may be judged incapable by reason of mental disorder, way of life or previous failure to carry out parental duties.

Once such a resolution has been made, a parent has no further rights over the child, except to refuse consent to a proposed adoption order – although the authority must bring up the child in his parents' religion.

What the authority must do When the resolution is passed, the authority must notify the parents – or anyone else who previously had parental rights – and tell them of their right to object.

The parent is then entitled to serve a notice in writing – a 'counter-notice' – objecting to the resolution.

The authority must bring the case to the juvenile court within 14 days because if it does not the resolution ceases to have effect. If court proceedings are started within that time, however, the resolution continues in force until the court decides the matter.

The resolution, if upheld or unchallenged, normally continues in force until the child is 18. However, the parents are entitled to apply to the court at any time for the resolution to be ended.

The local authority can itself decide to cancel it.

Appealing against a resolution The juvenile court's decision can be appealed against by either side, to the High Court. Notice of appeal must be given within 28 days.

If the child is adopted The authority's resolution ceases to have any effect if the child is adopted or if a guardian is appointed.

CHILDREN'S INCOME

Managing a young person's money

However young a child is, it can receive both earned and investment income in its own name. If the income, excluding any educational grant, is more than the single person's tax-free allowance, the balance is taxable. The rate of single person's allowance increases every year. *See:* INCOME TAX ALLOWANCES

When a child's income exceeds the tax-free limit, the parent or guardian is responsible for ensuring that a tax return is completed – provided that the child is unmarried and under 18 and living at home.

The child's income is assessed for tax in the same way as that of an adult, and the same allowances apply.

Effects on parents' tax

Income exceeding £5 from investments made by a parent for an unmarried child under 18 is taxed as part of the parent's income. If the investment is made by someone else – for example, a grandparent – the income is treated as the child's and may attract less tax. However, any advantage is lost if the grandparent or other person not a parent invests in a building society, as the tax deducted from the interest at source cannot be reclaimed.

ALL HIS OWN WORTH

No matter how young a child is, he is entitled to his own investment and earned income – say, from a paper round.

One of the best ways for a relative or friend to benefit a child not his own is by a covenant, an agreement to pay or invest a fixed sum annually for a period of more than 6 years on the child's behalf.

The arrangement requires the donor to deduct tax at the basic rate from the covenanted sum. The balance is given to the child, who may then recoup all or part of the deducted sum from the Inland Revenue, up to the amount of the single person's tax-free allowance. If the child has other taxable income, the sum that can be recouped under the covenant may be reduced.

There is no tax advantage for an unmarried child under 18 in a covenant made by a parent. *See also:* COVENANT

Supplementary benefit

The earnings of a child under 16 from a part-time job such as a paper round do not affect any parental claim for SUPPLEMENTARY BENEFIT. But other income received by a dependent child of any age living with its parents, including children over 16 and still at school, is treated as the parents' income and may reduce the benefit. Invested capital is regarded as belonging to the parents.

CHILDREN'S RIGHTS

The duties of society towards its future citizens

In general, children under the AGE OF MAJORITY – that is, under 18 – cannot exercise their rights of citizenship, for example by voting, standing for election, serving on a jury or owning their own home. But they do have most of the legal rights of adults, although they themselves cannot take steps to enforce them in law.

If court proceedings are necessary to secure a child's rights, they must be undertaken on the child's behalf by a 'next friend', who may be any adult who is usually a parent or close relative. The only exception is that a child itself may sue in the county court for wages it is owed – up to £2,000.

A child cannot sue in its own name in breach of contract or negligence but one of its parents can sue on its behalf as 'next friend'. If the child itself is sued, a guardian ad litem must be appointed to act for it.

Protecting and educating

If children are not supported by parents, guardians or relatives they will be cared for by the state. If the parent or guardian is killed in an accident, caused by someone else's negligence, the child – through a 'next friend' – can claim damages from that person.

The local authority of the area in which a child lives must provide education, and must also care for the child if it is neglected, abandoned or ill-treated by the parents. *See:* CHILD ABUSE; CHILDREN IN CARE; WARD OF COURT

The child's own money

Any child, however young, may have a bank account. The child can inherit property and titles, but cannot make a valid will unless on active service in the army, air force, Royal Navy or merchant navy. *See:* CHILDREN'S INCOME

When a child is old enough to take a job, it has special rights to protection in employment. It is also liable to income tax and may be made bankrupt. *See:* MINOR

Rights before birth

An UNBORN CHILD has no legal right to life up to the 28th week of pregnancy, but it is still a criminal offence to terminate a pregnancy except within the limits of the ABORTION Act 1967.

A child who is born disabled or deformed as a result of the negligence of someone other than its mother can – through a 'next friend' – sue that person for damages. For example, if a doctor

gives a pregnant mother drugs which he knows, or ought to know, can cause deformity in the child, the doctor can be sued, but only if the child is in fact born deformed or disabled, and only if it lives for more than 48 hours.

The child cannot usually sue its mother for negligence. If, for example, it is born deformed because its mother smoked to excess during pregnancy, she cannot be sued. The only instance where the mother can be sued is if the injury to the child was caused by the mother's negligent driving, in which case her insurance company pays.

CHILD'S SPECIAL ALLOWANCE
Aid in special circumstances

A mother who is bringing up her children on her own because she has been widowed, divorced or her marriage has been annulled, may be entitled to claim a special extra weekly allowance for her children. *See:* CHILD BENEFIT

CHIROPODY
Specialist treatment of foot problems

Free chiropody services are available under the National Health Service for pensioners, the physically handicapped, pregnant women and schoolchildren. Other people with minor foot ailments, such as ingrowing toenails or corns, may have to pay for private treatment.

Local chiropody clinics provide free treatment for those who qualify, and the area health authority will give the dates and places where the clinic is held, often at a hospital out-patients' department.

Information is available from area health authorities and local authority social services departments.

CINEMA ADMISSION
Rules that are intended to protect the very young

No child under 5 years of age can be admitted to a cinema, even when he or she is accompanied by a parent.

Cinemas are licensed by local authorities, who normally insist that films are classified according to rules laid down by the British Board of Film Censors.

If you believe that a cinema is not taking reasonable steps to enforce the restrictions on admission of children, you can complain to the local authority, which has power to withdraw the cinema's licence. *See also:* FILM CENSORSHIP

CITIZENS ADVICE BUREAU
A network of trained advisers

The Citizens Advice Bureau service provides free information and advice about almost any personal problem, especially in the fields of law and social welfare rights.

Each bureau in the nationwide network is supervised by the National Association of Citizens Advice Bureaux, and is staffed mainly by non-expert, but trained, volunteers. Some offices also employ full-time solicitors and other experts. Others have solicitors and financial experts who attend to give free advice on one day or evening each week.

Advice is offered at each office or by telephone. To find your nearest office, check the local telephone directory under 'Citizens Advice Bureau'. *See also:* CONSUMER ADVICE CENTRE

CITIZEN'S ARREST
What the man in the street can do

Every citizen has certain powers of arrest when someone commits a crime, but they are not as wide as police powers of arrest, and must be exercised with great care.

A citizen can arrest someone only for an 'arrestable offence' – usually one that carries a maximum penalty of 5 or more years' imprisonment – or for breach of the peace. He must be sure that the offence has actually been committed.

You cannot arrest someone on suspicion of a crime that you do not know for certain has been committed. Neither

> ## THE CITIZEN'S ARREST THAT FAILED
>
> *A person who makes a citizen's arrest must be sure that a crime has actually been committed.*
>
> Mr Walters ran a railway station bookstall. He also ran a private newsagent's shop, where he sold books.
>
> His bookstall employers found during stocktaking that books were missing. They set a trap by marking certain books.
>
> One of the bookstall company's staff bought a book from Mr Walters' private shop and discovered that it was a marked copy from the bookstall.
>
> He arrested Mr Walters on an accusation of theft. Mr Walters was sent for trial, but denied stealing. A jury acquitted him. He then sued the bookstall company for false imprisonment.
>
> ### DECISION
>
> Mr Walters won his case. He was awarded £75 damages because the company could not prove that the book had been stolen – by Mr Walters or anyone else.

can you arrest someone who is attempting a crime but who has not yet committed it (for example, you could not arrest someone you found prowling outside your house wearing nylon gloves and carrying a bag just because you suspected him of planning a burglary).

The police, on the other hand, are entitled to arrest someone they reasonably suspect of having committed some crime or whom they find attempting to do so.

Making an arrest

If you arrest someone, you must tell him why you are doing so. If he resists, you are entitled to use reasonable force, but must take him to a police station within a reasonable time, if the arrest is to be legal. The jury would be left to decide in any case what was reasonable force and if the arrested person had been taken immediately to the police.

Private citizens – including store detectives – who arrest people may lay themselves open to claims for FALSE IMPRISONMENT or for ASSAULT AND BATTERY if the offence is not an arrestable one, or if a court decides that no offence has been committed.

CITIZENSHIP

What it means to be a citizen of the United Kingdom

Almost everyone born in the United Kingdom – that is England, Scotland, Northern Ireland and Wales – the Channel Islands, Isle of Man and British colonies is a citizen of the United Kingdom and Colonies.

There are exceptions, however. For example, a child born to a foreign diplomat stationed in the United Kingdom or other relevant territory would not normally be a UK citizen.

On the other hand, a baby born on a ship, aircraft or hovercraft – civilian or military – which is registered in the United Kingdom or colonies is legally considered to have been born in the United Kingdom. The same applies to ships or aircraft belonging to the British armed forces.

Adopted children A child who has been adopted by a UK citizen, or by a couple of whom the husband is a citizen, becomes a UK citizen himself from the time of the adoption order.

Many people who were born in what are now independent Commonwealth countries are still citizens of the United Kingdom and Colonies – either because they were allowed to opt to remain citizens, or because they were not allowed to take up citizenship of the new state when it became independent.

Despite that citizenship, however, they have no free right of entry into this country unless they are classed as 'patrial'. *See:* PATRIALITY

Citizenship by descent

Someone born outside the United Kingdom and Colonies is a citizen if his father was a UK citizen at the time of the birth (or a British subject, if the birth was before December 1948) and if the child was legitimate at birth or became so by the parents' subsequent marriage. *See:* ILLEGITIMATE CHILD

Citizenship cannot normally descend in that way through more than one generation. A father can pass on his citizenship only if he himself was born, adopted, naturalised or registered as a UK citizen in the United Kingdom or colonies.

There are exceptions, however. A child can inherit citizenship, even though his father previously inherited it, if either:
1. The birth is registered at a British consulate within a year.
2. The father is on Crown service at the time of the birth.
3. The child or the father is born in a territory administered by the UK government.
4. The child is born in any Commonwealth country to whose citizenship he is not entitled.

A CHILD'S RIGHT TO UK CITIZENSHIP

Almost anyone born in the United Kingdom, or whose father is a citizen, has a complete right to citizenship and cannot be deprived of it.

A child born outside the UK cannot inherit UK citizenship as of right through its mother, even if it is illegitimate.

Citizenship by registration

It is possible to obtain citizenship voluntarily in two ways: by registration or naturalisation. Registration is the simpler, quicker and cheaper of the two: it should take only a few months and the fee is £25.

In some cases, however, the Home Secretary can refuse registration, even if the applicant qualifies for citizenship.
Married women Any woman who has been married at any time to a UK citizen is entitled to be registered, whether or not they are still married.

If she has at some time renounced UK citizenship, the Home Secretary has to be asked to approve the registration.

Commonwealth citizen The Home Secretary can, at his discretion, register a Commonwealth citizen or a citizen of Eire who has been ordinarily resident in the United Kingdom for the past 5 years, with no other qualification. He can also allow registration after a shorter period – or accept a period of 'relevant employment' instead.

A Commonwealth or Irish citizen aged 18 or more, and of sound mind, who has been settled in the United Kingdom – ordinarily resident, with no restrictions – since January 1, 1973, has a right to be registered.

A Commonwealth citizen, aged at least 18 and of sound mind, can be registered if:

● One of his parents was born to, or legally adopted by, a parent who at the time of the birth or adoption was a citizen by virtue of her birth in the United Kingdom, Channel Islands or Isle of Man, and:

● Has for the past 5 years been 'ordinarily resident' in the United Kingdom.

● Has been engaged in 'relevant employment'.

Ordinarily resident To be ordinarily resident the person has to be in the country lawfully, and have his home here. He can go away for holidays, even for several months, and he ceases to be ordinarily resident in the United Kingdom only if he leaves the country with the intention of making his home somewhere else even for a short period.

Relevant employment CROWN service, service in an international organisation to which the UK government belongs, or service in a company based in the United Kingdom are all relevant employment. An applicant is absolutely entitled to be registered as a citizen only if the employment is Crown service. In other cases the Home Secretary need register him only if it seems 'fitting'.

Children A legitimate child under 18 may be registered, at the Home Secretary's discretion, if the parent or guardian applies. Such an application is normally approved if the parents or guardian are already UK citizens. It is Home Office practice always to register any children under 16 of women who are themselves UK citizens by birth.

Stateless persons

There are special arrangements for registering a STATELESS PERSON who has some connection with the United Kingdom.

For example, someone who has been stateless from birth (perhaps through being born in a country where birth is not enough to give him citizenship there) will be registered as a UK citizen if his mother was a citizen of the United Kingdom and Colonies when he was born. *See:* NATURALISATION

Losing UK citizenship

No one who is a UK citizen by birth or descent can be deprived of his citizenship.

However, someone who has been allowed citizenship by naturalisation or being registered can have it taken away by the Home Secretary.

Anyone threatened with being deprived of his citizenship must be given notice by the Home Office and is entitled to have the matter investigated by a committee of inquiry. The committee is appointed by the Home Secretary and will have a chairman with judicial experience.

Who may be deprived The Home Secretary can take away citizenship from anyone who obtained it by fraud, a false statement or concealment of a material fact, if it is not considered to the public good that the person should remain a citizen.

A naturalised Briton may also be deprived of citizenship if within 5 years after naturalisation he has been sentenced, in any country, to a term of imprisonment of 12 months or more.

However, if the person has no other citizenship, and losing his UK citizenship would make him stateless, he will not be deprived of it.

A naturalised Briton who, in the view of the Home Secretary, shows himself disloyal to the Crown by act or speech, or who trades or communicates unlawfully with an enemy during wartime, can be deprived of citizenship, even if that would make him stateless.

Renouncing UK citizenship

To renounce his citizenship of the United Kingdom and Colonies, an applicant must complete a special Home Office form, R6, and have that declaration registered with the appropriate authorities.

In the United Kingdom, the appropriate authority is the Home Office. In other Commonwealth countries it is the British High Commissioner.

People who renounce their UK citizenship usually do so because they wish to acquire citizenship of another country that does not recognise, or does not encourage, dual citizenship.

For the renunciation to have any effect, the applicant must satisfy the Home Office that he is already a citizen of another country, or that he will become one within 6 months after renunciation.

If he does not become a citizen elsewhere within 6 months, he will still be a UK citizen and will be considered to have remained one throughout.

The provision is to prevent people making themselves stateless. But it does not deal with a situation (as happened in Uganda) where UK citizenship is renounced and citizenship of the new state granted – and later the new state cancels that citizenship.

Resuming UK citizenship

A person who renounces UK citizenship can resume it on certain conditions.

He must have renounced citizenship at a time when he was (or was about to become) a citizen of another Commonwealth country which would not let him do so without renouncing UK citizenship, or when he reasonably believed that if he did not do so he would lose his Commonwealth citizenship.

He must also have a 'qualifying connection' with the United Kingdom or, if the applicant is a woman, she must have been married to a man who had such a connection.

BRITISH SUBJECT

The expressions 'British subject' and 'British national' mean anyone who is a citizen of the United Kingdom or any other Commonwealth country.

People born in the United Kingdom or in territories which are still UK colonies (or who acquire citizenship there), are 'citizens of the United Kingdom and Colonies' as well as being British subjects.

A 'qualifying connection' exists if the applicant, his father or his father's father was born, registered or naturalised in the United Kingdom or in a place which – at the time he wants to resume citizenship – is still a British colony.

Anyone with all those qualifications has a right to be registered as a UK citizen. The Home Secretary also has power to register someone who has all the qualifications except the qualifying connection.

CLEAN AIR

Ensuring that the air is fit to breathe

A district council ensures that the air in its area is clean by introducing smoke-control regulations which prohibit the use of certain types of fuel. Anyone who fails to comply with the regulations may be prosecuted. *See:* AIR POLLUTION

CLEAN FOOD

Wide powers of inspection

If you are sold food that you believe is dirty or contaminated – or comes from unhygienic premises – you can report the seller to the local district council, which may prosecute him.

The maximum penalty for such an offence is 3 months' imprisonment and £100 fine.

Council environmental health officers have wide powers to inspect food shops and restaurants to ensure that both premises and staff are clean. *See:* FOOD

CLEARANCE AREA

A council's powers to deal with sub-standard housing

A local district council has the power at any time to declare that an area where most of the houses are unfit to live in is to be the subject of a slum-clearance scheme.

Someone who owns or occupies property in such an area is not entitled to object at that stage. But because the council **must ensure** that no one continues to live in a slum-clearance area, it will have to make a COMPULSORY PURCHASE order for all the properties. Objections can then be made.

Other actions a council can take

Apart from all-out clearance of a district, a council may deal with slums and 'twilight areas' by other, more selective methods: demolition (or closure) orders for individual houses, declaring a general improvement area or declaring a housing action area.

Demolition order The owner or tenant of a house which becomes the subject of a demolition or closure order is entitled to attend a council (or committee) meeting and put forward proposals for repairing or using the house, rather than having it demolished or closed.

If the council decides against him, he can appeal to a county court.

Anyone who is eventually forced to leave his home under a demolition or closure order is entitled to be rehoused by the council. *See:* HOMELESSNESS

A home loss payment is also made if the person has lived in the house for more than 5 years.

General improvement area The effect of declaring a general improvement area is that the council can acquire the land by means of a compulsory purchase order and then improve any homes on it. The houses need not be unfit to live in, but will usually have no modern amenities such as bathrooms or indoor lavatories.

The council can also give grants or loans towards improvements to homes which they do not own, in the improvement area. *See:* IMPROVEMENT GRANT

No one is entitled to object to the making of an improvement order.

Housing action area Once a housing action area has been declared, anyone who owns a house in it may be ordered to improve his property – but will be entitled to a grant towards the cost. If the owner decides to sell or let his house, the local authority must be given first refusal to buy or find a tenant.

The owner is also entitled to appeal to the local magistrates against an improvement notice concerning his property on the ground that improvement is unnecessary. The magistrates have power to quash the order.

A council is entitled to make compulsory purchase orders for any building or land in a housing action area.

CLOAKROOM

When you are entitled to compensation for theft

If the staff of a restaurant or meeting place take charge of your coat or other belongings, whether or not they charge you for doing so, you are entitled to expect the management to take reasonable care of your property.

The management will be liable for any loss unless they can prove that they had taken reasonable care.

Cloakroom conditions, on signs or tickets, which seek to exclude or limit the management's liability have no effect unless you are given reasonable notice of them, and unless they are fair and reasonable as defined by the UNFAIR CONTRACT Terms Act.

For example, British Rail conditions for handling left luggage say that the railway will not be liable for more than £100 compensation for articles left with them at any one time by the same customer.

Another condition is that the railway will not be liable for damage to fragile

LEAVING BELONGINGS IN
A CLOAKROOM

The management of any establishment which accepts charge of people's coats or other property may be held liable for any loss or damage, unless they can prove that they took reasonable care.

articles, even if the damage is caused by negligence of railway staff.

Both conditions would probably be held to be unreasonable under the Unfair Contract Terms Act.

A third condition says that in some circumstances, the railway may hand over articles to someone who cannot produce a receipt ticket, and that delivery of the articles will relieve the management from all claims for loss.

Since that condition appears to allow goods to be given away to the wrong person, it could also be considered unreasonable, if the railway staff were negligent – for example, if they did not ask enough questions before parting with the goods.

When you are liable If you hang up your own coat in a restaurant or meeting hall, without help from the staff, the management will not normally be responsible for looking after it.

CLOSE SEASON

The time when hunting is illegal

There are certain times during a year when the hunting of particular kinds of animals or birds and fishing for certain fresh-water fish is forbidden by law.
See: FISHING
GAME

CLUB

There are, in law, two types of club – members' and proprietary

A members' club may be formed by any group of people who get together for some social purpose and who each contribute towards running expenses. A members' club is not primarily operated to make a profit, so it is not a partnership, but it can be turned into a company, to give it legal advantages, particularly that of being able to sue in its own name. Members' clubs may have property of their own – for example, a golf course or tennis courts – or may meet by agreement in someone else's premises, like a chess or bridge club.

A proprietary club is run for profit. The proprietor owns it and charges the members fees for whatever privileges the club provides. The entertainment

---

JOINING AN ENTERTAINMENT CLUB

Entertainment clubs may make anyone a member without going through the formalities of nomination and written application if their rules permit. But people admitted to membership on simple demand must wait 2 days before they are legally allowed to enjoy any of the club's facilities.

Someone caught breaking the 2 day law might escape trouble if he was genuinely unaware of the rule, but a club that persistently flouted it would be committing an offence and the licence holder and every club officer would be guilty. The penalty would be a fine of up to £1,000 in the magistrates' court, or 2 years' imprisonment and an unlimited fine in the crown court. The club could also face police opposition to renewal of its licence.

A person injured at a club during the 2 day waiting period would not lose his right to claim compensation provided he had not deceived the club to obtain admission. If he used deception to get in, he would be committing a TRESPASS.

---

clubs which have supplanted music halls are usually proprietary clubs.

The importance of club rules

Clubs of both types are governed by their rules, which form part of the contract between the members, in the case of members' clubs, or between the members and the proprietor in proprietary clubs.

Membership

Generally, clubs are free to make whatever rules they like, although those with 25 or more members may not practise RACIAL DISCRIMINATION in admission, exclusions, allocation of club privileges or use of the facilities.

SEX DISCRIMINATION is allowed if the club is single sex, but if both men and women are allowed to join they must be given the same facilities.

A person who has the right qualifications to join a particular club, but who is refused membership, cannot compel the club to make him a member.

Expulsion

However, a member who is expelled may be able to get a court to declare that

---

the expulsion was not valid if he can show he was denied a fair hearing in accordance with NATURAL JUSTICE, or if the club broke its own rules over the expulsion. For example, if the club rules specified that its committee should decide on expulsions and a non-member of the committee took part in the decision, the expulsion would be void.

Club debts

Always read the club rules carefully before joining. You may find that they commit you to liabilities that you would not normally expect. If a members' club obtains goods on credit, for example, the person liable for the debt is usually the one who placed the order, together with anyone who authorised him to place it. In some cases, however, the rules of the club may state that all members are equally liable.

Debts incurred by proprietary clubs are treated in law in the same way as those of any other business. The proprietor is liable for what his agents do on his behalf.

If someone is injured

If someone is injured on club premises, anyone whose fault contributed to the injury may be sued. In addition, anyone who employs the person to blame may be liable. So if a club waiter spills scalding soup on someone, the waiter and the committee members who hired him could be sued. Members held liable for damages cannot demand financial help from other members unless the club rules specifically say so.

Changing club rules

Members of proprietary clubs have no control over the proprietor, and if they dislike the way he runs things there is little they can do. But those belonging to members' clubs may be able to secure changes. The first step is to study the club rules.

These may contain procedures for amending the rules themselves, if enough members agree. They also commonly lay down the way in which members must be notified of club meetings. If proper notice was not given, decisions taken at a meeting may be annulled.

If the committee is at fault it can be replaced, usually at an annual meeting. However, there is nothing in law to prevent a club giving the power to make decisions to only a few members, if its rules say so.

THE IMPORTANCE OF THE CLUB'S RULES

Always read the club rules carefully before you join. You may find that they commit you, for example, to meeting any financial losses.

'I'd never join a club that would have ME as a member.'

When liquor is sold

A club cannot supply intoxicating liquor to members or guests unless it has either a registered certificate from a magistrates' court or a justices' licence. Clubs are usually required to observe the general licensing hours of the area, but magistrates may allow an extension if meals are served, or if the premises have a MUSIC AND DANCING LICENCE.

COASTGUARD

Providing maritime protection

Her Majesty's Coastguard coordinates maritime rescue services, keeps watch for shipping hazards and warns mariners about bad weather.
See: LIFE-BOAT SERVICE
SEA

CODICIL

Alteration to a will

A WILL can be altered at any time after it has been made by means of a codicil – a separate document or even an amendment written on to the will itself. The codicil must be dated, signed and witnessed by two witnesses. Be-

neficiaries lose their benefit if they or their husband or wife sign as a witness, but the codicil remains valid.

The original will should always be referred to in a codicil and it is wise to add a clause confirming the provisions of the will and any earlier codicils.

A codicil (*see* p. 724) can be written to appoint a new executor where one has moved or died, to cancel or alter a legacy. If substantial changes are to be made, it is advisable to make a new will.

COHABITATION

When living together can mean losing money

Unmarried couples living together lose the right to a number of social security benefits through what is known as the cohabitation rule – under which the Department of Health and Social Security can decide that the couple are living as man and wife although they have no legal obligations to maintain each other.

Under the rule, a widow can lose her

> ### WIDOW ORDERED TO PAY BACK £5,000
>
> *The Department of Health and Social Security is likely to consider a couple to be cohabiting if they share a home for a long time and if the woman takes the man's name.*
>
> An anonymous telephone caller told a local social security office that a woman had been drawing widow's benefit while living with a man for years. The widow was ordered to repay £5,000.
>
> The couple insisted that the man was only a lodger, but the woman cooked for him. They denied any sexual relationship, and the woman said she had taken the man's name only to stop gossip.
>
> #### DECISION
>
> The tribunal ruled that because of the length of time they had lived together and because the woman had habitually taken the man's name, they must be considered to be behaving as man and wife. Therefore, under the cohabitation rule, the widow's benefit had to be repaid.

widow's benefit, including any increase for children, so long as she is cohabiting. However, the rule does not affect the woman's right to benefits to which she has contributed herself.

If a couple have been living together but are not legally married and the man dies, the woman is not entitled to widow's benefits or, if he is killed at work, to industrial injury death benefits, as a legal widow would be.

The cohabitation rule also affects supplementary benefits. A couple's needs and resources are added together as if they were married, and only the man is entitled to claim benefit on behalf of both of them. An unmarried, separated or divorced woman who begins to live with a man as his wife loses any supplementary benefit being paid for her or her children. *See:* COMMON LAW WIFE

In some exceptional cases, payments to a woman cohabiting with a man may continue. Where benefit is payable for the woman's children and the man is not their father, payments for the children's needs can continue for a 4 week 'adjustment' period if cutting off the benefit completely would reduce the household's income 'disproportionately' – and the adjustment period can be extended for another 6 weeks if the income is expected to increase.

If the couple's net income, after deducting any maintenance payments the man is making to a wife and children elsewhere, is below SUPPLEMENTARY BENEFIT level, the woman's benefit payments are continued indefinitely as if the couple were not living as husband and wife, but she will not get more than is needed to bring them up to supplementary benefit level.

The woman can also continue to receive supplementary benefit on grounds of urgent need, whether there are children or not, if the man refuses to support her. But she may have to repay the money if she is later in a position to do so.

COLLECTIVE BARGAINING

When employers and trade unions get round the table

Collective bargaining between trade unions and employers directly affects the pay and working conditions of about 15 million people in Britain, nearly 65 per cent of the working population.

There are hundreds of 'bargaining units'. The simplest, which involve only two people – a shop steward representing the employees and a foreman or

---

STRIKING A BARGAIN BETWEEN BOSS AND WORKER

The simplest form of collective bargaining involves only two people – the shop floor representative of the employees and a management spokesman, representing the employer.

---

supervisor appointed by the management – cover one section or department of a company. Such bargaining is not normally concerned with wages, but is confined to purely local matters such as the allocation of overtime work.

At the highest bargaining level, where national negotiations affect an entire industry, an employers' association usually represents the individual companies in that sector, and employees are represented by confederations of unions.

When agreements conflict

The number of levels at which bargaining can take place may lead to a conflict between the provisions of two or more agreements.

For example, a national agreement covering an entire industry may say that the normal working week is 40 hours, while a plant agreement for one factory may state that it is 56 hours.

A former employee from the factory who is claiming REDUNDANCY would get more money if the 56 hour provision

were applied. But if neither agreement stated which of the two took precedence, and if collective bargaining could not resolve the specific case, only a court or industrial tribunal could decide whether the normal work-week in the factory was 40 or 56 hours.

When agreements are enforceable

A collective agreement is not a legally enforceable contract between the collective parties who sign it – the employer or employers on one hand and the union or unions on the other – unless they expressly agree that it is.

If an agreement does not include a clause stating that it is legally enforceable, an employer is not entitled to sue a union, as an organisation, for breach of its terms. Similarly, the union cannot, in its own right, sue the employer.

However, many of the terms of collective agreements become legally binding on the employer and on his employees as individuals by being incorporated in each employee's EMPLOYMENT CONTRACT.

How individual contracts are affected

Collectively agreed provisions which deal with working terms and conditions – such matters as wages, hours, holidays, sick pay, pensions and maternity leave – can become incorporated into individual contracts explicitly or implicitly. They then affect all employees, whether members of a union or not.

In explicit cases, the terms may be written into an individual contract, or the contract may simply refer to the collective agreement so that it incorporates the terms of the agreement automatically.

If an individual contract says nothing about the incorporation of collective agreement provisions dealing with terms and conditions, they will become incorporated into it implicitly if they have been accepted to the point of becoming custom and practice in the company or industry concerned.

The only exception is if the collectively agreed provisions are 'unreasonable'.

If the collective terms cannot be regarded as custom and practice, either because they depart markedly from

previous arrangements or because they apply to only a small group of employees, they implicitly become part of individual contracts provided the employees affected are aware of them. If an individual is not aware of them, they may still be part of his contract. Court decisions in such cases have not been consistent.

Clauses in collective agreements dealing with purely procedural matters – such as the machinery for settling individual grievances – are rarely incorporated into employment contracts, though they could be important in, for example, UNFAIR DISMISSAL claims.

Unions' right to information

The law gives recognised trade unions the right to obtain from an employer non-confidential information about a company's affairs if it is needed for collective bargaining. *See:* TRADE UNIONS

The information is that which would normally be given 'in accordance with good industrial practice' or which, if not given, would materially impede the conduct of negotiations.

If the employer refuses to provide such information to a recognised trade union, the union can ask the CENTRAL ARBITRATION COMMITTEE to intervene.

The CAC cannot compel an employer to comply, but it can order him to concede the union's bargaining demands or to abide by other terms and conditions it may impose.

COLLEGES

The range of opportunities for advanced education

Comprehensive details of all colleges, courses and entry qualifications in an area can usually be obtained at the local reference library.

How to get into college

In most cases, to be accepted for study at a college of your choice you simply apply direct to that college.

One exception is any course aimed at teaching qualifications (and some other courses at colleges which mainly provide teacher-training). For those, apply through the Central Register and Clearing House.

Another exception is any course which is intended to lead to a degree in art and design. Such admissions are handled by the Art and Design Admissions Registry.

Who may apply You do not have to be a school-leaver to be accepted as a college student. Colleges often have special provisions for 'mature students' of any age.

It is up to each college to decide whom it will accept. A college maintained by the local education authority may reject you because it is full, or because you do not have the right qualifications. You can then appeal by letter to the college governors or the local education authority, but this is not often done.

How colleges are governed

Responsibility for running a college maintained by an education authority lies with its principal, the governors and the authority.

Governors are appointed under articles of government approved by the Department of Education. These recommend that governing bodies include representatives of staff, students and local commerce and industry; lay down conditions of appeal; and ensure students' rights in disciplinary hearings.

Normally, the governors are in charge of the general direction of the college and the principal is responsible to them for internal organisation and discipline. An academic board made up of staff and students is usually responsible for admissions and examinations.

Articles of government normally indicate to whom a student or would-be student may appeal, in any dispute with the college. If you feel that a college or its governing body has behaved unreasonably, you have a right of appeal to the Secretary of State for Education and Science.

Student discipline College governors are expected to make rules about discipline, giving students a right of appeal to a disciplinary committee comprising equal numbers of staff and students.

A student appealing to the committee should normally have the right to be accompanied by a friend or adviser.

Appointing staff The local education authority decides how many teachers its

maintained colleges should have and it is their direct employer.

Normally, senior posts are advertised and the candidates are interviewed by the college governors. Less important appointments are usually handled by the principal and the academic board. All appointments have to be confirmed by the local education authority.

Staff discipline All education authorities have a code laying down conditions of employment and disciplinary procedure for teaching staff.

If a teacher is threatened with dismissal, he has a right to be heard at the meeting of governors or education authority which is to consider his dismissal.

Governors can recommend dismissal, but it cannot be put into effect until the authority confirms it.

In a voluntary college depending on public funds, the governors act as employers, but the college must conform to the same principles as apply to maintained colleges. A teacher could not be sacked without approval of the local education authority.

COLLUSION

Agreeing the terms of divorce

Until 1963, a husband and wife who struck a bargain over terms for a divorce were guilty of collusion and, if the court came to know of their agreement, it would not grant a divorce. The law now regards it as being in the best interests of all the parties involved if such an agreement – about the conduct of the case – can be reached.

Any agreement about children must be approved by the court. *See:* CUSTODY OF CHILDREN

It is also advisable to ask the court to make an order confirming financial arrangements, such as MAINTENANCE, so that neither side can later go back on the agreement.

COMMITTAL PROCEEDINGS

The prosecution sets out its evidence to support a charge

Before a case is brought before a jury the prosecution must produce in a

magistrates' court all the evidence and witnesses it has gathered to support the charge or charges. *See:* CRIMINAL PROCEEDINGS

If the accused asks for trial by jury the prosecution usually needs to produce only the witnesses' written statements. The exceptions are when the accused is unrepresented, when identification is an issue or when a defendant refuses to agree to committal on the basis of the written statements.

At the end of the prosecution's presentation of its case the defence can ask the magistrates to dismiss the charge on the ground that the prosecution has failed to show that there is a case to answer.

The defence may request an old-style committal in which prosecution witnesses submit their evidence in person and are cross-examined by the defendant or his lawyer. The process is much longer, but the defence may think it worthwhile if it suspects the prosecution's case is weak.

If the magistrates agree, that is the end of the case. If not the accused is sent for trial to the higher court.

COMMON LAND

When an owner must allow the public to use his land

A common is a piece of land which the owner, by ancient custom confirmed by law, must allow other people to use. It may be called a common, village green, heath or recreation ground, but its status will be the same, and not every piece of land called a 'common' is in law a common, as common rights must be registered.

The owner of a common may be an individual, a company, a local authority or some body such as the National Trust.

Every common, and any rights attached to it, must have been registered by the local county council (or Greater London Council) before 1970. Any common not registered by then is no longer legally a common.

The rights of the public, the owner and people with the privilege of 'commoners' – those who own certain named property near the common – vary according to local custom.

THE COMMONERS WHO PULLED DOWN A SIGNPOST

Commoners have a complete right to stop trespassers from using or building on their land.

The parish council at Winford, Somerset, authorised a building company called Hayes Ltd, to put up a notice-board 6 ft by 3 ft on Felton Common.

The board was on poles sunk into the earth. The notice said 'HAYES Contractors'. An arrow pointed to the site of the company's work.

On the night of February 25, 1952, the board was wrenched off its supports and left on the ground, 100 yds away. The supports had been bent, but were too firmly fixed in the ground to be removed.

Seven commoners were charged with damaging the board, under the Malicious Damage Act, 1861.

They were tried at Somerset Quarter Sessions and convicted. All were conditionally discharged.

The seven appealed to the Court of Criminal Appeal. They admitted being involved in the notice-board incident, but claimed that the erection of the notice was a trespass which they, as commoners, were entitled to stop.

DECISION

The court held that the council had no power under the Commons Act 1899, to allow the erection of a notice-board that had nothing to do with the common itself.

Lord Chief Justice Goddard, presiding, commented: 'It is quite obvious that this board was much more of an advertisement than a direction post.'

The commoners therefore had a right to remove the board. Costs were awarded against the parish council.

OPEN SPACE OR AIRPORT RUNWAY?

Even when common rights have been abandoned – or usurped – for years, commoners can revive the legitimate use of an area of common land.

Since time immemorial, until the Second World War, people living around Yateley Common, in Hampshire, had been exercising their common rights to the land by grazing cattle on it and gathering heather.

This usage stopped during the Second World War, in 1942, when the government turned the common into a military airfield. And so it remained until 1960.

In 1973, the airfield site was sold to Mr Douglas Arnold who developed it into a busy and successful civil airport, called Blackbushe. Soon afterwards, a group of local people, claiming common rights, took the matter to the Commons Commissioner. He ruled that the land had been properly registered in the 1960s by Hampshire County Council as common land, and the commoners had the right to use it.

Mr Arnold took the case to the Appeal Court. He argued, among other things, that the common rights had been abandoned since the war and that, when he bought the land, there had been no explicit mention that the common rights transferred with it.

DECISION

The Appeal Judges said the fact that someone had abandoned his legal right was not enough. It had to be proved that he never intended to exercise his right again. That had not been proved, and how could it be when for many years the commoners had been prevented by law from exercising their rights?

As for the transfer of the common rights with the ownership of the land, that was a fact in law, no matter how little use the commoners made of their rights.

Mr Arnold's appeal was dismissed.

Rights of the public

Although not all commons are legally open to the public, most are. You are usually entitled to roam, picnic and play games on a common, but are not normally allowed to drive, park or camp, or cause a nuisance there.

You can find out your rights in a common by inspecting the county council's register.

Rights of an owner

The owner of a common may have the right to graze sheep or cattle, to take timber or minerals – such as sand or gravel – and to shoot or fish on the common.

But if he grazes animals on the common, in theory he must leave enough pasture for all the animals for which the commoners are entitled to grazing rights – even if they do not own that much livestock.

Furthermore, the owner cannot do just as he likes with his common land. He must not interfere with the rights of commoners. For example, he must not fence in or build on the common without permission from the Department of the Environment. If he does so, he can be sued in the county court for trespass, by any of the commoners affected.

If you notice any encroachment on a common, such as building work, report it to the county council. If the work has not got the required permission, the council can take legal action against the person responsible to end the encroachment and restore the common to its original state.

If the county council themselves are the offenders, a commoner could take proceedings in the courts against them.

Rights of a commoner

A commoner acquires 'rights of common' by owning property or land that is near the common and to which those rights have traditionally been attached.

Such rights exist now only if they appear in the register of commons and rights of common, kept by the county council or Greater London Council. Anyone who believes he has rights of common that are not in the register can submit his claim, with supporting evidence, to the Commons Commissioners who may order an amendment of the register.

A commoner, like an owner, may have the right to graze a specified number of animals on the common and to take timber for fuel, but not to shoot or fish without a licence from the owner.

If an owner unlawfully fences in a common, or does any building work – including the making of a car park – a commoner, but not any other member of the public, is legally entitled to remove the fence or structure even if by doing so he necessarily causes damage to it.

Alternatively, the commoner can sue the owner in the county court, to get the obstruction removed.

If a commoner sells the property to which his rights are attached, any registered rights pass to the new owner. Otherwise he cannot normally lose them, even if he has never chosen to exercise them.

Getting consent for building on a common

Anyone who wants to build anything on a common – for example, a local authority that owns the common and wants to build a games pavilion or a road on it – must get consent from the Secretary of State for the Environment (or for Wales).

The application must be advertised in a local newspaper and at least 28 days allowed for any objections to be made.

The Secretary of State, in reaching a decision, must take into account whether the proposed work would be for the benefit of the whole neighbourhood, and not just for a limited number of people.

There is no general right of appeal against the Secretary of State's decision, but he may be corrected by the courts if he makes an error of law in coming to his decision.

Permission has been given for the building of a house for a caretaker who looked after a common, on the ground that it was for everyone's benefit that the common should be properly cared for.

Consent was also given for the making of a paved netball pitch on a common, mainly for the use of a neighbouring primary school, because it was also to be made available for the public when not required by the school.

However, an application to build a private bungalow on common land failed, because it was not likely to benefit the neighbourhood.

COMMON LAW MARRIAGE

Do-it-yourself wedding on a desert island

In exceptional circumstances the English law recognises a marriage entered into under common law.

Before 1757, when the first Marriage Act was passed, a marriage could be contracted by the simple consent of the partners if no priest or authorised official was at hand. This no longer applies in England or Wales but it can still apply if, for instance, the couple are in a deserted country with no law, or in a country devastated by war. Once the couple have simply agreed to accept each other as man and wife, their marriage is as valid as any other and can be ended only by divorce.

COMMON LAW WIFE

Living with a man who is not your husband

A woman living with a man as his wife, but not legally married to him, is known as a common law wife. The name has no legal meaning and the woman has few of the rights of a lawful wife.

She cannot draw a social security retirement pension through her partner's contributions, nor a death grant as a legal widow can. The couple are taxed as single people and any children of the union are illegitimate.

The man is not legally liable to main-

COMMON LAW WIFE *continued on p. 106*

MARRIAGE OR COHABITATION
The advantages and disadvantages of living together without being married

	Married	Unmarried
Names		
Choice of name	Wife can use husband's surname and title even after divorce. Marriage certificate accepted as evidence of change of name. Men and women can call themselves by any surname. Documents are required only to prove identity or status (for example, married or single). Husband may use wife's surname if he wishes, but documentary evidence of change of name may be required as evidence of identity.	Woman or man may use the other's surname, but documentary evidence may be required as evidence of identity.
Business name	Wife may retain 'maiden' name for business or professional purposes, but she must register under Registration of Business Names Act.	No restriction if woman or man retains original name. But anyone who uses another name to carry on a business must register.
Sexual relationship		
Marriage	Marriage possible only between two people of different sexes; both 16 or over, both unmarried and not more closely related by blood than first cousins (step-parents and children and parents-in-law and children-in-law also prohibited).	Sexual relations permitted with partner of the opposite sex, if female aged 16 or over, whether or not married to someone else. Only sexual relations between parents and children, grandfathers and granddaughters and brothers and sisters prohibited. Homosexual relations between males allowed only if both are over 21.

Continued overleaf

MARRIAGE OR COHABITATION *continued*

	Married	Unmarried
Sexual relationship *continued*		
Refusing sexual intercourse	Refusal of intercourse by either partner can be ground for annulling or dissolving marriage. Husband cannot be found guilty of raping wife, even if she does not want intercourse, unless they are legally separated.	Woman or man has no obligation to take part in sexual intercourse. It is rape if the man has intercourse with his woman partner against her will.
Contraception	Husband's consent not needed for: ● fitting or supplying contraceptives for wife ● wife's abortion ● her sterilisation (Husband's consent not needed in law, but usually required in practice before the surgeon agrees to operate). Wife's consent is not needed for vasectomy. Depriving either husband or wife of a child might be ground for divorce and doctor might not act without consent of both.	No restriction.
Money		
Buying on credit	Wife is assumed to have husband's permission to buy food and other necessaries on his credit. Unless he gives notice to her, and sometimes to the shops with which she has been dealing, that she is not his agent, he may have to pay. A newspaper advertisement is not enough.	Woman living with a man assumed to have his permission to buy food and necessaries on his credit. Unless he gives notice that she is not his agent he may have to pay.
Household expenses	Wife can apply for court order if husband fails to support her and their children. Husband may also apply.	Neither party can apply for court order if other fails to give financial support.
Housekeeping allowance	Wife has right to half-share in any savings from housekeeping allowance made by husband or in things bought from savings. Husband has right to the other half.	Neither party has any right to share in savings from housekeeping unless in joint account to which both have contributed.
Loss of services	If wife is injured because of someone else's wrongdoing, husband can claim damages for loss of her services as a wife and mother. Wife cannot claim if husband injured, but may if he is killed.	No such claim is possible.
Income tax		
Basic principle	While husband and wife live together incomes are assessed together for income tax and treated as husband's. He must fill in tax return and pay any tax not collected under PAYE. Husband can set married man's allowance and, if wife earning, wife's earned income allowance against joint income. Even if wife is sole earner, both allowances are available.	Incomes separately taxed. Each can set off single person's allowance against own income. If only one income, only one allowance. If children, parent can claim extra allowance. If each has children and each earning, each gets extra allowance.
Separate assessment	Wife can choose to complete own tax return and be responsible for paying her share of their joint tax. Husband need not know her income, but income still added together. Allowances shared roughly in proportion to income, and total tax bill not affected. Higher tax rates payable if joint taxable income more than £11,250.	Always assessed separately. Each can have £11,250 taxable income before paying at higher rates.
Wife's earnings election	Couple can elect not to have wife's earnings added to husband's, avoiding higher tax rates. Each spouse can only claim one single person's allowance.	Income never added together for tax.
	Choice not possible for wife's investment income, which is always added to husband's total income and taxed at his highest rate. If joint investment income more than £5,500, investment income surcharge must be paid.	Investment income not added together. Each partner can have up to £5,500 before paying surcharge.
Business expenses	Husband or wife wishing to deduct other's salary – for example as secretary or chauffeur – as business expense must prove the expense is reasonable for duties performed.	Inland Revenue more likely to accept that employment genuine.

	Married	Unmarried
Income tax *continued*		
Additional personal allowance	Married man with child can claim extra allowance if wife totally incapacitated. Age relief if self or wife is over 65. Blind person's relief for self or wife.	No extra allowances on behalf of partner. Single parent can, however, claim additional personal allowance.
Covenants	One spouse cannot save tax by arranging covenanted payments to the other.	Tax can be reclaimed on deeds of covenant between partners.
Property		
Right to a home	Wife or husband has right to live in matrimonial home owned or rented by other, unless evicted by court order.	Neither party has right to live in home owned or rented by other unless there is a legally binding contract, or established joint ownership or tenancy.
Home in woman's name or joint names	Husband who buys property and puts it in wife's name is assumed to have given it to her. If he puts it into joint names he is assumed to have given her half. In the event of divorce the court can decide what share each should have irrespective of which owns it (see below).	If man or woman buys home and puts it into other's name or into joint names, original purchaser is entitled to all proceeds from sale unless the other can show that he/she contributed to purchase price or by physical work.
Mortgage relief	Relief is obtainable only once on joint mortgage.	Both man and woman can obtain relief on joint mortgage.
Selling a home	Wife or husband can prevent the other from selling or mortgaging matrimonial home by an entry on the Land Register or Land Charges Register.	Neither can prevent sale or mortgage unless part owner of the home.
Part ownership	Wife who pays mortgage instalments, deposit or household bills to help with purchase of a home, even if it is in husband's name, can claim share in proceeds of eventual sale. Generally same rule holds good for husband.	It is difficult for either party to prove that there was an intention to share ownership, especially if his or her contribution was confined to paying his or her own household bills.
	Wife or husband who makes extension or improvement to home owned by other can claim part ownership.	Difficult to establish part ownership unless partner making claim has done heavy physical work to improve the property or made substantial financial contribution to its purchase, for example, by paying mortgage instalments.
Second home	If husband and wife own two homes, capital gains tax must be paid on the profit from the sale of the second home.	Each partner can own a home and dispose of it without being charged capital gains tax.
Sale to other	If one spouse disposes of property to the other, capital gains tax not payable unless other spouse also disposes of it immediately.	Capital gains tax payable when unmarried partner passes property to the other.
Gift of property	If one spouse gives property to other, whether during life or at death or under court order on divorce, capital transfer tax not payable.	Capital gains tax may be avoided by a joint election for 'gifts relief' but capital transfer tax may be due.
Rates	Husband may be liable for rates on matrimonial home even if he no longer lives there, provided he has some financial interest in the property.	Only the occupier is liable for rates.
Distraint for rent arrears	Bailiff can seize goods belonging to wife of tenant.	Bailiff cannot seize woman's goods unless she is the tenant.

Continued overleaf

MARRIAGE OR COHABITATION *continued*

	Married	Unmarried
Social security		
Increases for women and children	Husband receiving national insurance benefit can claim extra allowance for wife and children. Wife receiving national insurance benefit in her own right can claim extra allowances for husband and children but only if husband cannot support himself.	Man cannot get extra allowance for woman alone, but he can for children plus woman if she looks after them. Woman receiving benefit in her own right can get extra for another woman (but not a man) looking after children.
Ex-wife's pension	Divorced or widowed woman or man can use ex-spouse's contribution record to help establish right to retirement pension.	Neither man nor woman can claim pension on other's contributions.
Widower's pension	Retired widower can claim retirement pension on contributions of wife who died over 60, if hers are better than his.	Man cannot claim pension on woman's contributions.
Wife's and widow's benefits	Wife who does not pay full contributions can claim some benefits from husband's contributions – for example, maternity grant, retirement pension and child's special allowance. Widow's benefits are paid only on husband's contributions.	Woman can claim only benefits from own contributions.
Invalid's pension	Non-contributory invalid's pension payable only to wife incapable of work and substantially incapable of normal household duties. Invalid care allowance not payable to wife.	Same rules apply to unmarried woman as to wife.
Supplementary benefit	If husband and wife living together, only husband can claim supplementary benefit for family. He must usually register for work; wife need not.	Same rules apply.
Duty to family	Spouse may be prosecuted for any deliberate failure to maintain only his or her own family and ordered to repay supplementary benefit paid to other spouse.	Man or woman can be prosecuted for deliberate failure to maintain only his or her own children. Partner cannot be ordered to repay supplementary benefit paid to other partner.
Immigration/Citizenship		
Right to join partner	Foreign or Commonwealth wife normally has right to join husband settled in Britain. Foreign or Commonwealth husband normally permitted to join wife.	Unmarried woman or man has no right to enter Britain to live with partner. Only permitted if genuine intention to marry. Could possibly enter as student or businessman.
Right to register	Wife of UK citizen normally has right to register as UK citizen.	No such right.
Children		
Child allowances	Child benefit, family income supplement and child's special allowance available.	Child benefit, family income supplement, but not child's special allowance available.
Child benefit	Wife has prior claim to child benefit even if children not hers.	Child's parent has prior claim to benefit.
Family income supplement	Husband can claim family income supplement if he has at least one child and his earnings are low. Wife cannot claim supplement unless they are separated and she has care of the children.	Woman can claim only if couple part and she has care of the children.
Child increases	Husband receiving national insurance benefits can claim extra allowance for dependent children. Wife can do so if husband incapable of self-support.	Either can claim.
Child's special allowance	If ex-husband maintaining children after divorce dies, ex-wife is entitled to child's special allowance on his contributions.	No state benefit if father dies.
Child maintenance	Either parent may be ordered to provide for the children.	Father can be ordered to provide for children only if paternity can be proved in affiliation proceedings.

MARRIAGE OR COHABITATION *continued*

	Married	Unmarried
Children *continued*		
Upbringing	Mother and father have equal powers over upbringing, e.g. religion, education, medical treatment, foreign travel.	Mother has parental powers, unless father obtains custody order.
Name of child	Parents must agree on choice of and any change in child's surname.	Mother can choose and change child's surname but is entitled to give it the father's surname.
Marriage of child	Agreement of both parents required for marriage of child under 18, unless parents are separated, when parent with custody must consent.	Only mother's agreement required unless father obtains custody order.
Adoption of child	Agreement of both parents required for adoption of their child, unless there are grounds, e.g. abandonment, ill-treatment or neglect, for dispensing with it. If one parent remarries after divorce, step-parent unlikely to be allowed to adopt their children, even if other natural parent agrees.	Only mother's agreement required unless father has custody order. If mother marries someone else, she and husband likely to be allowed to adopt the child even if natural father objects.
Child in care	Child in care may be discharged if either parent applies.	Only mother can seek discharge from care, unless father obtains custody order.
Citizenship	Legitimate child born abroad is UK citizen if father is UK citizen. Cannot claim UK citizenship through mother.	Child born abroad cannot claim UK citizenship from father. Can claim from mother if it would otherwise be stateless.
Custody	If parents separate, they or court can decide who shall have custody. Parent without custody will normally be allowed reasonable access.	Mother automatically has custody unless father obtains court order. Father may be allowed access.
Guardianship	Each parent can appoint guardian to act after his or her death.	Only mother can appoint guardian, unless father obtains custody order.
Inheritance	Legitimate children have automatic succession rights if relatives die without making a will.	Illegitimate children have automatic succession rights only from mother and father, not from grandparents, brothers and sisters, uncles and aunts.
	If the succession rights or the provision in will are inadequate, legitimate children can apply to court for reasonable provision from parents' estate.	Illegitimate children have same right.
Students		
Grants	If both spouses claim student grants, marriage reduces the total grant only if they have other income. If one spouse is mature student and other is working, the earner may have to make contributions normally made by parents.	Earnings of working partner do not affect assessment of other's grant. If both are students, total grant will not be affected by living together.
Extra grants	Married mature student can claim extra grant for dependent spouse and children.	Can claim for children, not usually for other adult.
Breaking up		
Eviction from home	Husband or wife cannot evict the other without a court order. If husband seeks order, court gives priority to needs of wife and children.	Sole owner or tenant can get partner out as a trespasser, unless home jointly owned or rented or unless there is a legally binding contract.
Domestic violence	Battered wife or husband can get court order excluding other from home – sometimes permanently – no matter which owns or rents it.	Battered woman or man can get order excluding other from home, temporarily, no matter which owns or rents it; but if the other owns or rents it, he/she can be excluded only for a limited period.

Continued overleaf

MARRIAGE OR COHABITATION *continued*

		Married	Unmarried
Breaking up *continued*			
	Maintenance payments	Either husband or wife may be ordered to pay maintenance to the other on separation or divorce. Wife unlikely to be made to support husband unless he is incapacitated and wife is much better off.	Neither can be ordered to support the other after parting, although a father can be ordered to support a child of the relationship.
	Sharing property	On divorce, all property owned by either husband or wife shared out as decided by court if not agreed between them. Even if wife paid nothing for the home, she may get one-third of its value, sometimes more, even outright transfer if she and children need the home and husband does not.	No legal shareout when relationship ends. Each entitled to own property, including share in joint property.
New relationship			
	Widow's benefit	Widow who remarries loses widow's benefit permanently.	Widow living with man loses benefit for period of cohabitation only.
	Private pension	Widow who remarries likely to lose private pension.	Woman unlikely to lose any private pension.
	Maintenance	Divorced person who remarries automatically loses right to maintenance payments.	Maintenance not automatically lost through cohabitation, but may be reduced or stopped if partner receiving maintenance is supported by the other.
Death and insurance			
	Share of estate	If either dies without leaving a will, the other is automatically entitled to first £25,000 of estate (if there are children) or £40,000 (if no children), and to a share in remainder. If necessary, surviving spouse can apply to court for reasonable share of estate.	No automatic share in other's estate. If either was dependent on the other immediately before the other's death she or he can apply to court for reasonable provision for maintenance out of estate.
	Life insurance	Either can hold insurance policy on own life payable to other. Survivor then gets the money, even if dead partner's estate is insolvent. Either can take out insurance policy on other's life.	No such possibility, unless one has an 'insurable interest' in the other, for example, if they are business partners.
	Accidental death	If either is killed in an accident, the survivor can claim compensation for loss of the breadwinner or housekeeper from person responsible.	No such claim by partner, but children can claim.
	Private pension	Occupational pension schemes normally provide for a widow's and sometimes for a widower's pension.	Less likely to provide for survivor even if he or she is a dependant.
	Widow's national insurance	Woman married before April 6, 1977 or widowed before April 6, 1978 may be able to pay reduced national insurance contributions.	Woman who is earning must pay full contributions.
	Widow's benefits	Widow may be entitled to widow's allowance, widowed mother's allowance and widow's pension on husband's national insurance contributions.	Woman entitled to no benefit when man dies.

COMMON LAW WIFE *continued from p. 101*

tain the woman, yet, because they live together as man and wife, she may lose benefits that would otherwise be available. *See:* COHABITATION

The woman does, however, have some rights, and where a partner is violent she can get a court order banning him from their home even if he is legally the tenant of the property.

A common law wife can also claim a share in the value of their home if she can show that she contributed to its purchase or improvement, either with money or simply by helping to complete improvement work on it. *See:* MATRIMONIAL PROPERTY

If a man leaves his common law wife with children he has fathered, she can claim for their maintenance. *See:* AFFILIATION ORDER

COMMUNITY HEALTH COUNCIL

Advice and help for patients

Each National Health Service district has a community health council – an advisory body, rather like a parish council, whose role is to keep under review the way the health service is operated in its district and to help and advise any patients who believe they have a complaint.

The council investigates the general details of a complaint but it has no power to demand confidential medical information. It can inspect health service premises and refer a complaint to the right official, or to the health service OMBUDSMAN, who does have access to confidential information – and to whom an individual can apply direct.

Some CHC secretaries will represent patients at local family practitioners committee hearings with complaints against GPs *See:* DOCTOR AND PATIENT

A council can point out faults in the service and suggest improvements to the area administrators. It can also represent public opinion in contentious matters, such as the closure of a local hospital. The Department of Health and Social Security must consult a local council before deciding.

Half the members of a community health council must be appointed or nominated by the local authority, one-third nominated by voluntary organisations and the remaining one-sixth appointed by the Regional Health Authority. No member of a Regional Health Authority or Area Health Authority can serve on a community health council.

Your local community health council will be listed under that name in the telephone directory.

COMMUNITY HOME

Housing children who are in need of care

Special homes, run either voluntarily or by local authorities, are available in all areas to house children in care.

COMMUNITY HOME SCHOOL

Education for children not living at home

Community schools, also referred to as community homes with education (CHE), have replaced the old approved schools. They are run by local au-

thorities or voluntary bodies to provide residential care with education for children who have been placed in care. *See also:* CHILDREN IN CARE

COMMUNITY OF PROPERTY

Who owns what in a marriage

Unlike in some countries, such as France, South Africa and parts of the United States, there is no community of property in Britain.

When someone gets married, he or she remains the sole owner of any belongings acquired before then. Wedding presents are generally regarded as belonging to the person whose family or friends gave them. A groom's gift to his wife would belong to her.

Even after the marriage, anything acquired individually, remains that partner's own property.

However, anything that a couple buy together – for example, furniture with money from a joint bank account, or with money contributed by both – belongs to both, usually in equal shares.

If there is a divorce, the courts can transfer belongings from one spouse to the other. *See:* MAINTENANCE

COMMUNITY SERVICE ORDER

When an offender can be sentenced to work for the community

Instead of fining or sending a convicted man to prison, a court may sometimes give him the choice of doing unpaid part-time work under a community service order. It applies only to offences which could be punished by imprisonment, usually the less serious ones.

Before imposing such a sentence, a court will get a social inquiry report from a probation officer, to find out if it would be a suitable punishment. The court cannot impose community service on someone who is not willing to accept it.

Community service can be ordered for not less than 40 and not more than 240 hours altogether. The work will be supervised by a probation officer.

The kind of work involved can vary

widely – from decorating and labouring to visiting the old and disabled. A community service order is made usually in less serious cases and when there are mitigating circumstances.

Work not done If the offender fails to carry out the work ordered, or if he does not do it properly, he can be brought before the magistrates, fined up to £50 and ordered again to do the work – or be given a different sentence altogether, such as imprisonment, for the original offence.

COMPENSATION

Financial award when you have suffered

If a person suffers through an action of another, he may be entitled to receive compensation for any injury or loss incurred. For example, if he is the victim of a crime and is injured, he may be entitled to CRIMINAL INJURIES COMPENSATION. He may also be entitled to compensation if he is out of work through REDUNDANCY or UNFAIR DISMISSAL.

See: DAMAGES
GOLDEN HANDSHAKE
PERSONAL INJURY

COMPLAINT

How the citizen can seek satisfaction

A customer has a right to expect that any goods or services he buys match their description and are adequate for the purpose for which they were intended. If not, he can complain and even take legal action to obtain compensation or damages. *See also:* pages 731–5.

See: DEFECTIVE GOODS
TRADE DESCRIPTIONS

COMPULSORY PURCHASE

Safeguards when an authority decides to buy land

Any public authority – for example, a council, government department or gas or electricity board – that wants to buy land or buildings despite the opposition of their owners is entitled to make a compulsory purchase order. But it must make sure that people directly affected have a chance to oppose the order.

When an authority makes a compulsory purchase order, it cannot act on the order immediately. The order must be advertised in two successive issues of the local press and a copy of the order must be sent to every owner and tenant of lands or buildings concerned. The order and a map of the premises must be deposited at the council offices.

Opposing an order

If you wish to oppose a compulsory purchase order – either because you own the land involved or object to the use proposed for it – start your campaign as soon as possible.

You must send your objection to the government department – usually the Department of the Environment – named in the notice of the order – within 21 days of the notice first being advertised.

Contact your local councillors. If it is the council which has made the order, try to persuade the councillors to have it withdrawn. If some other body has made the order, try to persuade the council to oppose it.

Enlist help from your neighbours and from local organisations such as civic societies and other pressure groups.

....

OBJECTION OVER-RULED

A house owner is unlikely to win a legal battle with a public authority that has decided to lay a pipeline or overhead cable across his land. It is best to try to reach agreement by negotiation.

If the land involved is a beauty spot or part of a green belt, ask for support from national bodies such as the Civic Trust and the Council for the Preservation of Rural England.

If an attractive building is at risk, approach the Georgian Group, Victorian Society or other organisation concerned with protecting old buildings. In addition, write to your Member of Parliament. A petition may help – but make sure that all signatures are genuine.

If the initial campaign fails to get the compulsory purchase order withdrawn, be prepared to fight at a public inquiry.

If you are affected by an order and lodge a formal objection, the government department involved will order one of its own inspectors to hold an inquiry in your area. If no one who is affected objects, there will be no such inquiry.

An inquiry must be advertised in a notice, posted in a conspicuous public place 2 weeks before the inquiry is held. Everyone affected by the order is entitled to attend and explain his or her opposition to, or support for, the order. Groups of protesters may find it useful to engage a solicitor or barrister to present their objections.

After an inquiry

When the inquiry ends, the inspector reports his findings to the government department concerned. The Secretary of State decides whether to confirm the compulsory purchase order, or whether to vary or quash it. Everyone directly involved is informed and can ask for a copy of the inspector's findings. The decision is also advertised in the local newspapers.

If an order is confirmed, it must then be displayed at the council offices for 6 weeks, during which time an appeal can be lodged.

Appealing against an order

It is possible in theory to appeal against an order in the High Court on the ground that the Secretary of State abused his powers, or that the rules were not observed. This is an expensive process, and unlikely to succeed.

What compensation

Any owner, lessee or mortgagee of land that is compulsorily purchased is entitled to compensation. If he believes he has not been offered enough, he can appeal to the Lands Tribunal and thereafter, if necessary, to the High Court.

Compensation should match the amount that the property would have fetched on the open market if no compulsory purchase order had been made. In addition, the owner is entitled to claim all his expenses – for example, money he has spent on professional advice and removal.

Losing your home If an order results in an owner or lessee losing the home where he has lived for at least 5 years, he will be entitled to a 'home loss payment' – usually three times the rateable value of the home.

The payment cannot be less than £150 or more than £1,500.

He may also be able to insist on being rehoused by the local council – especially if the compulsory purchase order makes him homeless. This rule can also apply to a tenant or a lodger in a compulsorily purchased house, but local authorities have varying attitudes.

Who qualifies

Compensation cannot be claimed by everyone affected by a compulsory purchase order.

However, you are entitled to claim if you have lost legal rights – if you are the owner, lessee or mortgagee of the property or are entitled to the benefit of a right of way or restrictive covenant, and the order deprives you of the property or other right.

You may also claim – even as a neighbour – if new public works produce noise, smell, fumes, vibration or some other physical factor that reduces the value of your property by at least £50.

House owners may in some cases have their home insulated against noise at public expense. There are, for example, special provisions for soundproofing houses near the major airports at Heathrow and Gatwick.

Limited right to cross land

Gas and electricity authorities and the Post Office have powers to lay cables, mains and other apparatus in or across privately owned land without the owner's consent. Water authorities can lay mains and public sewers on private land, but notice must be given, usually 1 month.

Large private companies may also have power to lay pipelines across someone else's land.

Opposing the authority If you object to such a proposal, unless the authority agrees to change its plans by negotiation, you are unlikely to be successful. You can demand an inquiry if the project is a pipeline, but not with other types of work.

Owners of land affected are entitled to compensation for any loss suffered. It is advisable to get professional advice from the outset: any fees properly incurred by a landowner can be claimed from the authority that carries out the work.

COMPUTER RECORD

The ever-increasing threat to privacy

Although many organisations, including government agencies, keep computerised records about individuals, the right to know what is recorded about you is very limited.

You have no legal right to check on computer files kept by most organisations, such as the police, Department of Health and Social Security, National Health Service or even your own bank.

The exception, in which the law helps the individual to find out what is on his computerised file, is in the case of information held by a CREDIT REFERENCE AGENCY, but that applies to all credit reference files – not just those stored on computer.

CONDITIONAL DISCHARGE

When the courts offer a second chance

Someone convicted of a crime may be offered another chance, by being given a conditional discharge.

The condition of the discharge will be that the offender commits no further offences for a stated period – up to 3 years. If he meets this condition he will not be punished for the offence just committed. But if he is convicted of another offence within the set time, he may be punished for both crimes.

Unlike a PROBATION order, a conditional discharge does not involve super-vision of the offender. It is also unlike suspended SENTENCES, in that there is no pre-determined penalty for the first offence if he breaks the conditions by committing another crime.

A conditional discharge also differs from a BINDING OVER order, which can be imposed on anyone who appears before a court, whether found guilty or not.

CONDITIONAL SALE

Agreeing to purchase by instalments

A conditional-sale agreement is one in which a customer agrees to buy goods by instalments, but will not own the goods until all instalments are paid.

It differs from HIRE PURCHASE in that the customer agrees to buy, and the trader agrees to sell, at the start of the transaction, whereas in a hire-purchase contract the customer exercises an option to buy only at the end.

Someone who buys goods that are already subject to a conditional-sale agreement may still be able to keep them if he was unaware of the agreement, or unaware that some of the instalments were still to be paid. If, on the other hand, he bought goods that were subject to an uncompleted hire-purchase agreement, he would be unable to keep them, and they could be repossessed by the finance company.

Conditional sale also differs from CREDIT SALE, in which the goods become the buyer's property at the start of the agreement and he can legally sell them before they are paid for – unless his agreement forbids him to do so.

A conditional-sale agreement has the same protection under the Consumer Credit Act as a hire-purchase contract. *See:* CREDIT AGREEMENT INTEREST CHARGE

CONDITIONS AND WARRANTIES

Protection for the buyer – always

When you buy something as a consumer, you have certain automatic rights which no wording in a contract, receipt or notice can take away. *See:* UNFAIR CONTRACT

A shopkeeper who sells you goods is in most cases automatically guaranteeing that they are of merchantable quality, fit for the purpose for which you are buying them and his to sell.

Even if the shopkeeper or trader says nothing about guarantee, those terms are implied by law, under the Sale of Goods Act 1979.

In addition, there may be written conditions or warranties guaranteeing the goods.

You have the right to cash compensation for any breach of a condition or warranty.

See also: DEFECTIVE GOODS
MANUFACTURERS' GUARANTEE

CONFESSION

When a confession may be used in evidence

A confession, written or oral, made by an accused person is normally accepted by a court as evidence of guilt even if it is later retracted.

Before it is accepted as evidence, however, the judge must be satisfied that the confession was given by the accused person without his being in any 'fear of prejudice or hope of advantage'. *See:* POLICE

An example of 'fear of prejudice' would be if the police extracted the confession by threatening to oppose bail, and an example of 'hope of advantage' would be if the police promised to get the accused a lighter sentence.

A confession would also be invalid if there was clear evidence that the balance of the accused person's mind had been disturbed at the time the confession was made by him.

A confession is not necessarily a statement made to the police. It can be made to any member of the public who, if the prosecution wishes, can be served with a witness summons and ordered to tell the court what the accused said. *See:* SUBPOENA

With one exception, it makes no difference that the confession was given in professional confidence – for example, to a doctor, a social worker or a priest, perhaps.

All the witness can do in such a case is to ask the judge's permission to decline to answer. If he is ordered to answer but

THE REPORTERS WHO WOULD NOT TELL

Professional ethics do not protect a witness from punishment for contempt of court if he refuses to answer.

Two journalists wrote stories in their newspapers about the behaviour of William John Vassall, an Admiralty clerk who became a spy.

In one article, Brendan Mulholland wrote: 'It was the sponsorship of two high-ranking Admiralty officials which led to Vassall avoiding the strictest part of the Admiralty's security vetting.'

Another reporter, Reginald Foster, wrote: 'Vassall had been buying women's clothes in the West End.'

A tribunal with legal powers was set up as a result to discover whether any civil servants or naval officers had been guilty of neglect in not discovering the spy in their midst.

Both Mulholland and Foster refused to give the tribunal their sources of information. The chairman said their answers were vital to the inquiry.

The Attorney-General asked the High Court to punish the two men as if they had been guilty of contempt of court. Mulholland was sentenced to 6 months' jail, Foster to 3 months. Both appealed.

The two reporters claimed that as journalists they were privileged from giving the source of their information. It was in the public interest that they should receive information and publish it. They said that if they did not keep their sources secret, that sort of information would no longer be available.

DECISION

The Court of Appeal dismissed both appeals. Lord Denning, Master of the Rolls, said: 'The only profession that I know which is given a privilege from disclosing information to a court of law is the legal profession, and then it is not the privilege of the lawyer but of his client. Take the clergyman, the banker or the medical man. None of these is entitled to refuse to answer questions when directed by a judge. The judge would not direct him unless it was relevant but also a proper and necessary question to be put and answered in the course of justice.'

WHEN THE SERGEANT MAJOR USED THREATS

A confession cannot be accepted in court if it is evident that the accused was coerced into making it.

In 1959 a regimental sergeant major investigating a fight that had resulted in a murder told troops that he would keep them on parade until he learned who was involved. Private Smith confessed.

DECISION

The court of appeal held that the confession was induced by threats and was not admissible at Smith's trial.

THE DOCTOR WHO KEPT A SECRET

Even doctors, who normally would be disciplined by their own professional body, have to answer questions fully in court. Their only loophole is to ask the judge's permission to remain silent.

A man and a woman were treated for injuries by Dr John David Hunter. The woman told him that they had been involved in a road accident, but he did not ask her for permission to tell the police.

Some days later, police officers investigating a complaint of dangerous driving asked Dr Hunter to tell them whom he had treated to help them to identify the driver. The doctor refused and said it would be a breach of professional conduct to give the names. He was summonsed for withholding information and fined £5 by the local justices. Dr Hunter appealed.

DECISION

The Divisional Court dismissed his appeal and ruled that there was no absolute privilege for a doctor over information between him and his patient.

Lord Widgery said: 'If a doctor giving evidence in court is asked a question which he finds embarrassing because it involves him talking about things which he would normally regard as confidential, he can seek the protection of the judge and ask if it is necessary for him to answer.'

THE PRIEST WHO REFUSED TO TALK

Most surprisingly, perhaps, is the rule that a priest must disclose the secrets of the confessional.

A husband who had started proceedings, suing his wife for divorce, served a subpoena on Father Francis Handley, who had met the couple as a marriage guidance counsellor.

Father Handley asked for the subpoena to be set aside because the only evidence he could give was evidence derived from his meetings with the couple as a counsellor.

DECISION

The Divorce Court ruled that there was no privilege for the priest or any other professional man. The privilege of communication between the priest and the husband and wife belonged to the husband and wife. It was for them to decide whether or not the privilege should be waived.

refuses he is guilty of CONTEMPT OF COURT.

Someone in that dilemma need reveal the information only in court, however. He is under no obligation to say anything to the prosecution or the police.

The only people who have an absolute right not to give evidence of such a confession are a solicitor or barrister acting for an accused person. They must tell the court only what their client wishes them to.

CONSERVATION AREAS

Protecting a treasured place

An area which has specially attractive or historic features may be protected against unsuitable development by being declared a conservation area by the local district council or county council.

If you own property in such an area, you cannot object to its being declared a conservation area. But if a declaration has not been made, you are entitled to suggest one to the district council. The effect is generally to increase the value of property within the designated area.

Once a conservation area has been declared, the council must warn the public of any application for PLANNING PERMISSION that might affect the appearance of the area.

Every planning application must be

published in a notice posted prominently on the site of the proposed work and in local newspapers.

Local residents have 21 days in which to send their comments to the council planning committee. All such comments must be considered by the committee or council before the application is decided.

In a conservation area, no building may be demolished and no trees cut down without the express consent of the council.

For illegally demolishing a building, there is a maximum £400 fine. The maximum penalty for cutting down a tree is a fine of twice the estimated value of the tree. *See:* PRESERVATION ORDER

CONSPIRACY

The crime of planning a crime

If two or more people agree to do something that will involve them in crime, they are guilty of conspiracy – even if they do not carry out the crime.

But if they do, they are guilty of the offence and of conspiracy as well. Usually they will be prosecuted only for the offence.

If the planned crime is a summary offence – one that can be tried only in a magistrates' court – a conspiracy charge can be brought only with the permission of the DIRECTOR OF PUBLIC PROSECUTIONS.

There must be at least two people

charged, even if one of them is a 'person unknown'. If one conspirator is acquitted, it does not follow that his co-defendants must also be acquitted – unless it would be inconsistent to convict one and not the other(s).

When one of two conspirators gives evidence against the other, his co-defendant cannot be convicted unless he himself is prosecuted. If one of three or more conspirators gives evidence against his fellows and the evidence makes it clear that he is also guilty, he will find it hard to avoid prosecution. In practice, the DPP would have to agree that he should not be charged.

There are many doubts about the scope and application of conspiracy. The prosecution does not have to provide evidence of a firm, detailed plan. Proving that the conspirators had a settled intention to carry out the act is enough to warrant a conviction.

But a conviction is unlikely when it can be shown that the crime conspired could not have been carried out.

Maximum penalty The penalty for conviction of any conspiracy charge is the same as would have been imposed for the commission of the crime itself.

CONSTRUCTIVE DISMISSAL

When resigning is the same as getting the sack

An employee who leaves his job because his employer's behaviour is a

> ## MANAGERESS WHOSE PAY WAS CUT
>
> *If an employee quits his job because his firm imposes conditions which make it difficult for him to continue he may be entitled to the same rights as a person who is unfairly dismissed.*
>
> Mrs Hill was manageress of premises on which the lease expired, and the company moved her to new premises. The manageress at the new place of work was on a lower salary than Mrs Hill, so the company reduced Mrs Hill's pay.
>
> The company intended to increase her wages under a general pay review. But Mrs Hill would not wait. She resigned and claimed redundancy.
>
> ### DECISION
> It was held that Mrs Hill's reduced pay amounted to constructive dismissal and she was awarded redundancy payment.

serious breach of a work agreement is said in law to have been constructively dismissed.

The victim has the same rights as other dismissed employees to compensation for UNFAIR DISMISSAL. If he is also actually redundant, he would be able to claim REDUNDANCY payments.

CONSUMER CREDIT

The different ways to buy now and pay later

There are many ways in which you can obtain goods or services on whole or part credit. You may borrow money to spend as you wish, or obtain a loan that is tied to the purchase of particular goods or services, often from a specified supplier.

As long as the sum borrowed does not exceed £5,000 – excluding interest, credit and installation charges – all credit arrangements are covered by the tight controls of the Consumer Credit Act, although in a few cases, not all the controls apply. If the sum borrowed is more than £5,000, the transaction is still covered by the Act's protection against extortionate terms.

> ## THE COCAINE THAT NEVER COULD BE
>
> *Conspiracy can be an offence only if the action resulting from the conspiracy would itself be unlawful and possible.*
>
> David Nock and Kevin Alsford were sentenced in January 1977 to 12 months for conspiring together 'to produce a controlled drug . . . cocaine'.
>
> In 1975 Alsford's home had been searched and chemical apparatus and a flask of white powder had been found. When questioned he had said: 'Yes, I admit everything. That's cocaine. I've just had it refined.'
>
> He admitted obtaining a sample of powder which friends had analysed, telling him that it was a mixture of cocaine
>
> and a legal substance called Lignocaine. He and Nock had then bought 5 lb. of the powder and had chemically separated what they thought was the cocaine.
>
> When the powder was analysed by the Metropolitan Police it was found to contain no cocaine.
>
> ### DECISION
> On appeal to the House of Lords the sentence was quashed. The agreement had been to produce cocaine from a powder which, however treated, could never have yielded any cocaine. Since the attempt would not have been unlawful the agreement could not have been a criminal conspiracy.

Two types of credit available to the consumer

Credit can be divided into two main kinds: 'purchaser credit' and 'loan credit'.

Purchaser credit covers the type of lending in which the person borrowing money buys goods or services from the lender or from a supplier who has a business arrangement with the lender.

A contract for such a loan is also known as a 'debtor-creditor-supplier' agreement. Under that type of agreement the lender, as well as the supplier of goods, can be sued if they are faulty. *See:* DEFECTIVE GOODS

Loan credit is a straightforward loan of money, not tied to the purchase of any particular goods or services. A contract of that type is also known as a 'debtor-creditor' agreement.

Under a debtor-creditor agreement, the lender is not liable for the quality of goods or services bought.

Both types of credit are covered by similar rules for the making, conducting and ending of the contract. They are treated differently, however, in some circumstances – for example, in the rules that control canvassing. *See:* DOORSTEP SELLING

Help for the jobless A sick or jobless person on SUPPLEMENTARY BENEFIT can sometimes have his credit purchase commitments paid for by the Department of Health and Social Security.

Help is usually given only if the goods involved are considered to be essential – for example, beds, tables, chairs or a cooker. The department would probably refuse to pay for commitments on a washing machine or television set, neither of which is considered essential, nor for clothes, included in the ordinary rate of supplementary benefit.

In deciding to pay someone's credit purchase instalments, the Supplementary Benefits Commission takes into account whether the person claiming is likely to be back in work soon. In the case, say, of a deserted wife, who is not likely to go back to work, the commission may make a lump-sum payment to complete the purchase. It may, however, decide that it is cheaper to make a grant for a second-hand replacement.

Anyone who disagrees with the commission's decision can appeal. *See:* SUPPLEMENTARY BENEFIT

CONSUMER GROUP

Forming a group to act for local consumers

Consumer groups are voluntary, independent associations formed to promote the interests of consumers in their own locality.

Most groups publish the results of their research work in magazines, newsletters or on local radio. Some act as pressure groups, concentrating on one particular topic of local concern at any one time.

The fields covered by consumer groups range from
● Comparative costings of goods in local shops.
● Expressing dissatisfaction with bus services or refuse collection.
● Explaining simply how new legislation affects consumers.

How to start a group

Contact the National Federation of Consumer Groups, 70-76 Alcester Road South, Birmingham B14 7PT which will put you in touch with your nearest area organiser or group.

The Federation can certainly advise the best tactics to use in a particular district, but the usual way is to form a small working party. Sound out friends, put leaflets in libraries and on noticeboards, inform the local newspaper and radio station.

When you have gathered some support, plan and hold a public meeting to draw in members, form a group and decide on priorities for action.

CONSUMER PROTECTION

A wealth of protective legislation that is still evolving

Any customer buying goods or services is entitled to a wide range of protection by law – much of which can be enforced by public officials at public expense.

Trading standards officers (or consumer protection officers) are employed by local councils to administer the Weights and Measures Act, Trade Descriptions Act, Consumer Safety Act and other laws that protect the consumer. Their job is to prevent traders from breaking those laws and to prosecute when an offence is committed.

A national official, the Director General of Fair Trading, administers the Fair Trading Act and Consumer Credit Act – which also concern criminal offences by traders.

If you have a complaint against a trader you should go to your local trading standards officer.

Your right to a fair deal is also supported by pressure groups such as the publicly financed National Consumer Council and the self-supporting Consumers' Association.

If your complaint is over breach of contract by a trader, or breach of the special rules about the sale of goods, you can enforce the civil law which deals with such matters, by going to court, if necessary. *See:* DEFECTIVE GOODS
FAIR TRADING
TRADE DESCRIPTIONS
TRADING STANDARDS
WEIGHTS AND MEASURES

CONSUMER SAFETY

Making a supplier pay for damage from unfit goods

If something you buy or hire is dangerous, and damage results, the supplier can be sued for compensation – and may also be prosecuted. Your entitlement to compensation is the same, whether you have bought the goods for cash or on credit, obtained them with trading stamps or hired them.

Take your complaint to the local trading standards officer, who can prosecute the supplier. If he is convicted of breaking the safety of goods law, he can be ordered by the magistrates' court to pay you compensation.

If no compensation is ordered, you can still sue the supplier in the county court or High Court, for breach of statutory duty.

As part of your case, you are entitled to give the civil court details of any successful prosecution.

Some goods are not covered by criminal law, but many others, including food, are listed in regulations laying down safety standards. *See also:* FOOD

It is a criminal offence for anyone

GOODS COVERED BY CONSUMER SAFETY LAWS

Goods that are subject to special regulations under the Consumer Safety Act 1978 fall into three classes: protection of children, protection against poisons and protection against fire and shock. Upholstered furniture must pass a fire test or bear a warning label.

Protection of children

Anoraks and other outer garments with hoods: the hood must not be adjustable by a cord.

Bags Plastic bags containing toys must have a printed warning about the danger of suffocation.

Carry-cots Stands must comply with size and strength regulations. The underside of the bottom of the carry-cot must be more than 17 in. above floor level and the cot must be retained in position by a guard-rail or rigid stops. The stand must be able to withstand a weight of 60 lb. The stand must have a durable label stoutly fixed to it, stating the maximum length and width of carry-cot which it is designed to take.

Babies' dummies All dummies must be made of plastic or rubber, must be resistant to damage and must be sold in a clean condition in a closed container with instructions for use.

Nightdresses must be of material difficult to set alight.

Toys Paint must contain no more than a specified amount of poisonous material – such as lead. Celluloid is prohibited, except in table-tennis balls.

Flammable pile fabric is prohibited.

Mains electricity must operate through a transformer at 24 volts or less.

Sharp metal points are prohibited.

Thin metal edges must be inaccessible to a child's fingers or be folded back.

Eyes, noses and other features on dolls and other toys should be secured so that they cannot be pulled off and be swallowed, or lay bare dangerous points.

Protection against poisons

Pencils, pens, crayons and similar items must contain no more than a stated amount of poisonous materials.

Cooking utensils, vitreous enamelware and glazed ceramic ware must comply with standards on content of lead or cadmium.

A flameproofing treatment for clothes which could cause cancer is banned.

Protection against fire and shock

Gas, electric and oil fires must always be sold with a fixed fireguard.

Oil heaters burning paraffin must be draught resistant and must carry a notice warning against:

● Using petrol as a fuel.
● Carrying the heater when it is alight.
● Refilling it with fuel when it is alight.
● Using heater in an unventilated place or where it may be exposed to draughts.

They must not be able to be tilted or overturned while they are alight.

Electrical goods must comply with detailed safety standards covering the insulation, earthing and accessibility of live parts. They must always be supplied with instructions for safe operation.

All equipment must have wiring coloured according to the official safety code. An explanation must be supplied.

---

who supplies goods in the course of a business to fail to comply with safety standards. Anyone found guilty can be fined up to £1,000 and imprisoned for up to 3 months.

A shopkeeper who is accused can escape conviction, however, if he can show that he took 'all reasonable steps' and exercised 'all due diligence' to avoid committing the offence. For example, a toy-shop owner who makes inquiries to satisfy himself that paint used on the toys complies with safety regulations can claim to have taken the reasonable steps required by law.

However, a manufacturer who uses poisonous paint is likely to be convicted. An importer of foreign toys may also be convicted, on the ground that he should take extra precautions against dealing in goods that do not comply with British safety laws.

Prohibiting dangerous goods

The supply of certain goods can be prohibited by the government, under the Consumer Safety Act 1978.

THE IMPORTER WHO DID NOT KEEP UP WITH THE LAW

Every individual shopkeeper has to make himself responsible for seeing that the goods he sells are not dangerous. Someone else's assurance may not be enough.

A toy sold by a shopkeeper in 1976 was found to have paint that contained an illegal amount of poisonous lead. The toy had been imported from France in 1971.

The importer was prosecuted under the Toys (Safety) Regulations 1974. The prosecution was brought in 1976.

It had been the importer's practice to make all orders from suppliers subject to a condition that their goods would comply with current British safety regulations. British suppliers and foreign manufacturers all gave such undertakings.

In addition, the importer had a standing invitation to the local trading standards department to take samples of goods for analysis, at any time.

At first, the magistrates dismissed the case on the ground that the importer had taken all reasonable precautions to avoid an offence under the Consumer Protection Act 1961.

The prosecution appealed against the decision, and the appeal was heard in the High Court.

DECISION

The magistrates were ordered to convict the importer.

The High Court judges held that the importer had no reliable guarantee of safety covering the particular toy involved. Regulations had changed in 1974 and the importer had done nothing to make sure that any of his goods complied with the requirements of the new rules.

An adequate precaution would have been to take one or more paint samples from toys in the relevant consignment and have the paint analysed. The importer's 'friendly relations' with the trading standards department did not absolve him from his responsibility for precautions.

The Lord Chief Justice, Lord Widgery, said that there were very few cases in which a company could rely on somebody else's certificate of compliance with the law, if it was possible for the company to have its own analysis made.

It can make an order prohibiting anyone from supplying specified goods that are considered dangerous.

It can also serve a prohibition notice on a particular supplier, prohibiting him from supplying specified unsafe goods.

The supplier can be compelled to publish, at his own expense, a warning about any unsafe goods he supplies or has supplied in the past.

It is a criminal offence to ignore a prohibition order or notice or to fail to publish a warning when required. The maximum penalty is 3 months' imprisonment and a £1,000 fine.

Anyone who suffers injury or damage because a supplier disobeyed a prohibition or warning order is entitled to claim compensation from him.

The shopkeeper would escape conviction if he could show that he took all reasonable steps and exercised due diligence to avoid committing the offence.

Safety standards for vehicles

It is a criminal offence to sell a motor vehicle, privately or by way of business, if it does not comply with the standards, laid down in the Motor Vehicles (Construction and Use) Regulations 1978. The maximum penalty for an offence is a fine of £100.

The fact that a vehicle has an MOT test certificate is not a sufficient defence.

It is also an offence to supply rear lights and reflectors for any motor vehicle, or crash helmets for motorcyclists, if they do not comply with minimum legal standards.

If a supplier is convicted of breaking the regulations, he may be fined up to £20, but the court can also order him to pay compensation to anyone who has suffered injury or damage because of his offence.

However, to obtain compensation in the civil courts, you must be able to show that the supplier was in breach of contract or guilty of negligence.

CONSUMMATION OF MARRIAGE

The legal significance of matrimonial sex

A marriage is legally valid from the moment the couple exchange their vows

whether it is consummated by an act of sexual intercourse or not. However, in law an unconsummated marriage is not a complete marriage and it can be declared null and void provided the nonconsummation is due to incapacity or wilful refusal. In the case of refusal, only the innocent partner can petition for NULLITY.

How the law defines consummation

A marriage is consummated once a single complete act of sexual intercourse has taken place after the marriage ceremony. Ejaculation and orgasm are not regarded in law as essential parts of a complete act of intercourse. Even if a husband practises coitus interruptus, a marriage will be considered consummated. The use of contraceptives is no bar to consummation.

If a child is born

It is possible for a couple to conceive a child without a complete act of intercourse.

Any child born of an unconsummated and nullified marriage is regarded as legitimate in law.

CONTEMPT OF COURT

The powers of a court to prevent any interference with justice

Three actions constitute contempt of court: misbehaviour in court, defiance of a court order and the publication of comments on a case while it is still before the court. Only factual reports on the proceedings are allowed: this is because any comment might be regarded as an attempt to influence the outcome of a case.

Both criminal and civil courts have the power to punish people for contempt. The purpose of the law is to ensure that cases are tried fairly and that there is no interference with justice.

English law regards a fair trial as more important than a free press so newspapers and broadcasters can be held guilty of contempt if they publicly discuss a case while it is still being tried. They cannot publish interviews with

PUBLISH – AND BE IN CONTEMPT

When it is known that a newspaper intends to publish an article that could prejudice a case, the people or companies threatened may be able to stop publication.

In 1974 several court actions were pending against the Distillers Company, makers of the drug Thalidomide, alleging that the company's negligence had led to babies being born deformed after their mothers had taken the drug.

The Sunday Times planned to publish an article about the testing and selling of Thalidomide allegedly setting out evidence that the company had been negligent. The High Court granted Distillers an injunction stopping publication of the article on the ground that its purpose was to mobilise public opinion so that Distillers would be forced to offer the deformed children higher compensation.

DECISION

The House of Lords agreed that an injunction preventing publication was right and held that although the article would not have affected the court or witnesses, it would have pre-judged the case.

BUT...

The Sunday Times then brought proceedings against the British Government in the European Court of Human Rights.

In April 1979 that court held that the House of Lords' injunction violated Article 10 of the European Convention on Human Rights, relating to freedom of speech. Its judgment said that it was more important that there should be freedom of expression in this case than the authority of the House of Lords should be maintained through the law of contempt.

Having held that the restriction was an unlawful one on the freedom of expression of *The Sunday Times*, the court left it to the parties to agree on the sum by which the British Government should reimburse *The Sunday Times* for all the expenses it had incurred in the English and European courts.

people involved in the case while it is being heard. They cannot speculate on the outcome. They cannot report evidence not given in open court. The reason for this is that juries must make their decision only on the evidence they hear.

Contempt of court can be committed in a criminal case even before a person has been charged. Comment about a person who is helping police inquiries and who may be about to be charged can constitute contempt.

Sometimes, at the request of the police, newspapers and broadcasters publish details about suspects, this happens especially in dramatic cases where there is a big search under way. Technically these reports could be held to be in contempt when the suspect is finally brought before a court.

It can be contempt of court to publish a photograph of a person involved in a case in which identification is at issue. This is because a witness seeing the photograph would find it hard to discuss it from memory in court.

But newspapers and television often show Identikit pictures of suspects issued by the police during their inquiries into a case. In theory a good likeness of a man who subsequently comes before the court could be contempt. In fact, the issue has never been put to a judge.

Judges' discretion

In all contempt cases judges have very wide discretion, and a judge could hold that the need for the police to pursue the suspect rigorously outweighed the possible contempt.

All photography inside a courtroom is forbidden. The publication of a photograph of an accused or anyone else involved in a case, including the judge or barrister, taken in the precincts of a court – for example, on the pavement outside – is also contempt. Sketches actually made inside a court cannot be published.

The penalty for contempt can be severe. Judges can gaol a guilty person for any period. And when the publication of comment has been held to prejudice a trial, the accused could be acquitted despite the fact that there is a 'cast-iron' case against him. In such cases the defence would submit that its client could not expect a fair trial because of the controversy.

After a verdict has been announced discussion of the case is allowed. Even the judge's decision can be criticised – provided that the comments are not abusive. Of course, saying that someone who had been acquitted was actually guilty could lead to a LIBEL action.

THE EDITOR WHO WAS GAOLED

Nothing is regarded more seriously in English law than behaviour that is likely to prejudice a fair trial. The punishment for contempt is severe.

In March 1949, John George Haigh was arrested, charged with the murder of Mrs Olive Durand-Deacon, and remanded in custody. Two days later the *Daily Mirror* published articles saying the vampire killer was no longer at large.

The articles did not name Haigh, but named Mrs Durand-Deacon and referred to a confession. They also said that four other murders were attributed to the man in custody and named the victims.

Haigh applied in the High Court for writs of attachment against the editor, Mr Sylvester Bolam, and the proprietors of the newspaper. He claimed that the articles were contempt of court and prejudiced his chance of a fair trial.

Mr Bolam did not contest the accusation of contempt. He said that it was widely known that certain named people were missing and feared dead.

He admitted that on the day before the articles were published he had received a confidential memorandum, sent to all editors by the Commissioner of the Metropolitan Police, warning that the case against Haigh was *sub judice*.

Mr Bolam said he had instructed his senior executives on how the case was to be reported. He realised he had been wrong and took full responsibility for a grave error of judgment.

VERDICT

Lord Goddard, the Lord Chief Justice described the articles, headlines, and pictures used with them as 'a disgrace to English journalism', violating every principle of justice and fair play that it had been the pride of the country to extend even to the worst of criminals. The article was not an error of judgment, but a matter of policy in pandering to sensationalism for the purpose of increasing the circulation of the newspaper.

He gaoled Mr Bolam for 3 months and fined the proprietors £10,000.

WHEN THE MAGAZINE WAS NOT IN CONTEMPT

Disclosing the secrets of a jury's decision in a specific case is not necessarily contempt of court.

A juror in the trial of Jeremy Thorpe told the *New Statesman* that he was willing without reward to divulge some of what had happened in the jury room. The *New Statesman* published his article.

It recorded that the jury was unwilling to convict on a charge of conspiracy to murder, because they could not accept the uncorroborated evidence of someone who would get more money from a newspaper if a conviction ensued. It further recorded that the jury agreed that the accused were guilty of a conspiracy of some kind.

The Attorney-General prosecuted the *New Statesman* for contempt of court.

VERDICT

The court found that there was no contempt. It would have been contempt only if the disclosure tended to imperil the finality of jury verdicts or to affect adversely the attitude of future jurors and the quality of their deliberations.

The *New Statesman* article was free from such tendencies.

CONTEMPT OF PARLIAMENT

Parliament itself is judge, jury and plaintiff

Anyone who says or does anything that undermines the authority of, or public respect for, the House of Commons or the House of Lords, is guilty of Contempt of Parliament.

Allegations of contempt are heard not by the courts but by each House's committee of privilege.

In the Commons, for example, the normal procedure is for an MP to make a complaint to the Speaker who decides whether to refer the case to the privilege committee. That committee, which consists of MPs appointed at the beginning of every parliamentary session, can if necessary issue a warrant for the accused's arrest.

When he appears before the committee the accused is not allowed to be represented by a lawyer, he is not allowed to ask questions and he has no right of appeal. The hearings are not open to the press or public.

The committee makes a recommendation to the House of Commons which usually adopts it.

If the offender is found guilty, he is summoned to the Bar of the House where he is expected to apologise. If he does so he is reprimanded by the Speaker and there is no further punishment, if the offence is a minor one. If it is a serious offence he could be expelled from the House.

If someone refused to apologise, he could in theory be sent to prison for an indefinite period.

CONTESTS AND COMPETITIONS

What the rules are for promoters and competitors

Competitions in which the results depend on the exercise of skill by competitors are legal. But if the result is decided by chance and some payment is required from competitors, the competition is a LOTTERY and may be illegal.

Examples of wholly legal competitions, whether or not there is an entry fee, are crossword, bridge, chess, and certain 'spot the ball' football contests.

If entry to a competition involves any payment and depends on chance – for example, by winning an entry ticket in a draw – it is a lottery.

When skill is needed in preliminary stages, but the final result depends on chance – for example, a draw to decide the winner in a short-story contest – the competition is a lottery.

Choosing the winner

If two or more competitors submit identical entries – for example, by completing a limerick with the same last line – the promoter is entitled to pick a winner 'out of the hat', provided that the competitors were told of that condition when the contest began.

Although a competition may depend on the entrants' exercising a particular skill – as with a crossword or short-story contest – they are not legally entitled to

expect the judges to be suitably skilled.

However, if a contest of skill is judged by someone wholly unsuitable, the result of the contest could be considered no longer to depend on skill, and to have become an illegal competition.

Finding out what won No one has an absolute right to be told what entry or answer won a contest, unless that is promised in the rules, but if the winning entry is not published when the contest result is announced, send a stamped, addressed envelope to the promoter or publisher and ask for a copy to be sent.

Disputing the result of a competition

Almost all competitions in publications are covered by the promoter's rules that his decision is final and that no correspondence will be entered into. There may also be a clause that says the entry is 'binding in honour only' – so that you are not entitled to sue.

By entering the contest you agree to abide by any such rules that are laid down and you are generally not entitled to complain if you disagree with the outcome.

However, on occasion, there may be an obvious mistake in the result. For example, a newspaper that has asked for 50-word humorous anecdotes may accidentally award the prize to someone who wrote more than 50 words. That would be a breach of contract with all competitors.

If something like that happens, and you believe that you would otherwise have won a prize – for example, if your entry was placed second and you complied with the contest rules – write to the promoter, pointing out the error and claiming the prize.

The promoter will either have to arrange for you to receive the prize – if it has not already been sent to the announced winner – cancel the result and re-judge all entries or compensate you with a similar prize or its cash equivalent. If he does not, you can, unless there is a 'binding in honour' agreement, sue for the breach of contract. Whether you sue in the county court or High Court depends on the amount.

Cash instead Many contests in which the prizes are goods or services have a rule that there will be no alternative cash prize. But if you are allowed to

---

> ## THE ACTRESS AND THE MEMORIAL CONTEST
>
> *When no skill is involved – for example when there is no means of arriving at the correct answer except entirely by chance – the contest is unlawful.*
>
> The renowned stage actress Ellen Terry died in 1928 at the age of 81. Two years later, two admirers organised a competition to raise money for an Ellen Terry memorial museum.
>
> People in the theatrical profession, and others chosen from *Who's Who*, were invited to buy books of 10s (50p) tickets and sell the tickets to friends.
>
> Competitors had to decide the order of popularity of ten roles played by Ellen Terry. That order of popularity in turn was to be decided by the choice of the competitors. Entrants whose lists came closest to the most popular choice of the competitors as a whole would be the winners.
>
> Three-quarters of the proceeds of the competition were to be distributed as prize money. The other quarter was to go to the museum project. The organisers were charged with running a lottery.
>
> The defence claimed that the contest had been restricted to a select group of people who would be able to exercise some skill in deciding their fellow-competitors' tastes in drama.
>
> The prosecution, however, maintained that since the 'select' group had been asked to distribute tickets, there was no telling who might buy them. It would be impossible, the prosecution said, to make a skilful forecast of the views of an unknown public about Miss Terry's acting roles. The case was dismissed, but the prosecution appealed.
>
> ### DECISION
> The High Court agreed with the prosecution. It noted that some of the competitors, even among the 'select' group picked from *Who's Who*, were too young to have seen Ellen Terry perform.
>
> The case was sent back to the magistrates with a direction to convict.

---

choose cash instead of the named prize, the amount, unless it is stated otherwise at the outset, must be equal to the retail value of the goods or services.

For example, if the prize is a car selling at £5,000 retail, the cash alternative, unless otherwise stated, must be £5,000 – and not any smaller amount that the promoter may have paid for it.

Sharing an entry under one person's name

When one person submits a competition entry on behalf of two or more people, there is a legally enforceable contract between the joint entrants.

If you take part in a joint entry submitted in someone else's name, and the entry wins a prize, you can sue the other person if he or she refuses to share the prize as agreed.

When you are 'entered' without warning

Many companies run two-stage competitions as part of their sales promotion campaigns. People, picked at random from mailing lists, are notified that they have been entered for a competition and may have won a first-stage gift. To claim that gift, the recipient returns a coupon, indicating either that he simply accepts the gift or that he also wants to take part in a competition for a bigger prize. That usually means ordering something from the company promoting the contest.

Such a scheme, involving no skill or other consideration, does not imply a contract between participant and organiser, and so anyone who agrees to enter cannot later sue the promoter over the result.

However, anyone who objects to receiving unsolicited material can ask the promoter to remove him from the mailing list, and under the Mail Order Publishers' Authority code of practice, that must be done.

CONTINUOUS EMPLOYMENT

How loyalty to an employer brings its own protection and rewards

Your rights as an employee improve the longer you work in any one job.

WHEN A CUT IN HOURS DID NOT COUNT

Length of service is assessed by the number of weeks in which you worked or had a contract to work at least 16 hours. But a temporary reduction to less than 16 hours will not affect your rights.

Jane Sheldrake had worked in a department store for more than 3 years. For about 6 weeks before being made redundant, her hours were reduced by her employers from 23 a week to 12. At the industrial tribunal hearing, the store said that trade had fallen off during that 6 week period and it was obliged to pay redundancy compensation only for the previous period when Jane had been working full time.

DECISION

The tribunal ruled that those 6 weeks were a temporary reduction in the hours that were normally worked, and counted towards Jane's weeks of continuous service. She received her full payment.

WHEN A 30 DAY BREAK DID NOT INTERRUPT SERVICE

Continuity of employment is not broken when a person goes on strike or is temporarily laid off.

After 40 years' service with a Tyneside ship repairer, a riveter was declared redundant and claimed payment based on that length of continuous work. However, his employers pointed out that there had been a gap of 30 days in 1964 when he and others were laid off owing to a shortage of work at the yard.

Although they had been taken on again, there had been no promise at the time that they would be re-employed, and in fact they had been told to seek other work. Had the riveter's service been broken?

DECISION

The Divisional Court decided it had not. The matter, it said, should be looked at in the light of what actually did happen, not what was expected to happen, when the riveter was laid off. It was a temporary cessation of work which did not break his continuity of service, and he won his fight for full redundancy payment.

After 4 weeks' continuous employment, you become eligible for minimum notice and guaranteed pay; after 52 weeks, you can claim compensation for UNFAIR DISMISSAL and written reasons for DISMISSAL; after 2 years you are eligible for REDUNDANCY payment and for MATERNITY rights.

Other periods of employment bring other rights. *See:* EMPLOYMENT PROTECTION

These rights will hold good, in many cases, even when there is a break in your continuity of service, or when there is a temporary reduction in the number of hours you work.

Length of service is assessed in working weeks – in which you work or have a contract to work at least 16 hours.

Meal-breaks do not count towards the number of working hours, but stand-by duties can – for example, if you have to remain on call at home or by a telephone elsewhere. Essential work done at home may count towards a working week.

How long someone has worked is usually calculated backwards from the date when he is actually dismissed.

An employer cannot artificially deprive someone of his rights, however, by dismissing him without notice just before those rights would have come into effect. Every employee is entitled to at least 1 week's notice, and this will count towards his period of continuous employment. *See:* NOTICE

Similarly, a woman who has the right to return to her job after having a baby, but is prevented from doing so, is regarded as having been continuously employed up to the date when she originally said she would return.

When a break in service does not count

Employment is continuous even when:
● A business changes hands, if the employee stays on in his own job or in some other capacity.
● An employee is transferred to an 'associated' employer. Two employers are

associated when one company is under the control of the other or both are controlled by a third.

● An employee changes jobs within a company.

● An employee is absent through sickness for up to 26 weeks, or even longer if his employer does not dismiss him. The period is also longer in the case of MATERNITY leave.

● There is a temporary cessation in someone's work, or he is absent through 'arrangement or custom'. Examples of this are when an employee is kept on the books so that he can qualify for pension rights, or is lent temporarily to another employer.

● An employer dies – provided that the employee is taken on by the dead man's representatives or trustees.

● An employer re-employs someone after a hearing for unfair dismissal, or by agreement with the official arbitration service, ACAS. An unofficial reinstatement may not guarantee continuity so ACAS should always be involved.

When service is broken by the employee

Employment is considered to be not continuous when:

● The employee leaves a company and rejoins later.

● When the employee receives redundancy payment after a business has been sold or taken over.

● When a temporary teacher's contract ends with one school term and starts again with the next, but does not cover the school holidays. The same rules may apply to someone who is an intermittent employee, for example, a footballer or cricketer engaged only during the season.

If you are laid off or take part in a strike

Going on strike does not break the continuity of service, but the weeks you are away from work do not count towards the total served and even a 5 minute strike counts as a whole week lost. If you are laid off you are still covered by the rules relating to temporary cessation of work or absence by arrangement and continuity is therefore not broken.

CONTRACEPTION

Getting help to prevent unwanted pregnancies

Women are entitled to obtain free contraceptive pills and appliances under the National Health Service. Any female can apply. She does not need to be married, over 16, nor to have her parents' consent.

If a woman does not want to consult her own GP or if her doctor is not able to offer contraceptive advice, she should consult the Medical List, which contains the names of all general practitioners in the area and indicates which are on the Contraceptive Services List. Although any GP can prescribe contraceptives the doctors on that list receive extra payment from the NHS for doing so, and are therefore more likely to be available. You will be asked to sign a form confirming that you are to receive contraceptive services from the doctor over the coming year. The list is always available at main post offices and public libraries.

Choosing a contraceptive

Contraceptives that can be prescribed free are the pill, intra-uterine device (coil) and diaphragm (cap), but not the sheath, although the sheath is sometimes provided free of charge by Family Planning Clinics.

The pill, in particular, is prescribed only if the doctor is satisfied that it is safe for the particular patient. Some types of pill, for example, are likely to aggravate certain medical conditions such as high blood pressure. Some are harmful in conjunction with other drugs.

If a doctor refuses to prescribe any pill, the patient is entitled to ask another

THE HUSBAND WHO WANTED A BABY

It can be grounds for divorce if either partner in a marriage denies the other's wish for a child without good reason, such as health or economic problems.

Mr and Mrs Forbes married when the husband was 26 and the wife a few months older. At the time of the marriage, the wife knew that her husband was fond of children, and she had never voiced any objection to having them.

Early in the marriage, she insisted that the husband use contraceptives to delay starting a family until they were older and had a home of their own. The husband agreed, reluctantly.

Later, the wife herself began to use contraception and after 5 years Mrs Forbes said bluntly that she would never have children.

Eventually, Mrs Forbes left her husband. Mr Forbes sued for divorce on the ground of cruelty, claiming that his wife's conduct had undermined his health.

DECISION

Mr Forbes was granted a divorce. The court held that it was cruelty for a wife to refuse, deliberately and consistently, to satisfy a man's natural and normal instinct to have children – so reducing him to despair and affecting his health.

THE WIFE WHO WANTED A BABY

There is no law forbidding a husband or wife from using some means of contraception without the consent of the other – but to do so may be grounds for divorce.

Mr and Mrs Knott lived together for 11 years. Mrs Knott wanted to have children, but Mr Knott practised the withdrawal method of contraception. Full intercourse never took place.

Eventually the couple parted. Mrs Knott sought a divorce on the ground of cruelty by her husband.

The court heard that when the marriage broke up, the wife was in a very nervous condition – although her husband had never been told by doctors that his sexual practice might injure her health.

DECISION

Mrs Knott was granted a divorce. The court held that Mr Knott's refusal to let her have a child and his use of the withdrawal method was 'a deliberate act, contrary to the laws of nature and one which any husband must realise must damage a wife's health'.

– but if there are good medical grounds for the first refusal, he is likely to reach the same decision.

Confidential treatment

Contraceptive advice and service is confidential between DOCTOR AND PATIENT.

Although the age of consent for sexual intercourse is 16, a doctor who supplies contraceptives or prescriptions for a patient under that age does not commit a criminal offence. Nor is he obliged to tell the girl's parents that she is seeking contraceptive help or that she has been given it, although the Department of Health and Social Security advises doctors that where possible the parents should be consulted.

If the girl is considerably younger than 16, the doctor might feel that it is in her interests for her parents to be told. If she is almost 16, he may decide not to tell. He should not, however, tell the parents without the girl's consent.

Husbands and wives

There is no law forbidding a husband or wife from using some means of contraception without the consent of the other – although doing so may give grounds for divorce.

A wife is entitled to take the pill, have a coil inserted, use the cap or be surgically sterilised without her husband's consent – or even his knowledge. A husband can use a sheath or have a vasectomy operation without his wife's consent.

In practice, most doctors insist on a husband's consent for a sterilisation and sometimes even for fitting an intrauterine contraceptive device, the coil. They may also ask for a wife's consent to her husband's vasectomy.

The normal rule of confidentiality applies to a wife or husband who seeks contraceptive help: a doctor who discloses that information to the other spouse against his patient's wishes would be guilty of unprofessional conduct.

Family planning clinics

Instead of consulting a GP about contraception, you can go to a family planning clinic – usually listed in the Yellow Pages of your local telephone directory under Family Planning Centre.
Informing your GP A family planning

clinic would normally inform your GP of any treatment or appliance prescribed – especially if you have been prescribed a contraception pill which could have an adverse reaction with some other drug.

You can, however, insist that the clinic does not contact your doctor.

When something goes wrong

A doctor who prescribed a contraceptive pill without carrying out adequate tests, or making enough inquiries about a woman's medical condition could be sued for MEDICAL NEGLIGENCE if the pill caused or aggravated an illness.

The manufacturers who supplied the pill could be liable for negligence to the woman who took it if they failed to give doctors adequate information about the drugs involved – either because insufficient testing had been done or because they feared that sales of their pill would be affected by such disclosure.

If you believe that your health has been affected by a pill negligently prescribed or supplied, you should seek legal advice. If a contraceptive fails to work, or, say, a coil causes serious trouble, a doctor can be sued only where negligence on his part can be proved.

CONTRACT

A legally binding agreement

An agreement does not normally have to be written down to be legally binding. Spoken words are enough to make most contracts enforceable in law, and it is even possible to enter into a

WHEN A CONTRACT MUST BE SIGNED

Some contracts cannot be legally binding unless there is a signed agreement or other document, such as a letter. They include:
1. A contract for the sale of a house or flat, or for a lease. But letting for 3 years or less is valid if agreed only by word or mouth. *See:* TEMPORARY LETTING
2. A contract to guarantee another person's debt. *See:* GUARANTOR
3. A HIRE PURCHASE agreement or any consumer credit agreement. *See:* CREDIT AGREEMENT

CAN A SHOPKEEPER REFUSE TO SELL?

A contract is made only when an offer has been accepted. This means that if a mistake has been made on a price ticket and goods are priced too low, you cannot insist on buying them at the price indicated. A shopkeeper who displays goods in his window with a price on them, is not, in law, offering them for sale. He is merely inviting the public to make offers to buy them. He may, of course, sell the goods at the mistaken low price for the sake of goodwill. What the shopkeeper cannot do is sell at a higher price than that at which he has advertised the goods. That is an offence under the TRADE DESCRIPTIONS Act for which he can be imprisoned.

contract by actions only, saying nothing.

For example, a housewife, shopping in her local supermarket, enters a legally binding contract when she takes goods from a shelf and pays for them at the check-out.

What matters is that both parties have accepted an agreement.

A contract is broken if, after the agreement is properly made, one party backs out of it – for example, if you agree to buy a television set from a dealer and then refuse to accept it on delivery. The dealer can take you to court for breach of contract. But the court would not order you to take the television set.

The usual decision when a contract has been broken is to award damages or compensation – in that case probably equal to the amount of profit the dealer has lost by your failure to buy the set.

When goods are faulty

The terms of a contract do not depend only on the words, spoken or written, of an agreement. Nothing may have been said about the quality of the goods bought, but it is an implied term of any contract of sale that goods will be fit for the purpose for which they are intended. By entering into the contract, the shopkeeper, in effect, guarantees that the goods he is selling are satisfactory.

The same rule would apply, for example, if a newly bought food mixer did not work. *See:* DEFECTIVE GOODS

If a house owner employs a decorator

to paint his house, there is an implied term in the contract that the decorator will take reasonable care and exercise reasonable skill in doing the work, even though nothing has been said about the quality of his workmanship. If the decorator fails to use reasonable care and skill the house owner can sue for breach of contract.

A hotel proprietor can claim damages from you if you fail to take up a booking once you have contracted to do so unless the hotel was full and he could have re-let the room. The amount awarded would generally be equal to the amount of profit lost. If you have paid a deposit, this sum would be taken into account by the court.

Damages, however, cannot be claimed for inconvenience or annoyance when a contract is broken – for example, a hotel room is not ready at the time for which it was booked. *See also:* EMPLOYMENT CONTRACT

Getting out of a contract

It is possible to get out of a contract if you can show that:
● The other contractor has broken the contract first.
● A false statement lured you into a contract, which you would not have made if you had been given a full account of the facts.
● There is a fundamental mistake in the contract and that it is therefore invalid.

SERVING YOURSELF WITH DRUGS

Putting goods on display in a shop constitutes what lawyers call an invitation to treat, not an offer. The offer comes when the customer offers to buy them. There is still no contract until the shopkeeper has accepted that offer – he is quite entitled to refuse.

The Pharmaceutical Society of Great Britain sued Boots the Chemist for selling drugs and medicine without the supervision of a qualified pharmacist as required under the Pharmacy and Poisons Act. The company ran a one-room, self-service shop in which customers helped themselves and paid unqualified staff at a cash desk. Drugs and medicines could be taken from a shelf in an area marked 'Chemists' Department' and paid for at the desk.

The company said that a qualified pharmacist was at the store and was authorised to stop a customer buying drugs and taking them away if he thought it was necessary to do so. The society argued that once the drugs had been put in a wire basket and taken to the cash desk the transaction could not be stopped.

DECISION

The court ruled that no contract of sale had taken place until the customer's offer to buy was agreed to by the acceptance of money at the cash desk at the entrance to the store. That acceptance took place under the supervision of a pharmacist. That constituted supervision under the Act, so the society lost its case.

the entry binding in honour only and did not constitute a contract.

The company had been within its rights to disqualify Mr Appleson's entry because under its rules the coupon had been posted too late.

THE LONELY HOLIDAYMAKER

A person who sues for breach of contract may be awarded more than the basic value of the goods or services which he failed to receive. He can also be compensated for disappointment or frustration.

Mr Jarvis booked for a 2 week winter holiday in Switzerland, described as 'Houseparty at Morlialp with special resident host'. The price included a welcome party, afternoon tea and cake, yodeller evening, bar and farewell party all for £63.45. It offered ski runs, ski kit for hire and a host who spoke English.

Mr Jarvis stayed from December 20, 1969 to January 3, 1970, and in the second week he was the only guest in the hotel. The owner did not speak English. The ski runs were a long way away, and kit was available on only 2 days. The afternoon tea comprised crisps and dry nut cake, and the yodeller was a local man in working clothes who sang a few songs very quickly and left. The bar opened once.

Mr Jarvis sued the tour operator who advertised the holiday. The trial judge awarded him £31.72, half the cost of the holiday. Mr Jarvis appealed on the ground that that was not enough.

DECISION

The Court of Appeal held that damages could be given for disappointment, mental distress, upset and frustration. Mr Jarvis had only one fortnight's holiday each year and he was entitled to compensation for the loss of it. The court increased his damages to £125.

THE CAR DEAL THAT STALLED

The damages awarded in breach of contract cases involving commercial transactions will often be directly related to the amount of profit lost.

The Robinson company signed an order form in 1965 for a Standard Vanguard car from the Thompson company and agreed to exchange an old car as part of the deal. Later, Robinson's said it did not want the car.

Thompson's sued for the sum of its lost retail profit, £61 1s 9d, claiming that the contract had been broken.

Robinson's denied the claim and said Thompson's could easily have sold the car to another customer or returned it to the suppliers.

DECISION

The court ruled that if there had been a short supply of Vanguard cars, damages would have been nominal because demand for the cars would have been high and another company would have filled Robinson's place for the sale. But both sides agreed that there were plenty of Vanguards to meet all local demand, so Thompson's had lost a potential profit. Damages of £61 1s 9d were awarded.

THE WINNER WHO LOST

A written agreement may contain conditions which specifically exclude it from being regarded as a legal contract.

Mr Appleson sued a football pools company for £4,335, the dividend for an all-correct line, which he claimed was on a coupon he had submitted.

DECISION

Mr Appleson lost his claim. The court ruled that wording on the coupon – that the transaction should 'not . . . give rise to any legal relationship, rights or duties . . . or be . . . the subject of litigation' – made

Paying for breach of contract

If the other contractor has suffered no loss through the breach of contract you would not have to pay.

CONTRACTOR'S LIABILITY

What you can expect when you employ an expert

Someone who contracts to do a job for you is bound in law to use reasonable skill and care. If he does the job badly, you can sue him for breach of CONTRACT.

In addition, if someone is injured or if property is damaged as a result of the bad workmanship, the contractor can be sued for NEGLIGENCE, even if you are not the person who suffers.

For example, if you pay a contractor to service an electric hedge-trimmer, and he does it badly, you are entitled to sue him for breach of contract.

If his bad workmanship results in injury to someone else using the hedge-trimmer, that person can claim damages from the contractor for negligence.

If a garage repairs your car badly, and as a result you have an accident with another vehicle, you can sue the garage for breach of contract – and the other driver can sue it for negligence.

A contractor cannot avoid liability by attempting to contract out of any responsibility for negligence which causes personal injury. *See:* UNFAIR CONTRACT

Using the right materials

A contractor must use materials that are reasonably fit for their purpose. If they are not fit, you can sue him for damages for breach of contract.

The contractor can include a term in the contract excluding or limiting his liability over materials, but if he is acting in the course of a business and you are not – for example, if you are a householder employing him to build a garage – such a condition is invalid.

When you may be liable

Although you are always liable for any harm caused by the negligence of one of your employees, you are not always held responsible for the wrongful actions of an independent contractor

THE TREE THAT WENT THE WRONG WAY

Deciding just who should bear the cost of damages in a dispute over contractor's liability can be complicated both by the number of people involved and by the location of the work.

Mr Woodland hired a contractor, Mr Coombe, to remove a 25 ft high hawthorn tree from his garden at Caterham, Surrey.

The tree was 28 ft from the road. Telephone wires ran across the garden and also crossed the road.

The contractor was instructed not to leave the tree stump in the ground. He dug a trench around the base of the tree, to sever some of the roots. Then he used a tractor and rope to pull the tree down.

The tree fell on to telephone wires and snapped them. As a result, the wires across the road sagged in a loop, to within 2 ft of the carriageway.

The work was being watched by Michael Salsbury, aged 21, the friend of a neighbour's son. He decided to coil up the wires dangling over the road.

Before he could do so, a car came along, travelling at 45 to 50 mph. Mr Salsbury jumped out of the roadway and fell face down on to the grass verge, breaking his fall with his hands.

Although Mr Salsbury did not know it, he had a small tumour on his spine. The fall made it bleed, and 3 days later, he became partly paralysed: his legs were numb.

Mr Salsbury sued the contractor, the contractor's employer and the car driver.

He claimed that the contractor had felled the tree in a negligent manner, so that it brought down the telephone wires. He also claimed that the householder, Mr Woodland, was responsible for the contractor's negligence.

In his claim against the driver, Ian Beresford Waugh, Mr Salsbury alleged negligence – on the ground that he either failed to see the dangling wires or failed to stop when he saw them.

DECISION

Mr Salsbury was awarded £6,500 damages against the contractor and the driver. The contractor was held one-third to blame and the driver two-thirds to blame.

The householder, Mr Woodland, was held to be not responsible for his contractor's negligence, since the work involved was not very dangerous, was not likely to create danger on the highway and did not count as work done near a highway.

THE FACTORY THAT BURNED DOWN IN THE NIGHT

When a contractor has acted so unreasonably as to break his contract altogether, he is not entitled to any protection it might have given him when the question of damages arises.

The Wayne Tank and Pump Co. Ltd., experts in the handling of industrial liquids, were contracted by Harbutts Plasticine to make heated storage tanks for an ingredient of Plasticine called stearine.

Stearine, which softens by the heat of the hand, is very flammable at high temperatures and becomes liquid at 120°–160°F.

Harbutts had been storing stearine in its solid form, so that it had to be melted before use. They wanted to be able to keep it melted in heated storage tanks and pass it through heated pipes to the Plasticine mixing machine.

The contractors decided to line the tanks with plastic, to prevent corrosion. The pipeline to the mixing machine was made of a plastic called Durapipe. It was contained in a heating pipe, threaded with wire.

The equipment was finished and ready for testing by the end of a working day in February 1963.

Because it was late, the contractor's men decided that the test should be done on the following day. Before leaving that night, they switched on the heating and told Harbutts that everything was connected and ready for testing next day.

In the early hours of the following morning, the pipe cracked, the factory caught fire and was burned to the ground.

Harbutt's insurers sued the contractors for breach of contract.

The court held that the entire system installed was wholly unsuitable for its purpose: Durapipe distorted at a temperature too close to that required for Harbutt's purposes and the electric heating pipe should not have been put round plastic.

It was also held that the heating should not have been left switched on all night.

DECISION

The contractors were held to have broken their contract, and damages were assessed at £146,581.

'

THE GRAVESTONE THAT FELL ON SOMEONE

When an injury is directly caused by faulty workmanship, the contractor must pay damages.

A 9-year-old boy was taking flowers to his grandmother's grave in a churchyard when a 5 cwt tombstone, recently erected, fell on him. The boy's leg was broken.

After an investigation, it was discovered that the tombstone had not been secured with metal dowels. The monumental mason who erected the tombstone, Mr Cotterill, was sued for negligence.

DECISION

Mr Cotterill, in failing to use metal dowels, had been negligent. He was ordered to pay the boy £117 damages.

working for you – for example, a taxi driver, garage man or property repairer.

That is because although in theory you can tell an employee how to do his job, you cannot give detailed instructions to an independent contractor you hire to do a specific task.

In some circumstances, however, you can be made to pay compensation for damage caused by an independent contractor. If you allowed an unqualified person to fit new brakes to your car, and as a result had an accident with another vehicle, you and the repairer would both be liable: you would have been careless in entrusting an important task to someone not qualified to do it.

Even if you are properly careful in choosing a contractor, you may be liable for his negligence if the job he is doing is considered exceptionally hazardous to other people. For example, if you employ a contractor to carry out alterations to a building on a busy street, you will be liable with him for any injury to a passer-by.

In such cases, the victim is entitled to recover damages from either of you, but the court will apportion the damages between you according to what is considered just.

Insurance

If the contractor has no money to pay his share, and is not insured against such liability, you will have to pay the entire sum. Before allowing potentially hazardous work to start, therefore, it is advisable to ask to see the contractor's receipt for a current insurance premium.

CONTRIBUTORY NEGLIGENCE

When a victim shares the blame for an accident

If someone crossing a quiet street on a pedestrian crossing is knocked down by a car that suddenly comes round a corner at high speed, it is a clear case of NEGLIGENCE, and the pedestrian is entitled to compensation for any injuries. *See:* PERSONAL INJURY

But if the pedestrian steps off the pavement without looking for traffic, and is hit by a vehicle travelling too fast to stop in time, he himself is guilty of contributory negligence.

Someone whose contributory negligence is partly to blame for his injuries may lose some of the damages which are assessed for his injuries.

The court first assesses the amount

THE DRIVER WHO DID NOT WEAR A SEAT BELT

Where a person is injured as a direct result of not doing something that a 'prudent' man would do, his damages are likely to be reduced accordingly.

Mr Froom was driving his car with his wife in the passenger seat and their daughter in the back seat. Neither Mr Froom nor his wife wore a seat belt.

The Froom's car was hit by another travelling towards them on the wrong side of the road. Mr Froom had a broken rib, chest bruises and abrasions to the head. He sued the other driver.

Damages of £1,792 were awarded to Mr Froom, but the other driver appealed for a reduction on the ground that Mr Froom himself had been negligent in failing to wear a seat belt.

In the Appeal Court, it was argued on behalf of Mr Froom that he and his wife did not 'believe in' seat belts on the ground that the belt could trap the wearer in the car if there was a crash.

If they honestly believed seat belts were unsafe, their counsel argued that proper respect should be paid to their belief.

DECISION

The Master of the Rolls, Lord Denning, in giving judgment said that he did not agree with the suggestion: a prudent man would wear a seat belt.

Damages were reduced to £350 and then further reduced by 20 per cent because of Mr Froom's contributory negligence.

THE PASSENGER WHO DRANK WITH HIS DRIVER

A passenger who drinks with someone who is later to drive a car is likely to be held partly responsible for any accident.

Mr Owens and Mr Brimmell were two young men in their early twenties who often went drinking together in pubs and clubs in Cardiff. They sometimes used Brimmell's car for their outings.

One night in August 1973, after each drinking 8 or 9 pints of beer, they got in Brimmell's car and set off for home. Neither wore a seat belt.

A few hundred yards along the road, Brimmell overtook another car at high speed and hit a lamp-post.

The passenger door burst open and the passenger, Owens, was thrown out. His injuries included fractures of several bones in the face, brain damage, loss of sight in one eye and a broken leg.

Owens eventually sued Brimmell over his injuries and in turn was accused of contributory negligence.

The judge was not satisfied that Owens' failure to wear a seat belt had contributed to his injuries. But, he ruled, Owens was negligent in going with his driver on a drinking spree, knowing that the drink would impair Brimmell's ability to drive and to appreciate the danger of driving while drunk.

VERDICT

The major responsibility for Owens' injuries rested with Brimmell, who was in charge of the car while drunk and was therefore in a position to do damage.

Damages were assessed at £57,208 – but reduced, by 20 per cent, to just under £46,000, because of Owens' contributory negligence.

DEFINING CONTRIBUTORY NEGLIGENCE

A judge's decision on how damages should be apportioned depends on how serious he thinks an injured person's own actions or omissions were.

For example, a driver who was injured in an accident after he had parked on a bend had his damages reduced by 80 per cent; and a steel erector who was severely injured because he was not wearing safety harness received only 10 per cent of the damages awarded.

The amount deducted by the judge to take account of the victim's own carelessness is rarely less than 10 per cent.

In cases decided by the courts, factors involving contributory negligence have included:

At work
● Worker suffering from dermatitis after refusing to use protective hand cream provided by employer.
● Steel erector not wearing safety harness.
● Machine operator removing safety guard to increase or speed production.
● Machine operator cleaning moving parts.
● Builder refusing to use crawling board on a fragile roof.

● Railway worker ignoring signal that train was approaching.
● Employee using ladder he knew to be defective.
● Window cleaner not securing sash.
● Dustman not wearing gloves provided when emptying glass from dustbin.

On the road
● Accepting a lift from a driver known to be so drunk as to be unfit to drive.
● Passenger refusing to use a front seat belt.
● Motor cyclist refusing to wear a safety helmet.
● Driving over a white line down the centre of a road.
● Not slowing down at crossroads.
● Ignoring a Stop sign.
● Parking on a bend.
● Not anticipating that a cyclist would move out into path of car.

On foot
● Stepping suddenly off pavement into path of oncoming car.
● Walking into an unfenced hole during daylight.
● Walking with back to traffic at night wearing dark clothing.

that would have been awarded if the accident was entirely the other person's fault and then decides what proportion of the blame can be attributed to the victim.

Damages are then reduced according to that proportion. For example, if the victim is held one quarter to blame for the accident, his compensation will be cut by 25 per cent.

Contributory negligence always makes it difficult to assess what an injured person is likely to be awarded in the end – and therefore difficult to decide whether to accept any out-of-court settlement that may be offered.

If an out-of-court settlement is accepted, costs are usually paid by the loser. If a settlement is not accepted, then the injured person must accept what the judge awards, even if it is less than the amount offered in an out-of-court settlement.

If the victim of an accident is very young or very old, the question of contributory negligence is judged on whether he was taking reasonable care for someone of his age.

CONTROLLED TENANCY

Low-rent housing until the law changed

Tenancies of houses or flats that were created or renewed before July 6, 1957, were known as controlled tenancies, provided that the rateable value of the premises was not more than £30 (£40 in London). The main consequence of control was that the landlord was unable to charge an annual rent for the property in excess of the total of:
● The gross value of the premises for rating purposes on November 7, 1956 (this figure would be doubled if the landlord was responsible for *all* repairs).
● The present year's rates (if paid by the landlord).
● A yearly amount agreed in writing (or determined by a court) as a fair and reasonable charge for any repairs and services (including furniture) provided.

Many controlled tenancies were, over the course of time, converted into regu-

lated tenancies as a result of various pieces of legislation. All remaining controlled tenancies ceased to exist, as such, on November 28, 1980, as a result of the Housing Act 1980. From that date they were all converted into ordinary regulated tenancies, for which the RENT OFFICER can fix a fair rent.

The rent payable by tenants under

CHANGED CIRCUMSTANCES

The conversion of a controlled tenancy to a regulated one does not automatically mean that the landlord can increase the rent. The rent officer however is likely to fix a fair rent that is substantially higher than the old controlled figure.

controlled tenancies was low, often as little as £2 per week. However, the conversion of controlled tenancies into regulated ones does not mean that the landlord can simply increase the rent.

To obtain a rent increase the landlord must request the rent officer to fix a fair rent. When that is done, the landlord can increase the rent to the new fair-rent level, but no higher, until the rent officer again increases the fair rent – which he cannot do within 2 years of his last adjudication.

CONVEYANCE

Transferring a house from one owner to another

The legal process of transferring land and buildings from one owner to another is known as conveyancing, and the legal document for doing it is a conveyance.

A document called a transfer is

CONVEYANCE

needed when a property is registered; such a transfer must then be noted in an entry at the LAND REGISTRY. But there are still many unregistered properties for which the traditional conveyance is used.

The draft conveyance, setting out details of the property and the rights and obligations that go with it, is drawn up by the buyer's solicitor and amendments are suggested by the seller's solicitor until both sides are agreed on the final wording. A fair version, known as an engrossment, is then produced by the buyer's solicitor.

The seller must sign the engrossment to transfer the property on completion of the sale but, if the buyer is entering into a COVENANT with the seller relating to the property, he should sign it too. Some solicitors acting for a buyer prefer

him to sign even if there is no covenant.

The unbroken chain of conveyance documents, stretching back into the past, forms the most essential part of the title deeds, establishing ownership of an unregistered property.

Because there is no record of ownership at the Land Registry, the physical safeguarding of the conveyances that make up the title deeds is vitally important. Loss or destruction of them does not destroy the owner's right to the property, but the difficulty of proving ownership could complicate a future sale or make it impossible to raise a loan with the property as security.

If the property is bought on mortgage, the building society or insurance company takes possession after completion of the new conveyance and the rest of the deeds until the mortgage is

GETTING IT RIGHT

The buyer's and seller's solicitors may have to exchange draft conveyances several times before a satisfactory document is agreed.

DOCUMENT THAT RECORDS A CHANGE IN OWNERSHIP
How a conveyance traces back the succession of buyers through the years

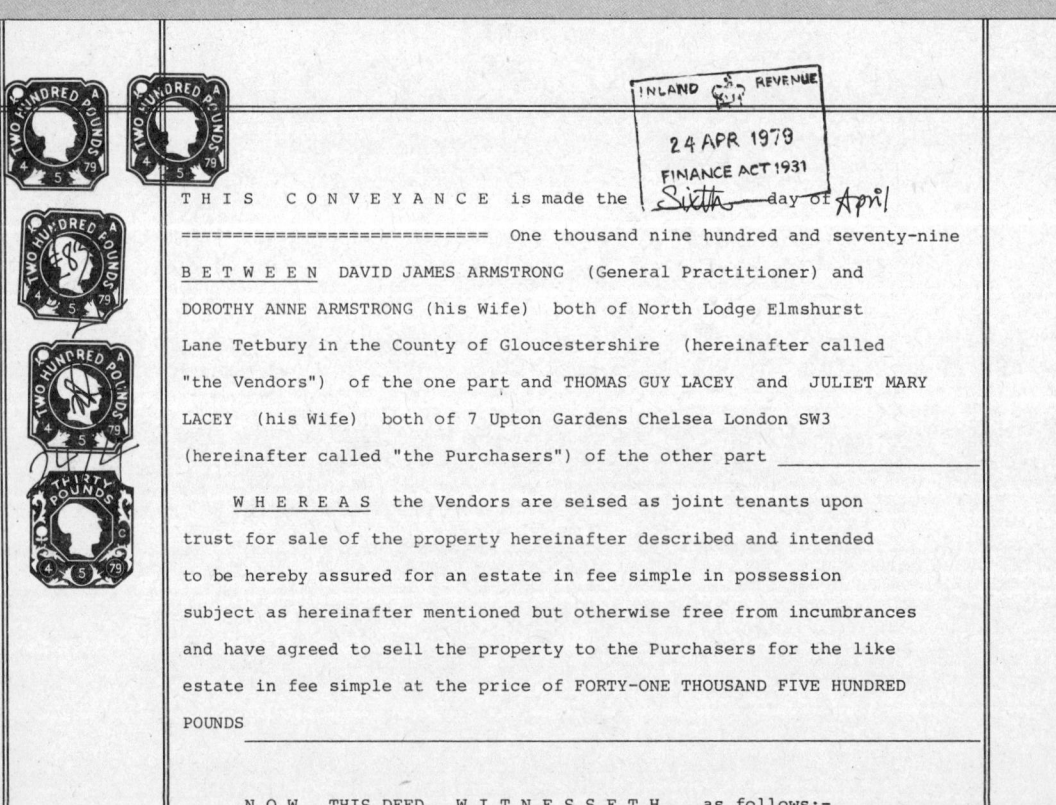

To transfer a property that is not yet registered at the Land Registry, you must draw up a conveyance, usually in traditional legal language

paid off.

If there is no mortgage the buyer can keep the deeds himself. If he is unsure that he has the facilities to keep them safe from loss, theft or fire, he can entrust them for safekeeping to his bank or solicitor. *See:* HOUSE BUYING AND SELLING

CO-OWNERSHIP

When an asset belongs to more than one person

Property, goods and financial assets can be held jointly or collectively under systems of co-ownership. The most common is the joint ownership of a house and goods by a married couple or a couple living together.

Many homes are bought in joint names because couples recognise the contribution each makes towards the purchase and repayment of mortgages and because they wish to share their assets. Even when a family home is not jointly owned, the law recognises, in the event of a separation, the wife's – or husband's – claim to a share of the assets. Judges will consider cash contributions towards the upkeep of a house and help in home improvements as justifiable claims to a share of the assets. *See:* DIVORCE; SEPARATION

Even after divorce or separation, co-owners have a legal right to continue to share their property, although county courts do have the power to order a co-owner out of a house where assault or a breach of the peace has been proved.

Two ways to share

A couple can share ownership of the family home or other assets in one of two ways – by joint tenancy, or by tenancy in common. Under joint tenancy the property is jointly shared and on the death of one co-owner his or her share passes automatically to the other.

A joint tenancy exists where a couple contribute equally to acquisition of the property and where a husband and wife hold a property in joint names even if their contributions are unequal.

When one joint tenant dies, his or her share goes automatically to the other tenant.

Tenancy in common exists when the property is bought in unequal shares and the shares are held separately, or when equal shares are held separately, not jointly. Each tenant in common can deal with his own share after a sale or leave it by will as he chooses. When no will is left, the share of a co-owner under tenancy in common will pass into his or her estate. *See:* INTESTACY

A joint tenancy can be easily converted into a tenancy in common. This is a regular practice when a couple fall out and intend to separate or to divorce. It can be done by either party without the consent of the other, merely by sending the other a simple letter stating: 'The property we own jointly will from now on be held in equal shares.'

It is not possible to convert a joint tenancy by stipulating in your will that after your death it is to become a tenancy in common, and naming someone to become a tenant in common. When one joint tenant dies, the property passes to the co-owner, no matter what the dead person's will may say.

Any number of people can be co-owners, but if the property involved is land, no more than four can legally act in selling it.

Those acting need not normally consult the others, unless a TRUST has been created expressly by some deed or document and it says that they must do

WHEN A COUPLE HAVE EQUAL
SHARES IN HOME OR PROPERTY

Many homes are bought in the joint names of husband and wife by couples who wish to share their assets. Even when that is not done, a wife's claim to a share may be upheld later if there is a legal dispute over ownership.

so. If the others have to be consulted, the sellers must accept a majority decision. If the land was bought and no trust has been created, the law imposes a trust, and consultation is necessary.

Co-ownership and housing associations

A group of people can form a HOUSING ASSOCIATION to buy flats, maisonettes or houses on long 100 per cent mortgages. The associations are controlled by the Housing Corporation and offer their members – the co-owners – many of the benefits of home ownership at little more than the cost of renting, and without the need to find a substantial initial deposit.

The housing association buys the land and property on a mortgage that may be spread over 40 or 60 years. Each member pays a small deposit – a percentage of the value of the property he will occupy – and then a monthly rent, based on the association's total mortgage repayment, repair costs, maintenance and insurance.

When a co-owner leaves the property, he is entitled to recover the deposit paid. If he stays more than 5 years he is also entitled to recover the contribution he has made to the block mortgage and to a share of any increase in the value of the property. The size of that share is related to the time he has stayed and is laid down in his agreement.

For example, someone may take over a flat valued at £15,000, pay a 5 per cent deposit and leave after 6 years – when the flat may be worth, say, £27,500.

When he leaves, he will be entitled to whatever he has paid towards the block mortgage and:

5% of £15,000	£750
plus	
Half the increase in value:	
$\dfrac{£12,500}{2}$	£6,250
	£7,000

Managing a co-ownership estate All co-owners are entitled to vote on the management of their estate. A co-owner cannot sub-let, or sell his property to anyone he chooses. The house or flat must go to the next person on the association's waiting list. If a co-owner dies, the tenancy agreement usually

GOOD NEIGHBOURS

Any group of people can form a housing association to buy flats or houses on long 100 per cent mortgages – which can greatly reduce the cost of home ownership, especially by eliminating the need for an initial deposit.

allows the husband or wife to take over.

High land prices and rising building costs have made the setting up of new co-ownership housing associations uneconomic in recent years, but housing association property still exists. All associations are controlled by the Housing Corporation.

Associations registered with the Housing Corporation may be eligible for grants to assist with their building programmes.

When goods are jointly owned

Ownership of goods is usually held jointly, but when there is a dispute one or other of the owners can seek a court order to have the object sold and the proceeds divided. This principle also applies to the two types of joint ownership of land.

Money in a joint bank account is held in law to be jointly owned by the co-holders of the account, and on the death of one party any balance in the amount passes to the surviving co-owner.

When investments are held in joint names, the company or unit trust usually takes instructions only from the first-named on its register. One holder with control in this way would have a legal responsibility to account to the others.

COPYRIGHT

Safeguards for writers, artists and composers

Anyone who writes a book, article, play, poem or words for a song, or who paints, draws or does sculpture, or composes music, is entitled to keep control over the use of his work by others. That entitlement is known as copyright.

The Copyright Act 1956, protects the creator of:
● Literary works, such as books of all kinds, short stories, poems, words of songs, articles and letters.
● Dramatic works, such as plays, mimes, operas and ballets.
● Musical works, such as songs and all forms of music without words.
● Artistic works, such as paintings, drawings, prints, photographs, sculptures, jewellery and pottery.
● Sound and visual recordings, radio and television programmes and films.

One work can involve more than one copyright. For example, a record of a song may have one copyright in the words, another in the music and a third in the sound recording. Each of those copyrights may be owned by a different person.

Copyright protection is given only to an original work, not one copied from someone else. Furthermore, the protection applies only to the form in which an idea is expressed, not to the idea itself.

For example, if someone makes a speech explaining his theory for doubling the world's food supply, he cannot prevent others from repeating his ideas, even if he is not given the credit for them. But if he sets out his ideas in writing, the written version is protected by copyright and cannot be copied without his permission.

If you invent a valve that works in a new way, your drawing of the valve is copyright, but not the invention itself. To protect an invention, a PATENT must be obtained.

A work does not have to possess literary or artistic worth to be protected by copyright: the protection extends to such items as football pool coupons and trade directories.

Making sure of your copyright

In most countries, including the United Kingdom, an original work is protected by copyright as soon as it is created. There is no need to register copyright, but it is advisable to indicate your claim to protection by marking your work with the international copyright symbol © and the date of publication or creation. For example © Reader's Digest Association Ltd, 1981.

If a work is not marked with the symbol it does not lose copyright protection, but use of the symbol gives notice to other people that you are aware of your rights, and that your permission is required for any commercial use of your work.

How long copyright lasts

The length of time that your protection lasts depends on the type of work you have created. For most published works, copyright lasts for the author's lifetime and for 50 years after his death.

If a work is first published after the author's death, copyright lasts for 50 years after first publication.

For photographs, prints, records and films, copyright protection lasts for 50 years from the date of first publication, whether or not the creator of the work is alive at that time.

Where a design is exploited commercially the copyright may expire 15 years after the design's first commercial use.

When the creator does not own a copyright

Although copyright usually belongs to the creator of the work, there are exceptions.

Someone who creates a work for an employer – for example, a photographer on the staff of a newspaper or magazine, or a staff poster-designer – is not entitled to the copyright. It belongs to his employer.

If you engage a freelance photographer to take pictures for you – for example, at a wedding – you will own the copyright of the photographs. However, if the photographs have not been commissioned – for example, if a friend takes them without payment – the photographer retains the copyright.

When a copyright work is performed

Anyone who creates a work that can be performed – whether dramatic or musical – has a right to prevent other people performing it in public without his permission. *See also:* PERFORMING RIGHTS

However, it is not a breach of copyright to perform the work in private – for example, in a school drama production to which outsiders are not admitted. But if parents were admitted, the performance would be public and be subject to copyright restrictions.

A performance to a private members' club or society – for example, a women's institute – is a public performance. So is playing records or radio music to workers in a factory.

Seeking permission A licence to perform a play in public should normally be obtained from the publisher of the printed version of the work. For music or records, the licence can be obtained from the Performing Right Society and Phonographic Performance Ltd.

Live performances A performer has no copyright in his live performance. If someone else imitates it, that person cannot be sued for breach of copyright.

It is a criminal offence – for which the maximum penalty is a £1,000 fine plus 2 years' imprisonment – to make a recording or film of a live performance for commercial purposes, without the writ-

ten consent of the performer. But it is not illegal to make a recording or film purely for private purposes.

If the recording or film has been made commercially, a crime is committed only by the maker, not by anyone who buys a copy, even if he knows it was illegally produced.

Taping an existing recording If you

ALL MY OWN WORK

The international copyright symbol helps to protect your work by advising copyists that you are aware of your rights.

---

make a tape recording of an existing record, you infringe copyright, even if the taped copy is for private use only.

A record company is not likely to take proceedings against someone who re-records for genuinely private use, even if it can trace the offender.

Recording television programmes If an event is broadcast live on television – for example, a cricket match or state ceremony – you are entitled to record it on video tape without permission.

You are not entitled to record any type of programme that includes copyright material, such as a film that is less than 50 years old or a concert or variety show in which any music played was written by someone who has been dead less than 50 years.

As with home sound-tape recordings, however, the copyright owner is unlikely to attempt to sue anyone re-recording his material purely for private use.

Using a photo-copying machine If you use a photo-copying machine to copy someone else's work for private research and study, you are not normally breaking the copyright law, provided you observe the rules of 'fair dealing'.

It is fair dealing, for example, to copy a few pages of a book for research purposes, but it would not be considered

---

WHO OWNS 'POPEYE'?

A businessman who admires a rival product must get permission to copy it.

A British toy manufacturer, O. M. Kleeman Ltd, applied to the American copyright holders for a licence to produce 'Popeye the Sailor' toys and dolls.

The copyright holders, King Features Syndicate Incorporated, had given permission to other British companies, but could not agree on terms with Kleeman's. Instead, Kleeman's imported a batch of 'Popeye' dolls, brooches and toys from a foreign manufacturer and produced copies of them.

King Features sued for breach of copyright. Kleeman's claimed that they had not infringed copyright. They said that they had copied, not from the original sketch but from a product not protected by a registered design – and as the designs should have been registered under the Patents and Designs Act, and were not, they were not entitled to protection.

The case was pursued through several

courts and ended as an appeal to the House of Lords.

DECISION

The House of Lords granted an injunction to stop O. M. Kleeman infringing copyright by import and manufacture.

It was ruled that a model could infringe the copyright of a sketch. In this case, it had done so by adapting the essential features of Popeye from the sketches. The Patents and Designs Act did not affect author's copyright. *See also:* PATENT

THE EXAM PAPERS THAT WERE COPIED

Original work is protected by copyright – it does not have to possess literary merit.

Examination papers published by the University of London Press were copied and published by a rival company, University Tutorial Press Ltd.

UTP, who had obtained 16 of the 42 test papers from a student who sat the

exams, were sued by the University of London Press and by two freelance examiners, Professor Lodge and Mr Jackson, some of whose questions had been used in the plagiarised papers.

In their defence, University Tutorial Press argued that the exams were not protected by copyright because they were neither literary nor original – the questions being fairly standard. They also claimed that the original publishers did not own the papers properly as they did not have authority in writing from the University Senate, only in an oral resolution.

DECISION

The High Court ruled: 'What is worth copying is worth protecting.'

The questions set were the product of someone's original skill and labour and were therefore protected by copyright. Since the papers were in print, they were protected as being 'literary'.

However, the court said University of London Press did not have written authority and found in favour of only Professor Lodge and Mr Jackson.

fair to copy the whole book, or to copy extracts to be circulated to an entire class of pupils.

Fair dealing has not been legally defined, but the Publishers Association and the Society of Authors have said that no permission is needed for an extract of up to 3,000 words, or a series of extracts totalling 8,000 words, provided that the total amount copied does not exceed 10 per cent of the entire work.

A librarian in an educational institution is entitled to make a copy of a complete article in a periodical, or of an extract from a book, for private study by any reader.

THE NYMPH WHO APPEARED WITHOUT WINGS

Copyright is infringed not only by the copier but by anyone who sells or imports the copy.

The August 1905 issue of 'Munsey's Magazine', an American periodical on sale at W. H. Smith bookstalls, contained an advertising competition. Readers were offered a 6 month subscription to 'The American Illustrator' if they could identify 40 per cent of some famous advertisements.

One of the illustrations was a picture, 'Nature's Mirror' by a German artist, Paul Thumann. The picture had been licensed to The White Rock Mineral Spring Company for use in its publicity.

On seeing this reproduction in a copy of the magazine bought from Smith's, the owner of the copyright of 'Nature's Mirror' – a fine art publisher named Hanfstaengl – complained to the booksellers.

He pointed out that where the original showed a draped female with butterfly wings – the goddess Psyche – gazing into a reflecting pool of water, the reproduction showed no wings and no reflections, and had no artistic merit.

W. H. Smith told its agents to tear the offending page from all outstanding issues of the magazine. Mr Hanfstaengl was not satisfied and sued Smith.

In the High Court, he claimed that the picture had been vulgarised in the magazine and would therefore damage his sale of fine reproductions. W. H. Smith maintained that the picture in the magazine was not a copy of the original.

DECISION

The court ruled that copyright had been infringed.

The judge said the picture in the magazine 'came so near to the original as to suggest the original in the mind of anyone seeing it'.

Mr Hanfstaengl was awarded a nominal one farthing damages, and costs.

THE WEDDING PICTURES THAT APPEARED IN THE MORNING PAPERS

If you engage a freelance photographer to take pictures at your wedding, you own the copyright.

When Donald Brian Williams got married in 1956, he hired Frank Settle, a former schoolfriend who had become a professional photographer, to take the wedding pictures.

Two years later, just as Mrs Williams was about to have a baby, her father was found murdered. Five days after the baby was born, the Williams' wedding photographs appeared in the *Daily Mail* and the *Daily Express*. Mr Settle had sold them for £15.

Mr Williams obtained an apology from the Press Council, an apology and undertakings from the *Daily Mail* and £52 10s damages and costs from the *Daily Express*. He then sued Settle for infringement of copyright.

The photographer admitted that the copyright belonged to Mr Williams, but claimed that he had an implied licence to give the negative to the newspapers.

The case was heard at Westminster County Court – where the maximum possible award at that time was £400.

The county court judge awarded Mr Williams £1,000 damages and costs on a High Court scale.

These, he said, were punitive damages and he added: 'Mr and Mrs Williams' wedding anniversary must always be marred by the thought of what these disgusting newspapers did.'

The photographer appealed against the imposition of punitive damages.

DECISION

The appeal failed. The Court of Appeal ruled that since the case had begun in the High Court, the judge could award more than the £400 maximum for a county court case.

The damages also were not too high. Mr Settle had violated not only Mr Williams' legal right of copyright but also his feelings, his sense of family dignity and his pride. It was a proper case for exemplary damages.

Copyright in a letter

The copyright in a letter belongs to the person who writes it. The person to whom it is sent is entitled to retain the letter itself, but not to publish the text without the writer's permission.

If you write to a newspaper or other publication the letter is assumed to be intended for publication and therefore not subject to copyright restrictions, unless you make it clear that publication is not intended.

Quotations from copyright material

An extract from a copyright work can be reproduced without a breach of copyright if it is done as part of a criticism or review of that work or another work, and is accompanied by an acknowledgment. Similarly, a series of illustrations, reproduced to show how an artist's style has changed, would not infringe his copyright.

Titles and slogans

The title of a work cannot be copyrighted, nor can a slogan, for the law considers very short phrases too insubstantial or trivial to be protected under the copyright law.

However, if someone copies the title of a well-known book, play or film, or an advertising slogan, it is possible to sue him for 'passing off' his work. *See:* TRADE MARK

When copyright is infringed

A private individual who infringes someone else's copyright is not likely to be sued. But anyone in business who does so risks an action for damages and a court order to prevent any further infringement.

It is good business practice to keep all the drawings relating to the products you manufacture. If your products are copied you may be able to sue for infringement of the drawings. If you are accused of copying, your drawings may prove that you designed the product independently. All drawings should ideally be dated and signed by the draughtsman.

A businessman who admires a rival product or advertisement, therefore, should seek legal advice before deciding to copy it.

Copyright may sometimes be infringed innocently – for example, when a publisher prints material which, unknown to him, has been copied by the supposed author from someone else's work. Publishers usually safeguard themselves by making the author responsible, in his contract, for any expense caused by an accidental infringement of copyright.

Copyright is infringed not only by the person who copies someone else's work, but also by anyone who sells or imports that copy, provided that he knows the material infringes copyright.

Copyright law is highly specialised, and anyone who considers that his copyright has been infringed should consult a solicitor. Do not delay before seeking legal advice as the law provides better remedies for those who act quickly. In most clear cases, a court will grant a temporary INJUNCTION to stop the infringer from carrying out further infringements.

If you have been accused of infringing someone's copyright you should seek legal advice as there may be many technical defences available to you. If you are in the wrong, stop copying at once. The plaintiff is always entitled to some damages, and your solicitor should be able to negotiate a reasonable sum in settlement of any claim.

CO-RESPONDENT

When a person is cited as a partner in adultery

Adultery is one of five reasons accepted by the courts as leading to the breakdown of a marriage, and the person with whom the adultery is committed is known as the co-respondent.

If a co-respondent is found by the court to have committed adultery, he or she may be ordered to pay some or all of the costs of the divorce.

The question of costs is a matter for the discretion of the judge, and they might not be ordered against a co-

respondent if the adultery took place after the marriage had completely broken down. Damages cannot be awarded against a co-respondent.

When a co-respondent is cited

A person accused of adultery in a divorce action must be served with a copy of the petition and answer questions on a document known as an acknowledgment of service. *See:* DIVORCE

He or she always has a right to appear in court and must be notified of the date of the hearing.

A co-respondent can file personally, or through a solicitor, a reply denying the adultery and asking to be dismissed from the suit.

Even when adultery is admitted, the co-respondent can appear at court to argue against paying costs. The adultery, for example, may have occurred long after the marriage had broken down or there may have been genuine reasons for believing that the respondent was not married.

In a divorce case where a CROSS-PETITION is served by the respondent, the man or woman said to be the adulterer is called the party cited. A party cited is in the same position as a co-respondent, and the same rules apply.

CORONER

The official who must investigate all unusual deaths

A coroner is a lawyer or doctor – or sometimes both – who investigates all deaths that are sudden, accidental, or suspicious. He is appointed by the local authority and must be informed of deaths where the deceased had not been attended by a doctor during the preceding 14 days; deaths resulting from accident, suicide, abortion or drugs; deaths occurring during a surgical operation; violent deaths; deaths caused by industrial poisoning; and deaths occurring in suspicious circumstances.

Only about one-fifth of all deaths in Britain come into one of these categories. In all other cases, the doctor attending the deceased issues a death certificate stating the exact cause.

In most cases, the coroner is notified by a doctor or hospital, but the police

and registrars of births, deaths and marriages who have not received a doctor's certificate giving the cause of death may also call his attention to a death.

Private citizens can also notify the coroner of any death which they believe should be investigated. His telephone number can be found in most telephone directories, or the police or your doctor will tell you how to find him.

What the coroner does

The coroner's officer, who is usually a policeman, questions doctors, policemen, relatives of the deceased and anyone else who can shed light on the circumstances surrounding the death, to discover whether there is an acceptable explanation for it.

In about three-quarters of cases, the coroner is able to satisfy himself without further action. If necessary, however, he orders a POST-MORTEM, a medical examination of the body, to establish the cause of death. It is usually followed by an INQUEST which is a public inquiry into the death.

An inquest may well involve delaying the funeral. A registrar cannot issue a disposal certificate until the coroner has given his formal notice that he is satisfied about the cause of death. An inquest may also prevent the use of the dead person's organs for transplant purposes. *See:* TRANSPLANT

CORPORATION TAX

The levy that some clubs and all companies have to pay

Corporation tax is a tax on the net profits of all companies. Social, sports and political clubs and associations are also liable to pay it on some of their profits.

Companies pay corporation tax at a fixed percentage rate on their net profits. The actual rate depends on how much profit they make. There are three rates, the small company rate, an intermediate rate, and then the full standard rate for companies making comparatively large profits. The level of profit and the rates of tax are varied from time to time.

An unincorporated association – that is an organisation that is not a partnership – such as a cricket club, dancing club or a business association, pays corporation tax only on investment profits or unearned profits. Those would include earnings from bank interest, building-society deposits or rent from letting property.

Earnings from bars, social events or other functions are exempt from corporation tax provided that the profits are used only for the benefit of the organisation and its members.

But a club that allows outsiders to directly use its facilities – without, for instance, being signed in only as a guest – is liable to pay corporation tax on all its profit from outsiders and members.

Money raised for charity

Charities do not pay corporation tax on their earnings. Any money raised by a club or organisation for charity would not be subject to corporation tax, even if the club has to pay corporation tax on some of its income.

CORRUPT GIFT

How the law tackles the use of bribes

A gift becomes a bribe in law if it is made with the intention of weakening the recipient's loyalty to his employer or to a public body for which he works or acts.

It does not matter whether a bribe is successful or not: it is the intention that makes the gift illegal.

A bribe need not be cash. It can be anything of value: a free holiday, the use of a car, theatre tickets, meals, drinks or the chance to buy goods at a specially low price.

Public corruption

The law is particularly concerned with bribery and corruption in public bodies. There are extremely strict controls on people in public life.

It is an offence for anyone to offer a bribe to someone who holds public office or works for a public body, in the hope that he will do, or refrain from doing, anything connected with his job or office.

The law presumes that any gift to an employee or officer of a public body is a bribe. It is up to the suspected person, either the donor or the receiver, to prove that it is not a bribe.

WHO BELONGS TO A PUBLIC BODY

The courts have given a wide interpretation to the term 'public body' over the question of bribery.

It includes any publicly owned body which has public or legally imposed duties and which is intended to benefit the public rather than make a private profit.

The list of people involved includes all civil servants and local-authority employees including teachers, social workers and traffic wardens; anyone working for a nationalised industry or the National Health Service, police, court officers and staff; MPs, local councillors and magistrates.

As a result, anyone who is involved in a public body should be very careful about accepting gifts from business acquaintances.

The gift may not even be intended as a bribe, or accepted as one, but that may be hard to prove later. If a gift is offered or given, it is wise to consult a senior official.

Private corruption

Bribery is also an offence in private business, but when corruption is alleged, the prosecution has to prove that any gift was intended to be a bribe when it was handed over.

A BRIBE IS ILLEGAL – EVEN WHEN REFUSED

It is an offence for anyone to offer a bribe to someone who holds public office or works for a public body, in the hope that he will do, or not do, something connected with his job or office. That is so, even if the offer is rejected.

Penalties for corruption

The maximum penalty for taking or giving bribes in a public body is 7 years' imprisonment. The bribe can be confiscated by the court and a convicted public servant may have to forfeit all or part of his pension rights.

Corruption in private business carries less severe penalties: the maximum is 2 years' imprisonment and an unlimited fine.

COSTS

Paying for legal services

Anyone who engages a solicitor to act for him if he is buying a house or fighting a court action will have to pay all the solicitor's expenses and a fee for his services – known as his costs. *See:* LEGAL COSTS

COUNCIL HOUSE SALE

When a tenant is allowed to buy his rented home

Most council tenants who have been in their home for at least 3 years, are entitled to buy it – if it is a house – or demand a long lease (at least 125 years' duration) if it is a flat. Tenants of old people's sheltered accommodation and accommodation adapted for disabled persons do not have that right. Joint tenants (for example, husband and wife) can exercise the right jointly, and up to 3 members of the tenant's family, even if they are not joint tenants, can exercise the right to buy jointly with the tenant, provided they are already living in the house.

Council mortgages

Tenants who buy are also entitled to mortgages from the local authority. The prospective purchaser can borrow up to the entire purchase price together with certain legal and other expenses. The exact amount he can borrow will depend upon the price of the house and his own earnings.

A tenant who finds he has insufficient income for a 100 per cent mortgage may still exercise his right to buy, provided he can pay the balance himself. Alternatively, he can pay a deposit of £100. He then has 2 years to complete his purchase, at the original price. During this period his earnings may increase so that, at the end of the 2 years' period, he will be earning enough for an increased mortgage.

Any mortgage granted will be for 25 years or less and will be an ordinary repayment mortgage.

If the tenant occupies a flat, and takes a long lease of it, his new lease will require the council to continue to maintain the structure and exterior of the building, accesses and services.

The legal formalities of buying your home

A tenant exercises his right to buy or to secure a long lease by serving a statutory notice on the council, telling it of the wish to buy. The council must tell the tenant the purchase price and how that figure was arrived at, give him information about the terms the council will insist on in the conveyance and how much the tenant may borrow on mortgage.

If the tenant wishes to claim a mortgage from the council, he has 3 months in which to do so, although both the council and the county court can extend this period.

Once everything has been agreed the council can serve a notice on the tenant, requiring him to complete the purchase within the period specified in the notice. If he does not do so, the sale is off (unless he has paid his deposit of £100, in which case he has 2 years in which to complete the purchase).

If the council refuses to consider your request to buy your council house, or is deliberately slow and obstructive in dealing with you, complain to the Department of the Environment. The Secretary of State has power to intervene and act on behalf of the council to transfer the house to you.

When a former tenant can sell again

A house that is sold to a tenant at a discount may not be re-sold within 5 years for more than the tenant paid for it, otherwise the difference between the original discounted price and the price the tenant received on the re-sale must

be refunded to the council. However, the amount to be refunded will be reduced by 20 per cent for each complete year after the original sale, until the 5 years is up. So, a tenant selling at the end of the 4th year after he purchased can keep 80 per cent of his profit.

If the owner sells the house, without consulting the council, the council can sue the owner for the difference between what he bought the house for and what he sold it for, less the 20 per cent allowance for each complete year after the sale. It can also recover this sum from a purchaser if the tenant has not repaid it himself.

If you are buying a house formerly owned by a council, you can find out how much you should have to pay by looking in the local land charges register, if the council sale took place before October 3, 1980, or in the Charges Register of the registered title to the house, if it took place on or after that date.

COUNCIL MEETING

How elected representatives deal with local affairs

All local authorities – including parish councils and community councils in Wales – must hold at least one meeting every year, in the spring.

A council may hold as many other meetings as it likes, but in practice, many councils meet once a month – usually on the same day of the month and generally in the evening, so that councillors with jobs can attend more easily.

Parish councils are not allowed by law to start meetings before 6 p.m.

The chairman of any council can call a special meeting at any time – on his own responsibility or at the written request of a certain number of council members. For the Greater London Council the required number is 20. For parish or community councils it is two. For other councils, five members must make the request.

How meetings can be called

All council meetings must be advertised by a notice at the council's offices at least 3 clear days before.

For a parish meeting, as distinct from a parish council meeting, at least 7 days' notice must be given and the notice must be posted in some conspicuous place in the parish. Everyone on the electoral roll can attend a parish meeting. The meetings are usually held in small parishes, where no council has been elected.

Apart from the public notices, each councillor must be given formal warning of a meeting. He must be sent a summons to attend, stating the business to be transacted, at least 3 clear days before.

If a councillor does not, for some reason, receive his summons to attend, the meeting is nevertheless valid.

No councillor can be excluded from a council meeting unless the chairman so orders on the ground that he is causing a disturbance which disrupts the council's business.

The public's right to attend council meetings

All council and committee meetings – though not sub-committee meetings – must be open to the public and the Press and should be held in a room big enough to accommodate a reasonable number of spectators.

However, if the council or committee decides that particular business should be conducted in private, the public and the Press can be ordered to leave – but the council or committee must first pass a resolution to that effect.

The chairman of the meeting is also empowered to order the removal of any member of the public who causes a disturbance which in his opinion prevents the council carrying on its business in an orderly manner.

After a meeting, the minutes of the proceedings must be recorded in a book, kept specially for just that purpose, and must be amended if necessary, in the light of any members' objections, and be signed at the next meeting.

Once the minutes are signed, any local government elector in the area is entitled to inspect them and make a copy of all or part of them, free of charge. Members of the public are not entitled to see the minutes before they have been approved. Many councils sell complete copies of their minutes, but they are not obliged to do so.

COUNCIL TENANCY
Renting a home from a local authority

Every citizen is entitled to be considered for the tenancy of a council house or flat in the area where he or she lives or works. However, most councils have far more applicants than homes available, and there is usually an extensive waiting list.

How priorities are decided

Some councils have a rule that applicants must remain on the list for a specified period – anything from 6 months to 2 years – before being given a house. In most London boroughs, for example, an applicant needs to have lived for at least 5 years in the Greater London Council's area.

Application forms for council tenancies can be obtained from the local housing department. The form will ask for details of present circumstances, present accommodation and size of family. Before dealing with an application the council frequently checks this information by visiting the applicant.

Someone whose home is being compulsorily purchased – for example, if it is in an improvement or CLEARANCE AREA – may be given priority for a council home, if he can find no other suitable accommodation, such as a private flat. Priority is also given to people whose homes are unfit for habitation, to the elderly homeless and to homeless people with small children. Nevertheless, an application must be made to the council in the normal way.

In other cases, the councils generally decide priorities by some kind of 'points' system – which means that applicants do not simply move up the list according to the length of time they have been waiting. The speed at which a person reaches the top of the list, and is offered a home, depends on the number of points his family can tot up, taking into account present housing conditions, and other circumstances, such as age and health.

Even after points have been allocated, some councils may take other factors into account. For instance, an applicant who has not paid his rent regularly in his present home may be pushed back on the waiting list.

A person who feels that his housing application has not been dealt with fairly, for whatever reason, is entitled to lodge a complaint with the local government OMBUDSMAN.

Councils are obliged to publish the details of their allocation procedures and 'points systems', and an applicant for a council house has a right to check the information kept about him on his file at the housing director's office to see that it is accurate.

Keeping in touch

Many councils expect applicants to re-register their application every year and to notify them of any change of address and circumstances. Failure to do so may lead to their being dropped from the waiting list.

Exchanging council homes

The tenant of a council house or flat will normally be allowed to exchange it for another – either in the same local-authority area or in another.

However, he will probably have to make his own arrangements, by finding another tenant willing to exchange. Some councils will advertise requests for exchanges in their office, but very few offer more help with such arrangements.

There may be some government money available to assist you with moving costs associated with an exchange or transfer. Ask at your local housing department whether a grant or loan is available to help.

One-way transfers

In exceptional cases a council may allow a tenant to move to another council home even when no exchange has been arranged – for example, when the children of a family grow up and the house becomes too big for the parents.

Rules that council and tenant must obey

Many councils require their tenants to sign a tenancy agreement; others simply include the conditions of tenure in the housing director's letter offering the tenancy and ask the new tenant to accept the terms in writing. If a rent book is issued, the tenancy conditions are usually set out on the cover. In all cases the terms are legally binding on both council and tenant.

Under the Housing Act 1980, councils must publish details and information about their tenancy agreements and also about their rules and methods of allotting their housing.

As a result of the Housing Act 1980, councils must consult with their existing tenants, and give them an opportunity to give their views, before making any decision on housing management, such as changing the letting agreements or the method of collecting rent.

Rent payments All council house rents are payable in advance. If a new tenant is required to pay a month's rent in advance he may be able to claim SUPPLEMENTARY BENEFIT or a RENT REBATE.

Tenants who find themselves in financial difficulties may also be entitled to these benefits. It is advisable to inform the council's housing department of any financial problem at an early stage.

Rent strikes Withholding rent payments is in most cases a breach of the housing agreement and can result in a tenant's eviction.

Organising a rent strike by a number of tenants could lead to a charge of CONSPIRACY.

Maintenance Every council is responsible for repairing its houses or flats and for outside maintenance. A tenant, for example, would not be allowed to paint the outside of his house in a colour of his own choice without council permission.

ANYONE CAN APPLY
FOR A COUNCIL HOME

Local councils generally have to decide priorities by some kind of 'points' system, which means that applicants do not simply move up the list according to the length of time they have been waiting.

"Sorry – nothing yet"

HOUSING DEP.

A tenant is normally expected to be responsible for inside decoration and perhaps minor repairs such as mending fuses and replacing tap-washers. He is also responsible for repairs to damage caused through his fault, such as broken windows. But major problems, such as blocked drains, are the council's responsibility.

If a tenant feels that the housing department has not done essential repairs, he can:

1. Complain to his local COUNCILLOR.
2. Give the council notice of his intention to do the repairs himself. He is then entitled to deduct the cost of the repairs from his next rent payment, although he should keep receipted accounts to prove that the repairs have been done.
3. Complain to a magistrate who has the power to order an inspection by the environmental health officer. For advice on how to start such an action, consult the clerk of the local magistrates' court. The health officer's report may be put to the magistrate at a court hearing and if the house is found to be unfit the council can be fined.

The magistrates can order the council to carry out repairs on the house and, if the order is ignored, the fine will be increased for each day the house remains unfit.
4. Start a county court action for damages arising from the council's neglect and seek a court order enforcing work that is needed. To start that kind of action, the tenant should seek the advice of a solicitor, particularly to find out whether LEGAL AID may be available in his case.

A council is not liable for any damage or injury caused by a defect in its buildings unless the authority or one of its maintenance staff has been told of the defect, or unless the fault was something which the council ought reasonably to have known about.

The council ought, for example, to be aware of faults such as leaking tanks or loose roof tiles, which its workmen should find in routine inspections.
5. Complain to the local government OMBUDSMAN.

Improving your home at your own expense

If you want to carry out improvements at your own expense to your council house, you may do so, provided you have the local authority's consent. You are entitled to go ahead with improvements if consent has been unreasonably withheld, although you should take LEGAL ADVICE.

The council cannot increase your rent because of improvements you have carried out at your own expense. Provided you had council consent you can obtain compensation when the tenancy ends to take account of the amount by which the value of the property has been increased.

Restrictions on sub-letting

A council tenant must not transfer his tenancy to anyone or sub-let part of his home without the council's written permission. Council consent is not needed before a tenant can take in a lodger. Provided the lodger observes the rules of the tenancy, the council cannot complain.

The council must be able to show that any refusal of consent to a sub-letting is reasonable. For example, if it can show that the tenants' proposals would result in overcrowding or would hamper any building work the council wished to carry out on the property, then refusal is reasonable.

A council refusing consent for a subtenant must tell the tenant why it is doing so. If the tenant (with appropriate professional help) thinks the council has withheld its consent unreasonably, he can go ahead and sub-let. Alternatively, he can seek a ruling from the county court.

Business use

A council house or flat can be used only as a place to live: business use, such as hairdressing or car hire, is generally forbidden.

Causing a nuisance

A tenant who uses his home for illegal or immoral purposes, or who causes a nuisance to neighbours – for example, by being noisy, keeping animals or storing refuse – is likely to be evicted.

A council tenant is usually specifically forbidden to obstruct a common driveway, park without permission, cut down trees or shrubs, or make alterations to the property, including putting up fences, garden trellis or television aerials, without permission.

Keeping animals

In theory, the keeping of pets or other livestock is usually forbidden under tenancy agreements. However, councils often allow pets to be kept unless they cause a nuisance to neighbours. Persistent offenders may risk eviction.

If the council wants to evict a tenant

Council houses let to council employees, or to homeless persons (unless they have been allocated the same house for at least 12 months), have no security of tenure apart from the council's legal obligation to behave lawfully and reasonably. All other council tenants now enjoy some security of tenure as a result of the Housing Act 1980. A tenant who pays his rent regularly, does not damage the property or cause nuisance, is entitled to live in his council home without interference.

If the tenancy is periodic – running, for example, from week-to-week or month-to-month, the council who wants a tenant to leave must first serve a notice to quit, in writing. When a house is let for a fixed term, a periodic tenancy – for periods the same as those for which rent was last payable under the first tenancy – automatically starts when the fixed term runs out. However, if the tenant refuses to leave when the written notice terminating the periodic tenancy expires, the council cannot evict him without a court order for possession of the premises – and such an order can be made only on certain limited grounds. The court cannot make an order for possession unless the council has first served the tenant with a notice telling him:

● The date after which proceedings will be taken against him.
● That the court will be asked, in those proceedings, to make a possession order.
● The grounds upon which possession will be sought.

The notice ceases to be valid (so that a new one must be issued) 12 months after the date on which proceedings may be started.

To obtain an order for possession of a council house, the council must convince the court that it is reasonable to make the order, that suitable accommodation will be available for the tenant when the order takes effect, and that at least one of these grounds applies:

1. The house has been specially designed or adapted for use by a physically disabled person, and the council needs the house for such a person and there is no longer such a person residing there at the time possession is sought.

2. The house is one of a group which the council normally lets to people with special needs which are catered for in the immediate locality (for example, special schooling for deaf or subnormal children or a social service facility), and there is no longer a person with these special needs living in the house – provided that the council needs it for occupation by someone with such needs.

3. The house is too big for the present tenant who has succeeded to it on previous tenant's death, and the present tenant has been informed more than 6 months but less than 12 months after the death of the previous tenant, that possession will be sought.

If the council can show only that it is reasonable to make the order (but not that other suitable accommodation will be available), the county court may still make an order for possession if the council can prove one or more of the following grounds:

1. That the tenant is in arrears with the rent or has broken some other important term of his tenancy agreement.

2. That the tenant, or someone living with him, has caused annoyance to neighbours or has damaged or neglected the property or the council's furniture.

3. That the tenant induced the council to grant the tenancy by fraudulently making a false statement (for example, as to the size of the tenant's family or the state of health of one of its members).

4. That the house was given to the tenant only as temporary housing while works were carried out by the council on his former council home, that those works are now finished and that the former home is available for re-occupation by the tenant.

There is no need to satisfy the court that it is reasonable to make the order, although the court must still be satisfied that alternative accommodation is available, if the council seeks possession on one of the following grounds:

1. That the house is overcrowded.

2. That the council intends, in the near future, to demolish, reconstruct or carry out major works involving the house, and cannot do so without gaining possession.

In deciding whether there is suitable other accommodation available for the tenant the court will consider:

● Whether the tenant will have security of tenure in his new home.

● The accessibility of his place of work and schools for the tenant and his family.

● The distance from the homes of other members of the family, where relevant.

● The needs of the tenant's family and their resources.

● If furniture was provided under the old tenancy, whether adequate furniture is to be provided with the new one.

Inheriting a council tenancy

It may be possible to inherit a council tenancy if it was, at the date of the former tenant's death, a periodic, not a fixed-term, tenancy. The successor must have been residing in the house and using it as his only or principal home at the time of the tenant's death and be either:

● The deceased tenant's spouse.

● Another member of the deceased tenant's family who has lived with the tenant for at least 12 months immediately before that tenant's death.

If there are two or more members of the tenant's family who qualify, they should agree between them who should succeed to the tenancy. If they cannot agree, the council will choose the successor.

When a council house family breaks up

Some councils let their homes to husband and wife jointly. In such cases when a marriage breaks down both partners are entitled to possession and both are liable for any rent arrears. So, if a husband walks out without having paid the rent, the wife will be responsible for arrears as well as the current rent.

But when one partner in a joint tenancy deserts the other, the deserted partner is entitled to stay in the home.

If a husband leaves home and the tenancy is in his name, his wife should arrange to have it transferred to her as soon as possible. As a first step she should make sure the rent is paid regularly and on time.

A wife who walks out can still claim the home, even if the husband is the sole tenant, if she can show that it is more reasonable for her to have the tenancy – perhaps because she wants to keep her children together. She should explain her position in full detail to the housing department.

COUNCILLORS

Getting elected to serve the community

Most citizens of the United Kingdom and Colonies who are at least 21 years old are entitled to stand for election to a county, district, parish or community council.

To qualify, however, a candidate must also have:

● Ensured that his name is on the local electoral roll, or

● Occupied land – even a field so long as it is used – in the area for the whole of the 12 months before he is nominated for election, or

● Worked or lived in the area for the whole of that time.

WHEN A PERSON CANNOT BECOME A COUNCILLOR

The following are not allowed to stand as councillors:

● Employees of the council for which the election is being held.

● Undischarged bankrupts.

● Anyone who within the past 5 years has been surcharged – ordered by a court or the district auditor to repay a sum of £2,000 or more which had been unlawfully obtained from any council.

● Anyone who within the past 5 years has been sentenced to at least 3 months' imprisonment.

For membership of a parish or community council, it is enough to have lived the 12 months within 3 miles of the parish or community boundary. A person can be nominated for more than one council at a time, provided he qualifies.

To stand for election, the candidate must be nominated on the appropriate form, available from the council, and be proposed and seconded by two local electors, with eight others also signing.

What a councillor can do

Once a person becomes a councillor – whether by winning an election or being returned unopposed – he is entitled to attend council meetings and take part in council business, and to sit on any committees to which his fellow-councillors elect him.

Most councillors probably attend one meeting per week. Committee chairmen have extra duties, such as office work, advising officials and seeing people, and some of them are virtually full-time councillors. All councillors may claim up to £14 for every day they do council work, and they are also entitled to expenses.

A councillor will generally deal with matters arising in his own ward or district, but he is not obliged to confine himself to that area.

He is entitled to see correspondence between the council and other persons, if information in it is necessary to enable him to do his duties as councillor.

No councillor, not even a committee chairman, is entitled to give instructions to any council staff unless the council has given him express permission to do so.

Conflict of interests If a council or committee is to discuss a matter in which a councillor (or spouse, if they are living together) has a financial interest, he must disclose that interest and take no part in the discussion or in any subsequent vote.

A conflict of interests would arise, for example, if an application for planning permission were made by a property owner for whom the councillor was acting as solicitor or estate agent.

Spending public money

If a local authority spends money without the legal power to do so – for example, using ratepayers' money to give a retiring chairman a 'golden handshake' – the district auditor can disallow the item.

The auditor can also apply to the courts for a declaration that the payment was illegal. If the declaration is granted, the councillors who voted in favour of the payment can be made to repay the sum involved.

Dishonest claims Any councillor or official who dishonestly obtains council money to which he is not entitled – for example, by making a false claim for travel expenses – can face criminal charges in court and can be ordered by the district auditor or council to repay the money.

If the sum exceeds £2,000, the councillor also becomes disqualified from council membership for 5 years.

Any councillor who accepts a gift as bribery is guilty of a criminal offence. It is an offence to accept a gift even when not carrying out the promise made in return for the bribe. *See:* CORRUPT GIFT

Giving up office

A councillor's term of office normally lasts 4 years (in some cases, the term is 3 years, however). When the term expires, if he wishes to remain on the council he must stand again.

Resigning office A councillor who wishes to leave the council before the end of his term can do so by writing a letter to that effect to the 'proper officer' – usually the clerk or secretary of the council.

Resignation by absence If a councillor misses all meetings of the council and its committees for a period of 6 months he loses his seat on the council unless the council approves a reason given for his absence.

COUNTRY PARK

Enjoying the open spaces

A country park, provided by a district or county council, and usually centred on some beauty spot, is open to any member of the public, whether he lives in the area or not.

Admission to the parks is free, but the council can make a reasonable charge for sailing, boating, fishing, picnicking, camping or similar activities.

COUNTY COURT

Where disputes between citizens are heard

Most civil court cases – where no crime is involved – are heard before a judge in a county court. For example,

disputes between a landlord and tenant, claims against a manufacturer for faulty goods or a claim for DAMAGES as a result of an accident are all heard in a county court. The county court cannot award more than £2,000, so larger claims are made in the HIGH COURT.

COURT MARTIAL

How servicemen can be tried for their crimes

Some offences committed by servicemen and women or by their families when overseas, are dealt with by Service court martial.

If the offence is a purely military one, such as mutiny or desertion, or if it was committed abroad, or if it was committed in the United Kingdom but the civilian authorities decided not to bring a charge, the serviceman or woman may be charged under military law and tried by court martial.

A serviceman who has left the forces can be court martialled for an offence committed while he was still under military law – but only if proceedings are brought within 3 years of his discharge. That same rule applies to a member of his family who has committed an offence whilst abroad.

A court martial has no jury. It is a panel of serving officers who are not connected with the accused person or his unit. They are advised on legal points, procedure and evidence by a judge advocate, who is a trained lawyer in the forces.

The judge advocate's role is something like that of a clerk to a magistrates' court. Rules of evidence and procedure in a court martial are similar to those in a civil court.

A serviceman facing a court martial can be represented by a Service lawyer if the charge is serious enough – such as mutiny. Otherwise he can be represented by an officer.

If the charge is one that is considered to warrant representation by an officer only, the accused can insist on being represented by a lawyer, but he must pay the cost.

What a court martial can do

The sentencing powers of a court martial are greater than those of a civil court. They are almost unlimited, ranging from a mere reprimand for lesser offences to the death penalty for mutiny, treason, or for desertion in war.

A court martial will not usually impose more than one punishment for one offence – except in the case of an officer sentenced to imprisonment who must automatically be cashiered (dismissed in disgrace).

Both verdict and sentence are subject to confirmation by a confirming officer. After confirmation, they may be reviewed by the Defence Council which can quash one or both – or uphold the verdict but alter the sentence.

A serviceman cannot be tried twice for the same offence. He may be tried by court martial or by a civilian court, but not both.

Appealing against the decision

A serviceman can appeal against his conviction – but not his sentence alone – to the Courts Martial Appeal Court, which consists of three High Court judges. However, he must first obtain that court's permission to appeal.

For this special hearing, he may be allowed LEGAL AID, depending on the size of his income and capital, but may be ordered to pay costs, which are deducted from his Service pay.

When a reservist commits a crime

Volunteer reservists are subject to military law, including court martial, when carrying out military training or when called out for permanent service.

Even if a reservist who has committed an offence has resigned he can be treated as subject to military law provided proceedings are brought within 3 years of his resignation and provided he is reasonably suspected of having committed the offence whilst subject to military law.

In practice, a volunteer reservist who seriously offends against civil or military law is invited to resign and does so. If the offence is a civil one he may then be prosecuted in a civil court. If it was against military law, no further action is taken.

When civilians are involved

If martial law is declared, all civilians can be tried by court martial – informal committees or tribunals of serving officers. When normal conditions are resumed the military may be liable to a civilian for unnecessary use of force or abuse of authority, but usually an Act of Indemnity is passed to exonerate the military personnel from liability.

COURT REPORTING

When public and Press may be excluded

Most courts of law are open to the public and the Press and broadcasters are free to report their proceedings, but not from inside the court.

However, there are exceptions in which the law intervenes to prevent publicity that might be harmful.

Matrimonial cases

In divorce, nullity and judicial separation cases, the Press can report only the names and addresses of the parties and witnesses, a concise statement of charges and defences, submissions on points of law – and the court's decision on them – the judge's summing-up (which may give details not otherwise reportable) and the judgment.

For domestic proceedings in a magistrates' court – such as a wife's application for maintenance or child custody – similar rules apply.

Juvenile court cases

Journalists and broadcasters must not, unless the court so directs, disclose the name, address or school of any child or young person under 17 years of age who appears in a juvenile court – whether as defendant or as witness, or as the subject of an application in civil proceedings.

It is also forbidden to reveal any other information that could enable the juvenile to be identified – for example, saying that his father is a local head teacher. If a child is involved in a non-juvenile sex case, the court has the discretion to order that the name be withheld from publication. In matrimonial and juvenile court cases, the public has no right to attend.

Committal proceedings

When CRIMINAL PROCEEDINGS start with a committal hearing in a magis-trates' court, to decide whether there is a case to answer at a crown court, the public can be admitted, but the Press and broadcasters may report only certain details to prevent pre-trial prejudice building up among potential jurors who read or hear reports.

The details permitted are: name of the accused person or persons, names of witnesses and lawyers, details of the court where the hearing is held, particulars of the alleged offence (but not of the alleged circumstances), the result of any application for bail or legal aid and the decision whether to send the case to the crown court.

If the magistrates dismiss the case, full details can then be reported. Even before they reach a decision, details may be reported in the normal way if the defendant applies for reporting restrictions to be lifted.

A defendant may make such a request in the hope that publicity will persuade witnesses to come forward.

If there is more than one defendant, reporting restrictions can be lifted at the request of any one of them. The others would be unable to stop the reporting.

If a request to lift the restrictions is made halfway through the hearing, or at the end, the whole of the hearing can be reported, including the part held while restrictions were in force.

Hearings in chambers

Any hearing in chambers – the judge's rooms – is private and the Press is excluded.

For example, in a divorce case, the judge announces the DECREE NISI in open court, and the parties conclude the financial and other details in chambers.

Old convictions

There are reporting restrictions on some old or 'spent' criminal convictions. *See:* REHABILITATION

COURT WELFARE OFFICER

The social worker who investigates problem cases

When a court has to make a decision about the future welfare of a child, the judge often directs the court welfare officer – a social worker or probation officer – to investigate the case.

For example, if a divorced couple dispute which of them should have custody of their child, the welfare officer may visit them to observe home conditions, assess the capacity of each as a parent, see the child and – if the child is old enough – talk to him.

The welfare officer also consults the child's teachers and anyone else who can provide information, and prepares a report for the judge. The parents have a right to see the report and obtain copies. The welfare officer may be questioned in court about his report.

The judge attaches considerable importance to a welfare officer's interview with a child, but is not bound to follow any of the welfare officer's recommendations – for example, a suggestion that the mother should have custody.

Another of the welfare officer's jobs may be to supervise a child who has been placed under a SUPERVISION ORDER by the court.

COVENANT

Enhancing cash gifts by tax rebate

A written and sealed undertaking to do something, or to refrain from doing something, is known as a covenant.

A common example is a written promise, or undertaking, by one person to pay another, or a charity, perhaps, a fixed amount of money each year.

If the undertaking, or deed, is properly drawn up the recipient can claim back from Inland Revenue all or part of the tax that the donor has paid on the covenanted sum.

The Inland Revenue treats the reclaimed tax and the net sum paid as part of the income of the person receiving money under a covenant. If he or she has other significant income, the covenanted money may bring his or her income above the tax-free amount allowed by the Inland Revenue and then

the advantages of the arrangement would disappear.

Such covenants, therefore, are of most benefit to people with low incomes – children, the chronically sick and the elderly. Charities also benefit.

To be effective under the tax rules, a covenant must be:

1. Capable of lasting for over 6 years. There is no tax penalty if the donor fails to maintain the payments for the whole period.

2. A legally enforceable deed, expressed in writing and signed, sealed and dated in the presence of a witness by the person making the payments. A copy should be given to the recipient.

3. Paid out of earned or investment income.

4. Freely made, not in payment for goods or services received.

If a parent makes investments for an unmarried child of his or hers under 18, the income they produce is treated by

A WAY OF AVOIDING TAX ON CASH GIFTS

By obeying four simple rules you can draft a deed of covenant that will make your gift worth more

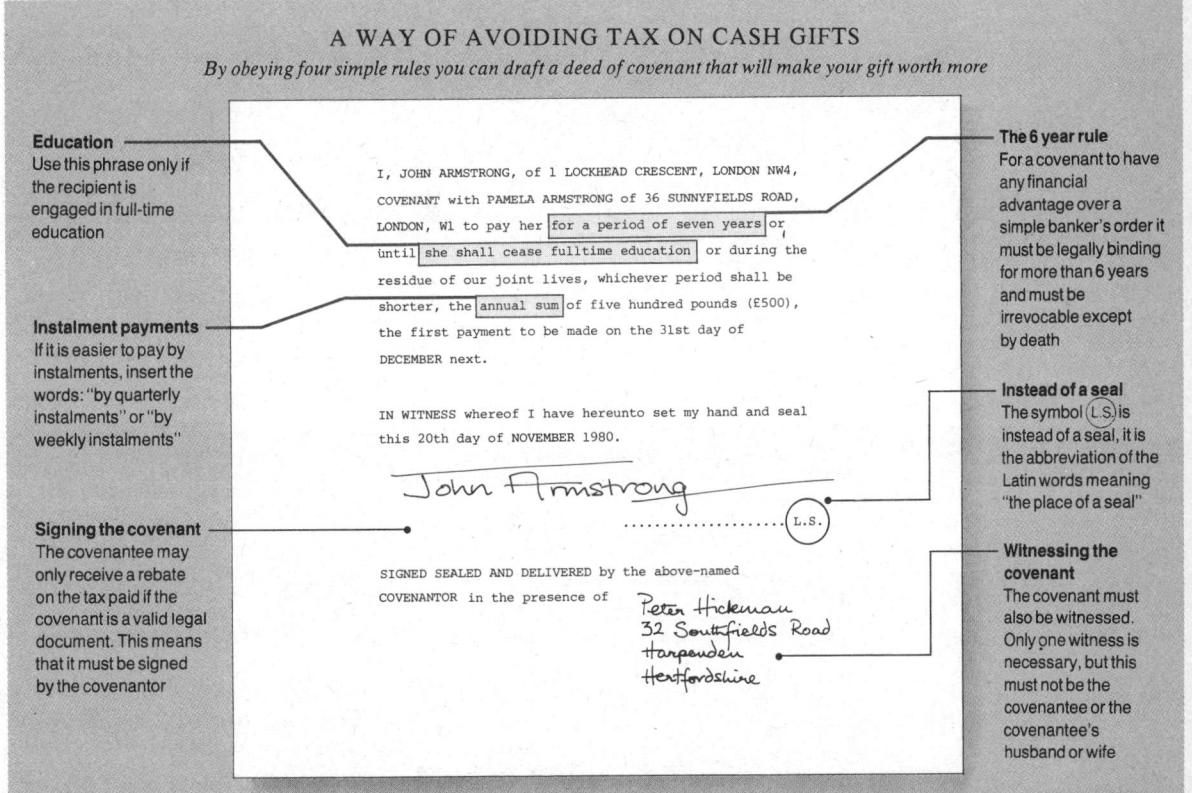

Education
Use this phrase only if the recipient is engaged in full-time education

Instalment payments
If it is easier to pay by instalments, insert the words: "by quarterly instalments" or "by weekly instalments"

Signing the covenant
The covenantee may only receive a rebate on the tax paid if the covenant is a valid legal document. This means that it must be signed by the covenantor

The 6 year rule
For a covenant to have any financial advantage over a simple banker's order it must be legally binding for more than 6 years and must be irrevocable except by death

Instead of a seal
The symbol (L.S.) is instead of a seal, it is the abbreviation of the Latin words meaning "the place of a seal"

Witnessing the covenant
The covenant must also be witnessed. Only one witness is necessary, but this must not be the covenantee or the covenantee's husband or wife

I, JOHN ARMSTRONG, of 1 LOCKHEAD CRESCENT, LONDON NW4, COVENANT with PAMELA ARMSTRONG of 36 SUNNYFIELDS ROAD, LONDON, W1 to pay her for a period of seven years or until she shall cease fulltime education or during the residue of our joint lives, whichever period shall be shorter, the annual sum of five hundred pounds (£500), the first payment to be made on the 31st day of DECEMBER next.

IN WITNESS whereof I have hereunto set my hand and seal this 20th day of NOVEMBER 1980.

John Armstrong .... (L.S.)

SIGNED SEALED AND DELIVERED by the above-named COVENANTOR in the presence of *Peter Hickman 32 Southfields Road Harpenden Hertfordshire*

Inland Revenue will repay any tax paid on money promised as a regular gift over a minimum of 6 years. The amount shown on the deed of covenant is the gross amount. Tax is recovered by sending form R185E, signed by the donor, to the covenantee's tax office, with his tax return. If the covenantee has no other income he will receive the amount of tax up to the value of the tax-free allowance to which he is entitled. If he has other taxable income he will get back only the amount that brings his income up to the tax-free limit.

the tax authorities as income of the parent. Therefore, there is no advantage in setting up a covenant for your own child under 18.

However, if the covenant is established by a grandparent or other relative or friend, the tax benefits remain. But you cannot get tax relief by giving a covenant to a friend's child, while your friend gives one to your child. A son or daughter over 18, or under 18 and married – for example, a student – may reclaim tax on sums paid by a parent.

Payments under a covenant

A person making payments under a covenant must deduct from them an amount equivalent to income tax at the basic rate before transferring them to the recipient.

So, if you want to pay an elderly aunt £1,000 a year and the basic tax rate is 30 per cent, you covenant to give her 'such sum as after deduction of income tax at the basic rate amounts to £700' – that is, £1,000 less 30 per cent.

You retain the other £300. If you are paying income tax at the basic rate or at higher rates, you will not have to do any more, because it is assumed that you have already paid income tax on the covenanted sum.

Your aunt can then apply to the Inland Revenue for repayment of the tax when completing her tax return. She must send with it form R185E, obtainable from any tax office, filled in and signed by you as the donor.

If she has no other source of income, she will receive the full amount up to the value of the tax-free allowance to which she is entitled. After that, any outstanding balance will be taxed. If she has other taxable income, she will get back only that amount which brings her income up to the tax-free limit.

Payments made to a charity under a covenant made after April 5, 1981 are allowable as a deduction from your taxable income provided your total of such payments in a tax year does not exceed £3,000.

To be valid for tax purposes, covenants to charity need only be capable of exceeding three annual payments (and not the 6 years applied to other covenants).

Restrictions on a householder

Restrictive covenants are often in-cluded in a CONVEYANCE when a house changes hands. Usually these were imposed by the original developer to maintain the amenities of adjoining properties. Each buyer generally relieves his predecessor of the duty to observe the covenants and assumes the responsibility himself – although the first buyer could be liable for ever.

The covenants usually cover such matters as refraining from putting up temporary outbuildings or cutting down trees or from using the house other than as a private residence.

Sometimes an old covenant may no longer seem relevant, but a planned development by the owner, say, an extension to the house, would be a technical breach of it. The owner can ask a court or land tribunal to set the covenant aside, but a quicker alternative is to take out insurance against the unlikely event of the covenant being invoked before going ahead with the development. Premiums are very low.

CRASH HELMET

Safety rule for motor-cyclists

All motor-cyclists and their pillion passengers – except followers of the Sikh religion wearing a turban – must wear crash helmets. Helmets must conform to one of the British Standards for helmets, and imported helmets must match these standards. The chin strap must be worn in the proper position. The maximum penalty is a £50 fine.

If a motor-cyclist or his passenger is injured through the fault of another road user and suffers serious head injuries as the result of not wearing a helmet, the damages will be reduced. *See:* CONTRIBUTORY NEGLIGENCE

CREDIT ABROAD

What happens if you shop in another country

If you buy something in a foreign country by using cash or your own cheque – with or without a CHEQUE GUARANTEE CARD – the transaction is governed by the laws of the country concerned.

If the goods are faulty, you can sue the supplier only in his own country. If a cheque is for some reason not honoured – if, for example, you stop it because of faulty goods – the supplier in turn can sue you in his own country or yours.

However, if you buy something abroad with a CREDIT CARD issued in Britain by a British company, the purchase is a linked transaction under the Consumer Credit Act and the card-issuing company may be liable for the quality of goods bought. The company that issued the card could be held liable for defects in goods bought abroad, and be sued in the British courts. If the overseas transaction took place after April 28, 1980, then the whole agreement will be exempt altogether from any of the provisions of the Consumer Credit Act and the company that issued the card cannot be held liable.

American-based companies, such as Diners Club or American Express, would count as British for the purposes of the Act. However, companies which – like those two – demand full payment of the current debt each month will not be liable for the quality of goods unless the card holder fails to clear the debt and so begins to pay interest.

CREDIT ADVERTISING

How a lender can describe his offer

Most advertisements offering credit must conform to rules laid down in the Consumer Credit Act. Only private advertisements – for example, in a shop window, newspaper or bargains magazine – are exempt. Anyone who advertises credit in connection with a business cannot be exempt.

It is a criminal offence for anyone to advertise credit facilities in a false or misleading way.

The rules cover all forms of advertising – in newspapers, magazines and other publications, on television or radio, in notices, signs, labels, showcards and price-lists, on display models or goods and so on.

Anyone who advertises credit for goods or services – either direct from him or through a third party, such as a finance company – must be prepared to tell the borrower the total costs of such an arrangement including interest, and the true interest rate.

An advertisement which contains any financial details such as 'credit up to 20 times your monthly payment' or 'only 2 per cent interest' must also give the true interest rate (expressed as a percentage-per-year), the total cost of the transaction, and the cash price of the goods. A trader cannot advertise goods or services on credit only. He must also be prepared to sell them for cash.

If you feel that a credit advertisement is false or misleading or may be breaking the rules, report the advertiser to your local trading standards department. If convicted, the advertiser can be fined up to £400.

Advertising to minors

People under the age of 18 are protected by law against touting by people who offer credit.

It is a criminal offence to send to anyone under 18 – with a view to financial gain – any document that invites him or her to borrow money, obtain anything on credit or hire or even apply for information about such facilities. The maximum penalty for such an offence is a £400 fine in a magistrates' court, or a year's imprisonment and an unlimited fine in a crown court.

The sender has a defence if he can prove that he had no reasonable ground to suspect that the recipient was under 18. However, if such material is sent to someone under 18 at a school or other educational establishment for minors, it is presumed that the sender knew the recipient's age.

CREDIT AGREEMENT

Safeguards for customers who borrow to buy

When you buy something on credit, or borrow money to make the purchase independently – even from a friend or relative – you have legal rights and wide protection whatever the type of credit arrangement you enter into.

Whether the deal is described as BUDGET ACCOUNT, CHECK TRADING, CONDITIONAL SALE, CREDIT SALE, HIRE PURCHASE or personal loan, the same legal safeguards will generally cover you – provided that the total amount borrowed is not more than £5,000.

Even if you borrow more than £5,000, if interest rates are extortionate, you are entitled to ask a county court to alter the agreement in your favour.

If you borrow money to be used for a specific purchase from a supplier who has a business arrangement with the lender, the person or company who lends the money is just as liable as the supplier if the goods are defective. *See:* DEFECTIVE GOODS

Even a hiring agreement, in which you do not arrange to become outright owner of the goods eventually, may come under the rules set out in the Consumer Credit Act 1974.

Making a credit agreement

The type of protection the law gives you depends largely on the stage you have reached in the contract and the way in which you made it.

Before you enter into any credit agreement, you must be given the following information:
● The total cost of your loan, including interest.
● The true rate of interest, set out as a yearly rate-per-cent of the money you owe. *See:* INTEREST CHARGE
● The cash price of any goods or services being bought by hire purchase or credit sale.

It is not enough for the lender to give this information in the credit agreement itself. The details must be set out in a formal price quotation, or an advertisement, notice, catalogue or price ticket. *See:* CREDIT ADVERTISING

Unless you are given the information in one of those ways, the lender cannot sue you or seek to repossess goods without a court order overriding his breach of the rules.

Reading the agreement

The agreement itself must contain a good deal more besides. Read it carefully before you sign. If possible take it home to study at greater length before you commit yourself.

The agreement form or document must be clear and legible. The regulations control such details as the size and style of lettering, the colour of the paper and how much of the agreement may be in handwriting, rather than in print.

You should be able to read all of the agreement, before you sign. There

should be no spaces left uncompleted and no part should be obscured by stamps, labels or signatures.

Any credit agreement you sign should include:
● Clear statements of your rights and duties in the transaction.
● The total cost of the loan, and true yearly rate of interest.
● Clear statements of the protection to which you are entitled and the remedies you can obtain if you are dissatisfied.
● Notice of whether, at what stage and how you can legally cancel.
● All the terms of the deal, apart from those that the law considers 'implied terms' – for example, the assumption that any goods will be fit to sell.

Do not sign simply on the basis of an assurance given by a salesman about the obligations being undertaken – for example, a verbal statement of the interest rate that you will be paying. All the terms, except those implied, must be stated in the written agreement.

If they are not – or if the agreement does not comply with other legal requirements – the lender cannot normally enforce the contract against you.

A court would allow a lender to sue a borrower over such a defective agreement only if the lender had been completely honest and open and the borrower appeared to have been dishonest.

Signing the agreement

When you are given a copy of the agreement to sign, it is generally not yet signed by the lender. At that stage, the 'agreement' is still merely an offer by you to enter into the contract: the lender, for example, will probably wish to make inquiries about your creditworthiness before he signs.

When you have signed, you must be given a copy to keep.

When the lender does accept your offer to borrow and signs the agreement, you must be given or sent – within 7 days of the lender posting or telephoning notification of his acceptance – a copy containing both your signature and his.

If you have not received that copy within 7 days, the lender cannot sue you or repossess goods. If you have still not received it after a full month, the sender may have committed a criminal offence for which he can be prosecuted.

If after you have inquired about the

copy it still is not sent, tell the local council's trading standards department.

The lender's acceptance of your offer to borrow, which marks the start of the credit agreement, takes effect when he posts his letter of acceptance or signed form – not when you receive it. The contract is then legally binding.

In some cases, the contract can be completed simply by a telephone call. If the lender informs you by telephone that he has agreed to lend the money you want, the agreement is legally effective even though you have not received his signed copy of the agreement form. The 7 day period during which he must send your second copy will start on the day of the telephone call.

You cannot be sued over the agreement, however, until you have received that form.

If the agreement has already been signed by the lender before you are asked to sign it, you are entitled to only one copy – but it must bear both parties' signatures, and the agreement will be binding the moment you sign.

Pulling out of an agreement

Once you have signed a credit agreement, there are three ways in which you may still pull out: by cancelling, withdrawing or terminating.

TIME TO CHANGE YOUR MIND

If you sign a credit agreement of any sort at home after discussing it orally with the salesman, you are given a 5 day 'cooling-off' period during which you can cancel the deal.

When you can cancel If you have signed a credit agreement of any sort at home, rather than in a trader's or lender's place of business, you may be entitled to cancel it during a 5 day 'cooling-off' period – provided that the negotiations that led you to sign the agreement were conducted orally and in your presence.

The 'cooling-off' period begins on the day after you receive your copy of the agreement signed by the lender.

You can send your notice of cancellation to the dealer or his agent, or directly to the lender.

If you cancel, the lender must give back any deposit and any part-exchange goods. You must return any goods already obtained under the agreement as soon as the lender gives back your deposit and part-exchange goods (or the part-exchange allowance in cash). Any cash loan must also be returned. But if you have borrowed money and spent it, and cannot repay at once, you may still be entitled to cancel. *See:* BORROWING

If you cancel an agreement for 'unrestricted use' credit – not tied to a specific purchase – the loan, and any interest due while any part of it is still outstanding, must be paid.

If you can arrange to pay off the whole debt within 1 month of giving notice of cancellation – perhaps by borrowing elsewhere at a lower interest rate – you need pay no interest at all under the credit agreement.

If you pay part of the sum within a month, you can pay the rest by instalments over the period originally agreed – and pay interest only on that balance.

When you cannot cancel If you sign a

IF YOU CANNOT KEEP UP THE INSTALMENTS

If you find that you can no longer afford to pay the hire-purchase or conditional sale instalments, but do not wish to hand back the goods, it may sometimes be in your interest to wait for the lender to make the first move.

As long as you have paid one-third of the total price, the company cannot take back the goods without a court order. Even if you have not yet paid one-third, the lender has no right to enter your property to take back goods without your permission or a court order. If he does so, you are entitled to sue him for damages.

For example, if someone has a hire-purchase car and leaves it parked in the street, the lender can seize it without his consent or a court order – but only if the buyer has failed to pay the instalments and has not yet paid one-third of the price.

But if the car is kept on the buyer's property, the lender cannot seize the vehicle without risking a trespass action.

Even if the car is left in a public street, the

lender cannot repossess it without first serving a default notice.

If you agree to hand back goods without a court order being made, you will be considered to have terminated the agreement voluntarily and must finish paying one-half of the total price.

However, if you believe that you will be able to pay within a reasonable time – or could cope with easier instalments – but the lender is not willing to depart from the strict terms of the agreement, it may be advisable to wait for him to take county court action.

If the matter goes to court, the judge can rearrange the credit terms in your favour, enabling you to keep the goods and pay by easier instalments – smaller sums, spread over a longer period. He may also order you to hand back the goods, but suspend the order for as long as you pay a specified amount of the arrears in a specified time.

A court may even, in rare cases, order a reduction in credit charges.

On the other hand, the court can decide

against you and allow the lender to repossess the goods without giving you an opportunity to pay more instalments. It may order you to pay the lender's costs and any other money he is owed.

When a default notice is needed

A creditor is not allowed to begin court action or try to enforce the agreement in any other way, without first serving a default notice – even if less than one-third of the total price has been paid.

The default notice warns the buyer that he has done wrong – for example, failed to pay the instalments, or perhaps unlawfully sold the goods which are not yet his to sell – and what steps he must take – pay the arrears, return the goods, or both. The notice will also say how much money the lender expects as compensation, as an alternative to having the goods returned.

Once you receive a default notice, you are allowed 7 days to act on it. If you fail to do so, the lender can sue.

credit agreement at a lender's or dealer's business premises, you cannot cancel it: there is no 'cooling-off' period. However, you may be able to withdraw – as opposed to cancel – before the contract becomes binding.

Even if you sign at your own home – or somewhere else, other than the business premises involved – you cannot cancel if negotiations which led you to sign were not conducted orally and in your presence.

If the agreement was made solely as a result of your reading advertising literature – for example, a mail-order catalogue – and there were no oral negotiations, you cannot cancel.

If there were oral negotiations but these were conducted by telephone, they were not carried on in your presence, so you cannot cancel.

However, if you feel that you have been misled by advertising or by telephone sales-talk, you can sue for MISREPRESENTATION and inform the trading standards department, who may prosecute the advertiser. *See:* CREDIT ADVERTISING

In any case, you cannot cancel if the credit is for £30 or less.

When you can withdraw Even if you sign a loan or hire-purchase agreement on business premises, you are not legally bound to go through with the transaction.

You can withdraw either by word of mouth or in writing, before the lender completes his side of the deal by posting or handing to you his signed copy.

If you do it by word of mouth, take someone with you as a witness. If you withdraw in writing, the withdrawal does not take effect until the lender receives it, so it is advisable to send the letter by recorded first-class delivery.

If you arranged the credit agreement through a retailer or the lender's agent – for example, a CREDIT BROKER – it is enough to notify the agent of your withdrawal.

Once you withdraw, any goods that you handed over in a part-exchange deal must be returned to you, within 10 days, in substantially the condition they were in when you parted with them. Otherwise you are entitled to the equivalent part-exchange allowance in cash.

If you are not promptly given back any deposit, part-exchange goods or cash allowance, you can sue the lender

WHEN TRANSACTIONS ARE LINKED

When the law says that you can cancel or withdraw from a credit agreement, it also allows you to pull out of secondary deals related to the main agreement – linked transactions.

For example, you have the right to cancel an agreement for the insurance or maintenance of a piece of equipment bought on credit, insurance against sickness leading to cancellation of a package holiday being paid for on credit, or the cash purchase of food for a freezer that is the subject of the main credit agreement.

Except for HIRE PURCHASE, any agreement by which the lender has a business connection with the seller of the goods automatically involves a linked transaction. The loan is the main agreement and the purchase is the secondary one. The borrower-buyer can sue the lender for defects in any goods bought under a linked transaction, just as he can over the main contract.

Even if a linked deal is agreed before the customer signs the main agreement – for example, if frozen food is ordered before the agreement to buy a freezer is signed – it is still a linked transaction which can be cancelled if the customer pulls out of the main contract.

Even if the two contracts name different companies, your protection is not affected, as long as those companies have a business arrangement with each other.

for the money and/or the value of goods in the county court.

When you cannot withdraw If you sign an agreement that has already been signed by the lender, it is binding on you immediately: you cannot pull out unless the contract includes a clause allowing you to cancel. In most hire purchase or conditional sale agreements, however, you may be able to terminate your contract later.

When you can terminate A hire purchase or conditional sale agreement can be terminated – ended before the due date – if you have paid at least half the total price plus the cost of any extras, such as installation charges for a domestic appliance or central heating.

If you have paid half the price and then return the goods, you need pay no more. If you have paid more than half, you cannot get anything back.

If you have paid half, but are behind with further instalments when you decide to terminate, you must still pay off the instalments due up to the date of termination.

When the credit charges are too high

If you feel that you are paying excessive credit charges, you can ask a county court to alter the terms of the agreement. You do not have to prove that the charges are extortionate: the lender must prove that they are not.

If the judge decides that the charges are extortionate, he can rearrange the agreement to make them fairer – provided that the borrower is an individual, not a company – even if the sum involved exceeds the normal limit, under the Consumer Credit Act, of £5,000.

Agreements made before the Act came into force are covered in the same way.

What is extortionate To decide whether a borrower's payments are extortionate, the court will compare them with interest rates that were generally being charged when the agreement was made. The judge will also consider whether apparently low-interest payments in fact disguise an inflated selling price.

Some of the borrower's personal circumstances will be taken into account – for example, his age, general ability to do business (including his degree of business experience), state of health when the agreement was made and any pressure that he might have been under, from any source, at that time.

On the lender's side, the court will consider the amount of risk which he accepted in making the loan, his relationship to the borrower – for example, if a family dispute is involved – and any other matter that the judge thinks relevant.

If a lender sues you for repossession, arrears or damages for breach of the credit agreement, and you consider his interest charges extortionate, you can respond by asking the court to intervene on your behalf and alter the terms.

Even if neither you nor the lender has started proceedings over your credit agreement, the size of the charges may still be considered by a court in any matter in which the debt is relevant.

For example, if a husband's means are being investigated in a family MAINTENANCE case, and a credit-agreement debt is a significant burden, the county court may rearrange the terms of the agreement. A magistrates' court dealing with maintenance cannot alter a credit agreement.

What the court can do If a credit agreement is ruled to be extortionate the court can do one of several things: set aside part of the contract, order money to be repaid to the borrower, alter the terms of the agreement and/or order the return of any security which has been paid to the lender by means of an arranged SURETY.

When you settle early

You are entitled to cut short a credit agreement by settling the debt before the agreed date – and to get some rebate of credit charges, because you will not be borrowing the money for as long as had been expected.

To arrange an early settlement, simply write to the lender saying that you wish to complete the agreement ahead of time.

Do not expect a large rebate: the lender is still entitled to a reasonable profit on the deal. You can check the amount you are entitled to, by inspecting special credit-rebate tables at a consumer-advice centre, council trading standards department or Citizens Advice Bureau.

Borrowing less than £30

A loan of not more than £30 – called a small agreement – is exempt from some of the rules of the Consumer Credit Act.

The formalities of making a credit agreement are not required and there is no 'cooling-off' period for the borrower. The lender in such a small agreement is not required to provide periodic statements of account, or copies of the agreement where new credit tokens are being issued.

However, no HIRE PURCHASE or CONDITIONAL SALE agreement can be classed as a 'small agreement'. Neither can any loan for which security has been taken in goods – for example, a PAWNBROKER agreement – or in cash. But a CREDIT SALE, or an arrangement in which the security is a written guaran-

tee or indemnity against failure to pay – as opposed to goods or money deposited with the lender – can be regarded as a small agreement.

WHEN THERE IS AN INSTALLATION CHARGE

If your credit agreement includes a charge for installing the goods – for example, plumbing in a dishwasher or putting up a television aerial – that charge must be treated separately if you decide to terminate the agreement or if the lender wishes to repossess the goods without a court order.

Terminating an agreement

To work out how much you have to pay before terminating, deduct the installation charge from the total and divide the balance by two. Then add the whole installation charge. The result is the minimum to be paid when terminating the agreement.

Example A dishwasher is bought for £300 including interest and a £60 installation charge.

Deduct £60 from £300	£240
Termination payment 50% of £240	£120
plus	
100% of installation charge	£60
Minimum payment to terminate	£180

Repossession of goods The lender can repossess his goods only if you have not yet paid one-third of the loan. To work out whether that proportion has been paid, deduct the installation charge, divide the balance by three, then add the whole installation charge.

If you have paid the resulting amount, the lender cannot repossess his goods without a court order.

Example A central-heating system costs £840 plus £120 installation charge.

Total price	£960
minus	
Installation charge	£120
equals	£840
Divide £840 by three	£280
plus	
Installation charge	£120
One-third payment for repossession purposes is therefore	£400

Short-term credit

Some agreements, by which a fixed sum is borrowed and is to be repaid in not more than four instalments, are also exempt. The exemption applies if the money is to be spent with the lender or with someone who has a business arrangement with him.

Under that rule, ordinary monthly trade credit – for example, the milkman's or newsagent's bill – will not be covered by the Consumer Credit Act.

Running account credit

Running account credit is an arrangement whereby the creditor usually obtains goods or services on credit, paying regular instalments off the debt, but not clearing the debt off altogether. As long as the agreed instalments are paid, the creditor can continue to have goods or services up to an agreed limit, as in a shop BUDGET ACCOUNT.

If the credit is running account credit, and the creditor must clear the entire debt each period (say monthly) in one payment, the arrangement is exempt from the Consumer Credit Act.

It will also be exempt if the money is borrowed from a lender who has no business arrangement with the person with whom the money is spent, provided the interest does not exceed the greater of 13 per cent or 1 per cent above the Bank of England's Minimum Lending Rate.

CREDIT BROKER

Introducing borrowers to lenders

Anyone who earns money by introducing customers to a money-lending company must have a credit broker's licence issued by the Office of Fair Trading, but he is not obliged to display this licence.

A licence is needed not only when credit broking is the main business – for example, mortgage broking – but also when it is secondary, as when a car dealer arranges hire purchase or when a solicitor, estate agent or accountant arranges a mortgage for a client.

If the credit broker has no licence, he is committing a criminal offence, and whoever lends the money is not legally entitled to make the borrower keep to the credit agreement, unless he can get an order to that effect from the Director General of Fair Trading. Without such an order the borrower is entitled to keep the cash and refuse to pay. However, if the goods are on hire purchase the lender may be able to sue for damages if the hirer parts with possession of the goods – if, for example, he sells them – but not otherwise.

If an introduction by a credit broker does not result in a credit or hire agreement within 6 months, no fee or commission of more than £1 is payable to him, whichever side decided not to proceed.

Under the Consumer Credit Act, the broker's client can sue in the county court to recover any commission of more than £1 already paid.

CREDIT CARD

Paying for your purchases without having to carry cash

If you have a credit card issued by a bank or credit-card company you are entitled to certain legal protection in your transactions with the bank or the lender of the money used for your purchases. Some credit-card agreements are fully protected under the Consumer Credit Act. Others are only partly protected.

Fully protected agreements

A credit-card agreement – such as Barclaycard and Access – by which you are allowed running account credit, paying only an agreed proportion of your total debt each month, has the full protection of the Consumer Credit Act.

The credit-card company, within 7 days of agreeing to issue you with a card, must send you a copy of your agreement.

When your card is renewed – probably once a year – a further signed copy of your agreement must be sent to you. If the company fails to send one, it cannot in theory recover any money you obtain or spend by using the card until you have been sent the copy agreement.

Furthermore, if a copy of the agreement is not sent to you within a month, the company commits a criminal offence, for which the maximum penalty is a £200 fine.

When a credit-card agreement is fully protected, anything you buy becomes the subject of a linked transaction, and the card-issuing company becomes as liable as the supplier for unsatisfactory goods or services.

Agreements partly protected

If your credit-card agreement does not automatically allow running account credit, so that you are required to clear your debt in full every month – as with American Express and Diners Club cards – the agreement is not fully covered by the Consumer Credit Act. The credit-card company is not liable for the quality of any goods you buy.

If you pay interest Although your agreement may say that you have to clear your debt every month, if you fail to do so, and are then charged interest or a 'service charge' on the money owed, the agreement becomes protected under the Consumer Credit Act. The credit-card company then becomes liable for the quality of goods bought after the interest charge is imposed.

If a credit-card company does not allow a customer to go into debt and pay

HOW THE CREDIT-CARD SYSTEM WORKS

The main difference between a credit card and a cheque guarantee card is that a credit card can be used by itself to buy goods or services from traders who have agreed to accept it, but a CHEQUE GUARANTEE CARD can be used only to guarantee that your cheque, up to a stated amount, will be paid by your bank.

A credit card cannot be used to guarantee cheques, except at specified banks. The exception is the dual-purpose card, such as Barclaycard, that can be used both to get credit and to guarantee a cheque.

Some cards, such as Barclaycard and Access, are issued free. Others, including American Express and Diners Club, charge a membership fee.

With certain cards, such as Access and Barclaycard, cash can be drawn at a bank without a cheque – but you start paying interest from the day you draw cash, whereas no interest would be payable on a cashed cheque.

With others, such as American Express and Diners Club, cash cannot be drawn without a cheque.

interest, but cancels the card and adds a penalty payment to the closing account, the penalty counts as interest and the agreement becomes fully protected.

The added interest will be subject to the controls of the Consumer Credit Act and the ex-card holder will be entitled to receive statements of what he owes, as well as to ask a court to decide at what rate he should pay the debt.

If you lose a credit card

Until you accept a card – by signing it, or by signing a receipt for it – you cannot be made liable for any use made of it. The receipt signed must be for the card itself, not just for the envelope in which it was sent.

Once you have accepted the card, you still cannot be made liable for debts totalling more than £30 which arise as a result of theft or unauthorised use. Even that maximum £30 liability applies only until you have given the credit-card company notice that you have lost your card.

In many cases, it may be enough to telephone the company as soon as you discover that the card is lost. If your agreement calls for the notice to be in writing, you can still give oral notice, for the sake of speed, and it will be effective at once, as long as you confirm it in writing within 7 days.

If you owe no money on the account when your card is lost or stolen, you are entitled to have any membership fee you have paid set off against any debt for which you are liable through unauthorised use.

For example, if you lose your credit card and someone uses it to run up a £20 debt, you may be liable for that debt because it is less than £30. But if you did not owe money when the card was lost, your membership fee of, say, £10 can be deducted from your £20 liability.

If you give or lend your card to someone else, you are liable for all debts incurred with it, provided that the original agreement gives a name, address and telephone number for notifying the company of a lost or stolen card.

When credit is stopped

The credit-card company, without warning you, can stop the use of your card by telling suppliers not to accept it.

However, unless the original agreement reserves the right to do so, or you have broken the agreement yourself by exceeding a credit limit or failing to pay your debts, the company will have broken its contract with you and you can sue in the county court for anything you have lost – for example, by having to go elsewhere for credit and pay higher interest.

CREDIT NOTE

When you want to return goods you have bought

If you take goods back to a shop, you may be offered a credit note rather than your money back.

You may be entitled to a full cash refund: that will depend on your reason for returning the goods.

Changing your mind If you return the goods because you decide you do not want them after all – for example, because the colour does not match something else, or your husband does not like them – you have no rights at all against the shop. It can refuse to take the goods even if you have not unpacked them, and it does not even have to offer a credit note.

Defective goods You are legally entitled to a full money refund, however, if the goods are defective and you return them promptly. You need not take a credit note.

Do not be deterred if a shop assistant says that it is not the company's policy to give cash refunds. *See:* DEFECTIVE GOODS

CREDIT REFERENCE AGENCY

Finding out what has been said about you

Anyone who tries to obtain credit is entitled to know what information about him has been filed away by a credit-checking agency, whether the credit is allowed or not.

To get the information, write to the company from whom you sought credit, asking for the name and address of any credit reference agency it has consulted about your financial standing. The request must be made within 28 days of the end of the credit negotiations.

The company must supply the information. If it fails to do so, it commits a criminal offence for which the maximum penalty is a £200 fine. There is no time limit for supplying information or for giving the name of the agency.

If a credit reference agency has not been used by the company, you are not entitled to find out what information it holds itself about you.

Checking your file Next, write to the agency asking to see your file. You must enclose a cheque or postal order for 25p, which is not recoverable even if the agency has no information about you.

If there is a file, the agency must send you a copy of all the information in it.

If the file is wrong You may discover that your file contains incorrect information. If so, you are entitled to insist that the incorrect information is put right or removed.

Within 28 days of your request for a correction or deletion, the agency must tell you in writing either that it has complied or that it has not.

If the agency says it has not complied, or if it fails to reply, you have a further 28 days in which to submit your own form of rewritten correction, which must not exceed 200 words.

If the agency says that it does not accept your correction, or if it fails to reply, you have a further 28 days in which to write to the Director General of Fair Trading whose staff suggests what further action you should take. They could, for example, order the agency to include your amendments.

A credit-checking agency can also ask the Director to intervene if it does not accept your suggested correction.

If you and the agency cannot agree, the Director can decide what should be done about the entry. If the agency fails to comply with the Director's orders, he can revoke the agency's licence.

Licence to trade A credit-checking agency must have a licence from the Office of Fair Trading. The penalty for trading without a licence can be 2 years' imprisonment for the company secretary or managing director and/or an unlimited fine on the company.

If a customer suspects that an agency is trading without a licence he can report the agency to the trading standards department. There is no penalty for a customer who uses an unlicensed agency.

CREDIT SALE

A more 'secure' alternative to hire purchase

If you buy goods on credit sale they become your property as soon as the agreement is made, not when the final instalment is paid – as with conditional sale – or when the customer takes up an option to buy, as at the end of a HIRE PURCHASE agreement.

The seller cannot repossess the goods at any stage. If a buyer fails to pay the instalments, the seller can only sue for what is owed. *See:* CREDIT AGREEMENT

The rules governing formation, cancellation, termination and interest rates are the same as those applying to any other credit arrangement governed by the Consumer Credit Act. *See also:* INTEREST CHARGE

CREMATION

The decision whether a body is to be cremated rests ultimately with the person responsible for the FUNERAL arrangements.

CRIMINAL COMPENSATION ORDER

If a person is injured or suffers loss through damage to his property as the result of a crime, he may be awarded compensation by the magistrates' court or crown court hearing the case, after the accused has been convicted.

The prosecution or the victim can apply for a compensation order; alternatively, the magistrates can make an order at their own initiative. *See:* CRIMINAL INJURIES COMPENSATION

CRIMINAL DAMAGE

How the law protects property

Anyone who damages or destroys another's property faces two possible court actions. The owner of the property may sue him for DAMAGES in a civil court, and the police may prosecute him for criminal damage.

> ## THE SQUATTER WHO WAS CARRYING A JEMMY
>
> *Under the Criminal Damage Act 1971, anyone who has anything 'in his custody' intending, without lawful excuse, to use it to destroy or damage property, is guilty of an offence.*
>
> A policeman saw David Buckingham leaving some unoccupied, boarded-up buildings in London, carrying a haversack. A jemmy was sticking out of the haversack.
>
> The policeman stopped Buckingham and asked what the jemmy was for. Buckingham said he worked for the squatters' movement and explained that he carried tools 'in case I have some trouble getting in'.
>
> The tools in the bag, apart from the jemmy, were a knife, two spanners, three screwdrivers and a torch.
>
> The policeman asked if they were all for breaking into premises. Buckingham replied: 'I only use them if I can't get in any other way.'
>
> Buckingham was charged with carrying the jemmy, intending to destroy or damage property. It was accepted that he had never intended to commit burglary. His defence was that at the time of his arrest, he had no improper intention of any kind.
>
> ### VERDICT
> Buckingham was convicted. The judge told the jury: 'Provided that the intention is in his mind, it does not matter how far in the future the event is going to take place.'
>
> ---
>
> ## THE TENANT WHO DAMAGED FIXTURES IN HIS FLAT
>
> *In certain cases, someone accused of criminal damage can successfully plead that he believed he was acting reasonably.*
>
> David Smith was the tenant of a flat which he improved by putting in new floorboards, ceiling material and wall partitions. He later decided to leave and asked if his brother could take over the tenancy. The landlord refused.
>
> Next day, Mr Smith pulled out the wiring of his stereo equipment, thereby damaging the floor, ceiling and wall partitions of the flat.
>
> He was convicted of causing criminal damage but appealed.
>
> His defence was that, because he himself had installed the flooring, the ceiling and the partitions, he was entitled, if he wished, to damage them.
>
> ### DECISION
> The court held that although the improvements had indeed been done by Mr Smith at his own expense, they were attached to the building, and so became the property of the landlord.
>
> But Mr Smith had honestly believed the property was his. Even though that belief was wrong, the court accepted that he had acted reasonably. He was cleared.

If someone is charged with causing damage, the prosecution has to show that he did it either intentionally or through reckless behaviour.

For example, if someone loses his temper in a public telephone box and smashes the receiver while trying to get a dialling tone he is guilty of recklessness, even though he wanted to make it work.

Maximum penalties If the cost of the damage exceeds £200, the defendant or the magistrates can insist that the case is heard in the CROWN COURT where the maximum penalty for criminal damage is 10 years' imprisonment and an unlimited fine.

If the damage costs less than £200, the case must be heard before the magistrates, who can impose a maximum penalty of 3 months' imprisonment and a £500 fine. The culprit may also be ordered to pay compensation to the owner of the damaged property.

Threatening or intending damage

Even if no actual damage is done, it is an offence to threaten someone else's property or to possess anything that could be used with intent to damage or destroy his property or belongings.

CRIMINAL INJURIES COMPENSATION

How the victim of a crime is financially recompensed

The victim of a crime may take action to obtain compensation for his injuries and losses in three ways:-

● He can sue the criminal for DAMAGES in a civil court action.

● He can be granted by the judge or magistrate at the criminal's trial a compensation order compelling the criminal to make some compensatory payment to him – either immediately or in instalments.

● He can apply to the Criminal Injuries Compensation Board for an award to be paid out of state funds.

The advantage of the last two methods is that the victim incurs no legal costs.

Criminal courts can award compensation for personal injury loss or damage resulting from the offence (except road traffic offences). They cannot make awards to dependants of someone killed as a result of a crime. In a magistrates' court, compensation is limited to £1,000. In other courts, there is no maximum.

Obtaining a compensation order

A person intending to claim compensation should tell the prosecution – usually the police – before the case is heard. He may be asked to complete a form giving details of his injuries, loss of earnings and expenses caused directly by the crime.

If the accused is convicted, the prosecution then applies to the court to make the order, although the court may make an award without any application being made.

The court must have regard to the means of the person against whom the order is to be made.

It may order him to pay an immediate lump sum into the court, or be given time to pay – or a combination of both may be ordered.

The figure assessed must take account of the physical and psychological suffering caused by the victim's injuries. Loss of earnings and expenses are added to that figure.

The court will limit the award to a sum that the criminal could reasonably be expected to pay over a 2 year period.

The award of compensation is a first charge taking precedence over any fine and legal costs, and if the offender defaults in payment, he will be treated as if he has failed to pay the fine and legal costs.

Any compensation awarded by the court is not necessarily all that the victim may be able to obtain, for – except in certain cases of common assault – he still has the right to pursue a civil claim (the civil courts will take into account any sums awarded by the criminal court or the Criminal Injuries Compensation Board).

Compensation orders are not restricted to the victims of assaults. Anyone who suffers loss or damage can seek an order, provided that the person responsible is convicted.

For example, if you are misled by a tour operator's brochure into taking a holiday which turns out to be well below the advertised standard you can ask for compensation.

However, you must first report your complaint to your local trading standards department – whose address is usually listed among the telephone numbers of the local district council – so that the tour operator can be prosecuted, if necessary, under the TRADE DESCRIPTIONS Act.

Applying to the board

An application may be made to the Criminal Injuries Compensation Board for compensation for personal injury directly attributable to a crime of violence that has been reported without delay to the police.

An application may also be made by:
● Anyone injured while arresting a suspect or helping a police officer to discharge his duties.
● Dependants of people killed as the result of a crime.

The board considers only those claims that it believes deserve compensation of at least £150. It excludes all claims for injuries resulting from traffic offences – unless the crime was deliberately running someone down or attempting to do so.

How to apply

A claimant must obtain, from the board's London office, 10–12 Russell Square, WC1B 5EN, a form on which he supplies full particulars of the case.

In the light of that and other evidence – including any available from the police – a member of the board decides whether or not the claim should be accepted in the first instance.

If the claim is accepted by the board

A successful claimant – or, if he is dead, his dependants – can be awarded an amount in part similar to that which it is estimated would have been given if he had instead decided to sue the criminal in the civil courts for damages. *See:* PERSONAL INJURY

The maximum compensation for loss of earnings is twice the national average of industrial earnings, and is paid as a lump sum.

If the claimant has been receiving social security payments, such as disablement benefit, those payments are deducted from the amount of compensation decided.

If the effect of an injury is prolonged, the board may make an interim payment.

When the victim has recovered, the case will be reviewed and a final award may be made.

If the claim is rejected at first

Anyone whose claim is at first rejected by the single member appointed by the board is entitled to have it reconsidered by three members of the board

---

A GUIDE TO THE COMPENSATION
A COURT CAN ORDER FOR CRIMINAL INJURIES
Amounts recommended by the Magistrates' Association

In deciding how much compensation to order a criminal to pay the victim of his crime, magistrates follow a guideline laid down by their own association. If, however, you sue for damages in a civil court action, compensation is assessed on a different basis. *See:* DAMAGES

The guidelines are designed to do nothing more than give a rough and ready basis for magistrates to work on in order that a victim may receive compensation and receive it quickly. They are starting points only, and – for example in the case of scarring – the damages might well be much higher.

Compensation for pain is increased when the injury is in a particularly sensitive area of the body and when the victim is elderly and infirm.

Compensation may be reduced when the injury is slight or if there was provocation of the offender by his victim.

Type of injury	Assessment of physical or mental suffering	Compensation suggested
Graze	Considerable pain for a few days; little after a week.	£10
Bruise	The closer the bruise to a bone, the greater the pain usually; pain likely for 2 weeks.	£20
Cut	Depending on size of cut and whether stitched; pain likely to have gone in 2 weeks.	£15–£50
Loss of tooth	Variable mental suffering, depending on position of lost tooth and on sex and age of victim; compensation greatest for front tooth of young female.	£25–£50
Sprain	Pain likely for at least 3 weeks.	£30–£50
Fracture	Depending on where; pain likely for 4 to 6 weeks.	£50–£100
Head injuries	Variable pain lasting, on average, for a month. Possibility of severe headaches.	£30–£100
Permanent scarring on face	Variable mental suffering, depending on position of scar, on sex and age of victim. Compensation greatest for young female.	£75–£150

and, at that stage, to produce witnesses in support of the claim.

After such a hearing, there is no further appeal against the board's decision except by judicial review on a point of law.

CRIMINAL PROCEEDINGS

How the court system works when a crime is alleged

Criminal proceedings start either with a person's arrest and charging by the POLICE, or with the issue of a SUMMONS to appear in a magistrates' court. Someone who is accused in either way has to work out how best to defend himself, or at least ensure the most lenient penalty.

Offences can be dealt with by magistrates – either unpaid justices of the peace or a full-time stipendiary – or by a judge and jury in a crown court.

The more serious cases are indictable – that is, they are generally tried by a crown court provided that the magistrates have first decided that there is a case to answer.

That means that the prosecution case is put, usually in the form of written statements by prosecution witnesses. The defendant can speak or cross-examine before the magistrates decide whether to commit him for trial at the crown court or, occasionally, free him on the ground that the prosecution, usually the police, has put forward a case that does not merit further examination.

Choosing the court

Less serious cases can be heard by the magistrates and in some instances the defendant may be able to choose which court will hear his case.

The magistrates are more likely to provide a speedy hearing if the defendant is pleading guilty. Most of their cases are tried within a month or so of charge or summons. In a crown court, the case is heard by a judge and jury. The rate of acquittal by magistrates and by jury is about the same. The sentence upon the convicted person can be heavier in the crown court.

In a magistrates' court, the defendant may not know in advance what the prosecution evidence is to be. For a crown

---

CHOOSING THE CROWN COURT

An accused person has the right in serious cases to choose to have the case heard in the crown court by a judge and jury – which may be more, or less, sympathetic than a bench of magistrates.

---

court case, the prosecution will have already supplied copies of the statements of their main witnesses by the time the case is heard. *See:* COMMITTAL PROCEEDINGS

The penalty he could receive is likely to be smaller in a magistrates' court – unless he is sent to the crown court for sentence.

Deciding how to plead

A defendant who believes himself innocent should plead not guilty. But if he is guilty he should admit his offence. If he lies on oath, he commits PERJURY, for which the maximum penalty is 7 years' imprisonment in addition to any penalty for the offence for which he is originally guilty. In most cases, however, a defendant is unlikely to be prosecuted for perjury simply because the court did not believe his evidence.

A defendant who pleads guilty will generally receive a lighter sentence, a sort of discount, than if he pleads not guilty and is found guilty.

In addition, a defendant who is convicted may have to pay part of the prosecution's costs – and those costs will be higher if the prosecution witnesses have had to attend court and give evidence in a 'not guilty' plea.

But if an accused person is innocent, he should plead not guilty: a charge is rarely so trivial that it is not worth an innocent person's while to contest it.

Pleading by post

Anyone who pleads not guilty to an offence should attend the court hearing – unless a lawyer represents him. Someone who pleads guilty must appear if:
● The offence carries a maximum penalty of more than 3 months' gaol.
● The case is one that could go to a crown court.
● The case is before a juvenile court.

If he does not appear, the case may be tried in his absence, or a warrant may be issued for his arrest.

In many minor cases tried in magistrates' courts, however – especially minor motoring cases – it is possible to plead guilty by post.

THE TWO COURTS THAT TRY CRIMINAL CASES

Magistrates' courts deal with less serious charges and use simpler and speedier procedures.

A crown court hears the more serious charges, in front of a judge and jury.

Some cases can be tried only in one court or the other, some can be tried in either court, and some can go from a magistrates' court to a crown court.

Magistrates' court only

Minor crimes – including most traffic offences – are dealt with only by magistrates if they are officially listed as 'summary' offences.

Usually crown court

Offences that are listed as 'indictable' are often tried in a crown court. Before an accused person goes for trial, however, a magistrates' court must find that the prosecution has the basis of a case against him. So while magistrates sometimes cannot try someone for an indictable offence, they can free him if they do not believe he has a case to answer.

Choice of courts

Many offences are listed as 'triable either way'. That means a defendant can choose to be dealt with by magistrates – if they are willing – or he can insist on going before a crown court judge and jury. If the magistrates find the basis of a case against him but do not want to deal with it, because of its apparent seriousness, he no longer has a choice. It goes to the crown court.

If a postal plea is allowed, the prosecution sends the defendant a 'Statement of Facts', containing a brief summary of the offence. The defendant completes the form and sends it to the court, enclosing his driving licence if a motoring offence is involved.

As well as completing the court form, a defendant is entitled to send a letter of mitigation, setting out any circumstances that he believes might persuade the magistrates to impose a lighter penalty. But if he wants the postal plea to be accepted, his mitigating letter must not contradict the Statement of Facts in any way whatsoever.

Deciding whether to engage a lawyer

Most defendants in magistrates' courts do not have a lawyer to defend them. It is often not difficult to conduct a case in person, although most laymen cannot expect to do the job as competently as an experienced barrister or solicitor. If the case goes to a crown court, the defendant should not attempt to represent himself.

The duty solicitor Many magistrates' courts, especially in the busy urban areas, have a duty solicitor scheme, run by local solicitors on a rota basis. The duty solicitor will give initial advice free. He will then represent you, if you wish, in the court, and will obtain LEGAL AID, where appropriate.

The duty solicitor is usually available at any time by telephone, and he is in the precincts of the court in the mornings. The court receptionists or ushers or other officials will tell you how and where to find him. If in difficulty, and if it is a serious matter, approach him for at least initial advice.

Being ready in time

If an accused person is not likely to be ready to defend the case on the date set for the court hearing – possibly because an important defence witness will be on holiday – he can ask for an adjournment.

The court is not obliged to grant an adjournment or remand – and is unlikely to do so if the request is not made until the day of the proposed hearing, and all the prosecution witnesses are in court, ready to give their evidence.

However, if the prosecutor (usually the police officer who is dealing with the case) is given as much notice as possible, he is unlikely to oppose a defence application for more time.

Trial in a magistrates' court

If a defendant does not attend court or send a lawyer to represent him in a case that can be tried in his absence, the magistrates will deal with it – if they are satisfied that the summons was served on him.

However, if the offence is one that could lead to a prison sentence, or if they are considering a driving disqualification, they may instead issue a warrant for the defendant's arrest.

When the case comes up, if the defendant is in court, he is asked to stand while the charge is read out by the magistrates' clerk. He is then asked whether he pleads guilty or not guilty. If a defendant does not wish or have to attend, he should inform the court in writing to avoid being liable for unnecessary witnesses' costs.

Pleading guilty

If the plea is guilty, the prosecuting officer gives a short summary of the facts. He also tells the court of the defendant's 'antecedents' – any relevant previous convictions recorded. In a motoring case, the defendant's driving licence is inspected.

The chairman of the magistrates then asks the defendant if he wishes to say anything. If the defendant feels he can say something to reduce his penalty, that is the time to do so. He should address the chairman of the magistrates as 'Sir' or 'Madam'.

The speech in mitigation should not dispute the substance of the police version of what happened, but it may include such points:
● Mitigating circumstances in the offence itself (for example, if the offence was damaging a burglar alarm, the fact that it was ringing all night near the defendant's bedroom window and the person responsible for it could not be found).
● Any family commitments and the defendant's financial circumstances.
● Previous good character.
● The fact of having pleaded guilty – 'making a clean breast of it'.

The magistrates then discuss the case

among themselves (retiring to a private room, if necessary). Then the chairman announces the SENTENCE.

If a term of imprisonment is possible, the magistrates may adjourn the case for a week or more, so that a social inquiry report, giving the home background of the convicted person, can be obtained. When a case is adjourned, the defendant is remanded either in custody or on bail.

Pleading guilty, then not guilty

A defendant is entitled to change his mind and plead not guilty after first pleading guilty. If he does so by post, the magistrates are not told of his previous admission.

However, the court clerk should be warned of his change of mind before the case is due to be heard, so that a new date for the hearing can be arranged to allow both prosecution and defence time to prepare their evidence and arrange for witnesses to be in court.

Pleading not guilty

When someone pleads not guilty the prosecutor – whether a police officer, solicitor or barrister – briefly summarises the facts of the case and then calls his witnesses to give their evidence.

The accused is not allowed to interrupt the witnesses, but each witness in turn can be questioned – 'cross-examined' – by the defendant or his lawyer.

If the cross-examination raises new matters of evidence, the prosecutor can put further questions to the witness, to clarify the points involved.

Then, if the defendant is not to be committed to a crown court, it is his turn to present his case.

He can simply ask the magistrates to dismiss the charge on the ground that there is no case for him to answer. Or he can give evidence on oath himself and call his own witnesses. He and his witnesses can be cross-examined by the prosecutor.

Closing speeches, summing up the case for each side, are made by prosecutor and defence – in that order, so that the defendant or his lawyer has the benefit of the last word.

The magistrates then consider their verdict. If the case is straightforward, they may stay in court and simply have a short discussion among themselves.

Otherwise, they retire to a private room.

The defendant stands to hear the chairman announce the verdict. If it is 'not guilty' he or his solicitor should ask for his legal costs, if any – although in practice he is unlikely to get them. *See:* LEGAL COSTS

If the verdict is 'guilty' the magistrates are told the defendant's 'antecedents' – any record of relevant convictions – before deciding the sentence.

Taking other offences into consideration

When a defendant has been convicted (or if he pleads guilty) he can ask for other offences, with which he has not been charged, to be 'taken into consideration'.

If the police do not object, the court may agree to take the extra offences into consideration in deciding the sentence. The advantage for the defendant is that he has then wiped the slate entirely clean, yet he cannot be given a higher sentence than the maximum for the one offence with which he was charged.

However, the other offences have to be similar to the one in the charge: a shoplifter can ask for other shoplifting offences to be considered, but cannot expect a court to take into account a more serious crime – say, burglary.

When a defendant is committed to a crown court

A defendant may be committed by a magistrates' court for trial by jury in a crown court in three ways.

Old-style committal All prosecution witnesses give their evidence verbally to the magistrates and are cross-examined by the defendant or his lawyer.

The evidence is written down by the court clerk and read out to the witnesses, who sign what they have said.

It is a long, slow process and is not normally used unless the defence believes that the prosecution case is especially weak, so that there is a good chance that the magistrates will agree to dismiss it, there and then.

There is, however, usually enough evidence to warrant a trial in the crown court, and the defendant is generally advised to keep the basis of his defence

a secret from the prosecution, until the trial.

Section 1 committal If the defendant agrees, and is legally represented, a simpler method of committal, allowed under Section 1 of the Criminal Justice Act 1967, can be used. It takes no more than a few minutes.

Instead of hearing the witnesses, the court receives their evidence in the form of typed depositions – with the accused's agreement. Copies of all the prosecution evidence are served on the defendant's solicitor, and, if the defendant agrees, the court formally orders committal.

Section 2 committal The accused agrees to have prosecution statements in writing but does not wish to accept committal.

There is a hearing, but without oral evidence by witnesses in court. Instead, the statements of the witnesses are read out and the magistrates then decide whether there is the basis of a case against the defendant.

After committal

There is usually a delay of several months between the committal and the crown court trial. During that time, if the defendant has not already applied for legal aid he should do so.

He or his solicitor should also try to get BAIL, if it has not already been granted by the magistrates.

If a defendant in a crown court case intends to rely on an ALIBI (evidence that he was elsewhere when the crime was committed), he must give notice to the prosecution not more than 7 days after being committed for trial and must supply details of any witnesses who are to support his alibi.

When the court issues a witness order

When a case is committed to the crown court, the magistrates order the various witnesses to attend the trial, by issuing 'full' or 'conditional' witness orders.

Under a full order, the witness must attend the crown court. Under a conditional order, when the defence does not dispute a particular witness's evidence, he need attend only if he is later notified that his evidence will be needed at the trial.

Trial in a crown court

The procedure in a crown court trial is similar to that in a magistrates' court, except that the case is heard by a judge and jury, usually in greater detail.

APPEALING AGAINST COURT DECISIONS

Defendants who are dissatisfied with a magistrates' court conviction or sentence or with the court's verdict on a point of law, may appeal in certain cases to the crown court and in others direct to the High Court.

Appeal against conviction
A defendant who is convicted after pleading not guilty is entitled to appeal to the crown court. The appeal takes the form of a complete re-hearing of the case by a judge sitting with at least two Justices of the Peace. There is no jury.

Appeal against sentence
Whether a defendant has pleaded guilty or not guilty, he is entitled to appeal to the crown court against the sentence imposed by the magistrates. The appeal is heard by a judge, sitting alone, or with magistrates, and he can increase or reduce the sentence.

Appeal on a point of law
If a defendant thinks that the magistrates have made a mistake on a point of law, he can appeal to the High Court, Queen's Bench Division, where the appeal will be heard by two or three judges.

If such an appeal fails, the defendant can attempt to take it to the House of Lords. But that can be done only if the case is considered to involve a point of law of 'general public importance' – and very few criminal cases get that far.

Crown court trial
A defendant convicted after pleading not guilty in a crown court can appeal against the verdict to the Court of Appeal, where the case is heard by three judges.
Appeal against sentence The Court of Appeal also deals with appeals against crown court sentences, whether the defendant has pleaded guilty or not.
Point of law The Court of Appeal deals with appeals on points of law and again the defendant has the right to take his appeal further, to the House of Lords. But again, very few cases get so far.

Trial in a crown court

The procedure in a crown court trial is similar to that in a magistrates' court, except that the case is heard by a judge and jury, usually in greater detail. The charges to be heard are set out in a document called an 'indictment', which need not be confined to those charges that were mentioned at the committal proceedings before the magistrates: it can contain any further charge that seems to be supported by the sworn statements of prosecution witnesses.

Each charge in an indictment is called a count. If an indictment contains charges against two or more people, any of the accused is entitled to ask the judge to 'sever the indictment' – that is, order that the applicant is tried separately from the other defendants.

The judge is not bound, however, to agree, even when one defendant is blaming another for the alleged crime.

CRIMINAL RECORD

How the police compile and keep information

Details of every person convicted of a serious crime in Britain are recorded and kept permanently under the supervision of the criminal records office, New Scotland Yard. Only the police have legal access to those records.

When someone is tried for a crime, the police supply the court with a list of any previous convictions – officially called 'antecedents', unofficially 'priors' or 'form'. If the person is found guilty, the list is given to his lawyer, who may make a final plea, and to the judge or magistrate so that it can be taken into account in passing sentence.

The provisions for REHABILITATION of offenders, which require most convictions to be forgotten in normal life after various times have elapsed, do not apply to police records. Previous offences can be recalled if a person is convicted again, no matter when.

Minor convictions under the Road Traffic Act, and for some other offences that the police do not classify as criminal behaviour – for example, drunkenness – do not go into police records unless the offender is already on file.

What else is kept on file

There is no legal restriction on the amount and type of other information the police can record. Details of people suspected of crimes, or even of potential criminal behaviour, are gathered from all parts of Britain and from abroad.

A citizen has no right to know what information, if any, is recorded about him. Police regulations, however, confine the use of such information strictly to the prevention or detection of crime.

CRIMINAL RESPONSIBILITY

When a child can be found guilty of an offence

A child under the age of 10 cannot be found guilty of a crime, in any circumstances, because the law presumes that anyone so young cannot know what is legally right or wrong.

A child under 10 who is involved in an offence can, however, be brought before a magistrates' court as being in need of care or control, and may be put into the care of the local authority. *See:* CHILDREN IN CARE

Between 10 and 14

Between the ages of 10 and 14, a child is still presumed not to know what is legally right or wrong, unless it can be proved otherwise. If it is proved that a child had the necessary knowledge, he or she can be convicted and put in care.

A boy aged under 14 cannot be found guilty of rape unless he acted in conjunction with someone else who was aged over 14 at the time.

Children over the age of 14 can be found guilty of any offence except cruelty to another child. Only someone over 16 can be guilty of child cruelty.

CROSS-PETITION

When a divorce is contested

When a marriage partner files a petition for divorce, nullity of marriage or judicial separation, the respondent, or other partner, will either not defend the petition or will file an answer denying the allegations made against him and asking for the petition to be dismissed.

In some cases, however, the respondent will make counter-allegations in the answer claiming that the petitioner caused the breakdown of the marriage, and that the respondent rather than the petitioner should be granted a divorce decree. This part of the answer is known as the cross-petition. *See:* DIVORCE

CROWN

The symbol of the power of the state

The term 'Crown' means more than the sovereign: in law it includes all central government departments and their agents. The term Crown liability, therefore, covers the action of civil servants, servicemen and other government employees.

The legal liability of the Crown is much the same as that of ordinary companies and individual people. So if the chauffeur of a Royal or official car knocks someone down, the injured person can sue for damages in exactly the same way as against any other person.

There are, however, a very few exceptions. A soldier who is hurt through the negligence of another serviceman or who is injured on Crown property cannot claim damages in the ordinary courts. *See:* ARMED FORCES

A civil servant or serviceman who is dismissed does not have the same right to claim for wrongful DISMISSAL as a worker in industry.

CROWN COURT

Where an accused person is tried by jury

All the most serious criminal cases, such as burglary, robbery with violence, rape, manslaughter and murder, are tried before a judge and jury in a crown court – which has replaced the ancient assize court and quarter sessions.

Anyone charged with an indictable offence – one serious enough to be tried by a jury – appears first before magistrates who decide if there is a case to answer. If they decide that there is, he is sent for trial to the crown court.

Less serious charges – for example, theft and assault – can be tried in a magistrates' court, but the defendant or magistrates may insist on trial by jury in a crown court. The least serious offences – called summary offences – cannot be tried in the crown court but must be tried in the magistrates' court.

If a defendant is convicted in a magistrates' court, but the bench decides that, because of his past record, he deserves a heavier penalty than they can impose, he can be sent to the crown court for sentence.

CUSTODY OF CHILDREN

When courts decide who should look after a child

When there is a dispute between parents about who should have custody of a child below the age of 18, it may have to be settled in court. Neither parent of a legitimate child has any greater legal claim than the other.

The court will always regard the welfare of the child as the first and most important consideration. That principle was laid down in the Guardianship of Infants Act 1925. Although in most

APPLYING TO THE MAGISTRATES

Magistrates' courts have wide powers, in domestic proceedings, to make custody orders. Whether or not one parent's complaint about the other is proved, the courts can make custody, supervision or care orders. *See:* CHILDREN IN CARE; MATRIMONIAL ORDER

However, when a person seeks custody of a child in the magistrates' court, the parties are not told, until the hearing, what allegations (if any) are to be made.

For that reason, difficult cases are often brought in the higher courts.

An appeal against a custody order made by magistrates goes to the Family Division of the High Court.

cases, courts commit children to the custody of an individual they also have power, and sometimes exercise it, to commit a child to the care of a local authority. *See:* CHILDREN IN CARE

When the parents separate

In the High Court or county court where a couple are seeking divorce, nul-

lity or judicial separation, the court may make orders for the custody and education of any 'child of the family', which includes any child – except an official foster child – who has been treated as one of the family.

Temporary custody After the proceedings have been started and the petition has been served on the respondent by the petitioner, there is usually some delay before the case can be dealt with. *See:* DIVORCE

During that period either parent may ask the court to decide the custody of any children of the family until the case is heard. The court will normally make what is called an interim order without going into full details of the case, and usually orders the child to remain with whichever parent had care of the child when the case was started. A full decision on who should have custody of the children is often postponed until after the DECREE NISI, although it can be made beforehand.

Even when the conduct of one parent has caused the breakdown of the marriage, the custody of the child will not necessarily be given to the other partner. In many cases the welfare of a young child requires that it should be looked after by its mother. In such cases the mother is unlikely to be deprived of custody because of her conduct, unless that conduct is likely to endanger the child's moral or physical welfare.

Agreement between the parties as to who should have custody and access is always preferable to a court order. It avoids any unpleasantness that might upset the child. But because the court must always consider the child's welfare as paramount it may sometimes disagree with these arrangements and make an order which is against the parents' wishes.

If there is a particularly bitter dispute between parents, the court may think it necessary for the child's interest to be represented separately at the hearing. In this case it will make an order for appointment of a GUARDIAN ad litem.

Access agreements When the court grants custody to one parent it will usually allow the other access to the child for certain periods, such as weekends. If no custody decision is made, either by agreement or by court order, the DECREE ABSOLUTE is unlikely to be granted. *See:* ACCESS TO CHILDREN

Special cases If there are exceptional circumstances which make it impractical or undesirable for either parent, or anyone else, to have custody, the court may make an order committing the child to the care of the local authority – provided only that the child is not over 17 and that the court has heard the view of social workers.

If one parent is given custody of a child and the court thinks that the parent needs advice and assistance in looking after the child, it may also make a SUPERVISION ORDER so that the child's progress can be monitored by the court welfare officer, who is a PROBATION officer.

In other complicated cases, divorce court judges can direct that a child should be made a WARD OF COURT, which means that the custody of the child is vested directly in the High Court and the question of the child's care is decided by a High Court judge.

Appealing against a custody order

Appeals against custody orders, whether made in a county court or the Family Division of the High Court, go to the Court of Appeal. Notice of appeal must be given to the other party and to the Court of Appeal within 14 days of the order being made. Because the procedure is complicated, it is essential to enlist the help of a solicitor and barrister.

The three Court of Appeal judges do not re-hear the evidence presented to the divorce court. Fresh evidence can be introduced only in special circumstances, if, for example, one of the parents was convicted of a serious offence since the original hearing. The judges read sworn statements, the welfare report and the divorce judge's decision and listen to arguments from both sides.

The court will allow an appeal only if it considers that the judge clearly made a wrong decision. If the court considers the original hearing was not properly conducted it can order a re-hearing, usually before another judge.

How a court hears a case for custody of children

Custody cases are heard by a judge in private, usually a county court judge. If

WHEN A THIRD PARTY MAY INTERVENE IN CUSTODY PROCEEDINGS

In most cases only a parent or guardian may apply to the court for custody of a child. But in divorce proceedings, when one or both parents claim custody of a child a third party – for example a grandparent – may ask the court for leave to intervene.

Permission can be given by a judge, but notice of the application for permission must be served on the other parties.

If the third person has good reason to be heard, his application is granted and he is called the 'intervener'. He can then make his custody application when the court hears the parents' application.

If he is not granted leave to intervene, or is unable to do so because the custody is not being decided in divorce, judicial separation or nullity proceedings, a non-parent may be able to seek an order for care and control by applying to the High Court in wardship proceedings.

---

there has been a defended divorce then it will be heard by a High Court judge, also sitting in private. The parties are usually legally represented, and LEGAL AID may be available.

Before the case is heard, the evidence is put in the form of sworn statements which are filed in the court and served on the parties so that they and the judge know what the issues are. The people who made the statements can then be cross-examined by the other party or their lawyers. It is often possible for much of the evidence to be agreed by both sides before the hearing.

To help the judge reach his decision, each divorce court has one or more welfare officers whose report is submitted to the judge before the hearing. The officer will be called to give evidence only if the contents of his report are seriously disputed or if the judge wants further information. *See:* COURT WELFARE OFFICER

At the hearing the lawyer for the party making the application makes an opening speech in which the facts are outlined and arguments in favour of the applicant's case are put forward.

The applicant will then give evidence and answer questions put by his own lawyer and by the lawyer for the respondent, or by the respondent himself if he does not have a lawyer.

The procedure is then reversed. The respondent or his lawyer sets out his case and calls witnesses, before addressing the judge. Finally, the applicant or his lawyer has a chance to sum up his case before any decision is made.

Custody without divorce

If a child's parents have separated but are not seeking a divorce, they can still ask a court to decide which of them is to have custody. The application can be made to a magistrates' court, a county court or the High Court.

Any court able to deal with custody cases can put a child in the custody not only of one parent or the other, but also of someone else – for example, a foster parent or grandparent.

However, an application to the court can be made only by one of the parents. Anyone else seeking custody, when divorce is not being sought, must start proceedings to have the child protected as a ward of the court.

Illegitimate children

The mother of an illegitimate child has full legal right to the custody of the child. That right can only be over-ruled by a court order or by the local authority taking the child into care. The father has no rights whatsoever but can apply to the court for an order for custody of the child.

Altering or revoking a custody order

Custody orders can be discharged or varied by the court and end automatically when the child is 18.

In practice, courts are reluctant to make any order against the wishes of a child old enough to know his own mind. They will not generally make or enforce orders against the will of any child over 16.

For example, if a custody order is made in favour of one parent when a child is 10, and the child decides when he is 16 to go to live with the other parent, the court is unlikely to order the child's return.

Foreign custody orders

If one partner in a broken marriage goes to live abroad, the partner remaining in Britain can apply for a custody order to prevent any children from being taken out of the country. *See also:* WARD OF COURT

If a partner who goes abroad obtains a rival custody order from a foreign court, the British courts will usually enforce that order if it is considered to be in the best interests of the child or children.

CUSTOMS DUTY

The tax a traveller pays on goods brought home

A traveller returning to Britain with foreign goods worth more than the permitted amount may have to pay customs duty on the excess goods.

Notices at the port or airport inform travellers which value of goods are duty-free, and a customs officer may ask a traveller if he has goods other than those to declare.

It is a criminal offence, carrying severe penalties, not to declare goods that are subject to duty. If you are in any doubt about goods you are carrying, ask the customs officer. The possible penalty for fraudulent evasion of customs

PAYING DUTY ON GOODS BROUGHT BACK FROM ABROAD

A traveller caught trying to bring undeclared goods into Britain can be heavily fined or even imprisoned. He cannot refuse to be searched by customs officers.

duty is a fine of three times the value of the goods involved or £100, whichever is the higher, and/or imprisonment of up to 2 years.

Duty-free allowance The duty-free allowance for each traveller in 1980 was: From non-EEC countries or if goods are bought in a duty-free shop:
1. 200 cigarettes; or 100 cigarillos (cigars weighing not more than 3 grammes); or 50 large cigars; or 250 grammes of smoking tobacco.
2. 1 litre of alcoholic drink more than 38.8° proof; or 2 litres of drink of 38.8° proof or less; or 2 litres of fortified wine (such as sherry) or sparkling wine; plus, in addition to any of these, 2 litres of unfortified, still (ordinary table) wine.
3. 50 grammes of perfume and 0.25 litre of toilet water.
4. Articles of any other description up to a value of £28.
From EEC countries and goods not bought in a duty-free shop:
1. 300 cigarettes; or 150 cigarillos; or 75 large cigars; or 400 grammes of smoking tobacco.
2. 1.5 litres of alcoholic drink more than 38.8° proof; or 3 litres of drink of 38.8° proof or less; or 3 litres of fortified wine or sparkling wine; plus, in addition to any of these, 4 litres of unfortified, still wine.
3. 75 grammes of perfume and 0.375 litre of toilet water.
4. Articles of any other description up to a value of £120.

These allowances apply also to day trippers abroad, but not if you just take a boat trip and do not set foot on foreign soil.

There are no tobacco and alcohol allowances for travellers under 17.

Search and seizure A customs officer, policeman, member of the armed forces or coastguard can stop and search a vehicle or vessel if he believes it may be carrying goods subject to duty. If undeclared goods are found, the vehicle or vessel containing them can be forfeited as well as the goods.

A customs officer can also search a person suspected of possessing undeclared goods. But the suspect can ask to be taken before a magistrate or the Chief Customs Officer, who must then decide whether there are sufficient grounds for a search. There is no legal right simply to refuse to be searched by a customs officer.

CYCLING

Rules for taking a bicycle on the road

Although a court cannot imprison or disqualify a cyclist, it can fine him as much as it does a motorist for certain offences. For example, a cyclist who disobeys a traffic sign or light is liable to the same maximum fine as a motorist – £100.

Cycling offences A cyclist must not hold on to motor vehicles in order to be towed. Nor must he carry a passenger – unless the bicycle is specially built or adapted to carry another person safely.

It is an offence to cycle carelessly or inconsiderately – for example, to pull out from a kerb or line of traffic without signalling, to ride too far from the kerb or to have insufficient control of the bicycle, perhaps through carrying something heavy under one arm.

Cyclists do not need to obey yellow 'no parking' lines, but it is an offence to leave a bicycle in a dangerous position, or on a footpath or traffic clearway.

The law treats a dismounted cyclist as a rider, not as a pedestrian. Therefore he cannot ignore a TRAFFIC SIGN or wheel his bicycle through traffic lights that are against him. A dismounted rider, however, is entitled to wheel his bicycle over a pedestrian crossing – whether to continue his journey or to cross a road as a pedestrian.

Lights Bicycles must be fitted at the back with a red light and reflector and at the front with a white light. The cyclist must have the lights on when riding at night or in poor visibility during the day. There is no need to have the lights on if the bicycle is stationary or if it is simply being wheeled along beside the kerb.

Brakes Bicycles with wheels that are more than 18 in. diameter must have a brake for each wheel. Bicycles with

PENALTIES FOR CYCLING OFFENCES
What it can cost to ride carelessly or unlawfully

	Offence	Maximum fine
Brakes	Riding or permitting use with defective brakes.	£50
	Selling or offering for sale bicycle with defective brakes.	£100
Lights	Riding or permitting use of bicycle with defective lights at night.	£100
	Riding or permitting use of bicycle with defective lights in poor visibility.	£100
Parking	Leaving bicycle in a dangerous position.	£100
	Leaving bicycle on footpath.	£100
	Leaving bicycle on clearway.	£100
Riding	On footpath.	£10
	Careless or inconsiderate riding.	£20
	Reckless riding.	£50
	Riding whilst unfit.	£50
	Taking hold of another vehicle.	£20
	Carrying a passenger.	£20
	Unauthorised racing.	£20
Signs and signals	Disobeying signal given by police constable or traffic warden.	£100
	Disobeying traffic signs, traffic lights or white lines.	£100
	Failing to accord precedence to pedestrian, or overtaking on approach to crossing.	£100

smaller wheels and bicycles with a fixed wheel need only one brake at the front. The police are entitled to check that a bicycle's brakes are working efficiently.

It is an offence to sell a bicycle with faulty brakes unless the seller can show that he had good reason to believe that the bicycle would not be used until the brakes were repaired.

Drunkenness It is an offence for anyone to ride a bicycle while he is incapable of controlling it properly because of drunkenness or the effect of drugs.

The police can arrest a drunken cyclist but they cannot test him with a Breathalyser or take a sample of his blood or urine. They may call a doctor to pronounce on the cyclist's fitness to ride, but if the doctor asks for a specimen of blood or urine, the cyclist has the right to refuse.

Even if the cyclist does supply a sample, it cannot be used in evidence against him. An alcohol level in a cyclist's blood above the legal level for a motorist is not considered necessarily to render a cyclist unfit to ride. The court's decision on whether the cyclist was unfit to ride is usually made on the evidence of the arresting policeman and sometimes on the opinion of a doctor.

Child cyclists A child of any age is legally allowed to ride a bicycle on a public road, but the parents of all child cyclists are responsible for ensuring that the child knows how to ride properly. If a child causes an accident because he or she is unfit to ride on a public road, the parent can be held liable. Parents are also responsible for ensuring that the brakes and lights on a child's bicycle work efficiently.

DAMAGES

Compensation for injury, loss or damage

If you suffer injury, loss or damage as the result of someone else's action or failure to act, you can claim damages, or compensation, from him if you can prove:

● That the defendant committed a wrong – either a TORT or a breach of CONTRACT.

● That the wrong directly caused your injury, loss or damage.

● That the harm to you was foreseeable by the defendant.

When someone is directly to blame

The issue of whether or not the defendant is directly to blame is usually straightforward.

When, through careless driving, a motorist knocks down a child and breaks its leg, the motorist is directly to blame for the injury.

When after you have paid someone £5 to mend your vacuum cleaner it still does not work, the repairer's breach of contract has directly caused you a loss of £5.

On the other hand, if a hotel at which you booked your holiday tells you at the last minute that it has no accommodation, and while you are driving to another hotel you are injured in a road accident, that is not the fault of the first hotel. The hotel's breach of contract is not the direct cause of your injury – you could have been injured in an accident even if you had been driving to the first hotel.

When the consequences were foreseeable

The issue of whether an injury, loss or damage was foreseeable is clear in principle. If a motorist knocks you down he can foresee that as a result you might lose earnings through being unable to work. But he cannot possibly foresee

> ### THE HERDSMAN WHO BECAME ILL
>
> *To make a successful claim for damages you have to prove that the defendant could foresee the consequences of his action or inaction.*
>
> William Tremain worked as a herdsman on a farm in Devon. Farmer Pike allowed his farm to become infested with rats, and Tremain, by putting his hands in a water trough infected by rats' urine, contracted a painful and debilitating disease. Tremain claimed damages against the farmer.
>
> #### DECISION
> The court held that Farmer Pike could have foreseen that the herdsman's food might become poisoned by the rats, but not that the rats might infect the water in the trough. It dismissed Tremain's claim.

that by knocking you down he has prevented you from posting a winning football coupon. You can claim damages from him for loss of earnings, but not for the fortune that you missed winning on the pools.

How damages are assessed

If a court is satisfied that the injury, loss or damage was a direct cause of the wrong and was foreseeable, it has to decide how much compensation should be paid.

The general approach, with a loss that is purely financial, is to restore the claimant to the financial position he would have been in if the wrong had not prevented him from earning.

In the case of defective goods, the compensation may be the cost of having the goods put into the condition they should have been in when the manufacturer or supplier sold them.

Some kinds of damages cannot be recovered. For example, there is no compensation for the grief of a relative after a FATAL ACCIDENT.

See also: CRIMINAL INJURIES
EMPLOYMENT CONTRACT
PERSONAL INJURY
REDUNDANCY

DANGEROUS ANIMAL

Anyone who keeps an animal is obliged by law to see that it does not cause injury or damage to other people. Most household pets, except dogs and dangerous animals, can be kept without a licence. *See:* ANIMAL

DANGEROUS DRIVING

The charge of 'dangerous driving' no longer exists in law. Someone who is accused of driving dangerously is usually charged with RECKLESS DRIVING.

DANGEROUS GOODS

Claiming from seller or manufacturer

Some goods are dangerous because they are unfit for their purposes. For example, if a child's cuddly toy has dangerous wires sticking out of it, the toy is not suitably made, and the buyer can claim his money back from the seller. If someone is injured because of a defect, the injured person can sue for damages. *See:* CONSUMER SAFETY; DEFECTIVE GOODS

Other goods may be dangerous because they carry insufficient warning about their potential harmful effects. A buyer who suffers injury or loss, as a result of using such goods, can sue the manufacturer.

UNSUITABLE FOR CHILDREN

A dangerous article may be one either unfit for its purpose or offering a potential hazard.

Toy Dept

> ### THE LABORATORY THAT EXPLODED
>
> In 1969 B.D.H. Chemicals supplied Vacwell Engineering Co. with a chemical in glass vessels. The vessels were labelled 'Harmful Vapour' but were not marked with any reference to the violent reaction of the chemical to water.
>
> A physicist who was washing the full vessels in a sink dropped one.
>
> There was an explosion, which killed the physicist and destroyed the laboratory.
>
> The engineering company sued the chemical manufacturers for supplying dangerous goods; it claimed £375,000 including £300,000 for lost profits.
>
> #### DECISION
>
> The court awarded the engineering company the damages claimed. However, the chemical manufacturers appealed and the matter was settled on agreed terms.

DAY CARE CENTRE

Daily companionship, therapy and care for people in need

Local authorities and voluntary organisations run day care centres for the old, the disabled, the mentally ill or mentally handicapped, people recovering from alcoholism or drug addiction and others in need.

The centres vary considerably in their activities. Those for the very old and frail feed and care for people unable to look after themselves but who do not want to go into an institution; they also offer support, advice and social activities. The centres provide transport from and to their homes.

Centres for the elderly or disabled provide, in addition to companionship and cooked meals, occupational therapy, discussion groups – and sometimes light industrial work for pocket money.

The only charges are small ones for meals and drinks.

Daily care is also provided by adult training centres – specialised, work-orientated training centres for adult mentally handicapped people.

To arrange for someone to attend a local authority centre, apply to the authority's social services department. Attendance at centres run by voluntary organisations is also usually arranged through that same department. However, you can approach such an organisation direct: addresses can be obtained from the local authority or a CITIZENS ADVICE BUREAU

DAY NURSERIES

Nursery care for children under five

Day nurseries provide care for children under 5 years of age – particularly those whose mothers go out to work. Most councils run nurseries, but there is no automatic right to a place in one, and demand is heavy.

Council authorities generally cater for the very few children whose parents are in especially difficult circumstances. Many other nursery places are provided privately by voluntary organisations and employers and private individuals.

Rules for council nurseries Most council-run nurseries open from 8 a.m. to 6 p.m., 5 days a week, including during school holidays. They can accept children from 6 weeks old, but in practice many nurseries will not take children under 2 years.

Children are allocated places by the local social services department, normally on the recommendation of a social worker.

Priority is always given to a child who might be at risk if the mother had to cope with him all day. A child whose mother is unsupported and has to go out to work may also be given a nursery place.

Charges at council-run nurseries vary from a flat £1 a day to a maximum of £25 a week, according to the parents' income and the council's policy.

Private nurseries A nursery that is not run by a council has to be registered and supervised by it.

Most councils insist that anyone who runs a private day nursery must be a trained nursery nurse, although the staff need not be trained. They also lay down health and safety regulations that must be followed and specify the maximum number of children for each member of staff – the ratio is usually between eight and ten children to one staff member.

There is normally a flat-rate charge for all children, fixed by the nursery and not by the council. Some private nurseries give full-time care, but others offer only a part-time service.

Every council social services department has a list of day nurseries.

Employers' nurseries Some companies run nurseries at work, and these are subject to the same controls as private nurseries. The nursery is usually subsidised by the company, although parents pay a fee.

Setting up a nursery

Anyone who wishes to set up a private day nursery must apply to the local authority social services department. The department will check the premises for health and fire risks and general suitability.

The council will also require evidence, such as a diploma or references, of the training and experience of the person who is to run the nursery.

Meals provided

Nurseries provide equipment for play suitable to the age of the children in their care. The children play, if possible, outdoors and indoors. They should be given a break, a cooked lunch and tea in the course of the day.

DEAFNESS

Help and training for those who cannot hear

Someone who becomes deaf or hard of hearing should ask his doctor to refer him to a specialist, called an audiologist. All treatment, including the provision of a hearing aid, is available free under the National Health Service.

Deaf or partially deaf people may be entitled to DISABLEMENT BENEFIT, and to additional social security allowances if their disability prevents them from working. The benefits can be claimed from a local social security office on form BI 100A.

To find out about the special facilities for deaf people in your area, contact the local social services department.

Volunteers who help

Few authorities have social workers specially trained to help the deaf, but in most areas voluntary organisations such as the Royal National Institute for the Deaf (RNID) and the Royal Association in Aid of the Deaf and Dumb (RADD) are available to help. If there is no local office in your area, contact the head office at the Royal National

---

HOW THE STATE PROVIDES FOR THE UNDER-FIVES

Council facilities to take care of young children when mother is at work

Local councils are responsible for the safety and welfare of children in private day nurseries as well as of children in their own centres. They must satisfy themselves that the premises are adequate and inspect them frequently. A suitably qualified person must be in charge, and a limit is fixed on the number of children for which the nursery can cater. At all times, one helper must be in attendance for every 8 or 10 children – whatever proportion the council has laid down. There must also be enough toys and equipment suited to the ages of all the boys and girls attending the nursery. If the children attend all day, there must be facilities for a properly cooked meal and periods of rest. Where possible, councils usually seek to provide playing space out of doors as well as inside, but they do not always succeed in doing so in inner city areas.

Institute for the Deaf, or the Royal Association in Aid of the Deaf and Dumb.

When a child is affected

To enable a deaf child to learn to speak, his hearing impairment must be found as early as possible. Local child health clinics test babies' hearing from 6 weeks old as part of their regular checks on the development of infants. There is a second test at the age of 6 months and a third, more comprehensive, examination at the age of 8 months.

Advice and guidance for parents of deaf babies are available from health visitors and the child health clinic. If no qualified social worker is available, the parents can be referred to organisations such as the National Deaf Children's Society, which provides information, advice, financial help, holidays and special toys and equipment. They also arrange local groups so that parents can meet and support one another.

Education

The local authority education department is responsible for the education of deaf children. If it does not provide special facilities in its own schools, it can pay for children for whom it is responsible to attend schools run by voluntary organisations for the deaf. Children who live in rural areas may have to become boarders.

Some schools for the deaf have nursery units, and accept children from the age of 2. *See:* SPECIAL EDUCATION

When an adult is deaf

Some local authorities run free lip-reading classes and social clubs for the deaf, but in most areas the services for adults are provided by the voluntary organisations such as the RNID and the RADD. They offer information and advice on finding employment and all the other problems of deafness, as well as arranging many social activities. All these services are free.

The address of the nearest branch of either organisation can be found in the telephone directory, or be obtained from the local authority social services department.

Special help for the elderly

Local authorities must provide residential accommodation for the elderly, including those who are deaf. Such homes have staff specially trained in communicating with the deaf, and many run social activities aimed at improving communication. For details of help in your area, contact the council's social services department.

If the person concerned prefers to enter a special home run by a voluntary organisation – for example, if he or she is Jewish and wants to be in the care of others of the same faith – the local authority, subject to a means test, may contribute towards the cost.

DEATH

What must be done when a life ends

Only a registered doctor is legally entitled to decide that someone has died and to give evidence in legal proceedings about the fact of the death and what caused it.

A doctor who finds neither pulse nor breathing in a body can normally presume that the person is dead.

However, if the doctor fails to carry out the tests, or if he does them inadequately, he may wrongly decide that a live patient is dead, and necessary medical treatment may be ended.

If he does so, and the patient dies or suffers damage, the doctor can be sued for MEDICAL NEGLIGENCE – either by the patient's dependants or by the patient, if he survives. *See also:* LIFE SUPPORT SYSTEM

Certifying a death   When someone dies, the death and its cause must be certified by a doctor and reported to the Registrar. If the doctor is suspicious about the cause of death it must be reported to a CORONER for investigation. *See also:* DEATH, Registration of

What happens to property

When someone dies, all that he possesses – even his body – passes to his personal representatives. If he has left a will, at least one representative acts as his EXECUTOR. If there is no will his representatives are called administrators.

The executors or administrators have an absolute right to decide what is to happen to the body – whether it will be cremated, if not, where it will be buried, with what funeral rite, and whether any organs can be donated to a hospital. *See:* TRANSPLANT

Any wishes expressed in the will, as to the disposal of the body and any transplant, are generally carried out, but the personal representatives are not obliged to do so.

If the dead person carried a card permitting organs to be used in transplants, or made such a provision in his will, the representatives could still forbid a transplant. A surgeon, however, could safely overrule their objections, because the representatives would be entitled only to sue for damages, and a transplant would not have caused any damage to the estate. Nor would he have committed any criminal offence.

WHEN A BRITON DIES ABROAD

When a British citizen dies abroad, the death must be registered in accordance with the laws of the country in which he dies. It should also be registered with the BRITISH EMBASSY or consul.

Some countries require immediate burial or cremation. Otherwise, the executors or next-of-kin may decide to bring the body back to Britain. To make local arrangements abroad, ask the British consul.

When a body is brought back to Britain, the CORONER for the district in which the body is to be buried must be informed before the burial.

In cases where he wishes to ascertain the cause of death, the coroner will require an inquest to be held before allowing the burial to go ahead. Even if there has been a foreign inquest he can hold another if he is not satisfied.

When a foreigner dies in Britain

The death of a foreigner in Britain must be registered at the Registry of Deaths here like any other death. If the relatives wish to take the body out of the country, they must inform the local coroner – who may already have been informed of the death by a doctor who examined the body. The coroner has 4 clear days, after being notified of a death by next-of-kin, to decide whether the body can be removed. If he decides that it cannot, because he has not fully satisfied himself as to the cause of death, he can detain the body for as long as he wishes, and hold an inquest.

HELP IN THE HOME WHEN SOMEONE IS DYING

When someone is dying and being nursed at home by the family, a wide range of services is provided by the local council and the health authority.

Assistance includes visits by social workers, health visitors, nurses and home helps. Special beds, back rests, bed tables and hoists may also be supplied, as well as incontinence pads and an incontinence laundry service.

Social workers may give advice to the dying person's family and continue to visit for some time after his death.

Claims and contracts

Death has many legal consequences. It usually ends certain types of contract, including the right of a spouse or ex-spouse to MAINTENANCE, for example. In some cases, however, the courts can order maintenance to be paid to a widow, widower or child out of a dead person's estate.

In most cases, any proceedings concerning the status of a dependant – such as DIVORCE, SEPARATION, NULLITY or legitimacy – end if one or other party to the proceedings dies. Death also ends LIBEL AND SLANDER proceedings – whichever party has died.

It is, however, in certain rare cases, possible to seek a declaratory judgment even after death to have a legitimacy dispute settled or to have a marriage declared void.

If a legal claim by or against a person is outstanding when he dies, it can continue, but only if brought on behalf of, or against, his estate.

When someone dies financially insolvent, a trustee in BANKRUPTCY may be appointed to distribute whatever assets are available from the estate.

Death caused by negligence

If someone is killed by another person's NEGLIGENCE – for example, by careless driving – his executor or administrators can, within 3 years, sue for damages on behalf of his estate.

Claims can be made for loss of expectation of life and for FUNERAL expenses and also by dependants for loss of future support. Courts do not award large damages for loss of life, even if the person was young and healthy before the incident that led to his death. But dependants may be awarded substantial damages for the loss of financial support that they could have expected if the person had lived. *See:* FATAL ACCIDENT

Death after an assault If someone dies as a result of a criminal assault, the person responsible can be charged with MURDER only if death occurs within a year and a day of the assault. If death occurs after a year and a day the assailant would be charged with causing grievous bodily harm or attempted murder.

If someone dies alone When someone dies after living alone, and has no known relatives, and no one has arranged burial or cremation, the local council must do so. It can also dispose of the deceased's estate.

DEATH, Registration of

Legal procedures when someone dies

Any death must be reported within 5 days, to the registrar of births and deaths for the area in which it occurs.

Three certificates must be obtained:
1. A medical certificate of death, issued free, stating the cause of death and completed and signed by a doctor who has examined the body.

If for any reason the doctor does not issue a certificate of death immediately, a relative who was present at the death or during the last illness – or who lives in the same registration district as the dead person did – has a right to insist on one.

If someone dies in hospital, the hospital staff generally arranges for a doctor to examine the body and prepare the certificate. When someone dies outside hospital, a doctor should be called immediately – preferably one who has treated the dead person in his or her last illness.

If a different doctor is called, the death – however it occurred – is reported to the district CORONER and there may be an INQUEST, delaying registration and funeral.
2. A disposal certificate allowing the body to be buried or cremated, issued free of charge by the registrar for the district where the death occurred.

Without the disposal certificate, an undertaker cannot legally carry out a funeral. The certificate will not be issued without a medical certificate.
3. A death certificate, also issued by the registrar on production of a medical certificate.

The death certificate is a copy of the entry in the official Register of Deaths, and is needed, for example, to claim life-insurance benefits. It costs £1.50.
Finding the registrar The address of the local registrar should be supplied by the doctor who issues the medical certificate of death. It can also be found in the telephone directory, under 'Registration'.

Whoever is responsible for registering the death must do so in person. If that is not possible within 5 days – for example, because the responsible person is ill – send the registrar written notice of the death, with the medical certificate issued by a doctor.

If the registrar decides that the death does not have to be reported to the coroner, he may immediately issue a disposal certificate, permitting burial, but not cremation.

WHO SHOULD INFORM THE REGISTRAR

The following people, in order of precedence, are legally obliged to have a death registered. Anyone responsible for registering a death who fails to do so may be fined up to £100 or sentenced to 6 months' imprisonment.

If death occurs in a house or in hospital
● A relative of the dead person, who was present at death.
● A relative of the dead person, in attendance during the last illness.
● A relative of the dead person living or present in the registration district in which death occurred.
● Anyone present at the death.
● Anyone living in the same premises.
● The person responsible for having the body buried or cremated.

If death occurs elsewhere
● Any relative of the dead person who knows any of the details that need to be registered.
● Anyone present at the death.
● Anyone who found or took charge of the body.
● Anyone responsible for having the body buried or cremated.

The person responsible for registering the death must then go to the registrar within 14 days of the death, to complete the registration.

What the registrar requires

If you have to get a death registered, take the Notice to Informant and the dead person's Health Service medical card to the registrar – and also the medical certificate, if the doctor hands it to you instead of sending it direct.

The registrar will ask you the full names of the dead person, his or her place and date of birth, occupation, place and date of death and the address where the person normally lived.

You will also be asked if the person was receiving a pension or allowance from public funds and – if he or she was

married – the age of the surviving widow or widower.

Once the registrar has that information, he will register the death and issue the disposal certificate. Take the certificate to the undertaker.

Provided that the necessary documents are available and the death does not have to be reported to the coroner, it is possible for a death to be registered on the day that it happens.

When a death is reported to the coroner

The medical certificate of death not only confirms that the person is dead, but must also state the causes from which he or she died.

If the causes are uncertain, or if death

resulted from an accident or violence, or occurred in suspicious circumstances, the fact must be reported to the district coroner. He may then decide that further investigation is needed in the form of a POST-MORTEM and inquest.

Once the coroner has been notified of a death, no death certificate can be issued and no funeral can take place until the coroner has given permission.

Anyone who feels a death should be investigated can report it to the district coroner, whose address appears under 'Courts' in the local telephone directory.

The doctor conducting the medical examination may decide the coroner should be notified. If he does, he will mark the medical certificate in Box A, signifying that it cannot be used to have

---

WRITTEN EVIDENCE OF THE CAUSE OF DEATH

A doctor's duty to examine a person who has died and state the reasons for his death

The doctor also informs the registrar on the back of the certificate whether he has notified the coroner of the death

Decisions on holding post-mortems rest with the coroner, but much depends on the information given to him by the doctor in the case

The death should be registered by a close relative, anyone present when it happened, the head of the household, or the person arranging the funeral

If a doctor signs the death certificate without informing the coroner, the registrar of births, marriages and deaths issues a certificate for burial straight away. If the doctor has not attended the patient in the 14 days before the patient's death, however, or if he is not satisfied about the cause of death, he must inform the coroner. In that case, the registrar issues a burial certificate only after the coroner tells him to.

the death registered until the coroner has finished his investigation. However, legal responsibility for notifying the coroner of a death rests with the registrar of births and deaths. He must refuse to register, and must report, any death if:

● The dead person was not attended by a doctor during his last illness.

● There is no properly completed medical certificate of cause of death.

● The doctor who signed the medical certificate did not see the dead person after death, nor in the 14 days before death.

● The cause of death is unknown.

● Death was unnatural, or the result of violence or neglect, or of abortion, or occurred in suspicious circumstances.

● Death occurred during an operation, or before recovery from the effects of an anaesthetic.

● Death was due to industrial disease or industrial poisoning.

Sometimes a doctor may make a mis-

THE CERTIFICATE THAT THE DEATH HAS BEEN REGISTERED

When a dead person's particulars are entered in the official Register of Deaths and a copy of the entry issued

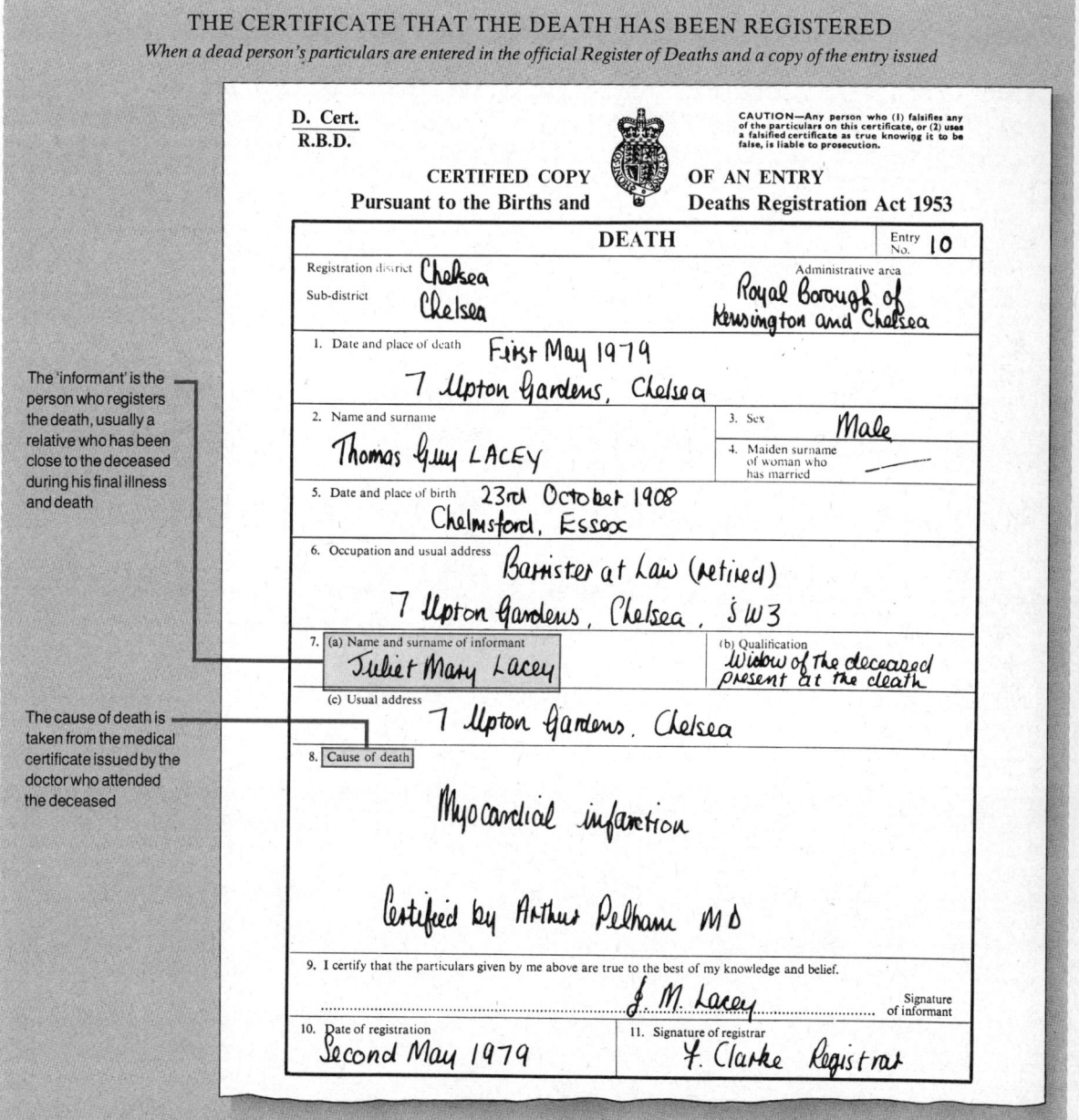

The 'informant' is the person who registers the death, usually a relative who has been close to the deceased during his final illness and death

The cause of death is taken from the medical certificate issued by the doctor who attended the deceased

D. Cert.
R.B.D.

CAUTION—Any person who (1) falsifies any of the particulars on this certificate, or (2) uses a falsified certificate as true knowing it to be false, is liable to prosecution.

CERTIFIED COPY OF AN ENTRY
Pursuant to the Births and Deaths Registration Act 1953

DEATH   Entry No. **10**

Registration district *Chelsea*   Administrative area *Royal Borough of Kensington and Chelsea*
Sub-district *Chelsea*

1. Date and place of death *First May 1979 7 Upton Gardens, Chelsea*

2. Name and surname *Thomas Guy LACEY*   3. Sex *Male*

4. Maiden surname of woman who has married —

5. Date and place of birth *23rd October 1908 Chelmsford, Essex*

6. Occupation and usual address *Barrister at Law (retired) 7 Upton Gardens, Chelsea, SW3*

7. (a) Name and surname of informant *Juliet Mary Lacey*

(b) Qualification *Widow of the deceased present at the death*

(c) Usual address *7 Upton Gardens, Chelsea*

8. Cause of death *Myocardial infarction*

Certified by Arthur Pelham MD

9. I certify that the particulars given by me above are true to the best of my knowledge and belief.

.... *J. M. Lacey* .... Signature of informant

10. Date of registration *Second May 1979*

11. Signature of registrar *F. Clarke Registrar*

A person who is responsible for registering someone's death must give particulars of that person, including his or her full name, place and date of birth, occupation, date of death and where that person lived, to the local registrar of births, marriages and deaths. The registrar notes the details in the official Register of Deaths and provides a copy of that entry as a death certificate before issuing a certificate for burial.

Copies of fictitious register entries supplied by and reproduced with the approval of the Registrar-General.

take in the medical certificate. If he does so, the registrar can refuse to accept it and may withhold the death and disposal certificates until a new medical certificate is issued. If that happens, and the delay causes financial loss – through postponing an already-arranged funeral, for example – there may be grounds for suing the doctor for damages.

Obtaining the coroner's permission

If a death is reported to the coroner, the next-of-kin need do nothing for the time being.

After preliminary investigation, the coroner may decide that no detailed informal inquiry, or formal inquest, is needed. He will then either notify the registrar, giving permission for him to issue the death and disposal certificates, or give the next-of-kin his notice of the natural cause of death.

The person responsible for registering the death then gives the notice to the registrar and obtains the death and disposal certificates.

If the coroner notifies the registrar direct, he will also tell the next-of-kin about his decision – by letter or by telephone.

When an inquest is held

If the cause of death is not immediately known, the coroner may order a post-mortem examination of the body. Until the result of the examination is known, he will not permit the death to be registered.

If the post-mortem shows that death was not natural, an inquest will be held. If more time is needed to complete the investigation, the inquest may be adjourned, but the coroner can issue next-of-kin with an order for burial, or certificate for cremation, which – like a disposal certificate from a registrar – permits a funeral to take place.

The order or certificate must then be taken to the undertaker or crematorium.

If there is no delay in the inquest, the coroner sends the registrar a certificate permitting the death to be registered. The registrar then issues the death and disposal certificates.

In such a case, the next-of-kin need do nothing about registering the death, because the coroner is the 'informant'.

When a body has not been found

In some deaths – for example, an air crash, or shipwreck – a body may not be found. Therefore no medical certificate of death can be issued.

Special rules apply in each case and, depending on the circumstances, it may be several years before the person assumed to be dead can be officially registered as dead.

DEATH GRANT

How the state helps people to meet the cost of a funeral

A death grant is a lump sum paid by the Government to whoever pays, or has agreed to meet, someone's funeral expenses. If the cost is met by the armed services or a burial society, the grant can

> ### WHO CAN AND CANNOT GET A DEATH GRANT
>
> The lump sum death grant is given to whoever is paying for the funeral.
>
> **Full grant payable**
> ● For death of man or woman who has paid (or been credited with) 25 national insurance contributions between July 25, 1948 and April 5, 1975, OR who actually paid contributions in one tax year on at least 25 times the lower earnings limit for that year.
> ● For death of spouse, widow, widower of someone with similar insurance record.
> ● For death of handicapped person unable to work but with close relative with similar insurance record.
>
> **Half grant payable**
> ● For death of man born between July 5, 1883 and July 4, 1893; woman born between July 5, 1888 and July 4, 1898.
>
> **Reduced grant payable**
> ● For the death of a child of someone with the appropriate national insurance record:
> Age under 3, grant £9
> Age 3–5, grant £15
> Age 6–17, grant £22.50.
>
> **Grant not payable**
> ● For death of man born before July 5, 1883; woman born before July 5, 1888; stillborn child.

still be paid to the dead person's next of kin. The amount of the grant varies with the age of the deceased. In 1980 it ranged from £9 for a child aged under 3 to a maximum of £30.

Qualification for the death grant depends on NATIONAL INSURANCE CONTRIBUTIONS paid by, or credited to, the dead person or a close relative. Contributions paid abroad are sometimes taken into account.

If a hospital or local authority arranges the funeral for someone who has no relatives, or none willing to pay for the funeral, it is paid any grant for which the dead person was eligible.

The Department of Health and Social Security makes special payments, equivalent to the full death grant, towards the funeral expenses for anyone who received a war disablement pension but is not eligible for the death grant.

The department will, alternatively, arrange a simple funeral for anyone receiving a war disablement pension who dies as a result of the disablement. Next-of-kin should inquire at the local war pensions office.

When the grant is payable for a death abroad

A grant is payable for a death outside the United Kingdom if it happens in another EEC country or in Austria, Cyprus, Jamaica, Jersey, Guernsey, Norway, Spain, Turkey or Yugoslavia.

If it occurs elsewhere abroad and the deceased was receiving United Kingdom social security benefit – such as retirement pension – at the time of death, or if he was ordinarily resident in Great Britain and died within 13 weeks of going abroad, the death grant is also payable.

How to claim

A person claiming death grant must do so within 6 months after the death. He or she should take along to any social security office the death certificate, the marriage certificate, if the claimant is the widow or widower of the deceased, and the undertaker's account or estimate, if the claimant's claim is based on the fact that he has paid, or has agreed to pay the funeral expenses.

Even when those documents cannot be obtained within the 6 months, the claim form should still be filled in.

A PAYMENT TOWARDS THE UNDERTAKER'S BILL

How a person can claim financial help from the state towards the expenses of a funeral

The grant is normally payable if the dead person qualified while he was alive for some kind of national insurance benefit

As payment of a death grant is based on the dead person's national insurance contributions, the number helps to establish eligibility

If the claim is made for a dependant, the person on whose national insurance contributions the claim is based must be eligible

The grant is also payable for the funeral expenses of people who, because they are minors or are disabled, were unable to work

Reduced grants are payable when a child has died. Claims can be made for newly born children who did not survive, but not for a stillbirth

Particulars of the Deceased

1 Full name (BLOCK CAPITALS PLEASE) *Surname last*

Mr/~~Mrs/Miss~~ THOMAS GUY LACEY

His/her National Insurance number, if any	Letters	Figures	Letter
	PT	23 04 62	B

If a woman, state whether single, married, widow or divorced

Last home address 7, UPTON GARDENS, CHELSEA, LONDON S.W.3.

2 Date of death FIRST *(day)* MAY *(month)* 1979 *(year)*

3 Date of birth TWENTY-THIRD *(day)* OCTOBER *(month)* 1908 *(year)*

If the date of birth is not known, please state the approximate age of the deceased

4 Was any benefit, pension or allowance (including war pension or allowance) being paid to the deceased by this Department, or was payment for the deceased as a dependant being made to you or to any other person or is any such claim currently under consideration?

(Yes or No) YES

If YES, (1) give particulars

STATE RETIREMENT PENSION

Please return any order book or Girocheque still held

(2) Say whether you wish to claim any outstanding arrears?

(Yes or No) YES

To be completed only if the deceased was a child

9 Were you receiving Child Benefit for any child up to the date of the death?

(Yes or No) _____

Were you also receiving Child Benefit Increase? *(Yes or No)* _____

If the answer to either or both questions is YES, please send the Child Benefit (and if appropriate the Child Benefit Increase) order book(s) unless the deceased was a newly-born child for whom you have not claimed Child Benefit in which case please give the allowance number shown on the front cover of the order book CHB.................

If you are not receiving Child Benefit, please send the child's birth certificate (if you have it) or give the following information

Place of the child's birth _____

Names of parents (BLOCK CAPITALS PLEASE) *Surname last*

Father _____

Mother _____

To be completed only if the claim is based on the contributions of someone other than the deceased

10 Particulars of person on whose contribution record the claim is based

Particulars of Claim

5 Did the deceased leave a Will? *(Yes or No)* YES

If YES, give the name and address of the Executor(s)

RONALD SIMPKINS, ℅ SIMPKINS, FLETCHER & CO., SOLICITORS, 33, BLAKE CRESC., CHELSEA, S.W.3

6 IF THERE IS NO WILL, have Letters of Administration (in Scotland, Confirmation) been obtained or are they being obtained? *(Yes or No)*

7 IF YOU ARE NOT THE NEXT OF KIN and if you have answered NO to both questions 5 and 6 give the name and address of the next of kin. The order of priority is normally: widow/widower (but not if a decree of judicial separation was in force), children, father or mother, brothers or sisters, other relatives.

Relationship of next of kin to the deceased

8 If the funeral expenses have been (or will be) paid by someone other than yourself, or if a local authority or hospital authority is arranging (or has arranged) the burial, give the following information

Name and address of authority or person

11 If you have any of the following documents please send them with this form, but if they are not available do NOT delay making your claim: please tick the box for any which you send with this form.

☑ Any order book or Girocheque issued by this Department for the deceased

☐ Undertaker's receipted account

☐ _____

☐ Any contribution card, certificate of age exception/earner's non-liability or certificate of election/reduced liability of the deceased

If the deceased was a child:

☐ Child Benefit order book (but see item 9)

☑ Marriage Certificate (if claim is made by widow or widower)

☐ Child Benefit Increase order book

☐ Any Welfare Foods Service books for the child

When there is no will give the name and address of any person acting as administrator of the deceased's estate

If the deceased left a will, the claimant should supply the name and address of the executor(s)

The grant can be paid to someone who did not pay the funeral expenses. But the claimant must state who paid the expenses

If there is no executor or administrator and you are not the next of kin, give his or her name and address

Even if relevant documents such as NHS cards are not available, you should send the completed claim form within 6 months

The undertaker usually helps bereaved relatives to make an application for the death grant, as well as with the registration formalities. He normally supplies a copy of form BD 1 on which the application is made, but it can also be obtained from the local office of the Department of Health and Social Security, to which it should be returned when completed and signed. Application can also be made on the back of the free certificate of registration of death along with the undertaker's account or estimate.

DEBT

How a creditor can try to recover money from a debtor

It is not a crime to owe money, and a debtor cannot be prosecuted for refusing to pay up. He can be sent to prison by a civil court but only if he ignores a court order to pay:
- Maintenance for a wife or child.
- A fine or legal aid contribution.
- Arrears of income tax or national insurance.

A debtor who is not a minor can be sued for almost any debt. Exceptions are gambling debts or debts arising from any contract against public policy – such as a bill for some kind of immoral services.

A creditor can use the courts to try to regain his money by various means, but if all these fail he simply has to write off the debt.

The risks involved in suing

If someone owes you money, write formally to him, setting out in detail what you think he owes you and trying to find out why he has so far failed to pay.

If you are sure your debtor has no means of paying, you may well be advised to go no further. If he does seem to have money, and yet offers no good reason for not settling with you, you can consider suing him.

There are, however, disadvantages in suing. The courts generally agree to repayment in small instalments, so you may have to wait a long time to get back all you are owed. Furthermore, you will have to pay some of your legal fees, even if you win – and all of them if you lose or if the debtor has no money.

A lawyer's fees are set by a scale which fixes the maximum amount a debtor is liable for. If the debtor has no money, or if the fees are in excess of the debtor's liability, which is usually the case, the creditor must pay the solicitor. *See:* LEGAL COSTS

What a creditor should not do

It is a criminal offence to harass a debtor or his family by, for example, threatening violence, publicity or criminal proceedings.

It is also an offence to obtain, or try to obtain, money from a debtor by pre-

tending to have official sanction from a court – for example, by producing some official-looking document that has no legal validity.

These laws are aimed primarily at controlling the activities of debt-collecting agencies, but they apply also to individuals. It is illegal, for example, for a newsagent who is owed money to threaten violence, or to make frequent demands in a manner likely to cause the debtor or his household alarm, distress or humiliation – for example, by parking a van marked 'Debt Collector' outside his home.

The maximum penalties for harassing a debtor are £100 on first conviction; £400 subsequently. *See:* BLACKMAIL; DEBT COLLECTOR

If you decide to sue

Most debt cases involving sums of no more than £2,000 are heard in the county court. Claims for arrears of maintenance, income tax, national insurance and rates can be heard in a magistrates' court.

Cases involving sums over £2,000 are heard in the High Court – but that does not mean only in London. The High Court sits also in provincial centres.

To start county court proceedings to recover a debt, you or your solicitor must issue a default summons – sent by the court to the debtor and requiring him to admit or deny your claim within 14 days.

What happens next will depend on

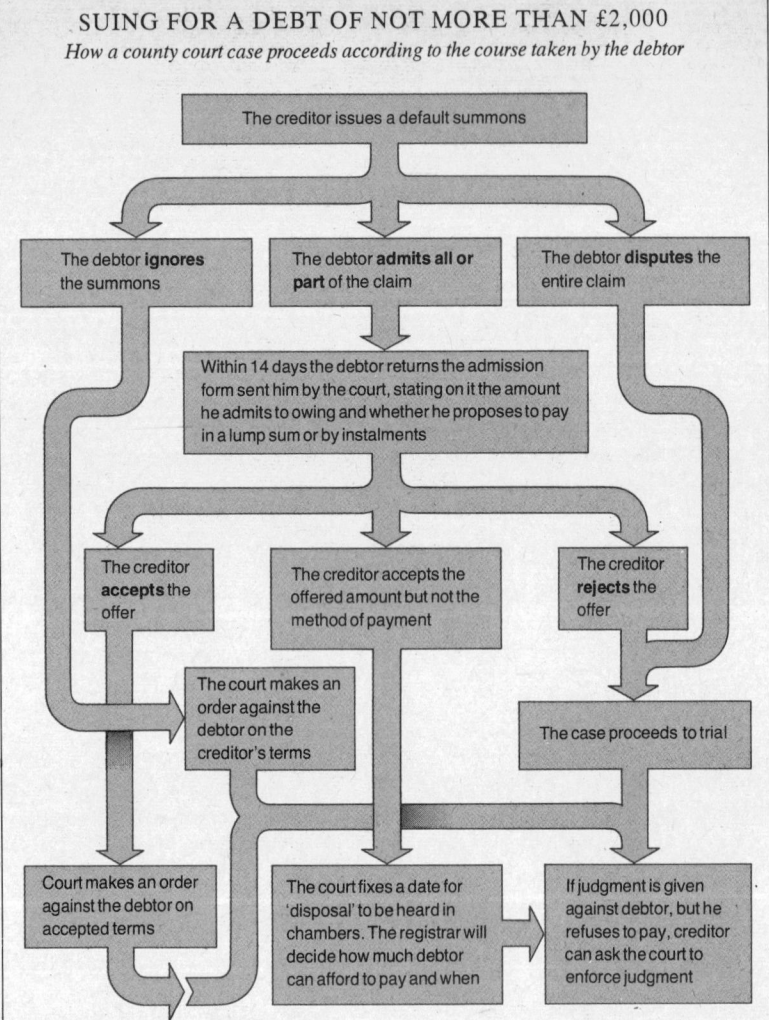

SUING FOR A DEBT OF NOT MORE THAN £2,000
How a county court case proceeds according to the course taken by the debtor

The creditor issues a default summons

The debtor **ignores** the summons | The debtor **admits all or part** of the claim | The debtor **disputes** the entire claim

Within 14 days the debtor returns the admission form sent him by the court, stating on it the amount he admits to owing and whether he proposes to pay in a lump sum or by instalments

The creditor **accepts** the offer | The creditor accepts the offered amount but not the method of payment | The creditor **rejects** the offer

The court makes an order against the debtor on the creditor's terms

The case proceeds to trial

Court makes an order against the debtor on accepted terms | The court fixes a date for 'disposal' to be heard in chambers. The registrar will decide how much debtor can afford to pay and when | If judgment is given against debtor, but he refuses to pay, creditor can ask the court to enforce judgment

HELP FOR A DEBTOR ON SUPPLEMENTARY BENEFIT

If a debtor who is receiving supplementary benefit is in danger of, say, eviction because he cannot pay his rent, or of having his fuel supply cut off because he has not paid the bill – he may be able to get help from the Supplementary Benefits Commission.

In especially urgent cases, such as when there is an illness in the family or an unforseen emergency, the Commission may make a lump sum payment. Otherwise, it is likely to help only by paying part of the debtor's weekly supplementary benefit directly to the creditor, until the debt has been cleared.

The Commission is more likely to make a lump sum payment if the debt was built up during a period when the debtor could have claimed an addition to his benefit, but failed to do so – for example, if the claimant had extra heating costs, but had not been aware that he could get state help to meet them.

Low-income debtors The Commission may also help a debtor who has been entitled to supplementary benefit, but who has not claimed it. It may even help someone who is working full time, but only if the need is urgent and his income is below or close to the level of supplementary benefit. Even then he may be expected to repay the help given.

the debtor's reaction – whether he admits the claim, disputes it or ignores it.

If the case goes to trial, you may be given judgment – official confirmation that the debtor owes you money. The debtor may decide to pay up, but he may ignore the judgment – perhaps because he has no money. If the debtor writes a letter to the creditor saying he cannot pay, he will still be ignoring the judgment.

Forcing a debtor to pay

Getting a judgment in your favour is usually only the first step towards recovering your money. The next step is to have the judgment enforced. That can be done by having the debtor's goods seized and sold or by intercepting his wages or any debts due to him.

Seizing a debtor's goods You can ask for the debtor's goods to be seized by a BAILIFF to be auctioned off to meet the debt. Often, the mere threat of that will induce him to pay, and it can be a particularly effective method against a company.

The major disadvantage is that the money raised by auctioning the seized goods may not be enough to justify the outlay of the court fee. The court fee in the county court is 15 per cent of the amount claimed, subject to a minimum of £2.10 and a maximum of £20.

The bailiff is not allowed to seize goods that do not belong to the debtor. If the debtor claims that certain items belong to his family, the bailiff will probably not risk seizing them. Nor will he take goods which are on HIRE PURCHASE because they are the property of the finance company.

A debtor is allowed to keep clothes, bedding and tools of his trade.

Intercepting his wages The court can make an attachment of EARNINGS order, requiring the debtor's employer to make regular deductions from his salary.

That is effective only if the debtor has a steady job.

Intercepting money due to him If the debtor is in business, he himself may be owed money by others. If so, you can ask the court to make a garnishee order, requiring them to pay the money direct to you instead. Similarly, if your debtor has a bank account, the court can make a garnishee order instructing the bank to pay you.

Organising a debtor's affairs

When a debtor has other judgments against him and if his total debts exceed £500, the court can make an administration order, helping the debtor to organise his affairs and deciding the amount and regularity of the instalments to be paid to each creditor. Usually the instalments are small.

An administration order can be made only at the request of the debtor.

Making the debtor bankrupt You can ask the court to make the debtor bankrupt only if the debt exceeds £200. The disadvantage of BANKRUPTCY proceedings is that if several people are owed money, you may find that some have claims which take precedence over yours and that eventually you would recover only a few pence in the pound, if anything at all.

DEBT COLLECTOR

The right not to be bullied

A person or company employed to collect unpaid debts is not entitled to harass a debtor by making frequent or threatening demands for payment, or threats to sue for payment. Comments such as 'You will hear from us further' could constitute a threat.

The debt collector is also forbidden to make demands accompanied by publicity – for example, parking outside a debtor's home in a vehicle boldly marked 'Debt Recovery Service', or by mentioning the debt to local shopkeepers.

It is illegal for a shop to display a 'shame list' of debtors.

The debt collector should make a polite request for payment. If payment is not made he should start court proceedings to recover the debt.

In any case, a debt collector must have a licence from the Director General of Fair Trading. To operate without one is a criminal offence.

Trade organisations can exchange lists of debtors privately provided that the exchange is not intended to coerce a debtor into paying.

A trader can act without a debt collector but he is bound by the same rules.

Any debt collector convicted of working without an Office of Fair Trading licence can be fined up to £400 by magistrates, or fined an unlimited sum (or sentenced to 2 years' imprisonment) by a crown court.

A debt collector convicted of any form of harassment can be fined up to £100, on conviction by magistrates, for a first offence, and up to £400 on conviction for a second or subsequent offence. *See also:* DEBT

DECEPTION

Dishonestly obtaining goods or money from someone

The offence of deception falls into five main categories, all of which are punishable in law. For a person to be guilty the deception must have been made deliberately, or recklessly, and must be shown to have had the effect of deceiving the victim.

Obtaining property by deception

Anyone found guilty of obtaining property by deception is liable to a penalty of up to 10 years' imprisonment and an unlimited fine. Property can be money as well as goods. For instance, if a window cleaner falsely claims to have cleaned windows while the householder was out and asks for payment, he can be charged with the offence. So, too, can a person who pays for goods with a cheque which he knows will not be honoured by his bank.

Obtaining pecuniary advantage by deception

The offence of obtaining pecuniary advantage by deception covers any monetary advantage achieved dishonestly, although four particular types of benefit are specifically included:

- Obtaining an overdraft.
- Securing an insurance policy.
- Increasing earnings.
- Winning monetary bets.

It can, for example, be an offence not to divulge details of a recent criminal conviction in order to get a job. Not only can the applicant be dismissed; he can also be prosecuted for obtaining pecuniary advantage by deception. *See also:* REHABILITATION

The penalty for this use of deception is imprisonment for up to 5 years and an unlimited fine.

Obtaining services by deception

The offence of obtaining services by deception means evading payment for the use of an item or somebody's services – such as those of a solicitor or accountant – by obtaining them through deception. To be guilty of this offence – for which the penalty can be 5 years' imprisonment and an unlimited fine – there must be no intention of paying for the services obtained. For instance, if a person poses as a newspaper reporter to gain free entry into a football match or a theatre for which he would normally have to pay for a ticket, he could be charged with the offence. So, too, could a person who produced a false driving licence to hire a car. But if he borrowed a car from a friend on a free loan, he would not be committing the offence by deceiving the friend with a false licence as there was no intention to pay for the use of the car.

Evading liability by deception

Anyone who uses deception to avoid paying a debt that he has no intention of ever paying, can be charged with evading liability by deception. The offence covers three situations:

- Using deception to persuade the creditor to forgo all or part of the debt. For instance, telling a false hard-luck story or insisting that the debt has already been paid.
- Using deception to stall payment – such as giving a worthless cheque or arranging to pay at a later date, but with no intention to do so. Stalling is not an offence if there is intention to pay.
- Using deception to obtain services at a reduced rate. For instance, falsely applying for concessionary fares or for a rent or rate rebate.

The penalty is up to 5 years' imprisonment and an unlimited fine.

Making off without paying

Bilking, as this offence is commonly called, covers such things as driving off from a garage without paying for petrol, or leaving a restaurant without paying the bill – and having no intention of paying. If a person obtains these services but pays with a worthless cheque so as to avoid payment, he would be committing the more serious offence of obtaining property by deception.

The penalty for making off without paying is up to 2 years' imprisonment and an unlimited fine.

POSTMAN OVERDREW ON GIRO

It is deception to draw cheques when there is no money in a bank account to meet them.

A strike left postman Kishor Lalbhai Patel short of money. After a wage cheque was paid into his Post Office Giro account in January 1971, nothing more was received before March 2. By that time Patel's account was £108 overdrawn, although he knew he had no permission to overdraw.

He was charged with three offences of dishonestly obtaining £10 from the Post Office by falsely pretending he was entitled to be paid that sum.

Patel pleaded in court that there was a genuine intention to repay the money, so no offence had been committed. North London magistrates dismissed the charges. The Post Office appealed.

DECISION

The Appeal Court held that Patel had no reason to believe that any funds would reach his account in time to meet the cheques he had cashed at the post office. He knew he had no funds in his Giro account, he knew he had no right to overdraw, and he knew he had no prospect of providing the funds in time. The magistrates were ordered to convict him.

STOLEN BY DECEPTION . . . A PIECE OF PAPER

Some material thing must be obtained by false pretence for a person to be guilty of deception.

Three people completed a false mortgage application form and submitted it to the Greater London Council.

The three – Ignatius Chima Duru, Mohammed Asghar and Yaseen Khan – were charged with obtaining money by deception and were gaoled for 18 months in 1973. Duru and Asghar appealed against conviction, and all three appealed against sentence.

They claimed in the Appeal Court that there had been no intention to deprive the council of any property and none had been obtained from the council. Nor was there any intention to deprive the council of any money, because any mortgage loan would be eventually repaid.

VERDICT

The court held that they had clearly had an intention to deprive the council of the piece of paper which gave the right to receive the money. The appeals were therefore dismissed.

DECREE ABSOLUTE

When a marriage is finally over

A decree absolute is the last stage of a DIVORCE. When it is granted, the marriage is officially at an end, and both parties are free to remarry.

The decree absolute is not normally granted until at least 6 weeks after the DECREE NISI. The time limit can however be shortened if one of the parties produces evidence that it is desirable – for example, if a child is about to be born and the petitioner wants to remarry. Such an application, with the evidence in AFFIDAVIT form, accompanied by a medical certificate giving the expected date of the birth, should be made at the time of the hearing of the decree nisi.

Applying after 6 weeks

After the 6 week period, the petitioner – the person applying for the decree – can obtain an application form from the court registry. When completed it should be returned to the court.

If the petitioner does not do that, the respondent may do so after 3 months. The decree absolute is never granted automatically, and the parties remain married, subject to the decree nisi, until one of them applies for it to be made absolute.

Even after a decree absolute has been granted, and one of the parties has remarried, a divorce can still in very rare circumstances be revoked and the subsequent marriage declared invalid.

That would happen only if there had been an extreme irregularity in the conduct of the divorce case.

THE DOCUMENT THAT STATES THAT A MARRIAGE IS FINALLY DISSOLVED BY LAW

Once a decree absolute has been granted, a married couple are free to remarry

Certificate making Decree Nisi Absolute (Divorce)

MATRIMONIAL
CAUSES RULES   In the COWLEY County Court.
Rule 67(2)

No. of matter 80 (b) 555

BETWEEN .... Mary Elizabeth BARTON .... *Petitioner*

AND .... John Frederick BARTON .... *Respondent*   (SEAL.)

AND .... *Respondent*

Referring to the decree made in this cause on the 30th

day of   April   1980 , whereby it was decreed that the marriage

solemnised on the   3rd   day of   August   1966

at the Church of the Holy Trinity, Mallowfield, in the County of Wessex

between   Mary Elizabeth BARTON   the Petitioner

and   John Frederick BARTON

                                              the Respondent

be dissolved unless sufficient cause be shown to the Court within six weeks from

the making thereof why the said decree should not be made absolute, and no such cause

having been shown, it is hereby certified that the said decree was

on the 18th day of   June   1980   made final and absolute and that the

said marriage was thereby dissolved.

            Dated this 18th day of June 1980

                                      D. PRICE,
                                      Registrar.

Former partners free to remarry after date shown

No valid objection made; so divorce can be made final

A decree absolute ends a marriage. If a serious legal irregularity is discovered later the decree can still be revoked – and any remarriage annulled – but such a case would be extremely rare, and only if there had been an irregularity during the divorce case.

DECREE NISI

When a divorce is given provisional approval

When a DIVORCE court is satisfied that breakdown of marriage has been proved – either by sworn statements to the registrar or by verbal evidence in court – a divorce decree nisi is granted by a judge.

Until the decree nisi becomes a DECREE ABSOLUTE, however, neither husband nor wife is free to remarry. If one of the couple dies before the decree is made absolute, the survivor inherits the other's property as though they were still married.

The decree nisi states the date and place of the marriage, the names of the parties and the ground on which the marriage is held to have broken down. Copies are sent to both parties.

Grounds for cancellation

The decree nisi is normally in operation for 6 weeks. During that time, the court can cancel the divorce either because the couple have both changed their minds or because some irregularity in the original divorce proceedings has been discovered – for example, if the respondent's consent had been proved with a false document.

If such an irregularity happens – for example, if a husband wrongly obtains a decree without his wife's knowledge – the other party to the marriage can appeal to the court against the decree.

During the 6 weeks, the respondent may also notify the court that he or she wishes to oppose the granting of a decree absolute – usually for financial

THE DOCUMENT THAT SAYS A MARRIAGE IS ALMOST OVER

When a marriage has broken down but the husband and wife are still legally bound for 6 more weeks

Notice of Application for Decree Nisi to be made Absolute.

MATRIMONIAL CAUSES RULES
Rule 65(1)

In the   COWLEY County Court

No. of matter   80 (b) 555

BETWEEN   Mary Elizabeth BARTON   Petitioner

AND   John Frederick BARTON   Respondent

AND   Respondent

SEAL.

TAKE NOTICE that the Petitioner   Mary Elizabeth BARTON

applies for the decree nisi pronounced in his (her) favour

on the 30th day of April   1980 , to be made absolute.

Dated this   15th day of   June   1980 .

The form solicitors use when they apply for a decree nisi to be made absolute. A letter to the court after 6 weeks is just as acceptable. An application form can also be obtained from the court registry.

A successful appeal in a defended case, a reconciliation or the discovery of some legal defect could stop the divorce

A judge has power to reduce the waiting time in specially urgent cases – for example, when a child is expected. Or it may be extended if financial negotiations are still going on

Decree Nisi - Dissolution (Section 1 (2) (b))

MATRIMONIAL CAUSES RULES
Rule 55

IN THE   COWLEY   COUNTY COURT

No. of matter   80 (b) 555

Between   Mary Elizabeth BARTON   Petitioner

and   John Frederick BARTON   Respondent

SEAL

Before His Honour Judge Smithson

sitting at   the County Court, Cowley, Mercia

On the   30th day of April   1980 ,

the Judge held that

the respondent has behaved in such a way that the petitioner cannot reasonably be expected to live with the respondent, that the marriage solemnised

on the   3rd day of August   1966 ,

at the Church of the Holy Trinity at Mallowfield in the County of Wessex

between   Mary Elizabeth BARTON   the Petitioner

and   John Frederick BARTON   the Respondent

has broken down irretrievably and decreed that the said marriage be dissolved unless sufficient cause be shown to the Court within six weeks from the making of this decree why such decree should not be made absolute.

After 6 weeks the petitioner applies for the divorce to be made final. Unless complications have arisen the decree absolute is then granted promptly by the court. It is posted to both parties. The divorce may be cancelled, however, if the couple change their minds during the 6 weeks or if it is discovered by the court that some irregularity has taken place in the earlier divorce proceedings.

reasons. However, that can be done only if the case is based on the fact that the couple have lived apart for 2 years or 5 years.

Once such a notification is filed, the decree absolute cannot be granted until a settlement has been approved by the court.

The respondent in a case that is not based on separation cannot delay the granting of a decree absolute on financial grounds.

Before a decree absolute is granted, the court must be satisfied with arrangements made for any children of the family. If a child is born between the granting of the decree nisi and the issue of the final decree absolute, it is assumed to be the husband's unless that is disproved. The court can make CUSTODY OF CHILDREN and MAINTENANCE orders over it.

DEED POLL

You are entitled to call yourself by any name you choose, provided that it is not done for a fraudulent reason. The official way to change your name is by deed poll. *See:* NAME, Change of

DEFECTIVE GOODS

Knowing what a 'defect' is and how to claim for it

A trader who sells a customer goods that are defective, faulty or otherwise unsatisfactory must pay compensation or refund his money in full if:
● The goods do not match the seller's description.

● The goods are not fit for their common, everyday usage.
● The goods do not do the specific job for which they were bought.

When goods are not as described

Goods are defective if they do not match any oral or written description attached to them at the time of the sale.

If, for example, a ring described as 'solid gold' turns out to be gold-plated, the trader has broken a term of his contract with the buyer and is liable to compensate him.

Similarly, if goods are chosen from a sample – for example, wallpaper or carpets – they must conform to the sample in style, colour and texture. *See:* GUARANTEE; SALE OF GOODS; TRADE DESCRIPTIONS

THE HOUSEWIFE WHO DID NOT TAKE NO FOR AN ANSWER
Persistence pays off when you claim a refund for goods that do not do their job properly

1 Mrs S buys a new toaster from the local branch of an electrical goods chain. It is a low-priced model, and the manufacturer's guarantee covers only electrical faults. Mrs S relies on the shop's 'Money Back If Not Satisfied' sign.

2 The lever that ejects the toast is stiff and soon becomes difficult to operate. One morning it jams completely. With the toast burning, Mrs S uses more force – and breaks a spring in the mechanism. Now the toaster is useless.

3 Mrs S takes the toaster straight back to the shop. The manager says it can be repaired, but she must pay because she caused the damage. Mrs S tells him that the toaster was faulty all along and demands a refund. He refuses.

4 A friend suggests that Mrs S consult the consumer advice centre run by the local council. One of its staff contacts the shop manager, who explains that his head office does not allow refunds on goods that are wrongly used.

5 The consumer advice centre starts a long correspondence, first with the shop manager and then with his head office in London. The company will not budge, so the advice centre arranges for the toaster to be examined. A technician confirms that the lever mechanism was never properly fitted. The advice centre helps Mrs S to prepare a case to sue the company in the county court. The senior officer at the centre goes with her to the court. At a simple hearing – closed to the public – the court registrar hears her claim, and the shop manager's defence that Mrs S misused the toaster. Convinced by the technical evidence, the registrar orders the company to pay the refund.

‘

THE BOY WHO LOST AN EYE

A customer can claim compensation from a trader for any damage or injury caused by defective goods.

Nigel Godley, aged 6, bought a plastic toy catapult from Mr Perry's newsagent's shop in 1958.

Three days later the catapult broke as Nigel was firing a stone from it. The elastic snapped back and a sharp piece of plastic hit his left eye. As a result he lost the eye.

Nigel, through his father, sued the newsagent – claiming that the catapult was not fit for its normal purpose and was therefore not of merchantable quality. In evidence, a chemist said the toy was dangerous because of the plastic's fragility and tendency to 'dogtooth' fracture.

DECISION

The court held that, even although the newsagent could not reasonably have known about the catapult's defects, he was liable to pay compensation. Nigel was awarded damages of £2,500.

The newsagent in turn sued the wholesalers who had supplied him, and they sued the company that had imported the toys. Both claims succeeded, so ultimately it was the importers who paid for Nigel's injury.

Goods not fit for their purposes

Any article you buy must be reasonably fit for the purpose to which people usually put goods of that kind – what the law calls of 'merchantable quality'. In addition, if you have told the trader you want an article for a specific purpose or job, it must be suitable for that.

Merchantable quality Goods need not be perfect or without blemish to satisfy the 'merchantable quality' condition. The test is whether a reasonable person, knowing their condition and their normal, everyday usage, would still buy them for the price.

But a trader cannot escape his obligation to provide goods of merchantable quality simply by labelling them 'seconds' or 'defective'. They must still be as suitable for their general purpose as it is reasonable to expect 'seconds' to be.

If they turn out to be less than suitable, the trader can escape liability to pay compensation only if he pointed out, at the time of the sale, the particular defect that later caused complaint.

Specific suitability An article can be of merchantable quality but be unfit for the specific purpose you have in mind. A length of material, for example, could be used to make curtains or a skirt or cover an armchair.

If you wanted to use it for upholstery, and it proved unsatisfactory for that, though it was suitable for its other purposes, you would have no claim against the trader unless you had told him why you wanted the material.

When a trader need not pay

When you take goods back to a shop on the ground that they are not of merchantable quality, your claim will not succeed if:

● The trader pointed out the specific defect before you bought the article.

● You noticed the defect or examined the article closely enough to have been able to notice it.

● You may claim that the goods are unfit for a specific purpose. The trader need not pay compensation if he can show that you ignored his recommendations and bought something he had advised against.

Asking for your money back

Assuming the trader *has* broken one of the conditions of sale, you must still act quickly if you want to return defective goods and get your money back.

● Do not keep the goods longer than is reasonably necessary to discover the defect.

● Do not tell the trader that the goods are satisfactory and that you are keeping them.

● Do not consume any of the goods.

You are entitled to some delay, however, if the goods you bought – tinned food, for example – could not be fully examined until you came to use them.

Claiming compensation

Even if you do not reject the goods promptly, you have the right to claim compensation for up to 6 years from the date of purchase – unless you are claiming compensation for personal injury caused by the goods. In that case the limit is 3 years.

There are two main types of compensation, both of which are intended to put a claimant in the same financial position as if the goods had not been defective:

● If the defect can be put right by having the goods repaired, the trader must pay any reasonable repair cost.

You are not obliged to give the goods back to the retailer or manufacturer. You can have the repair work done anywhere.

● If the goods cannot be repaired, you can ask the trader to pay you compensation in the form of a partial refund. In effect, he pays you the difference between the true value of the defective goods and the amount you originally gave him for them. *See also:* MANUFACTURERS' LIABILITY

DEFECTIVE PREMISES

Avoiding injury to others

The law expects the occupier of any premises, private or commercial, to keep them in good repair. Otherwise, he may be liable to pay damages to a visitor who is injured.

See: OCCUPIERS' LIABILITY
PROPERTY INSURANCE

DEMONSTRATION

How to go about organising a protest

Freedom of speech is a basic British right, and anyone can hold a demonstration or organise a procession in the streets.

Demonstrations may give rise, however, to various offences, for example, breach of the peace, obstructing the police, obstructing the highway, using threatening, abusive, or insulting words or behaviour, and unlawful assembly. It is also against Britain's RACE DISCRIMINATION laws for any demonstrator, speaker or banner to incite people to racial hatred.

Restrictions on marching

If you are organising a demonstration and intend to have a PROCESSION, discuss it with the police beforehand. They have the right to regulate your route. Check also with the local authorities whether there are any bye-laws to be observed in the streets through which you plan to walk.

For example, a bye-law may say that you must tell the police of your plans, in advance.

If the local chief officer of police has reason to believe that the march could give rise to public disorder he can impose whatever restrictions he feels necessary. He may, for example, forbid the use of flags, banners and emblems. No particular march can be forbidden, but the Home Secretary can give the police permission to prohibit certain types of procession in their area for up to 3 months.

Anyone who disobeys lawful police instructions about a demonstration can be fined £50 and imprisoned for 3 months.

Restrictions on meetings

If your demonstration is to include a PUBLIC MEETING, you should go to the town hall and find out whether there are any local Acts or bye-laws that have to be observed.

Many places open to the public – parks and public squares, for example – are owned and controlled by the local authority and in many of them meetings are banned altogether or at certain times.

It is advisable to tell the police when and where your meeting is to be held, even if you are not legally obliged to do so – especially if you expect any opposition or a large attendance.

When a meeting can be banned

The powers of the police to prohibit a demonstration in advance are very limited. The fact that the meeting may constitute trespass or cause obstruction is not sufficient excuse. The police or local authority may refuse permission for the demonstration to take place only if their permission is required under a bye-law or if the authority owns the site. The police have wider powers covering processions.

Putting up posters

Planning permission from the local authority is not required for putting up posters – if the meeting is political, re-

---

‘

THE 400 UNINVITED GUESTS

An assembly becomes unlawful if those involved begin to behave in a way that makes others fear a breach of the peace.

A dinner dance was held at the Garden House Hotel in Cambridge during Greek Week in 1970. A man called Caird and about 400 other people assembled in the garden of the hotel in an anti-Greek demonstration.

They later forced their way into the hotel: furniture was damaged and guests and police were injured. Caird was sentenced to 18 months' imprisonment. He appealed.

DECISION

The Appeal Court held that however peaceable the original demonstration had been, it became an unlawful assembly once the demonstrators began acting in a common purpose that caused citizens to fear a breach of the peace. The sentence on Caird was upheld.

’

---

ligious, social or educational, if the posters are not more than 6 ft square and if they do not obstruct the highway.

Who is responsible for what happens

An organiser of a demonstration cannot be punished for any offence that happens during the demonstration, unless he was personally responsible for the incident. Anyone taking part in the demonstration must be careful to obey lawful police instructions. Anyone who causes a breach of the peace by using threatening, abusive or insulting words or behaviour is liable to be arrested.

Using a loudspeaker

If you intend to use a loudspeaker, you must give the police 48 hours' notice. You can be prosecuted for making unreasonable noise or for creating a public nuisance.

When property is damaged

A property owner may be able to claim compensation from the police authority if his premises are damaged during a demonstration, and if he can show

---

that the damage was done by at least three people who were behaving riotously – that is, using violence of an alarming nature in pursuit of a common cause.

However, a businessman who for safety's sake decides to close premises on a demonstration route cannot claim compensation for any resulting loss of trade.

Most private house insurances specifically exclude compensation for damage caused by RIOT.

A person who is injured during or because of a demonstration may be able to obtain CRIMINAL INJURIES COMPENSATION.

DENTIST

Your rights to dental treatment

A dentist, whether working privately or within the National Health Service, is under no obligation to accept a new patient.

If he has begun a course of treatment, he must finish it. Otherwise he is not obliged to continue treating any particular patient.

How to find a dentist

Not all dentists accept National Health patients. Those who do can be found on a list at any main post office or at the offices of the local Family Practitioner Committee, the address of which is on your medical card. *See:* DOCTOR AND PATIENT

Once you find a dentist, establish at the outset whether he is taking you as a private or health service patient. Legally, it is his choice as well as yours.

If he accepts you as a health service patient, he will ask you to sign a form stating that you want treatment under the health service. That enables him to claim payment from the state for the treatment he gives you.

A patient's right to treatment

Under the Health Service, most dentists take the patient's wishes into account, but you have no right to demand any specific treatment. The dentist has the final say although you are entitled to refuse any treatment.

With the most common types of work – X-rays, fillings, extractions, dentures

DEPENDANT

WHEN YOU HAVE TO PAY FOR NHS DENTAL TREATMENT

The most a National Health Service patient ever has to pay for any necessary treatment is £54, if it includes dentures. If not, the maximum is £8 for a course of treatment. Typical charges are:
- Fillings – from £1.70 to £2, including local anaesthetic.
- Extractions – from £2.20 to £7.40, including local anaesthetic.
- De-scaling – £2.40.
- Dentures – from £17 for a single resin denture with one tooth, to £50 for more than one denture in metal or porcelain.

There is no charge for an initial check-up, for stopping bleeding, for repairs to dentures, for the dentist's travelling time and expenses if he has to come to your home, or for treatment in a dental hospital.

Exemptions No charge is made to:
- People who are receiving some measure of SUPPLEMENTARY BENEFIT or FAMILY INCOME SUPPLEMENT.
- People getting free prescriptions or free milk and vitamins because of low income.
- Children under 18.
- Young people aged 18 or over, who have not left school.
- Expectant mother or a woman who has had a baby in the last 12 months.

Dentures are free for those aged 16–18 who are in full-time education.

Exemption and refunds

Anyone with a net income just above supplementary benefit level may claim exemption or reclaim the charges he has paid. Others with a slightly higher income may pay a reduced charge or reclaim part of the charges.

Claim forms can be obtained from the dentist or social security office.

and one or perhaps two crowns – the dentist can proceed at once.

If you want more expensive treatment than is strictly necessary – a gold filling, inlay or crown, or a more costly denture or bridge – he must first have the approval of the local dental estimates board, and you will have to pay in full for the extra work.

Any other form of 'luxury' work can normally be obtained only as a private patient.

If the estimates board refuses to approve more expensive work, or sets a price which you or the dentist regard as excessive, write to the board, asking for the decision to be reconsidered, or to the Secretary of State, or to your MP.

How to complain

If you think a dentist has been guilty of unprofessional behaviour – for example, misusing drugs, working while drunk or making sexual advances to a patient – write to the General Dental Council in London.

If your complaint is about negligence – for example, if the dentist pulled out the wrong tooth – you can either complain to the Dental Council in a serious case or sue for DAMAGES.

If you were treated in a dental hospital, you may have to sue the hospital rather than the dentist.

If you are a health service patient and think that the dentist's general service has been poor – for example, that conditions were unhygienic, treatment inadequate, or the dentist was rude, ask the Family Practitioner Committee to investigate.

When dentures do not fit You have the right to reject NHS false teeth that do not fit, and to refuse payment. If a denture causes you any pain or injury, you may also sue the dentist for negligence.

Under private treatment only, the dentist has a contract with you that is covered by the SALE OF GOODS Act, and you can claim against him in the same way as anyone who buys DEFECTIVE GOODS.

DEPENDANT

When extra social security benefits can be claimed for a family

Anyone who is eligible for a social security benefit receives more money if he has dependants.

There are four categories: children, wife or husband, certain relatives and certain housekeepers.

Children

A person entitled to INDUSTRIAL INJURY BENEFIT, INVALIDITY PENSION, MATERNITY allowance, WIDOW'S BENEFITS, SICKNESS BENEFIT or UNEMPLOYMENT BENEFIT, can claim extra for any child or children under 16 for whom CHILD BENEFIT is payable.

If the father of an illegitimate child is living with the mother of that child, or if he can prove that he has been paying at least half the cost of maintaining the child during the preceding 6 months, he is entitled to extra social security benefit, even if child benefit is not payable.

Anyone who has a child who is not living with him but for whom child benefit is being paid, qualifies for an increase only if his contribution to the child's support equals or exceeds the increase and child benefit combined.

For example, to qualify for a £1.25 increase in unemployment benefit for a dependent child, he must, if child benefit is £4.75 a week, have been regularly contributing at least £6 a week to the child's support.

When a husband and wife living together are both entitled to claim extra, the husband's claim takes priority.

In other cases of double claim, the minister decides who receives the increase. *See:* OVERLAPPING BENEFITS

The only circumstance in which a wife who is living with her husband can claim extra for dependent children instead of her husband, is when the husband cannot support himself because of physical or mental disability.

Wife or husband

Any man entitled to INDUSTRIAL INJURY BENEFIT, INVALIDITY PENSION, SICKNESS BENEFIT or UNEMPLOYMENT BENEFIT can claim extra benefit for a wife provided that she is living with him or, if not, that the amount he pays for her support equals or exceeds the increase in benefit. A husband cannot claim extra for a wife if she is earning more than the increase.

A woman receiving any of the above benefits, or a maternity allowance, can claim extra for a husband only if he cannot support himself.

Relatives

Only certain relatives, apart from children, qualify as dependants for the purpose of social security benefit: parents, grandparents, grandchildren, brothers and sisters, half-brothers and half-sisters and the parents-in-law of a widow or widower.

172

The relative, moreover, must live with or be maintained by the claimant and must be over 18. If the relative is a man, he must be incapable of supporting himself, and a woman must not be earning more than the extra that can be claimed.

Housekeepers

A housekeeper qualifies as a dependant only if she is over 18; looks after a child or children for whom the claimant is entitled to draw child benefit; lives in the same house as the claimant; costs the claimant at least the amount of the increase in wages or maintenance; and is not earning more than the increase from another job.

The current rates of social security benefits for dependants are given in Department of Health and Social Security leaflet NI 196.

DEPORTATION

When someone is ordered to leave the country

No one who is a patrial UK citizen can be deported to another country (though he may be extradited to face trial for crimes committed abroad).

If a person who has been deported returns without permission he can be fined £200 and imprisoned for 6 months.

Deportation can be ordered by the Home Secretary if:
1. Someone persistently breaks the IMMIGRATION rules and does not leave the UK when asked to do so.
2. Someone aged 17 or over who is convicted of an offence punishable by imprisonment and the court recommends that he be deported. (The Home Secretary has to consider all the circumstances, particularly the person's age and domestic circumstances; the strength of his links with and length of his residence in the UK; his character, conduct and employment record; the nature of the offence of which he has been convicted and any compassionate circumstances.)
3. The Secretary of State thinks it conducive to the public good to deport someone – usually because the person has been convicted of serious or repeated offences or because his activities are officially thought to be undesirable.
4. Someone in the person's immediate family is to be, or has been, deported. For example, if a man is being deported, his wife and children under 18 will also be told to leave; if the person being deported is a woman, only her children under 18 are also affected.

A wife who is no longer living with her husband is not treated as a member of his family.

Before deporting a dependent relative, the Home Secretary takes into account whether a wife can support herself and her children in Britain even if her husband is deported; and whether she has ties with Britain quite separately from her husband.

If children are involved, the Home Secretary considers what effect deportation might have on their education and whether realistic plans have been made for their care and maintenance after one or both of their parents have left the country.

A child approaching 18, or one who has left the family home and is financially independent, is not normally deported. A child who has been deported in this way can apply for readmission when he or she is 18.

A deportation order cannot be made against a family member if more than 8 weeks have passed since his relative was deported from the country.

When an order will not be made

A deportation order is not enforced if the only country to which a person can be deported is one to which he would be unwilling to go because of a well-founded fear of being persecuted for reasons of race, religion, nationality or political opinion.

No Commonwealth citizen or citizen of Eire is liable to deportation if he has been ordinarily resident in Britain since January 1, 1973. That rule does not apply if he has become a Commonwealth citizen only since then.

His immunity from deportation is not affected by his having left the country during this period so long as he did so for some temporary reason, such as holidays, business or family illness. But a person who obtained readmission to the UK by giving the immigration officer false information about his status

WHEN YOU HAVE NO CHOICE

Someone on whom a deportation order has been served can be kept in prison or police custody until he leaves the country if there is a risk he may disappear.

in the UK would run the risk of being regarded as an illegal entrant.

There is one pitfall. If a decision to deport is made with or without the person's knowledge within the 5 year period, he has no immunity even though he has since completed the 5 years' residence.

No alien – except a citizen of Pakistan who is regarded by the Home Office as a Commonwealth citizen for these purposes – is immune from deportation, no matter how long he lives in the UK.

In practice, the Home Office gives indefinite leave to remain in the UK, to those immune from deportation, but that is not a legal right.

Appealing against deportation

If the Home Office serves a notice of intention to deport, the individual has the right of appeal to an adjudicator on the question of whether it is right to deport him, as well as the right to object to being deported to the country the Home Office had specified.

If the deportation is recommended by a magistrates' court, he can appeal to a crown court against the recommendation as a sentence, but if the recommendation is upheld, he has no right to appeal, except over the choice of country to which he is to be sent.

If all else fails, he can ask his MP to intervene on his behalf, and put forward any claims he might have to be allowed to remain in Britain – such as being married to a woman settled here.

Arrest and detention

The Home Office can authorise the arrest and detention in prison of anyone on whom notice of intention to deport has been served. After a deportation order has been made, moreover, the person named may be detained until he eventually leaves Britain, or is allowed to stay – a process that may take several months. While an immigration appeal is pending, there is the right to apply for bail to an appeals adjudicator.

But a recommendation by a court that someone be deported does not automatically mean that he is kept in prison until the Home Office decides. Magistrates are expected to grant bail unless there is a serious risk that the defendant will disappear.

Where can a deportee be sent?

The Home Secretary must direct that the person being deported should be sent either to a country of which he is a citizen, or one to which there is reason to believe he would be admitted. Someone who wishes to go to another country will have to show good reason and will also have to prove that he will be admitted to the country of his choice.

The cost of the deportation is paid by the Government.

The status of diplomats

Foreign diplomats are not subject to our immigration laws, and can come and go freely so long as they are members of a diplomatic mission. This applies also to any member of the diplomat's family who forms part of his household. Domestic servants of such households are given permission to remain by the Home Office without the necessity to apply for work permits, but only for 12 months at a time; they will be given further extensions of stay only if they remain members in the diplomat's employment.

DEPOSIT AND PART-PAYMENT

Whose is the money when there is no sale?

If you put money down on goods – for example when they are temporarily out of stock – make clear to the shop or trader that you are making a part-payment, not paying a deposit. To be sure of your rights, ask the trader to mark the receipt 'cash returnable if no sale'.

When it is clearly understood by both sides that the money was intended as a part-payment, and the buyer then pulls out of a sale he may be able to have his money refunded in full, if it is acceptable to the trader for him to pull out.

When money is paid as a deposit, it is immediately the property of the shop or trader. If the buyer later withdraws from the sale, he is not entitled to have the deposit refunded, although the trader may give a refund for goodwill.

If the sale goes through, however, the deposit counts as a part-payment which is deducted from the total price to be paid. The customer is not entitled to interest on money held as part-payment unless it is agreed that he should be.

If goods have been specially made for you, and you reject them without good reason, the trader is entitled to sue you for breach of contract. You in turn are entitled to sue to get your money back if you reject the goods because they were not properly made.

A deposit paid under a CREDIT AGREEMENT must be returned in full if you cancel or withdraw from the contract within the time allowed.

DESERTION

A husband and wife have a duty to share their lives

A partner who, without consent or good reason, withdraws from any of the joint arrangements of a marriage – with the intention of being apart permanently – is in desertion.

That does not necessarily mean leaving a particular place. One partner can desert the other simply by insisting on living in a separate part of the same house and refusing to eat meals together or share household tasks.

When the 'deserter' stays

If a husband or wife causes the other to leave unwillingly – by force, say, or by order – or if he or she prevents the other from entering their home, that partner can be held to have deserted. So can one whose behaviour is so gravely offensive that the spouse feels forced to leave.

But causing a spouse to live apart is not desertion if there is justification for it – such as a reasonable belief that the spouse is committing adultery.

An unwilling departure caused, for example, by imprisonment, illness or war is not desertion. Nor is a SEPARATION to which both parties agree. If both partners sign a separation deed, neither is guilty of deserting the other while the deed is in force. *See:* MATRIMONIAL ORDER

Desertion and divorce

Proof of desertion for at least 2 years is a reason for DIVORCE. The petitioner must prove that the parties have separated, and that his or her partner intended to end their living together.

The respondent can oppose the petition by showing that the petitioner consented, or behaved in such a way that the respondent was justified in leaving.

If the respondent tries to return and is unreasonably prevented, he or she can CROSS-PETITION on the ground that it was the petitioner who deserted.

The 2 years apart must be strictly proved. But to encourage reconciliation attempts, a couple may resume their life together for periods totalling not more than 6 months.

Those periods are added to the 2 years apart, so if a couple lived together for a total of 3 months a divorce petition cannot be filed until 27 months after the original desertion.

Complaint to a magistrate

Desertion is one of the grounds for seeking a Magistrates' MATRIMONIAL ORDER requiring a husband or wife to pay MAINTENANCE.

Such an order can be made even if desertion has not continued for 2 years: the desertion need only exist when the complaint is issued and at the time of the hearing.

DEVELOPMENT LAND TAX

Rates of taxation on the sale of developed land

If you sell land or buildings the value of which has increased as a result of property development, you may have to pay Development Land Tax. It is charged in addition to any CAPITAL GAINS TAX and INCOME TAX or corporation tax for which the seller may be liable, but credit is given against any or all of those taxes.

The tax is levied as follows:
● The first £50,000 of development value in a financial year exempt (though one or more of the other taxes will still have to be paid).
● Profit above £50,000 taxed at 60 per cent.

The tax is assessed by the Development Land Tax Office, a branch of the Inland Revenue.

There are several exemptions from the tax. If the developed house was the main home of the seller, or his wife, or was occupied rent-free by a dependent relative, it will be free of the tax provided that the size of the house and garden combined is not more than 1 acre.

Houses with larger gardens may also be exempt if the garden is 'in character with the house'.

DILAPIDATIONS

Deciding who is responsible for repairs to a rented home

When a property is leased for 7 years or more, the question of who is responsible for making good any dilapidations – that is damage caused by natural ageing, weathering or normal wear and tear – is decided by the wording of the tenancy agreement. *See:* LANDLORD AND TENANT

However, most tenancies are for shorter periods than that and although an agreement may allocate repairing obligations to either landlord or tenant, in most cases common law imposes obligations on the landlord to carry out certain repairs.

When the landlord is responsible for repairs

When the tenancy agreement is weekly, monthly, quarterly or for a fixed term of less than 7 years, the landlord must carry out all structural and exterior repairs and undertake any necessary painting or other protective work that goes with maintenance of the structure. That obligation is imposed on the landlord by law, regardless of anything contained in the agreement on the subject of repairs.

Roofing, brickwork and stonework, repairs to exterior doors, windows and staircases come into that category.

The landlord must also keep gas, plumbing and electrical fittings in good order. He must maintain water-heating and space-heating systems, but is not responsible for portable electric fires and heaters.

When property is damaged by accident the tenant or his insurance must normally pay.

When the house or flat is rented furnished, the common law requires the landlord to ensure it is fit to live in at the start of the tenancy.

That rule applies also to unfurnished property with a rent of less than £80 a year in London or £52 a year in the rest of Britain.

However, with all types of tenancy, the landlord cannot be held responsible for damage caused by his failure to do repairs, if he has not been told about them. The tenant must tell him.

When the tenant is responsible for repairs

The tenant's obligations, which are usually specified in the tenancy agreement, may include all internal decorations – including wallpapering – and any small internal repairs, such as replacing tap washers and fuses, mending broken locks and handles, easing doors and re-fixing unstable fittings.

If the agreement requires the tenant simply to keep the property 'in good repair', he must maintain it at least in the condition in which he found it. He could even be held responsible for small repairs that needed doing before he moved in, if he made the mistake of taking over the property in a dilapidated condition.

If an agreement does not make clear a tenant's responsibility for repairs, his obligations are simply to do those small jobs about the house that are necessary to his own enjoyment of the premises – for example, repairing fuses, locks, tap washers, broken windows and so on. He must not deliberately damage the premises.

If the tenant fails in his obligations, he can be sued for breach of the tenancy agreement and evicted. If he is leaving anyway, the landlord can sue him for damages.

Forcing a landlord to do necessary repairs

If a landlord has been told that repairs which are his responsibility are needed, but fails to carry them out, pressure can be put on him by both the tenant and the local council.

When the neglected repairs are a health hazard or nuisance – such as damp, a blocked lavatory, broken sash-cord or leaking roof – the council can ask the local magistrates for an order under section 91 of the Public Health Act, compelling him to do the necessary work.

If he ignores the order, the council can do the work and then recover its costs by suing him.

Alternatively, the tenant can seek such an order from the magistrates by issuing a private summons under section 99 of the same Act. If that fails, he can seek an order from the county court, but at the same time he must start a civil action for damages. This could be long and costly.

If all else fails, the tenant is entitled to do the repairs himself and deduct the cost from his rent – provided that he can prove conclusively that he gave the landlord sufficient notice. Before taking that drastic step, however, it is advisable to consult a solicitor.

Seeking a rent reduction because of dilapidations

Instead of taking legal action against the landlord for his failure to do repairs, the tenant could go to a rent tribunal or RENT OFFICER to have his rent reduced. That would not get the repairs done, however, and further dilapidation of the premises could be just what the landlord wanted.

If a property deteriorates too badly, the local council would have to order its closure and the tenant would be forced to leave. That could be convenient for a landlord who wanted to redevelop the property.

In any case, the rent officer will take account only of repairs for which the landlord is clearly responsible. He will not consider repairs arising from damage caused by the tenant.

DIPLOMAT

The immunities granted to official representatives

An embassy in Britain has the same legal status as if a small part of the country it represents had been deposited on British soil.

Only its own staff are automatically entitled to enter it. It cannot be searched by the police. Its post and telephone calls are protected by international law from interception, and its diplomats and other staff stand almost entirely outside British law.

The same privileges apply to consuls and to representatives of international organisations.

Diplomatic immunity

A foreign diplomat in Britain cannot be arrested or prosecuted for any criminal offence. His person and property, including his car, cannot be searched; and he or his chauffeur can disregard

PROTECTION OF DIPLOMATS

It is a serious offence to interfere with a diplomat, whether by attacking him or by taking him hostage. Under the Internationally Protected Persons Act 1978, British courts can deal with not only offences occurring in Britain, but also offences against diplomats anywhere in the world.

It is the duty of the host state to protect all foreign diplomats against such attacks. In 1980 the International Court of Justice and the United Nations Security Council ruled that Iran was in breach of international law in allowing the American Embassy in Teheran to be seized and the diplomats to be taken and kept hostage.

A host state cannot enter an embassy without the permission of the foreign state. For example, when the British authorities wanted to send the Special Air Service into the Iranian Embassy in London to seize the hostage-takers and free their hostages, the permission of the Iranian government had to be obtained.

THE CLERK WHO TRIED TO GIVE UP HIS IMMUNITY

Diplomatic immunity does not belong to an individual and a person employed as a diplomat in a foreign country has no power to waive it.

Mr Madan was a clerk on the staff of the Indian High Commission in London when police arrested him for trying to get a railway ticket by false pretences.

He told police that he waived the diplomatic immunity that went with his job, and was put on trial.

At the trial his lawyer tried to stop the case, saying that Madan's diplomatic immunity still prevailed. The court overruled the argument and convicted Mr Madan. He appealed.

DECISION
The Appeal Court ruled that diplomatic immunity belongs to a country, not an individual. Madan had no power to waive it and was therefore immune at the time of his trial. The conviction was quashed.

parking and other regulations. If the car is not showing CD plates to indicate a diplomatic car, a diplomatic pass may have to be shown to prove immunity if questioned.

A civil action can be brought against him only if it concerns land he owns privately in Britain, his entitlement or assumed entitlement to a dead person's estate, or professional or commercial activities outside his official functions. However, he remains subject to his own country's law, and a claimant might be able to take civil action against him in the courts of that country. *See:* INTERNATIONAL LAW

Diplomatic privileges

Apart from such cases, a diplomat does not have to give evidence in court and he is exempt from jury service. He does not have to pay British income tax, customs duties or national insurance contributions.

All members of a foreign diplomat's family have exactly the same privileges. Administrative and technical staff of an embassy have the same immunities, except protection against most civil actions; they can be sued on any matter unconnected with the embassy. If British nationals are members of the administrative and technical staff they are immune during working hours.

The only exemptions granted to the domestic staff of an embassy are that they do not have to pay income tax or national insurance contributions, provided that they are covered by a social security scheme in their own country.

A diplomat does not have a free hand to act as he wants, however. If he seriously abuses his privileged status, the Government can demand his removal

from Britain. If he is suspected of being a spy, he is declared persona non grata, and made to leave the country, perhaps within 24 hours. No reason need be given for the suspicion.

International officials

Senior foreign or British officials of international organisations receive the same immunities as diplomats, whether living in Britain or just visiting it.

High-level representatives protected in this way include the Secretary-General of the United Nations and his deputies, and judges of the European Court of Justice. Lower-ranking officials have correspondingly fewer privileges.

Consuls and honorary consuls

Many of the privileges granted to diplomats extend also to consuls and honorary consuls, but in addition to the civil actions that can be brought against diplomats, consuls may also be sued in connection with traffic accidents or contracts signed by them otherwise than on behalf of their state.

Consuls can also be prosecuted for criminal offences and they can be called to give evidence in court. If they refuse to attend, they cannot be penalised, however.

British diplomats abroad

British diplomats abroad have the same privileges and immunities as foreign diplomats in Britain. If Britain went to war with the foreign country, the diplomat would be withdrawn immediately.

If there were any delay, the country would protect the diplomat. *See also:* FOREIGN EMBASSY

DIRECTOR

*Employers who may also be
employees of a company*

Both private and public companies
must have at least one director. *See:*
BUSINESS, Starting a

There can be two types of director in
a public company: full-time and part-
time. A part-time director receives a
relatively small fee and is expected
merely to appear at occasional board
meetings.

A full-time working director is an
employee, and is entitled to the same
protection as other employees against
unfair dismissal and redundancy.

If the company fails If a company becomes insolvent and ceases to trade,
an employee-director becomes entitled
to a redundancy payment which is
met entirely by the State. *See:*
REDUNDANCY

If a director is dismissed

A company director who is dismissed
is entitled to seek compensation
through an industrial tribunal. *See:*
UNFAIR DISMISSAL

However, the maximum he can claim
is £16,090 and it may be better to sue
through the courts for wrongful dismissal instead.

National insurance contributions

Company directors have to pay
Class 1 NATIONAL INSURANCE
CONTRIBUTIONS. The percentage contribution depends on whether, as a
member of his company's occupational
pension scheme, a director is contracted
out of the additional provisions of the
state scheme.

Class 1 contributions are payable by
both the company and the director.
Where he has a number of separate
directorships with different companies,
each of the companies is responsible for
paying Class 1 contributions in respect
of his earnings from each directorship.
If he is a director of various companies
within one group, and only one of them
pays his total remuneration, contributions are calculated on the single
payment.

A professional person, such as an accountant or solicitor employed on his
own account, may be appointed a director for his professional services.

Whether the fees are paid to him or to
his firm, Class 1 contributions are payable. If he has made some arrangement
with the Inland Revenue whereby he is
paid without deduction of PAYE tax,
he is liable for Class 4 contributions.

A director who is a married woman or
widow is also liable to pay Class 1 contributions on her earnings, whether she
is active or inactive in the business.

Income tax

A director who receives any FRINGE
BENEFIT is taxed on what it costs his
company to provide the benefit unless
he is a full-time employee owning no
more than 5 per cent of the share capital
and earning less than the relevant
amount. Those few directors who fall
within the exception are taxed on the
amount of money they could get by
selling the benefit at its second-hand
value.

DIRECTOR OF PUBLIC PROSECUTIONS

The nation's chief prosecutor

The Director of Public Prosecutions
is the government's chief prosecutor for
England and Wales. He is appointed by
the Home Secretary and works under
the Attorney General.

Some crimes – for example, serious
forgeries and offences under the Official Secrets Act – must be referred to
him by the police. Some cases – including offences by solicitors, gun and drug
crimes, incest, bankruptcy and Companies Acts offences – can be started
only with his consent.

DISABILITY PENSION

*Regular payment awarded to disabled
ex-servicemen and women*

Anyone who is disabled or is unable
to take normal work because of injury
or damage suffered during military service is entitled to a special disability
pension. *See also:* WAR PENSIONS

How to make a claim

If you think you are entitled to a
pension, ask for form MPB 214 at your
local social services department, or ob-

tain one from your army welfare officer,
complete and send it to the Department
of Health and Social Security.

If your application is rejected, you
must be told why, and you have the right
to appeal to a pensions appeal tribunal.
But you must do so within 12 months.

The local office of the Department of
Health and Social Security will tell you
how to make an appeal and where to
find the tribunal.

If you are awarded a pension but
disagree with the amount awarded you
can ask the tribunal to review the award
– within 12 months.

When contributory negligence is alleged

If the Secretary of State agrees that
the disability was caused by the applicant's military service, but that the serviceman was wholly or partly responsible for his injury because of negligence
or misconduct, an award can be refused
or reduced. The applicant can appeal
to the pensions appeal tribunal within
12 months.

Appealing to a tribunal

A pensions appeal tribunal must have
at least three members, all of them appointed by the Lord Chancellor's office.
At least one member must be of the
same sex and have served in the same
arm of the Services as the claimant.

If the appeal is against refusal of a
pension, the tribunal must include a
barrister or solicitor and a doctor. If the
appeal is against the assessment of disability, the tribunal must include two
doctors.

When an appeal is heard, the tribunal
may pay the applicant's travelling expenses and any expenses incurred by
him in obtaining medical reports and
certificates and the attendance of expert
medical witnesses.

The decision of a tribunal is usually
final, but if the appellant considers that
a decision is wrong on a point of law, he
may ask the tribunal for leave to appeal
to the High Court. If such an appeal is
heard, the tribunal may pay any costs
incurred by the appellant – for example,
if he cannot afford to pay.

The right to a pension

Once a pension has been awarded to
an ex-serviceman, payment continues

as of right unless the Secretary of State varies or revokes the award. The Secretary is allowed, by law, to do this – under powers granted to him by Royal Warrant or Order in Council. If that happens, the pensioner can appeal to the pensions appeal tribunal.

DISABLEMENT

Help available to disabled and chronically sick people

A disabled person is someone who, because of physical or mental impairment, or loss of limbs, is unable to function properly in a society designed for fit people.

In Britain, the Chronically Sick and Disabled Persons Act 1970 makes every local authority responsible for finding out how many disabled people live in its area, and for providing whatever aids and facilities it considers each disabled person needs to help him to lead a fuller life.

A disabled person does not have to be formally registered to qualify for the benefits available, but if he is permanently or severely disabled he can ask to be assessed for inclusion on the Handicapped Register and so qualify for the extra benefits available in some areas only to registered people.

If you are disabled, ask your doctor or the social services department of your local council, whose address you can find in the telephone directory, to arrange for a social worker to visit you. The social worker will assess your disability and your needs and also put you in touch with any voluntary organisation concerned with your particular handicap.

If you disagree with the social worker's assessment you can appeal to the adviser on services for the disabled at your social services department.

Many of the benefits for the disabled – disability pensions, artificial limbs, home nursing, for example – come from central government or the National Health Service and depend upon the assessment of a family doctor or hospital doctor and not a local government social worker.

Most disabled people qualify for more than one benefit or service, so you should check your rights carefully. Your local social security office, social services department, hospital social worker or Citizens Advice Bureau will help you to do this.

Leaflets HB 1 *Help for handicapped people* and HB 2 *Aids for the disabled* – obtainable from your local social security office or post office – will also help you to know what is available.

Services available through the National Health Service

Your health needs – such as treatment by a GP, hospital doctor, chiropodist or district nurse – or any necessary health aids and appliances such as hearing aids, incontinence pads or artificial limbs, are generally covered by the National Health Service.

Your doctor If you need advice about your general health, consult your family doctor. He will see that you get treatment and will also tell you what services are available.

Hospital treatment If your doctor thinks that you need hospital treatment he will refer you to a hospital or ask the specialist to visit you at home. You cannot demand hospital treatment or the services of a specialist. *See:* HOSPITAL

Prescriptions If you need continuous drug treatment or other items on prescription, such as bandages, or if you are on a low income, you may be able to get your prescriptions free or at a reduced rate. For information about such concessions get leaflet M 11 (low-income exemption) or forms FP 91 (medical exemption) or FP 95 (season ticket) from a post office.

Health visitor If you are suffering from a long illness, or if you have a handicapped child, a health visitor can visit you regularly, to advise on health matters and nursing aids and equipment.

District nurse Your family doctor can arrange for you to be visited by a district nurse. The nurse will also give you any injections you need, help you with bathing, bandages and other nursing requirements and arrange for you to get special nursing aids – such as a bedpan or lifting hoist.

Chiropody treatment If you have foot trouble, ask your doctor or district nurse to arrange for you to see a chiropodist – who can visit you at home, if necessary. If you cannot afford a chiropodist's fee, or if you are a pensioner, you can be treated free of charge.

Artificial limbs and appliances Some surgical appliances are supplied, maintained and replaced free of charge through the National Health Service on the recommendation of a hospital consultant. The hospital will make arrangements for you to visit the nearest limb fitting or artificial limb and appliance centre where you can be fitted with a limb or appliance and taught how to cope with it.

Other needs The National Health Service can supply most of your medical needs – sometimes free – so if you need a hearing aid, wig, artificial eye or anything else to help you to lead a fuller life, ask your doctor to refer you to a specialist.

A wig is supplied free usually only if the patient is prematurely bald or has extensive head scars – caused, for example, by an accident or illness.

How your local social services department will help

Every local authority has a social services department that provides a wide range of non-medical services – in and outside the home – for the disabled. These services may vary from area to area so contact your local office to see what is available to you.

Home help If you cannot cope with your housework, washing or shopping, ask your GP or hospital to contact your local authority. Some authorities provide such help free. Others make a charge if the disabled person can afford it. The social services department will assess your income and decide whether you have to pay.

Hot meals Councils in most parts of the country provide a hot midday meal on two or more days a week for disabled people who would otherwise not get one. Housebound people can get theirs from a meals on wheels service – run either by the council itself or by a voluntary organisation such as the Women's Royal Voluntary Service.

People who can get about can go to a day centre or luncheon club if there is one in their area. Transport will be provided if necessary. A small charge is made for all meals.

Telephone Some local authorities pay for the installation of a telephone for

ADAPTING A HOME TO HELP A DISABLED PERSON

How to find out about the hundreds of aids and appliances that are available

Getting out of bed
Getting in and out of bed can be made easier by using an electrically operated hoist which slides along tracking fixed to a gantry or to the ceiling. Alternatively, a 3-position bed enables an invalid or disabled person to sit in a chair without the problem of getting out of bed

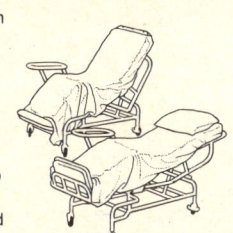

Raised lavatory seat
A removable seat, held in the desired position by plastic pads, raises the lavatory to a comfortable height. The surround which is portable enables the handicapped person to help pull himself on and off the seat

Taking a bath in private
An automatic chair lift is one of the many ways in which a handicapped person can lift himself in and out of a bath

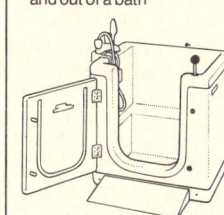

In a portable bath closet the disabled person can take a bath in a sitting position in waist-high water

Making a ramp
A wheelchair can be manoeuvred easily into a house with the aid of a wooden ramp

Widening a doorway
If an existing doorway is too narrow for a wheelchair to pass through, it can be widened and a wider door fitted

Indoor wheelchair
A battery-operated indoor wheelchair allows the user to move freely around the house

Adapted telephone
The Post Office has a large range of specially designed equipment for adapting a telephone to suit any type of disability

Travelling upstairs
A chairlift, on which the handicapped person can sit or stand, can be fitted to an existing staircase

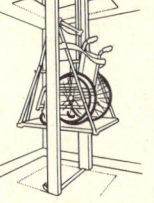

An electrically operated hoist carries a handicapped person in a wheelchair through a trap door to a higher or lower floor level without him leaving the chair

Coping in the kitchen
Kitchens can be adapted to wheelchair users with the help of built-in and low-level equipment

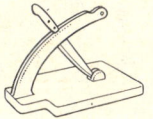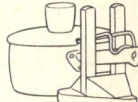

Gadgets, such as the one on the left with which to guide a knife, and the saucepan clamp on the right, help those with limited use of their hands

The long-handled helping hand grips items which would normally be beyond reach of the handicapped person

handicapped people or for the parents of handicapped children. They may also pay the telephone rent – but you must pay for the calls yourself.

Cheap travel Bus passes are issued by some councils entitling registered disabled people to cheap or free travel. Blind people can also get concessionary fares from British Rail and London Transport and on British Airways domestic flights.

Parking badge If you are blind or have difficulty in walking and use a car – either as driver or passenger – you are entitled to an orange badge which allows you to ignore certain parking restrictions. The badge allows you to park at a parking meter without a time limit and without paying. You can also park on a yellow 'no parking' line, provided that you do not cause a traffic obstruction and that you keep to a locally prescribed time limit. The orange badge is valid anywhere, except for an area of central London which has its own scheme for disabled people who live or work in the borough where they wish to park.

Holidays Many local authorities provide holidays for mobile disabled people and people in wheelchairs who do not need nursing care. The holidays, which are free or at a reduced cost, are usually provided at holiday camps or centres run by voluntary organisations. Transport to and from the holiday centre is provided. Day outings, particularly for people living alone, are also provided.

Home aids Councils lend aids – such as raised lavatory seats, hoists, alarm signals, geriatric chairs and commodes. They also carry out adaptations to the home – for example, fitting handrails or ramps. Minor alterations are usually provided free. If major adaptations are required – such as a downstairs lavatory or a lift – they may help towards the cost.

Other services Many social services departments install specially adapted radios and televisions free of charge. Some have a free laundry service and home library service. Others run day centres to provide social contact and recreation. Transport to and from the centres is usually provided. Some areas have visiting occupational therapists for disabled people who cannot get to a centre.

SPECIAL HELP FOR DISABLED CHILDREN

Many area health authorities keep a register of 'at risk' children who could become handicapped – that is children whose mothers have had illnesses in pregnancy, babies who have shown abnormal reactions or babies born to families who already have a handicapped child.

When a child is on the register, the authorities keep a check on its development and advise the parents on where to get treatment for the child.

Assessment centres If you are concerned about your child's development ask your GP to refer the child to an assessment centre or to a specialist at a hospital. If your doctor is unsympathetic, contact the local hospital or area health authority direct. You can find the address in the telephone book.

Health clinics All local authorities have child-health clinics which treat disabled children and give advice to parents.

Nursery care Many social services departments run day-care nurseries for disabled children.

Financial help Children over the age of 2 who need a lot of looking after are entitled to an attendance allowance. Children over 5 who are unable to walk, or can walk only with help, can be paid a mobility allowance. Parents of a disabled child can claim a grant from their local housing depart-

ment to help them to adapt their home for the child's needs. They may also be entitled to help from the Department of Health and Social Security.

If you are the parent of a disabled child ask the social services department of your local council to explain what services and financial help you are entitled to receive. *See:* FAMILY FUND

Education Under the Education Act 1944, it is the duty of every local education authority to find out which children in its area need special education. Any education authority will arrange a medical examination for a handicapped child over the age of 2 and advise the parents on its educational needs.

The authority must arrange where the child is to be sent – either to a special class in an ordinary school or to a special school devoted to a particular handicap. If a child is severely handicapped, home tuition may be provided.

The education authority may also provide aids for education, such as Braille equipment for a blind child or an interpreter for a deaf and dumb child.

If a school or education authority is unhelpful, the parents can ask a local councillor or their Member of Parliament to apply to the Department of Education and Science.

Local housing help

Local councils have several types of housing specially designed for disabled people. They also have IMPROVEMENT GRANT schemes to help those who need to adapt their own homes. Such schemes cover only part of the cost involved. There is no means test for the grant.

If you cannot cope in your own home as it is at present, get in touch with the housing department at the council headquarters and ask for a visit by one of its staff.

If you cannot afford the adaptation cost despite receiving a grant, the council social services department may pay the balance, but that will involve a means test.

Rent and rate rebates If you are a registered physically disabled person and your income is limited, you are entitled to a rent rebate or allowance and rate rebate under the Housing Finance Act. Even if you are not regis-

tered, you may get a rebate if you are not receiving supplementary benefit; but registered disabled people get bigger rebates. Apply to the rent and rates rebate office of your local council.

What financial help is available

There are many financial benefits payable by the Department of Health and Social Security to disabled people and their families. The amount you get depends upon the cause and effects of your disablement.

Sickness benefit If you cannot work because of your disablement you can claim SICKNESS BENEFIT for up to 28 weeks provided you are of qualifying age and have paid the qualifying number of insurance contributions.

If you are still unable to work after 28 weeks, your sickness benefit automatically becomes an INVALIDITY PENSION and an INVALIDITY ALLOWANCE is added to the benefit.

If you do not have enough national insurance contributions you can claim a non-contributory invalidity pension provided that you are of working age, are not a married woman and have been incapable of work for 28 weeks.

If you are a married woman of working age and incapable of both paid work and your normal household duties you may be entitled to a housewife's non-contributory pension.

Industrial injury benefit If you cannot work because of an accident at work or because you are suffering from an industrial disease you may be entitled to claim INDUSTRIAL INJURY BENEFIT or DISABLEMENT BENEFIT. Disablement benefit can be paid even if you are able to work.

Attendance allowance An ATTENDANCE ALLOWANCE is payable for anyone over the age of 2 who is severely disabled – physically or mentally – and has needed a lot of looking after for at least 6 months. Anyone – other than a wife living with or supported by her husband – who stays at home to look after such a person may be entitled to an INVALID CARE ALLOWANCE.

Mobility allowance If you are under pension age and unable to walk – or can walk only with help – you may be able to claim a MOBILITY ALLOWANCE.

When a disabled person is capable of working

If you are capable of working but have difficulty in finding a job, contact the disablement resettlement officer at your local employment office or job centre. He will help you to find suitable employment or recommend a course at an employment rehabilitation centre if he thinks you need to regain your confidence to work.

The courses usually last for 6 weeks. You will not receive wages during your training, but you will be paid a tax-free living allowance and all your expenses.

If you show potential for training for a particular job, the resettlement officer will arrange for you to take a course at a skill centre or other training establishment and will tell you what allowances you get during training.

Disabled register If you are severely handicapped, the resettlement officer will invite you to register as a disabled person. Registration is voluntary, but it

does have advantages. For instance, employers of more than 20 people are legally bound to employ registered disabled people to make up at least 3 per cent of their total payroll.

Sheltered employment If someone is too handicapped to work under ordinary conditions the resettlement officer may be able to arrange 'sheltered' employment for him. Sheltered employment means that the individual competes only with other handicapped people, and does not have to cope with the work standards of people with no disability. The main sources of sheltered employment are Remploy, who have 87 factories throughout Britain, local authorities and voluntary organisations, subsidised by the Government.

Help with fares If you are severely disabled you may be able to claim up to 75 per cent of your fares from the Manpower Commission. To qualify you must be registered under the Disabled Persons (Employment) Act and you must be physically unable to use public transport. If you think you may be eligible for help of this kind apply to the resettlement officer at your job centre or employment office.

How mentally handicapped people can be helped

Mentally handicapped people are entitled to many of the same benefits and services as the physically handicapped. *See:* MENTAL DISORDER

WHEN SUPPLEMENTARY BENEFIT IS PAYABLE
Special rules governing extra financial help for the disabled

Any disabled person over the age of 16 – except a married woman living with her husband – can claim supplementary benefit if his income is below a certain level. Although benefit is not normally paid to people who are still at school or in full-time employment, there are some exceptions for the disabled.

Still at school

Anyone still at school and so severely handicapped as to be unlikely to get a job can claim benefit from their 16th birthday.

In full-time work

A self-employed person whose earning power is substantially reduced by disablement, compared with other people doing similar work, can claim benefit.

If you can work

If you are able to work but have no job you must sign on – that is register – as an unemployed person at the local office of the Department of Employment. If you do not do so, you will not receive benefit. But you may not have to sign on if your disability makes it unlikely that you will find a job.

If you cannot work

If you are unable to work, you do not have to sign on at the employment office, but you must submit medical certificates to the social security office.

Rates of benefit

The amount of benefit you receive depends upon what other income you have.

If you are getting an ATTENDANCE ALLOWANCE or MOBILITY ALLOWANCE your supplementary benefit will not be affected.

Up to £4 of a DISABILITY PENSION can also be ignored, but the rest of a disability pension and any other national insurance benefits will be deducted in full from your entitlement.

If you received a lump sum payment as compensation for an injury it will be treated as capital, but you are allowed £2,000 savings (excluding the value of your own home). If you have more, you cannot claim supplementary benefit.

If the money is held in trust it will be treated as yours if the trustees are empowered to make payments to you or for your benefit.

Extra benefit

If you have additional expenses because of your disablement – you may have abnormally heavy wear and tear on clothing or shoes, for instance, or you may need a special diet, extra heating or domestic help – ask your social security office if you qualify for either occasional lump sum special payments, or 'exceptional-circumstances' additions to your weekly benefit.

If you are getting an attendance or mobility allowance, you will automatically be assumed to need extra heating.

If you receive supplementary benefit for longer than 1 year, you will qualify for extra long-term benefit provided that you have not had to register for work in the last 1 year.

DISABLEMENT BENEFIT

How to get compensation for injury at work

If, as a result of an ACCIDENT AT WORK or INDUSTRIAL DISEASE, you suffer a personal injury that means you can no longer enjoy a normal life to the full – called 'loss of faculty' – you are entitled to disablement benefit.

Your entitlement is not governed by your earning capacity – for example, disfigurement, even although it caused no bodily handicap, would qualify.

You do not need to have paid any national insurance contributions to be eligible, but you must have been in employment when you sustained the injury or industrial disease.

Self-employed people do not qualify for disablement benefit.

Even if the accident or disease makes you incapable of work, you cannot draw disablement benefit until 26 weeks after it happens.

During that time you can draw INDUSTRIAL INJURY BENEFIT and you may be entitled to other industrial injury benefits such as unemployability supplement, constant attendance allowance and special hardship allowance. If after the first 26 weeks you are still incapable of work SICKNESS BENEFIT or invalidity pension may be paid as well as any disablement benefit.

However, even when you are not prevented from working you should claim disablement benefit immediately after the injury.

How to claim

Claim at your local social security office, using:
● Form BI100A for accidents.

HOW AN APPLICANT'S DEGREE OF DISABLEMENT IS CLASSIFIED

Working out the level of compensation that should be awarded for the loss of limbs or faculties

Injury	% degree of disablement	Injury	% degree of disablement
Very severe facial disfiguration	100	*Amputation:*	
Absolute deafness	100	of one foot	30
Loss of:		*Loss of:*	
both hands	100	vision of one eye	30
a hand and a foot	100	three fingers of one hand	30
both legs or a leg and other foot	100	two fingers of one hand or of thumb end	20
sight	100	all toes of one foot	20
Amputation:		whole great toe	14
through shoulder joint	90	whole index finger	14
at hip	90	whole middle finger	12
of both feet	80–90	part of index finger	5–11
below hip and above knee	70–80	four toes of one foot, excluding great toe	9
below shoulder	60–80	part of middle finger	4–9
at knee	60–70	whole ring or little finger	7
Loss of:		three toes of one foot excluding great toe	6
a hand, or of the thumb and four fingers of one hand	60	part of ring or little finger	2–6
four fingers of one hand	50	two toes of one foot excluding great toe	5
Amputation:		part of great toe	3
below knee	40–50	any other toe	3
Loss of:		part of four toes of one foot, excluding great toe	3
one eye	40	part of three toes of one foot, excluding great toe	3
thumb	30–40	part of two toes of one foot, excluding great toe	2
all toes of both feet	20–40	part of any other toe	1

An official percentage tariff is used by the independent medical board to decide an applicant's degree of disablement. For example, loss of both hands rates 100 per cent, loss of one hand is 60 per cent and the amputation of a fingertip without loss of bone rates 2 per cent. An applicant is compensated according to the tariff of compensation rates unless the nature of his injury makes this unreasonable.

● BL100 (Pn) for pneumoconiosis and byssinosis.

● BI100 (OD) for deafness.

● BI100B for other industrial diseases.

If your injury or disease is accepted by the Department of Health and Social Security as an industrial one, an independent medical board of two doctors appointed by the Department decides whether you have suffered a loss of faculty as a result and assesses the degree and the duration of your disablement.

If you can travel, you are told where and when to go for a private medical examination, and your expenses are reimbursed. If someone is unfit to travel alone, a companion's expenses are paid as well.

If you are not fit to travel you are examined at home or in hospital.

It would be useful to you to have a report about your disablement, so you should ask your GP or hospital doctor to make one for you.

The board expresses the degree of disablement as a percentage. If it is less than 20 per cent the benefit will be paid in a lump sum. If it is 20 per cent or above it is paid as a weekly pension.

Not all cases are straightforward. The claimant may have had a congenital defect or some pre-existing injury which made the effects of the accident more serious. He may suffer multiple injuries or have a succession of accidents. These cases – which are not covered by the tariff – are dealt with under separate regulations.

How to appeal

Anybody who is dissatisfied with the decision of the medical board can appeal to the medical appeal tribunal. If you wish to do so you should inform your local social security office within 3 months of the medical board's decision and state your reasons for doing so.

The tribunal consists of two doctors and a lawyer chairman. You can be represented by anyone you choose, but if a lot of money is at stake it would be advisable to get a solicitor who specialises in industrial injury claims. He would be best able to assemble the necessary medical evidence and he would know whether it was worthwhile getting a specialist's report. It may be possible to get legal aid from your trade union.

DISAFFECTION

The law against inciting members of the forces to rebel

It is an offence to attempt to seduce any member of the armed forces either verbally or otherwise, from his duty or allegiance, or even to possess a document that, if distributed, would constitute such an attempt.

The normal public right to distribute pamphlets becomes restricted if the pamphlets are given to members of the armed forces.

It is not an offence to distribute a leaflet that merely gives information – for example, you are entitled to tell a soldier how he can lawfully obtain his discharge. But you are not allowed to encourage him to desert or to neglect his duty in some other way. A member of the armed forces is forbidden to join a trade union.

PACIFIST LITERATURE
IS FORBIDDEN

You may give propaganda literature to a member of the armed forces but you must not encourage him to neglect his duty.

Anyone convicted of incitement to disaffection can be sentenced to 2 years' imprisonment and/or fined an unlimited amount.

DISCIPLINE AT WORK

How a worker who misbehaves may be punished

Employees must behave themselves at work, take care in what they do and conduct themselves in a reasonable

manner. All of those obligations are imposed by English common law, and if an employee fails to observe one of them, his employer can discipline him.

Dismissal is the only punishment that is generally recognised under common law. Others – for example, fines or a period of suspension without pay – may be unlawful unless they are specifically allowed under the EMPLOYMENT CONTRACT. If they are not in the contract, the employee may sue for breach of CONTRACT or, if he resigns in protest, he may be entitled to claim constructive DISMISSAL.

The Employment Protection (Consolidation) Act 1978 requires employers to give every employee details of his employment contract in writing within 13 weeks of his starting work, but there is no direct punishment for anyone who does not do so.

On the other hand, both employer and employee can benefit from having disciplinary rules and procedures written down rather than relying on custom and practice. An employer is more likely to resist claims for breach of contract or unfair dismissal if he can show that the grounds for disciplinary action were clearly set out in writing and accepted by the employee when he joined the company. In particular, the right to suspend an employee without pay is not likely to be upheld by a court or an industrial tribunal unless it is specifically written into the contract.

If an employee is sacked for a trivial offence, he can claim UNFAIR DISMISSAL. Even if the offence is serious, the employee may succeed in an unfair dismissal claim if he can show that the employer acted unreasonably. That may occur in several circumstances, of which the most common are:

● If company disciplinary rules and procedures were not properly followed.

● If the employee was not given an adequate chance to explain his version of events.

● If the employee could not be reasonably expected to know that the offence could lead to dismissal.

In such cases, the compensation will be reduced if the employee's behaviour contributed to his dismissal.

Following the ACAS code

Even when disciplinary rules and procedures are clearly stipulated in a

> ## THE NIGHT WORKER WHO FELL ASLEEP
>
> *An employer who wants to be able to dismiss employees for a specific offence – for example, falling asleep at work – must ensure that they have been given clear warning that it is an offence. He must follow proper disciplinary rules and procedures, and must be consistent in his treatment of offenders.*
>
> Mr Ayub was a production worker at Vauxhalls, the vehicle manufacturers. Working on a night shift, he finished all the work allocated to him, and then fell asleep. He was dismissed, and claimed unfair dismissal.
>
> ### DECISION
>
> The dismissal was unfair, as Mr Ayub's offence did not amount to gross misconduct. However, the decision might have been different had employees been clearly warned that falling asleep might cost them their jobs. The industrial tribunal was told that another employee, who had committed the same offence 3 days earlier, had only been suspended.

written employment contract, accepted by both employer and employee, they can be discounted by an industrial tribunal if it decides they are unreasonable.

The general standard by which an employer's disciplinary arrangements may be judged is one of the ADVISORY, CONCILIATION AND ARBITRATION SERVICE (ACAS) codes of practice, No. 1 *Disciplinary Practice and Procedures in Employment*, available from Her Majesty's Stationery Office.

Although not legally binding, the code is intended to apply to all employers or companies of whatever size, suitably adapted to meet specific circumstances.

When dismissal is justified

Misconduct justifying dismissal in one set of circumstances may not do so in another. For example, the use of bad language at work may be unacceptable in a department store, but of less concern on a building site.

Drinking at work Drinking or being under the influence of alcohol does not generally justify dismissal for a first offence unless the job is hazardous – for example, construction work – or if the employee is a pilot, a nurse or a public transport worker.

If an employer wants to be able to sack an employee who is not in a position of such responsibility for a first drinking offence, he should write a provision into the disciplinary rules.

Disobeying safety rules A serious breach of safety rules justifies summary dismissal – that is, immediate dismissal without notice or warnings – although, as always, the employee must be given a chance to explain himself. It makes no difference whether the safety rules are laid down by the Government or by the company. But if the infringement is not serious, or if its consequences are not obvious, the employee may succeed in claiming unfair dismissal.

Clocking-in offences Dishonest timekeeping, such as clocking in at work on behalf of someone else, can normally be punished by summary dismissal only if that is clearly stated in the employment contract, in the company's disciplinary

DISCIPLINARY RULES THAT SHOULD BE OBSERVED

The ACAS code recommends that disciplinary rules should be:
1. Reasonable and adequate for both employer and employees.
2. Drawn up only after consultation with the employees, if possible through their trade union representatives.
3. Clear and concise – capable of being understood by employees and not written in legal jargon, or expressed so generally as to be meaningless.
4. Precise in their statement of penalties, with a clear indication of the type of conduct that may lead to summary DISMISSAL.
5. Known and understood by the employees. (ACAS says that the employer must not only ensure that employees are aware of the rules, but should explain what they mean.)

The code further suggests that disciplinary procedures should allow:
● Careful and prompt investigation by a manager or supervisor before any action is taken, even in serious cases where misconduct would justify summary dismissal.
● The suspension of the employee on full pay to allow an investigation into any allegation that could lead to summary dismissal.

● Both sides to put their cases fully.
The employee should be informed of the complaint against him and be allowed to defend himself, in person or through a union representative or fellow employee, before any decision on disciplinary action is reached. (Failure to allow a worker to present his side of a complaint is one of the most common reasons that employers lose claims for unfair dismissal.)
● A clear and unmistakable written warning to offenders.

It is not enough for a manager to write 'further conduct of this sort may lead to your dismissal'. He should write 'further conduct of this sort will lead to your dismissal'. Only those guilty of the most serious offences should be dismissed without a previous written warning.
● An agreed procedure for appeals.
ACAS says it is the duty of the employer, when an employee is disciplined, to inform him that he can appeal and to tell him how to do it.
● Full disciplinary records to be kept.
Employers should make written records of the nature of any breach of discipline, the action taken, the reason for it, whether

an appeal was lodged and, if so, the outcome of the case.

The code does not suggest that employers should make copies of disciplinary records available to the employees concerned, but there is nothing to prevent an employee asking to read or take notes from his disciplinary file.
● A period of limitation, negotiated between management and staff, after which a warning becomes 'spent' if the employee concerned has behaved satisfactorily in the intervening period.

Once a warning is spent, it should not be used to justify further disciplinary action. The ACAS code does not suggest how long the period of limitation should be, but in some companies it is 1 year and sometimes longer, depending upon the nature of the offence.
● Special attention to certain cases.

Such cases could include the disciplining of trade union officials, in which the employer might be accused of hampering union activity, or of staff on night shifts or in remote depots, when senior managers are not available to take part in the disciplinary procedures.

rules or in a notice posted beside the time-clock.

Falsifying time-sheets If there have been clear warnings to staff that dishonest completion of time-sheets will be punished by dismissal, an employer is entitled to sack offenders provided that the allegations are thoroughly investigated and that the employees are given the chance to explain.

If an employee tried to justify his behaviour by claiming that 'everyone is doing the same thing', he must be able to show that the claim is true. If it were, and the employer turned a blind eye to other offenders, a dismissal would be unfair, unless the person sacked had already been given written warnings.

Lateness for work Employees are required by law to do a full day's work according to the terms of their employment contracts. But in practice some leeway is allowed.

If an employer is concerned about someone's persistent lateness for work, and is considering dismissal, he must

---

WHEN AN ARGUMENT LED TO THE SACK

If a worker is to be dismissed for fighting, the employer must ensure that there was actually a fight, not simply a row or a disagreement.

Till and Walters were working together when they started arguing. The discussion became extremely heated, but no blows were struck. Both were sacked and both claimed unfair dismissal.

DECISION

The tribunal held that their dismissals were unfair because 'there was not a fight, merely a tussle'.

---

warn the employee of the consequences – in writing if possible. An industrial tribunal may not regard general comments about timekeeping or even specific requests to arrive on time as

sufficient warning to justify dismissal.

Absenteeism Persistent or prolonged absence from work without informing the employer or without proper reason may be grounds for dismissal. But the employer risks having to pay compensation for unfair dismissal if he does not ask the employee concerned for an explanation, or if he fails to follow the company's disciplinary rules, before dismissing him.

Fighting at work An employee can be expected to know that fighting at work cannot be allowed, but he cannot know the consequences unless they are pointed out to him.

So the company's disciplinary rules should make it clear if fighting can lead to dismissal, particularly if the penalty is summary dismissal.

The status of the person who is attacked may affect a decision on whether a dismissal for fighting is fair. A mild attack on a foreman or supervisor is more likely to justify dismissal than a similar attack on an equal.

THE GIRL WHO CLOCKED IN FOR HER SISTER

It is unlikely that an industrial tribunal would uphold a summary dismissal for a clocking-in offence, even when it involved dishonesty, if the worker had not had clear warning of the consequences.

When Vivien Gomersall clocked in at the factory, she did so also on behalf of her sister Susan and two other employees. The company's disciplinary rules warned that clocking-in offences would 'render the employee liable to dismissal'. Vivien and her sister were sacked.

Vivien claimed unfair dismissal because the rules were ambiguous – they did not definitely state that employees would be sacked for the offence but simply that they were liable to be sacked.

DECISION

Unfair dismissal. Disciplinary rules should be clear.

Rules on clocking-in must be applied reasonably and fairly. They will not be upheld by an industrial tribunal if an employee is dismissed for a petty breach, or if he had no dishonest intention.

Mitigating circumstances should always be taken into account before an employee is dismissed summarily. His version of events should be checked thoroughly.

THE NIGHT WATCHMAN SACKED FOR VANDALISM

If an alleged theft or act of vandalism is being investigated by the police, an employer does not need to wait until the end of the inquiries or for the outcome of the trial before deciding to dismiss the employee concerned. Provided the employer has enough evidence to be sure that the person concerned is guilty, the dismissal is not unfair, even if no criminal charges are brought or if a court eventually acquits the employee.

Mr Conway, a part-time night watchman at a factory, was charged by the police with malicious damage after windows in

the premises were broken. Several weeks later, Mr Conway's employer asked the police if the charge still stood. He was told that it did and, as a result, he dismissed Mr Conway at once.

When the police eventually dropped the charge, Mr Conway claimed unfair dismissal.

DECISION

The dismissal was fair. Although the charges were eventually dropped, the employer had, on the evidence, reasonable grounds to believe that Mr Conway had broken the windows.

AN ERROR AT THE CHECKOUT

In any case involving dishonesty, an employer must give the employee a chance to defend himself or herself before a decision on dismissal is taken.

Mrs Hill, who worked at a supermarket checkout, failed to ring up 18 items, worth a total of £7, in a large quantity of goods bought by a customer. Asked about the incident by a checkout controller, she replied she had felt unwell. The police were called, and they took Mrs Hill away to the police station for questioning. Later the

same day, the company decided to dismiss her from her post.

The police decided not to bring charges against Mrs Hill, and she claimed unfair dismissal.

DECISION

The dismissal was unfair. Mrs Hill had been unwell when questioned by the controller. She should have been given a further chance to explain a few days later. The proper disciplinary procedures had not therefore been fulfilled.

THE FITTERS WHO WENT ABSENT

In some jobs, absence for reasons other than SICKNESS *may be inexcusable, particularly if it affects safety.*

Two maintenance fitters, both long-serving employees with excellent records, took 2½ hours off one afternoon. Despite their records, they were summarily dismissed for unauthorised absence, in keeping with company policy explained in notices throughout the factory.

DECISION

The dismissals were not unfair, for the warning notices were clear. More important, the men held responsible and important jobs, and were paid to be on call at any time.

THE FORKLIFT TRUCK DRIVER WHO DRANK

Industrial tribunals considering claims of unfair dismissal for drinking at work usually ask whether there was a specific no-drinking rule, and whether it had been brought to the worker's attention.

McAllen, a forklift truck driver, liked a few drinks at lunchtime – 4 pints of beer and a brandy. The employer knew of McAllen's habits and tolerated them for 3 months. Then, without any formal warning, McAllen was dismissed for being drunk. He took his case to an industrial tribunal.

DECISION

The dismissal was unfair. The employer should have warned McAllen.

Theft and damage If a worker can be proved to have stolen from his employer or workmates, or to have deliberately damaged his employer's property, he can be dismissed without notice.

Even when an employer has no direct proof, only suspicion, he can sack a worker if there are 'reasonable grounds' for believing he committed theft or vandalism, and the evidence shows he is guilty 'on a balance of probabilities'.

If the dismissed worker takes the case to an industrial tribunal, the employer will have to be able to show the evidence he had and prove that proper disciplinary procedures were followed.

Offences outside work If an employee is convicted of a crime committed outside the workplace, his employer may be entitled to dismiss him, depending mainly on the nature of the crime and the nature of the job.

Dismissal is fair if the conviction undermines the employer's confidence in the employer's suitability for the post he holds, or if it adversely affects the employer's own reputation. For example, a shopfitting company was held by an industrial tribunal to be justified in sacking a fitter who stole goods from a client's shop.

Financial crimes by employees regularly handling sums of money are generally grounds for dismissal. So, in many circumstances, are sexual offences.

Local and national government employees, and those who work for public corporations such as the Post Office, are more likely to be dismissed for a conviction than their counterparts in private industry – particularly if it involves dishonesty.

Lack of co-operation An employee has a duty to co-operate with his employer and to do his job in accordance with his contract. If he does not – for example, by refusing to work overtime when he is obliged to do so by his contract – he can be disciplined.

But he is under no obligation to like his employer, or even to be friendly towards him. Surliness or deliberate awkwardness may fall short of disciplinary offences. In such cases, the employer should attempt to discover and, if possible, remove the causes of the employee's attitude.

If the surliness develops into rudeness and the awkwardness into a refusal to carry out orders, the employer can follow the disciplinary rules and procedures, giving the worker a chance to discuss the problem. Any warning should be in writing and make the consequences of continued misbehaviour clear. An employer may also be able to dismiss an employee whose personality is creating serious unrest among staff.

HOW EMPLOYEES MAY BE DISCIPLINED

An employer has the choice of several disciplinary methods even within the recommended rules and procedures.

In ascending order, the most usual forms are:

1. An oral warning. By itself, an oral warning carries little legal weight and, alone, it cannot be relied upon to justify a later dismissal, although it is often the first step in formal disciplinary procedures. A summary of the conversation in which a verbal warning has been given should be kept in the company's disciplinary records.

2. A written warning. A copy of the letter to the employee, and of the employee's reply, should be filed in the employer's disciplinary records.

3. Suspension with full pay. An employer is usually allowed to suspend an employee on full pay for disciplinary reasons – perhaps while the case against him is being investigated. However, in some jobs, for example, acting or piloting an aircraft, the EMPLOYMENT CONTRACT says or implies that the employee is entitled to be given work to do, and suspension, even with full pay, might be unlawful.

4. Fines or suspension on reduced pay or without pay. None of these measures is lawful unless it is specifically authorised in the employment contract or by disciplinary rules that can be said to form part of the contract.

5. Demotion. Unless demotion for disciplinary reasons is authorised by the employment contract, the employee may be able to claim constructive DISMISSAL. However, an employer and employee may agree upon demotion, with or without a reduction in pay, as an alternative to sacking.

6. Dismissal. The dismissal of a worker for disciplinary reasons is justified only in the most serious cases, and may be held to be unfair unless the offence is grave or unless the employee has received previous written warnings for similar misconduct.

Any dismissed worker who has completed 1 year's service with his employer can bring a claim for unfair dismissal. The employer must then prove that the dismissal was fair and that the proper rules and procedures were followed.

If an employee is sacked before he has served 1 year, he can claim only the wages due for his period of NOTICE if they have not already been paid.

DISCOUNT

If a store or manufacturer offers reduced prices, you have a right to demand the discount as advertised. However, the supplier is not obliged to sell to you – though if he does, it should be at the discount price.

See: FAIR TRADING
PRICE REDUCTION

DISINHERITANCE

When a will does not provide property for a dependant

A dependant who does not receive reasonable provision for his maintenance under someone's will may be entitled to ask a court to make an order giving him a share of the estate, provided that the person who left the will lived permanently in England or Wales.

If there is no will, the rules of INTESTACY may produce a result that a dependant considers does not make adequate provision for him or her. He can make a claim for reasonable maintenance in the same way as a dependant appealing against a will.

The term dependant, for this purpose, covers:
● A wife or husband.
● An ex-wife or ex-husband who has not remarried.
● A child or anyone who has been treated as though he or she were a child of the deceased.
● Anyone wholly or partly maintained by the dead person immediately before his death.

Before going to court, the claimant should ask the EXECUTOR if he will meet his claim. If those who benefit under the will are all over 18 and all agree to the claim, the executor could meet the claim without going to court. If, however, the beneficiaries do not agree, or if any of them is under 18, the claimant would have to start court proceedings.

If the dead person's net ESTATE (that is, the estate after all liabilities have been met) is not more than £15,000, the claimant must apply to the county court, otherwise to the High Court.

Application must be made within 6 months of the date on which the will was proved as the last will of the deceased, unless the court allows a later application. A court would grant a later application only for a very serious reason – for example, if illness or an accident prevented the claimant from making a claim within the 6 months, or if he had been abroad and did not know about the will until after it had been proved.

The court decides whether the claim is justified and, if so, what would be a reasonable provision for the claimant. In doing so, it considers:
1. Any written or spoken statement by the dead person, whether in his will or not, that has any bearing on the disinheritance.
2. The size and nature of the estate.
3. The comparative needs and resources of the claimant and the people who already benefit under the will.
4. The dead person's comparative obligations towards the claimant and the beneficiaries.
5. Any mental or physical disability of the claimant or of any of the beneficiaries, if it affects the disabled person's capacity to work or involves payment for treatment or care.
6. Any relevant conduct of the claimant or of any of the beneficiaries – for example, a long period of selfless nursing by any of the parties, or, at the other extreme, a selfish disregard of a moral obligation to the deceased.
7. When the claimant is a husband, wife, ex-husband or ex-wife, the claimant's age, the length of the marriage, and – if there was a family – how the claimant fulfilled his or her responsibilities as a spouse and parent.
8. If the claimant is a child of the deceased, the court would take into account the age of the claimant. The younger the child, the more provision the court is likely to make.

If the court decides that the claimant is entitled to money from the estate, it orders the executors of the estate to make that provision.

The order specifies what form the provision is to take: a lump sum, periodical payments, a transfer of property, or some other form. The claimant can state in what form he would like the provision to be made, but the court makes the final decision.

In the case of a widow or widower only, the award can be for more than just maintenance – it can be for a reasonable overall provision.

A will altered in that way by a court remains valid in all provisions not affected by such an alteration.

DISMISSAL

What happens when an employee is sacked

An employer can end an employee's contract at any time, simply by sacking him. But if the employer does not follow certain procedures, or if he does not have valid reasons for the sacking, he may face a claim for WRONGFUL DISMISSAL or UNFAIR DISMISSAL.

Dismissal with notice

The procedures for dismissing an employee are generally stated or implied in his EMPLOYMENT CONTRACT. They provide for a period of notice, from when the employee is informed of his dismissal to the time it takes effect.

Minimum notice periods are laid down by law for most categories of workers, but not for all. The main exceptions are: those who have been in the job for less than 4 weeks; part-timers; and people who perform their duties abroad. *See:* EMPLOYMENT PROTECTION

The statutory minimum notice period for an employee with more than 4 weeks' service, but less than 2 years', is 1 week. After 2 years' service, the notice period increases by 1 week for each complete year of service, up to a maximum of 12 weeks after 12 years or more in the job. Those minimum periods may be increased by the employment contract, which may also grant a right to notice to employees excluded from the statutory provisions. *See:* NOTICE

The employer must continue to pay wages during the notice period. The employee may be required to continue to work, but if he is not he must still be paid wages 'in lieu of notice'.

An employee is entitled to leave while under notice – for example, to start another job – as long as he gives the employer some notice, no matter how short, of his intention to do so. He is not entitled to any payment for the period of notice he does not work, but he does not forfeit his right to claim unfair dismissal or REDUNDANCY.

Giving notice Some individual employment contracts and most collective agreements require notice of dismissal to be given in writing. If there is no such requirement, oral notice of dismissal is just as valid as written notice. But it is in the interests of an employer to write the notice down in case of a future dispute.

Some employers send dismissal notices by recorded delivery, or require the employee to sign and return a copy of the letter as proof of receipt. However, an employee cannot be compelled to sign the letter.

Written notice should state clearly the date from which it takes effect and the length of the notice period or the date by which the employee is expected to leave. The notice period cannot start until the employee has been informed that he is under notice. If payment is to be made in lieu of notice, that should be stated.

Getting written reasons for dismissal

An employer who dismisses someone is not always obliged to give his reasons for doing so at the time. But most employees are entitled to be given the reasons in writing, and should insist upon them if they are considering a claim for unfair dismissal or redundancy.

The main groups of workers who are not entitled to written reasons are:
1. Those who have been employed continuously by an employer for less than 26 weeks at the time the employment contract ended. The statutory notice period is taken into account in calculating the 26 weeks. For example, an employee who works for 25 weeks and is then given 1 week's pay in lieu of notice can demand a written explanation for his dismissal. But if he had worked for only 24 weeks, he would have no such right.
2. Part-timers working fewer than 16 hours per week. See: PART-TIME WORKER
3. People who normally work outside Great Britain. See: EMPLOYMENT PROTECTION

An employee who is entitled to ask for written reasons for his dismissal should put his request in writing. Once the employer has received it, he has 14 days in which to reply. If he fails to do

so, and there is no good reason for his failure, or if the reasons for dismissal appear untrue or incomplete, the employee can complain to an industrial tribunal.

The employer's reply does not have to be completely exhaustive, but it must be self-explanatory, so that anyone reading it can understand from it the essential reasons for dismissal. Provided that the reply meets that condition, it can refer to other documents – for example, previous written warnings as well.

The employee's complaint must be submitted to the industrial tribunal on form IT1, obtainable from any local job centre, within 3 months of the end of the employment contract, or the tribunal will almost certainly refuse to consider it. If the tribunal upholds the complaint it declares what it considers to be the reasons for dismissal, and orders the employer to pay 2 weeks' extra wages to the employee.

Each party involved in the hearing has to pay his own costs.

Dismissal without notice

An employer is entitled to dismiss an employee summarily – on the spot, without notice – if he is guilty of gross misconduct clearly amounting to a fundamental breach of his contract.

The employee is entitled to demand the reasons for dismissal in writing, provided that he is qualified to do so. He retains the right to claim wrongful dismissal to try to obtain his notice pay, and to claim compensation for unfair dismissal or redundancy if he disputes his employer's action.

Only the gravest offences justify summary dismissal. They include embezzlement, deliberate vandalism, theft at the workplace and violent assault upon a superior. Isolated misbehaviour or a breach of discipline which, while serious, cannot be described as gross misconduct is not enough.

When dismissal is not clear

If notice of dismissal is given in writing, it is generally clear to the employee that he is being dismissed. But sometimes notice is given orally and it is not immediately obvious whether the employee has been sacked – and therefore may claim wrongful or unfair dismissal – or has resigned, when he may forfeit his

rights to legal redress. Industrial tribunals consider all the circumstances surrounding a possible dismissal before determining whether it is one or not.

An employee who stopped work arguing that he had been dismissed, simply because his employer had told him angrily to 'get lost' would be unlikely to have a claim upheld by an industrial tribunal. It is in the employee's interest to wait for confirmation of dismissal before stopping work.

If an employee is, or thinks he may have been, dismissed orally, he is entitled to demand written reasons in exactly the same way as if the dismissal notice were in writing,

When dismissal is wrongful

If an employer fails to observe all the terms of the contract – perhaps by failing to give proper notice – the employee may claim wrongful dismissal to secure compensation for the breach of contract. Compensation in cases of wrongful dismissal is normally restricted to the amount of money to which the employee is entitled under the employment contract had proper notice been given. Further damages are rarely awarded.

For example, if the employee were entitled to 6 months' notice, but his employer gave only 3 months' notice, the employee could claim wrongful dismissal to obtain the remaining 3 months' money.

Wrongful dismissal claims are normally heard in county courts. But if the sum involved is more than £2,000, the case is heard in the High Court. The employee can obtain LEGAL AID.

An employee who sues for wrongful dismissal may, if justified by circumstances, also bring a separate claim for unfair dismissal before an industrial tribunal, which may take into account the lack of notice in awarding compensation.

If an employee is dismissed because the company is reducing its activities and he is not to be replaced, he may be entitled to claim REDUNDANCY.

Constructive dismissal

If an employee is forced to resign from his job because of some act by his employer that amounted to a serious breach of the employment contract, he may be able to claim he has been 'constructively' dismissed and obtain compensation from a tribunal for unfair dismissal.

For example, if an employer decides arbitrarily to cut an employee's wages, or to switch him to work entirely different from what he was hired to do under his employment contract, the employee would have a good chance of winning compensation.

He would not be likely to succeed if the change was provided for in the employment contract.

When outside circumstances end a contract

Sometimes an employment contract is ended as the result of outside circumstances.

Death The death of the employer or of the employee automatically ends their contract. If the employer dies and the employee is laid off work as a result, he can claim redundancy, but not unfair dismissal unless he was under notice or had left the job before his employer's death. *See:* EMPLOYEE, Death of; EMPLOYER, Death of

Bankruptcy If an employer goes bankrupt or into liquidation and the employees are dismissed as a result, they can claim redundancy, but not unfair dismissal.

They are entitled also to claim unpaid wages, outstanding holiday pay and up to 4 months' paid pension contributions to an over-all total of £800 as preferential creditors, and any balance as ordinary creditors. Alternatively, they can submit the claim, through the receiver or liquidator, to the Department of Employment. *See:* BANKRUPTCY

When a contract is 'frustrated'

When an employer decides to get rid of an employee because of his prolonged absence from work – for example, through illness or imprisonment – he may be able to show that the employment contract has been 'frustrated' by the employee's inability to fulfil his contractual duties.

Courts and tribunals are reluctant to accept frustration of contract as grounds for ending someone's employment, because the principle would, if too broadly interpreted, greatly undermine employees' legal rights. But if a court or tribunal does decide that a

---

THE GARDENER WHO USED BAD LANGUAGE

Even if an employee has been guilty of misconduct, his summary dismissal may not be upheld if the incident was an isolated one, unrelated to his general behaviour and performance. A single act is rarely grounds for summary dismissal unless it involves a serious crime – for example, embezzlement or large-scale theft.

Mr Wilson was employed as a gardener by Mr Racher. He was diligent and efficient, but Mr Racher criticised him for trivial reasons. One day, Mr Wilson turned his back on his employer to avoid unjustified criticism. But the criticism continued. Mr Wilson retorted with obscene language, which was heard by Mr Racher's wife and children. Mr Racher sacked him on the spot, without notice. Mr Wilson contested the dismissal.

DECISION
Summary dismissal was not justified by one use of obscene language, particularly as Mr Wilson was diligent and efficient.

THE WORKER WHO RECEIVED A 12 MONTH SENTENCE

An employee who loses his job because his employment contract has been frustrated cannot claim unfair dismissal because he has not been 'dismissed'.

Mr Hare was sentenced to 12 months in prison for unlawfully wounding someone in an incident unconnected with his work.

His employers claimed that, as Mr Hare could not perform his duties while he was in prison, the employment contract had been ended.

He disagreed and sought to bring a claim for unfair dismissal.

DECISION
The contract had been frustrated by Mr Hare's imprisonment. The tribunal ruled that he was not therefore entitled to an award for unfair dismissal.

Even if a period of imprisonment is not long enough to frustrate the employment contract, an employer may be justified in dismissing an imprisoned employee if the nature of his offence can be seen to have a bearing on his work. *See:* DISCIPLINE AT WORK

WHEN THE REASONS WERE A DAY LATE

Industrial tribunals strongly uphold the rights of employees to receive written statements of the reasons for dismissal.

Mr Keen was dismissed from his job as regional sales manager. He asked his employer for written reasons, and they were posted to him 12 days after he made the request.

However, they took 3 days to reach Mr Keen, arriving on the 15th day. He asked an industrial tribunal to award him 2 weeks' pay because of his employer's 'unreasonable refusal' to supply the written information within 14 days of his request.

DECISION
Mr Keen was awarded 2 weeks' pay.

THE EMPLOYEE WHO WAS TOLD 'DON'T BOTHER TO GIVE NOTICE'

Industrial tribunals take into account the underlying intention of the employer when determining whether an employee's departure from his job is resignation by him or dismissal by the employer.

Mr Bishop was a foreman who got into dispute with his employer about the length of his lunchbreak.

During their arguments, Mr Bishop said he wanted to leave, giving a week's notice. His employer retorted: 'Don't bother to give notice. Leave now!' Mr Bishop did, and claimed unfair dismissal.

DECISION
The employer's comments amounted to a dismissal. The claim was upheld.

contract has been frustrated, the employee cannot claim unfair dismissal because, legally, he has not been dismissed.

Illness An employee who is absent for a long time because of illness may lose his job through frustration of contract. Many employers define the maximum period during which they will grant sick pay in the written particulars of employment that they give to employees.

If they do so, they are unlikely to be able to claim frustration of contract during the period specified. But once that period has expired, the argument that the contract has been frustrated may be upheld.

Imprisonment If an employee is imprisoned for a long time, he cannot perform his duties and the contract is ended. The courts have not defined exactly how long a prison term must be to frustrate the employment contract. One or two months might not be enough. A sentence of 12 months probably would be.

Fixed-term contracts

When a fixed-term contract expires, neither the employer nor the employee needs to give notice of dismissal unless that is specifically stated in the original agreement. However, if the period of the contract was 52 weeks or more, the employee may be entitled to claim unfair dismissal if it is not renewed. If it was for 2 years or more he may be able to claim redundancy. However, an employer offering a fixed-term contract of 1 year or more may insist that the employee waives his right to claim redundancy and unfair dismissal. *See:* EMPLOYMENT CONTRACT

A full-time employee whose contract was for more than 26 weeks and who worked in Britain is entitled to ask his employer to state, in writing, why the contract was not renewed.

When contract provisions still apply

Some employers require employees to sign a written agreement that, after leaving, they will not set up in competition with their former company, or reveal trade secrets to rivals.

Such clauses are not enforceable if they unreasonably restrict the former employee's right to earn a living or if the restriction would be against public policy. If the matter is brought to court by either party, the onus is on the employer to prove that the clause is reasonable.

Employers are expected to follow agreed rules and procedures, outlined in a code drawn up by the ADVISORY, CONCILIATION AND ARBITRATION SERVICE, when disciplining employees. In all disciplinary cases, including those involving summary dismissal, the employer should investigate, and should allow the employee to give his version of events. If the employer does not follow the procedures, he may lessen his chances of successfully defending a claim brought against him by the dismissed employee. *See:* DISCIPLINE AT WORK

Courts and industrial tribunals have come to regard summary dismissal as an extreme punishment, to be used only in exceptional circumstances. Because of the difficulties of knowing whether a particular summary dismissal will be upheld, many employers make a payment in place of notice even though they believe that, legally, they are not obliged to. The employee cannot then claim wrongful dismissal. To help him defend any unfair dismissal claim, the employer should put a note with the wages in place of notice, stating that they are paid 'without prejudice to our view that you are not entitled to your wages because your conduct justifies us in summarily dismissing you'.

DISTRESS WARRANT

How a debtor's goods can be seized

Once a county court or magistrates' court has ruled that a debt is owed, the debtor should pay it or agree with his creditor to make a settlement within a stated time. If he does not, his goods may be seized under a distress warrant to pay off the debt.

A distress warrant, which is issued by the court, gives a BAILIFF power to enter the debtor's home between sunrise and sunset for rent arrears (or at any reasonable time for other debts), except on a Sunday, and to seize goods which can be auctioned to pay the debt. A bailiff cannot use force to get into a house or flat, but he can enter through an open window, for example. Once inside, he can force or break down any inside door to reach the debtor's property.

Similarly goods that are being bought on hire purchase or which belong to someone else can be taken if the bailiff is executing a warrant for rent arrears, but they are protected if the debt is for rates. It is the duty of the rate payer, however, to inform the hire purchase company or other owner so that it or he can claim the goods from the bailiff.

If, meanwhile, the bailiff has sold the goods, the rate payer will be liable to the owner for their value.

Goods can be seized only by a bailiff and not by the creditor himself. If the bailiff takes something that does not belong to the debtor, he has not committed any criminal offence, as long as he took the goods in good faith and did not know that they belonged to someone else. The true owner can claim the goods back in a civil court.

If a sale realises more than the total debt, the balance is given to the debtor.

DIVORCE

When a marriage cannot be mended

Irretrievable breakdown of a marriage is the only ground for divorce. It can be proved by the partner who wants the marriage dissolved – the petitioner – satisfying a court on one or more of five points:

1. The other partner – the respondent – has committed ADULTERY and the petitioner finds it intolerable to live with the respondent for any reason – not necessarily the adultery.

2. The respondent has deserted the petitioner by withdrawing from the marriage without consent for 2 years – but not necessarily by leaving a particular place. *See:* DESERTION

3. The couple have lived apart for a total of at least 2 years, and the respondent consents to a divorce. The SEPARATION need not be continuous: the couple may attempt RECONCILIATION for up to 6 months. Living apart usually means living at separate addresses, but a couple can conduct separate households under one roof.

THE WIFE WHO COULD NOT PUT UP WITH THE BAD TIMES

Enjoyment of the good times of a marriage does not oblige a wife to put up with the bad.

Anne and Brian Ash married in 1963. In 1966 Brian started a public relations job with much higher pay and what the judge called an 'almost unlimited' expense account. It led to his excessive drinking. He resigned 2 years later and was unemployed.

Anne took a job, leaving Brian to look after the house and children. His drinking increased and he became abusive and violent to her. Her petition, filed in 1971, claimed that she could not reasonably be expected to live with Brian because of his behaviour. He opposed the divorce, blaming his conduct partly on Anne's lack of understanding.

The judge had to decide whether he was dealing with an ordinary, reasonable spouse, or whether he must look at Anne's particular character and personality, having regard to her own behaviour during the marriage.

DECISION

The judge remarked on Anne's 'penchant for self-dramatisation' and malevolent attitude, but ruled that although she had enjoyed the good times with Brian, she was genuinely unable to tolerate the bad. She won her decree.

THE BRIDE WHO COULD NOT BRIDGE THE AGE GAP

Talking down to a young wife can be judged sufficient cause to allow a marriage to end.

Herbert was 56 when he married Brenda in 1969. She was only 24. Throughout the 4 years of their marriage, she claimed, he was highly critical and treated her 'like a child'. She told the court: 'My life was not my own. I dreaded hearing his key in the door.'

The court had to decide whether or not it was intolerable to a woman of Brenda's particular character and temperament to have to live with Herbert, even though other women might have coped.

DECISION

The judge found that Herbert had been self-opinionated and critical in trying to educate his wife to conform to his own standards. He ruled that she could not reasonably be expected to tolerate it, and granted the decree.

4. The couple have lived apart for 5 years. The respondent's consent to a divorce is not required, but it can be opposed by showing that it would cause grave hardship – for example, a wife's loss of widow's pension rights. In such a case the husband would get his divorce if he made provision to compensate her, or if the judge decided that their divorce was in the public interest – for example, because he had another family.

5. The respondent has behaved in such a way that the petitioner cannot reasonably be expected to live with the respondent. In undefended cases the court usually accepts the petitioner's view of what is intolerable behaviour. When a petition is opposed the judge must decide what a reasonable person would expect that particular petitioner to put up with in those particular circumstances. Each case stands on its own facts and on the personalities of the parties.

For example it may not be reasonable to expect a neurotic woman to put up with overbearing conduct by her husband. But a healthy, well-balanced woman might be expected to cope with exactly the same behaviour.

Persistent drunkenness and violence are typical grounds for complaint. Less obviously objectionable behaviour may also be intolerable if the petitioner is deeply affected. Sometimes nagging can amount to intolerable behaviour. So can habitual refusal of sexual intercourse, or refusal to have children.

When a divorce can be sought

A petition is not accepted unless at least one partner has lived in England or Wales for a year or is domiciled here, and – in most cases – until the couple have been married for 3 years. A judge can allow proceedings before 3 years if the petitioner is suffering exceptional hardship or the respondent's behaviour is exceptionally depraved. Such a claim can be opposed by denying it or by contending that the circumstances are not exceptional.

A woman whose husband brought another woman into their home within weeks of the marriage was given leave to petition immediately. So was a man who married a woman when she was

DIVORCE continued on p. 194

DOCUMENT THAT STARTS DIVORCE
Why a marriage should end

IN THE   COWLEY

COUNTY COURT

No. 80 (b) 555

IN THE DIVORCE REGISTRY*

BETWEEN

Mary Elizabeth BARTON

Petitioner

and

John Frederick BARTON

Respondent

DIVORCE PETITION

Full name and address of the petitioner or of solicitors if they are acting for the petitioner.

James, Sutton and Knowles
Central Chambers
Cowley

Court number allotted to each petition identifies the case on all documents

Petition forms are supplied at county court offices or at the Divorce Registry in London. Detailed notes on how to complete them are also provided.

THE DOCUMENT THAT TELLS HOW A MARRIAGE HAS BROKEN DOWN

A petitioner sets down the reasons why a marriage should end and gives evidence to support his claim

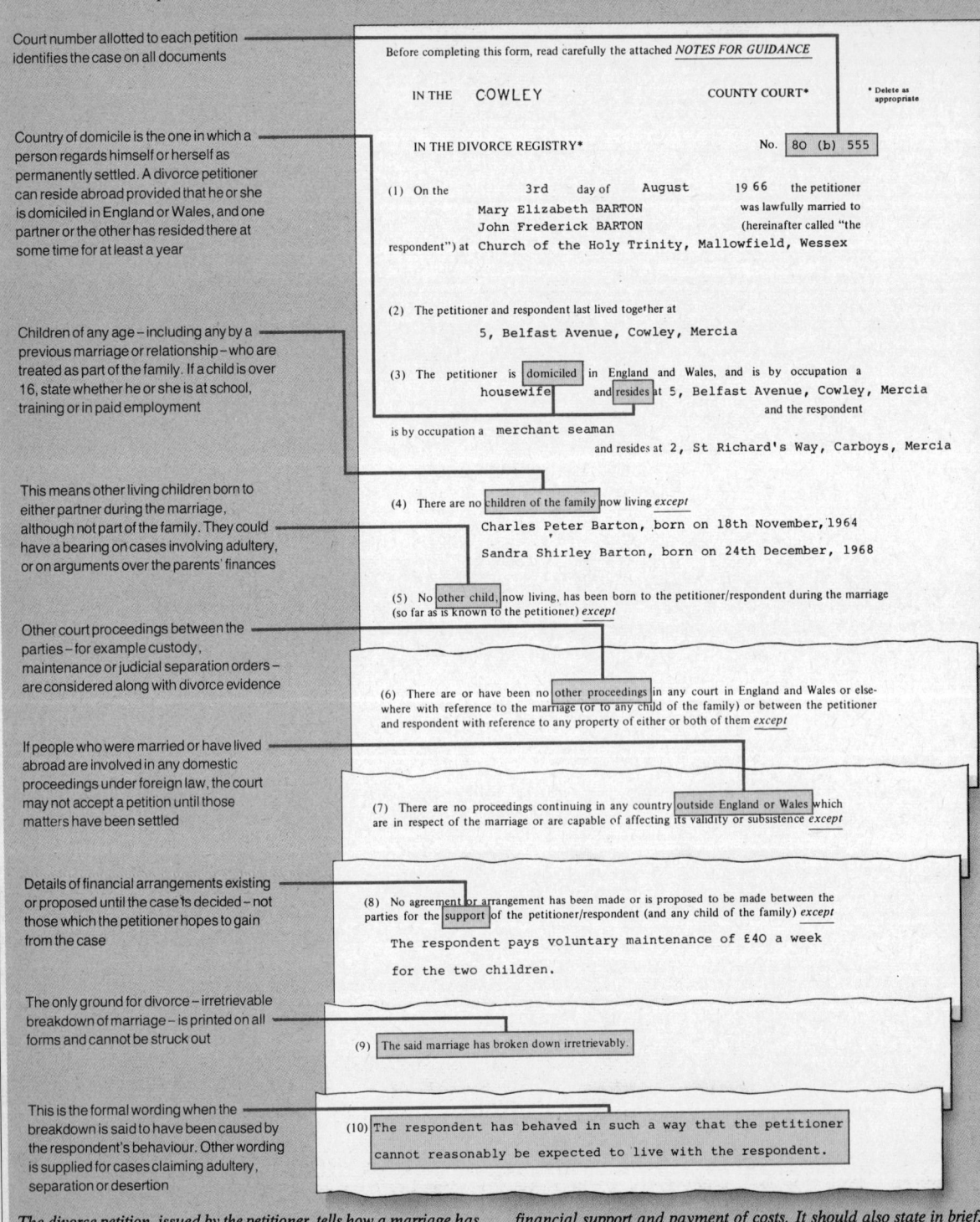

Court number allotted to each petition identifies the case on all documents

Country of domicile is the one in which a person regards himself or herself as permanently settled. A divorce petitioner can reside abroad provided that he or she is domiciled in England or Wales, and one partner or the other has resided there at some time for at least a year

Children of any age – including any by a previous marriage or relationship – who are treated as part of the family. If a child is over 16, state whether he or she is at school, training or in paid employment

This means other living children born to either partner during the marriage, although not part of the family. They could have a bearing on cases involving adultery, or on arguments over the parents' finances

Other court proceedings between the parties – for example custody, maintenance or judicial separation orders – are considered along with divorce evidence

If people who were married or have lived abroad are involved in any domestic proceedings under foreign law, the court may not accept a petition until those matters have been settled

Details of financial arrangements existing or proposed until the case is decided – not those which the petitioner hopes to gain from the case

The only ground for divorce – irretrievable breakdown of marriage – is printed on all forms and cannot be struck out

This is the formal wording when the breakdown is said to have been caused by the respondent's behaviour. Other wording is supplied for cases claiming adultery, separation or desertion

Before completing this form, read carefully the attached *NOTES FOR GUIDANCE*

IN THE **COWLEY**   COUNTY COURT*   * Delete as appropriate

IN THE DIVORCE REGISTRY*   No. 80 (b) 555

(1) On the   3rd day of   August   19 66   the petitioner Mary Elizabeth BARTON   was lawfully married to John Frederick BARTON   (hereinafter called "the respondent") at Church of the Holy Trinity, Mallowfield, Wessex

(2) The petitioner and respondent last lived together at 5, Belfast Avenue, Cowley, Mercia

(3) The petitioner is domiciled in England and Wales, and is by occupation a housewife and resides at 5, Belfast Avenue, Cowley, Mercia and the respondent is by occupation a merchant seaman and resides at 2, St Richard's Way, Carboys, Mercia

(4) There are no children of the family now living *except* Charles Peter Barton, born on 18th November, 1964 Sandra Shirley Barton, born on 24th December, 1968

(5) No other child, now living, has been born to the petitioner/respondent during the marriage (so far as is known to the petitioner) *except*

(6) There are or have been no other proceedings in any court in England and Wales or elsewhere with reference to the marriage (or to any child of the family) or between the petitioner and respondent with reference to any property of either or both of them *except*

(7) There are no proceedings continuing in any country outside England or Wales which are in respect of the marriage or are capable of affecting its validity or subsistence *except*

(8) No agreement or arrangement has been made or is proposed to be made between the parties for the support of the petitioner/respondent (and any child of the family) *except* The respondent pays voluntary maintenance of £40 a week for the two children.

(9) The said marriage has broken down irretrievably.

(10) The respondent has behaved in such a way that the petitioner cannot reasonably be expected to live with the respondent.

The divorce petition, issued by the petitioner, tells how a marriage has broken down and states the petitioner's claims for child custody, financial support and payment of costs. It should also state in brief, some evidence of the breakdown of the marriage which may include

(11) PARTICULARS

The respondent frequently drank to excess during the marriage and when drunk often used violence on the petitioner. Recent examples of such behaviour are given below.

(a) On Christmas Day, 1978, the respondent while drunk threw food at the petitioner and threatened to cut her throat with a carving knife.

(b) On 14th June 1979 the respondent while drunk destroyed the contents of the petitioner's wardrobe and punched her when she tried to restrain him.

(c) On 2nd December 1979 the respondent when drunk broke the family's television set, struck the child Charles Peter across the head and told the petitioner to get out of the house. When she refused to go he struck her to the ground and kicked her.

The respondent left the family home on 3rd December 1979 and has not resided there since then.

Brief evidence of a breakdown of marriage: examples of behaviour, dates of separation or desertion, or names, dates and places if adultery is alleged

PRAYER

The petitioner therefore prays:—

(1) That the said marriage be dissolved.

(2) That the petitioner may be granted the custody of

Charles Peter Barton

Sandra Shirley Barton

(3) That the   respondent   may be ordered to pay the costs of this suit.

(4) That the petitioner may be granted the following ancillary relief:

(a) an order for maintenance pending suit
a periodical payments order
a secured provision order
a lump sum order

(b) a periodical payments order
a secured provision order   } for the children of the family
a lump sum order

(c) a property adjustment order

Signed

The names and addresses of the persons to be served with this petition are:—

Respondent:— John Frederick Barton

2, St Richard's Way, Carboys, Mercia

Co-Respondent (adultery case only):—

The Petitioner's address for service is:— c/o James, Sutton and Knowles,
Solicitors,
Central Chambers, Cowley

Dated this   10th   day of   March   1980

Address all communications for the court to: The Registrar, County Court, COWLEY

The Court
office at   } 4. The Square, Cowley

is open from 10 a.m. to 4 p.m. (4.30 p.m. at the Divorce Registry) on Mondays to Fridays.

Various benefits to the petitioner and/or children can be ordered by the judge at the respondent's expense. A petitioner can ask for one or more of the following:
● Maintenance pending suit – support until the case is decided
● Periodical payments – a set sum to be paid at regular intervals, usually monthly
● Secured provision – assuring future payment: the purchase of a policy giving the wife an annuity when her ex-husband dies, compensating her for loss of a widow's pension
● Lump sum payment – a cash transfer making periodical payments unnecessary, or in addition to periodical payments
● Property adjustment – right to ownership of property jointly owned or owned by the respondent

To be completed only when a third party is identified in a case alleging adultery. That person – the co-respondent – then is sent a copy of the petition by the court

examples of a partner's intolerable behaviour, dates of desertion or separation, or names, dates and places if adultery is alleged. At least two copies of the petition must be completed, but if adultery is alleged and a third party involved, a third copy of the petition is needed.

DIVORCE *continued from p. 191*

pregnant by another man and accepted the child – but was then deserted by his wife. Other cases in which leave to petition ahead of time would probably be granted include those in which one party is convicted of murder, rape or serious sexual perversion.

Proceedings for NULLITY of marriage can start before 3 years and in some cases must do so.

How a divorce petition is filed

A petition for divorce can be filed in the Divorce Registry in London or in most county courts. Petition forms are available, with explanatory notes, from the registry or court office free of charge.

The petition and at least two copies must be completed legibly. If a third party – called the co-respondent – is cited in the case, a third copy is needed.

The petition should be as brief as possible. It is not necessary to record in detail every incident of allegedly intolerable behaviour. Dates, times, places and some description of recent serious incidents are sufficient.

If the petition form is completed by a solicitor it should be checked by the petitioner before signing. Correction can be made after filing only by application to the court, which can cause delay and expense.

When there are children in the family – not necessarily only the children of the marriage – who are under the age of 16, or under 18 and still being educated or trained, a separate form must be completed setting out the arrangements proposed for their care.

The petitioner must also provide a copy of the MARRIAGE CERTIFICATE. If the marriage took place outside England and Wales further details may be required later.

All the documents must be taken or sent to the court or divorce registry with a filing fee of £20. Court officials are not allowed to help to complete forms or to give legal advice, but they undertake to try to serve all relevant documents on other parties.

The court posts a copy of the petition to the respondent and, if appropriate, the co-respondent. It also sends a form of acknowledgment which the respondent is expected to sign and return within 8 days.

If the respondent fails to acknowledge receipt, the petitioner can ask the court to send a bailiff to the respondent's address, to serve the documents personally. If all reasonable attempts to find the respondent fail, the court may order newspaper advertisements to serve him notice of the petition, or abandon attempts to contact him.

When a petition is unopposed

If a respondent decides not to contest a divorce petition, the case can be concluded quickly and cheaply. If there are no children, neither party has to go to court.

When the court office receives the respondent's acknowledgment of receipt of the documents, stating that he or she does not intend to defend the case, it notifies the petitioner how, where and when the hearing will be dealt with. The court also sends a form of AFFIDAVIT asking questions to confirm the contents of the petition. When the petitioner has completed it, he or she must swear to the truth of its contents.

The oath can be sworn before a solicitor, who will charge a £1 fee, or at the court office where no fee is charged.

The case is then listed by the court in a 'special procedure' list and the documents are examined by the registrar.

If he is satisfied that the marriage has broken down irretrievably, and that all the facts have been proved, he signs a certificate and a date is fixed by the court office for a DECREE NISI to be pronounced by a judge in open court.

It is not usually necessary for either party to appear before the registrar, but if he is not satisfied with the affidavit he may require the petitioner to provide further evidence or clarification by post or in person.

When children are involved, the registrar makes an appointment for the proposed arrangements for their future to be considered before a judge in private.

If the registrar considers that the petition has not been proved, he removes it from the 'special procedure' list and directs that it be heard in full before a judge in open court.

When a case is defended

It is no defence to a divorce petition for the respondent to say that the dissolution of the marriage is offensive on moral or religious grounds. Nor can a respondent resist divorce merely to stop the petitioner remarrying.

The only way in which the respondent can stop a divorce is by showing that the marriage has not broken down irretrievably or that the facts relied on to prove breakdown in the petition have not been proved. In cases based on 5 years' separation, there is also a defence of grave hardship.

A respondent who wants to fight the case should complete the 'acknowledgment of service' form accordingly and return it to the court at once.

Within 29 days of receiving the petition, he or she must send to the court an 'answer', stating whether he or she

---

HOW MUCH A DIVORCE WILL COST

The expenses of a divorce may be shared between the petitioner and respondent, but in a defended case they may have to be paid entirely by the party who loses. The amount depends on the complexity of the case and whether lawyers are engaged.

A do-it-yourself divorce petition costs £20. If the petition is unopposed and there is no dispute over the custody of children, there need be no extra cost.

If a solicitor is engaged in an undefended case, costs rise to between £60 and £150, depending on how much work has to be done. If there are disagreements over money or the custody of children it will take longer and cost proportionately more – usually about £100–£150 for each day

of a solicitor's time, depending on the experience of the solicitor.

When a barrister is engaged

A defended case in which a barrister is also engaged costs at least £400 – many cost much more. If a court hearing lasts a long time or if expert witnesses have to be called, the bill could run into thousands of pounds.

LEGAL AID may be available for preliminary advice and to help prepare petition documents and related applications. Aid may also be available to conduct defended proceedings. The £20 filing fee can be waived for petitioners qualifying for legal aid or SUPPLEMENTARY BENEFIT.

ARRANGEMENTS FOR THE CARE OF CHILDREN
Evidence of how any children involved will be affected if a divorce is granted

Between	Mary Elizabeth Barton	Petitioner
and	John Frederick Barton	Respondent
and		Co-Respondent

The proposed arrangements for the children of the family under 16 and those over 16 but under 18 who are receiving instruction at an educational establishment or undergoing training for a trade, profession or vocation are as follows:—

(i) residence

Where each child is to live, who else lives there and who is to look after each child. Presence of other adults could help to show that a child will always be supervised – or it could indicate overcrowded conditions

Charles Peter Barton, born on 18th November 1964 and Sandra Shirley Barton, born on 24th December 1968, reside with the petitioner at 5 Belfast Avenue, Cowley, Mercia, in a three-bedroomed detached house owned jointly by the petitioner and the respondent. It is proposed that the children should continue to reside there with the petitioner and that she should continue to look after them. No other person resides there.

(ii) education etc.

Where each child goes to school, or what job training is given

Charles Peter Barton attends Cowley Comprehensive School. Sandra Shirley Barton attends Cowley

(iii) financial position

Who supports each child, how much is provided, and whether any court application is intended

The respondent pays the petitioner voluntary maintenance of £40 a week for both children. The petitioner proposes to make an application to the court for a... increasing payments

(iv) access

Proposed opportunities for the other parent to be with children

The respondent spends about three hours each Saturday afternoon with the children. It is proposed that this arrangement should continue.

Any physical or medical reasons why a child needs special care

State whether or not the said child(ren) are suffering from serious disabilities or chronic illness or from the effects of such illness.

Neither child suffers from any serious disability or chronic illness or from the effects of such

If children are the subjects of an official care order, neither parent has a claim to custody

State whether or not the said child(ren) are under the care or supervision of a welfare officer or officer appointed by a local authority or other person or organisation.

Neither child is under the care or supervision of a welfare officer or officer appointed by a local authority or other person or organisation.

Immediately a divorce petition is filed, the court seeks details of the arrangements proposed for any children in the family – not just children of the marriage. Even when a child has been fathered by another man and born before the marriage, he must be provided for, if he has been treated as a member of the family. The age limit is 16 – or 18 if a child is still at school or in training.

admits breakdown of marriage and setting out the facts on which his or her case is based.

If the respondent alleges that it was the petitioner who caused the breakdown, he or she may CROSS-PETITION for divorce, or may simply defend to stop the other party getting a decree.

When there is a cross-petition, the judge may allow the case to be shortened by granting cross-decrees – giving each party, if both agree, a divorce against the other. For example, the wife may be granted a divorce based on the husband's behaviour, and the husband a divorce based on the wife's.

With the 'answer' the respondent must also set out any orders that he or she wants the court to make – for example, for maintenance costs or custody of children.

As soon as an 'answer' has been filed, the case is transferred to the High Court where it is eventually heard in open court by a judge. Each party is normally represented by a barrister, instructed by a solicitor, but they can choose to speak for themselves. Both sides give evidence and can call witnesses.

If a respondent or co-respondent returns the acknowledgment of service with an indication that the case will be defended, but fails to file an 'answer' within 29 days, the case stays in the undefended lists. Late filing requires special leave of the court.

When the decree is granted

When hearings are completed or when the documents in an undefended case are approved by the registrar, the judge grants a DECREE NISI, which means that unless further action is taken within 6 weeks a DECREE ABSOLUTE will dissolve the marriage.

A respondent can normally appeal only in a defended case. But even in an undefended case the decree can be set

---

WHEN A DIVORCE PETITION IS OPPOSED

The other partner can put up an argument against the petition – in open court if necessary

IN THE COWLEY COUNTY COURT   No. of Matter: 80(b) 555

B E T W E E N :-

        MARY ELIZABETH BARTON   Petitioner

        - and -

        JOHN FREDERICK BARTON   Respondent

The respondent in ANSWER to the petition filed in this suit says that:-

1.   So far as is known to the respondent there is no other child now living born to the petitioner during the said marriage save for the children set out in paragraph 4 of the petition.

2.   No agreement or arrangement has been made or is proposed to be made between the parties for the support of the petitioner or the children of the family except a voluntary payment of £40 a week for maintenance of the children.

3.   He agrees that the said marriage has broken down irretrievably, but denies that such breakdown can be attributable to his behaviour as alleged in the petition or at all.

4.   He denies that he has behaved in such a way that the petitioner cannot reasonably be expected to live with him. Save as expressly admitted in the following paragraphs he denies every allegation in paragraph 11 of the petition.

5.   He admits that he has struck the petitioner on about three occasions but says that on every such occasion the petitioner provoked him by shouting abuse at him, and scratching and kicking him.

6.   He admits that in December 1979 he ordered the petitioner to leave, but says that he was justified in doing so as over the past two years she had neglected him, had refused him sexual intercourse and nagged him and humiliated him so that he could no longer bear to live with her.

THE RESPONDENT THEREFORE PRAYS:-

(1)   That the prayer of the petition may be rejected;

(2)   That the said marriage may be dissolved;

(3)   That he may be granted the custody of the child of the family Sandra Shirley Barton;

(4)   That the petitioner may be ordered to pay the costs of this suit.

Objection to any part of a divorce petition must be made in an 'answer' document within 29 days of receiving the petition.

The respondent need not be opposed to the divorce – he or she may simply wish to dispute the proposals for children, or to deny allegations in the hope that financial arrangements will be more favourable.

aside on grounds of fraud, non-service or lack of jurisdiction. Notice must be given to the Court of Appeal and to the other party within 6 weeks.

In an undefended divorce, only the decree is made in open court. In a defended case, the public and Press can hear all the evidence, but only certain details can be published or broadcast.

Making the best tax arrangements

If a married couple get divorced or become permanently separated, they are no longer treated as one person by the Inland Revenue. The husband keeps his married man's allowance for the full tax year, which starts in April, even if the separation comes near the beginning of that year. In the following year, he reverts to the lower single person's allowance, unless he is still wholly maintaining his wife and she has no other income.

If a wife is working, separation can bring her an immediate tax advantage in the year in which it happens. She qualifies both for a full year's wife's earned-income relief and for a full year's single person's allowance.

The earned-income relief is set against any income she earns up to the date of separation. The single person's allowance is set against income earned after the separation.

So for a wife, the date of separation can be especially important. To gain the maximum tax advantage, she should have earned at least as much as she would be allowed against tax in each part of the tax year.

In many cases, September – halfway through the tax year – is the best time to separate. Unless the wife has a high income, a separation near the beginning of the year does not allow enough time to use up the wife's full earned-income allowance. A separation near the end of the year means that the wife's allowance is wholly used up but the single allowance is not.

Example: A wife earns £3,000 a year, with a wife's earned-income allowance of (say) £1,100. Assume a tax rate of 30 per cent.

If husband and wife do not separate

Wife's salary for full year	£3,000
less	
Earned-income relief	£1,100
Amount to be taxed	£1,900
Total tax for the year (at 30%)	£570

If husband and wife separate in September

Wife's salary for 6 months to date of separation (April–Sept)	£1,500
less	
Earned-income relief for full year	£1,100
Amount to be taxed	£400
Tax on 6 months' salary (at 30%)	£120
Wife's salary for 6 months after separation (Sept–April)	£1,500
less	
Single person's allowance for full year	£1,100
Amount to be taxed	£400
Tax on 6 months' salary (at 30%)	£120
Total tax on full year (£120×2) is therefore	£240

---

7. The petitioner has behaved in such a way that the respondent cannot reasonably be expected to live with her.

After answering the petitioner's claims, the respondent announces that he has complaints of his own

PARTICULARS

(a) The petitioner has habitually abused the respondent and often when in a temper scratched and kicked him.

(b) On Christmas Day 1978 the petitioner repeatedly criticised and nagged the respondent and threatened to "kick him out" in front of the children of the family.

(c) On 14th June 1979 the petitioner tore the respondent's clothing during an attack on him.

(d) On 2nd December 1979 the petitioner kept the respondent out of the house for two hours in freezing weather.

(e) During the years 1978 and 1979 the petitioner neglected and ill-treated the respondent as set out in paragraph 6 above.

He gives examples of behaviour by his wife which, he says, makes it unreasonable for him to be expected to live with her

The husband's cross-petition

If the respondent is defending the case his denial of allegations in the petition may be followed by a plea to dismiss the petition. Or he may acknowledge that the marriage has broken down but blame the petitioner. When an 'answer' makes such allegations and seeks a decree in favour of the respondent it is a cross-petition.

All defended cases are argued in open court and both parties should have legal advice. They are usually represented by a barrister who is instructed by a solicitor, but the parties may choose to speak for themselves in the court hearing.

If husband and wife separate in early May

Wife's salary for 1 month (April–May)	£250
less	
Earned-income allowance for full year	£1,100
Amount to be taxed	nil
Tax already paid	£46
Refund to wife	£46
but	
Earned-income allowance not used up is £1,100 *less* £250	
Allowance wasted (£1,100 *less* £250) is therefore	£850

Allowances for children

If a child lives with one parent after a separation, that parent is entitled to the additional Personal Allowance.

If the child lives partly with one parent and partly with the other, the allowance can be apportioned between the two. That arrangement can also be made, if the parents agree, whether the child is 'shared' or not. To arrange this, the parents should write a letter to the local Inspector of Taxes.

Maintenance – voluntary or contractual

If one spouse or ex-spouse pays voluntary maintenance to the other, he or she does not normally get tax relief on the payments and the recipient does not pay tax on them.

That rule applies also to voluntary maintenance paid for a child.

For a wife who is herself a taxpayer, voluntary maintenance is usually better than contractual maintenance, which is taxable.

However, the Inland Revenue sometimes seeks to insist that voluntary payments of equal sums made at regular intervals amount to contractual maintenance and are therefore taxable. If that happens, specialist advice from a solicitor or accountant should be sought.

If maintenance is paid under a formal contract, that is not a court order, the payer is entitled by law to deduct tax at the basic rate before passing on the payment.

The recipient must then declare the whole amount as income.

For example, a husband who formally agrees to pay his wife or ex-wife £40 a week, and who is paying tax at 30 per cent can deduct £12 (30 per cent of £40) as tax relief and pay her the balance, £28.

The same rule applies to maintenance paid for a child.

The wife must declare the maintenance as earned income. If she already pays tax, or if the maintenance makes her liable to do so, she will have to pay her appropriate rate of tax on the £28 payments.

At the end of each tax year, the person paying maintenance must supply the recipient with an official tax certificate on form R. 185 obtained from the Inland Revenue, showing the total maintenance that was payable, and the amount of tax that he has deducted before payment.

The recipient must produce the tax certificate when she submits her own tax return to the Inland Revenue.

If the recipient is not liable to pay the tax that is being deducted from the maintenance before she receives it, she can claim it back at regular intervals on a repayment claim form obtainable from the local collector of taxes' office.

If the payer is already liable for tax at the basic rate, he will not normally have to pay any extra because of the deductions that he has made. But if he deducts tax at source when he was not liable to tax – or deducts more from the maintenance than he proves to be liable for – he must pay any excess amount deducted to the Inland Revenue. He is not entitled to keep it.

Small payments under a court order

Tax must not be deducted at source from 'small maintenance payments' – that is payments of less than £33 a week (£143 a calendar month) for a spouse or ex-spouse and £18 a week (£78 a month) for a child.

Paying maintenance direct to a child

Contractual maintenance for a child need not be paid as income to the parent with whom the child is living. It can be income for the child in his own right, and that may carry a tax advantage.

If, for example, the child's mother has remarried, to a man who pays a high rate of tax, any maintenance for the child paid to her would be taxed at her new husband's high rate. But if it is paid as the child's income, the tax is likely to be lower – if any is due at all.

Example: A father pays £1,200 a year maintenance for a child living with the divorced mother, who pays tax herself. Assume single person's allowance of £1,100 and tax at 30 per cent basic rate.

WHEN CHILDREN ARE INVOLVED

Even when a couple are divorcing by agreement, the divorce is not made final until a judge approves arrangements for children of the family under the age of 16, or under 18 if they are still being educated or trained, or of any age if they are in need of special care.

He considers a document from the petitioner setting out where and with whom the children are to live, who is to support them, where they are to be educated and what arrangements are proposed for access by the other parent. If a child has a serious illness a medical report must be attached.

If the petitioner claims or already has custody and the respondent does not object, the registrar makes an appointment for the petitioner to see a judge in private – 'in chambers' – to discuss arrangements for the children. The respondent may also attend. *See:* CUSTODY OF CHILDREN

In a dispute over child-care arrangements, the judge may offer suggestions to resolve it. He may adjourn the hearing for further consideration, and may also call for information from a COURT WELFARE OFFICER.

Eventually the judge will rule on the arrangements and either make an order declaring them satisfactory, or refuse to do so until they are improved to his satisfaction.

If custody itself is disputed, the court will consider the effect of parental conduct on a child. Adultery would not deprive a parent of custody unless he or she was thought to be a moral danger to the child – for example, through involvement in prostitution. On the other hand a history of violent or perverted marital conduct might well affect a custody decision.

If maintenance is treated as the mother's income, and she pays 30% basic rate, tax due on £1,200 .... £360

If maintenance is child's income and it has no other, tax is paid on £1,200
    less
Personal allowance £1,100
Total amount £100
Tax at 30% on £100 .... £30

Tax saved by paying as child's income is therefore £330

Example: The mother is remarried to a man paying tax at 70 per cent.

If maintenance is paid as income of mother, tax due is 70% of £1,200 .... £840

If maintenance is child's income, tax is paid on £1,200 *less* £1,100 .... £100
Tax at 30% on £100 .... £30

Tax saved by paying as child's income is therefore £810

If you do decide to make maintenance payable in such a way – so that it is your child's own income – it is advisable to make sure that the arrangement is part of a court order. If the agreement is not precisely worded, Inland Revenue may contest a claim, and tax relief may be lost.

Maintenance under foreign court order

Tax relief is allowable only on a British court order. Someone paying maintenance under a foreign court order while living in the United Kingdom is not entitled to tax relief on the payments. Anyone who receives maintenance from abroad, while living in Britain, is liable to pay British tax on the amount received.

For example, if a couple divorce in Australia, the husband may be ordered

---

HOW THE OTHER PARTNER IS BROUGHT INTO A DIVORCE ACTION
Even if the other partner does not intend to defend the petition, many questions have to be answered

TAKE NOTICE that a ⬚ petition for divorce has been presented to this Court. A sealed copy of it and a copy of the petitioner's proposals regarding the children is/are delivered with this notice.

1. You must complete and detach the acknowledgment of service and send it so as to reach the Court within 8 days after you receive this notice, inclusive of the day of receipt. Delay in returning the form may add to the costs.

2. If you intend to instruct a solicitor to act for you, you should at once give him all the documents which have been served on you, so that he may send the acknowledgment to the Court on your behalf. If you do not intend to instruct a solicitor, you should nevertheless give an address for service in the acknowledgment so that any documents affecting your interests which are sent to you will in fact reach you. Change of address should be notified to the Court.

1. Have you received the petition for divorce delivered with this form?
2. On which date and at what address did you receive it?

Space normally blank. It is used only when there are amended or supplementary petitions

Date of receipt marks start of 8-day period to acknowledge petition and 29 days to answer it

3. Are you the person named as the Respondent in the petition?
4. Do you intend to defend the case?
5. Even if you do not intend to defend the case do you object to paying the cost of the proceedings?
   If so, on what grounds?

If yes, a formal document must set out the respondent's case. If the respondent intends to have a lawyer prepare it – advisable in all defended cases – the lawyer should complete this form as well

If a strong reason is given why the petitioner should pay all costs, an appointment will be made for a judge to hear the claim in private. If the respondent is willing to pay some costs but not all of them, the answer to give now is no – an objection can be raised later

6. Even if you do not intend to defend the case, do you object to the claim in the petition for custody of the children?
7. Do you wish to make any application on your own account for:
   (a) custody of the children?
   (b) access to the children?

In an undefended case the respondent can dispute arrangements for children by sending a statement to the court with this form. In a defended case the respondent's counter-proposals form part of the 'answer' document sent later

The court is responsible for serving the petitioner's claims on the other partner, the respondent. His or her rights are fully protected only if he or she acknowledges receiving the papers and indicates what action is intended. If the petition is to be defended, the respondent must prepare a detailed 'answer'. If the respondent fails to acknowledge the papers, the petitioner may ask a bailiff to serve the documents.

HOW DIVORCE AFFECTS NATIONAL INSURANCE CONTRIBUTIONS AND SOCIAL SECURITY BENEFITS

A woman who gets divorced while under age 60 is immediately treated as a single woman for national insurance purposes. This means that, if you are employed, you have to pay class 1 NATIONAL INSURANCE CONTRIBUTIONS at the full rate once your weekly earnings go over the LOWER EARNINGS LIMIT (£27 in 1981-2). If you are self-employed, you must pay class 2 and, if appropriate, class 4 contributions. These contributions become due immediately following the decree absolute, if you are working. You do not have to pay national insurance contributions if you continue working after age 60.

On reaching retirement age (60), a divorced woman can get a retirement pension, based partly on her former husband's national insurance contributions. It works like this.

If your former husband's contribution record is better than your own (it will be if you have not been working, for example) you can take his contributions as your own for either:

● All the tax years of your working life up to the one in which your marriage ended.
● All the tax years of the marriage.

To that, you add any national insurance contributions of your own – for example, if you work after the divorce. If then both you (for the time after the divorce) and your husband have full contribution records, you should get a full RETIREMENT PENSION. But if, for example, you do not work after the divorce, or your husband does not have a complete contribution record, you may not have enough contributions to qualify for a full pension and will get, therefore, a reduced one instead.

If you remarry before reaching 60, you cannot use your first husband's national insurance contributions any longer. You must rely on your second husband for your pension. In the case of a second divorce, it is the second husband's contributions which are taken into account when you apply for a retirement pension.

There are special arrangements to help divorced women who have not been working or who have not been paying full national insurance contributions to qualify for benefits such as those for sickness or unemployment. These operate when after your divorce you have paid class 2 contributions equal to 25 times the minimum weekly contribution, or 25 class 1 contributions, or a mixture of both. These must be paid in any income tax year after April 1975. And a divorced woman who was still married 11 weeks before she has a baby can claim the £25 MATERNITY grant on her former husband's contributions.

A woman divorced after age 60 can get a retirement pension immediately using her former husband's contributions. She can get this pension even if her husband has not retired. To do so she can use his contributions in all the tax years of the marriage up to the end of the tax year in which she reached 60, or all the tax years in her working life up to the age of 60, whichever is more favourable to her. A woman who has been married more than once can only use her last husband's contribution record.

---

by the local court that decides the case to pay maintenance. If he subsequently comes to live in Britain and continues to pay the maintenance, he cannot claim tax relief in Britain.

If the wife comes to Britain, and continues to receive maintenance from her ex-husband in Australia, the money is treated as the wife's taxable income. *See:* INCOME TAX ALLOWANCES

When maintenance ends

When a woman remarries, her ex-husband's duty to maintain her ends, but he must continue to maintain his children. *See:* MAINTENANCE

DOCTOR AND PATIENT

Your relationship with your general practitioner

If you have moved home and need to find a new doctor, your new neighbours may be able to help. If they cannot, consult the local medical list at the public library or main post office. The list gives the names of all GPs in the area and states whether they are on the Obstetric List, which means they have additional training in maternity services, or

the Contraceptive Services List. *See:* CONTRACEPTION

When you have chosen a doctor, ask at his surgery whether you can join his list.

The doctor's right of refusal If a GP refuses a new patient, it usually means that his practice already has its permitted quota of patients. In exceptional cases, and when a patient has simply moved from one part of an area to another, the GP may refuse to accept him because he has an unsatisfactory reputation with other doctors. The GP need not give his reason for refusing.

The right to be registered Every citizen in Britain, however, has the right to be registered with a GP. If a patient is unable to find a doctor prepared to accept him, he can obtain one by contacting the local family practitioner committee. Its address is on the front of the National Health Service medical card, and can also be obtained from any doctor's surgery.

The family practitioner committee (a part of the area health authority which deals with GPs) must refer the patient's request for a GP to its allocation joint committee. After looking into the case, the committee orders a GP to accept the patient.

The GP must take the patient when instructed, but he can later have that patient removed from his list. While the committee is dealing with the matter, the patient is entitled to immediate and necessary treatment for up to 14 days from any GP that he approaches, even if he has refused to accept him on his list.

To have a patient removed from his list, the GP must give notice to the family practitioner committee. Removal then takes effect automatically after 8 days or when the patient is accepted by another GP – whichever is sooner. The patient has no right of appeal, but if he is undergoing a course of treatment, it must be completed before he can be removed from the list.

Registering as a temporary patient

If you are living temporarily away from home, you are entitled to register with a GP where you are staying. To do so, fill in form FP19 at the new doctor's surgery.

If you cannot give your National Health Service number, as given on the front of your medical card, the GP is entitled to charge you a fee for treatment – though in practice few GPs do.

If you do have to pay, ask for a receipt so that you can later reclaim the money from the family practitioner committee for the area in which you are staying.

If registration with the new GP lasts 90 days or more, you should transfer from the list of your previous GP to that of the new one or that of another GP in the area. If you are temporarily away from home and need emergency treatment, any local GP who is summoned must attend you. You will be given a form to sign to enable him to claim payment from the family practitioner committee. Only if you require further treatment will you be required to register as a temporary patient.

Seeing your doctor

If a GP operates an appointments system, he is entitled to refuse to see any patient who arrives at the surgery without an appointment provided that no appointments are available in the remaining surgery period and he is satisfied that the patient's health will not be at risk. The GP must ensure that the patient is offered an appointment within a reasonable time.

If you do not have an appointment and a receptionist refuses you access to the doctor, you are entitled to insist that he at least knows of your presence to decide for himself whether your health may be jeopardised by delay.

If the receptionist does not inform the GP or if she refuses you an appointment without the GP's knowledge, you have a ground for complaint to the local family practitioner committee.

If your doctor does not have an appointments system he must designate the times at which he will be available at his surgery. If you arrive at one of those times he must see you, unless he is occupied with an emergency case.

If your doctor refuses to see you during surgery hours, report him to the family practitioner committee. If harm is suffered as a result of his refusal, you can sue him for damages.

Home visits and emergencies

If you or a relative ask your doctor to see you either outside surgery hours or at your home, he should ask for any information necessary to enable him to decide whether treatment is urgently needed.

He may, after considering the information, decide not to see you until the next convenient surgery, or he may feel that more urgent treatment is called for, in which case he must attend personally or arrange for another doctor to do so or arrange for your admission to hospital.

If he is asked to attend an accident victim he must do so, even if the victim is not his patient, unless the doctor is elderly or infirm, or another doctor can attend immediately.

If your doctor has handed his practice over to a locum – a replacement – or a deputy, for a holiday or at weekends or during the evenings, you have no right to insist on seeing your own doctor. You have, however, the same right to treatment from the locum or deputy as you would have from your own doctor.

A GP or a locum who fails to attend one of his patients once he has been told that the patient is seriously ill or the victim of a serious accident would almost certainly be in breach of his contract with the family practitioner committee, and you are entitled to complain to the committee. Make your complaint against the regular doctor because it is his responsibility to provide an adequate locum.

The confidentiality of medical records

Doctors have a professional and a legal duty to respect the confidentiality of the information they acquire about their patients.

A doctor should allow further access only to others involved in treating the patient – and even then, they should receive only the information essential for carrying out their part of the treatment.

For example, if a woman has a child in hospital under the care of an obstetrician and then needs psychiatric treatment because of severe post-natal depression, the obstetrician can pass on to the psychiatrist any confidential information that he believes will help the psychiatrist to help her to recover.

A patient, however, has the right to insist that nothing he or she tells one doctor shall be disclosed to another.

After the doctor has done his duty by pointing out that such rigid confidentiality may hinder treatment, he must respect the patient's wish.

A GP would be entitled to dismiss his receptionist if he discovered that she had wrongly revealed information about patients.

A doctor employed by a company to provide medical examinations for its employees has the same responsibilities to his patients as if they were private or NHS patients. He should limit disclosures of confidential information to the company to stating whether someone is or is not fit for the work he is doing. He should not pass on any clinical information, or anything relating to the general physical or mental health of the employee.

However, the doctor does have to pass on to the Department of Health and Social Security detailed information on, for example, hospital inpatients or women having smear tests, to help compile medical research statistics. Sometimes this can be done by clerks without the doctor's knowledge.

Also, doctors have to notify cases of suspected drug addiction and certain contagious diseases.

Children's rights A doctor treating a patient under 16 normally informs the parents or guardian of everything about the child's condition that he believes they ought to know. However, he can withhold information from them if he thinks fit.

For example, the Department of Health and Social Security has advised GPs that they have no obligation to inform the parents of a girl under 16 that contraceptives are being prescribed for her.

A child attains a legal right to refuse or consent to medical treatment at 16. From that age a child is entitled to have everything he or she tells the doctor to be treated as confidential, and not to be passed on even to its parents.

Doctors in court Outside the medical profession, a court of law is the only place where a doctor may disclose confidential information about a patient. Like all witnesses, except a SOLICITOR, he must answer fully all questions put to him.

When confidentiality is broken Apart from the circumstances outlined above, a doctor who discloses confidential information about a patient, or whose receptionist does so, can be sued for damages.

In addition, such a breach of confidence is a disciplinary offence, for which the patient or anyone else affected can report the doctor to the General Medical Council.

When you are dissatisfied with your general practitioner

If you are not satisfied with the treatment you are receiving from your GP, first discuss your complaint with the GP. If you remain unconvinced, you can ask him to arrange for a second opinion. If he refuses, you can change your doctor.

Changing your doctor First you must find a GP who is prepared to add your name to his list. This may not be as easy as it sounds. The new GP may find your decision to leave your original GP unreasonable and refuse to accept you. Or professional loyalty may decide him against taking a patient from another doctor's list.

If you find another GP prepared to accept you, ask him to transfer your name to his list.

Suing a doctor If you have suffered injury or a deterioration in health, or if a member of your family has died, because of what you believe to be incompetence on the part of a doctor, you can sue him for MEDICAL NEGLIGENCE.

In a case of negligence by a locum, you can sue your regular doctor, the locum, or both.

But never try to pursue such an action without seeking professional legal advice, for nearly all doctors belong to a medical defence organisation to protect them against actions for negligence.

Making a complaint against a doctor

There are two ways to complain about a doctor who treats patients under the National Health Service.

Serious professional misconduct A doctor is guilty of serious professional misconduct if, for example:
1. He carries on an 'adulterous or improper' relationship with a patient.
2. He indecently assaults a patient.
3. He shows gross professional negligence – by, for example, failing to attend a sick patient.
4. He performs illegal abortions.
5. He advertises his services.
6. He issues sickness certificates without making sure that the patient is ill.

7. He attends a patient while under the influence of drink or drugs.
8. He makes an unwarranted disclosure of confidential information.

Any complaint of serious professional misconduct must be made to the Registrar of the General Medical Council – the body that supervises the medical profession.

If the council decides to investigate the matter, the complainant has to make a written statement setting out in detail the grounds for his allegation. Eventually, he may be asked to attend a hearing of the council's disciplinary committee and give evidence on oath. He can claim any expenses he incurs.

If his allegations are found to be wrong, he can be sued by the doctor for defamation – but only if it can be shown that he made the complaint maliciously – for example, because of a personal grievance.

Poor service or treatment Although National Health Service GPs are not employees, they are bound by contract to provide their patients with a proper medical service. If you believe that your GP's practice falls short of what is required, you can complain to the local family practitioner committee.

The COMMUNITY HEALTH COUNCIL provides help for anyone who wishes to do so.

A complaint must be made in writing within 8 weeks of the incident that gave rise to the complaint – otherwise it may not be accepted. However, the committee takes into account delays caused by absence or illness. If you want to appeal against a refusal to accept a late complaint, you can write to the Secretary of State for Social Services – but an extension is rarely given.

Minor complaints If the complaint is not serious and there is a chance that relations between doctor and patient can be restored, the family practitioner committee tries to resolve the complaint informally – perhaps by getting doctor and patient together to discuss the problem in the presence of a medical member of the committee and an outside chairman.

When you have a serious complaint against a doctor

If the complaint is serious, or if the complainant insists on having it investigated formally, it is referred to a service committee, consisting of members of the family practitioner committee.

The service committee interviews the complainant and the doctor. If it decides that there is a case to answer, it calls a formal hearing of three or more of its members.

The complainant and doctor attend the hearing and are allowed to produce witnesses. Neither complainant nor doctor can be represented by a paid lawyer but each can be helped by an unpaid adviser. The secretary of the local community health council will sometimes help complainants.

The report of that hearing goes to the full family practitioner committee, which decides whether the doctor has broken his contract with the NHS. If he has, the committee may decide to caution him or – if the breach is serious – fine him by withholding part of his NHS payment.

Both the complainant and the doctor can appeal against the decision to the Secretary of State for Social Services.

See also: MEDICAL NEGLIGENCE
PRIVATE MEDICINE

WHEN THE 8-WEEK RULE WAS ENFORCED

Ignorance of the rules is not a sufficient reason for setting aside the time limit.

A patient wrote to the Secretary of State after his complaint, submitted 3 months after an incident, had been rejected. He said the reason for the delay was that he did not know of the limit.

He received the following reply: 'The Secretary of State cannot accept lack of knowledge of complaints procedures and the time limits as sufficient reason for not making a complaint in time.

'In this regard he has taken into account the fact that there is a note about the time limits for complaints on the medical card which is issued to every NHS patient.

'The time limit of 8 weeks after the event giving rise to the complaint is intended to meet normal difficulties on the part of the sick and bereaved people.'

DOG CONTROL

How other people can be made to keep their dogs under control

If a dog is not being kept under proper control, and causes nuisance or danger, you can complain to the police or your local authority.

You have a right to bring a private prosecution yourself against the dog-owner, but it is advisable to consider doing so only if the authorities refuse to act.

If you do decide to bring a private prosecution, the procedure is straightforward. Simply go to the local magistrates' court office and say that you wish to make a complaint under Section 2 of the Dogs Act 1871.

When a dog is dangerous

It can be difficult to prove that a dog is dangerous. The court will hear evidence of its known temperament – for example, evidence that it frequently snaps at children. But the magistrates often want evidence that the animal has been a danger on some occasion before the one that led to prosecution.

The prosecutor must prove not only that the dog is dangerous but also has not been kept under proper control.
Lack of control It is for the magistrates to decide whether there was proper control. If a dog that was not kept on a lead or muzzled, attacked someone, that would be proof of insufficient control.

There is no need to show that the dog is dangerous to humans: it is enough to prove that it is dangerous to other animals. Nor is it necessary to show that the owner knew that his dog was dangerous.
Control order If the owner is convicted of having a dangerous dog not kept under proper control, and the magistrates order him to keep it under control in future, he has no right of appeal against the order.
Destruction order If the magistrates order the dog to be destroyed, the owner can appeal to the crown court. The appeal must be lodged within 14 days.
Switching ownership Sometimes a dog-owner tries to avoid being convicted of owning a dangerous dog by transferring ownership to someone else just before the court hearing.

PROVING A DOG IS DANGEROUS CAN BE DIFFICULT

The court will hear evidence of a dog's known temperament. But magistrates often want proof that the animal has been a danger on some previous occasion.

If it is a genuine sale or gift of the dog, the court (although it may be suspicious) cannot make a control or destruction order against the owner originally summonsed.

However, an order can be made against the new owner – although a fresh summons would probably need to be issued, naming him as owner.

When a dog is not wearing a collar

If a dog is off the lead and on a highway or in a 'place of public resort' – for example, on a cricket field – the owner must ensure that it is wearing a collar bearing the name and address of its owner.

An owner who lets his dog out without a collar can be fined up to £400. Only a local authority can prosecute for that offence, but a member of the public is entitled to ask the council to do so, under the Control of Dogs Order 1930. The council need not agree to prosecute. If an owner is prosecuted and fined, he has the right of appeal.

When a dog is not on a lead

An owner who lets his dog roam in streets that have been designated by the local authority as roads in which dogs must be on leads can be fined up to £20. Such designated streets usually have relevant notices attached to lamp-posts or other street equipment.

Only the local authority can prosecute, but a member of the public is entitled to urge the council to do so, under the Road Traffic Act 1972.

Although a driver should not swerve because of a dog on the road, it is an understandable reflex action. If an accident and injury or damage results, the owner of the dog can be found wholly or partly to blame, and be liable for damages, if he has not taken proper control of the dog and if he should have foreseen the possibility of an accident – for example, by taking an ill-disciplined dog into a street full of traffic and people.

When dogs foul the footpath

In most areas it is an offence under council bye-laws for a dog-owner to allow his dog to foul a footpath. Any citizen is entitled to prosecute an owner who does so. But it is generally advisable to ask the police or council to act.

If eventually you decide to prosecute privately, first check with your local authority whether there is a bye-law that makes the fouling of a footpath an offence. If there is such a bye-law, in asking for the summons, refer the magistrates to it, according to the details supplied by the local authority.

A dog-owner accused of letting his dog foul a footpath will not be convicted if he can show that he was not guilty of 'culpable neglect or default'.

If he proves that he tried to take the dog to the roadway or gutter as soon as it became apparent that the animal was about to foul the pavement, he will not be guilty.

If the dog fouls a private garden, the owner would not be guilty of this offence as the garden is not a public place. But the garden-owner could sue the dog-owner for trespass and damage if he could show that the dog was encouraged to use his garden.

When a dog is too noisy

Noisy animals, including dogs, are controlled by bye-laws in many areas. Usually the bye-laws prohibit the keeping of a noisy animal in any premises if 'serious nuisance' is caused to people living near by. Ask at your local council offices to find out if such a bye-law exists in your area. If it does, you are entitled to bring a private prosecution to end the nuisance.

"

WHEN A DOG FOULED THE GRASS VERGE

An owner accused of letting his dog foul a footpath will not be convicted if he can show that he tried to take the dog to the roadway or gutter.

Mrs Green's dog fouled a grass verge between the pavement and the roadway. She was prosecuted under a local bye-law, which prohibited dogs from fouling the footway.

However, Mrs Green argued that the verge was not a 'footway', because it was not part of the pavement provided for people to walk on.

DECISION

Mrs Green's argument was upheld. The case was dismissed.

"

If you prosecute Once you decide that you may have to bring your own prosecution, you should serve a formal notice, in the form of a letter, on the keeper of the dog.

The notice should warn that the dog is noisy and causing a serious nuisance. It is advisable to describe the type of nuisance being caused – general disturbance, interference with sleep, distress to children and so on.

The notice should state that court proceedings will begin unless the nuisance is stopped within 14 days. It must be signed by at least three householders who live within earshot of the dog.

The notice can be served either by handing it to the keeper of the dog or by sending it by recorded-delivery post.

If the nuisance does not stop within the 14 days, the keeper can be prosecuted by the person or persons who served the notice. On conviction, the keeper of the dog can be fined up to the maximum laid down in the local bye-law – usually the same amount as for allowing a footpath to be fouled.

If a dog worries livestock

An owner whose dog attacks or chases sheep, cows, horses or other livestock on agricultural land can be prosecuted by the police, local authority or an individual. If the worrying may reasonably be expected to cause injury or suffering to the livestock, the dog's owner can be fined up to £200.

Destruction or control order If a dog can be shown to have injured cattle or poultry, or to have chased sheep, the magistrates can treat the dog as dangerous and order the owner to keep it under control – or have it destroyed.

If a dog is found straying

Anyone who finds a stray dog has a legal duty to take it – or report it – to the police. There is a maximum fine of £25 for failing to do so.

If you find a stray dog and would like to keep it, you can tell the police so when you take it to them. Unless the owner is traced the dog will be handed back to you, after 1 month, and you must, by law, keep it for at least 1 month afterwards.

If you do not want the stray dog that you have found, the police can sell or destroy it within 7 days of picking it up unless the owner is traced. If the owner is traced the police can destroy the dog if the owner does not claim it within 7 days of the police notifying him that they have the dog.

When a dog is abandoned

Anyone who abandons an animal, including a dog, temporarily or permanently, can be prosecuted if the abandonment is likely to cause the animal unnecessary suffering, and unless there is reasonable cause or excuse.

Prosecutions can be started by the authorities, the RSPCA or an individual.

If the owner of the animal is convicted, he can be fined up to £50 and imprisoned for up to 3 years.

A dog-owner convicted of the offence can also be disqualified from owning a dog for a specified period.

If someone is cruel to a dog

The law forbids cruelty to any animal kept as a pet, and there are special rules about keeping dogs.

Anyone convicted of causing a dog unnecessary suffering through ill-treatment can be fined up to £50 and/or sentenced to 3 months' imprisonment.

A prosecution can be brought by the authorities or by an individual.

He can also be banned from keeping a dog for a specified period – even for life. If during that period he keeps a dog – or even applies for a dog licence – he can again be fined £50 or sent to prison for up to 3 months.

The convicted dog-owner can appeal against disqualification to the crown court. He can also go back to the magistrates after not less than 6 months, if still disqualified, and ask for the disqualification to be reviewed.

If the application to the magistrates is rejected, the convicted person must wait at least 3 months before applying again, unless his disqualification expires during that time.

Danger from guard dogs

Guard dogs trained to defend trade premises or building sites against intruders must be kept under specially strict control.

Under the Guard Dog Act 1975, a guard dog on commercial premises must either be kept secure – in a kennel or tied or chained up – and unable to roam either inside or outside the premises, or must be under the immediate control of a dog handler. There must be a clear warning notice outside the premises. Anyone breaking the law on guard dogs can be fined up to £400.

The restrictions do not apply to guard dogs in people's homes or on farms.

When a dog licence must be obtained

Every person who keeps a dog above the age of 6 months must get an annual licence. A licence is needed for each dog. The fee, $37\frac{1}{2}$p, can be paid at any post office.

It is an offence, punishable by a fine of up to £10, to keep a dog without a licence or to fail to produce a licence when asked by a policeman. The onus of proving that the dog is not 6 months' old or that it does not belong to the person who is looking after it or on whose premises it is found, is on the accused.

DOMESTIC HELP

Employing someone to work around the house

The moment you pay someone to work as cleaner, handyman or gardener, you become an employer. You have to pay NATIONAL INSURANCE CONTRIBUTIONS if you pay more than the LOWER EARNINGS LIMIT, no matter how many hours are worked. Contributions must be paid even for workers from overseas.

If someone works for more than one employer, a separate contribution has to be paid for each employment in which the earnings limit is exceeded. No contributions need be paid for any employment in which the lower earnings figure is not reached – even when several separate amounts added together total more than the limit.

No national insurance contributions are payable by the householder when a window-cleaner, contract gardener, decorator or outside caterer, for example, is hired on contract terms.

Who pays for injuries?

Anyone employed as a domestic help can claim INDUSTRIAL INJURY BENEFIT for any injury incurred during that employment, even if national insurance contributions are not paid by the employer.

The householder can be held liable for NEGLIGENCE if dangerous or unsafe equipment has been provided for the employee's work. For example, a part-time gardener who was injured when trimming a hedge with a faulty electric trimmer could claim damages.

But a domestic help who injures herself by tripping over a vacuum-cleaner cable would have no claim against her employer. She could claim industrial injury benefit, whether national insurance contributions were being paid or not.

Social security help

The Department of Health and Social Security may sometimes assist in paying for domestic help for anyone who is sick or old and who is already receiving supplementary benefit.

The Department can grant an exceptional circumstances addition, such as the full cost of a HOME HELP, when that help is arranged privately. If a home help is supplied by the local authority, the service is normally free, subject to a means test. The DHSS will not pay any local authority charges.

If, as a result of old age, illness, disablement or heavy family responsibilities, a person receiving supplementary benefit needs help with ordinary household tasks such as cleaning or cooking, extra benefit is payable to meet a reasonable charge for essential domestic help. But benefit is not paid to cover the cost of help provided by a close relative who incurs only minimal expenses, or to cover charges made by a local authority for providing a HOME HELP.

A pensioner or a younger person on the long-term rate of supplementary benefit is expected to pay the first 50p of the cost of domestic help out of the normal weekly benefit. No additional benefit is paid for window cleaning or errands.

DOMICILE

The country that is your 'legal home'

An individual's marriage status, his liability for certain taxes on capital and even his legitimacy at birth are all determined not by where he is permanently resident but by the country in which he is legally domiciled.

A person can be domiciled in England and therefore be subject to English law in those matters, yet live permanently elsewhere.

How domicile is decided

Everyone has a domicile. A child is born with a domicile, but when he becomes an adult, he can decide on a new domicile. He can never have more than one domicile at any time, however.

Domicile of origin Every child is born with a domicile of origin, which is inherited from one or other of the parents. In English law, a child takes the domicile of its father if the father is alive and married to the mother at the time of birth. If the father is dead, the parents divorced or the child illegitimate, it takes the domicile of the mother.

That is so even if the child is born in another country. A child born, say, in France, has an English domicile of origin if the father's domicile at the time of the birth is English. It does not matter where the father is living at the time.

Domicile of origin is important for although a person can change his domicile by choice at any time, he reverts to the original automatically if he abandons a chosen domicile without choosing another.

Domicile of choice A person changes his domicile by moving to a new country and deciding to stay there for the rest of his life. He does not have to make any declaration and it does not have the same public recognition as an acceptance of NATIONALITY or CITIZENSHIP.

A court deciding whether someone has changed his domicile of origin has to take into account factors such as:
● The person's permanent home and length of time living there.
● The country where most of his assets are.
● Where most of his family live.
● Where he made his will.
● What impression he has given to other people about where he intends to retire.

For example, a person contesting a claim by the Inland Revenue in England for CAPITAL TRANSFER TAX on a parent's will, would have to convince a court that the deceased parent had chosen domicile in another country.

Minors cannot choose their domicile, and until they become adults, their domicile of origin is legally known as domicile by operation of law.

That applies also in some countries where a wife takes her husband's domicile on marriage. Under English law, a woman who marries keeps her own domicile – which means that it can be different from that of her husband.

A child whose parents change their domicile by choice also has his domicile changed. A boy, for example, born to a cook with Scottish domicile working in Paris would have Scotland as his domicile of origin.

If the father moves to London and becomes domiciled there by settling permanently while the boy is still a minor, the boy then takes his father's domicile of choice – England.

If, when he is 18, the boy decides to travel the world he immediately reverts to his domicile of origin – Scotland. And if he finally settles to work in Brussels, for example, his domicile becomes Belgium by choice.

The effect of domicile

The question of a person's domicile arises only in legal matters such as disputes in which it is necessary to settle a person's marriage status, in disputes over a person's liability to certain taxes on capital or in inheritance disputes.

There are no set rules which determine domicile. The court with jurisdiction over the matter decides the question. Depending on which country he is in and which domicile he claims, a person may be able to appeal.

Tax liability Someone whose domicile is England has to pay tax on any capital transfers made in England or elsewhere, and his estate is liable to these taxes. Domicile does not, however, make a person liable for income tax. That is determined by residence and a person does not have to be resident in his country of domicile.

Marriage and divorce

Domicile is also important in questions of marriage status and divorce. A woman, for example, married polygamously in a country which recognises polygamy as legal, may have her marriage recognised in a country where polygamy is not legal, provided she can establish the first country as her country of domicile.

That, in turn, can settle the legitimacy of any children born of the marriage and their rights to share in the FAMILY ASSETS.

DOORSTEP CREDIT

How the law controls canvassing of credit

Canvassing – an unsolicited visit to your home by a salesman trying to sell credit facilities – is strictly controlled by the Consumer Credit Act.

A visit is solicited if you ask for it in writing. If you write – or fill in a coupon – merely asking for further details of a credit offer, you are not soliciting a visit. If a salesman calls as a result, he is canvassing.

If he telephones to arrange to visit you, any resulting visit will legally be unsolicited, and so he will be canvassing.

On the other hand if he simply telephones, unsolicited, to do business by telephone, he is not canvassing.

A canvasser, or his company, must have a licence from the Office of Fair Trading. A licence will not be granted for soliciting debtor-creditor agreements, in which there is a straightforward loan and the lender has no business connection with the supplier of any goods bought with that loan. *See:* CONSUMER CREDIT

NO FOOT IN THE DOOR

It is illegal for a credit salesman to make unsolicited visits to people's homes. The penalty could be that his company would have its licence revoked by the Office of Fair Trading.

'GOOD morning, madam'

If you receive an unsolicited visit, and a straightforward money loan is made as a result, the lender cannot sue you or make you repay any money borrowed.

Licensed canvassing If the credit being offered is of the debtor-creditor-supplier type – in which the lender has a business connection with the supplier of goods – and the borrower defaults, the lender can sue for the money.

He can also repossess the goods, provided that he is also the supplier of those goods and the agreement is one in which he retains ownership until the debt is paid – as with hire purchase.

However, the borrower will still be protected by the rules allowing him to pull out of a transaction.

Types of business that can legally be canvassed by someone who is licensed include insurance, hire purchase, mail order, check trading, conditional sale agreements and rentals.

Even if the business can legally be canvassed, anyone who does so without a licence cannot sue or repossess goods without an order from the Office of Fair Trading, which is unlikely to be given.

DOORSTEP SELLING

The householder's right to fair dealing and privacy

The door-to-door salesman has the same legal obligations as any other trader. He must make no false claims about his goods and he must refund the money or pay compensation if the goods are defective.

However, a common problem with buying on the doorstep is that later, when a complaint arises, the salesman may be difficult to find. Before parting with money or signing an agreement, insist on seeing proof of the salesman's identity, his address or the address of his company.

See: CREDIT AGREEMENT
DEFECTIVE GOODS
SALE OF GOODS
TRADE DESCRIPTIONS

DRAIN

Who has to pay when something goes wrong

If your house drain becomes blocked and you cannot clear it yourself, you are entitled to call your local council's environmental health department to undertake the work.

If the blockage is in a main sewer, you do not have to pay for any work done. But if the trouble lies in your drain – especially if a section of drain has to be dug up – the council is likely to charge you for the work.

The difference between a drain and a sewer is generally that a drain serves only one property, and a sewer serves more than one.

If the drain runs under your neighbour's land before joining a main sewer, you may be entitled to a contribution from him towards any charge made.

If the blockage has clearly been caused by the neighbour – perhaps for example, by digging in his garden – he will have to pay the whole cost. The council will decide who is responsible for the blockage. If either party is dissatisfied they can take the matter to court. There is also nothing to stop the owner of the drain going on to his neighbour's land to do the repair himself.

In the case of rented property, responsibility for drains is stated in the terms of the lease and is usually the landlord's.

When you have no main sewer

If your house drain runs into a cesspit or septic tank instead of a main sewer, you have to pay the local council or a contractor to empty it regularly.

If there is a public sewer near your home, you are entitled at any time to have your drain connected to it. But you must inform the council and give it the opportunity to do the work, for which it will make a charge.

The water authority is not entitled to charge for sewerage service if your property is not drained directly or indirectly into a main sewerage system.

DRINK AND DRIVING

Penalties for a motorist who takes too much alcohol

The law is particularly severe on any motorist convicted of a drinking-and-driving offence. A motorist can be prosecuted for any of the following offences:

1. Driving or attempting to drive with excess alcohol in the blood.
Maximum penalty: 6 months' imprisonment, a £1,000 fine and compulsory disqualification for at least 12 months.
2. Being in charge of a vehicle (as opposed to driving or attempting to drive) with excess alcohol in the blood.
Maximum penalty: 3 months' imprisonment, a £500 fine and possible disqualification for 6 months.
3. Failing, without reasonable excuse, to provide a specimen of breath.

ONE LONG BREATH

The breath-test equipment should be inflated with a single breath of not less than 10 and not more than 20 seconds. However, inflation of the bag by several short breaths or puffs – for example, if the driver is a bronchitic – is valid.

Maximum penalty: a £50 fine, but no disqualification or licence endorsement.
4. Failing, without reasonable excuse, to provide a specimen of blood or urine.
Maximum penalty: 6 months' imprisonment, a £1,000 fine and compulsory disqualification for at least 12 months.
5. Driving, or attempting to drive, when unfit through drink or drugs.
Maximum penalty: 6 months' imprisonment, a £1,000 fine and compulsory disqualification for at least 12 months.
6. Being in charge of a motor vehicle (as opposed to driving, or attempting to drive) while unfit through drink or drugs.
Maximum penalty: 3 months' imprisonment, a £500 fine and possible disqualification for 6 months.

Most drinking-and-driving prosecutions are brought under the law that makes it an offence to drive, or attempt to do so, on a road or other public place with an excessive amount of alcohol in the blood – that is, more than 80 milligrammes of alcohol to 100 millilitres of blood or 107 milligrammes of alcohol in 100 millilitres of urine, as proved by a blood or urine test.

'Public place' can include a garage forecourt and public-house car park during licensing hours.

When a breath test can be required

If a motorist is suspected of a drinking-and-driving offence, the first step towards possible prosecution is a roadside breath test – not in itself proof of guilt, but a method by which a police officer can establish whether the motorist should be arrested and be required to give a blood or urine sample.

It is, however, only the blood or urine sample that is very strong evidence of whether the amount of alcohol in his blood is legally excessive.

The breath test is administered by a police officer using an Alcotest or similar tube filled with chemical crystals that react to alcohol. The tube is attached to an inflatable bag, and the motorist must blow through the tube sufficiently to inflate the bag.

Since it is a roadside test, the motorist cannot expect privacy. However, he may be invited to take the test inside a police vehicle.

RULES FOR THE BREATH TEST

The breath test must be properly administered or it is invalid and any subsequent action, including an arrest, has no legal effects.

1. At least 20 minutes should elapse between the motorist's last drink and his taking the test. Otherwise the reading may be artificially high. It is for the motorist to explain when he last had a drink. The police should normally wait 20 minutes to ensure an unchallenged reading.
2. A motorist who is smoking should be told to stop doing so a short time before the test, because tobacco fumes can discolour the crystals brown.
3. The breath-test equipment must be correctly assembled, though a second test can be required if the equipment was wrongly assembled for the first.
4. The instructions say that the inflatable bag on the breath-test equipment should be inflated with a single breath of not less than 10 or more than 20 seconds. The courts have held, however, that it is enough for the police to tell the motorist to blow into the bag with one long, deep breath.
5. When the bag has been inflated, the police officer must inspect the crystals before making an arrest.

The police are entitled to require a breath test only if they suspect that:
1. The motorist has alcohol (not necessarily an excessive amount) in his body.
2. He has committed a moving traffic offence (for example speeding, but not, say, failing to have a licence plate illuminated). But if he is lawfully stopped because of a defective light, say, and the police officer then smells alcohol, he may suspect that the motorist has alcohol in his body.
3. He has been involved in a traffic accident.

Although random breath tests are not allowed, the police are entitled to stop any vehicle at random. If they then suspect that the driver has alcohol in his body, a breath test can be required.

'Drunk in charge'

Even if the vehicle is parked, and has not been in an accident, the driver can be required to take a breath test, provided that he has been seen driving or is suspected of having been involved in an accident.

If he is merely in charge of the vehicle, has not been seen to drive it and is not suspected of having been involved in an accident, he cannot be required to take a breath test. He can, however, be arrested without a warrant and taken to a police station, where he must be offered a breath test. He is entitled to refuse a breath test, but he must supply a blood or urine sample.

If the sample is shown to be positive, he can be prosecuted for being in charge of a vehicle while unfit through drink, and will have to prove that there was no likelihood of his driving in that condition – for example, because he had handed his key to someone else.

A motorist who is still in possession of his ignition key is still liable to arrest for being in charge of his vehicle even if he is on the back seat sleeping off the effects of drink. He might awake, wrongly believe he is then fit to drive again, and in fact drive when he is unfit to do so.

If there has been an accident, the police do not need to have witnessed it before requiring a breath test from a driver who is suspected of having been involved. They must, however, have reason to believe that the motorist was driving, or in charge of, a vehicle which was involved.

Who can require a breath test

Only a constable in uniform – of any rank, and including a special constable – is (legally) entitled to ask for a breath test. He must not be in plain clothes, but his uniform need not be complete, provided that he is readily identifiable.

If, for example, a police officer is not wearing his helmet or cap, but his uniform is otherwise complete, the demand for a breath test is legal.

The officer who stops a vehicle, for whatever reason, need not be uniformed, but if he wants to have the motorist breath-tested he must get a uniformed officer to do so.

If a suspect motorist has been injured, the police are entitled to require a breath test unless he is in hospital – if, for example, he is on his way to hospital by ambulance. The consent of the ambulance crew is not needed, but once he reaches hospital a breath test cannot be given without the consent of the doctor in charge of the case.

How soon a test must be given

In general, the police are not obliged to carry out a breath test within any time limit. But it must be administered in time for any subsequent blood sample to show the level of alcohol as it was at the time when the motorist was driving.

The law says only that when a moving traffic offence has been the reason for stopping the motorist, the breath test must be given 'as soon as reasonably practicable'.

Where the test can be given

A breath test must be given at the place where the driver is stopped, 'or near by'. The courts have held that a test administered 160 yds from where a driver had been stopped was too far away to be legal. Each case, however, is likely to be decided on the circumstances involved.

If a driver attempts to put time or distance between the police and himself

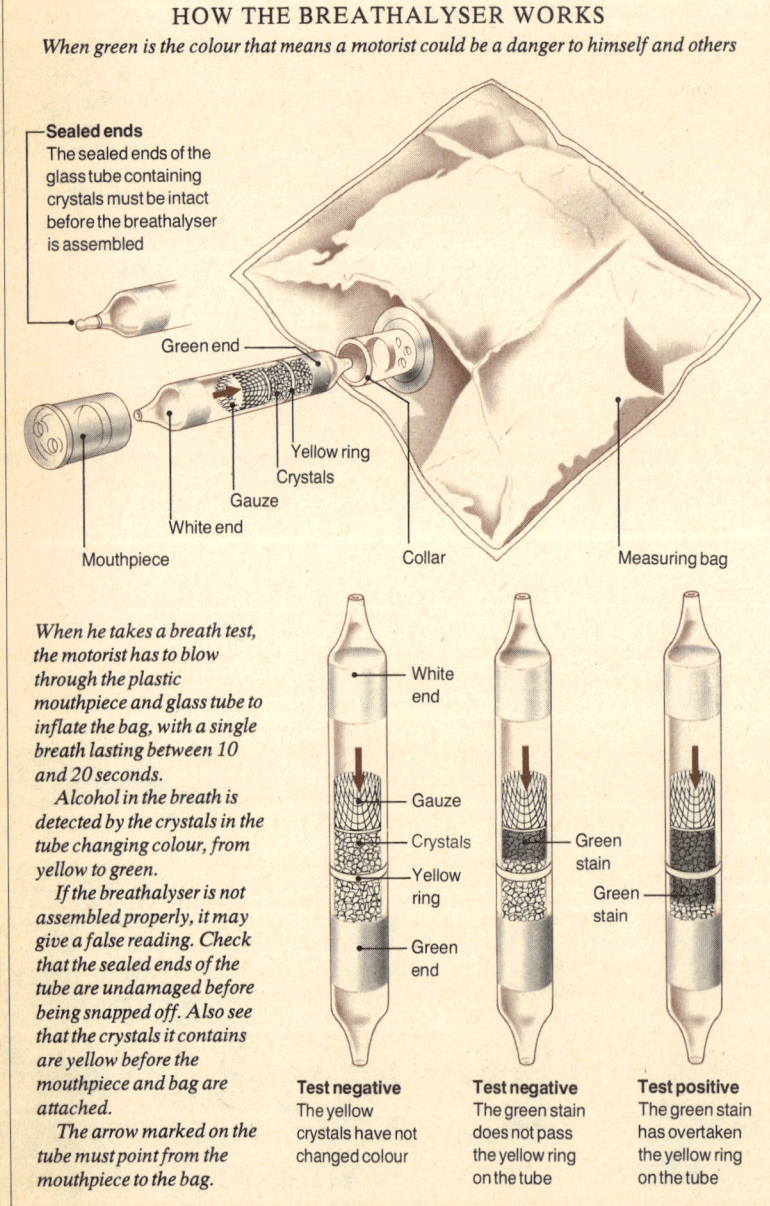

HOW THE BREATHALYSER WORKS

When green is the colour that means a motorist could be a danger to himself and others

Sealed ends
The sealed ends of the glass tube containing crystals must be intact before the breathalyser is assembled

Green end

Yellow ring
Crystals
Gauze
White end

Mouthpiece

Collar

Measuring bag

When he takes a breath test, the motorist has to blow through the plastic mouthpiece and glass tube to inflate the bag, with a single breath lasting between 10 and 20 seconds.

Alcohol in the breath is detected by the crystals in the tube changing colour, from yellow to green.

If the breathalyser is not assembled properly, it may give a false reading. Check that the sealed ends of the tube are undamaged before being snapped off. Also see that the crystals it contains are yellow before the mouthpiece and bag are attached.

The arrow marked on the tube must point from the mouthpiece to the bag.

White end
Gauze
Crystals
Yellow ring
Green end

Green stain
Green stain

Test negative
The yellow crystals have not changed colour

Test negative
The green stain does not pass the yellow ring on the tube

Test positive
The green stain has overtaken the yellow ring on the tube

by rushing away from his vehicle, he can legally be pursued – even on to private property – and still be required to give a breath test when he is caught. He can also be prosecuted for obstructing the police – an offence punishable by a maximum fine of £100.

However, there must be no interruption in the chain of events between the time when a police officer witnesses an offence and the time when he makes an arrest.

THE POLICEMAN WHO GAVE A BREATH TEST TOO SOON

If a breath test is given less than 20 minutes after the driver's last drink it may not be valid. But a second test, given after the 20 minutes, is valid, provided that the chain of events leading to the second test is unbroken.

Mr W was seen stumbling out of a public house at Kettleby, Leics. He then got into a car and drove off. He was followed by a uniformed constable in a police car. The constable could find no fault with Mr W's driving.

Mr W drove into a private yard, stopped and got out of his car. The constable gave him a breath test. Mr W, asked when he had last had a drink, said that it was 10 minutes earlier. The test proved positive.

However, a sergeant who arrived on the scene advised the constable to wait 20 minutes and then take a second test. That test was also positive and Mr W was arrested.

A blood test showed that Mr W had more than twice the legal limit of alcohol in his blood.

At Melton Mowbray Magistrates' Court, he was convicted of driving with excess alcohol in his body, fined £35 and disqualified from driving for 1 year.

Mr W appealed to a quarter sessions court, on the ground that the breath tests were unlawful since at the time they were taken he was not driving or attempting to drive, and that therefore the constable had no power to arrest him without a warrant.

The appeal was upheld. The prosecution, however, then asked the High Court to rule whether the constable had power to require the second test that led to the arrest.

DECISION

The court held that the second test was valid. The first test had not broken the chain of events between Mr W's starting to drive and the request for a second test. Mr W was therefore still legally considered to be driving when the second test was taken.

The conviction was upheld.

THE MOTORIST WHO STOPPED FOR A SNACK

A driver legally ceases to drive once he stops and does something that is not connected with driving.

Mr R, driving with his wife, stopped his car in a roadside layby, switched off the engine, removed the ignition key and, leaving his wife in the passenger seat, walked towards a fish and chip shop to get a snack for them both.

He had walked about 10 yds from the car when he was stopped by a police constable in uniform who thought he had been drinking and was required to take a breath test. The test proved positive.

Mr R was subsequently found to have 190 milligrammes of alcohol to 100 millilitres of blood in his body.

At Bedford Crown Court, he was convicted of driving with excess alcohol, fined £80 and disqualified for a total of 21 months, after previous endorsements had been totted up.

Mr R appealed, on the ground that when breath-tested he was not driving or attempting to drive – and that buying fish and chips was not an incident of his driving.

DECISION

The conviction was quashed by the Appeal Court. It ruled that for Mr R to be still legally driving, what he did after stopping and leaving his car would have to be connected with driving – for example, filling up with petrol or wiping the windscreen.

Going to a shop for food was not an incident of his driving, but an incident of the journey.

THE DRIVER WHO TRIED TO ESCAPE

A motorist pursued by the police on suspicion of a drinking and driving offence must take a breath test if requested at the end of the pursuit, even though he is no longer attempting to drive.

Mr S was driving at a speed in excess of 50 mph which alerted the attention of a police car at Hove, East Sussex. When the police car drew in front of him and warned him to stop he escaped by driving on the pavement and subsequently on either the kerb or the off side of the police car.

On arrival at his home, he stopped and got out of his car. He was offensive and obstructive to the police and smelt of alcohol and when asked he refused to take a breath test.

Later, Mr S agreed to a breath test, which proved positive. A subsequent blood test showed a result of 163 milligrammes of alcohol to 100 millilitres of blood, and he was charged with having excess alcohol in his body.

He elected to go for trial by jury and was convicted at East Sussex Quarter Sessions, fined £75 and disqualified for 12 months. He appealed against the conviction.

In the Court of Appeal, the conviction was upheld, but Mr S was given leave to appeal further, to the House of Lords, on a point of law of public interest. This point was the question whether, when a person suspected of having alcohol in his body is pursued by the police, he can be required to take a breath test at the end of the pursuit, when he is no longer driving or attempting to drive.

DECISION

The Lords ruled that an offence committed while someone is driving or attempting to drive can be proved only at a later time. It had never been contemplated that a breath test should be given while the offence was being committed or at the moment when the officer first suspected an offence.

To accept that a motorist must still be driving or attempting to drive when the breath test is required would lead to an absurd result and would prevent the law being enforced. The test must, however, be given near by.

THE NIGHT A DRIVER'S MOTHER SHUT OUT THE CONSTABLE

A motorist who does anything to frustrate the drink and driving law can be convicted of an attempt to defeat the course of justice.

Mr B was seen speeding in his car late at night and a constable in a police car signalled to him to stop. He did not do so. The policeman chased Mr B to his mother's home.

When Mr B got out of his car, the constable required him to give a breath test. Instead, Mr B ran to the door of the house, hammered on it and shouted to his mother, 'Quick, Mum – get me a drink! And don't let that copper in!'

The mother refused to let the policeman into the house. A second policeman was called: the two officers entered the house and were able to see Mr B raising a bottle of beer to his lips.

Mr B, told that he would be arrested for refusing a breath test, replied: 'I am not leaving this house ... I have had a drink since driving, so you can't touch me for that.'

If after you have ceased to drive you have a drink and the breath test is applied, the test is ineffective. He was, therefore, charged with attempting to defeat the course of justice.

At Bristol Crown Court, Mr B was convicted and fined £200 with the alternative of 6 months' imprisonment. He appealed.

Mr B claimed that there were well-established categories of the offence of attempting to defeat the course of justice, and those categories ought not to be extended so as to make it unlawful to do something which in itself was lawful but which was done in order to frustrate an Act of Parliament. If he had committed an offence, it was argued, it was not the one with which he was charged, but was the obstruction of a police officer in the course of his duty.

DECISION

Mr B's appeal was dismissed by the Appeal Court.

The judges held that once the police constable had begun the procedure laid down under the Road Safety Act 1967 by asking for a breath test, any action that the motorist deliberately took with a view to frustrating that procedure could be considered an attempt to defeat the course of justice.

By deliberately taking extra drink, Mr B had attempted to frustrate the legal procedure.

Testing a driver at home If a police officer is told of an accident that he himself has not witnessed, he is entitled to visit a suspect motorist's home, even hours after the accident and request permission to enter and administer a breath test, but he cannot do so if permission to enter is refused, because he would then be a trespasser.

The motorist, however, would be entitled to put forward the defence that he had been drinking after he returned home – for example, in order to get over the shock of an accident that happened when he had not been drinking.

A motorist who refuses to take a breath test will be arrested.

If a test is positive

A breath test is positive, indicating excess alcohol in the blood, if the crystals turn green beyond a yellow ring marked on the tube. The motorist is generally allowed to see the test result, but he is not legally entitled to do so.

A motorist whose breath test is positive can be arrested, without a warrant, and taken to a police station. He must, however, be told clearly that he is under arrest because of suspected drinking and driving.

He must be left in no doubt that he is under restraint and not free to leave at will. A polite request to accompany a police officer to the station, and a motorist's offer to do so, have been held

not to constitute an arrest. Unless the arrest is properly carried out, any subsequent prosecution may fail.

At the police station

If a driver fails or refuses a breath test, he must again be offered one at the police station. If that is positive, or if the motorist refuses to take the test, the police can demand the blood or urine sample.

The driver can choose which to give, but he must be warned that if he refuses both, he is liable to imprisonment, a fine and driving disqualification just as if he

had given a sample containing excess alcohol. If the driver is in hospital – for example, after being injured in an accident – a blood or urine specimen must not be taken without permission from the doctor in charge of the case.

Choosing which sample to give

One advantage of choosing to give a urine sample rather than a blood sample is that the motorist does not have to wait for a doctor to arrive at the police station. He need be detained only for as long as it takes him to supply two urine specimens – one to empty the bladder of

THE BREATH-TEST BAG THAT HAD A HOLE IN IT

A motorist cannot be arrested on a result obtained from a defective breath-test apparatus.

Mr R, a motorist, was stopped by a Hampshire police constable and required to take a breath test. He blew into the bag for several seconds, but it did not inflate. The constable then realised that there was a hole in it.

The constable also saw that the crystals had turned green, indicating a positive result, and offered Mr R a second device to blow into. He refused.

Mr R was then arrested, on the basis of the positive result from the faulty device. He subsequently refused to supply a

blood or urine sample and was charged with failing to supply a specimen of either, without reasonable excuse.

A magistrates' court convicted Mr R, but he appealed.

DECISION

The High Court upheld his appeal. It ruled that a bag with a hole in it is not a bag, so that the device used to test Mr R was not of the type approved by the Secretary of State.

As a result, the first request for a breath test was not valid. The police could have arrested Mr R for refusing the second test, but not because the test with the faulty bag proved positive.

urine that may not give a correct reading, the second to be analysed.

But a urine test can be less satisfactory than a blood test for both the motorist and the police. Although alcohol takes longer to affect the urine than it does the blood, it also takes longer to be eliminated from the urine.

In the early stages of drinking, or soon afterwards, there is a lower level of alcohol in the urine than in the blood. Then a urine test may not indicate the full amount of alcohol in the body.

Giving blood

If a motorist chooses to give a blood sample, the police will call a doctor to take it.

The sample is usually taken in a room set aside for the purpose. Before taking a blood sample, the doctor may make an examination or ask if he is suffering from any disease to ensure that the driver does not need immediate medical attention.

The driver is entitled to call his own doctor (or solicitor) at that stage, but the police do not have to delay taking a sample to await the arrival of either.

The police doctor tells the driver where he proposes to take the blood from. Normally the specimen is taken from a vein in the left arm, but it may also be taken from a finger or ear lobe.

The driver cannot choose where the specimen is to be taken from, except for some good medical reason. If the doctor asks for a sample from the vein, and the driver consents only to having it taken from the finger, this is considered an unreasonable refusal.

Extracting blood from the vein with a syringe is simple and painless and removes any chance that the alcohol reading will be made misleadingly high because of alcoholic contamination of the skin.

Enough blood must be taken to fill two small plastic containers. Each is labelled by the doctor and each label is countersigned by the police officer in charge of the test.

One container is put in an envelope that is sealed and signed by the doctor and police officer. The other must be offered to the motorist, for private analysis.

THE DRIVER WHO WAS WATCHED ON A ROUNDABOUT

Even if a motorist believes there is no reason for him to have been asked for a breath test, if it is later proved that a test was justified, he has no defence against a charge of refusing one.

Mr D was watched by two policemen as he negotiated a roundabout on the Great North Road in his car. The officers followed him and found him, some distance along the road, stopped at a garage, filling up with petrol.

When the policemen stopped to speak to Mr D they told him that his breath smelt of alcohol and asked him to take a breath test. He replied that he did not agree.

Mr D was taken to a police station. There he explained that he had refused a breath test because he had not committed a moving traffic offence. He also refused to give a blood or urine sample when asked to do so.

He was charged with failing to provide a blood or urine specimen without reasonable excuse. The police justified their requests for specimens by Mr D's behaviour on the road while negotiating the roundabout and by the smell of alcohol on his breath.

At Durham Quarter Sessions, Mr D was convicted, fined £20, or 1 month's imprisonment in default, and disqualified for 1 year. He appealed.

DECISION

The Appeal Court dismissed Mr D's appeal. It was held that although a motorist may refuse a request for a breath specimen if he believes that no circumstances have arisen which justify the request, he refuses at his peril.

If the police subsequently prove that they had the required grounds under the law for making the request, the motorist's opinion is no answer to the charge.

A DRINK OF BRANDY AFTER THE ACCIDENT

A motorist who has innocently taken a drink to get over the shock of an accident may be entitled to refuse a breath test.

Mr F was involved in an accident between his car and another and was taken to hospital at Wakefield, West Yorkshire. Shortly before 1 a.m. – about 2½ hours after the accident – he was discharged from the hospital and told to return later for an X-ray.

Mr F was arrested after refusing a breath test and was taken to Wakefield police station. There, at 1.33 a.m., he refused again.

At 1.34 a.m. he was asked for a blood specimen and warned that to refuse was an offence. He refused and was charged.

At the magistrates' court, he explained that before the accident he had spent 2 hours at a miners' welfare club, playing snooker. He said he had drunk 1½ pints of beer there.

In the accident, he said, he had suffered a leg injury and shock. On the way to hospital he was given brandy by one of his passengers, a woman who had said she always carried a bottle of brandy in her handbag. At the hospital he had another drink from the bottle.

Mr F pleaded that his arrest and the requests for breath, blood and urine samples were not valid, because when first asked for a breath test he was still a hospital patient and the hospital doctor should have been consulted.

He also pleaded that he drank the brandy innocently, at a time when he did not know that he was under suspicion by the police. He was in a state of shock.

The case was dismissed, but the prosecution appealed.

DECISION

Mr F's acquittal was upheld in the Queens Bench Division. It was held that the taking of brandy, which would have made specimens unreliable, was a reasonable excuse for refusing tests.

In that case, however, there was evidence that Mr F had been given the brandy by someone else and that he had taken it innocently.

In a later case, in 1973, the Court of Appeal did not follow the High Court's judgment and ruled that taking alcohol after ceasing to drive was not a reasonable excuse for refusing to take the breath test or provide a specimen.

The motorist need not take his sample away at once: it will be kept for him at the police station if he wishes to collect it later, or if he at first refuses and then changes his mind. If the motorist is not offered a sample, the police sample cannot be used.

Giving urine

A driver who chooses to provide a urine sample must give two specimens, within an hour of each other, in the presence of the police officer who required the specimen. Normally a policewoman is available, but if there is no woman officer in the station, a woman driver is not entitled to demand that one be brought. But she could lawfully refuse to provide a sample if she was not offered conditions of reasonable propriety and decency.

Privacy cannot be allowed because of the need to guard against any attempt to dilute the sample.

After the first sample has been given and discarded, the driver is told to wait until he is ready to pass another sample. He is not expected to pass more than the small amount required for analysis.

If he succeeds in providing a second specimen within the hour, the procedure is as with a blood sample. The urine sample is divided into two and put in bottles.

The bottles are labelled and sealed with tape in the presence of the driver, who is asked to initial the labels. He is then offered one of the bottles to take away for independent, private analysis.

THE MAN WITH 'DIVINE GIFTS' IN HIS BLOOD

A driver's personal or religious beliefs are not sufficient ground for refusing to give a blood sample.

Mr J was stopped by the police for speeding and was given a breath test that proved positive. A second test at the police station also proved positive.

He refused to give a blood specimen, on the ground of a belief that his blood contained divine gifts which provided him with faith-healing powers.

Mr J gave a urine sample that was thrown away according to the prescribed procedure. He was, however, unable to provide a second urine sample to be analysed.

He was charged with failing, without reasonable excuse, to give a blood sample. At Middlesex Crown Court, he was convicted, fined £40 with the alternative of 6 months' imprisonment and disqualified for 1 year.

Mr J appealed.

DECISION

The appeal was dismissed. The Appeal Court held that the law on drinking and driving had been introduced in the interests of the public as a whole, and that it limited individual rights.

If a motorist was able to set up a defence that he refused to give a blood sample because of a sincerely held belief, it would make him judge of his own cause.

The only excuse for refusing a blood sample under the Road Traffic Act 1972 was that the motorist was unable to do so through some mental or physical condition. A personal or religious belief could not be accepted as a sufficient excuse for refusing.

THE MOTORIST WHO WAS UNABLE TO BREATHE INTO THE BAG

A driver with a reasonable excuse for not taking a breath test must still provide a blood or urine specimen.

Mr K was stopped by the police because he had been driving fast and erratically. His breath smelt of alcohol and he was required to take a breath test.

He refused, on the ground that he had a physical disability – a tracheotomy, or incision in the throat – that prevented him doing so. He also refused a blood or urine test, believing that he was entitled to do so if he had not been able to take a breath test.

He was charged with failing to provide breath, blood or urine samples.

At Inner London Sessions, Mr K was acquitted of failing to take a breath test because his medical condition was a reasonable excuse. However, he was convicted of failing to supply blood or urine.

He was sentenced to 9 months' imprisonment and disqualified from driving for 3 years. The judge certified the case fit for appeal on a point of law on whether Mr K had failed to give a breath specimen.

DECISION

The conviction was upheld by the Court of Appeal, but Mr K's sentence was reduced because of his infirmity. He was released immediately.

THE WOMAN DRIVER WHO WAS TOO SHY

A driver who is too embarrassed to give a urine sample cannot refuse a request for a blood sample.

Police, called to a house after reports of a disturbance, saw Joan T drive away. They suspected that she had taken alcohol, stopped her and asked her to take a breath test. She refused and was taken to a police station where she again refused a breath test. She was dishevelled and in a nervous and distressed state and clearly the worse for drink. She was violent, at one time grabbing a bottle and throwing it, and also refused to give a urine or blood sample. There was no policewoman or doctor present.

Joan T was charged with failing to give a urine or blood sample. At Luton Magistrates' Court she pleaded that because only male police officers were present to superintend the taking of a sample, she was too embarrassed to give either a urine or blood specimen. She said: 'I consider embarrassment a reasonable excuse.'

The charge was dismissed, but the prosecution appealed.

DECISION

The High Court upheld the appeal. It was ruled that even if embarrassment was an excuse for not giving a urine sample, that excuse did not apply to refusing a blood specimen. The case was sent back to Luton Magistrates' Court with an order to convict.

THE ALTERNATIVE CHARGE– DRIVING WHILE UNFIT

A motorist can be prosecuted for driving or attempting to drive while unfit through drink or drugs, without taking a breath test – or even if he takes a test and passes it. He does not need to have committed any traffic offence or to have been in an accident.

If the driver's behaviour clearly shows that he is unfit to drive, he can be arrested and must be offered a breath test at the police station. He is not obliged to take it.

A doctor can be called to ensure that there is no medical explanation for signs of apparent drunkenness, such as unsteady gait or slurred speech. If the driver consents, the doctor can examine him and apply traditional tests, such as asking him to pick up coins, walk a straight line and answer simple questions. Such expert evidence, however, is not essential to a prosecution for driving while unfit.

If a breath test has proved positive or has been refused, the police can require a blood or urine test: it is an offence for the driver to refuse.

The result of the blood or urine test can be used in evidence by either side. If it shows that the motorist was over the legal limit, but by only a little, it may help him to convince a court that his ability to drive was not impaired.

On the other hand, a driver who is charged with having excess alcohol in the blood, as opposed to being unfit through drink, cannot escape conviction if he is even marginally over the legal limit.

Being unfit through drugs

A driver can be prosecuted if he drives or is in charge of a vehicle while unfit through any drug, including any type of medicine – for example, an overdose of insulin prescribed for a diabetic. Maximum penalties are the same as for being unfit through drink.

Evidence of unfitness through drugs includes speech difficulty, sight difficulty, dilated pupils, sweating, inability to do simple sums and traces of a drug in a urine sample.

A driver accused of being unfit through drugs can plead either that he was not under the influence of a drug or that the drug did not make him unfit to drive or be in charge of a vehicle.

Failing to give the sample A driver who has refused a blood sample and then fails to provide the required urine samples within an hour must be required to give blood. If he again refuses, he will be charged with failing, without reasonable excuse, to provide a specimen.

Only extreme injury or physical incapacity are accepted as a reasonable excuse for giving neither blood nor urine.

Some drivers refuse all tests in the hope that they may escape the very long disqualification that would probably be imposed if evidence of analysis, showing a very high alcohol level, were available to the court. They cannot, however, escape a minimum of 12 months' disqualification.

After the test

Once a blood or urine test is complete, the driver will be allowed to leave the station provided that the officer in charge is satisfied that he does not intend to drive or that he is fit to drive.

If the police station breath test proved positive, and the driver wishes to drive away after the blood or urine test, he will be given a further breath test before being allowed to do so.

Alternatively he can leave his car keys at the police station and continue his journey by some other means.

Getting a private analysis

A motorist who decides to have his blood or urine sample analysed privately should do so as quickly as possible. Until the analysis can be carried out, the sample should be kept in a refrigerator, but not a freezer.

Private analysis can generally be done within 48 hours, compared with approximately 3 weeks taken by the police. The cost of private analysis may be about £25.

The analyst's report will usually give full details of the condition and packing of the sample, as well as the alcohol content found. Few police analyses, however, are successfully disputed.

About 20 per cent of specimens tested by police analysts show an alcohol level below the legal limit. Motorists who have provided those are informed by post.

The remaining 80 per cent, whose alcohol level exceeds the legal limit, must be told the test result at least 7 days before court proceedings start.

DRIVEWAY
The right of access across a pavement

Everyone has the right to drive over a pavement in order to reach the driveway of his home. However, if, to obtain access, you have to mount the kerb or cross a grass verge, the local highway authority – usually the county council – can insist that a 'carriage crossing' is constructed at your expense, by lowering the level of the kerb at that point.

The authority will serve a notice on you to that effect and may impose conditions on the use of the crossing – for example, that no vehicles exceeding a certain weight may use it.

If it is a private street, you are allowed to carry out the work yourself, provided that you do not cause a danger or nuisance to pedestrians. If the street has been adopted by the local authority, the authority's consent is necessary before a private contractor can be employed, and the council's exact requirements must be met. If the council do the work and you fail to pay the charges within a reasonable time, the authority may charge interest.

If you object to the crossing – perhaps because you think 'the works proposed are excessive or simply unreasonable' – you may, within 28 days of receiving the notice, send a written objection to the highway authority.

The authority must send a copy of your objection to the Secretary of State for the Environment who makes the final decision. Reinforce your objection by sending details to the Secretary of State, letting the highway authority have a copy.

Closing a driveway

In some exceptional cases – for example, when your driveway leads on to a road that is being converted into a motorway or a motorway-access road – the Secretary of State may serve notice on you to close the driveway. In such a case, he must, at no expense to you, provide for your vehicle an alternative means of access to a public highway. If that is not convenient to you, you have the right to object, and the Secretary of State will usually order a local inquiry before making a final decision.

DRIVING DISQUALIFICATION

How a motorist can lose his licence

Disqualification from driving is automatic for some motoring offences and can be imposed at the court's discretion for all endorsable offences. *See:* ROAD TRAFFIC OFFENCES

When a driver is disqualified he must hand his licence over to the court and it is retained by the issuing authority until the period of disqualification expires. For the most serious offences, where disqualification is compulsory, the minimum ban is 12 months, with no upper limit. Discretionary disqualification has no minimum or maximum period but in most cases it is for 6 months or less.

Courts have no power to disqualify for offences that are not endorsable – for example, parking on a yellow line, disobeying a 'one-way street' sign, having a defective silencer or no MoT certificate – regardless of the driver's previous record. If an offence is endorsable, it is also disqualifiable.

When a driver must be disqualified

The offences for which disqualification for a minimum of 12 months is compulsory are:
● Drink-and-driving offences.
● Manslaughter.
● Causing death by reckless driving.
● Racing on the highway.

Reckless driving on its own involves compulsory disqualification only if the driver has already been convicted of a similar offence within the previous 3 years.

Offences involving DRINK AND DRIVING – including refusal to give a blood or urine specimen – are by far the most common reasons for compulsory disqualification, but if the motorist was only 'in charge' of the vehicle and was not attempting to drive, the court need not disqualify him.

The Magistrates' Association recommends suspension for longer than 12

months if the blood-alcohol level is more than 50 per cent above the legal limit of 80 milligrammes of alcohol to 100 millilitres of blood.

Special reasons against disqualification

In rare cases, the courts can set aside a compulsory disqualification or reduce the period for 'special reasons'.

In a drink-and-driving case, a motorist can plead special reasons against disqualification if, for example, he can prove that his drink was 'laced' without his knowledge, or if he was affected by a combination of drink and medicinal drugs whose effects he could not be expected to know.

However, the court can still disqualify even if the special reason has been proved. In the case of a laced drink the court may decide that the driver was neglecting his responsibilities by not taking sufficient care to ensure he was given a suitable drink.

A court may also take the view that it is well known that many drugs, particularly sleeping pills and tranquillisers, should never be mixed with drink – and that ignorance of their effects is not an acceptable excuse.

Special reasons have been accepted when a motorist has driven because of an emergency – for example, if he had to take an injured person to hospital. But the rules are strict, and the motorist must show that he was unable to obtain an ambulance or taxi or to get someone else to drive.

The distance driven in excess-alcohol cases is normally irrelevant – although a man who has done nothing more than move his car from outside his house into

---

THE INVALID WHO DRANK AND DROVE

The number of circumstances for which the rule of automatic disqualification will be waived have been steadily reduced by the courts in recent years.

Mr Mullarkey, who had artificial legs, was convicted of driving his invalid car after drinking. He said that disqualification would cause appalling hardship because he could walk only a very short distance.

DECISION
The magistrates ruled that Mr Mullarkey's circumstances did not amount to a special reason and he was disqualified.

THE AMBULANCE THAT CRASHED

Ambulance and other emergency service drivers have no immunity from disqualification, but can claim mitigating circumstances.

An ambulance driver taking a woman in premature labour to hospital crossed a red light and collided with a motor scooter. The scooter driver was killed.

The ambulance driver was convicted of causing death by dangerous driving.

DECISION
The magistrates said that the life of the baby and the mother depended on the speed at which they reached hospital. The driver was discharged unconditionally and was not disqualified.

THE MOTORIST WHOSE DRINK WAS LACED

In drink and driving cases, the courts may accept a 'special reason' for not disqualifying an offender. In general, only the fact that a driver did not realise how strong his drink was will be accepted.

Car salesman Samuel Messom demonstrated a new car to a couple and afterwards they invited him for a drink. He asked for a small whisky with ginger ale but was actually given a large brandy. He was given a breath test which showed an alcohol level in excess of the legal maximum, but claimed he did not know how strong the drink had been because the taste was masked by the ginger ale.

DECISION
Mr Messom was disqualified for 12 months at Middlesex Crown Court but the ban was lifted on appeal because his excuse amounted to a special reason.

his drive may possibly escape disqualification.

Special reasons cannot be pleaded on the ground that driving ability was not impaired, that lack of food affected the alcohol level or that the alcohol level was above the limit only because more alcohol was absorbed after he stopped driving.

When a driver is likely to be disqualified

A court's power to disqualify a motorist for any endorsable offence is rarely used in routine cases of, for example, speeding or minor careless driving. But a motorist who does 60 mph or more in a 30 mph zone and is convicted of speeding may well be disqualified even if he has no previous record of driving offences.

Danger to other people is one of the most important factors when a court is deciding whether to disqualify, so disqualification is regularly imposed for reckless driving and driving without insurance. Disqualification is sometimes imposed in a careless-driving case.

In many endorsable offences the driver can plead guilty by letter, but if the court is considering disqualification it will warn him in writing so that he can attend in person or instruct a solicitor.

'Totting up' offences for a disqualification

A driver who collects three endorsements on three occasions within 3 years is liable to automatic disqualification. The 3 year period is calculated from the date of the first conviction – not the date of the offence – up to the date of committing the third offence.

Totting up applies only when the two previous endorsements have been imposed on separate occasions, either at the same court or at different courts. Several endorsements on a single occasion count as only one in totting up.

Totting-up disqualification arises only if:
1. A motorist is convicted of an endorsable offence.
2. On the day he committed that offence he had two endorsements on his licence, imposed less than 3 years before.
3. Those two endorsements were imposed on different days either at the same court or at different courts.

For example, a motorist is stopped for speeding in January 1980, but not convicted until October that year, when his licence is endorsed. He receives another endorsement in 1981, for careless driving. In August 1983 he is again accused of speeding. The case is not heard until February 1984, when his licence is again endorsed, but he is still subject to totting-up because his third offence was committed less than 3 years after the first endorsement.

The period of totting-up disqualification is 6 months, for each endorsable offence on the third occasion. The periods run consecutively.

For example, a motorist who already has two endorsements and who is charged with driving with excess alcohol, careless driving and disobeying a red light, must usually be disqualified for at least 2½ years. That is 12 month minimum for the excess alcohol, plus 6 months' totting-up disqualification, and two further consecutive periods of 6 months' totting up for the other two offences.

Reasons for not disqualifying

Disqualification can be for less than 6 months or may not be imposed at all if there are mitigating circumstances. The minor nature of an offence – for example, parking on the approach to a pedestrian crossing – or a long interval between offences, may influence the court not to disqualify. But the most common ground is hardship.

A lorry driver or travelling salesman who would lose his job if he could not drive might avoid disqualification. So might an invalid, or someone living in a remote area with poor public transport. The court can also consider hardship that might be caused to others – for example, a disabled member of the driver's family, who might suffer if the driver was disqualified.

When a driving test may be ordered

A motorist convicted of an endorsable offence can be disqualified until he passes a driving test again. For example, a motorist convicted of reckless driving may be disqualified for 12 months and ordered to take a driving test. He must not drive at all for 12 months. Thereafter he can only drive if he obtains a provisional licence and is subject to the regulations for learner drivers.

Appealing against a disqualification

A motorist can appeal against disqualification even if he has pleaded guilty to his offence – and even if the offence involved a compulsory or totting-up disqualification. The period of disqualification takes effect immediately but the motorist can ask the court to suspend it until his appeal is heard. Such applications are often rejected.

Getting a disqualification removed

Disqualification need not last for the full period imposed by the court. After a time the motorist can apply to the court that disqualified him to have the ban lifted. Normally, he will need some special reason – for example, a new job that requires him to drive.

If the disqualification was for between 2 and 4 years he can apply to end it after 2 years – the minimum time that must elapse before any such application. If disqualified for between 4 and 10 years, he can apply after half the period has elapsed. If the disqualification is for more than 10 years, he can apply after 5 years.

A motorist cannot apply for the disqualification to be removed if it was for less than 2 years.

The clerk of the court notifies the police of every application, so that they can oppose it if they wish. The court considers the circumstances of the original offence, and the present position of the offender, especially whether he requires his licence for work.

If an application is refused, it can be renewed every 3 months. If granted, the disqualification can be ended at once, or at a future date fixed by the court.

If a motorist has been disqualified for a series of consecutive periods, he may have no right to apply at all. If, for example, he is banned for 2 years for driving with excess alcohol plus two further periods of 6 months under the totting-up rules, he cannot apply after 2 years, because he will just be starting another 12 month disqualification which is treated as a separate period.

DRIVING INSTRUCTION

Standards of teaching required by law

Anyone with a full driving licence can legally give lessons to a learner. But no one can charge for such lessons unless he is registered as a Department of Transport approved driving instructor, or holds a special licence issued by the Department to trainee instructors.

A car dealer is not allowed to give free lessons unless he is registered as an instructor. That is to prevent him including 'free' lessons as part of the purchase price of a vehicle, and then giving unqualified instruction to the purchaser.

A learner should ask to see the instructor's certificate of registration – or, if the instructor is a trainee, the special licence.

Anyone who takes payment for giving driving lessons while unregistered can be sentenced to 4 months' imprisonment and fined £100. A learner who knowingly pays for lessons from an unregistered person can be liable as an accessory to the instructor's offence and subject to similar punishment.

DRIVING LICENCE

Who can drive what, and what happens when the rules are broken

No one may drive a motor vehicle on British roads without a valid licence. The type of licence needed, and your entitlement to it, depends on:
● The vehicle you want to drive.
● Whether you have passed a driving test.
● Your age.
● Your health.
● Your nationality.
● Your driving record.

How to apply

All licences are issued – and all drivers' records kept – by the Driver and Vehicle Licensing Centre.

But do not apply to the licensing centre immediately. First, you must obtain an application form from any post office or the nearest local vehicle licensing office.

The form, which covers all cases except heavy goods or public-service driving, asks for information about yourself, the type of licence you want, the details of your last licence, if any, and whether you have been, and remain, disqualified or convicted of any 'endorsable' motoring offences.

Giving false information or failing to reveal a current endorsement or disqualification is an offence, carrying a maximum penalty of a £200 fine.

When you have completed the form, send it to the Swansea centre – the address is on the form – with the appropriate fee, and your previous licence or pass certificate from your driving test.

BEING MEDICALLY FIT TO DRIVE

You should tell the licensing centre about any medical or physical illness that could make you a danger to other road users – not only when you first apply for a licence, but also later on, if you become aware of a potentially dangerous condition.

Any illness that causes fainting, giddiness or blackouts, or which severely restricts a driver's use of his arms and legs, should be reported.

Examples are epilepsy, diabetes, a stroke, multiple sclerosis, Parkinson's disease, heart disease, high blood pressure, arthritis, drug addiction, alcoholism and any mental illness.

Reporting such an illness does not necessarily mean that you will be refused a licence. The licensing centre will accept advice from your doctor about your physical competence to drive, but it may grant a licence for a limited period of, say, 1 or 2 years.

You need not report an illness or injury which is not expected to last more than 3 months. If in doubt, consult your doctor.

Standard of eyesight

Every driver must be able to read a standard number plate from a distance of 75 ft in good daylight. If you need spectacles or contact lenses to do so, you should wear them every time you drive.

Getting a provisional licence to start driving

A provisional driving licence is a temporary one, lasting for a year, to enable a learner to drive a motor vehicle before passing a test. It is valid for any vehicle except heavy goods and large passenger vehicles.

If you already have a full licence to drive one type of vehicle, you may not need a provisional licence to drive another type.

A qualified car driver, for example, does not need a provisional licence to learn to ride a motor cycle. Nor will a qualified motor cyclist require a provisional licence if he decides to learn to drive a car.

All provisional licence holders and anyone driving a vehicle for which he has not passed the test, must display 'L' plates at the front and back.

He must also be accompanied by a qualified driver unless it is a vehicle built to carry only one person, or a motor cycle with or without a sidecar.

A learner motor cyclist must not carry anyone on his pillion unless the passenger is himself a qualified motor cyclist.

Nor is he allowed to drive a solo motor cycle that has an engine capacity of more than 250 cc. With a sidecar, there is no limit.

Getting a full licence when you have passed the test

A driver may apply for a full licence provided that he has held one at any time in the past 10 years or has passed the test for the vehicle he wants to drive, and is not disqualified.

A full licence normally runs until your 70th birthday. But if you are 67 or older, it will be issued for 3 years or less – depending on your state of health – and will have to be renewed yearly.

The cost of a full licence is usually £5.

Getting a duplicate licence

If you lose your licence, or it is destroyed or defaced, you may apply for a duplicate at a cost of £2.

If the original licence is later found, and is still valid, you must return it to the licensing centre and keep the duplicate. Do not return the duplicate and keep the original.

HOW TO CHECK WHETHER YOUR LICENCE IS VALID FOR THE VEHICLE YOU WANT TO DRIVE
Understanding the vehicle coding on your driving licence

When a driver passes a test, the full licence he receives contains a capital letter or letters in a box. The letter indicates the group of vehicles he is entitled to drive.

Other vehicles

A driver needs an additional licence to drive either a heavy goods vehicle or a public service vehicle.

Group letter	Type of vehicle
A	Any vehicle, other than in group X
B	Any vehicle with automatic transmission, other than group X
C	Motor tricycle, other than an invalid carriage, weighing not more than 410 kg. unladen
D	Motor bicycle, with or without sidecar
E	Moped
F	Agricultural tractor, mounted on wheels
G	Road roller
H	Track-laying vehicle steered by its tracks

An HGV licence is for a goods vehicle whose maximum weight exceeds 7.5 tonnes, including the weight of a trailer.

A PSV licence is for a vehicle used for carrying passengers for hire or reward.

In both cases, the driver should apply to his local Traffic Area Office, whose address is listed in the local telephone directory, for details of licensing and testing.

Group letter	Type of vehicle
J	Invalid carriage
K	Mowing machine or pedestrian-controlled vehicle
L	Electrically propelled vehicle, other than an invalid carriage
M	Trolley vehicle
N	Vehicle exempted from Excise duty because it travels no more than 6 miles a week on roads and then only between pieces of land in its owner's possession
X	Motor bicycle which is not electrically propelled; road roller; vehicle steered by its tracks; invalid carriage; trolley vehicle

Exchanging a licence

If you pass a test, or become qualified by age, to drive additional groups of vehicles, you can obtain an exchange licence.

For example, if a qualified motor cyclist passes a test to drive a road roller, he is entitled to an exchange licence that records the new information. So is a fully licensed car driver who, at the age of 18, becomes automatically entitled to drive other types of vehicle.

The other reason for applying for an exchange licence is to have previous endorsements removed. That can be done only 4 years after the date of an endorsement – or 11 years, if the endorsement was for a drink-and-driving offence.

Driving abroad

A full British driving licence is enough for most Western and several Eastern European countries. Elsewhere, you need an international driving permit, which can be obtained from the Automobile Association, the Royal Automobile Club or the Royal Scottish Automobile Club.

You can apply in person at one of their local offices – taking your full British licence and a passport-sized photograph – or you can send a completed application form and a photograph. If you apply in writing you do not need to produce your driving licence, but you must give its number. The permit costs £1.50 and lasts for a year.

The motoring organisation will also tell you the specific licence requirements of any country you intend to visit.

It is an offence for a British driver whose licence has expired, or who has been disqualifed, to use an international permit to drive in Britain. But it is not illegal for him to use one to drive abroad.

Special rules for drivers from abroad

A tourist coming to Britain can use his own national licence or an international permit for up to a year. He must then take out a provisional licence and pass the appropriate test to qualify for a full British licence.

Anyone who has held a full licence issued within the past 10 years in Northern Ireland, the Isle of Man or the Channel Islands is entitled to a full British licence without taking a test.

Endorsements for driving offences

Many motoring offences carry an automatic endorsement which is recorded in code on the driver's licence.

For example, someone convicted of exceeding a 30 mph speed limit will have the fact stamped on his licence with the dates of offence and conviction, the penalty and a code number identifying the court.

There are more than 50 endorsable offences, each with its own code reference. The full list is to be found on form INS1, at any local vehicle licensing office.

Under a 'totting-up' system, three endorsements within 3 years brings an automatic disqualification, unless the court decides that there are special reasons for it to allow the offender to continue driving. *See:* DRIVING DISQUALIFICATION

If someone commits a motoring offence, but has no current licence or is

RULES FOR DISABLED DRIVERS

A full licence to drive an invalid carriage or specially constructed vehicle does not entitle a disabled person to drive any other type of vehicle. If he wants to learn to drive something else, he must take out a provisional licence for it.

However, a licence issued to a disabled driver often stipulates that the driver must be able to operate all the controls effectively at all times. The stipulation applies to any vehicle that the driver wants to learn to drive.

WHAT YOUR LIFE-LONG DRIVING LICENCE QUALIFIES YOU TO DRIVE
Understanding the legal restrictions on drivers who have even a 'full' licence

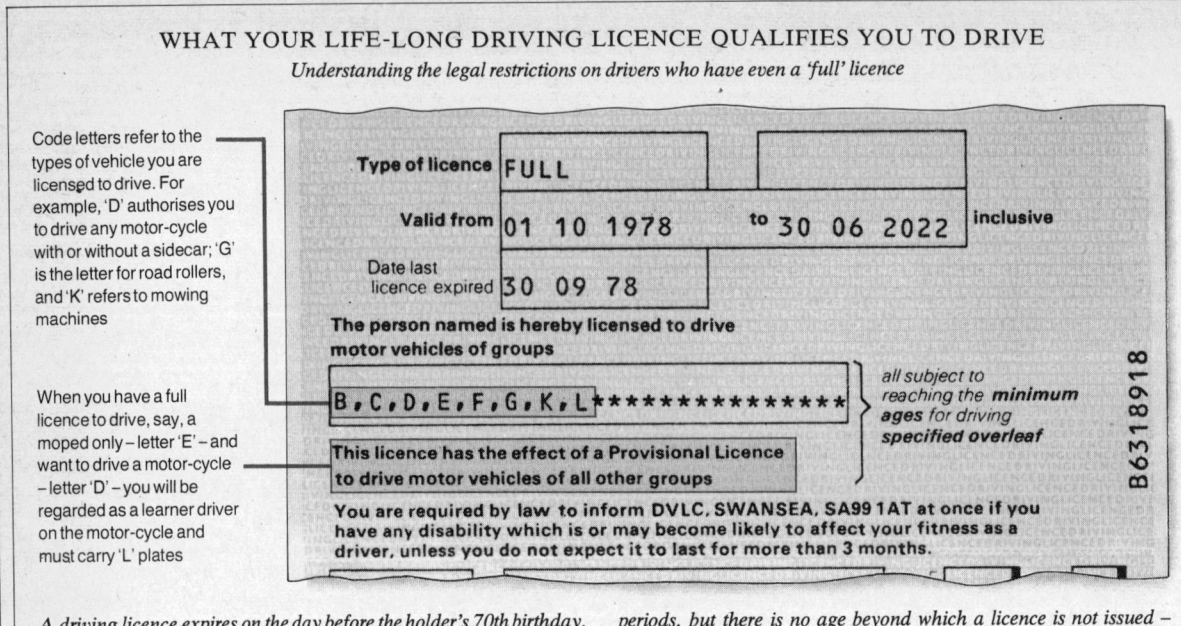

Code letters refer to the types of vehicle you are licensed to drive. For example, 'D' authorises you to drive any motor-cycle with or without a sidecar; 'G' is the letter for road rollers, and 'K' refers to mowing machines

When you have a full licence to drive, say, a moped only – letter 'E' – and want to drive a motor-cycle – letter 'D' – you will be regarded as a learner driver on the motor-cycle and must carry 'L' plates

Type of licence **FULL**

Valid from **01 10 1978** to **30 06 2022** inclusive

Date last licence expired **30 09 78**

The person named is hereby licensed to drive motor vehicles of groups

B, C, D, E, F, G, K, L**✱✱✱✱✱✱✱✱✱✱✱✱✱✱✱**

} *all subject to reaching the minimum ages for driving specified overleaf*

B6318918

This licence has the effect of a Provisional Licence to drive motor vehicles of all other groups

You are required by law to inform DVLC, SWANSEA, SA99 1AT at once if you have any disability which is or may become likely to affect your fitness as a driver, unless you do not expect it to last for more than 3 months.

A driving licence expires on the day before the holder's 70th birthday. For anyone who has reached 67, renewal is possible for only 3 year periods, but there is no age beyond which a licence is not issued – unless there are medical reasons for stopping someone driving.

too young to obtain one, the details of any endorsement or disqualification are recorded at the licensing centre and will appear on any licence he later obtains.

When the police stop a driver

Anyone driving a vehicle or supervising a learner is obliged to show his licence when asked to do so by a police officer.

When there has been an accident or motoring offence, the police can also demand to see the licence of anyone they believe to have been driving at the time.

If a driver does not have his licence with him, he must produce it, in person, at a police station of his choice within 5 days of being asked to show it, including Sundays. He must go to the police station that he has named.

DRUGS

How the law controls their use and abuse

Unlawful drugs – that is drugs whose use and distribution are 'controlled' under the Misuse of Drugs Act 1971 – are divided into three groups, A, B and C, indicating their degree of danger,

Those in group A are regarded as the most dangerous and those in group C as the least dangerous.

Possession of drugs

It is an offence to possess or take any controlled drug except by doctor's prescription. The maximum penalty is 7 years' imprisonment. However, penalties of up to 14 years can be imposed for trafficking – producing, supplying, importing or exporting drugs.

When a blood or urine test reveals a controlled drug in someone's body, he is regarded as being 'in possession', just as

HOW DRUGS ARE CLASSIFIED

Class A 99 drugs including heroin, morphine, dextromoramide, medicinal opium, dipipanone, levorphanol, cocaine, LSD, injectable amphetamines and mescaline.

Class B 13 drugs including purple hearts, cannabis, cannabis resin and benzedrine.

Class C 10 drugs including several amphetamine-type substances and Mandrax.

if the drug were in his pocket. A person who pleads that he did not know he was in possession of a controlled drug, or that he had taken it, must satisfy the court as to his ignorance.

What the police can do

The police can stop and search anyone they reasonably suspect of possessing a controlled drug – without a warrant. But to search a person's home, or any other premises, a SEARCH warrant is needed.

Vehicles can be stopped and searched for drugs – without warrant – and the police and Customs and Excise officers can search all ships and aircraft.

Substances suspected of containing a controlled drug can be seized for analysis. While awaiting the laboratory report, the police may give a suspect BAIL and order him to report regularly to the police station.

If someone is found with drugs on your premises – for example, a lodger who has a room to himself – you are not involved in the offence provided that you were unaware of it. It would be for the police to prove that you did know.

When someone is an addict

Anyone who knows or suspects that someone is a drug addict – for example, a son or daughter – should urge the person to seek medical help, but is under no obligation to report the matter, or to report suspected possession of drugs whether legal or illegal.

However, if a doctor has reasonable cause to believe that a person is addicted to a controlled drug, he has a legal obligation to inform the Home Office, in writing, within 7 days.

Some doctors are licensed by the Home Office to prescribe controlled drugs for registered addicts. A doctor who is not so licensed, and who cannot treat a patient by any means apart from prescribing controlled drugs, can refer the patient to a specialist drug clinic. An addict can go directly to such a clinic without consulting a doctor.

There are 18 drug clinics in the Greater London area and about 50 elsewhere in Britain. Addresses of the clinics can be obtained from family doctors, hospitals, local authority social services departments, or the police.

When prescribed medicine causes harm

If you have been harmed by a prescribed drug, you can seek compensation by suing the doctor who prescribed it, the chemist who dispensed it, the company which manufactured it, or all three – depending on the circumstances.

If the doctor prescribed the wrong drug for your illness, or if there were medical reasons why you should not have been given the prescribed drug, or if he gave the wrong dosage, you can sue him on grounds of MEDICAL NEGLIGENCE. You can also complain against him to the local family practitioners committee, which can punish the doctor but cannot award you compensation. *See:* DOCTOR AND PATIENT

If you were given a harmful drug in hospital, you should sue both the doctor who prescribed it and his employer, the local health authority.

The only grounds for suing a pharmacist over an NHS prescription are if he dispensed a drug other than the one prescribed, if he wrote incorrect instructions on the label, or if he had stored or prepared the medicines in such a way that they were damaged.

If, however, you have been harmed by drugs dispensed on a private prescription, or sold without a prescription – if, for example, you asked the pharmacist to recommend an ointment for a rash, but found it caused the irritation to spread – you can sue the chemist for selling faulty or incorrect goods. You might also be able to sue for negligence. *See:* DANGEROUS GOODS; DEFECTIVE GOODS

If the drugs were bought for you by someone else, you could sue only if the chemist had been negligent in preparing or storing them, or in advising on the appropriate medication.

If you were harmed as a result of incorrect manufacture of the drug, or if you can prove that it had been inadequately tested, you could sue the manufacturer for negligence.

In general, however, negligence by a manufacturer would be difficult to ascertain as drug companies test their products extensively and must satisfy stringent government safeguards before the drugs can be marketed.

Never pursue an action against a doctor, pharmacist, health authority or manufacturer without taking professional legal advice. If you lose the case, your legal costs will be heavy, while those you are suing will usually have insured themselves against claims of this nature. *See:* LEGAL ACTION

DRUNK AND DISORDERLY

When someone is 'incapable' in public

When the police charge someone with being drunk in public, they do not need the evidence of a breath test. It is enough for a police officer to tell the magistrates that the accused showed 'the typical symptoms of being drunk' – for example, inability to stand up straight, a strong smell of drink, slurred speech and drowsiness. In fact, the police cannot insist on breathalysing a non-motorist and do not, in practice, try to do so.

The maximum penalty for being drunk and disorderly is a £50 fine.

To prove disorderliness, however, the prosecution must show that the accused was also unruly, noisy or uproarious – which includes behaving in an unseemly manner. If disorderliness cannot be proved, the accused may be found guilty of being found drunk in public. The maximum penalty for this lesser offence is a £25 fine.

DRUNKENNESS AS A DEFENCE

When drinking can cause 'insanity'

The actions of a drunk person are judged in law by the same standards as would be applied to those of someone who is sober. Someone who deliberately makes himself drunk before committing a crime cannot successfully argue later that he acted without his normal knowledge of right and wrong.

The only occasions when drunkenness can be a defence are when a man becomes so drunk as to be incapable of committing a crime or as to be temporarily insane.

DRY CLEANER

Who is responsible for damaged clothes

When a dry cleaner accepts clothes for cleaning or pressing he accepts a responsibility to take all reasonable care of them. If they are lost or damaged the cleaner is liable to pay compensation unless he proves that the loss was not the result of negligence or lack of skill.

To guard against such claims some cleaners issue receipts with printed conditions limiting their liability.

These conditions may not always be legally enforceable. A condition that says that no liability at all is accepted for loss or damage may well be held to be unreasonable. On the other hand, a condition limiting liability to a fixed amount would probably be said to be reasonable if that condition had been brought to the customer's attention.

Dry cleaners do not generally promise to remove all stains.

Conditions printed on the receipt may give the cleaner power to sell clothes if they are not collected within a reasonable time, such as 6 months. He is entitled to keep the cost of cleaning and the cost of selling the clothes out of the price he receives, but any surplus must be kept available for the customer if he eventually demands it.

EARNED INCOME

How income is defined for tax purposes

For income tax, earned income is strictly defined in law:

1. Salary and wages from a job and any taxable benefits from it – such as free medical insurance, a suit or a car.

2. Any earnings from self-employment in a trade or profession, including any partnership in which you are actively engaged.

3. Income from most pensions or any retirement annuity from a scheme approved by the Inland Revenue.

4. State retirement pension paid to a widow or a person over 65.

5. Sums of money paid to a person after leaving a job – for example, taxable compensation for loss of office.

6. Any income from the creation of a copyright or patent.

7. Maintenance payments made by a marriage partner to the other partner, or to the child of both or either – or by a natural father to his child.

EARNINGS, Attachment of

Forced deductions from a debtor's wages

A creditor who has been unable to get money owed to him by someone earning a wage or salary can ask a county court for an attachment of earnings order. That order instructs the employer to make regular deductions from the debtor's earnings until the money owed is paid.

An order can also be made by any court against a husband who has fallen behind in payments – ordered by a court – to his wife or children. *See:* MAINTENANCE

Getting a county court order

First, obtain a county court DEBT judgment. If the debtor still refuses to pay or a bailiff is unable to recover the money because, for example, all his goods are on HIRE PURCHASE, an attachment order can be sought.

You must apply in the county court for the area in which the debtor lives, on application form No. 402, obtainable from the court. Send the form, when completed, to the court together with the judgment order already obtained.

The court sends the debtor a notice of the application, a copy of it and a reply form. He then has 14 days in which to give the court full details of his employment on the reply form.

He must state his job, place of work, basic pay, overtime, bonus payments, total take-home pay, and any income from any other source. He must also list his dependants and total outgoings, such as mortgage repayments or rent, rates, hire-purchase commitments, regular costs such as food and heating, and any other court orders against him.

The court can order the debtor to appear and explain why he will not give the required information. Failure to do so then would be CONTEMPT OF COURT and he could be fined or imprisoned.

Alternatively, the court registrar can estimate the man's earnings and the court can make an attachment order for what is considered a suitable weekly amount. That amount may be more than the debtor can in fact afford, so it is in his own interest to disclose his true financial position at the outset.

A debtor who has provided the information should suggest on the reply form an amount that should be deducted from his wages.

Fixing the deductions The debtor's reply is sent to the creditor, who can accept the repayment sum offered or he can ask the court to order a higher rate.

The registrar then arranges a private hearing with the debtor. If the debtor fails to appear, a new date is fixed. If the debtor fails to appear at the postponed hearing without good cause, he can be fined up to £25, imprisoned for 14 days, or both.

At that hearing the registrar seeks to establish the debtor's 'protected earnings' – the basic amount he needs to meet his essential outgoings.

If necessary, he can order the debtor's employers to send a statement of the debtor's earnings.

The registrar sets the normal deduction rate: a sum of money which the court considers should be put aside from the debtor's earnings, each week, month or other period, to meet his liabilities. An attachment of earnings order is then made. This must specify

---

A DEBTOR SHOULD DISCLOSE HIS TRUE FINANCIAL POSITION

If the court registrar has to guess a debtor's earnings – because he has not given the information required – the amount he pays under an attachment order might be more than he can afford.

---

both the protected earnings and the normal deduction rate.

What the employer has to do After an attachment order has been made, a copy is sent to the debtor's employer who must immediately start deducting the amount stated from the debtor's weekly or monthly wages. An employer who fails to do so can be fined up to £25, or gaoled for 14 days.

The amount deducted must be sent to the court registrar, who passes it on to the creditor.

When earnings fluctuate If a debtor's earnings vary – for example, if they are higher in some weeks than they were at the time the attachment order was made – he still pays only the amount fixed by the court.

If, however, his earnings drop, the amount deducted can be reduced, because the employer cannot take anything from the debtor's protected earnings.

For example, a debtor earning £45 a week may have protected earnings of £35 and an attachment order for the remaining £10. If he earns £50 in one week, the deduction remains at £10. However, if his income falls to £42, his employer can deduct only £7 – the amount remains in excess of the £35 protected earnings. The shortfall of £3 cannot be carried forward to another week to make his payment for that week £13, even if his earnings will rise. The £3 is not, however, written off – it is still owing. That principle does not apply to maintenance arrears.

Special rules apply when an employee is paid in lump sums or has irregular earnings. The rules can involve complicated calculations, and it is advisable to obtain a pamphlet – *The Attachment of Earnings Act, 1971: An Explanatory Booklet for Employers*, published by HMSO.

When a debtor changes jobs If the debtor moves to a new job, the attachment order for earnings becomes void. However, the debtor must tell the court at once of his new employment. If he fails to do so, he can be fined up to £25, imprisoned for 14 days, or both. When details of the debtor's new job are received, the court issues a new attachment order to the new employer.

A debtor does not have to notify the court of a change of address as long as he continues to work at the same place.

Varying the order The sum to be deducted from the debtor's earnings can be altered by the court on application from either the creditor or the debtor. Evidence has to be given of any alteration in the debtor's circumstances.

EARNINGS-RELATED SUPPLEMENT

Extra money that may be available for the sick or jobless

If you become unemployed or are laid off because of illness, injury or pregnancy, you may be entitled after 2 weeks to claim an additional social security benefit called earnings-related supplement. Widows are entitled to it immediately, without waiting for 2 weeks to elapse.

The payment is additional to normal sickness or unemployment benefit and is related to how much you earned in the relevant tax year. It means that the higher your income – and therefore the higher your national insurance contributions – the more you receive.

To qualify, a man must be under 65 – a woman under 60 – and must have paid Class 1 insurance contributions on earnings of at least 50 times the LOWER EARNINGS LIMIT in the relevant tax year.

The self-employed and people of pensionable age, even if still working, are not entitled to the supplement.

The amount you are entitled to is based on your total 'reckonable' earnings in the previous tax year – that is the earnings on which you paid PAYE. If you were off work for some weeks, the total earnings figure is reduced. Other earnings are not taken into account.

To find out your entitlement in 1981, divide the yearly total for 1979–80 by 50 to give an average weekly 'reckonable' wage, then subtract £19.50 from the average. So for a person who was earning an average of £30 a week the supplement would be: £30 less £19.50, leaving £10.50. One-third of that is £3.50.

A person who averaged more than £30 weekly still gets that £3.50 plus a sum equal to 10 per cent of the average by which earnings exceeded £30.

On an average £60 a week, for example, the supplement is calculated as:

£60–£30	£30
10% of £30	£3

Total earnings-related supplement is therefore
£3.50 + £3 .... £6.50

The maximum payable during 1981 is £14 for those who averaged £135 a week or more.

Earnings-related supplement continues to be paid for 156 days, excluding Sundays.

The Government has announced that earnings-related supplement will be abolished in 1982. It will not be paid for new claims made from January 1982 onwards.

As with other claims for benefit, if you disagree with the amount awarded, you can appeal. The Department of Health and Social Security will provide a chart which it uses to check its calculations. *See:* SOCIAL SECURITY APPEALS

EDUCATION AUTHORITY

How schools are run and paid for

Parents who have a school problem and have failed to solve it with the head teacher or governors, should next approach the local education authority.

These authorities provide and staff all state schools and lay down general rules – such as whether or not caning is allowed. They also have the power to dismiss head teachers or staff, but are unlikely to interfere with the internal management of a school.

Parents who disagree with a school's rules – for example, about uniforms or caning – can protest to the education authority. They can also try to persuade it to spend more on books or reduce numbers in classes. Most complaints to education authorities, however, are often about the choice of SCHOOL.

How it works The education authority is usually the county council. But in large towns it may be the metropolitan district council. In outer London, the education authority is the borough; for the 12 inner London boroughs and the City of London it is the Inner London Education Authority.

The way in which an education authority spends its funds is decided by its education committee, which consists mainly of councillors – although other people with a special interest in education may be co-opted.

The political party with a majority on the council has a majority on the committee and on any sub-committees which deal, for example, with finance, staffing, buildings and handicapped children.

The names of education committee chairmen and members are published in the Education Committees Yearbook which can be seen at most local libraries. Some councils also publish lists of sub-committee members.

You are entitled to attend meetings of your education committee. If you are on the local ELECTORAL REGISTER, you are entitled to ask your authority for minutes of meetings. In many areas, meetings of sub-committees are also open to the public, although they do not have to be, and minutes may also be available.

All education committee decisions must go before the full council for confirmation – except in the case of inner London where the ILEA has the powers of a full council.

Influencing the authority If you want to influence or change the policies of your local education authority – for example, get them to spend more on equipment – you will need to persuade the councillors who make the policy decisions.

Many councillors hold regular sessions at which an individual can explain his or her problems and seek help.

Special problems Full-time staff of local education authorities have considerable freedom to deal with day-to-day matters. Parents in dispute with head teachers or school governors should approach them first.

The officials can often settle disputes over the range of subjects taught, the choice of school, rules on dress and methods of punishment. Some authorities are split into divisions: parents should approach their local division.

A parent who takes a problem to local authority staff can seek the support of a councillor: that may be advisable if a question of policy is involved.

Councillors can sometimes get information not available from a local official – for example, a copy of local regulations about corporal punishment or a

document that discloses how children are chosen for a particular secondary school.

Neither councillors nor parents, however, have a right to see a child's school record, even if they have reason to believe that the record may not be fair. However, some councils, such as Manchester, do allow parents to see their child's record. *See:* SCHOOL RECORDS; SCHOOL REPORT

Duties of the authority Education authorities have certain responsibilities that they must carry out by law.

An authority must provide enough schools for all the children – including handicapped children – in its area. They must also provide student grants, religious education, school meals, milk for primary school children, boarding accommodation for children who live in such remote areas that they cannot otherwise get to school, and transport for all children who live outside a prescribed distance from the nearest school.

A local authority is not entirely free to run schools as it pleases. It cannot raise enough money from RATES alone to pay for all local education requirements. The rest of what is needed comes in a subsidy, known as a rate support grant, from the government.

Although the grant is provided as one lump sum for all types of council expenditure, the local authority has to get approval from the Department of Education and Science for its spending plans. As a result it must take into account the Department's national education policy.

Making an appeal

If you cannot get satisfaction from the education authority, you can appeal to the Secretary of State for Education and Science.

He can intervene, under Section 68 of the 1944 Education Act, if he feels that a school or education authority has acted unreasonably or is proposing to do so. That applies whether or not the authority is exercising discretionary powers. Most appeals under Section 68 are over the choice of school.

The Secretary of State can intervene if a local authority fails to carry out its duties under the Education Act or departmental regulations. Under Section 99 of the 1944 Act, he can give 'such

directions as appear to be expedient' to ensure that authorities do what they should. In a case brought by parents in Haringey, London, in 1979 against the local education authority for failing to provide education during a caretakers' strike, the High Court ruled that parents can seek a remedy before the courts if they believe that the local education authority is in breach of its statutory duty.

This is the first case of its kind, and it is uncertain in what other circumstances a court would interfere when a local education authority had failed to perform a statutory duty – such as providing enough books and equipment to give children an education suitable for their age and ability.

The 1944 Act says that local authorities must provide a varied and comprehensive service, that efficient education must be available for the needs of the local population, with schools 'sufficient in number, character and equipment' to provide suitable education for all children in the area, and that no fees should be charged for education in schools.

Parents therefore should not be asked to pay for basic needs – for example, books and equipment essential for the education process – but they can be invited to subsidise supplementary provisions, such as additional courses or facilities.

To appeal to the Secretary of State, write to the Department of Education and Science, setting out your grounds for appealing.

If possible, mention the Department's regulations or circulars in support of your appeal. Copies can be obtained from the Department, and from larger reference libraries.

ELDERLY PEOPLE

Help available to those who have retired

Elderly people are generally considered to be those who have reached retirement pension age – that is, 65 for men and 60 for women.

Services available to elderly people fall into six main categories: money, health, housing, help in the home, outside activities, work and leisure.

Financial help

Most elderly people are entitled to a State RETIREMENT PENSION, to which they have contributed during their working lives. But that pension by itself is not normally sufficient. Anyone whose income is below a certain level – decided from time to time by the Government – may claim a supplementary pension from the local social security office. *See:* SUPPLEMENTARY BENEFIT

To claim, the pensioner must obtain form SB1 from any post office or social security office, and send it completed to the local social security office. State on the form if you would prefer to call at the local office rather than have an officer to call on you to discuss your claim. **If you have savings** Provided that your savings are not over £2,000, the amount of supplementary pension you get will not be affected.

The supplementary pension is paid with your retirement pension, one pension book covers both.

Anyone receiving a supplementary pension will also qualify for other benefits, such as free dental treatment and free spectacles.

Medical help

Apart from the usual National Health Service treatments, and help with the cost of spectacles, hearing aids and dental treatment, elderly people are entitled to free medicine on prescription.

To get free medicines complete the appropriate section on the back of the prescription form. In some areas a free chiropody service is provided by the local authority.

Elderly people often suffer from more than one complaint at the same time and, for that reason, most general hospitals have special geriatric units, which allow an elderly person to be treated without having to be transferred from one department to another.

In many areas, day hospitals provide medical treatment, physiotherapy and occupational therapy to enable elderly people to continue to live at home despite their disabilities.

Transport between home and hospital is generally available free by hospital car or ambulance. Otherwise, people on low incomes can claim a refund of fares, by completing form H11 – obtainable at the hospital – or by showing the supplementary benefit or Family Income Supplement order book at the hospital.

Health visitors call on some elderly people at home, giving advice on such matters as health, nutrition and keeping warm. The district nurse also visits patients and gives any nursing attention required – including injections, surgical dressings and bathing.

Help with housing

Most elderly people are able to continue to live in their own homes. Even the disabled can usually do so with the help of family and friends who live near by, and with practical aids provided by the local authority.

To help to meet the cost of maintaining a home, rent and rate rebates are available to people who are on low income but not receiving supplementary benefit. Details can be obtained from the council offices.

If an elderly person becomes too in-

firm to continue to live alone, or if the house in which he lives is too large to heat or keep clean, he is entitled to apply to the local authority for one or other of the housing schemes available.

Residential houses

Also available are residential homes, where people may have to share a bedroom – although more and more separate rooms are being provided.

Do not accept, however, that an elderly person needs to go into a residential home until all other possibilities have been investigated. The local council provides a wide range of services that may enable the person to remain in his or her own home.

Other accommodation available to the elderly are almshouses – owned usually by charities and let free or for a very small sum, to people who have followed a particular religion, trade or profession – residential homes provided by local authorities and voluntary organisations, and flats or bed-sitting-room units provided by voluntary housing associations.

Details can be obtained from the local authority housing or social services departments or from the local Citizens Advice Bureau.

Help in the home

Many services and appliances are available from the local authority to help elderly people to retain their independence in their own homes. Applications should be made to the local authority social services department.

Those who cannot cope with housework or washing and shopping may be provided with a home help, and housebound people who find cooking for themselves difficult can receive meals on wheels. A charge may be made for both these services, depending on the applicant's financial circumstances.

Many local authorities provide linen and a free laundry service for people who cannot cope with soiled sheets. Application for those services should be made by the family doctor, or the hospital if the elderly person has recently been receiving hospital treatment.

Among the aids and appliances available are handrails on stairs and in bathrooms and lavatories, seats, rails and grip-mats for baths and 'helping hands' (long-handled grips for reaching high).

SPECIAL CONCESSIONS FOR THE ELDERLY

Pensioners qualify automatically for many cost concessions. The ones most commonly available include:
● *Transport* Reduced fares are charged for travel by British Rail, the London Underground and most bus services.
● *Holidays* Many travel organisations allow pensioner rates for holidays in Britain or abroad. But you should make sure that the saving offered is not cancelled out by a demand for a specially high medical insurance premium.
● *Entertainment* Many cinemas and theatres offer reduced charges or special

performances for pensioners. Museum and exhibition charges may also be reduced.
● *Services* Pensioners often benefit from price concessions at hairdressers, swimming baths, leisure centres, libraries and so on.
● *Investment* Special National Savings certificates, the repayment on which is linked to the cost-of-living index, are available only for men over 65 and women over 60. Some finance houses and insurance societies offer special terms for the elderly.

Some local authorities provide telephones for elderly housebound people or, if a telephone is already installed, pay the rental. But they do not pay for calls.

Local authorities have a legal obligation to provide many of these services if they consider you need them, and to go on providing them for as long as your need exists. They also have a duty to publish information about the services and to make sure that anybody using one of them is told of any others he may need.

If in doubt about your rights, consult a Citizens Advice Bureau, Age Concern branch or disabled people's organisation.

If you are severely disabled and someone stays off work to look after you, he or she may be entitled to claim certain benefits, such as INVALID CARE ALLOWANCE and SUPPLEMENTARY BENEFIT. If so, their pension rights will be protected, at least in part, by 'home responsibilities protection'.

If you are over 65 and a relative looks after you, even though you are not an invalid, he will be able to claim a dependent relative's income tax allowance.

Taking part in outside activities

One of the main fears of the elderly, especially the 24 per cent who live alone, is isolation from the social life of the community. Being cut off from the mainstream of activity can lead to depression and an avoidable general decline in health.

To avoid that, many local authorities and voluntary organisations, such as churches, the Red Cross and WRVS, organise clubs and day centres that provide a variety of social activities.

Day centres Many local councils provide or support clubs for elderly people living in their area. Members take part in a wide range of social activities for all or part of the day.

Lunch is sometimes provided, for a small charge, and free transport is generally available for those who cannot make their own way to the club.

For the elderly infirm, many day centres provide bathing, chiropody and laundering facilities as well.

Luncheon clubs Local authorities, sometimes in conjunction with volun-

tary organisations, run luncheon clubs to provide a well-balanced meal for people who can get about, but who might not bother to cook for themselves. Often there is some social function after the meal.

A small charge is usually made, and the clubs generally have a waiting list.

To join a day centre or luncheon club, apply to the local social services department.

Holidays Most councils provide a limited number of holidays each year for old people who can get about. The holidays in seaside guest houses or houses run by voluntary organisations are often free or greatly subsidised.

Apply as early in the year as possible to the local social services department. Priority is often given to people who have not had a holiday for a long time.

Infirm elderly people may be considered for a holiday for the disabled. For those recovering from a physical or mental illness a convalescent holiday may be available.

A family doctor or local social worker is the best source of detailed information.

Work and leisure

Many people who reach retirement age choose to carry on working, sometimes on a part-time basis. Others even decide to begin a new career. Up to the age of 70 – 65 for women – they can earn a certain amount a week (£52 in 1981) without reduction of retirement pension. After those ages, there is no earnings limit.

Government job centres try to help pensioners in most areas to find suitable work. Many towns also have special voluntary employment bureaux to help people over pensionable age to find jobs. Some local authorities and voluntary bodies run work centres providing light work for pensioners for 2 or 3 hours a day.

For pensioners who wish to follow their hobbies, or take up new interests, the council's education department or the local branch of Workers' Educational Association run classes for pensioners at reduced rates.

Addresses and details of these services can be obtained from most local libraries, Citizens Advice Bureaux, or council offices.

ELECTION
The people's right to choose a government

British people have a legal right to choose their own national and local government in free elections. Voting for district and county councils normally takes place separately from a general election, when Members of Parliament are chosen, but the principles are the same. People casting their vote must be able to do so in secret and candidates must be prevented from using bribery or unfair means to influence the result.

Who can vote?

Anyone over the age of 18 who is on the ELECTORAL REGISTER can vote unless he or she is a peer (who can vote in a local government election only), an alien, a criminal serving a gaol sentence or a person certified as being of unsound mind. But every person must take his own steps to see that his name is on the local electoral roll.

Rules for a parliamentary election

A general election must be held at least every 5 years, but the Prime Minister can ask the Queen to dissolve Parliament at any time during its 5 year life – even if he still has the support of the majority of members.

When Parliament has been dissolved, writs, or orders, to hold a general election are issued from the office of the Clerk of the Crown in Chancery to the returning officer – usually the town clerk or chief executive – at each of the country's 635 constituencies. Each constituency must return one member to Parliament, but any number of candidates can contest the seat.

How candidates are nominated

When a returning officer receives a parliamentary election writ he must publish the date of the election by putting up posters at public places such as town halls and libraries within 2 days. A time is fixed during which nominations for candidates can be accepted by the returning officer. Polling must by law take place on the ninth day after nominations have closed.

Candidates can be nominated only

with their consent, and each must be supported by at least 10 registered electors, including a proposer and a seconder.

The candidate does not have to belong to any political party, nor does he have to live in the constituency where he is seeking election. Nominations must be made on a special form obtainable from the returning officer.

Every nomination must be backed by a deposit of £150, returnable only if the candidate polls at least one-eighth of the total vote at the election.

Every candidate must appoint an agent, usually unpaid, and the amount of expenses they can spend during their election campaign is limited by law.

In a county constituency the allowance is £1,750 plus 2p for every elector; in towns it is £1,750 plus 1½p for every elector. The personal expenses of the candidate are not limited, and he can have as many unpaid volunteers and supporters helping him as he can muster.

It is an offence for anyone to bribe or attempt to bribe a voter, to attempt to intimidate a voter, or to impersonate a voter. Any person found guilty could be imprisoned and the election could be declared void.

Objecting to a candidate Only a candidate or his proposer or seconder can object to another candidate, and then only on the grounds that the candidate is not qualified to stand for election. *See:* MEMBER OF PARLIAMENT

Rules for local elections

The rules for parliamentary elections apply generally to local elections, and no one can vote unless he is registered on the current electoral roll for the parliamentary constituency in which he lives.

England has 6 metropolitan counties – Tyne and Wear, Merseyside, West Midlands, Greater Manchester, South Yorkshire and West Yorkshire – and 39 non-metropolitan counties. In London, there are the Greater London Council, 32 boroughs and the City of London Corporation.

Wales has 8 counties.

Beneath those councils are 332 district councils in England, and a further 37 in Wales, with powers over local planning, housing and refuse-collecting.

When elections are held

Polling for county councils takes place every 4 years from 1973. The election is usually held on the first Thursday in May, unless Parliament issues an order changing it, because, for example, a parliamentary election is being held at about the same time.

A county council is elected for 4 years and it cannot be dissolved during that term. If any members resign they can be replaced in by-elections. At the end of the 4 years a councillor can, if he wishes, submit himself for re-election.

Members of district councils are also elected for 4 years but in most cases only one-third are elected or re-elected each year – except in the year when there is a county council election.

Casting your vote

Before polling day at a parliamentary election – but not at a local election – each registered voter receives by post from the local returning officer a note of his voting number and the polling station at which he should vote.

Polling stations must be open from 7 a.m. until 10 p.m. on the day of the election. At the station, each voter is given a ballot paper, and his name must be crossed off the list of registered voters so that it is impossible for him to vote a second time.

The ballot paper contains the names of all the candidates in alphabetical order and a description of their politics in not more than six words, such as the party to which they belong, or their main campaign issue.

The voter should put an X against the name of the candidate he wishes to see elected.

He should then fold the paper and place it in the sealed ballot box.

If any other mark is put on a ballot paper it can be discredited as a 'spoiled paper'. The voter can, however, ask for a second paper, provided he has not already put the first into the ballot box.

Every voter must leave the polling station as soon as he has deposited his paper in the box.

Secrecy Voting in Britain has been secret since 1872 and the returning officer, the presiding officer, who supervises the poll, and all poll clerks must make a declaration of secrecy.

Postal voting Some electors are allowed to vote by post in both parliamentary and local elections:
● Anyone unable to go to the polling station because of old age, illness or physical disability.
● Any registered voter who has gone to live permanently in another constituency.
● A worker required by his job to be away from home on election day.
● A serviceman who has been moved to a new station and his wife and any dependants who have been moved with him and are entitled to vote.

No voter is allowed a postal vote if he is away on holiday. Nor is anyone who

ELECTING YOUR EUROPEAN MP

Since 1979, members of the European Parliament have been elected by the voters of the countries of the European Community. Britain, France, Italy and West Germany each return 81 members. Holland returns 25, Belgium and Greece 24, Denmark 16, the Irish Republic 15 and Luxembourg 6.

In Britain, the normal parliamentary constituencies have been grouped into larger European constituencies, each with about 500,000 voters – 66 in England, 8 in Scotland, 4 in Wales and 3 in Northern Ireland.

Candidates must be aged at least 21 years, of sound mind and must not have spent more than 3 months in prison during the 5 years before nomination.

Bankrupts and employees of the Crown cannot stand, but peers, Church of England clergymen and members of the House of Commons can do so. Candidates pay a £600 deposit, which they forfeit if they poll less than 12½ per cent of the total number of votes cast.

Everyone on the normal electoral roll can vote, as well as peers and citizens of the Irish Republic resident in Britain. The voting procedure is the same as in a national election.

In England, Scotland and Wales the candidate in each constituency who polls the most votes is elected. In Northern Ireland the province as a whole elects all three members, using the system of a single transferable vote.

ELECTION

has emigrated to another country but is still on the electoral roll.

To get an application form for a postal vote write to the electoral registration officer at the local council in the constituency where you are entitled to vote. Anyone who is refused a postal vote can appeal to a county court. If a postal vote is allowed on the grounds of an elector's occupation or physical incapacity it is valid for as long as his name remains on the electoral roll. In other cases, it is valid for one election only.

Voting by proxy Someone who expects to be out of the country on business at the time of an election can ask to have his vote cast by proxy – that is, have someone else make the vote for him.

Application for a proxy vote must be made to the registration officer at the local council offices at least 12 full days, not including Sundays and Bank Holidays, before a parliamentary election and 14 days before a local election.

THE FORM THAT SECURES YOUR RIGHT TO VOTE
How the head of a household lists the eligible voters on his premises

Address

No. of flat, room or floor (where applicable)	No. of house (or name if not numbered)	Name of street or road	Remainder of address including post code
	48	SUNNINGTON ROAD	LONDON N18 8PR

Residents eligible to be included (see notes 1 and 2 on the left)

Surname and title (Mr, Mrs, etc.) (BLOCK LETTERS)	Full Christian names or forenames (BLOCK LETTERS)	If 18 or over by 16th February 1980 enter a ✓ in this column	If under 18 on 16th February 1980 but 18 by 15th February 1981 give date of birth (see note 1)	If a merchant seaman enter "M" (see notes 1 and 2)	Jury Service (see note 5) If over 65 by 16th February 1980 enter a ✓ in this column
LACEY	JAMES EDWARD	✓			
LACEY	PAMELA WINIFRED	✓			
LACEY	JULIET MARY	✓			✓
THOMPSON	EMMA JANE		18.1.63		

Other residents

Is any part of your house/flat *separately* occupied by persons not entered above? *Please answer Yes or No:* **No**

Declaration

I declare that to the best of my knowledge and belief the particulars given above are true and accurate, and all those whose names are entered above are British subjects or citizens of the Irish Republic and will be 18 or over by 15th February 1981.

Electoral registration forms are sent to every known household in Britain, addressed to 'the occupier'. It is the duty of the head of each household – usually the husband in a married relationship, or the main breadwinner in other groups – to see that it is completed correctly. If it comes with an envelope, it must be returned. Otherwise it will be collected.

The voter must give his reasons for absence from the constituency on polling day and the names of a first choice and second choice proxy.

The registration officer contacts the first-choice proxy, and if that person agrees to cast the absent elector's vote, the officer confirms the appointment in writing. If the first-choice proxy does not agree to cast the vote, the officer contacts the second choice.

You can change your mind about having your vote cast by proxy – but not after the vote has been cast.

Counting votes After polling has ended, the votes in an election must be counted as soon as practicable. Apart from the clerks officially conducting the poll, the candidates and their agents and up to 10 nominated counting agents, no one is allowed in the counting room.

The returning officer supervises the count and he decides whether a paper is spoiled, but his decision is subject to review on an election petition.

If a poll ends in a tie, with two candidates having exactly the same number of votes, lots are drawn to decide who is the winner. After the returning officer announces the result, he must send it officially to the Clerk of the Crown at the High Court in London.

Challenging the result of an election

Any elector has a right to challenge an election result because:
● The person elected was not qualified or not properly elected.
● Corrupt or illegal practices took place.

The procedure is complicated. A number of forms have to be obtained, from the clerks to the Queen's Bench Division of the High Court. These should be filled in with the help of a lawyer, then lodged at the court.

The petition is heard by an election court. If the appellant is successful, the elected candidate can be disqualified and the person who came second can be declared elected in his stead, or the election can be declared void and a new election ordered.

Penalties for electoral offences

The maximum fine for voting twice in an election is £100. An offender can also be barred from voting for 5 years. The maximum penalty for personation – claiming to be someone else in order to vote – is 2 years' imprisonment.

ELECTORAL REGISTER

How to register to vote

The right to vote in a parliamentary or local council election in Britain is open, with certain exceptions, to people over the age of 18. In order to use that right, however, your name must appear

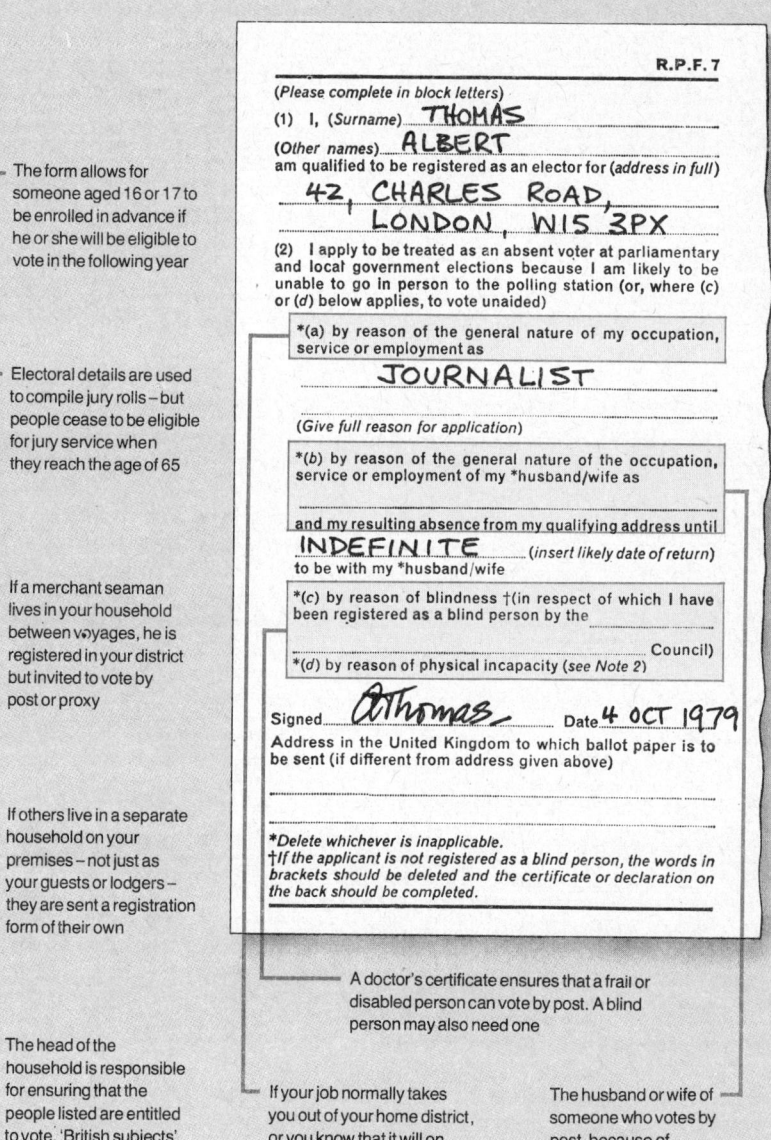

The form allows for someone aged 16 or 17 to be enrolled in advance if he or she will be eligible to vote in the following year

Electoral details are used to compile jury rolls – but people cease to be eligible for jury service when they reach the age of 65

If a merchant seaman lives in your household between voyages, he is registered in your district but invited to vote by post or proxy

If others live in a separate household on your premises – not just as your guests or lodgers – they are sent a registration form of their own

The head of the household is responsible for ensuring that the people listed are entitled to vote. 'British subjects' include Commonwealth citizens

A doctor's certificate ensures that a frail or disabled person can vote by post. A blind person may also need one

If your job normally takes you out of your home district, or you know that it will on election day, you are entitled to vote by post

The husband or wife of someone who votes by post, because of employment, can also vote by post

Form contents:

R.P.F.7

(Please complete in block letters)

(1) I, (Surname) **THOMAS**

(Other names) **ALBERT**

am qualified to be registered as an elector for (address in full)

42, CHARLES ROAD, LONDON, W15 3PX

(2) I apply to be treated as an absent voter at parliamentary and local government elections because I am likely to be unable to go in person to the polling station (or, where (c) or (d) below applies, to vote unaided)

*(a) by reason of the general nature of my occupation, service or employment as

JOURNALIST

(Give full reason for application)

*(b) by reason of the general nature of the occupation, service or employment of my *husband/wife as

and my resulting absence from my qualifying address until

INDEFINITE (insert likely date of return)

to be with my *husband/wife

*(c) by reason of blindness †(in respect of which I have been registered as a blind person by the

Council)

*(d) by reason of physical incapacity (see Note 2)

Signed *A.Thomas* Date **4 OCT 1979**

Address in the United Kingdom to which ballot paper is to be sent (if different from address given above)

*Delete whichever is inapplicable.
†If the applicant is not registered as a blind person, the words in brackets should be deleted and the certificate or declaration on the back should be completed.

If, when you register your name for voting, you know that your occupation will keep you away from your home area at election time, you should ask for form RPF 7, on which you can claim your right to vote by post. So can people who are blind or disabled.

on the electoral register for the constituency in which you live.

Each autumn the electoral registration officer sends a form to every house in his constituency. The householder has a legal duty to write on it the name of every person over the age of 16 years and 8 months living in the house on October 10, and to return it to the registration officer. It is an offence not to do so and the penalty is a fine of up to £50.

Who qualifies

The electoral register comes into force on February 16 each year and should include all names sent to the registration officer the previous autumn. Your name should be on the roll if you are:
● A citizen of the United Kingdom, the Republic of Ireland or an independent country in the Commonwealth.
● Living in the constituency (occupying business premises is not enough).

Who does not qualify

Certain people do not qualify for a vote and would not normally appear on an electoral roll:
● Aliens.
● People of unsound mind.
● Anyone serving a gaol sentence or convicted of corrupt or illegal electoral practice.

Peers, who cannot vote in a parliamentary election, are included on the electoral roll but are listed as local government electors only.

The rights of teenagers A person is entitled to vote immediately he or she becomes 18, so a teenager's name should appear on the electoral roll for the year in which the 18th birthday falls. If an election is held before the 18th birthday, however, he or she is not entitled to vote then.

When a name is omitted from the register

However long a person has lived in the same house, he or she should complete and return a registration form for the electoral roll every year. The names of all people eligible to vote should be included, even if they are the same names, year after year.

Failure to return the form is not only an offence, but may also lead to your name being left off the electoral roll. That does not automatically happen, however: even if you do not send in a form, provided that your name continues to appear on the electoral roll, you are still entitled to vote.

On November 28 each year, a provisional list of electors is available for inspection in each constituency at public libraries and local post offices. If your name does not appear on the list for your street or area, and you believe it should, you have until December 16 to ask the local registration officer to add it to the list.

It may be that the householder where you live accidentally left your name off his form, or that the form has been lost. If the registration officer refuses to add your name to the list, he must give his reasons. You can appeal to the county court against his refusal.

Special rules for students

Someone studying at a college away from his home constituency is entitled to be registered on the electoral rolls of two constituencies – the one where he lives and the one where his college is.

He can vote in both constituencies in local elections and parliamentary by-elections, but for a parliamentary general election he can vote only once.

Working away from home

People working temporarily away from home, including merchant seamen, can register for a vote at the address where they would usually live – even if the house is sub-let to someone else while they are away.

When a voter moves People who move home remain on the electoral roll in their former constituency until new rolls are drawn up, the following February. Then they qualify for inclusion in the electoral roll of their new constituency.

In any intervening election, local or parliamentary, they can vote – either by post, or personally – only in the constituency in which they are registered. *See:* ELECTION

ELECTRIC WIRING

Safety laws designed to protect equipment users

When the electric wiring on domestic equipment that works on mains electricity has an earth wire, the three wires must be coloured differently. The mains lead must have attached to it when it is bought a label or tag of the type shown below.

It is a criminal offence to sell electrical equipment without such a notice or to sell equipment that is not correctly wired.

Maximum penalty: Fine of £1,000 and 3 months' imprisonment under the Consumer Safety Act 1978. *See:* CONSUMER SAFETY

A DOWN-TO-EARTH LAW ON ELECTRICAL APPLIANCES
When equipment must carry instructions on correct fitting

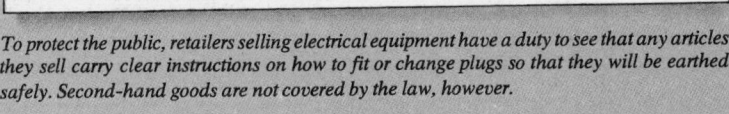

WARNING—THIS APPLIANCE MUST BE EARTHED

IMPORTANT The wires in this mains lead are coloured in accordance with the following code —
Green-and-Yellow: Earth   **Blue: Neutral**
Brown: Live

As these colours may not correspond with the coloured markings sometimes used to identify the terminals in a plug, connect as follows —
The wire coloured green-and-yellow must be connected to the terminal marked E or by earth symbol ⏚ or coloured green or green-and-yellow.
The wire coloured blue must be connected to the terminal marked N or coloured black.
The wire coloured brown must be connected to the terminal marked L or coloured red.

RH4

To protect the public, retailers selling electrical equipment have a duty to see that any articles they sell carry clear instructions on how to fit or change plugs so that they will be earthed safely. Second-hand goods are not covered by the law, however.

ELECTRICITY SUPPLY

*Your right to have power
in your house*

Anyone who owns or occupies a property connected to an electricity main is entitled to be supplied with electricity, provided he has paid all his previous electricity bills, and that the premises, wiring and appliances are safe.

If a local electricity board fails to give a supply it commits a criminal offence for which it can be fined £50 by a magistrates' court and a further £50 for every day that the offence continues.

To obtain a supply of electricity, get a contract form from your local board office. On it you must estimate the maximum amount of electricity and the range of appliances that you expect to use, so that the appropriate tariff can be applied. The contract form contains details of the amount of electricity used by different appliances, to help you make your estimate.

A board is entitled to ask an applicant for a deposit, and is especially likely to do so if he has been a bad payer. The amount can vary up to about £50.

If you buy a house or flat, particularly if it is old, arrange a survey of the electricity circuits, by the local board. It is your responsibility to make sure that your system meets the board's standard and you will have to pay an electrical contractor or the electricity board for any repairs necessary.

Getting connected

If your house is not connected to a main, but is within 50 yds of one, you can require the board to connect your property to it.

The board may ask you to pay the cost of providing any line longer than 20 yds between your home and the main, as well as the cost of any other lines laid on your land not included in the 20 yds – for example, a line from your front gate to the house, when the front gate is 20 yds from the main.

If there is no main near by, six or more householders in a street can insist that the board lays a new main. The board will require those demanding the main to sign for an electricity supply. Once the contracts are signed the board must lay the main. If it fails to do so, it can be prosecuted by any or all of the householders and if convicted fined up to £50 for each day that the failure continues.

Paying for your electricity

Electricity is paid for either by putting coins in a slot meter – for which the customer pays a rental which is included in the cost of electricity – or on credit, with bills submitted every 3 months according to the total units of electricity shown on the credit meter.

A credit meter is installed at the customer's expense and this can vary, depending on the amount of work involved in the installation.

Domestic electricity bills include a minimum quarterly charge, which is a standing charge for using electricity, as well as a charge for the number of electricity units used during that quarter.

If the board's meter reader finds no one at home he will usually leave a card so that the customer can make his own reading and record it. Otherwise the bill may be estimated. The estimate is based on your bill for the equivalent quarter of the previous year.

If an estimate seems unusually high, insist on your meter being read before you pay. There is no need to make an offer to pay if the estimate seems low. If anyone fills in his card incorrectly and over or undercharges himself, the error will be adjusted on the bill following the next official meter reading.

Challenging a meter reading

A meter may sometimes register more fuel than has in fact been used. If you suspect such a fault, ask your local electricity office to have the meter tested.

An electricity meter is deemed to be accurate if it runs fast by no more than $2\frac{1}{2}$ per cent or slow by no more than 3 per cent. If your meter is found to be running too fast, you will be repaid the amount of the over-run, if this can be checked, otherwise a reasonable estimate. If the meter is running too slow, you may be asked to make up the underpayment, depending on the circumstances.

The board will send an official to check your appliances and meter. He

HOW TO READ YOUR ELECTRICITY METER
Dial or digital, the figures read from left to right

DIAL METER

10000   1000   100   10   1 kWh. PER DIV.

The pointer has passed the figure 1; note down 1

The pointer has not reached the figure 9; add an 8 to read 18

The pointer has passed the figure 5; add a 5 to read 18,5

The pointer covers the figure 6: as the pointer on the dial to the right is between 9 and 0, add a 5 to read 18,55

The pointer has passed the figure 9, so add a 9 for the final reading, 18,559. The lower dial shows tenths of a unit

$\frac{1}{10}$

DIGITAL METER

0 1 3 8 1 4

10000   1000   100   10   1   1/10

Read from left to right, ignoring the right-hand figure. The reading is, therefore, 1,381

Both types of meter show the total number of electricity units used since the meter was installed. To find out how much you have consumed and still have to pay for, deduct the total of units already charged for, shown on your last bill, from the new reading.

AVOIDING POWER BILLS CAN BE AN OFFENCE

Any person who tries to avoid paying for electricity by diverting the supply so that it cannot be registered by a meter is committing the crime of theft and can be charged.

may test your meter with his own portable check meter, which clips on to your credit meter and measures its accuracy. Alternatively, he may install a check meter to run alongside your own meter, for about a fortnight.

Even if your meter is found to be running correctly, you will not have to pay for a test. A charge of £2 per visit is made only if someone habitually asks for a meter to be read.

If after a test you are still not satisfied that your meter is working properly, ask your local electricity office for an independent inspection to be made by a Department of Energy inspector. He will check the meter and issue a certificate showing its degree of accuracy. There is no charge for an independent inspection.

The same inspection and payment system operates if you have a coin-slot meter in your home.

Changing your meter

A customer is not automatically entitled to change from one type of meter to the other, but he can apply to the local electricity board office to do so. The board then decides whether to make the change.

A board will not replace a credit meter with a slot meter unless the customer can show genuine hardship or that his finances are in a mess and he is

unable to budget for quarterly bills. There is no general rule for deciding hardship: each board will consider each application on its merits.

Electricity offences

No one should ever tamper with a meter or attempt to alter a reading or feed it foreign coins.

Anyone who, with intent to avoid paying, diverts an electricity supply so that it is not registered by the meter, commits THEFT.

Anyone who tampers with a meter, even if he intends to pay for electricity, or disconnects it without giving notice to the board also commits an offence. *See:* CRIMINAL DAMAGE

When something goes wrong with the service

If you are dissatisfied with any aspect of the board's supply, charges, goods or service, complain personally to the manager at your local electricity office or in writing to the board area manager.

If that fails to produce a solution, contact a local representative of your regional consultative council, which is independent of the electricity board and whose members are appointed by the Department of Trade.

Names and addresses of the local representatives on your council can be obtained from your local board office or from the consultative council itself.

The council's address is given on your electricity bills. It can also be obtained from the local library, post office or telephone directory.

When your home can be entered by an electricity official

An electricity board official is not entitled to enter your home, or to try to use force to enter it, without your consent, unless he has obtained a warrant authorising the entry from a magistrate.

The warrant must state why entry is required:
- To enable an official to inspect apparatus.
- To check how much fuel has been used by the consumer.
- To remove apparatus thought to be dangerous.
- To disconnect the supply.

Unless there is an emergency – for

example, if it is believed that overloading of the mains may cause a fire – at least 24 hours' notice of intended entry is required.

An official who enters your home, whether under a warrant or otherwise, must leave your home as secure as he found it. If he leaves it insecure and someone else then enters and steals something belonging to you, you can sue the electricity board for the loss arising from his negligence.

If the official causes any damage by entering the property, he must make it good. If he does not do so, claim compensation from the board – or sue it.

Unless the official has a warrant or there is an emergency, it is not an offence to refuse to allow him to enter your home. But if he has a warrant or it is an emergency, it is a criminal offence to obstruct him. The maximum penalty is a £5 fine.

When the supply can be cut off

Electricity boards have the right to disconnect a supply, or to refuse to connect a new supply, if:
- The customer has not paid his bills for electricity used.
- The premises or electrical wiring or appliances are unsafe.
- The customer is using electricity dishonestly – bypassing the meter.

The supply cannot be disconnected on the ground that the customer has failed to pay for equipment obtained from the electricity board.

Pensioners who have not paid their electricity bill must not be disconnected by the boards between October 1 and March 31 – unless it is clear that they have means to pay and have not done so.

Under a code of practice concerning

IF A POWER CUT CAUSES LOSS OF BUSINESS

An electricity board cannot be sued for damages if lack of electricity supply causes someone a business loss. A board would not, for example, have to pay for a loss suffered by a factory at which production stopped because the electricity supply had been cut off due to industrial strife. Nor can a householder sue for the inconvenience of not being able to use a washing machine.

disconnection, agreed between the electricity board, the Department of Energy and the National Consumer Council, no board should disconnect any customer's supply if it can make a firm arrangement for payment of any arrears and a guarantee of future payments. For example, once a local social services department has agreed to pay the bill direct, or a bank standing order has been made out, the supply should not be cut off.

When the customer cannot pay, or the supply has already been cut off for non-payment, he should contact the local social security office or the council social services or housing department. One or other of them may pay the bill or make arrangements for it to be paid. *See:* FUEL BILL

When a landlord resells electricity to his tenant

A landlord is entitled to resell electricity to his tenant. He can do so by using his own slot meter or credit meter or fitting a slot meter for his tenant, or by including the cost of electricity in the rent. If he includes it in the rent, a special section should be set aside in the rent book stating the rates charged for electricity.

If a tenant is supplied through the landlord's meter, any money due at the end of the tenancy belongs to the landlord and not to the electricity board.

A tenant can ask his local board to be supplied direct, provided that he has not made an oral or written agreement with the landlord to pay the landlord for electricity.

A tenant who is supplied by his landlord, and who has difficulty in paying for it, will receive the same consideration from the local social security office or local authority as if he were supplied direct by the electricity board.

What a landlord is entitled to charge

A landlord who resells electricity to a tenant must not charge more than the maximum resale price fixed by his area electricity board. He can, however, make two extra charges – a small, daily 'availability charge' to cover the cost of providing a meter and wiring, and a charge for each electricity unit used.

A typical permitted resale price is the normal domestic rate plus 0.2p per unit, plus a daily charge of up to 2.5p.

Ask your landlord for a proper bill showing the amount of fuel used, the dates of meter readings and the charges made, and check the charge against the table of permitted charges.

A tenant can find out the approved local maximum price from a leaflet entitled 'Electricity – how much can landlords charge?'

The leaflet, prepared by the Department of Energy and obtainable at any electricity board office, gives the rates for the area and a table of the maximum extra charges allowed.

If a tenant discovers that his landlord is overcharging him for his electricity, the electricity board will not help him to recover the money, but he can sue the landlord in the county court for the excess.

A landlord who disconnects a tenant, or refuses to provide electricity, as a means of forcing him to leave the premises, can be prosecuted for HARASSMENT, and the tenant can also sue him for breach of contract. *See:* CONTRACT

Arranging to end the electricity supply

Anyone leaving a property should give at least 24 hours' notice in writing to the local electricity board office. Failure to do so can make him liable to pay for all the electricity used on the property until the next meter reading, or until the board has been informed by a new occupier requesting a supply that the property has changed hands.

EMERGENCY POWERS

When danger threatens society

A state of emergency can be declared at any time if the Government fears that services essential to people's lives are threatened by strikes, civil upheaval or natural causes.

The Government can make regulations and use the armed forces and the police to ensure the supply and distribution of food, water, fuel, electricity and transport.

A state of emergency is proclaimed by the Queen on the advice of the Gov-

ernment and remains in force for 1 month. It can be revoked earlier or be renewed after a month.

New offences can be created temporarily during an emergency. Fines of up to £100 or sentences of up to 3 months' imprisonment can be imposed on anyone who disobeys new regulations – for example fixing food prices or requisitioning property – but the right to strike cannot be taken away, conscription cannot be introduced and the right to a trial remains.

Emergency powers in time of war

When Britain is in a state of war, regulations can be imposed to limit a citizen's usual freedom. In modern times they have been authorised by special Acts of Parliament. But in theory the ancient measure of martial law could still be enforced.

The armed forces have a continuing right under common law to take whatever measures they consider necessary to control the population and defend the realm. A person's right to his own property or to public access could be overruled in the national interest, even if an emergency proclamation had not been made. *See also:* TERRORISM

EMIGRATION

When people want to start a new life abroad

Anyone in Britain has the basic right to leave the country and live elsewhere. No permission is needed from the Government, although there are controls on the transfer of money, and a person's normal freedom of movement can be restricted for other legal reasons.

For example, people can be prevented from leaving Britain if they are:
● Subject to criminal proceedings.
● Serving a sentence of detention.
● Required to remain as a condition of bail, probation or parole.
● Compulsorily detained because of mental disorder.
● Serving in the armed forces and travelling without leave.
● Restrained by a court injunction because their departure would infringe someone else's rights.

Under many of those legal restraints a person can be compelled to give up his or her passport, or can be refused an application for a passport. Someone who has been granted government funds to return to Britain on a previous occasion cannot use his passport until the money is repaid.

A passport is not legally necessary to leave Britain – but it is practically impossible to go anywhere else without one. International airlines and shipping companies are unlikely to carry a passenger without a passport, and in most cases they must also be satisfied that a traveller will be allowed to enter his country of destination.

Other countries' rules

No nation in the world allows unlimited immigration. Each has its own laws that can keep out non-citizens because of poor health, criminal behaviour or even political activity, and further rules that restrict the flow of people eligible for long residence or permanent settlement.

Emigration to Europe is relatively easy because most UK citizens have the right to enter any other EEC country to seek or take up work. They are given temporary permission to stay, followed by a residence permit if their work continues. *See:* EUROPEAN COMMUNITIES; PATRIALITY

Other countries' immigration restrictions vary, and any country's rules can change at short notice. In general a person's chances of being accepted, assuming that he or she is in good health and has had no serious criminal convictions, depend on:
● Employment prospects.
● Financial means.
● Age.
● Family.

Inquiries about settling in another country should be made to that country's diplomatic mission in Britain. Almost every foreign nation has an embassy or consulate in London, and Commonwealth states have high commissions there. Some countries also have consular offices in other major British cities.

Diplomatic missions usually give general information about conditions in their country, although it is advisable not to rely entirely on that. A country's leading newspapers are a good alternative source of information, and most diplomatic offices have them available.

Diplomatic missions also provide enough explanation of their immigration rules to indicate whether a person could qualify to settle there. If that seems unlikely there is little point in making a formal application, which can be complicated and costly.

Applicants must provide extensive documentary evidence and character references. For example, an application to settle in the United States must include a police report from every country in which the applicant has spent 6 months or more since the age of 16.

Depending on the country to which he hopes to go, a migrant may have to show that he has a job waiting for him. If he is a family man, he may need a guarantee of accommodation. A migrant and any dependants travelling with him will almost certainly have to undergo a medical examination before their final acceptance, which may also be subject to police or security clearance.

A person can be sure of his right to settle in another country only when an immigration entry permit or visa is stamped in his passport. It is unwise to give up a job, sell property or transfer funds before then.

The money an emigrant can take

Special EXCHANGE CONTROL regulations apply to people going to live permanently outside the United Kingdom, Eire, Channel Islands, Isle of Man and Gibraltar. A family resident in the UK intending to stay abroad for 3 years or more is allowed to take or send £200,000. If a family is going to work in an EEC country, more than the basic allowance can be transferred.

That allowance covers the whole of a family – husband, wife and unmarried children under 18 – but children over 18 or married children of any age qualify for their own allowance. The basic sum excludes fares paid for in Britain, and up to £2,000 per person is allowed for travel.

Although assets in excess of the allowance are normally restricted, it is usually only necessary that they remain within the Scheduled Territories (not just Britain).

Only certain assets (for example, the documents of title to securities) must be deposited with an authorised deposi-

tory and, although permission is required for restricted assets to be dealt with in any way, banks are able to effect certain transactions without applying to the Bank of England.

Restricted funds can normally be transferred abroad within the 4 year period only through the investment currency market, which entails an extra payment – unofficially called the dollar premium – over the normal currency exchange rate.

An emigrant is normally entitled to receive British life or endowment assurance payments abroad, and any pension payments due to him. Income from assets held in Britain – for example, rents, dividends, interest or premium bond prizes – can be received abroad, even if the assets themselves are restricted.

If an emigrant dies within the 4 years of exchange-control restriction, the control ends and money held in Britain can be sent abroad to beneficiaries of his estate.

An emigrant who experiences unexpected hardship after his departure can apply through his British bank for the release of restricted funds, but permission is not granted to meet expenses which should have been foreseen – for example, the cost of housing.

Buying a house Provided a prospective emigrant who wishes to purchase a property abroad for his private use does so before his redesignation as non-resident, no charge is made against his emigration allowance in respect of any part of the entitlement to official exchange (£100,000) used for this purpose. After redesignation, however, he would not normally be permitted to use restricted funds for this purpose unless they were transferred through the investment currency market.

People who are exempt Anyone who immigrated to Britain can leave with all the assets he brought, including any income from them, and any savings from other income in Britain. Exchange control applies only to capital assets – for example, business premises or equipment – that are bought in Britain. UK residents cannot be exempt, nor can any gifts from UK residents.

How to apply An emigrant who wants to take or transfer money to his new country should apply to his own bank, which provides the necessary form and can give advice on completing it.

THE STEPS YOU MUST TAKE IF YOU DECIDE TO EMIGRATE

The long, painstaking process may daunt all but the most determined families

1 The first need of every would-be emigrant is for information, and making a visit to the embassy of the country of their choice is their first step.

2 From the material produced by governments, the family start to plan their new life, balancing the excitement of the unknown and the reality of their needs and ambitions. Usually they have jobs to go to; if not, it is unlikely that they will be accepted as immigrants. They complete and return the application forms.

3 Eventually – weeks or even months later – the whole family is asked to go to talk to the embassy's migration officer. Meanwhile, their references and histories have been checked carefully; and the officer has made sure that none of them has a criminal record. Their medical examinations are arranged.

4 When the embassy has approved their application, the family begin to wind up their British life, selling their home and settling accounts.

5 From the first glimmerings of the idea that they should make their future in a new country to the moment when they walk across the tarmac to their aeroplane or up the gangway to their ship, taking in what may be their very last impressions of Britain, many months have elapsed. It is in that period that they have had a chance to have second and even third thoughts about what they may stand to gain and lose by their journey. No country wishes to have new citizens who will shortly want to return home. They have decided, however, on the basis of all the help, advice and cautioning available that they do want to go and that the country and the jobs of their choice are right for the entire family.

The form includes a statement of all the assets – in any country – and liabilities of the emigrant and his family. Depending on the amount involved, the bank issues an authority and arranges to make the money available, or it forwards the application to the Bank of England for approval. Permission remains valid for 3 months.

An emigrant's tax position

If an emigrant family's main income was from employment and it stops before the end of the tax year on April 5, the taxpayer is likely to be owed a refund of part of his INCOME TAX deductions. Personal tax allowances are granted for the whole year, even if the income is for only part of a year.

A refund can be claimed by declaring that employment has ceased, on a form obtainable from any tax office. Repayment can be made before the emigrant leaves Britain if he can show proof of his travel arrangements.

A self-employed person is unlikely to be owed a refund of tax. The last half-year's instalment of tax demanded by assessment may be reduced if he produces evidence that his British income is ceasing.

Profit from the sale of an emigrant family's only home is not normally liable to CAPITAL GAINS TAX.

Income from investments left in Britain remains liable to tax, but an emigrant can claim a proportion of the usual personal tax allowance, called the 'world income fraction'. Allowances are granted in the same ratio as the emigrant's British income bears to his total income from all countries.

If the holder of British Government securities becomes a permanent resident abroad, the interest from them ceases to be liable to British income tax. Many emigrants switch to that form of investment to improve their tax situation.

National insurance rights

A person already entitled to a retirement pension or widow's benefit who goes to live abroad, retains the right to receive it. They can normally be paid anywhere abroad. But the recipient will not be given any increase in the rate of pensions, which are granted after he or she has gone abroad. However, these increases can be paid in EEC countries and in other countries with which Britain has reciprocal agreements – Austria, Bermuda, Cyprus, Gibraltar, Israel, Jamaica, Jersey and Guernsey, Malta, Spain, Switzerland, Turkey, the United States and Yugoslavia.

An emigrant, who wishes to maintain his entitlement to a pension on reaching retirement age or to provide a pension for his widow, may continue to pay contributions voluntarily. He may do this by completing form CF83, obtainable from any social security office. He should state on the form whether he is paying by direct contributions from abroad, by direct debit of an account with a United Kingdom bank, or by arranging for an agent in the UK to pay on his behalf.

Health services abroad

National Health Service treatment is available only in Britain. Emigrants cease to be eligible for treatment because they are not ordinarily resident.

Emigrants must rely on whatever health services are provided in their new country. In most cases that means they must be prepared to buy health insurance, or else pay the full cost of medical attention, drugs or hospital treatment.

A new country's laws

Anyone who settles in a new land is completely bound by its laws and obliged to accept its legal system, which may be altogether different from Britain's. Behaviour that is acceptable in Britain may be heavily punishable somewhere else – for example, taking an alcoholic drink is an offence for which you can be flogged in some Islamic countries.

Until an emigrant is granted CITIZENSHIP of a new country, he is liable to DEPORTATION if he does not comply with that country's law. In many places a court conviction is not necessary to expel a non-citizen.

While an emigrant retains British citizenship he can appeal for help from Britain's diplomatic mission in his new country, or from the Foreign Office. But if an emigrant knowingly breaks the law and is dealt with according to the country's recognised legal system, Britain is unlikely to protest unless the punishment is exceptionally harsh.

British representatives will attempt to aid citizens who appear to be unjustly deprived of their rights – for example, imprisoned without trial. *See:* BRITISH EMBASSY

As long as he retains British citizenship, an emigrant who runs out of money and cannot support himself is entitled to apply to a British diplomatic mission for repatriation as a destitute citizen. That means the Government pays the cost of getting him and his family home. But their passports are confiscated so that they cannot travel abroad again until the money is repaid.

Legal rights in Britain

An emigrant loses none of his legal rights under British law – but he cannot claim them from abroad. A legal action can be started only in the country over which a court has jurisdiction. If an emigrant wants to deal with a legal problem in Britain, he must arrange for a British lawyer to act on his behalf. If that is not practicable, his only choice is to return to Britain.

For that reason it is essential for an emigrant to make sure that arrangements over which there could be a legal dispute – for example, the sale of a house or the shipment of household goods – are completed if possible before he leaves.

He must also be sure that he leaves behind no obligations over which he could be sued, because he might have no opportunity to defend the action, and whoever sues him could win possession of assets left in Britain. An emigrant who foresees any legal problem should discuss it with a lawyer before leaving the country.

An emigrant is not immune to prosecution for an offence committed in Britain. He can be arrested if he returns to a British territory within 7 years, and depending on the nature of the crime and the country to which he goes, he may be liable to EXTRADITION.

EMPLOYED PERSON

How the law decides whether someone is an employee

English law distinguishes between employed persons, or employees, who work under what is called a 'contract of service', and the self-employed, whose

BEING YOUR OWN BOSS BRINGS EXTRA RESPONSIBILITIES

Self-employed people have to record their business expenses, pay all their national insurance, and if their turnover is £10,000 per annum, pay Value Added Tax – with all the extra paperwork and administrative work that that involves.

'Self-employed, Schedule D'

relationship with clients and customers is bound by what is termed a 'contract for services'.

Employees enjoy far wider rights in the course of their work than the self-employed. They are more extensively covered by the EMPLOYMENT PROTECTION rules. If they lose their jobs, they may claim UNFAIR DISMISSAL or REDUNDANCY, and are entitled to UNEMPLOYMENT BENEFIT – rights that the self-employed do not have.

The two types of worker are treated very differently by Inland Revenue and under the national insurance regulations.

Employees pay income tax on Schedule E, deducted from their wages at source under the Pay As You Earn system. Part of their weekly national insurance contribution is paid by their employers.

Self-employed people pay income tax on Schedule D the year after the income is earned. Because they are allowed to deduct more business expenses when calculating their liability, their tax bills may be lower than those of employees. But they have to meet the whole cost of national insurance contributions themselves and, if their turnover is more than £10,000 a year, are liable for VALUE ADDED TAX as well. *See:* SELF-EMPLOYED

Deciding who is an employee

Most people fall quite clearly into the category either of employee or of self-employed person. But there are borderline cases. When such a case arises – for example, in a claim for unfair dismissal or redundancy, or in a tax dispute – the court or industrial tribunal applies a series of tests.

None of these tests, by itself, is conclusive proof of whether someone is an employee. Courts and tribunals reach their decisions by looking at all the circumstances surrounding the person's work, and are not always consistent in their conclusions. However, there is agreement on one point – the description 'employee' or 'self-employed' adopted by the individual himself, or

---

THE SELF-EMPLOYED LECTURER WHO WAS DISMISSED

Although someone pays income tax and national insurance as a self-employed person, he may not be self-employed under the employment protection rules if in most other respects his working terms and conditions are like those of colleagues who are employees.

Mr Davis was a lecturer engaged in 1971 by the New England College of Arundel on an annual lecturing contract. Originally, the college deducted his income tax at source and paid national insurance contributions on his behalf. Later, after appointment, he asked to be treated as self-employed for national insurance and tax purposes, and the college no longer made the deductions.

Eventually, Mr Davis was dismissed and he tried to claim unfair dismissal. The college argued he was self-employed and therefore could not make the claim.

DECISION

The Employment Appeal Tribunal said that Mr Davis was an employee. He asked to be treated as self-employed for tax purposes but that did not alter the relationship. He could claim unfair dismissal.

THE PART-TIME RESEARCHER WHO WORKED TO ORDER

Someone who works from time to time under the detailed control of another is not classed as self-employed simply because the employment is irregular.

Mrs Irving was a market research interviewer who, from time to time, was given work by one particular company. She was free to turn it down or to work for other employers when available. But if she accepted the job, she was expected to follow detailed instructions on how to do it and to complete it by a specified date. The social security authorities claimed that Mrs Irving was an employee and that the company should be paying national insurance contributions for her, which it had not been doing.

DECISION

Whenever Mrs Irving accepted work from the company, she became its employee until the work was finished. She was not self-employed.

THE MANAGER WHO FORMED HIS OWN COMPANY

In deciding whether someone is self-employed or an employee, courts and tribunals take into account the intentions of both parties to the contract under which he works.

Mr Massey was a branch manager for the Crown Life insurance company. His accountant told him that he would pay less income tax if he could persuade his employers to treat him in future as self-employed.

Crown Life agreed to the idea. In 1973 Mr Massey formed his own company, John L. Massey Associates, which contracted to supply his services as a branch manager to Crown Life. He paid tax and national insurance as a self-employed person.

But in 1975 Crown Life ended its agreement with Mr Massey. He claimed unfair dismissal.

DECISION

Mr Massey was not an employee of Crown Life and therefore could not claim unfair dismissal. The Court of Appeal held that both Crown Life and Mr Massey had genuinely intended to change his status from employee to self-employed.

> ## THE DRIVING INSTRUCTOR WHOSE CONTRACT CHANGED
>
> *Even if a contract for services between a company and a self-employed person has many of the same features as a normal employment contract, that person is not an employee if both parties intend that he should not be.*
>
> In 1974 the British School of Motoring was reorganised. A series of smaller companies was formed, each of which entered a contract for services with a driving instructor who had previously been an employee of BSM.
> Mr Thorn worked for BSM (1257) Ltd. His contract specifically stated that he was self-employed and gave him no basic pay – only commission. He paid his own national insurance stamp as a self-employed person. However, the company held his national insurance card, and deducted the contributions on his behalf from his earnings.
>
> Mr Thorn was required to work a certain number of hours each week for BSM (1257). The company provided the car, oil and petrol, and made the bookings with pupils. But Mr Thorn was free to take other work if he wanted to, and the company did not try to tell him in detail how to conduct his lessons on its behalf.
> The Department of Health and Social Security maintained that Mr Thorn was not self-employed, but an employee, and that BSM (1257) should pay employers' national insurance contributions for him. The company contested the claim.
>
> ### DECISION
> Mr Thorn was self-employed. The High Court held that, although some terms of his contract were more appropriate to the contract of an employee, there was nothing in it that was inconsistent with his being self-employed.

attached to him by those for whom he works, is not necessarily correct in law.

As a first step, the court or tribunal looks at previous arrangements for paying tax and national insurance, to establish whether they have been made for an employee or a self-employed person. It also examines whether the person gets holiday pay. If he does, he is likely to be an employee.

The court or tribunal then asks:
Is the work controlled? If a worker is free to decide how to do the job, without specific guidance or control by someone else, he may be self-employed. If someone else controls his work, he is likely to be an employee.

However, that test does not always provide a satisfactory answer. For example, a hospital surgeon decides how to operate on a patient. His employers do not tell him how to do it. But although the surgeon controls his own work, he is an employee.
Is he part of someone else's organisation? If someone is an employee, his work is likely to be an integral part of the company or organisation that employs him. If he is self-employed, he is likely only to be an accessory to the organisation.

For example, a company may have its own chauffeurs to drive some executives, and hire cars, with drivers, for other employees, as and when necessary. The chauffeurs are employees: the hired-car drivers are not – even if they work for the company regularly.

EMPLOYEE, Death of

When an employee dies

Although the death of an employee automatically ends his EMPLOYMENT CONTRACT with his employer, the employee's executors or administrators can generally continue to pursue any unsettled claim for REDUNDANCY or UNFAIR DISMISSAL. Wages or other payments to which the employee had become entitled before his death, but which he had not received, form part of the estate. *See also:* ACCIDENT AT WORK

EMPLOYER, Death of

How an employer's death affects employment contracts

When an employer dies, any EMPLOYMENT CONTRACT he has entered into as an individual automatically ends. An employee who loses his job as a result of his employer's death – for example, if the business then closes – may be entitled to claim REDUNDANCY payment from the employer's estate. However, he cannot claim UNFAIR DISMISSAL unless he was already under notice when the employer died.

If the employer is a company, the death of one or more of its officers – for example, the managing director – does not in itself interrupt employment contracts. In the case of partnerships, the effect of the death of one partner depends on whether the contract was with the dead person as an individual, or with the partnership as an entity.

EMPLOYER'S LIABILITY

When an employer is liable for the actions of his staff

An employer is liable for any wrong done by a member of his staff if it is done in the course of that person's employment. Anyone who suffers loss as a result of civil wrong, or TORT, committed by an employee may therefore be able to recover damages from the employer.

For example, if you are knocked down by a bus, you can sue the bus company for the driver's negligence. If a solicitor's clerk absconds with your deposit for a house, you can sue the firm of solicitors.

When the employer is not liable

The employer is not liable, however, when an employee does something wrong outside the normal course of his employment as it has been defined by the employer.

If a sales representative goes a mile or so off his business route to buy cigarettes, and while off that route has an accident with his car, through negligence, he will probably be considered to have committed a wrong within the course of his employment: his employer will be liable for any damages. But if he has an accident after driving 20 miles off his route without his employer's permission to visit friends, that will probably be regarded as being outside the course of his employment, and he, not his employer, will be liable.

Even when an employer has expressly forbidden an employee to do something but the employee ignores the in-

> ## THE MILKMAN WHO ENGAGED A BOY ASSISTANT
>
> *Even when an employer takes precautions – by issuing notices to his staff, for example – he may not evade liability if he is sued.*
>
> Mr Plenty was a milkman who agreed to pay Leslie Rose, aged 13, to help him deliver milk. He did so despite notices at the depot which forbade the use of children on rounds.
>
> One day, Mr Plenty drove his milk float too near the kerb. Leslie's leg was dangling over the side, and his foot got trapped between the float and the kerb.
>
> Leslie's father sued Mr Plenty and the dairy company for damages. The court found Mr Plenty liable, but held that the employers were not liable, because of their prohibitory notices about the employment of children. Mr Rose appealed on his son's behalf, claiming that the company was liable for the acts of their roundsmen.
>
> ### DECISION
>
> The Court of Appeal decided that despite the notices, the employers were liable for Leslie's injuries. The boy had been taken on to carry out the employer's business, and, although prohibited, Mr Plenty's act was done in the course of his employment and for the employer's purposes.
>
> ---
>
> ## BUS CONDUCTOR WHO TRIED TO HELP
>
> *An employer is not liable for the negligence of an employee who goes outside the scope of his employment, against instructions.*
>
> Mr Carberry, a bus conductor, had a firm instruction in his rule book that he must not drive buses.
>
> One day his bus was blocking the path of another, in the bus depot at Streatham, London. Mr Carberry's driver was not present, so Mr Carberry got into the cab of his bus and attempted to move it.
>
> Mr Carberry had never driven a bus before and did not know how to do so.
>
> The bus crushed and injured the driver of the other bus, Mr Mohammed Iqbal, who was standing at the back of his vehicle.
>
> Mr Iqbal sued their employers, the London Transport Executive, for injuries caused by Mr Carberry's negligence.
>
> ### DECISION
>
> The employers were held not to be liable. Although Mr Carberry had only been trying to help his absent driver when he moved the bus, doing so was outside the scope of his employment, which was collecting fares and not driving buses.

struction, the employer may be liable for any accident that results.

If his instruction or prohibition merely told the employee to do his job in a certain way, the employer will still be responsible if the instruction is ignored.

If, however, his instruction or prohibition restricted the scope of the worker's employment, he can avoid liability.

For example, if a garage owner has a young hand, whose job is to push cars around the garage – not drive them, because he is not a qualified driver – the owner will be responsible for any injury or damage caused if the hand ignores an order not to drive. That is because his prohibition has done nothing to restrict the scope of the hand's employment, which is moving cars around the garage.

But if an employer made it a condition of a van driver's job that he should not give lifts, and the driver then picks up a passenger, the driver will himself be personally liable if he has an accident through negligence and the passenger is injured. That is because the employer clearly limited the scope of the employee's job.

Liability for an independent contractor

In certain circumstances, someone who engages an independent contractor, who is therefore not his employee, will still bear liability for the contractor's actions, as if he were an employer.

For example, if someone hires a taxi and tells the driver to turn down a drive that does not belong to him, the owner of the property can sue the passenger for TRESPASS.

Similarly if a motorist employs a garage that he knows is not technically qualified to do a brake repair on his car, and subsequent brake failure results in the death of a pedestrian, the motorist is liable for the garage's defective repair, because he was aware of the garage's incompetence. *See:* CONTRACTOR'S LIABILITY

Insuring against liability

Most employers insure themselves against liability for their employees' actions. Public authorities engaging independent contractors also do so. *See:* LIABILITY INSURANCE; PUBLIC LIABILITY

EMPLOYMENT AGENCY

How the law protects people who use a private organisation to find – or fill – a vacancy

Privately run employment agencies are strictly controlled by law to protect people who use them to try to find a job and employers who engage them to fill a staff vacancy.

An employment agency cannot operate without a licence from the Department of Employment. It costs £108 a year and has to be renewed annually. The penalty for running an agency without a licence is a fine of up to £400.

The licence must be prominently displayed on the agency's premises. It can be refused if the Department regards the agency proprietor as an 'unsuitable person', or if he or she is under 21, and an application for renewal can be rejected on the same grounds. In such cases, the applicant may appeal to the Secretary of State for Employment, on forms provided by the Department of Employment.

In addition, someone planning to open an employment agency must post a notice on or near the intended premises at least 21 days before the application is submitted. The notice must be in a position that allows it to be read easily by members of the public, and must state the name and address of the proprietor, the address of the proposed agency and a description of the type of work it will do. The proprietor must also advertise in the Press his intention of applying, so as to give the public an opportunity to object.

The Department of Employment has a list of approved newspapers, and that can be obtained, together with a licence application form, from any of the Department's local offices.

There is no set form for objecting to an application. Objectors should write to the Secretary of State.

Once a licence application has been granted, the agency's premises and records can be checked by a Department inspector at any time. The penalty for obstructing an inspector in the course of his duty is a fine of up to £50. If he is refused information to which he is entitled, it is up to £100.

Agency fees to job-seekers

Employment agencies are not allowed to charge fees to people looking for jobs. The penalty for doing so is a fine of up to £400, and the agency's licence may not necessarily be renewed.

However, there are two exceptions to that general rule:

1. Fashion models, actors and others in the entertainment industry may be charged fees by their agents, by agreement between the two parties.

2. An agency may charge a fee to an AU PAIR seeking a family with whom to live. The charge may not exceed 1 week of the au pair's payment.

Agency fees to employers

There are no legal restrictions on the fees employment agencies may charge to employers seeking staff. The equivalent of 1 week's wages is common for secretarial or administrative personnel. For executive positions, the fee may be substantially higher, and may include consultancy charges as well.

EMPLOYMENT APPEAL TRIBUNAL

How to lodge an appeal in a case involving employment law

The Employment Appeal Tribunal hears appeals on decisions reached by an INDUSTRIAL TRIBUNAL on matters of employment law such as UNFAIR DISMISSAL, REDUNDANCY payment, equal pay, RACIAL DISCRIMINATION and SEX DISCRIMINATION at work.

It sits only in London and in Glasgow, and cases are heard by a judge, and two laymen – one representing employers and the other representing unions.

The tribunal is a court of law, but its procedures are less formal than those of other courts. Nevertheless, it is advisable for anyone who is bringing or facing a case before the tribunal to be represented by a solicitor or barrister.

When you can appeal

An appeal can be brought before the tribunal only if it is based on a point of law, not if it is simply a question of fact. The tribunal cannot interfere with an industrial tribunal's decision on the facts of a case. *See:* EVIDENCE

Industrial tribunals are required, however, to give reasons for their decisions, so an appeal may be based on the argument that 'no tribunal, properly directing itself' could come to the decision that it did on the evidence before it. The facts of the case then become relevant, although in theory the appeal is still on a point of law.

Making the appeal

Either side in an employment dispute can appeal to the tribunal against the decision of an industrial tribunal. The appeal must be lodged within 6 weeks of the industrial tribunal's ruling, using Form 1, obtainable from any office of the Department of Employment.

Who pays for the appeal

Although LEGAL AID is not available to take a case before an industrial tribunal, an appellant can apply for financial help when an appeal is lodged with the Employment Appeal Tribunal. All or part of the costs may be met by legal aid.

Both parties to the appeal have to pay their own attendance expenses, and those of any witnesses they call.

Generally, the tribunal does not award legal costs to the winner of an appeal. So each side has to pay its own. However, the tribunal can award costs if the appeal is 'unnecessary, improper or vexatious, or there has been unreasonable delay or other unreasonable conduct'. Someone who makes a completely unjustified appeal can be penalised.

EMPLOYMENT CONTRACT

Defining the relationship between employer and employee

Every employed person has a legally binding employment contract that defines his relationship with his employer and their obligations to each other. Under the basic terms of the contract, the employer agrees to pay wages for work performed, to provide a safe work place and to ensure that any other employees are competent. The employee agrees to carry out the work, to co-operate with the employer and to render loyal service.

The contract also defines the terms and conditions of the job – for example, working hours, holiday entitlement and sick-pay arrangements.

An employment contract does not have to be in writing to become legally binding. An employer may simply tell a job applicant: 'The pay is £60 a week and you get 3 weeks' holiday a year. You can start on Monday.'

If the applicant replies 'I agree', or with some similar phrase, the contract is as valid as if it were written down.

In cases of dispute, a court or INDUSTRIAL TRIBUNAL would then have to work out the implied terms of the contract, taking into account the nature of the job and the custom and practice in the company or industry concerned.

A written employment contract greatly reduces the chances of a dispute between employer and employee over what exactly has been agreed.

The ADVISORY, CONCILIATION AND ARBITRATION SERVICE (ACAS) encourages employers to set out full details of the employment contract in writing.

The Employment Protection (Consolidation) Act 1978 requires employers to provide a written summary of the main terms of an employee's contract – though not the contract itself – within 13 weeks of his starting work.

The code for contracts

ACAS has endorsed the provisions dealing with employment contracts in the Code of Practice that accompanied the Industrial Relations Act 1971. Although that Act is no longer in force, parts of the code are still used by ACAS as a guide to good industrial relations.

The code's provisions on employment contracts are voluntary. Employers are not legally obliged to follow them, and cannot be prosecuted if they do not.

However, in cases of disputes over contracts, courts and industrial tribunals use the code as a standard by which to judge an employer's behaviour. If he has not followed the code he will find it more difficult to resist an employee's claim. *See:* CONTRACT; DISMISSAL; REDUNDANCY; UNFAIR DISMISSAL

The code recommends that each employee should be informed of:

1. The requirements of his job and the person to whom he is directly responsible.

2. The company's disciplinary rules and procedures and the circumstances that can lead to his suspension or dismissal.

3. The trade union representation in the company.

4. The opportunities for training and promotion.

5. Company social and welfare facilities.

6. Fire prevention and safety rules.

The Health and Safety at Work Act 1974 obliges an employer to provide employees with safety information. *See:* HEALTH AND SAFETY AT WORK

7. Any company suggestion schemes.

Legal requirements for written contracts

Under the Employment Protection (Consolidation) Act 1978 most employers must give each employee a copy of a document setting out the main terms and conditions of his employment. *See:* EMPLOYMENT PROTECTION

The employer can simply refer in the written particulars to other documents, provided that they are easily accessible to the employee. For example, the particulars may refer an employee to a collective agreement for details of pay,

hours and holidays; to a works rulebook for disciplinary rules and procedures, and to a pension booklet for details of the company pension scheme.

There is no criminal penalty for an employer who fails to provide written particulars. But if the information is not set down in writing, the employer may find it more difficult to defend himself against any future claim for breach of contract or unfair dismissal. The employee may ask an industrial tribunal to give him a correct written statement if his employer has failed to do so.

A set of written particulars provided to an employee under the terms of the Employment Protection Act is not legally an employment contract, but only a summary of the contract's most important ingredients.

If there is no other written record,

IF THE CONTRACT IS UNWRITTEN OR INCOMPLETE

Some employers do not provide written employment contracts. Those who do may omit some provisions through oversight. The written particulars required by the Employment Protection (Consolidation) Act are not a complete record of the agreement between employer and employee.

If a dispute arises over an unwritten provision of an employment contract, the court or industrial tribunal looks at the surrounding circumstances to determine what, in its view, the contract implied.

Obvious terms Some terms of an employment contract are so obvious that they go almost without saying.

For example, an employer may hire a van driver without specifically stating that it is part of his job to ensure that he holds the appropriate driving licence at all times. If the van driver is found to be disqualified from driving, the employer can dismiss him without being in breach of contract. In such circumstances, a claim for unfair dismissal would be unlikely to succeed.

Custom and practice What is considered the usual practice in a company or industry can help to decide any unwritten provisions of an employment contract.

For example, if a factory customarily closes down entirely during the first 2 weeks of July, it is an implied part of the contract that workers must take 2 weeks of their holiday entitlement then, unless specifically asked not to.

Collective agreements Some written employment contracts state that employees are bound by the terms of collective agreements negotiated between the employer and a trade union. But many do not.

In working out the application of a collective agreement to an individual contract, courts and tribunals generally ask: 'Has the employee accepted the terms of that agreement, or of similar ones, previously?'

If he has, the agreement is usually held to apply, whether the employee concerned is a member of the union or not. So if a non-union member accepts pay rises and other benefits negotiated by the union, he may be in a weak position if he tries to dispute other terms of a collective agreement.

Any employee, whether a union member or not, is entitled to try to prevent a provision in a collective agreement from becoming part of his individual contract. To do so, he must register his objection in writing to his employer immediately he learns of the provision.

However, he stands little chance of success. If the employer refuses to accept the objection, and dismisses the employee, or disciplines him in accordance with the proper procedures, a court or tribunal will almost certainly refuse an unfair dismissal claim. *See:* COLLECTIVE BARGAINING

Previous conduct If an employee has previously accepted a reasonable order or decision by his employer without objection, he may be obliged to accept similar future decisions or orders as part of his contract.

For example, if an employer asks an employee to move from one office or factory to another, and the employee does so without objecting, but later declines a second

move, he may be in breach of contract. In such circumstances, if he is dismissed for refusing the second move, he might not succeed in a claim for unfair dismissal.

However, one acceptance of a reasonable order or decision is not, by itself, conclusive proof that the employee is obliged under his contract to accept others of the same sort. Courts and tribunals examine all the surrounding circumstances.

Work rules and disciplinary codes

Employers are expected to have comprehensive disciplinary rules and procedures. Provided that the rules and procedures are prominently displayed in the workplace, or made easily accessible to employees – for example, as a booklet – they will form part of the employment contract, even if they are not referred to in it.

However, in considering disciplinary rules, courts and tribunals take into account whether they are 'reasonable' and whether an employee could be aware of them. *See:* DISCIPLINE AT WORK

An employer who simply pins the rules on the company notice board, but who takes care to point them out to new and existing employees, can assume that they form part of the employment contract.

However, if he pins up new rules at random without mentioning them to all employees, a tribunal might decide that the additions do not form part of the contract unless there is a written provision to the contrary, or unless they had been negotiated with a trade union.

SPECIAL RULES FOR FIXED-TERM CONTRACTS

Employment contracts that last for a pre-arranged period only – fixed-term contracts – are governed by similar rules to those of contracts of indeterminate length.

If a fixed-term contract is not renewed when it expires, the employee may be entitled to claim UNFAIR DISMISSAL, provided that he has completed 1 year's service with the employer. The only exception to that rule is when the contract is for 1 year or more and the employee has agreed in writing not to make an unfair dismissal claim. A similar agreement in a contract of less than 1 year is not legally enforceable.

If an employer sacks an employee be-fore the fixed-term contract expires and without good reason, thus breaking the contract, the employee can sue for WRONGFUL DISMISSAL – to obtain damages equal to the wages he would have earned if the contract had run its full term minus any other wages he has been able to earn – and for unfair dismissal.

Some fixed-term contracts include a provision allowing either party to end them at any time by giving notice of, for example, 1 month. Provided that the employee has completed 1 year's service, he still has the right to claim unfair dismissal if he is given notice. However, he could not claim wrongful dismissal.

He then has clear evidence, if the matter is ever raised before a court or industrial tribunal, of what he regards as the terms of his employment contract.

If an employer refuses to give written particulars

If you have been more than 13 weeks in your job and have not received written particulars of the terms and conditions, either separately or as part of a written employment contract, you are entitled to demand them – unless you are a part-timer or in one of the occupations not covered by the 1978 Act. *See:* EMPLOYMENT PROTECTION

However, if your employer refuses to supply the particulars, the law gives you little redress.

You could take the matter to an industrial tribunal and ask it to draft the particulars for you. But that takes time, legal aid is not available to pay any lawyer's fees and you risk seriously antagonising your employer. If you have worked for him for less than 1 year, you

however, the particulars will be accepted by a court or tribunal as good evidence of what was agreed between employer and employee.

In practice, many companies consolidate the particulars and any other relevant information into a letter of appointment which they give to each new employee as soon as he starts work. That letter becomes the basis of the employment contract. However, it may still be possible to prove that implied terms not specifically mentioned in the letter form part of the contract, through custom and practice.

If the written particulars are inaccurate

As written particulars drawn up under the employment protection law are usually the best evidence of the terms of the employment contract, they must be as accurate as possible.

The employee should check the written particulars carefully as soon as he receives them. If there are inaccuracies, he should point them out, in writing, to the employer and ask for them to be corrected. If there are any provisions to which he objects, he should challenge them immediately, writing to the employer and keeping a copy of the letter.

Unless the employee challenges a provision immediately he becomes aware of it – and can produce evidence of having done so – if he later becomes involved in a dispute over that provision, he may be held by a court or tribunal to have accepted it by default.

If an employer refuses to change a provision to which a new employee objects, the employee must decide what further action to take. He may resign or refuse to accept the job. He may pursue the point in other ways – for example, by getting his trade union to take it up. Or he can reserve his position by repeating his objection, again in writing.

WHAT THE WRITTEN PARTICULARS MUST SAY

According to the 1978 Act, the written particulars must set out:
1. The names of employer and employee.
2. The date on which employment started.
3. The rate of PAY and how often wages are paid: if the employee is paid at piece rates or on commission, the basis for calculating payments must be explained in detail.
4. The hours during which the employee is normally expected to work: an employee is not obliged to work overtime unless required to do so under the terms of his employment contract.
5. The holidays to which the employee is entitled, the method of calculating his entitlement and the pay he receives while on holiday. *See:* HOLIDAY ENTITLEMENT
6. The company rules governing absence through illness and sick pay. *See:* SICKNESS
7. The terms of any company pension scheme.
  If there are no paid holidays, sick pay or pension scheme, the written particulars should say so.
8. The period of notice that either employer or employee must give to end the employment contract. If the length of notice stipulated in the written particulars is shorter than that required by law, the legal minimum applies. *See:* NOTICE
9. The employee's job title. The Employment Protection Act does not require the employer to describe the employee's duties in writing, but to do so is an added precaution against future disputes.
  In particular, if the employee may later be required to do a different job, to do overtime or to move to different premises, it is in the employer's interest to state that fact in the written particulars. Otherwise, if the employee later refuses such a change and is dismissed, he might succeed in a claim of unfair dismissal.
10. The disciplinary rules and procedures that apply to the employee and the way in which he can appeal against disciplinary action. *See:* DISCIPLINE AT WORK
11. Any special provisions for defining the employee's length of service. Such provisions most commonly apply to groups of companies, in which an employee may transfer from one subsidiary to another. If service with associated companies is counted for calculating holiday or pension entitlements, it may also be counted in establishing EMPLOYMENT PROTECTION rights – for example, MATERNITY leave, REDUNDANCY payments and awards for unfair dismissal.

are not protected by the law on unfair dismissal.

When you have checked that you are entitled to the particulars, and that they are not set out in some other document – for example, works rules – to which your employer has already drawn your attention, write to him. Ask for 'the written particulars of my contract of employment, as required by Section 1 of the Employment Protection (Consolidation) Act'. Keep a copy of the letter.

If you feel that the matter may not be straightforward, send the letter by recorded delivery, so that there is proof that your employer has received it.

If you do not get a satisfactory reply, you could try drafting the particulars yourself. Send a copy to your employer, with a covering letter explaining what you have done and why. Say that unless he provides his version of the written particulars, you will assume that he accepts yours as correct.

That may persuade him to act. But if he does not, and fails to reply, he will find it difficult to deny the accuracy of your version later.

Changing the employment contract

Every time an employee gets a pay rise or extra holidays, his terms of employment change. The Employment Protection (Consolidation) Act 1978 obliges employers to give written particulars of changes in a contract within 1 month of their taking effect. However, there is no criminal penalty if an employer does not do so, and in practice the rule is often ignored. The alteration simply takes effect by mutual consent between employer and employee.

In some circumstances, an employee might object to a proposed change in the terms and conditions of his employment. Whether he is entitled to do so or not depends upon:

1. Whether the change is provided for in a written contract or in written particulars of employment. For example, if the particulars state that the employee 'may be required to work in any of the company's offices in the United Kingdom', he cannot resist a transfer from one place to another. He must either accept or resign and cannot claim unfair dismissal.

2. Whether, in the absence of a written agreement, the employee has accepted similar changes in the past.

A change not previously provided for, either in writing or by implication, must not, however, be so fundamental that it puts the employer in breach of the employment contract. A reduction in pay, a demotion or a cut in the working week that leads to loss of earnings are all fundamental changes. An employee facing such a change without any previous expressed or implied condition in his contract can resign, claiming that he is a victim of constructive DISMISSAL by the employer.

EMPLOYMENT PROTECTION

How the law safeguards people's jobs

Many rights aimed at protecting employees from unfair treatment at work and at safeguarding their interests if they lose their jobs have been drawn together in the Employment Protection (Consolidation) Act 1978.

The main items covered by the Act include: DISMISSAL; the EMPLOYMENT CONTRACT; LAY-OFF and short-time working; MATERNITY leave; NOTICE; PAY; REDUNDANCY; TIME OFF WORK; TRADE UNION rights; and UNFAIR DISMISSAL.

Both men and women have protection under equal pay and SEX DISCRIMINATION legislation. People of all races are protected, at work as elsewhere, by the law on RACIAL DISCRIMINATION.

Employers who are exempt

All employers, no matter how few people they have working for them, are generally bound by the employment protection rules.

However, in a husband-and-wife business in which one spouse technically employs the other, many of the spouse-employee's rights are lost – though not those relating to equal pay and notice of dismissal.

Employers with 5 or fewer employees are exempt from the duty to reinstate an employee after maternity absence where it is not reasonably practicable for them to do so and there is no suitable alternative employment.

Employees who are excluded

Several categories of employees are excluded from at least some of the employment protection rules:

● Part-timers. People employed for fewer than 16 hours a week have little protection. But if they have worked for the same employer for 5 years or more, they are not classed as part-timers unless they work fewer than 8 hours a week. *See:* PART-TIME WORKER

● People who have reached retirement age. Traditionally, retirement age is 65 for men and 60 for women. But if the agreed retirement age for a particular job is lower, the employee has no right to claim redundancy or unfair dismissal once he has reached it. Conversely, if the agreed age is higher, unfair dismissal rights are not lost at 60 or 65. For instance, a woman teacher with a contract to 65 could claim unfair dismissal if dismissed at 60.

● People on fixed-term contracts of 12 weeks or less. Someone who is taken on for a specific project that is expected to last for 12 weeks or less and which is completed within that time is also excluded. A worker whose contract is for longer than 12 weeks is covered by the employment protection rules.

● People who normally work abroad. If an employee's contract requires him ordinarily to work abroad, he may lose his United Kingdom employment protection rights.

● Crown servants. Anyone who works for or under a government department is also excluded from full protection. Crown servants include members of the armed forces, civil servants, judges and 'industrial' employees of the Crown – for example, Forestry Commission workers.

● Domestic servants. A domestic servant is excluded if he or she is a close relative of the employer and works only in his private household – not in other premises, for example, a family shop. 'Close relative' means a parent, grandparent, step-parent, child, grandchild, brother, sister, half-brother and half-sister.

● Registered dock workers.

● Merchant seamen.

Employment abroad

Taking a job abroad with a foreign employer usually results in your rights

HOW THE LAW PROTECTS AN EMPLOYEE'S RIGHTS
Special time limits in some cases – and exceptions, too

Employee has a right to:	If he or she has worked for:	Employees who may not be entitled to protection								
		1	2	3	4	5	6	7	8	9
Written particulars of contract. *See:* EMPLOYMENT CONTRACT	13 weeks		X	X	X	X		X	X	X
Notice of dismissal. *See:* NOTICE	4 weeks		X	X	X			X	X	X
Written reasons for dismissal. *See:* DISMISSAL	26 weeks				X	X		X		X
Claim for unfair dismissal. *See:* UNFAIR DISMISSAL	52 weeks (Employers with 20 employees or less, 2 years)	X			X	X		X	X	X
Redundancy payment. *See:* REDUNDANCY	2 years and been dismissed as redundant	X	X		X	X	X	X	X	X
Redundancy consultation. *See:* REDUNDANCY	Any time, but employee need consult only with recognised independent trade union				X	X		X	X	
Maternity pay. *See:* MATERNITY	2 years and was employed until 11th week before confinement, and gave employer at least 3 weeks' notice before leaving because of pregnancy					X		X	X	X
Reclaim job after pregnancy. *See:* MATERNITY	2 years and was employed until 11th week before confinement; gave employer at least 3 weeks' notice before her absence began and notified employer at least 3 weeks in advance of her intended return; returned within 29 weeks of confinement.					X		X	X	X
Itemised pay statement. *See:* PAY	Any time			X		X		X		X
Guaranteed pay on short-time or lay-off. *See:* LAY-OFF	4 weeks and provided that at least one 'workless day' was not caused by trade dispute and the employee not refusing suitable alternative work				X	X		X	X	X
Equal pay. *See:* SEX DISCRIMINATION	Any time			X				X		
Payment on insolvency of employer. *See:* DISMISSAL	Any time			X	X	X		X		
To belong to a trade union and to participate actively. *See:* TRADE UNION	Any time					X		X		
Time off for union duties. *See:* TRADE UNION	Any time provided that the union is recognised and independent					X		X		X
Time off for public duties. *See:* TIME OFF WORK	Any time but only certain public offices are included			X		X		X		X
Time off for training or to look for work. *See:* TIME OFF WORK	2 years and has been given notice of dismissal because of redundancy			X	X	X		X		X

The chart summarises employees' rights under employment protection laws.

To qualify for some rights, the employee must have worked for the employer concerned for a specified time. The length of the qualifying period, which starts from the first day of employment, is shown in column 2.

In exceptional circumstances, previous service with another employer may be taken into account in qualifying for some of these employment rights, although that normally occurs only when the previous employer is directly associated with the new one, or when the original business has been taken over by the present company or employer as a going concern.

The rights from which some classes of employee – for example, part-timers – are excluded are listed in the chart according to the type of employment.

Retiring age	1
Crown servants	2
Merchant seamen	3
Registered dock workers	4
Husband or wife of employer	5
Domestics who are close relatives	6
Employee ordinarily works outside UK	7
Fixed-term contracts for 12 weeks or less	8
Part-timers (usually under 16 hours per week)	9

as an employee being governed by the law of the country concerned. However, some multi-national companies may make express provision in the EMPLOYMENT CONTRACT as to which laws will operate.

The employment rights of someone working abroad for a British company are usually governed by English law. The Employment Protection Act rights, however, do not cover those who ordinarily work abroad.

ENGAGEMENT

Rights and obligations when a couple decide to marry

A couple who agree to become engaged are not entering into a legal contract. Either can call off the engagement and the other has no claim for damages. Such claims ended in 1970, when the law on BREACH OF PROMISE was changed. Even a woman who has sexual intercourse with a man only because he has promised to marry her cannot ask for damages if the wedding does not take place.

When a couple break off an engagement, each is entitled to a share of any property they have acquired, in proportion to his or her contribution.

If, for example, the couple bought a house and the man paid £1,500 in deposit and mortgage repayments, and the woman spent £500 in money or labour on decorations, the value would be shared 75 per cent to the man and 25 per cent to the woman.

If a couple cannot agree on how to share the proceeds either can take action in the county court or High Court as if they had married – within 3 years of the end of the engagement.

Giving back gifts

Presents given to the couple during the engagement are treated as if they are wedding presents: gifts from the woman's family or friends are her property and gifts from the man's friends are his. However, presents that are given to the couple only on the understanding that a wedding will eventually take place should be returned to the people who gave them.

Presents given by one partner to the other for the matrimonial home – for example, a washing machine – should be returned to the giver.

The engagement ring is considered to be the girl's property, even if she calls off the engagement, unless the man can prove it was given conditionally.

NO DAMAGES FOR A
JILTED LOVER

Either party can call off an engagement, and the other person cannot ask for damages because the wedding will not take place. Usually, the girl can keep the ring.

'It's all off!'

A man who wants the ring to be returned if the engagement ends should make that clear at the outset, either in writing or by telling the girl in the presence of witnesses. That might be necessary, for example, when a ring is a family heirloom used only for engagements.

Money spent on wedding preparations cannot be reclaimed by either party. The bride may have paid for the bridesmaids' dresses, the groom for the honeymoon hotel, the bride's father for the wedding reception. There is no legal way to recover the money.

ENTRY, Right of

When an official needs a pass or warrant to enter your home

Thousands of officials have the right – given in Acts of Parliament – to enter your home. However, they must, if you challenge them, produce proof of that right. Unless there is an emergency with which they have to deal, they commit a TRESPASS, for which you can claim damages, if they persist in entering.

Checking credentials

If anyone claiming to be an official wishes to enter your home, ask him first to produce his official pass or warrant and then ask him why he claims the right to enter. If you have any doubt about whether the official is genuine, do not let him in until you have checked his credentials with the office from which he claims to come. If the office cannot satisfy you, call the police.

If you refuse entry to a genuine official who has produced the necessary documents, he can apply to the local

> ### THE EJECTED INSPECTOR
>
> *You can demand 24 hours' notice of a public health official's intention to enter your home. If he enters without proper notice he commits a trespass.*
>
> Mrs Stroud received a Public Health Act notice to renew a drain at her bungalow, in Herne Bay, Kent, but failed to do so.
>
> A Herne Bay Urban District Council clerk wrote informing her that since she had not had the work done, the council would do it at her expense.
>
> Three months later, as Mrs Stroud had still failed to renew the drain, the council sanitary inspector and a builder called at the bungalow to do the work. The council had not given the statutory 24 hours' written notice of intended entry.
>
> Mrs Stroud's husband, armed with a spade and clothes prop, ejected the inspector and the builder from the property. The council then charged Mr Stroud with obstructing the sanitary inspector in the execution of his duty. He was convicted and fined, but appealed against the verdict.
>
> DECISION
> The Divisional Court quashed the conviction. Lord Goddard, giving judgment, said that the council had not given 24 hours' written notice of intended entry: the council's letter 3 months earlier was not proper notice. The inspector was therefore a trespasser. The householder – 'with all the rights of a free-born Englishman whose premises were being invaded' – was justified in using reasonable force to eject him.

magistrates for a warrant. When he returns with the warrant, you must then let him in. If you continue to refuse to admit him you can be prosecuted. However, if he goes beyond the specific powers stated in the warrant, he commits a trespass.

If a public health or housing official wishes to inspect your home you may insist that 24 hours' notice be given of a proposed visit.

Landlords' rights The rights of a landlord to enter a tenant's premises are governed by the lease or tenancy agreement. Usually, the lease or agreement allows the landlord to enter and inspect the premises after reasonable notice and at a reasonable time. If the landlord enters at any other time, the tenant can sue him for trespass.

A landlord never has the right to enter a tenant's premises and evict him by force. If the landlord has lawfully ended the tenancy but the tenant refuses to leave, the landlord must obtain an EVICTION order from the court. A court bailiff can then evict the tenant.

WHEN OUTSIDERS CAN ENTER A HOME WITHOUT CONSENT
Understanding the occasions on which any of several thousand people can legally ask to 'come in'

	Grounds	Time	Authorisation needed	Notice required	What happens if the householder refuses entry
Landlords	To inspect the property	Reasonable hours	The terms of the lease or tenancy	According to the agreement	Landlord can seek permission in the courts
	Eviction: Landlord has no right to evict except through the courts				
Neighbours	To repair or maintain common services or walls	Reasonable hours	Deeds sometimes give specific rights of access	Reasonable	Force cannot be used; police will not assist. Neighbours must take court action
Electricity board officials	To check fittings, read meters or cut off supply	Reasonable hours	1. Official pass	None	Official can apply for a warrant
			2. Magistrate's warrant	None	Entry by force if necessary; board must repair damage or pay cost
	To check equipment or mend a fault when danger to life or property is suspected	Day or night	Official pass	None	Official cannot use force; he may ask policeman to accompany him to prevent a breach of the peace
Gas authority officials	To check fittings, read meters or cut off supply because of unpaid bills	Reasonable hours	1. Official pass	Disconnection: 24 hours. Otherwise none	Official can apply for a warrant
			2. Magistrate's warrant	None	Entry by force if necessary; board must repair damage or pay cost
	To check equipment or mend a fault when danger to life or property is suspected	Day or night	Official pass	None	Official cannot use force; he may ask a policeman to accompany him to prevent a breach of the peace
Water authority officials	To check fittings and see if water is being wasted, misused or polluted	Reasonable hours	1. Official pass	24 hours	Official can apply for warrant to inspect meter, or supply can be cut off from outside property
			2. Magistrate's warrant	None	Entry by force if necessary
Post Office officials	To inspect or remove telephones	Reasonable hours	Official pass	None	Post Office engineer cannot force entry
	To check that householders using TV sets have a TV licence	Reasonable hours	1. Official pass	None	Inspector can apply for a warrant
			2. Magistrate's warrant	None	Inspector can ask police to accompany him to prevent a breach of the peace

Continued on next page

	Grounds	Time	Authorisation needed	Notice required	What happens if the householder refuses entry
Post Office officials *continued*	To investigate unlicensed broadcasting	Day or night	Magistrate's warrant	None	Cannot gain entry by force. Must apply for warrant which must be used within 1 month of issue
Local authority officials (health or housing inspectors)	To investigate breaches of the Public Health Acts, bye-laws or building regulations	Reasonable hours	1. Official carries a letter of authority	None	Single occupancy: 24 hours' warning; after second refusal, inspector can apply for a warrant. Multiple occupancy: no second chance
			2. Magistrate's warrant	24 hours	Entry by force if necessary; householder liable to fine of up to £20
	To examine with a view to orders for compulsory purchase, demolition, closure, clearance or repairs	Reasonable hours	Official carries a letter of authority	None	24 hours' warning; if entry still refused, liability to £20 fine. Official cannot obtain a warrant or force entry
Police	To prevent a breach of the peace or make an arrest	Day or night	Officer's warrant card	None	Police may use what force they consider necessary
	To carry out investigations	Day or night	1. Officer's warrant card	None	Police cannot force entry without magistrate's warrant, except when searching for stolen property
			2. Magistrate's warrant	None	Warrant allows police to use force as necessary
	To return children, mental patients or others, subject to special orders to the appropriate authority	Day or night	Warrant by constable accompanied by medical practitioner and mental welfare officer	None	Police may use what force they consider necessary
	To seize goods or publications	Day or night	Magistrate's warrant	None	Warrant allows police to use force as necessary. Must seize goods and show them to magistrate
	To investigate VAT or motor tax offences	Reasonable hours (at night if good reason)	1. Official pass	None	Police can apply for warrant
			2. Magistrate's warrant		Force can be used as necessary when investigating motor tax offences
Firemen	To put out a fire, to protect from fire or to rescue people or property	Day or night	Any fireman on duty	None	Firemen can force entry and the householder is liable to prosecution if he refuses, with penalty up to £25
Customs officers	To search for contraband	Day or night	Writ of Assistance or magistrate's warrant	None	Doors, windows and containers can be opened by reasonable force. Between 11 p.m. and 5 a.m. a policeman must attend
Court officers (sheriffs and bailiffs)	To carry out court orders by seizing goods	Day or night but not Sundays	Judgment summons, court order or distress warrant	None	Officers cannot break in; they must enter through unlocked doors or windows

Continued overleaf

WHEN OUTSIDERS CAN ENTER A HOME WITHOUT CONSENT *continued*

	Grounds	Time	Authorisation needed	Notice required	What happens if the householder refuses entry
Court officers (sheriffs and bailiffs) *continued*	To carry out court orders by seizing particular goods	Day or night but not Sundays	Warrant for delivery or writ of delivery	None	Officers can use what force they consider necessary to enter and carry out the goods or documents
	To evict a tenant or squatter	Reasonable hours	Warrant for possession or writ of possession	None	Officers can use any force needed to secure eviction
	To seize anyone charged with contempt of court; to take possession of premises by court order	Day or night	Court order	None	Officers may use reasonable force
Certificated bailiffs	To carry out court orders by seizing goods and selling them to pay rent, rates or taxes	Between sunrise and sunset, but not Sundays	Distress warrant issued by landlord (rent), local authority (rates) or Inland Revenue (taxes)	None	Certificated bailiffs cannot force entry into private homes unless distress has already been levied
Valuation officers (Inland Revenue)	To value property for rates or estate duty	Reasonable hours	Official pass or written authority	24 hours	Liability to £5 fine and demand based on estimate. Forced entry not permitted
Collectors of taxes	To levy distraint warrant for non-payment of tax	Daytime	Inland Revenue warrant	None	Force can be used to gain entry and police can be called to assist
VAT inspectors	Any purpose in connection with administration of VAT	Reasonable hours	Official pass	None	Can apply for magistrates' warrant allowing him to use force and remove documents

EQUAL OPPORTUNITIES

How the Government monitors its sex equality laws

Anyone who feels unfairly treated because of his or her sex can seek advice from the Equal Opportunities Commission. It helps people to exercise their rights under the SEX DISCRIMINATION and Equal Pay Acts, and in some cases takes action on its own.

The commission helps to settle disputes, and provides free legal advice if conciliation fails. If a case is complicated or tests a new point of law, it may provide legal representation if you:
● Sue in a county court over sex discrimination in education, housing, goods, facilities or services.
● Take an equal pay or employment claim to an INDUSTRIAL TRIBUNAL.

Equal pay claims can cover overtime rates, holiday rights, sick leave entitlement and bonuses if they form part of an employment contract.

Unfairness in matters outside a contract, such as other bonuses, recruitment and promotion, is dealt with as sex discrimination.

ESPIONAGE

An offence against the interests of the state

Anyone convicted of espionage or spying may be imprisoned for up to 14 years under the OFFICIAL SECRETS Acts 1911–39.

A person commits such an offence if he approaches, inspects or is in the neighbourhood of a prohibited place for any purposes that are held by a court to be prejudicial to the safety or interests of the state.

The term 'prohibited place' includes military, naval and air force establishments, munitions factories, docks and power stations. The Government may add establishments to the list at any time.

Sketches and notes

Anyone who makes a sketch plan, model or note or who obtains official records or documents which could help an enemy, is also guilty of an offence of spying.

However, other activities that are not directly connected with spying but may be considered to be prejudicial to the interests of the state, also come under the Acts – for example, in 1962 nuclear-disarmament demonstrators were convicted of spying under the Official Secrets Acts for planning to enter an air force station at Wetherfield in Essex in order to prevent aircraft from taking off or landing.

ESTATE

What is left when someone dies

The property of someone who has died – known as his estate – does not pass immediately to the heirs. It goes first to the personal representatives of the deceased – the EXECUTOR of his will, or his administrators in a case of INTESTACY.

When little is left after a death

If there is only a small amount of cash and possessions of limited value such as clothes and furniture, the estate can be divided informally, without official action. The relatives share these effects according to the will or, if there is no will, to the special rules of intestacy.

Assessing the value of the estate

The worth of an estate is calculated as its value on the date of death. Interest due on all loans, debts, shares and deposits must be calculated to that date, as must all taxes and rent owed by or to the dead person.

The value of property can be estimated by the personal representatives – for example, by checking newspaper advertisement columns for the price of similar cars or houses. Or it can be professionally valued for specialist items such as antiques.

Stocks and shares are valued at their Stock Exchange middle price on the date of death, or if it was closed on that date, on the next day that the Exchange was open. To find the value of shares in a private company, ask the company accountants to certify a figure.

Having assessed the total value, and all debts and expenses, the executors or administrators must submit a tax account to the Inland Revenue. Any CAPITAL TRANSFER TAX will then be levied, unless postponement can be claimed.

The rate of capital transfer tax is estimated from the size of the estate plus any chargeable gifts made during the dead person's lifetime.

After tax and debts have been paid, the remainder is divided in accordance with the will or intestacy rules.

Valuing the home

If the house is jointly owned, the surviving widow or widower has the right to stay on. Normally, in such cases, the value of half of the house – in fact, a reduced market value taking into account the presence of an owner occupier – is assessed as part of the estate, both for tax and for distribution of the assets. If, however, the home was only in the name of the spouse who died, the value of the house with full vacant possession is taken. If it was bequeathed in the will to someone else, the occupant can be evicted by court order, unless he is a protected tenant. *See:* EVICTION

Valuing a business If the dead person owned or was a partner in a business, an accountant will have to be engaged to value it. His assessment must take into account the stock, property and goodwill of the business.

Valuing personal belongings The value of personal items is what they would fetch if sold second-hand.

When a beneficiary is not yet 18 years old

A legacy left to someone under 18 is normally transferred to trustees until the heir comes of age. The trustees may also be the GUARDIANS. They should open a joint bank account from which money can be drawn by cheques signed by the trustees or otherwise invest the money until the heir is 18, when it must be handed over to him.

ESTATE AGENT

Buying and selling property through a third party

An estate agent is a go-between for people buying and selling property. He does not have to be professionally qualified, although many are.

If you decide to go to an estate agent, choose one who belongs to an official body, such as the Royal Institution of Chartered Surveyors, the National Association of Estate Agents or the Incorporated Society of Valuers and Auctioneers.

A qualified estate agent has a code of conduct to observe and is covered by a scheme to protect deposits so that if the agent goes bankrupt the deposit will be refunded to a buyer or handed over to a seller: whichever would have occurred in the normal course of events.

What an agent does

An agent can advertise property in various ways – on a board outside the property, on a card in his own office window, in a list sent to inquirers or in the Press.

He can advise on the best method of sale, the right asking price and the best time to sell. He may visit your home to inspect the property and fittings, measure rooms and take photographs for advertising purposes.

The agent is not legally required to do any of those things. If you want your property advertised in a particular way, discuss it with the agent and make sure he understands what you want him to do to earn his commission. The agent is paid only when a sale is completed.

You can instruct more than one estate agent to work for you. But an agent deals with many properties at the same time, and is unlikely to give priority to yours if another agent also has a right to sell it.

There are two ways in which to give an agent exclusive rights – by giving him either sole agency or sole selling rights. Before agreeing these terms, make sure that your solicitor approves.

What sole agency means

If you agree to give an estate agent sole agency, you must not allow another one to try to sell or rent your property. If you do so, and the second agent finds a purchaser for your home, you will have to pay commission twice over – once to the agent who introduced the purchaser and again to the firm to whom you gave sole agency.

The principal reason for appointing a sole agent is to encourage him to be more active in finding a purchaser for your property. But appointing a sole agent does not always ensure that you get better service.

If you appoint a sole agent, impose a time limit – say, 2 months. If the agent has not found a purchaser by then, you are free to instruct someone else. Even if you have given someone sole agency, you are still free to try to sell your property yourself. If you find a purchaser yourself, then – provided that no other agent is involved – you do not have to pay commission.

A sole agent sometimes appoints another as his sub agent, to try to ensure a faster sale of your property. Even if you then have two or more agents trying to sell your property, you pay commission only to your sole agent: it is for him to share it with sub agents.

What sole selling rights mean

If you give an agent the sole selling right, as opposed to sole agency, you must pay him when the property is sold, even if you yourself found the purchaser and the agent appeared to have made little effort. Stipulate a time limit after which the sole selling right expires. The limit should be at the most 2 months, and preferably shorter.

An agent's duty to a seller

An estate agent has a duty to obtain the best possible price for your property: he is employed by you, and not the

---

THE AGENTS WHO FAILED TO PASS ON A NEW OFFER

All offers must be passed to a client until he has made a contract to sell.

Mr Keppel owned a block of flats at Walham Green in London. He went to a firm of estate agents, Wheeler & Atkins, in May 1925, and asked them to find a purchaser at £6,500. He said he would be prepared to consider an offer of £6,000.

The agents got in touch with a Mr Essam, who next day made an offer of £6,150. A partner in the firm of estate agents, Mr Atkins, at once went to see Mr Keppel who told him to accept the offer 'subject to contract'.

Mr Keppel and Mr Essam consulted their respective solicitors who started to prepare the formal written contract for their clients to sign. Contracts were exchanged on June 11, 1925: until then, Mr Keppel was not bound to sell to Mr Essam, but was free to accept any higher offer.

On June 3, before contracts were exchanged, Wheeler & Atkins received a higher offer from a Mr Daniel, who was prepared to pay £6,750 for the property.

The agents did not tell Mr Keppel of that new offer. Instead they got in touch with the buyer, Mr Essam, and asked if he would be willing to re-sell the property at a profit as soon as he bought it. Mr Essam eventually agreed to sell the property to Mr Daniel for £6,950.

Mr Keppel heard about that deal only after he had exchanged contracts on June 11. He refused to pay Wheeler & Atkins any commission and also sued them for £800 damages – the difference between what Mr Essam paid him and what Mr Essam received from selling the flats to Mr Daniel.

The estate agents counter-claimed for their commission.

In the High Court, Mr Justice Finlay held that once the estate agents had introduced Mr Essam and his offer of £6,150 had been accepted subject to contract, the firm had done all they were employed to do and were no longer under any duty to Mr Keppel.

He gave judgment against Mr Keppel, who appealed.

DECISION

The Appeal Court judges reversed the decision about Mr Keppel's claim for damages. They ruled that estate agents had a duty to disclose offers to Mr Keppel until he was bound by his contract.

As Mr Keppel could still have changed his mind about selling to Mr Essam, the estate agents should have passed on Mr Daniel's offer of £6,750 on June 3, so that their client could decide what to do. They were in breach of their duty to Mr Keppel.

The agents were ordered to pay him £600 damages – the difference between the £6,150 that he received on the sale to Mr Essam and the £6,750 that Mr Daniel had first offered.

However, as the estate agents had genuinely believed they were entitled to do what they did, and were acting honestly, the Appeal Court said they were entitled to their commission.

THE SELLER WHO GREW TIRED OF WAITING

A seller who signs an agreement to pay commission when a buyer is found, must pay even if the sale falls through.

Mr Ware-Lane wanted to sell his leasehold house in Sidcup for £2,250. He went to a firm of estate agents, the Drewery and Drewery Organisation, in December 1958. When he called at the estate agent's office 1 month later he was told that a Mr Sinho was prepared to pay £2,160. Mr Ware-Lane said that was acceptable and the estate agent produced two forms for him to sign.

The first form, the 'vendor's agreement', stated that Mr Ware-Lane agreed to sell the house to Mr Sinho at a price of £2,160 'subject to contract'.

The second form was called a 'letter of authority' and stated: 'I instruct and authorise you to offer the above property for sale.' It included the following words: 'I agree to pay you commission . . . if and when:

● (a) A prospective purchaser signs your "purchaser's agreement".

● (b) I sign your "vendor's agreement".'

On the same day, Mr Sinho signed the estate agent's 'purchaser's agreement', stating that he agreed to buy the house from Mr Ware-Lane at £2,160 'subject to contract'.

The words 'subject to contract' meant that neither agreement so far signed was a binding contract and that either party could change his mind and call off the sale at any time.

Mr Ware-Lane did change his mind. Mr Sinho was trying to get a mortgage and Mr Ware-Lane became impatient because the sale did not proceed. He therefore found another purchaser and backed out of the sale to Mr Sinho.

The estate agents sued Mr Ware-Lane in the Dartford County Court for £66.50 commission. Judge Wingate Saul held that Mr Ware-Lane must pay the commission. Mr Ware-Lane appealed to the Court of Appeal.

DECISION

The decision was upheld by the Court of Appeal judges. They held that the 'letter of authority' Mr Ware-Lane had signed was quite clear. He had agreed to pay commission if and when two documents were signed. The documents had been signed and it did not matter that they did not have the legal effect of making a sale. The commission was still payable.

prospective buyer, to whom he owes no allegiance or duty.

If you have accepted an offer from a purchaser and a higher one arrives before you have contracted to sell, the agent is legally bound to tell you.

What an agent can charge

An estate agent's commission is paid on a sliding scale according to the price received for the property. It includes all his out-of-pocket expenses, such as postage and advertising: he cannot ask you to pay separately for those unless you have specifically agreed to do so.

If the property is not sold, the estate agent receives no commission and has to pay his own expenses – unless you have agreed to do so.

There is no uniform commission rate: different agents may charge different rates. An example of an agent's rate is 5 per cent on the first £500 of the sale price, 2½ per cent on the next £4,500 and 1½ per cent on the remainder.

Always ask an estate agent for his scale of charges and compare them with those of other firms in the area before you agree to let him act for you. Under the Estate Agents Act 1979 (when it comes into force) an estate agent must tell clients what his charges will be, or how they will be calculated. If he fails to do so, he may lose his legal right to his charges, even if he is successful in arranging a sale.

The court will take into account whether the client suffered any loss or damage by the agent's failure to give the necessary information and whether the agent acted deliberately or not.

When commission is paid

Commission is not usually paid until the sale is completed. The seller's solicitor then normally pays the commission to the agent direct from the purchase price.

Sometimes an agent may try to get his commission before the sale is complete. Do not agree to any terms which state that commission is payable before a sale is completed – 'on exchange of contracts' or 'on introducing a person ready, willing and able to purchase'. If you do so, the agent may claim commission even if the sale falls through.

If, after exchanging contracts the buyer withdraws, the seller can sue him for breach of contract and the damage

involved and the losses incurred. But he cannot normally sue the buyer for any commission paid to an agent.

Under the Estate Agents Act 1979, an estate agent must give to his client information about the circumstances in which the client becomes liable to pay his charges. There is no control over what these terms are! They remain a matter for agreement by the client.

Read carefully any form or letter that you receive from the estate agent, whether the firm has signed it or not. If you do not agree with what a document says, or are not sure what it means, write to the firm and say so at once.

If you sign something or are sent a form and do not reject it, you may find you are bound by unacceptable terms to pay premature commission.

Buying through an estate agent

A prospective buyer may engage an estate agent to find him a suitable house or may simply ask for a list of available properties. There is no charge for the estate agent's services or for a supply of his property lists, unless you have specifically agreed to pay.

An agent paid by a seller could not seek payment from a purchaser as well – he can serve only one of them. If he is hired by the buyer he owes him a duty of good faith and competence.

The estate agent is paid by the seller and is not legally obliged to tell a prospective buyer everything about a property. He need not, for example, point out defects in a property or answer your questions about it. But anything he does choose to tell you about a property must be true.

For example, he need not mention that roof tiles need replacing, but he must not falsely describe the roof as being in good, sound condition.

When a suitable property is found, an estate agent may ask the prospective buyer to pay an immediate deposit. That payment is a 'goodwill' deposit, usually about £50 to £100, and its purpose is psychological – to assure the seller that the buyer is seriously interested in the property.

A prospective buyer is not legally obliged to pay a 'goodwill' deposit. If he does pay, and then decides not to buy the property, his money must be returned, provided he has not signed a binding contract to buy the property.

The binding contract usually requires the buyer to pay a deposit of 10 per cent of the purchase price, when the contracts are exchanged.

He hands the money to the seller's estate agent, who may act as stakeholder. The agent cannot then pass the deposit to the seller without the buyer's permission, and cannot return it to the buyer without the seller's permission.

Often, even if an estate agent is involved, the solicitor for the seller or the buyer acts as stakeholder. He puts the money in a special account reserved for clients' money.

Solicitors and estate agents have to put the money in a client account at a bank to keep the money separate from their own. If the money earns interest, they can usually keep it for themselves.

When the Estate Agents Act 1979 comes into force, an estate agent must not take a deposit unless his insurance covers for loss of clients' money. If he does not have approved cover he is guilty of a criminal offence if he takes a deposit. The maximum penalty is a fine of £1,000 if he is convicted in a magistrates' court, and of an unlimited amount on conviction after a trial by jury.

ESTIMATE

Finding out what a contract for work will cost

If you need some work done – for example, house decorating or repairs – ask the contractor for a quotation. Once you accept, the quotation forms a CONTRACT between you both.

In that way, a quotation differs from an estimate, which gives only the approximate, probable cost of the work: the eventual bill can be much higher.

Both a quotation and an estimate should be in writing. If a contractor is prepared to give only an oral estimate or quotation, try to have a witness present when you agree on the price.

It is advisable to include in your request for either a quotation or an estimate full details, in writing, of the work to be done. It is possible, though not usual, for a contractor to ask for a fee before surveying what is involved and supplying the quotation or estimate.

Unless you have agreed in advance to

pay a fee, you are not obliged to pay anything for a quotation or estimate supplied.

Contractor's conditions

The contractor, in supplying either, may attach certain conditions limiting his responsibility for damage to property or for defective work – or even reserving the right to increase the suggested price, in certain circumstances, such as a rise in the cost of materials.

You can ask the contractor to alter or delete any such conditions before you accept the quotation or estimate, but once you accept them, you are bound by them, unless they appear to be unfair.
See: UNFAIR CONTRACT

Even if you are given an estimate, you can try to fix the cost of the work by asking if, once accepted, the estimate will be regarded as a firm price.

If the contractor agrees, get the reply in writing. If he says that it will not be a firm price, try to set a maximum charge for the work – and get that agreed in writing.

When changes are made during the work

If you ask for additional items while the work is being done, or if you want some of the agreed work changed, you will usually have to pay extra. Before agreeing to any changes or extras, get a new firm price, in writing, from the contractor.

If extra work is done without your agreement, you are not obliged to pay for it.

Charging more than the quotation

If a contractor tries to charge you more than the price in his quotation, or more than an estimate which he has agreed will be a fixed price, or more than a maximum price that you and he have agreed, pay him only the amount due under your agreement.

Occasionally, an estimate may bear the letters E. & O. E. – meaning 'errors and omissions excepted'. If they are on an estimate that does not give a firm price, they are simply a reminder that the price may be different if something has been overlooked or if a mistake has been plainly made. They do not entitle

the contractor to disregard his estimated price altogether.

If they appear on an estimate giving a firm price they entitle the contractor to charge more only if there is an obvious error – say £300 instead of £3,000.

EUROPEAN COMMUNITIES

How laws made elsewhere affect our lives

Life in Britain is increasingly subject to the laws and regulations of the three European communities to which the United Kingdom belongs. They are:
● The European Economic Community, or Common Market, which was established in 1957, under the Treaty of Rome, to improve and bring into line the economies and living standards of its member countries and to bring the states politically closer together.
● The European Coal and Steel Community, set up in 1951 to establish a common market in coal and steel.
● The European Atomic Energy Community (Euratom), formed in 1957 to develop the peaceful use of nuclear power.

The countries with which Britain is linked in all three European communities are Belgium, Denmark, France, the Federal Republic of Germany (West Germany), the Irish Republic, Italy, Luxembourg and the Netherlands. Greece became the tenth member on January 1, 1981.

By far the most wide-ranging of the three communities, and the one that has the greatest direct effect on the everyday lives of British citizens, is the European Economic Community.

Under the Treaty of Rome, its governing bodies have power to make laws on trade, agriculture, transport, tax and other economic matters. They also can enforce the free movement of people and goods between member countries and the right of workers from each country to work in any other EEC state.

Abolishing customs duties

Britain's membership of the EEC means that it no longer has the right to impose restrictions – called quotas – on the goods it imports from other member countries: and it no longer charges customs duty on most goods brought into

Britain from them. But the new rules do not apply yet to duties and quotas imposed on alcoholic drinks, tobacco, perfumes and other articles bought for private use by citizens from one member state on a visit to another member state.

A step towards abolishing such duties is Britain's two-tier arrangement, under which a UK citizen returning from an EEC country is given a greater duty-free allowance on goods bought in an ordinary shop than on goods bought in a special duty-free shop. For example, a Briton is allowed to bring in 1.5 litres of whisky duty free if he bought it in a French shop, because he has already paid French duty. If he bought the whisky in a duty-free shop – at an airport or on a ferry, for example – he is allowed only 1 litre free of UK duty.

Controlling content and quality

Each member country in the EEC is entitled to make rules controlling the standard of goods sold within its borders. For example, sausages on sale in Belgium must have a higher meat content than is legally necessary in Britain.

Gradually, however, the EEC is harmonising its product quality rules so that all countries will require the same standards. New international standards already govern the quality of cars, crystal glass, textiles, paints and measuring instruments.

Labelling Precise rules about how dangerous substances are to be labelled in EEC countries are being prepared, and there are already regulations setting out how food is to be labelled if it is made in one member state and sold in another. All such items must carry a list of ingredients and the date by which they must be sold.

Free markets Companies are dissuaded from setting up agreements to divide the European market among themselves – by selling sole trading or manufacturing rights for example – in conflict with the EEC principle of free movement of goods.

Travelling in the EEC

All citizens of EEC countries are entitled, under the Treaty of Rome, to travel freely among member countries – for business or for pleasure. In practice, however, there are still restrictions on that right.

Passports Under EEC rules, a citizen

> ## THE UK CITIZEN WHO WAS BARRED FROM ENGLAND

Although the Treaty of Rome allows citizens of any EEC member-state to move freely between all of them, it does not prevent a national court from restricting the movement of one of its own citizens within national borders.

Vera Saunders was found guilty of theft by Bristol Crown Court. She was not sentenced, but she signed a recognisance promising to go (home) to Northern Ireland and not to set foot in England or Wales for 3 years.

She broke her promises and appeared again at Bristol. The judge asked the European Court of Justice whether the ban on her entering England or Wales was against Community rules on freedom of movement.

DECISION

The ban was a penal decision, involving a British citizen and a crime committed on British soil. It was therefore purely a national matter and did not break Community rules.

of a member state does not need a passport when travelling to another member state. But he must be able to prove his identity and nationality.

Most EEC countries issue identity cards to their citizens, but Britain does not. For UK citizens, therefore, a Visitors' Passport is normally needed. For a 'no passport' day trip to the Continent from an English Channel port, travel companies arrange temporary identity documents carrying a photograph of the bearer. *See:* PASSPORT

Motor insurance Checks on motor insurance at national frontiers are eventually to be abolished, and a motor-insurance policy issued in any member

state already gives the legal minimum cover in all other EEC countries.

But the main disadvantage is that a UK policy, for example – even if comprehensive – does not provide more than third-party cover in another EEC country. To secure comprehensive protection while motoring in Europe, arrange special cover before you leave Britain. *See:* MOTORING ABROAD

If a motorist is involved in an accident in an EEC country, he must provide proof of insurance. The most easily recognisable proof is the International Motor Insurance Card – known as the Green Card – although it is no longer compulsory in EEC countries.

Illness Any resident of the United Kingdom who pays NATIONAL INSURANCE CONTRIBUTIONS at the employed person's rate (Class 1) is entitled to medical treatment and medicine in another EEC country on the same basis as a citizen of that country.

Self-employed people are similarly entitled, provided that they have been insured as employees at some time. Someone who no longer works is also entitled to full medical benefits, provided that he has paid enough UK national insurance contributions to earn a full-rate pension at retirement.

To claim medical benefits in another EEC country, you must produce proof that you are entitled to them. That means in most countries, you must produce your passport and form E111, which you should get from any office of the Department of Health and Social Security before you go abroad.

Form E111 is not needed by UK citizens visiting Denmark or Ireland.

Living and working in Europe

A British citizen can live and work in any other EEC country, without a work permit. However, you must have a valid full passport (not a British Visitors' Passport) endorsed with the words, 'Holder has the right of abode in the United Kingdom'.

THE TYPES OF LAW THAT RULE THE EUROPEAN COMMUNITIES

In the European Economic Community, Euratom and the Coal and Steel Community, EEC laws are more important than those of any single member state. If there is a conflict between Community law and national law, Community law prevails.

New Community laws can be made in three ways:
● Regulations passed by the Council of Ministers or the Commission have direct legal effect in all member states and on people and companies in those states, once they have been published in the EEC's *Official Journal.*

For example, one regulation says that lorry drivers with vehicles of more than a certain loaded weight may not work more than a stated number of hours during a set period. Member states, companies based in those states and drivers employed by the companies are legally obliged to obey those rules.

Regulations passed by the Council do

not have to be confirmed by the national parliaments in order to become legally binding in each country. But in Britain, for example, parliamentary committees examine all Community regulations and if a regulation involves a change in British law, Parliament may decide to cover that change by passing a new Act, or by approving a new ministerial regulation.

The British Government can legally refuse to put a Community regulation into effect, only if it can show that the regulation is against the Community's own rules. The final decision then rests with the European Court.
● Directives, also passed by the Council of Ministers or the Commission. They are binding only on the member states, and do not apply to people or companies in Britain until put into effect by a British Act of Parliament or British ministerial order.

A directive outlines a broad aim which member states must achieve by a stated

date – usually 2 to 5 years after the directive is passed. Each national government is left free to put a directive into effect in its own way. For example, a directive ordering member states to introduce Value Added Tax was given effect in Britain by the passing of the Finance Act 1972.

A country that fails to meet the deadline for a directive without good reason – for example, a severe economic crisis – may be brought before the European Court by the European Commission or by another EEC member, for failing in its obligations.
● Decisions, addressed by the Council of Ministers or the European Commission to a member state, a company or even an individual citizen. They are completely binding on whoever they are addressed to.

A decision may be a fine on a company that has broken Community rules on unfair trading, or it may be the setting up of a specialist committee to deal with a particular subject, such as employment.

If that endorsement is not already printed in your passport, ask a passport office to stamp it in your passport before you move abroad. Without the endorsement, you may not be allowed to stay.

In all EEC countries, except Ireland, you also need a residence permit which is issued after you have arrived. The timing varies from country to country. Consult the London embassy of the country in which you want to settle.

Reporting to the police

Once abroad, you must register with the police in the area where you will be living – in theory, immediately you arrive, but in practice within a few weeks. You must produce your passport and – if you are an employee – a certificate of employment signed by your employer.

Self-employed people and students must also register with the police, and

may be required to produce evidence to justify their stay and to show that they can support themselves. Such evidence may include a certificate of professional qualifications, a client's contract for services, a lease or freehold on commercial premises or a note from the university or college where a student is to study.

Residence permit

When the police have checked your documents, they issue a residence per-

---

HOW THE COMMON MARKET IS GOVERNED

The European Economic Community is administered by four institutions set up under the Treaty of Rome:

● **The Council of Ministers** The Community's main body for making major decisions, which consists of government ministers from each of the member states.

It usually meets in Brussels and can make laws and rulings that bind not only the member states but also organisations and individuals in any of those states.

It can decide many issues by majority vote, although the most important decisions – for example, whether a country should be allowed to join the EEC – must be agreed unanimously.

In practice, the majority vote is rarely used, and no member state is outvoted on an issue that would affect its own vital interests. If there is a critical disagreement, the Council puts off reaching a decision until it can be unanimous, rather than risk driving any member to leave the Community. That practice, in effect, gives each member nation a power of veto far wider than any laid down in the Treaty of Rome.

The makeup of the Council of Ministers is not fixed. Each member state sends the government minister most concerned with the topic to be discussed at a particular session. If it is a matter of general policy, for example, the council will consist of the foreign ministers – or, occasionally, the prime ministers – of the member states. If the subject is food, the representatives will be the agriculture ministers.

● **The European Commission** The Community's civil service, which has its headquarters in Brussels. It has two main functions: suggesting how to make the Treaty of Rome work in practice, and carrying out measures approved by the Council of Ministers.

The Commission is also responsible for enforcing EEC rules that forbid unfair trading practices, such as market-sharing agreements, monopolies or price rings. It can order a company to end such arrange-

ments and if the company fails to do so, the Commission can impose a maximum fine of about £500,000.

Commissioners – who must act independently of their home governments – are appointed from all the member nations. Britain, France, Italy and Germany each provide two, and the other members provide one each.

● **The European Court of Justice** Based in Luxembourg, which deals only with matters of Community law. It is not a court of appeal for cases that involve the laws of individual nations. *See:* HUMAN RIGHTS

The court has 10 judges – one from each member state – and four advocates-general, whose job is to summarise both sides of a case during a hearing.

The three roles of the European Court of Justice are:

1. To interpret Community law. If a national court cannot decide what an EEC law means, on any particular issue, it may ask the European Court for an interpretation which will then become part of that law, for all nine countries in the Community.

2. To make sure that the EEC institutions act lawfully. The Council of Ministers, the Commission or any of the member states can challenge a Community law or other decision, on the ground that it conflicts with the principles of the Treaty of Rome. If the court upholds the complaint, it can cancel all or part of the measure complained about.

Individuals and companies can also challenge Community laws or decisions. To do so, however, they must first show that the measure being challenged is of 'direct and individual concern' to them. A company fined by the European Commission for unfair competition, for example, can appeal to the European Court against the decision of the amount of the fine, but someone who merely reads about the fine and is not directly involved has no right to intervene.

3. To ensure that member states respect

their obligations to the EEC. If any member state fails to enforce a Community law or other ruling, the European Commission – or another member nation – can draw the court's attention to that failure.

If the court upholds the complaint, it can order the country involved to comply with the law. It cannot impose fines or other penalties on any state. But a Community institution that acts unlawfully can be ordered by the court to pay damages to those who suffer as a result.

No such order has yet been made, and there is no machinery for enforcing payment of damages.

A company or individual disobeying a Community rule can be punished only by the courts of the nation concerned, under that nation's laws dealing with EEC matters.

● **The European Parliament** Meets in Strasbourg and Luxembourg and is directly elected by voters in each of the EEC countries. *See:* ELECTION

It has no power to make laws, but debates laws being prepared by the European Commission and the Council of Ministers.

The Council of Ministers is not bound by the opinions of the European Parliament, but many proposed Community laws have been amended after debate in the parliament.

The European Commission can be questioned orally or in writing by the parliament, and is obliged to answer the questions.

The parliament can – by a two-thirds majority vote – dismiss the whole group of 14 European Commissioners, although that right has never been used. Commissioners cannot be discharged by the parliament individually.

The European Parliament has power to reject the Community's annual budget. It can only alter 25 per cent of the spending, because 75 per cent is spent on the agricultural policy, but it has power to delay this expenditure.

HOW THE EUROPEAN COMMUNITY MAKES LAWS
Civil servants propose, but governments decide

EUROPEAN COMMISSION

The heads of the Commission, the European Commissioners, formally adopt draft proposals for new Community laws drawn up by their civil servants. When a draft proposal has been adopted, it is submitted to the Council, which circulates it to other Community bodies. Once the Commission has received comments on the draft, including those from Coreper, it is re-submitted to the Council, if necessary after being revised

The main law-making body of the European Economic Community – the Common Market – is the Council of Ministers, in which the governments of the member states, including Britain, are represented.

The European Commission, the Community's civil service, has limited law-making powers delegated to it both by the Council of Ministers and by the treaties setting up the Community.

Most Community laws, other than those dealing with agriculture, follow a procedure of discussion and amendment that may take several years to complete.

COREPER

The Committee of Permanent Representatives, Coreper, consists of senior officials of ambassador rank representing the governments of the member-states. They do the detailed work of the Council

4 Revised proposal

1 Draft proposal

3

COUNCIL OF MINISTERS

The Council of Ministers sends the draft proposal to other Community bodies and delegates its own study of the draft to Coreper.

The Council may adopt the draft as Community law, request the Commission to amend it, reject it or simply take no decision.

The Council can adopt its own version, rather than the one proposed by the Commission, only by unanimous agreement

2

ECOSOC

The Economic and Social Committee, Ecosoc, consists of representatives of employers and trade unions and a third group that includes other professional interests like farmers and consumers. The Commission is not required to amend proposals for new laws in the light of Ecosoc's comments, but it may do so

EUROPEAN PARLIAMENT

The Parliament is not a law-making body; its role is purely consultative. The European Commission must submit draft proposals to it, and its opinions must be noted – but not necessarily acted upon. However, it has power over part of the budget and can also question the Commission and the Council on their handling of Community matters

5

The Council issues laws in the form of: directives, which the member-states must implement through their national law-making systems; regulations, which automatically have full force in all member-states; and decisions, addressed to a member-state, a company or an individual, which are binding in every respect

National governments or parliaments can influence Community law-making by instructions to their minister at the Council of Ministers

Individuals and groups can influence Community law-making by representation to members of Ecosoc

Individuals and groups can influence Community law-making through representation to their European MPs

6

EUROPEAN ECONOMIC COMMUNITY

Most Community laws are applied to people living in the 14 member–states, including Britain, through their national legal system, in the same way as national laws, over which they take precedence

EUROPEAN COURT OF JUSTICE

The European Court is the final arbiter on Community law, but it is not an appeal court that can overrule a national court. It may, if requested by a national court, give an interpretation of Community law which the national court is then bound to apply.

The Court may amend Community rules

7

if they are incompatible with Community law. It can hear cases brought by member-states or individuals against the Community institutions and by the institutions against the member-states. It cannot impose fines or prison sentences to reinforce its decisions

mit, which is equivalent to the identity card issued to local citizens and which you can use instead of a passport when crossing frontiers within the EEC.

In some areas, you may be given only a temporary permit which you must renew as it expires until your full permit is available.

The police can refuse a permit if they believe an applicant might be a threat to public order or break some local law – for example, if they know that he has a recent criminal record.

Someone who is refused a residence permit can appeal only through the courts of the country concerned. He cannot take legal action in Britain, say, to try to obtain a permit in France.

Taking the family

A UK citizen who goes to live and work in another country is entitled to take with him (or her) his wife (or her husband) and any children under the age of 21, provided that their passports state their right of abode in the United Kingdom and that the police of the host country are told of their presence.

If the children are over 21, their applications for registration with the police are treated separately from those of the other family members.

A child born abroad, whose father is a British citizen, is entitled to British nationality. To ensure proof of his nationality the parents should register the birth with a British consul within a year. *See:* CITIZENSHIP

Paying taxes in the EEC

A British citizen who lives and works in another EEC country is liable for all its local taxes, including income tax, capital gains tax (or its local equivalent), property tax, local authority tax and value added tax.

Income tax A British citizen who becomes liable to income tax in another EEC country may escape British tax on his earnings, even if he sends part of the income back to the United Kingdom.

Provided that you are out of Britain for at least 365 consecutive days – which can be interrupted for short visits home – you do not have to pay any UK tax on your earnings abroad. *See:* FOREIGN INCOME

All EEC countries operate a form of pay-as-you-earn tax system for employed persons, and assess the tax-

payer's final liability once a year. Although all the systems are broadly similar to that of the UK, the tax-free allowances vary from country to country.

Some of the member states – Bel-

SOCIAL SECURITY IN THE EEC

A British citizen who goes to live and work in another Community country must normally pay contributions into the local social security scheme, and stop paying them in the UK.

However, if the employing company has a place of business in the UK, and if the employee knows that he will be working abroad for fewer than 52 weeks, he is obliged to continue his UK payments and need not pay into the foreign scheme.

In such circumstances, complete form CF83, available from any office of the Department of Health and Social Security. If your contributions to the UK scheme are not automatically deducted by your employer, you can pay them through an agent, or as a lump sum at the end of the period you are abroad.

Under Community rules, contributions made in any Community country count in any other. So if you return to Britain after 3 or 4 years in, for example, France, you are entitled to benefits as if you had been in Britain all that time.

A British citizen living and working in another Community country can claim the same social security benefits as citizens of that country, provided that he can show that he would have been entitled to the corresponding benefits at home.

To do so, obtain a certificate from the Department of Health and Social Security, showing that your national insurance contributions were up to date when you left Britain.

Unemployment benefit, however, is not normally paid to a British citizen in another EEC country unless he can show that he has had a job, and paid social security contributions, in that country. The rule may be waived at the discretion of local social security officials, but not without good reason.

For example, if a British citizen and his wife move to France, where the husband has a job but his wife cannot work because her professional qualifications are not accepted there, benefit may possibly be paid to the wife.

gium, France, Ireland and the Netherlands – offer extra allowances to foreign residents at the discretion of the local tax inspector and subject to certain conditions.

Rates of income tax vary throughout the Community. If you go to work in Denmark, you will pay higher rates than in Britain, whatever your income group. In Germany and the Netherlands, tax rates start lower than in Britain, but move sharply upwards for the higher paid worker.

The rights of professionals

Under the Treaty of Rome, all Community citizens have a right to set up in business anywhere in the EEC. However, that rule is not yet in force for all professions, because member states have not yet been able to agree on the relative worth of professional qualifications earned in the various countries.

Doctors, dentists and state-registered nurses can work in all Community countries provided that they can pass a test to satisfy the host country's professional institutions that they are sufficiently familiar with the local language.

Accountants, teachers, journalists and entertainers are allowed to work in any EEC country without taking a local examination, but cannot expect to be given a job that requires knowledge of the language, if they are not familiar with it.

Barristers and solicitors are entitled to offer legal advice and may appear in court in any Community country.

Engineers' qualifications are not yet formally recognised in EEC countries outside their own.

Rights of workers

Apart from guaranteeing the free movement of workers, the EEC has laid down rules for many aspects of workers' rights.

Equal pay The Treaty of Rome directs all member states to introduce EQUAL PAY for men and women doing similar work. In Britain, this was put into force by the Equal Pay Act 1970.

Dismissals Another directive, put into effect in Britain in the Employment Protection Act 1975, now amended, said that any employer dismissing 10 or more workers within a period of 30 days must give them 30 days' warning, and inform the Department of Employment

30 days ahead. If 100 or more workers are involved, the period is 90 days.

Looking for work

If you go to look for work in another EEC country and you have been receiving UK unemployment benefit in this country, you can continue to get this for up to 3 months elsewhere in the Community. To qualify, you must have been registered as available for work (normally for 4 weeks) at a UK unemployment benefit office or careers office.

Unemployment benefit continues only as long as you register for work in each country in which you are seeking employment.

As long as you register in the new country within 7 days of ceasing to be available for work in the Community country you have just left, benefit can continue to be paid.

After receiving UK unemployment benefit in another EEC country, you cannot get it again for another period of unemployment abroad unless you have worked in the UK in the meantime.

If you fall sick while looking for work in another EEC country, you can get UK SICKNESS BENEFIT instead of unemployment benefit as long as the time for which you would have got unemployment benefit has not run out.

You can also get sickness benefit from the UK if you are working in another Community country but have continued to pay contributions to the UK national insurance scheme.

EUTHANASIA

Ending the life of a person who is constantly in pain

Euthanasia, or mercy killing, is the deliberate termination of someone else's life by medical means, such as an overdose of drugs or withdrawal of life-support treatment, to end suffering. In law, such an act is regarded as murder.

Bringing on death by failing to call for essential medical assistance can, as a crime of omission rather than commission, lead to the lesser charge of manslaughter.

In either case, it is no defence to prove that the person who was suffering had pleaded to have his or her life ended.

Helping a person to end his own life – by, for example, fetching him a lethal drug – or encouraging him to do so, is not euthanasia, but the crime of assisting or encouraging SUICIDE.

Suicide itself is no longer a crime, but the maximum penalty for helping someone else to commit suicide is up to 14 years' imprisonment.

Pain-killing drugs A doctor who gives a mortally ill patient drugs to relieve extreme suffering is not guilty of any crime even if the drugs also hasten the patient's death.

EVICTION

When a tenant can be made to leave his home

Although no one can be evicted from his home without a court order, tenants of some houses and flats are specially protected under the Rent Act and Protection From Eviction Act. If a tenancy is protected, the tenant cannot sign away that protection.

A tenancy, whether furnished or unfurnished, is normally protected if:
1. It is privately owned and has a rateable value falling below certain limits.

If first let before March 22, 1973, the rateable value at the time must not have exceeded £400 in Greater London or £200 elsewhere.

If first let between March 22, 1973, and April 1, 1973, rateable value must not have exceeded £600 in Greater London, £300 elsewhere.

If first let on or after April 1, 1973, the rateable value must not have exceeded £1,500 in Greater London, £750 elsewhere.
2. The rent payable is at least two-thirds of the rateable value.
3. The premises are not let as holiday accommodation and were not bought by the landlord to be his eventual home on retirement.
4. The landlord does not live on the premises.

The tenancy is not normally protected if:
1. It is a COUNCIL TENANCY, a CROWN letting (unless the landlords are the Crown Estates Commissioners) or a letting from a registered HOUSING ASSOCIATION. (Some council and housing association tenants have security of tenure, but the rules protecting possession by them of their homes are slightly different from those governing Rent Act protected tenants).
2. The rent is less than two-thirds of the rateable value.
3. The accommodation is let by a college or university to a student.
4. It is a holiday letting.
5. The landlord lives on the premises and it is a furnished letting, or is an unfurnished letting begun since August 14, 1974.
6. The landlord is an owner-occupier and has always given notice that he would want the premises at the end of the tenancy for himself or members of his family who were already living with him on the premises before the letting commenced.

The court will grant possession even where the owner-occupier has died and the house is required either as a residence for a member of his family living with him at his death or by his successor to sell with vacant possession.

An owner-occupier can recover possession even if neither he nor a member of his family intends to live in the house, but he can convince the court that it is not reasonably suitable to his needs, bearing in mind his place of work, and that he needs to be able to sell with vacant possession to buy a more suitable house.
7. The accommodation goes with a person's job.
8. The rent includes payment for board or other services provided to the tenant personally – for example, room cleaning or porterage.
9. The letting is a SHORT TENANCY.

What a landlord must do

If a tenancy is 'periodic' – running, for example, from week-to-week or month-to-month – a landlord who wants the tenant to leave must first serve notice to quit, in writing.

When premises are let for a fixed period, and the tenancy is protected, the landlord does not need to serve notice to quit.

However, if the tenant refuses to leave when the fixed term runs out or when his written notice expires, the landlord cannot evict him without a court order for possession of the premises – and such an order can be made only on certain very limited grounds.

The grounds for possession

To obtain an order for possession of any premises where there is a protected tenancy, the landlord must establish at least one of these grounds:

1. That he can give the tenant suitable alternative accommodation – which can include a council's certificate that it will provide an alternative home in the same district. A council house or flat in a different district would be unlikely to be considered acceptable by the court.

If the landlord cannot produce such a certificate, it must be shown that the tenant, if moved to new accommodation provided or found by the landlord, will have the same legal protection there as he already has in his present home.

If the new accommodation is council housing, the landlord is not required to show such protection, because council tenants do not have security of tenure.

The court may consider that a new tenancy of part of the premises already occupied by the tenant would be sufficient, provided that all his reasonable requirements – such as cooking, sleeping and access – would be met.

2. That the tenant is in arrears with the rent or has broken some other important term of his tenancy agreement.

3. That the tenant, or someone living with him, has caused annoyance to neighbours or has damaged or neglected the property or the landlord's furniture. These are grounds for eviction even when the damage has been put right or the nuisance ended.

4. That the landlord wants to move into the house or flat and suffers greater hardship by not being able to do so than the tenant would suffer by having to move out. This claim cannot be made if the landlord bought the premises subject to the tenancy, after March 23, 1965.

5. That the house went with a job which the tenant has left – and the house is needed for another employee.

6. That the landlord has retired and wants to live in the rented home – and the tenant was told of that possibility before taking up the tenancy.

7. That the premises have been used for immoral purposes, such as prostitution.

8. That the tenant previously gave notice that he was quitting and the landlord – relying on that notice – has contracted to sell the house.

If the court is satisfied, it can make an order giving the landlord possession of the property in 28 days. But in most cases the judge has discretion to refuse an order or to make a suspended order, so that the tenant need not leave immediately.

For example, if possession is claimed on the ground of rent arrears, the order may be suspended if the tenant can satisfy the judge that he is likely to pay regularly in future and reduce the arrears.

If the tenant gets into arrears again, the landlord can go back to the court and ask for the suspended order to be put into force. The court may or may not consent: it will depend on how serious are the new arrears.

Even if the premises have been used for immoral purposes, provided that the tenant can show that he himself was largely innocent, the court may suspend the possession order until another incident of immoral use can be proved. The court would take into account whether or not the tenant took any steps to prevent use of the premises for immoral purposes, or reported it.

When a tenant is not protected by law

If an owner claims possession so that he – or a member of his family who lived with him on the premises when he last occupied them – can live there again, the court must make an order, giving possession in 28 days – provided that the owner told the tenant at the start of the letting that he might want the premises for himself in the future.

Possession must also automatically be given if:

● The property is furnished (or unfurnished and first let since August 14, 1974), and the landlord lives on the premises, or

● The rent includes a payment for board or personal services.

However, the landlord must get a court order before attempting to evict. The court has power to suspend the possession order for up to 3 months but, in suspending possession it will order the tenant to pay any arrears of rent owing, unless the tenant can persuade the judge that to do so would be un-reasonable or cause him or her exceptional hardship.

Any landlord who attempts eviction without the court's authority can be accused of the offences of unlawful eviction and HARASSMENT.

A tenant who refuses to leave after a possession order has been made can be forcibly evicted by a court BAILIFF.

Protection by a rent assessment committee

Some tenants, whose tenancy agreements took effect before November 28, 1980, and who were not protected tenants under the Rent Act, may be entitled to ask a rent assessment committee to suspend the operation of a notice to quit.

If a tenant, whose tenancy began before this date, agrees with his landlord a change in the terms of his tenancy (for example, about the rent he pays, the services or furniture provided or the number of rooms taken) after November 28, 1980, the rent assessment committee has no power to grant him any security. The same applies to a tenant whose fixed-term tenancy ended before November 28, 1980, but who remained in possession, paying rent, after that date.

If a tenant has a periodic tenancy – as opposed to a fixed-term one – and receives a notice to quit, he should write to the local rent assessment committee, the address of which can be obtained from the town hall, a housing-aid centre or Citizens Advice Bureau or the telephone directory.

The application must normally be made within 28 days of the notice to quit coming into effect: if the notice has expired, the committee cannot help.

The application should not be simply for a delay in the proposed eviction: as a technicality, the tenant must also apply for a reasonable rent to be fixed for the property.

When the committee receives the application, the notice to quit is automatically suspended. The committee inspects the property then holds a hearing as soon as possible, usually within 6 weeks, though there is no time limit.

At the hearing, the landlord can object to the tenant's application, and the tenant must attempt to convince the committee that his application is justified – for example, by showing that he has been a good tenant and would suffer undue hardship if he were forced to leave.

The tenant can present his case personally or he can choose to be represented by a solicitor or surveyor or even by a friend with no professional qualification.

If the rent assessment committee thinks the application is justified, it can give the tenant security from eviction for any period up to 6 months. It may or may not also fix a new, higher or lower, rent. Before that period expires, the tenant can apply for an extension.

There is no limit in law to the number of times a tenant can apply to a rent assessment committee, but it would rarely grant more than a second, successive period of security.

If the first application is refused, the suspended notice to quit starts to operate again. However, 7 days must elapse before the notice can expire.

Tenants whose agreements took effect after November 28, 1980 cannot claim any security from the rent tribunal. However, in the case of a periodic

WHAT A NOTICE TO QUIT MUST STATE
How tenants must be informed of all their legal rights under the Rent Acts

The notice must be a clear directive to leave the whole of the premises and surrender possession to the landlord or his agent

Four weeks is the minimum notice for ending any tenancy. The period can be much longer, however, depending on the terms of the agreement. A quarterly tenant, for example, is entitled to a quarter's notice. In the case of yearly tenancies, at least 6 months' notice must be given

If the tenant does not leave the dwelling, the landlord must get an order for possession from the court before the tenant can be lawfully evicted. The landlord cannot apply for such an order before the notice to quit has run out

The tenant who does not know if he has any right to remain in possession after a notice to quit has run out or is otherwise unsure of his rights, can obtain advice from a solicitor. Help with all or part of the cost of legal advice and assistance may be available under the Legal Aid Scheme. He should also be able to obtain information from a Citizens Advice Bureau, Housing Aid Centre, a Rent Officer, or a Rent Tribunal Office

To   James Ernest Baldwin:

I the undersigned as landlord hereby give you notice to quit and deliver up to me or to whom I may appoint possession of the premises known as 14 Sunnington Road, London, N.W.12., which you hold of me as tenant thereof on 23 May 1981 next or at the end of the week of your tenancy which will end next after the expiration of four weeks from the service upon you of this notice.

I hereby draw your attention to the information contained in the Schedule hereto being information prescribed for the purpose of section 5 of the Protection from Eviction Act 1977 by the Notices to Quit (Prescribed Information) (Protected Tenancies and Part VI Contracts) Regulations 1975.

SCHEDULE

1. Even after the notice to quit has run out the landlord must get an order for possession from the court before the tenant can lawfully be evicted.

2. If the tenant does not know whether his tenancy is a protected tenancy, or is otherwise unsure of his rights, he can obtain advice from a solicitor. Help with all or part of the cost of legal advice and assistance may be available under the Legal Aid Scheme. He can also seek information from a citizen's advice bureau, a housing aid centre, a rent officer or a rent tribunal officer.

Dated the 17th day of April 1981   James Rowntree

If a landlord wishes to give a tenant notice to quit, he must do it in writing. If he does not draw the document up correctly, the tenant can safely ignore it. It is not enough simply to reclaim possession of the premises. The landlord must include in the notice information about the tenant's rights under the Rent Acts and where he can go if he is unsure about his position.

letting, a proper notice to quit (at least 4 weeks) must still be served, and a court order is always needed. The court can suspend the order for possession for up to 3 months, subject to the payment of all rent arrears (unless the tenant can show that such payment would be unreasonable or cause him exceptional hardship).

When a long lease runs out

If a tenancy is not covered by the Rent Act because the rent is less than two-thirds of the rateable value – which normally means that the lease is of 21 years or more – the tenancy still has some protection. When the lease runs out, the tenant cannot be evicted without a court order. Until the tenant leaves, the tenancy continues as before.

If the landlord does not want to continue the tenancy or agree a new one, he can ask the county court for a possession order on any of these grounds:
1. The tenant has failed to pay rent, rates or insurance premiums for the property.
2. The premises are reasonably required for the landlord, his children over the age of 18, his parents or his parents-in-law. (The landlord cannot rely on such a ground if he bought the property after February 18, 1966 or if the tenant would suffer greater hardship by having to leave.)
3. The tenant is allowing the premises to be used for illegal or immoral purposes.

Because a complicated set of notices must be served by both sides, keeping to strict time limits, tenant and/or landlord should seek legal advice.

It may be possible to inherit a statutory tenancy – one that was a protected tenancy under the Rent Act – if the original tenancy agreement has expired and the landlord has not won possession on any of the permitted legal grounds.

If the tenant who has died was married, the statutory tenancy goes to his or her spouse, provided he or she was living with the tenant at the time of that tenant's death.

If the deceased tenant was unmarried, or not living with his or her spouse at death, any member of the tenant's family who was living with the tenant for at least 6 months before his or her death is entitled to take over the tenancy if he or she can establish a claim to do so. If there is more than one member of the family with a claim and they cannot reach agreement then the dispute must be settled by the county court.

If that relative then dies, another relative can inherit the tenancy, but the succession ends after that.

A statutory tenant, that is, a tenant remaining in possession by virtue of statutory protection, rather than under his original tenancy agreements, must keep physical possession of the home. If he moves away – except for normal holidays or business trips – or attempts to sub-let the entire rented premises, his tenancy is ended and the landlord is entitled to possession. But he must get a court order.

EVIDENCE

Facts a court hears in order to decide a case

Evidence in a court case consists of the facts of the case as given on oath, or affirmation, by witnesses for both sides, as well as the statements of children too young to swear an oath and material items, or exhibits, that have a bearing on the case.

There are seven basic rules:
● Burden of proof. The party bringing the case must produce enough evidence to prove it. In criminal cases, where the standard of proof is stricter than in civil cases, the prosecution has to prove the accused guilty 'beyond reasonable doubt'. In civil cases the plaintiff has to prove the defendant liable only 'on a balance of probabilities'.

Because of these different standards of proof, a motorist who caused a road accident may be acquitted in a criminal prosecution for careless driving, yet be successfully sued for damages in a civil case over the same incident.
● Leading questions. A leading question is one so framed by a lawyer as to whittle down the witness's range of possible answers to a mere 'Yes or No' and so produce the desired reply. For example, it is a leading question to ask 'Were you frightened?' rather than 'What were your feelings?' A leading question suggests the answer.

A lawyer can put leading questions to the opposition but not to his own client or witnesses.
● Opinion. The sole task of all except expert witnesses is to present the facts of the case as they know them and not to draw conclusions from the facts. It is for the court or jury to draw conclusions.

A witness to a road accident may tell the court that he saw a motorist driving at what he assessed to be a certain speed, but he may not add, 'I thought he was driving recklessly' – which is an opinion.

The court, however, does listen to the opinion of an expert witness – for example, a doctor who gives his opinion on a victim's chances of recovery from an injury.
● Hearsay evidence. Evidence that is hearsay or second-hand is generally inadmissible in court.

If Mr Brown told his wife that Mr Jones had just told him that he had killed someone, Mrs Brown's account of the conversation would not be allowed as evidence – it is only hearsay. Only Mr Brown or Mr Jones could give admissible evidence.
● Child witnesses. A child is allowed to give evidence in court, but the court has to decide whether the child is able to comprehend the facts. The court may also need the child's evidence to be corroborated by a responsible witness.

'

THE INJURED WIFE WHO REFUSED TO GIVE EVIDENCE

One spouse cannot be compelled to give evidence against the other in a criminal case.

In 1978 Edward Hoskyn was charged with wounding his mistress Janis Scrimshaw. But 2 days before Hoskyn was due to be tried at the Old Bailey, Miss Scrimshaw married him.

When Hoskyn was tried, his wife refused to give evidence against him but was ordered to do so by the court.

Hoskyn was convicted but appealed against the verdict.

DECISION
The House of Lords ruled that Mrs Hoskyn should not have been compelled to give evidence against her husband and quashed the conviction against Hoskyn.

'

STUDENTS WITH SPECIAL PROBLEMS

The examination supervisors – invigilators – must, as part of their job, report to the examining board anything that might affect the performance of the students during the test. A fire alarm or similar disturbance could seriously affect students' concentration. Any such event should be reported to the board, which will always take it into account when the papers are marked.

A student may have a particular personal problem that affects his performance – for example, a sudden attack of asthma, recent illness or family bereavement. It should be reported to the invigilator at the time of the examination and not left until the results have been published.

Obviously, a candidate cannot have as much as, say, 20 per cent added to his original mark, but in a borderline case he may be given the benefit of the doubt. This could mean an improved grade or a pass rather than a fail. Produce a medical certificate if possible.

Second chance Every examination board has its own rules about allowing examinations to be taken again. Some boards permit a student to re-sit an examination within a few months instead of taking an entire course a second time. Others have limits within which an examination cannot be re-taken.

Arriving too late Most boards set a time during which the examination must be taken. Anyone who arrives late is unlikely to be allowed extra time to complete the paper. However, check with the invigilator.

Someone whose examination should have been completed in the morning, but who does not arrive until the afternoon, may nevertheless, in some circumstances, be allowed to sit the test in the afternoon.

The invigilator must, however, be convinced that there are good reasons for the delay such as a strike of public transport or extremely bad weather conditions. If there is a clash in the examination timetable, alternative arrangements can normally be made beforehand. The invigilator must be satisfied that the candidate has had no contact with anyone who has already sat the paper.

Anyone who appears at the centre on the wrong day is not allowed to take the examination.

● Circumstantial evidence. When evidence does not directly establish the existence of the vital facts in a case but indirectly points to their existence, it is known as circumstantial evidence, evidence by inference.

That can be given in court, but the degree of reliance the court places on it depends on how convincing it is and what other facts are given in the case.
● Evidence by a husband or wife. In criminal cases, a husband or wife cannot be made to give evidence against the other but can do so if he or she wishes.

EXAMINATION

The conditions that govern tests

A school can refuse to let a child sit a GCE or CSE examination if the head teacher and the child's teachers consider that he or she has little chance of passing.

Parents who feel that their child should take the examination, despite the decision of the school, should discuss the matter with the head teacher.

Schools and local authorities try to be helpful in such cases. Some will agree to enter the child provided that the parents pay the examination fees.

If after discussion the school still refuses to enter the child, the parents have no legal power to get the decision changed.

The parents can approach their local MEMBER OF PARLIAMENT or the OMBUDSMAN, but neither has any legal power to enforce a change of attitude. They can use only their influence.

An alternative for a parent is to enter the child as a private candidate at another examination centre.

Challenging a result

It is possible to appeal to an examining board after an examination – on the grounds, for example, that the questions were unfair, or the marking was unjust or, occasionally, because the candidates have followed the wrong syllabus. But there is no recognised system of appeal and the board is not obliged to consider an appeal.

If you feel that an examination was in any way unfair, first approach the head of the centre where you took the examination. His support, or the support of his staff, is essential if an appeal is to be considered, and it is best if the appeal is made by the head or by the centre, rather than by the person who took the examination.

In cases in which students have followed the wrong syllabus, boards have sometimes returned examination fees, even when the mistake was not their fault. It is most unlikely that they would alter a result for such a reason.

Re-checking papers Most boards are prepared to re-check examination papers, but they usually charge a fee to do so, and it is very rare for the marks to be altered.

A re-check can be asked for when, for example, a student has done noticeably less well than he or his school expected, or suspects that his name may have been confused with another student's.

A request for re-marking or re-checking of a GCE or CSE paper has to come from the head of the school or college where the examination was taken, and cannot be made by an individual. If the head of a centre refuses to pursue an appeal, the student can approach the school governors, who can discuss the case with the head.

Penalties for cheating

If someone is caught cheating during an examination, his or her paper will automatically be disqualified by the examining board.

Some boards rule out all papers taken by a person who has cheated; others rule out only the paper in which he or she was found cheating. Some boards refuse to allow anyone who has cheated to take any further examination conducted by them.

When there has been collusion or copying between two students during an examination, both students are likely to be disqualified, on the ground that the boards and invigilator cannot easily decide who copied from whom.

A student who feels unjustly penalised over someone copying his work can appeal to the board.

Impersonation It is a criminal offence for a person to be impersonated in an examination. Both the impersonator and whoever is impersonated can be charged with deception. The maximum penalty for each person involved is 5 years' imprisonment or an unlimited fine. *See:* DECEPTION

Other examinations

Examinations for professional qualifications – for example, in law or engineering, or for grades in piano-playing – are conducted by special boards. Each board has its own regulations, which can be obtained from the board concerned. Lists of examining boards are available at most public libraries.

EXCHANGE CONTROL

No restriction on moving money into or out of Britain

All restrictions on taking money into or out of Britain or obtaining foreign currency were removed in 1979, after more than 40 years of tight restriction.

British citizens and companies are free to open foreign bank accounts, buy and keep gold bullion and coins, buy foreign shares and property. It is also possible to write a cheque on a British bank account in dollars, francs, marks or any other foreign currency. Similarly, a British cheque can be used to settle bills abroad. Foreign currency brought into Britain no longer has to be changed back into British money.

Nevertheless, the Exchange Control Act 1947 is still law, and the Government has the power under that law to impose strict limits again.

Many other countries continue to impose limits on the amount of money that can be taken from their territories.

EXCHANGE OF CONTRACTS

When a property transaction becomes binding on both sides

One of the most critical stages in the long process of HOUSE BUYING AND SELLING is the point at which the buyer's solicitor sends the seller's solicitor an agreed deposit (usually 10 per cent of the purchase price) and a copy of the contract signed by the buyer.

When the seller's solicitor receives these, he gets his own client to sign another copy of the contract (which was originally drawn up by the seller's solicitor), and that is sent to the buyer's solicitor.

CRITICAL EXCHANGE

The most critical stage in buying or selling a house is the point at which the seller's solicitor sends the buyer's solicitor the copy of the contract which has been negotiated.

'Sorry. Almost sold. Just awaiting exchange of contracts'

When both contracts have been exchanged in that way, the deal between buyer and seller is legally binding. Until that moment, either side can decide to withdraw from the transaction, no matter what oral, or even written, promises had been given. *See:* GAZUMPING

A written promise to exchange contracts might, however, give a claim for damages if broken.

EXCLUSION CLAUSE

When a contract condition is invalid even if it is accepted

Any condition in a contract that seeks to limit or take away a person's basic legal rights – say, to compensation for death or injury caused by someone else's negligence – is likely to be void, even if the contract has been signed and accepted.

Under the UNFAIR CONTRACT Terms Act 1977, some of these conditions – usually called exclusion clauses – are automatically invalid:

● If they seek to exclude one party's right to compensation for death or injury caused by the negligence of the other party or one of his agents – say an employee acting in the course of his work.

● If they try to evade or weaken a dealer's obligation to see that the goods

he sells are of suitable quality and fitness for the purpose for which they are required.

That second category applies only to sales direct to consumers, however. It does not cover goods that are sold by way of trade – including goods bought by ordinary consumers at trade discount prices.

When a clause may be upheld

Some exclusion clauses and conditions may be held to be valid by the courts if they can be shown to be fair and reasonable, if they were known by the party who is penalised by them and if both sides had similar bargaining strengths when the contract was devised. *See:* UNFAIR CONTRACT

EXECUTOR

Winding up a dead person's estate

When you make a will, you should name one or two people to be responsible for carrying out your wishes after your death. These personal representatives, called executors, will take charge of your affairs, collect everything belonging or owing to you, pay all debts and taxes and divide what is left among your chosen heirs according to your wishes. Make sure that the people you nominate agree to act as executors – they have a right to refuse.

Executors are allowed to benefit under the will, unlike the witnesses to the will who may not share in the estate.

Whom to choose

When most of an ESTATE is to be left to one person – such as the widow or widower – he or she is usually the best choice as executor. To have someone else responsible for winding up your affairs could seem an intrusion into the beneficiary's private affairs. Moreover, the task of handling the estate may help to relieve their grief.

If the person who will benefit most under the will is not suitable – because of frailty or language difficulties, for example – appoint another relative or close friend, preferably someone with good business sense and who is on good terms with the other heirs. But do not appoint executors who are much older than you, as they may die first.

If your executor is not one of the heirs, it is a good idea to award him in the will a small sum for undertaking the responsibility.

A second executor It is always safer to name more than one executor – in case one is ill or abroad at the time you die. Another advantage is that two people may find it easier to reach joint decisions – such as how to dispose of property to the satisfaction of all the heirs – than one executor working alone. A widow may well welcome the support of a sympathetic relative or friend as her co-executor.

When young children are among the heirs, part of the estate is usually put in trust for them until they come of age. In such cases, two executors – who can also act as trustees – are required. The GUARDIAN may be a good choice, but is not essential.

If your estate is to be divided among several people, or if you own a business or have complex financial dealings, you should ask your solicitor or accountant to be co-executors, working with your personal executor. Whereas personal executors are unpaid, professionals will require a fee which must be deducted from the estate. It is normal practice to insert a clause in the will, awarding them their fees.

Another circumstance in which you might appoint an impartial professional as executor is when the heirs are on bad terms with each other and would not accept a relative's decision.

Professional executors Some banks and insurance companies advertise professional executor services, offering skill and experience, easy access for you and your heirs and continuity of service – unlike individuals, the bank does not die, become ill or go on holiday. A professional service may be the best choice when a long-term TRUST is set up under the will – for example, granting your widow the income from your estate during her lifetime, but sharing the property among your children after her death.

If your will and affairs are uncomplicated, you may find the cost of a professional service disproportionately high: perhaps between 2–4½ per cent of the value of the estate before tax, depending on its size, with a minimum fee of £450, plus VAT. In addition, you may also have to pay legal fees.

WHEN THERE IS NO EXECUTOR

If someone dies without making a will, or if no executors have been appointed, or if they have died or are unavailable, the nearest relatives apply to the local probate registry – you can find out its address from a Citizens Advice Bureau – for the grant of 'letters of administration'. Once these are granted, their duties and authority are the same as the executor's.

If no relatives apply, the Treasury Solicitor's department administers the estate for the Crown. *See:* INTESTACY

The Public Trustee The Government operates a non-profitmaking executor service which is cheaper than those of the banks and insurance companies. It charges 1–4½ per cent of the gross value of the estate with a minimum of £250 plus VAT. However, the Public Trustee can function only in England and Wales and – though its officials do travel – it has only one office, in London, and local professional help may be more convenient.

Keeping your executors informed

When people or companies have agreed to act as executors, you should tell them what you own and where they can find essential documents. From time to time, particularly if your situation changes radically, keep them informed about the state of your finances and property.

The duties of an executor

● Locating the will. If someone has died and appointed you his executor, you will need to obtain his will which is your formal appointment – though not a legal authority – to handle his affairs. The will also directs you how to settle those affairs. Most important immediately, it may indicate what the dead person wanted done with his body.

● Arranging the funeral. Your first duty as executor is to organise the FUNERAL. Although the dead person may have left instructions for disposing of his body, you are not bound in law to accept them – though normally they are carried out where possible. However, if the body has been donated for scientific or medical use – in a signed and witnessed declaration – you must hand it over to the named hospital or institution. *See also:* CREMATION; DEATH GRANT; DEATH, Registration of; TRANSPLANT

● Finding out what has been left. If the dead person kept his papers together and up-to-date and informed you regularly about his financial state, finding out what is left may be a simple process requiring only a rough assessment of the value of his belongings, before you can proceed to the next stage.

Normally, however, you need to examine his personal papers and consult his bank manager, accountant or solicitor.

Passbooks for banks, building societies, cooperative societies and similar institutions must be sent off to be made up to the date of the death. You may be asked to produce a copy of the death certificate and the will, before the dead person's bank or professional adviser agrees to disclose confidential information.

You should be able to value some of the property yourself – for example, the house and car – by comparing the items with others advertised in local newspapers. But you would have to call in an expert valuer to estimate the worth of specialist objects such as antiques.

● Finding out what debts are owed. When you have compiled an account of the value of everything the dead person has left behind, you should deduct from it the sum of his debts – including his bank loans, mortgages, rent, rates, telephone, gas and electricity bills, tradesmen's bills, hire-purchase payments and any amounts due on credit cards. The undertaker's account for the funeral is also considered a debt of the estate.

If you suspect that there are outstanding debts that you cannot trace, put an advertisement in *The London Gazette* and a local newspaper, calling on all creditors to come forward with their claims within a given period, say 2 months. Such a measure protects you – as executor – from having to pay bills that come to light after you have distributed the estate.

If you are a main beneficiary, you may – with the others who benefit – decide not to advertise since you would have to pay bills that come to light after the estate is distributed.

The list of debts should take into

account any taxes that are owed – such as personal income tax, if the dead person was self-employed.

● Applying for authority to wind up the estate. When you have worked out the extent of the property, apply for the legal authority to collect it, sell whatever necessary and pay out legacies according to the will. That authority – called 'grant of probate' – is obtained from your local probate registry. Apply to the personal application department at the address listed in the local telephone directory.

To obtain grant of probate, you must complete several forms, take an oath to

honour all your duties as executor and deposit cheques to cover the amounts you have estimated to cover CAPITAL TRANSFER TAX and probate fees. These documents must be approved by an officer of the probate registry and by the tax authorities before probate is granted, a process that normally takes between 1 and 3 weeks – but longer if your tax assessment is queried.

You have to go to probate registry in person at least once – to take the oath – and perhaps more often to answer queries.

When you receive the grant, ask the registry for photocopies – you will need

to send them to all institutions that hold the dead person's property, as proof of your authority to gather in his belongings.

● Raising a loan to pay the tax. Until probate is granted and executors are empowered to deal with the estate, the dead person's money and property are 'frozen' at the banks or institutions where they are deposited. To pay the capital transfer tax and probate fees, therefore, it is usually necessary to raise a short-term loan.

If the dead person had a bank account with enough capital to cover the loan and the interest charged on it, it is

THE RULES TO OBSERVE WHEN APPLYING FOR GRANT OF PROBATE
What executors must do to obtain authority to wind up an estate

Please complete in BLOCK CAPITALS

At which office do you wish to attend? (See list of Probate Registries on pages 2 and 3 of Form PR48 and list of Probate Offices on Form PR48A)	LONDON — ADELPHI JOHN ADAM ST.
The Deceased Full Name	THOMAS GUY LACEY

If any item belonging to the deceased is not held in the full name, state below the name in which

Address	7 UPTON GARDENS, CHELSEA, LON
(For official use only)	*Please leave blank*
Date of death	1 MAY 1979
Occupation	BARRISTER AT LAW (RETIRED)
Status (married, widower, widow, bachelor, spinster or divorced—state which).	MARRIED
The Applicant or Applicants Full Name(s)	1. JULIET MARY LACEY 2. JAMES EDWARD LACEY
(For official use only)	*Please leave blank*
Postal Address(es)	1. 7 UPTON GARDENS, S.W.3 2. HOUSE OF COMMONS, S.W.1
Occupation	1. HOUSEWIFE 2. MEMBER OF PARLIAMENT	If a woman, state whether spinster, married, widow or divorced
Relationship to deceased	1. WIFE 2. SON	If widow or widower of deceased state date and place of marriage

If there is no valid will, the estate is divided according to the rules of INTESTACY. A surviving husband or wife would be awarded most of what is left, with the remainder going to close relatives in a strict order of priority: first, the dead person's children and their descendants, then his parents, then his brothers, sisters, uncles and aunts and their families

If a different address appears in the will, probate registry officials insert it here

Under the rules of intestacy, illegitimate children have the same rights as legitimate. Likewise, when an illegitimate person dies intestate and without marrying, his parents can inherit

When executors and administrators have worked out the extent of a dead person's possessions, they must apply for official permission to pay his debts and share out his estate. To do so, they must complete an application for grant of probate and several other forms which list the value of the estate. Then they make an appointment at the local probate registry where they must hand over cheques for the amount of

easiest to get credit from the manager of that bank. If there is not enough money left, you may have to give another part of the estate – the deeds to the house, for example – as security for a bank loan. Sometimes the bank asks the executor to take personal responsibility for repaying the loan.

When the dead person's bank agrees to a loan, you should open an executorship account at that bank and draw your cheques for probate against that account.

If the dead person did not have a bank account, try to raise the loan from your own bank or other sources – such as friends – using the estate as security.

If the dead person left premium bonds or National Savings funds or certificates, you can apply to use that money to pay capital transfer tax. Ask for an application form at the probate registry and, if your application is approved, the money will be paid direct to the registry by the Department for National Savings.

● Assets that can be dealt with before probate is granted. Some matters can be settled before grant of probate, though mostly they do not involve the executors directly.

Joint bank or building society accounts, for example, pass automatically to the surviving partner.

Life-insurance policies that are payable to someone else can be claimed by that person simply by producing a copy of the death certificate. Such money would not be taxed as part of the estate, but the executors must disclose if a policy existed, so that the Inland Revenue can check whether capital transfer tax is payable on it.

However, if the life-insurance policy was an 'own life' scheme, insuring the dead person for his own benefit, it cannot be cashed before probate is granted and is taxed as part of the estate.

Friendly and provident societies pay up to £1,500, before probate is granted, to those nominated by the dead person to receive payments on his death. Anything over £1,500 is only paid after probate.

● Gathering the assets. When you have obtained grant of probate, you must register it with all institutions that hold the dead person's assets – banks, building societies, mortgage companies, stockbrokers, storage firms and so on – by sending each of them a copy of the grant and asking them to transfer the assets and property to your name.

Alternatively, you can have specific items transferred directly to those who are to receive them under the will. For example, if the dead person has left a block of shares to one of the named beneficiaries, you can have them put straight into his name – if they are not needed to pay off debts.

● Clearing the debts. All debts must be settled before any legacies can be given to the heirs. If the debts exceed the assets, consult a solicitor.

The funeral bill takes priority above all others and must be paid out of the estate. But the grave and a headstone, or any other memorial, must be paid for by those who wish to provide them.

Include among the debts any expenses you have incurred in handling the estate – for example, travel, postage, solicitor's fee for consultation – and the fees of any professional executors appointed in the will.

Paying all the debts may take a long time, particularly if there is an outstanding tax bill – for example, if the dead person was self-employed, his tax for several past years may need adjusting. There may also be many queries from

---

Did the deceased leave a will?	YES/~~NO~~	If "YES" and the applicant is not named in the will under 18?

If the applicant is an executor, and other executors named in the will are NOT now applying, complete this section by giving their names and deleting whichever reasons do not apply.

DR. D. J. ARMSTRONG
(name—another executor)

is dead	
does not wish to apply or to act as executor	✕
does not wish to apply now, but may wish to do so later	

_____
(name—another executor)

is dead	
does not wish to apply or to act as executor	
does not wish to apply now, but may wish to do so later	

Did the deceased leave a husband or widow?	YES/~~NO~~

Please state number of relatives who survived the deceased

Sons or daughters under 18			—	Grandchildren
Sons or daughters 18 or over			/	Grandchildren who are children of pre-deceased children
Daughters under 18 but married			—	
Parents			—	Grandparents
Brothers or sisters under 18				Nephews or nieces who are
Brothers or sisters 18 or over			/	children of pre-deceased brothers or sisters

Has any relative of the deceased been adopted?	~~YES~~/NO/~~NOT TO MY KNOWLEDGE~~

THIS SECTION NEED NOT BE ANSWERED IN CASES WHERE A WILL IS BEING PRO
NOR IN RESPECT OF AN ILLEGITIMATE PERSON WHO HAS BEEN ADOPTED
Answers are necessary in other cases because under the Family Law Reform Act, 1969, certain rights ar
and to the parents of illegitimate persons.

Was the deceased **illegitimate**?	YES/NO/NOT TO MY KNOWLEDGE
If so	
Is the mother of the deceased alive?	YES/NO
Is the father of the deceased alive?	YES/NO/NOT TO MY KNOWL
Did the deceased leave any **illegitimate** sons or daughters?	YES/NO/NOT TO MY KNOWL
Did the deceased have any **illegitimate** children who died leaving children of their own?	YES/NO/NOT TO MY KNOWL

tax likely to be due and for probate fees. They must also take an oath to honour their duties as executors. When the papers have been approved by High Court and tax officials, probate is granted, usually within 3 weeks.

EXECUTOR

the capital transfer tax office over the value of various items in the estate and over new assets that come to light.

When land or a house is involved, the Inland Revenue insists on a valuation by the district valuer before setting a figure for capital transfer tax.

When the tax authorities have been satisfied, apply to the Inland Revenue for a clearance certificate showing that all tax due has been paid.

● Distributing the estate. It is not legally necessary for executors to read out the will after a funeral and it is seldom done nowadays. However, you may well decide – even before grant of probate – to tell the main beneficiaries the likely size of the estate and of their legacies.

No one is entitled to demand that information, although anyone – even unrelated members of the public – can obtain a copy of the will, after grant of probate, from the registry.

Similarly, you are not required to hand over any items or money to the heirs until you have cleared all possible problems and debts of the estate. But executors often decide to make quick payment of small gifts, or pay small amounts on account of a larger legacy, as soon as they know that they are not needed for paying debts.

For example, if the dead person has left his treasured fishing tackle to a fellow-angler, it is likely that he would have wished it to be handed over promptly. The widow may also welcome such gifts – even though her own legacy will be tied up for sometime.

All legacies have equal priority – unless one or other is given precedence in the will, which is most unusual. They must be paid in full, before the residue can be awarded.

An heir can accept a cash legacy in another form – a block of shares of equal worth, for example, or a car of the same value as the money he would have received – but must pay the difference into the estate if the value of the object exceeds the amount of his legacy. The value of such assets must be taken at the date of transfer, not at death.

If specific objects are left as gifts, the recipient must pay the cost of packing, transporting and insuring them, unless the will says otherwise.

● Transferring land. If the dead person left land or a house, you will have either to sell it or to transfer it into the name of one of the heirs.

To carry out the transfer you need to complete a document called an 'assent', which must be signed by the executors. Since the assent forms part of the title deeds to the land, it is best to have it prepared by a solicitor or qualified conveyancer.

Unless the will makes it clear that the bequest of a house or land is free of all taxes and liabilities, the beneficiary has to pay the proportion of capital transfer tax due on the property.

He is also liable for all of its debts – such as a mortgage.

If the property you are transferring to an heir carries a mortgage, you should confirm – before completing the assent – that the building society is prepared to continue the mortgage with the new owner.

● Preparing a final account and dividing the residue. Having paid all the legacies – and before you share out what is left – prepare a set of accounts listing all the assets and debts of the estate and all payments and transfers you have made. Take care to include interest that has accumulated on assets which took a long time to distribute and make adequate provision for taxes for which you – as executor – may be liable, such as the interest on the executorship account.

Give a copy of the accounts to each of the people who are to share in what remains of the estate – the residue – which you must divide among them when they have approved your accounts.

If the will instructs that a trust should be created with the residue, from which the heirs can draw regular interest and dividends, you will probably find that you have been appointed trustee.

When the residue has been divided, you have, in all probability, completed your duty as executor. However, if a new asset comes to light years later, you may be called in again to handle it. If you are no longer alive, the responsibility devolves on the executors of your own will.

PAYING LEGACIES IN FULL

Mr Lacey dies leaving property and goods worth £20,000. After tax and debts have been paid, £6,000 remains to be divided among his heirs.

Mr Lacey's will awards £3,000 to his son, £1,500 to each of his two grandchildren and the residue – or remainder – to his widow.

As the legacies to the children have to be paid in full, Mrs Lacey receives nothing.

If there is not enough money to pay the legacies in full, the total sum is divided into proportionate amounts – so that if Mr Lacey had left only £3,000, his son would receive £1,500 and each grandchild £750, with Mrs Lacey again receiving nothing. On the other hand if Mrs Lacey had been bequeathed a fixed amount, instead of the residue, she and her son and grandchildren would have shared whatever was available.

However, if Mrs Lacey has not been provided for otherwise – for example, by lifetime gifts from her husband – she can seek a court order to grant her a share of the estate. *See:* DISINHERITANCE

IF YOU NEED TO RAISE MONEY TO PAY DEBTS

You must also decide whether you need to sell any part of the estate to pay debts, repay the capital transfer tax loan, cover the expenses of administering the estate and pay cash gifts specified by the will.

You have complete authority to decide what must be sold, but you may not sell items that have been specifically granted to someone in the will unless there is not enough cash without them to meet all the debts and expenses.

Remember that premium bonds qualify for draws for 12 months after the holder's death. It may be wise to keep them.

An order of priority for selling off the assets to meet the debts is laid down by law:
First, any property that has not been disposed of in the will.
Second, the 'residuary estate' – whatever you calculate will be left after all debts and legacies have been paid.
Third, whatever property was named in the will to be used for meeting debts.
Fourth, the cash fund, from which you would distribute legacies of money.
Finally, items that have been specifically granted to someone in the will.

264

EXEMPTION CLAUSE

When a trader, manufacturer or any other individual or organisation tries to take away rights that you might otherwise have, he or it usually does so by using a special clause – called an exemption clause – in a notice, contract or other document.

In many cases, the clause may be ineffective. *See:* UNFAIR CONTRACT

EXPENSES

When the Inland Revenue allows expenses to be free of income tax

Expenses can be set against income tax both by employees and by self-employed people. Claims must be made each year on the taxpayer's INCOME TAX RETURN.

Expenses of employees

Employees can off-set against tax only expenses that they have incurred 'wholly, exclusively and necessarily' in carrying out their duties. All expenses must have been absolutely essential.

Among the expenses that are allowed against income tax are:
1. Essential tools that have to be provided by the employee himself.

Inland Revenue interprets 'essential' strictly and may not allow certain items, arguing that if they were essential, the employer would provide them. For example, an office worker might not be allowed to claim for the cost of a briefcase.

However, many trade unions agree set allowances for tools or protective clothing, or for other working materials, that members can claim without query.
2. Protective and special clothing – for example, overalls, laboratory coat, footwear or helmet.

Most employees cannot claim for clothes just because they are required to look smart while at work. But some people in the entertainment industry are allowed to claim for clothing, make-up and hairdressing.
3. Business use of an employee's own car, including capital allowances.

Business use does not include travelling to and from work.

Any contributions made by the employer to the running costs of the vehicle must be deducted from the amount claimed.

The AA Schedule of Estimated Running Costs for different cars is accepted by Inland Revenue.
4. Business use of the employee's own telephone.

He is entitled to charge for all business calls plus part of the rental in proportion to the amount he uses the telephone for business. He must deduct any contributions the employer makes.
5. Subscriptions and fees to professional associations relating to his employment.

Union subscriptions are covered if the union concerned is more than a mere negotiating body. But if it produces professional periodicals and concerns itself with codes of conduct, the Inland Revenue may allow part of the subscription. The amount is frequently negotiated between the union and the tax authorities.

The cost of studying for additional qualifications and the cost of obtaining professional magazines are not allowable expenses.
6. Business travel and subsistence expenses.

The cost of getting to and from work and expenses reimbursed by the employer are not claimable.

The cost of meals at work is not allowable even if, for example, an employee is kept late in an emergency. Meal expenses while working away from home, if it is necessary to stay

---

WHAT YOU CAN CLAIM

The expenses that can be offset against income tax are carefully defined. Receipts are not always necessary but should be included for expenses incurred at home.

'Sorry, he's busy working on his expense account'

---

elsewhere overnight, can be claimed.
7. An employee's contributions to a superannuation scheme operated by the employer.

If the job does not offer a pension, an employee's private contributions to a retirement annuity policy are allowable.
8. Business entertainment.

Entertainment expenses are allowable only if they cover 'reasonable entertainment' of overseas customers. An employee cannot claim such entertainment expenses against the tax on his salary if they are reimbursed by the employer and he has already claimed expenses tax relief against trading profit. Expenses tax relief cannot be claimed twice – once by the employer and once by the employee.

An employee can claim other expenses not reimbursed by his employer.

When employees regularly incur expenses on their employer's behalf, Inland Revenue normally allows them to draw the expenses from the employer untaxed – provided that the employer guarantees that they were all genuine expenses.

If an employee then claims the same expenses against his taxable income he is technically guilty of attempted fraud and could be fined or imprisoned.

One way to show that expenses are necessary in the course of the job is to have them written into the contract of employment – for example, by having a paragraph in your letter of employment stating that you are expected to make business telephone calls from home or that you are expected to provide meals for clients at home.

Expenses of the self-employed

Self-employed people can claim many more deductions than can people who are employees. The Inland Revenue's requirement for the self-employed is that the expenditure be 'wholly and exclusively' for the purpose of the business. The word 'necessarily' is not mentioned.

Expenses that can be offset against income tax are:
1. Cost of stock bought for resale and other business materials, including discounts allowed on sales and bad trade debts.
2. Cost of employing staff – wages, national insurance, pensions and redundancy payments.

3. Cost of maintaining, running and repairing equipment.

The capital cost of buying equipment is not allowable.

4. Costs of running premises: rent, rates, heat and light, insurance, cleaning and maintenance.

Improvements, such as extensions, are not allowed, and if any part of the rates and rent is claimed, CAPITAL GAINS TAX may have to be paid if the premises are sold.

5. Delivery, carriage and postage costs.

6. Office expenses, such as stationery, telephone and printing.

7. Professional revenue charges – for example, audit fees, the legal costs of debt collection, preparation of contracts and the settling of trade disputes.

8. Cost of business travel and hotel bills. The cost of travelling to the business address is not included.

9. Cost of entertaining overseas customers.

10. Gifts to customers – provided that the gifts are not worth more than £2 each and that each gift contains a conspicuous advertisement for the donor.

The gift must not be food, drink or tobacco unless the donor trades in, or manufactures, these items.

11. Interest payments on money borrowed for use in the business, including interest on overdrafts and hire-purchase contracts.

12. Donations to charity.

Expenses not allowed against income tax include:

● All private payments – for example, expenses connected with family or domestic activities.

The Inland Revenue always looks closely at wages paid to members of a proprietor's family. For example, if someone's wife is paid £50 a week to answer the telephone and it is found that a commercial rate for such duties would be only £10, £40 will be added to the business's taxable profit.

● A proprietor's own withdrawals from business income, regarded as taxable profit. When he withdraws cash and spends part of it privately and part on the business, only the business expenditure can be claimed.

● Capital expenditure, fines and legal costs, political and charitable donations and payments of tax – other than PAYE and national insurance contributions – on behalf of the employees.

When landlords can claim

Landlords can claim:

1. The cost of repairing and maintaining their property – including the cost of gardening if that is specified in the lease. They cannot claim the cost of property improvement.

2. Regular expenses such as rates, ground rent, lighting of common passageways and insurance.

3. The cost of managing the property, including rent collection, advertising, accountancy and legal charges.

4. Interest on the mortgage of any property let, or available for letting, throughout the year.

5. The cost of providing any services, and the wear and tear of any furniture, provided that the lease makes the landlord responsible for such services and for the good condition of furniture.

EXTRADITION

Sending a person to another country for trial

Someone accused of committing a serious crime in one country and who has gone to another country may be sent back to face justice.

The process, called extradition, operates only between countries that have special treaties. Britain, for example, has extradition treaties with 44 countries, and special arrangements, which work in virtually the same way as extradition, with Commonwealth countries, dependencies and Eire.

Commonwealth The surrender of accused persons between Commonwealth countries and British dependencies is governed by the Fugitive Offenders Act 1967. Though technically not extradition the procedure is similar.

Eire A warrant for arrest issued in Eire can be used in Britain simply by having it endorsed by a magistrate in the area where the accused person is believed to be. This applies to any indictable offence or one punishable by at least 6 months' imprisonment.

Like extradition, the procedure cannot be used for political offences.

The crimes for which a person can be extradited are listed in Schedule 1 of the Extradition Act 1870. It covers most crimes punishable by imprisonment.

Britain also has additional arrangements with countries with which it has no extradition treaty to cover hijacking and other crimes specifically connected with aircraft.

Asking for extradition

In Britain a request to have a person extradited must be approved by the Home Secretary who then asks a magistrate to issue an arrest warrant.

The magistrate must be given evidence that would be enough to send the person for trial if the offence had been committed in Britain.

The person to be extradited will normally be held in prison until he is either handed over to the country making the request, or he is freed. If that takes longer than 2 months he can apply to the High Court to be released.

Anyone facing extradition can apply for legal aid and, in theory, for bail, though it is seldom granted.

To appeal against extradition the accused must lodge an application for an order of HABEAS CORPUS within 15 days of the magistrates' court decision.

People who cannot be extradited

A person cannot be extradited if:

1. The offence of which he is accused is political. In English law that means any offence committed in connection with or as part of a political disturbance. That definition applies only in cases of extradition, however. In common law there is no political crime.

2. He can show that, although the crime for which extradition is sought is not political, the country seeking the order really wants to punish him for a political offence.

3. The country seeking the order does not have a law preventing a person who has been extradited for one offence from being punished for some other offence until he has had the opportunity of returning to the country that surrendered him.

4. He is in his own country and it has a separate treaty prohibiting the surrender of nationals. Britain and Denmark, for example, have an arrangement that excludes the return of Britons to Denmark and Danes to Britain.

5. The accused person has diplomatic immunity or is a member of certain international organisations, such as United Nations agencies.

FAIR TRADING

*How the state supervises
sales methods*

The Office of Fair Trading is a state-supported organisation set up to ensure that traders carry on business fairly and that the public interest is not harmed by unfair trading practices.

The Office, which is independent of the Government, and headed by a director-general, also controls the administration of the Consumer Credit Act 1974. *See:* CONSUMER CREDIT

To protect the public, the Office of Fair Trading looks for monopolies and company mergers that create a monopoly that might restrict competition and lead to unnecessarily high prices, where the value of the assets taken over is more than £5 million.

Under the Fair Trading Act, a monopoly – the domination of the market in particular goods or services by one supplier or group of suppliers – exists if at least one-quarter of the goods or services being considered is supplied by, or to, one person or group of companies.

If there is any doubt about the fairness to the public of a monopoly or proposed merger, the director-general of Fair Trading may ask the Monopolies and Mergers Commission to report on whether the arrangement is against the public interest.

Restrictive practices The Office of Fair Trading is also responsible for compiling a register of agreements made between traders which fix prices or restrict supplies. The agreements are then referred to the Restrictive Practices Court which decides whether they are in the public interest. If they are not – or if they are not registered – they are void.

How the consumer is protected

To protect the economic interests of consumers the Office of Fair Trading constantly keeps under review the commercial activities of traders. There are three particular functions of the Office relating to consumer protection.

Codes of practice A wide range of codes of trading conduct, negotiated with trade associations, establishes provisions to protect the customer. Among them are those dealing with electrical appliances, electricity supply, radio, electrical and television retailers, travel agents, shoe sales and repairs, laundries and cleaners, mail-order suppliers and motor traders.

New laws If the Office of Fair Trading finds some widespread trading practice that misleads, confuses or adversely affects the right of consumers, the Office may recommend that the practice should be made a criminal offence. This would be done by an order of the Secretary of State for Prices and Consumer Protection. Among the orders already made are those banning the use of certain exemption clauses and requiring information to be given in mail order advertisements. *See:* MAIL ORDER; UNFAIR CONTRACT

Action against traders If a trader persists in committing a criminal offence under the Trade Descriptions Act 1968, or breaking contracts, the director-general of Fair Trading, in addition to prosecuting him, can ask for an assurance that he will trade fairly.

If he refuses – or gives an assurance and then breaks it – the director-general may ask the Restrictive Practices Court to make an order forbidding the trader to continue his unsatisfactory conduct. Breach of such an order amounts to CONTEMPT OF COURT, and the trader can be imprisoned.

If you wish to complain about an unfair trading practice, write to, or telephone, the Office of Fair Trading, Field House, Breams Buildings, London EC4 1PR.

The Office of Fair Trading has already obtained assurances from restaurants and hotels that they will comply with the food hygiene regulations, and from shops and suppliers of services that they will no longer supply defective goods or carry out defective workmanship and will promptly return money to dissatisfied customers.

FALSE IMPRISONMENT

*Compensation for a person
wrongfully detained*

It is an infringement of someone's civil liberty to detain him without legal cause in a cell, room or any other confined space against his will. He can claim compensation in the High Court or county court for false imprisonment.

A policeman commits false imprisonment if he places someone under arrest without a legal right to do so. If he unlawfully detains someone against their will, not necessarily in the cell of a police station, but even in the interviewing room, that, too, is false imprisonment.

Private charge If the police wrongfully arrest someone on the basis of information received from a private citizen – for example, a store security man – the informant cannot be held responsible for false imprisonment.

But if you report someone to the police, and they will act only if you make a CITIZEN'S ARREST and only if you sign the charge sheet at the police station, then you are liable for a claim for false imprisonment if the arrest is not justified.

> ## DAMAGES FOR A WORKER HELD BY SECURITY GUARDS
>
> *A security guard who detains a worker against his will is guilty of false imprisonment if the worker is proved innocent.*
>
> In 1918 the Graham-White Aviation Company suffered several thefts of aircraft construction materials from its factory at Hendon. Police found certain items in a house where one of the company's employees, an apprentice called Meering, was a lodger.
>
> Later, two members of the company's security force told Meering he was wanted for questioning by the police and he was escorted to a waiting room at the company's offices. The two security men waited outside. When the police arrived Meering was arrested and charged with receiving stolen property.
>
> At the court hearing Meering produced receipts showing he had bought all the items. He was found not guilty. He later sued the company for false imprisonment and malicious prosecution.
>
> ### DECISION
>
> The judge ruled that from the moment he met the security men Meering was no longer free. The security men were acting as private persons and had no power to detain someone on mere suspicion. Meering was awarded £250 damages for false imprisonment and £1,250 for malicious prosecution.
>
> The company appealed. The court said that the company had not authorised the guards to imprison Meering and could not be held responsible. The damages were reduced to 1 shilling for false imprisonment by the company's servants, though the award for malicious prosecution was upheld.

Other kinds of arrest

Not only the police can be guilty of false imprisonment. A store detective who holds a suspected shoplifter against his will is also guilty if the person is subsequently found innocent. So is a factory security guard who detains an innocent workman without his consent.

It is also false imprisonment for a patient to be kept against his will in a mental institution without having been found insane under the proper procedure. *See:* MENTAL DISORDER

Taking action

Anyone who believes himself to be wrongfully held should make it clear to those concerned that he will sue for false imprisonment. Such a warning may in itself secure release.

If you decide to sue it is often not sufficient to prove that you were innocent of the offence for which you were detained. You must show that you were held without your consent. It will frequently be the defence of the person sued that you agreed to be detained.

Compensation The courts award compensation for the indignity, mental anguish and, when appropriate, the damaging publicity of being falsely imprisoned. They also compensate for any loss of earnings.

A large number of civil actions against the police for false imprisonment succeed. Most are settled out of court to protect the reputation of the police. If they do reach court and it is shown that the police acted in an arbitrary or oppressive manner, the plaintiff may be awarded exemplary or punitive damages to emphasise the court's disapproval.

The police, however, are always justified in holding a person against his will, even if he is later found not guilty, if they had proper cause to ARREST him. *See:* POLICE

FAMILY ASSETS

Who owns what in the home

Each member of a family is entitled to his or her own property and has no claim on the property of any other member of the family. But a court may order either husband or wife to maintain the other.

The position changes when a marriage breaks down. Then, a husband or wife has a right to claim support from the other spouse and may be entitled to a share in the family home and other property. A child has a legal right to be supported by one or both parents. *See also:* MAINTENANCE; MATRIMONIAL PROPERTY

Family assets then become an important factor. The home, plus any savings made by the husband or the wife, the contents of the home, motor cars, stocks and shares and jewellery, paintings and books, record player and records are all family assets, no matter who bought them.

Any court deciding financial orders after SEPARATION or DIVORCE will take into account all the family assets and has the power to re-distribute them among the family. The court takes into account the needs of each member of the family and his or her contribution to the welfare of the family as a whole.

Even if one spouse is the sole owner or tenant of the matrimonial home, the other spouse will be entitled to live there if the court decides that it is reasonable. And either spouse may be given a share of the value of the home, depending on contributions made to buying it and to the welfare of the family, and on personal need.

No member of a family has any absolute legal right to share in the family assets. The law lays down that family assets can be shared or adjusted entirely at the discretion of the court, but only after divorce, NULLITY, judicial separation, or the death of the husband or wife. *See:* INHERITANCE

A husband and wife in dispute over property can ask a court to decide ownership even if they have no intention to get divorced or separated or before they begin to do so.

WHOSE BELONGINGS?

Each member of the family is entitled to his or her own property except when a marriage breaks down.

FAMILY FUND

Special help for handicapped children

The Family Fund, government financed, provides special help for severely handicapped children under the age of 16, who live at home. It is independently administered by a private charity, the Joseph Rowntree Memorial Trust.

The aim of the Family Fund is to give help not normally provided by the statutory services. Such help includes providing telephones, washing machines, driving lessons, holidays, clothing and recreational items.

Application can be made to the fund by any family which has in its care a child suffering from a very severe handicap causing severe subnormality or functional loss of more than one limb, major communication problems or serious management difficulties.

How a family may be able to qualify

There is no formal means test for applicants to the Family Fund, but no help is given to families unless they are in financial need.

The trust takes into account the family circumstances – the type of job and probable income of the father, and the type of house the family lives in. A well-paid worker with only one child would be unlikely to receive help.

People on supplementary benefit will have to apply to the social security office before asking the fund for help. No benefit will be lost. *See:* SUPPLEMENTARY BENEFIT

Grants from the fund of less than £50 are not usually made.

Write to The Family Fund, P.O. Box 50, York YO1 1UY.

FAMILY INCOME SUPPLEMENT

Extra money for low-wage households

A family living on a low wage from full-time work may be entitled to cash benefits known as Family Income Supplement. To qualify there must be at

WHEN YOU DO NOT WORK FOR AN EMPLOYER

A self-employed person working for at least 30 hours a week can claim Family Income Supplement.

least one child in the house and the breadwinner must be working for at least 30 hours a week (24 hours in the case of a single parent).

In normal family circumstances, it is the man who must be working, but a one-parent family with the mother working can also qualify.

If a man and a woman are living together as husband and wife but are not married they are treated as a two-parent family for Family Income Supplement purposes and the man must be working to qualify. The adults in the household need not be the parents of the children so long as they are providing for them; but foster children do not count because foster parents are already paid for keeping them.

Self-employed people working for at least 30 hours a week (24 hours for a single parent) can claim Family Income Supplement.

How to make a claim

Claims are made on leaflet FIS 1 obtainable from any post office or social security office. Normally, claims are dealt with entirely by post without a home visit or interview. If you think you are entitled, claim at once, even if you cannot give all the details asked for on the form. You can always send the details later. But if you claim late, the payments will not be backdated.

The amount To qualify for Family In-

come Supplement the family's normal income must be below a 'prescribed amount' laid down for each size of family. The amounts during 1981 were:

Number of children	Prescribed amount (per week, gross before tax)
1	£67
2	£74
3	£81
4	£88
5	£95

More than 5 children, add £7 for each child.

Maximum payments There is a limit to the amount of supplement that a family can claim, depending on the number of children. For a one-child family the maximum is £17 a week and it increases by £1.50 for each additional child. These figures, which include extra help towards heating cost, are raised from time to time.

Income To work out a family's normal income take gross earnings before tax and insurance deductions. Add the wife's income but do not include:

● The children's income, other than maintenance payments from an absent parent.
● Child benefit.
● Educational maintenance allowances.
● Rent allowance from the local council.
● Attendance allowance.
● Mobility allowance.
● The first £4 of a war pension.
● Payments for foster children.

If the total income is less than the prescribed amount the Family Income Supplement payable is roughly half the difference. For example, the prescribed amount for a family with 3 children is £81. If total income is £71, the difference is £10 and the Family Income Supplement payment would be £5 a week.

For a wage or salary earner, the supplement is based on earnings for the last 5 weeks, or 2 months for those paid monthly. But if recent earnings were higher than usual it is important to say so on the claim form because the lower the normal earnings the higher the Family Income Supplement payment.

For the self-employed, Family Income Supplement is based on net profit. This is normally the profit shown in the latest accounts, but if the figure is abnormally high an estimate of current profit should be submitted.

How long Family Income Supplement payments are normally awarded for 52 weeks and will continue at the same rate even if income rises or falls or the size of the family changes.

Anyone who falls sick or loses his job can go on drawing Family Income Supplement on top of any national insurance benefits until the end of the 52 week period, but Family Income Supplement will be taken into account in deciding if the family is entitled to SUPPLEMENTARY BENEFIT.

Extra benefits Any family receiving Family Income Supplement is automatically entitled to a number of other benefits – free milk and vitamins for children under 5 years 1 month and expectant mothers, free school meals, dental treatment, glasses and prescriptions, and payment of fares for hospital treatment. So it is worth claiming Family Income Supplement even if the family's income is not much below the prescribed amount.

Appeals Anyone who disagrees with the Family Income Supplement awarded can appeal to the local SUPPLEMENTARY BENEFIT appeal tribunal.

FAMILY WELFARE ASSOCIATION

Extra help for people in distress

People in distress from such problems as bereavement or marriage difficulties can get help from a voluntary organisation, the Family Welfare Association.

It consists of trained social workers who either visit people in their homes or see them in the offices of an official welfare agency.

The association works among people such as the handicapped, the isolated, the unemployed, or those who have problems with children.

Help is given by the association on its own or in liaison with the social services departments of local authorities. Its members can give intensive assistance in cases of a specialised nature, when the departments do not have the re-

sources to give enough attention to the problems.

People in distress can contact the association directly. The local address can usually be obtained from the social services department, a CITIZENS ADVICE BUREAU, or the telephone directory.

FATAL ACCIDENT

The rights of relatives to claim damages

If someone is killed because of another's negligence, the person responsible can be sued for damages – by dependent relatives or, if there are none, by the deceased's executor or administrator.

If the death occurs through an accident at work, the relatives may qualify for INDUSTRIAL DEATH BENEFIT.

Claims by relatives

Dependent relatives entitled to claim damages under the Fatal Accidents Act include wife or husband (but not someone cohabiting with the victim without being married), parents, children (including any adopted and illegitimate children), stepchildren, grandparents, grandchildren, brothers, sisters, uncles and aunts.

Damages are awarded for loss of cash benefit, not for grief, so awards for the death of a child are rare.

All claims for damages must be made within 3 years of the death, and NEGLIGENCE has to be proved.

HOW DAMAGES ARE ASSESSED AFTER A FATAL ACCIDENT

Mr Crosby was a car passenger who was killed when the driver negligently drove into a lamp-post. He was survived by a widow and young children. The court assessed the total damages payable to his dependants as follows:

Calculating Mr Crosby's net annual income

Pay after tax, national insurance contributions and union dues	£3,000
Income from investments	£100
Increase in the value of his home by do-it-yourself work	£100
Total financial contribution	£3,200

Calculating Mr Crosby's annual expenditure

Travelling, lunches, clothes, entertainment	£1,000
Share of family housekeeping bill	£500
Payment towards family holiday	£100
Life insurance	£100
Total expenditure	£1,700
So the gross annual dependency of family is	£1,500
Investments inherited by the family	£100
Net annual dependency of family	£1,400

Applying the multiplier

The judge decides that, as a fit 32-year-old, Mr Crosby would probably have worked until he was over 60. Because that is close to the maximum possible allowance, the judge multiplies the net annual dependency by 15:

£1,400 *multiplied by* 15	£21,000
Add the funeral expenses	£250
Total damages	£21,250

How damages are assessed

The court decides how much a claimant loses by the victim's death as follows:

● Deduct from the dead person's annual earnings at the time of death any tax payable and normal outgoings. (The court takes into account any rise in earnings that the deceased would have had between the death and the court hearing, but does not allow for any future rises.) The result is called the net annual dependency.

● Multiply that net annual dependency by a figure based on the number of years the person would have continued to provide support, taking into account his age and health. The maximum multiplier for a person with, say, 40 years' work ahead of him is 16. It might be only 2 or 3 if he was old and ill with a work expectancy of only a few years.

● Add any funeral expenses. The result of that calculation gives the total amount of damages.

How damages are reduced

If a dependant has benefited from the death by, for example, inheriting money or stocks and shares, that amount will be deducted from the damages awarded.

No deduction is made for life insurance or social security benefits paid on the victim's death. Nor is there any deduction when a relative, who is making the claim, inherits the home in which the deceased and the relative lived.

Damages awarded to dependent children are paid into the court, which supervises the money in the interests of the children.

If the dead person was partly responsible for the accident in which he was killed, the damages are reduced in proportion to the degree to which he was to blame. *See:* CONTRIBUTORY NEGLIGENCE

If there are no relatives

Even if an accident victim leaves no dependent relatives, damages can be claimed on behalf of his estate by his executor or administrator.

The claim can be made for:
● Funeral expenses.
● Compensation for any pain and suffering and medical expenses sustained by the deceased in any interval between the accident and death.
● Loss of deceased's potential future earnings less his estimated living costs.
● Damages of up to about £1,000 for loss of expectation of happiness by the cutting short of life.

FAULTY GOODS

When goods do not function as they should

If you buy goods that are faulty or cause injury or damage because of a defect, you have legal rights against the seller – provided that the seller was acting in the course of a business.

Provided you act promptly, you can reject the goods and claim your money back. Or you can choose not to reject them and instead claim compensation from the seller to make good the difference between what you paid and what the goods are worth.

You can also claim compensation from the seller if injury or damage has been caused because of the fault. *See:* DEFECTIVE GOODS

FENCE

One of the most common reasons for disputes between neighbours is the ownership of – and the liability therefore to repair and maintain – BOUNDARIES, WALLS AND FENCES.

FIDELITY INSURANCE

Protection against theft by an employee

A company whose employees regularly handle large sums of money can take out an insurance fidelity policy against fraud or theft by any of them.

Such a policy can cover all employees of a particular type – for example, wage cashiers or staff who take bets in a betting shop.

A more limited policy is one that gives cover for one particular, named employee. It is suitable for a small business or for a sports club in which one official deals with subscriptions and fees, and for holiday or Christmas savings clubs.

On the proposal form, you must state the precise duties to be carried out by the person in respect of whom you wish to insure. The insurance company must be told if he or she has any criminal convictions and if the business or club applying for the policy has ever lost money through anyone's dishonesty.

The insurance company may want to know if any references were checked when the person concerned was first employed or first took up his present duties. If they were not, the insurers may make their own inquiries.

All relevant facts must be declared on the proposal form, otherwise the insurers may later disclaim liability. *See:* INSURANCE POLICY

If you (the employee) are refused a fidelity policy, you may be sacked. If this occurs within 6 months of the day you joined the company, you cannot claim UNFAIR DISMISSAL. You have no legal right to know why the insurance company refused.

Taking precautions against loss

An insurance company issuing a fidelity policy may insist that the employer – or club committee – makes an effort to prevent the loss of cash by dishonesty.

For example, a regular check of cash tills, or regular inspection of club or business accounts or bank statements, may be required. Failure to take such precautions when required by the conditions of a policy would enable the insurers to avoid liability.

The insurers must also be notified of any change in the employee's duties as soon as it takes place. A cashier, for example, may be promoted to manager, or a club treasurer may resign and be replaced. If the insurers are not told of any such change, they can avoid liability for any subsequent loss.

Some insurance companies stipulate that the policy-holder must tell them at once if there is a suspicion that an employee is being dishonest. When told, they can demand that the police be informed, or – if so agreed in the policy – that the employer sue the suspected person for fraud or theft. In such cases, the insurers usually undertake to pay the employer's legal costs should the prosecution result in a conviction.

An employee whose suspected dishonesty is reported to an insurance company could sue his employer for libel. But he is unlikely to win the case unless he can prove that the report was made out of spite, as the court would normally accept the employer's plea of 'qualified privilege' – that he was obliged by contract to inform his insurers of such suspicions.

When money is lost

A fidelity policy lays down a maximum sum that can be claimed in case of loss. Some policies require the employer to take out a private prosecution – if evidence is available and the police do not prosecute – and to make all possible attempts to recover the money.

The insurers will pay only for money lost while a policy is in force. If a theft is committed before the policy is taken out, but discovered only when it is in force, no compensation is paid.

FILM CENSORSHIP

How standards in the cinema are controlled

Every cinema that shows films to the public must be licensed by the local authority. In practice, that means that the council can decide what sort of film can be shown in its district and whether there will be any restriction on who should see it.

If a cinema ignores the wishes of the council it could have its licence revoked.

In most areas, the committee of councillors responsible for vetting films is likely to take guidance from the British Board of Film Censors, an independent body, whose work has government approval, but which has no legal powers.

The councillors can also vary the board's recommendations. For example, they can rule that a film with an X certificate is suitable for showing to anyone over 14 in cinemas in their area, or they can decide that an A certificate film is not suitable for anyone under 18.

A council committee can allow the public showing of a film for which the board had refused a certificate.

A filmgoer has no legal right to appeal against the decision of a local authority or against a certificate issued by the Board of Film Censors. The only

HOW THE CENSORSHIP BOARD WORKS

The Board of Film Censors, set up more than 60 years ago by the film industry itself, views every film intended for public showing, and decides whether it should be cut, shown only to restricted audiences or not shown at all. Its verdict cannot be enforced, but is intended to guide or persuade distributors and local authorities.

Since 1923 the Home Office has recommended that local authorities should note the board's decisions in their rules for cinema licensing. But they do not do so in all respects. For example, no film is ever approved as being fit to show a child under 5 years of age. So in theory a child of that age could never legally be taken into a cinema during a performance if the local authority accepted the censorship board's recommendations.

The board gives a certificate to every film which it approves for public showing.

Every film that is to be shown in British cinemas is submitted by its distributors for examination by the board. Each is seen by at least two examiners who are expected by the board to take into account changing public attitudes.

They may in very rare cases decide not to give a certificate at all if they consider that a film merely exploits sex or violence. Yet they may approve one that they consider approaches responsibly a serious problem of sex and morality in society. In some cases independent experts are consulted by the examiners and even invited to see the film.

When the examiners do not agree, the film may be seen by two other examiners.

 The film is approved as suitable for showing to the public in general

 Parents may not want children under 14 to see some of this film

 The board thinks no person under the age of 14 should see the film

 The film is suitable only for adults and no person under 18 should be admitted

course of action is to write complaining to both the council and the board.

Rules for film clubs

A cinema club can be run without a licence from a local authority.

A club can show a film which has no certificate from the Board of Film Cen-

---

WHEN THE CENSOR CAN BE OVER-RULED

The local authority may decide that a film is suitable for children after all.

sors, and may have been banned by the local authority, but it does run the risk that it could be prosecuted under the Obscene Publications Act if it shows a banned film that is judged to be obscene.

The police can bring a prosecution against any club or cinema under the same Act, even if the film shown has been given a Board of Film Censors' certificate and has been approved by the local authority. The consent of the Director of Public Prosecutions is required.

FINANCE HOUSE LOAN

A cash loan from a finance company or other money lender is subject to the same rules as any other CREDIT AGREEMENT, as long as it does not exceed £5,000.

Even if the sum borrowed does exceed £5,000, however, if you believe that the interest being charged is unfairly high, you can ask a county court to alter it in your favour. *See:* INTEREST CHARGE

FINE

Making an offender pay

A fine is a financial penalty imposed on an offender. It is the most common sentence handed out in the magistrates' and criminal courts. The offender is ordered to pay a specified sum within a fixed period with the possibility of going to prison if he fails to do so.

For some offences there is a maximum fine that can be imposed. If no maximum is laid down the court can order as large a fine as it wants, though there is an absolute limit of £1,000 in magistrates' courts.

The amount of the fine, which is not tax deductible, usually reflects the gravity of the offence and sometimes the defendant's financial circumstances. The court is unlikely to impose a large fine on a person of inadequate means.

Time to pay

Only rarely will a court order a fine to be paid immediately. Usually the defendant is given time to pay, and may also be allowed to do so by instalments.

If the court thinks the defendant is incapable of managing his affairs well enough to save money for the fine, it can make a fines supervision order under which a probation officer will be ap-

---

TIME TO PAY

In most cases, a court will allow a convicted person time to pay any fine imposed.

'Thanks, guv! Time to pay?'

THE PRISON SENTENCES FOR UNPAID FINES

As a last resort, courts can gaol an offender who refuses to pay a fine. The maximum length of the sentence depends on the amount owed.

Amount due	Gaol for up to
Up to £25	7 days
£25 to £50	14 days
£51 to £200	30 days
£201 to £500	60 days
£501 to £1,000	90 days
£1,001 to £2,500	6 months
£2,501 to £5,000	9 months
over £5,000	12 months

---

pointed to help him. But in this case the fine must still be paid to the court, not the probation officer.

There are exceptional cases in which the offender can be ordered to pay the fine immediately or go to prison:
1. If the offence is punishable by imprisonment and the defendant has the means to pay immediately.
2. If it is thought that the offender may leave the country.
3. If he is already serving, or is about to serve, a prison or detention sentence.

Failure to pay If the fine is not paid by the date set, the defendant will be ordered to attend a means inquiry at the court. His circumstances may have changed for the worse since the fine was imposed, in which case the amount may be reduced or even cancelled. Often he will simply be given more time to pay or the instalments will be reduced.

However the court also has various sanctions which can be used against defaulters:

Search The court can order the defendant to be searched on the spot. Any money found on him can be used to pay the fine or any amount due in compensation or costs.

Prison Committal to prison is rarely used unless all other methods of enforcing a fine have failed. In any case it can be ordered only if the original offence was punishable by imprisonment and if the defendant has the means to pay the

fine but refuses to do so.

A persistent defaulter may be given a suspended prison sentence which will take effect only if the fine remains unpaid.

Detention When the unpaid fine is only a small amount, a court is likely to order the defendant to be detained in the cells for the rest of the day as an alternative to prison. He must be released by 8 p.m. That wipes out the fine.

Attachment A person who is working can have an unpaid fine deducted by instalments from his wages. The court will order his employer to do this. *See:* EARNINGS, Attachment of

Community work A person who fails or refuses to pay a fine may be given the chance of doing unpaid community work as an alternative, but that is not automatic. *See:* COMMUNITY SERVICE ORDER

Fines on children The maximum fine that can be imposed on a defendant aged 10 to 13 is £50. From age 14 to 17, the maximum is £200.

The fine can be enforced by a SUPERVISION ORDER, by attachment of earnings, or by making the parent or guardian responsible for payment – in which case the adult becomes subject to the same penalties for non-payment as the offender.

If someone who has been fined reaches the age of 17 before it has been paid, he can be dealt with thereafter as if he were an adult.

Other kinds of fines that may be imposed

A penalty imposed by a council lending library on someone who fails to return a book or record on time can be enforced in a magistrates' court, provided that the council has a BYE-LAW permitting such fines.

If there is such a bye-law someone who fails to pay a library fine can be prosecuted for breaking it. If there is no such bye-law, the council can sue the person in the county court for debt – although it is unlikely to do so over a small sum.

Trade union 'fines' A financial penalty imposed by a trade union on a member who has broken its rules cannot be enforced in the courts. Failure to pay, however, can result in expulsion from the union. *See:* TRADE UNION

FINGERPRINTING

*When the police have a right
to take your fingerprints*

The police can take fingerprints from anyone over 14 who gives consent or

HOW FINGERPRINTS ARE KEPT

When someone is convicted his fingerprints will be taken and they are kept permanently on file.

who has been ordered by a magistrate to be fingerprinted.

They may fingerprint a child under 14 only with his parents' consent.

When fingerprints have been taken by consent, and the person is acquitted, the police automatically destroy the prints.

Confirmation that they have been destroyed will generally be given by the officer in charge of the case.

THE WOMAN DRIVER WHO BIT THE POLICE

If a magistrate orders fingerprinting of a person on bail, it can be done only on court premises.

Mrs Jones, who suffered from arthritis, was beaten for a parking space in Kingston-upon-Thames, Surrey. She drove her car into the one that had occupied the space.

A police constable who saw the incident accused her of a driving offence. When Mrs Jones disputed the allegation, the constable called for assistance and she was taken to a police station.

Bail was granted, but the officers wanted fingerprints. Mrs Jones refused.

The police obtained a court order, then attempted to take her fingerprints by force – at the police station. After she had bitten two of them, they gave up and charged her with assaulting them in the execution of their duty, as well as dangerous driving.

Mrs Jones was found guilty at Kingston Crown Court, but appealed against her conviction on the ground that the jury was misdirected.

DECISION

Mr Justice Pain ruled that the police had no power to take Mrs Jones's prints at the station – only at the courthouse where the order was made. So their use of force was a criminal assault, and she was entitled to bite them to resist it.

Mrs Jones's convictions were quashed.

Prints taken to eliminate innocent people from criminal inquiries – for example, those of a family whose home has been burgled – are also destroyed as soon as the case is over.

When an arrested person refuses to be fingerprinted

The police can apply for a magistrate's order only after summonsing or arresting a person and charging him with an offence for which he could be imprisoned. A condition of the order is that prints must be destroyed if the person is not convicted.

Fingerprinting by court order can be done only on court premises, if bail is granted, or at a prison or remand centre if a person is held in custody. If he resists, reasonable force can be used.

What happens to fingerprints after a trial

When someone is convicted, fingerprints taken by court order are kept permanently in police files. If prints have not already been taken, the criminal is fingerprinted after being admitted to prison. So if a convicted person is given a suspended sentence or put on probation, he cannot be fingerprinted then.

Even when a convicted person's prison sentence is ended, he cannot ask for his fingerprints to be destroyed.

If there is a complaint against the police

Someone who later claimed that his fingerprints had been taken illegally – without true consent, or outside the powers granted by a court order – could make a formal POLICE complaint, or attempt an action for trespass. If force was used, he might allege assault.

Although, in theory, damages could be awarded, and the court could order the prints to be destroyed if the complainant were eventually acquitted, no alleged irregularity in the fingerprinting procedure can affect their admissibility in evidence.

WHEN THE POLICE CAN PHOTOGRAPH YOU

The police have no special right to photograph anyone, unless he is in prison awaiting trial and they have obtained an order from a magistrate.

There is, however, no law forbidding the police or anyone else from photographing people, and the police cannot legally be forced to destroy photographs taken without consent.

If the police take a photograph of someone who is being questioned, without his consent, he is entitled to complain to a senior officer, but normally he has no legal right to stop the photography.

If, however, they were to use force or some subterfuge – such as asking the suspect to step into a room, and taking a picture as he does so – he might have grounds for an official POLICE complaint or an action for ASSAULT or TRESPASS.

Photographing the public at large

It is not a TORT to photograph people while they are taking part in a demonstration, and the police can legally keep a file of the resulting pictures.

It would, however, be an offence to take photographs of people entering a court building to attend the trial of anyone charged with offences arising out of the demonstration.

If that happened, the trial judge should be informed, so that he could summon the photographer before him. The photographs would almost certainly be destroyed by judge's order.

HOW FINGERPRINTS CAN SOLVE A CRIME
When a criminal is caught because he left his mark at the scene of his offence

1 When entering a home, a burglar may be leaving clues to his identity on every window or piece of furniture that he touches during the course of the burglary.

2 After the crime, the police are called to investigate. While one officer talks to the owners of the house to find out if they saw or heard anything, the fingerprint officer 'dusts' the windows, doors and furniture with a special powder that will reveal any fingerprints left by the burglar.

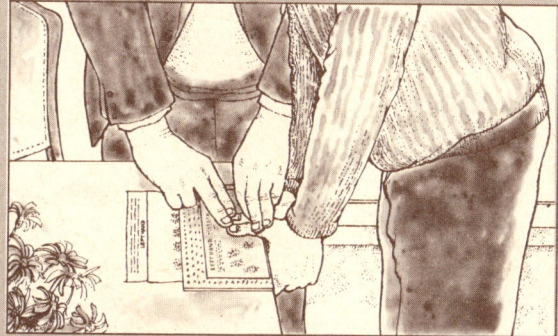 

3 To eliminate the marks left by people who live in the burgled house, or who are known to have been there recently, legitimately, all their fingerprints are taken. They will be destroyed later. When the police have a suspect, the police will take his prints or – if he refuses – ask a magistrate to allow them to do so.

4 When the police have no suspect, and have eliminated the prints of the family who have been burgled, and any friends or visitors, an expert compares any fingerprints unaccounted for with similar prints already filed on the central microfilm register of the National Fingerprint Collection.

5 The police can use the evidence of the fingerprints when the suspect is brought to court. If he is convicted, his fingerprints are kept permanently in police files. Even when he has finished his sentence, he cannot ask for them to be destroyed. If he is acquitted and his fingerprints were taken only by magistrate's order, they must be destroyed.

FIRE

When a careless person burns someone's property

Anyone who, by negligence, starts a fire that harms another person or his property, is liable for damages.

This is so even if the person did not actually light the fire, but caused it by, for example, storing petrol and highly inflammable material together. He is also liable if the fire was started by someone authorised to be on his property – for example, a plumber using a blowlamp carelessly. In such a case, the plumber is also liable for damages.

Even when the victim of the fire has FIRE INSURANCE, the person responsible for the fire may still have to pay damages. The insurance company is entitled to sue him for recovery of the sum that it paid out to the insured.

Anyone who intentionally burns someone else's property is dealt with under a CRIMINAL DAMAGE charge.

Bonfires It is an offence to light a bonfire in a smokeless zone. Neighbours seriously inconvenienced by a bonfire can sue whoever is responsible.

See: AIR POLLUTION
NUISANCE

FIRE INSURANCE

How to protect yourself against loss by fire

By taking out a householder's INSURANCE POLICY, you insure your building and its contents against damage by fire – as well as against other risks. Although it is more usual to insure some properties – for example, a granary – against fire only, most usual dwellings are covered against fire by comprehensive policies.

Fire insurance under a household comprehensive policy covers damage or destruction by fire, lightning, earthquake and explosion. Such a policy also covers other risks. *See:* PROPERTY INSURANCE

Taking out fire insurance

When you complete the insurance proposal form – whether for a comprehensive policy or, in rare cases, for fire only – take care to set a proper value on your building and possessions. Describe them in detail and make sure that the insured value is enough to cover rebuilding of the property if it is completely destroyed.

In completing the form, you must also disclose all material facts. For example, if you have ever suffered loss by fire, you must disclose that to the insurers. You must also tell them if another company has refused to insure you or your property, or to renew any type of policy for you.

Even matters not related to fire or insurance – such as a criminal record of any kind – must be disclosed, if they would be relevant to the reliability of a policyholder.

If a policyholder has lied about any fact, or has withheld relevant information, the insurers are entitled to refuse any claim that he makes.

Understanding the conditions of the policy

Every policy contains conditions which, if you break them, entitle the insurance company to reject your claim: read the conditions carefully before signing the proposal. If necessary, ask for a copy of the type of policy that will be issued to you.

For fire insurance, there are usually conditions entitling the company to avoid paying compensation:

THE EX-ROBBER WHOSE HOUSE BURNED DOWN

Anyone taking out fire insurance must disclose any criminal conviction that he may have, even if he is not directly asked to do so.

Mr W was convicted in 1960 on a robbery charge. The following year, he bought a house. He obtained a mortgage of £12,000 from the Bristol and West Building Society, which insured the property on his behalf with the Sun Alliance and London Insurance Ltd.

In 1974 the house burned down. Mr W claimed the insurance, but the insurers refused to pay. Mr W sued them in the High Court.

The insurance company maintained that when Mr W knew that the building society was applying for insurance on his behalf, he should have disclosed his criminal past, even though such information was not specifically demanded in the building society's insurance application.

Mr W, it was said, should have given the information when answering the question, 'Are there any other matters which you wish to be taken into account?'

Mr W had replied, 'No'.

DECISION

The court upheld the insurers' refusal to pay. It ruled that anyone who applies for insurance is bound to disclose any facts that a reasonable and prudent insurer would regard as material – even if those facts are not specifically asked for.

THE WOMAN WHO HID HER MONEY IN THE FIREPLACE

Anything that is burned by accident – no matter how or where – can properly be claimed for.

Mrs Flora Harris became nervous about her valuables after burglars tried to break into her flat in Putney, London. On December 2, 1939, when she was about to go out, she wrapped up her jewellery and £128 in notes in a newspaper and hid them in her fireplace, under an unlit fire.

Next morning, she lit the fire. By the time she remembered her hoard in the grate, most of the money and jewels had been destroyed.

Mrs Harris claimed their value under her Lloyd's fire-insurance policy, but was refused. She then sued the Lloyd's underwriter, Mr Poland, who had sold her the policy.

In the High Court, Mrs Harris maintained that, as the hoard had been ignited accidentally and had not been intended for fuel, the fire was covered by her policy. Lloyd's contended that as the fire had been in a grate and had not spread beyond, it could not be covered by fire insurance – but only under an 'all-risk' policy.

DECISION

Lloyd's were ordered to pay. The court ruled that since the property had been burned accidentally, it did not matter that it was the property – and not the fire – that was not in its proper place.

● If you have not notified the insurers of damage to, or destruction of, the property.

● If you have disposed of the property.

Making a claim

A fire-damage claim must be submitted within 30 days of the fire. The claim should give full details of the damage and how it was caused. If there is any difficulty about complying with that requirement, ask your insurer to extend the time limit.

What you can claim for after a fire

Any accidental fire damage is covered by fire insurance, whether or not there has been negligence – even if it was negligence by the insured person.

Fire insurance can in theory be claimed only if there has been ignition, although ALL-RISKS INSURANCE may cover damage caused by heat alone – such as scorching. In any case, despite the wording of a comprehensive or fire-only policy, the insurer normally pays compensation for scorch damage.

Damage by smoke You can claim for smoke damage caused by a fire that breaks out in your home or near by, but not for damage caused by smoke leaking from a faulty heating stove.

If a fire brigade causes damage while putting out a fire – if, for example, carpets and decorations are drenched in water or chemical foam – you can claim. You are also covered for any damage caused to property while it is being removed from the path of the fire.

If your house has to be demolished to prevent flames spreading from a neighbouring property to other houses, that is regarded as a loss by fire – even though the flames have not touched your house – and you can claim.

How much you can claim

When making a claim, you must prove the value of your loss. If, for example, your house is insured for £40,000 and is then totally destroyed by fire, you should receive the full sum, provided that you can prove that the property was worth that amount. You can do so by proving the purchase price and allowing for any general rise in prices that has occurred since you bought the property. The insurance

company's assessor can also be shown any similar properties in your immediate neighbourhood.

If you can prove only a value of, say, £35,000, that is the maximum sum you can recover.

A householder's policy occasionally contains a clause – known as an 'average' clause – to protect the insurers against under-insuring. If your property is under-insured, you will receive only a proportion of the cost of the damage.

If, for example, a property is worth £80,000 but is insured for only £40,000, the most you can recover from the insurer is half the value of the damage. If the property is insured for £60,000 – three-quarters of the value – you can claim up to three-quarters of your loss.

Whether there is an average clause or not, you can expect to be asked to declare on the proposal form that you have stated the full value of the property.

If such a declaration is given, and you subsequently make a claim, the insurer may be able to show that you were under-insured. If so, the insurer may refuse to pay.

If no average clause applies, which is the usual position, and the declaration

does not apply for the future the insurer may or may not be entitled to insist on 'averaging' and refuse to pay. You should resist any attempt to compensate you for less than the amount for which you have insured.

Loss of business If fire causes you loss of business – for example, if your shop burns down – you can claim for that loss of business only if you have taken out consequential loss insurance.

Deliberate fire raising If someone deliberately sets fire to your property, you are still entitled to claim on your insurance. The only bar to such a claim would arise if a policyholder knew that the fire was to be started. *See:* ARSON

When a home is made uninhabitable

If your home burns down or is made uninhabitable by fire, then – provided that you have consequential loss insurance – you can claim the cost of alternative accommodation as well as the cost of the damage. A comprehensive policy usually includes that benefit, but a fire-only policy seldom does.

An accommodation claim is covered by a section of the policy usually called

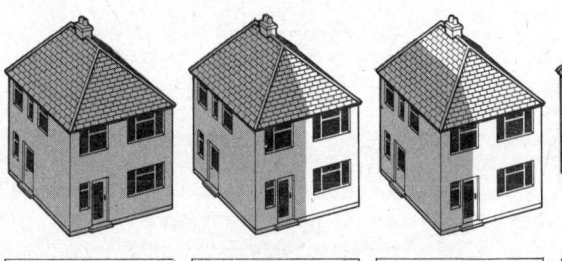

WHAT HAPPENS WHEN YOU ARE UNDER-INSURED
How an 'average clause' in a household contents policy can work

HOUSE CONTENTS ACTUALLY WORTH	HOUSE CONTENTS INSURED FOR	CONTENTS LOST ACTUALLY WORTH	INSURANCE COMPANY WILL PAY ONLY
£10,000	£5,000	£3,000	£1,500

Check your policy carefully to ensure that it does not contain an average clause. Such a clause is unusual in general household comprehensive policies, but if your insurer includes one, you must be sure to declare the full value of the property and its contents each time you renew the policy. If the house contents are insured for only a proportion of their full value, the insurers will pay only that proportion of the value of any claim for loss. For example, if the full value of the contents is £10,000, but they are insured for only £5,000, and goods worth £3,000 are stolen, the insurers will pay only £1,500.

'loss of rent', which allows an extra 10 per cent on top of the total insured value for the cost of housing you until your property has been restored.

However, the insurance company will not pay to accommodate you at a higher standard of living than you are used to. It will normally meet the bill for an enforced stay at a reasonable hotel – deducting from the bill what you would have spent if you had still been living at home. You would be entitled to stay in a luxury hotel only if there was no other accommodation available.

If you are put up by relatives or friends, the insurer will pay towards the expense of staying with them, provided that you can produce receipts.

You are normally expected to pay your hotel and rent bills and claim for them afterwards. However, the insurance company may agree to make an advance payment before the final settlement.

Landlord's loss If a tenant is forced out of his home by fire damage, his landlord can claim 'loss of rent' compensation provided that the landlord has taken out consequential loss insurance. The tenant should generally insure against loss of accommodation as well as loss of his belongings.

FIRE SERVICE

Calling the brigade in an emergency

It is the duty of the local fire brigade to answer all emergency calls at any time to attend a fire. Anyone can call the brigade free of charge by dialling 999 on the telephone.

You may be asked for your address or telephone number and the fire brigade headquarters may call you back to check details.

It is a criminal offence to make a false call. The maximum punishment is 3 months' gaol and a £100 fine.

The fire brigade will also undertake rescue work, especially when life is in danger. They can be called to road accidents, industrial or building-site accidents – for example, when a ditch caves in and buries someone – or home accidents.

Putting out a fire Firemen on duty have a right to force their way into any property at any time of the day or night

in order to put out a fire. No notice need be given to the owner of the premises. Anyone who tries to stop a fireman entering a building which is on fire commits an offence and can be fined £25. *See also:* FIRE INSURANCE

When you have to pay

The local fire authority can charge for any service other than putting out fires, but in practice no charge is made in any emergency when life is in danger. A charge is also unlikely when suffering or injury has been caused.

For example, parents would probably not get a bill for the rescue of a child whose head was trapped in railings.

However, the fire brigade will almost certainly charge for rescuing a trapped pet, such as a cat caught in a tree.

The bill is payable by whoever calls the brigade: if that person is not the owner of the animal, he must pay and then try to claim from the owner. The charge will cover a hire fee for any vehicle used, as well as an hourly rate for each man taking part in the rescue. Whoever calls the brigade is usually told in advance what the charge is likely to be.

The rescue service will almost certainly be free if a valuable farm animal is at risk – if, for example, a pedigree breeding cow or thoroughbred stallion is trapped in a ditch.

Pumping out floods Firemen will pump out flooded homes or factory premises, but a charge may be made. In practice, a company is usually charged, but private homes are often pumped out free of charge – especially if the occupier is old or disabled.

Fire prevention The local fire authority will advise private householders or firms in business premises on methods of fire prevention. They will also check private fire hoses and extinguishers. A charge is negotiated in advance for such a service.

FIREGUARDS

Compulsory protection for fires and heaters

All gas and electric fires and oil heaters offered for sale must be fitted with a proper fireguard when they are offered for sale. That regulation includes any

SAFETY RULES

A guard on a fire or a heater, to comply with the law, must pass strict tests laid down by the British Standards Institution. It must:
● Stand up to 11 lb. pressure for at least 1 minute and still meet all other safety requirements.
● Spring back to its original position automatically, if it is a hinged guard.
● Give at least $1\frac{1}{4}$ in. of clearance from the flame or element.
● Be far enough away from the element or flame to prevent a piece of material, placed against the guard, from bursting into flame in less than 10 seconds.
● Stand a hammer blow, if made of glass.
● Be accompanied by a warning, on the appliance, that the guard should not be removed.

fire using liquid gas or gas in a portable container. Any trader or supplier who puts a fire or heater on sale without a guard is committing an offence under the Consumer Safety Act 1978, and can be gaoled for up to 3 months and fined up to £1,000. The trading standards officers of local authorities are responsible for enforcing the regulations. *See:* CONSUMER SAFETY

If someone is injured or if his property is damaged because a fire or heater has been sold without a proper guard, he can claim damages under the Consumer Safety Act.

When a child is hurt

It is not an offence for a person to use a heater or a fire in the home without a proper guard. But if a child under 12 is killed or seriously injured by a fire or heater which is insufficiently protected, the person in charge of the child can be prosecuted under the Children and Young Persons Act.

Exempted heaters A fire or heater specially made for industrial use does not have to be fitted with a safety guard if the appliance is not suitable for heating residential premises.

Other heaters exempted include electric fires designed only to fit on a ceiling, and any heater so designed that the flame or element is completely enclosed within the structure of the appliance, so that there is no danger of personal injury from contact with the flame or element.

FIREWORKS

How safety laws apply

It is a criminal offence to let off fireworks in a street or public place, even if there is no danger and no one is frightened or annoyed by them. The maximum penalty is a £200 fine.

Factories where fireworks are made must be licensed by the Health and Safety Executive of the Department of Employment. Anyone who makes fireworks on unlicensed premises can face a £1,000 fine in a magistrates' court or an unlimited fine in a crown court.

Fireworks and explosives must not be sold to anyone who appears to be under the age of 16, whether by a shop or an individual. The maximum penalty for that offence is a £200 fine.

Fireworks may not be sold or exposed for sale in a street or public place: the maximum fine is £2.

All fireworks except sparklers, jumping crackers, 'throw-downs' – which explode on hitting the ground – and fireworks weighing less than ⅛ oz. or intended for export, must be marked with the name and address of the manufacturer. The maximum penalty for failing to do so is a £10 fine.

FISHERMAN

Special benefit for self-employed

A self-employed fisherman whose income includes a share of the gross earnings or profits derived from a boat's catches, pays a higher rate of Class 2 NATIONAL INSURANCE CONTRIBUTIONS than other self-employed people. In return, he qualifies – unlike other self-employed people – for unemployment benefit.

He does not get benefit for the first 3 days' unemployment, but is paid thereafter for each working day on which he is not employed. If he makes a fresh claim within 3 months of the first, he does not have to wait 3 days before beginning to receive benefit.

To claim unemployment benefit, the fisherman must have done no fishing on the days concerned – and must not have refused any reasonable opportunities of fishing work.

Fishermen liable for the higher Class 2 contribution also pay Class 4 contributions – a percentage of their annual profits. *See:* SEASONAL WORKER

FISHING

Where permission must be obtained to go fishing

Everyone has the right to fish at any time in the sea and in tidal waters, except where local laws forbid it.

Tidal waters extend upstream to where fresh water begins, or to where normal tides no longer move the water. To fish off a pier, you must obtain the permission of the owner – usually the local council.

Freshwater fishing You may not fish in a freshwater river or stream, a lake, a pond or a canal without permission from the owners of the fishing rights.

The rights in a river belong to those who own the land next to it – whoever owns the river bank also owns the half of the river bed on his side. Fishing rights on lakes and ponds belong to the owner of the surrounding land.

Information about fishing rights on canals can be obtained from the Fisheries Officer at the British Waterways Board.

The simplest way to obtain freshwater fishing rights is to join an angling club.

When a licence is needed

As well as getting permission from the owner of the fishing rights, an angler usually needs a licence.

It is obtained from the fisheries officer of the local water authority, or from certain post offices, fishing-tackle shops and angling clubs. The fee varies from area to area. A licence is essential for salmon or trout fishing in all areas of Britain.

Anyone with this licence can automatically fish for all other freshwater fish and eels.

A licence is needed to fish for freshwater fish other than salmon or trout in all areas except Cornwall, Cumberland, Devon, Hampshire, Mersey and Weaver, and the Shropshire Union Canal and the area of the Hertfordshire Lee.

A licence usually authorises only one named person to fish and to use only one rod. But someone with exclusive fishing rights on a stretch of water can obtain a licence which enables him to authorise other anglers to fish in his waters. This authority must be given to each angler in writing.

It is an offence to fish without the necessary licence and maximum penalties range from a £100 fine, for a first offence, to 2 years' imprisonment. *See:* POACHING

An angler who accidentally hooks a fish for which he does not have a licence does not commit an offence provided that he returns it to the water at once.

FISHING WITHOUT THE
RIGHT LICENCE

If you hook the wrong fish it is not an offence provided you throw it back right away.

Protected species Burbot, dolphins and porpoises can be protected by conservation laws against any unlicensed killing or catching, in the same way as animals in danger of extinction.

Close seasons There is no close season for sea-fishing, but periods have been set aside in which it is forbidden to fish inland, to allow fish to breed in safety. The exact dates can be obtained from the river authority, but, in general, close seasons are:

Salmon	November 1 – January 31
Trout	October 1 – February 29 (except rainbow trout, which are a matter for bye-law)
Coarse fish	March 15 – June 15

Illegal fishing Explosives, poisons and electrical devices may not be used for fishing, either inland or at sea. It is also an offence to use a light for taking fish. Fish roe may not be used as bait and there are various instruments – for example a firearm, gaff, spear, wire or snare – that may not be used to hook fish.

FIXTURES AND FITTINGS

*What a tenant can take
when he leaves*

A tenant may not carry out improvements to the property by adding to or altering the landlord's fixtures and fittings or erecting television or radio aerials, without the landlord's consent, although the landlord cannot withhold his consent unreasonably. *See:* LANDLORD AND TENANT

A tenant with a lengthy lease who has improved his home by installing new fittings may be able to take most of the fittings he has had installed when he leaves the property.

Any article that can be removed without causing serious damage to the building or land to which it is attached is a removable chattel, and the tenant has an automatic right to take it with him.

A light bulb, for example, is a removable fitting, but the socket is not. A can opener screwed to the wall could be taken away, but not a sink, which could leave a gaping hole if taken out.

Domestic fixtures In recent years courts have allowed tenants to remove fixtures installed for domestic convenience or ornament, such as split-level cookers, decorative chimney pieces, wall cupboards, panelling and even central-heating pipes from a greenhouse, but not the boiler. The courts' main concern has been to ensure that the removal did not cause extensive damage. But what constitutes extensive damage is a matter of opinion.

Increasing property value Any permanent improvement by the tenant to the property that has increased its rateable value – such as the erection of a sun lounge, verandah or greenhouse – is the sort of improvement likely to be regarded as the landlord's possession.

The tenant is allowed to remove it only if he is prepared to provide the landlord with a replacement, but that will not often be possible. If, for exam-

WHAT ADDITIONS MAY GO – AND WHAT MUST STAY
A tenant's rights depend on how much damage he would cause

Anything that is built into or attached to the structure of a building is legally a fixture. That means that a tenant cannot normally remove it when he leaves, even if he paid for it. But the courts allow tenants to take some fixtures that they have added for ornamental purposes or for domestic convenience – provided that their removal causes no more than superficial damage to the fabric of the house or flat. Even that damage must be put right at the tenant's expense if the terms of his lease require him to 'deliver up the premises in good and decorative repair'.

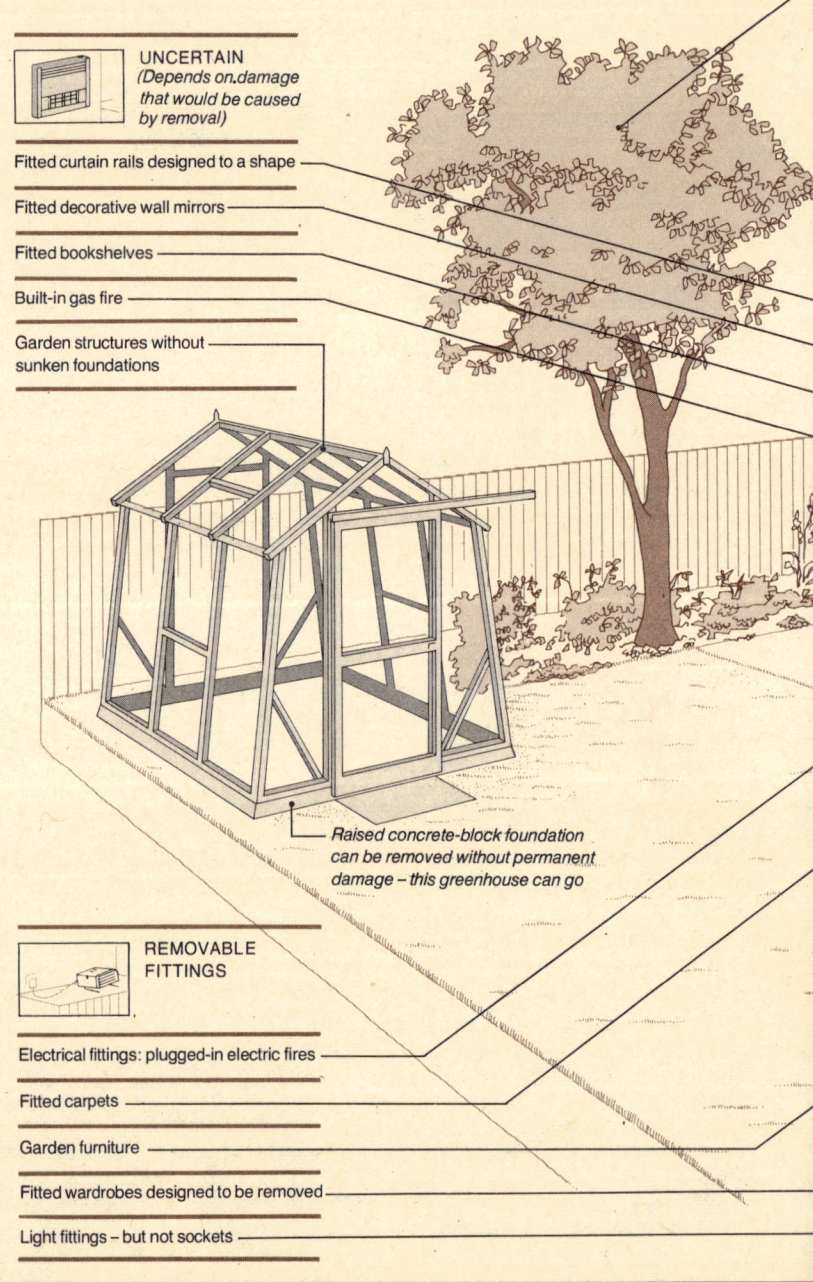

UNCERTAIN
(Depends on damage that would be caused by removal)

Fitted curtain rails designed to a shape

Fitted decorative wall mirrors

Fitted bookshelves

Built-in gas fire

Garden structures without sunken foundations

Raised concrete-block foundation can be removed without permanent damage – this greenhouse can go

REMOVABLE FITTINGS

Electrical fittings: plugged-in electric fires

Fitted carpets

Garden furniture

Fitted wardrobes designed to be removed

Light fittings – but not sockets

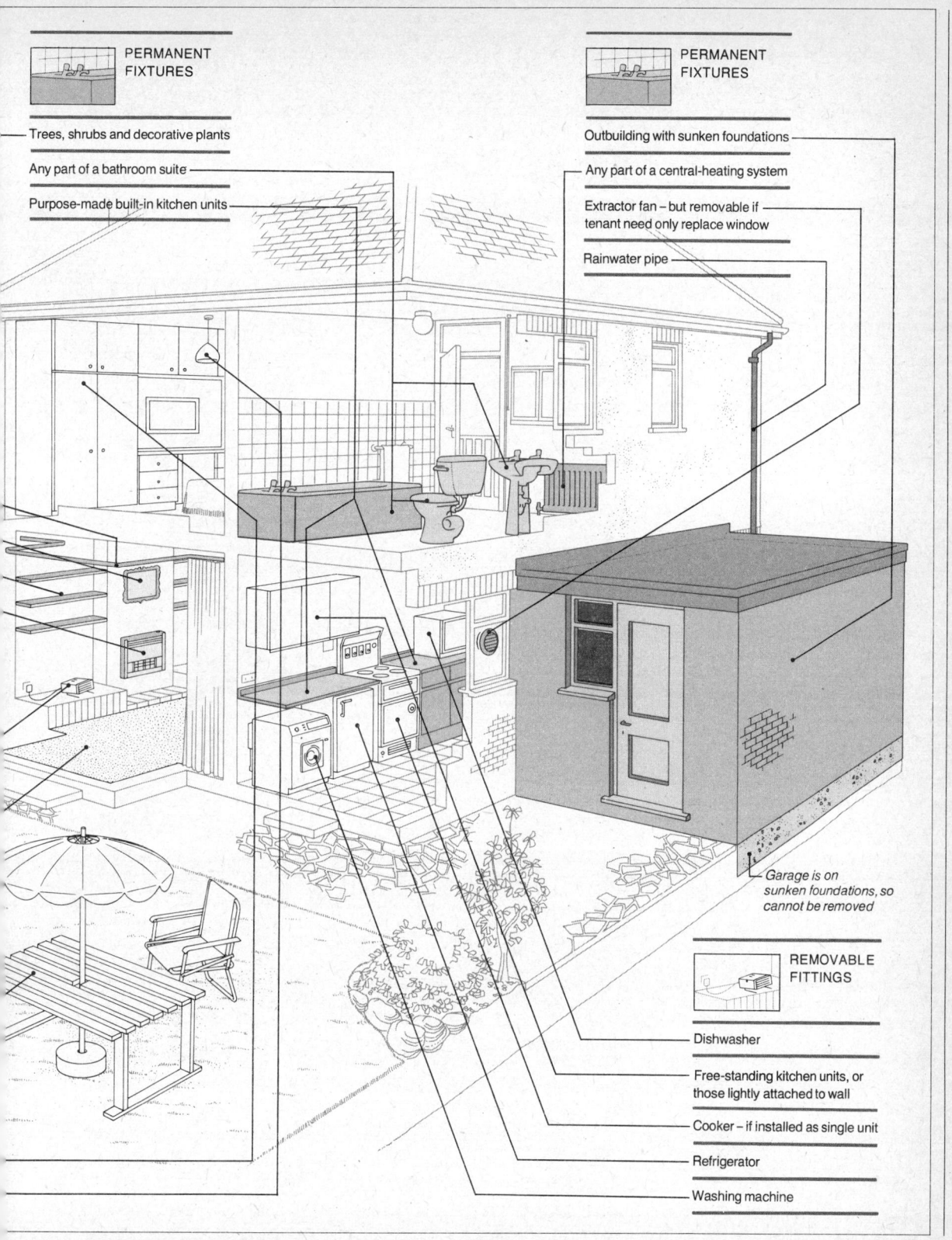

Trees, shrubs and decorative plants

Any part of a bathroom suite

Purpose-made built-in kitchen units

PERMANENT FIXTURES

Outbuilding with sunken foundations

Any part of a central-heating system

Extractor fan – but removable if tenant need only replace window

Rainwater pipe

Garage is on sunken foundations, so cannot be removed

REMOVABLE FITTINGS

Dishwasher

Free-standing kitchen units, or those lightly attached to wall

Cooker – if installed as single unit

Refrigerator

Washing machine

YOU CAN TAKE IT WITH YOU
WHEN YOU GO

A house seller can take anything he has installed providing it can be removed without causing serious damage and that he has agreed the removal with the buyer.

ple, a tenant has replaced a sun lounge with a new, expensive one, he can take it away and refit the landlord's original structure.

The tenant must remove any fixtures he wants before the landlord takes repossession of the property – otherwise the tenant forfeits them automatically at the handover.

Legal action A tenant who is in doubt about the permissible amount of damage caused by removing a fixture should consult a solicitor.

If a tenant removes a fixture which a landlord believes he has no right to take, or if a landlord prevents a tenant from taking a fixture to which the tenant believes he is entitled, then either can sue the other in the county court.

Effects on rent Improvements a tenant makes to the property he is renting do not affect the rent he is liable to pay.

If a rent officer calls to fix a fair rent, the tenant should tell him of any improvements he has made outside the terms of the lease. The officer will ignore them in assessing the rent.

FLAT

Making sure who is responsible for what

People living in flats as tenants have their rights protected by the Rent Act

and the laws governing the relationship between LANDLORD AND TENANT.

But there can be complications for anyone planning to buy a flat – mainly because of the sometimes conflicting interests of neighbours.

Buying a leasehold flat

Freehold flats, where the owner also has complete possession of the land on which they are built, are rare. Most are bought leasehold, usually for 99 or 999 years. *See:* LEASEHOLD LAND

The lease governs the relationship of the flat-owner with the owner of the whole block or building and the other residents.

Always read it carefully – and if possible have it checked by a lawyer – to see that it gives access to passages and stairways, rights to water, sewage and power and use of communal services such as lifts and TV aerials.

If it does not make these matters clear, the value of the flat may be reduced and it may be difficult to re-sell or raise a loan on the property.

The lease will usually require the flat-owner to contribute to a block insurance policy. If so, check it carefully to make sure exactly what is covered and for how much.

Repairs and decoration by landlord or tenant

The lease should make clear whether you must repair the main walls of your flat or decorate the exterior, and whether the other flat-owners must do the same.

Make sure that the arrangements for repairs and decoration cover the whole building: if someone is not made responsible in the lease, no one may be responsible in law, and part of the building may fall into disrepair.

Ideally, the lease should make one person responsible for structural repairs, decoration of the exterior and common areas and maintenance of boilers, lifts and similar equipment.

In many cases such repairs and maintenance will be the responsibility of the company or individual who owns the block, possibly through a managing agent.

Alternatively, a management company or residents' association may have been set up to provide services.

When tenants and owners are liable for service charges

Both private tenants and owners of flats will normally have to pay a share of the cost of providing the common services and facilities. The proportion may vary with the size or rateable value of the flat and should be fixed in the lease.

A provisional payment for the services – based on actual costs for the previous year or a current estimate – is generally collected every 6 months. A balancing payment is collected later when the full figures are known.

The lease may also provide for special payments to build up a reserve fund for costly jobs, such as replacing lifts.

When a flat changes hands special arrangements must be made to apportion the buyer's and seller's share of the service charges and reserve funds.

How charges can be controlled

People who pay service charges have several rights:
- They are entitled to a copy of the annual accounts showing how the service charges are calculated.
- Residents can challenge the reasonableness of both the services and the charges in the county court.
- If any service item costs over £500 or £25 multiplied by the number of flats in the building, whichever is the greater, at least two estimates must be obtained, including one from an independent source.
- Any work falling within the above figures must be notified to the residents, who should be given at least a month to put their views on the matter to the landlord. Unless the work is urgent, it cannot start until these views have been considered by the landlord.
- If there is a recognised residents' association for the building the proposals must be discussed with them.

Members of residents' associations providing services control the charges through the association.

FLATSHARING

Protecting your rights in a tenancy agreement

When two or more people decide to share a rented house, they often arrange matters between themselves informally, and only one of them has dealings with the landlord. It is generally wiser, however, for each to ensure that he is protected under the Rent Act by establishing a JOINT TENANCY.

If the group does not do that, any member other than the one in whose name the accommodation is leased, may be regarded in law as a sub-tenant, a LODGER who can be asked to leave at any time, or even as a trespasser. *See:* SUB-TENANCY; TRESPASS

When a flatsharer seeks supplementary benefit

Anyone living in shared accommodation and claiming SUPPLEMENTARY BENEFIT may find that the kind of sharing arrangement they have affects the amount of benefit they get.

The basic difference is between those classed as householders – which includes tenants – who are entitled to maximum help in paying rent, rates, mortgage interest and other items connected with housing, and those classed as non-householders, who receive proportionately less.

A person living with a close relative but not responsible for paying the rent, is a non-householder and is entitled only to a fixed amount towards the rent – £2.15 a week in 1981.

If he is paying his way as a lodger and is not living with close relatives supplementary benefit will cover board and lodgings – so long as they are not unreasonably expensive – and an allowance for personal expenses.

When two or more people – other than those living as husband and wife – are joint tenants living as a single household they are treated as non-householders, but they receive a share of the householder rate.

If they are joint tenants not living as one household – the usual test is whether they share meals – each qualifies for the householder rate plus his share of the rent.

FLOWERS

When picking a bloom is theft

Anyone who picks wild flowers or mushrooms without permission from the owner of the land – including a common – and who then sells them, is guilty of theft.

If the person does not sell the flowers or mushrooms, he is not guilty of theft, but can be sued by the landowner for damages.

It is an offence to uproot any wild plant without the owner's permission. The maximum penalty is a £100 fine. *See:* PLANTS AND FLOWERS

FOOD

How the law safeguards what you eat and drink

It is a criminal offence in Britain to sell for human consumption any food that is not of the nature, substance or quality demanded by the buyer.

Under the Food and Drugs Act 1955 anyone selling food that is usually consumed by humans, but which proves unfit for human consumption, is guilty of a criminal offence, even if:
● He took precautions to avoid the offence.
● He was not negligent.
● The food sold is proved to be not injurious to health – for example a mouldy but harmless pie.

The maximum penalty is 3 months' imprisonment and a £100 fine.

It is also a criminal offence to interfere with food or drink by adding or removing any substance so as to make it injurious to health. The maximum penalty for that offence is 3 months' imprisonment and a £100 fine.

WHEN THE FOOD YOU BUY IS UNSATISFACTORY

The trading standards office may make a test purchase at the shop you name and send it to the public analyst.

If you think that the food you buy is not satisfactory, complain to the local council's trading standards office, which may decide to make a test purchase at the shop you name and send the sample to the public analyst.

If you are given food that you suspect to be dirty, complain to the council's environmental health officer. He may decide to prosecute the seller under the Food and Drugs (Control of Food Premises) Act 1976.

In both cases you, as the buyer, stand to gain nothing from any prosecution – although in rare cases the magistrates may decide that you should be awarded some damages or compensation for any

HOW TO READ DATE CODES ON PACKAGED FOODS

The code dating of perishable packaged food allows a shopkeeper to know how long it can safely be kept without being sold. Code dating is a voluntary arrangement between manufacturers and retailers and it is not an offence to sell food after the expiry date shown, unless the food is unfit for human consumption.

The code does not tell the retailer when the food was manufactured or the date by which it must be sold. It indicates the date on which the food left the manufacturer and the last date by which it should have been delivered to the retailer. The retailer must then decide, according to conditions in his own shop, how long he can safely keep the food on sale.

A typical date code might read DS 01 1.

The letters DS are the manufacturer's code, indicating which factory the food came from. The figures 01 denote the week of the year in which the food left the factory – 01 represents the first week of the year: 52 would be the last. The final figure represents the day of the week that is the last permitted day of delivery to a retailer. The days are numbered from Saturday (1) to Friday (7). Code-dating calendars are issued by some manufacturers to shops.

injury or suffering that you have been caused.

Cleanliness where food is sold

Hygiene regulations under the Food and Drugs Act are administered by the local council and cover all places where food is prepared or sold for human consumption. It is a criminal offence for a shop, stall or restaurant not to comply with the regulations. The maximum penalty is 3 months' imprisonment and a fine of £100.

● Premises must be clean and sanitary and free from vermin and insects.

● Clean handbasins and lavatories must be available to staff. They must have adequate supplies of soap, nail brushes and clean towels.

● Staff must not smoke or spit while handling food.

● Any open injury – say, a cut finger – must be covered with a waterproof dressing while staff are handling food.

THE WOMAN WHO FOUND A NAIL IN ONE OF HER SWEETS

It is no defence to a charge of selling food not of the nature, substance or quality demanded, that every reasonable precaution was taken.

A woman who bought sweets at a shop in Leeds, West Yorkshire, found a nail in one of them. She complained to the Leeds Public Health Department.

An inspector investigated and brought a prosecution against the manufacturers, George W. Horner and Company for selling a sweet that was not of the nature, substance or quality demanded.

The Leeds magistrate decided that the nail had got into the sweet during manufacture, but that the manufacturers had used every reasonable precaution to prevent it. They were found not guilty, and the inspector appealed.

DECISION

The High Court ruled that the manufacturer must be convicted. When someone is accused of being responsible for the sale of food not of the nature, substance or quality demanded, it cannot be a defence to plead that the nail had got into the sweet without any negligence on his part.

The court said that in this case, the manufacturer had clearly committed an offence under the Food and Drugs Act. The High Court judges sent the case back to the magistrate with a direction to convict the manufacturer and impose an appropriate penalty.

THE RESTAURANT THAT SERVED CAUSTIC SODA IN A LEMONADE BOTTLE

A soft drink can be regarded as 'food' if a prosecution is brought under the Food and Drugs Act for selling a drink that was unfit for human consumption. Others beside the seller may be prosecuted.

Mr Graham Lansley was employed by Carlsberg to install and maintain equipment for the supply of draught lager in public houses and restaurants in southeast England.

On July 15, 1975 he visited the Kashmir Restaurant at 20 Palace Street, Canterbury and cleaned the pipes of the lager equipment with a cleaning fluid that contained 20 per cent caustic soda – a solution stronger than paint stripper. He then called over a waiter and showed him how to clean the pipes.

Mr Lansley next poured some of the cleaning fluid into an empty lemonade bottle. He crossed out the word 'lemonade' on the label with one line of ballpoint pen, and wrote the word 'cleaner' at the bottom of the label in letters, the highest of which was about $\frac{1}{4}$ in. tall.

Mr Lansley left the bottle under a counter in the bar and service area: it was the only lemonade bottle there. He showed the waiter where he had put the bottle.

The next day, a Mr Studer took his family to the Kashmir Restaurant for lunch. He ordered food and some drinks: lager for himself, cola for Mrs Studer and lemonade for each of his children – Cornelia, aged 7 and Jurg, aged 4.

The waiter who served them filled two glasses from a lemonade bottle that was standing with other lemonade bottles on the floor at the back of the bar and service area. The drinks were served to the family.

As soon as they had drunk part of their drinks, the children started to scream that their mouths were burning. The waiter produced the bottle from which he had poured the children's drinks and it was discovered that the word 'lemonade' had been crossed out with the word 'cleaner' written at the bottom of the label.

The children were taken to hospital.

Canterbury Council prosecuted the owners of the Kashmir Restaurant for selling two glasses of lemonade which were not of the nature demanded by the purchaser and for selling food that was unfit for human consumption.

The three owners of the restaurant, in turn, brought a prosecution against Mr Lansley, alleging that the offence was his fault. The cases were heard in the Canterbury magistrates' court on January 23 and January 25, 1976.

The magistrates found the owners of the restaurant and Mr Lansley all guilty. All appealed to the High Court.

The owners of the restaurant argued that they had not sold food to the purchaser. Mr Lansley argued that the object of the Act was to regulate people who sell food, and as he did not sell food, he was not governed by the Act.

DECISIONS

The High Court upheld all the convictions. One of the judges hearing the appeal, Mr Justice Wien, said that a sale of supposed lemonade constituted a sale of food, even though something different was mistakenly supplied.

The court, upholding Mr Lansley's conviction, said that if someone who sold food could show that the offence was someone else's fault, that other person could be convicted even though he had not sold any food.

The owners of the restaurant were fined £100 and ordered to pay £79.80 towards the cost of the prosecution. Mr Lansley was fined £100 and ordered to pay £25 costs.

In separate civil proceedings, in the High Court in October 1977, compensation was awarded to the Studer children.

Cornelia Studer, whose injuries resulted in her needing regular throat treatment for 2 years after the incident, was awarded £43,000. Her brother, who suffered only minor injuries, was awarded £200.

The damages were awarded against the proprietors of the restaurant and the company responsible for servicing the bar equipment, but not against Mr Lansley.

● Shops displaying food must ensure that it cannot easily be contaminated.

● Unwrapped food, other than vegetables, must be displayed at least 18 in. from the floor.

Outdoor stalls

Market food stalls, like shops, are controlled by the local authority. Regulations are more lenient than for fixed shops, but a fish stall, for example, must be screened on three sides and there must be facilities for waste and a water supply near by.

Restaurant rules

A caterer convicted of a hygiene offence can be imprisoned and fined but he can also be prohibited by the court from using the unhygienic premises for any kind of catering for up to 2 years.

A court can also make a closure order that prohibits anyone from using the premises for selling food until all danger to health has been removed.

It is a criminal offence to disobey a closure order, which must be displayed prominently on the premises. The maximum penalty is a £400 fine.

Controlling what goes into your food

A trader or shop can be prosecuted for selling food not of the nature, substance or quality demanded. Whether what was supplied was the food demanded must always be decided by the court. There are three separate offences:

● The 'substance' refers to the ingredients.

● The 'nature' refers to what is made out of the ingredients.

● The 'quality' refers to different grades.

If a restaurant sells margarine when butter is ordered, it can be convicted of selling food not of the substance demanded, unless the waiter has made clear what he is serving.

The composition of some foods is controlled by food standards orders under the Food and Drugs Act. In other cases, codes of practice are agreed between representatives of the trade.

Sometimes the code of practice is more specific than the legal regulations. For example, the law says that a fish 'spread' must have 70 per cent of the

FOOD INGREDIENTS THAT NEED NOT BE LISTED BUT MUST CONFORM TO REGULATIONS

Some prepacked foods – for example, chocolates, sweets, ice cream and bread – must be labelled with an accurate description but they do not, like many other prepacked foods, have to bear a list of ingredients in weight order.

They are, however, subject to other regulations.

If a manufacturer claims that his produce provides energy, calories, proteins, vitamins or minerals, the claims must be clear and he must be able to substantiate them with scientific evidence if he is later challenged.

Nothing can be called a 'slimming aid' unless it has been proved to help slimming.

Bread over 10 oz.	Must be sold by weight
White bread	Must have vitamins, iron and chalk for calcium content
Brown or wholemeal	At least 0.6% fibre and up to 5% soya or rice flour
Wheatgerm	10% processed wheatgerm
Protein bread	22% protein
Milk bread	6% milk solids
Starch reduced bread	Under 50% carbohydrate
Eggs	By law, sold in seven grades: size 1 – 70 grams or more; size 7 – under 45 grams

THE MOCK SALMON 'CUTLETTES' THAT DID NOT HAVE ENOUGH FISH

If food is given a novel name it does not alter the regulations concerning the standard of ingredients in the food.

Victor Value, at their shop at 43 High Street North, East Ham, London, were selling what were described as 'mock salmon cutlettes'.

An environmental health inspector, visiting their shop after a complaint had been received from a dissatisfied customer, bought a sample and sent it for public analysis. The analyst found that the 'cutlettes' contained 33 per cent of fish. The Food Standards (Fish Cakes) Order 1950 requires that fish cakes contain at least 35 per cent of fish. There was, however, no standard for fish 'cutlettes'.

East Ham council prosecuted Victor Value for selling mock salmon 'cutlettes' that were not of the substance demanded. Victor Value, in turn, brought a private prosecution against Piper Products of Poole, the manufacturers, claiming that if an offence had been committed, as the council alleged, it was the manufacturer's responsibility.

The case was heard by East Ham magistrates, and each company offered the same defence – that no offence had been committed because there was no standard for fish 'cutlettes' that contained 33 per cent of fish.

A public analyst gave evidence saying that as 'cutlet' usually meant a small cut of meat or fish, a fish 'cutlette' should contain a substantial amount of fish and should have more fish than a fish cake.

If the 'cutlettes' had been sold as fish cakes they would have been deficient in fish, and they were therefore deficient in fish when sold as 'cutlettes'.

The magistrates dismissed the case against both the seller and manufacturer. The council appealed.

DECISION

The High Court accepted the evidence of the public analyst that any food described as cutlets should contain more than 33 per cent of fish and that therefore the 'cutlettes' sold were not of the substance demanded.

They sent the case back to the magistrates at East Ham with a direction to convict Victor Value of an offence under the Food and Drugs Act, and then to consider whether that offence was due to any action or lack of action by the manufacturers of the 'cutlettes'.

named fish, but fish 'paste' must have 70 per cent of fish, without specifying a minimum quantity of the named fish.

The code of practice further lays down a minimum amount for different kinds of fish paste: salmon 'spread' must, by law, contain 70 per cent of salmon. Salmon 'paste' must, by law, contain 70 per cent fish. But the code goes further and lays down that the 70 per cent of fish in the 'paste' must have 25 per cent salmon in it.

When a customer has a doubt about the content of food, the public analyst, if requested, will for no charge give a detailed analysis.

FOOD STANDARDS AND LABELLING

Under the Food and Drugs Act 1955, regulations have been made laying down standards for many foods. They include the following, which must contain a minimum proportion of certain ingredients, as listed here:

Sausage rolls	At least 10¼% meat
Meat pies	At least 25% meat
Fish cakes	At least 35% fish
Beef sausages	At least 50% beef
Pork sausages	At least 65% pork
Meat paste	At least 55% meat
Fish paste	At least 70% fish
Fish spread	At least 70% of the named fish
Suet (shredded)	At least 83% suet
Suet (block)	At least 99% suet
Jams	Varying from 25% minimum fruit content for blackcurrant, 38% for strawberry and 40% for some mixed jams
Marmalade	At least 20% citrus fruit
Mincemeat	At least 30% dried fruit and peel
Coffee	A label 'French coffee', a coffee-chicory mixture, must have a minimum of 51% coffee
Viennese coffee	85% coffee and 15% figs
Liquid coffee essence	At least 4 lb. of coffee to 1 gallon of essence
Coffee-chicory essence	2 lb. of coffee to 1 gallon of liquid
Milk and cream	Jersey, Guernsey and South Devon, at least 4% butter fat
Dried milk	Labels must state the number of pints of liquid milk
Condensed and evaporated milk	At least 9% milk fat and 31% milk solids
Cream	Containers marked with net weight
Double cream	At least 48% milk fat
Single cream	At least 18% milk fat
Butter	At least 80% milk fat, a maximum of 2% solids, natural colouring only, and not more than 16% water may be added. If it has more than 3% salt, it must be labelled 'salted'
Margarine	May be blended with up to 10% butter, not more than 16% water, and must have added vitamins in the mixture of vegetable, animal and fish oils used

If someone sells you short measure

If you have been given short weight in a shop or at a market stall, keep the bag with the purchase and contact the trading standards officer, who will make a test purchase.

If the customer is prepared to give evidence in court, the shop can be prosecuted under the Weights and Measures Act 1963. The maximum penalty for a first offence is a £100 fine, and for a second offence a fine of £250.

WHAT THE PUBLIC ANALYST IS AND HOW HE WORKS

Every borough and district council appoints at least one public analyst – a chemist who has passed an examination set by the Royal Institute of Chemistry. The analyst deals not only with borough complaints but also with matters referred to him by district or parish councils.

In addition to food, his work deals with other consumer protection and trade description matters and also public health hazards – for example, poisonous waste.

When dealing with a complaint about food, the public analyst examines one-third of a test sample obtained from the premises facing a complaint. The remaining one-third samples are handed to the council trading standards inspector investigating the case and to the seller of the food, who may arrange for his own independent analysis.

In a prosecution, evidence from the public analyst is often sufficient evidence of the nature, substance or quality of the food sample tested.

However, the evidence can be challenged – for example, on the ground that the sample had deteriorated by the time the analyst was able to examine it.

A defendant is entitled to call the analyst as a defence witness, if he is not appearing as a prosecution witness.

FOOT AND MOUTH DISEASE

Official powers when animals are infected

Wide emergency powers are available to the Ministry of Agriculture and inspectors of local authorities when an outbreak of foot and mouth disease is discovered among farm animals.

People can be banned from using fields and footpaths in a large area around the farm where an infected herd has been kept. All dogs within a 5 mile radius have to be kept inside, chained up outside, or kept on a lead.

Failure to comply with the regulations is a criminal offence and police have powers of arrest. The penalty can be prison for up to 2 months and a fine of up to £100.

Farmers are entitled to compensation from the Ministry of Agriculture for any loss they suffer when they have to destroy an infected herd.

FOOTBALL POOL

How the law controls the promoters

A football pool is a form of pool betting in which all money staked and all winnings paid are part of a common pool. Football pool promoters must be registered with the local authority for the area in which they have their headquarters.

Parliament has laid down strict requirements for the conduct of the pools. Prizes must be available to all entrants. If one entrant bets twice as much as someone else, his winnings must be twice as high. The amount won must depend on the accuracy of the forecast. The promoter must appoint a chartered accountant, approved by the local council, to verify all figures.

If there is a dispute

The entry form that you sign after filling in the coupon says: 'I agree to abide by the company's rules, which govern all entries, and agree that this transaction is binding in honour only.'

That 'honour clause' prevents your taking the company to court in case of a dispute, although members of the Pool Promoters' Association will investigate complaints and, if a mistake is proved, will pay the complainant what he should have won.

It is for the pools competitor to ensure that he completes his entry correctly and legibly, and that it is sent to the pools company in plenty of time.

Entries that are in any way incorrect –

A WINNING ENTRY MUST ARRIVE ON TIME

The pools competitor must ensure that his entry is completely correct and legible and that it is posted in time.

'But did I post his coupon?'

for example, if the coupon is not signed – will not be accepted. Nor will those delivered to the promoter after matches have begun. They must reach the promoter by noon on Saturday, and proof of posting is not proof of delivery. Late entries are disqualified – and you cannot sue the Post Office over a delayed entry, because it is protected by law against such claims.

Dealing with collectors

As an alternative to posting the coupon yourself you can hand it to an official collector whose job it is to pass entries in bulk to the promoter. He may do so in person, by using the railway or a road parcels delivery service, or he may post the entries.

Although a collector is paid a commission by the promoter, he is regarded as the competitor's agent, so if he fails to ensure that your entry arrives in time, you cannot sue the promoter.

There is no formal contract between the competitor and the collector. You could take him to court and, if you prove he has been negligent, you might be awarded damages. But that would be worthwhile only if his negligence deprived you of a substantial win, and if the collector could pay.

Locally organised pools

Pools run locally – usually to raise funds for charity – are subject to the special provisions of the Pools Competitions Act 1971. The promoter must be

FORMING A SYNDICATE

A pools coupon can be submitted by a group of people who form a syndicate to share the entry fee, postal order and postage costs, and any winnings.

The advantage of a syndicate is that it allows for a relatively large stake to be placed, thus theoretically increasing the chance of a win.

If an entry wins, each member of the syndicate is entitled to a share of the winnings, the amount depending on how much he has contributed. As a rule if there are, say, 10 in the group the winnings will be divided into 10 equal parts.

The syndicate organiser is not entitled to take a larger share, unless he has invested more than other members or has an agreement with them giving him a larger share. Any such agreement should be in writing.

If you belong to a pools syndicate whose entry wins a prize and you are not paid your proper share, you can sue for the money. The 'honour clause' in the coupon applies only to the transaction with the pools company and not to the agreement between the syndicate members.

If someone under 18 is in a winning syndicate he is legally entitled to his share. He is not legally liable to the rest of the syndicate for his promised share of the stake money.

registered with the local authority and also needs a licence from the Gaming Board. *See:* GAMBLING

The Board can attach conditions to the licence, such as the number and type of competitions to be held.

FOOTPATH

Where walkers' rights are protected

A footpath is a public RIGHT OF WAY which may be used only by pedestrians. Anyone found driving on one can be fined up to £20, and riders and cyclists can be sued for TRESPASS.

Public rights on many footpaths have been established over centuries and most – though not all – are signposted. But the only way to be certain of your rights is to check a recent Ordnance Survey map, where footpaths are shown by a thin red line, or to ask at the nearest county council for its 'definitive map' of public rights of way, which is available to the public during normal office hours.

Local authorities should signpost public footpaths at the point where they leave a metalled road, but are not legally obliged to do so. If there is no signpost, complain to the council – but you cannot enforce your complaint.

Keeping a footpath open

If you find that a public footpath has been obstructed, notify the surveyor's office at the local county or town council, whose duty it is to preserve and protect public rights of way. They should, if necessary, take court action against the landowner to remove the obstruction and repair the path, or clear it themselves and sue him for the cost.

If the council does not take action, you can apply to a magistrates' court for an order enforcing the authority to keep the way in repair, but this may prove expensive if you are unsuccessful.

If a fence or barbed wire has been erected across a public footpath, you are entitled to cut it sufficiently to give yourself free passage. But keep damage to a minimum: the fence belongs to someone and he could sue you for damages. If you find a 'No Through Way' sign on a public footpath, report it to the local authority – but do not take it down yourself. The council can have the sign

---

A BULL SHOULD NOT BE
LOOSE NEAR A FOOTPATH

If a farmer refuses to move a bull from where it is a danger to users of a footpath, the local authority may be able to do so and sue the farmer.

WHO MAY USE A PAVEMENT

Pavements, like footpaths, are provided exclusively for pedestrians. You may not ride, drive or cycle along them. It is an offence to park a vehicle of more than 3 tons on a pavement.

A local authority, although not obliged to do so by law, should provide pavements alongside a carriageway, wherever they are needed for the safety of pedestrians. Anyone who damages a pavement can be sued by the local authority for the cost of its repair.

Local authorities sometimes provide 'walkways' through privately owned built-up areas, such as shopping precincts. The public have a right to walk in such areas, subject to conditions – such as hours of opening – displayed at the entrance.

---

removed and prosecute whoever put it up. He could be fined up to £20.

If the path is blocked by a large object – a fallen tree, say – you may walk around it across adjoining private land. But your detour must be no more than is necessary to avoid the obstacle.

Most county councils have bye-laws forbidding farmers to keep bulls loose near a footpath. If you are prevented from using a footpath by a bull, ask the farmer to remove it. If he refuses, contact the local authority – if a bye-law exists, they can remove the bull and prosecute the farmer.

Stiles and gates along a public footpath must be maintained by the landowner. If you find them in poor condition, complain to the local authority who are obliged to enforce their upkeep – often, they will carry out the work themselves and recover the expense from the landowner.

Ploughing up a footpath

A farmer who wants to plough up a public path that runs through his land must give 7 days' notice to the local authority. If he fails to do so, he can be fined £10. When ploughing is completed, he must restore the path within 6 weeks if he gave notice, 3 weeks if he did not. If he fails to do so, he can be fined up to £200 – and would have to pay the cost if the council lays a new path. If, after conviction, he still refuses to repair the path, he can be fined £1 for

---

each day the offence continues. You still have right of way while the path is ploughed up, provided you keep to the line of the path, walk in single file and take care not to damage crops.

Hazards on footpaths

The local authority is responsible for the safety of footpaths. It can obtain court orders requiring neighbouring landowners to remove dangerous objects – such as a barbed wire fence bordering the path – but, if injured by such a fence, you can claim damages only from its owner.

However, if you suffer injury because the path has fallen into disrepair, sue the council for damages. It can escape liability only if it can prove it took reasonable care to safeguard the path, or that you were behaving unreasonably or carelessly when the accident occurred.

Closing a footpath

When a local authority wants to close a public path, it must prove either that the path is unnecessary or that it can provide a more convenient detour. To do so, it applies for an order from a magistrates' court. Two magistrates will normally inspect the path and, if they find there is a case for closing it, will arrange a hearing.

The authority must give at least 28 days' notice of the hearing to everyone whose land adjoins the path, and must publish details of its application in a local newspaper at least once a week in each of the 4 weeks before the hearing. Copies must be displayed on parish notice boards and on the path itself.

If you object to the closure, write to the council or give evidence at the hearing. Having heard the council's case and any objections, the magistrates either make the order for closing the path or dismiss the application. Their ruling can be appealed against in the crown court.

If a local authority or individual wants to close a public path for any other reason – if, for example, it wanted to build on it – it must write to the Secretary of State for the Environment. If he finds that the application is reasonable, his department will advertise the plan locally and invite objections to it. If there are none, he can order the closure. Otherwise, department inspectors will hold a public hearing at which all sides can give their views. The Secretary of State will receive a report from his inspector and will approve the application only if he is convinced that the public interest has been protected.

There is no right of appeal against a Department of Environment ruling. If it has infringed a point of law, however, it can be challenged in the High Court.

FOREIGN DECREE

Divorces that are recognised in Britain

A couple married in England (or Wales) can be divorced in certain circumstances in another country. A divorce or a legal separation is recognised in England if it is effective under the law of the country in which it was granted and if one of the couple lives there habitually or is domiciled there or is a national of that country. *See:* DOMICILE

It is also valid if one of the couple is domiciled in a country which recognises the decree. A husband, for example, who is domiciled in California can get a divorce in Mexico from his wife living in London – even though a Mexican divorce is not recognised in England. A Mexican divorce is recognised in California and, because the husband is domiciled there, it is valid in England.

A foreign decree will not be recognised in England if it is granted under conditions contrary to the British concept of justice. A husband or wife must, for example, be given a reasonable opportunity to appear in court to object to the decree. A court in England settling a dispute over MATRIMONIAL PROPERTY would take this into account. *See:* DIVORCE

For example, a husband who obtains a quick divorce in Reno, Nevada, where residential qualifications are minimal, may find the decree invalid in England unless he gives his wife sufficient time to get there.

FOREIGN EMBASSY

Protecting the interests of citizens abroad

An embassy is a government office set up in a foreign country to represent

THE HUSBAND WHO GOT 'SECRET' DECREE IN BOLIVIA

A foreign divorce is not recognised in England if one of the spouses is not given proper notice of the proceedings, and a reasonable opportunity to take part in them.

Mrs K, a Cypriot national, married Mr K, a member of the Royal Air Force, in the British sovereign base area of Akrotiri, Cyprus, in 1964. They had three children during the marriage.

For most of their married life, Mr K served abroad, at first with the RAF and later as an employee of a communications company.

In 1972, Mr K was sent to Bolivia. His wife joined him, but the marriage by then was unhappy. Mrs K went back to Cyprus to stay with her parents – taking the children with her, because of their schooling.

Before Mrs K left Bolivia, her husband got her to sign documents which, he said, were needed to enable her to take the children out of the country. The documents were in Spanish. Mrs K spoke a little Spanish, but did not attempt to read them.

Mr K said he would join his wife in Cyprus when his job in Bolivia ended, in August 1974. During that year, however, there was unrest in Cyprus, and Mrs K and the children moved to England and settled in a house that had been bought in the couple's joint names, early in their marriage.

That August, Mr K did not leave Bolivia. He wrote telling his wife that his company could not find a replacement for him, but that he would definitely rejoin her in August 1975.

When he eventually arrived in England, Mr K disclosed to his wife that he had divorced her and married someone else – and that he had a daughter by the other woman.

That was the first time, according to Mrs K, that divorce had been mentioned between them.

She discovered that a divorce decree had been made in Bolivia in August 1975, showing her as the petitioner on the ground of severe physical cruelty. There were two sworn statements by witnesses who described physical assaults on her by her husband.

Mrs K petitioned the High Court Family Division for a declaration that the Bolivian decree was invalid and that she was still married to Mr K.

The court heard a sworn statement by a Bolivian lawyer who said that it was possible for a petitioner to obtain a divorce in Bolivia without attending the hearing, provided that the petitioner signed an authorisation or power of attorney.

However, the court also heard that the decree contained false statements to the effect that there were no children of the marriage, that Mrs K went out to work and that neither party owned any property.

A decree obtained by Mr K in Bolivia would be recognised in England only if the wife had been given notice of the proceedings and a reasonable opportunity to take part, and if recognition of the decree would not be against public policy.

DECISION

Mrs K was granted the declarations that she sought. The court held that the divorce proceedings in Bolivia were obtained by deceiving the lawyers involved – possibly with the collusion or connivance of Mr K, or at his instigation. The divorce was contrary to public policy.

the government's interests in that country and to look after the interests of its citizens working or travelling there.

An embassy is headed by an ambassador – or occasionally a chargé d'affaires – who keeps diplomatic contact with the country in which he is stationed. There are also commercial staff to deal with matters of trade; registry officials to record births and deaths of their nationals living in the country; and officials to deal with passports, stranded holidaymakers and people arrested or in prison.

The embassies of Commonwealth countries in Britain are known as high

commissions, but they do the same job. Most embassies are situated in the capital city of a country, but many bigger nations also have consulates – which are, in effect, branch offices – in other important ports and cities.

Only a few countries do not have embassies in London. They usually ask another country with an embassy to look after their interests.

Embassy duties The main purpose of a foreign embassy is to act as an intermediary between its own government and the government of the host country.

The commercial department works to encourage trade between the two coun-

HELPING NATIONALS WHEN
THEY ARE ABROAD

The embassy will help you if you lose your money and see you get home safely.

tries. The consular department can renew passports, and it also has the power to administer the foreign estate of any of its nationals who die in the country.

It issues visas and looks after the day-to-day interests of its nationals, visiting or resident in the country, advising them about health regulations or legal restrictions.

It can help, for example, with problems of illness or with visitors who have lost their money, and it will usually see that they get back safely to their country.

For legal purposes an embassy is regarded as the territory of the country which it represents. British police, for example, have no powers to enter, say, the Russian embassy and arrest a Russian citizen suspected of crime. But they can ask for the person to be handed over.

Under this diplomatic immunity a person can seek political asylum in an embassy. Foreign staff at an embassy also have protection from the laws of the country in which they are stationed. *See:* DIPLOMAT

Arrested aliens When a foreign national is arrested in Britain, the police should inform his embassy – or he should be allowed to do so himself.

The embassy has a right of access to its nationals held in custody and a right to arrange legal representation if the prisoner so wishes. If he is sent to pris-

on, embassy officials can pay regular visits and the prisoner is allowed to contact them.

Addresses of embassies, consulates and high commissions can be found in any public library.

FOREIGN INCOME

Tax owed on money earned abroad

If you are a citizen of the United Kingdom, and therefore liable to British tax, but travel abroad as part of your job, you may be entitled to tax relief on the part of your earnings that arises from your work overseas.

There are two levels of relief:
● Partial, which can be claimed by people who usually go abroad on business for at least 30 days in a tax year – that is April 6 to April 5.
● Total, which can be claimed by people who work abroad for a continuous period of more than 1 year.

Both types of relief can be claimed by employees of British or foreign-owned companies, and partial relief by the self-employed.

If you believe you qualify, you should claim when you submit your annual tax return. The tax return form 11P contains a section for detailing earnings from duties performed abroad. *See:* INCOME TAX

Your tax inspector may ask for proof

REDUCING YOUR TAX BILL

When you spend more than 30 days abroad in any tax year, you do not have to pay UK tax on a quarter of the earnings you make abroad.

that you have worked overseas – an employer's declaration, or travel receipts if you are self-employed.

Claiming partial relief

If you spend 30 days or more abroad on business in a tax year, you can obtain tax exemption on 25 per cent of your overseas earnings for the time you are away. For an employee, earnings from duties performed abroad are generally calculated according to a formula in which the salary during the tax year is divided by 365 days and then multiplied by the number of days overseas.

Example: Mr Y is a salesman earning £7,000 a year. During one tax year he spends 70 days abroad on business.

The proportion of his salary arising from duties performed abroad is:

$$\frac{£7,000}{365} \times 70 \text{ days} = £1,342.47$$

He does not have to pay tax on 25 per cent of that amount – £335.62.

The same formula is applied to self-employed people.

In either case, any capital allowances to which they are entitled are deducted from their gross earnings before the exemption is applied.

How the 30 days are calculated

The 30 overseas days needed to claim tax relief on earnings from duties overseas do not have to be continuous. You can make several short trips – for example, 5 trips of 6 days each – and, provided that they are all in the same tax year, you will qualify.

The days must be 'complete' – those on which you were outside the UK at midnight. If you fly from London to Paris at 7 a.m. and return at 11 p.m. on the same day, that does not count as a day abroad. However, if the flight from Paris arrives in London after midnight you will have accrued one day.

Time spent travelling outside the UK towards your foreign destination counts as time away.

If you are outside the UK on business for 7 or more consecutive days, Saturdays and Sundays may be included in your total, even though you did not work over the weekend. If you take an occasional weekday off for local sightseeing, that counts towards the total, too, provided that the main purpose of the trip was business.

Claiming extra relief

Although the basic formula for calculating earnings from duties abroad is directly related to the number of days spent overseas, the tax authorities may accept a claim for higher relief in some circumstances. The decision is left to local tax inspectors and must be negotiated with them. But if you think you are entitled to higher relief, say so on your tax return.

Extra relief might be granted if, for example, you were sent abroad for 9 months to work on a specific project, but were required to come back for a few days each month to report on progress to your employer. You should claim the full 9 months' relief.

The Inland Revenue may also grant extra relief if it can be shown that an employee's main duties are performed abroad, and that the time he spends working in the UK is only incidental. An engineer whose chief task is servicing his company's installations overseas, but who returns to the UK between assignments, might come into that category.

In such cases, it greatly helps the employee's claim for relief if he has a 'split contract', with separate sections in it to cover, respectively, his work in the UK and that overseas.

He must still declare his total earnings to the Inland Revenue, but the overseas section of the contract is evidence of the extent of his duties abroad. If a service engineer receives £3,000 – one-third of his total salary – for waiting time in the UK and £6,000 for his main duties overseas, he can argue that he is entitled to relief on the £6,000 – even though he may have spent more than one-third of the year in the UK.

The Inland Revenue accepts the principle of 'apportionment' in split contracts – higher payment for work overseas because of higher wage rates in the foreign location – provided that it appears 'reasonable'. But if there is no specific provision for that in the contract, the tax authorities are unlikely to accept a claim for extra relief based on the argument that local pay rates are higher than those in the UK.

Companies cannot avoid the tax rules by a split contract that makes a UK resident technically an employee of an associated foreign concern while he is working abroad. If there is any link between the two employers, he must pay tax on his earnings from both.

Expenses Travel and accommodation expenses paid by an employer for an employee on business overseas are not liable to tax, provided that the employee is not saving money by having them paid.

Claiming total relief

Someone who works for a period of at least 365 days outside the UK for a British or a foreign employer pays no UK tax on his earnings abroad during that time. However, he must still pay any tax due from income arising in the UK – for example, if he has let his house, on the rent.

The 365 day qualification period does not have to be continuous, but:
1. No single return visit to the UK can be longer than 62 consecutive days.
2. The total number of days spent in the UK must not exceed one-sixth of the total time of his employment abroad.
Example: An engineer working in the Middle East spends 170 days there and then comes home for a holiday of 40 days before returning to his job.

His employment abroad on the day he goes back to the Middle East has lasted (170+40)=210 days, of which the holiday in the UK represents about one-fifth.

To reduce the proportion to one-sixth and keep his tax relief, the engineer must remain in the Middle East for at least a further 30 days, because:

$$\frac{40\text{ days' holiday}}{(170+40+30\text{ days' employment})} = \frac{40}{240} = \frac{1}{6}$$

An employee who works abroad for more than 365 days can bring all his earnings back to the UK afterwards. They are not liable to UK tax.

People who cannot claim relief

Civil servants and members of the armed forces cannot claim relief on earnings from duties overseas. Gas and oil rigs in the UK sector of the North Sea do not qualify as 'overseas'.

Paying local taxes on money earned abroad

A British resident who works abroad and who is paid there may be taxed locally on his income. Whether he is or not depends on the foreign country's tax rules.

If his earnings for duties performed abroad are taxed overseas, he can claim tax relief in the UK, so that the total amount paid in tax is not more than the amount due in the country – the UK or the one where he worked – that has the higher tax rate. That is called double taxation relief. In some cases double tax agreements will provide that he pays tax in one country only.

The UK has double taxation agreements with all major overseas nations except the USSR, and with most smaller ones.

Example: A lecturer is promised a gross fee of £500 for speaking at a conference overseas. Under the rules of the country in which the conference is held, tax of £140 is deducted before the fee is paid – giving a net foreign income of £360.

UK tax applied at the standard rate to £360 would be £165, leaving a final net figure of £195.

However, by claiming double taxation relief, he can offset the £140 paid abroad against the £165 due in the UK. His UK tax liability is then (£165−£140)=£25, and the net amount he finally keeps is (£360−£25)=£335.

If the amount paid in tax abroad is higher than that payable in the UK, no further UK tax is due – but the difference between the two amounts cannot be reclaimed.

Foreign investments

Since October 1979, UK residents who have dividends accruing to them in a foreign currency can decide to keep the money abroad or bring it back to Britain in whatever form or currency they wish.

The EXCHANGE CONTROL regulations that formerly made it necessary for the dividends to be repatriated in sterling were abolished on October 23, 1979.

The payments are liable to income tax, and basic income tax may be deducted by the British bank receiving them. If tax has already been deducted in the country from which the payments come, double taxation relief can be claimed. Sometimes double tax relief is given in advance by reducing the rate of tax deducted by the British bank.

Pensions from abroad

The first 10 per cent of a foreign pension paid to a UK resident is not liable to income tax. Pensions for service in former or existing colonies that have become the responsibility of the Crown Agents also get the 10 per cent relief, provided that they became payable before April 1973.

German government pensions paid to victims of Nazi persecution are not taxed in the UK.

FOREIGN MARRIAGE

When a wedding abroad is valid in England and Wales

If a British subject gets married abroad, the validity of the marriage depends on the law of the country in which the parties claim DOMICILE, unless it is conducted under English law.

It will be recognised in England and Wales, provided it is recognised in the country of domicile of each of the parties and is conducted according to the law of the country where it took place. If you have a church wedding in France, you must have a civil ceremony as well, for your marriage to be recognised in France and so in England and Wales.

However, if English law recognises a divorce granted to one of the parties, one exception to this rule is that he or she will be free to remarry although the country of domicile does not recognise that divorce. For example, a Spaniard obtaining a divorce recognised in England would be regarded by English law as free to marry, even though Spain did not regard the divorce as dissolving the previous marriage.

The laws of marriage of the country of domicile must be observed. A man wishing to marry his cousin cannot do so if either of them is domiciled in a country where the marriage of cousins is illegal.

Provided it was legally performed in the country of domicile, a polygamous marriage is legally recognised in England for many purposes although it cannot be conducted in this country.

Children of such a marriage are legitimate and English courts will make orders, such as maintenance for any of the wives, and maintenance and cust-ody of the children. *See:* POLYGAMY

A polygamous marriage contracted by a man or woman domiciled in England will not be recognised by the English courts even though it is recognised in the country in which it takes place.

Under English law

A marriage can be conducted abroad under English law if one of the parties is English by domicile. It is legal if carried out by an 'authorised marriage officer' – for example, a British ambassador, embassy official, high commissioner or British consul.

A serviceman abroad can be legally married by a chaplain to the forces or by anyone nominated by the serviceman's commanding officer. A Service marriage can also take place on a Royal Navy ship in foreign waters, if the ceremony is conducted by a chaplain.

A marriage conducted on any vessel moored in English waters must conform to English law.

Anyone married abroad or under foreign custom who is in doubt about the validity of the marriage can apply to the High Court for a declaration that the marriage is valid.

A petition asking for such a declaration must be filed at the Divorce Registry, in London.

If the court refuses a declaration, the marriage is not valid in England. If it makes a declaration of validity, the marriage is binding in the normal way.

Magistrates are then able to hear any dispute about the marriage, and neither party can go through another marriage ceremony without committing bigamy.

If the marriage is declared invalid, the partners will have no claims to maintenance or property and INHERITANCE will be affected.

Dissolving the marriage A marriage contracted in another country can be dissolved in England or Wales, under English law, provided that at least one partner has been resident in Britain for at least a year. *See:* FOREIGN DECREE

FORESHORE

The freedom to use beaches for pleasure

Most of Britain's beaches – the foreshore between high and low-tide marks – belong to the Crown and are administered by local councils.

Powers of the local council

Normally anyone is entitled to use a beach for recreational purposes. However, a council can pass a BYE-LAW regulating the use of a beach up to 1,000 metres out to sea from the low water line as measured on a map. The council does not have to put up markers to show the boundary line.

Swimming areas may be restricted – for safety or nature conservancy – or part of the foreshore may be allotted for the use of certain groups, such as nudists. Cars or camping may be banned at the council's discretion.

However, a council cannot legally prohibit people from walking along a foreshore, except for safety reasons – for example, because of a rock fall.

Private beaches

A private landowner whose land runs alongside a public beach cannot keep the public off the foreshore. He can however prohibit people from crossing his land to reach the foreshore, unless there is a public RIGHT OF WAY, and he is entitled to remove a trespasser, if necessary by using reasonable force. *See:* TRESPASS

You have few legal rights to take things you find on or in a beach. *See:* BEACHCOMBING; WRECK

Some stretches of Crown foreshore have been sold or leased for private use – mainly by holiday companies and the National Trust. An owner or tenant of such a private beach is generally entitled to exclude the public but he cannot legally refuse to allow anyone to land from a boat.

A beach that has a sign claiming it as private may in fact not be. You can find out whether it is genuinely private by asking the local council. If it is not, you are entitled to use the beach as far up as the high-tide line.

Beaches in government control

Some stretches of foreshore are used exclusively by government departments – for example, by the Ministry of Defence, as a gunnery range.

A government department is entitled to prohibit the public from going on its beach and to prevent boats from landing there.

FORGERY

The criminal offence of falsifying a document

It is forgery to falsify a document with the intention of using it to defraud or deceive. That rule applies whether or not the document is ever used for such a purpose.

Anyone who makes an exact copy of a bank note is guilty of forgery, even if he has no intention of using it for fraud or deception.

It is forgery to make an exact replica of a cheque with intent to defraud or deceive, or to make a material alteration – for example, to a name or date – on a cheque or other document with the same intention.

Forgery must involve a document – which includes any letter – or a seal, such as those used by some official bodies and officers, such as the Registrar General.

The term 'document' covers official forms and records, such as certificates of birth, marriage or death; other official papers which may confer an advantage or benefit, such as immigration papers, prescriptions for drugs, licences of any kind, ballot papers and job references; and documents of financial value, such as money orders and insurance policies.

A copy of a famous painting cannot be a forgery because it is not a document. Someone pretending that a copy

---

FALSIFYING A DOCUMENT WITH INTENT TO DECEIVE

An exact replica of a bank note is a forgery whether you use it or not.

THE ACCOUNTANT WHO TRIED TO TRICK THE TAX MAN

Falsifying the date of a document to obtain an advantage for someone is forgery.

A solicitor, Mr H, executed a financial settlement in March 1936 in favour of his son Peter, aged 6. It was of a kind that could be revoked at a later date: at the time, a revocable settlement was subject to income-tax relief.

However, in May that year, the Government published a Finance Bill under which a revocable settlement would not be subject to tax relief if it was made after April 21. Since Mr H's settlement, on April 21, was revocable, it would cease to be tax-deductible once the Finance Bill became law.

To obtain continuing tax relief on the settlement, Mr H and a trustee – Mr W, a chartered accountant – executed a further deed that made the settlement irrevocable. Although the deed was not executed until May, it was dated April 21.

The Finance Bill became law in July 1936. Mr W, as trustee, had applied for a further tax refund and negotiations with the Inland Revenue were continuing.

To prove that the settlement was tax-deductible under the new law, Mr W eventually sent it, with the backdated deed, to the Inspector of Taxes.

By chance, an Inland Revenue official realised that although the deed amending the settlement was dated April 21, that was the date on which it had been posted back from the tax office to Mr W, so that it could not have reached him, and so could not have been amended, until at least the following day. Mr W and Mr H were prosecuted.

At the trial at the Central Criminal Court in London, Mr H was acquitted but Mr W was convicted of uttering a forged document. He was sentenced to 17 days' imprisonment, but appealed.

In his appeal to the High Court, he argued that no crime had been committed. The deed was not a false document within the meaning of the Forgery Act 1913 because when it was made, the Finance Bill was not necessarily going to become law and so the date of the deed was immaterial.

DECISION

Mr W's conviction was upheld. The High Court held that if a deed purports to have been made at a false time, and the only reason for choosing that false time is to obtain an advantage to the parties to the deed, the time could not be described as 'immaterial'.

---

was the original would probably be guilty of DECEPTION.

Maximum penalties for different kinds of forgery

● Forging the Great Seal of the United Kingdom, or the seal of the Registrar General or other government officer or body – life imprisonment.

● Forging the seal of a register office; a certificate of birth, marriage, death or cremation; a document of title to land or power of attorney, a share certificate, debenture warrant, promissory note, insurance policy or any valuable security; a bank note, cheque or bill of exchange; a postal or money order, building society book or receipt; possessing forged bank notes, seals or dies; demanding property on forged documents – 14 years' imprisonment.

● Forging a court seal or document, affidavit or dividend warrant; possessing or making paper or implements for forgery – 7 years' imprisonment.

● Forging an examination certificate or drug prescription – 2 years' imprisonment or an unlimited fine.

● Forging a ballot or election nomination paper, hackney carriage licence, driving examiner's certificate or records; possessing or making paper for forging Treasury bills – 2 years' imprisonment.

● Forging a road fund licence or vehicle registration document – up to 2 years' imprisonment in a crown court.

● Forging immigration documents – 6 months' imprisonment and £1,000 fine.

● Forging a reference for a job – £50 fine.

When money is counterfeit

A forged banknote is worthless and must be handed over to the police or Bank of England. If you discover that a banknote in your possession is forged, do not try to use it. That would be a criminal offence, carrying a maximum penalty of life imprisonment.

If you were given the note in payment

for something, you are entitled to claim its face value from the person who gave it to you. Even if he did not know it was forged, he is assumed in law to have represented it as worth its face value when he passed it to you.

If he knew it was forged, he can be prosecuted, and he still owes you that sum of money. If you received forged money as a gift, you have no legal claim against the person who gave it to you.

If you pay someone with a forged note unknowingly, you have committed no offence, but, you must pay again.

FOSTERING

Parents who take someone else's child into their home

Couples who take other people's children to live in their own homes and bring them up as if they were their own children are known as foster parents.

They have all the responsibilities of normal parents to take care of the children; but the real parents can insist on having the children returned to them.

No person who has been convicted of causing or permitting bodily harm to a child can become a foster parent, nor can a person who lives in a house where there is a person with such a record.

People are also barred from fostering if an order has been made removing a child from their care, or if they have advertised for foster children giving a false name and address.

These restrictions apply whether a parent intends to foster privately or under a local authority scheme.

Foster parents can arrange to take children privately or by arrangement with their local council. In either case the child in their care must be under the supervision of local social workers.

Private fostering

Any person who looks after a child to whom he or she is not related for more than 27 days is fostering the child, and must notify the local authority. An exception is made in the case of persons who are fostering continuously and have already notified the local authority of the first child they took. Otherwise anyone who fails to give notification – no matter what arrangements have been made with the parents – is guilty of

a criminal offence and can be gaoled for up to 6 months and fined up to £400.

It is wise for a couple who want to foster children to contact their local authority first. There they can obtain advice about their legal responsibilities and the accommodation they will need to provide. Having done so, there is nothing to stop them making a private fostering arrangement either through friends or by advertising.

Approved fostering

Many fostered children are in the care of the local council before they are put out to foster parents. Local councils welcome inquiries.

If they find home conditions satisfactory they will register couples as approved foster parents. Children can be placed with these families at short notice.

How to apply Write direct to the social services department of your local authority and ask for arrangements to be made for a social worker to visit the home.

Some local authorities hold group meetings for couples interested in fostering. Discussion is held on the responsibilities and the problems of looking after foster children.

Vetting The local authority will want to know full details about the home life of prospective foster parents. They will be asked for details of work, type of accommodation available, how many children are already living in the home.

A social worker then visits the prospective foster parents in their home to try to learn something of their relationships with their own children. References are required and permission is sought to approach the family doctor, and the police.

Placing a child Social workers prefer to place a fostered child with a married couple, although some single or widowed women are given children to foster. It is unlawful for a child to be placed for fostering with an unmarried man, unless he is a close relative.

Once a couple have agreed to take a child they have to sign a declaration that they will bring up the child as if it was their own and encourage the child to follow its own religion.

Supervision The fostering family have to give an undertaking to the local authority that they will look after the

child's health and allow council social workers to see the child on request at regular intervals.

On visits, the social worker will discuss with the child any problems it may have either at home or at school.

The social worker can also remove the child from the house at any time without notice if he feels that it is in the child's interests. Official foster parents have no right of appeal to a court, but private foster parents can appeal against this in the local JUVENILE COURT within 14 days. If the appeal is rejected they have 21 days in which to appeal to the CROWN COURT.

The local council can make strict regulations about the number of children allowed at any one time in a foster home and the amount of accommodation that should be available. It can also ban a particular family from fostering children, but private foster parents can appeal against the ban to the juvenile court.

Short-term fostering

Some couples prefer to foster children on short-term basis only, keeping the children for periods of up to 8 weeks at a time. Because children can always be taken away from their foster parents, the short-term schemes avoid the emotional involvement that is unavoidable when a child has lived for a long time with the same family.

Children placed for short-term fostering are usually children in some sort of crisis, such as children about to be adopted, children in need of care while their mothers are in hospital, or children under a Place of Safety order. *See:* CHILDREN IN CARE

Parents who foster short-term are usually ready to cope with children of any race and sometimes of a different religion. They are given full details of a child's background and behaviour pattern before the child is placed with them. It is entirely up to the foster parents to decide whether or not they could cope with a handicapped child.

Long-term fostering

Some couples take foster children on a permanent basis and agree to look after them indefinitely, often until the child is 16, the present school-leaving age, when it is no longer subject to regulations as a foster child. However, if the child is subject to a care order, the local authority may wish him to remain under some regulations until 18 or 19.

The child's real parents are often involved in the placing of their child and meet the foster parents before the child moves in. The child normally spends a few introductory weekends with its prospective foster parents before permanently settling with them.

These children often keep in touch with their real parents throughout the period they are fostered, but if it is to be a long-term fostering, there is usually no initial intention of returning the child to its real parents. The parents do, however, have a legal right to claim their child back at any time, provided the child is not in care.

Removing a child

A child in council care who has been placed with foster parents can be removed from the foster parents at any time if the council considers it is in the child's interests.

If, however, the child was placed voluntarily in care, then the real parents can remove it from a foster home at any time up to 6 months. After that if the natural parents want to have their child moved from a foster home they may have to give the local council 28 days' notice.

A child placed in care by a court cannot be removed from foster parents except by the local authority or by a revised order from the court.

When adoption is planned by foster parents

Local authorities do not encourage couples to look upon child fostering as a short step to ADOPTION. But foster parents who have looked after a child for more than a year can ask for an order of custodianship with the consent of one of the real parents. They can do so without the parents' consent if they have fostered the child for 3 years or more.

Some foster parents do successfully adopt the children in their care. If they have looked after a child for 5 years or more and they then apply for an adoption order, neither the real parents nor the local authority can remove the foster child without a court order. But the foster parents would still have to convince the court that there were grounds

for dispensing with the parents' agreement to the adoption.

What payment is involved

Parents fostering children through private arrangements make their own terms for payment for the keep of the fostered child. Local authorities fix rates which they pay to their approved foster parents. These rates vary widely from one council to another.

In fixing the rate to be paid, councils take into account the age of a child and the cost of feeding and clothing it. Rates for teenagers, for example, are usually much higher than those for a child under 5 years old.

Foster parents also receive from most local councils additional allowances to pay for birthdays, holidays and Christmas extras for the children in their care.

Professional foster parents offering special care

Many local authorities offer substantially increased rates, some even a salary, to couples who are prepared to offer a home to children with special needs – for example, badly handicapped children.

The couples chosen usually have experience in professional child care – for example, teaching or nursing; most would already have experience of bringing up a family themselves with older children.

These 'professional' foster parents receive increased support from the local authority through frequent social worker visits and group support through contact with other professional foster parents at regular meetings. Grants are available to adapt houses to meet the needs of a handicapped foster child. In many cases professional foster parents may also be eligible for ATTENDANCE ALLOWANCES.

FRAUD

There is no offence known as fraud, but the term is often used to describe crimes of DECEPTION which are dealt with under the general law of theft. The offence of 'fraudulent conversion' has been abolished, and the charge now used is 'obtaining pecuniary advantage by deception'.

FREE MILK
Help for families with low incomes

Families who are drawing supplementary benefit or family income supplement or who have a low income are entitled to 1 pint of free milk a day for each child under school age and for an expectant mother. They are also entitled to free supplies of vitamins A, D and C.

A parent not receiving supplementary benefit or family income supplement who believes that the family income may be low enough to qualify should obtain leaflet M11, which gives the income limits, from any post office or social security office. Fill in the attached claim form and post or take it to the local social security office. They will decide if the family qualifies.

How to obtain tokens for free milk

Families who qualify for free supplies receive tokens from the Department of Health and Social Security. The tokens can be exchanged with a milkman for a pint of milk a day for an expectant mother and for each child under 5 years 1 month.

If a child is under 1 year old and is bottle-fed, the family can use its tokens to obtain dried milk from a maternity and child health clinic or from a welfare food centre. Details can be obtained from the clinic or health visitor.

At the clinic or centre, families can also exchange tokens for vitamin tablets (for an expectant mother) and vitamin drops (for children under 5 years 1 month).

Families on supplementary benefit or family income supplement receive the tokens by post when they are sent their order books by the Department of Health and Social Security.

If these are not sent, parents should write to the local social security office or, if they are receiving family income supplement, to the Department of Health and Social Security, Family Income Supplements, Poulton-le-Fylde, Blackpool FY6 8NW.

Milk for children in day care

Children attending a day nursery or play group approved by the local authority, or being looked after by an approved child minder, are entitled to one-third of a pint of free milk on each day that they attend for 2 hours or more. Day-care milk is given in addition to any free milk the family may already be getting.

Organisers of day nurseries and play groups and child minders should apply to the local social services department. *See also:* SCHOOL MEALS AND MILK

Children of 5 to 16 who are too severely handicapped to attend an ordinary or special school are entitled to a pint of free milk a day. To claim, obtain form FW20 from the local social security office.

FREE SAMPLE

When goods are given away free

Anyone who receives a free sample of goods is not entitled to replacement or compensation for its value if the sample is faulty. A free sample is not a sale, for no money is paid or payable. The recipient does not therefore have any of the rights of a buyer.

However, if the free sample is so faulty as to cause injury or damage, anyone who suffers may be able to sue the manufacturer or supplier if they have been negligent.
See: NEGLIGENCE
PREMIUM OFFER

NO CATCH

When a free sample is given, the recipient has few of the rights of someone who buys goods. On the other hand, there is no obligation to purchase.

'It's free. Honest. No catch.'

FREE SCHOOL

How people can run their own classes

Parents with their own ideas on how children should be educated can set up their own school, financed by voluntary fund-raising, provided that they can satisfy the local education authority that they are fulfilling the legal obligation to see that their children are being educated. *See:* HOME TEACHING

YOU CAN SHOW THE
SCHOOL INSPECTOR THE DOOR

Provided that a free school is registered the local education authority has no right to inspect it.

'School Inspector – 1944 Act'

You do not need to notify the authority before opening a free school, but if you intend to teach five children or more over the age of 5 you must register the school with the Department of Education and Science. Write to the department, telling it of your proposal and it will send you the appropriate forms to fill in for registration.

At first, a free school is provisionally registered. The Department of Education and Science then inspects the school. If the school is considered satisfactory, it is put on the permanent register.

Anyone who runs an unregistered school can be fined £50 for a first offence. And he can be sentenced to 3 months' imprisonment and fined £50 for any subsequent offence.

Free schools for children of all ages have been set up in a number of deprived areas. There is no head teacher.

The teachers share the work of taking lessons, cooking, cleaning the premises and doing the accounts. No fees are charged, and the staff work for very small salaries, or for nothing.

The pupils may take part in decisions about how the school should be run.
School inspection Provided that a school is registered, the local education authority has no right to inspect it or to instruct it to teach any particular courses. Some free schools may, however, receive help from the local education authority because they are known to be working with deprived or difficult children.

FREEHOLD LAND

Land that is freehold was held originally in England and Wales by freemen, rather than by villeins. Today, it means simply that the landowner has no obligation to pay any rent or charge to a landlord. *See:* LEASEHOLD LAND

FRINGE BENEFIT

When tax must be paid on extras

Many firms give their employees fringe benefits in the form of cars, accommodation, medical insurance, luncheon vouchers and cash handouts. Tax should be paid on almost all of these benefits, though the form in which they are given can reduce the tax liability.

In general, tax liability is reduced when the benefit consists of an article or gift rather than cash.
Secretary's dress An employer buys his secretary a new dress or outfit for £50 so that she will look smart at the office. She wears it – but he remains the owner of the dress.

After 12 months the employer gives the secretary the outfit. Its value then as second-hand clothing is £30 – and that is the amount on which the secretary should pay tax.

When two levels of taxation apply

Employees are divided into two groups for the taxation of fringe benefits, and different rules apply for each group.

1. Higher-paid employees – anyone earning over a certain amount (the amount is increased from time to time) and any director, irrespective of his earnings, unless he works full-time for the company, has 5 per cent or less of the shares and earns under the relevant amount.

2. Lower-paid employees – anyone earning less than the higher limit.

Higher-paid employees are taxed on what it costs the employer to provide the benefit. Lower-paid employees are taxed on the amount of money that they could get by selling the benefit at its second-hand value.

In the case of higher-paid employees, when an asset is loaned to the employee rather than given to him, the annual benefit is measured as 20 per cent of the cost of the asset to the employer. Thus, if a television costing £400 is loaned by the company to an employee, the annual taxable benefit is £80. The rules are different for the loan of a company car.

The significance of a company car

A company-owned car that is also used privately is treated as a taxable benefit only if issued to a higher-paid worker. A lower-paid worker does not have to pay tax on a company car unless its provision is related to a cut in pay.

The basic measure of benefit is called the 'scale', which quantifies the annual benefit according to engine size or cost of the car, and its age. These benefits are revised from time to time.

If the car is used for only 1,000 miles or less of business use a year, the benefit is one and a half times the scale rate. Second and subsequent company cars are also charged at one and a half times the scale benefit, irrespective of business use.

If the first car is used for more than 1,000 miles business use in a year, the benefit is only the scale rate. If the business use in a year is 18,000 miles or more, the scale benefit is halved.

Petrol bills Petrol supplied by a company or bought on a company account for use in a company car is not taxable. However, if the employee first buys the petrol himself and the company later reimburses him, the cost of the petrol used for private motoring is liable for tax.

HOW TAX IS ASSESSED ON PRIVATE USE OF A COMPANY CAR

Scale rates apply to cars used for more than 1,000 miles a year for business purposes. One and a half times the scale rate applies in certain other cases

The Inland Revenue puts an annual cash value on the private use of a company car, the amount depending on the car's usage, age, engine capacity or original cost.

CARS ORIGINALLY COSTING UP TO £9,600

	Cylinder capacity	Taxable benefit
Vehicle less than 4 years old	1300 cc or less	£230
	1301 – 1800 cc	£300
	Over 1800 cc	£450
Vehicle more than 4 years old	1300 cc or less	£155
	1301 – 1800 cc	£200
	Over 1800 cc	£300

CARS ORIGINALLY COSTING £9,600 – £14,400

	Cylinder capacity	Taxable benefit
Under 4 years old	Any	£660
Over 4 years old	Any	£440

CARS ORIGINALLY COSTING MORE THAN £14,400

	Cylinder capacity	Taxable benefit
Under 4 years old	Any	£1,050
Over 4 years old	Any	£700

When a house is provided with the job

Self-contained accommodation provided for a worker is tax free only when it is essential for the worker to occupy the house in order to do his job.

For workers such as hotel staff who live on the premises, the accommodation is tax free if it is provided free. But if a deduction is made from salary for the cost of the accommodation, the gross salary is taxed, with no allowance against the accommodation charge.

Take for example, the head waiter of a holiday hotel who lives on the premises and is paid £6,000 a year salary. If, say, £600 a year is deducted from his salary for accommodation, he pays tax on the full £6,000.

If, however, he is paid only £5,400 a year and is given free accommodation, he will be taxed only on £5,400. It is always better to have the free accommodation and the lower salary.

When medical insurance is provided by the company

Employees' subscriptions to medical funds and insurance schemes are free of tax, but the employee must pay tax on any medical bills met from an insurance scheme, or paid by the company. An employer's private medical insurance contributions are taxable and normally charged to the employee.

When the cost of removal may be reimbursed

No tax is payable on removal expenses paid by a company to an employee who is moved to a new area.

Such tax-free expenses can include legal costs for buying and selling a house, removal services and refitting of carpets – or even new carpets if he has to fit larger rooms.

If an employee is moved to an area where housing is more expensive than where he previously lived, he can be paid a reasonable rent allowance, tax free, for about 5 years.

When free meals are provided

If an employer provides subsidised or free meals in a staff canteen, the employees are not taxed on the value of those meals – provided that the service is available to all members of the staff irrespective of rank, and there is no attempt to provide better facilities for certain groups such as directors and senior management.

If a dining-room is provided for the exclusive use of the directors, therefore, they should declare the value of the meals they receive and pay tax.

When a meal allowance is paid by the employer

When an employer reimburses an employee in cash for the cost of meals incurred by him even while on duty, the employee must pay tax on the amount received.

Thus, if a clerk is required to work overtime and is paid, say, £1.50 by his

ON THE FRINGE

Most fringe benefits received by employees are taxable. The amount of tax payable depends on the kind of benefit received and the employee's level of earnings.

"Not another fringe benefit, Carstairs."

HOW THE TAXMAN TREATS COMPANY 'PERKS'
Different taxation levels depending on type of benefit

If an employee receives fringe benefits from his company in addition to his wage or salary, in nearly all cases he is liable to pay income tax on all or part of their value, depending on the type of benefit being enjoyed and the employee's earnings.

Benefit	How it is taxed
Firm's car used not more than 1,000 miles a year for business, by a 'higher paid' employee	1½ times scale benefit (see p. 297).
Firm's car used more than 1,000 miles a year for business, by a 'higher paid' employee	Scale benefit (see p. 297).
Pool car	No tax payable.
Loans from employer at favourable rates of interest	Tax payable on the difference between the commercial rate charged unless it is less than £200, or if the interest is allowed as tax relief.
Housing or accommodation paid for by firm	Tax payable on the gross annual value of the tenancy, plus any costs paid by the firm such as rates and heating. Tax free if the employee has to live in the house to do his job.
Television sets, washing machines or other consumer goods	Tax is payable on the amount paid by the employer for the article if it is new, but on the value at the time if the gift is secondhand. A different, less favourable, method may apply on secondhand goods given to 'higher paid' employees.
Medical insurance	Tax payable on the employer's premium.
Working clothes	Tax free.
Luncheon vouchers	Taxable over 15p.
Cash vouchers	Full value is taxable.
Staff canteen meals	Tax free if the canteen is open to all staff without distinction of status.
Travelling and entertaining expenses	Tax free if the whole amount is spent on the employee's behalf.
Removal expenses	Tax free.

employer to reimburse him for the cost of buying an evening meal near his office, the £1.50 is taxable, and the employee cannot claim for any tax relief for the cost of the meal he has purchased.

In some cases, however, when standard payments are made to employees regularly obliged to buy meals away from home and the employer's base, Inland Revenue may agree with the appropriate trade union or professional body to allow some part of the payments tax free.

When overnight expenses are reimbursed

An employee's expenses for a stay away from home overnight are not taxable when they are reimbursed by his employer. This would cover the cost of accommodation, travel, reasonable entertainment, evening meal and breakfast. Inland Revenue does not normally allow the cost of lunches as tax free – even when the employee is away overnight.

Any vouchers other than luncheon

vouchers – for example, cash vouchers or those for specific goods and services – are taxable on their full value.

FUEL BILL

What to do if a bill cannot be paid at once

Anyone who cannot pay a gas or electricity bill should contact the accounts officer at the local gas or electricity office and suggest paying on easier terms.

The local gas or electricity office will give advice on easier-payment schemes. For example, payment can be made through a budget account, by which the probable cost for the year is divided into monthly instalments and any balance on either side is cleared at the end of the year. Otherwise, special savings stamps, produced by the gas and electricity authorities, can be purchased and collected in a book by the customer, to be put towards paying a bill.

Help from social services or social security

Someone who cannot even pay on easier terms should consult his local authority social services department or the local social security office.

If he is unemployed, he may find that he is entitled to claim supplementary benefit at his local social security office.

Someone who is in full-time work and not entitled to claim supplementary benefit, and who cannot pay a fuel bill, should go to the local authority social services department. If lack of heating or lighting will cause hardship to a family with young children – to the extent that they might have to be taken into care – the authority can make an emergency lump-sum payment to meet the bill. Local charities may, on the advice of a council social worker, make a payment to clear a fuel bill for an elderly or disabled person.

A lump-sum payment – in the form of a cheque paid direct to the fuel board – is unlikely to be made if the applicant's income is much more than that of a supplementary benefit claimant. Someone in full-time work who receives a lump-sum payment from the local authority may be asked to repay it.

Local authorities are sparing in their use of the power to make payments: each case is considered on its own merits.

Extra supplementary benefit

Anyone on supplementary benefit may be entitled to extra help with heating bills. This can take one of three forms:

Increases in weekly payments Weekly supplementary benefit payments are increased in cases where fuel costs are likely to be heavy. If this is because there is an elderly person or a young child in the household or because someone needs extra warmth as a result of illness or restricted mobility, the increase is usually £1.40 a week, but in cases of serious illness or severe disability it is £3.40.

Someone whose house is difficult to heat is also entitled to extra benefit, in addition to any increase for sickness or restricted mobility – provided that the increases do not total more than £3.40 a week.

Weekly increases are also given where the home is centrally heated. The amount depends on the number of rooms. If there are not more than 4 rooms, not counting a bathroom, lavatory or hall, the increase is £1.40. For more than 4 rooms it is £2.80. But a central-heating increase will not be paid in addition to an increase given for other reasons. Only the higher of the two increases will be given.

The increases are revised annually to keep them in line with rising fuel prices. The categories of people entitled to them are also liable to change.

Lump-sum payment A person receiving supplementary benefit whose fuel bills come to more than the amount he has put aside to pay them as a result of abnormally high consumption in a period of exceptionally severe weather, is entitled to a lump-sum payment to cover the excess over normal consumption.

A lump sum is also payable where the reason for not putting aside enough to pay the fuel bills is the cost of running an unfamiliar heating system. In this case, the lump sum is half the fuel costs incurred during the first 6 months' use of the new system.

If a person has not been getting supplementary benefit which he could have claimed – for example, he may not have realised he was entitled to an increase for heating – and, as a result, money aside for fuel bills has been spent on other needs for which an extra payment could have been made, a lump-sum

INCREASES IN WEEKLY BENEFIT PAYMENTS TO PROVIDE FOR EXTRA HEATING

Ill or elderly beneficiaries qualify for more help

If someone who is receiving supplementary benefit has to pay higher heating bills because of illness or frailty, or because a house is unusually difficult to keep warm in winter, say, he or she should ask for an extra allowance.

Reason for extra heating	Increase
Mobility restricted because of old age or frailty	£1.40
Chronic (long-term) illness	£1.40
Accommodation difficult to heat – for example, because it is damp	£1.40
Accommodation exceptionally difficult to heat	£3.40
Housebound, or unable to go out without help	£3.40
Serious illness	£3.40
Suffering from serious illness that requires constant day and night room temperature	£3.40
Confined to bed, or unable to walk without help, and in need of extra heating day and night	£3.40

payment for fuel must be made.

If somebody on supplementary benefit has got into difficulties with fuel bills, a payment will be made to cover the charge for installing a pre-payment meter, if it is considered necessary, or for reconnection of the fuel supply where arrangements have been made for payment of the debt either by a lump-sum payment or by deductions from the weekly benefit.

Although lump-sum payments are normally made only to people already getting supplementary benefit weekly, they can also be made to a person who is entitled to weekly payments but has not claimed them.

Direct payment to the fuel board

If a person on supplementary benefit has failed to budget for the cost of fuel, and owes £22 or more to the gas or electricity board, which cannot be cleared by a lump-sum payment, the supplementary benefit officer may decide that part of his weekly benefit should be deducted and paid direct to the fuel board. This can be done either at the person's own request or at the discretion of the benefit officer, but only if in the benefit officer's opinion it would be in the interests of the person concerned and particularly those of his dependants.

The deduction consists of a payment, which is usually £1.10 a week, towards the debt and payment of the estimated cost of current weekly consumption.

Preventing disconnection of gas and electricity

The electricity and gas industries operate a code of practice aimed at preventing needless disconnection of fuel supplies over unpaid bills.

The code states that if the family breadwinner is drawing supplementary or unemployment benefit, or if all the people in the house are pensioners, he or she should tell the gas or electricity office that there is difficulty in paying. Then contact the local Department of Health and Social Security office.

If someone has a child under 11, or is drawing FAMILY INCOME SUPPLEMENT, and is in difficulty with his bill, he should also tell the gas or electricity

office and contact the local authority social services department.

If someone moves without paying the bill

If you move into a house, flat or other accommodation, and the previous occupier has left without paying a fuel bill, you are not responsible for seeing that the bill is paid. The gas or electricity authority is not entitled to disconnect your supply on the ground that the previous occupier failed to pay.

When you move out, you should give the gas or electricity authority at least 24 hours' notice. If you fail to do so, you may have to pay for any gas or electricity used on the property until the meter is next read or your change of address has been notified by a new occupier requesting a supply.
See: ELECTRICITY SUPPLY
GAS SUPPLY
SUPPLEMENTARY BENEFIT

FUNERAL

Making the arrangements after a death in the family

No one has a legal right to insist on how his or her body should be disposed of after death. Those who have to arrange a funeral are not bound to carry out any wish expressed, such as a preference for cremation or burial – even if the wish is set out in a will. In practice, however, such wishes are usually respected.

If you have a special request about the disposal of your body after death, put it in writing – either in your will, or in a letter to the EXECUTOR and your family – and tell them about it orally.

If you want part or all of your body to be used for medical purposes, you must say so in a declaration written separately from your will and signed by two witnesses, who can be members of your family. The declaration is legally binding on your heirs and executors, and you should send a copy of it to any hospital or institution to which you have made a specific bequest.

If you particularly do not want your body to be so used, make your wishes clear in your will. Executors or next of kin cannot give permission for the

medical use of your body if you have made your objection known. *See:* TRANSPLANT

Making the arrangements for a funeral

A body must not be disposed of until a registrar's certificate or coroner's order has been issued. *See:* DEATH, Registration of

If a dead person has left a will, it is the duty of his executors to arrange the funeral. If there is no will, or if the executors are not immediately available, the funeral must be arranged by the person – whether owner or tenant – who occupies the premises in which the body is lying.

If the body is in a public institution, such as a hospital, those in charge of the institution normally ask the dead person's relatives to take responsibility – and will arrange the funeral only if that request is refused.

When there are no relatives or executors, and the person did not die in a hospital or other public institution, it is the duty of the local council's social services department to arrange a funeral.

Restrictions on where a funeral can be held

A funeral, by burial or cremation, can be public or in private: it can be held at sea, or by any other method of disposal that does not cause a nuisance or health hazard. It is usual to employ an undertaker or burial society, but executors or relatives can organise the funeral themselves.

What to look for when choosing an undertaker

Having decided what type of funeral is required, the executors or relatives should seek itemised cost estimates from several undertakers and compare their charges and services. The basic minimum offered by undertakers – a simple coffin, hearse, bearers and the services of the undertaker in arranging ceremonial details and the necessary certificates – costs from about £150 upwards. That does not include the burial fee – which is payable to the cemetery or church – or the cost of accompanying

AN UNDERTAKING BY THE UNDERTAKERS

Since 1979 the public has been protected by a code of practice that the 2,200 members of the National Association of Funeral Directors agreed in consultation with the Office of Fair Trading. Members of the association are pledged to:
● Offer a basic, simple funeral service.
● Give a written estimate of all funeral charges and an itemised invoice.
● Ensure that advertising is clear, honest and in good taste.

● Provide full and fair information about services and prices and offer guidance on certification and registration of death, social security benefits and the application of insurance policies in each case.
● Provide speedy and sympathetic handling of complaints.
● Provide suitable training for management in client relations.
● Display the association's symbol on the premises.

cars, flowers, a headstone and other extras.

If you have been unable to compare undertakers' costs and subsequently feel that you have been overcharged – or if the undertaker has been negligent – complain to the National Association of Funeral Directors, if he is a member.

The association's disciplinary and conciliation committee will hear your case and can recommend damages or a refund.

If the undertaker is not a NAFD member, or if you are not satisfied with their decision, complain to the trading standards officer at your local council offices.

When embalming is required A body can be preserved, usually for cosmetic purposes, by replacing the blood with a chemical, formalin. The executor or relative arranging the funeral should tell the undertaker if they specifically object to the process.

Embalming must not be carried out until the registrar's certificate or coroner's order has been issued, as it may obscure the cause of death.

Paying for the funeral

The government DEATH GRANT – a maximum of £30 – covers only a small part of the cost of a funeral, but other financial help is often available to those in need. See: FATAL ACCIDENT; SUPPLEMENTARY BENEFIT

The undertaker's bill has priority over all other debts of the ESTATE and must be paid by the executors before they distribute any legacies. For tax purposes, it should be submitted as a debt of the estate, even though it was not incurred by the dead person himself.

If a funeral is arranged by a hospital or local authority – in the absence of relatives or executors – it is entitled to recover the cost from the estate, if any.

Arranging a burial in a churchyard

Everyone is entitled to be buried in the churchyard of the parish in which he had his home, or in which he dies – whether or not he was a Christian – provided that there is room for the burial. He is also entitled to a Church of England burial service, unless he died by suicide or without having been baptised.

However, he is not entitled to a memorial or to exclusive use of a particular part of the churchyard without permission – known in church law as a faculty – from the church authorities.

Normally, a faculty is granted by the vicar for a fee, which varies according to the location of the burial plot and the size of the memorial. But if the requirements are unusual – for example, insistence on a black headstone where all the other monuments are white – the vicar refers mourners to the Diocesan Registrar, who then seeks permission from the Chancellor of the Diocese, normally a High Court judge.

The church decides the position of the grave and receives a burial fee of £11. The cost, including the charge for a burial service, is £17. The vicar must approve the inscription before a headstone is set up.

Any extras – such as the services of an organist, choir or bell-ringers, or heating the church at a time when it is normally unheated – are provided for an additional fee which is worked out by agreement between the vicar and those responsible for the funeral.

A vicar can allow someone who did not live in the parish to be buried in his churchyard, but may charge a higher fee which he agrees with the mourners.

Other types of burial

Other burial grounds are run by other religious denominations, by charities, or privately.

Public cemeteries are provided by local authorities. See: CEMETERY

A burial outside a cemetery – for example, in a dead person's garden – must be approved by the local planning authority, health department and the Department of the Environment. If there are objections – from neighbours, for example – the body must be buried at a recognised site.

Even when the dead person has stated in writing that he wanted to be buried, not cremated, his executor or next-of-kin is entitled to rule otherwise after his death.

Special rules for cremation

Special safeguards, however, must be observed before a body can be cremated to ensure that there are no unresolved doubts about the cause of death.
When death is not reported to the coroner When someone has died in ordinary, unsuspicious circumstances, there is no need to report the death to the CORONER. Instead, if the body is to be cremated, ask the undertaker for a copy of Form A, the application form for cremation.

It must be completed by the deceased's executor or by the person arranging the funeral and it has to be counter-signed by a householder to whom the applicant is known.

The doctor who treated the deceased during his last illness, although not necessarily the one who signed the death certificate must identify the body and complete Form B, giving information about the deceased's treatment and stating whether the doctor benefits financially from the death.

A confirmatory certificate, Form C, must be completed by an independent doctor who has seen the body and made a careful external examination. The doctor who completes Form B normally arranges for another to complete Form C. The two doctors must sign a separate declaration that they do not suspect that the deceased died a violent or unnatural death, or that the cause of death is unknown, or that an INQUEST is required. If they do not do so, an inquest must be held before the body can be cremated.

The certifying doctors are entitled to charge a fee which is paid by the undertaker who adds it to his total funeral bill. In practice, the undertaker handles most of the paperwork.

When the death is reported to the coroner

If the doctor who attended the deceased is not available, the death has to be reported to the coroner who issues Form E, authorising cremation, if he sees no reason to hold an inquest. If a death is reported by the doctor or by the registrar of deaths, the coroner makes his own inquiries and may hold an inquest or order a post-mortem before issuing Form E.

Form F, the authority to cremate, is the final stage. This form is issued by the medical referee to the crematorium after he has seen Forms B and C or E. Each crematorium has a medical referee – a local doctor appointed by the Secretary of State for Health – who checks all applications for cremation. If the medical referee is not satisfied with the information on the forms he can refuse permission to cremate.

FURNISHED LETTING

How the law protects tenants

Since August 1974, all new tenants have had certain minimum legal protection under the provisions of the Rent Act – whether they rent furnished or unfurnished property. *See:* EVICTION

There are, however, certain rights, for both landlord and tenant, that apply only to furnished lettings.

A landlord offering a flat or house to let furnished implies in his offer that the premises are fit to live in. If a tenant, on moving in, discovers that they are not, he will not be liable for any rent or use of the premises he has had, and he can sue the landlord in the county court for damages for any loss he has suffered.

Property is considered unfit if it is

badly affected by damp, infested with bugs or contaminated by an infectious disease.

A tenant, without endangering his security of tenure, can complain to the local council's environmental health department. Its officers can ask the local magistrates for an order compelling the landlord to put the property in order, or the council can do the necessary work itself and charge the cost to the landlord. If it chooses, it can also obtain a closing order prohibiting the landlord from letting the property. The tenant can then sue the landlord for breach of CONTRACT.

How furnished is defined

Part of the rent for a furnished flat is legally considered to be in payment for the use of the furniture provided.

In any disputes over a tenant's liability for wear or tear, or in any claim by the tenant for a RENT ALLOWANCE, it may be necessary to prove whether or not the property is furnished.

There is no strict definition of what qualifies a house or flat to be considered furnished, but one or two pieces of second-hand furniture bought at a local junk shop would not be enough. The

proportion of rent attributable to use of furniture has to be 'substantial' – say, 15–20 per cent.

A landlord has to provide at least the bare essentials to enable a property to be lived in – for example, a cooker, table, chairs, a bed, curtains and possibly even a carpet.

When a premium is required

Some landlords ask prospective tenants to pay a deposit, often described as 'returnable', against any loss or damage to furniture during the tenancy. The tenant can refuse to pay it, because the Rent Act prohibits the taking of premiums, but if he does, he may not get the property. *See:* KEY MONEY

It is best to pay and then claim the money back from the landlord. If he refuses to pay, the tenant should make clear that he knows that he is protected against exploitation by the terms of the Rent Act, and he should say that he is willing to take court action to recover his money.

It is within the law, however, for a landlord to sell the furniture in the flat or house to the tenant at a reasonable price. The property would then fall under the definition of unfurnished.

WHEN A LANDLORD IS RESIDENT

Tenants who occupied their rented, furnished property before August 14, 1974 and who have a resident landlord, do not have the same security against eviction as people who have taken tenancies since.

Tenants with agreements made before then, and whose landlord is resident, will have to leave the premises when the agreement expires if the landlord wants them to. The most a tenant in that situation can hope for is an extension of his tenancy fixed by a rent tribunal for, usually, a 6 month period, renewable indefinitely.

The only other course for the tenant is to try to prove to the rent tribunal that the property is unfurnished.

Many tenancies taken out as furnished before August 14, 1974 consisted of rooms with the barest minimum of furniture. These may not now meet the requirements of furnished property as sufficient to enable the property to be lived in.

If the tribunal decides that the property is not furnished, the tenant has the same protection against eviction as a tenant whose agreement was made after August 14, 1974.

A tenant of furnished premises, with an agreement that was signed before that date and that has not yet expired, and with a resident landlord, can challenge any proposed rent increase at a rent tribunal, or can ask for an existing rent to be lowered.

A tenant can install his own furniture in place of his landlord's, provided that he has made a written agreement with his landlord to do so. The agreement may state that he must use the landlord's furniture.

If he is allowed to use his own, the landlord's furniture must be stored on the premises – for example, in the attic – and not elsewhere. It must also be properly looked after. When a tenant moves out he must remove all his furniture and put back the landlord's.

An agreement for a tenant to use his own furniture is not a ground for a reduction in the rent.

A tenant of furnished premises, with an agreement made before August 14, 1974, but who has no resident landlord, is now a fully protected tenant within the Rent Act.

When property is damaged

A tenant is not liable for any damage or repair necessary because of wear and tear through normal use of the furniture or fittings. He has to pay, however, for any deliberate damage or damage caused through negligence, and the landlord can sue for compensation in the county court.

FURNITURE STORAGE

When you leave furniture in a depository

If you leave furniture at a warehouse or depository for storage you enter into a CONTRACT with the owners. Before doing so, look carefully at their conditions of storage as they may try to restrict your rights and increase theirs.

The conditions are normally printed on the quotation you receive and they

CHECK THE CONTRACT
FOR EXEMPTION CLAUSES

Usually the depository is liable for breakages, but you should insure against fire and theft.

may be repeated on the agreement form you eventually sign. Conditions to beware of particularly are those that seek to exclude any liability for loss or damage.

Although the depository is bound to take reasonable care of your furniture, you should make your own arrangements for insuring it against fire and theft, and any other likely or possible risk that you may be aware of, such as flooding, while it is in store – unless the storage company agrees to arrange such cover for you.

It will not be liable to compensate you if the furniture is damaged in a fire that is not the fault of the company or its servants. Nor will it have to reimburse you if the furniture is stolen – provided that it can show they took reasonable precautions against theft.

Even if the loss or damage is the storage company's fault, it may try to shelter behind an exemption clause in its printed conditions. That can be effective only if the clause is fair and reasonable under the UNFAIR CONTRACT Terms Act 1977.

GAMBLING

Where and when you can place a bet

It is legal to bet on cards, horse and greyhound racing, bingo games, dice games, a FOOTBALL POOL, prize competition or properly licensed lottery, but there are complicated laws governing how you can bet, and restricting the places where gambling can be carried on.

It is illegal, for example, for any type of betting to be carried on in the street, and no one under the age of 18 can bet – except privately in his own home.

In general, the law aims to restrict gambling to such places as casinos, horse-race courses, dog tracks, betting shops, bingo halls and private clubs that have been licensed by the local authority and are controlled by laws aimed at protecting the gambler.

Gambling is permitted in public houses only on games of skill such as darts, shove ha'penny or chess and on games of chance such as cribbage and dominoes.

There are two ways to bet:
● Gaming – which is betting with other players in a game of chance, such as roulette or cards, or in a pool, such as a football pool, from which a fixed, or unfixed, sum will be paid to any winner. Debts incurred can be recovered by law.
● Wagering – which is a bet struck between two people on the outcome of an event, such as a horse race or a general election, in which one of them will win and the other will lose. Debts incurred cannot be recovered through the courts.

CONTROLLING THE PEOPLE WHO CONTROL GAMING

The Gaming Board was set up by the Government in 1968 to control all gaming in Britain's casinos and clubs.

The board has 40 full-time inspectors who keep a thorough check on the personal and financial background of all the people involved – of the operators themselves, the financial backers, the croupiers and the dealers.

Casinos need a certificate of consent from the Gaming Board before they can apply to the local magistrates for a gaming licence. The board issues certificates only to casinos where the operators and staff have its approval.

The board can withdraw its consent later if it finds it was given any false information, and can order a casino to re-apply for consent if it changes hands or if any major changes are made at the club.

The board – and anyone else – can also object when the casino makes its annual application for a renewal of its gaming licence.

A person or company applying for a certificate of consent from the board can apply at a personal hearing and be represented by a solicitor. If the board refuses consent it does not have to give any reasons and can keep confidential any information given to it by private individuals.

OBJECTING TO A CASINO LICENCE

Gaming licences are renewed annually by the local licensing magistrates. Applications are usually heard in May, but the club must advertise its application in the local Press in March.

Anyone who wants to object must send two copies of a statement, briefly outlining his reasons, to the magistrates' clerk before April 15. He is then told the date of the hearing which he can attend in person or through his lawyer.

An objector has the right to organise opposition to a licence – perhaps by lobbying councillors or writing to the local Press for support.

The magistrates can reject a gaming licence application for a number of reasons, including noise, nuisance, unsuitable premises, inadequate parking facilities or the existence of other gaming clubs in the area. They can also take objections into account by granting a licence but imposing specific restrictions on it.

Someone making a frivolous objection may be ordered to pay costs.

Gambling in a casino

Casinos are gambling clubs in which only the players taking part in games of chance can lose: the clubs can never lose. They must have a certificate from the Gaming Board and a licence from the local magistrates.

Casinos operate two types of betting games:

Unequal chance Games such as roulette, blackjack and the various forms of baccarat (punto banco, chemin de fer), in which the casino, or 'house', runs the bank. This acts like a bookmaker, offering odds to the players, who bet with the bank on the outcome of the game. The odds always favour the bank.

In roulette, for example, there are 36 numbers to choose from, but there is also one zero on the wheel which a gambler can also bet on. The odds against any number's coming up are, therefore, 37 to 1. The greatest odds the house ever offers is 35 to 1. In the past some roulette wheels had two zeros on them, which put the odds more in the house's favour, but that system was outlawed by the Gaming Act 1968.

Equal chance Games such as backgammon, poker and dice games in which all the players have a mathematically equal chance of winning. If there is a bank, each player must be given an equal chance of holding it by being offered the bank.

The employees or operators of a casino offering games of equal chance are forbidden by law to take part in the games, except as a banker.

Who can play Anyone wanting to play in a casino must be at least 18 and must have been a member for at least 48 hours. He must also have signed, at least 48 hours before he can play, an 'intent to gamble' declaration.

Those rules do not apply to members' guests, however, and there is no legal restriction on the number of guests a member may take into a casino. Each club usually imposes its own limits.

The permitted hours of play vary from area to area.

Casino members pay an annual subscription and may also be charged entrance and table fees.

No credit available

Casino operators and their staffs are forbidden to lend money or give any form of credit to allow someone to gamble or cover his losses. But anyone not connected with the club can lend money for such purposes.

A gambler can buy gambling chips at a casino and pay for them by cheque, but the casino must pay the cheque into its own bank account within two days. If the player wins, he must not be given back his own cheque, but must be paid in cash or given a cheque by the casino management.

Failure to observe that basic rule can lead to a casino's losing its gaming licence – and so its closure.

If a player's cheque is not honoured by his bank, the casino can sue him for the money, and if a casino fails to pay a winner, the winner can sue for his winnings.

Gambling in a proprietary club

Some commercial, privately owned gaming clubs specialise in just one or two games, such as backgammon and baccarat, and are not generally known as casinos. However, they need a full casino licence if they want to charge a profitable entry and participation fee.

Without a licence, they are limited to a total charge of 10p per person per day.

Betting with a bookmaker

Bookmakers are companies or individuals who take wagers from the public. They do not need a certificate from the Gaming Board, but they do need a licence from local magistrates to open a betting shop.

Bookmakers make their own odds and offer bets on horse racing, dog racing, football matches, beauty contests, general elections – in fact almost anything where the outcome is still to be decided.

A gambler can bet with a bookmaker on credit, by telephone or by post, or at a racecourse. Or he can walk into a betting shop and place a cash bet. Because his bet is struck only with the bookmaker, and because one of them has to lose, it is a wager and therefore neither party has any way of enforcing payment by law.

If a gambler lays a bet by credit with a bookmaker and loses, the bookmaker cannot sue him. He may, quite legitimately, send debt collectors to get the money from him, but he must make sure that the collectors do not harass or threaten the client.

If the bookmaker defaults

If a bookmaker refuses to pay out on a win, there is nothing the punter

---

THE CARD PLAYERS IN A RAILWAY CARRIAGE

Gambling is prohibited in unauthorised public places, but they have never been precisely defined in law. Each prosecution is therefore considered separately.

Travelling down from Waterloo to the races at Kempton Park one day, a Mr Archer and two other men were found playing cards for money in a compartment of the train.

Mr Archer had been winning considerable sums of money from the other two at 'Find the Lady'. Three cards are put face down in a row; one is a queen. The dealer – in this case Mr Archer – shuffles them rapidly. Bets are then laid on the position of the queen.

The police charged Mr Archer with gaming in a public place.

In court, it was argued on his behalf that a railway carriage was not open to the public as the public had to pay to enter it.

VERDICT
This defence was rejected and Archer was found guilty. Payment for entry was not considered to make the train a private place.

THE BOOKMAKERS WHO LOST £1,000

Neither a bookmaker nor an individual gambler can take legal action to recover any money he alleges is owed to him as a result of a wager.

The rule of a firm of bookmakers was that all betting done with them must be on a cash basis. Mr Brendan Campbell, an employee, accepted credit bets from a customer totalling £1,000. The customer lost and failed to pay.

The bookmakers sued Mr Campbell for breach of his contract of employment and claimed £1,000 damages.

DECISION
The High Court rejected the claim, arguing that, in reality, it was not for damages but for a 'sum of money . . . alleged to have been won by the bookmakers upon a wager'.

Under the betting and gaming laws, it was a wagering contract and therefore not a matter for the courts to decide.

THE CROWDED BETTING SHOP

To secure the conviction of a bookmaker who has allegedly allowed someone under the age of 18 into his premises, the police must show that he knew the youth was there and knew that he was under age.

Two police officers saw Russell Laver, who appeared to be under 18, trying to hide in a group of about 20 people in a betting shop. They charged the manager, John Mallon, with unlawfully admitting and allowing Laver to remain.

Mallon was behind the counter and claimed that the crowd prevented him from seeing that Laver was in the shop.

DECISION
The magistrates found Mallon guilty, but the High Court quashed the conviction on appeal.

can do legally to get the money from him. In practice, failure to pay by a bookmaker is unlikely – unless the bookmaker has gone bankrupt or disputes the validity of the bet.

One of the functions of the National Association of Bookmakers is to uphold its members' reputation. It can order a member to pay out a winning bet. If he still refuses, he can be expelled from the association, and be blacklisted.

A blacklisted bookmaker would find it virtually impossible to get permission to take bets on a racecourse, and he would almost certainly be refused a magistrates' licence to open a betting shop.

Similarly, any gambler who refused to settle his account with a bookmaker may find himself listed by the association, making it impossible for him to lay a bet with an official bookmaker.

When there is a dispute

Any dispute over horse-race betting is adjudicated by Tattersall's Committee, a semi-official body set up about 200 years ago and consisting of members of the public and people from the racing world.

Both bookmakers and gamblers can take disputes to the committee. It cannot legally enforce its decision, but it can tell the bookmaker and gambler whether the bet was valid, and it can ask the loser to pay.

Because of the committee's close connection with the authorities who run racing and because its opinion is held by them as final in any dispute, a gambler or bookmaker who failed to obey a committee ruling could be banned from all British race tracks.

A gambler or a bookmaker who takes a dispute to Tattersall's has to pay a fee of between £1 and £75, depending on the amount at stake in the disputed bet.

Most horse-race tracks where bookmakers operate have a man known as a ring inspector, who can adjudicate in any dispute, and who can have a bookmaker or a gambler expelled from the course.

Greyhound tracks also have advisory committees to settle disputes, with powers to ban bookmakers and gamblers.

Betting on the Tote

The Totalisator Board is a state-run betting agency which operates POOL BETTING on horse races, and is subject to different rules from those that apply to bookmakers.

The Tote cannot lose, because it deducts a fixed amount for running costs from the total amount of money bet on any one race, and shares out the remainder among all the winning bets placed with it.

Tote betting is not legally a wager, so any money won or lost on the Tote can be claimed in the courts. Any profits the Tote makes are reinvested in racing.

Greyhound tracks run their own totalisator betting pool. These bets, too, are legally enforceable.

How betting shops are controlled

A bookmaker needs a local magistrates' licence to open a betting shop. Applications are heard usually every 3 months, and are advertised first in the local Press.

An objector has 14 days after the day of the advertisement to send two copies of a statement to the magistrates' clerk. Otherwise he is not allowed to attend the hearing.

The magistrates can refuse a licence on various grounds – for example, if a sufficient number of other bookmakers are already in business in the area or if there is a church or school near by.

No one under the age of 18 is allowed in a betting shop. But to secure a conviction, the prosecution must show that the bookmaker or his staff knew the youth was on the premises and knew, or ought to have known by his appearance, that he was under age.

Betting shops may be used only for betting. Refreshments, music, dancing and other entertainments are forbidden. So are radio and television unless they are in a back room and cannot be heard by the customers in the shop. The Exchange Telegraph 'blower' service, a private, subscribers' service which relays commentaries and results from the race-course, is allowed.

Restrictions on private gambling

Betting by telephone or through the post is permitted and so are wagers between members of a private club or between people who live or work on the same premises. A hospital in-patient, for example, can lay a bet with a porter, and so can a hotel resident with a waiter.

But betting in the street or in other unauthorised public places, even between private individuals, is illegal. A public place for the purpose of gambling has never been defined by law, and the term is open to interpretation in every new case that arises.

Unless you are at home, it is an offence to bet with anyone under the age of 18 or to employ anyone under that age to place or negotiate bets.

In a members' club Clubs that are run by and for the benefit of the members themselves need licences only to sell alcohol, for entertainment or for gaming machines.

However, before any club can operate gaming, it must have at least 25 members; it must not be temporary; and gaming must not be the principal reason for the club's existence.

Even within these broad definitions, the attitude of the licensing authorities varies from area to area.

In a public house Games of chance can be played for money only with the permission of the local magistrates. And even if they grant the publican a licence, they invariably set a very small limit on the stakes – perhaps 10 or 20 pence.

Licensed lotteries, sweepstakes, raffles and gaming machines are allowed, but any other form of betting or wagering, including the passing of betting slips and the payment of any winnings due, is illegal.

Gaming is allowed in private rooms on licensed premises, provided that the public is not admitted. An organisation may hire a room for that purpose or the landlord may hold a private gambling session.

At home Domestic gambling is entirely free from legal control, but anyone running a game in his own home would be guilty of a criminal offence if he tried to make a profit, by charging an entry or table fee, for example.

In a card club Privately owned clubs which deal exclusively in bridge or whist can charge a maximum of £3 per person per day.

When a syndicate gambles

If two or more people form a partnership or syndicate to gamble, they can take legal action against each other to recover their winnings. If, however, the member of the syndicate entrusted with the job of placing the bet fails to do so, the others cannot sue him.

Gambling by machine

Coin-operated gambling machines where predetermined combinations of symbols constitute winning bets can be installed in cafes, public houses, hotels, clubs, casinos and works canteens, but the operator must have a licence from the local magistrates.

Fruit machines, as they are known, have fixed percentage pay-outs, so only players can lose. Most of them are cash machines. *See:* GAMING MACHINE

GAME

Shooting animals and birds for food

Two types of game are hunted in Britain:
● Ground game – that is rabbits, hares and deer.
● Game birds – pheasant, partridge, grouse, snipe, woodcock and capercaillie.

Game is protected by law. You need a game licence to shoot game birds, deer and rabbits, but not rooks, pigeons or wildfowl; and you need the landowner's permission. At certain times of the year it is an offence to hunt game.

Hunting ground game

Rabbits and hares must not be killed at night, and hares must not be killed on Sundays or on Christmas Day. Hares must not be sold between March 1 and July 31.

The maximum penalty for breaking any of these rules is a fine of £20, even if the hunter owns the land on which the animals are killed and the shooting rights over that land.

Otherwise, anyone who owns or rents enclosed arable land can kill rabbits or hares at any time of the year. On the other hand, the owner or tenant of moorland or arable land that is not enclosed cannot kill rabbits or hares by any means between April 1 and August 31. Nor can he shoot them between September 1 and December 10.

Deer can be hunted only with the permission of the landowner, and the hunter must usually have a game

BETTER TO BE A HARE

Hares are safe on Christmas Day and on Sundays, but rabbits can be killed with the permission of the landowner.

licence. This is not required, however, for hunting with hounds or for hunting on enclosed land by permission of the owner or occupier. It is also illegal to hunt certain deer at certain times of the year.

Red deer	Stags, May 1 to July 31 Hinds, March 1 to October 31
Fallow and Roe deer	Bucks, May 1 to July 31 Does, March 1 to October 31

It is an offence to hunt any deer from 1 hour after sunset until 1 hour before sunrise.

Many game birds are bred simply to be released and shot, but there are strict controls over when they can be killed – even when the birds are privately reared.

No game bird can be shot from 1 hour after sunset until 1 hour before sunrise at any time of the year. In addition there are special close seasons – times when it is illegal to kill them – for each species.

Shooting wildfowl

No game licence is needed to shoot ducks, geese and wildfowl.

It is illegal to kill them, however, between February 1 and August 31 inland and between February 21 and August 31 on the foreshore.

When hunting is illegal

Anyone on land with either a gun or a dog can be asked to produce a game licence. He can be challenged by a police officer, by a gamekeeper, by the owner or occupier of the land, by an official of the local authority or by anyone who has a game licence himself.

If the person challenged does not have a licence with him, he must give his name and address and state the place where the licence was taken out. *See:* POACHING

A motorist who accidentally kills

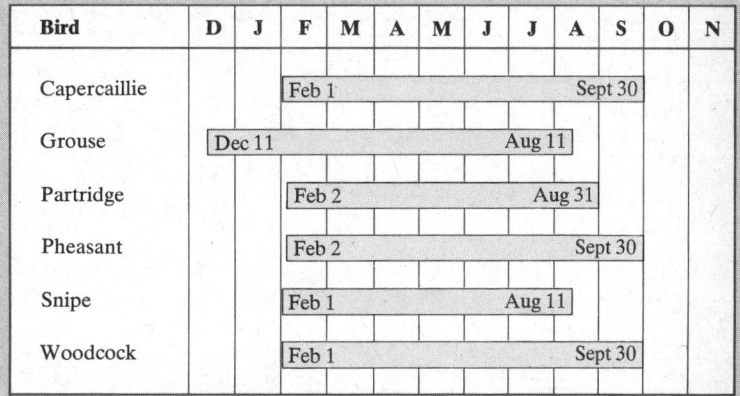

WHEN A GAME BIRD MUST NOT BE SHOT
The calendar that tells a hunter to hold his fire

Bird	D	J	F	M	A	M	J	J	A	S	O	N
Capercaillie			Feb 1							Sept 30		
Grouse	Dec 11								Aug 11			
Partridge			Feb 2						Aug 31			
Pheasant			Feb 2							Sept 30		
Snipe			Feb 1					Aug 11				
Woodcock			Feb 1							Sept 30		

A hunter risks a £20 fine if he shoots one of Britain's six varieties of game bird during its close season. He risks the same penalty for attacking them by night at any time of the year.

OBTAINING A GAME LICENCE

Anyone who hunts game without a licence can be fined up to £20, even if he shoots nothing.

There are three different types of game licence, all obtainable from post offices or the head offices of local authorities.

Red licence	Lasts for a year from July 31
Green licence	From August 1 to October 31
Blue licence	From November 1 to July 31

It is also possible to take out a licence for a specified period of 14 days.

Gamekeepers have to apply for a special licence which lasts for a year.

Anyone intending to use a gun should also have a firearms certificate. *See:* GUN

game, either birds or ground game, is not legally entitled to take the animal he has killed unless he has a game licence. A driver who does so without a licence is breaking the law and can be fined up to £20.

You can sell game if you have a game licence, and then only to a licensed game dealer.

GAMING MACHINE

Controlling the robots that offer fun and profit

A gaming machine is any machine on which a game of chance, or skill and chance combined, can be played for gain or amusement by putting in a coin or token.

That definition covers pinball machines, fairground 'penny-in-the-slot' machines and the many kinds of 'one-armed bandit' or fruit machine, on which a predetermined combination of symbols – often pictures of various fruits – constitutes a winning bet.

Under the 1968 gaming laws, there are three categories: machines that pay out big cash jackpots, machines that pay small prizes in cash or in kind, and machines played only for pleasure.

When there is a jackpot

The strictest controls are on fruit machines offering large cash prizes – known in law as 'jackpot' machines.

They can be operated only in premises that already have a full casino licence, in a BINGO CLUB or in a proprietary or members' club registered with the local authority. *See:* GAMBLING

No more than two machines are allowed, a single 'play' must cost no more than 10p and prizes must be in cash, not tokens.

There is no limit on the jackpot, but in practice it is rarely more than £100. The gaming machine manufacturers – through their organisation, the British Amusement Catering Trades Association – have reached a private agreement with the Gaming Board not to exceed that amount.

The association has also agreed with the board that all jackpot machines will pay back at least 73 per cent of the money staked.

When there is no jackpot

The second and largest category of gaming machines is what the law calls amusement-with-prizes machines. Like jackpot machines, they are almost always 'one-armed bandits' or fruit machines.

These can be installed in places open to the public, such as public houses, cafes, hotels and arcades. Their operators – with the exception of people who run travelling shows and fairs –

HOW FRUIT MACHINES ARE CONTROLLED

You win by getting a correct combination of fruit symbols but the prize must be paid out in cash, not tokens.

HOW THE OPERATORS ARE SUPERVISED

The sale and distribution of gaming machines is supervised by the Gaming Board. Anyone who supplies machines on hire, or sells or maintains them for a living, needs a certificate from the board, which investigates his background and that of his principal associates.

The certificate lasts for 5 years, but can be revoked at any time. The board's inspectors check from time to time on the activities of those involved in the business.

Any private individual with a reasonable objection to the way a gaming-machine business is being run should complain to the board or the police.

must obtain a permit from the local authority, which takes each case on its merits when deciding how many machines to allow. The permit lasts for 3 years.

There is a maximum stake of 5p and a maximum cash prize of 50p. If the prize is in the form of tokens or valuables, it can be worth up to £1, and a player must be able to exchange his tokens for goods or non-cash prizes.

The Gaming Board has agreed with the trade association that the pay-out on amusement-with-prizes machines should be no less than 70 per cent of the money staked.

When there is no prize

No permit or licence is needed for a machine that does not offer a prize – for example, a pin-ball or penny-in-the-slot machine or a mechanical horse race in a fairground or amusement arcade.

The most the player can hope for is to do well enough to win a free game or his money back.

Gaming for charity

Anyone running a charity function or non-commercial entertainment such as a bazaar, fête, dinner-dance or sporting event, can provide gaming machines – including jackpot machines – without a permit, but only if none of the proceeds, after expenses, is for private gain.

The machines must be incidental to the entertainment: they must not be the main or only inducement for people to attend.

GARAGE

When servicing or repairs are badly done

Work on your car by a garage must be done with reasonable care and skill. The garage is liable for any loss or damage caused by lack of care or skill and for the cost of having faulty workmanship put right elsewhere.

It is also liable for any personal injuries that result, either to you or anyone else.

If a garage refuses to put right faulty work, and you decide to sue, always obtain an independent opinion about the work from another garage or from a qualified engineer – possibly from one of the motoring organisations.

When new parts are provided

Parts or materials supplied by a garage must be reasonably fit for their purpose – which means that the garage is liable if any part proves unsuitable or defective and results in loss or injury, even if the defect is not the garage's fault.

However, a garage's liability to pay

WHEN YOU RENT A PRIVATE GARAGE

A written agreement is not usual or even necessary when you rent a garage from a friend or neighbour. In such an arrangement, the landlord has few duties. Once he has made the garage available, his only obligation in law is not deliberately to injure the tenant or damage any property he is keeping in the garage.

The landlord has no liability if the car or property is wrecked or damaged by fire, nor if the car or property is stolen – even because of a faulty lock on the garage.

The tenant cannot claim any damages if, for example, he trips on an uneven floor and injures himself – even if the landlord has been negligent.

If, however, the tenant takes someone else into the garage, and that person is injured in some way, that person can claim damages from the tenant – even if the injury results from negligence by the landlord. The tenant has no duty to carry out any repairs caused by fair wear and tear, but he is liable for any deliberate or negligent damage.

Working in a garage

It is important to tell the landlord what the garage is to be used for. A tenant cannot, for example, carry out any business activity – such as commercial repair work – if he has rented the garage for domestic use. If he did break his agreement, he would certainly have to relinquish his lease.

If the tenant intends to carry out repairs to his own car he should tell the landlord, for such work could be noisy and a nuisance to neighbours.

He should also tell the landlord if he intends to wash his car at the garage. That could make the landlord liable for additional water rates. *See:* WATER SUPPLY

Paying the rent

Although a rent book is not needed for the hire of a garage, some record of rent payment should be kept to avoid any subsequent dispute. Payment by cheque is usually enough because clearance of the cheque is evidence of payment.

Either landlord or tenant can give notice to quit, orally or in writing. The length of notice should be the same as the rental period – weekly, monthly or yearly.

A garage owner who tries to stop a tenant using the garage without proper notice could be sued.

GARAGE FIRE WRECKED A CUSTOMER'S CAR

Mr Hollier's car was badly damaged by a fire in March 1970 at the garage of Rambler Motors (AMC) where it was being repaired. Mr Hollier sued.

DECISION

The case went to the Court of Appeal. The garage agreed that the fire was started by faulty electric wiring and did not appeal against a finding of negligence. But it denied liability because of an exemption clause displayed on its invoices which said: 'The Company is not responsible for damage caused by fire to customer's cars on the premises. Customer's cars are driven by staff at owner's risk.'

The court ruled that the notice did not make it clear that it was warning customers that the garage would not accept liability even in the case of negligence. Mr Hollier was awarded damages.

Under the Unfair Contract Terms Act 1977 any attempt by a garage to absolve itself from liability for loss or damage due to negligence could well be invalid.

GARAGE THAT WAS SUED OVER FAULTY MATERIALS

A garage is liable for any loss or damage caused by defects in spare parts fitted while a car is being repaired or serviced.

The Brent Cross Service Company fitted six new connecting rods into the engine of a car owned by G. H. Myers and Company in 1932. The rods were supplied by the makers of the car. The following month one of the rods broke causing damage to the engine. Myers therefore sued the garage.

DECISION

When the case went to appeal, it was ruled that there was an implied condition that the rods were reasonably fit for their purpose, even though the garage had no means of discovering the defect. The garage was ordered to pay compensation.

A PUNCTURE REPAIR THAT CAUSED AN ACCIDENT

Even a passer-by hurt in an accident which is caused by faulty workmanship can claim compensation from the garage.

Mr Hancock had a puncture on his lorry repaired by Mr Peters's garage in 1937. Later, while the lorry was being driven down the High Street in Yiewsley, the flange which kept the tyre on the wheel came off. The flange mounted the pavement and hit a pedestrian, Mrs Stennett, on the leg.

Mrs Stennett sued Mr Hancock and Mr Peters for damages over her injury.

DECISION

The High Court dismissed the claim against Mr Hancock because it was reasonable for him to rely on the work done by Mr Peters's garage. Clearly, the flange had come off because of negligence by one of Mr Peters's workmen. Mrs Stennett was awarded £150 damages against Mr Peters.

compensation for faulty parts is limited to the car owner. Third parties cannot claim unless the garage has been negligent.

When your car is damaged

The garage has a responsibility to take reasonable care of your car while it is being repaired or serviced. If it is damaged or stolen due to the garage's negligence you can claim compensation. It is for the garage to prove that it was not negligent if it wishes to avoid paying your claim.

Garages often try to absolve themselves from liability by displaying notices on the premises or printed on order forms saying that cars are left at the owner's risk. Such notices have no legal weight if they are unfair and unreasonable. *See:* UNFAIR CONTRACT

No such clause can take away your rights to compensation for death or personal injury in the case of NEGLIGENCE.

Code of trade practice

Some garages belong to a trade association – for example, the Motor Agents' Association and the Society of Motor Manufacturers and Traders – and therefore may observe a code of practice approved by the Director General of Fair Trading. *See:* REPAIRER

GAS SUPPLY

Your right to have fuel piped into your home

When you move into a house or flat that is connected to a gas main you are entitled to obtain a supply of gas – provided that the property and equipment is not unsafe and that you do not owe money to any local gas authority for previous supplies elsewhere.

Go to your local gas office or showroom and complete a standard form of contract, listing the type and probable number of appliances you intend to use and estimating the amount of gas you will need, so that an appropriate tariff can be charged. Gas authority officials will help you to work out the estimate.

British Gas can demand a deposit – sometimes as much as £50 – from an applicant, and is especially likely to do so if he or she has been a bad payer.

If it refuses to provide gas without

good reason – for example if there is no question of unsafe premises or outstanding debts – it can be fined up to £20 and be ordered to supply gas by the local magistrates.

Making a connection

If your house is not connected to a Gas Corporation mains, but is within 25 yds of one, you can insist on your house being connected to it. If more than 10 yds of piping is required, you may be asked to pay the extra cost.

A house owner whose property is more than 25 yds from the nearest main cannot insist on connection. A local gas authority can refuse to link the house to the mains or it can ask the house owner to pay the full cost of the connection. In some country areas that can be very expensive.

Paying for your gas

Houses supplied with gas may be fitted with a credit meter, supplied by British Gas, which monitors the amount of gas used. Gas is measured in cubic feet by a meter, but charged to the customer at a fixed price for each British thermal unit (a standard measurement of the heat produced by a fuel) provided by the gas supplied.

Most meters are read every 3 months by a gas authority employee, and a bill for the number of therms used is sent to the customer.

A customer may have a coin-slot meter instead, which allows him to pay coins for his gas as he uses it.

If the official meter reader finds no one at home, he will usually leave a card so that the customer can make his own reading and record it. Otherwise the bill may be estimated. The estimate is based on your bill for the equivalent quarter of the previous year.

If an estimate seems unusually high you have the right to insist on your meter being read before you pay. There is no need to make an offer to pay more if the estimate seems low.

If anyone fills in his card incorrectly and over or undercharges himself, the error will be adjusted on the bill that is sent after the next official meter reading.

Challenging a meter reading

A gas meter may be registering more fuel consumption than has in fact been

used. If you suspect such a fault ask your local gas office to have the meter tested.

A gas meter is considered accurate if it runs fast by no more than 2 per cent or slow by not more than 3 per cent. If your meter is found to be over the limit for fast running you are entitled to be repaid the amount by which the meter has over-run on your last two bills, but no more.

If the meter is found to be running slow, you will have to make up for any underpayment on your last two bills.

The same inspection and payment

CHECKING A COIN METER

How to be sure that your money buys the right amount of gas

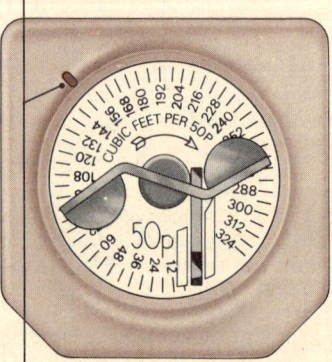

Read the figure on the dial opposite the setting mark. This shows the number of cubic feet of gas the meter gives for one coin, for example 15 cu. ft for 5p, 150 cu. ft for 50p. Check at your local gas showroom that this is the correct rate

Every coin-in-the-slot gas meter has a setting mark to show how many units a coin should buy. If the price changes, the landlord alters the setting.

system operates if you have a coin-slot meter in your home.

If you ask for a test, the local gas office will arrange for a new meter to be fitted, and your meter will be removed and sent to the Department of Energy for testing. A test certificate showing the degree of accuracy of the old meter will be sent to you, but the meter itself will not be refitted. The Department also has power to examine the meter in use.

If the old meter is found to be faulty you will not be charged for the test; otherwise a small fee is charged to cover disconnection and reconnection.

Changing your meter

A customer cannot insist on changing from one type of meter to another. A gas authority may, however, agree to replace a credit meter with a slot meter if the customer can show genuine hardship or if he is in financial trouble and so he is unable to budget for quarterly bills. The local gas authority will consider each application on its merits.

Gas offences

It is an offence to tamper with a meter, insert foreign or counterfeit coins or attempt to alter the readings. The maximum penalty is a £100 fine.

Anyone who tampers with pipes or fittings without giving notice to the corporation also commits an offence. *See:* CRIMINAL DAMAGE

When something goes wrong

The Gas Corporation must supply gas of a minimum pressure and calorific value. It can be fined up to £400 for failing to do so. Regular checks are made by independent examiners from the Department of Energy.

If you have a complaint about the supply or about any service, contact the manager at your local gas office or write to the area manager, whose address is given on each bill.

If you are still not satisfied contact your regional gas consumers' council. You can get the address from your local gas offices or Citizens Advice Bureau.

If you find or suspect a gas leak

If you suspect a gas leak, turn off your supply immediately at the mains and tell your local gas service department. The gas mains tap is normally near the meter. The emergency number of the nearest available service department is always listed in the telephone directory under 'Gas'.

By law, the Gas Corporation must repair a gas leak within 24 hours unless there are exceptional circumstances that prevent its immediate attendance. If it fails to do so, it can be prosecuted by the occupier of the premises where the leak has been found or by the local authority. The maximum penalty for such a failure is a £100 fine.

If your house is destroyed by a gas explosion the local authority has a duty to rehouse you, and you may be able to claim under a household insurance policy. *See:* FIRE INSURANCE; HOMELESSNESS

Taking safety measures

Any gas user who fails to comply with safety rules laid down by law can be fined up to £400.

You must not use, or let anyone else use, a gas appliance on your premises if it is known or suspected to be dangerous. Only competent and qualified workmen are allowed to install or ser-vice any gas appliance. You can sue the Gas Corporation for negligence if one of its employees services or installs appliances incompetently.

Contractors listed by the Confederation for Registration of Gas Installers work only under strict safety conditions and are qualified to service and install appliances.

The van symbol that shows that a workman who installs or services gas appliances is qualified to do the work safely. CORGI stands for Confederation for Registration of Gas Installers.

When your home can be entered

A gas official is not entitled to enter or try to use force to enter your home without your consent, unless he has obtained a warrant authorising entry from a magistrate.

The warrant must state why entry is required:
● To inspect apparatus.
● To check how much gas has been used.

WHEN A LANDLORD SELLS GAS TO A TENANT

A landlord is entitled to resell gas to a tenant through his own meter or by fitting a special meter or by including the cost of gas in the rent charged.

If he includes it in the rent, a special section should be set aside in the rent book stating the rates charged for gas.

If a tenant is supplied through the landlord's meter any money due at the end of the tenancy belongs to the landlord and not to the Gas Corporation.

A tenant can ask his local gas office to be supplied direct, provided that he has not made an oral or written agreement with his landlord to pay the landlord for gas.

A tenant who is supplied by his landlord and who has difficulty in paying for the gas, will receive the same consideration from the local authority or local social security office as if he were supplied direct by the Gas Corporation.

What a landlord can charge

A landlord who resells gas to a tenant must not charge more than the maximum resale price fixed by the Gas Corporation.

The tenant can check the approved local maximum price from a leaflet *Gas – how much can landlords charge?* obtainable at any gas office. The leaflet, prepared by the Department of Energy, contains a table of the maximum extra resale charges allowed.

Ask your landlord to provide a bill showing the amount of fuel used, the dates of the readings and charges made and check the charge against the table of permitted charges.

When there is a dispute

If a tenant discovers that his landlord is overcharging him for gas, the corporation will not help him to recover the money, but he can sue the landlord in the county court for the excess.

A landlord who refuses to provide gas to a tenant or disconnects the supply as a means of forcing him to leave the premises, can be prosecuted for HARASSMENT and the tenant can also sue him for breach of contract. *See:* CONTRACT

● To remove apparatus thought to be dangerous.

● To disconnect the supply.

Unless there is an emergency, at least 24 hours' notice of intended entry is required.

An official who enters your home, whether under a warrant or otherwise, must leave your home as secure as he found it. If he leaves it insecure and someone enters and steals from you, you can sue the Gas Corporation for the loss arising from his negligence.

If the official causes any damage by entering the property he must make it good. If he fails to do so, claim compensation from the corporation – or sue it.

Unless the official has a warrant or there is an emergency, it is not an offence to refuse to allow him to enter your home. But if he has a warrant or it is an emergency it is a criminal offence to obstruct him. The maximum penalty is a £5 fine.

When the supply can be cut off

A local gas authority has the right to disconnect a supply, or refuse to connect a new supply if:

● A customer still owes money 28 days after a written demand has been made and after a further 7 days' notice of disconnection has been given.

● Appliances or piping on the premises are unsafe.

● A user has tampered with the meter or supply pipes.

The supply cannot be disconnected on the ground that the customer has failed to pay the bill for equipment obtained from British Gas.

Under a code of practice covering disconnection, agreed between the Gas Corporation, the Department of Energy and the National Consumer Council, no local gas authority should disconnect a supply if it can make a firm arrangement for the customer to pay arrears and guarantee future payments.

For example, if a local social services department has agreed to pay the bill direct, or a bank standing order has been made out, the supply should not be cut off.

A pensioner who has not paid his or her bill must not be disconnected between October 1 and March 31, unless it can be shown that the pensioner has the means to pay but has not done so.

Anyone in genuine hardship should contact the local social security office or housing department. *See:* FUEL BILL

Arranging to end the supply

Anyone leaving a property should give the local gas office 24 hours' notice in writing. Failure to do so can make him liable to pay for any gas used on the premises until the next meter reading or until a new occupier requests a gas supply.

GAZUMPING

When a seller of property raises the agreed price

In times of property shortage, when prices are rapidly rising, a house buyer may commit himself in principle to buying a property at an agreed price and then find that the seller refuses to go ahead with the sale unless the price is increased. He may threaten to sell elsewhere.

Such a breach of their agreement – popularly known as gazumping – is morally wrong, but not illegal. A legal obligation to sell is made only when signed contracts have been exchanged.

The buyer can do little to prevent gazumping, even though he may have spent money on initial legal costs. If he cannot agree with the seller on a price, he must drop the transaction.

The best protection against being

....

A RISK OF HOUSE-BUYING

An agreement to buy or sell a house is not binding on either side until written contracts have been exchanged – usually by their solicitors.

....

gazumped is to try to ensure that once an offer is made, there is no unnecessary delay before contracts are exchanged and the seller is bound to sell at the agreed price.

When property for sale is plentiful and there is a shortage of buyers, the seller may be 'gazumped' by a prospective buyer.

After an initial agreement has been reached, but before a binding contract has been made, the buyer may demand a reduction in price before proceeding with the purchase. *See:* HOUSE BUYING AND SELLING

GIFT

Making sure that a present does not go wrong

Someone who is 18 or older, and who understands fully what he is doing, can legally make a gift of any property, including money, to anyone he chooses, provided that the property is his to give.

If, however, the gift is a substantial one, it is advisable to make it properly, according to law. Otherwise, if the giver dies, or becomes bankrupt or mentally incapable, the person for whom the gift is intended cannot insist on having it.

Getting a receipt

One way of demonstrating that property has changed hands is to get a receipt for the gift. For example, the giver can make a written note recording the nature and date of the gift and lodge it with his bank.

A receipt might be valuable evidence that property has changed hands if, for example, a debt judgment has been given against a husband and bailiffs call to seize his goods.

But documentary evidence of ownership is not necessarily accepted by bailiffs. If a husband whose goods are being seized claims that he gave his car to his wife, the wife may have to hand over the vehicle and then sue for its return – producing what evidence she can, as to the genuineness of the gift.

If the husband claims that a television set was given by him to his wife, again she may have to prove the fact in court. It is not enough merely to have the television licence in her name: a licence is merely a permit to use a television receiver on the premises, not evidence of ownership of the set.

Gifts from a bankrupt If someone makes a gift and then becomes bankrupt within 2 years, the recipient can be made to hand it over to be sold for the benefit of creditors – even if there is satisfactory evidence that the gift was genuine. *See:* BANKRUPTCY

Money and investments

A gift of money, in the form of a cheque, can go wrong if the giver dies before the cheque reaches his bank, and is cleared. The money immediately becomes part of his ESTATE and cannot be disposed of without the consent of the EXECUTOR or administrators of the estate.

Money kept in a post office, building society or other savings account can be given away simply by completing the appropriate forms to transfer it to someone else's savings or bank account and by lodging the forms with the giver's own savings pass book.

The recipient can collect his gift in cash direct, provided that he can produce the account-holder's pass book and that the giver has sent written instructions to the post office, building society or other savings management.

Stocks, shares and trust units are transferred to a new owner by signing a transfer form obtained from the trust managers and handing it over, with the unit certificate. The gift is not legally completed until the company (for stocks or shares) or the trust managers have registered the change of ownership.

In some cases, however, the courts have ruled that although the giver died before change of ownership could be registered, the gift could stand because he had done all that was required of him.

Land and buildings

The only way legally to give away land and buildings is to transfer them by a deed. It is not enough to hand over the title deeds of the property, with a note confirming the gift. *See:* CONVEYANCE

Tax on gifts

A gift creates a liability for CAPITAL GAINS TAX or CAPITAL TRANSFER TAX: a gift of land or shares and other sec-

urities may also be subject to stamp duty at a maximum of 2 per cent.

When undue influence is alleged

A gift is sometimes challenged on the ground of undue influence exercised over the giver. For example, a doctor may be accused of persuading a sick and elderly patient to make him a gift; a solicitor may be alleged to have used his position to induce a client to make a will in his favour, or an elderly parent may be said to have made a gift to a grown-up child who had exercised undue influence.

If a gift is challenged on such grounds when there is some such special relationship, it is for the recipient to prove that there was no undue influence. He must produce evidence that the gift was freely given. A solicitor, for example, whose client wishes to include him in a will, should have the will witnessed by another, independent solicitor who is satisfied that the gift is being properly made.

In any other case in which undue influence is alleged, when there is no such special relationship, it is for the person making the allegation to prove it.

GOLDEN HANDSHAKE

Reducing the tax bill after losing a job

If you lose your job through redundancy or dismissal, and receive a 'golden handshake' lump-sum payment in compensation, you may receive the money tax free – or at least taxed only at a specially low level – provided that you are not entitled to the payment under your employment contract.

Only payments made under the terms of a contract are taxed as normal income, which would generally result in heavy taxation.

In general, the first £10,000 of any non-contractual golden handshake is free of tax. Whether the remainder of the payment is taxed, and if so, to what extent, depends partly on what the payment is called.

Payments may be described as statutory redundancy payment, compensa-

HOW YOU CAN MINIMISE YOUR TAX

1. Although tax on your compensation is not affected by what you earned in your job before leaving, it is increased by any earnings you make afterwards, within the same tax year.

Therefore, when redundancy or dismissal has been decided, and if you are to receive more than £10,000, try to persuade your employer to put the redundancy or dismissal into effect as late in the tax year as possible. Even if you then immediately take a new job, provided that it is near the end of a tax year, you will not have time to earn much money that can be added to your compensation and possibly take you into a higher tax rate.
2. If your compensation is more than £10,000 and you would benefit by claiming standard capital superannuation benefit, ask for an ex gratia payment rather than any other form of handshake.
3. Do not accept pay in lieu of notice or compensation for loss of office, if you can have an ex gratia payment instead.

tion for loss of office, pay in lieu of notice, or ex gratia payment.

Statutory redundancy payment

Any compensation for REDUNDANCY under the Employment Protection (Consolidation) Act 1978 is tax free. But if other payments are also

A GOLDEN HANDSHAKE MAY BE TAX FREE

The first £10,000 compensation for loss of office is tax free unless a redundancy payment is also made.

made, the redundancy payment uses up part of the £10,000 tax-free limit.

Example: A man becomes redundant and is paid a total of £12,000. The sum is described as being £4,000 statutory redundancy pay and £8,000 compensation for loss of office. Since only the first £10,000 is tax free, he must pay tax on £2,000.

The amount left to be taxed should not however be taxed as heavily as if it was an addition to his salary in the year he left the job. Anybody made redundant is entitled to the benefit of an arrangement known as 'top slicing relief' – so called because the calculations ignore income that would make the top slice of your total income subject to very high tax rates.

Compensation for loss of office

Payment for loss of office is normally the amount that you and your employer agree you could get if you sued him – for example, if you alleged UNFAIR DISMISSAL. The term also covers any payment made under a court order after an action for wrongful dismissal or breach of contract by the employer.

The first £10,000 compensation for loss of office is tax free, unless a statutory redundancy payment is also made – in which case the redundancy payment is deducted from the tax-free amount. On compensation over £10,000 you are entitled to top slicing relief.

Payment in lieu of notice

When an employee is asked to leave his job without serving whatever period of notice is laid down in his individual contract, or by custom and practice, he is normally entitled to the wages he would have earned in that period.

Payment made 'ex gratia'

Any payment that is not compensation for loss of office, or pay in lieu of

---

HOW TOP SLICING RELIEF WORKS

Top slicing is a special method of assessing income tax on redundancy or dismissal pay-offs. It reduces liability at the high end of the tax scale – the top slice of income – instead of at the basic rate.

To work out what top slicing relief you may be entitled to on a taxable compensation payment:

● First divide the payment by six, for an ex gratia payment, or – if it is compensation for loss of office which is not due under the contract – by the number of unexpired years in your contract (counting a part year as a whole year).

● From the figure arrived at, deduct your personal allowances for the full year.

● Then – ignoring your income from the job, but taking into account other income for the year – work out the tax you would have had to pay on the sum that remains, using the table of tax rates normally supplied by the Inland Revenue with your annual tax forms. (If your compensation payment is divided into more than one sum, under more than one description – apart from statutory redundancy pay, which in any case is tax free – you cannot set your personal allowances against more than one of those sums.)

● Next, multiply the tax figure you have arrived at by six, for an ex gratia payment, or by the number of unexpired years in your contract, if the sum is compensation for loss of office or pay in lieu of notice.

● The result is the amount of tax you should pay on the taxable part of your compensation money.

Example: A man aged 57, due to retire at 60, becomes redundant. He leaves his employer at the end of September, having earned £6,100 during that tax year. His personal allowances for the full year total £1,000. Assume 1978–9 tax rates. The man has no other income for that tax year.

The compensation is made up of:

Statutory redundancy payment	£5,800
Compensation for loss of office	£9,200
Pay in lieu of notice (paid under contract)	£900
Total compensation paid	**£15,900**

Of the three sums, statutory redundancy payment is tax free, pay in lieu of notice is taxed as normal income. Compensation for loss of office is partly taxable, but benefits from top slicing relief.

To find the taxable amount of compensation for loss of office:

From tax-free limit	£10,000
deduct Tax-free statutory redundancy payment	£5,800
Total	**£4,200**
From compensation payment	£9,200
deduct Tax-free balance	£4,200
Therefore taxable amount before top slicing relief is	**£5,000**

To calculate top slicing relief:

divide Taxable part of payment	£5,000
by number of years' unexpired service (3)	£1,667
(If ex gratia payment divide by 6) *deduct* One year's personal allowance	£1,000
Net taxable amount is	**£667**

Calculate tax on £667 as if it were the only taxable income at, for example, 25% | £166.75
multiply by
Number of years' unexpired service (3) | £500.25
(If ex gratia payment, multiply by 6)

Therefore tax on £5,000 compensation for loss of office after top slicing relief is	£500.25

(Tax on £5,000 without top slicing relief, at appropriate 1978–9 rates would be £1,857.)

Total tax payable on the £15,900 golden handshake:

On statutory redundancy (£5,800)	Nil
On compensation for loss of office (£9,200)	£500.25
On pay in lieu of notice (£900) taxed at highest rate paid by recipient, say 33%	£297.00
Therefore total tax is	**£797.25**

If instead of compensation for loss of office, the sum of £9,200 is an ex gratia payment:

Taxable amount as before	£5,000
Divided by 6	£833
less One year's personal allowances	£1,000
Total	**£167**
Multiply by 6	£1,002
Therefore tax payable	**Nil**

notice, is an ex gratia payment – that is, one made as a favour.

At least £10,000 of it is exempt from income tax. If the standard capital superannuation benefit – a calculation based on average recent earnings and the number of years' service – comes to more than £10,000, the higher figure is tax-exempt.

Even after standard capital superannuation benefit has been used, the remaining amount to be taxed is still subject to the benefit of top slicing relief.

If your total compensation exceeds £10,000 and is divided under more than one heading, you must choose either the automatic £10,000 tax-free limit or standard capital superannuation benefit. You cannot claim both on the same golden handshake.

When payment is made

If you are made redundant or dismissed, your compensation payment has to go through the usual PAYE tax system which automatically allows for the £10,000 tax-free payment, but possibly not for any top slicing relief to which you may be entitled on larger sums.

COMPENSATION THAT IS FREE OF TAX

Certain compensation payments are free of tax, no matter what the amount:
● Ex gratia payments on the termination of a job caused by death or disability of employee.
● Terminal grants to members of the armed forces.
● Ex gratia payments at the end of a job in which the employee worked abroad for 75 per cent or more of his entire service or for the whole of the last 10 years.
● Ex gratia payments when the employee has served more than 20 years, at least half of them abroad, including any 10 of the past 20 years.

As a result, your payment may be over-taxed initially.

Some large employers, faced with dismissing large numbers of workers, make an informal arrangement with the Inland Revenue to take account of some top slicing relief when PAYE is deducted from the golden handshake. But a small company dismissing a single worker, or only a few, is not likely to have such an arrangement. In that case, you must claim any excess tax back from the Inland Revenue. The full details may not be settled until long after the end of the tax year in which you leave your job. As soon as the tax year ends, on April 5, ask your Inspector of Taxes for a written assessment of your liability on the lump sum. Ask for a separate account of any top slicing relief that has been given.

When you can claim interest

If the Inland Revenue deducts too much tax and does not repay for an exceptionally long time, you may be entitled to claim interest.

The Inland Revenue does not have to pay interest, however, until it has held your money for one clear tax year. For example, if tax is over-deducted in November of one year and repaid the following November, you are not entitled to interest, because the year runs from April to April.

If the repayment is made in May, 17 months after the over-deduction, however, you are entitled to interest. But it is reckoned only from the beginning of the new tax year, so on a repayment made in May, you get only 1 month's interest.

GOODS, Carriage of

Someone who carries goods for money is legally bound to take reasonable care of them, but he is not liable for any loss or damage unless that is due to some negligence on the part of his employees or himself. If you have valuable goods to send somewhere, insure them. *See:* CARRIAGE OF GOODS

GOODS, Defective

A person who buys goods that do not match the way they are described in the shop or advertising material or are unfit for the purpose for which they are intended, has rights against the seller. Sometimes he can return the goods and get his money back. Sometimes he has to keep the goods but can claim compensation if they need repairing or are worth less than he paid. *See:* DEFECTIVE GOODS

MAKING THE MOST OF A PAY-OFF
How to calculate tax relief on a voluntary payment

Standard capital superannuation benefit is a special income tax relief that applies only on golden handshake payments that are made 'ex gratia' – voluntarily, not as a statutory or contract obligation.

It enables some employees who retire, or who accept dismissal as an early retirement, to escape tax on a higher figure than the usual £10,000 limit.

Someone on a high income who is offered early retirement should persuade his employer to keep any legally required payments to a minimum, and pay as much as possible voluntarily.

The benefit is worked out by taking the average of your last 3 years' salary before you left the job – calculating back from the date of leaving. Multiply the average by the total number of years you were employed by that company – treating a part year as a full year – and divide the result by 20.

The answer is the amount that will be tax free with a minimum of £10,000.

Example: A salesman loses his job and retires after 18 years' service. He receives an ex gratia payment of £17,500. In the 3 years up to his premature retirement, he earned £10,500, £11,500 and £14,000.

To work out standard capital superannuation benefit:

Add 3 years' salary	£36,000
Divide total by 3 to find the yearly average earnings	£12,000
Multiply that yearly average by the number of years' service:	
£12,000×18	£216,000
Divide result by 20 to find tax-free amount:	
$\frac{216,000}{20}$	£10,800
Deduct tax-free amount from total ex gratia payment:	
Total ex gratia payment *less*	£17,500
Tax-free amount	£10,800
Therefore amount to be taxed is	£6,700

GOODS, Ownership of

A buyer's right to goods he has paid for

Ownership of goods is not always easy to prove, and a person who loses property, or has it stolen, may not be able to reclaim it.

There are no title deeds with ordinary, movable goods. When valuable articles, such as jewellery or an expensive watch, are bought, it is wise to get and to keep a written receipt.

Buying goods

Normally, goods become the property of a person after he has made a CONTRACT with the seller and agreed to pay money for the goods. If, however, the goods did not belong to the seller in the first place they may not legally become the property of the buyer.

That is true even if the seller and the buyer both genuinely believed that the sale was a valid one. The goods may have been stolen and passed to the seller without his knowing. In that case, they still belong to the person from whom they were stolen. If he can trace the goods and prove ownership, he can recover them without payment – but that rule does not always apply.

COMPENSATION FOR RECLAIMED GOODS

Anyone who has goods reclaimed from him by an original owner after he has bought them from someone else has a right to get back the money he paid for them.

The Sale of Goods Act 1979, lays down that the seller must legally have had a right to sell the goods. If he did not, the buyer can sue him for the full amount paid – even if he has had use of the goods for some time.

Buying at a market Any goods sold at a market established by law become the legal property of the buyer and cannot be recovered under any circumstances, even if they can be proved to have been lost or stolen.

That ancient, legal rule is known as market overt. It does not apply to a market which is not legally constituted nor to ordinary shops – except in the boundaries of the City of London.

STOLEN CANDELABRA SOLD BEFORE DAWN

Goods bought at a market before sunrise are not protected by market overt, and they can be reclaimed by the original owner.

Thieves broke into Mr Desmond Reid's home in Chelsea in 1969 and stole a pair of Robert Adam cut-glass candelabra. In February 1970, an art dealer, Mr Cocks, saw the candelabra in a cardboard box at the New Caledonian Market in Southwark, south London.

Mr Cocks paid £200 in cash for the candelabra to a man who was putting up his stall. It was 7 a.m. and the sun had not yet risen.

Later, a friend of Mr Cocks agreed to display the candelabra, priced at £800, in the window of his shop in Belgravia.

The following month Mr Reid was discussing his lost candelabra with a dealer. The dealer told him to go to the shop in Belgravia. Mr Reid did, and when he saw the candelabra he called the police.

Police took possession of the candelabra. Mr Cocks protested that he had no idea that they had been stolen. The police refused to hand the candelabra back to Mr Reid.

In May 1972, Mr Reid sued the Metropolitan Police for the return of his candelabra. Westminster County Court ruled that the goods were sold in a market authorised by Act of Parliament. The sale, the judge decided, was protected by the ancient legal rule of market overt and Mr Cocks was the rightful owner. Mr Reid appealed.

DECISION

The Court of Appeal agreed that New Caledonian Market was protected by market overt. But the sale had taken place before sun up. In a case in 1596 it had been ruled that for market overt to apply the sale must not be in the night. Mr Reid remained the owner of the candelabra and the police were ordered to return them to him.

There, any shop selling goods in which it normally trades, is protected by market overt. Certain rules apply:

● The sale must be carried out in accordance with any special customs or rules of the market – for example, no credit.

● The market must be open so that members of the public can see what is going on.

● The sale must take place between the hours of sunrise and sunset.

● The buyer must not have knowledge at the time of the purchase that the goods were previously lost or stolen.

Selling through an agent

Goods sold through an authorised agent become the property of the buyer even if the original owner never gets the money for them.

For example, if someone leaves a table with a secondhand furniture dealer, and it is eventually bought, there is no legal way that the original owner can reclaim the table from the buyer if the middleman – the secondhand furniture dealer – refuses to hand over the money or is unable to do so. The original owner's only legal course of action is to sue the dealer for the money he received for the table.

A recognised agent in the business of buying and selling can sell goods left with him even if the owner did not ask him to sell them. In such a case, the goods become the property of the person who buys them from the dealer.

That can happen when an article, say a valuable painting, is left with an auctioneer for valuation, and the painting is sold at the next auction. The original owner can claim against the auctioneer.

Selling a car A car owner can guard against having his vehicle sold without his authority by holding on to the vehicle registration certificate.

GOODS, Sale of

The legal contract between buyer and seller

When goods are sold, the seller and the buyer enter into a contract which confers rights and imposes obligations on both parties. The contract need not be in writing.

Quality of goods

There is no law governing the quality of goods sold by a private individual, but if you buy something from a business, such as a shop or tradesman, you are entitled to goods of 'merchantable quality' – which means that they must be reasonably fit for their usual purpose. *See:* DEFECTIVE GOODS

Goods sold under a specific description must correspond exactly with that description. If they do not, the seller – even a private individual – can be sued under the Sale of Goods Act.

Ownership of goods

The seller must own the goods or at least have a right to dispose of them. If he does not, and the true owner later demands the return of the goods, the buyer is entitled to recover his money from the seller. *See:* GOODS, Ownership of

Collection and delivery

Unless there is a specific agreement about delivery, it is a buyer's responsibility to collect the goods. If a seller

> ### THE MAN WHO BOUGHT A STOLEN CAR
>
> *A person who sells must be the owner of the goods or have the right to dispose of them. Otherwise an innocent buyer, who is later forced to hand the goods over to the true owner, is entitled to his money back from the person who sold them to him.*
>
> Mr Divall bought a car from Mr Garbett and then re-sold it to Mr Rowland for £334. Mr Rowland, a car dealer, subsequently sold it to Colonel Railsdon for £400.
>
> Five months after the original purchase, police said that it was a stolen car and seized it. Mr Rowland refunded the £400 to Colonel Railsdon and then sued Mr Divall for the £334.
>
> The judge in the High Court in London said that Mr Rowland was not entitled to all his money back because he and Colonel Railsdon between them had had the use of the car for 4 months. Mr Rowland appealed.
>
> DECISION
> The Court of Appeal said that the Sale of Goods Act laid down an implied condition on the part of the seller that he had a right to sell the goods. Mr Divall had broken that condition. Mr Rowland was entitled to a full refund.

agrees to deliver he can ask the buyer to agree to pay extra.

If a specific time is fixed for the goods to be handed over and they are not ready by then, the buyer has the right to cancel the agreement. When no time is fixed, the buyer is entitled to the goods within a 'reasonable' period, but he must give the seller a specific deadline – say 1 or 2 weeks – by which the goods are to be produced before he can cancel the agreement.

Paying the price

A seller can refuse to hand over the goods until the agreed price has been paid, unless the buyer and seller agreed beforehand that payment could be made later or by instalments. If the buyer fails to pay, the seller can give notice of his intention to sell them elsewhere. If he does so and gets less than the original agreed price, he can claim the difference from the buyer who let him down.

A seller can sue for the price of goods that have been delivered, but he cannot sue for the price of goods that have simply not been collected unless there is a specific agreement for payment to be made on a certain date regardless of delivery.

Return of goods

If you have reasonable cause to reject goods that have been delivered to you – for example, if they are faulty, or if the wrong quantity is delivered – you can insist that the seller collects them. You are not bound to return them, provided you tell the seller you reject them.

However, you cannot reject the goods once you have told the seller you have accepted them. Nor can you reject them if you keep the goods for longer than you need to examine them without telling the seller that you are dissatisfied, or if you treat them as your own – for instance by building some electrical parts into your house. In such cases you can sue for damages if the goods are defective.

GOODS RENTAL

The strict laws covering hire agreements

There is no legal difference between

renting, leasing or hiring goods. All differ from HIRE PURCHASE in that the customer never becomes the owner of the goods, no matter how much he pays or how long the rental agreement lasts.

The Consumer Credit Act covers hire purchase, and gives protection to rental customers as well. The legislation applies to most rental agreements lasting 3 months or more in which the total payments do not exceed £5,000.

Understanding the agreement form

The legislation lays down strict rules about the way the rental contract must be set out, how it should be signed and the number of copies the hirer should receive. An agreement is probably unenforceable if these rules are broken. *See:* CREDIT AGREEMENT

Read your rental agreement carefully to see that it does not impose conditions you find unacceptable. It may, for example, insist on a minimum period of hire before you can terminate the agreement, though in most cases the law stipulates that the minimum period cannot be longer than 18 months.

A hirer may also be required to keep the goods at a particular place. For example, a television rental agreement may insist that the set is not moved from the hirer's address or, in the case of car hire, that the vehicle should be housed in a garage.

Even when there are no such explicit conditions, the hire company is entitled to ask at any time for information about where the goods are. The maximum penalty for refusing to give this information is a £50 fine.

A hirer must take reasonable care of the goods he is renting. If anything happens to them because of his negligence he must pay compensation. It is advisable, therefore, to insure the goods for their full value. Some hire agreements may insist on insurance. If you are in doubt about the actual value, ask the hiring company.

Condition of hired goods

Goods that are hired must be adequate for the purpose for which they are wanted and they must match any description given in advertisements or in the agreement itself.

Some agreements stipulate specific

arrangements for the company to maintain or service the goods and those arrangements may be subject to various conditions. None is valid, however, if it seeks to absolve a hire company from its duty to supply a consumer with goods in adequate condition.

If you fail to pay

When a hirer fails to pay the rental the hire company can repossess its goods without a court order, though it cannot insist upon entry into private premises without a court order.

WHEN NO PAYMENTS ARE MADE

A rental company is entitled to repossess its goods – without a court order – if the hirer does not keep up the payments. He must, however, first be served with a default notice.

'We'll tell the neighbours it's for repair, not repossession'

However, before attempting to repossess its property, the hire company must serve a default notice on the hirer, otherwise he can sue for damages for loss of enjoyment of the goods.

A county court has wide powers to help hirers who face claims. It can allow extra time to pay debts or refuse to allow repossession.

Indeed, if a county court judge decides that the hire payments, when added to the value of the goods to be repossessed, yield an excessive profit, he can order some of the money to be repaid to the hirer.

If a hirer finds it difficult to continue payments, therefore, he is well advised to allow the case to go to court and to appear himself to ask the judge to vary the rental agreement in his favour.

Ending an agreement

Your right to pull out of a hire agreement is restricted. You can terminate the agreement ahead of time only if it has run for at least 18 months – unless a shorter time is stated in the agreement. You must then give 3 months' notice that you wish to end the rental. If the hire charges have been paid more often than once every 3 months you need give only one rental period of notice.

A hirer whose payments exceed £300 a year cannot terminate the agreement ahead of time unless the agreement itself says he can do so. If he terminates, he must return the goods immediately.

When a rental agreement breaks the law

Any person or company hiring goods to the public must hold a licence from the Office of FAIR TRADING. If not, he or it cannot take legal proceedings against a hirer who breaks the terms of the agreement without the special permission of the Office.

Such permission is rarely given but it might be granted if, for example, a trader had applied for a licence but had not yet received it or if he had previously held a licence but failed to renew it.

An unlicensed trader can be prosecuted and fined up to £1,000. On indictment in a crown court he can be imprisoned for 2 years and be fined an unlimited amount.

GRADUATED PENSION

An earnings-related supplement to retirement pension

Graduated pension was an earnings-related pension scheme introduced by the Government in April 1961 and wound up in April 1975. All employed people had to pay into the scheme a weekly contribution directly related to their earnings.

The number and size of their contributions determined the amount of graduated pension they were entitled to at retirement, in addition to the normal weekly retirement pension covered by flat-rate national insurance contributions.

Calculating the amount When the graduated scheme ended, the Department of Health and Social Security issued to each contributor form GR20, which informed him of the total amount of his contributions. From that figure, he can work out the weekly amount of graduated pension to which he or she is entitled.

Every contribution of £7.50 for men and £9 for women bought the contributor a weekly graduated pension payment of $2\frac{1}{2}$p. For example, a man who paid £177 in contributions over the years would have contributed $23\frac{3}{5}$ units of £7.50, and with the units rounded up to 24, would have received on retirement 24 times $2\frac{1}{2}$p a week – that is, 60p a week.

Increase in rate Since 1978, graduated pensions are increased each year in line with price rises. This, for example, means that what would have bought a 60p addition now (1981) carries an entitlement of 85p.

The maximum number of units that could have been earned during the graduated pension scheme is 86 (men) or 72 (women).

In 1981 the maximum weekly payments of graduated pension are £3.04 (men) and £2.55 (women).

How payment is made

Graduated pension is ordinarily paid with retirement pension. People not entitled to a retirement pension because they have not paid enough national insurance contributions – or, in the case of a married woman, because her husband has not yet retired – can obtain any graduated pension to which they are entitled as a separate payment.

A wife receives nothing from her husband's graduated pension contributions, but a retired widow of 60 or over is entitled to half the graduated pension earned by her husband. A retired man of 65 or over is similarly entitled to half the graduated pension earned by his late wife.

Where graduated pension is not paid with retirement pension, it is paid by quarterly Girocheque. The earnings rule does not affect graduated pension.
See: RETIREMENT PENSION

Extra pension Any man who decides not to retire at 65 (or a woman at 60) and not to draw any pension, can earn extra graduated pension. The amount due is increased by $7\frac{1}{2}$ per cent per year for each complete year that retirement is postponed.

If you need information

If you have lost form GR20, which tells you the total amount of the contributions you paid, or if you wish to challenge the amount stated, contact your local Department of Health and Social Security office.

Be prepared to provide, if possible: your national insurance number, the names and addresses of your employers between April 1961 and April 1975, the dates you worked for them and any works or staff number you had, the amounts of graduated pension contributions that you believe you paid, and details of any occupational pension schemes into which you were contracted out from the graduated pension scheme.

GRAFFITI

Sometimes amusing, but always an offence

It is an offence intentionally or recklessly to destroy or damage another's property. *See:* CRIMINAL DAMAGE

Anyone who paints graffiti on walls, whether the property is public or private, or inscribes on them in other ways so that it is costly to remove, commits this offence. Anyone who sees the crime committed can make a CITIZEN'S ARREST.

If a bystander sees someone standing by a wall with a bucket of paint and a brush about to paint graffiti on the wall he could make a citizen's arrest, because it is also an offence to have something under your control intending to use it to damage property.

When these offences are tried in a CROWN COURT, the maximum penalty is 10 years' imprisonment and an unlimited fine. Magistrates can impose a maximum penalty of 3 months' imprisonment and a £500 fine. Where the damage costs less than £200, the case must be heard before magistrates.

The culprit may also be ordered by the court to pay CRIMINAL INJURIES COMPENSATION.

The owner of a wall on which graffiti is inscribed can also sue the offender in the COUNTY COURT, claiming damages

for TRESPASS. He will be awarded whatever it costs to repair the damage.

GUARANTEE

When a manufacturer promises to compensate you

If you buy goods from a retailer, there is no direct contract of sale between you and the manufacturer. That means that your rights if the goods do not work properly are against the retailer, not against the maker. *See:* DEFECTIVE GOODS

It is only when defective goods cause foreseeable injury or damage that a manufacturer has a direct liability to pay compensation – to anyone who suf-

----

UNDER GUARANTEE?

Not all goods are covered by a manufacturer's guarantee, but in certain fields – particularly electrical equipment and cars – it is customary for the makers to back up the retailer's legal duties by promising to put right any fault or replace the goods.

----

fers, not only the individual purchaser of the goods. *See:* MANUFACTURERS' LIABILITY

But injury or damage caused by defective goods is not as common as defective goods that need repair or replacement. Although the buyer has rights against the retailer where goods need repair or replacement, the retailer may not be as skilled in servicing the goods as the manufacturer, or have as large a stock of spare parts.

Even if he is skilled and does have the

stock, it is the manufacturer's reputation which is affected by the defect. For that reason, many manufacturers do accept that they have a responsibility to deal with defects by issuing a guarantee or warranty with the goods, particularly electrical equipment and cars.

The words guarantee and warranty mean the same – car manufacturers seem to prefer the word warranty.

Your rights under a guarantee

Your rights under a guarantee depend on the precise wording of the guarantee document.

Most guarantees cover defective components and defective workmanship. There is usually a promise to repair faulty parts or faulty goods or to replace them if the manufacturer prefers.

Sometimes the guarantee says it does not cover labour costs, and there is often a statement that it is the consumer's responsibility to pack the goods properly and to pay for their carriage to the manufacturer's place of business.

A guarantee is usually for a fixed period – 6 months or 12 months, perhaps – from the date of sale, or for a certain amount of usage, such as 10,000 miles in the case of a car.

Whether a guarantee gives you legal rights against the manufacturer which you can enforce in the courts is uncertain: there has so far been no legal ruling, largely because manufacturers generally honour their guarantees.

Sending back a card

A guarantee may legally set conditions that must be complied with before it operates – for example, that it depends on the customer's completing and returning a postcard to the manufacturer within 10 or 14 days of buying the goods.

That means that the manufacturer could insist on this having been done before he honours the guarantee. In practice many do not bother to check on returned cards before repairing faulty goods if it is clear that the goods are still within the guarantee period, or if the customer has a retailer's receipt. They use the cards mainly to gain statistical information about sales.

Until 1977, there was a good reason why guarantee cards should not be returned: some contained an exemption clause, stating that in return for the benefits of the guarantee the consumer would agree to give up his legal rights against the manufacturer to claim damages if personal injury or damage to property was caused by the manufacturer's negligence. The card to be returned required the consumer to sign that he accepted that clause.

Under the UNFAIR CONTRACT Terms Act 1977, however, such clauses are no longer valid. Even if there is one in your guarantee, and even if you sign a card saying that you accept the clause, it can not take away your legal right to sue the manufacturer if you suffer injury or damage because of the negligence of the manufacturer or any of his employees. *See:* NEGLIGENCE

As a result, there is no longer any disadvantage in signing and returning a guarantee card. As a manufacturer could refuse to comply with the guarantee if a card had not been returned, it is advisable to complete and return it.

How the retailer is affected when goods are defective

Under the Sale of Goods Act 1979, a buyer has legal rights to compensation from the retailer if the goods are defective even if the defect was not the retailer's fault. *See:* DEFECTIVE GOODS

Nothing in a guarantee can take away or diminish those rights. It must not contain any wording that purports to have such an effect, and it must contain a clear statement that the buyer's rights under the Sale of Goods Act (usually described as his statutory rights) are not affected.

Even if a guarantee says that the consumer is to be responsible for labour costs or for the cost of returning the goods to the manufacturer, he is still entitled to be compensated for such expenditure by the retailer.

In many cases it is possible for a consumer to combine the enforcement of his statutory rights against the retailer and his rights against the manufacturer under the guarantee. If goods are defective he can complain to the retailer who may advise him to take advantage of the guarantee.

If the buyer agrees to do so it does not relieve the retailer of his obligations under the Sale of Goods Act, and if exercising rights under the guarantee involves the buyer in expense the retailer is responsible for compensating him.

GUARANTOR

Agreeing to accept liability for someone else's debt

Someone who agrees to stand as guarantor for another person's debt becomes personally liable if the money is not repaid. If you sign such a guarantee you are promising that if he does not pay, you will.

Only written guarantees are enforceable. If you are asked to sign a document in connection with credit which is being given to someone else, read it carefully. Never sign a guarantee unless you are willing and able to pay up if the worst comes to the worst.

Remember that the person for whom you are standing as guarantor does not have to be dishonest for the debt to fall on you. He may just have bad luck, become ill or lose his job.

If the debt is being paid by instalments the guarantor is liable not simply to keep up the regular payments but to settle the whole account in a lump sum. Even one missed payment could result in the entire debt falling on the guarantor.

The person or company that advanced the credit does not have to sue the original debtor before claiming from the guarantor.

A guarantor who does have to pay can sue the original debtor to recover the money.

Credit agreements

If you have agreed to act as guarantor in a credit transaction regulated by the Consumer Credit Act, you are relieved of all your obligations if the person for whom you are providing financial backing legally withdraws from or ends the deal. *See:* CREDIT AGREEMENT

If the Consumer Credit Act applies, you cannot ever be made to pay more than the person for whom you are standing guarantor would have had to pay. Nor can you be made to pay in a different way – for example, if the agreement stated that the amount due could be paid by cheque, you cannot be made to pay cash.

GUARDIAN

The role of a person legally appointed to act as a parent

A guardian is a person legally appointed to act as a parent to an unmarried child under the age of 18, who is deprived of one or both parents through death.

A guardian has the power, as if he or she were a real parent, to:
● Refuse a child under 18 permission to marry.
● Choose the child's education.
● Control the child's property and money.
● Stop the child being adopted.
● Retain custody of the child, and generally supervise its upbringing.

A guardian can be appointed by one or both parents while both are alive, or named in a will to act after the death of one parent. Both parents have an equal right to appoint a guardian and may choose separate guardians.

A guardian can also be appointed by a court.

Appointment by a court

If a parent dies without appointing a guardian, or if the person he or she appointed refuses to act as guardian or also dies, there are certain circumstances in which a court will appoint a guardian to act jointly with the surviving parent.

For example, the surviving parent may be irresponsible or unable to look after the child without help, or may travel abroad because of his or her job, or may leave the child in danger or neglect him.

In any of these cases, either the

WHEN AN ADULT CAN HAVE A GUARDIAN

An adult can be received into guardianship if he is suffering from mental illness or a MENTAL HANDICAP. That would happen particularly when a mentally handicapped person has lived at home, but his parents become unable, perhaps through age or infirmity, to take responsibility for his well-being. A White Paper has proposed extending the arrangement for chronically ill patients discharged from hospital.

parent might apply to the court to appoint a guardian, or someone else with an interest in the child, such as a relative, can apply to have himself appointed as guardian.

When one parent is dead

On the death of one parent, any appointed guardian acts jointly with the surviving parent.

If the surviving parent objects to the guardian, either the parent or the guardian can apply to the magistrates' court, county court or High Court for an order that either should be sole guardian or that both should be joint guardians. The guardian can similarly ask the court to confirm his position.

If the surviving parent and the guardian disagree on a point of upbringing – whether, for example, a child should receive private or State education – the dispute can be settled by a court order. The surviving natural parent does not have a right to over-rule the other, appointed guardian.

When both parents are dead

If both parents die and have appointed separate guardians, both guardians have joint custody and care of the child, subject to any court order obtained by one of the guardians.

If a child is homeless, and its dead parents have not appointed guardians, the local authority may take the child into care. See: CHILDREN IN CARE

It is still open for any person to apply to the court to be appointed guardian of the child.

If a widow remarries and then dies, leaving a child from her first marriage, the step-father does not have parental rights and should apply to the magistrates' court, county court or High Court to be appointed the child's guardian, unless the mother has appointed him guardian in her will.

Rights of a guardian If a child's parents have died suddenly and the child has been taken into care by the local authority, a legally appointed guardian is entitled to require the authority to hand over the child to his or her care. That does not apply, however, if the child has been put in the authority's care by a court order.

A guardian has the right to give or refuse consent to the ADOPTION of his ward. But if a court regards the refusal

as unreasonable, it can allow the adoption without his consent.

The guardian administers any property owned by the child, but can be asked by a court to account for any profits that are made from the property.

Guardianship continues until the child attains majority at 18, or marries before reaching that age.

Removing a guardian by order of the court

A guardian can be removed from his position only by an order of the High Court. The application can be made by the child itself or by any other person concerned about the welfare of the child.

The court will remove the guardian if satisfied that it is in the child's best interest to do so, and can then appoint another guardian.

GUARDIAN'S ALLOWANCE

Additional benefit for someone who is looking after a child

A person who is receiving CHILD BENEFIT for the child in his care may also be entitled to a guardian's allowance (£7.50 a week in 1980) if one of the child's parents was born in the United Kingdom or lived in the United Kingdom for at least 52 weeks in any 2 year period after the age of 16 and if:
● The child's parents, natural or adoptive, are both dead.
● The child's parents are divorced and one is dead and the other does not have custody of the child and does not maintain it.
● The child is illegitimate and the mother has died.
● The whereabouts of the child's parents remain unknown despite efforts to trace them.
● One parent is dead and the other is serving a term of at least 5 years' imprisonment.

How to claim

To claim the allowance, the applicant should obtain form BG 1 from a social security office. An applicant cannot claim if he is already receiving a boarding-out allowance for the child.

GUN

Police control over the use of firearms

Anyone who owns a gun of any sort – including a shotgun, rifle or pistol – should normally have a certificate issued by the police. Only low-powered airguns can be used without police permission.

There are two kinds of certificate:
● Shotguns – covering all smooth-bore weapons with barrels that are 24 in. or more long.
● Firearms – covering all other guns that can inflict injury – even if, like starting pistols, they were not designed to do so.

A firearms certificate specifies the type of arms and the ammunition which the holder can buy and use.

Anyone hunting or shooting GAME must have a firearms certificate even if he already has a game licence.

No one under the age of 14 can be allowed a shotgun or firearms certificate, and the police may also refuse an application by anyone they consider unfit to have a gun. Anyone refused a certificate can appeal to the local crown court. There is no appeal against that court's decision.

When a certificate is not needed

Some people do not require a firearms or shotgun certificate:
● Anyone shooting at an artificial target at a time and in a place approved by the police. That includes most members of rifle clubs on club premises.
● Anyone without a certificate who borrows a gun from a person who has a certificate, provided that he fires the gun on land owned or rented by the holder of the certificate, and in the presence of the owner of the gun.
● People who carry guns for a certificate holder under the holder's instructions. They are not, however, allowed to fire the guns.
● Collectors who keep antique guns as ornaments – even if they are in working order – and the holders of low-powered air guns.

Obtaining a certificate

Application forms for shotgun and

firearms certificates are usually available at police stations. The maximum penalty for making a false statement in an application is a £200 fine and 6 months' imprisonment.

Temporary permit The police can issue a temporary permit for a shotgun or firearm in certain circumstances – for example, to the executors of a dead person's estate to cover possession of any guns until they are sold or handed over to their eventual new owner.

When a gun is missing Owning and using a gun of any sort can be dangerous and there are several penalties for misuse.

A gun must be kept in a safe place, and the police should be told immediately if a gun is missing or stolen. They must also be told if anyone holding a certificate changes address.

A person holding a valid certificate can sell, give, lend or hire his gun only to someone who also has a valid certificate or is a registered firearms dealer.

When a gun is sold, the police who issued the certificate must be told within 48 hours. Otherwise the buyer commits an offence by having a firearm without a licence.

Police do not always need a warrant to search premises for firearms, and they can arrest anyone suspected of possessing a firearm without a warrant.

Sawn-off shotguns It is a criminal offence for anyone other than a registered firearms dealer to shorten the barrel of a shotgun to less than 24 in. without police permission.

sites required is the responsibility of county councils and London borough councils. They can use compulsory purchase powers to acquire land.

Local authorities must advertise proposals for any gypsy site in the Press to give residents time to object.

Complaining about council policy

Complaints about the kind and quantity of accommodation should be made to a local councillor.

If you feel that a local authority is not providing enough accommodation for gypsies you can also complain to the Secretary of State for the Environment, who could order a council to fulfil the minimum requirements.

Where gypsies cannot camp

The Secretary of State for the Environment can designate an area – usually at the request of the council responsible – as having adequate gypsy accommodation. When that happens, gypsies must then camp only on authorised sites within that area. They can be moved on by the police if they camp anywhere else, except in cases of illness, breakdown or other emergency.

In an area that has not been designated as having adequate sites, the police can move gypsies only if they are breaking the law – for example by obstructing or camping on the highway, including verges and footpaths.

The maximum penalty for camping on a highway is a £50 fine. In the case of

obstruction the fine can be £50 for each day the obstruction continues.

When gypsies occupy a common they are likely to be breaking a bye-law and can be prosecuted. The council can also ask a county court for an order to recover possession of the land.

Anyone who allows gypsies to keep a CARAVAN on his land – unless he is a farmer for whom they are working – must obtain planning permission and a caravan site licence from the council.

Gypsies who set up camp on private property and refuse to leave can be evicted by the landowner or tenant – by force if necessary. He is entitled to tow a caravan away, but not to use any unreasonable means, such as overturning the caravan or setting fire to it.

A landowner can also sue for TRESPASS, even if the offence amounts only to an ABANDONED VEHICLE or other rubbish being left on his land.

Preventing unsightly activities

The law of NUISANCE can be used to end unsightly activities such as carbreaking, and to prevent noise, smell or insanitary conditions. If the nuisance is being committed in a public place, such as a roadside verge, any member of the public can ask the local authority to issue an abatement notice, ordering the gypsies to stop doing whatever is causing concern. If they ignore such a notice, they can be prosecuted and fined £20.

Any local authority also has powers to declare a specific trade offensive so that it may not be carried on without the authority's written consent.

GYPSIES

Where they can and cannot camp

Gypsies are subject to the same laws as other citizens, but some legal provisions have been made to take special account of their way of life.

Under the Caravan Sites Act 1968, local authorities must provide adequate accommodation for gypsies – defined as 'persons of nomadic habit of life, whatever their race or origin'.

Metropolitan counties and London boroughs are not required to provide more than 15 spaces for gypsy caravans in any district. But every council has the right to provide more if it chooses.

Assessment of the number of gypsy

WHEN THE COUNCIL HAD TO PAY

Anyone can ask the local authority to provide sites for gypsy caravans. If it does not do so, and the gypsies then cause him nuisance, he can sue the authority for the amount of his loss or damage.

In 1973, Epsom and Ewell Borough Council leased part of the Nonsuch Estate to Page Motors Ltd, so that the company could build a garage for the sale and repair of cars.

Many gypsy caravans came on the estate, which the council continued to own. The council was unwilling to provide sites for the caravans under the Caravan Sites Act, and Page Motors complained that

the gypsies burned rubber tyres, obstructed access to their premises and allowed dogs to attack customers.

Customers and suppliers were frightened off, so that their turnover largely declined.

The garage sued the council for allowing a nuisance.

DECISION
The court found against the council and directed an inquiry into the extent of the business loss which the nuisance caused.

The council had to pay the garage whatever that loss amounted to.

HABEAS CORPUS

The historic safeguard against wrongful imprisonment

A writ of habeas corpus – which means in Latin 'You have the body' – is an historic procedure that safeguards people in Britain against wrongful imprisonment by police, prison authorities, hospital officials or any other person or group.

The writ, which begins with the words 'Habeas corpus', can be issued by any High Court judge. It demands that the person named in it be brought before the judge, who then decides whether the person is being unlawfully imprisoned or detained.

A habeas corpus writ can be asked for by the person who believes he is wrongfully held, by his friends or relatives or by anyone else who is interested.

For example, if someone has been kept at a police station without being charged, his friends can seek a writ of habeas corpus, ordering the police to bring him before a court, so that the circumstances can be investigated.

The procedure is normally used when someone has been detained for a long time – perhaps several days or more. The writ can however be sought after any period of detention, however short.

Although a judge can adjourn or delay his decision for a day or two, so as to allow the police to decide whether to charge the person named in the writ, the request for a writ in practice forces them to free the person or charge him without further delay.

Apart from police cases, examples of situations in which the habeas corpus procedure can be used are:
● Where a person is held unlawfully in a mental hospital (against the person in charge of the hospital).
● Immigration officials where a person is detained on suspicion of having entered the country illegally.

How to apply

Anyone applying for a writ of habeas corpus must produce an AFFIDAVIT before the judge, explaining the circumstances of the person's detention. He can make the application without having direct knowledge of what has happened to the detained person – if, for example, the police will not confirm or deny they are holding someone.

A habeas corpus application must normally be made to the court office of the Queen's Bench Division of the High Court, in London. If the court is not sitting – at a weekend or vacation – you can apply to any High Court judge, wherever he is, at any time of night or day. Court officials will give you the whereabouts of the duty judge.

What happens in court Once the writ has been issued, the detained person and whoever is holding him or her appear in court, so that the judge can decide whether the detention is legal.

The judge has power to order the person to be freed, and, if an order is made, he must be released at once. Failure to do so is CONTEMPT OF COURT, and the person responsible for the continued detention can be imprisoned for an indefinite time.

Anyone who succeeds in a habeas corpus claim might also sue for FALSE IMPRISONMENT, and claim damages.

HACKNEY CARRIAGE

Special protection for passengers who travel by taxi

A whole range of legislation controls the running of TAXI-cabs in English towns and cities – some still aimed at protecting the interests of the hackney cab's original power source – the horse.

HAIRDRESSER

Legal protection against incompetent treatment

No qualification or registration is needed to set up in business as a hairdresser, but anyone who does so has a legal responsibility to show reasonable care and skill in treating his customers'

> ## THE WAITER WHO WAS GOING GREY
>
> *A hairdresser must use care and skill not only in dressing hair but also in choosing the right materials for the job.*
>
> Mr Watson, a Manchester waiter, found that grey hairs made it harder for him to find work. From time to time, therefore, he went to Mrs Buckley, a hairdresser, to have his hair dyed.
>
> On one visit she suggested that he should try a new dye. Soon after she applied it, Mr Watson developed dermatitis and had to go into hospital.
>
> It was found that the dermatitis was caused by an excessive amount of chromic acid which had got into the new dye accidentally. Mr Watson sued Mrs Buckley for damages.
>
> DECISION
> The judge ordered Mrs Buckley to pay damages. Mr Watson, he ruled, was entitled to expect that any materials used by Mrs Buckley were reasonably fit for their purpose.

IF SOMETHING GOES WRONG

A customer who is caused actual suffering because of a hairdresser's negligence or lack of care can sue him for damages.

"I said leave it long at the back"

hair. A customer who is caused suffering because of the hairdresser's lack of care or skill can sue for damages.

Special hours of business for hairdressers

Although other shopkeepers and traders are restricted to opening and closing at certain times, hairdressers are specifically allowed to do business by visiting clients in their homes or in their clubs or hotels outside the normal approved hours. *See:* SHOPS

HALF-BROTHER AND SISTER

When marriage is allowed and forbidden

Men and women cannot marry their half-sister or half-brother – that is someone to whom they are related only through their mother or father. But you can marry the half-sister of a deceased wife or the half-brother of a deceased husband. *See:* MARRIAGE

HALLMARK

When 'gold' must indeed be gold

When a trader describes something as being gold, silver or platinum, examine it carefully to see whether it is hall-marked – punched with a series of special marks to prove what quantity and quality of the precious metal it contains. If there is no hallmark, the article must be described as rolled gold, plated gold, plated silver or plated platinum, unless it is very small or so thin that it cannot be hallmarked.

With that exception, it is a crime to give an unhallmarked article a trade or business description indicating that it is wholly or partly made of gold, silver or platinum. The maximum penalty is an unlimited fine and 2 years' imprisonment.

The only other circumstances in which a trader is entitled to use the descriptions 'gold' and 'silver' is when he is referring simply to the colour of an article. Then he must make clear that it is only colour that is being described.

Any trader who deals in articles of precious metal must display in a conspicuous part of his premises an official notice issued by the British Hallmarking Council, explaining the hallmarking system. The maximum penalty for not doing so is an unlimited fine and 2 years' imprisonment.

Altering a hallmark

It is also a criminal offence for anyone, whether in the course of trade or business or not, to alter or repair a hallmarked article without the written consent of the office that hallmarked it originally – called the assay office. Nor may anyone remove, alter or deface a hallmark, except to batter an article so that it is fit only to be remade entirely.

The maximum penalty for those offences is an unlimited fine and 2 years' imprisonment.

The maximum penalty for counterfeiting or forging a hallmark is 10 years' imprisonment.

When you have a complaint

If you believe that you have been defrauded over the purchase of a hallmarked article, complain to the local council's trading standards office and ask it to refer the complaint to the assay office whose mark is stamped on the article.

To test the quality, the assay office will remove, imperceptibly, a sliver of metal, and it will report its findings to the trading standards department.

WHAT A HALLMARK TELLS YOU

Hallmarks give buyers of gold and silver a guarantee of quality and origin. The maker's, or sponsor's, mark indicates the name of the manufacturer; the standard mark guarantees the metal content; the assay office mark indicates where the article was tested and marked; the date letter shows when it was marked.

A MODERN SILVER HALLMARK

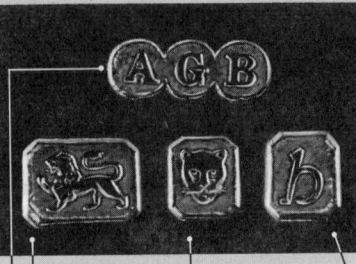

Sterling silver
The English mark is a lion. Formerly its head was turned and crowned

London assay
A leopard head has been used since AD 1300. Early on, it was crowned

Maker's mark
Each individual smith or firm in the trade can register a punch at the assay office based on initials

Date letter
Each assay office designs a distinctive letter for each year. The ornate B shown is for 1957

Anyone who counterfeits or alters a hallmark, or possesses a die for doing so, can be sent to prison for up to 10 years on conviction.

MAKERS' MARKS

Makers punch their own mark on articles before sending them for assay. The solder, as well as the metal, must be of the required quality.

QUALITY MARKS

SILVER

Britannia silver

London
Birmingham
Sheffield
Edinburgh
after 1975

Foreign silver
mark after 1904

Sterling silver

London
Birmingham
Sheffield
after 1975

Edinburgh
after 1975

Edinburgh
Glasgow
before 1975

Common control
mark after 1975

Foreign silver
after 1904

Foreign
mark

PLATINUM

London
Birmingham
Sheffield
after 1975

Common control mark

Assay offices started to hallmark platinum only in 1975. The figure 950 refers to the number of parts of pure platinum out of 1,000

22, 18, 14, 9 carat
after 1975

Common control
mark (18 carat)

Foreign
mark

From AD 1300 the standard for gold was 19½ carats. The maker's mark came in 1363

GOLD

	Modern	Old	Foreign	
22 carat	916	22	22	916
18 carat	750	18	18	750
14 carat	585	14·585	14	585
9 carat	375	9·375	9	·375

Carat standards were first introduced in 1477. The new standards indicate the number of parts per 1,000 of pure gold

DUBLIN

22 carat

20 carat

18 carat

The main concern of hallmarks has always been the proportion of pure metal to alloy, and the maintenance of standards has long been regarded as a prerogative and duty of the state. Until 1976 it was a domestic matter in Britain, and, even then, the common control mark that was agreed internationally extended outside the country only to Austria, Finland, Sweden and Switzerland.

OFFICE MARKS

BRITISH ARTICLES

London gold and silver

Edinburgh gold and silver

Birmingham silver

Birmingham gold before and after 1975

Sheffield silver before 1975

Sheffield gold before 1975

Sheffield gold, silver and platinum after 1975

Chester gold and silver closed 1962

Dublin silver

Dublin gold

Glasgow gold and silver closed 1964

Since 1842 there have been special hallmarks for foreign plate. Articles that can be shown to be more than 100 years old are exempt

IMPORTED ARTICLES

	London	Birmingham	Chester	Dublin	Edinburgh	Glasgow	Sheffield
Gold	Ω	△	🌿	ℳ	X	⊞	Ω
Silver	Ω	△	🌿	ℳ	X	⊞	Ω

DATE LETTER

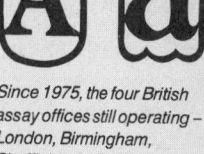

Since 1975, the four British assay offices still operating – London, Birmingham, Sheffield and Edinburgh – have all adopted the same date letter

Collectors of antique plate encounter marks of assay offices that have long been closed, each with its own system of date marks. Exeter and Newcastle closed in 1883, Norwich by 1701, York in 1857, Chester in 1962 and Glasgow in 1964. Dublin marks struck before April 1, 1923 are recognised as British. The Dublin harp is always accompanied by the figure of Hibernia.

HARASSMENT

Forms of pressure that are against the law

Harassment can consist of physical violence or the threat of it, creating a constant din, sending abusive letters – anything in fact that causes the victim persistent distress.

It is most commonly carried out by landlords who want to evict tenants or creditors who want to recover their money. *See:* DEBT

When a tenant is harassed there are four main steps that the victim can legally take.

Suing for damages The most effective and speedy remedy is to sue the harasser for damages and at the same time apply to the county court for an INJUNCTION ordering the harasser to cease his unlawful activities.

When the harassment is severe, you may be able to obtain an injunction within 24 hours of the application. LEGAL AID may be available to cover some, or even all, of the costs of the applications.

Calling the police Harassment can be difficult to prove – when, for example, it takes the form of distressing noise or abusive behaviour. The police are usually reluctant to intervene in such cases unless there is clear evidence that the harasser has committed a crime. *See:* ASSAULT AND BATTERY

Private prosecution A victim of harassment may be able to bring a private prosecution against the harasser, if the harassment is severe and consists, for example, of abusive words and behaviour, assault, behaviour likely to cause a breach of the peace, or if it is part of an attempt by a creditor to recover a debt.

Private prosecution also has the disadvantage of being a slow remedy for someone facing severe harassment: there is usually a delay of several weeks before a case can be heard.

But if the court convicts the harasser, it can make him, by a criminal compensation order, pay compensation to the person he was harassing. This would usually be limited to financial loss such as for a broken window.

Complaining to the local council A tenant may decide to prosecute his landlord privately or he can ask the

---

THE LANDLORD WHO HARASSED HIS FEMALE TENANTS

Mr B, a landlord, harassed three women tenants, one of them very elderly, in an attempt to make them leave his property so that he could re-let it at a higher rent.

He damaged their flats, insulted them, and cut off their gas and electricity and use of the lavatory.

The local authority prosecuted him for harassment.

VERDICT

Mr B was convicted, sentenced to 2 years' imprisonment and ordered to pay a total of £1,600 compensation to the three tenants.

---

local authority's tenancy relations officer to take up his case. The officer can prosecute any landlord, or any of his employees, who harasses a tenant. The harassment must be severe – such as cutting off gas or electricity, or intimidation by thugs or fierce dogs – and the tenant must be able to produce clear evidence of it.

Such prosecutions also take a long time to come to court.

Alternatively, it may be enough for a tenant to ask the tenancy relations officer to issue a warning to his landlord that legal action will be taken if the harassment does not stop.

Maximum penalties For harassment of a tenant, a £1,000 fine and 6 months' imprisonment if the case is heard in a magistrates' court or an unlimited fine and 2 years' imprisonment in a crown court.

A local authority can prosecute a landlord who severely harasses his tenants – but the legal process may be lengthy.

HARE COURSING

A blood sport with dogs that is legal

Using greyhounds to pursue and kill hares in the field – the sport known as coursing – is a lawful pastime. No licence is needed, only the permission of the person over whose land the coursing is to take place.

Anyone who goes hare coursing on private land without the permission of the owner or tenant can be prosecuted for POACHING. It is also an offence to kill hares at night or on a Sunday or Christmas Day.

Because hare coursing is a legal pastime, anyone attempting to interfere can be prosecuted for BREACH OF THE PEACE or ASSAULT AND BATTERY. There are no laws to prevent gambling on hare coursing.

HEALTH AND SAFETY AT WORK

Making sure your workplace is safe – your rights and responsibilities

Everyone is entitled to a safe and healthy place of work, and it is the employer's duty to provide one. If he fails to do so, he can be prosecuted and anyone who is injured can sue him for damages. *See:* ACCIDENT AT WORK

Safety at work is governed by more than 30 Acts of Parliament, but under the Health and Safety Act 1974 a commission was established to replace all the existing laws by more comprehensive general rules backed by codes of practice worked out within industries.

What an employer must do

Employers have a legal duty to ensure 'so far as is reasonably practicable' the health, safety and welfare at work of all employees. In particular, they must provide and maintain:

● Safe machinery, plant, tools and equipment – including guard-rails where necessary.

● A safe and healthy working environment.

● A safe working system, including secure handling, storage and transport.

● Safe entry and exit arrangements – a proper fire exit, for example.

● Information, training and supervision necessary to ensure the safety of employees.

In addition, an employer has a general duty for the safety of non-employees – such as visitors to his company, or neighbours and passers-by outside. For example, he must take steps to prevent the emission of poisonous or unpleasant waste outside his premises as well as within.

HEALTH AND SAFETY RULES FOR SHOPS, OFFICES AND RAILWAY PREMISES
How the law protects and imposes duties on employees

Area	What the law says
Cleanliness	Floors and steps must be cleaned at least once a week. Refuse must not be allowed to accumulate in work areas.
Overcrowding	40 sq. ft or 400 cu. ft must be allowed for each employee in every room.
Ventilation	Adequate supplies of fresh or purified air must be in circulation.
Temperature	The premises must have a reasonable temperature: not less than 60°F after the first hour's work, not more than 80°F. A thermometer must be displayed prominently on each floor.
Lighting	The premises must have enough suitable lights.
Toilets	There must be enough suitable and clean toilets – separate for men and women. The number depends on the size of the workforce. For example, 5 WCs for men and 5 for women would be needed for a staff of 100, though fewer would be needed for the men if urinals were provided.
Washing facilities	Enough suitable basins must be provided for men and women, on the same scale as toilets. Hot and cold, or warm, running water, soap and drying facilities must also be available.
Drinking water	Staff must have adequate, accessible drinking water, with either a cup or fountain provided.
Clothes storage	There must be room for hanging up outdoor clothing and reasonably practical arrangements for drying them.
Seating for rest periods	There must be reasonable facilities for sitting down, where work is not disturbed. Shops must provide at least one seat for every three employees.
Seating for work	Where work can or must be done sitting down, a seat with proper support, suitable both to the worker and to the type of work he or she is doing, must be provided.
Eating facilities	Where shop or office workers eat meals at work, suitable facilities must be available to them.
Lifts	Both the lift and its gates must be safe. They must be thoroughly examined by a competent person at least once every 6 months. The lift's maximum load – such as '6 persons or 900 lb.' – must be prominently displayed in the cabin.
Fire precautions	Most places of work must have a valid fire certificate from the local fire authority, granted only when its safety conditions – such as sufficient exits and extinguishing equipment – are met.
First aid	Every place of work must have a first aid box or cupboard, containing only first aid equipment, in the charge of a responsible person. If there are more than 150 employees, another box must be provided for each additional 150. Each box must contain sterilised dressings of various sizes, triangular bandages, adhesive plaster and dressings, cotton wool, safety-pins, a sterilised eye-pad and a first aid leaflet. The amount of dressings depends on the number of people employed and the type of shop or office. Anyone in charge of first aid should have received recognised training and should requalify every 3 years. Names and locations of first aid supervisors should be displayed prominently.

An employer may not charge his workers for any health or safety arrangements required by law – they could not, for example, be asked to contribute towards the cost of protective clothing stipulated in regulations.

Self-employed people must provide for themselves a safe and healthy workplace which also gives no danger or risk to the health of anyone else.

What employees must do

Employees have a legal obligation:
● To take reasonable care to avoid injury to themselves and to others.
● Not to interfere with or misuse any safety equipment.
● To co-operate with their employer in complying with safety regulations.

An employee (or employer) who flouts safety regulations, even if he does not cause an accident, can be prosecuted and fined up to £1,000 in a magistrates' court. Very serious cases could – in theory – be sent to a crown court, where the penalty would be an unlimited fine. Altogether the law is hard on breakers of safety regulations.

For example, if a metal welder refused to wear protective goggles, stipulated in regulations, and injured a fellow worker as a result of dropping his tools because he had himself been injured by flying particles, the welder could be:
● Disciplined by his employer.
● Refused compensation for his injuries.
● Prosecuted by the Health and Safety Executive.

However, the employer would still be liable for claims for damage from anyone injured in such an accident because he is liable for his employees' negligence.

The trade union rôle

When a company recognises a trade union, that union is entitled to appoint safety representatives from among the company's employees. The employer has no right to veto an appointment. Such representatives – who are normally shop stewards – must have been employed by the company for at least 2 years, or have 2 years' experience in similar employment. Their function is to represent the staff in discussions with the employer on health and safety, to investigate any staff complaints or accidents and to carry out regular inspections of the workplace.

Safety representatives have no special legal responsibility to ensure safety, apart from their normal duties as employees.

They are entitled to time off work with pay to carry out their function and to receive relevant training. The Government recommends that safety representatives should keep themselves informed about the law on health and safety, their employer's policy and the hazards associated with their work. They are entitled to information from employers on safety performance and plans and any research into likely hazards.

There is no limit to the number of safety representatives that may be appointed, but it should correspond to the size of the workforce and the dangers involved in the industry.

An employer must set up a safety

HOW COMPANIES ARE OBLIGED TO PREPARE A SAFETY POLICY
General rules that should be laid down and published prominently – for everyone's protection

Anyone employing more than five people must prepare a safety policy and display it prominently. It must be revised and such changes must also be displayed prominently.

Although some flexibility is generally possible, the policy should:
● State the company's intention to provide safe and healthy working conditions.

RULE 1
NO SMOKING

YOU MAY NOT SMOKE IN ANY AREA WHERE **NO SMOKING** NOTICES ARE DISPLAYED

Although smoking is permitted in most parts of the factory there are some places where the risk of fire is so great that the practice cannot be allowed. A match or cigarette end carelessly thrown away in such places might easily cause a fire or explosion which could endanger lives and everyone's job.

RULE 2
HORSEPLAY

HORSEPLAY IS PROHIBITED

Practical joking or horseplay in a factory can be extremely dangerous. As applied to your job it means throwing things, tripping up other people, directing a compressed air jet at someone or any act which may startle or distract other employees.

RULE 3
USE OF GUARDS & SAFETY DEVICES

Employees must make use of guards and safety devices fitted to the machines they operate. Under no circumstances may a guard be made inoperative or be removed from a machine.

Guards are provided for the benefit of employees and if the guards on your machine are not in good order you must report the matter to your Supervisor at once.

RULE 4
TRUCK DRIVING

Unless you are an authorised driver you must not drive a fork-lift truck or other power-operated factory vehicles.

Power-operated trucks require specialised knowledge and training to operate them safely and unauthorised operation by untrained people could cause a serious accident.

RULE 5
PERSONAL PROTECTIVE CLOTHING

You must wear protective equipment on jobs for which it is provided.

Safety spectacles, safety footwear, gloves etc., are provided for some jobs because experience has shown the need for them. Refusal to make use of them is a breach of safety rules.

RULE 6
REPORTING INJURIES AND OBTAINING TREATMENT

You must seek immediate medical treatment for any injury you receive no matter how slight it may seem to be. On returning from the medical department you should report the incident to your supervisor.

Immediate medical treatment may be the means of avoiding complications such as infection which can easily result from an apparently trivial injury. Failure to report your injury at once may prejudice your claim to Industrial Injury Benefit or other compensation to which you might otherwise be entitled.

committee, comprising managers, supervisors and safety representatives, if any two safety representatives ask him (in writing) to do so. Such committees are designed to promote employee involvement and management-union co-operation on safety.

As safety representatives are usually

shop stewards, they can use union power to enforce their demands.

More important, however, is the powers of the factory inspectorate. When a safety representative is aware that the rules are being broken, he should report the breach to the local inspector.

How safety at work is enforced

If you think that conditions or methods at your work are unsafe or unhealthy, do not wait for an accident to happen: report the matter immediately to the head of your department. If no action is taken, get in touch with the

● Describe rules and arrangements made for health and safety.
● List the names and phone numbers of executives responsible for safety and of employee safety representatives.
● Give details of safety training and supervision schemes.
● Define the responsibility of the company and of individual employees for maintaining safety.

If the company recognises a trade union, the safety representatives that it nominates must be consulted before a safety policy is formulated.

When no union is recognised by a company or individual employer, there is no legal rule that the workers must be consulted about safety, but many employers find it useful to do so.

RULE 7
PERSONAL CLOTHING

When working on or around machines do not wear loose fitting clothing or dangling neck ties. Always wear good sound shoes. Women employees should not wear high heels.

Loose clothing and long hair can be caught up in moving machinery much more easily than most people realise. Light shoes invite a serious foot injury.

RULE 8
AUTHORISED PERSONS ONLY

Unless you receive a direct instruction from your supervisor you must not:—

1) Enter an Electric Sub Station, Transformer Room or other enclosure containing electrical equipment.
2) Enter a Gas Meter House.
3) Go on to the Factory Roof.
4) Climb on any machinery or up girders.

Admission to certain parts of the factory is restricted to employees who have occasion to go there in the cause of their normal duties. Generally these places present some danger which may not be readily apparent to people who have not received specialist training and instruction.

RULE 9
RUNNING

DO NOT RUN IN THE FACTORY

Running in the factory is an extremely unsafe practice and many accidents are caused through it. Because of the hazards involved it is expected that all employees will exercise good common sense and not run – even in case of fire, walk to the nearest exit.

THIS IS THE LAW
FACTORIES ACT 1961

It is not generally realised that there are requirements in the Factories Act which apply to EVERY PERSON employed in a factory and cases of legal action by H. M. Inspector of Factories are not unknown.

The Factories Act places a responsibility on every employee in a factory not to damage, remove or interfere with guards or safety devices and to make proper use of the safety equipment for his benefit. Employees who knowingly and wilfully act in any way which endangers themselves or other employees are guilty of an offence for which they may be prosecuted and fined.

local office of the Health and Safety Executive – the address can be found in the telephone book – and ask for the factory inspector who deals with your branch of industry. Your name will not be given to your employer unless you agree.

If you belong to a union recognised by the company, report the hazard to your safety representative. If you do not know who that is, ask your shop steward to pursue the complaint with the management.

Factory inspectors are entitled to visit a workplace at any time and to enforce health and safety regulations. They can, for example, remove or destroy any article that they believe is causing imminent danger of personal injury.

If an inspector finds that a law has been broken, he can serve the employer with an improvement notice, directing him to make certain changes within a set time, or a prohibition notice, requiring him to end a dangerous practice. In cases of serious danger, he can order a piece of machinery, a workshop or, in theory, even a whole factory to be closed until the risk has been remedied.

An employer can appeal – within the period of the notice – to an INDUSTRIAL TRIBUNAL against an improvement or prohibition notice, which may be suspended during the course of the hearing. If the appeal fails, he can appeal against the tribunal's decision – only on a point of law – to the EMPLOYMENT APPEAL TRIBUNAL. In most cases, the industrial tribunal would be likely to uphold the inspector's order, but may, exceptionally, give the employer longer in which to comply.

Anyone who fails to comply with such a notice can be prosecuted in a magistrates' court and fined up to £1,000 and £50 for each day that the offence continues. If the offence is tried in the crown court, the penalty is up to 2 years' imprisonment and an unlimited fine.

In addition, anyone who was injured because health and safety regulations were neglected can sue the company for damages. When a company is prosecuted for contravening an improvement or prohibition notice, any director or manager who consented to the offence is also guilty and may be punished separately.

When you have a complaint

If you decide to leave your job because you feel you have been exposed to risk due to your employer's failure to maintain health and safety standards, you may be able later to obtain compensation for UNFAIR DISMISSAL. Similarly, someone who has been dismissed can claim unfair dismissal if he can prove the employer neglected health and safety.

If you live near, or regularly pass by, a factory or building that constitutes a risk to health or safety – for example, by emitting foul fumes, or leaving dangerous obstacles in the public's way – contact the Health and Safety Executive, which can enforce the regulations. If you have been injured by an organisation that has neglected health and safety, you can sue for damages. *See:* NEGLIGENCE

In certain sectors – principally non-industrial activities such as shops and offices – health and safety legislation is enforced by the LOCAL AUTHORITY. The Health and Safety Executive can refer you to the appropriate council officer.

HEALTH CENTRE

Putting many medical services under one roof

In many areas, health centres are provided by the area health authority to bring various aspects of health care under one roof. The size of the centres varies: the larger ones may include not only doctors and dentists, but also health visitors, district nurses, social workers and physiotherapists.

Doctors and dentists who join a health centre pay rent and contribute to its running costs, but the main expenses are paid by the health authority.

If a doctor or dentist gives up his individual practice and moves to the better facilities of a health centre, his patients are not consulted in advance. They must however be given notice.

If you do not wish to attend a health centre – if, for example, it is too far away – you are entitled to change to another doctor.

If you stay with your present doctor, your rights to his services, including home visits, are not affected. But on moving to a health centre he may enter into partnership with other doctors. In this case you would normally be expected to accept treatment from whichever doctor was on duty when your own was unavailable.

See: DENTIST
DOCTOR AND PATIENT
HEALTH VISITOR

THE SUPERMARKET THAT FAILED TO SHUT DOWN A LIFT KNOWN TO BE UNSAFE

It is an employer's duty to ensure that all plant and machinery is safe.

A goods lift at the Safeway supermarket in Kilburn High Road, London, frequently broke down – often as a result of staff members riding in it.

Engineers were summoned three times in a year to examine the lift and each time found it to be unsafe. They recommended that it be turned off and its main fuses be removed.

The supermarket manager, Richard Bailey, passed on the reports to his head office, but was told to keep the lift in service and to make sure that it was used for goods only. He warned his staff several times – on threat of dismissal – not to ride in the lift and posted a notice forbidding passengers to use it.

In March 1978, 2 weeks after engineers condemned the lift for the third time, 15-year-old Anthony Johnson, a boy who did casual work for the shop on Saturdays, was killed while using the lift.

Camden Council sued Safeways and Richard Bailey under the Health and Safety at Work Act for failing to maintain the lift in safe condition.

The supermarket pleaded guilty to the charges, but claimed in mitigation that it had been forced to continue using the lift – despite the engineers' warnings – in order to shift its supplies. It had forbidden staff to use it and, when found once riding the lift, Anthony Johnson had been given 'a very severe warning indeed'.

The prosecution withdrew the case against the manager.

DECISION

Hampstead magistrates' court fined Safeways £940 for failing to maintain safe premises.

HEALTH SERVICE COMMISSIONER

A channel for your grievances about health care

Complaints of maladministration in the Health Service are handled by the Health Service Commissioner and his staff. They are concerned with all regional and area health authorities, family practitioner committees, the Health Service Board and its Welsh Committee, hospital boards of governors and the Public Health Laboratory Service Board. *See:* OMBUDSMEN

HEALTH VISITOR

How they supplement the medical services

No one is forced to see a health visitor but most family doctors welcome their aid.

Health visitors are always qualified nurses (usually female) who provide a wide range of advice and practical help to augment the services of doctors, specialists and hospitals. Among their main jobs are visits to the homes of mothers-to-be, nursing mothers, elderly people and patients who have just come out of hospital.

Often the health visitor will call without a request from the patient. It may, for example, be at the suggestion of a family doctor. A call is usually made automatically to nursing mothers after the health visitor has been notified of the birth by the area health authority. The visitor will check that mother and child are progressing and give advice.

A health visitor who gave incorrect advice might be guilty of NEGLIGENCE if as a result the patient suffered any harm. When attached to a family doctor's practice, health centre or hospital, the health visitor must inform the doctor in charge of the case about patients whose symptoms call for further attention. Failing to do so could also lead to a negligence action, as the patient could be denied essential treatment.

Child-care

Health visitors advise on immunisation for children and run clinics where children can have hearing, eyesight and other aspects of their development checked.

Helping the elderly and the handicapped

Home contact with elderly people enables health visitors to check that they are claiming the full range of state benefits and entitlements, and to arrange for services such as meals on wheels and attendance at day centres and clubs.

Health visitors call on handicapped people in their homes to give advice and help and arrange for supportive services.

Health education

Health visitors sometimes run anti-smoking and obesity clinics and advise on family planning.

HIGH COMMISSION

Embassies of the Commonwealth

Britain and other Commonwealth nations do not have embassies in each other's countries. Instead, they have High Commissions, which perform the same basic functions.
See: BRITISH EMBASSY
FOREIGN EMBASSY

HIGH COURT

All major non-criminal court cases are heard by one or other of the three divisions of the High Court – Chancery, Family, or Queen's Bench.

The High Court also has overall control on the conduct and jurisdiction of all criminal cases tried by magistrates and over tribunals. When it hears cases from the lower courts, the High Court is known as the Divisional Court.

HIGHWAY CODE

The road users' guide to safety

The Highway Code, produced by the Department of Transport, is a guide to all road users. But it is not law, and disregarding the code is not in itself an offence.

The code can however play an important part in legal proceedings. If someone charged with a driving offence can be shown to have disobeyed the code, the court can take that as evidence in assessing his guilt.

For example, a motorist who has knocked down a child who ran out from a parked ice-cream van, and who is then prosecuted for driving without due care, may plead that the child darted out without warning. But clause 15 of the code warns motorists, 'Be careful near a parked ice-cream van – children are more interested in ice-cream than in traffic,' and it emphasises the point with a photograph.

The prosecution could invoke that clause of the code as evidence that the motorist should have taken particular care when passing the van.

On the other hand, if someone charged with a driving offence can show that he was conforming to the code, the court can take that into account in his favour.

Civil actions The code has the same

> ## THE PEDESTRIAN WHO WAS KNOCKED DOWN AT A JUNCTION
>
> *A motorist must bear the Highway Code in mind when a pedestrian is in the road.*
>
> In 1963, 73-year-old Mr Alfred Frank started to cross a street in the City of London at a junction controlled by traffic lights that were in his favour. He had almost reached the central refuge when he was knocked down and seriously injured by a car that had turned right into the street when the lights changed in its favour.
>
> The court ordered the driver of the car, Mr Peter Cox, to pay Mr Frank compensation of £3,547.
>
> Mr Cox appealed, on the ground that Mr Frank should have looked out for his car.
>
> DECISION
> The court dismissed the appeal, invoking the section of the Highway Code that says that a motorist turning at a road junction must give way to pedestrians who are crossing the road into which the motorist is turning.

function in civil actions over road accidents. If you have been injured in a road accident and are claiming compensation for negligence, it helps your case if you can show that the person you are suing disregarded the Highway Code. Conversely, if you ignored the code, that may be taken to be CONTRIBUTORY NEGLIGENCE on your part.

HIRE AGREEMENT

Anyone who hires goods without intending to become the outright owner is protected by the Consumer Credit Act over cancellation of hire agreements, methods of repossession by the hirer and difficulties over payment of hire fees. *See:* GOODS RENTAL

HIRE PURCHASE

The hiring that ends with a sale

A hire-purchase contract is a special form of instalment purchase. It takes the legal form of an agreement to hire goods with the intention of eventually owning them outright.

The hirer pays a deposit and regular instalments to cover the purchase price and INTEREST CHARGE on that sum. The final payment includes a nominal amount by which the hirer takes up an option to buy.

If a finance company is involved when you buy goods on hire purchase you make a direct contract with that company, not with the trader who supplies you with the goods. That is because, technically, the finance company has bought the goods from the trader and therefore owns them.

As a result, the trader who supplies the goods cannot be sued for any defect in them unless he was negligent and damage or injury was caused. You must normally sue the finance company, and in any case it is usually better to do so because the finance company has equal liability and is more likely to be able to pay if you win your case.

If a company sells you something on hire purchase, it automatically promises that:
1. It owns the goods offered to you.
2. The goods will be delivered in sound condition.

3. You will be allowed to enjoy the use of the goods without interference from the company provided that you pay the instalments promptly.

In return, you as 'hirer' and would-be purchaser, undertake to:
1. Accept delivery of the goods ordered, unless there is something wrong with them.
2. Take care of the goods.
3. Keep the goods insured, where required by the agreement.
4. Not sell or pawn them, or deal in them in any way, without the company's permission. In most cases, anyone who buys goods that are still on hire purchase has no right to them and will lose them if the legal owners find out they have been sold.

One exception is when someone as a private individual – not a company or car dealer – buys a car, not realising that the vehicle is on hire purchase and that it still belongs to a third party. In that case, the buyer has a legal right to the car he has bought. *See:* CREDIT AGREEMENT

The only other exception is when hire-purchase goods are sold in 'market overt'. *See:* GOODS, Ownership of

HOAX CALL

The penalties for mischievously raising a false alarm

A hoax telephone call or some other kind of bogus message which creates false public alarm or causes needless

> ### THE HOAX TIME BOMB
>
> *A hoax causing general alarm is viewed as a serious public nuisance.*
>
> Seven young men placed what looked like a time bomb in a London street. A passer-by telephoned the police who closed the street. A bomb expert examined the 'bomb' and discovered it was a hoax.
>
> The seven men were prosecuted for conspiring to cause a public mischief.
>
> #### VERDICT
> They were given 2 years' conditional discharge.

WHEN A HOAX IS NOT AMUSING

It is an offence to waste the time of the police by making a deliberately false report.

inconvenience or work is treated seriously by the law.

The five main offences are:
● Threatening to damage or destroy property. Maximum penalty – 10 years' imprisonment.
● Placing or sending a hoax bomb or sending a warning about a hoax bomb by telephone or writing. Maximum penalty – 5 years' imprisonment.
● Wasting the time of the police by making a deliberately false report that causes alarm. Maximum penalty – 6 months' imprisonment and £200 fine.
● Sending a false message by telephone to cause inconvenience or needless anxiety. Maximum penalty – £50 fine.
● Causing a public mischief. No maximum penalty laid down.

HOLIDAY ACCOMMODATION

When a short-term tenant can be forced to leave

The tenant of holiday accommodation, unlike the tenants of other accommodation that is not also occupied by the owner, has no security of tenure.

At the end of a landlord's valid notice to quit, which must be at least 4 weeks, or – if a fixed-term letting has been granted – at the end of the term, the holiday tenant has no right to remain on the premises.

However, if the tenant fails to leave at

the end of the notice period, the landlord cannot physically evict him from the property without first obtaining a court EVICTION order. Provided that it is a genuine holiday letting, the court must grant the order – and the tenant will probably have to pay the legal costs.

When the agreement is a sham

There is no legal definition of a holiday letting. The court decides on the facts of the individual case. If the letting is for a short period – say, 3 months or less – and is described in the tenancy agreement as a holiday letting, the court will normally accept it as such.

Some landlords, however, trick a tenant seeking normal accommodation into signing a lease or agreement that describes it as a holiday letting, in order to deprive the tenant of his security of tenure under the Rent Act.

If a tenant signs such an agreement and realises only later that he has signed away his protection under the Act, then the only way in which he can resist the landlord's eventual notice to quit or can obtain the intervention of a RENT OFFICER is by producing evidence to show that the agreement is a sham.

He would need to show, for example, that he had told the landlord that he did not want the property as holiday accommodation – or that the landlord told him initially that the agreement was merely a device to avoid the Rent Act, and would not be enforced.

The tenant would need to produce evidence – such as a witness who heard

NO SECURITY OF TENURE

A landlord cannot evict a holidaymaker unless he has an eviction order.

what the landlord said – to contradict the wording of the sham agreement.

Out-of-season lettings

A tenant who rents accommodation normally let as holiday accommodation has security of tenure under the Acts – provided that he rents it outside the holiday season and that he has not mistakenly signed a lease or agreement that he is renting the property for a holiday.

But there is one exception. It applies if the lease stated that the letting was to be for no more than 8 months, and if the landlord gave the tenant at the time of letting written notice that he might want to repossess the property. If these two conditions have been met, and provided that the property has been occupied as holiday accommodation within the previous 12 months, the landlord has the right to repossession.

HOLIDAY ENTITLEMENT

Your right to an annual vacation

Almost all full-time employees in Britain get at least 3 weeks' paid holiday a year, not counting bank holidays. More than one-third of them get 4 or more weeks' holiday. But there is no general law that gives employees the right to holidays, with or without pay, or even to a day off on bank holidays.

For most people, holiday entitlement is fixed by the EMPLOYMENT CONTRACT, which may be written or implied. In law, an employer is free to offer any holiday arrangements he wishes when engaging a new employee. If the employee accepts, the arrangements become legally binding upon both parties to the contract.

Custom and practice

In practice, holiday entitlement is generally established by collective agreement or by custom in the company or trade concerned. If there is no written employment contract, or holidays are not specifically mentioned, an employee's entitlement can be deduced from a collective agreement or by custom and practice.

No matter how holiday arrangements are established, an employer cannot arbitrarily reduce them once they have

become part of a written or unwritten employment contract. He may be in breach of contract if he tries to do so.

Protected groups

Farm workers and employees in trades and industries covered by a WAGES COUNCIL – for example, hairdressing – have minimum holiday entitlements that are defined by law. They are laid down in orders prepared by the Agricultural Wages Board (for farm workers), or by the appropriate Wages Council, and approved by Parliament.

The only other group of workers whose holiday rights are laid down, in part, by law are women and people under the age of 18 who work in factories. The Factories Acts say that they must be given bank holidays off, or a day off later instead.

Qualifying periods

Most employers insist on a qualifying period before a new recruit is allowed to take a holiday with pay. They are legally entitled to do so, provided that the qualifying period is an explicit or implicit part of the employment contract.

One common qualifying arrangement allows 1 day off for each month worked in the preceding 'holiday year' – which, in many companies, is calculated from April to April – to be taken after at least 6 months' service.

For example, an employee who starts work on September 1 will complete 7 months' service by the end of the 'holiday year' on the following March 31. He may then be permitted to take 7 working days off for that year's summer holiday.

Many employers increase holiday entitlements according to length of service – for example, by agreeing to an extra week for an employee who has completed 5 years with the company.

When holidays may be taken

The time of year when holidays can be taken is sometimes decided by custom and practice. For example, if a factory shuts down for 2 weeks every August, it is an implied condition of employment that employees should take their holidays at that time.

An employer is entitled to restrict the amount of holiday that may be taken at one time, either by writing that condition into individual contracts, or by

YOUR RIGHT TO CLAIM SOCIAL SECURITY BENEFITS WHILE YOU ARE ON HOLIDAY

If you take a holiday from your job, with or without pay, you are not entitled to claim unemployment benefit during your vacation. That rule also applies to enforced breaks that are a recognised feature of the job – for example, school holidays in the case of teachers. For that reason, a part-time teacher whose school does not pay him during holidays cannot claim unemployment benefit when he is not working, if he has arranged to go back to his job when the holidays are over.

Unemployed people claiming benefit who go away on holiday may lose their entitlement, because one condition for getting benefit is that the recipient must be available for work. However, benefit is not always stopped for that reason.

An unemployed person intending to go on holiday should inform his local employment office in advance of his holiday address and telephone number. If his destination is in Britain, Northern Ireland or the Isle of Man, he may still receive benefit, because he could return immediately to take up any job that became available. The benefit is paid on return from holiday. It must be claimed on form UB567H from the claimant's usual employment office.

If an unemployed person cannot give a holiday address because he is camping or touring, he is not eligible for benefit, as he cannot easily be contacted if work should become available for him. He may, however, arrange for the payment to continue on condition that he telephones his local office every morning or as requested.

Benefits are not normally payable if the holiday is outside Britain, Northern Ireland or the Isle of Man, but they may be continued during a short trip abroad to an EEC country but not elsewhere to seek work. *See:* UNEMPLOYMENT BENEFIT

Sickness benefit If an employee falls sick just before or during his holiday, he may claim SICKNESS BENEFIT in addition to any holiday pay from the employer. He does not have to pass on the benefit to his employer unless that is stipulated in his employment contract. If the illness or injury is not serious enough to stop him going away, he can still collect the benefit, provided that he remains in the UK.

making a company rule that becomes, by inference, part of those contracts.

A typical restriction for employees entitled to 4 weeks' holiday might be that they can take no more than 2 weeks at once, that at least 1 week must be taken outside the period June–September and that holidays not taken before a certain date cannot be carried over into the next year. In such a case, it is the employee's responsibility to ensure that he receives his full holiday.

If permission for a holiday is refused

An employer may refuse permission for a holiday at a particular time because of pressure of work or some other factor that makes it inconvenient. Whether or not he is entitled to do so depends on the contract and the circumstances.

Provided that the employer gives adequate advance warning that certain dates are unacceptable – for example, when the holiday schedules are drawn up or when the request for time off is first made – he is within his rights. If, however, he gives permission but withdraws it at the last moment, he may be in breach of contract.

If an employee is dismissed for taking a holiday when permission has been given and then withdrawn, he may be entitled to make an UNFAIR DISMISSAL claim. However, such a claim will fail if the employee has not sought permission, or has not given advance notice of his absence.

If in such circumstances the dismissal is held to be fair, he will probably be disqualified from Unemployment Benefit for up to 6 weeks.

In deciding such cases, courts and tribunals examine the behaviour of employer and employee to decide whether it was reasonable in the individual circumstances. They also take into account the employee's contractual duty to cooperate with his employer.

When payment is taken instead of holidays

Some employers offer employees extra pay to continue working during part of their holiday entitlement, but that practice is not approved by the trade unions. An employee cannot be compelled to work during the holiday to which he is otherwise entitled unless that is a specific or implied term of his employment contract.

If an employee leaves his employer before taking holidays to which he is entitled, he can claim extra pay as compensation – an additional day's wage for each day's holiday not taken – if that is provided for in his employment contract.

However, if there is no specific provision, or if the contract lays down qualifying conditions – for example, a minimum period of service – and the conditions have not been met, the employee is unlikely to succeed in a claim for extra money. If he takes the matter to court, he will have to prove that he is entitled to accrued holiday pay.

Special rules for workers who are part-time employees

Generally, a PART-TIME WORKER is not allowed a paid holiday, although the precise arrangements depend on the individual's employment contract, which, if it is not in writing, can be decided according to custom and practice.

HOLIDAY HOME

Special rules and restrictions on a second home

Anyone who has acquired a second home in the country or at the seaside for use at weekends and for holidays is faced with particular legal problems that do not affect the single home-owner.

The first difficulty is insurance. Insurance companies do not normally cover property that is likely to stand empty for considerable periods, unless some special arrangement has been made. If you do not inform the insurance company that the property you are asking it to insure is a holiday home, the insurance company will terminate the policy and not pay out on a subsequent claim, as soon as it discovers the true position.

The insurer must be told the value of the property, the number of occasions during the year when it is likely to be occupied, its precise location and any other fact you think might be relevant. You will almost certainly be charged an additional premium.

Full cover is always expensive. The insurer normally insists that all services are turned off when the property is unoccupied, and that satisfactory arrangements are made for security checks on the property from time to time. In particular, liability for damage by water and frost is likely to be excluded.

Liability for rates You do not have to pay rates on property that stands empty for 1 month or more, but you must be able to show that the property is unoccupied. Even to have furniture or personal belongings in the house would suggest that it is occupied – in law. So, although you may be able to get rate relief from the time you buy your holiday home to the time you first move in, once you have moved in, the property is fully rateable – even if you are not living there all the time.

Mortgage relief

If your holiday home has been bought with the help of a loan or mortgage you are not usually entitled to claim tax relief on the interest payments, even if you do not have a mortgage on another property. That is because tax relief is available only on mortgage payments secured on a main or principal home.

The one exception is the case of a taxpayer whose employment requires him to live elsewhere – for example, in a house provided by his employer. In those circumstances, the employee can buy one home as his own and (provided the loan does not exceed £25,000) claim tax relief on the interest payment even if he only uses the home for holidays.

When the holiday home is sold

When you sell a holiday home you may have to pay CAPITAL GAINS TAX on any profit you make. The only profit that is exempt is what you make on selling your main residence. However, if you rent or live rent free (for example, as an employee) in your main residence, you can choose to treat your holiday home as your main residence to claim exemption from capital gains tax. If you own two homes, you may choose one to be treated as your main residence for exemption. If it is likely that the sale of your holiday home will make a greater

taxable gain than the sale of your second house, choose the holiday home.

To establish which home you wish to be considered tax-exempt, inform the Inland Revenue in writing within 2 years of buying the second home. Otherwise, the question will be decided according to which home is your main residence at the time you sell one or other of the properties. If that question cannot be agreed between you and your tax inspector, it will be decided by the Appeal Commissioners. *See:* INCOME TAX ASSESSMENT

A house that is always let to tenants cannot be selected for exemption, although one that is only let occasionally might still qualify.

Television licence

If you have a television in your holiday home you must have a licence for it. Failure to have a licence can lead to a fine of up to £200 plus any arrears of licence fees due. If you have only one portable set which you carry with you to your second home for use while on holiday then, provided you already have a licence for the set for use in your main home, you will not need another one to cover use at the holiday home as well.

However, if you have two sets, one at home and one installed in the holiday accommodation, then you must have a second licence, even if you brought the second set on holiday with you – unless you can show that the set you left at home was not used at all during your absence.

If you rent your holiday home, you still need a television licence, and that is your responsibility, not the landlord's. A landlord who installs a television in a holiday flat does not have to buy a licence for it. It is the responsibility of the user to supply the licence. If the user has a licensed set at home, his licence covers the use of a set in his holiday accommodation, provided the set at home is not used during the holiday period.

Renting a holiday home

If a tenant rents his holiday accommodation, and it is let specifically for a holiday, the tenant has no security of tenure beyond what is granted in the tenancy agreement – that is, the period for which he has agreed to rent. At the end of the period for which the tenant

agreed to take the holiday accommodation, if it is a fixed-term letting, or at the end of the landlord's valid NOTICE TO QUIT, if it is a periodic letting, the tenant has no right to remain. However, if the tenant fails to leave at the end of the notice period, the landlord cannot physically evict him without obtaining an EVICTION order.

Provided the letting was genuinely for holiday purposes and the tenancy has been validly ended, either by the service of a valid notice to quit or by the end of the fixed period of time for which the accommodation was granted, the court must grant the landlord the possession order, and the tenant may have to pay both his and the landlord's legal costs.

When the owner wants his property back

The Rent Act provisions that make it difficult for a landlord to regain possession of rented property do not apply in the case of an owner-occupier who wants to rent his holiday flat or cottage for short periods when he does not want to occupy it himself.

A tenant has no security of tenure of accommodation let to him for a period of 8 months or less, provided that the accommodation was, at some time within the 12 months before the tenancy started, occupied for holidays by either the landlord himself or tenant. To have such protection, however, the landlord must serve a special notice on the tenant saying that he 'might seek, at a later date, to recover possession of the dwelling in the ground set out in Case 13 of Schedule 15 to the Rent Act 1977'.

If the notice, served in writing, includes exactly that form of words, the landlord can recover possession of the property at the end of the period of the letting provided only that he fulfils three conditions:
● The notice must be served on or before the granting of the tenancy – not afterwards.
● The landlord must be able to show that the property was occupied for holidays at some time during the 12 months before giving notice.
● The landlord must be able to show the tenant was not given any right to occupy the premises for a continuous period of 8 months or more.

HOME HELP

*Assistance in the home for the sick
and the infirm*

A home help is somebody paid by the
local authority to help with the cooking,
cleaning and shopping in a household
where the housewife – or anyone else
who normally looks after the home – is
unable to cope.

The reason for that inability may be
illness, pregnancy, convalescence, or
the fact that the person normally in
charge of the home is simply too old or
infirm. Help is also generally available
to clean a long-neglected home.

Obtaining a home help

To apply for a home help, contact the
organiser of the service at your local
social services department. The organiser will visit your home and assess the
amount of help needed – from a few
hours a week to daily attendance. There
is often a waiting list for help, but urgent
requests receive priority.

In some areas the home help service
is free. In others, there is a charge which
may be a flat rate or be based on
income.

HOME IMPROVEMENT

*When you need permission to make
changes in your home*

Most major home improvements
must be approved by two separate departments of your district council. The
planning department is concerned with
outward appearance and the effect of
the locality of any new building work.
The BUILDING REGULATIONS department is concerned with the safety and
health of the persons who live in the
building.

Planning control is mainly achieved
by planning officers exercising their
judgment as to the suitability of any
proposed building for its locality. It is
impossible to lay down hard and fast
rules that would apply to every development, although there are rules describing minor work that does not require
planning permission. Such work is
known as 'permitted development'.

Building regulation control is more
precise and is operated by building in-

IF IN DOUBT, ASK!

*Not all home improvements require
council permission, but if you are in
doubt, ask.*

'You don't need planning
permission for
a dog kennel'

---

spectors who are responsible for ensuring that the constructional work and the
installation of certain fittings complies
with the regulations. (In inner London
the safety of design, building standards
and materials used are controlled by
bye-laws instead of the building regulations.)

If your house has been classified as
being of special architectural or historic
interest, you will also require Listed
Building consent for any alteration that
may affect its character. Such permission is applied for and granted together
with a planning application. *See:*
PRESERVATION ORDER

If the property is LEASEHOLD LAND
or even freehold with a covenant or
agreement not to make alterations
without consent, you may also need the
consent of the landlord or person entitled to enforce the covenant.

How to get your improvement
plans approved

If approval is required, you must
apply separately to the planning and
building regulations departments. The
two often work closely together and
application forms for both can generally
be obtained from either. You can return
the forms to the one office – with
enough drawings for both. The drawings that have to be prepared for building regulation approval will usually be
suitable also for obtaining planning approval – or can easily be made so.

If building regulations approval is refused, it is normally easy to obtain approval by amending your plans. But if
PLANNING PERMISSION is refused,
there may be no way of gaining approval except, perhaps, by appealing to the
Secretary of State for the Environment.
If you have any reason to think that
planning approval might be withheld, it
would be wise to apply at first only for
'outline planning approval'. You will
then know whether to go ahead, or
change your plans – or abandon the
proposal.

The planning and building regulations departments may suggest amendments to your scheme before the
council consider it.

Appealing against a refusal

Planning applications are normally
considered once a month, but if the
council has a heavy backlog there may
be a delay of several weeks. Once
granted, planning permission is valid for
5 years; it lapses if work has not started
by then.

If planning permission is refused –
and you do not wish to amend your
plans – you have the right of appeal to
the Secretary of State for the Environment, within 6 months of receiving
notice of disapproval.

If he considers the appeal justified, he
will arrange for an inquiry to be held.
This may be by written representation
or public hearing. You, the council and
any other interested party will be invited to give evidence. On the basis of
the findings, the Secretary of State will
grant or reject your application.

If you do not obtain the appropriate
permission or do not carry out work
strictly according to the plans approved,
the council can serve you with an enforcement notice, ordering you to demolish the unauthorised work and to
rebuild it in accordance with the approved plans or otherwise to council
approval – at your own expense. If you
ignore that notice, you can be prosecuted and fined up to £400.

Obtaining building regulations
approval

You are entitled to a decision on a
building regulations application within
5 weeks of its submission. If your plans
are complicated, however, the council

HOME IMPROVEMENTS THAT NEED APPROVAL

Understanding when you have to notify the district council of work that you wish to undertake

Many minor home improvement jobs are automatically permitted – you do not need to tell the council what you intend to do or wait for permission. But major additions and alterations, or work that could cause danger or inconvenience to others, are likely to be governed by planning permission or building approval rules. Starting without a permit could be costly.

Type of work	Is planning permission needed?	Is building regulation approval needed?
Any extension that is to project in front of the house or above the rooftop	Yes	Yes
A small porch, more than 2 m back from the front fence or boundary	No	Yes
Any extension that is less than 50 m³ or one-tenth the size of the house, whichever is greater, up to a maximum of 115 m³	No	Yes
Any extension bigger than 50 m³, or one-tenth the size of the house, whichever is the greater	Yes	Yes
Any extension that is larger than 115 m³	Yes	Yes
A shed in front of the house	Yes	No if less than 30 m³ and situated more than 2 m away from the house
A shed of limited size (with ridge roof up to 4 m; other roof up to 3 m) not in front of the house	No	
An oil-storage tank in front of the house	Yes	No
An oil-storage tank of up to 3,500 l capacity not in front of the house	No	No
A fence or garden wall higher than 1 m on a boundary to a road having vehicular traffic, or 2 m on any other boundary	Yes	No
A front fence lower than 1 m or a back or side fence (other than one to a road with vehicular traffic) lower than 2 m	No	No
A new or altered access from a trunk or classified road	Yes	No
A new access for any extension that required planning permission	Yes	No
A new access for an extension that did not need planning permission	No – unless it is from a trunk road	No
Alterations to existing structural work	No – unless external	Yes
New or altered stairway	No	Yes
New or extended habitable rooms	No – unless extension is in front of house	Yes
New or extended drainage, internal or external	No	Yes
New, altered or replaced flue pipes	No	Yes
A new toilet	No – unless extension is in front of house	Yes
Replacing existing sanitary and heating appliances	No	No – if no structural work is required
Fitting new solid fuel heating appliances	No	Yes
Fitting new electric heating appliances	No	No
Fitting new gas heating appliances	No	No – if the work is done by the Gas Board and no structural work is required
Installing fitted furniture, such as wall cupboards	No	No
General repairs	No	No
Painting the inside or outside of the house	No	No

can ask for longer to deliberate – up to 2 months from the date of submission. Should you not agree, it may reject your plans immediately if they do not comply with the regulations.

If work is not started within 3 years of the date of submission the council may withdraw the approval. If you do not build in accordance with the building regulations you can be made to demolish and rebuild at your own expense. You may also be fined up to £100, and up to £10 for every day you fail to comply, if the council is successful with a prosecution.

The council must state its reasons for rejecting plans. If it says that a building regulation is contravened there are several courses open to you.

First, discuss the matter with the building inspector and find out if the council would be likely to relax any regulation contravened, on the ground that your proposal is a reasonable one. You can apply for a relaxation without the building inspector's support, but without it your chances of success would be much reduced.

If there is little chance of obtaining a relaxation, your best course is to amend the plans so that they comply with the regulations. The building inspector will advise you, but you do not have to adopt his suggestions if you do not like them. There may be other ways of satisfying the regulations. The professional advice of an architect or surveyor might enable you to succeed quickly.

You can appeal to the Secretary of State for the Environment against a refusal of the council to relax a regulation or to the local magistrates against a rejection of your plans by the council, but you would need to feel very strongly about your proposals, and to have adequate professional support, before attempting to do either.

As building work proceeds you may have to give notice that work has been done or is about to be done. You will find particulars in the building regulations, but you can more easily obtain the necessary information from the building inspector.

Obtaining approval in inner London

Planning permission in inner London is obtained in the same way that it is elsewhere. The building regulations, however, do not apply; instead, all building work in inner London has to comply with the construction bye-laws of the Greater London Council. It is the responsibility of the district surveyor for your area to ensure that you comply.

You cannot have plans approved in advance in inner London; instead there is a simple requirement that all construction must comply with the requirements of the bye-laws. The onus is on you to see that this is done. However, notice must be given to the district surveyor at least 48 hours before starting work.

In practice, it is common to give longer notice and to discuss plans with the district surveyor before starting work, to reduce the risk that he will reject any of the work when it has been done. You can be ordered to demolish work that does not comply.

You have to pay a fee to the Greater London Council for the district surveyor's services. It is based on the value of the work and is on a rising scale currently starting at £5 for a £100 job.

All drainage work must comply with the drainage bye-laws of the Greater London Council. Enforcement of the bye-laws is the responsibility of the local borough council. All drainage work requires prior approval from the borough council, and the council's own inspectors will visit the site at intervals to ensure that the work complies with the bye-laws.

Raising money for home improvements

Most people need help to meet the cost of repairing or extending their home – often as much as several thousand pounds, even for a do-it-yourself job. You may be able to obtain an IMPROVEMENT GRANT or repairs grant from your local council to cover part of the cost, but you could also need a loan to pay the rest of the bill.

Interest on loans for home improvement is eligible for income tax relief – the lending institution or your local tax office can explain how to claim it. If, for example, you have taken a loan of £1,000, to be repaid in 8 quarterly instalments of £150 – and assuming you are paying tax at the standard rate of 33 per cent and have enough taxable income to absorb the relief – you can save £67 out of the total interest charge of £200.

Where to get a loan

● If you have a council mortgage, or have obtained a local authority grant for improving your property, you can ask the council for a loan to meet the outstanding expense. Such loans are given at a preferential rate and usually take the form of a second mortgage on the residence.

● Building societies give home-improvement loans to clients who have a savings account or MORTGAGE with the society. The loan can be short or long term; the amount given and the rate of interest depend on the state of the society's finances, but are usually more favourable than other lending institutions.

● If you do not have a building society account, ask your bank manager. Most banks offer loans for home improvement, but usually only for 3 year terms and against solid security.

● If you cannot get a loan from your bank manager, you can borrow from a finance house at a higher interest rate. Finance houses – many of whom advertise nationally – demand less security than banks, but charge more.

● Insurance companies lend money to people who have policies to offer as security. Their rates are relatively low, but the loan may affect the amount of protection offered by the policy – so read the loan agreement carefully before signing it.

The hidden cost of home improvement

By improving your home, you will have increased its value: by the same token, you will have increased its rateable value. When the work is completed, the council is entitled to reassess your property and raise your annual RATES bill – although you have paid for the work.

HOME TEACHING
When a child is educated at home

Every child who is of compulsory school age – that is, 5 to 16 years – must receive efficient full-time education 'either by regular attendance at school or otherwise'. It is the parents' duty to see that he does so.

Education must start as soon as possible after the child's 5th birthday, and must continue until he is 16. *See:* SCHOOL-AGE

Special rules when a child does not go to school

If a parent chooses to educate his child at home, either himself or by employing a teacher, he is entitled to do so provided that he can show the local education authority that the education provided is efficient.

Some parents decide to educate their children at home because they are against schools on principle: others do so because they are dissatisfied with local schools.

Whatever the reason, if you decide on home education you must be consistent. You cannot keep a child at home in the summer and send him to school in the winter, or provide some lessons at home and send him to school for others.

In certain circumstances – for example, if a child is psychologically unable to face going to school, or if a girl pupil is pregnant and the school is reluctant to let her attend classes – the local education authority has the power to provide the child with free home teaching for up to 5 half-days a week.

NO EASY OPTION

When a parent decides to educate his child at home, he must be able to prove to the local authority that the teaching is efficient.

'And I'll test you on it when I come back from shopping'

When a parent chooses home education

If your child is not sent to school the local education authority will want to know why. It will want proof, such as samples of work and lists of books being used, that the teaching you are providing is systematically organised – and evidence that the child has opportunities for sport and games and mixing with other children.

It may ask for a formal timetable of subjects and the qualifications of the teacher – although it is not legally necessary for the teacher to be qualified.

The authority will send an inspector to check on the child's progress, and is more likely to be satisfied with the education being provided if the parent has obtained details of the education authority's own school schedules, and has made the home education fit in with them. Careful records should be kept to show what the child has done.

If the local authority is not satisfied

If you fail to convince the local education authority that you are giving your child a satisfactory education, it will issue a notice warning you that it is making a SCHOOL ATTENDANCE order against you.

If you do not comply with the order you will be taken to the magistrates' court by the local authority, who alone can prosecute in such cases. You can then argue your case for educating your child at home and can call witnesses to support your methods. The court will then decide whether your child is being satisfactorily educated.

If you lose the case you can be fined up to £20 and ordered to comply with the attendance order. If you continue to keep your child at home you are liable to further court appearances with more penalties.

When a child cannot go to school

If a child cannot go to school at all because of serious illness or because a place at a suitable school cannot be found for him – perhaps because he is severely handicapped – the local educa-

tion authority has a duty to provide a home teacher.

If you think your child qualifies for home teaching you should contact your local education authority. You can find its address in the telephone directory.

If the authority decides that a home teacher is necessary but it cannot supply one, you can advertise for one at current rates. If you are successful, the teacher could be employed by the local authority to teach your child. If all attempts to find a teacher fail, the authority may be prepared to pay for a correspondence course from an accredited correspondence college.

Home teaching is used only as a last resort as local authorities like to get children back to school as soon as possible. That applies even when a child has had a serious illness or accident, or is severely handicapped.

If a child's home is a long way from a suitable school, that is not in itself a reason for it to receive home teaching. In such a case the local authority is obliged to find and pay for board and lodging for the child near the school.

HOME WORKER

How the law affects you if you work from home

If you regularly work from home, either as an employee or as a self-

CLAIMING YOUR COSTS

Home workers are entitled to claim some of their home running costs against their income tax liability.

'And that's my husband – he's self-employed'

employed person, you can claim income tax relief on the running costs of that part of your house or flat that you use for your job, provided that you pay those costs yourself and are not reimbursed for them by an employer or client.

To establish your right to claim relief, you must first satisfy the tax inspector, either in a letter or by visiting him, that a significant part of your working time is spent at home. If you are an employee who occasionally brings a file home to study in the evening, you will not qualify. On the other hand, if you have set aside facilities – a desk and filing cabinet, for example – for weekend and evening work, you may obtain a nominal allowance of £25–£30 a year for the expense involved.

Keeping records

The Inland Revenue requires all self-employed people to produce annual accounts of income and expenses, whether they work from home or from other premises. *See:* SELF-EMPLOYED

If you are an employee who works from home and you intend to claim income tax relief on expenses for which you have not been reimbursed, keep a careful record of those expenses, with bills and receipts, to submit to the tax inspector when you complete your annual tax return. There is space on the return form 11 for an expenses claim.

What you may claim

The items that someone working from home may set against tax vary according to the circumstances. The tax inspector decides what they are, but if you disagree with his assessment you can appeal against it. *See:* INCOME TAX

In submitting your claim, you should list all expenses that can conceivably relate to business. The inspector will eliminate any that do not qualify for relief, but he may not offer to include any you have forgotten to mention.

The items for which relief may be claimed fall into three categories:
1. Raw materials – for example, wool or fabrics used in knitting or dressmaking.
2. Business equipment – for example, a typewriter, sewing machine or vehicle used for business.
3. Operating expenses – including electricity bills, telephone accounts,

stationery and postal costs, local authority rates, accountant's fees, advertising costs and insurance premiums to cover business equipment. Travel expenses arising from business may also be claimed.

A home worker may seek tax relief under any or all of those heads, whether he is an employee or self-employed. However, many of the items are normally reimbursed by employers and, if they are, they do not qualify for an additional allowance.

How relief is assessed

Once the tax inspector has accepted a list of items on which he will allow relief, he determines the proportion of the cost of each that can be offset against tax. If you disagree with his decision, you can appeal against it.

Some items are obviously business expenses. If your work involves typing and you have to buy your own paper and carbon paper, you can normally offset most of the cost. However, the inspector needs to satisfy himself that the record of your outlay is accurate – so you should ask for, and keep, receipts – and that the amount is reasonable in the light of your job.

Household running costs are less straightforward, because the bills do not generally distinguish between domestic and business expense. In deciding the proportion of such expenses that can be

....

CAUTION CAN CUT COSTS
FOR THE HOME WORKER

If a home worker is obviously using his home extensively for business purposes, he may have to pay higher rates. Caution is advisable.

....

set against tax, the inspector takes into account the amount of time spent working from home and the facilities set aside at home for business use.

For example, if you live in a 6-room house, work entirely from home and have set aside one room mainly for business, the inspector starts his calculations by assuming that a sixth of your household running costs qualify as business expenses.

However, he may adjust that proportion up or down according to circumstances. He might argue that you would have had to heat and light the room even if it were not used for work and reduce the allowance. On the other hand, if your work involves electrical equipment you may succeed in persuading the inspector that your electricity bill is higher than it would otherwise have been and that your allowance should therefore be increased.

If you work at home only occasionally, you will normally obtain only token relief of £25–£30.

The arrangements for offsetting the cost of business equipment against tax also vary according to the circumstances and according to the nature of the equipment itself.

For example, typewriters and calculators must be offset in the year in which they were bought. But you cannot claim more than 25 per cent of the price of a car in any one tax year.

The inspector may reduce the allowance on business equipment if he thinks it fulfils a domestic function as well. If you use your car both for business and for pleasure, he will want to know the proportion of motoring time devoted to each. Typewriters, sewing machines and electric drills are presumed to have a domestic use.

Avoiding capital gains tax

If you work mainly from home and set aside part of your house or flat solely for business, the Inland Revenue may charge you capital gains tax when you sell the premises. The tax would be levied on the proportion of the profit from the sale equal to the proportion of the premises used for your work.

However, the tax is payable only if there is exclusive business use of the room or rooms. You can avoid it if you can show that there was some domestic use as well. So get the children to do their homework in your office or study, or keep it as a spare bedroom for guests. If you have a workshop, store your own decorating materials and household equipment there.

If you have previously claimed that part of the house was set aside solely for business to obtain income tax relief, you will be charged capital gains tax on it. So in claiming income tax relief, always qualify the claim by saying that there is occasional private use as well.

When the rates may be affected

The General Rate Act 1967 says that only premises 'used wholly for the purposes of a private dwelling-house' attract the domestic rate. Those used for business or commerce are liable to higher charges. *See:* RATES

The term private dwelling-house is, however, interpreted broadly. You do not have to pay higher rates if:
● You let one or two rooms to lodgers.
● You use a garage or outbuilding for some commercial purpose, provided that it was not built or altered for that reason. Someone who repairs cars from home and adds an inspection pit to his garage to help him does not have to pay extra rates. But if he put in a counter and a sales window to sell spare parts to customers, his rates would be increased.
● Someone living in the house uses a room or rooms for some commercial purpose, provided that it is not set apart entirely for that reason. If you convert your front room into a shop or waiting room, your rates would be increased, but if you and your family use it from time to time for business typing or sewing they would not.

The rates authorities consider the nature and extent of the business, any physical alterations to the premises and the degree to which the business is publicised in determining whether additional charges must be paid.

However, a home worker who makes only minor alterations to the premises – for example, by converting a spare room into an office – is not obliged to tell the rates department and cannot be penalised for failing to do so. Major alterations – for example, the building of an extension to serve as a waiting room – require planning permission. If the home worker does not inform the rates authorities, the planning department almost certainly will.

WHEN PLANNING PERMISSION IS NEEDED

If you regularly work from home and that involves a 'material change of use' of the premises from a private dwelling, you must obtain prior PLANNING PERMISSION for the alteration from the planning department of your local council. If permission is refused, you can appeal to the Department of the Environment.

According to the courts, a material change of use is a matter of fact and degree, determined by all the circumstances. If you use a spare bedroom as a study or sewing room, you are unlikely to need planning permission. But if you convert your front room into a shop or a taxi call office, permission would probably be necessary. If in doubt, ask your local planning department for guidance.

The nature of the work

In deciding whether a material change of use is involved, planning departments consider the nature of the work being done at home, the likely volume of business, the physical alterations to be made to the premises and the degree to which the existence of the business is made public through advertising or signs.

Someone who occasionally cuts the hair of friends and acquaintances at home is unlikely to need planning permission. But if the same person advertises his or her services with a sign on the house, in the local newspaper or in shop windows, the planning authorities may decide that there has been a material change of use.

Noise and vibrations

If a home worker installs business or industrial machinery – for example, a lathe, a knitting machine or a printing press – he may be breaking the laws on noise, even though he has not altered the material use of the premises, and has therefore not contravened planning regulations.

Anyone disturbed by the noise or vibrations of machinery may seek a notice from the local authority environmental health department or an order from a magistrates' court restricting or forbidding the use of the machinery concerned.

If you do not own the premises

Someone who rents a house or flat and works from home may be breaking the terms of his tenancy agreement. Such agreements do not normally forbid occasional light work – for example, typing or sewing – provided that it does not disturb other tenants, but the exact wording should be checked.

Insuring business assets when you work from home

If you work from home, a normal household contents insurance policy is sufficient to protect you against the loss of inexpensive business items – for example, a pocket calculator – but you may need to make special arrangements for any more valuable articles – an electric typewriter, stocks of goods for resale, large quantities of cash and business files and documents – that you think you may eventually have to keep at home. Check the terms of your household contents policy carefully and, if in doubt, ask the insurance company.

Contents policies are devised for private dwellings. If you are regularly visited by numbers of clients or customers, you may be required to pay a higher premium. The additional cost is a tax-deductible business expense. *See:* INSURANCE

Employment protection rights for home workers

A full-time employee who works from home instead of from his employer's premises does not lose any of his EMPLOYMENT PROTECTION rights and his EMPLOYMENT CONTRACT is governed by the same rules as those applying to other employees.

Most of the regulations on HEALTH AND SAFETY AT WORK do not apply. But if the home worker uses a machine provided by his employer and is injured because of a defect in it, he can sue the employer for NEGLIGENCE.

People who work for fewer than 16 hours a week – or fewer than 8 hours if they have been with the same employer for 5 years or more – are excluded from most employment protection rules. *See:* PART-TIME WORKER

A home worker has the same liability to pay national insurance contributions and the same right to social security benefits as other employed and self-employed people.

HOMELESSNESS

*The council's duty to provide
accommodation or advice*

Any homeless person – apart from a vagrant – and anyone threatened with homelessness, is entitled to assistance from the local housing authority.

The legal definition of a homeless person includes:
● Evicted tenants.
● People turned out by their relatives.
● Those made homeless by fire, flood or some other disaster.
● Battered women likely to suffer violence if they return home.
● People who have a mobile home or a houseboat but no site or mooring.
● Immigrants who are allowed to enter Britain, but who have nowhere to live.

People entitled to be housed

The housing authority is legally obliged to provide accommodation for homeless people who have a priority need – for example, families with dependent children, pregnant women, households where there is an elderly or mentally or physically handicapped person, and people homeless as a result of fire, flood or other disasters.

Priority applicants are usually given a council house or flat, but a council can instead help the homeless to buy a house, find private rented accommodation or move to another area. Whatever accommodation is given, it must be legally adequate for the people concerned.
Emergency accommodation People who are suddenly made homeless may be sent temporarily to a local authority reception centre or hostel, or they may be given a short-term lease on an empty house. Whenever possible, provision is made for the whole family staying together. As a last resort the housing authority may arrange temporary accommodation in a guest house or hotel.

When more than one council is involved

If a council decides that a homeless person has closer connections with another area, it passes responsibility to that housing authority. That happens in particular in London where families frequently arrive at rail or coach terminals, or at Heathrow Airport, with nowhere to go. If two authorities disagree as to which should be responsible, temporary accommodation must be provided in the area where the family arrived, until the matter is settled.

Whatever happens, one council or another has to accept responsibility. If the person has no local connections – if he is from another country, for example – the authority to whom he first applies is legally responsible.

A battered woman may need to be housed in another area to reduce the risk of violence from her husband, and in such cases local authorities usually co-operate.

When a home need not be provided

Homeless people who fall outside the priority categories or who have become homeless intentionally do not have a legal right to accommodation, but the housing authority does have a duty to give them advice and assistance. Those cases include most single homeless people and childless couples.

Some councils also classify tenants evicted for non-payment of rent as being intentionally homeless. Anyone classified in that way can appeal to his local councillor, MP or local ombudsman.

The assistance in such cases may include registration on the housing waiting list, advice on rent rebates and mortgages and practical help to find accommodation. Some councils own housing aid centres with lists of accommodation agencies, hostels and lodgings. The council may also advise on the possibility of moving into accommodation licensed for SQUATTING.

Challenging a decision

A homeless person who feels he is not getting the assistance to which he is entitled should contact a local councillor, MP or the local ombudsman.

An organisation of housing charities, the Joint Charities Group, has advice centres in some cities. Look in your telephone directory or consult a Citizens Advice Bureau.

Protection of property

Every housing authority must take reasonable steps to protect or store the property of homeless people in priority need. The authority is entitled to charge for such a service, depending on the income of the homeless person. Non-priority cases may get help to protect property at the council's discretion.

Applying for supplementary benefit

Homeless people are as entitled to SUPPLEMENTARY BENEFIT as those who have a home. Benefit should never be refused solely because a claimant has no fixed address.

If a single person with nowhere to stay calls at the social security office, he is normally paid enough money to enable him to get a bed for the night. Once he has a place to stay he is entitled to benefit in the usual way.

If there is reason to think that a cash payment will be misspent, or that a claim is fraudulent, a voucher – instead of cash – is issued, to be presented at a particular hostel or lodging house.

Such vouchers are usually issued for only a few days, after which payment is made by Girocheque, posted to the claimant.

When accommodation is provided

If a homeless family is provided with temporary accommodation by the local authority, supplementary benefit is payable in the usual way.

If meals are supplied, the benefit will cover the board and lodging charge, the cost of any meals that are not provided, and a small allowance for personal expenses.

HORSE RIDING

*Traffic laws that must be obeyed
by riders*

Anyone who rides a horse in a public place is not bound by all the laws that apply to wheeled traffic. For example, someone on horseback does not commit an offence merely by ignoring traffic signs – including parking restrictions – and police signals. But to disregard them might be considered evidence of NEGLIGENCE in a civil claim.

No licence is needed to ride a horse on the highway and there is no age limit for anyone who wishes to do so. However, it is usually an offence to ride or lead a horse on a footpath, and anyone who does so can be fined £10.

In some areas, council bye-laws also prohibit horse riding on roadside grass verges.

It is also an offence to be drunk in charge of a horse on a highway: the maximum penalty is a £10 fine or 1 month's imprisonment.

Anyone who rides a horse in the street 'furiously, to the obstruction, annoyance or danger' of residents or passers-by, also commits an offence. The maximum penalty is £20.

A person who rides a horse recklessly and in doing so injures someone can face an ASSAULT AND BATTERY charge. It is not, however, an offence to be in charge of a horse that deposits manure on a highway.

Riding schools Anyone who wishes to run a horse-riding school must obtain a licence from the local council. If the application is rejected, the applicant can appeal to a magistrates' court.

Once a licence is issued, council officers will inspect the riding-school premises, to ensure that they are suitable for horses.

The licence-holder must have an insurance policy covering him against liability for any injury sustained by anyone who hires a horse or who, in return for payment, uses one of his horses in the course of riding lessons. Injury or damage to any other person during the hire or use of the horse must also be covered.

HOSPICE

Comfort and care for the terminally ill

Hospice care is an organised system of nursing and other help for patients who are known to be dying.

The care is provided either in a hospice centre or in the patient's own home. Emphasis is placed on the control of symptoms and prevention of pain through the use of drugs, and on support and guidance for the family both before and after the patient's death.

There are about 40 centres in Britain specialising in the care of such patients. Some are run by the National Health Service, others privately by religious or voluntary organisations.

In many areas, hospice services are free through the National Health Service. In others some payment may be necessary. Anyone seeking advice on the availability of hospice services should ask his or her family doctor or local health authority.

HOSPITAL

The rights of a person receiving hospital treatment

Under the National Health Service, a doctor is legally obliged to send a patient to hospital if the patient needs treatment that only a hospital can provide.

Except in an emergency, such as an accident or sudden illness, hospitals will accept only patients sent by a doctor. No one can just walk in and demand treatment.

There is, though, no right to receive hospital treatment. The courts have held that the provision of hospital services must be subject to availability of resources. The only prospect of bringing a successful claim against a health authority would be to show that staffing levels are totally inadequate, or if treatment was refused because of an incorrect diagnosis by a duty doctor.

But once in hospital, a patient has a right to be treated with reasonable skill and care and can sue for damages if he does not get it.

If you are referred to hospital

Most patients are referred to hospital by their family doctors. The doctor writes to the hospital for an appointment, or gives the patient a letter to take to the doctor in charge of the relevant clinic, and the patient makes his own appointment.

A hospital does not have to accept a patient sent by a family doctor. A doctor or patient cannot insist that the patient should see a particular consultant.

Treatment as an outpatient A doctor at the hospital decides if a person is to be treated as an inpatient or outpatient.

Outpatients are treated by a clinic doctor. Any prescriptions should be taken to the hospital pharmacy. The system of charging – or exempting people from prescription charges – is

the same as at an outside chemist. If a patient needs a special item, such as an artificial limb, leg brace or wig, the doctor will refer him to the appropriate specialist or limb-fitting centre. *See:* DISABLEMENT

Treatment as an inpatient Most hospitals have a waiting list for beds, and except in exceptional cases, such as a person whose condition suddenly worsens, referred patients wait their turn.

The hospital admissions department will inform you by letter when a bed is available, and tell you where to report. They will also send you a hospital handbook giving visiting times and rules.

Patients are not limited to hospitals in their own area. They can ask to join the waiting list of a hospital elsewhere, even though their doctor might not agree. Sometimes this can lead to speedier admission and, therefore, treatment.

When a patient's consent is needed

A patient can refuse any form of treatment, so the hospital doctor needs the patient's consent before he can do anything. The patient can tell the doctor – orally or in writing, voluntarily or in answer to the doctor's question – that he is willing to have the treatment offered.

He can also imply consent, for example, by rolling up a sleeve and offering an arm for an injection, or opening his mouth for the doctor to examine his throat. A patient treated without his consent or against his wishes may be able to sue the doctor for assault.

If a patient refuses a particular treat-

FORCING A PERSON TO GO INTO HOSPITAL

No one can be forced to enter hospital unless:
● He is mentally ill and has been ordered to do so under the Mental Health Act 1959.
● He has a notifiable disease, such as smallpox or tuberculosis, and has been ordered into hospital under the Public Health Act 1939.
● He is unable to look after himself because of chronic illness or old age and has been ordered into hospital under the National Assistance Act 1946. *See:* INFECTIOUS DISEASE; MENTAL DISORDER

YES – BY IMPLICATION

A doctor is entitled to assume that a patient has given his consent to treatment if he behaves as if he had no objections – for example, by opening his mouth for examination.

'There. The patient is implying consent'

ment he can be asked to leave the hospital, unless that would clearly jeopardise his health.

When written consent is needed

Doctors usually ask for written consent before any surgery or hazardous treatment, such as radiation therapy or electro-convulsive therapy.

The patient, or the parent or guardian in the case of a minor, is asked to sign a form which gives details of the intended operation or treatment. This says that the person has been told what treatment is to be carried out and fully understands it. The Department of Health and Social Security has recommended a standard form of consent, but hospitals are not obliged to use it.

When a patient is unable to sign his own form – he may be unconscious, confused or mentally retarded – it can be signed on his behalf by his next-of-kin, guardian or a relative.

Signing the form Do not sign the form until the doctor has explained clearly what he intends to do. Any dangers or side-effects should be explained.

A doctor may be justified in not telling a patient everything only if he believes that the full knowledge could endanger the chances of recovery.

When the risks of an operation are too high – such as a 50–50 chance organ transplant – a doctor would not be justified in holding anything back.

DECIDING TO CLOSE A HOSPITAL

When an Area Health Authority plans to close a hospital – or part of it – it must consult the local Community Health Council.

If the Community Health Council agrees to the proposal it can be carried out. If the council disagrees, the matter must be referred to the Secretary of State for Social Services.

Opposing a closure

If you object to the closure of a local hospital, contact the Community Health Council giving your reasons.

It is unwise to sign a consent form that gives the doctor permission to carry out any surgery or treatment he considers necessary.

Patients are sometimes asked to do this when they are undergoing an exploratory operation. If the surgeon finds diseased organs, he can then remove them without further consent. If you have not signed, the surgeon must get your permission to perform anything other than the exploratory opera-

THE WOMAN WHO WAS STERILISED WITHOUT HER CONSENT

If a patient signs a consent form when he or she is not in a fit state to do so, the consent is invalid.

A woman went into hospital for a caesarian section for the birth of her fifth child. Her four previous deliveries had all been by caesarian section and the doctors believed that, in view of her gynaecological condition, further pregnancies could endanger her life. They tried to persuade her to be sterilised, but she refused.

Just before the operation, when she was under the effects of the first anaesthetic, the woman was asked to sign a form authorising sterilisation. Believing the form authorised only the caesarian section she signed.

She later discovered that she had been sterilised. She sued the doctors and the area health authority. She maintained that her consent was invalid as she was given the form when she was not in a state to comprehend fully what she was signing.

DECISION

The judge found that the woman had signed a consent form when she was not in a state to understand it. Consent to the sterilisation was invalid. She was awarded damages of £3,000.

THE OPERATION THAT WENT WRONG

Consent to an operation can be valid when a doctor has held back facts which could cause distress and jeopardise the success of the operation.

Mrs Hatcher was a lady who occasionally broadcast for the BBC. She went into St Bartholomew's Hospital suffering from a toxic thyroid gland, and an operation was advised.

She asked if there was any risk to her voice. She was reassured by the doctors.

In the course of the operation, the nerve was so badly damaged that she could not speak properly. She could not broadcast again.

She sued Dr Black, the physician, and Mr Tuckwell, the surgeon, for advising the operation and Mr Tuckwell for damaging the nerve.

At the trial, Lord Denning told the jury that Mr Tuckwell had admitted that on the evening before the operation he told Mrs Hatcher that there was no risk to her voice, when he knew that there was some slight risk. He had done so for her own good because it was of vital importance that she should not worry.

'In short, he told a lie, but he did it because he thought in the circumstances it was justifiable.

'You should find him guilty of negligence only when he falls short of the standard of a reasonably skilful medical man, in short, when he is deserving of censure – for negligence in a medical man is deserving of censure.'

DECISION

The jury found for the defendants and judgment was entered against the plaintiff with costs.

tion. That means more than one operation, but you have the right to choose.

If there is anything to which you would never give your consent, you can write this on the form.

When consent is not given

A patient, who refuses consent cannot be treated, even in an emergency, no matter how serious the consequences are likely to be.

If the patient is unconscious – after an accident for example – and his life or future health is in jeopardy, a doctor can treat him even if he knows that the patient would have refused.

Next-of-kin or relatives should be asked to consent – but even if they refuse, the doctor is legally entitled to do whatever is necessary to save the

OBJECTING ON RELIGIOUS GROUNDS

The wishes of a patient who objects on religious grounds to any particular treatment must be respected by the doctor. However, if a patient needing an operation refuses a blood transfusion the surgeon may refuse to operate – or he may refuse to promise that a transfusion will not be given.

patient's life and prevent permanent harm. He is not entitled to do more than that.

When treatment such as the amputation of a limb is necessary, the doctor should wait for the patient's consent. But if he believes delay would cause, or probably cause, the patient's death he is legally justified to go ahead and give whatever treatment he thinks necessary in that case.

Consent of spouses There is no legal obligation for a husband or wife to obtain the other's consent for sterilisation, abortion or the fitting of a contraceptive device, although some doctors are reluctant to proceed in such cases without the agreement of the other spouse.

Mental patients If a patient has been detained under the Mental Health Act 1959, consent to treatment is not necessary for treatment designed to alleviate or cure the mental disorder or its consequences.

Examination by students

Patients should be warned if students are likely to be present when they are

---

WHEN CHILDREN UNDER 16 GO INTO HOSPITAL
How attempts are made to keep life as normal as possible to facilitate recovery

Consenting to treatment

Parents – or guardians – must give their consent, orally or in writing, before a child under 16 can be treated in hospital. If the child has been taken into care, consent can be given by the local authority or whoever has custody of the child.

If the parents refuse consent, or cannot agree, no treatment will be given, even though the child may want it. If, however, the child's life is in danger, emergency treatment can be given without consent of the parents.

If the parents refuse consent to treatment essential to the child's health, they may be charged with the crime of wilful neglect of a child. If the child dies as a result of their refusal, the parents might face a charge of MANSLAUGHTER.

If the child refuses

If the parents give their consent, but the child refuses treatment, the doctor may be reluctant to proceed unless the child's life or future health is in danger. But he is legally protected if he goes ahead.

In an emergency

If a child needs emergency treatment and the parents cannot be contacted, a doctor can treat the child without consent.

Religious objections

If the parents refuse consent on religious grounds a doctor is legally entitled to carry out whatever treatment is necessary to safeguard the child's health. Even if the

parents' refusal to consent to treatment for their child is based on religious grounds, then if the child suffers because of the lack of treatment the parents might face a charge of wilful neglect, and if he were to die could face a manslaughter charge.

Visiting children

Hospitals are recommended to allow unrestricted visiting in children's wards and to provide accommodation for mothers, particularly of young children.

If accommodation is not provided and you are determined to stay with your child at night, you should be firm and tactful about your intention. If the night sister is unhelpful, see the hospital secretary.

The National Association for the Welfare of Children in Hospital will also help.

Providing education

The local education authority is responsible for the education of children in hospital. The authority is obliged to provide teachers, accommodation, books and equipment.

Starting a school

If there are usually 25 or more school-age children in a hospital, the local authority is expected to set up a hospital school with its own head teacher and board of governors.

The Education Act 1980 will make it obligatory for the governing body to include governors representing parents.

If there are not enough children for a

hospital school, the authority must provide teachers or correspondence courses for the children.

Maintaining the idea of going to school

Hospital schooling should be regular and interrupted as little as possible by ward routine. The idea of going out to school should be preserved, even if this simply means a child moving to a special part of the ward for lessons.

Specialist teaching

Children in hospital should be provided with the same kind of specialist teaching that is available in ordinary schools. Exams can be taken in hospital.

Parents and teachers

Local education authorities encourage parents to take an interest in the hospital school and to have the same relationship with the teachers as in an ordinary school.

If a child is allowed to leave hospital for a home visit, the visit should be arranged so as not to interfere with his schooling.

Worried parents

If you are worried about the education being provided for your child in hospital, you should contact the local education authority and the governors of the hospital school. The local community health council or the National Association for the Welfare of Children may also help.

examined or treated, and this happens even in hospitals which are not teaching ones. Everyone has a right to refuse to have students around their bed, without prejudice to treatment. A patient who agrees to be treated or examined by or in the presence of students, can later change his mind.

If a patient is led to believe that he is being examined or treated by a qualified doctor, when in fact he is not, any consent will be invalid.

Dental hospitals In a dental hospital most types of routine treatment are carried out by students. Anyone has a right to refuse to be treated by a student, but this may mean a delay of a few weeks before he can be seen by a qualified dentist.

Seeing your case notes

A patient's hospital record is the property of the area health authority. Patients have no legal right to see case notes, X-rays or results of laboratory tests. A doctor is not legally bound to tell a patient what is wrong with him or to reveal the results of tests or X-rays.

If a patient decides to sue a doctor or hospital, for wrong diagnosis or negligence, for example – or even before he decides to sue – he can ask a court to order the hospital to make available for copying all relevant documents.

Paying for peace and quiet

Some hospitals provide amenity beds – beds in a small room rather than in a large ward – for National Health Service patients who prefer privacy. A charge is made for the beds, and this varies according to the hospital and the facilities provided.

Allocating the beds There is no legal obligation for a hospital to supply such beds, but if it does it allocates them when patients are admitted – they cannot be booked in advance.

If a patient needs privacy for medical reasons his doctor will try to get one, and in such cases there is no charge.

Discharging a patient

Any patient except one compulsorily detained under the Mental Health Act 1959 can discharge himself from hospital at any time, but the hospital will not discharge him until his treatment is completed and the doctor in charge of his case considers it is safe for him to go.

WHEN SOMEONE NEEDS TREATMENT IN A HOSPITAL AT SHORT NOTICE

If your doctor decides you need urgent hospital treatment, he can call an ambulance to take you there.

A doctor at the emergency department will decide what treatment you need and whether to admit you as an in-patient. If there is no bed available, he should inquire whether there is one at another hospital.

If you are taken by ambulance or make your own way to a hospital that does not have an emergency department, the hospital is entitled to refuse you even if it means a long delay in your being treated.

If you have been injured in an accident or suddenly taken seriously ill, you are entitled to go to a hospital emergency department without an ambulance or referral by your doctor.

Self discharge If a patient leaves hospital against the doctor's advice he will be asked to sign a form stating that he is leaving against the advice of the hospital. But if he refuses to sign he cannot be prevented from leaving. The signed form relieves the hospital of liability should the patient suffer harm from his discharge. If he refuses to sign, it will be harder for the hospital to deny liability.

Discharge by doctor A doctor will discharge a patient only when treatment is complete, and when he believes the patient is well enough to go. The patient should check that he has a supply of any drugs needed; whether he has to return to the outpatient department; and if any sickness certificates are needed for his employer and social security office.

A person who does not feel fit enough to be discharged, or feels that he should remain in hospital for any other reason – perhaps there is no one at home to look after him – should ask the doctor if he can stay longer.

Early discharge If a patient is discharged before it is medically safe, and he suffers injury as a result, he may be able to sue the doctor for negligence. It is also negligent to discharge a patient being treated after a suicide attempt, if there is a likelihood that he will make another attempt unless given further treatment.

Visiting patients in hospital

Many hospitals have open visiting – that is, usually any time between limits fixed by the hospital, for example, 10.30 a.m. and 8 p.m. But visitors may be asked to leave at meal times.

If a patient is very ill, or in need of rest and quiet, visiting may be restricted at the discretion of the ward sister.

A visitor asked to leave a ward should do so. No one has a right to stay on hospital premises without permission, and anyone who does so is guilty of trespassing.

You should not take food or drink to a patient without first asking the ward sister if you may do so.

When a person with a social security benefit goes into hospital

If you are receiving a social security benefit it may be reduced while you are in hospital. The reason is that social security benefits are intended to help with the ordinary needs at home, or special needs arising from disablement. While in hospital some of these needs are met by the National Health Service. Benefits are therefore reduced or withdrawn altogether.

If you are in hospital privately, and are meeting the entire cost of your up-

---

WHAT A SISTER SAYS GOES

Visitors are allowed into hospital at the discretion of the doctors and nursing authorities. They must observe any rules laid down.

'For purely medicinal purposes, Sister'

keep, *no* reduction is made in any social security benefit you may get, except INVALID CARE ALLOWANCE.

If you get:
- RETIREMENT PENSION
- WIDOW'S ALLOWANCE or WIDOW'S PENSION
- SICKNESS BENEFIT
- INVALIDITY ALLOWANCE or non-contributory INVALIDITY PENSION
- INDUSTRIAL INJURY BENEFIT or industrial injury unemployability supplement

your benefit will be reduced after 8 weeks in hospital by £5.45 (during 1981) if you have a dependant, or by £10.90 if you have not.

After a year in hospital, you may find that your benefit will be reduced again, or alternatively, paid in part to a dependant. But you will then start to build up an entitlement to a resettlement benefit which would be paid on your discharge from hospital. This resettlement benefit is, in fact, part of the money that stops when you are in hospital. In certain circumstances, there can be another reduction after 2 years in hospital.

Other benefits which are affected are: ATTENDANCE ALLOWANCE or CONSTANT ATTENDANCE ALLOWANCE. If you get either benefit, it stops after 4 weeks in hospital.

Invalid care allowance That stops 12 weeks after you, or the person you look after, goes into hospital.

Supplementary benefit That is reduced (to £5.45 plus an allowance for rent and rates or mortgage interest) as soon as you go into hospital, if you are a single person. If you are married, any extra payments you have been getting for a special diet, laundry, domestic help and so on, stop at once (payments for extra heating may continue, for both married and single patients, depending on the grounds on which they were awarded). A further reduction of £5.45 is made after 8 weeks. If you are still in hospital after 2 years, you are treated as a single person, and benefit is paid separately for your wife and children.

If a claimant's wife is admitted to hospital, the effect on their supplementary benefit entitlement is the same.

A single person's housing costs will usually be met for up to a year if he is likely to be returning home within a year or so. If he is paying a retainer for lodgings, it will normally be included in his benefit for at least 8 weeks.

Extra benefit may be payable for the cost of visiting a member of the family in hospital.

Benefits for dependants Benefit paid for the support of a dependant may also be stopped or reduced if that dependant goes into hospital.

WHAT TO DO IF YOU WANT TO MAKE A COMPLAINT

Every Area Health Authority has its own method of dealing with complaints. This is usually shown in the hospital handbook given to patients before they enter hospital.

Minor complaints

Complaints about routine matters can be dealt with by the ward sister, or out-patient clinic sister.

Serious complaints

If you have a serious complaint, say, about treatment, you can take it up with the consultant in charge of your case. If you are not satisfied with his response, you can write to the hospital secretary or a district official – such as the Sector Administrator or the District Administrator in charge of the hospital – at the Area Health Authority. You can get the address from the telephone book.

If you are still not satisfied write to the Area Administrator at the Area Health Authority.

Very serious complaints, such as alleging injury or deprivation of medical care, can be dealt with at area level from the start.

If the Area Administrator's response is unsatisfactory, complain to the Regional Health Authority, or the Health Ombudsman.

The Regional Authority can appoint an independent inquiry to investigate, or the Secretary of State for Social Services can order an official inquiry.

Help with complaints

If you need advice on making a complaint contact your local COMMUNITY HEALTH COUNCIL or the Patients' Association.

Careless treatment

If your complaint is a legal one, such as alleging careless treatment by a doctor, it will not be dealt with by the Health Authority. *See:* DOCTOR AND PATIENT; MEDICAL NEGLIGENCE

Help with hospital fares

If you have to travel to hospital for treatment as either an out-patient or an in-patient, or if you are leaving hospital for good, you may be able to get help with your fares, and the fares for someone to accompany you.

If you get FAMILY INCOME SUPPLEMENT or SUPPLEMENTARY BENEFIT, show your order book at the hospital. If you do not get one of these benefits but have a low income, claim on the form attached to DHSS leaflet H11, which you can get at the hospital or at a DHSS office. If you visit hospital to see a patient who is a close relative and you need help with fares, ask at the

---

' THE PATIENT WHO WAS NOT CONSOLED

A hospital has a duty to consider the care of its patients in every aspect – mental as well as physical.

Mr Eric Hyde, aged 37, was admitted to Ashton-under-Lyne Hospital in January 1972 suffering from acute neck and shoulder pain. As the pain increased, his mental condition deteriorated because he feared he had cancer.

Believing that the hospital was indifferent to his condition, he tried unsuccessfully to discharge himself. He became increasingly depressed, but his consultant was not informed and no psychiatric consultant was called in.

Eventually, after 2 weeks, Mr Hyde threw himself from a window on to the road below his ward. He sustained terrible injuries which left him a tetraplegic, unemployable and wholly dependent on his wife. He eventually decided to sue the area health authority for negligence.

DECISION

Mr Justice Lincoln held that the hospital was negligent in failing to observe and diagnose his mental condition, and should have foreseen that its inadequate treatment and lack of care created a risk of his attempted suicide. He awarded Mr Hyde £200,000 damages. '

local social security office.

Going home

If you occasionally go home from hospital during a spell of in-patient treatment when your benefit has been reduced, you may be able to get it increased again on being allowed home for a few days. Tell your local DHSS office of any time you are at home.

When you are ready to leave hospital for good, tell the local DHSS office in good time so that your full benefit can be restored. Ask at the hospital if you need money for the journey home.

HOTEL

When a traveller must be given food and shelter

Any establishment that is defined in law as a hotel must try to provide food, drink and accommodation for any customer who is in a fit state and who appears to be able and willing to pay. The proprietor is relieved of that legal obligation only if he has no food or drink available or if all rooms have been taken. The penalty for refusing service without good reason is imprisonment or a fine.

The law, however, distinguishes between a hotel – or common inn as it used to be described before the Hotel Proprietors Act 1956 – and private or residential hotels, boarding houses or public houses without accommodation.

NO FIT STATE

A hotelier must provide food, drink and accommodation only for customers who appear to him to be in a fit state and able and willing to pay.

To qualify for the legal status of a hotel, the establishment must be willing to give service to travellers 'without special contract'.

The owners or staff of any other kind of 'hotel' can – within the limits of the Race Relations Act and Sex Discrimination Act – refuse to serve anyone without giving reason.

If the bill is not paid

Anyone who dishonestly leaves any category of hotel without paying the bill and with intent to avoid payment can be imprisoned for up to 2 years. A proprietor or his staff can arrest the absconder without warrant on a charge of theft.

The proprietor of a common inn has extra rights, however. He can exercise what is called a lien by holding any luggage brought to the hotel by the guest – even if it does not belong to him – until the bill is paid.

If a bill is not paid after 6 weeks, the proprietor can sell the luggage by public auction. The only condition is that he must advertise the auction in both a national and local newspaper at least a month before it is held.

If the sale raises more money than is needed to pay for the bill and auction expenses, the excess belongs to the guest.

The law does not allow a hotel proprietor to seize or sell any vehicle or property left in a vehicle, or any live animal.

Looking after a guest's property

When a guest takes sleeping accommodation at a 'common inn' hotel, the proprietor is normally fully liable for any loss or damage to his property – even if that loss or damage is not caused by the hotel staff's NEGLIGENCE.

The hotel can, however, reduce its liability by displaying a special notice under the Hotel Proprietors Act. Then it is liable for loss or damage only up to a total of £100 with a maximum of £50 for any one article. But it is still fully liable, without any limit, if the property was stolen, lost or damaged through the negligence or wilful act of its staff, or if it was deposited for safe custody.

A hotel proprietor can also avoid liability if he can show that the loss or damage did not take place during the period beginning at midnight before the

HOW A HOTEL LIMITS ITS LIABILITY TO GUESTS
If you have anything valuable, ask for it to be put in the safe

NOTICE

LOSS OF OR DAMAGE TO GUESTS' PROPERTY

Under the Hotel Proprietors Act 1956, an hotel proprietor may in certain circumstances be liable to make good any loss of or damage to a guest's property even though it was not due to any fault of the proprietor or staff of the hotel.

This liability however—

(a) extends only to the property of guests who have engaged sleeping accommodation at the hotel;

(b) is limited to £50 for any one article and a total of £100 in the case of any one guest, except in the case of property which has been deposited, or offered for deposit, for safe custody;

(c) does not cover motor-cars or other vehicles of any kind or any property left in them, or horses or other live animals.

This notice does not constitute an admission either that the Act applies to this hotel or that liability thereunder attaches to the proprietor of this hotel in any particular case.

A hotel is protected against guests' claims only if it displays this special notice – printed in plain type and positioned conspicuously near the reception area or entrance. If it does not do so, it can face claims for the whole amount of a guest's loss.

guest arrived and ending at midnight after he left.

Hotels that do not display the special notice under the Hotel Proprietors Act, but instead still display a notice under the Innkeepers Liability Act 1863 are not protected from legal claims if property is lost or damaged. The 1863 Act was repealed in 1956.

A hotel is liable for loss or damage to a guest's vehicle, to property left in a vehicle or to any live animal, only if its staff is negligent.

Displaying the prices of rooms

Every hotel in the 'common inn' category – if it has 4 or more bedrooms or 8 or more beds – must display a price notice. The maximum penalty for not doing so is a £200 fine. Bedrooms and beds normally occupied by the same person for more than 21 nights do not count towards these qualifying totals.

The notice must be displayed in a prominent position in the reception area or at the entrance, where it can be read easily by anyone seeking sleeping accommodation at the hotel. It must be legible and state the current prices payable per night for:
● A bedroom for occupation by one adult.
● A bedroom for occupation by two adults.
● A bed other than in a room for one or two persons; and this must state whether it is in a dormitory or a room to be shared with other guests.

If different rooms have different prices it is enough to state the lowest and highest price in each category.

If a service charge is made, the price list must give details. It must also state whether the prices include VAT. If they do not, the amount of VAT payable must be stated as a sum of money.

If the price of meals is included – whether or not they are taken – the tariff must say so. The meals affected must be identified – for example, 'including breakfast' or 'including breakfast, lunch and evening meal'.

The notice may include additional information – such as whether morning tea is provided, or if there is a laundry service – but that extra detail must not detract from the prominence to be given to the compulsory information.

If you feel that a hotel is not displaying an adequate notice, complain to the trading standards department of the local authority, which is responsible for seeing that hotels comply with the rules.

HOUSE BUYING AND SELLING

How ownership of a property is transferred

An agreement for one person to buy a house from another is similar to any other CONTRACT, except that it must be in writing to be legally binding. In practice, a sale is usually conducted in three main stages:
● Both parties agree a price, but make clear they are not legally bound by the deal.
● Both sign contracts committing themselves legally to the sale at the agreed price on an agreed date.
● On the agreed date the sale is completed and the buyer acquires the property from the seller.

Buying or selling ultimately is the personal decision of the individuals, although they may take advice from an estate agent, surveyor and solicitor.

There is nothing to prevent either party from conducting all the legal formalities himself. He can also go to a commercial or voluntary organisation that works at cut-price rates.

Most people, however, go to a solicitor. The main advantage is that, if a solicitor makes a careless mistake that results in a loss to his client, the client can claim compensation from the solicitor's insurance. Moreover, co-operation between solicitors can help the transaction to go through smoothly.

Buying property abroad

A person buying or selling property or land in a foreign country is governed entirely by the laws of the country con-

---

THE THIEF WHO WALKED IN – AND OUT WITH A SUITCASE

The proprietor of any hotel offering accommodation – including a private hotel or boarding house – has a duty to take reasonable care of his guests' property. If he does not, and property is lost or damaged, a guest can claim damages.

In 1945 Mrs Olley was staying at the Marlborough Court Hotel in London. One morning she left her room and hung the key on the key board at the reception desk and went out.

During the day a man entered the hotel, took the key from its hook and went upstairs. Later, he came down carrying a suitcase and went out.

When Mrs Olley returned in the afternoon and found that her key was not on the board she called the porter, who let her into her room with a pass key. She then discovered that over £300 worth of furs, jewellery and clothing were missing. Mrs Olley sued the proprietors of the hotel.

The High Court judge ruled in favour of Mrs Olley and awarded her £329. The proprietors of the hotel appealed against the decision.

DECISION
The Appeal Court judges affirmed the decision in favour of Mrs Olley. The hotel was negligent in failing to keep proper watch to see that strangers did not help themselves to keys. Mrs Olley was not to blame, as she was entitled to expect that reasonable precautions would be taken by the hotel staff.

It was also held that the hotel was not in any way protected by a notice behind the door in the bedroom, which said: 'The proprietors will not hold themselves responsible for articles lost or stolen unless handed to the manageress for safe custody. Valuables should be deposited for safe custody in a sealed package and a receipt obtained.'

The hotel had not drawn Mrs Olley's attention to this when she registered at the reception desk, and as she could not have seen the notice until she later went to her room it was too late for it to become part of the contract that had been made when she registered. And even if it had become part of the contract it was not clear that it was intended to exclude liability for negligence. Lord Justice Denning said: 'Ample content can be given to the notice by construing it as a warning that the hotel proprietor is not liable in the absence of negligence. As such it serves a useful purpose. It is a warning to the guest that he must do his part to take care of his things himself.'

cerned and can enforce his rights only in the courts of that country.

The only time your rights in a foreign property agreement can be enforced in a British court is if the other party lives in Britain or, if it is a company, has an office here.

See also: CONVEYANCE
LAND REGISTRY
MORTGAGE
PROPERTY INSURANCE
SOLICITOR
STAMP DUTY

BUYING LAND OR A HOUSE AT AUCTION

Large, unusual properties or those with a high redevelopment value or needing modernisation are often sold by auction. If you intend to bid for a property at auction:

1 Collect the printed auction particulars from the auctioneer and go to see the property, making sure, as far as you can, that the features listed are in fact there.

2 Have your solicitor check the sale conditions mentioned in the auctioneer's particulars. Instruct him to make local searches.

3 Have the property surveyed, if necessary by specialists in such things as woodworm and dry rot. Make sure that you are satisfied by all the ensuing specialist reports.

4 Decide how much you can afford to bid and resolve not to be tempted to go beyond that amount. Auctions generate a lot of excitement and it is easy for the inexperienced bidder to forget his limits.

5 Next obtain a firm offer in writing of the loan you will need from a building society or other lender. The offer should relate to the particular property you are after.

6 If your bid is accepted at the auction, you will immediately have to pay a 10 per cent deposit and sign a document recording the sale. In some areas you may also have to pay part of the sale costs.

7 The period until the sale must be completed will be laid down in the agreement and is normally about a month. It is as well to check this before the sale if you must move at a specific time.

A step-by-step guide to
BUYING AND SELLING A HOUSE

IF YOU ARE A BUYER

Finding a house See as many houses as possible to get an idea of prices. Remember, however, that sellers often ask for more than they expect to get. If a house seems overpriced, offer a lower figure.

Agreeing a price If you pay a small de-

Buyer agrees the price with seller

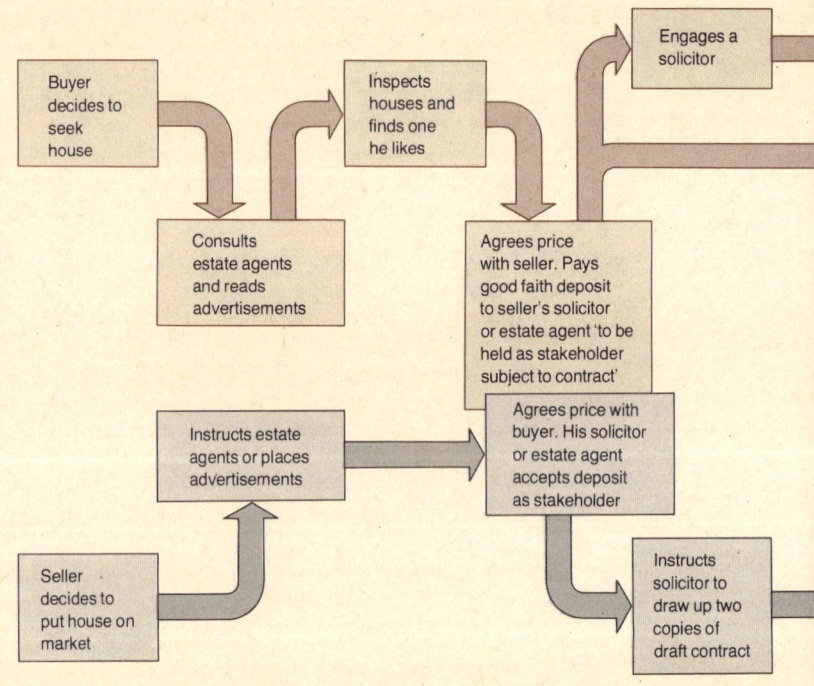

IF YOU ARE A SELLER

Finding a buyer A householder who decides to sell his property can advertise it and conduct any negotiations with potential buyers without professional help. Most people, however, instruct an estate agent who can usually find a buyer more

quickly – often at a higher price than the seller would have negotiated himself. The agent's fee is usually 2 or 2½ per cent of the sale price, and value added tax (VAT) has also to be paid by the seller. In some areas, agents charge the client for advertising.

Make sure you are not committed to paying a fee unless and until the sale is completed. Insist on a small returnable deposit of, say, £50–£100 from the buyer

posit to show your offer is a serious one, make sure your receipt includes the words 'subject to contract and survey'. At that point the sale is not binding on either party; if it never happens, your deposit is returned.

Most buyers have to negotiate a mortgage and cannot commit themselves until they are certain that the building society or insurance company will advance the necessary amount of money. The building society orders a valu-

Buyer commissions his own survey

ation of the house, but you do not normally see the report. If you want a survey, you have to instruct a surveyor yourself – which is advisable in most cases and *essential* if the house is an old one. The report may disclose defects so serious that you decide to withdraw. If they are less serious you can ask the seller to put them right or ask him to lower his price.

When your solicitor has received the draft

Continued overleaf

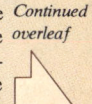

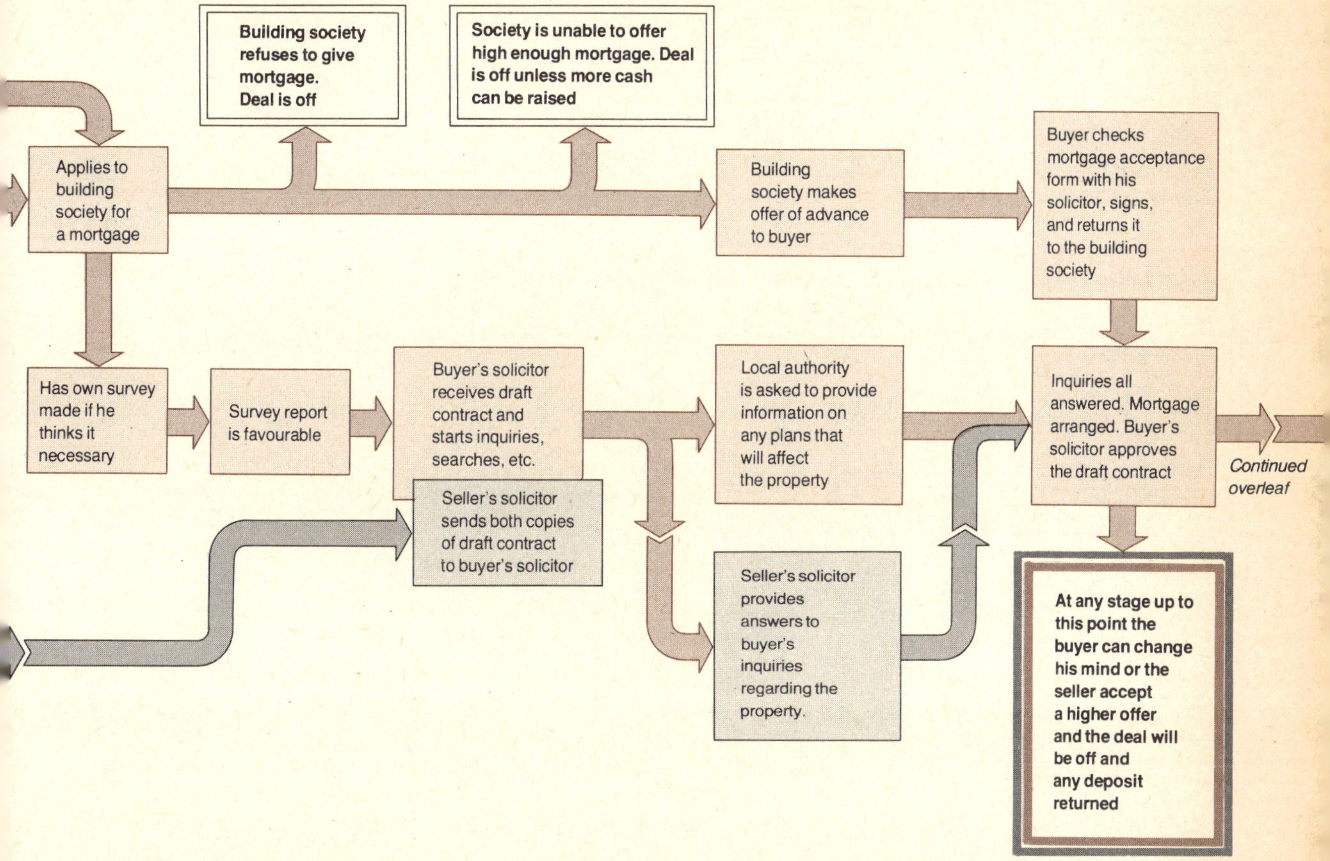

Building society refuses to give mortgage. Deal is off

Society is unable to offer high enough mortgage. Deal is off unless more cash can be raised

Applies to building society for a mortgage

Building society makes offer of advance to buyer

Buyer checks mortgage acceptance form with his solicitor, signs, and returns it to the building society

Has own survey made if he thinks it necessary

Survey report is favourable

Buyer's solicitor receives draft contract and starts inquiries, searches, etc.

Local authority is asked to provide information on any plans that will affect the property

Inquiries all answered. Mortgage arranged. Buyer's solicitor approves the draft contract

Continued overleaf

Seller's solicitor sends both copies of draft contract to buyer's solicitor

Seller's solicitor provides answers to buyer's inquiries regarding the property.

At any stage up to this point the buyer can change his mind or the seller accept a higher offer and the deal will be off and any deposit returned

---

'subject to contract'. Its payment means that the buyer is more likely to let you know quickly if he decides not to proceed with the purchase.

Helping your solicitor If you plan to use the 10 per cent deposit you receive on exchange of contracts to pay a deposit on another house in a simultaneous transaction, make that clear to your solicitor at the outset. If it is not agreed with the buyer, you may have to

borrow your deposit from the bank, which adds another expense.

Your solicitor sends a draft contract and details of your title to the property to the buyer's solicitor, but the sale is still not legally binding. If you receive a higher offer for the house, it is a matter entirely for you to decide whether to accept it or abide by your acceptance of the earlier offer. Your solicitor receives a list of 'preliminary inquiries' from

the other side about such things as boundaries and repairs to the property and needs your help in answering them.

Alternative offers You may be prepared to stand by your acceptance of the buyer's offer and have no wish to 'gazump' him – which means demand a price higher than the original offer on the ground that the market has risen. Remember, however, that just as you are not legally bound to sell, the buyer is not

Continued overleaf

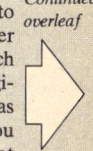

A step-by-step guide to
BUYING AND SELLING A HOUSE (continued)

Continued from previous page

contract from the seller's solicitor, he has to establish that there are no serious legal drawbacks, such as a money claim by the local authority, attached to the house. He also inquires from the local council whether there is any planned development that could affect the house. Remember, however, that the solicitor does not normally visit the house. It is your responsibility to raise with him any questions you have after inspecting the prop-

Buyer signs contract

erty, such as the state of the fences or where the drains run. Also make sure he is clear about what you have agreed with the seller about what is and is not included in the sale – for example, fixtures and fittings or a removable tool shed. Until you sign the contract and your solicitor sends it to the seller's solicitor, you can still change your mind.

Legal paperwork In the period between exchange of contracts and completion of sale,

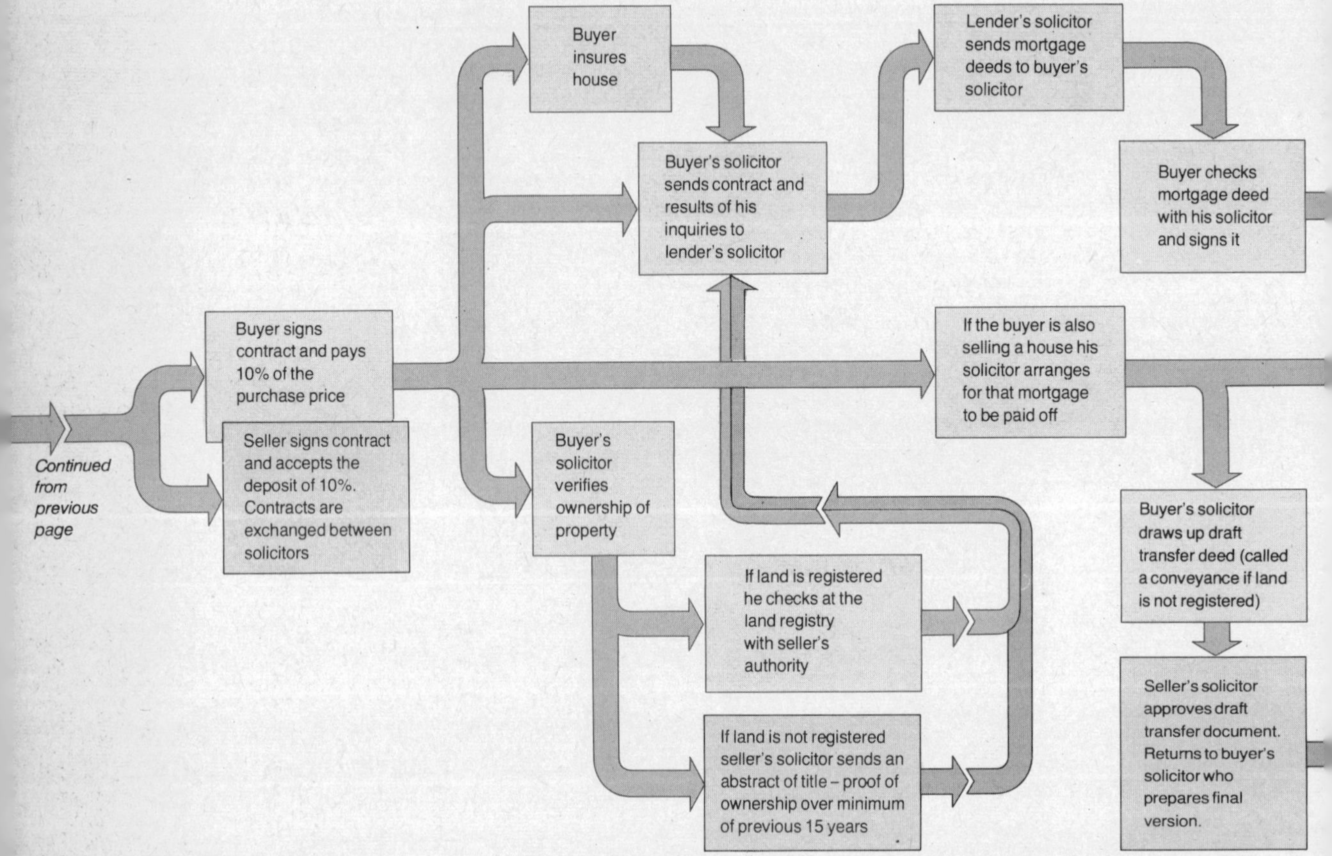

Continued from previous page

Buyer insures house

Lender's solicitor sends mortgage deeds to buyer's solicitor

Buyer's solicitor sends contract and results of his inquiries to lender's solicitor

Buyer checks mortgage deed with his solicitor and signs it

Buyer signs contract and pays 10% of the purchase price

Seller signs contract and accepts the deposit of 10%. Contracts are exchanged between solicitors

Buyer's solicitor verifies ownership of property

If the buyer is also selling a house his solicitor arranges for that mortgage to be paid off

If land is registered he checks at the land registry with seller's authority

Buyer's solicitor draws up draft transfer deed (called a conveyance if land is not registered)

Seller's solicitor approves draft transfer document. Returns to buyer's solicitor who prepares final version.

If land is not registered seller's solicitor sends an abstract of title – proof of ownership over minimum of previous 15 years

---

Continued from previous page

legally bound to buy. He may find a property that suits him better, be deterred by his surveyor's report or not raise enough money. Instruct your estate agent or agents to continue to report any further offers, telling those later prospective buyers that the house is under offer but that their offer will be considered if the original one fails. It is as well to have alternative offers on hand until contracts have been exchanged.

Seller signs contract

Risk of penalties As soon as contracts have been signed and exchanged, both sides are firmly committed to the sale. If the buyer fails to complete the purchase, he forfeits his 10 per cent deposit. If your loss is more you can sue for the balance. If you fail to complete, the buyer can ask a court to order you to complete, whatever the cost or inconvenience to you, or to compensate him for any loss he has incurred through your failure to

the buyer's solicitor makes sure the seller really owns the property and prepares the transfer deed which will transfer ownership. He sends a draft to the seller's solicitor for approval then draws up the final deed – a standard form if the house is registered at the Land Registry but one that must be prepared specially if it is not. He also completes mortgage details.

Moving in You have that intervening period to make arrangements for moving. Besides hiring removal contractors to transfer your furniture, see that you will be supplied with services such as gas, electricity and telephone. Ask several removal companies for tenders; their charges vary considerably. When you make the arrangements allow time to collect the keys to your new home. They may not be handed to you until you have paid the full price.

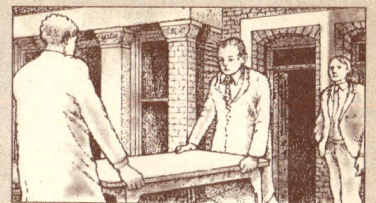

The final stage: moving in

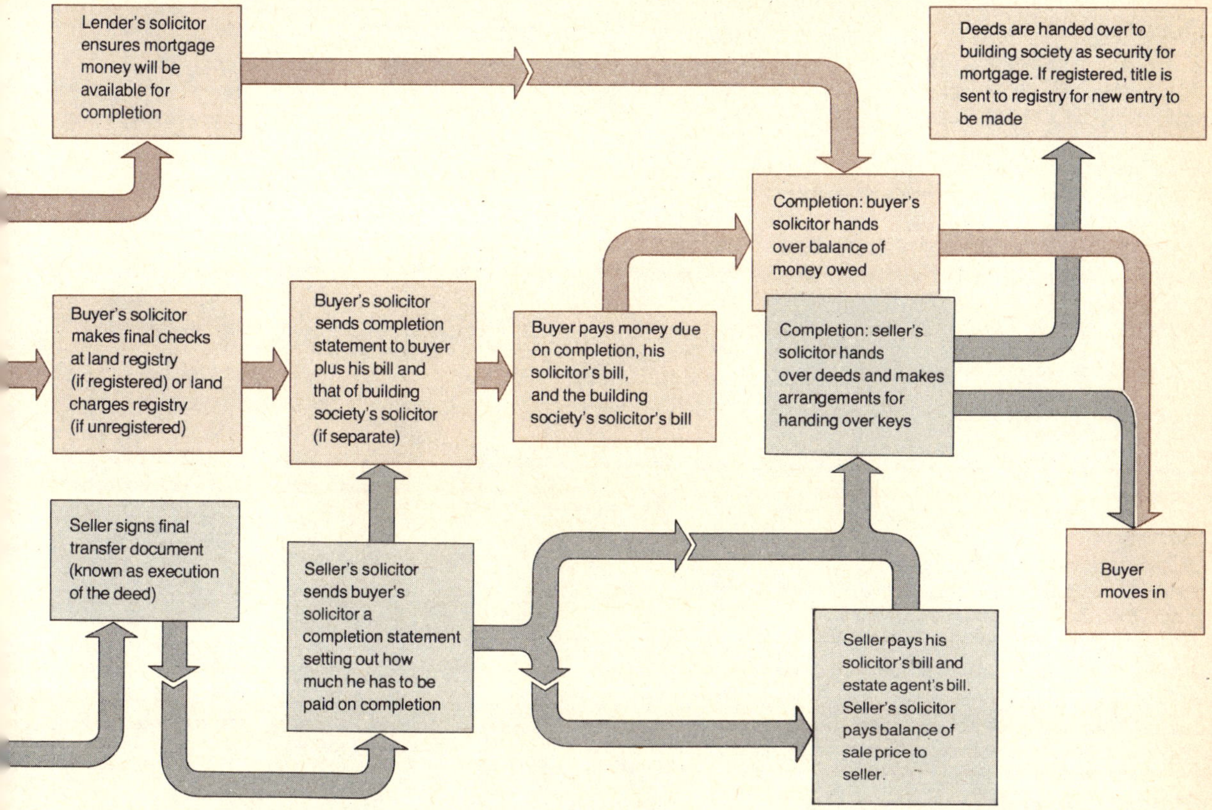

Lender's solicitor ensures mortgage money will be available for completion

Deeds are handed over to building society as security for mortgage. If registered, title is sent to registry for new entry to be made

Completion: buyer's solicitor hands over balance of money owed

Buyer's solicitor makes final checks at land registry (if registered) or land charges registry (if unregistered)

Buyer's solicitor sends completion statement to buyer plus his bill and that of building society's solicitor (if separate)

Buyer pays money due on completion, his solicitor's bill, and the building society's solicitor's bill

Completion: seller's solicitor hands over deeds and makes arrangements for handing over keys

Buyer moves in

Seller signs final transfer document (known as execution of the deed)

Seller's solicitor sends buyer's solicitor a completion statement setting out how much he has to be paid on completion

Seller pays his solicitor's bill and estate agent's bill. Seller's solicitor pays balance of sale price to seller.

complete. If he can show that he has had to pay more for a comparable house, you may have to pay him the extra, plus any other amounts he might be out of pocket.

If either party is late for completion he will have to pay all expenses – for example, hotel bills, storage charges or bank charges on a BRIDGING LOAN – or interest (even if the other party has not incurred any expenses).

Seller's solicitor checks transfer deed

Signing the transfer After your solicitor has approved the final transfer document and a fair copy has been made, your solicitor asks you to sign it. He keeps it and sends the buyer's solicitor a statement showing the outstanding amount.

Granting access Once the balance of the price has been paid and ownership of the house has been transferred, you can hand over the keys for the buyer to move in.

HOUSEKEEPING MONEY

Paying the household expenses

Traditionally, a husband as wage-earner gives his wife a regular sum to pay the household expenses. But she has no legal right to a share of his income as long as they are living together. Similarly, a husband has no legal right to a share of money earned by his wife.

That situation alters only if the couple separate, or if one of them applies to the magistrates for a court order on the ground that the other has failed to provide reasonable maintenance. *See:* MAINTENANCE

If a wife saves money from the housekeeping and buys something with it, that purchase is treated in law as belonging equally to both. For example, if a wife wins the pools with an investment from housekeeping money the husband is entitled to half the winnings.

If money saved out of the housekeeping is put into a bank or other savings account, the couple have an equal right to share it.

HOUSING ASSOCIATION

An alternative to private landlords and councils

Housing associations are non-profit-making organisations that exist to provide accommodation either through CO-OWNERSHIP or by renting.

Most of those that provide rented homes are registered with a government body, the Housing Corporation, and receive financial help from it. Some cater for specific social groups, such as students or single-parent families. There is usually a selection process from a waiting list similar to that for council housing. The associations' estates are usually administered by professional housing managers.

The associations tend to be more flexible in their attitudes than local authorities, however, and set out to meet the needs of people who cannot find what they want in the rest of the private and public housing sectors.

How to apply

The address of the nearest housing association can be obtained from any Citizens Advice Bureau or Housing Aid Centre. Write to the association's letting officer, who will explain the procedure for his association and send an application form. The associations have no legal duty to house anyone, however, and it is entirely for them to decide whether to offer a tenancy to an applicant.

Assessing a fair rent

A housing association registered with the Housing Corporation must charge a tenant a rent fixed by the local Rent Officer as a fair one. Sometimes, however, either by accident or design, an association fails to have its rents registered.

The register can be inspected at the offices of the Rent Officer: there is a separate section that covers housing-association rents. *See also:* RENT REGISTRATION

If a tenant finds he is paying more than the fair rent, he can tell the association that he intends to deduct the excess that he has already paid, from future rent.

If he finds that no rent has been registered, he should ask the Rent Officer to register one.

When a housing association rent can be increased

Unlike a private landlord, a housing association can increase rents at any time if it obtains the approval of the local Rent Officer. It must give its tenants at least 4 weeks' notice of an increase, or longer if the terms of the tenancy lay down a longer period.

Security of tenure

Tenants of registered housing associations or charitable housing trusts have, under the Housing Act 1980, some security of tenure. If the tenancy is periodic – running, for example, from week to week or month to month – the tenant cannot be made to leave by his association landlord unless he has first been served with a written NOTICE TO QUIT.

If his house has been let to him on a fixed term tenancy, when that tenancy runs out he is entitled, automatically, to a periodic tenancy, for periods the same as those for which rent was last payable under the original fixed-term.

If, after being served with a notice to quit, the tenant refuses to leave, the association cannot recover possession of the house or flat without getting a county court order. The court will not make an order unless the association has served the tenant with a notice telling him:
● The date after which proceedings will be taken against him.
● That the court will be asked, in those proceedings, to make a possession order.
● The ground upon which possession will be sought.

This notice ceases to be valid (so that a new one will have to be served) 12 months after the date stated on which court action is to be taken.

Points that the association must prove

To obtain an order for possession the association must convince the court that it is reasonable to make the order, that suitable accommodation will be available for the tenant when the order takes effect, and that at least one of these grounds applies:

1. The house has been specially designed or adapted for use by a physically disabled person, and the association needs the house for such a person and there is no longer such a person living in the house.

2. The association has provided the housing for persons whose circumstances (other than financial) make it especially difficult for them to obtain suitable housing – for example, elderly people, ex-prisoners or drug addicts – and there is no longer anyone living there with such requirements, and the association needs the house to allocate to someone else who does satisfy the special qualifications.

3. The house is one of a group which the association normally lets to people who need to live in that particular locality (because, for example, there is special schooling or a social service available there and there is no longer anyone with need to call on these local resources living in the house). The association must have someone else on its list to whom it wishes to allocate the house who does have these special needs.

4. The house is too big for the present tenant, who has succeeded to the tenan-

cy on a previous tenant's death, and the present occupant has been informed, at least 6 months but less than 12 months after the previous tenant's death, that possession will be sought.

If the association can show only that it is reasonable to make the order (but not that other suitable accommodation will be available) the county court may still order the tenant to leave if the association can prove any of the following:

1. That the tenant is in arrears with the rent or has broken some other term of his tenancy agreement.

2. That the tenant, or someone living with him, has caused annoyance to neighbours or has damaged or neglected the property or the association's furniture.

3. That the tenant induced the association to grant the tenancy by making fraudulent or false statements.

4. The house was only given to the tenant as temporary housing while works of repair or improvement were carried out by the association on the tenant's former home; that these works are now finished and the former home is available for re-occupation by the tenant.

There is no need to satisfy the court that it is reasonable to make the order, although the court must still be satisfied that alternative accommodation is available, if the association seeks possession because:

1. The house is overcrowded.

2. The association intends, in the near future, to demolish, reconstruct or carry out major works involving the house, and the work cannot be done without gaining possession.

Other accommodation

In deciding whether there is suitable other accommodation available for the tenant, the court considers:

● Whether the tenant will have security of tenure in his new home.

● The accessibility of his place of work and schools for the tenant and his family.

● The distance from the homes of other members of the tenant's family (for example, aged parents) where this is relevant.

● The needs of the tenant's family and their resources.

● If furniture was provided under the old tenancy, whether adequate furniture is to be provided in the new home.

A housing association tenant has no security of tenure if he has:

● A long tenancy granted for a fixed term of more than 21 years.

● A tenancy granted to him as a homeless person under the Housing (Homeless Persons) Act 1977, unless he has been allocated the tenancy for more than 12 months.

● The tenancy was granted to him as temporary accommodation to enable him to work within the boundaries of one of the London Boroughs or district council areas and to find permanent accommodation there, and the tenant was notified of this when he took on the tenancy.

Inheriting a housing association tenancy

It may be possible to inherit a housing association tenancy if it was periodic when the former tenant died. The successor must have been residing in the house and using it as his only or principal home at the time of the tenant's death and be:

● The deceased tenant's spouse.

● Another member of the deceased tenant's family who has lived with the tenant for at least 12 months immediately before that tenant's death.

If there are 2 or more members of the deceased tenant's family who qualify they should agree between themselves who should succeed to the tenancy. If they cannot agree, then the association will choose the successor.

Complaints

Associations must give tenants an opportunity to state their views before making any decision affecting them.

If a tenant feels he has been treated unfairly by an association and cannot obtain satisfaction, he should write to the Housing Corporation.

Buying the lease

The tenants of certain housing associations (mainly those that are not charities or not registered under the Industrial and Provident Societies Act 1965) have, if they are tenants of houses, the right to buy the freehold lease. They also have the right to a mortgage from the Housing Corporation. The rules are similar to those relat-

ing to the purchase of council houses.
See: COUNCIL HOUSE SALE

HUMAN RIGHTS

When an individual can resort to international law

Britain does not have a written constitution or any single law that lays down the citizen's rights, overriding all other legislation. But Britons can, in certain circumstances, seek to enforce the European Convention on Human Rights and Fundamental Freedoms.

The convention is not directly enforceable through British courts because Parliament has not enacted it into British law. But it is binding on signatory countries, including Britain.

The convention confers on the citizens and residents of the signatory countries the general right to:

● Life, liberty and security of person.

● Fair administration of justice.

● Respect for private and family life, home and correspondence.

● Marriage and founding a family.

● Education.

● Enjoyment of possessions.

● Free elections at reasonable intervals.

The convention also generally guarantees freedom of:

● Thought, conscience and religion.

● Expression and opinion.

● Assembly and association with others.

and freedom from:

● Torture, inhuman and degrading treatment and punishment.

● Slavery, servitude and forced labour.

● Retrospective criminal legislation.

In guaranteeing all those rights, governments are not expected to discriminate on grounds of race, colour, origin, sex, language, religion, opinion, birth, ownership of property or other status.

Anyone who feels his own rights or those of someone else have been violated can complain to the European Commission of Human Rights, Strasbourg 67007, France.

The right to life

It is not a violation of the right to life to kill someone in order to:

● Defend someone else from unlawful violence.

● Make a lawful arrest.

● Prevent a lawfully detained person escaping.

● Act lawfully to quell a riot or insurrection.

The convention also permits the lawful execution of offenders.

The right to liberty

The convention does not guarantee the right to liberty to:

● Lawbreakers convicted by a competent court.

● Detainees held so that they can be brought before a court on reasonable suspicion of having committed an offence, to prevent their committing one or to prevent their escaping after committing an offence.

● Minors whose education needs to be supervised (for example in a Borstal or remand school).

● People who need to be isolated to prevent the spread of infectious diseases.

● Alcoholics, drug addicts, vagrants and people of unsound mind.

● Illegal immigrants or people subject to deportation or extradition.

Freedom from slavery

The right to freedom from slavery, servitude and forced labour does not apply to:

● People required to work during detention (a prison sentence with hard labour, for example), or during conditional release from detention (for example, work carried out under a Community Service Order).

● Members of the armed forces or those performing alternative service as conscientious objectors.

● Citizens required to perform compulsory service during an emergency threatening the community – for example, war, a natural disaster, or other state of emergency.

● Anyone obliged to perform normal civic duties – such as jury service.

The right to justice

The right to fair administration of justice, liberty and security of person entitle a detained person to be told promptly, in detail and in a language he understands, the reasons for his detention and what charges he faces.

He must be promptly brought before a magistrate or someone else with judi-cial power and is entitled to trial within a reasonable time or to release pending trial, subject to guarantees being provided that he will appear for trial.

Everyone is entitled to take court proceedings to establish speedily whether his detention is lawful and to be released – with a right to compensation – if it is not.

Everyone is entitled to a fair hearing,

THE 18-YEAR-OLD WHO WAS BIRCHED

Birching is a 'degrading punishment' banned under the European Convention on Human Rights.

Anthony Tyrer, 18, was found guilty by an Isle of Man juvenile court of assault and – after the finding was confirmed on appeal – he was given three strokes of the birch.

He complained to the European Commission of Human Rights that birching breached Article 3 of the European Convention on Human Rights, which bans torture and inhuman or degrading punishment or treatment.

Although Anthony later withdrew the complaint because of the time taken to deal with it, the commission referred the case to the European Court of Human Rights.

DECISION

The court ruled that birching was a degrading punishment and upheld the complaint, 6 years after it was made.

The British Government asked the Isle of Man Government to repeal the law allowing birching. Although it has not yet done so, courts on the island have been told that birching contravenes the convention and no one has been punished in this way since the Court of Human Rights' ruling. The European Commission of Human Rights has declared itself satisfied with the British Government's remedial action.

THE EUROPEAN COURT OF HUMAN RIGHTS

The Court of Human Rights – which is also based in Strasbourg – consists of one judge from each member state of the Council of Europe. But they act independently of the state which nominates them for election by the council's Constituent Assembly.

Usually, seven judges sit at one time, although, exceptionally, cases may be heard by all members of the court.

Cases are usually heard in public, but the court can go into closed session if it decides to do so. The court's decisions, and the reasons for them, are published. They are referred to the Committee of Ministers, which must see that the court's judgments are carried out.

How jurisdiction is limited

There are two important restrictions on the court: it can only accept a case if the state or states involved accept the jurisdiction of the court. Most Council of Europe members – Britain among them – do so. Secondly, each case is referred to the court as a dispute between states arising out of the alleged breach of an agreement between them – that is, the convention.

For this reason, an individual complainant does not take part in the proceedings, unless called as a witness. Nor is his case argued by a lawyer, although his lawyer may be asked to 'assist the court' and is often invited to join the team which presents the commission's report to the court.

Proceedings, based on the report, at first take place by means of written submissions and replies between the parties. The case is then examined at a hearing.

If the court decides that the convention has not been breached, the case is closed. There is no appeal.

When damages can be awarded

When the court rules that there has been a violation of rights, it can 'afford just satisfaction to the injured party' – which means that damages or costs can be awarded. The court can require parties to the case to 'take such action as is necessary to give effect' to its judgments. This may mean that reparation must be made to the injured party under the terms of national law or, as in the case of Committee of Ministers' rulings, it can lead to a change of practice by the offending government.

When a government against which a complaint has been made takes remedial action before the court has made judgment, the court can strike a case off its list. The same can happen when a settlement is reached during its deliberations.

within a reasonable time, and by an independent and lawful tribunal, of any criminal charge against him, or to determine his civil rights and duties.

Generally, trials must take place, and judgment be pronounced, publicly. But the Press and public may be excluded from all or part of a trial:

● In the interest of morals, public order or national security.

● When the interests of juveniles or the protection of the private lives of the parties requires (for example in divorce or custody cases).

● When, in the court's opinion, publicity would prejudice the interests of justice.

The convention says that everyone charged with a criminal offence has the right:

● To be presumed innocent until lawfully proven guilty.

● To have adequate time and facilities to prepare his defence (including access to a lawyer).

● To defend himself in person, through a lawyer of his own choice or through free legal assistance.

● To call and examine witnesses on his own behalf under the same conditions as witnesses against him.

● To have a free interpreter if he cannot understand or speak the language used in court.

One article bans retrospective legislation, but it does not rule out conviction for any act or omission which, when it occurred, was criminal according to the general principles of law recognised by civilised nations – for example, terrorism, piracy, hijacking, genocide and war crimes.

The right to privacy and family life

Men and women of marriageable age have the right to marry and found a family according to national laws governing these rights.

Everyone has the right to respect for his private and family life, his home and his correspondence. No public authority may interfere with that right, unless it is lawful and necessary to do so in the interests of:

● National security – for example, telephone tapping to detect a spy.

● Public safety and the prevention of crime or disorder – for example, open-

ing of letters in some cases.

● National economic well-being – to prevent tax evasion or flouting of exchange controls, for example.

● Health – when a child is taken into official care, and parental rights are denied, for the sake of the child's psychological well-being.

● Morals – perhaps to prevent the pornographic use of children within a family, although such an example has not been tested.

● The rights of others.

Freedom of thought

The freedom of thought, religion and conscience includes the right to change one's belief and the right of religious practice, worship and teaching, in private or in public, alone or with others.

That right is subject to the same limitations as the right to respect for private and family life, except that it cannot be limited on grounds of national security.

Freedom of expression

The right to freedom of expression and of opinion also gives people the right to receive and impart information and ideas without official interference and regardless of frontiers.

But governments are not prevented from requiring broadcasting or cinemas to be licensed.

Like several other rights, it can be limited to:

● Maintain national security and territorial integrity – for example, under the Official Secrets Act.

● Preserve public safety and prevent crime and disorder – for example, through restrictions placed on communications by prisoners.

● Protect health and morals – through national laws controlling pornography, for example.

● Protect the reputation and rights of others – by the libel laws, for instance.

● Prevent the disclosure of information received in confidence – for example, industrial secrets.

● Maintain the authority and impartiality of the judiciary – to prevent remarks which would be contempt of court, say.

The right of assembly and association

The right of peaceful assembly and freedom of association includes the

right to form and to join a trade union, but does not prevent lawful restrictions barring members of the police, the armed forces and people in state employment from belonging to unions. It is uncertain whether the trade union rights of civil servants are protected.

This right too is subject to limitation in the interests of national security, public safety, prevention of crime or disorder, and protection of health, morals and the rights of others.

The rights of freedom of expression, freedom of assembly and association, and freedom from discrimination are guaranteed even to aliens living in a signatory country.

The right to enjoyment of possessions

The convention states that individuals and organisations shall not be deprived of their possessions, except lawfully – for example, by a court order, in the public interest, or through a compulsory purchase order on land.

The right to education

No one shall be denied the right to education and the state must respect the right of parents to ensure that their children are educated in conformity with parents' religious and philosophical convictions.

However, it has been held by the Court of Human Rights that this right is not violated by the provision of sex education in schools against parents' wishes.

The right to an effective remedy

The convention provides that anyone whose rights are violated shall have an effective remedy before a national authority, even if the violation is committed by someone in an official capacity.

Signatory states are permitted to repeal most of their obligations under the convention during war or other emergency – such as terrorism – but they may not do so, however, if it would break international law.

A state cannot repeal its obligations to protect the right to life – except during warfare declared under the Geneva Convention – or its obligations concerning the use of torture and retrospective legislation.

Any measures repealing a state's obligations must be notified to the Secretary General of the Council of Europe, and he must be told when they cease to operate.

Conditions that must be met when making a complaint

Before a complaint about an alleged violation of one or more of these rights can be considered by the European Commission of Human Rights, the commission must be satisfied that it meets several conditions for admissibility.

The complainant must first have exhausted all available remedies within the country where the violation of rights is alleged to have taken place.

A complaint against the prison system in Britain, for example, would need to have been finally rejected by the Home Secretary before it could be submitted to the commission.

The commission must receive a complaint within 6 months of the final decision within the country concerned.

Conditions for individuals

Five further conditions apply to any complaint made by an individual, but not if it is made by one government against another government. The complaint must not be:

● Anonymous – although the commission may decide to keep a complainant's name secret.

● Substantially the same as a matter already dealt with by the commission, or already submitted to another system of settling international disputes – for example, arbitration machinery set up under a treaty between two countries such as Britain and Ireland.

● Incompatible with the provisions of the convention – for example, by using the convention to prevent another person from obtaining something to which he is entitled under national law.

● Manifestly ill-founded – for example, if a complainant's interpretation of his rights is obviously not reasonable.

● An abuse of the right to petition the commission – for example, as part of an election campaign.

In many cases, the commission goes so far as to consider written or oral arguments by all the parties concerned before deciding whether a complaint is admissible.

HOW TO MAKE A HUMAN RIGHTS COMPLAINT

If you feel that your rights under the European Convention have been violated by any member government which accepts the right of individual petition – including Britain – you can complain directly to the European Commission of Human Rights in Strasbourg.

A complaint – called an application – can be made by any individual, group or organisation.

If the alleged violation occurred abroad and the country's government does not accept the right of individual petition, you will need to persuade the British Government, or any other signatory government, to complain on your behalf.

To do this in Britain, write to your Member of Parliament asking him to take the matter up with the Foreign Secretary, who has the power of deciding whether Britain should pursue a case.

Any complaint should set out the facts of the case, reasons for thinking there has been a violation of rights and details of the steps taken to get the matter put right. This information is needed to prove that you have exhausted all means of redress available in the country concerned – one of the conditions of admissibility laid down by the convention.

You would need, for example, to give details of letters, phone calls or meetings with officials, and of decisions by courts or government ministers.

There are no fees to pay for making a complaint. No costs will be awarded against you if your complaint is not upheld or if it is ruled inadmissible.

If the complaint raises legal complexities or involved factual questions, or you are uncertain whether it is admissible, it may be useful to be represented by a lawyer who is familiar with the convention and its machinery. But you do not have to have legal representation.

Free legal aid is available to complainants whose limited financial means would otherwise prevent them from pursuing a complaint. The commission has not published details of how much financial aid may be provided or of how limited a complainant's means have to be to qualify.

How complaints are dealt with by the commission

When it receives a complaint, the Commission of Human Rights first decides whether the complaint is relevant to the convention. It then invites written observations from the government against which the complaint has been made. The complainant has the right of reply to these comments.

With the information provided by both parties, the commission decides whether the complaint is admissible and gives both parties the reasons for its decision, which is final.

Once a complaint has been ruled admissible, the commission starts its full investigation of the facts of the case. It can interview the complainant, witnesses and officials involved, and visit places concerned in the case.

Having established the facts, the commission must try to achieve a settlement between the government involved and the complainant. Any settlement must be approved by the commission.

If an acceptable settlement is reached, the commission draws up a report, briefly recording the facts of the case and the solution achieved. The report is published by the Secretary General of the Council of Europe, and the case is closed.

If no acceptable settlement is reached, the commission gives a longer factual report to the Council of Europe's Committee of Ministers, together with an opinion on whether the convention has been breached.

Governments concerned in a case also receive this information, but the complainant does not. It is for the Committee of Ministers to decide whether the report and opinion should be published. They are automatically published if the case is brought before the European Court of Human Rights.

Sometimes a complainant withdraws his complaint after it has been ruled admissible but before the commission has issued an opinion. The commission can – if it feels that the case raises issues on which an opinion would clarify the meaning of the convention – continue to consider the case and give a report and opinion in due course. The commission itself can decide to publish this information in such cases.

After it has given an opinion on a complaint still outstanding, the commission asks either the Committee of Ministers or the European Court of Human Rights to decide whether there has been a breach of the convention.

How a government can be punished

The European Convention was agreed in 1950 by members of the Council of Europe – a political, economic and social forum to which any democratic state in Europe can belong.

The convention is legally binding on the 21 governments that have signed it. Not all signatories, however, recognise the right of individuals, groups and organisations to complain to the Commission of Human Rights about alleged contraventions. Some only accept complaints made by other signatories.

Some states do not accept the jurisdiction of the European Court of Human Rights over complaints. In that case, complaints can be judged only by the Committee of Ministers, the Council of Europe's main political body.

Any government that does not comply with a decision of the committee – or of the court, if its jurisdiction is accepted – can be suspended from

membership of the Council of Europe. For the same reason, the convention is enforceable only against a government that has undertaken to be bound by it, and not against other bodies or individuals. If they violate someone's rights, he can only try to prove that a government did not fulfil its obligations to guarantee his rights.

Which countries individuals can complain against

Although 21 countries have accepted the European Convention, not all of them accept all of its provisions.

The right of individuals, groups and organisations to complain to the European Commission of Human Rights is recognised by Austria, Belgium, Britain, Denmark, the Federal Republic of Germany (West Germany and West Berlin), Iceland, Ireland, Italy, Liechtenstein, Luxembourg, Netherlands, Norway, Portugal, Sweden and Switzerland, but not by Cyprus, France, Greece, Malta, Spain and Turkey.

Countries which do not accept the jurisdiction of the European Court of Human Rights are Cyprus, Greece, Malta, Spain and Turkey.

Britain has extended its acceptance of the convention to Bermuda, Belize, the Cayman Islands, Channel Islands, Falkland Islands, Isle of Man, St Helena, Brunei, the Turks and Caicos Islands, British Virgin Islands, Antigua, Montserrat and St Christopher.

HUNTING

Restrictions on your right to ride to hounds

No licence is needed to hunt with hounds for foxes or deer, but you must have the consent of the occupier of the land over which you intend to ride.

If a hunt enters land without permission, the occupier can sue the Master of the Hunt, and any individual huntsman he can identify, for TRESPASS. He can also sue the Master and any identifiable huntsmen for any injury or damage caused, whether by the hunt itself or by followers of the hunt – unless the Master can prove that he instructed the followers not to enter the land.

Anyone can bring a private prosecution against a huntsman who causes unnecessary suffering to any animal.

THE COMMITTEE OF MINISTERS

The Committee of Ministers is a political body consisting of one representative from each member state of the Council of Europe. Its decisions on complaints under the convention require a two-thirds majority. They are reached in camera, there is no appeal against them, and they are binding.

The commission can decide to refer a case to the court for judgment instead of itself considering it. Any government involved in a case can also bring it before the court. But the Committee of Ministers must consider a case if it has not been referred to the court within 3 months of an opinion being given by the commission.

If, after considering a case, the Committee of Ministers decides that there has been no breach of the convention, the parties involved in the complaint are informed. No further action is taken.

When a violation is proved

When the committee decides that there has been a violation of rights, it sets a time limit for the offending state to change its law or policies so that there can be no

further similar breach of the convention.

If the state does not do so, the committee decides how to give effect to its call for remedial action. The convention does not specify how this can be done, other than by publication of the commission's report. But signatories to the convention undertake to carry out the committee's decisions, and if they do not, they can be suspended from membership of the Council of Europe.

Political pressure to conform to the convention is the ministerial committee's strongest sanction: often a member state brings its practices into line with the convention before it has been required to do so.

Austria, for example, in 1962 repealed a law which allowed criminal appeal hearings to take place without the presence of the appellant and his counsel. A number of appellants complained that this violated the right to a fair trial. The Committee of Ministers agreed, and welcomed the introduction of repeal legislation, which took place while the complaints were being considered by the commission.

THE VILLAGERS WHO SUED FOR TRESPASS

If a hunt enters land without permission the occupiers can sue for trespass.

In 1969, the hounds of Hambledon Hunt, Hampshire, entered gardens in the village of Curdridge. They killed a cat and were said to have terrified an infant boy.

Mr and Mrs David Pearce sued Lieutenant-Colonel Frank Mitchell, the Master of the Hunt, for trespass and the loss of the cat, and they also sought an injunction to restrain the hunt from further trespassing in the gardens. Mr and Mrs Christopher Chapman also sued for trespass.

DECISION

The judge awarded the Pearces £5 for trespass and £7 for the loss of the cat, and he awarded the Chapmans 1s. for trespass. He refused to grant an injunction, on the grounds that the hunt had behaved itself well for 170 years.

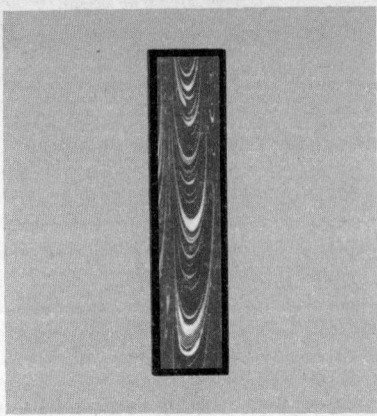

IDENTIFICATION PARADE

Safeguarding a suspect against false identification

If the police suspect a person of a crime and have a witness to the incident, they may ask the suspect to take part in an identification parade. A person is entitled to refuse to take part just as the police are entitled to refuse to organise a parade if a suspect asks for one.

There must be at least eight people in an identification parade. They must be similar in appearance, age and race.

The suspect is entitled to have a solicitor or a friend present at the parade and to seek legal advice before going on the parade. He may stand where he chooses in the line-up, change his appearance – for example, by taking off his glasses. He is also entitled to object to any member of the line-up if he considers the other person's appearance is not similar to his own and to ask any other member to remove his glasses or jewellery.

When you are a witness

If a person is called as a witness, he must not be allowed to see a suspect before the identification parade takes place, nor be told anything about the suspect by the police.

A witness who has inspected the parade must be kept apart from those who have not. Any witness is entitled to request a member of a parade to put a hat on, walk or say a particular phrase.

If a witness cannot identify anyone in the line-up, he should tell the police, and they should record that no positive identification has been made.

If he identifies someone he should touch the person on the shoulder and say that is the person.

Other ways to identify a suspected person

When the police do not know the identity of the person they are seeking, they may ask witnesses to look through books of photographs of people who have been convicted of similar crimes in the past. The witnesses must not be helped to identify any person.

If a witness is later asked to identify the main suspect in an identification parade, the police must not show his photograph again.

ILLEGITIMATE CHILD

Rights of someone whose parents are unmarried

A child born to parents who are not married to each other at the time of the birth is illegitimate. But if its parents marry later, the child automatically becomes legitimate, from the date of the marriage.

If the marriage is void, the child will be illegitimate, unless at the time of conception either parent believed they were legally married. *See*: NULLITY

If one of the parents marries someone else – not the other parent – the child remains illegitimate, even if the marriage takes place before the birth.

However, if the child is adopted by the married couple, it immediately becomes their legitimate child.

Rights of an illegitimate child

For most practical purposes, illegitimate children have equal rights in law with those who are legitimate.

If a parent makes a will or executes a deed giving property to his children, the term 'children' includes any illegitimate as well as legitimate children. An illegitimate child also has the same rights as a legitimate child to share in the estate of a parent who has died without making a will.

Someone who is illegitimate can also claim to be maintained out of its deceased parents' estate, whether there is a will or not.

However, an illegitimate child has no right to share in the estate of any relation other than a parent unless he is mentioned by name in the will.

Wills made before 1969 If the parent of an illegitimate child made a will before July 25, 1969, the question whether the child is legitimate is still important.

An illegitimate child whose parent died before that date, and who was not mentioned by name in the will, still has no claim on the estate, despite the change in the law.

Honours and titles An illegitimate child cannot inherit an honour or title, or inherit an entailed estate.

An illegitimate child can claim compensation for a relative's FATAL ACCIDENT in the same way as a legitimate child.

Rights of the parents

The father of an illegitimate child has fewer rights than the father of a legitimate child. For example, his consent is not needed for the child's ADOPTION. The mother's consent is required as it is for the adoption of a legitimate child.

The father of an illegitimate child has no automatic right to the custody of the child; this initially lies with the mother. But he may apply to the court for custody or access and the court will be guided by what is in the child's best interests.

All fathers find it difficult to obtain custody of young children but a natural father may be granted access. If the mother neglects or abandons the child and the father cannot provide a home, it may be taken into care.

If the father is given custody of the child, he has the right to appoint someone other than the mother to be the child's GUARDIAN after his death. His consent will also be necessary for the child's adoption.

The father has no right to insist on the child taking his surname or having his name on the birth certificate.

The mother of an illegitimate child has the right to financial assistance from the father to bring up the child, and can obtain from the magistrates' court an order to make him pay maintenance.

Social security benefits are normally the same in respect of an illegitimate child. CHILD BENEFIT is payable for an illegitimate child, and extra may be claimed by a person entitled to INDUSTRIAL INJURY BENEFIT, INVALIDITY PENSION, MATERNITY allowance, widow's benefits, SICKNESS BENEFIT or UNEMPLOYMENT BENEFIT for any such child for whom child benefit is payable.

GUARDIAN'S ALLOWANCE is payable where the mother of an illegitimate child is dead, unless the identity of the father is established when a claim is dependent on the claimant proving that the father is dead, in prison or missing. The right of a parent bringing up his or her child alone to an extra personal INCOME TAX ALLOWANCE extends to the parent of an illegitimate child.

Children of a foreign marriage

A child may be regarded as legitimate even if his parents' foreign marriage is not valid in this country – provided that he is considered to be legitimate by the laws of the country where both parents are domiciled.

When his parents have different domiciles his legitimacy under the laws of either country may be enough to make him legitimate in Britain.

IMMIGRATION

When permission is needed to enter Britain

The right to enter Britain at any time and stay without restriction depends on

PATRIALITY. Most patrials were born in Britain or have gained CITIZENSHIP through residence. They travel on United Kingdom passports.

Some non-citizens, travelling on Commonwealth passports, have patriality if either parent was born in Britain, or if they are married to a patrial. On the other hand, many people who were born in former British territories, although they hold 'UK and Colonies' passports that describe them as UK citizens, are not classed by the law as patrials.

Patrials have what is called the right of abode: they cannot be refused entry and are not liable to DEPORTATION. Anyone else needs official permission to enter Britain and official approval to remain. However an EEC citizen is entitled to come for up to 6 months to look for work and to stay on if he or she finds a job.

How permission varies

The terms on which a non-patrial traveller, his wife and their children under 18 are allowed to enter Britain vary according to their origin, purpose and financial situation. Permission can be given for:
● A short temporary stay.
● A limited period, but on the understanding that if things go well they will be permitted to settle here.
● An indefinite stay.

Settlement means a person has his home in Britain, without restriction on the length of his stay or on his right to work. But settled people do not have a patrial right of abode until they gain citizenship. They remain liable to deportation, and if they leave Britain for more than 2 years, they can be refused re-entry.

The three stages of control

Government immigration policy is laid down in a set of rules that must be applied by entry clearance officers, immigration officers and Home Office staff.

Entry clearance officers check the applications that most immigrants have to make before setting out. They work in British embassies, high commissions and consulates abroad, as employees of the Foreign and Commonwealth Office.

Immigration officers are stationed at airports and docks to decide whether

THE MAN WHO STAYED AWAY TOO LONG

A settled immigrant has a right to leave Britain and return – but not if he is away for more than 2 years. The limit is extended only if the immigrant's closest ties are in Britain and he has spent most of his life in the country.

Dharam Bir Taneja, an Indian accountant born in 1934, came to Britain in 1962 and stayed until May 1970, when he left to study in the United States. He returned in April 1972 – within the time limit for admission as a returning resident – but after a week went back to the United States.

In March 1974 Mr Taneja again applied for readmission and was granted an entry certificate by the clearance officer at the British consulate-general in Chicago. But he did not use it.

When Mr Taneja applied once more in November 1974 – 7 months after his latest time limit had expired – he was refused entry clearance.

In an appeal to an immigration adjudicator, a lawyer argued on Mr Taneja's behalf that the rules gave the officer power to relax the time limit. He should have done so in Mr Taneja's case because illness had prevented him from using the first entry clearance, and because his life was in Britain – he had gone to study in America only so that he could further his career in Britain, not to set up permanent residence.

The entry officer forwarded a report by Mr Taneja's own doctor that apart from bouts of depression there was no evidence of real illness. He argued that Mr Taneja had lived in Britain for only 8 of his 42 years, and had no close relatives in Britain. The appeal was dismissed.

When the case was taken to the Immigration Appeals Tribunal, it had to decide whether the adjudicator could have been wrong in law to rule that the circumstances did not allow the use of a discretionary power.

DECISION

The appeal was dismissed. Mr Taneja was obliged to return to India as soon as he had finished his course of study.

and on what terms travellers can be admitted. They are employed by the Home Office and advised by Health Department medical officers.

If a person breaks any condition of their stay they can normally be prosecuted or, alternatively, the Home Office may decide to deport him or her on that ground (though in that case there would be a right of appeal).

Obtaining preliminary clearance

Anyone subject to immigration controls who wants to enter Britain can apply for clearance in his own country. In some situations he will not be admitted to the UK unless he has done so, and as a result airlines and shipping companies will not accept bookings for him.

For example, a person coming to settle here on the basis of relationship to a person already settled here must have an entry clearance. So must a person coming to engage in business here, or a person of independent means.

The only people who do not need entry clearances nowadays are visitors (including people coming for medical treatment) and other people who are essentially coming only for a very limited period, such as au pairs and working holiday-makers. Anyone who is coming with the intention of later getting permission to live here permanently must have an entry clearance.

Entry clearances are not compulsory for students, but most students would find it very difficult to gain admission without one.

Forms of application vary with the country of departure and the traveller's purpose. The applicant must prove his or her identity and may be asked for proof of family relationships, occupation or financial situation.

The entry clearance officer must be satisfied that the facts in the application are correct – a requirement that can take years to meet if it depends on proving a family relationship in India, Pakistan or Bangladesh. If the officer considers that the immigration rules allow entry for the stated purpose, he stamps the applicant's passport with either an entry certificate – for people from British Commonwealth countries – or a visa, for aliens.

Entry clearance officers abroad can

SPECIAL GROUNDS FOR REFUSING ENTRY

A traveller who would otherwise qualify at least for temporary admission can be refused entry if:
● A medical inspector advises that he should be excluded.
● He refuses to be medically examined.
● He is under a current deportation order.
● He has been convicted of an extraditable crime in any country.
● His exclusion is considered 'conducive to the public good' because of his character, conduct or associations – a provision used mainly to prevent criminal, subversive or terrorist activities.
● He cannot convince the immigration officer that he will be admitted to another country after staying in Britain.

also issue patriality certificates, exempting the holders from control.

When the traveller arrives in Britain

An immigration officer must admit a person holding an entry clearance, unless:
● He believes it was obtained by misstatement or concealment of facts – whether or not the holder knew about the deception.
● Changed circumstances disqualify the application – for example, if a woman already in Britain rejects a man who says he is coming to marry her.
● He finds grounds for refusal for medical reasons or because a traveller's presence is considered likely to harm the community.

Unless there is a deportation order against them, the wife or children under 16 of any Commonwealth citizen settled in Britain cannot be refused admission.

No one whose usual home is in Britain and who returns after an absence can be refused admission on medical grounds alone.

A medical officer's role

Anyone who wants to stay in Britain for more than 6 months can be referred by the immigration officer to a medical inspector. So can anyone, even if coming for a shorter period, who seems to need medical treatment or who mentions that he has a medical problem.

If the medical inspector reports that a traveller's admission is not desirable – for example, because he or she has a notifiable disease – or that an immigrant may not be able to support himself or his dependants because of his condition, the immigration officer normally refuses admission.

If the person needing treatment is a returning resident who cannot be refused entry on medical grounds, he or she can be ordered by the immigration officer to report to a medical officer of health so that treatment can be arranged.

OFFENCES AGAINST THE IMMIGRATION LAWS

An immigrant breaks the law if he:
1. Knowingly enters Britain without permission or in breach of a DEPORTATION order.
2. Obstructs or misrepresents facts to an official executing the Immigration Act, or refuses to answer questions or produce a required document.
3. Alters or falsifies a passport or entry certificate, or possesses a forged document with the intention of using it to gain entry.
4. Knowingly remains beyond the time limit of his permission to enter, or breaches any other condition of that permission – usually a prohibition against taking employment.
Maximum penalty: £200 fine and 6 months' imprisonment, with a recommendation for deportation if the court thinks fit. But in many cases offenders are detained and expelled by the Home Office without prosecution.

It is an offence for any person to give shelter to an immigrant who he knows or has reasonable cause to believe is an illegal entrant or has broken a condition of his stay.

If an overstayer marries, his wife can be convicted of harbouring him, although prosecution is unlikely. The maximum penalty is a £400 fine and 6 months' imprisonment.

The most serious immigration offence is to be concerned knowingly in arrangements to bring an illegal entrant into Britain. The maximum penalty is 7 years' imprisonment.

If entry is refused

If an immigration officer refuses entry, he must give the traveller a printed notice, carrying the authority of a chief immigration officer or immigration inspector and showing the reason for refusal. The notice must state the time limit for appealing, and an appeal form must be supplied with it.

The right to appeal can usually be exercised only after a traveller has left the country – unless he arrived with a valid entry clearance. Then he is entitled to remain in Britain until an appeal is heard.

An immigration officer has the power to order the detention of a person who is refused admission, while outward travel is arranged. A passenger can also be held in custody while his or her claim to admission is investigated or an appeal is heard. Special detention accommodation is provided at or near Heathrow Airport, London, but a detained traveller may be sent to PRISON if other secure accommodation is not available.

After 7 days' detention a person must be told of his or her right to apply for BAIL. Applications are decided by government-appointed appeals adjudicators at hearings that are open to the public.

Instead of detaining a traveller whose claim to admission is being investigated, an immigration officer can allow temporary entry on condition that the person hands over his or her passport and reports back by a specified time. Restrictions can be imposed on the traveller's movements – for example, residence at a certain address.

When a stay is limited

A non-patrial who does not qualify for immediate settlement can be admitted for a limited time. Immigration officers have wide powers of choice when granting temporary stays, and the time allowed could be anything from a day to 12 months, provided that the traveller can support himself without working for the period that he wants to stay. The maximum period is normally 6 months.

Someone who qualifies only as a visitor and is given a limited stay will be forbidden to take employment – paid or unpaid – without obtaining the consent of the Department of Employment, or to engage in a business or profession without the Home Office's consent.

Extending a limited stay

A person who wants to stay longer than the time limit stamped in his or her passport, or wants to have a ban on work removed, should send the passport to the Home Office immigration department with a letter explaining the claim. A personal approach is likely to involve hours of waiting.

Application for an extension must be made before the time limit expires –

TRAVELLERS WHO MUST GO HOME

People with no prospect of qualifying for permanent residence can be admitted to Britain for a limited time. They have the right to ask for extensions, but must leave the country eventually or risk expulsion, prosecution or both.

Strictly temporary admission is granted to:
● Visitors with enough money to meet all expenses, including the cost of outward travel. A visitor will be forbidden to take employment or to engage in a business or profession. A person entering for medical treatment must have funds to pay for it. Foreigners will be refused medical care except in genuine emergencies. Reciprocal agreements for free emergency care exist with all EEC countries, Austria, Bulgaria, Czechoslovakia, Malta, New Zealand, Norway, Poland, Romania, Sweden, Russia and Yugoslavia.
● Students enrolled for full-time courses at institutions recognised by the Home Office. They can be admitted for periods of 12 months at a time. A person hoping to enrol can be given a shorter time limit, extendible if he or she succeeds. The maximum total period is 4 years. Students are normally forbidden to take employment but consent may be given if they apply to take part-time or vacation work. A student must have funds to support himself and dependants – he can bring a wife and children under 18.
● AU PAIR girls.
● Working holidaymakers between the ages of 17 and 27 who may take incidental jobs – but not make a career – while travelling in Britain. In practice this provision is available almost exclusively to young Canadians, Australians and New Zealanders, who are given 6 or 12 month stays, extendible for up to 2 years.

even if only 1 day before. It automatically gives the applicant the right to remain for 28 days after a decision is made, or until the end of any extension granted, which could be for a period shorter than 28 days.

The length of extension is normally similar to the period allowed on entry, if the applicant still appears to be capable of self-support, but the total visit can never be for more than 12 months.

Anyone who applies for extension before a time limit has expired is entitled to appeal against a refusal.

If someone on a limited stay fails to apply for an extension before the time is up, he is likely to be refused the extension – even if it would have been allowed otherwise – and has no right to appeal against refusal. He can be prosecuted and gaoled for up to 6 months for overstaying his time limit, or the Home Office could decide to deport him for some breach of his conditions. He then would have a right of appeal.

When a limited stay can be made permanent

A traveller seeking permanent settlement can be admitted for a limited period at first, on the understanding that if he meets certain conditions he will be given extensions of time and will eventually qualify by length of residence. He must, however, have an entry clearance for admission.

Extendible entry on that basis can be granted to:
● Self-employed artists and writers.
● People of independent means (who must have at least £10,000 capital and also meet certain other conditions).

The Home Office seldom allows extension of a stay for a purpose that was not stated when a traveller arrived. Someone who comes as a visitor but could qualify to settle – for example, a man who sees an opportunity to start a business – will have to leave when his time is up, and make a new application.

Special rules for businessmen

People who can support themselves by self-employment or by business activities can be admitted initially for 12 months. Their permission to stay can be renewed year by year until they qualify for permanent residence after 4–5 years.

Anyone who wants to enter to start a business must prove to the entry clearance officer that he has enough money or other assets to meet expenses and potential liabilities, and that his profits will maintain him and any dependants with him.

A man who intends to earn his living by investing in an existing business must show that it needs his money and services. His investment must be in proportion to the return he will gain – not simply a disguise for paid employment.

A self-employed artist or writer must satisfy the entry clearance office – and the Home Office when he applies for extensions of his stay – that his work is genuinely freelance and is enough to maintain him and any dependants.

Independent means

Someone with enough capital or stable income to support himself and his family without working can be granted an entry clearance as a person of independent means; but he will have to show that he has at least £100,000 in capital or income of not less than £10,000 under his control in the UK, and also that his admission is in the 'general interests' of the UK or that he has close connection with the country (for example, that he has relatives here or has lived here for a long time in the past).

PROVING HER INTENTION
IS HONOURABLE

A fiancée may be admitted without an entry certificate if she can convince the immigration officer that she is definitely to marry.

'Here's each year's Valentine he's sent me since he settled here'

Intention to marry

A woman who convinces an immigration officer that she intends to marry a British patrial or a settled immigrant is given permission to stay for 3 months.

As soon as the marriage has taken place, the woman will be given indefinite leave to remain in the UK, unless she is a Commonwealth citizen who has married a patrial, in which case she automatically becomes patrial herself.

A man who wants to marry a woman settled here will not be allowed to live here unless the woman he plans to marry is a UK citizen who was, or one of whose parents was, born in the UK. Even then he will not be able to come if he has not met his prospective wife, or if the entry clearance officer suspects that he is marrying primarily to get into the UK. The same applies to a man who is already married to a UK woman.

If the entry clearance officer thinks that the couple do not intend to live together permanently he will refuse. A man who is admitted or allowed by the Home Office to remain here on marriage will only be given 12 months' leave to stay initially (though he will be allowed to take work). He will be allowed to settle here after that time.

When an indefinite stay is allowed

Two classes of people are admitted to Britain for indefinite periods – no limit is stamped in their passports – although they do not have the rights of patriality or citizenship:

● Diplomats and their official staff, who are exempt from immigration control as long as the British Government continues to recognise their diplomatic status.

● Commonwealth citizens with any grandparent born in Britain. They are officially admissible if they intend to seek or take up employment, and in practice they can remain even if they do not find it, and can settle permanently. They remain liable to deportation unless they qualify for citizenship.

How the settlement quota system works

A restricted number of immigrants is allowed into Britain with immediate right of settlement. They are people who were born in former British territories and still hold United Kingdom and Colonies passports.

All such people have the right to settle in Britain but they must wait in their present country of residence for entry clearance before they travel. Their flow from the Indian subcontinent and East Africa is regulated by an annual quota of entry clearances.

Quota clearances are issued only to heads of households, so in families where husband and wife have different citizenship, the passport of the husband usually decides their right to settle. If he has given up his UK citizenship and only his wife holds a UK passport, the whole family is excluded.

Widows, divorced women and wives who are family breadwinners because their husbands are disabled can qualify as heads of households in their own right. If they hold UK passports they and their children are admitted, along with a disabled husband. Single people over 18 of either sex are treated as heads of households if they hold UK passports.

Entry for permanent settlement is also allowed occasionally to REFUGEES or to people who arrive seeking POLITICAL ASYLUM.

The relatives who can follow

Only a person settled in Britain without restriction on his or her stay has the right to be joined by relatives, and then only by:

● A wife.
● A husband.
● Children under 18.
● Unmarried daughters and dependent unmarried sons under 21.
● Dependent parents and grandparents.
● Elderly or disabled near relatives living alone.

In each case, the person already settled, officially called the sponsor, must be able to show that he or she can and will support and accommodate the relatives without the help of public funds.

The only exception to that requirement is made when the sponsor was settled in Britain on January 1, 1973, and is being joined by a wife or children under 18. Any relative wanting to join a settled immigrant must have an entry clearance before setting out for Britain.

Wives joining husbands A wife who applies to join her husband after he has settled in Britain need not have been dependent on him, but must show proof of the marriage. If it took place in an area without an adequate system of registration she must produce extensive supporting evidence and may have to undergo medical examination to help establish her identity. The difficulty of proving a marriage on the Indian subcontinent, for example, can lead to a delay of years before an entry clearance is issued.

Husbands joining wives It is now impossible for a husband to join a wife who has settled in the UK, unless she or one of her parents was born here, and she is a UK citizen.

Children under 18 A child under the age of 18 is entitled to enter only if both parents are already settled in Britain or are being admitted for settlement at the same time. 'Parents' can mean stepparents, adoptive parents or the parents of an illegitimate child, but all relationships have to be proved.

If one parent is alone in Britain, he or she can sponsor a child only if the other parent has had no responsibility for the child's upbringing, or if it can be shown that exclusion will harm the child – for example, because its living conditions with the parent in the home country are undesirable.

When an application is made for a child to enter Britain from a country with no adequate system of birth registration, the child is questioned by an entry clearance officer and may be required to undergo medical examinations, including X-rays, to confirm its age and parentage. If a child's answers to questions about family relationships differ from those of the mother or other children, the officer can refuse all the entry clearances because he is not satisfied that they are related. On the Indian subcontinent, checking procedures can take so long that when a refusal and appeal are also involved, a boy applying at the age of 10 might be 15 before his case is closed.

Children who are under 21 A son of 18 years or older cannot normally be admitted to join parents settled here, but must qualify in his own right. A daughter over 18, but under 21, may perhaps be admitted if she is unmarried and fully dependent, was living with the family overseas, and has no other close relatives in the country of origin to turn to.

Parents and grandparents Elderly parents (at least one must be over 65), or widowed mothers of any age may be able to qualify to join children settled here if they can prove that they are dependent on these children, but they will also have to prove that they have no other close relatives in their own country to turn to.

A sponsoring child must show that he or she can accommodate and maintain not only the parents or grandparents, but also any further people who might be admissible later as dependants of them. An entry clearance officer will want evidence that the sponsor has been sending money regularly to cover most of the upkeep of parents or grandparents. In practice very few parents or grandparents are admitted.

Other near relatives Brothers, sisters, aunts or uncles of settled immigrants

THE IMMIGRANT WIFE WHO DID NOT KNOW HER PASSPORT WAS FALSE

An immigrant can be expelled if the original claim to entry was not correct – even one who did not know that the passport she carried was not her own.

Ijaz Begum Khan, the third wife of a Pakistani settled in Britain, entered the country on the passport of his second wife. She did not know – she could not read or write.

When it was discovered later that the name she used in Britain was not the name she entered by, she was arrested and detained as an illegal entrant.

Appeals to an adjudicator and to the Immigration Appeals Tribunal failed, and her case was taken to the High Court by application for a writ of HABEAS CORPUS. That was refused.

In a final effort to avoid expulsion, Mrs Khan appealed again. The Court of Appeal had to decide whether her detention and expulsion were legal if she did not know that she had committed an offence.

DECISION
The judges ruled that although 'guilty knowledge' must be proved in a criminal prosecution, it is not a requirement when dealing with illegal entry. The appeal was dismissed and Mrs Khan was flown home to Pakistan.

THE LITTLE GIRL WHO HAD TO SHARE HER BED

For a child to be allowed to leave one parent and join the other, undesirable conditions at home must also be proved to be unavoidable.

Monica was 12 when an application was made on her behalf to the British High Commission in Kingston, Jamaica, for clearance to join her father in Britain. He had left Jamaica when she was 6 months old.

The entry clearance officer refused because immigration rules say that both parents should be in Britain. Exceptions are made only when the sponsoring parent has had sole responsibility for the child's upbringing, or if 'family and other considerations' make the child's exclusion undesirable.

In an appeal to an immigration adjudicator, a lawyer argued that overcrowding in Monica's home, where she shared a bedroom and apparently a bed with a sister and two older half-brothers, was a danger to her welfare. It was also alleged that her stepfather, who had little income, resented her being in his house when her father could well afford to take her.

The entry clearance officer, defending his decision, argued that Monica was better off in a familiar environment than with a 'virtual stranger' who had been back to Jamaica for only 4 weeks, when she was 11.

The adjudicator noted that Monica had a grandmother in the same neighbourhood. She had lived with her until she was 9, and still visited her. He concluded that Monica's situation could be remedied in Jamaica, and dismissed the appeal.

The Immigration Appeals Tribunal consented to a further appeal on behalf of Monica – by then 14. It had to decide whether the adjudicator was right to rule that undesirable circumstances must also be unavoidable.

DECISION
Monica's appeal was dismissed. She had to stay in Jamaica.

are admitted only in a narrow category of 'distress'. They must:

● Be over 65 or severely disabled.

● Be living in poverty compared with similar people in their home country.

● Have no relative to help them in their own country.

When an immigrant can appeal

Almost any ruling under the Immigration Act can be challenged by the person it affects. The only people who have no right of appeal are those who are:

● Refused extension of their stay in Britain after disobeying a time limit.

● Refused entry by order of the Home Secretary on grounds of public good.

● Deported on grounds of public good, if the Home Secretary certifies that the decision was made for political reasons or in the interests of national security. In that case the Home Secretary can appoint a committee to hear arguments before the deportation order is carried out, but it cannot be legally challenged.

Anyone else can have a decision on his or her case reviewed by an immigration appeals adjudicator. Adjudicators sit at various centres in Britain, but not abroad, so appeals by people who are refused entry or who are expelled have to be heard in their absence. However, someone who arrives with a valid entry clearance and is then refused entry on special grounds has the right to remain in the country – usually in detention – until the appeal is heard.

An appeal against an adjudicator's decision can be made to the Immigration Appeals Tribunal in London, but only on arguable points of law or if a person being expelled claims to be a political refugee who should not be returned to his own country.

A few cases involving deportation on grounds of public good, or deportation of the family of a person being deported, go directly to the tribunal.

In any immigration appeal the only issues are whether the ruling appealed against was made within the law, or whether an official's power of discretion – for example, in deciding whether a family relationship is satisfactorily proved – was properly exercised. No appeal authority has the power to say that someone should be allowed into Britain or be allowed to stay if the case falls outside those limits.

THE TIME LIMITS FOR IMMIGRATION APPEALS

Immigration decisions against which there is a right of appeal, and the time limits in each case, are shown below:

Refusal of entry clearance abroad	3 months
Refusal of entry on arrival – no clearance issued abroad	28 days after leaving UK
Refusal of entry on arrival – clearance issued abroad	Lodged immediately by passenger claiming right to wait in Britain
Refusal of patriality certificate abroad	3 months
Refusal of patriality certificate by Home Office	14 days
Refusal to extend time limit on stay or to cancel other conditions such as work ban	14 days
Refusal of stay for person previously exempt, such as a diplomat who resigns his post	14 days
Deportation	14 days from notification of intention to make order. No appeal against order itself
Removal – when legality of expulsion is challenged	28 days after leaving
Removal – when appellant objects to country to which he is being sent	14 days. Destination is normally country of nationality, but Home Secretary can direct removal to any country he thinks likely to admit person removed
Refusal to allow re-entry by cancelling an earlier deportation order	28 days

Late appeals An immigration appeals adjudicator may accept an appeal lodged after the time limit if he thinks there are special circumstances. But once an adjudicator has given his decision on an appeal and stated a time limit on any further right of appeal, a late claim is not permitted in any circumstances.

Although there is no direct right of appeal to the courts, the High Court has the power of judicial review. That means that if judges find that a decision by an official authority such as the Immigration Appeals Tribunal is clearly wrong in law, they can make an order quashing the decision – declaring it invalid.

How the appeal system works

Any official who refuses an application under the Immigration Act must issue a notice stating his reasons, and telling the applicant of his or her right of appeal and the time limit for lodging an appeal. Whenever there is a right of appeal, a 'notice of appeal' form with directions on how to complete it must also be issued.

The completed form must be returned within the time limit to the official who made the decision. It is his duty to forward it as quickly as possible, with a statement of the facts and his reasons for the decision, to an appeals office which arranges hearings.

An appellant – the person making the appeal – has the right to be represented by a lawyer, or he may be represented by someone else with the appeals adjudicator's permission. Many people who do not know a suitable British lawyer seek the help of the United Kingdom Immigrants Advisory Service, a government-funded but independent organisation which provides free legal advice and representation to appellants abroad or in Britain.

The time taken for a case to be heard depends on the type of appeal and the area where it arises. Entry clearance appeals lodged on the Indian subcontinent can take up to 2 years – but the appeal of someone who is refused entry after arriving with an entry clearance is likely to be heard within a week. Such a person has the right to wait – in detention – until his case is decided.

The appeals office notifies the appellant or his representative of the time and place of the hearing, giving usually 4–6 weeks' notice. It also sends copies of the official's explanatory statement and any other documents – for example, medical reports – which make up his case. If the appellant wants to submit documentary evidence of his own, he should send it to the appeals office at least a week before the hearing.

Hearings are public and can be reported – though it is rare for the Press or any people not involved in the case to be present. An adjudicator can exclude the public from hearing certain evidence, or prohibit its being reported, if he believes that it is in the interests of one of the parties. The immigration official's evidence is contained entirely in his statement and supporting documents, but the appellant is free to give spoken evidence – interpreters can be provided at government expense – and to call witnesses. The decision is normally given in writing, usually within 1 month, and posted to the appellant. He is informed of his limited right to appeal further to the tribunal, and of the time limit on that. No costs are awarded to either side for appeals to the adjudicator or the tribunal.

Immigrants' tax and national insurance obligations

Immigrants have the same obligations as any other British resident. They must pay INCOME TAX on any taxable income, and must pay NATIONAL INSURANCE CONTRIBUTIONS out of any earned income.

On income from British sources, an immigrant can claim a whole year's personal tax allowance even if he or she starts work partway through the tax year.

Income from overseas sources is fully taxed if the immigrant makes his home in Britain – even if he has not been granted permanent residence. But if his stay is temporary he is taxed only on income sent into the country. A lump sum payment from a former employer overseas is not taxed in Britain.

Immigrants must pay CAPITAL GAINS TAX on any profit from the sale of overseas assets if they become permanent UK residents. Those assets are also liable to CAPITAL TRANSFER TAX if they are given or bequeathed to others.

Interest on British Government securities, which is tax-free if held by overseas residents, becomes liable to income tax when an immigrant makes his home in Britain.

Social security benefits

The qualification rules for most social security benefits make no distinction between British citizens and immigrants. Any immigrant can apply for SUPPLEMENTARY BENEFIT, and if an immigrant has paid enough national insurance contributions he can apply for other SOCIAL SECURITY BENEFITS that are subject to contribution conditions. For non-contributory benefits it is usually necessary to have lived in Britain for a minimum period.

IMMUNISATION

Society's first line of defence against the 'killer' viruses

Immunisation, which includes inoculation and vaccination, is the most successful method yet devised to protect communities against the spread of serious contagious and infectious diseases.

Large numbers of people can be made immune quickly and effectively by inoculating or vaccinating. Strictly, inoculation means introducing an infective substance into the body by breaking the skin. Vaccination is injecting with cowpox to combat smallpox. 'Vaccination', however, is generally used to describe inoculation.

Immunisation is voluntary and is generally available free under the National Health Service, especially for children and whenever an epidemic breaks out.

Adults may sometimes have to pay – for example, if you plan to visit a foreign country where certain diseases are always found. You are entitled to free immunisation only if the foreign country requires it because of an outbreak of disease in Britain, and not if it is merely a routine requirement.

When an adult is required to pay for immunisation for foreign travel, any children must also be paid for.

Many foreign countries ask for proof that you have been immunised against any disease that is prevalent there (for example, cholera), or that may have recently broken out in Britain (for example, smallpox).

In 1978 after an isolated case of smallpox in Birmingham, people from the Midlands area found that many countries would not let them in without an international vaccination certificate.

The necessary form can be obtained from your GP or from a travel agent or local health authority office. The vaccination will usually be administered by the GP, who will then enter the details on the certificate, and stamp it.

There are also private clinics where you can be vaccinated for a fee. There is one at Heathrow Airport, for instance. If you want to find one ask your travel agent for details when you make your initial booking arrangements.

Once stamped, the certificate will not be valid for a few days. You must wait 8 days before a primary smallpox vaccination certificate is valid, 10 days in the case of yellow fever, and 6 days with cholera. But they are then valid for 3 years, 10 years and 6 months respectively.

Protecting the young

Babies, infants and children are particularly susceptible to some diseases,

---

NOT TO BE OVERLOOKED

The Department of Health frequently issues reminders to parents of when children should be immunised.

'There, there – it's all over bar the screaming'

such as tuberculosis. Other diseases, such as German measles, are more dangerous in adults. To meet both needs, the health authorities provide immunisation from an early age, free of charge.

From time to time, the Department of Health and Social Security issues leaflets to remind parents of the vaccinations required by children and of the procedure for obtaining them under the National Health Service.

Usually, parents are told of a suitable age at which their children should be taken to the family doctor. If they are at school, a day is set aside for vaccination by a medical officer.

The course recommended by the Department of Health and Social Security is to be immunised first against polio, diphtheria, whooping cough and smallpox. Inoculations against measles, tetanus, tuberculosis and, for girls, German measles, are given later. Parents are entitled to refuse to allow their children to be inoculated.

Immunisation for adults

Adults who were not vaccinated as children against polio and tetanus can receive the treatment free under the National Health Service.

Women of child-bearing age can receive a free inoculation against German measles. Otherwise, adults are normally required to pay for immunisation unless a disease of epidemic proportions has broken out in Britain or in a country they are intending to visit.

There is no entitlement to free treatment before the outbreak of an epidemic, even if it is known to be imminent.

Dangers of immunisation

Because immunisation involves infecting the body with weakened strains of a disease, there is always a danger in agreeing to be vaccinated or inoculated.

In certain circumstances, which a doctor should foresee, whooping cough vaccine may be dangerous to a child and German measles to an unborn child. No pregnant woman therefore should be vaccinated against German measles.

A doctor who fails to warn parents before vaccinating a child against whooping cough or who fails to check a woman for pregnancy before immunising her against German measles, can be liable for DAMAGES for negligence if a child is damaged or if a woman gives birth to a handicapped child. *See also:* VACCINE DAMAGE

IMPOTENCE

When a husband or wife cannot consummate a marriage

Impotence – sexual incapacity, in legal terms – can be a ground for a NULLITY decree ending a marriage. That applies, however, only if the incapacity has been present from the beginning of the marriage and only if it cannot be cured by some reasonable treatment.

In a man, impotence is an inability to have or sustain an erection. In a woman, it is either a physical defect or a nervous condition of vaginal spasms preventing intercourse.

A husband or wife who is impotent with his or her spouse may be able to have full intercourse with another partner. That, however, does not affect the granting of a nullity decree. *See:* CONSUMMATION OF MARRIAGE

IMPROVEMENT GRANT

How house owners and tenants can obtain financial help

The owner of a house that needs improvements can in certain circumstances obtain a grant from the local council towards the cost of the work. A tenant whose tenancy is protected under the Rent Acts or even a secure tenant of a council house may also qualify for a grant, provided the tenant has the consent of his landlord.

The applicant may be required to produce confirmation from his solicitor that he is the owner or holds a lease for a sufficient time.

There are three types of grant:

Intermediate grant If a house or flat lacks any basic amenities, the owner or tenant is legally entitled to a lump sum from the council to help pay for installing the amenities.

The size of the grant is a proportion of the total cost of the work. The proportion varies from area to area, but is never more than half the actual cost or the prescribed maximum, whichever is the less.

An owner or tenant qualifies for a grant only if the dwelling has been without the amenities for at least 12 months. But councils make an exception when a

TAKING ADVANTAGE OF THE FREE PROGRAMME OF IMMUNISATION AGAINST DISEASE

Children – and in some cases adults – can receive free immunisation against certain diseases. The health authorities recommend specific age periods for the different vaccines and intervals of time between each inoculation.

Age	Vaccine	Interval
First year	Three doses of polio vaccine *and* three doses of triple vaccine (whooping cough, diphtheria and smallpox) sometimes without the whooping cough	6–8 weeks between the first and second dose; 4–6 months between the second and third
Second year	Measles	At least 3 weeks after the last polio and triple vaccine
4–5 years	'Booster' dose of polio and double vaccine (tetanus and diphtheria)	About 3 years after previous dose of polio and triple vaccine
11–13 years	Tuberculosis and, for girls, German measles vaccine	The German measles vaccine should be at least 3 weeks after that for tuberculosis
Adulthood	Polio and tetanus vaccine	No recommended interval

THE INTERMEDIATE GRANTS THAT ARE AVAILABLE

Amenity	Maximum grant
Fixed bath or shower	£180
Hot and cold water supply to the bath or shower	£230
Wash-basin	£70
Hot and cold water supply to the wash-basin	£120
Sink	£180
Hot and cold water supply to the sink	£150
Lavatory	£270

registered disabled person needs a special amenity. The council usually stipulates that the dwelling should be in a good state of repair and have an expected life of 15 years.

Improvement grant If an owner is making major improvements to a house or flat that has a rateable value of not more than £225 (£400 in London), the local council can, at its discretion, make a grant of not more than half the total cost of the improvements, provided that the cost does not exceed £5,000.

Because grants are not intended for owners to create luxury dwellings but to enable them to put older houses into a satisfactory modern condition, improvements must be of such a kind as inserting a damp-proof course, renewing the wiring or providing an indoor lavatory. But councils will not approve a damp-course grant for a self-contained flat built after October 1, 1961 without the special permission of the Department of the Environment, as all necessary amenities had to be provided after that date.

Councils rarely make grants for installing double glazing – although some do for french windows – or central heating. *See also:* AIR POLLUTION; INSULATION GRANT

A council will pay no grant at all if the cost of the improvement scheme exceeds £5,000. To qualify, an owner must revise his scheme and bring the total cost below the limit.

Repairs grant In housing action areas – districts declared by councils as having generally poor living conditions – and general improvement areas – districts that are to be smartened – a house owner or tenant can apply to the council for a grant to pay for repair. In a housing action area the grant is 75 per cent; where there is social need, 60 per cent, and where there is proven hardship, 90 per cent of the total.

The applicant must be someone of limited means who would suffer hardship if he had to pay for the repairs himself. The repair grant is £1,500 maximum, and the council always makes the grant at its discretion, depending on circumstances.

Conversion into flats An owner may also be able to obtain a grant towards converting a large house into two or more flats, or converting an even larger building, such as a barn or warehouse, into one or more dwellings. The total cost of the conversion must not exceed £5,800, and the house must have an existing rateable value in London of not more than £600 a year (£350 elsewhere).

Applying for a grant

Applications for all grants are made on a form obtained from the Housing Department or Technical Services Department of the local council.

Councils generally relax the conditions for making a grant if it is to help improve the accommodation of a disabled person.

If the council refuses – at its discretion – an application for an improvement or repairs grant, the applicant has no right of appeal but can lobby individual councillors who can recommend his case. A councillor's backing of an application may help to alter the council's decision.

The council makes a grant only on condition that the owner or tenant will occupy the dwelling for at least 4 years either by himself or by a member of his household or close family.

A landlord must let the dwelling as a residence, and not a holiday home – which does not fall within the Rent Act – to persons other than his own family if the grant is made.

When the grant is paid

A council normally pays a grant only when the work has been completed to its satisfaction. In some instances – again, at the council's discretion – it may pay the grant by instalments while the work is being done. On improvement grants there would be three interim payments, and the work would be inspected periodically by an environmental health officer.

Councils usually insist on the work being carried out within a year of their making the grant.

INCEST

When sexual intercourse is prohibited

It is a criminal offence for a male of 14 or over to have full sexual intercourse with a female whom he knows to be his:
- mother
- daughter
- granddaughter
- sister
- half-sister (legitimate or illegitimate).

He is also committing an offence if he incites to have sexual intercourse with him a girl under 16 who is his granddaughter, daughter or step-sister.

The law presumes that a boy under 14 is incapable of intercourse.

It is also an offence for a female of 16 years of age or more to have intercourse voluntarily with a male whom she knows to be her:
- father
- son
- grandfather
- brother
- half-brother (legitimate or illegitimate).

If one of those has intercourse with her against her consent he can be charged with RAPE as well as incest. And if the female is under 16 he can also be charged with unlawful intercourse.

If a child is involved in an incestuous relationship, the local authority may apply for the child to be taken into care. *See:* CHILDREN IN CARE

Maximum penalties 7 years' imprisonment. For a male aged 14 or over who has intercourse with a girl under 13, life imprisonment.

INCITEMENT

The offence of encouraging others to commit a crime

It is a criminal offence to incite someone else, by threats, persuasion or other pressure, to commit a crime – even if the crime is never carried out.

If the crime incited is an indictable offence – one serious enough to have to be tried in a crown court – the incitement is also an indictable offence.

THE SPEEDING-TRAP DETECTOR

It is a criminal offence to incite anyone or everyone to break the law.

Invicta ·Plastics manufactured Radatic, an electronic device which would detect police radar traps for catching speeding motorists. Anyone using the device would be committing a breach of the Wireless Telegraphy Acts.

The company published an advertisement showing a speed-restriction sign seen through a car windscreen to which Radatic was attached. The advertisement invited readers to write for the address of their nearest stockist of the device.

VERDICT

The company was convicted of inciting the public to break the law.

If the offence is a less serious offence, and one that can be tried summarily by magistrates, the incitement is also tried summarily.

Maximum penalty The penalty for incitement is the same as that for the intended offence, even if the offence is not committed.

INCOME TAX

How personal circumstances and occupation decide your tax liability

In principle, the more income you receive for work done in the United Kingdom, the greater the proportion the tax man can claim.

INCOME THAT THE INLAND REVENUE CANNOT TAX
When money or acquired assets are yours entirely

You do not have to pay any income tax on:
● Pools dividends, lottery and competition prizes, racing wins and other betting profits.
● Premium bond wins.
● Interest on national savings certificates, bonuses on Save As You Earn contracts, and maturity bonuses on British savings bonds.
● Defence bonds and national development bonds on redemption.
● Voluntary payments from relatives – including from husband to wife and children after DIVORCE or SEPARATION.
● Educational grants.
● Local authority housing improvement grants.
● Gifts from employers to mark special occasions – for example marriage, birth of a child, or retirement – unless an amount is so large that the Inland Revenue sees it as a disguise for wages.
● Bonuses – but not wage or salary increases – from employers for gaining educational or professional qualifications.
● Part of retirement or REDUNDANCY lump-sum payments.
● National Savings Bank interest up to a set limit – £70 in 1979–80.
● The capital part of purchased annuities.

● Certain allowances and gratuities in the reserve or auxiliary armed forces.
● Compensation to victims of Nazi persecution, if exempt from German tax.
● Unemployment benefit.
● Sickness or invalidity benefit.
● Maternity allowance, benefit and grant.
● Family income supplement.
● Industrial injury benefit.
● Child benefit.
● Supplementary benefit.
● War-widow's pension.
● Death grant.
● Widow's special child allowance.
● Guardian's allowance.
● Wound or disability pension.
● Disablement benefit.
● Special hardship allowance.
● Invalidity allowance paid with invalidity pension.
● Attendance allowance for disabled.
But some social security payments are taxed or partly taxed:
● Retirement pension.
● Widow's allowance or pension.
● Widowed mother's allowance.
● Invalid care allowance.
● Invalidity allowance when paid with retirement pension.
● Mobility allowance to disabled.
● Industrial death pension to dependants.

But tax liability differs from person to person because:
● Income from some sources is exempt from taxation.
● Some income is not taxed because of the way it is spent.
● Personal allowances are made for individual needs before tax is charged.

People whose whole income is exempt from taxation – for example, diplomats – or those whose taxable income is less than the tax relief and personal allowances available, pay no tax at all.

Tax is calculated on the amount of income left after exemptions and allowances in each tax year, which always runs from April 6 to April 5. It is charged at rates set by the Government each year on a rising scale: higher incomes are taxed at higher rates.

The different sources of taxed income

The law does not define 'income'. Instead it lists the sources of payments that may be liable to be taxed. The source of your income decides how you are taxed – by PAY AS YOU EARN deductions, by half-yearly instalments, or on demand after the tax year is over.

Taxable income sources are grouped in the following schedules:
● Schedule A – profits from land and buildings.
● Schedule B – commercial woodlands.
● Schedule C – interest on government securities.
● Schedule D
Case I – trading profits.
Case II – professional or vocational profit.
Case III – interest and other annual payments (not covered in Schedule C).
Case IV – interest on foreign securities.
Case V – foreign assets or trading profits.
Case VI – any other profits, including furnished letting.
● Schedule E – employment earnings, including wages, salaries, bonuses, fees and the value of benefits not paid in cash and pensions.

● Schedule F – dividends and other company distributions.

Building society interest and income received from trusts and settlements are taxable, but they are not listed in any schedule.

Most personal income is earned from employment – Schedule E – and is taxed as it is paid, under the PAYE (pay as you earn) system.

Tax is also deducted from many annual payments before they are made – particularly those under Schedule F – but only at the basic tax rate, so people on higher incomes may have to pay more when their total income for the year is known.

People who earn business, trading or professional income under Schedule D are responsible for paying their own tax.

How PAYE works

Most tax on income earned through employment is deducted before the employee gets his or her money, under the PAYE system.

The employee's estimated tax liability for the year is divided into approximately equal instalments corresponding with each pay period, and the employer is responsible for deducting and passing these to the Inland Revenue.

A wage or salary earner taxed under PAYE should not have to pay any extra to complete his liability at the end of a year unless he has other income, or unless his employer has failed to deduct enough. But an employee who stops work or whose family responsibilities increase during a tax year is likely to be owed a refund of overpaid tax.

Tax on some annual payments – for example, MAINTENANCE received under a court order – and on some INVESTMENT INCOME such as company dividends, is also deducted in advance. But only the basic rate of tax is applied at this stage, so someone with a high taxable income may have to pay more when the year is over.

A person whose only income is a wage or salary taxed under PAYE need not make an income tax return each year, but may be required to make one occasionally to confirm that his or her circumstances have not changed.

Anyone who is taxed under PAYE has the right to ask his Inspector of Taxes to make a check on the tax paid if it seems too high.

Being taxed without PAYE

Tax on the earnings or personal profits of SELF-EMPLOYED people, on FOREIGN INCOME, and on any other income not already taxed, is calculated by the Inland Revenue after the taxpayer sends in an INCOME TAX RETURN. Under that method of charging, known as assessment, it is the taxpayer's duty to pay the sum demanded within certain time limits. He does, however, have a right of appeal against an assessment.

INCOME TAX ALLOWANCES

Personal allowances that help you keep more of your money

Everyone is entitled to earn some money without paying tax on it. The amount allowed varies because the law accepts that your personal responsibilities affect your ability to pay. So a family man can claim more than a single person.

The cash value of each type of allowance is set each year, along with tax rates. When tax is deducted through PAYE, the employer is told how much to take from the taxpayer's wages through a coding system. The code number allocated depends entirely on the information submitted to the tax office by the taxpayer. When he wants to claim further allowances – or stop claiming those to which he is no longer entitled – he must do as the self-employed taxpayer does each year: submit an INCOME TAX RETURN, giving details of his earnings and circumstances, or write to his tax office – for instance when he is getting married.

Anyone who is liable to pay income tax – even a baby – qualifies for a basic personal allowance. Widowed, divorced or separated people are classed as single. So are married couples if husband and wife are both working and choose to be taxed separately on their earned incomes; each is entitled to a single allowance.

Married allowance

A man's personal allowance is increased, generally by at least 50 per cent, if he is married and his wife lives with him.

It does not matter whether or not she works, unless they choose to be taxed separately on earned income and retain a single allowance each. But the allowance cannot be claimed in full in the year in which he is married.

When a husband first claims the increased allowance he must send his marriage certificate to the tax office, if it is asked for. A man who lives with a woman but is not legally married to her cannot claim.

A divorced or separated man can

THE BEST TIME TO MARRY AND SAVE INCOME TAX
How even a day's difference can lose or save a great deal of money

A tax year always starts on April 6, so tax months start on the 6th of each calendar month.

Because every married man is entitled to a higher tax allowance than a single man, a man who marries partway through the tax year qualifies for part of the increase. His share is calculated in monthly portions – one-twelfth of the annual increase is allowed for each month he has been married.

A wedding on, say, September 6 is no different from one on October 5 – both dates fall in the same tax month. But a bridegroom who marries one day earlier, on September 5, gains an extra part of the increased allowance because he qualifies in the previous tax month.

Say the marriage allowance is £900 higher than the single person's allowance, and the rate of income tax is 30 per cent. This would give him an extra tax allowance of £75 a month, and a saving of tax of £22.50.

If he applies immediately for a change of PAYE tax code the saving is made through lower deductions from his pay packet.

Otherwise he qualifies for a refund when the tax year is over.

Time of year The best time to marry is towards the end of the first month of the tax year – on or just before May 5 – so that the husband receives the full year's married allowance.

If either husband or wife does not use up all their allowances in the tax year of marriage, the balance can be transferred to the other spouse – but not if they marry on the first day of the tax year, April 6.

claim the increased allowance if he is wholly and voluntarily supporting his wife or ex-wife. He cannot claim if she has any other form of income. And if he pays her under any formal, legally enforceable arrangement – for example, a court order for MAINTENANCE – he does not qualify for a married allow-

ance. Instead he can gain tax relief by claiming his payments as an allowable expense on his tax return.

When a man marries A newly married man is granted one-twelfth of the increased allowance for each month or part-month of marriage in the first tax year.

The only men who gain no immediate tax advantage from marriage are those who already have charge of children – for example, widowers. Claiming the married allowance disqualifies such a man from receiving a special child-care allowance that is granted for the whole year. Rather than give up a full allow-

TWO WAYS A COUPLE CAN BE TREATED SINGLY BY THE TAXMAN
Deciding between separate assessment and separate taxation

There are two ways in which a wife's tax affairs can be handled individually: by separate assessment or separate taxation.

Separate assessment does not change the amount of tax a couple have to pay. The wife is responsible for making her own return and paying her own tax, and she is entitled to any refund of tax she overpays.

An application for separate assessment is generally made when a husband wishes to avoid liability for tax on his wife's income.

Separate assessment can be arranged by applying in writing at any time up to 3 months before or 3 months after the start of the tax year on April 6. Either partner can apply – the other's consent is not needed.

Arranging separate taxation
Working couples on higher incomes may benefit by claiming separate taxation of the wife's earnings. The husband remains responsible for their joint tax return and liability, but the wife is treated as a separate individual on her earned income. She receives a single tax allowance, and her earnings above that amount are taxed at their own rate rather than being added to her husband's. So in effect her income starts at the bottom of the tax scale instead of being taxed at her husband's highest rate. Unearned income – for example, interest on savings – is still taxed at the husband's rate.

The husband loses his married allowance and his wife's earned income relief, so the claim only becomes worth while when a certain level of income is reached. The level can vary from year to year.

A claim for separate taxation – which must be signed by both partners – may be made at any time from 6 months before the tax year starts to 12 months after it ends.

The effect on tax
The point at which a couple will start to save money by having their earnings taxed separately depends on the tax scales and allowances set by the Government.

Example: A husband earns £10,000 from employment and his wife £5,000. His unearned income from investments is £500,

her bank interest is £600. The marriage allowance is £1,815 and the single person's allowance and wife's earned income relief are £1,165.

A joint tax return would show:

Husband – all income	£10,500
Wife – all income	£5,600
Total income	**£16,100**
Less	
Marriage allowance £1,815	
Wife's earned income relief £1,165	£2,980
Net taxable income	**£13,120**

Tax levied on £13,120:

£1,500 @ 25%	£375.00
£8,500 @ 30%	£2,550.00
£2,000 @ 40%	£800.00
£1,320 @ 45%	£594.00
Total tax	**£4,319.00**

But under separate taxation the same couple's return would show:

Husband

Earned income	£10,000
Unearned – self and wife	£1,100
Total income	**£11,100**
less single allowance	£1,165
Net taxable income	**£9,935**

Wife

Earned income	£5,000
less single allowance	£1,165
Net taxable income	**£3,835**

By this method the tax levied on each is:

Husband

£750 @ 25%	£187.50
£9,185 @ 30%	£2,755.50
Total tax levied	**£2,943.00**

Wife

£750 @ 25%	£187.50
£3,085 @ 30%	£925.50
Total tax levied	**£1,113.00**

	£2,943.00
	+ £1,113.00
	£4,056.00
Saving	£4,319.00
	– £4,056.00
	£263.00

But if either of them had earned £2,000 less, a claim for separate taxation would have been foolish.

Their combined tax bill would have been £3,373.00, while the total of their separate bills, because of the loss of the husband's married allowance, would have been £3,606.00.

On the figures used for tax rates and allowances in this example, separate taxation is an advantage only when the couple's total earned income is approximately £14,500 or more.

In practice this cut-off point varies from year to year because of changing tax scales introduced in each Budget.

When a husband stops earning
If a working couple are both taxed by PAYE, the husband's code takes into account most allowances and other forms of tax relief, such as mortgage interest rebate.

The wife's code includes only her earned income relief, if they are taxed jointly, or her single allowance if separately.

If a husband is no longer employed, a working wife may apply to have the family's allowances transferred on to her code so that her PAYE deductions are reduced immediately.

Otherwise, when the tax year ends, the allowances are automatically offset against the wife's earnings on a joint income tax return.

ance in exchange for a part-year one, he should delay his claim until the following tax year.

When a woman marries The Inland Revenue regard a woman as single until the end of the tax year in which she marries. She remains responsible for her own tax liability.

Unlike her husband she does not qualify for any new tax allowance – although if she gives up her employment she will receive a refund of part of the year's PAYE deductions.

The next year Unless a couple arrange to be assessed separately, a husband is held responsible for his wife's tax liability from the start of the first full tax year after marriage. The rate at which she is taxed depends on the size of their two incomes added together.

Wife's earned income relief

When a wife's earnings are taxed with her husband's, he gains a tax relief equal to an extra single allowance – in addition to the married allowance he can already claim – except in the year in which they get married.

That extra tax relief applies only to EARNED INCOME. If the wife's earnings are less than the amount of the allowance, the difference cannot be offset against any other income she has, or against her husband's income.

Additional personal allowance

An extra personal allowance may be available to a taxpayer who is bringing up a child alone. This allowance is equal to the increase a married man is granted on the single allowance. It is usually claimed by people who are widowed, divorced or separated, or by unmarried mothers. But a married man can receive the extra allowance – in addition to his married allowance – if his wife's physical or mental condition makes her completely unable to care for their child. A medical certificate is needed in such a case.

Claiming the extra allowance disqualifies a taxpayer from claiming an allowance for the employment of a housekeeper or someone else to care for children.

Housekeeper allowance

A widowed person who has a resident relative or employee as a housekeeper is entitled to a small allowance – £100 in 1980–81. If the housekeeper is a married female relative, the claimant must certify that her husband is not receiving a marriage allowance for her.

The same allowance is granted to a single taxpayer who has a relative living in the house to care for a brother or sister, provided that the claimant already qualifies for the child allowance.

Age allowance

An increased personal allowance is granted to a taxpayer aged 65 or over – subject to an income limit which is set each year. The allowance rates, which also vary from year to year, usually represent an increase of 30–40 per cent over normal single or married allowances.

The age allowance is given to single taxpayers – including widowed, separated or divorced people – as soon as they are 65, and to married men when either they or their wives become 65. It is payable for the full year and can be claimed on the income tax return form at the beginning of the tax year. The tax office will then adjust the tax-payer's code, and he will be awarded a refund.

Income limit When a taxpayer is earning more than the limit set for the present tax year his age allowance is cut by two-thirds of the excess.

For example if a couple's income is £6,200 and the limit is £5,000 – an excess of £1,200 – the allowance is reduced by £800. On high incomes, this method of reduction can remove the age allowance altogether. But it cannot remove a taxpayer's right to a basic single or married allowance, granted regardless of income. Qualification for the age allowance does not stop a taxpayer claiming other allowances.

A wife's earned income relief still applies to married couples – even when the wife has retired, if she receives a pension paid for by her own national insurance contributions.

Retirement pensions

Pensions, whether State or private, are taxable income and must be declared to the Inland Revenue. There are a handful of exceptions – for example, pensions paid to victims of Nazi persecution are tax-free.

The only circumstance in which you are entitled not to pay the tax is when it was not claimed because of a fault by the Inland Revenue, the failure to pay was discovered more than a year after the end of the tax year in which it was due and your income is less than £4,000 (in 1980) a year. However, if an old-age pensioner is presented with a large bill for unpaid tax, he is unlikely to have to pay interest to the Inland Revenue for the period of underpayment.

A woman who receives an old-age pension in her own name – as a result of having paid her own national insurance contributions – is entitled to a separate tax allowance from her husband, known as wife's earned income relief. The allowance is claimed by stipulating the separate contributions on the tax return form.

Lump-sum payments Tax is not due on lump-sum payments from an OCCUPATIONAL PENSION approved by the Inland Revenue. Ex-gratia retirement payments from an employer of up to £10,000 and possibly more are also tax free.

Investment income A retired person whose income is below the tax threshold can obtain a rebate of tax deducted at source on certain investment income – for example, company dividends and interest on some government securities. But tax deducted from building society interest can only be offset against tax due and cannot be repaid. Building societies are not good investments for people who do not pay income tax.

Child's services allowance

A taxpayer forced by age or ill health to depend on the services of a daughter or son can claim a small allowance – £55 in 1980–81. The child must live with and be maintained by the claimant. A widowed person can benefit by claiming instead a housekeeper allowance, which is usually worth about twice as much.

Dependent relative allowance

Taxpayers can claim a special allowance for any dependent relatives – including in-laws – who live with them or are partly supported by them. The relative can be a widowed, divorced or separated mother, any relative over 65 or any relative incapable of looking after himself or herself.

If the relative's taxable income is more than the basic single rate of old age pension, the claimant's tax allowance is reduced. It goes down £1 for every £1 of excess income, and can be removed entirely. A taxpayer can often gain more benefit by paying a covenanted sum to the relative instead of seeking the dependent relative allowance. *See:* COVENANT

Blind allowance

A blind person registered with the social services department of a local council can claim an additional tax allowance – £180 in 1979–80. But it is reduced by the amount of any social security disability benefit, and it disqualifies the person from claiming a child's services allowance.

A married man can claim the blind allowance on his tax return if his wife qualifies as a blind person. If husband and wife are both blind, they can claim two allowances. *See:* DISABLEMENT

Widow's bereavement allowance

When a man entitled to the married man's allowance dies, his widow will be entitled (for the remainder of that tax year) to an allowance equivalent to the difference between the married and single allowances. *See:* WIDOW'S TAX

INCOME TAX ASSESSMENT

When the tax man works out how much you owe

If tax on some or all of your income was not deducted before you were paid, it is charged against you by assessment. That means that Inland Revenue works out how much is owed and sends a demand for payment.

An assessment is also used to confirm the accuracy of deductions under PAYE or to check the claims of people who believe that they have paid too much tax.

Calculations are based on the INCOME TAX RETURN completed by the taxpayer, plus any other information the Inland Revenue might receive from people who have paid income to the taxpayer.

If no return is made, or an inspector of taxes thinks that a return is incomplete, he is entitled to guess what the taxpayer owes. His guess is likely to favour the Government, and the taxpayer may also be prosecuted for tax evasion.

Whenever an assessment shows that tax has been underpaid or overpaid, a notice of assessment is sent to the taxpayer. It is a form intended to explain how the taxable income was calculated after taking allowances into account, the rates at which tax is levied, and how the tax figure compares with the amount already paid for the year.

If an inspector of taxes finds that PAYE coding was accurate and the amount deducted is right, no notice of assessment is sent. But the taxpayer has the right to ask for one.

When assessment shows that tax has been overpaid, a refund is sent with the notice of assessment.

If an employee whose main income is taxed by PAYE is found to have underpaid, and the amount owed is not large, the tax office usually arranges for the employer to recover it by adjusting PAYE deductions in the following year.

When an assessment shows that tax is owed which cannot be recovered by PAYE adjustments – usually because the taxpayer is self employed or retired – the notice of assessment serves as a demand for payment.

The taxpayer has 30 days in which to appeal against the assessment, or else must pay the amount demanded directly to the tax office. Time limits for payment vary according to the type of income, and interest charges are added – at 12 per cent a year from February 1, 1980 – for later payment.

Tax inspectors have the additional power to make revised assessments if they discover that not enough tax was paid in an earlier year. Reassessments cannot normally go back more than 6 years, but if a tax inspector believes that the underpayment was intentional, he can seek an appeal commissioner's consent to go back as far as 1936–7.

Reassessment of an earlier year is most commonly called for because a tax inspector has underestimated the profits of a self-employed person. Estimates are often needed when annual accounts are not ready by the time of the original assessment.

Another likely reason for reassessment is a reconsideration of the way of treating certain income. This happens, for example, when a profit treated as a private capital gain, not large enough to be taxed, is later seen to be a taxable business trading profit. Such reconsideration is not likely to arise under PAYE unless an undisclosed source of

THE TIME LIMITS FOR MEETING A TAX DEMAND

When tax is demanded in a notice of assessment, and has to be paid directly rather than by an adjustment of future PAYE deductions, the inspector of taxes also sends a notice stating the time limit for payment. In many cases the amount owing is split up, and different time limits are applied in the following way:

Type of income	Payment due
Self-employed profits	Half by January 1 in tax year. Half by following July 1
Investment income received without deduction	All by January 1
Investment income received net, with basic rate tax already deducted	All by following December 1

Example: A taxpayer meets his tax liability for the 1980–1 tax year – from April 6, 1980 to April 5, 1981 – by making payments in the following order:

1. Employment earnings – deducted under PAYE.

2. Self-employed profits – half by January 1, 1981.

3. Self-employed profits – second half by July 1, 1981.

4. Bank interest received without deduction – by January 1, 1981.

5. Company dividends and public loan interest, basic rate tax deducted at source – by December 1, 1981.

If an assessment is not raised in time for the normal payment dates to be met, then tax is payable 30 days after the date the assessment is issued.

Interest is charged on late payments.

other income is discovered, or unless through some mistake the taxpayer's allowances were too high.

When you can appeal

If you disagree with the amount of tax demanded in the assessment, you can lodge an objection within 30 days of the date on it. An appeal form may be sent with the notice. If not, ask for form 64-7 from any tax office.

On this form you can give notice of your intention to appeal against the amount of income assessed and against the amount of tax demanded. You are required to say how much tax you believe is being overcharged, and any postponement of payment applies only to that amount. Any amount that is not being challenged must be paid within the normal time limit.

Most appeals are made because an inspector of taxes has based his assessment on estimated figures – for example, when a self-employed person's annual accounts are not ready. As soon as the actual figures are supplied, there is automatically a reassessment. In these cases, giving notice of an appeal is simply a way of gaining more time to get the figures ready.

If a tax demand is disputed after final figures have been taken into account, it is usually because of a disagreement over the allowance for some item of expenditure, or over whether certain income is taxable. The inspector who assessed the tax must try to settle the dispute informally, by letter or in a personal discussion with the taxpayer.

Going for a hearing

The inspector has an obligation to try to settle the appeal informally. If this cannot be done, he must bring it for hearing before a tribunal of commissioners.

Generally the taxpayer has the right to choose between the special commissioners (a panel of full-time tax experts) or the general commissioners appointed in local areas. The latter are chosen from the business and professional community and are paid only their expenses.

Certain technical appeals must go to the special commissioners.

A hearing before commissioners is conducted along the lines of court proceedings, but is not open to the public

and cannot be reported. The taxpayer, who can be represented by an accountant or a lawyer, is responsible for his own costs even if the appeal succeeds.

Either side can make a further appeal on a point of law to the High Court, then to the Court of Appeal and finally to the House of Lords. The successful side can claim costs from the other if a tax appeal reaches a court.

INCOME TAX REFUND

When the tax man has to give some money back

If too much tax is taken from your income by deductions during the year, you are entitled to a refund.

Under PAYE, most overpayments occur when employees die, stop work or qualify for new allowances part way through a tax year. In other cases, taxpayers discover that allowances that should have been claimed in some previous year were overlooked. Refunds can be claimed up to 6 years later.

Where the person or company responsible for paying some part of someone's income also deducts tax – for example, company dividends, public loan interest, trust income and maintenance payments – the recipient may have been overtaxed, particularly if he or she has little or no other income.

A self-employed person can offset a business loss against other income, reclaiming tax already paid. But although a reduction of United Kingdom tax liability may be claimed on foreign income if tax has already been paid abroad, it can never be the basis of a repayment.

How to claim a refund

If changed circumstances entitle you to an extra personal allowance and you are taxed by PAYE, notify the tax office which handles your deductions. Your employer will give you the address if you do not have it. Be prepared to prove your claim – for example, with a marriage certificate.

As well as changing your tax code so that deductions will be lower in future, your employer will be authorised by the Inland Revenue to return overpaid tax to you, either in a lump sum or by offsetting it against your tax instalments for the rest of the year.

People who are regularly entitled to a tax refund are often paid quarterly automatically.

'You never know – it may be a refund'

If you have been out of work for 4 weeks or more, if you retire permanently, or if you are a married woman giving up work for the rest of the tax year, ask the tax office for a refund claim form. Your refund will be sent by post.

If you receive payments that are already taxed, other than by PAYE, give the details in your income tax return and attach evidence – the warrants that come with company dividend or public loan interest cheques, or the certificate (form R185) that the payer of trust income or maintenance is obliged to give you. Any overpayment of tax will show up in your assessment, and a refund follows automatically.

The tax that is deducted from interest payments to building society investors is never refunded.

People who regularly qualify for refunds – for example, pensioners, divorced mothers, and children with investment income – may not need to wait until the end of the tax year. In many cases their tax office will make refunds in quarterly instalments.

If you are seeking a refund of tax paid in an earlier year, rather than the current year or the year just ended, start your claim by telephoning or writing to the inspector of taxes at your tax office.

Interest on refunds If a tax refund is delayed for more than 12 months after the end of the tax year in which tax was overpaid, the Inland Revenue are obliged to pay interest on any amount over £25. The annual interest rate was set at 12 per cent from February 1, 1980.

When a taxpayer goes on strike

Any significant loss of income during a strike will probably mean that an employee's PAYE deductions before the strike will prove to have been too high.

If the dispute is settled and he resumes work during the same tax year, his employer adjusts his remaining PAYE deductions to compensate for the previous overpayment, or he may be authorised by the Inland Revenue to make a lump sum repayment.

There is no legal provision for refunding tax before the end of a tax year to someone who is still on strike, but the Government can authorise the Inland Revenue to make a special arrangement.

INCOME TAX RETURN

When and how to complete your tax return

A taxpayer uses an income tax return to declare all amounts and sources of income and make all claims to tax relief and allowances. That information enables Inland Revenue to calculate how much should be paid in any tax year.

Income details and claims for tax relief are accepted only on the printed

---

RETURN IT – OR BE FINED

It is an offence not to complete and send back an income tax return form within 30 days of issue.

'At least the return postage is prepaid'

---

return forms supplied by the Inland Revenue.

If you receive business or professional income, bank or loan interest, maintenance or trust payments, or other investment or foreign income in any tax year, you must make an income tax return for that year. People who receive such payments regularly can expect to be sent a return form each year.

If your income requires you to make a return and you do not receive a form by the end of the tax year, it is an offence not to notify the Inland Revenue that you are liable for tax. You can be fined up to £100.

If your only income is from employment, and all of it has been taxed under PAYE, you may be sent a return form only once every 3 years, to confirm that your source of income and personal circumstances have not changed.

Anyone who is sent a return form is required to send it back completed within 30 days of the issue date shown on it. Failure to do so is an offence for which he can be fined £50, plus tax unpaid, or £10 for each day overdue.

In practice the Inland Revenue takes no action unless a return is not received by mid-June. After that a reminder notice is sent. If it is ignored, a tax inspector can obtain an order for payment of tax and fines from an appeal commissioner. The defaulter is then liable to be proceeded against for recovery of a legal DEBT.

A PAYE taxpayer who does not receive a form should ask for one if he or she is likely to be entitled to a new allowance in the coming year.

A husband is responsible for declaring his wife's income details in his own return if they live together, unless one of them has arranged with the tax office for separate assessment. If an unmarried child under 18 is living at home and has taxable income, a parent or guardian is responsible for its returns.

INDECENCY

Forcing someone to take part in sexual activity

Any form of sexual activity that is forced on another person without that person's consent is an indecent assault, and the offender can be imprisoned.

It is indecent assault to kiss a woman or girl, or touch her body, without her consent or against her will – or merely to suggest sexual intercourse to her.

The maximum penalty in a crown court for indecent assault on a female is 2 years' imprisonment and an unlimited fine. The offence can however be tried in a magistrates' court if magistrates and defendant agree. The maximum penalty there is 6 months' imprisonment and a £1,000 fine.

A woman can be charged with indecently assaulting another female. If the victim is under the age of 13, the maximum penalty is 5 years' imprisonment: if she is over 13, the maximum is 2 years.

A man or woman convicted of indecently assaulting a man can be imprisoned for up to 10 years in a crown court. In a magistrates' court the maximum penalties are 6 months and a £1,000 fine.

Before sentence is passed in an indecent assault case, the court usually studies medical or social reports on the defendant.

Indecency with a child

An adult who indulges in sexual behaviour with a child of either sex under the age of 16 commits an act of indecency, whether or not the child agrees to the activity.

A man who has intercourse with a girl under 16 years of age can be charged with unlawful sexual intercourse, even if she agreed to intercourse. The maximum penalty for a man who commits any indecency with a child is 10 years' imprisonment and an unlimited fine.

A woman who has sexual intercourse with a boy under 16 can be charged with indecent assault. The maximum penalty for a woman convicted of indecent assault or indecency with a child is 2 years' imprisonment and an unlimited fine.

The courts are reluctant to convict an adult of indecency if the child is the only prosecution witness. They usually require some corroboration, which may include medical evidence.

Indecent exposure

A man who exposes his genitals to a woman – publicly or in private – can be charged with indecent exposure. It must be proved that the man wilfully intended to insult the woman. If she saw him merely by accident, he has committed no offence.

The maximum penalty for indecent exposure is 3 months' imprisonment or a £25 fine for the first offence and 1 year's imprisonment for any subsequent offence. A first offender, however, is often given an absolute discharge, provided that he agrees to seek medical help.

If a woman exposes her body in public in an indecent way, she can be charged with a breach of the peace and can be imprisoned for up to a year. She could also be charged with the old Common Law offence of indecent exposure.

Outraging public decency

The act of sexual intercourse in public, witnessed by two or more people, can lead to a charge of outraging public decency and an unlimited term of imprisonment.

INDEPENDENT SCHOOL

Educating a child outside the state system

Parents who send their children to an independent school – one outside the state system, such as a public school or a church school not subsidised by the state – have a contract with the school owners and are considered to have accepted the conditions of entry and the school rules.

Such rules often include a condition that parents must give a term's notice of withdrawal or pay a term's fees in lieu of notice. However, if you can show that the school has failed to keep its side of the contract – for example, by not giving a service it had promised to provide – you may be able to ignore such a condition.

Independent schools have the same duty as state schools to look after their pupils. Teachers act in the place of parents while the children are in school.

The school must keep an admissions register and, except for boarding schools, an attendance register. It must notify the local education authority about pupils who fail to attend regularly, or who are absent for more than a fortnight without a medical certificate.

The local authority can, if it chooses, provide milk, meals and clothing for an independent school as it does for its own schools, and it may decide to allow the school to use library, swimming pools and other facilities. The school health service may provide medical and dental treatment.

Independent schools have more freedom to expel pupils because, unlike a local education authority, they do not have to provide an alternative place at another school. However, the courts have held that the power of expulsion must be exercised reasonably.

Registering and running an independent school

Any school providing full-time education for five or more pupils of compulsory school age must be registered with the Department of Education and Science. The premises must be suitable and the education adequate for the ages and abilities of the pupils. The proprietors and teachers must be morally and physically fit to have charge of children.

The Department of Education and Science can refuse to register a school, or can remove it from the register, if those conditions are not met.

The maximum penalty for continuing to run an unregistered school is a £50 fine on the first conviction and 3 months' gaol with a £50 fine for any subsequent conviction.

> ### SCHOOL THAT EXPELLED AN INNOCENT BOY
>
> *Independent schools have more freedom to expel pupils than state schools, but the power of expulsion must be exercised reasonably.*
>
> After a series of thefts at Haileybury College in 1888, the school authorities planted a marked half-crown in one of the studies. The coin was found next day in Henry Hutt's desk. He denied stealing it and said he did not know how it came to be in his desk.
>
> The headmaster, Mr James Robertson, had the boy locked in the sickroom for the next 2 days until he was expelled. His housemaster wrote to Henry's father: 'He has been caught stealing. Suspicion has long been directed to him. Short of actually being caught in the act no boy was ever convicted on clearer evidence.'
>
> Mr Hutt sued the college for breach of contract, assault and false imprisonment (locking him in the sickroom) and libel and slander.
>
> #### DECISION
>
> The judge said that it was wrong for any boy to be 'branded for life by expulsion' on the authority of one master.
>
> The jury decided that the boy had not stolen the half-crown and that the expulsion was unreasonable. The college agreed to pay £100 to Mr Hutt and to attach a note to the record of Henry's expulsion saying that he was not guilty of theft.
>
> On the other claims it was decided that the masters had reasonable grounds for suspicion and their actions and remarks were made innocently.

When there is a complaint

If the Secretary of State believes that an independent school is unsatisfactory on any of four grounds, a notice of complaint can be served on the school stating full details of the complaint, any measures needed to remedy the deficiencies and a time limit for carrying these out. The four grounds are that:

● All or part of the school premises are unsuitable for use as a school.

● The accommodation provided on the premises is unsuitable, taking into account the number, ages and sex of the pupils.

● Deficient and unsuitable instruction is being given.

● The proprietor or any teacher employed there is not a fit person to be the proprietor of an independent school or a teacher at any school.

The school is given 1 month to appeal against the complaint. If it does so, the appeal is heard by the Independent Schools Tribunal, selected from legal and educational panels nominated by the Lord Chancellor and the Lord President of the Council.

The appellant may be represented by a barrister or solicitor, and the proceedings are usually heard in public.

After hearing the evidence, the tribunal can make an order to:

● Annul the notice of complaint.

● Strike the school off the register.

- Strike the school off unless measures recommended by the Secretary of State are carried out.
- Disqualify the premises as unsuitable, or limit the number of pupils.
- Disqualify the proprietor from being a proprietor of a school or a teacher from teaching in any school.

If the school does not appeal, the Secretary of State can make any of the orders the tribunal might have made.

People who fail to obey the terms of an order can be prosecuted. The Secretary of State can remove a disqualification if circumstances change.

Assisted places scheme

Under the Education Act 1980, the Department of Education and Science will subsidise some places at independent schools for children whose parents could not otherwise afford the cost. Independent schools participating in the scheme will charge lower fees, and possibly make a grant towards boarding expenses.

The amount of the reduction will depend on the parent's income, but is unlikely to cover the whole cost. The scheme is expected to come into operation in time to help children entering independent schools in the autumn of 1981.

INDUSTRIAL DEATH BENEFIT

Who is entitled to payment – and in what circumstances

Industrial death benefit is payable when someone dies as a result of an ACCIDENT AT WORK or an INDUSTRIAL DISEASE. Most claimants are widows, but it may also be paid to children, parents and other dependent relatives.

When a widow can claim

Widows who qualify should always claim industrial death benefit rather than widow's benefit because the rates are higher. The amount of the benefit varies. The highest rate – £38 a week in 1981 – is paid during the first 6 months after the death and in that time an EARNINGS-RELATED SUPPLEMENT may also be payable. After 6 months the benefit is paid at either a high or a low permanent rate.

The high rate – £27.70 a week in 1981 – is paid to the widow if:
- She is also entitled to an allowance for a child.
- She lives with a child under 19 for whom the deceased was entitled at his death to draw CHILD BENEFIT.
- She is over 40 when she no longer satisfies those first two provisions.
- She was over 50 at the date of death.
- She was permanently incapable of supporting herself when her husband died.
- She is pregnant by her late husband.

In all other cases the low permanent rate – £8.15 in 1981 – is paid.

If the deceased had been drawing constant attendance allowance there is no need to prove that industrial accident or disease caused death.

When a marriage had broken down

A woman separated from her husband at the time of his death can claim only if she was receiving or was entitled to receive (and actively seeking to enforce payment of) regular sums of money from him.

Industrial death benefit ceases when a widow remarries. Instead, she receives a gratuity equal to 1 year's benefit.

When there are children

An extra allowance is paid for children for whom child benefit is already being received. If the widow is drawing widow's pension she receives the highest allowance – £7.50 for each child per week in 1981.

All other claimants – who, if they are not the widow, must be contributing to the child's upkeep – receive a lower allowance, which in 1981 was £1.25 a week for each child. If the widow remarries she is still entitled to benefit for the child at the lower rate.

When others can claim

A husband can claim benefit if his wife dies as a result of industrial injury or disease provided he was permanently incapable of supporting himself at the time of her death and his wife had been contributing at least half of his maintenance. The rate awarded is the higher permanent one.

Parents may claim only when they

have been receiving a regular amount of weekly maintenance from the deceased.

Other relatives who may be entitled to benefit are grandparents, great-grandparents, children, step-children, grandchildren, great-grandchildren, brothers, sisters, half-brothers, half-sisters, step-brothers, step-sisters and even parents-in-law.

Anyone who is such a relative by ADOPTION, or would be but for illegitimacy, is also included.

The relative must have been receiving at least half the cost of his maintenance from the deceased or be permanently incapable of supporting himself. If the relative is a married woman she may qualify if her husband is permanently incapable of supporting either of them.

The amount of benefit paid to relatives depends on the amount of support they were receiving from the deceased and on whether they are permanently incapable of self-support.

A woman looking after the deceased's children and living with him at the date of the accident or onset of the disease may claim benefit as long as she continues to look after the children after his death and does not marry or live with a man as his wife.

How to claim

Claims for industrial death benefit for widows and children should be made on form BW1, obtainable from your local social security office. Other claimants should use form B1200, also obtainable from the social security office.

All claimants must be able to produce a death certificate in respect of the deceased; widows also need a MARRIAGE CERTIFICATE and a BIRTH CERTIFICATE for any children. Others will have to produce evidence of their relationship with the deceased. But do not wait until you have collected all the evidence you need. Delay can affect your rights, so put in the claim and follow up with the evidence as soon as possible.

INDUSTRIAL DISEASE

Compensation for illness contracted at work

Anyone who is incapacitated by a

disease he contracted at work may be entitled to compensation under the system of INDUSTRIAL INJURY BENEFIT.

To qualify, the person must be suffering from one of about 50 prescribed diseases, contracted in specified industries, listed on DHSS leaflet NI2.

The list includes:
● Pneumoconiosis.
● Dermatitis.
● Poisoning by lead, manganese, arsenic and other industrial chemicals.
● Certain skin and eye diseases.
● Cancer caused by asbestos, nickel compounds and other substances.
● Tuberculosis.
● And even chronic cramp due to prolonged typing.
● Anyone entitled to this benefit should not merely claim SICKNESS BENEFIT, because the rates for industrial injury benefit are higher.

INDUSTRIAL INJURY BENEFIT

When you can claim compensation for injury or illness

If you suffer personal injury in an ACCIDENT AT WORK or from an INDUSTRIAL DISEASE you may be entitled to an industrial injury benefit (in 1981, £23.40 a week).

If the accident or disease makes you incapable of work you are entitled to benefit for 6 months from the date of the accident or from when doctors agree that the disease started.

Injury benefit is not taxable and may be increased for DEPENDANTS or by an EARNINGS-RELATED SUPPLEMENT. It is paid at a higher rate than SICKNESS BENEFIT, so if you are incapable of work claim injury benefit also when you claim sickness benefit.

A claim is not affected if you are paid by your employer when you are incapable of work. Your employer may be entitled, under your contract of employment, to deduct from your wages or salary the amount of benefit to which you are entitled – whether or not you have claimed the benefit. Some employers automatically do so.

Disablement benefit

Anyone who, because of an industrial accident or disease finds that his power

WHEN A MEDICAL EXAMINATION IS NEEDED

Before it can be decided whether someone is incapable of following his pre-accident occupation, he is usually examined by a doctor nominated by the Department of Health and Social Security.

If a claimant disputes the special doctor's report, he should obtain medical evidence himself.

If he belongs to a trade union, the simplest procedure is to seek the help of its industrial injury experts who can arrange for him to be examined independently. The authorities that deal with social security appeals then reach a decision based on the reports from the Department of Health and Social Security and the independent consultant. *See:* SOCIAL SECURITY APPEALS

to enjoy a normal life is impaired – for example, by the loss of a hand or even a finger – is entitled to DISABLEMENT BENEFIT after injury benefit ceases to be payable.

If, in spite of the disablement, the victim can carry on working, he should claim disablement benefit immediately, since he is not eligible for sickness or injury benefits paid only to someone incapable of working.

Anyone who is unable to work should claim injury benefit for the maximum possible of 6 months, then claim disablement payments.

If he is still unable to work after 6 months, sickness benefit, invalidity benefit or non-contributory invalidity pension may be paid – simultaneously with disablement benefit.

The amount of disablement benefit you will get depends on the degree of disablement. For a small degree of disablement – less than 20 per cent – a lump sum is paid. For any greater degree of disablement, benefit is paid weekly, as a pension.

Disablement benefit is paid regardless of whether earning capacity has been affected.

If earnings have been reduced by the disablement, a range of extra payments may be made. In 1981, the 100 per cent rate was £44.30 a week and the 20 per cent rate was £8.90 a week.

Special hardship allowance

This is the most important of the extra payments, and is received by about 150,000 incapacitated people. To qualify, you must be currently assessed as less than 100 per cent disabled. You must either:
● Have been incapable of following your regular occupation, or suitable equivalent employment, since the end of the injury benefit period.
● Be, and be likely to remain, permanently incapable of following your regular occupation and incapable of suitable equivalent employment.

When a claimant cannot work at all, he is entitled to the maximum special hardship allowance in addition to any

THE INJURED MINER WHO GREW TOO OLD TO WORK

Special hardship allowance paid because of a drop in earning power is still payable even after retirement age.

A coal miner, Mr S, injured his right knee at work and had to take a less well-paid job. He was awarded special hardship allowance to cover the drop in earnings.

Two and a half years later – after passing the compulsory retirement age for coal miners, 65 – he continued to claim special hardship allowance, as well as drawing retirement benefit.

The Department of Health and Social Security opposed his claim, on the ground that whether or not he had been injured, obesity and old age would have prevented his working as a miner.

Since he was drawing retirement benefit, the Department contended, he should not also get special hardship allowance. A national insurance tribunal was asked to decide the dispute.

DECISION

The tribunal held that Mr S was entitled to continue to claim special hardship allowance, based on the difference between what he would be earning if still a miner and what he would be earning if still doing the lower-paid job.

other benefits for which he qualifies, provided that the allowance and disablement pension together do not exceed the 100 per cent disablement rate.

When a disabled person can still work, but only at a job that pays less than he was earning before his injury, he is entitled to claim. If he has a job, the authorities find out how much he is being paid, and also ask his former employers what he would have been earning with them. Subject to the maximum figure, the allowance is the difference between the two. If the claimant is not working, the authorities have a harder task. They must decide what job he is capable of doing and how much he would earn at it.

Special hardship allowance can be drawn, even after retirement age. The fact that old age, apart from injury, makes someone unfit for his former work is not taken into account.

Unemployability supplement

Anyone who, because of industrial injury or industrial disease, is likely to be permanently unable to work, or to earn more than a specified weekly sum, can claim unemployability supplement. The amount of the supplement depends on the age at which the applicant first becomes entitled to it and is payable at the same rate as invalidity allowance. *See:* INVALIDITY.

Increases are paid for dependants, but unemployability supplement and special hardship allowance cannot be paid together for the same period. The supplement can, however, be paid with the constant attendance allowance and the exceptionally severe disablement allowance.

Constant attendance allowance

Anyone who is so badly handicapped as the result of injury or disease at work, that he or she needs constant care and attention, is eligible for constant attendance allowance.

The allowance is available, for example, to someone who is blind, paralysed or bedridden – provided that daily, regular attendance by someone is shown to be needed over a long period. It is not enough that the patient simply needs help to dress and undress. It is enough, however, to prove unpaid attendance by a relative or someone else.

The claimant must either be receiving

a 100 per cent disablement benefit; or he must be getting some benefit plus payment from another disablement scheme – such as a war pension – which together bring his payments to the level of a 100 per cent disablement benefit.

The need for someone to be in constant attendance is considered automatically when a claimant is medically examined on first applying for disablement benefit. A separate claim for constant attendance allowance on form BI 104 is required only when the need for a constant companion arises later on.

If the need for constant attendance is likely to be permanent, the victim may qualify for extra payments if he can prove what is officially called exceptionally severe disablement.

Hospital treatment allowance

Anyone who receives a DISABILITY PENSION at less than the full rate while he is undergoing hospital inpatient treatment for his industrial injury, is entitled to a hospital treatment allowance to raise the pension to the 100 per cent rate. Normally the local social security office invites a claim from anyone who is eligible.

If you are not invited to claim, but believe that you are entitled to do so, ask the social security office for an application form.

When someone incapable of work wants to claim benefit

All claims for industrial injury benefits, invalidity allowance or sickness benefit are dependent on the applicant proving that he is incapable of work.

The claimant must obtain a doctor's certificate – form Med 3 – advising that he should not go to work. But the Department of Health and Social Security does not always regard the certificate as conclusive proof that a claim is valid.

When an illness or injury is prolonged, or if the claimant has a long record of unverifiable ailments, the department may refer him to one of its own doctors. If a claimant returns to work before the department's doctor can examine him, his claim for benefit is not necessarily accepted.

An independent official – called the Insurance Officer – can decide, subject to appeal, that despite the claimant's certificate he was capable of work and

that the claim is therefore invalid.

If the department's doctor disagrees with the claimant's doctor, the Insurance Officer decides whether to allow the claim. The claimant can appeal against his decision to a NATIONAL INSURANCE LOCAL TRIBUNAL and ultimately to the NATIONAL INSURANCE COMMISSIONERS. *See also:* SOCIAL SECURITY APPEALS

INDUSTRIAL TRIBUNAL

The 'courts' that hear most employment cases

Industrial tribunals are statutory bodies, similar to courts, which decide upon many cases arising from employment law.

They deal mainly with legal disputes between employers and employees and sometimes those between employers and official bodies – for example, industrial training boards. But most of the cases involve REDUNDANCY or UNFAIR DISMISSAL.

Some employment matters are outside the tribunals' scope and are dealt with through the ordinary courts. They include:

- Claims for wage arrears.
- WRONGFUL DISMISSAL claims.
- Prosecutions under the HEALTH AND SAFETY AT WORK rules.
- Claims for personal injury.
- Cases involving social security payments.

HOW TRIBUNAL MEMBERS ARE APPOINTED

Each tribunal has three members – a legally qualified chairman, appointed in England and Wales by the Lord Chancellor, and two other people, who do not have to be legally qualified, but who are chosen for their 'knowledge or experience of employment in industry or commerce'.

One is usually drawn from a list of candidates put forward by the Confederation of British Industry, representing employers, and approved by the Secretary of State for Employment.

The other is chosen from a similar panel of names suggested by the Trades Union Congress, representing employees.

Industrial tribunals sit in most cities and large towns. Their hearings are normally open to the public, but a tribunal can hear a case in private at the request of one of the parties. Such requests are rarely granted and never without good reason – for example, if the evidence might contravene the Official Secrets Act or reveal business secrets to rivals.

Tribunal proceedings are less formal than those of ordinary courts, but their decisions are just as binding. Like courts, they can order witnesses to attend and can require the production of documents as evidence. Failure to comply with a tribunal order carries a penalty of £100 and, if the person concerned is a party to the case, the claim or defence may be struck out.

Legal representation at tribunal hearings

Either party involved in a hearing can choose to be represented by a lawyer. But LEGAL AID is not available to meet lawyers' fees for appearing at a hearing and, whatever the outcome of the case, each party usually has to pay his share of the costs. As a result, many people plead their own cases, sometimes with the help of their employers' association or trade union.

In cases involving equal pay or SEX DISCRIMINATION, the EQUAL OPPORTUNITIES Commission may assist with the presentation and the costs. In hearings arising from RACIAL DISCRIMINATION, the Commission for Racial Equality sometimes gives similar help. To obtain the assistance of either commission, write to it with details of the case.

How to apply to a tribunal

The procedures for applying to an industrial tribunal are the same whether the applicant is an employer or an employee.

1. Before making the application, check that:

● You are entitled to do so. A full-time employee who has been in his job for less than a year cannot claim unfair dismissal. Two years' service is necessary to claim redundancy. Part-timers who work less than 16 hours a week have fewer employment-protection rights than full-time staff. *See:* EMPLOYMENT PROTECTION

● An industrial tribunal is the correct place to take your case, and that it is not one – for example, a claim for wage arrears – that is outside the tribunal's scope.

Employers' associations or trade unions can give general advice on whether a claim to a tribunal might be justified. Your local job centre, employment office or unemployment benefit office can supply a series of free leaflets containing information to help you decide

THE CASES AN INDUSTRIAL TRIBUNAL CAN HEAR
How the awards that can be made are limited by law

Industrial tribunals are responsible for deciding many types of cases involving employment law. In addition to making financial awards, they can issue declarations of application – the way in which a law should be applied in a particular case.

Type of case	Maximum award
Appeals against health and safety improvement and prohibition notices	Declaration of whether justified or not
Appeals against levies under the Industrial Training Act	Declaration of whether justified or not
Employees' rights when employer is insolvent	Declaration of entitlement. *See:* BANKRUPTCY
Employer's claim for redundancy rebates	Declaration of entitlement. *See:* REDUNDANCY
Equal pay claims	Back-dated earnings entitlement for up to 2 years
Failure to provide itemised pay statement	Compensation equal to undefined deductions for up to 13 weeks. *See:* PAY
Failure to provide written particulars of employment contract	Declaration of terms of employment. *See:* EMPLOYMENT CONTRACT
Failure to provide written reasons for dismissal	2 weeks' pay. *See:* DISMISSAL
Guarantee payments	£40 in any 3 months
Maternity pay	90 per cent of wages for up to 6 weeks. *See:* MATERNITY
Protective award if employer does not observe redundancy procedures	If fewer than 10 employees, 28 days' pay. 10–99 employees, 30 days' pay. More than 100 employees, 90 days' pay. *See:* REDUNDANCY
Racial discrimination	£6,250. *See:* RACIAL DISCRIMINATION
Redundancy	£3,600. *See:* REDUNDANCY
Sex discrimination	£6,250. *See:* SEX DISCRIMINATION
Time off for trade union activities	26 weeks' pay
Time off to look for alternative employment	Two-fifths of week's pay. *See:* TIME OFF WORK
Trade union membership: discrimination by employer	52 weeks' pay
Unfair dismissal	Basic compensation: £3,600. Compensatory payment: £6,250. Failure to comply with order for reinstatement or re-engagement: £6,240. *See:* UNFAIR DISMISSAL

whether to make an application and how to do so.

Leaflet ITL1 – Industrial Tribunals Procedure – is a broad guide to the way in which tribunals work. Other leaflets offer more specific information on claims for unfair dismissal and redundancy and on other applications under the rules on job protection, as well as those involving sex discrimination, race relations and trade union rights.

2. Check the time limit within which your application must reach the tribunal. Claims for unfair dismissal must be submitted within 3 months of the date on which you left the job. If the application is not submitted within that time, it is unlikely to be heard.

3. Ask your job centre, employment office or unemployment benefit office for form IT1 on which to submit your claim. On it, you must give your name and address, the name and address of the person, company or organisation whose action you are disputing and the grounds on which you are seeking a tribunal decision. If someone else is to represent you at the tribunal hearing, you must give his name and address on the form.

If you belong to a trade union or a trade or professional organisation, it may be able to advise you on how to complete the form. Alternatively, the local CITIZENS ADVICE BUREAU can give general guidance, or you can seek the help of a solicitor. You may be entitled to financial assistance in meeting the solicitor's fees for help in completing the form though not for his attendance at the hearing. *See:* LEGAL ADVICE

4. When the claim form has been completed, make a copy and send the original to the Central Office of the Industrial Tribunals.

When the claim has been submitted

When the central office receives an application for a hearing, it allocates the case to a tribunal in the applicant's area. The local tribunal acknowledges receipt by sending the applicant form IT5 which includes the case reference number.

The tribunal sends a copy of the application form IT1 to the other party in the case – called the respondent – with form IT3, called a notice of appearance. The respondent must complete form IT3, stating whether he intends to contest the application and, if so, on what grounds, and return it to the address shown on it within 14 days.

If the respondent intends to fight the case, it is in his interests to keep his declaration of the grounds for doing so as simple as possible, to avoid giving the claimant information that he may use in evidence in the hearing. He can, for example, merely say that the facts cited by the applicant are untrue.

A respondent should return form IT3 whether or not he disputes the claim. If he does not send it back, he may lose his right to take part in the tribunal proceedings and therefore to have any influence on the amount of any award made against him.

If it is not possible to return the form within 14 days, it should be sent as soon as possible with a note explaining the reason for the delay. The tribunal can, if it wishes, extend time allowed.

A copy of the completed form IT3 is sent to the applicant.

Obtaining more details of the defence

If the details of the respondent's defence are vague, the applicant can ask the tribunal to issue an order requiring 'further and better particulars'. To obtain the order, he should write to the tribunal specifying the information that he requires.

Fixing the date of the hearing

When the tribunal has fixed a time and place for the hearing, it notifies the parties concerned at least 14 days in advance.

If either party has nominated someone else to represent him at the hearing, the notice is sent to that representative. Each party is responsible for informing any witnesses that he may be calling of the time and place of the hearing.

If you cannot attend

If for any reason you cannot attend a hearing on the date fixed, tell the tribunal immediately. It may then decide to rearrange the hearing on a new date. Alternatively, you can, with the tribunal's permission, submit your side of the case in writing. But if you do so, you will not have the opportunity to question witnesses.

Settlements and conciliation

In most cases involving industrial tribunals – though not those arising from redundancy payments – copies of the application and the respondent's reply are sent by the tribunal to the Advisory, Conciliation and Arbitration Service (ACAS) well before the hearing. An ACAS officer may then contact the parties to try to help them reach a private settlement.

Neither is obliged to accept an ACAS offer of help. To refuse it does not prejudice the outcome of the hearing.

If the offer is accepted, information given to the ACAS officer cannot be admitted as evidence at a later hearing without the permission of the person who provided it.

Because of the volume of work involved, ACAS cannot take up all the cases of which it is informed. If you believe that it can help, contact the ACAS director for your region. You can get his address from any employment office.

If the parties to a dispute reach a private settlement, with or without ACAS assistance, before the hearing, they must immediately inform the industrial tribunal in writing. Before an employer makes a voluntary settlement in a dispute arising from a redundancy payment, he should consult the Depart-

BRINGING THE SIDES TOGETHER

The Advisory, Conciliation and Arbitration Service exists to bring both sides together.

ment of Employment. If he does not do so, he may lose his right to have part of the payment offset through the redundancy rebate scheme. The settlement should be approved by an ACAS conciliation officer, otherwise it will not be binding.

Calling witnesses

Either party to a dispute can call witnesses to appear on his behalf at the hearing. They may be required to give their evidence on oath or affirmation.

The person summoning a witness is responsible for informing him of the date and place of the hearing and for providing conduct money to cover travelling expenses. Part of the money can be recovered from public funds after the hearing, provided that the tribunal considers that the witness's presence was necessary.

If a witness is reluctant to appear – perhaps because he fears to do so might prejudice his own job – the person wanting to call him can ask the tribunal for a witness order compelling him to attend.

To obtain a witness order, write to the tribunal giving the case reference number, the name and address of the witness and a brief summary of the type of evidence he would be called upon to give. If an order is issued, the person summoning the witness is required to serve it.

The penalty for defying a witness order is £100.

The rules of evidence in an industrial tribunal are broader than those in other courts. Hearsay, for example, may be admitted, although it is given less weight than direct evidence. Someone knowingly giving false evidence on oath or affirmation is subject to the law on PERJURY.

Documentary evidence

Once a case is raised before an industrial tribunal, the tribunal is required to consider all matters arising from it that come within its scope, whether or not they are specifically mentioned in the original application.

A claim involving redundancy payment may, for example, raise the circumstances surrounding the applicant's dismissal, and the tribunal will examine whether or not it was fair.

Therefore both parties to a dispute

THE DOCUMENTS YOU SHOULD TAKE TO A HEARING

Any documentary evidence that may be of assistance to the industrial tribunal in deciding a case should be taken to the hearing. The documents should include:

1. The contract of employment or written summary of its terms and any other documents relating to it – for example, the company rule book.
2. Details of pay in the employment – wage slips or the company paysheets.
3. Details of pay in any new employment.
4. Documents relating to other benefits received from the employer and from any new employer – for example, travelling expenses, vehicle allowances and subsidised housing.
5. Any booklets or memoranda giving details of pension and superannuation schemes.

6. Details of any expenses incurred in taking up a new job – for example, bills for removals.
7. Documents relating to income tax paid or refunded and to unemployment and other benefits received.

If the case involves a dismissal or redundancy, both parties should take their copies of the notice of dismissal and other relevant correspondence – for example, a written warning for misbehaviour if one has been given, previous commendations for good work and any references given on leaving.

If the company issues written job descriptions and standards of performance – the criteria by which an employee's ability is assessed, for example – those should be taken, too.

---

should take with them to the hearing all documents relating to the employment.

If documents are not released

In preparing his case, an employee in dispute with his employer may want to study company documents of which he does not have a copy – for example, written rules or a personal file. If the employer refuses to make them available, the employee can apply to the tribunal for an order requiring their production at the hearing or for an opportunity to allow him to study them beforehand.

To obtain the order, he should write to the tribunal stating which documents are required.

If the tribunal agrees that the request is reasonable, it serves notice on the employer, giving a date by which he must comply. If he fails to do so, he may be fined up to £100.

Attending the hearing

Most industrial tribunal hearings are scheduled for 10 a.m. or 11 a.m. Those due at 11 a.m. are not heard until the earlier ones are finished. All those involved in a hearing should be there well beforehand.

The tribunal clerk normally explains the procedure before the hearing. The tribunal itself decides the order in which evidence is to be heard and witnesses are to be called.

The parties – or their nominated representatives – may give their own evi-

dence, question their own witnesses and those of the other party, and address the tribunal. The tribunal members can question the parties and witnesses to elicit relevant facts.

Usually, the tribunal announces its decision, with reasons, at the end of the hearing. However, it may decide to postpone a ruling until a specified later date. In both cases, the parties eventually receive a written summary of the decision and the reasons for it.

If the tribunal decides that further witnesses must be called or additional documents produced, it can decide upon an adjournment until a specified later date.

When an award is made

If the tribunal awards financial compensation, the person or organisation against whom the award is made must pay it directly to the other party within 42 days.

If it has not been received within that time limit, the applicant may start proceedings to recover it through a county court.

Tribunals do not normally award costs against the loser of a case: each party has to meet his own. However, a tribunal may award costs if it decides one party has acted frivolously or vexatiously, or if a hearing is adjourned or postponed because of some action or failure by one party and the delay causes financial loss to the other.

In cases involving unfair dismissal, a

tribunal can order the applicant to be reinstated in his old job or re-engaged by his former employer in some other capacity. If the employer cannot tell the tribunal immediately whether reinstatement or re-engagement is feasible and the hearing has therefore to be adjourned, he must pay the costs arising from the adjournment.

The tribunal can order the loser of a case to pay the other's costs if he has acted unreasonably.

How to appeal

Either party can appeal against a decision by an industrial tribunal on an issue of law, but not of fact. They must do so in writing to the EMPLOYMENT APPEAL TRIBUNAL in London within 42 days from the issue of the written summary of the tribunal decision. Information on how to appeal is sent with the written decision.

In certain circumstances, an industrial tribunal can review its own decision and, if necessary, amend it. It will do so if:

● There has been an error by the tribunal staff.

● Notice of the hearing has not been sent to one of the parties or a witness.

● One of the parties or a witness whose presence is essential is not there.

● There is new evidence, the existence of which could not reasonably have been foreseen when the hearing began.

● The interests of justice have not been served.

A request for a review may be made orally to the tribunal at the end of a hearing, or in writing within 14 days from the issue of the written summary.

Claiming expenses

Part of the costs of attending a tribunal hearing can be met from public funds, provided that the tribunal is satisfied that the attendance of the person making the claim was justified.

Both parties in the case and all witnesses, on whichever side, can claim expenses. So can representatives of the parties involved, provided that they are not full-time officials of a trade union or an employers' association, barristers or solicitors.

Expenses should be claimed from the clerk of the tribunal immediately after the hearing.

Travel Second-class rail fare, if the

place of the hearing is more than 6 miles from home or place of work in the United Kingdom, or more than 6 miles from the point of arrival in the UK. If a motor vehicle is used, a mileage allowance of from 2.7p per mile to 6.6p per mile, depending upon engine capacity, may be claimed.

An additional allowance of 0.5p per mile is granted for any passenger in the vehicle who is eligible to expenses for attending the hearing.

Subsistence If the period of absence from home to attend the hearing is less than 2½ hours, no subsistence allowance can be claimed. Other rates are:

2½–5 hours' absence 63p
5–10 hours' absence £1.25
More than 10 hours' absence £3

If absence from home overnight is unavoidable for any of the parties or witnesses, there is an allowance of £15.90 per night, or £17.80 if the hearing is within a 5 mile radius of Charing Cross, London.

Loss of earnings Employees and self-employed people who actually lose earnings as a result of attending a hearing may claim the amount lost, up to a maximum of £14 per day. No extra allowance can be paid, however, if the work concerned is advanced or deferred and the earnings are therefore made up.

Unemployed people who lose their benefit through attending a hearing may also claim up to £14 a day as compensation.

Records of tribunal cases

Details of applications to an industrial tribunal, including the names and addresses of the parties, are entered in a register open to public inspection. It is kept at the Central Office of the Industrial Tribunals in London. There is no fee for consulting it.

The tribunal decision, or the withdrawal of an application, is also recorded in each case.

INFECTIOUS DISEASE

Controlling the natural spread of disease

Any doctor who treats a patient suffering from one of the infectious diseases must notify the district commu-

nity physician so that the patient can, if necessary, be isolated and all likely contacts traced.

They are:

acute meningitis	malaria
acute poliomyelitis	measles
	relapsing fever
anthrax	scarlet fever
cholera	smallpox
diphtheria	tetanus
dysentery	tuberculosis
food poisoning	typhoid fever
infective hepatitis	typhus
lassa fever	whooping cough
leprosy	yellow fever

If someone who is suffering from or carrying an infectious disease refuses to be medically examined, the district community physician can obtain an order from a magistrate in a private hearing for compulsory examination. The patient can also be required to provide blood or urine specimens and to submit to any tests necessary for the diagnosis of his condition.

The magistrate can also order an individual to be detained in hospital.

He can be restrained from leaving — by force, if necessary. There is no right of appeal against such orders. However, if someone believes that he has been wrongfully detained on a magistrate's order, he can sue the district community physician for negligence, in the county or High Court. Alternatively he can complain to the Health Service ombudsman if his detention was due to maladministration by the district community physician.

Acting on the advice of the district community physician, local authorities have power to disinfect premises occupied by someone suffering from an infectious disease. If refused entry, they are entitled to break in. *See:* ENTRY, Right of

If any damage is caused as a result of the disinfecting work, the authority can pay the owner compensation, but is not obliged to do so.

Arriving from abroad

Anyone with a notifiable disease who attempts to enter Britain from abroad can be prohibited from leaving his aircraft or ship, or can be sent to a quarantine hospital, detained for medical examination or required to have his person and clothes disinfected.

If there are not sufficient grounds for

taking such measures, but it is nevertheless suspected that the person is a carrier of an infectious notifiable disease, he can be required to undergo surveillance for a period that will depend on the nature of the suspected disease.

Surveillance involves notifying the port or airport medical officer of any move from the address to which the person is first going and being available for medical examinations when required.

Penalties for offences

It is a criminal offence for someone who knows that he is suffering from a notifiable disease to go to work, travel on public transport or appear in any public place where he might spread the disease. The maximum penalty is a £10 fine.

Anyone ordered to stop work by the district community physician because of a notifiable disease is entitled to compensation for loss of earnings from the local authority. A worker failing to obey such an order is liable to prosecution for going to work, knowing that he is suffering from a notifiable disease.

Parents who send a child to school when told by the district community physician not to do so, because the child has an infectious disease, can be fined up to £25 for each breach of his order.

Someone who disobeys a surveillance order after arriving from abroad can be deported.

INHERITANCE

Dependants can claim for support

Although anyone can direct who is to inherit his money and other property (after tax), by making a will, the courts have power to protect the interests of dependants who are not properly provided for.

They are not bound by a deceased person's stated reasons for cutting a dependant out of his will. Where provision is seen to be unreasonable at the time of death, the courts will override his wishes.

English law does not require a will automatically to provide for a widow and children. They may therefore have to claim in court for a share of the estate. If there is no will the inheritance normally goes to the wife or husband, children, parents or relatives in the order laid down by law. All children are equally entitled to share in a parent's estate – including adopted or illegitimate children. *See:* INTESTACY

Who can claim

Any dependant who feels he was not reasonably provided for in a will or under the intestacy rules can apply for an order for maintenance or a lump sum. Applicants may be:

● The wife or husband of the deceased.
● A previous wife or husband who has not remarried.
● Children of any age, including those adopted, illegitimate or unborn at the date of the death.
● Any other person treated by the deceased as a child of the family. *See:* MAINTENANCE
● Anyone else wholly or partly maintained by the deceased at the time of death.

The court takes into account the financial position of the applicant and of the beneficiaries of the estate. It also considers the obligations the deceased had to the applicant and the conduct of the applicant.

If a widow, widower or former wife or husband applies, the court takes into account the applicant's age and the contribution he or she made to the marriage. Where a maintenance order was in effect at the time of the death the court will normally order a similar amount to be paid out of the estate, so far as the needs of the beneficiaries (such as a second wife and family) allow.

Time for application

Claims for provision out of an estate must be made within 6 months of the grant of probate, where there is a will, or where there is no will, within 6 months of the appointment of an administrator. Ignorance of the death may be accepted as a ground for applying after 6 months have elapsed.

A solicitor should be employed to prepare the application, which must be accompanied by a sworn statement and any relevant documents. Legal aid can be applied for.

Costs of an application are usually paid from the estate, but if the estate is very small and the application is ruled to be not justified, the costs must be met by the applicant.

Where the applicant's needs are urgent, the court can make an interim order before its investigations are completed.

WIDOW WON EXTRA SHARE IN A WILL

The provisions in a will can be altered by the High Court if the judge considers that the dead person did not reasonably provide for his dependants.

Stanley Goodwin died in 1964 and left the residue of his estate to his second wife. It amounted to £1,550 after estate duty had been deducted.

The other part of his estate consisted of a half share of a trust in certain lands and buildings. He left this share and the income from it to the five children from his first marriage.

Most of the wife's share consisted of a £1,100, interest-free loan made to her son. It was repayable at £2.50 per week.

In 1968, the widow asked the High Court for a reasonable provision to be made to her from the estate. She pointed out that duty on the entire estate, including the shares left to her step-children, had been charged against her share of the will, and that because of illness her son had been unable to make any repayment of the interest-free loan for a year.

All Mrs Goodwin had was the house which she and her husband had jointly owned, £120 in the bank, and her rights under the will. She was 82 and unable to work.

The defendants – the step-children and their spouses – said that the son's loan was legally repayable and should be called in. The judge said this was unreasonable because of his illness.

DECISION

The judge said that the only thing that mattered was whether or not the widow had been reasonably provided for under the will. He awarded Mrs Goodwin £8 a week until her death or remarriage, charged on the capital and income of all the estate other than that to which she was already entitled.

The final order may take several forms:
● Periodical payments.
● A lump sum, which may be paid by instalments.
● Transfer of property – for instance, the house in which a divorced wife is living.
● Variation of an existing trust, such as a marriage settlement.

If an applicant dies before he can receive any money or property awarded to him, it reverts to the other beneficiaries of the original will, not to those of his own estate.

Widows and widowers can remarry without forfeiting a payment ordered by a court, but such payments to a divorced wife or husband end with their remarriage.

How a title is inherited

Hereditary peerages and baronetcies pass usually to the eldest son. If there is none, the title goes to the dead peer's nearest male relative – possibly a distant cousin – but only on his father's side of the family.

No one may inherit a title unless he is directly descended through the male line from the original holder of the title.

The older a title, the more extensive are the number of descendant relatives of the original title-holder, so the more likely a remote relative may inherit. Sir Winston Churchill, for example, could have succeeded to the dukedom of Marlborough if the 9th duke had had no son. But Anthony Eden's title of Viscount Avon can only pass from son to son because no one else so far can be a direct descendant.

No adopted or illegitimate son can inherit a title. Nor can inheritance be claimed through a parent who was illegitimate or adopted.

INJUNCTION

How the courts can prevent a wrongful action

An injunction is a court order forbidding some action or conduct that appears to be illegal or wrongful. It can, for example, prevent a publisher from distributing a book if it seems to be defamatory, compel a landlord to take back a tenant who may have been un-justly evicted or order a neighbour to stop making what appears to be excessive noise.

An application for an injunction must be made to the High Court or the county court. The evidence does not have to be as complete as in a full court hearing but the applicant must show that he has the basis for a successful case. If a full court hearing later decides that the action was legal after all, damages for losses due to the injunction may have to be paid.

> ## A DISPUTE OVER THE GARDEN WALL
>
> *A court will grant an injunction only when no other remedy is sufficient. If the plaintiff can be compensated by damages, the court simply orders the defendant to pay, without granting an injunction.*
>
> Mrs B and Mrs T were neighbours. Mrs T erected a building which intruded 3 ft on to Mrs B's land. Mrs B did not complain, however, until cracks caused by the building appeared in her own wall. She asked for an injunction stopping Mrs T from trespassing.
>
> ### DECISION
> The injunction was refused because Mrs B had not taken action immediately. By the time she did so, it would have been unreasonable to have the building demolished. She was granted damages instead.

Applying for an injunction is a complex procedure and a lawyer should always be engaged. LEGAL AID is generally available only for emergency cases involving, for example, wife battering or eviction.

The defendant is normally entitled to be given notice of the intention to ask for an injunction – 48 hours in the High Court, 24 hours in county court cases.

In an emergency

In an emergency – for example, if a battered wife is threatened with further violence or a tenant faces wrongful eviction – an interim injunction may be granted immediately and without the defendant's knowledge.

It will probably be valid for about a

> ## WHEN THE BANK WAS IN THE WRONG
>
> *Even when the defendant is willing to pay compensation for the inconvenience his behaviour is causing, a court may decide to order him to stop.*
>
> When the National Westminster Bank in Cardiff decided to make some essential repairs to its Bute Street branch, it found that the work could be done most cheaply and effectively by trespassing on the adjacent property. Its neighbour refused permission.
>
> The bank instructed its contractor to go ahead and trespass, and the neighbour sought an injunction.
>
> The bank argued that it was unreasonable to stop the work and was willing to compensate the neighbour for any loss.
>
> ### DECISION
> The judge ordered the bank and the contractor to stop trespassing, remove any scaffolding over the neighbour's property and take away all debris.
>
> He said that the bank would have to make its premises safe by work carried out within its own boundaries, however expensive that might be.

week, and a date will be fixed for a further hearing when a permanent injunction can be sought, and the defendant can put his case.

Anyone who disobeys an injunction is in CONTEMPT OF COURT, but the plaintiff has to apply to the court for the defendant to be punished for such a breach. He cannot ask the police to enforce an injunction unless the judge specifically includes a 'power of arrest' in the order.

INQUEST

A coroner's inquiry into the cause of a death

All deaths that are sudden, accidental or suspicious must be reported to a CORONER, who will then decide whether to hold an inquest – a public inquiry into the cause of death.

An inquest must be held if there is

reasonable cause to suspect that someone has died a violent or unnatural death, has died suddenly from an unknown cause or has died in prison. The coroner must also summon a jury when a death has occurred in circumstances that would be prejudicial to public health and safety if they were to continue or happen again – for example, if someone has been killed at a dangerous crossroads which has no warning signs, or if a death is thought to have been caused by a policeman using a heavy cosh.

All cases of murder, manslaughter, suicide, fatal road or industrial accidents, and some deaths arising from alleged medical negligence, must be investigated.

The public has a right to attend an inquest and the proceedings can be fully reported by Press and broadcasters. *See:* COURT REPORTING

If, however, someone has been charged with a criminal offence connected with the death, the inquest is normally adjourned until the criminal proceedings are over.

A coroner must always see the body, if available, before opening an inquest. If he has not done so, the inquest is void. He must also decide whether to hold a POST-MORTEM examination of the body before the inquest.

Disposing of a body

If a coroner decides that an inquest is necessary, the body cannot be released for disposal until the inquest has been opened and formal identification received. If the inquest is to be concluded at one sitting, the coroner issues a disposal certificate at the end of the hearing. Otherwise, the certificate is usually issued as soon as formal identification has been made.

When death has been caused, or probably caused, by a criminal act for which someone has been arrested, the coroner cannot issue a disposal certificate until the arrested person, or his lawyer, consents.

Inquest by jury

Once a coroner has decided that an inquest is necessary, he can either hear the case alone, or summon a JURY, which must consist of not fewer than 7 and not more than 11 members.

Close relatives or personal represen-

tatives of the deceased must be informed of the time and place.

A jury must be summoned, for example, if the death occurred in prison or was the result of a traffic or industrial accident. Jurors can claim compensation for financial loss caused and can also claim a subsistence allowance.

An inquest cannot usually be held unless the dead person's body is available. If, for example, someone is believed to have been murdered and the body secretly disposed of, there can be no inquest – as opposed to a criminal trial – unless the body is found.

If someone is believed to have drowned at sea, and no body has been found, no inquest can be held. However, an inquiry is held by the Department of Trade. If a body is found in the sea, an inquest is held by the coroner for the nearest district on shore.

If, however, a body has been destroyed in a fire or if someone has died in a mining accident after which the body cannot be recovered, an inquest may be held.

In every case, the inquest must be opened as soon as possible after the death. If necessary – for example, if a criminal charge connected with the death is pending – the coroner can adjourn the inquest as soon as formal evidence of identification of the body has been given.

WHEN AN INQUEST INVOLVES A CRIME

An inquest verdict must not be allowed to prejudge any issue of criminal or civil liability. Since the Criminal Law Act 1978, nobody can be charged at an inquest with murder or manslaughter, and the coroner must not declare that any named person is guilty of killing someone, or that a driver was responsible for a fatal accident.

If there is evidence pointing to murder or manslaughter, the coroner can adjourn the inquest and notify the DIRECTOR OF PUBLIC PROSECUTIONS of that evidence. If someone is then charged, the inquest is further adjourned until after his criminal trial.

The police, or the Director of Public Prosecutions, can ask for an inquest to be adjourned while they are making their own inquiries.

Witnesses A coroner has the power to summon as a witness anyone he considers able to contribute relevant evidence. If someone summoned to give evidence refuses to attend an inquest, the coroner can impose a sentence of 3 months' imprisonment or an unlimited fine.

Inquest witnesses can claim expenses for attending a hearing, and can also claim for loss of earnings according to a set scale. In the Greater London area, for example, a maximum of £12.40 a day loss of earnings can be claimed, with £1.65 subsistence for attendance up to 8 hours, and transport costs up to a maximum of £21.60.

Legal representation Anyone who gives evidence at an inquest can be represented by a solicitor, but the lawyer can ask only questions that are relevant to the evidence given. He must not make a speech or submit legal arguments. The coroner decides what questions to allow.

Witnesses may be questioned by close relatives of the deceased, representatives of his insurance company, anyone who stood to benefit from his life assurance, anyone who might have been responsible for the death and trade union representatives if the death was caused by an industrial accident or disease.

An inquest does not continue once someone has been charged with an offence involving the death. Instead, the coroner adjourns the hearing until any criminal proceedings have been disposed of.

How an inquest verdict is decided

When all the evidence has been heard, the coroner, or his jury, will deliver a verdict. A jury verdict does not have to be unanimous, but it cannot be valid if more than two jurors disagree.

Verdicts generally open to a coroner or his jury are:
● Lawful killing.
● Unlawful killing.
● Suicide.
● Accidental death (when death occurs by some mischance that was not the dead person's fault: for example in a road accident).
● Misadventure (when someone has died in an accident that appears to have been partly his fault).

● Death from industrial disease.

● Natural causes.

● Open verdict – when there is not enough evidence to decide how death occurred. That is not necessarily a final verdict: if new evidence becomes available at any time, the inquest can be resumed.

The coroner, when delivering a verdict, indicates the principal cause of death and any additional medical conditions that could have contributed.

Appealing against the verdict

It is possible to challenge a coroner's verdict, although such challenges are extremely rare, and can be made, except for suicide, only on a point of law.

An appeal can be made on the ground that:

● The coroner followed a wrong procedure.

● New evidence has come to light.

● The evidence presented at the inquest did not support the verdict.

Complaining about a coroner's conduct

An inquest is not a criminal or civil trial and the coroner is therefore not allowed to suggest that any particular person is responsible for a death.

A coroner is not legally liable for remarks that he makes in his court, provided that any criticism of anyone is related strictly to the case being heard. If it is not, anyone aggrieved by a coroner's remarks is entitled to sue him.

INSANITY AS A DEFENCE

When a person cannot be held responsible for a crime

A person facing a criminal charge can plead insanity as a defence if at the time of the offence he was suffering from a disease of the mind, to such extent that he did not know what he was doing or did not realise that it was wrong.

Conditions such as epilepsy, cerebral tumour and blood clot on the brain are serious enough to be accepted by a court as evidence of insanity.

When a defence of insanity succeeds, the accused is found not guilty by reason of insanity and is sent to be detained in a mental hospital for an indefinite period.

The test of insanity

The criminal case which established insanity as a defence was that of Daniel McNaghten, who, in 1843, shot and killed Edward Drummond, private secretary to the then Prime Minister, Sir Robert Peel.

McNaghten was found not guilty on the grounds of insanity. The House of Lords put a series of questions to judges, and their answers have provided a guide ever since to testing insanity in the courts.

That guide is known as the McNaghten Rules. There are four:

1. The accused is sane in law until it is proved that he is not.

2. Evidence must be given in court that the accused was insane at the time of the offence.

3. The court must be convinced that at the time of the offence the accused did not know what he was doing.

4. If the court finds the accused insane the verdict must be 'Not guilty by reason of insanity', and he must be detained for an indefinite period in a mental hospital.

In murder cases there is a special rule for defendants who are disturbed but not within the McNaghten Rules. *See:* DIMINISHED RESPONSIBILITY

Unfit for trial A person who is suffering from mental disorder which makes it impossible for him to understand the nature of court proceedings, and to exercise his rights in court, cannot be tried.

The defence has to produce evidence of the accused's state of mind. If the defence of being unfit to stand trial is accepted by the court, the accused person will be found not guilty and committed to a mental hospital for an indefinite period.

If he returns to sanity, the case can be reopened.

INSECTS

How the law safeguards tiny creatures

Some insects and other kinds of invertebrate animals are protected by English law because they are becoming so rare that there is a danger of their becoming extinct.

It is an offence to kill, injure, take or possess any protected animal, or to disturb its sleeping refuge (except where it is in a private house). The maximum penalty is a fine of £500.

The protected species are:

Beetles	Rainbow leaf
Butterflies	Chequered Skipper Heath Fritillary Large Blue
Dragonflies	Norfolk Aeschna
Grasshoppers	Field Cricket Mole Cricket Wart-biter
Molluscs	Carthusian Snail Glutinous Snail Sandbowl Snail
Moths	Barberry Carpet Black Veined Essex Emerald Reddish-Buff
Spiders	*Dolomedes plantarius*

INSULATION GRANT

Help to pay for the cost of saving heat

Council grants are available to help to pay to insulate the roof space and water supply of private houses – for example, by using systems that incorporate glass fibre, granular expanded polystyrene and foamed polyurethane.

CHECKING THE WORK

When a grant is made, the local council always sends an inspector to check the insulation work.

The maximum grant is 66 per cent of the cost, or £50, whichever is less. It is given to all genuine applicants whatever their income. People who get a supplementary pension, a rent rebate, a rent allowance or a rate rebate can get a higher grant of 90 per cent of the cost of loft insulation.

Apply for the grant to your local council as soon as you have a contractor's estimate and before work is started. The council will send an inspector to look at the premises before and after the work has been completed.

Grants may also be available from the council for double-glazing and other forms of insulation and improvements, particularly for the elderly, disabled and those in bad health or on low incomes.

INSURANCE

Buying protection against the hazards of life

Almost everyone requires insurance at some time. In every case there is a risk of something happening that would impose a financial burden, so people make a contract to pay money (the premium) to an insurance company and in return the company agrees to pay them a lump sum should the risk materialise.

In some cases insurance may be compulsory. For example, it is illegal to drive a car on the road without MOTOR INSURANCE, and a building society will not advance a mortgage on a property unless PROPERTY INSURANCE has been taken out.

Most forms of insurance are not compulsory but are often advisable. If holidaymakers fear the possibility of being ill abroad, having to cancel the booking or having their luggage stolen, they can take out travel insurance. Everyone runs the risk of causing loss to others by a TORT: a tile from the roof of a house might fall on a passer-by or a dog may cause a road accident. To meet these risks LIABILITY INSURANCE is available.

Breadwinners in families have heavy financial commitments which they meet out of earnings. If they die prematurely these commitments can still be met if LIFE ASSURANCE has been taken out. Anyone accident prone can take out PERSONAL ACCIDENT INSURANCE.

YOU MUST HAVE
AN INTEREST

To insure something legally, you must have what the law calls an 'insurable interest' in it.

People are free to insure against any conceivable risk if they find an insurer willing to provide for it. But insurance is not a form of gambling, so the insurer must have an insurable interest in the subject of the insurance. If you own the favourite for next year's Derby, you can insure against the risk that he might be unfit to run. However, if you are not the owner and merely place an ante-post bet on the horse, you cannot hedge your bet by asking an insurance company for cover similar to that they would give to the owner.

On the other hand, if you are organising a summer fete you can insure against the risk of a wet day.

Using a broker

Anyone planning to take out insurance can either deal directly with an insurance company or go to an insurance broker who will know the terms offered by several rival companies and who can advise on which is best suited to individual needs. A broker's services are free. He gets his income as commission from the company whose policy the client eventually chooses. Despite that commission, he has a duty to act in the best interests of the client.

The proposal form

Taking out any kind of insurance involves filling in a proposal form. The questions you have to answer enable the insurance company to assess the risk

and decide on what terms it will offer you cover.

You have a duty to supply all relevant information. If someone seeking PROPERTY INSURANCE, for example, has had a fire in the past, he must say so on the form.

The consequences of misrepresentation or failing to disclose relevant information can be serious. The company could refuse to pay out on a future claim if relevant information is not given correctly on the proposal form. *See:* INSURANCE CLAIM

You also have a duty to tell the insurance company if your circumstances change after you have completed the form. For example, someone who took out FIRE INSURANCE on his house would have to tell the company if he subsequently replaced his tiled roof with thatch. If he failed to notify the company and the house was burned down, the company would be unlikely to pay out.

The small print

After receiving a completed proposal form, the insurance company issues an INSURANCE POLICY, which constitutes the terms of the contract. Before that stage is reached, you should ask to see the policy and read the fine print carefully. If you have a broker, consult him and ask his advice. The document will contain many conditions which define the circumstances in which liability will be accepted and the extent of that liability.

Make sure that the risks you want to be covered against are specified and that the amounts you can claim are adequate. For example, a person who insures against the theft of valuable jewellery should make sure that the small print does not exclude items above a certain value. He should also decide whether to accept any excess clauses that might, for example, prevent him from claiming the first £50 of any loss.

Paying the premium

Most forms of insurance are kept in force by the payment to the company of regular premiums, usually once a year. It is the responsibility of the insured to pay each premium when it is due, although most companies allow a few days' grace for the premium to be paid before cancelling the cover.

If the event you have insured against should occur, you must make an INSURANCE CLAIM in writing. If you cannot agree with the company on the sum to be paid in settling the claim, the dispute can ultimately be resolved by court proceedings.

INSURANCE AGENT

*The person who is paid
to sell insurance*

An insurance agent, unlike an INSURANCE BROKER, works for only one company, or at best for a small number of companies. Insurance companies employ agents as salesmen to promote their policies over those of rival companies.

An agent will normally represent no more than say three companies, so he is not someone from whom to seek impartial advice when choosing insurance. That is the role of a broker.

Many insurance agents are part-time and it is not uncommon to find solicitors, accountants, travel agents, garages and others acting as agents.

INSURANCE BROKER

*Free help available when you choose
an insurance policy*

When you are seeking insurance you can choose a company and policy yourself, but the range is so vast that it is usually better to obtain the advice of an insurance broker. He has knowledge of several or many companies and should be able to recommend one best suited to individual needs.

Eventually no one will be able to call himself an insurance broker unless he is registered, under the Insurance Brokers (Registration) Act 1977, with the Insurance Brokers' Registration Council. Registration is expected to be completed by the end of 1981.

Among the registration requirements is the need to have professional indemnity insurance.

Not even a broker gives impartial advice over the entire range of insurance companies. He earns his livelihood mainly from commission paid by companies whose policies he sells, as agent.

Most of a broker's services are free to the customer, including help to complete the proposal form. Ask about any fee before you engage him.

An insurance broker charging someone who is taking out insurance must, under the Insurance Brokers' Registration Council code of conduct, disclose that charge to his client in advance.

If a broker is to recover uninsured losses for a client, he must disclose in advance the basis or scale of his eventu-

> ### THE GUITARIST WHO WAS A BAD RISK
>
> *An insurance broker must exercise professional care in helping a customer to complete a proposal form.*
>
> Mr McNealy was a property repairer by trade but also played guitar in a part-time group. He went to an insurance broker to insure his car and, on his advice, filled in a proposal form for an insurance company, giving his occupation as property repairer. There was no question on the form about part-time jobs.
>
> After an accident in the car Mr McNealy was sued successfully for damages by a passenger who was injured through his negligence. A court upheld the insurance company's refusal to pay out on the policy on the ground that Mr McNealy's failure to disclose that he was a part-time musician rendered the policy void.
>
> #### DECISION
>
> The Court of Appeal held that the broker was negligent in not asking Mr McNealy about part-time jobs when he knew the policy would not be available to someone like a part-time musician. The broker was therefore liable to compensate Mr McNealy in full for all the damage to his car, the damages awarded to the passenger and all legal costs.

al charges.

Like other professional advisers, an insurance broker can be sued for PROFESSIONAL NEGLIGENCE if he gives you poor advice which results in your suffering damage or loss.
See: INSURANCE AGENT
MOTOR INSURANCE

INSURANCE CLAIM

*Obtaining compensation as
smoothly as possible*

If you suffer a loss against which you think you are insured, inform your insurance broker or company as soon as possible. In fact your policy may require you to report the loss within a given time, and some policies require you to notify the police or fire brigade.

If you have any doubt about whether your insurance policy covers you for a particular loss, claim. But remember that making a deliberately fraudulent claim – for example, saying that you lost something in a fire that you did not even possess – is a criminal offence and may also cancel any genuine rights you have under a policy.

When you inform your insurance company, you are sent a claim form, asking for details of how the loss occurred, with dates and times, who was to blame, and a detailed account of the items lost or damaged and their value.

Assessing your claim

In settling a claim, the insurance company applies the principle that you are not entitled to profit from misfortune. If, for example, you insure a new bicycle for £50 and it is stolen 3 years later you can claim only its current value – possibly well below £50. So while it is foolish to be under-insured it is pointless to insure something for more than its true value.

If the sum you are claiming is small – less than £20, say – the insurance company normally sends you a cheque within a few days. With larger claims, the company may ask an independent assessor – called a loss adjuster – to inspect the damage or consider the loss and decide what amount should be paid.

If you disagree with an assessment you too can seek the advice of a loss assessor. You do, however, have to pay for his services, so unless you feel the company's assessment is grossly short of the true value it may not be worthwhile.

When a claim is settled

When an insurance company settles a claim it usually asks you to sign a form of discharge absolving the company from further responsibility in the claim. If you later discover that you could have

> ## DEATH DOES NOT PAY A DIVIDEND
>
> *If a court finds that a dead man committed a criminal act, his survivors' insurance claim might not be successful.*
>
> Mr C had 261 milligrams of alcohol in 100 millilitres of blood when he killed himself driving his car. His insurers refused to pay out under a personal accident policy on the ground that they were not liable for any claim that arose from 'the insured person's own criminal act'.
>
> ### DECISION
> The court found that Mr C was killed as a result of driving dangerously under the influence of drink. The policy, therefore, was void.

claimed more, do not hesitate to pursue the extra claim even if you have signed the form of discharge. Most companies accept any reasonable claim – no matter how much later.

When there is a dispute

Most insurance claims are settled quickly and satisfactorily, but if you have grounds for complaint, ask the British Insurance Association to take up your case with the company. If that approach fails, you must consider taking legal action.
See: INSURANCE

LIFE ASSURANCE
PROPERTY INSURANCE

INSURANCE POLICY

Why it is important to read the policy document carefully

An insurance policy is a legal contract made between you and your insurance company.

As soon as you receive it you should read every line carefully. If it contains anything you object to or omits anything you want to have included, write to the company immediately.

Most insurance policies have five parts:
● Preamble – a generalised introduction to the policy stating that an agreement has been reached between the company, the insurer, and you, the insured.
● What is insured – describing exactly what is insured against what eventualities.
● Exceptions relieving the insurance company from liability – the type of exception clauses varies according to the class of insurance. For instance, in a fire insurance policy there is normally an exception for loss or damage by earthquake, but this would not usually be included in a motor-insurance policy.
● Conditions – the really vital terms of the policy. If you do not comply with them, the insurance company can avoid liability. Conditions vary according to the type of insurance. A burglary policy may stipulate that a burglar alarm should be set; an employer's liability policy may require certain precautions to prevent accidents. *See:* LIABILITY INSURANCE

A MOTOR INSURANCE policy may insist on proper maintenance of the car. Important conditions relate to making a claim. *See:* INSURANCE CLAIM

The burden of proving a breach of a condition lies with the insurance company.
● Schedule – which includes the basic details that apply only to your policy: the policy number, your name and address and other personal information, what is insured for how much, when the premiums are payable, the date the pol-

----

UNDERSTANDING THE SMALL PRINT OF THE POLICY

Make sure that you understand your insurance policy. As soon as you receive the document, go through it line by line. If there are any sections that disturb or surprise you, consult your broker at once.

----

icy begins and the period of insurance.

Once a policy has been issued no material alteration can be made without the consent of both parties. Changes and additions are made by a new document, known as an endorsement, being attached to the existing policy.

Assigning an insurance policy

Most insurance policies include a clause determining whether the policy and its benefits can be passed – that is, assigned – to someone else.

In most cases you must have the insurance company's written agreement if you want to assign a policy – and you must also hand over the goods or property insured to the person who is to benefit. So if you want to give your household fire insurance policy to someone else you have to give them the house as well.

Assignment happens automatically when an insured person dies. The policy passes to his representatives or next of kin. Similarly, in bankruptcy the policy passes to the debtor's trustees.

Cancelling a policy

A policy may include a condition allowing the insurance company to cancel the policy at any time, and setting out how this may be done and what premium will be returned. The company may do this, for instance, because of the number of claims being made under the policy. As a policy holder, you can cancel only if the policy authorises you to do so, except that certain rights to cancel are given by law in respect of LIFE ASSURANCE.

When a policy lapses

Motor-insurance policies have to be renewed before the existing policy expires. Other types of policy often allow a period after the premium is due (days of grace), for payment and renewal of the policy. But failure to renew makes the policy lapse; and no claim in respect of an event occurring after the lapse will be successful. Normally the insurance broker or agent will remind you that your next premium is due. But if no such reminder reaches you and you fail to renew, the policy still lapses.
See: INSURANCE
INSURANCE CLAIM
LIFE ASSURANCE
PROPERTY INSURANCE

INSURANCE PREMIUM

Paying to protect yourself against possible risks

The premium is the amount paid by an insured person to the insurers in return for their willingness to accept the risk being insured against – for example, the risk of a house being destroyed by fire or of injury to the insured person.

The amount to be paid varies greatly according to the market rates. For example, car-insurance premiums are higher if a vehicle is to be driven in London rather than in the provinces. Similarly, higher premiums are generally charged each year to account for inflation.

The premium is usually payable either when the proposal form is sent to the insurers or when the proposal is accepted. If a premium is not paid on time – for example, on the renewal date of a policy – the insurance lapses, and no claim will be accepted.

In certain cases you may be able to claim back part of the premium you have paid – for example, when there has been double insurance.

INSURANCE PROPOSAL FORM

The vital first step in arranging cover

The first step in taking out any kind of insurance is to fill in a proposal form. The form is supplied either by the insurance company direct, or by a broker. It contains questions that enable the insurer to assess the risk and decide how much premium you will be charged.

An insurance proposal form, however, is not merely an application for cover. It forms part of the eventual insurance contract and should not be signed until the policy has been carefully read.

Anyone who makes untrue or misleading statements on a proposal form, or who conceals any relevant information in completing it, risks the rejection of any claim he may make later under his insurance policy. The person seeking insurance must volunteer any fact that could affect the company's judgment, even if the form does not include a question on that point.

For example, a FIRE INSURANCE proposal form may not ask whether the applicant has a criminal record of any kind. But if he has served a prison sentence for any type of crime, he must mention it on the form. Otherwise, if his house later burns down, the insurance company may refuse to pay.

In practice, British Insurance Association companies and Lloyd's have agreed not to deny liability over a private – as opposed to business – policy, provided that any defect in the information is innocent and that the correct information, if known, would not have materially influenced the insurer's judgment.

INTELLIGENCE TEST

How a child's educational potential is assessed

Most schoolchildren have their intelligence quotient, or IQ, tested at least once, to establish how their ability compares with the national average and, in some cases, to form the basis for 'streaming' – dividing an age group into separate classes according to ability.

Parents are not usually informed of the results of IQ tests and do not have any legal right to demand the result.

There is no right of appeal against the consequences of an IQ test. For example, if a child is placed in a non-languages course because of an IQ re-

---

NO RIGHT TO KNOW

Parents are not generally told the result of school IQ tests, and they have no legal right to demand the results – even for their own child.

'What do you mean by IQ 140?'

---

sult, the parents cannot force the school or the EDUCATION AUTHORITY to reallocate him.

Tests where concern is felt When a child's behaviour or pattern of learning causes concern, his school may arrange for an individual IQ test to be given by the local authority's educational psychologist.

The Department of Education recommends that parents should be given the opportunity to accompany the child – though not to be present during the test – and to be given a full explanation of the results. But the parents have no right in law to demand them.

If test results lead to a decision to send the child to a special school, the parents can appeal to the Secretary of State for Education who will order an inquiry. *See:* SPECIAL EDUCATION

Arranging a private test

If you are concerned about your child's ability, you can have his IQ tested privately by an independent psychologist – the local education authority or the British Psychological Society can supply a list of practitioners.

Do not insist on being told the score – most psychologists believe that the test result has to be expertly interpreted to be of any value. Ask instead for details of the child's strengths and weaknesses shown up by the test.

Challenging the results

When a parent feels that his child's ability has been misrepresented by the results of an IQ test, there are several possible grounds for questioning their validity:

● IQ tests can easily identify children of exceptionally high and low ability. They are less accurate at discriminating among the 80 per cent of average performers.

If, for example, your child is placed in a lower stream because of a poor IQ test score but has done well in other recent exams, ask the school to ensure that the IQ test is not the sole basis for selection. Request that the other results and teachers' assessments be taken into consideration.

If those requests are refused, ask that the child be allowed to sit another IQ test. Results of an average child can vary by as much as 10 points from one day to the next.

● IQ tests contain a social and cultural bias, with questions that are familiar to most of the children in the country, but might not be known by an ethnic minority. If you belong to such a minority, therefore, you can challenge an IQ test for its majority bias.

● Some IQ tests have not been revised for years and overlook many recent social developments. One well-known test asks: Where do you buy meat/fruit/bread? The child is supposed to answer: At the butcher/greengrocer/baker. If he said 'at the supermarket', he would get no marks.

Ask your child what questions he was asked in the test; if they seem outdated, challenge the results on that ground.

Children usually receive some preparation for an IQ test, by working on sample questions before they are set the real paper. Such coaching is known to improve performance. If your child did not get enough coaching ask for a properly coached re-test.

INTEREST CHARGE

A trader must state the real cost of buying on credit

Anyone who borrows money or buys goods or services on credit is entitled to know the full cost of the arrangement.

A CREDIT AGREEMENT must show the true annual rate of interest – not merely the flat rate that is charged. An advertisement that quotes an interest rate must include the true rate. For example, a couple buy a £100 refrigerator on credit. They agree to pay £110 – a flat rate of interest of 10 per cent – in 11 monthly instalments of £10. Their debt is reduced by each monthly payment, but the interest charge is not. The couple are paying 10 per cent on money they no longer owe.

A true interest rate is based on a calculation of the average time a borrower has the use of money on credit. In that example, the couple pay a true annual rate of over 21 per cent.

True rates vary not only according to the cash amount charged, but also according to the repayment arrangement. The rate on a debt repaid in weekly instalments would be even higher, because the borrower has less use of the full amount of the loan.

A credit customer who believes that he has been misled should ask his local authority TRADING STANDARDS office to check the agreement.

Local authorities have the power to prosecute traders who mislead the public on interest rates. The offence carries a maximum fine of £400 by a magistrate, or an unlimited fine and/or up to 2 years' imprisonment on conviction in

---

MAKE SURE YOU ARE NOT
BEING OVERCHARGED

In law, you must be told the true rate at which you are paying interest on any credit transaction.

'Clever dick here, asking for the true interest rate'

---

the crown court. A county court has the power to order a reduction of interest if it is found to be excessive.

When a trader or lender quotes the total charge or cost of the credit taken, he must include not only the true annual rate of interest, but also the other charges the debtor must pay under the agreement, even if they are not payable for the use of the credit as such – for example, insurance premiums, service charges, or the lender's surveying charges on a mortgage.

INTERNATIONAL LAW

Deciding which country's laws will settle a dispute

As more and more people travel, work or take holidays abroad, their rights after an accident, loss of property, or a dispute may involve the laws of both England and a foreign country. Scotland has a completely separate

legal system to England and Wales, and so when you have a legal problem Scotland has to be treated as a foreign country.

A set of rules, known as private international law, has been developed to determine which country's laws operate in different situations.

In some cases you can enforce your rights in an English court, even though foreign laws may help you to decide what your rights are. In other cases you would have to go to a foreign court.

When a foreign dispute can be settled in England

Legal action to claim your rights in a dispute arising in another country, or involving a foreign resident or company can be taken in the English courts if:

● The other party in the dispute remains in or comes to England long enough to be served with a writ. But if it would be completely unfair to the other party to allow a trial in England a judge may stop proceedings.

● A company with an office in England is involved. A writ can be served on the company at that office.

● Everyone involved agrees to having the case heard here.

● There are very good reasons why it should be held here – for example, if, despite the involvement of a person or persons from abroad, or the fact that the dispute arose abroad, there are still strong connections between the dispute and England; and provided that the case falls within English court rules of procedure.

That might happen, for example, when an accident occurs in England but the person responsible is a foreigner and leaves England before he can be served with a writ. In that case you can ask a judge to allow a trial in England. The other party must be told that proceedings are being taken.

When disputes must be settled abroad

When you cannot serve a writ in England, and the other party refuses a trial in England, then – unless your dispute is one that a judge can allow under the court's rules of procedure – you have to go to the relevant foreign court to seek compensation or enforce your rights.

WHEN YOU MUST GO ABROAD

If you cannot serve a writ in England, you must generally take action for breach of contract in a foreign court.

When a contract is involved

There are detailed rules governing your rights when an 'international' contract gives rise to a dispute.

When an agreement is reached with a foreign company or individual, or when one of the promises in the agreement is to be performed abroad, the contract may specify which country's laws should operate if there is a dispute. Otherwise the laws of the country that is really most closely connected with the agreement and its performance will operate. To decide which law that is, you must take account of where the parties live, where the agreement was finalised and where it is to be carried out.

Legal aid is available to help you to obtain advice on whether the law of a foreign country or of England governs your rights. You can also seek legal aid to enforce your rights in England. In cases where you can enforce your rights only by going to a foreign court, however, you cannot get further assistance from the English legal aid funds. Ask at the embassy of the country concerned to see if legal aid is available to you under its domestic system.

INTERNATIONAL WATERS

Offshore legal limits

British law extends only to the limit of United Kingdom territorial waters – 3 nautical miles off shore. Beyond that lie international waters where limited British law applies only on British ships and oilrigs. *See:* SEA

INTESTACY

When someone dies without leaving a valid will

If you do not make a will, your property must be distributed after your death according to the rules of intestacy laid down in the Administration of Estates Act 1925. The rules were based on a survey of the usual provisions of wills and are adjusted from time to time to allow for inflation.

Although the rules may work perfectly adequately when small amounts of property are involved, they can never be as satisfactory for larger estates. Only by making a will can a testator arrange his affairs to reduce the amount of CAPITAL TRANSFER TAX payable on his death. And only by a will can he give his heirs freedom to make best use of their inherited property.

Choosing the administrator

If you die intestate – that is, without leaving a valid will – your closest relatives are entitled to apply for legal authority, known as 'letters of administration', to wind up your affairs. The authority is issued by the local probate registry – whose address and phone number can be obtained from a Citizens Advice Bureau – after the intended administrators have provided an account of the ESTATE, paid court fees and capital transfer tax, and sworn an oath to undertake their duties.

A surviving wife or husband has first claim to that authority. Thereafter it can be claimed by the dead person's children over 18, his parents, brothers or sisters and their children, half-brothers and sisters and their children, his grandparents and uncles and aunts.

If the nearest relative does not want to apply – if, for example, he or she is too frail, or inexperienced in business matters – he or she can renounce his or her right by completing a 'form of renunciation', obtainable from the probate registry – without forfeiting his inheritance. The right to become administrator passes to the next in line.

If several relations are of equal standing – for example, if a widower dies leaving several children – they have equal priority and usually select an administrator amicably among themselves.

However, they all have a right to apply and the authority is usually granted to the first suitable applicant.

If – because of a family row, say – he is unacceptable to the other heirs, they can in theory challenge the appointment in the High Court – but such action is rarely necessary.

A maximum of four administrators may be appointed, but one is usually enough. Two must be appointed if a TRUST is to be set up for the surviving husband or wife or for any of the heirs who is under 18.

When someone dies leaving neither a will nor relatives, his estate passes to the Crown and is administered by the Treasury Solicitor's Department.

What the administrator does

When an administrator has accepted responsibility for winding up an estate, his tasks are similar to those of an EXECUTOR appointed under a will. He must:

● Calculate the total value of everything left by the dead person.
● Subtract all of his debts.
● Work out the amount of capital transfer tax due on the amount remaining.

If the dead person's affairs are complex, the administrator may need to consult an accountant or solicitor.

He should then make an appointment with the local probate registry to seek the necessary legal authority to handle the estate.

At the registry, he must show proof of his eligibility as an administrator – the dead person's death certificate, his own birth certificate and any necessary forms of renunciation should be enough. He must also give his account of the value of the estate and cheques for capital transfer tax and probate fees.

He will probably have to raise a bank loan against the security of the estate, to cover the cheques. Having provided all the information required by the registrar, he has to take an oath swearing it to be true and undertaking to fulfil the duties of administrator.

Once approved by probate registry and the tax authorities – who may question his assessment and demand addi-

THE RULES OF INTESTACY

How the law restricts the way in which an estate can be divided when there is no will

Surviving relatives	Division of property
1. Widow/er only – no children, grandchildren, parents, brothers, sisters or their children	Widow/er takes the whole estate.

2. Widow/er, no children, but parents, brothers. sisters or their children	Widow/er takes personal belongings and up to £55,000 – with 4 per cent interest until it is paid. He also receives half of the rest of the estate.
	    The other half goes to the parents, in equal shares if they are both alive.
	    If both are dead, it is divided equally among the brothers and sisters, or their children if they have died.

3. Widow/er or children and grandchildren	Widow/er takes personal belongings and up to £25,000 – with 4 per cent interest until it is paid.
	    Half of the remainder is divided equally among the children, or their children if any have died.
	    The other half is put in trust, from which the widow/er receives the interest during his lifetime, and which the children share equally among themselves when he dies.
	    Alternatively, the children can redeem the trust by paying the widow/er a lump sum in exchange.

4. No widow/er but children or grandchildren only	The property is shared equally among the sons and daughters of the dead person, or their children if any of them have died. Large money gifts to his children in the dead person's lifetime are deducted from the sum they receive from the estate.
	    Awards to children under 18 must be held in trust for them until they come of age. But the trustees – who are usually the administrators – are empowered to spend up to half of the trust on the child's maintenance and education.
	    Illegitimate children have the same rights as legitimate heirs if their parent died intestate; the legitimate children of an illegitimate child can inherit if he or she has died.
	    Step-children cannot benefit under the intestacy rules.

5. No widow/er or descendants, but parents still alive	The parents take the whole estate, shared equally. If only one survives, he or she takes all.
6. No widow/er, descendants or parents, but other relatives alive	The estate is divided equally among the dead person's brothers and sisters, or their children if any have died. If there are no brothers, sisters, nieces or nephews, the following order of priority applies: ● Half brothers and sisters, or their descendants. ● Grandparents – but not descendants of dead grandparents. ● Full uncles and aunts, or their descendants. ● Half uncles and aunts, or their descendants.
7. No relative surviving	The estate passes to the Crown. It is administered by the Treasury Solicitor's Department, which can grant benefits to any dependants or other people who might claim part of the estate.

tional payment – he will receive by post his 'letters of administration'. He must then pay all debts of the estate, before distributing what is left among the family, according to the rules of intestacy.

How an estate is divided

The distribution of the estate depends on whether there is a surviving widow or widower and which other relatives are alive.

The widow or widower has particular privileges – the right to all personal belongings including furniture, cars, horses, paintings, jewellery, clothing and all household goods, but not any items that were used for business, such as a tradesman's van.

He or she can insist on having the former matrimonial home as part of his or her share and is entitled to demand that – if part of the estate has been put in trust for his or her lifetime – any trusts should be redeemed by the other heirs. In such cases – which involve only estates worth more than £25,000 – the other heirs must pay the widow/er a sum that takes into account the size of the trust and the number of years he or she is likely to enjoy it, and then share the trust themselves.

Members of an equal group of relatives – such as the dead person's brothers and sisters – receive equal shares of the estate. If one dies, his descendants are entitled to his share.

Example: John Smith dies intestate, leaving neither widow, children nor parents. After tax and debts are paid, his estate is worth £3,000.

He is survived by his brother Frank and sister Ethel; another brother

George is already dead. Frank and Ethel will receive £1,000 each and each of George's two children is entitled to £500.

However, George's son had been killed in a road accident, leaving two young daughters of his own: £250 will be put in trust for each of John Smith's great-nieces until they reach 18, when they may claim it.

Contesting an administration

If you believe you have a just claim on the estate and have not been adequately provided for in its administration, you can ask a county court – or the High Court if the net estate is worth more than £15,000 – to make an order giving you a fair share. The principal ground for such a claim would be if a claimant had been a dependant of the dead person – his stepchild or his mistress, for example – but is not eligible to inherit under the rules of intestacy. *See:* DISINHERITANCE

Partial intestacy When a will fails to dispose of all the dead person's property, a state of 'partial intestacy' is created. That, however, does not require administrators to be appointed. Instead, the executors take charge of undisposed assets and use them to pay the debts and expenses of the estate. Then the remainder is distributed under the intestacy rules but taking into account any benefits under the will.

INVALID CARE ALLOWANCE

Benefit paid to persons caring for disabled relatives

If you are caring for a severely disabled relative you may be entitled to an invalid care allowance (£16.30 a week in 1981). To qualify you must:
● Be between the ages of 16 and 65 (60 if you are a woman).
● Spend at least 35 hours a week looking after the disabled person.
● Not be earning more than £6 a week.
● Not be attending full-time school or college.
● Normally live in the United Kingdom.
● Be present and have been present in the United Kingdom for at least 26 weeks out of the 12 months before receiving benefit.

To qualify, the disabled person must be your:

parent	step-brother
step-parent	brother-in-law
parent-in-law	sister
grandparent	half-sister
child	step-sister
step-child	sister-in-law
son-in-law	uncle
daughter-in-law	aunt
grandchild	nephew or
brother	niece
half-brother	

And he or she must be receiving an ATTENDANCE ALLOWANCE, a constant attendance allowance at the maximum rate or an allowance for total disablement for INDUSTRIAL DISEASE.

When the allowance will not be paid

The allowance is not payable to a married woman who is living with her husband, or is separated from him but is receiving maintenance from him at least equal to the amount of the allowance. Nor is it paid to a woman living with a man as his wife.

You will not be eligible for the allowance if you are receiving another social security benefit that is as much as or more than the allowance. If the other benefit is less than the allowance, you can claim the difference.

Even if you are already receiving SUPPLEMENTARY BENEFIT you can claim the allowance – but it replaces the supplementary benefit in whole or in part.

Increased allowance payable for dependants

You can claim an increase in your allowance for:
● Any children for whom CHILD BENEFIT would normally be payable (£7.50 a week in 1981).
● Your wife if she is living with you and is not earning more than £9.80 a week or receiving any other social security benefit.

If you cannot claim for a wife, you can claim for a housekeeper if:
● She lives with you.
● She has care of children for whom you claim an increase.
● She does not earn more than £9.80 a week – apart from what you pay her.

How to calculate your earnings to make a claim

When you calculate what you or your dependants earn for the purpose of claiming this allowance, you should deduct reasonable expenses connected with the employment. For instance – fares, overalls, tools, trade union subscriptions and luncheon vouchers up to a maximum of 15p a day.

What happens to your allowance when you retire

The allowance ceases to be payable when you reach the age of 65 – 60 if you are a woman – and draw a retirement pension.

If you do not qualify for a retirement pension of at least as much as the allowance, you can continue to draw the allowance up to the age of 70 (65 for a woman) provided you still satisfy the qualifying conditions. After 70 (65 for a woman) you can continue to draw the allowance even if you are no longer caring for the disabled person.

How to make a claim for an invalid care allowance

If you think you qualify for the invalid care allowance get leaflet NI 212 from your local social security office and complete the claim form – DS 700 – which is attached to it. Send this form back to the social security office without delay.

Claims cannot be backdated for more than 3 months unless there is good cause for the delay, and in no circumstances for more than 12 months.

If you are refused an allowance you can appeal to a social security appeal tribunal against the decision. The reason for refusal and details of how and where to appeal will be explained in the notification sent to you by the social security office.

How other benefits are affected

You are not liable to pay NATIONAL INSURANCE CONTRIBUTIONS while you are not working. But to protect your right to other social security benefits, you are credited with a Class 1 national insurance contribution for each week in which you receive invalid care allowance. These credits count towards other benefits, such as those for sickness, unemployment and retirement pension.

If, for some reason, you find in any tax year that your contribution credits are not enough to qualify for RETIREMENT PENSION (you need 52 contributions credited in a year), you may then apply for home responsibilities protection – whereby the number of years of contributions you need for a retirement pension can be reduced. When your pension is being worked out, the number of years for which you get home responsibilities protection is deducted from the number of qualifying years of contributions you would normally need for a pension. You can get a full pension as long as the reduced number of qualifying years does not fall below 20.

If you are male and stay at home to look after someone, your wife may in the same way find it easier after your death to get a full WIDOW'S PENSION and WIDOWED MOTHER'S ALLOWANCE. In that case, the number of qualifying years required for full pension can be reduced to less than 20 provided it is at least half of the years normally required.

You do not have to apply for home responsibilities protection during any time you receive invalid care allowance – contribution credits count instead.

If you cannot work regularly because you have to stay at home to look after someone and do not get an invalid care allowance then you may get home responsibilities protection. You qualify for any tax year in which you:
● Look after someone who is already receiving an attendance or constant ATTENDANCE ALLOWANCE for at least 35 hours a week.
● Get supplementary benefit so that you can stay off work to look after an elderly or sick person at home.

If you are looking after someone who is getting an attendance or constant attendance allowance you must apply at the end of each tax year, on a form obtainable from the local social security office. If you are getting supplementary benefit to look after someone at home, there is no need to apply: protection is granted automatically.

You may also have a claim for SUPPLEMENTARY BENEFIT to look after a sick person at home.

If any relative of yours is incapable of looking after himself or herself and is living with you, you as a taxpayer can claim a special dependent relative allowance. Make sure also that the invalid in your care is claiming all the benefits to which he or she is entitled.

INVALIDITY ALLOWANCE

Additional benefit paid with an invalidity pension

If you are receiving an INVALIDITY PENSION and were under 60 – 55 if you are a woman – on the first day of the 168 days you needed to qualify for a pension, you are entitled to an invalidity allowance. It should be paid automatically, but if you do not receive it write to your local social security office.

How much you get

The amount of allowance depends upon how old you were when your incapacity began. In 1981 the weekly rate of invalidity allowance payable with invalidity pension was:

For incapacity beginning:

Under age 40 or before July 5, 1948	£5.45
Under age 50	£3.45
Under age 60 (men) Under age 55 (women)	£1.75

Invalidity allowance payable with retirement pension
For incapacity beginning:

Under age 40 or before July 5, 1948	£5.70
Under age 50	£3.60
Under age 60 (men) 55 (women)	£1.80

Once you have been granted an allowance you continue to draw it at the same rate throughout your period of incapacity even though you may enter a different age group.

For example, if you were aged 34 when you first received your allowance and were still incapacitated and unable to work at 54 you would at that time still receive the under-35 allowance.

When someone incapable of work wants to claim benefit

All claims for industrial injury benefits, invalidity allowance or sickness benefit are dependent on the applicant proving that he is incapable of work.

The claimant must obtain a doctor's certificate – form Med 3 – advising that he should not go to work. But the Department of Health and Social Security does not always regard the certificate as conclusive proof that a claim is valid.

When an illness or injury is prolonged, or if the claimant has a long record of unverifiable ailments, the department may refer him to one of its own doctors. If a claimant returns to work before the department's doctor can examine him, his claim for benefit is not necessarily accepted.

An official of the department – called the Insurance Officer – can decide, subject to appeal, that despite the claimant's certificate he was capable of work and that the claim is therefore invalid.

If the department's doctor disagrees with the claimant's doctor, the Insurance Officer decides whether to allow the claim. The claimant can appeal against his decision to a NATIONAL INSURANCE LOCAL TRIBUNAL and ultimately to the NATIONAL INSURANCE COMMISSIONERS.

INVALIDITY PENSION

Benefit paid to disabled people who cannot work

Anybody of working age who is unable to work because he or she is disabled may be entitled to an invalidity pension – after 28 weeks of incapacity – whether or not he or she has paid national insurance contributions.

There are three kinds of pension:
● Contributory – payable in place of SICKNESS BENEFIT to men and women who have paid enough insurance contributions.
● Non-contributory – for men and single women who have not paid enough contributions to receive the contributory pension.
● Housewives' non-contributory – for married women who are incapable of doing both their own household duties and paid work.

INVALIDITY PENSION

Contributory invalidity pension

The contributory pension is paid in place of and at a higher rate than sickness benefit. To qualify you must have been incapable of work – and eligible for sickness benefit or maternity allowance – for a total of 168 days, not counting Sundays. That can be one continuous spell of 168 days, or several periods of fewer days, provided you do not work for more than 8 weeks between each period.

How to claim

Claim in the same way as for sickness benefit – that is by completing a sickness certificate and sending it to your local social security office. If you are already receiving sickness benefit, invalidity pension will be substituted after the qualifying 168 days, and will be sent to you together with any INVALIDITY ALLOWANCE to which you may be entitled.

You must continue to send doctor's certificates regularly to your social security office to ensure that your pension is not delayed or forfeited.

If you are refused an invalidity pension you can appeal against the decision to a social security appeal tribunal. The reason for refusal and details of how and where to appeal will be explained in the notification sent to you by the social security office.

How your benefit could be affected

While you are receiving benefit you must not:
● In any way delay your recovery.
● Leave your present address without saying where you can be found.
● Do any work unless the social security office has told you that it will not affect your benefit (up to £15 wages per week).
● Refuse to be medically examined by a regional medical service doctor.

If you break any of those rules without good cause you could be disqualified from receiving invalidity benefit for up to 6 weeks.

How much you may receive

The amount of benefit you receive depends on the number of dependants for whom you claim. For example, if you have no dependants you will get the invalidity pension plus any invalidity allowance to which you are entitled. If you have dependants, such as a wife, husband, children, mother, father, brother, sister, grandmother, grandfather – either natural or in law – you will get the pension, plus any invalidity allowance and dependants' increase for which you may be eligible.

If your wife earns more than £45 a week, the increase for her will be reduced.

Invalidity pension benefits are reviewed, and usually increased, in November of each year. The current rate is always given in leaflet NI 196, which you can get from your local social security office.

Invalidity pension is £26 a week (in 1981). You can qualify for £15.60 for a dependent wife and £7.50 for each dependent child for whom you are receiving child benefit.

Non-contributory pension

The non-contributory invalidity pension is for men and single, divorced or widowed women of working age who are unable to work, but who are not entitled to sickness or invalidity benefit because they do not have enough national insurance contributions. In 1981, the rate is £16.30.

A married woman is not eligible unless she is living apart from her husband and receiving maintenance worth less than the pension. She may, though, be entitled to the non-contributory invalidity pension for married women.

To qualify you must:
● Be under 65 – 60 if you are a woman – and have been incapable of work for 168 consecutive days, excluding Sundays.
● Have been living in the United Kingdom for the whole of that time.

You must also have been living in the United Kingdom for a total of at least 10 years in the last 20 and have been present for at least 26 weeks during the 12 months before payment begins.

This pension is paid at a lower rate than the contributory invalidity pension, but the rules are similar.

WHAT HAPPENS WHEN YOU RETIRE?

If you retire at 65 – or 60 if you are a woman – and draw a retirement pension, your invalidity pension ceases. But your retirement pension is increased by a higher amount of INVALIDITY ALLOWANCE, provided that your pension is based on your own insurance contributions.

The same rule applies when you reach the age of 70 – or 65 if you are a woman – if you continue to work until that age. Invalidity pension is not payable after 70.

When you choose late retirement

If you do not retire at 65 or 60 but will be entitled to a retirement pension on your own contributions when you eventually do retire, you are entitled to draw an invalidity pension – up to the age of 70 or 65 if you are a woman – when you are incapable of work.

If you are drawing a retirement pension and then cancel your retirement between the ages of 65 and 70 – 60 and 65 if you are a woman – you can draw an invalidity pension if you become incapable of work.

In both cases, to take account of the fact that invalidity pension is not taxable while retirement pension is, the invalidity pension and allowance you would get is at the corresponding lower rate. Days for which you receive invalidity pension do not count as working days for which extra pension is paid.

Increases for dependants

You can claim an increase for a dependent wife and children in the same way as if you were drawing a retirement pension. If no increase is payable for a wife you may be able to claim for a woman caring for any children.

Widow's benefit

If you are a widow entitled to a basic retirement pension on both your own and your husband's contributions, you may be able to choose to receive an invalidity pension based on the higher of the two rates. If the higher rate is on your late husband's contributions, you should contact your local social security office to explain the position.

What happens about income tax

Invalidity pensions and allowances are not taxable. But if you are receiving a retirement pension which has been increased by the amount of invalidity allowance you were receiving before you retired, that increase is taxable.

If you think you qualify get leaflet NI 210 from your local social security office and complete the claim form – BF 400 – which is attached to it. If you are refused a pension you can appeal to a social security appeals tribunal against the decision. Young disabled people aged between 16 and 17 can count time on NCIP towards qualifying for the higher long-term rate of SUPPLEMENTARY BENEFIT.

Non-contributory invalidity pensions for married women

A non-contributory pension is available to:
● A married woman who is living with her husband.
● A married woman who is living apart from her husband and who is receiving maintenance payments equal to or more than the amount of the pension.
● A single woman living with a man as his wife.
To qualify you must:
● Be over 16 – 19 if you are still at school or full-time college – and under 60 when payment begins.
● Have lived in the United Kingdom for at least 10 years during the past 20 years.
● Have been in the United Kingdom for at least 26 weeks during the 12 months before payment begins.
● Have been in the United Kingdom for at least 28 weeks before your application.
● Have been continuously incapable of normal household duties and paid work for 28 weeks.
Periods of more than 28 days' incapacity abroad do not count.
If you think that you are entitled to the non-contributory pension ask for leaflet NI 214 at your local social security office and complete the claim form – BF 450 – which is attached to it. Send this form back to the social security office, who will ask a doctor – usually your own GP – to visit you in your own home to assess the circumstances of your household.
If you are refused a pension you can appeal against the decision. The reason for refusal together with a copy of the doctor's report and details of how and where to appeal will be sent to you by the social security office. You can bring any evidence you like – medical or otherwise – before the appeal tribunal. The tribunal will consider the doctor's report, your evidence and the evidence of anybody you choose to call in.

You do not qualify merely because there are some normal household jobs which you can no longer do. You have to prove that you cannot do normal household duties to a substantial extent and also that you are incapable of paid work. For instance, your heart condition may stop you from washing clothes, lifting heavy pans and cleaning windows, but if you can still prepare meals, order the shopping and do light dusting you will be unable to claim.

The rate in 1981 is £16.30.

INVENTIONS BY EMPLOYEES

When an employee invents something as part of his job

If an employee invents something as part of his job there are two sets of circumstances in each of which the employer is entitled to claim ownership to the invention:
1. If the employee makes his invention 'in the course of his normal duties', it belongs to his employer. The Patents Act 1977 does not define 'normal duties' and there is as yet little case law. But, for example, a research worker who invented something related to a project that he had been asked to undertake by his employer would not be able to claim the invention for himself, although he might be entitled to a 'fair share' of any proceeds.
2. If, because of the employee's work and responsibilities, he has a 'special obligation' to further his employer's interests, anything he invents as the result of his job belongs to his employer. That rule is aimed particularly at senior staff – for example, a director of research and development might not be actively engaged in research, but he would be expected to put his full skill and knowledge at his employer's service.

In all other circumstances the invention belongs to the employee and he is entitled to patent it and to receive any royalties arising from it.

If the employer patents an invention made by one of his employees but which belongs in law to the employer, the employee-inventor is entitled to be named as the inventor on the patent.

Contracts and collective agreements

Many companies put rules about employees' inventions into their employment contracts. Provided that the employee could reasonably have expected to be aware of the rules when he entered the contract, he is bound by them, and the terms on which the employer claims his invention will be upheld.
However, the employer cannot use the rules to secure the right to an invention that has nothing to do with the employee's job.
Any rule which seeks to deprive the employee of his rights in inventions belonging to him is void and unenforceable. Nor does the employer have the automatic right to an invention that, while partly related to the employee's job, does not arise directly from it and was worked upon by the employee in his own time, using his own materials and off his employer's premises.

Claiming a share in the proceeds of an invention

If an employee invents something that, by law, becomes the property of his employer, he may be entitled to a 'fair share' of any profits.
To succeed in his claim, the employee must show that his employer has derived 'outstanding benefit' from patenting the invention. The size and nature of the employer's business are taken into account when deciding if the benefit has been 'outstanding'.
Some collective agreements deal with employees' rights to patent inventions and collect royalties from them. Collective agreement provisions on inventions are legally binding upon members of the union that signed the agreement. Non-union members are not bound in the same way unless the arrangements are specifically incorporated in their individual employment contracts.
If the employer and the employee cannot agree on what is a 'fair share', the employee can apply to the Comptroller General of Patents, Designs and Trade Marks or to the Patent Court, a branch of the High Court, for an order requiring his employer to pay him compensation.

The employee can lodge a claim for compensation at any time during the life of the patent on the invention concerned – 20 years – or within 1 year of the date on which the patent expired.

Patent law is highly specialised. Anyone considering a claim should consult a specialist solicitor.

INVESTMENT INCOME

'Unearned' money that carries an extra tax liability

Investment income is not clearly defined in tax law, but is taken generally to mean anything other than earned income.

Most investment income is liable to an additional rate of tax known as the investment income surcharge which is levied over and above normal income tax.

In practice, investment or 'unearned' income falls into one of six main categories:
● Company dividends.
● Interest from government and local authority securities and loans.
● Bank interest.
● Building society interest.
● Rents from property.
● Income from trusts and settlements.

The surcharge rates vary from year to year. For 1980–1, they were:
First £5,500 of investment income ....Nil
Over £5,500 ....15%

How the surcharge is worked out

With some types of investment income – mainly company dividends and interest from building societies, and certain government or local authority securities and loan stock – what the taxpayer actually receives is a *net* amount.

The basic rate of income tax has already been deducted at source.

To assess any investment surcharge that is still to be paid, the net amount is 'grossed up' – converted back to what it was before the deduction of the basic income tax.

The surcharge is then worked out on the full, untaxed sum.

Allowances Personal tax allowances cannot reduce a person's liability to pay the investment income surcharge unless he has little or no earned income. His personal allowances would have to exceed the total of his earned income and the part of his investment income that is free of surcharge.

However, the taxpayer may be able to reduce his liability to surcharge by deducting some 'annual charges' from the investment income. These include mortgage interest, interest on money borrowed to buy commercial property or for use in a family business, and maintenance payments.

Mortgage interest and maintenance payments may be set against earned income in the PAYE coding notice, but the taxpayer may get greater tax relief if they are set instead against investment income.

IRISH CITIZEN

When a person holding an Irish passport comes to Britain

Since the partition of Ireland in 1921, anyone born in the six Counties of Northern Ireland – that is, Antrim, Armagh, Down, Fermanagh, Londonderry and Tyrone – is a citizen of the UK and Colonies, but he is eligible also to obtain a passport issued by the Republic of Ireland.

Entry to the United Kingdom

An Irish citizen does not need a passport or any kind of permission to enter any part of the United Kingdom, including Northern Ireland. He has the right to live and work permanently in the United Kingdom and to vote in all British elections. He is entitled to stand as a candidate in British and European elections.

When he can be sent home

An Irish citizen, who is not also a UK citizen, can be excluded from the United Kingdom and sent to Eire if:
● He is convicted of an offence involving imprisonment within 5 years of his taking up residence in the United Kingdom, and a court recommends his exclusion. He cannot be excluded if he had lived in the United Kingdom for 5 years or more when he was convicted.
● He took up residence after January 1, 1973, and the Home Secretary considers his exclusion to be conducive to the public good. He cannot be sent away for the public good if he was normally resident in the United Kingdom before January 1, 1973.
● The Home Secretary or Secretary of State for Northern Ireland decides that he has been involved in the 'commission, preparation or instigation of acts of terrorism'.

Someone born in Northern Ireland can be excluded from Great Britain to Northern Ireland unless he has lived in Great Britain for the past 20 years.

Becoming a British citizen

If an Irish citizen, who has been ordinarily resident in the United Kingdom for 5 years, wishes to become a British citizen, he can apply for registration with the Home Office. *See also:* CITIZENSHIP

Obtaining an Irish passport

Under Irish law, an Irish citizen – or someone whose father, grandfather or grandmother was an Irish citizen – is entitled to apply for a passport issued by the Republic of Ireland.

JOINT TENANCY

Protection against eviction for people sharing accommodation

Anyone sharing a rented house, flat or other living accommodation may have only limited security of tenure unless he can show he is either the tenant or a joint tenant. *See:* LANDLORD AND TENANT

A joint tenancy exists where two or more people share the use of rooms in a flat or house and act as a group in paying their rent and in their dealings with the landlord.

As joint tenants they can be turned out of the property only for such reasons as failing to pay the rent or causing a nuisance or if the landlord has a genuine need of the premises.

But if each occupier shares common rooms and no occupier is entitled to exclusive occupation of any part of the house, there is no tenancy at all. One or all of them can be told to leave at any time and there is no protection from the Rent Tribunal.

When the existence of a joint tenancy is disputed

When the occupants of a residential property challenge a threat of EVICTION, a county court will generally accept that a joint tenancy exists – no matter what evidence exists of what was agreed when the property was first let – if, for example:

● Some or all of the rooms are shared by the occupants and the landlord does not live on the premises.

● Rent is paid by one person or by each occupant in turn.

● Repairs, such as mending fuses, replacing tap washers and decorations, are done by the occupants.

● Bills for gas, telephone and electricity are paid by the occupants.

● Any departing occupants are replaced by someone chosen by the people sharing the premises.

It is advisable, however, to establish with the landlord at the outset that the tenancy is a joint one.

A tenancy cannot be joint if:

● Separate agreements are made between the landlord and each of the occupants.

● None of the occupants has exclusive possession of any particular part of the house.

● Departing occupants are replaced by the landlord.

● Rooms are also shared by the landlord, who lives on the premises. *See:* FURNISHED LETTING

Ending a joint tenancy

Many joint tenancies are held in the name of one person who signs the agreement with the landlord and pays the rent on behalf of himself and the other tenants. If that person quits the premises, however, the remaining tenants are protected from eviction by the Rent Act.

Tenancies fixed for a definite term, such as 6 months or a year, cannot be ended by one joint tenant alone even if that tenant is the one who acts for the sharers and who signed the agreement. *See:* FLATSHARING

When money is owed

Each joint tenant can be held responsible for payment of the whole of the rent. If a landlord can trace only one of the joint tenants, that person is liable for the full amount owing.

If a joint tenant leaves a flat or house owing money for gas, telephone or electricity bills, the landlord or other tenants can make him pay only by persuasion or by suing him for DEBT.

JOY RIDING

Driving someone's car without permission

It is an offence to take a conveyance for your use or someone else's use without the consent of the owner or other lawful authority.

The conveyance is usually a car, but the law also covers buses, lorries, vessels, aircraft and (in some circumstances) cycles.

When a 'joy rider' abandons a car he is not guilty of stealing it, although the petrol used has been stolen.

Just getting into a car is not a crime. An accused must have been in control and have moved it – for example, by driving off, or by releasing the handbrake and steering it down a hill. Just getting in a car, however, may constitute the offence of attempt.

Anyone with a 'joy rider' also commits an offence if he or she knows the circumstances. Maximum penalty: £1,000 fine and 6 months' imprisonment or both; endorsement and possible disqualification.

JUDGE

When a judge can be criticised openly without penalty

As long as judges are 'of good behaviour' and act within their jurisdiction they cannot be sued.

Their decisions are based on their own interpretation of Acts of Parliament but are strongly influenced by previous decisions in similar cases, known as case law or 'precedent'.

> ## WHEN CRITICISM WENT TOO FAR
>
> *When a criticism is clearly not directly connected with a judge's decision, however, the law protects him from unwarranted personal abuse.*
>
> In 1900 Judge Darling warned the Press during an obscenity case that if any indecent matter given in evidence was published he would see that the law was enforced.
>
> The editor of the *Birmingham Daily Argus* wrote: 'The terrors of the Mr Justice Darling will not trouble the Birmingham reporters very much. No newspaper can exist except upon its merits, a condition from which the Bench, happily for Mr Justice Darling, is exempt. There is not a journalist in Birmingham who has anything to learn from the impudent little man in horse-hair, a microcosm of conceit and empty-headedness, who admonished the Press yesterday'. The editor of the *Argus* was prosecuted for contempt.
>
> ### VERDICT
> He was found guilty, fined £100 and ordered to pay costs.
>
> ## THE JUDGE WHO WAS ACCUSED OF PREJUDICE
>
> *A judge who is known to hold firm religious views is still able to be impartial even in cases where his views are directly concerned.*
>
> When the editor of the *Morning Post* sought damages in a libel case against the early advocate of birth control, Dr Marie Stopes, the action was heard by Mr Justice Avory. Damages of £200 were awarded.
>
> The *New Statesman* wrote that the judge had allowed his Roman Catholic convictions to prejudice his summing up to the jury, and that 'an individual owning to such views as those of Dr Stopes cannot apparently hope for a fair hearing in a court presided over by Mr Justice Avory'. The editor was charged with contempt.
>
> ### VERDICT
> The editor was convicted but the court accepted his unreserved withdrawal and apology.

When a judge may be criticised

Everyone is free to express his honest opinion on any sentence pronounced by a judge and on the manner in which he conducted a case. That right extends to conversation, in print, to broadcasts, and it allows the critic to use strong terms if he wishes. Public criticism of a judge's decision is not barred even when an appeal is pending.

You are not allowed, however, to imply that a judge reached a decision because he was corrupt or was influenced by extreme political views. That would be a CONTEMPT OF COURT, punishable by a fine or imprisonment.

JUDGES' RULES

The legal code for police when dealing with a suspect

A fundamental principle of English law is that any statement or confession by a suspect to the police can be given in evidence in court only if it has been given voluntarily.

The 'Judges' Rules and Administrative Directions to the Police' are guidelines to govern the questioning, arrest, charging and detention of anybody suspected of a crime. There is a copy of the judges' rules in every police station, but copies are not supplied to individual policemen.

The rules do not have the force of law. A police officer who ignores or breaks them cannot be prosecuted unless his infringement is in itself a criminal offence – for example, assault. But he runs the risk of having his evidence rejected in court and – in serious cases – faces possible suspension or dismissal from the force.

Rules governing questioning

The police can question anyone regardless of whether he is suspected of a crime, if they think he may have useful information. They can do so without arrest, but are not entitled to take him to a police station without his consent.

General questioning – for example, questions as to a suspect's whereabouts at the time of a crime – can continue to the point at which the suspect is charged or told that he may be prosecuted. The suspect is not obliged to answer any of the questions.

Children and the handicapped Young people under 17 and adults who appear to the police to be mentally handicapped must be interviewed only in the presence of a parent, guardian or someone other than a police officer – a social worker, for example. When a child is being interviewed, however, the witness must also be of the same sex.

A child may be questioned on school premises only with the consent and in the presence of the head teacher or someone nominated by him.

The rules emphasise that great care must be exercised when a mentally handicapped person is interviewed. The police should always be aware that the answers may not be reliable. If they do not exercise care, they may fail to persuade a court to accept a confession.

Foreigners When a foreigner is being questioned, an interpreter should be used to take down his statement in his own language. The foreigner should sign only that statement and not the English translation of it.

The right to silence Nothing in law compels anyone – whether or not he has committed a crime – to answer police questions. Except in a court witness box, everyone has a complete right to remain silent – but even in court an accused person may choose to remain silent by electing not to go into the witness box.

Cautioning a suspect

The judges' rules state that as soon as a police officer has evidence that someone has committed an offence, he must warn, or caution, him before putting any further questions. The caution must be precisely these words: 'You are not obliged to say anything unless you wish to do so, but what you say may be put in writing and given in evidence.'

However, anything said before the caution – whether spoken or written – can be given as evidence in court, provided that it was voluntary.

A second caution must be given as soon as a suspect is charged or told that he may be prosecuted. It is almost exactly the same as the first caution except that the police must begin by asking: 'Do you wish to say anything?'

If the suspect says nothing, he does not put himself at a disadvantage in any subsequent prosecution. If, however, he is innocent, it may be advisable to say so at the earliest opportunity.

After the second caution, the police must stop questioning unless it is necessary – under the judges' rules – 'for the purpose of preventing or minimising harm or loss to some other person or to the public, or for clearing up an ambiguity in a previous answer or statement'. If the police do want to put further questions on those lines, they must give a third caution, similar to the previous two.

Taking a written statement

There are detailed guidelines to the police about how a written statement should be taken after a caution.

A suspect must be offered the chance to write his own statement. If he agrees to dictate one, it must be reproduced exactly as it was spoken and he must be given the chance to read and correct or add to it.

When the process of taking a written statement has begun, the police must not question or prompt the suspect, except to make the statement more coherent, intelligible or relevant.

No one is compelled to sign a statement, whoever wrote it.

The charge When the police have charged someone, they must give him a written copy, including particulars of the offence or offences with which he is charged.

Providing facilities in custody

The police can force no one to go to a police station or to remain there, except by arresting him. If he has not been arrested he is entitled to leave.

At any stage of a police investigation, the suspect is entitled to communicate and consult privately with a lawyer. That rule applies even if the person is in custody – unless the police can show that such consultation could hinder the processes of investigation or the administration of justice.

The judges' rules further state that someone in police custody should:
● Be supplied with writing materials on request.

● Be allowed to telephone friends.
● Have letters or telegrams sent without delay at his own expense.
● Be informed orally of those rights and have his attention drawn to notices in the police station describing them.
● Be provided with reasonable comfort and refreshment – excluding alcohol – while he is being questioned.

JURY

When a citizen must help to administer justice

Anyone accused of a serious crime is entitled to be tried by a jury of fellow citizens. To maintain that right, the law imposes on most adults in Britain the duty to serve as jurors, when required.

It is an offence to ignore a jury summons or to fail to attend court when required. The maximum penalty is a £100 fine.

In general, any man or woman aged 18 or over, and under 65, can be called for jury service.

People who are not eligible

A citizen is ineligible for, or disqualified from, jury service if he or she falls into one of three categories:
● Professional – magistrates, coroners, barristers, solicitors, legal executives, prison governors, prison officers, probation officers, police officers (including special constables), clergy, nuns, ministers of religion and anyone in a comparable job.

Any such person remains ineligible to serve on a jury for 10 years after leaving the occupation that disqualifies him. A judge, once appointed, can never serve on a jury.
● Criminal – anyone who has served 3 months or more in prison or Borstal in the previous 10 years or who has at any time been sentenced to 5 years' or more imprisonment.
● Non-residential – anyone who has not been resident in the United Kingdom, Channel Islands or Isle of Man for at least 5 years since the age of 13.

If, by mistake, someone who is not eligible or who is disqualified is summoned to serve on a jury, he should inform the returning officer immediately.

Anyone summoned for jury service is

sent a list of categories of people not allowed to serve.

To accept a summons and sit on a jury when ineligible can lead to a maximum fine of £100.

If the disqualification is because of a past prison sentence, the maximum penalty is a £400 fine.

When someone can be excused

Some people may be excused jury service if they wish – for example, peers, Members of Parliament, doctors, dentists, nurses, midwives and members of the armed forces.

Anyone who has served on a jury – apart from a coroner's jury – within the previous 2 years is also entitled to refuse a jury summons.

Unless you fall into any of those categories, you cannot be excused jury service without a particular valid reason: general inconvenience is not sufficient.

If you do wish to be exempted from service, you should go to the court at the time stated on the jury summons. Ask the court officials to inform the court of your wish to be excused and say why.

Whether you are allowed not to serve is a matter entirely at the court's discretion.

Examples of what is legally considered a 'good reason' are:
● Illness, deafness or blindness.
● Pregnancy.
● Holiday arrangements.
● Having to nurse a sick relative.
● Having a one-man business to run.
● Inability to find a child minder.

Even if a 'good reason' is accepted, the person applying is not exempted from jury service for all time. Another jury summons can be issued in the near future.

How jurors are chosen

Jurors usually receive their summonses about 6 weeks before they are due to serve. Their names are chosen at random from the local electoral register, by the clerk of the court. Jurors are selected to serve in a particular court building, but are not allotted to a specific case until after they arrive.

The summons gives the date on which jury service is to begin, but not when it is to end – because it is often impossible to know when a trial may finish.

WHEN POTENTIAL JURORS ARE INVESTIGATED

Jury vetting is the practice of checking the background of members of the panel from which a jury will be chosen before a trial. The investigation is usually done by the police, who notify the trial lawyers.

The rules on jury vetting are not clear. The Court of Appeal has held that it is proper for panels to be vetted to see if they include disqualified persons, or those with relevant criminal convictions. But another Court of Appeal said that vetting was unconstitutional. The Attorney-General has ruled that full investigations should take place only with the permission of the Director of Public Prosecutions in serious cases, such as organised crime, cases with political motives, or official secrets cases. Then, jurors' names are checked for criminal records, relationships with known criminals and any other available information.

The prosecution may use that information to ask a juror to 'stand by' without disclosing the reason.

Judges have power to order vetting in other cases, including vetting by the defence.

A potential juror who refuses to serve because of objections to vetting may be guilty of CONTEMPT OF COURT.

However, the summons may indicate a minimum period of service – usually about 2 weeks.

Calling a panel

The summonsing officer calls a panel of more than 12 people for any given case, on the assumption that some will have good reason for not attending and others will be rejected, or successfully challenged, by the defence or prosecution.

The final jury of 12 is chosen from the panel, on the first day of the trial, by ballot. All names are put in a box: the first 12 drawn by the clerk of the court form the jury – but they may be rejected if there are objections, or challenges, from defence or prosecution.

As each name is read out, the juror takes a seat in the jury box. When all 12 are seated they take the oath in turn.

Peremptory challenges The defence can challenge up to three jurors without giving a reason: that is called a peremptory challenge. The defence lawyer simply says 'Challenge' – and the judge tells the juror that he or she will not be needed for that trial.

A peremptory challenge may be made for many reasons: do not take it as a personal affront. It is part of a defence lawyer's role to try to select a jury that he thinks will give his client the best chance of acquittal.

A juror who has been rejected for a particular trial returns to the general jury pool and waits to be empanelled for another case – unless his period of service is coming to an end.

Standby challenge The prosecution is not allowed to make a peremptory challenge, but can ask a juror to 'stand by for the Crown'.

The juror then goes to the back of the panel list and will not sit on that jury unless there are not enough others to make up a full jury.

Challenge for cause Both defence and prosecution can challenge any number of jurors 'for cause', if they think that the fairness of a trial could be jeopardised by the presence of any of those jurors.

A challenge for cause can be made, for example, if it is thought that a juror knows someone involved in the case, or has heard or read something about it that might influence him.

It is for the judge to decide whether such a challenge is valid. Once the challenge has been made, he may question the juror himself – or allow the defence or prosecution to do so.

Taking the oath After any challenge, the jurors, one by one, take an OATH or make an affirmation. Penalties for breaking the oath or affirmation are severe. For example, a juror who supports a particular verdict because of being bribed, or through fear, can be imprisoned for up to 2 years.

During a trial

When the jurors have been sworn, the clerk of the court tells them the charge against the accused, and the trial begins.

At some stage before a verdict is reached, the jurors must choose a foreman to be their spokesman. There is no fixed point in the trial when this is done, but it is frequently arranged after the evidence and closing speeches – before the verdict is discussed.

The jury must listen to everything that is said – the opening and closing statements by prosecution and defence, the evidence and cross-examination of witnesses and the judge's summing up, in which he directs the jury on points of evidence and law.

The judge may send the jury out of court to the jury room if there are matters that they ought not to hear – for example, if the prosecution or defence

---

THE JUROR WHO WENT AWAY ON HOLIDAY

A crown court judge has the power to dismiss a juror while allowing the case to continue.

The trial of Cyril Hambery, a household-goods salesman accused of theft and false accounting, dragged on longer than expected in 1977.

The judge at Croydon Crown Court did not begin his summing up until Friday morning, and after lunch he warned the jury that they would probably have to return to the court on Monday.

One woman juror explained that she was due to go on holiday. The judge decided that under the Juries Act 1974, he could release her, and he did so. The remaining 11 jurors returned on the Monday and found Hambery guilty of all the charges. He was sentenced to 12 months' imprisonment.

Hambery appealed. He claimed:
● The judge had no power to discharge the juror.
● If he had the power he had used it wrongly.
● The Appeal Court could review any discretion the judge had to discharge a juror.

DECISION

Hambery's appeal was dismissed. The court held that the judge did have the power to discharge a juror, and it had no reason to criticise his use of that power. The court ruled: 'If the administration of justice can be carried on without inconveniencing jurors, it should be.'

THE ROLE OF A JURY IN A CRIMINAL COURT CASE
How a jury is chosen to hear evidence and reach a verdict in a case

1 A panel of more than 12 jurors is selected for each case. The court usher calls them all into court where they are called to the jury box, one by one. The prosecuting or defending counsel may challenge any juror. In that case he or she leaves the court and returns to the general jury pool to await selection in another case.

2 If a juror is accepted he takes an oath on the New Testament or makes an affirmation that he will listen to the evidence involved and give a true verdict.

3 When 12 jurors have been sworn in, the clerk of the court tells them the charge against the accused. The jury listens to the opening statements of the prosecution and defence, to the evidence and cross-examination of witnesses and to closing statements by both sides. Jurors may take notes during the case and may ask a question of any witness, provided that the question is written on a note and passed to the judge. Once the judge has summed up the evidence and arguments for the jury, the usher swears on oath to look after the jurors, then leads them to the jury room to discuss a verdict.

4 In the jury room the jurors, if they have not already done so, choose a foreman to chair their discussions and act as spokesman. They discuss the evidence and must stay together until they have managed to reach a verdict in the case.

5 A jury should try to reach a unanimous verdict, but if it cannot do so, a majority verdict of at least 10–2 must be reached. The jury returns to the court where its foreman tells the judge what verdict it has reached.

lawyers want to ask the judge whether it is in order to refer to a previous conviction of a defendant or a witness.

Coping with the evidence

Jurors are not normally allowed to have copies of the evidence that they have heard, but they are entitled to take notes during the case, to help them to assess the evidence. It is particularly advisable to do so during a long and complicated trial.

If no writing materials have been supplied, ask the court usher for some. If that does not produce results, ask him to ask the judge. If he refuses to do so, raise your hand in the jury box and put the request to the judge himself.

Asking questions Jurors are not allowed to ask witnesses questions, for fear that they may put inadmissible questions and produce inadmissible replies that could make it necessary to begin the trial again.

But a question from a juror can be conveyed by passing a note to the judge, who will either answer the question himself or put it directly to the witness, on the juror's behalf, or to one of the lawyers concerned in the case. Alternatively, he may say that the question cannot be asked.

If the witness has already left the witness box, the judge may recall him to deal with the juror's question.

Leaving the courtroom If a juror wishes to leave the courtroom other than during an adjournment – for example, to go to the lavatory – he should speak to the usher or pass a note to him, or through him to the judge. The judge can then order a short adjournment.

However, repeated interruptions are a source of irritation, and jurors are usually given unofficial advice not to drink a lot of liquid before the hearing starts or resumes.

At the end of each day's hearing, jurors go home.

If for any reason a juror is unable to continue with a trial, it does not have to be abandoned, provided that at least 9 of the 12 jurors remain.

A judge can discharge a juror for various reasons, including sickness, some prior arrangement or some unforeseen inconvenience.

Reaching a verdict

After the evidence and closing

HOW A JUROR IS REIMBURSED

Jurors receive no wage or fee for their service, but they can claim certain cash allowances.

The allowances are not large and most jurors who are in business or who lose pay can expect to suffer a financial loss during their jury service.

Subsistence
The amount of the subsistence allowance, covering meals and other expenses, depends on the length of time, each day, that the juror is away from home. The maximum, in 1981, was just £4 for a 10-hour day.

Travel
A juror who travels to and from court by public transport may claim the second-class rail or bus fare. Taxi fares are paid only if there is no alternative transport.

Jurors who use their own cars or motor cycles may claim a mileage allowance. For cars, the 1981 rates ranged from 14.1p to 18.7p per mile, depending on the size of the engine and whether there was any alternative. For motor cycles, the allowance ranged from 3.5p to 7.6p per mile.

Financial loss
Jurors may claim a daily allowance for loss of earnings. In 1981, the maximum was £14 a day for the first 10 days and £28 for each subsequent day.

An employer is not obliged to pay a juror's wages or salary while he is absent on jury service.

But if an employer dismisses someone because of that jury service absence he could face a strong claim for UNFAIR DISMISSAL and possibly a CONTEMPT OF COURT charge.

---

speeches by prosecution and defence, the judge sums up the evidence and arguments for the jury. The usher then leads the jurors into their jury room and locks them in so that no one can interfere with their discussions.

Choosing a foreman Unless the jury has previously chosen a foreman, it must do so immediately before discussing its verdict. The foreman, who can be a woman, becomes the jury chairman and spokesman until the end of the case, and announces its verdict to the court.

There is no set procedure for choosing a foreman: it is for the jurors themselves to decide how they will choose, and whom they will select.

Nor are there any rules about how a jury should arrive at its verdict. Their discussions, however, are confidential.

Queries and delays If jurors are in doubt about a point of law or evidence, they should ask the usher to take a message to the judge. He can recall the jury and give the question and answer in open court.

Although jurors go home at the end of each day's hearing during evidence, argument or summing up, they no longer do so once they have begun to consider their verdict. They must stay together until the verdict is reached.

If they cannot reach a decision by the end of the first day, they are given overnight accommodation, usually in a hotel.

Majority verdicts A jury must try to reach a unanimous verdict, but if it has not done so within 2 hours, the judge can recall the jurors to tell them that he will accept a majority. He need not, however, recall the jury for that purpose until he feels it necessary.

If the jury cannot reach a unanimous verdict, it can decide by a majority. But the majority verdict must be supported by at least 10 of the 12 jurors. If the jury has been reduced to 11 or fewer, a verdict cannot be returned with more than one juror dissenting.

Failure to agree There is no time limit for reaching a verdict, but if a jury cannot even reach a majority verdict, and the judge decides that no further discussion will produce one, he discharges the jurors and orders a new trial.

Juries in non-criminal cases

Trials of civil actions in the High Court by jury are not common, for the right to claim a civil jury is limited to cases of LIBEL AND SLANDER, FALSE IMPRISONMENT and MALICIOUS PROSECUTION, on the application of either party, or on the application of any party against whom fraud is alleged.

Even in those cases a jury may be refused if the court considers that the trial will involve a prolonged examination of documents or accounts or a scientific or local investigation.

In civil jury trials, if the jury finds in

favour of the plaintiff, it decides how much damages to award.

Coroner's jury

Whenever a coroner holds an inquest he can decide to have a jury sit with him. He must have one if there is reason to suspect that the death:

● Occurred in prison.

● Was caused by an accident, poisoning or disease that is required by law to be notified to a government department.

● Occurred in circumstances whose continuance or possible recurrence would be prejudicial to the health or safety of the public.

No precise qualifications are laid down for coroner's jury service, and there is no age limit. The coroner has an officer, usually a policeman, who summons jurors – generally from the electoral register. A juror is given 6 days' notice of his service. If he fails to attend he can be fined up to £5.

A coroner's jury must have between 7 and 11 persons, at the coroner's discretion. If the majority of the jury wants to do so, it must be shown the body.

A coroner's jury must record a verdict on the cause of death: it need not be unanimous.

Although it can add a comment, or rider, to its verdict, that comment is not legally part of the verdict, and the coroner must not record it unless he thinks it is designed to prevent the recurrence of similar fatalities.

Juries are paid travelling expenses and compensation for loss of earnings at rates laid down by the Home Secretary.

JUVENILE COURT

Magistrates and the young offenders

A juvenile court is a special type of magistrates' court which handles cases concerning children and young persons under the age of 17.

The court usually comprises three magistrates, members of a special panel drawn from the main bench, assisted by a clerk.

The procedure is less formal than that in courts dealing with adults, and except for the Press only people directly connected with the case being heard are admitted.

Press and broadcast reports of juvenile court proceedings may not identify the juvenile.

When a young person is accused of an offence, a parent or guardian is usually required to attend the court and the summons naming the juvenile normally includes his parents. If they do not attend, a warrant can be issued for their arrest.

Sent to a higher court for trial

A juvenile does not have the same right as an adult to elect to be tried by jury. But if he is over 14 and under 17 and is charged with a serious offence such as murder, manslaughter or rape, or he is jointly charged with an adult, he must be tried in the adult magistrates' court with the adult. On a serious charge, the adult could be tried in the crown court and the juvenile in the juvenile court.

In practice, both are likely to be tried in the crown court, but if a juvenile is charged jointly with an adult who chooses to be tried before magistrates, they will both be tried by an adult magistrates' court.

When the juvenile is not sent to the crown court, but is found guilty by the magistrates, he is usually sent back to the juvenile bench for sentence. He must be sent back unless the adult court thinks he can be dealt with by fine, binding over, or conditional or absolute discharge.

How the case is heard

The trial of a criminal case in a juvenile court begins with an explanation, in simple language, of the charge. The juvenile is then asked whether he admits or denies the police accusation.

If the charge is admitted, a police officer or a lawyer acting on behalf of the police presents the facts. If further information is required, the magistrates can adjourn the case to await reports on

the juvenile from the social services department of the local authority or a probation officer. Such reports give details of his background and other matters that may be relevant.

The magistrates ask the juvenile, his parent, guardian or lawyer whether any of them has anything to say about the offence. After that the court decides what action to take.

Legal representation

If the juvenile denies the charge, the hearing of the case is similar to that in adult criminal proceedings, but if he is not legally represented, his parent or guardian will be allowed to assist in conducting his defence. That includes cross-examining witnesses.

Recording a guilty verdict, but no conviction

The term 'convicted' is not used in juvenile courts; instead the accused may be found guilty. If there have been any previous findings of guilt, the police will inform the court before any order is made. Before it announces its decision, the court must inform the parent or guardian and the juvenile to allow them to make representations.

Orders and fines The magistrates cannot send a juvenile to prison or to a borstal, but if the case is a serious one, they may decide to commit him to the crown court where he may, if he is over the age of 15, be sentenced to a term of borstal training.

If a juvenile is over 14 the magistrates can order that he attend a detention centre for 3 months or between 3 and 6 months depending on age. Alternatively, they may make a SUPERVISION ORDER, order him to attend an attendance centre or pay a fine (up to £200 for each offence).

They can also grant an absolute or conditional discharge or bind a juvenile or his parents over to keep the peace.

A juvenile may apply on his own account or through his parents or guardian for LEGAL AID to be represented by a lawyer in the juvenile court.

KEY MONEY

*When payment is expected
in return for a tenancy*

Key money is a lump sum demanded in exchange for the tenancy of a house or flat, or as a returnable deposit against damage to the premises, its furnishings or fittings. It is often demanded illegally.

The words key money, or premium, also describe a payment made by an incoming tenant to settle an outgoing tenant's rent arrears or as an inducement to the latter to surrender his tenancy to the landlord.

It is a criminal offence, punishable by a fine of up to £100, for anyone to demand a premium for any tenancy

WHEN KEY MONEY IS ILLEGAL

If a premium is charged by the landlord illegally the tenant can deduct the amount from future rent payments.

protected by the Rent Act or the limited protection of the Rent Tribunal who has registered a decision of a 'reasonable rent'. *See:* EVICTION

If a tenant finds himself to be the victim of such a demand he should report the matter to the local council's harassment or tenancy relations officer. If he paid the premium to the outgoing tenant he can sue in the county court for its return or, if it was paid to the landlord, he can deduct the amount from future rent payments.

Charging for fixtures and fittings

The most obvious kind of premium is cash, but an illegal premium may be demanded or paid in other ways, such as in goods or an excessive price for fixtures, fittings or furniture.

Fittings and furniture It is quite lawful for a landlord or outgoing tenant to make it a condition of a tenancy that the incoming tenant should purchase fittings, such as curtains or carpets, and furniture. But only a fair price may be asked.

Anyone who tries to make an incoming tenant pay for furniture must provide the tenant with an inventory of the furniture and the price being asked for each item. Failure to do so is a criminal offence, punishable by a fine of up to £100.

If a person so badly needs a home that he accepts unreasonable demands he can dispute the unreasonableness with the landlord or outgoing tenant once he has secured the tenancy. In the last re-

sort he can ask a county court to decide whether any payment made was illegal. This may cost him money in legal fees but once his tenancy is secure there is no risk to it by insisting on his rights.

Fixtures The position is slightly different where fixtures, such as cupboards or double-glazing, are concerned. Such items become part of the premises and so belong to the landlord. An outgoing tenant is not entitled to remove them, but he may charge an incoming tenant, to whom he has transferred his tenancy, the amount it cost him to install them – or the amount he paid a previous tenant for them. But a landlord is not obliged to pay for improvements voluntarily made by the tenant.

An outgoing tenant is also permitted to charge what it cost him to do structural alterations to the premises. He can, in addition, charge for any outgoings such as rates or telephone rentals he has paid in advance for the period after he has left the premises. *See:* FIXTURES AND FITTINGS

When a landlord asks for a deposit

It is illegal for a landlord to demand a loan from the tenant as a condition of granting him the tenancy, but the courts have held that a landlord does not commit the criminal offence of demanding an illegal loan if he takes a deposit from an incoming tenant, provided it is returned to the tenant at the end of the tenancy.

A landlord may demand a deposit from an incoming tenant to cover damage or rent arrears. Such a payment will be quite legal so long as it does not exceed $\frac{1}{6}$ of the annual rent.

If the tenancy is for less than a year, the rent must be converted to an annual one in order to make this comparison. The sum demanded must also be reasonable in relation to the potential liability of the tenant which it is deposited to cover.

KIDNAPPING

*It is a serious offence to carry off
a person against his will*

No one has a right to carry off another person by force or to hide someone away against his or her will. Anyone who does so commits the crime of kidnapping and can be sent to prison for life or ordered to pay an unlimited fine.

Most kidnapping offences are carried out to extort ransoms from relatives or business friends of the kidnapped person. But it is kidnapping to 'steal, carry away and hide' anyone, whatever the motive. A man who forcibly takes his wife away from the place where she wishes to be can be guilty of kidnapping.

Child snatched by parent Parents who are parting, or who are already separated or divorced, may disagree over custody of their children and one may try to take away the children from the other, and even out of the jurisdiction of the courts.

No parent can be accused of abduction or kidnapping his or her own child. But if a court has granted one parent custody of a child and the other parent takes the child away, without the consent of the one with custody, that parent is guilty of CONTEMPT OF COURT and can be sent to prison.

If no custody order has been made and the child has been taken away by one parent, the other parent can either apply to a court for custody, or apply to make the child a ward of court. *See:* WARD OF COURT

A parent who fears that his or her child may be taken away by the other parent can apply to make the child a ward of court whether or not the child is in his or her custody.

Once that is done, any parent who removes the child will be guilty of contempt of court even if there has been no custody order.

If a child is made a ward of court and there is real danger that it may be taken out of the country, the court can ask the Home Office to notify seaports, airports and the Passport Office so that the child cannot leave the country. A parent can ask for LEGAL AID for an application to make a child a ward of court. *See also:* ABDUCTION

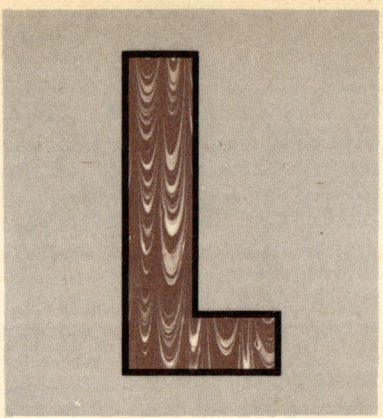

LABELLING

It is against the law to sell some goods without description

Pre-packed foods, proprietary medicines and some potentially dangerous domestic equipment must carry a label when they are offered for sale. If they do not, the person selling them is committing an offence.

Many other goods can be sold without a label, but if a manufacturer or trader decides to attach a label to them voluntarily, the information given must be accurate.

Anyone who sells goods of any sort with a label that gives false or misleading information is committing a criminal offence and can be fined or imprisoned. *See:* TRADE DESCRIPTIONS

A shopper who buys goods that do not comply with a description on the label, on which he relied, has a legal right to reject the goods and demand his MONEY BACK.

Special, even more stringent rules apply to food. A storekeeper selling food that is wrongly labelled can be prosecuted under the Food and Drugs Act. The maximum penalty is 3 months' gaol and a fine of £100.

A trader prosecuted under the Trade Descriptions Act can be gaoled for up to 2 years and face a fine of any amount.

Goods that can be dangerous

Certain goods such as electrical equipment to be used in the home, or paraffin heaters, must carry accurate information telling the buyer how to use them safely.

For example, refrigerators, toasters and electric fires must carry the colour code for wiring and instructions on how to fit a plug correctly; paraffin heaters must give an explanation of the safe way to operate them; and nightdresses that are flammable must have a label saying 'Warning – keep away from fire'.

The maximum penalty for failing to display a safety label on goods for sale is 3 months' imprisonment and a fine of £1,000.

SPECIAL RULES FOR FOOD LABELLING

Every label on pre-packed food must carry the usual name of the product or an accurate description of what it is. Ingredients, except water, must be listed, and should be given in correct order by volume or weight – with the ingredient that makes up the largest part first.

If, however, the weight of each ingredient is given, they can be listed in any order.

Exemptions

Pre-packed goods which do not have to carry a list of ingredients are: bread, pastries, biscuits, chocolate, sweets and ice cream.

Other goods

The following goods must also carry labels showing their weight or measure: perfume, soap, toilet preparations, toothpaste, detergents.

LAND REGISTRY

Simplifying property transfers

Since 1862, a system of public registration of property titles has been developed in England and Wales to make it easier to transfer legal ownership when houses are bought and sold. Starting with the City of London, registration has been introduced compulsorily district by district as properties change hands. There are now some 5 million properties registered.

THE WIFE WHO REFUSED TO BUDGE

A houseowner who fails to go through with the sale of his house after exchanging contracts can be liable for any loss to the buyer because of a rise in property values.

Mr Edmund Tyler decided he wanted to sell his bungalow in Ashford, Surrey, on his retirement and move to Norfolk. His wife and daughter were 'very cool' on the idea but raised no overt objections. Indeed, Mrs Tyler even showed prospective buyers round the bungalow.

The day after Mr Tyler signed a contract to sell the house to a Mr Wroth for £6,050, however, Mrs Tyler entered a notice at the Land Registry under the Matrimonial Homes Act 1967, that prevented a house-owner from evicting or excluding his or her spouse from the home.

Mr Tyler was therefore unable to sell the house with vacant possession as long as his wife refused to move. Mr Wroth asked a court to order Mr Tyler to fulfil his contract or pay damages in lieu.

DECISION

The court decided that an order making Mr Tyler fulfil his contract would force him to bring an action against his wife and might break up the family. It ruled, however, that Mr Wroth was entitled to be put in as good a position as if the contract had been fulfilled. Accordingly, it ordered Mr Tyler to pay £5,500 damages to reflect the increase in the value of the bungalow between the completion date and the time of the judgment.

Each property title is given a number and recorded on three separate registers:
● Property register – which gives a description of the property, with a reference to a plan or the registry general map. It also states whether the property is freehold or leasehold, giving details of the lease.
● Proprietorship register – which gives the name and address of the person registered as the owner. Each time the property is sold, the registry staff strike through the name of the seller and enter the name of the buyer as the new owner.
● Charges register – which records rights or claims that people other than the owner have on the property. The two most common are mortgages and covenants restricting the use of the property – for example, to preserve the amenities of an estate of which it forms part.

Other charges can be recorded, but some – claims by the local authority, say, for the cost of essential work on the property – are recorded in a separate register kept by the district council.

A wife or husband can also enter a notice under the Matrimonial Homes Act 1967, to prevent the other from excluding her or him from the house – which effectively prevents any sale of the property with vacant possession.

All three registers are private; no one is allowed a copy of an entry without the owner's written permission. A member of the public can find out only if a property is registered and what its number is. The registry will not tell him who the owner is or any other details.

The owner is given a Land Certificate, a copy of the register. If he mortgages the land, that certificate is retained in the registry and the lender is given a Charge Certificate. When the mortgage is paid off, the Charge Certificate is taken back and the Land Certificate is returned to the owner.

If the owner wants a second mortgage on the property, he has to give written permission for the finance company to inspect the register so that it can satisfy itself that he really is the owner and see what sums of money have already been advanced against the property.

When the owner sells, he authorises the buyer, or his solicitor, to inspect the registers so that he can investigate the title. A day or two before completion,

the buyer's solicitor obtains a search certificate which gives his client 20 working days' priority to be registered as the new owner, without any other changes in the registers.

LANDLORD AND TENANT

Special rules when you rent where you live

Most rented houses and flats are let by the agents who manage the property, but some are advertised by the landlord. When you have registered with an ACCOMMODATION AGENCY, you can be charged a fee only when you agree to take one of the properties on its list. It is illegal for an agency to demand payment for registration or for access to its list of vacant properties.

If you rent directly from a landlord, he is not allowed by law to demand a special premium payment in addition to normal rent, nor may he impose an excessive charge for furniture, fixtures or fittings. It may also be illegal, in some circumstances, for a landlord to demand KEY MONEY.

If you have been obliged to pay any such extra sum, you can sue for its return in the county court or, if it was paid to the landlord, you can deduct it from your rent payments.

Always view the premises before agreeing to rent them. Make sure that everything is in working order before you move in – if not, ask the landlord to have repairs made.

Signing an agreement

Although a tenancy is entirely legal without a written contract, the landlord or his agents may ask you to sign an agreement outlining your obligations as a tenant. Read it carefully before signing. Pay particular attention to conditions concerning repairs, payment of rates, permission to sub-let and the period of the lease, and if you have any doubts that you cannot resolve by talking to the landlord, go to a Citizens Advice Bureau or a solicitor. *See:* DILAPIDATIONS; LEASEHOLD LAND

If you accept any conditions – for example, about keeping pets – and break them later, the landlord can sue you for damages. He could also obtain an order for your EVICTION if he can

READ CAREFULLY BEFORE SIGNING.

If you are asked to sign an agreement, read what it says about the period of the lease, rates, repairs and sub-letting

persuade a court that you have broken the agreement in a serious or persistent manner.

The landlord or agent may reserve the right in the written agreement to enter the premises at reasonable times to satisfy himself that you are keeping them in good condition. He must always give warning of such visits, which should not be too frequent. If good reason for them cannot be shown, he could be guilty of HARASSMENT.

The agreement will usually state the amount of rent and the dates on which payment is due. The sum may have been agreed between you, or it may have been registered by the RENT OFFICER.

If, after signing the agreement, you find you are paying an excessive amount compared to other local rents, you can apply for RENT REGISTRATION, which may mean that your rent will be reduced. But if your claim is unfounded, you may end up paying an even higher rent. *See also:* RENT LIMIT

Paying rent

Tenants who pay rent weekly must have a rent book, containing the name and address of the landlord and his agent, the amount of rent and rates due and details of local RENT ALLOWANCE and RATES rebates schemes. If a landlord refuses to provide a rent book, complain to the harassment officer at the local council, who can prosecute him.

Tenants who pay at longer intervals are not entitled to a rent book, but should ask for receipts if they are paying rent in cash.

If there is no rental agreement, these receipts or the bank's record of a tenant's cheques to the landlord may be the only available proof that he is the legal tenant.

Rent should be paid promptly – failure to pay within 21 days is one of the principal grounds on which a landlord can sue for eviction. However, if a tenant pays all arrears before the case comes to court, the landlord is unlikely to get a possession order but will probably be awarded costs.

Maintenance and repairs

One of the most frequent causes of dispute between landlord and tenant is the cost of repairs to the premises. Sometimes, this is covered in the rental agreement.

An obligation to 'put in repair' requires the tenant to undertake all repairs from the onset of tenancy. If a tenant has promised to 'yield up in good repair' he must leave the premises in a well-maintained condition, even if it was badly kept when he entered.

FIXING A FAIR RENT
How a tenant may object if he thinks his rent is too high

1 When a landlord decides he wants to increase a tenant's rent, he visits his tenant to tell him so. Even when a tenant does not object, the landlord has to apply to the local rent office for a rent increase if the rent was already registered.

2 The rent office sends a copy of the landlord's application to the tenant and if the tenant objects to the increase, he is invited to write to the rent office. However, before outlining his objections, the tenant may visit the rent office to study the books in which recent rents are registered for properties similar to his. He may find that his rent is lower and the increase is justified.

3 If the tenant still objects, he is visited by the rent officer and a referencer. The referencer measures the rooms to make a plan of the premises, while the tenant points out any defects he thinks make an increase unjustified.

4 The landlord and tenant meet at the rent office for an informal discussion with the rent officer, who decides whether the rent is to be increased. He fixes the size of the new rent and then notifies both parties.

But agreements normally allow for 'fair wear and tear', meaning that the tenant does not have to repair damage arising from normal use or natural ageing.

Whatever the agreement states, in tenancies due to last for less than 7 years – even when they are renewed – the landlord is required by law to repair the structure and exterior of the home and maintain the heating systems and the plumbing and gas and electric fittings. It is the tenant's duty to report defects and to repair minor internal breakages and faults – such as handles and fuses.

WHEN THE LIGHTS GO OUT

The tenant should report defects to the landlord but he must repair minor breakdowns, like fuses, himself.

A landlord can be compelled by the local council and the courts to make necessary repairs.

A tenant can be sued by his landlord for neglecting or causing damage to the property. *See also:* DILAPIDATIONS; OCCUPIERS' LIABILITY

Landlord's obligations In addition to his responsibility for repairs, the landlord is required to leave the tenant alone so that he can, in the words of the law, 'quietly enjoy' his occupation of the premises. The landlord is relieved of that obligation only if the tenant breaks the terms of their agreement or fails to pay rent – when he may be sued for damages or evicted by court order.

If you are persistently disturbed by your landlord, report him to the harassment officer at the local authority. If the harassment was serious, you should sue for damages and obtain a court INJUNCTION.

Making improvements

No tenant may carry out improvements to his property – for example, add to or alter fixtures and fittings belonging to his landlord, erect television or external radio aerials, or carry out external redecoration – without his landlord's consent. However, this consent must not unreasonably be withheld, and it is up to the landlord to show that it was not. A landlord will not be regarded as withholding consent unreasonably if the effect of the tenant's proposals would be to make the house less safe, involve the landlord in increased expenditure or reduce the sale or letting value of the house.

If the landlord is asked for consent to an improvement and he does not reply, he is presumed to have refused his consent. But a landlord who refuses consent must give his reasons for doing so in writing. Where a landlord's refusal of consent is unreasonable, a tenant can go ahead with the improvement.

Sub-letting rented property

Most short-term tenancy agreements contain an absolute ban on sub-letting – and the tenant can therefore not sub-let without breaking the agreement and risking action by the landlord.

However, other agreements may forbid sub-letting 'without the consent of the landlords'. In such cases, the landlord cannot refuse permission unreasonably, if the property is being sub-let to responsible people. If the landlord refuses consent unreasonably, the tenant can sub-let.

If there was no tenancy agreement and the landlord did not forbid sub-letting orally when the tenancy began, the tenant may sub-let without his permission. Although there would be no legal requirement in such a case that the sub-tenant should have good references and be able to pay the rent, for his own peace of mind the tenant should satisfy himself on these two matters before granting the sub-tenancy.

Sub-tenants of a landlord whose agreement allows him to sub-let will not be evicted if their immediate landlord is ordered to give up the property. They would, however, face eviction if their landlord has sub-let without authority. This could apply, for example, to a tenant of a landlord whose mortgage agreement forbids him to let part of the property.

Ending a tenancy

If a tenant wants to leave, he must give 4 weeks' notice in writing if he pays rent weekly or monthly. Quarterly tenancies require 3 months' notice and in tenancies of longer period the amount of notice is usually set down in the tenancy agreement.

In the case of yearly tenancies, the parties may have agreed that the rent is to be paid at shorter intervals. Nevertheless the tenancy can only be ended at the end of the year. Generally 6 months' notice will be required unless you can agree a shorter period of notice with the landlord.

If rent is paid at longer than monthly intervals and the tenant wants to give up the property, the landlord may insist that he pays rent until the end of his tenancy period, or until he can find a new tenant.

You can give up tenancy simply by moving out and returning the keys to the landlord – by accepting them, he implies that he has agreed to your leaving.

But if there is risk of dispute with the landlord over your departure, you can formalise the ending of the tenancy by sending him a written note 'surrendering' the property.

If the house was let for more than 3 years, a deed, drawn up by a solicitor, will have to be used for surrender. If a landlord wants his tenant to leave, he must serve him notice to quit at least 4 weeks in advance, or more, depending on the length of the tenancy.

However, the tenant does not have to leave – even if his period of tenancy has ended – unless the landlord applies for and obtains a county court order for his EVICTION.

To obtain such an order, the landlord generally has to satisfy the judge that:
● The tenant has refused to pay rent or broken an important term of their agreement.
● He can provide the tenant with suitable alternative accommodation.

But even when those conditions are met, the judge may rule it unreasonable to make a possession order.

However, if the landlord lives on the premises or provides certain services – such as meals – a judge must automatically give him a possession order at the end of a period of tenancy.

See also: COUNCIL TENANCY
FURNISHED LETTING
LODGER

LAUNDRY

The code that guarantees care of your belongings

You are entitled to expect a commercial laundry or dry-cleaner to take reasonable care of articles that it accepts, and to use skill in cleaning and pressing them. A laundry is not liable for loss or damage if it can show that it took reasonable precautions. A legal claim for compensation can succeed only if it was negligent.

But the Association of British Launderers and Cleaners, to which more than 90 per cent of laundry companies belong, offers further safeguards that should make legal action unnecessary. Its code of practice, drawn up in consultation with the Office of Fair Trading, requires members:

● Not to use any EXEMPTION CLAUSE to avoid legal liability.
● To reprocess on request, free of charge, any article that is unsatisfactory due to the laundry's fault.
● To pay fair compensation for loss or damage caused by negligence, fire or burglary.
● To display prices for processing standard articles.
● To complete orders by the time stated, unless prevented by exceptional circumstances.

High-value items Although the code forbids exemption clauses, association members may ask a customer to state the value of an expensive or unusual item, and quote a special price.

Owner's risk If a launderer or cleaner expects damage to an article no matter how much care is taken, he can warn the customer that the article is accepted only at the owner's risk. That stipulation should be printed or written on the customer's receipt. It does not relieve the laundry from liability if it is negligent.

Fire and burglary A laundry is not liable to pay compensation for loss or damage from fire or burglary, if there was no negligence on its own part. But

under the association's code, members pay compensation to any customer who is not covered by his own insurance.

When there is a dispute

The association's consumer advisory service helps to settle disputes between customers and its members. Independent laboratory tests to resolve technical questions are arranged without charge, provided that customers agree to abide by the findings.

Faulty goods Provided that it is not negligent, a laundry is not liable for damage caused by faulty manufacture – for example, colours that run – unless it could reasonably have been aware of it before starting work.

Nor is it responsible if goods are labelled with wrong cleaning instructions, or easily damaged because of misuse by the customer – for example, a towel with threads cut while drying razor blades.

Assessing compensation If an article is lost, or damaged beyond repair, you do not have a right to the full cost of replacement. Previous wear and tear is taken into account – so if an article is lost halfway through its assumed useful life, a customer is entitled to only half the cost of replacing it.

Dealing with launderettes

Launderette companies and other operators of self-service washing or dry-cleaning machines are legally responsible for the safety and efficiency of their equipment, and for the reliability of their staff.

They must conduct their business with reasonable care – with the degree of supervision, maintenance and skill that a reasonable person could expect.

A customer who can show that a launderette proprietor failed in that duty, and that his negligence caused personal injury or damage to clothing, is entitled to compensation. If a claim is rejected, the proprietor can be sued.

Notices saying that the proprietor accepts no liability protect the proprietor only if they are fair and reasonable. They can never protect him if his negligence caused personal injury.

'Service' washing If a customer pays a special charge and leaves clothing to be attended to by staff, he or she is entitled to expect a reasonable standard of cleaning as well as reasonable care.

Compensation can be claimed for loss or damage if the attendant is negligent – but not if the customer fails to warn that an article needs special care.

LAY-OFF

When an employee's job is temporarily cut back

An employer facing a temporary decline in business – for example, because a strike has interrupted the supply of essential materials – may not be able to provide the usual amount of work for his employees. If he cannot afford to pay full wages while work is slack, he may decide to lay off, or suspend, some or all of his employees. Usually that means that he tells them not to report for duty until asked to do so and he reduces or stops their pay during their enforced absence.

Alternatively, he may introduce short-time, cutting the number of hours that employees are required to work each week and therefore the amount he must pay them.

When lay-offs and short-time are unlawful

An employer is not entitled to lay off an employee, or put him on short-time, unless the arrangement is provided for in the EMPLOYMENT CONTRACT. If it is not, the employee can leave his job and apply to an INDUSTRIAL TRIBUNAL for compensation. He can also sue for his wages for the proper period of notice.

If the claim is upheld, the tribunal will make an award either for UNFAIR DISMISSAL or for REDUNDANCY, depending on the circumstances. Compensation for unfair dismissal, which can be claimed by full-time employees after they have completed 1 year's service with their employer, tends to be higher than that for redundancy, which can be claimed only after 2 years' service. However, unfair dismissal compensation can be reduced because of conduct – for example, leaving a job too hastily. Redundancy pay cannot be.

An employee who is laid off or put on short-time and who is eligible for both types of award should mention both on his tribunal application. The tribunal will then decide which is appropriate.

WHEN LAY-OFFS AND SHORT-TIME ARE PROVIDED FOR IN THE CONTRACT

Even if an employee has a provision in his employment contract requiring him to accept being laid off or put on short-time, he may still have the right to seek a redundancy payment, though not to claim unfair dismissal.

He may do so only if there is a reduced amount of work for him to do and:

● He has been laid off for 4 consecutive weeks or for at least 6 weeks during the previous 13 and has not been paid anything other than the statutory guaranteed payments.

● He has been on short-time for 4 consecutive weeks or for at least 6 weeks during the previous 13, and his weekly earnings have been less than half the normal amount.

Before making an application, the employee must tell his employer, no later than 4 weeks after the end of period of short-time or lay-off, that he is going to do so. He must also give his employer NOTICE that he intends to leave. The notice period must be at least 1 week, or longer if that is required by the contract.

Once an employee has given notice of his intended redundancy claim and his departure, he can apply to an industrial tribunal for an award.

However, if the employer believes that normal work is likely to be resumed soon, he can reduce the chance of the claim succeeding. To do so, he must give notice, within 7 days of learning of the employee's intended application to the tribunal, that there is a 'reasonable expectation' that, within the next 4 weeks, the employee would start a period of 13 weeks' full employment.

A PART-TIME WORKER cannot claim unfair dismissal or redundancy. However, if he is paid off or put on short-time in breach of his contract he can leave and sue his employer for WRONGFUL DISMISSAL to recover any earnings to which he is entitled. Employees over the normal retirement age in the company or industry are also ineligible for redundancy or unfair dismissal awards, although they may sue for wrongful dismissal.

When a claim is too hasty

An employee who leaves when he is told he is to be laid off or put on short-time for only 2 or 3 days is unlikely to obtain compensation, even though his employer has technically broken the employment contract.

Tribunals consider whether the person making a claim has acted reasonably in the circumstances. Someone who leaves because of the loss of a few hours' earnings would be held to have contributed to his own dismissal.

However, if the lay-off or short-time working lasts, or is likely to last, for several weeks, or if the employer persistently introduces 1 or 2-day lay-offs or short-time, the employee is justified in leaving.

When the contract is not clear

An employment contract need not be in writing. If it is not, or if some details are missing, the terms can be agreed orally between employer and employee, or be derived from a relevant collective agreement or from custom and practice in the company or industry.

However, an employer will find it difficult to prove his right to lay employees off or to put them on short-time unless there is a clear written provision on the subject, either in a summary of the employment contract given to all workers or in a collective agreement covering his company. In cases involving lay-offs and short-time, courts and tribunals tend to side with the employee unless the employer can show why they should not. *See:* EMPLOYMENT CONTRACT

In some occupations – for example, among casual agricultural workers – there is an accepted custom of not paying workers who cannot do their jobs because of bad weather. But in many others, the procedure, though common, is not sufficiently established to count as custom.

Accepting a voluntary cut in earnings

Many employees accept being laid off or put on short-time when there is no requirement in their contract to do so, in the hope that business will soon pick up and their full earnings will be restored.

They do not necessarily forfeit their right to make a claim against their employer if the lay-off or short-time is extended beyond the period originally agreed.

For example, an employee may accept that he is to be laid off for 3 or 4 weeks. If he is then told that there will be no work for him for 3 or 4 weeks more, he can still succeed in a claim for redundancy or unfair dismissal.

An employee may agree to be laid off or put on short-time on one occasion, but refuse on another, without losing his right to make a claim. However, if he accepts more than once or twice, his employer may argue that the arrangement has become an implied condition of the contract through practice.

To safeguard his rights, an employee who agrees to a lay-off or short-time should write to his employer, keeping a copy of the letter, in which he states that, while he accepts the decision for a specified period, he does so reluctantly and it is not a condition of his contract.

Guaranteed work agreements

More than half of Britain's manual workers and many employees in white-

---

CUSTOM AND PRACTICE WAS NOT ENOUGH

Courts and tribunals are unlikely to accept that lay-offs or short-time working can be justified by custom unless that custom is well known and widespread.

Mr Jones worked for a company of bookmakers. During one winter, all horse racing was cancelled for a time because of bad weather and an outbreak of foot-and-mouth disease.

Mr Jones's employers laid him off, arguing that it was an implied term of his employment contract, according to custom and practice in the betting world. Mr Jones disagreed and so he took the matter to a tribunal.

DECISION

The company was not justified in laying Mr Jones off. The so-called custom was not sufficiently well known and was too vague.

collar jobs are covered by guaranteed work agreements, known as GWAs, negotiated between trade unions and employers.

GWAs define the circumstances in which employees may be laid off or put on short-time and stipulate the minimum weekly wages that must be paid until full earnings are restored.

Once a GWA has been reached through collective bargaining, it automatically becomes part of the individual employment contract of workers in the company or sector concerned.

Most GWAs specify a minimum qualifying period – for example, 4 weeks' employment – before a worker becomes covered by its provisions. Most also allow the employer to insist that workers must carry out alternative jobs if they are available.

Being paid during lay-offs

A worker who has been in his job for more than 4 weeks may be entitled to payment from his employer if he is laid off, even though there is no guaranteed work agreement.

Under the Employment Protection (Consolidation) Act 1978, employers must make guarantee payments to employees who lose at least 1 full day's work through being laid off. The arrangement does not apply to short-time working.

To qualify, the employee must have been laid off either:
● Because of a reduction in the employer's demand for the type of work the employee normally does; or
● Because some other occurrence – for example, a strike at a supplier – has affected the business.

Employees laid off because of an industrial dispute involving other members of their employer's staff, or staff in an associated company, are not eligible for the payment.

Neither are part-time workers, employees who are the husband or wife of the employer, those who normally work outside Great Britain, members of the police and armed forces, dock workers or share fishermen. *See:* EMPLOYMENT PROTECTION

How much can you get?

An eligible employee is entitled to a guarantee payment for up to 5 days in any period of 3 months.

THE WORKER WHO REFUSED TO DO HIS OLD JOB

An employee who is laid off is not entitled to a guarantee payment under the Employment Protection (Consolidation) Act 1978 if he unreasonably refuses an offer of suitable alternative work from his employer.

Mr Purdy was a coach trimmer. Business was slack, and as an alternative to being laid off he was offered work in the finishing shop, where he had previously been given a job for 5 months because other employment was not available.

He refused and claimed a guarantee payment from his employer through an industrial tribunal.

DECISION

Mr Purdy was not entitled to the payment, because his refusal to do another job was unreasonable. Although the job offered was outside his normal trade, it was suitable in the circumstances.

THE FOREMAN WHO FOUND ANOTHER JOB

If an employee is laid off for several weeks and finds another job in that time, he does not forfeit his right to claim compensation from his former employer.

Mr Smith was a foreman. Because of a shortage of work, his employers told him he was to be laid off, initially for 2 or 3 weeks and perhaps for up to 7 weeks. He left the job, found another within a fortnight and then sought a redundancy payment from his former employers.

DECISION

Mr Smith was entitled to a redundancy payment. His employment contract did not provide for him to be laid off and, as he had not agreed to the arrangement, he was within his rights to regard himself as having been dismissed.

The basic entitlement is normal daily pay up to a maximum of £8 a day, to a total of $20 \times £8$ a year, or £160.

There are complicated rules for calculating hourly and daily pay rates from the basic working week and customary overtime.

Example: Ann Evans is a machinist. She earns £1.50 an hour for a basic 42 hour week worked over 5 days. She also works 5 hours' overtime each week, at £2.50 per hour.

Basic and overtime hours and payments are added together to obtain the hourly rate used to establish guarantee pay:

$$\frac{(£1.50 \times 42 \text{ hours}) + (£2.50 \times 5 \text{ hours})}{42 \text{ hours} + 5 \text{ hours}}$$

$$= \frac{£63 + £12.50}{47} = £1.61 \text{ hourly rate}$$

To establish the length of Ann's working day, her basic and overtime hours are added together and divided by the number of days she works per week:

$$\frac{42 + 5}{5} = 9.4 \text{ hours per day}$$

Her daily rate, for the purpose of the scheme, is therefore the hourly rate multiplied by the length of the working day:

$$£1.61 \times 9.4 = £15.13 \text{ per day.}$$

However, as the scheme has a ceiling of £8 per day, that is the amount to which she is entitled.

Claiming guarantee pay

Under the employment protection rules, an employer is responsible for making guarantee payments to eligible workers. He cannot recover the cost from the state.

If the employer does not make a payment, eligible employees can complain to an industrial tribunal up to 3 months after the date on which the money should have been received. The tribunal can order the employer to pay, though it cannot fine him for not having done so.

Claiming social security benefits

Someone who is laid off or put on short-time may be entitled to claim UNEMPLOYMENT BENEFIT, provided that he meets the qualifying conditions. If he is laid off and registered as unemployed, he becomes entitled to the standard benefit after he has not worked for

3 consecutive days. If he is on short-time, he must not have worked for 2 consecutive days, and for 1 complete day in the following 6 days, excluding Sundays and holidays.

Unemployment benefit is not payable for any days for which guarantee payments are received, nor if the lay-off is the result of a STRIKE in which the employee is involved.

To claim the EARNINGS-RELATED SUPPLEMENT, the employee must not have worked for a total of 18 days – at least 6 of which must have been consecutive – a condition that rules out most people on short-time.

Few workers on short-time are eligible for SUPPLEMENTARY BENEFIT, but those who are laid off may meet the qualifying conditions.

LEARNER DRIVER

Restrictions on motorists who have no full licence

A learner driver who has not passed the Department of Transport driving test holds only a provisional driving licence and must display an L-plate on the front and back of any car he drives. He must be accompanied, when he drives, by a qualified driver who holds a licence valid for the type of vehicle being driven. He cannot drive on a motorway until he has a full licence.

A learner motor cyclist does not have to carry a qualified person, but he must have L-plates. If a learner motor cyclist does carry a passenger, that passenger must have a full licence and be qualified to ride a motor cycle. A learner must not ride a motor cycle of more than 250 cc.

L-plates can be bought at most motor accessory shops or they can be home-made, provided that they conform to the regulations – a red letter measuring 4 × 3½ × 1½ in. on a white background 7 in. square. Always remove L-plates when a qualified driver is at the wheel, as recommended in the Highway Code. It is not, however, an offence to fail to remove the plates.

What a supervisor must do

If you are a qualified driver overseeing a learner you must try to prevent him from 'acting unskilfully or careless-

LOOK, NO L-PLATES!
If you pass your test you can drive immediately without L-plates; you do not need to obtain a full licence first.

ly'. If your driver commits an offence you may be prosecuted for 'aiding and abetting' if you are encouraging him in unsafe manoeuvring.

You may be prosecuted for careless driving yourself if you are in control, or partly in control – for example, if the vehicle has dual controls – and you fail to take proper precautions and preventive action.

Driving test

All applicants for provisional licences are sent a copy of *Your driving test – and how to pass it.* It is sent free when you apply for a provisional licence.

If you pass the test, you are given a certificate of competence and you can drive immediately without L-plates. You are not obliged to apply for a full licence until your provisional licence expires, but you must carry your certificate with your licence. If you fail the test, you must wait at least a month before taking another test. You can, however, apply for a firm date at once. There is no limit to the number of tests that you can take.

LEASEHOLD LAND

Conditions that may be imposed by a landlord

A lease lays down the conditions under which a landlord allows the use of land or property for a specified time. The period may range from a weekly

tenancy of a flat or house to what amounts to the ownership of a building under a lease lasting hundreds or even thousands of years.

The conditions in a lease may include an obligation on the part of the tenant to do certain repairs and decoration and can lay down restrictions – for example, forbidding certain alterations or uses of the property or not allowing sub-letting.

Enforcing a lease

If a tenant breaks the terms of the lease the landlord can sue for damages or seek a court injunction to prevent him from continuing to break the conditions – or, in some cases, compel him to fulfil a particular condition.

A lease often contains a forfeiture clause under which the landlord can end the lease for a breach of the conditions. In the case of unpaid rent the landlord can seek to end the lease, sue for the arrears in court or instruct a bailiff to seize goods on the property and sell them to recover the amount owing. The process is known as 'levying distress' and, except for dwellings protected under the Rent Acts, does not need a court order.

In cases other than those for unpaid rent, a landlord who wants to invoke the forfeiture clause must first give the tenant notice, stating the complaint and asking the tenant to put matters right.

The tenant can apply to the court for more time – for example, to carry out repairs – or he can ask the court to rule that he should not lose the lease.

Ending a lease

A lease may be for a fixed period of time or it may be on a weekly, monthly, quarterly or yearly basis. Such a lease does not automatically end after the period specified. Either landlord or tenant must give notice. The length of the notice may be stated in the lease. If not, it depends on legal rules. A minimum of 4 weeks' notice must be given for a dwelling; otherwise the notice must equal the duration of the lease, up to a maximum of 6 months – so a month's notice would have to be given to end a monthly lease and 6 months' to end a yearly, or longer, lease.

The length of the notice is the same for landlord and tenant. The notice must state the correct date for ending the lease. For example, if a monthly lease runs from the 1st of the month and the tenant does not want to renew it, he must give a month's notice, stating specifically that the lease is to end on the last day of the next month.

The Rent Acts extend the life of tenancies of many houses and flats, and other Acts give protection to business tenants and agricultural tenants.

Buying the freehold

A leaseholder who wants to buy the freehold of his house when the lease comes to an end must meet certain tests:
1. The lease must originally have been for over 21 years.
2. The ground-rent (ignoring any service-charge element) must be within certain limits laid down by Parliament.
3. The house must be under a stated rateable value.
4. Only houses are affected, and not flats. The test is whether any part of a 'unit' is built above or below some other 'unit'; if it is, the unit is a flat.
5. The claimant must have lived in the house as 'his only or main residence' for 3 years. He can count any time he lived there as a member of the family of the householder from whom he took over.

If the householder qualifies, he can serve notice of his wish to buy – or to take an extended lease for 50 years from the end of the current lease. The form of the notice is laid down by the Leasehold Reform Act 1967.

The freeholder can challenge the householder's qualification. Similarly, if the freeholder is the Crown or the National Trust, the rights do not apply.

Certain public authorities can refuse to sell the freehold, if they need the house for redevelopment within 10 years and can obtain a certificate from a government department to that effect.

At what price?

A new lease is at a modern ground rent, calculated on market values when it is to start, on the assumption that the freeholder owns the land but the house-holder owns the buildings. The price for the freehold is the price of the property as if such a lease had been granted – so, in effect, it is the investment value of that income. If agreement is not reached, disputes are settled by leasehold valuation tribunals. The householder must pay the freeholder's legal fees and surveyor's costs.

LEGAL ADVICE

Sources of advice and help

Britain has no single national policy on the provision of legal services. As a result different official and voluntary agencies can sometimes overlap in the assistance they provide.

This assistance falls into two categories. LEGAL AID is for court cases. Legal advice and assistance are for work outside the courts and for representation in certain magistrates' court proceedings.

If you want free legal advice start by checking whether you qualify under the Law Society's green form scheme. In most cases, a client has to pay some contribution towards the solicitor's bill – unless he is receiving SUPPLEMENTARY BENEFIT or FAMILY INCOME SUPPLEMENT.

Some offer completely free advice:
Citizens Advice Bureaux give advice on all sorts of legal problems, at no cost whatever the inquirer's means. There are more than 700 CAB offices in Britain, staffed mainly by trained volunteers, but with some professional full-time workers, including lawyers, in the large cities. There is a central office in London to which advisers can refer for information on legal matters.

The Citizens Advice Bureau has detailed knowledge of which solicitors in its area do what work best, although it is generally cautious when giving advice in case it is thought to be favouring one against another.
Neighbourhood law centres In some city centres, local councils have set up neighbourhood law centres, financed from local funds and staffed by legally qualified people – including solicitors.

Law centres concentrate on the sort of cases which often arise in deprived city areas and which private solicitors are reluctant to take – for example, immigration, housing, employment, social security and consumer problems.

The service is generally free, but clients are sometimes asked to contribute towards costs. If a law centre decides to take up a case, it will handle the matter in exactly the same way as a private solicitor would do.
Legal advice centres, unlike law centres, only give advice or help not involving court work. They are staffed

by volunteer, but qualified lawyers.

Because the lawyers attend on a rota, it can be difficult for a client to see the same person twice in succession. Since secretarial facilities are limited it may be difficult for one lawyer to keep track of a case. Generally the lawyers will advise on all legal problems, but act only on some. For example, they will act on housing problems but not on those involving commercial transactions.
Trade unions often provide legal services for their members, occasionally through a lawyer on the union staff, but usually by referring members to a firm of lawyers retained on a consultancy basis. Most often the union helps with employment problems – for example, accident claims, redundancy claims and entitlement to industrial injury benefits.
Housing advice centres, operated by some local authorities and some independent bodies such as Shelter, specialise in housing matters. They can help to house or re-house the homeless and have lists of solicitors who specialise in housing problems.
Consumer advice centres, run by some local authorities, provide advice on consumer law and tell shoppers their rights. Some centres do undertake to write to shopkeepers on a consumer's behalf, and if that fails tell the 'customer' how to go about taking action in court.

Organisations such as the National Council for Civil Liberties, Release, and, for motoring problems, the AA and RAC may be able to help.

The Law Society List, available in your public library, will tell you what kind of cases each of your local firms of solicitors will handle. Telephone one or two firms and ask them if they undertake the type of work you want done. If they do, ask for an estimate.

The fixed-fee interview

About three-quarters of the firms on the Legal Aid Solicitors' List will give half-hour interviews to anyone for a flat fee of £5. But remember that it is only an 'introductory offer' and that subsequent interviews or action are likely to cost more. In most cases both client and lawyer can tell within half an hour whether it is worth continuing.

If you do want to take advantage of the scheme make that clear when you telephone for an appointment. Otherwise you may find yourself charged at the normal, higher rate. *See:* LEGAL COSTS

The green form scheme

The Law Society's green form scheme, so called because of the colour of the form the client has to complete, covers the first £45 of the solicitor's fee, for all work for which legal aid is appropriate.

If it is necessary to do more than £45 worth of work, it can be extended as necessary, for instance to provide another £25 worth.

Originally, the green form scheme was designed to cover non-court work only, but there is now one exception to this. The green form scheme can finance 'domestic proceedings' in the magistrates court, for instance, applying for an AFFILIATION ORDER, for a MAINTENANCE order, or for an exclusion or protection order against a violent husband. *See:* MATRIMONIAL ORDER

Otherwise, court proceedings are outside the green form scheme and the proper course of action is to apply for LEGAL AID.

How to qualify under the scheme

Entitlement to help under the green form scheme depends entirely on the amount of disposable income and disposable capital an applicant has.

Disposable income is what is left from a person's weekly earnings after deducting tax, national insurance and allowances for husband or wife, children, or other dependants. In 1981, the allowances were:

● £10.95 for each child up to 10 years of age.
● £16.35 for each child of 11–15 years of age.
● £19.65 for each dependant (or child) of 16–17 years of age.
● £25.60 for each dependant of 18 or over.
● £24.45 for a husband or wife.

Disposable capital is the total value of a person's assets after the value of his home, furniture and tools of trade has been deducted. If a person has no dependants, and disposable capital of £600, he cannot get help from the scheme, however small his income. The limit rises to £800 if he has one dependant, £920 if he has two, £980 for three and £60 for each further dependant.

A person with few capital assets and a disposable income of between £40 and £85 per week, has to pay a contribution assessed on a sliding scale.

The resources of husband and wife are added when the figures are being assessed, except where they have a contrary interest – for instance, divorce.

How to use the scheme

If you think you are eligible, tell your solicitor. Not all solicitors operate the scheme and if yours does not, you will have to go elsewhere.

If he does undertake green form work, the solicitor completes the form, giving information about your income and capital. He tells you how much you have to pay, if anything, asks you to sign the form, and probably asks for the amount due at the same time.

When those formalities have been completed the solicitor investigates your legal problem, with as much professional care as if you were a private client paying his normal rate.

When the solicitor has given £45 worth of advice, however, the client must pay any additional fees incurred, unless an extension can be arranged by the solicitor under the green form scheme.

If the green form scheme is being used in connection with domestic proceedings in a magistrates' court, then there is no £45 limit.

In undefended divorce cases, the green form limit is £55 – to compensate for the fact that full legal aid is no longer available for such work. It means you can get a lawyer to help with the preliminary work, although in court you must act for yourself or pay.

If a solicitor recovers money for his client as a result of working under the green form scheme, he is entitled to ask for payment from it to meet all the extra legal costs. This is called the statutory charge. Your lawyer can use the money to pay his own fees. For example, if you have already had to contribute £10 towards £45 worth of advice, and you gain £70 as a result of your lawyer's efforts, you may be asked to pay £35 of the proceeds to make up the 'green form' balance. But if your lawyer has only done £25 worth of work, your payment would be only £20; and in this case, if your earlier contribution had been £50, you would be entitled to a refund of £5.

Each case is considered separately. If it would cause hardship to make a contribution from the money won, the charge is waived.

Some of the fruits of the case are exempt from being used to pay the legal costs – in particular, maintenance payments and most welfare benefits.

So if a solicitor negotiates a settlement of a maintenance claim, he cannot take his legal fee from the maintenance payment. Instead he is paid by the Law Society and the client pays no more.

LEGAL AID

How you can get money to pay the lawyers

People involved in civil or criminal cases can often get financial assistance to help pay court costs and legal fees under the legal aid scheme. Generally, assistance in non-court cases is known not as legal aid but LEGAL ADVICE.

Legal aid is given only to people whose total disposable income and capital assets fall within strict limits.

Who qualifies for aid Anyone involved in a court case who believes he has insufficient money to pay the legal costs can apply for legal aid. The rules used for working out whether or not a person qualifies are similar for civil and criminal cases. (A criminal offence is one which harms public interests and is usually prosecuted by the state for punishment and retribution. A civil case is a dispute between individual parties, one of which is trying to obtain benefit for itself.)

Assessing disposable income

Everyone who applies for legal aid either to the magistrates' court or Law Society legal aid office must co-operate in a means test which falls into two parts. First it establishes how much disposable income the applicant has – that is, the amount of spare cash left over after specified living costs have been paid. If that falls below a fixed limit, the person qualifies for legal aid – subject to the second test.

The second test is to establish the size of the applicant's disposable capital assets. If that figure falls below a fixed limit, the applicant qualifies for legal aid, unless the court or legal aid committee rules that his case does not merit aid. In any case, he may be asked to pay part of the legal costs.

The means test To apply for legal aid in a civil case, get a form from a solicitor's office or Citizens Advice Bureau. Anyone seeking legal aid in a criminal case gets the form from the magistrates' court.

If you are involved in a civil case, state on the form what earnings you expect to have in the next 12 months, including your spouse's income unless you are in legal dispute with him/her. From your total gross income, deductions are made for tax, national insurance contributions, mortgage repayments or rent, cost of travel to and from

work, and for any dependants. What is left is your disposable income – the money you would normally spend on your own food, clothes, holidays, entertainment and savings.

If your disposable income exceeds £4,075 in a year, you will have to pay your own legal costs. If it is less than £1,700 in a year then you qualify for legal aid to cover the full cost of your court action.

If your income is between the two figures, you will get some legal aid but you must pay a contribution yourself – usually a quarter of the amount by which disposable income exceeds £1,700 a year.

If your income is below £4,075 you must apply the second test before the legal aid is finally granted.

Stricter financial levels apply in applications for criminal legal aid.

Working out your assets The second part of the form asks you to fill in the total value of all your assets – excluding the value of your house and furniture, car, clothes, and tools or trade equipment.

If your court action is a civil case involving a dispute over an article, such as a boat or a piece of land, you do not add the value of that particular item to your list of assets.

The disposable value of your capital is the total value of all other assets, such as your boat, savings, investments, valuable jewellery and the amount you could borrow against an insurance policy. Capital allowances, which may be deducted from this total, include: any debt likely to be repaid from capital in the next 12 months, such as rent arrears. If the final total is more than £2,500, you will not usually qualify for legal aid. However, in certain high-cost cases the 'capital' rules may be waived.

If your disposable capital is less than £1,200, you qualify for legal aid in full. If it is between £1,200 and £2,500 you will have to pay some part of your legal costs – probably the amount by which your capital exceeds £1,200, but the total of your disposable income is taken into account.

Placing your application Once you have completed the relevant forms they must be sent, in civil cases, to the local office of the Law Society, in criminal cases, to the clerk to the magistrates' court. The address of the Law Society's

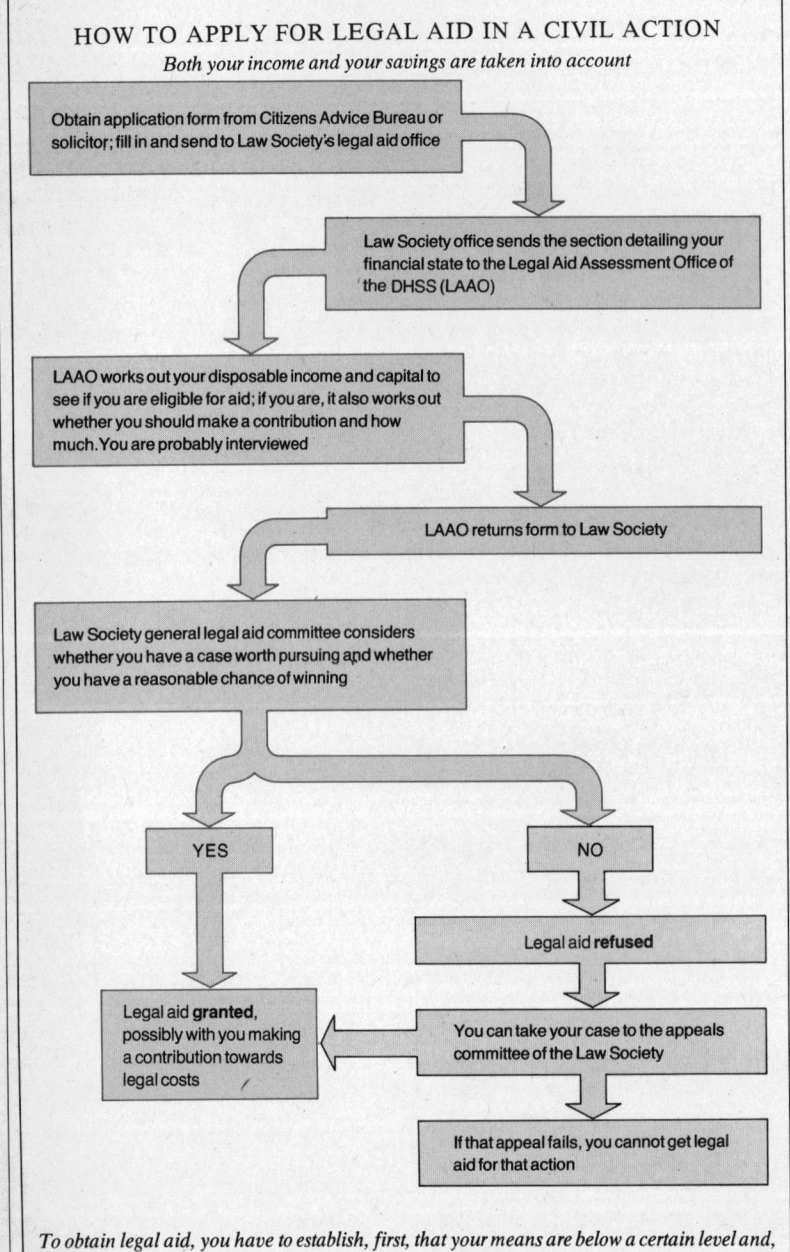

HOW TO APPLY FOR LEGAL AID IN A CIVIL ACTION
Both your income and your savings are taken into account

Obtain application form from Citizens Advice Bureau or solicitor; fill in and send to Law Society's legal aid office

Law Society office sends the section detailing your financial state to the Legal Aid Assessment Office of the DHSS (LAAO)

LAAO works out your disposable income and capital to see if you are eligible for aid; if you are, it also works out whether you should make a contribution and how much. You are probably interviewed

LAAO returns form to Law Society

Law Society general legal aid committee considers whether you have a case worth pursuing and whether you have a reasonable chance of winning

YES — NO

Legal aid **refused**

Legal aid **granted**, possibly with you making a contribution towards legal costs

You can take your case to the appeals committee of the Law Society

If that appeal fails, you cannot get legal aid for that action

To obtain legal aid, you have to establish, first, that your means are below a certain level and, secondly, that you have a good case. In actions on behalf of children it is the means of the adult through whom they are suing that are assessed.

local office can be found in the local telephone directory. Your solicitor will tell you where it is.

Even in routine civil cases it is advisable to see a solicitor first to seek advice on the strength of your application and your prospects of getting legal aid. He will know how best to fill in the form and will be able to point out weaknesses in your application.

If you do consult a lawyer you may have to pay for his help. This can be done under the Green Form scheme or under the £5 fixed fee procedure. You agree to pay £5 for a half-hour interview with a lawyer to discuss your case, so that he can decide if he can pursue it further.

This fee cannot be met by legal aid.
See: LEGAL ADVICE

Checking a claim

When your application has been sent in, the Law Society sends that part containing financial details to the Legal Aid Assessment Office of the Department of Health and Social Security for inquiry and assessment. The LAAO investigates details of the applicant's capital and income, partly from the infor-

WHEN LEGAL AID MAY BE AVAILABLE IN CRIMINAL CASES
A system of financial help operated by the courts themselves

Legal aid in a criminal case is administered by the court in which the trial is to be heard, and not by the Law Society. Anyone facing prosecution should therefore apply for aid to the court. Special forms are available at the court office. An accused is granted criminal legal aid only if he comes within the financial limits, and if the court thinks it right that he should receive legal aid.

Magistrates' court Aid can be granted by the magistrates or by their clerk. But the clerk cannot refuse a criminal legal aid application – only the magistrates can do so.

Crown court Aid can be granted by the magistrates when they commit an accused for trial in the crown court. Alternatively, it can be granted on application to the crown court itself.

Generally, criminal legal aid is only granted in the more serious cases. Lord Chief Justice Widgery recommended in 1973 that legal aid be granted if it is a grave charge, in the sense that the accused is in real jeopardy of losing his liberty or livelihood, or of suffering serious damage to his reputation.

Criminal legal aid is also recommended for cases in which there are substantial legal issues raised, or if the nature of the defence involves the tracing and interviewing of witnesses or expert cross-examination.

The effect of these rules is that usually all crown court defendants are granted legal aid, subject to their passing the means test. But in the magistrates' court the position is more confused: different courts apply different standards, and an application that would succeed in one court will fail in another.

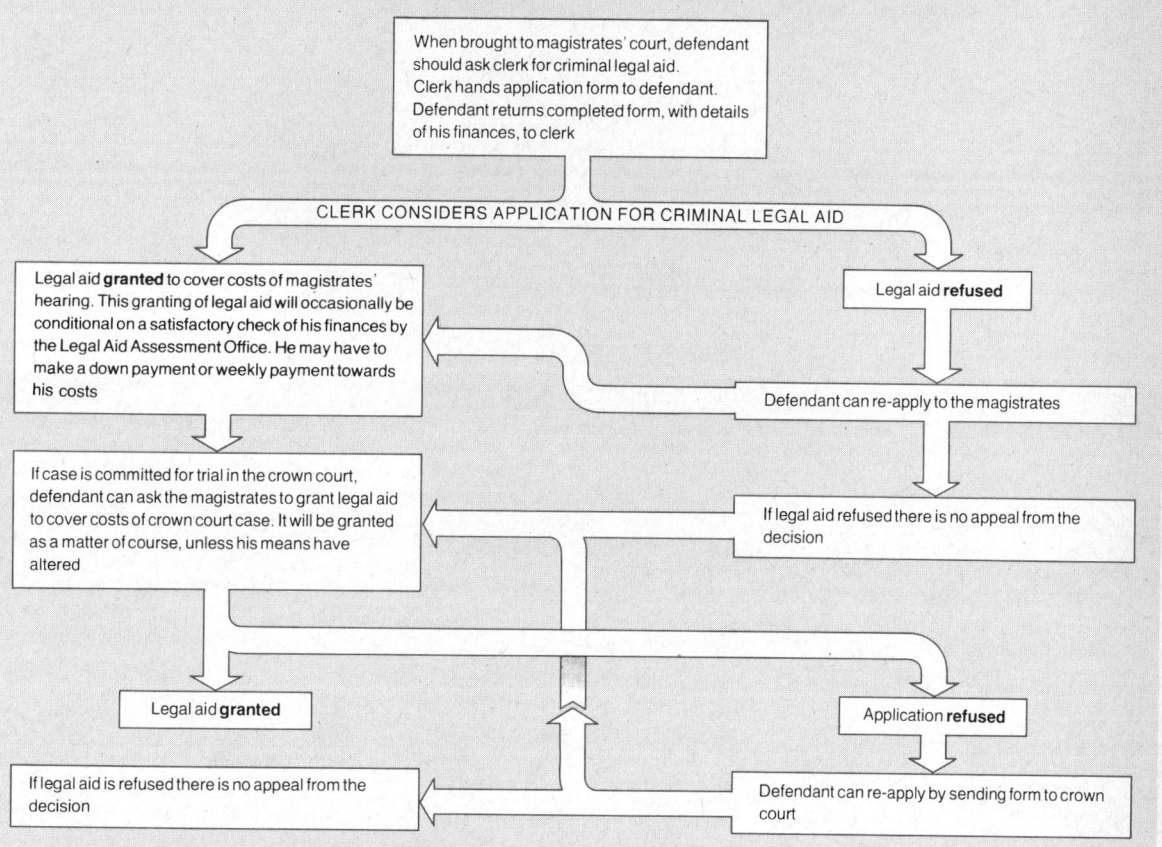

When brought to magistrates' court, defendant should ask clerk for criminal legal aid. Clerk hands application form to defendant. Defendant returns completed form, with details of his finances, to clerk

CLERK CONSIDERS APPLICATION FOR CRIMINAL LEGAL AID

Legal aid **granted** to cover costs of magistrates' hearing. This granting of legal aid will occasionally be conditional on a satisfactory check of his finances by the Legal Aid Assessment Office. He may have to make a down payment or weekly payment towards his costs

Legal aid **refused**

Defendant can re-apply to the magistrates

If case is committed for trial in the crown court, defendant can ask the magistrates to grant legal aid to cover costs of crown court case. It will be granted as a matter of course, unless his means have altered

If legal aid refused there is no appeal from the decision

Legal aid **granted**

Application **refused**

If legal aid is refused there is no appeal from the decision

Defendant can re-apply by sending form to crown court

mation given and partly from further inquiries. In criminal cases, legal aid applications are often made to the magistrates or their clerk, who grants aid conditionally. Applications are passed to the commission only in diffi-cult cases or at the applicant's request.

Applicants are usually interviewed by a supplementary benefits officer. When

HOW TO WORK OUT WHETHER YOU ARE ELIGIBLE FOR LEGAL AID IN A CIVIL ACTION

A step-by-step guide to assess means against possible needs within the state scheme

Start here with **CHART NO. 1**. Only if you are eligible under Chart No. 1 need you go on to Chart No. 2

Income

Enter your weekly gross income, including that of your spouse (unless you are in dispute with the spouse – e.g. defended divorce), and any child benefit you receive		£114.00 **(A)**

But you are allowed certain deductions:

Weekly NI and tax payments	£28.08
Work expenses (e.g. cost of travel, tools, trade union dues, childminding)	£5.50
If you live with your husband or wife and also maintain him or her, you can also deduct	£20.92

For each dependent child you can also deduct an amount equal to the current supplementary benefit allowances	Age	£	£7.81
	0– 5	7.81	
	5 – 10	7.95	
	11 – 12	10.33	
	13 – 15	11.93	
	16 – 17	14.33	
	over 18	18.68	

Weekly rent or mortgage payments	£15.00

Add up all these deductions	£77.31 **(B)**
This is your **'weekly disposable income'** (deduct **'B'** from **'A'**)	£36.69 **(C)**
Now multiply **'C'** *by 52*	× 52
This is your **'annual disposable income'**	£1,907.88 **(D)**

If **'D'** exceeds £4,075, you are not eligible for legal aid

If **'D'** is less than £1,700 then you are eligible for legal aid. You will not have to make any contribution towards your legal costs, unless you have more than a certain amount of capital. Turn to Chart 2 to see how much capital you must have before you might be asked to make a contribution

If **'D'** is between £1,700 and £4,075 you are eligible for legal aid, but you will have to pay a contribution towards the cost. This contribution could be as much as ¼ of the amount by which **'D'** exceeds £1,700. In addition, you may have to pay an extra contribution, depending on the amount of capital you have: turn on to Chart 2, to see how much that could be.

Income contribution in the example above is:
£1,907 *minus* £1,700 .... £207.00
Divide £207 by 4 .... £51.75

Maximum income contribution **£51.75**

the commission reports back it states how much the applicant should be expected to pay towards his costs.

Even if all these inquiries show that you qualify financially for legal aid, it will not automatically be granted.

In civil cases, the Law Society's legal aid committee may consider that your case is not worth fighting. It may decide

This is **CHART NO. 2**. You should only refer to this chart if you have already been through Chart No. 1

Capital

List the value of all your assets. But you need not include your house, furniture, clothes, tools, trade equipment, or any item which is the subject matter of the dispute

Cash, savings, bank accounts, national savings certificates, shares, etc	£950	
The amount you could borrow on the security of an insurance policy you have	nil	
The fair, realisable, value of your assets	£650	
If you have a business, write down the amount that you could reasonably take out of it, without impairing its profitability	nil	
Add up all your assets. This is your **'disposable capital'**		£1600 **(E)**

If **'E'** exceeds £2,500 the Law Society has a discretionary power to refuse you legal aid

If **'E'** is less than £1,200, then you cannot be expected to use any of your capital to contribute towards your legal fees. Whether or not you will be eligible for legal aid, and whether or not you will have to make a contribution to your legal costs will depend entirely on the amount of your income. Refer to Chart 1

If **'E'** is between £1,200 and £2,500, the Law Society has a discretionary power to ask you to make a contribution towards your legal fees. This contribution will be the amount by which **'E'** exceeds £1,200

Capital contribution in this example is:

£1,600 *minus* £1,200 .... £400.00

So maximum contribution is:

Maximum income contribution £51.75
    plus
Capital contribution £400.00

Maximum contribution **£451.75**

Two factors are involved in deciding whether the state is prepared to give you financial help in a civil action. A local panel of the Law Society must be satisfied that you have a good case that is worth pursuing. If it does not think so, you can appeal to the central legal aid committee. But you must also qualify financially for legal aid. Such qualification depends both on your income and on any *capital assets you have built up, other than your home and furniture and tools and equipment that are essential to you earning your living. In the case of children under 18 years old who can sue only through an adult 'next friend', it is the financial position of the next friend that is considered when an application for legal aid is submitted on the child's behalf.*

that you have little chance of winning, or will not gain much if you do win – for instance if the defendant is known not to have extensive assets – and that it is not worth advancing the money.

You can appeal against this decision to the society's appeals committee. If the appeal is rejected you can take the matter no further.

Legal aid cannot be obtained to pay for legal advice unconnected with a court case, nor for cases involving libel, slander, or tribunal cases, such as unfair dismissal or redundancy.

When legal aid is granted in criminal cases

In criminal trials, legal aid is granted only in the more serious cases, such as where an accused person may lose his liberty or livelihood, or suffer serious damage to his reputation. It is also granted in cases which raise important legal issues and for applications for bail pending trial.

In effect, this means that all defendants to be tried in crown courts are granted legal aid by the magistrates, provided they pass the financial means test.

In magistrates' courts defendants are granted legal aid only at the discretion of the magistrates or their clerk. But if the magistrates refuse and the defendant is subsequently sent to the crown court, he can re-apply for legal aid to the crown court. If this is rejected, there is no further appeal.

When a limited certificate is granted

Sometimes in civil cases the aid granted will be a 'limited certificate', which means that the solicitor is authorised to go only to a certain stage in the action – to obtain a medical report or counsel's advice, for example.

When that stage is reached, the Law Society committee looks again at the case to see if the provision of more legal aid is justified.

When you have to make a contribution

If the Legal Aid Assessment Office calculates that you are able to pay some of your own costs, you are told how

---

MEETING YOUR LEGAL BILLS

Anyone involved in a court action may be able to receive financial help through the legal aid system for any court costs or legal fees incurred.

---

much when the firm offer of aid is made to you.

You do not necessarily have to pay the full amount of that assessed contribution.

If the estimated costs are less than that maximum, you need only pay the amount of the estimate.

At the end of the case you may be asked for more (but still only to the maximum sum quoted to you earlier), or alternatively there may even be a refund if the costs are less than you paid.

Paying by instalments

When you are paying your contribution out of 'disposable income' you can pay it by instalments, as your salary reaches you on a monthly or other regular basis over 1 year. That is not possible, as a rule, with contributions from 'disposable capital'.

No one is forced to agree to the contribution demanded, but if you refuse, legal aid will not be granted.

In theory an applicant for legal aid has no right of appeal, but in practice the Law Society can ask the LAAO for details of the assessment. The office may review and reduce the amount of contribution. Even when it does not, you can always refuse to pay – if you decide to drop the case.

In criminal cases the accused often has to make a down-payment or a weekly payment to cover a possible order that he contributes towards his costs.

Changing solicitors

If you are on legal aid you are entitled to change solicitors if you have a valid reason, for example if you moved to a new area or your solicitor moved to another firm and you wanted him to continue handling your case. Then you would transfer to the new firm.

The old solicitors must give the papers relating to your case to the new firm, and their costs up to the time of transfer are paid when the Legal Aid Fund pays the bill.

If you are paying your solicitor from your own funds, you can change for any reason, but your original solicitor need not hand over your file until you have paid him.

When legal aid ends

Civil legal aid is not generally awarded for a specific period of time unless the certificate says so. But there are two ways that it can be taken from you.

If as the case goes on it seems that you have no prospect of success, it may be 'discharged' by the Law Society on the ground that the expense is unreasonable. You cease to be legally aided from the date of discharge.

If you refuse to co-operate with the LAAO after you have been granted legal aid, your legal aid certificate may be revoked which means that you have, legally, never been entitled to legal aid. You must therefore repay the Law Society for all work done on your case.

How the solicitor is paid

Your solicitor sends his bill to the local legal aid office. You are not even told how much he is paid. In crown court cases the court decides how much the lawyers are paid.

When a legally aided civil case comes to an end

The general rule in civil cases is that the loser pays the winner's costs, as well as his own lawyer's fees and expenses. *See:* LEGAL COSTS

If the loser is on legal aid, however, the amount he pays towards his legal costs is limited to the total 'contribution' he was asked for when granted aid. But he may still have to pay something towards the winner's costs. If the legally aided person wins, then the amount contributed by the Legal Aid Fund can be deducted from the damages he is awarded if the loser does not pay the winner's costs for him.

LEGAL COSTS

*What your solicitor can
include in his charges*

When a businessman or tradesman talks of costs, he means his overheads, the cost of running his business before giving himself profit. When a solicitor does so, he is including all his expenses plus the fee for his professional services – his profit.

By custom any bill for legal services is in two sections – disbursements and profit costs. Disbursements are expenses incurred on the client's behalf. For example if you are buying a house, your solicitor has to pay for local authority searches, land registry fees, and stamp duty, in addition to basic office expenses such as stationery, postage and telephone calls. All those he will charge to your account. Profit costs are his fee for handling the case, and represent his charge for the work completed. On top of that there is VAT to pay.

Payment for work done out of court

For all work not involving an appearance in court, solicitors must legally charge no more than a 'fair and reasonable' amount. What is 'fair and reasonable' depends on:

● The complexity of the matter.
● The degree of skill involved.
● The number and importance of the documents.
● The circumstances in which the work is done.
● The time spent. The fact that a proposed purchase falls through, for example, does not mean that the solicitor should not be paid. He can claim for all the work he has done.
● The value of the money and/or property at stake; for example, handling the sale of a £100,000 house justifies a larger fee than handling one selling for £10,000, because if he makes a mistake the solicitor's liability is much greater.

● In conveyancing matters, whether the land is registered or not. If it is, costs are lower.
● The importance of the matter to the client.

Non-court work includes buying and selling houses and businesses, drawing up leases, administering estates, drafting wills and drawing up contracts.

How the solicitor's bill is calculated

Most solicitors have some form of time-keeping system whereby they record daily the actual time spent on each case they are handling. They then charge the time at an hourly rate.

That rate is more for a senior than a junior, so a client who demands the services of a firm's senior partner has to pay more than the one who is content to have the same job handled by an assistant solicitor.

Because of the differences in rates chargeable, it is advisable not to insist that your affairs be handled by a solicitor instead of one of the firm's clerks. Clerks are often experienced and very competent.

The hourly rate must also reflect a firm's overheads. Offices and staff in central London cost more than in a country town, for example. Such costs must be reflected in the fees – albeit indirectly.

A solicitor is likely to charge between £15 and £30 an hour for non-court work. Under the green form LEGAL ADVICE scheme, and for LEGAL AID work in the magistrates' court, solicitors are paid £22 an hour for court appearances, £18 an hour while advising the client and preparing the case, £1.50 for each letter written, and £1.50 for each phone call. Many solicitors regard those fees as unprofitable.

If a case presents any special problems, they add an extra sum and so arrive at their fee. To that figure they add out-of-pocket expenses, and the two together make up the final bill plus VAT.

Seeking an estimate

It pays to telephone several firms for a rough estimate before you decide to engage a solicitor, even although none can give a precise figure at the outset. Check that you are comparing like with

like. For example, one firm may include VAT in its estimate, while another may itemise those amounts separately later. Even more importantly, one firm may include disbursements while the other may not.

It may be possible to find a solicitor who is willing to offer a binding quotation of what your action will cost. If so, the agreement must be in writing and signed by you. Such an agreement is not 100 per cent binding on the client, who can ask the court to reduce it if he considers it unreasonable.

If you think your solicitor has not been 'fair and reasonable' in charging for non-court work, you should ask him for an explanation of the bill. If he refuses, you can ask for a remuneration certificate from the Law Society and/or ask that the bill be 'taxed' by the High Court.

Asking for a remuneration certificate

When you ask your solicitor to apply to the Law Society – which controls all solicitors in England and Wales – for a remuneration certificate for the work he has done on your behalf, he is obliged to send his file of papers on your case to the society. Its officials then decide whether the bill is 'fair and reasonable'.

Even if the decision is against you, you have lost nothing. The Law Society cannot increase the fee and it costs you nothing to have the papers examined.

However, that usually takes 3 or 4 months, during which the solicitor is kept waiting for his money. Depending on how strongly he feels about the case, the solicitor may agree to a small reduction in his fee rather than wait for the society to reach a decision.

If you are unhappy with the charge assessed by the society, you need not pay. Ask the High Court to 'tax' the bill.

If you have already paid the solicitor before you decide that you have been overcharged, you cannot ask for a remuneration certificate. Instead you must ask for the bill to be taxed.

However, if your solicitor simply deducts his fee from any money he has to give you – for example, when you are the beneficiary of a will or when you have deposited money with him – you are not limited in that way. The bill was paid without your approval, so you can ask the Law Society for a remuneration certificate. But act quickly, otherwise your inaction will be taken as agreement of the bill.

Taxing in court

To have a bill taxed means that it goes before a court official who decides whether it is 'fair and reasonable'. If the solicitor has declined to reduce his fee and the Law Society has agreed with him, it is unlikely that a court official will find in the client's favour.

The court, moreover, has the power to increase the amount charged. For those reasons it is advisable not to opt for taxing unless you feel extremely strongly that you have been overcharged.

If the solicitor's bill is increased, left as it was, or reduced by less than one-fifth, you must pay for the costs and inconvenience of taxation. If one-fifth or more is deducted from the bill, the solicitor must pay for the taxing procedure. If his bill is reduced by more than half, the Law Society is notified and may investigate in case the solicitor has been guilty of unprofessional overcharging.

A basic difference between the two methods is that whereas a request for taxation can follow an application for a remuneration certificate, if the client asks for taxation first he cannot then request action by the Law Society. Taxation, therefore, is a last resort.

When a solicitor can sue

In non-court cases, a solicitor must follow a set procedure before he can sue a client for unpaid fees.

He must give the client written notice that he, the client, is entitled to apply to the Law Society for a remuneration certificate and that he can have the bill taxed.

The client has only a month from when he receives the solicitor's letter in which to call for a certificate. If he does not ask the solicitor to obtain a remuneration certificate in that month he loses his right to do so and is left with taxation as the only alternative. Technically, the court can deny even that procedure after a month, but it seldom does so.

At the end of the month following his letter to the client, the solicitor can sue for non-payment.

TIMING YOUR BILL

Most solicitors have some means of calculating how much time is spent by themselves and their staff on every client's case.

'Right! My costs start as from – NOW!'

When court work is involved

In any civil court case – where one person or company is suing another – the loser pays the winner's legal costs as well as his own. The winner of a civil action is denied costs only in very exceptional cases – for example, if his case was unmeritorious or won on a technicality.

Even when the loser pays, however, he does not have to compensate the winner for all his costs – known as 'solicitor and client costs'.

He must pay only those that were 'necessarily or properly incurred for the attainment of justice', called 'party and party costs'.

Any other costs incurred by the winner's lawyers that were not strictly necessary must be paid by the winner.

For example, if a Q.C. has been briefed when a less senior barrister would have been enough, or unnecessary diagrams and plans for the scene of a road accident have been prepared, those costs would have to be paid by the winner of the case as 'solicitor and client costs'.

When a case has been decided and the court orders the loser to pay the winner's costs, the winner's solicitor sends a summary of the costs to be paid to the loser's solicitor.

If they cannot agree a figure, the winner's solicitor may apply to the registrar at the county court involved or the taxing officer in the High Court for the costs to be 'taxed'.

He prepares a detailed bill of the costs for an informal discussion between himself, the loser's solicitor and the registrar or taxation officer when the taxing officer decides whether to disallow or reduce parts of the bill.

For some types of work there are set limits on what the loser can be charged. Often though, inflation has made the limits well out of date and the winner's solicitor will want to charge more. If so, the difference between the set rate and what is actually charged must be borne by the winning client.

The loser – landlord or tenant – would have to pay the excess amount owed to his lawyer.

Legal aid costs

If a person who has been granted legal aid wins his case, his solicitor's costs are paid for on what is known as a 'common fund basis' by the Legal Aid Fund.

If a court orders the loser to pay costs, they are usually only the 'party and party costs' that have been necessarily incurred by the winner's solicitor during the case. Any further costs are paid for on the common fund basis out of the Legal Aid Fund.

However, if the costs incurred by the winner's solicitor exceed those paid on a party and party basis by the loser, the winner has to make up the difference.

Usually, the amount is deducted from the winner's original contribution to legal aid, but it may also be deducted from any damages that the winner has been awarded.

The loser sends any damages awarded to the winner's solicitor. He sends the money to the Law Society so that the Legal Aid Fund may be reimbursed if necessary.

If a person who has been ordered to pay costs after a losing a case is unable to do so – for example, because he has gone bankrupt – any common fund costs that have been paid to the winner's solicitor by the Legal Aid Fund will have to be repaid to the fund by the winner out of the winner's contribution to Legal Aid, or from any damages awarded to him.

If you lose a legally aided case, you seldom actually have to pay the winner's costs in full, although the court could order you to do so. Because you are legally aided, it usually fixes a maximum sum for you to pay – generally the same as your initial contribution.

So all you have to pay, probably, is no more than twice the amount of your contribution. If your opponent as a result faces financial hardship, the Legal Aid Fund pays the balance.

When costs have to be paid in criminal cases

In criminal cases, where someone faces a charge that could lead to his being fined or imprisoned, the general rule that the loser pays the winner's costs seldom applies.

Although an individual is presumed innocent until proved guilty, the fact that he may be proved innocent does not mean that it was wrong for him to be prosecuted. Whether an acquitted person is awarded his costs often depends on which court he was tried in.

After trial in a crown court an acquitted defendant normally receives costs – unless there are strong reasons for withholding payment. For example, it may happen that there is an indication of guilt but the court is obliged to acquit on a technicality. In that case he would get nothing.

An acquitted defendant is less likely to recover his costs in a magistrates' court. As a rule he will be refunded only when the evidence against him has been very flimsy, which means the prosecution should not have been brought.

Costs are usually paid out of public (central government) funds, but if a court believes the prosecution should never have been brought, the prosecutor may be ordered to pay – for example the local police authority. In this case the money comes from the ratepayers.

Costs in a small claim case

If you sue for no more than £200 do not expect to recover your costs even if you win. On the other hand you are not usually ordered to pay if you lose.

When a barrister has to be paid

Barristers' fees are not fixed. Usually they are negotiated by their clerks with the instructing solicitors.

If a negotiated fee is considered by a court to be too high for the case just heard, it can order the loser to pay only

a 'reasonable' amount. But the winner is still liable to pay the full fee. In practice, the solicitor is personally liable for the barrister's fee and so will ask the client for the amount negotiated before giving instruction to the barrister.

A barrister cannot sue either his client or the solicitor for non-payment.

DOCTOR PAID FOR THE CASE HE WON

It can sometimes be more expensive to win a case than to lose it.

A German called Dr Dering was accused by novelist Leon Uris in his book *Exodus* of taking part in 17,000 experimental operations in the Nazi concentration camp at Auschwitz. Dr Dering sued for libel.

DECISION

Dr Dering won his case. He proved that although he had taken part in some operations he had not taken part in 17,000. The court awarded Dr Dering ½d damages – and ordered him to pay the costs for both himself and the author.

WIDOW WON HER CASE BUT LOST HER MONEY

Legal costs can be so high that the person who wins a case may be worse off than he or she was before.

Mr Parkinson died in 1976 and left his 61-year-old widow his house and other assets, worth about £4,000 – but only for the remainder of her lifetime. After that everything was to go to the RSPCA.

The value of that lifetime interest in the house and the assets was not enough to meet the costs of living in the house. Mrs Parkinson appealed in the county court for 'reasonable provision' to be made from the estate. The court refused to alter the will and she appealed.

DECISION

The Court of Appeal upheld Mrs Parkinson's plea. But Mrs Parkinson had to pay the costs – there was no one else to pay except the estate. The costs of both hearings were £1,000 – a quarter of the whole estate. To pay, she had to sell the house – the very thing she had gone to court to claim.

But he can make a complaint against the solicitor to the Law Society.

Paying a solicitor

Unless a solicitor knows you very well, it is likely he will ask for an advance payment, called money on account, before he agrees to take your case. Similarly he is likely to ask for the amount of the fee agreed for the barrister, if one is to represent you.

When a solicitor's final bill is submitted, it is payable immediately. If you want to pay by instalments, arrange that with the solicitor at the outset.

If you do not settle his bill, the solicitor is entitled to retain all the papers relating to your case – which means, for example, that you cannot change solicitors and continue your action.

If a solicitor holds more than £500 for more than 2 months on a client's behalf, he must pay interest at the level currently being paid to depositors by clearing banks. If the amount is less than £500 the interest is agreed between solicitor and client. A dispute can be referred to the Law Society.

LEGAL TENDER
When money must be accepted

Debts and purchases must be paid for in cash of legal tender unless the creditor or seller is willing to accept payment in another form such as a cheque or postal order.

Bank of England £1 notes and coins struck by the Royal Mint are legal tender throughout the United Kingdom – notes and gold coins for any amount, other coins to restricted limits:
● 50p and 25p coins (crowns) are legal tender for payment of amounts up to £10.
● 10p, 5p and 6d coins are legal tender for amounts up to £5.
● 2p, 1p and ½p coins are legal tender for amounts up to 20p.

Bank of England notes of £5, £10 and £20 denominations are legal tender only in England and Wales.

The law requires payment of the exact amount owed; the creditor cannot be forced to give change. If you wish to purchase an item costing £7 and have only a £10 note the seller can give you the option of paying £10 or not buying.

In practice this right is rarely exercised.

Scottish and Northern Ireland banknotes are not legal tender anywhere.

After notes and coins have been 'called in' they cease to be legal tender.

LEVEL CROSSING

Where a railway line crosses the road

There are three kinds of level crossing in Britain:

● Open level crossings, at which the driver must look and listen for the approach of a train before proceeding.

● Crossings with gates or full barriers, usually operated either by an attendant or by remote control.

● Crossings with half-barriers which drop automatically when a train approaches.

There are warning signs before all level crossings, often accompanied by double white lines to prevent overtaking. Drivers should approach a level crossing at moderate speed, keeping a good distance from the car ahead, and cross with care only if the road on the other side is clear.

Some crossings have flashing red lights, or amber lights and bells, to warn that a train is near. You must stop at these lights, but, if you are already on the crossing when they begin to flash, keep going ahead.

To cross on a red light, or when the gates begin to close or the barriers to descend, is an offence. You could be prosecuted for failure to observe a traffic sign and be disqualified from driving and fined. *See also:* RECKLESS DRIVING

LIABILITY INSURANCE

How you can insure against having a claim against you

Businessmen, traders and other employers can take out liability insurance to safeguard themselves against claims for damages in respect of accidents involving employees or the public:

1. Employer's liability Virtually all private employers are legally obliged to take out insurance to provide at least £2 million cover against claims arising for their legal liability for the death or injury of any employee. The only circum-

stances in which such cover is not compulsory are when the employee is a close relative or domestic servant. *See:* EMPLOYER'S LIABILITY

Every employer is required to display copies of his insurance certificate in a prominent position at each place of business. The maximum penalty for not doing so is a fine of £50.

2. Public liability A businessman or trader can if he wishes insure against the risk of claims from members of the public – for example, from a customer who slips and injures herself in a shop. *See:* PUBLIC LIABILITY

LIBEL AND SLANDER

When writing or speaking too freely can be dangerous

The reputation of any man or woman, in law, is entitled to protection against unfair or malicious attack. Anybody who accuses or criticises another person – and so damages his or her reputation – risks being sued for defamation.

If the offending remarks are in writing or some other permanent form, the defamation is libel. If they were only spoken, it is generally slander. The exception is when the offending words are broadcast on radio or television. The defamation is then treated as if it were in permanent form, like writing, even if the broadcast is not a recording.

For a libel or slander action to stand a chance of success, the person bringing

the case, the plaintiff, must prove that what was said:

● Was defamatory.

● Referred to him.

● Was communicated to a third person.

Even if those three conditions apply, however, a libel or slander action can still fail, against one of several defences: justification, fair comment or privilege.

What makes a statement defamatory

The law does not strictly define what is a defamatory statement – whether it is spoken, written or in the form of a picture. It is for a jury to decide.

There is a general principle, however, that a statement is libellous or slanderous if it damages the reputation of the plaintiff, or tends to lower him in the eyes of ordinary men and women.

From that standpoint, some types of comment are more risky than others. It is particularly dangerous, for example, to criticise someone's morals or honesty, or accuse him of criminal behaviour or professional incompetence.

For example, it may be safe to write that a television actor's performance was unsatisfactory, and even to write the same about subsequent performances. But it is libellous to suggest that he is generally incompetent as an actor.

Defamation by innuendo A statement that seems innocent can still lead to a libel or slander action, if people reading or hearing it are able to draw an inference that is defamatory.

THE 'PLOT' WITHIN A PLOT

When a statement of fact is alleged to be defamatory, it is no use pleading 'fair comment' in defence. The defendant must show that what he said was substantially true.

Coral Browne, Anthony Quayle, Anna Massey and Corin Redgrave were the four leading actors in the West End production of *The Right Honourable Gentleman*. They each gave in their notice to the impresario Emile Littler who was putting on the play.

Mr Littler believed it was a plot engineered by Mr Lew Grade, one of whose companies managed the four artists. He believed that Mr Grade wanted the play

to close so that he would be able to put on his own production of another play at the same theatre.

Mr Littler wrote to all four artists about his suspicions and was sued for libel by Mr Grade.

DECISION

The Court of Appeal held that the letters were defamatory. To accuse someone of a plot was a statement of alleged fact, and so Mr Littler could not rely on the defence of fair comment. The only defence was that the statement had been true and he had failed to prove that.

He was ordered to pay damages of £2,250 and costs.

For example, it may seem harmless for a newspaper to publish a photograph of a man and woman, with a caption announcing their engagement. But if it transpires that the man is in fact already married, his wife can successfully sue on the ground that, to people who knew her, the caption carries the innuendo that she is merely the man's mistress and has been pretending to be his wife.

Identifying the person defamed

An action for defamation cannot succeed unless the offending statement either names the plaintiff or is put in such a way that ordinary people know to whom it refers.

If, for example, a writer on food says that an Italian restaurant in a certain town is infested with mice, and there is only one Italian restaurant in that town, he can be sued. But if he writes that every restaurant in the town cheats in its bills – and there is a large number of restaurants – a court is likely to rule that the statement is a generalisation and that no individual restaurant has grounds for action.

A group of people cannot sue as a group, unless as a company or partnership. Each member of a defamed group must sue individually and be able to show that he or she was clearly the subject of the defamatory statement.

Defaming the dead

Only a living person – or a company that is still trading – can sue. A dead person is regarded as being beyond damage. His surviving friends or relatives cannot sue on his behalf.

Publication must be proved

For a libel or slander action to succeed, it must be shown that the defamatory material was published – that is, communicated to a third person – in writing or pictures, or by word of mouth or in gestures.

If someone accuses you of dishonesty, but does so to you personally, in total privacy, you cannot sue him. But if he raises his voice and someone else overhears the accusation, that is defamation.

It is not necessarily a defence to show someone accused of defamation did not intend his statement to be communicated to a third party. For example, if you receive a letter containing libellous material, and it is opened by someone else – for example, a secretary – you may be able to sue whoever sent it. That

POSSIBLE DEFENCES AGAINST AN ACTION FOR DEFAMATION

Three main defences are open to anyone accused of defamation: justification, fair comment or privilege.

Justification
The best defence against an action for libel or slander is to prove that the statement complained of was true. It is often difficult, however, to establish the truth of a defamatory statement. The law assumes that such a statement is false unless the defendant can prove that it is substantially true.

Fair comment
Anyone making a defamatory statement that consists of comment, as distinct from an allegation of fact, can protect himself by ensuring that the comment is made honestly, that it is on a matter of public interest and that he has no improper motive, such as malice.

For something to be a matter of public interest, and therefore subject to 'fair comment', it does not necessarily have to be of general interest to the public. It must, however, be a matter in which the public is entitled to take an interest because it is of genuine public concern.

A local newspaper may write, for example, that rates are unnecessarily high because the chairman of the finance committee has an inadequate grasp of local government budgeting.

If the chairman sues for libel, the newspaper must prove that it was an honest comment on his performance as chairman of a public body. That defence will not succeed if the chairman can prove that the newspaper editor – or, unknown to the editor – a reporter was motivated by malice in publishing the report.

Comments on the sexual morality of private – or even public – individuals are not likely to be considered matters of public interest, however 'fair' those comments may be.

A comment does not, however, cease to be fair merely because most people disagree with it. If a fair-minded person could have made it honestly – and it was in fact honestly made – then it is fair comment.

For example, if a critic writes a scathing review of a book, it is an expression of opinion that he is entitled to make, provided that there is no improper motive – such as personal vendetta against the author.

Privilege
There are two types of privilege: absolute and qualified.

Absolute privilege A statement covered by absolute privilege is protected against an action for defamation in all circumstances. For example, a member of the House of Commons or Lords can say whatever he likes during a parliamentary debate. Witnesses giving evidence in court are similarly protected and so are newspapers and broadcasters reporting parliamentary or judicial proceedings.

Absolute privilege also protects statements made by a client to his solicitor and reports made by officers of the armed forces to their superiors.

Qualified privilege The second category safeguards someone who makes a defamatory statement only if these conditions apply:
● The person who makes the statement has a legally recognised interest or duty to do so.
● The person to whom he communicates the statement also has a legally recognised interest in it, or duty to receive it.
● The person making the statement is not motivated by malice – that is, any dishonest, improper or other ulterior motive.

Someone who, for example, reports a burglary to the police and who claims – mistakenly – that he recognised the burglar, is protected by qualified privilege from being sued for defamation by the person he identifies, provided that he can show he made the claim in good faith.

Again, a ratepayer who complains to his local town hall that he has seen refuse collectors idling when they should have been working may be mistaken, but the collectors cannot sue him because as a ratepayer he has a proper interest in speaking out – and even has a duty to do so.

However, if someone were to telephone a laundry and allege that one of its delivery men had spent the last hour in the home of a woman customer, the defence of qualified privilege would not be available.

What the delivery man did is not the business of the person who made the call, and unless he can prove that both what he said and what he implied by making such a statement were true, he has no defence to an action for defamation.

THE COUNCILLORS WHO CLASHED
OVER A PIECE OF LAND

THE COUNCILLORS WHO CLASHED OVER A PIECE OF LAND

It can be a defence to a defamation action to show that what was said, even if untrue, was made on a privileged occasion and was not motivated by malice.

At a meeting of Bolton Borough Council, the leader of the local Labour Party, Councillor Lowe, criticised Councillor Horrocks of the Conservative Party in his capacity as a member of the Management and Finance Committee.

He accused Councillor Horrocks of being underhand and dishonourable over some land in which Mr Horrocks was professionally interested.

Councillor Horrocks sued and, at the trial, was awarded damages of £400 and costs estimated at £9,000. Councillor

Lowe then successfully appealed to the Court of Appeal, whereupon Councillor Horrocks appealed to the House of Lords.

DECISION

The House of Lords accepted that Councillor Lowe's speech might have been defamatory and untrue. However, because it was a matter of local concern, the occasion was one of qualified privilege. Although Councillor Lowe was no doubt prejudiced, and had refused to apologise, he did honestly believe what a more rational person might reject. Therefore he was not actuated by malice and the defence of qualified privilege prevailed. The appeal was rejected.

---

is because, even though the letter was addressed to you, personally, there was always a chance that it could be opened in error, or be otherwise seen by a third party.

Proving financial loss

Anyone who sues for libel is entitled to damages, if he proves defamation, without having to show that he has suffered a financial loss.

The same is also true in a slander action, if the offending statement:
● Disparages someone in his job.
● Suggests that someone has committed a crime.
● Accuses a woman – though not a man – of acting immorally.
● Suggests that someone has a contagious or infectious (especially venereal) disease.

When any other type of slander is involved, the plaintiff must prove financial loss.

What to do if you are libelled or slandered

Never enter into a defamation action lightly. Libel or slander proceedings can be very costly and you cannot get legal aid.

If you feel seriously aggrieved about what you believe to be a libel or slander, consult a solicitor at once. If he agrees that there are grounds for action, he may suggest that you should be content

with an apology, if one can be obtained. A newspaper or other publication that agrees to apologise in suitable terms will normally also pay your legal costs.

If, however, the matter is too serious to be dealt with in that way, the solicitor can seek not only an apology but also damages. Most such cases never reach trial in court, but are settled by lawyers acting for the two sides.

The agreement reached normally settles a sum of damages and the wording of the apology, usually announced in open court, which means that the wording can be publicly reported.

Going to court If the action is not settled out of court, it must either be

....

WIFE OR MISTRESS?

If a man is already married and his engagement is announced in the newspaper his wife can sue because the innuendo is that she is only his mistress.

....

dropped or go to trial – usually before a judge and jury.

If the complainant proves libel or slander, he can be awarded damages ranging from a nominal halfpenny to many thousands of pounds.

The judge does not give the jury any guidance as to what has been awarded in previous similar cases, so the amount of damages is difficult to predict. A retrial can be ordered if the Court of Appeal considers the award unreasonable.

When libel is a crime

Libel (but never slander) can also be a criminal offence. Criminal proceedings should be taken only where the libel is likely to cause a breach of the peace or is a serious attack on the victim's character.

Prosecution for criminal libel can be brought by any individual as well as by the authorities, but it is rare, because the person libelled cannot get damages as he can in action for ordinary libel.

A prosecution for criminal libel cannot be brought against the owner or editor of a newspaper – or anyone else responsible for publishing the newspaper – without permission from a judge.

Once a criminal-libel prosecution gets into court, it may succeed in circumstances in which an ordinary civil libel action might fail.
● Justification, on the ground that the statement was true, is no defence, unless the statement is shown to have been in the public interest, and without malice.
● A criminal libel does not have to be communicated to a third party: it is enough that it was communicated to the person defamed.
● Criminal libel proceedings can be brought even though the person defamed is dead.

LIEN

When goods are held until a customer pays his bill

Lien is the legal term given to the right that a tradesman has to hold another person's property if it was brought to him to work on and if the work is not paid for.

For example, a watch repairer need not let a customer have his watch back until the repair charge is paid – even though the watch is worth much more than the charge. If no price was agreed beforehand, the repairer can hold the watch until a reasonable price is paid. If there is a dispute over what price is reasonable, a customer should seek legal advice from a solicitor or from a consumer advice centre.

The lien of a tradesman, or of a company offering a service such as laundry or dry-cleaning, extends only to the item of goods on which money is owed. For example, a garage proprietor cannot hold a lien on a car because the owner has not paid for repairs to a motor mower that he has already collected.

The holder of a lien must take reasonable care of the property and is liable if the goods are damaged through his negligence.

Professional lien

Lawyers, accountants, bankers and some other professional men have wider powers of lien. If they are owed money by a client they can hold documents or securities even though they do not relate to services for which the money is due.

LIFE ASSURANCE

How a tax concession cuts premiums

Since April 1979, income tax concessions on most life-assurance premiums have been deducted directly from the premium instead of from the tax liability of the person paying the premium, as was previously the case.

Provided the person paying is resident in the United Kingdom, other than in the Channel Islands or in the Isle of Man, a flat $17\frac{1}{2}$ per cent is deducted from the premium. The concession applies even if the person paying does not pay income tax.

If you are taking out a new insurance policy, make sure that it qualifies for relief. You are entitled to demand a certificate from the insurance company saying that it does.

Example If your premiums total £500 a year, you are entitled to £87.50 relief, so you pay only £412.50.

You can couple a policy with a housing loan so that you qualify for relief on premiums as well as on interest instalments. *See:* MORTGAGE

Premiums qualify for relief if:
● The policy is on the life of the person paying the premiums or of that person's husband or wife.
● The premiums do not total more than a sixth of your income or £1,500 a year, which ever is the greater.
● There is a capital sum payable at death.
● The sum assured is at least 75 per cent of the total premiums.
● The paying term is at least 10 years.
● Premiums are payable at intervals of a year or less.

In the case of some small policies, when premiums are paid weekly or every 4 weeks, payments are not reduced. Instead, the sum assured is increased.

Example If you take out a policy with premiums based on an assured sum of £1,000, the value of the policy is increased to £1,212.

LIFE SUPPORT

A doctor's duty to try to save a seriously ill person

A seriously ill person can sometimes be saved from death by the use of an artificial respirator, or life-support machine. The decision whether to use one rests entirely with the doctor.

It is also legally his decision alone when a life-support machine is to be switched off. He must, however, be sure that the patient is clinically dead – which means that his brain is no longer functioning. When organs are to be removed for transplant, he may keep the machine operating after death to prevent deterioration.

The doctor normally discusses the decision in advance with the next of kin, but is not legally obliged to do so.

A doctor who switches off a life-support machine while a patient is still alive can face a charge of murder. If he fails to carry out the proper tests to establish if life is extinct, or misjudges the results, he can be charged with manslaughter. The machine can be switched off only if the tests show beyond doubt that the patient is dead.

When a patient can choose

Most patients ill enough to be placed on a life-support machine are not likely to be conscious. Those who are have an absolute right to refuse treatment by a life-support machine even if this means their certain death.

In some cases, however, a doctor would be entitled to decide that illness has seriously damaged the patient's mental faculties and that the patient shows no sign of being able to understand the situation. In that case, the doctor can couple the patient to a life-support machine, even though the patient had refused.

No right to insist A patient, however ill, has no right to insist on treatment by a life-support machine even if one is available. He can merely ask; the decision whether to use it rests with the doctor.

If a doctor refuses to use a life-support machine when one is available, and the patient subsequently dies, the doctor can face proceedings for NEGLIGENCE.

When relatives are involved

Relatives of a seriously ill person have no more right than the patient to insist that a life-support machine should be used. Nor have they any right to insist that the machine be turned off.

Although relatives cannot prevent a doctor from switching off a life-support machine, he usually informs the next-of-kin when tests indicate that the patient is dead and the life support is to be withdrawn.

If the relatives have good reason to disagree, their only course is to apply to a court for an INJUNCTION restraining the doctor from switching off the machine.

In practice, however, after discussion with the relatives, the doctor would normally allow them to get a further opinion, from a doctor of their own choosing.

LIFE-BOAT SERVICE

Help for people in danger at sea

The life-boat service round the shores of Britain is provided by the Royal National Life-boat Institution, a private charity supported by voluntary contributions.

The RNLI maintains enough off-shore boats, usually crewed by volunteers, so that a boat can reach any point within 30 miles of the coast within 4 hours, and stay there for at least a further 4 hours. During the summer extra high-speed inshore boats are also stationed in busy areas.

The service exists to save, without charge, the life of anyone who is in danger at sea. Whenever possible a life-boat will answer any request for help – such as for life-saving, rescue, medical assistance. The secretary of the local life-boat committee is responsible for authorising the launching of a boat, usually at the request of the coastguard, who co-ordinates all search and rescue operations using life-boats, helicopters and any nearby vessel.

Claiming property salvage

The whole purpose of the RNLI is to save life. It does not claim salvage for rescuing property.

However, members of life-boat crews are entitled to make claim themselves, but rarely do. In 1977 only one claim was made.

Under the Merchant Shipping Act 1894, anyone who saves or helps to save property at sea is entitled to make a claim for salvage. The law makes no distinction between crews of life-boats and other people.

If a crew member does make a claim, he forfeits the payment he would otherwise have received from the RNLI for the rescue. He also has to pay for the fuel used and any damage done to the boat or equipment.

LIQUOR OFFENCES

The penalties for breaking the licensing laws

Several countrywide laws control the sale and consumption of intoxicating liquor in public houses – and in addition there may be local bye-laws governing opening hours and the granting of extensions and special licences.

Among the offences that can be committed by a customer are:

● Drinking after hours – that is still being in possession of your glass with drink in it more than 10 minutes after the last bell.
Maximum penalty: £100 fine.
● Buying alcoholic drink when under 18, or buying it for someone under 18.
Maximum penalty: £50 fine.
● Being drunk, violent, quarrelsome or disorderly, and refusing to leave a public house when asked to do so.
Maximum penalty: £25 fine.

Offences that can be committed by a publican include:
● Selling alcoholic drink without a licence.
Maximum penalty: £200 fine and 6 months' imprisonment.
● Selling alcoholic drink to someone, knowing he is under 18; or to someone knowing that it is being bought for someone under 18.
Maximum penalty: £200 fine and, on a second subsequent conviction, loss of licence.
● Allowing drinking after hours.
Maximum penalty: £100 fine.
● Supplying alcoholic drink on credit (but not, for example, in accepting payment by credit card for a meal and drink).
Maximum penalty: £50 fine.
● Selling liquor to someone who is already drunk.
Maximum penalty: £25 fine (£50 on second or subsequent conviction).
● Allowing illegal gaming in the public house, or knowingly allowing prostitutes to meet there.
Maximum penalty: £25 fine (£50 on a second or subsequent conviction).
● Permitting drunkenness, or violent, quarrelsome or riotous conduct.
Maximum penalty: £25 fine (£50 on second and subsequent conviction).
● Employing someone under 18 to work behind the bar.
Maximum penalty: £5 fine (£25 on second or subsequent conviction).

See also: DRUNK AND DISORDERLY
OFF-LICENCE
PUBLIC HOUSE

LITTER

When it is unlawful to dispose of rubbish

Whether or not there is a warning notice, it is an offence to throw down, drop or deposit general litter, such as

KEEPING BRITAIN TIDY

It is always an offence to drop litter in any open-air public place – even when no suitable rubbish bins are provided.

cigarette packets, sweet wrappers, beer cans or bottles, in an open-air public place, such as a street or park. It is not an offence under the Litter Act 1958 to drop litter in a shop or theatre. However, some local authorities have their own bye-laws which may make it an offence to litter places other than those covered by the Act.

The maximum penalty for dropping general litter is a fine of £100.

When large items are dumped in the open air

It is an offence to dump furniture, mattresses, television sets and dismantled parts of cars or whole cars. *See:* ABANDONED VEHICLE

It does not matter whether the dumping place is public or private property, provided that it is in the open air, and it is not an authorised dump.

The maximum penalty is a fine of £100 for the first offence and £200 or 3 months' imprisonment for subsequent offences.

What happens when someone is prosecuted

A litter prosecution can be started in a magistrates' court up to 6 months after the offence is committed.

In deciding on a penalty, the court takes into consideration the type and amount of litter deposited, the risk of injury to other people and the need to deter others from dropping litter. For example, a person who drops jagged metal or broken glass will usually have to pay a larger fine than someone who drops a cigarette packet – and someone who drops broken glass in a children's playground will be punished more severely than someone who does so on unused land.

Special rules about poisonous substances

Special laws apply to the dumping of poisonous substances. Under the Deposit of Poisonous Waste Act 1972 it is an offence to dump substances such as cyanide or asbestos except at specially designated dumping places.

The maximum penalty is a fine of £1,000 and 6 months' imprisonment. Under the later Control of Pollution Act (1974), however, the term of imprisonment that a court can order is increased to 2 years.

LIVING APART

When a married couple have separate homes

A man and woman who are married to each other have a duty to live together, but it is not enforceable by law and they commit no offence if they decide to live separately. However, they are still bound by the rights and duties of marriage, particularly that of MAINTENANCE for each other and for their children.

A couple who decide to live apart should try to agree on the amount of maintenance to be paid and should then apply to a magistrates' court for a maintenance order – on which tax relief can be claimed. If they are unable to agree, they will have to ask the magistrate or the county court to decide what the order should be.

If one partner has left the other without financial support, the deserted partner can apply to the magistrates' court for a MATRIMONIAL ORDER to set and enforce maintenance.

Custody and property

If they are likely to be living apart for a long while, they should make arrangements to divide their property and share custody of their children. Such agreements can be either spoken or written or formalised in a deed of separation, but the terms would not necessarily be enforced by law. *See:* SEPARATION

Living apart, whether by agreement or not, is one of the principal grounds for DIVORCE. The marriage can be ended after 2 years of separation, if both partners want a divorce, and after 5 years if one of them opposes it. *See:* BREAKDOWN OF MARRIAGE

A husband or wife who has custody of children and is living apart from his or her partner can claim extra CHILD BENEFIT, provided they are not living with another person.

LOCAL AUTHORITY

How local services are administered

The work of a local authority affects your day-to-day life whether you live in a city, town or in the country. Its services range from running schools and libraries, looking after the elderly, providing housing and transport to issuing licences for the local cinema, collecting refuse and burying the dead.

A local authority is run as a separate legal entity from central government. It appoints and pays its own officers and staff. But it has no powers except those granted by ACT OF PARLIAMENT.

Control by central government

If a local authority wants to take action in a way that means extending its powers, it must seek the approval of the Secretary of State concerned. For example, if an authority wishes to introduce a bye-law covering slaughterhouses in its area, the bye-law must be confirmed by the Minister of Agriculture and then printed so that copies are available at the authority's offices for members of the public to inspect or buy, before it is enforceable.

A local authority consists of an elected body of members who form the council and a separate group of paid officers, staff and workers who are employed by the authority. The members of the council, who are unpaid but entitled to claim allowances for attending meetings up to a maximum of £10 a day, decide the policy of the authority and the action it intends to take, and the officers advise the councillors and carry out their policy.

How local government is organised

Between 1972 and 1974, local government in England and Wales was reorganised. The number of counties was reduced from 58 to 53 and the 1,400 or so borough, urban and rural councils were replaced by 369 district councils.

The six most heavily populated areas in England outside London – Greater Manchester, Merseyside, South Yorkshire, Tyne and Wear, West Midlands and West Yorkshire – are now known as 'metropolitan areas'. Each has its own metropolitan county council, and is further divided into metropolitan districts, each with its own council. There are 36 metropolitan district councils in England.

The rest of England is divided into 39 non-metropolitan counties. Each has a county council and is further divided into districts, each with a district council. There are 296 non-metropolitan district councils in England.

Wales has 8 counties, each with a council, and 37 districts, each with a district council.

In certain rural areas there is an additional bottom tier of local government in the form of a parish council or parish meeting. There are over 9,000 parish councils or meetings in England. In Wales, where they are called community councils or community meetings, there are 842 community councils.

London's local government system, reorganised in 1965, is headed by the Greater London Council and has 32 London borough councils as its second tier. The City of London is the equivalent of a borough but it has its own special rules.

Shared responsibility

The local authority tiers divide some of the services they provide. A county council, for example, is responsible for maintaining all roads – except motorways and trunk roads – in its area while a district council looks after all housing services itself. Other responsibilities are shared between county and district councils – for example, the running of museums and art galleries and aspects

THE GRASS-ROOTS LEVEL OF LOCAL GOVERNMENT

Local government in rural areas is the responsibility of parish meetings or parish councils (community councils in Wales). After the reorganisation of local government between 1972 and 1974, some of the smaller urban and rural districts, with a population of under 20,000, became parish councils. If they had a mayor before reorganisation, they could retain the post and the title of 'town council', although their powers became those of a parish council. The areas with the smallest populations hold parish meetings as they have no parish council. Other areas have both a meeting and a council.

Setting up a council

If a parish has more than 200 local government electors in its area, its district council must, by law, establish a parish council. However, a parish meeting is entitled to request its district council to establish a parish council, provided that there are at least 150 electors in its area.

Alternatively, if there are two or more small parishes in an area with less than 150 electors in each, their district council is entitled to group them together under a group parish council, provided that each parish meeting agrees to join a group.

A district council must, by law, periodically review its parish or community electoral areas. It may decide that a new parish or community council should be set up in an area to make services more efficient.

However, the district council must seek the permission of the Home Secretary before the status of a parish can be altered.

The district council also decides the size of its parish councils and the number of electoral wards in each parish. Parish councillors are elected for 4 years. They are elected at the same time and retire together and elections take place at the same time as district council elections. Most parish councils have a staff of, at least, a secretary or clerk and a treasurer.

A parish or community council must hold an annual meeting and elect a chairman and hold at least three other meetings in a year. The chairman can be re-elected for another year at the next annual meeting. He is also entitled to call an extraordinary meeting of the council at any time, but at least three other councillors must attend before the meeting is legally constituted. At least 3 days' notice to members of the council and to the public is required before any meeting of the council can be held.

Who may attend

Any person who is entitled to vote and lives in a parish, may attend a parish meeting. At least one parish meeting must be held each year, by law, and if the parish has a council, the council chairman is chairman of the parish meeting. Otherwise, the meeting elects its own chairman. At least 7 days' notice of a parish meeting is required. However, if the parish meeting has been

called to establish a parish council, then at least 14 days' notice of the meeting must be given to members of the parish. Members of the Press are entitled to attend parish councils and meetings.

Community councils and community meetings in Wales follow the same rules, although a community council is required to hold only one meeting in a year at which a chairman is to be elected.

Shared services

Both types of meeting or council share their services and duties with their district council. They are responsible, along with district councils, for: allotments, bus shelters, cemeteries and crematoriums, footway lighting, museums, off-street parking with the consent of the county council, parks and open spaces, recreation and physical-training facilities, public conveniences, roadside seats, signposting and maintenance of bridleways and footpaths, swimming baths, traffic signs and village halls and community centres.

A council or meeting has the right to be consulted by district and county councils over any planning decisions that may affect its area. It may also institute bye-laws through its district council who must seek the consent of the Secretary of State concerned before the bye-law can be enforced.

A parish or community council or meeting is not entitled to levy rates. That is the responsibility of the district council.

of planning. Parishes provide services in collaboration with district councils.

The county council

The top tier of local government is the county council. The largest councils in the metropolitan areas have an average of around 100 members each, while the non-metropolitan county councils average around 80 members.

Each county is divided into electoral areas, known as electoral districts, each of which provides one COUNCILLOR for the council. Elections take place every 4 years, and all the councillors are elected at the same time. They all retire together after the 4 year term.

A county council must hold an annual meeting and elect a chairman and vice-chairman from its members. They hold office for 1 year and retire at the next annual meeting and continue as ordinary councillors.

The council holds as many subsequent meetings as it thinks are necessary during a year, although a county council usually meets every 6 weeks.

Many county councillors are members of the district councils in the area, but any person is entitled to stand for election to a county council, provided that he is over 21, a British citizen, and not disqualified from election for any reason.

In the metropolitan counties, education, housing and social services are undertaken by the district councils. In London, housing and social services are the responsibility of borough councils. However, education in the 12 Inner London boroughs and the City of London is the responsibility of the Inner London Education Authority. Otherwise, the other London borough councils are responsible for education.

In the rest of England and Wales,

education, housing and social services are run by county councils.

The district council

The two types of district council have an average 60 members each, although there are some very much smaller non-metropolitan councils – for example, Rutland District Council has only 20 members serving an area with a population of about 30,000 (1978).

Each district is divided into electoral areas called wards. The title of alderman, given to senior councillors, was abolished when local government was reorganised, and all elected members are known as councillors.

Councillors stand for 4 years, but metropolitan district councils elect a number of councillors for each ward that is divisible by 3. Every year, one-third of the council retires and has to stand for re-election. There are no dis-

Many pre-1972 councils were granted the status of a borough by a Royal Charter, which entitled them to have a mayor and deputy mayor instead of a council chairman and vice-chairman. Some larger areas were granted the title of 'city' with a lord mayor instead of a mayor.

Such authorities were also entitled to grant the title of freeman of the borough or city to a person who was entitled by birth or marriage to the title and 'honorary freeman' to a person who had served the area well.

A district council created since 1974 is entitled to apply for borough status. To do so, a council must convene a special meeting and pass a resolution, by a majority of two-thirds of the whole council, to petition the Crown to grant a Royal Charter. A committee of the Privy Council considers the petition and advises the Queen whether to grant a charter.

If a district receives borough status, its powers and services are not altered, but its chairman and vice-chairman become mayor and deputy mayor and there may be certain ceremonial privileges – for example, the mayor may be preceded by a mace-bearer.

Any parish council in England or community council in Wales is entitled to resolve that the parish has the status of a 'town'. The chairman and vice-chairman are then known as the town mayor and deputy town mayor and the council meeting is known as the town meeting. However, there is no added power involved, and no charter is granted.

trict elections in the fourth year when county council elections take place instead.

The non-metropolitan district councils were allowed to choose their system of representation when they were reorganised. They could either choose the same system as the metropolitan councils and re-elect one-third of their members every year or elect all the councillors at the same time and have them retire together after their 4 year term. About two-thirds of the councils chose to elect all their councillors at the same time.

Every district council must, by law, hold an annual meeting and elect a chairman and vice-chairman from among its members. They retire at the next annual meeting and become ordinary councillors. The council can hold as many meetings as it thinks are necessary to carry out business, although most districts meet once a month or every 6 weeks.

How a local authority operates

In all types of local authority, the full council considers the most important matters of policy and decisions at its meetings. Otherwise, the business is carried out by committees consisting of councillors, usually selected to reflect the political balance of the council. Only the full council can decide how many committees it has and who may sit on them.

It is entitled to appoint as many committees and sub-committees as it wants. A typical housing committee, for example, may have three sub-committees to deal with council tenancies, new properties and existing properties.

There are, however, certain committees that a council must establish by law. If it is responsible for education or police, it must set up a committee to run each department. The membership of those committees is also laid down by Act of Parliament.

Every education committee must include some people with experience of education in the area. If the members of the council have no experience, then up to half the number of committee members can be co-opted, non-elected members. The police committee must have two-thirds councillors and one-third magistrates.

Most committees are entitled to invite, or co-opt, outsiders to join them, provided that at least two-thirds of their members are councillors. Any committee that deals with finance, however, can have only elected councillors. Sub-committees do not need to have any legal minimum number of council members.

A team of full-time, paid council officers works alongside the councillors and advises the committees and sub-committees. A council is entitled to appoint as many officers as it thinks it needs to run its services, but there are certain posts that must be made by law.

For example, a non-metropolitan county council which has responsibility for education, the fire service, social services and trading standards, must appoint a chief education officer, a chief fire officer, a director of social services – with the permission of the Secretary of State for Social Services – and trading standards inspectors.

The local authority's team of officers is led by a chief executive, who carries out the duties formerly executed by the town clerk – the council's legal adviser and organiser of its administration. There may, however, be a separate council solicitor.

There is often some form of co-ordinating committee in a local authority, usually known as the policy and resources committee. It consists of councillors – the majority drawn from the strongest political party in the full council – and includes the chairmen of the other committees. It will be advised by the chief executive and his management team, and may be chaired by the council chairman.

All the business considered by the other committees should come before this committee, so that the work and the policy of the authority is co-ordinated.

The policy committee may be served by several sub-committees – for finance, personnel, land and buildings, and one to monitor the performance of the authority's departments, for instance.

How a local authority is financed

A local authority receives its income from two main sources – by levying RATES on all property in its area, to be paid by householders and others, and by grants received from central government.

District councils are the only authorities in the local government system allowed to levy a rate. A county or parish council, a joint board, a water authority or a combined police authority must raise any income it needs by asking the appropriate district council to add its requirements to the rate it is levying.

The district council's financial department works out an estimate of expenditure at the start of the financial year, taking into account what it expects in government grants and any revenue raised from its own trading services – for example, its municipal bus service. The amount remaining is the sum that has to be raised through the rates. The district adds the precepts from its county and parish councils and other authorities, and the total is considered by the policy and resources or finance committee before being put before the full council for approval. The other main source of income is the rate support grant from central government, which is divided into three types of aid:

● Needs element – payable to an authority with heavy expenditure on its services.

LOCAL AUTHORITY *continued on p. 439*

THE SOCIAL SERVICES PROVIDED BY A LOCAL AUTHORITY
How county and district councils share the burden of necessary administration

The services provided by a local authority range from running schools and providing housing and transport to issuing licences for the local cinema. Those services are divided between county councils and district councils – for example, a county council is responsible for maintaining all roads, except motorways and trunk roads, in its area, while a district council looks after all housing services. Other services, such as the many aspects of planning, are shared by both types of councils in an area.

Service	Provided by	What the service entails
Education	Metropolitan district and non-metropolitan county council	Provide an adequate number of primary and secondary schools for the area, fully equipped to ensure a full-time education for all pupils
		Appoint a chief education officer
		Appoint boards of governors
		Ensure school attendance
		Ensure there is a daily act of worship and regular religious instruction
		Provide free transport for schoolchildren where necessary
		Provide further education including establishing or assisting colleges of education
		Keep accounts of any monies spent
		Arrange medical inspections and free medical attention in schools
		Provide milk, meals and other refreshments for pupils
		Prepare a development plan for education in the area to be submitted to the Secretary of State for Education
		Provide special training for handicapped children and those in need of special care
		Provide boarding accommodation where necessary
		Provide areas for recreation and physical training
		Provide student grants
		Supply reports for the Secretary of State for Education where required
Environmental health	County council	Control animal disease
		License sites for disposal of industrial waste
		Dispose of refuse
		Ensure trading standards (formerly the work of Weights and Measures departments) and consumer protection, including labelling and the standard of food
	District council	Enforce building regulations by council inspectors
		Provide cemeteries and crematoriums
		Collect refuse (see note **1**)
		Control air and noise pollution
		Enforce food hygiene standards including inspecting meat (see note **2**)
		Inspect factories, offices, shop and railway premises
		Provide sites for markets and fairs

Service	Provided by	What the service entails
Environmental health (continued)	District council	Provide sewage service (acting as agents for regional water authority) (see note **3**)
		Prevent nuisance
		Provide slaughter houses and knackers' yards
		Undertake protection of the coast-line
Fire and police	County council	Act as fire authority for its area by providing an equipped and trained fire brigade and obtaining information about buildings in the area and water supplies for fire fighting, and arranging advice on fire prevention
		Act as police authority by establishing a police committee consisting of two-thirds county councillors and one-third magistrates and financing half of the police expenditure from the rates (see note **4**)
		Make arrangements to maintain essential services in the event of an enemy attack by drawing up a plan for civil defence in the area
Footpaths and bridleways	County council	Carry out surveys
		Maintain and protect footpaths and bridleways
		Provide signposts
	Shared by county and district council	Construct, alter or close footpaths and bridleways
Housing	District council	Undertake house and area improvements
		Undertake management of council flats and houses, rents, rent-rebate schemes, implement a rent review periodically, sale of council homes
		Provide loans for mortgages or home improvements and grants for home improvements or repairs
		Undertake slum clearance including compulsory purchase of property
Leisure services	County council	Issue minor licences (theatres)
		Provide smallholdings
	District council	Issue local licences (cinemas, taxis, small lotteries and pet shops)
		Provide allotments
	Shared by county and district councils	Provide parks and open spaces including camping sites
		Provide recreation and physical training including community centres, playing fields and sports centres
		Provide swimming baths
Libraries	Metropolitan district and non-metropolitan county councils and 4 district councils in Wales	Provide facilities for borrowing or making reference to books, magazines and other printed material, records, pictures or films for children or adults
		Provide advice and information to encourage the use of library facilities and co-operate with other library authorities
Museums and art galleries	Shared by county and district councils	Establish and maintain museums and art galleries in the area and encourage private museums or galleries by providing grants
Personal social services	Metropolitan district and non-metropolitan county councils	Appoint a director of social services, subject to the approval of the Secretary of State for Social Services, and establish a social services department and council committee to provide and run services for:
		Children – adoption service, fostering service, provision for receiving children into care, preventing and managing child abuse, provide community homes for children in trouble through neglect or ill-treatment or who have broken the law, day-care services for under 5's, including day nurseries, playgroups and child minders (note **5**)

Continued on next page

SOCIAL SERVICES *continued*

Service	Provided by	What the service entails
Personal social services (continued)	Metropolitan district and non-metropolitan county councils	**The disabled** – register disabled persons and provide information on the services available. Assist in the home by arranging for homes to be adapted to suit a person's needs and providing help in obtaining recreational facilities (library books, television and radio) and meals at home. Assist outside the home by providing assistance for travel, recreational facilities (outings or lectures), help for taking holidays, public convenience facilities, help with employment
		The elderly – co-operate with local voluntary organisations to provide meals at home (Meals on Wheels), day centres, home help service including sitters-in and night attendants, inspect old people's homes, residential accommodation, transport facilities
		The mentally handicapped – adult and junior training centres, day-care facilities, employment, residential accommodation (children's homes, hostels, fostering, group homes)
		The mentally ill – day centres, residential accommodation including hostels for short-term intensive-care patients, and staffed homes for patients after long-term hospital treatment, and group homes without staff but with close support from social services department
		Emergency help – providing accommodation and other assistance for one-parent families, the homeless and battered wives
Planning	County council	Draw up a structure plan for the area outlining the plans for the physical and economic development of the area and the council's aims and policies. The plan must include areas where major development or re-development is to take place – known as action areas – and must be made available to the public (see note **6**)
		Provide facilities within national parks, for example, refreshments, camping sites and parking
	District council	Draw up a local plan for the area which is in line with the county 'structure plan'. A plan may include action areas and must be available to the public
	Shared by county and district councils	Acquire land by agreement or compulsory order or dispose of land for development or re-development
		Provide caravan sites
		Maintain conservation areas and supervise historic building controls
		Reclaim derelict land
		Enforcement of planning control
		Oversee planning applications and general development
		Undertake tree preservation
		Register local land charges
Rating	District council	Levy rates on all property in its area taking into account the financial requirements of county and parish councils and other bodies
Town development	Shared by county and district councils	Provide buildings for industry and commerce
		Provide facilities for public worship
		Provide housing accommodation
		Provide public services
		Provide recreation facilities
Transportation	County council	Act as Highways Authority by planning, constructing and maintaining all highways, including private roads (see note **7**)
		Act as passenger transport authority by planning and co-ordinating the transport systems in the county

Service	Provided by	What the service entails
Transportation (continued)	County council	Control parking and traffic
		Provide public transport undertakings, for example, a county bus service and any concessionary fares involved
		Oversee road safety, including studying road accidents and providing advice and information to road users
		Provide street lighting, which may be delegated to district councils
	District council	Provide off-street parking, for example, on waste ground, subject to county council approval
		Provide public transport undertakings, for example, a municipal bus service and any concessionary fares involved
		Remove and dispose of abandoned vehicles, including providing dumps for unwanted vehicles
	Shared by county and district councils	Run airports
		Provide footway lighting
Youth employment	Metropolitan district and non-metropolitan county councils	Provide a career advisory service for those about to leave school and an 'employment' service, giving information on job opportunities to school or 'further' education college leavers

Notes

1. In Wales, district councils are responsible for the collection and disposal of refuse.
2. Milk and dairies are the concern of the Ministry of Agriculture, Fisheries and Food.
3. Sewage, water supply and river pollution are the responsibility of 10 regional water authorities covering England and Wales. Some districts make special arrangements with the authority to maintain and lay sewers.
4. In some areas the police are governed by a special police authority responsible for a combined force covering more than one county; for example, Devon and Cornwall, Avon and Somerset.
5. In many areas, county and district councils form a joint committee to carry out their planning functions.
6. A social service department works closely with its housing department to provide accommodation where necessary.
7. Motorways and trunk roads are the responsibility of the Department of Transport.

LOCAL AUTHORITY *continued from p. 436*

● Resources element – payable to an authority which falls short of the national average rateable value per head of population. The grant makes the authority's rateable value up to the national standard. About 90 per cent of all the rating authorities receive a resources grant.

● Domestic element. Under the General Rate Act 1967, all rating authorities must reduce the rate levied on dwelling houses by a specific number of pence in the £. In return for that relief for the domestic ratepayer, the authority is reimbursed by the Government through the domestic element grant.

The central government makes two other sorts of grant:

● Special grants for particular service – for example, the Government pays 50 per cent of an authority's bill for running its police force; 90 per cent of any student grants; and 100 per cent of the cost of building and maintaining any roads due to be made into trunk roads.

● Supplementary grants for particular services – for example, the National Parks Supplementary Grant for counties in national park areas, or councils having considerable numbers of immigrants.

When a council is negligent

A local authority performs many functions during which an injury may be inflicted on a member of the public. The authority, like everyone else, is liable for NEGLIGENCE whether on its own part or on the part of one of its employees.

For example, if an employee drives a council vehicle carelessly and is involved in an accident, the authority will have to compensate any road accident victim. If a teacher is careless when supervising children, he may be held responsible for an ACCIDENT AT SCHOOL. If a council builds houses defectively so that occupants are hurt, it will have to pay damages and if it grows trees in the park with alluring berries that are poisonous, it will be answerable to the parents of children who become ill through eating them.

Even when an authority is carrying out a duty imposed by Act of Parliament, it is still governed by the law of negligence.

When the negligence consists of merely omitting to act – known in law as nonfeasance – an authority may still be liable for any ensuing loss. For example, if a council fails to take reasonable measures to repair a pavement and a pedestrian stumbles, the authority may have to pay compensation. When Parliament issues a statute, it is telling a local authority to undertake a service and to undertake it carefully so no one is harmed.

If you are dissatisfied with any aspect of your local authority's service, complain in person or in writing to the officer in charge of that service or to the authority's chief executive, if you do not know the chief officer concerned, or to your local councillor.

If you want to find out who the chief officers, councillors or committee members are, ask at your local authority municipal buildings or offices. Many local authorities have a special depart-

HOW A COUNCIL'S POWERS ARE RESTRICTED – AND INCREASED

A local authority is an administrative body with no powers to pass laws – only to enact bye-laws with the authority of Parliament. All its powers are conferred upon it by ACT OF PARLIAMENT.

The Acts, known as 'general Acts', may be:
● Mandatory – compelling a local authority to carry out a particular service – for example, providing residential accommodation for the elderly.
● Adoptive – where an Act gives an authority power to carry out a certain function – for example, to levy a rate on unoccupied property – but the authority has to make a resolution to adopt the Act before it applies in that area.
● Permissive – granting new powers to an authority but leaving it to the authority to take the power or not. For example, all authorities can use their public parks for entertainment – holding a pop concert, for example – but it is a matter for each individual authority if it chooses to do so.

If an authority does not carry out the requirements of a mandatory Act which contains a default clause, the Secretary of State may declare the authority to be 'in default' and transfer its duties to another authority or to himself.

For example, Clay Cross Urban District Council refused in 1972 to raise council rents as required by the Housing Finance (Fair Rents) Act 1972. The Act contained special powers for the Secretary of State for the Environment to declare an authority who did not carry out its duties to be in default in discharging its functions.

The Secretary of State appointed a housing commissioner who carried out the council's duties at the council's expense.

How affairs are scrutinised

The work of all local authorities is also scrutinised by central government departments, who advise on how services can be run and who appoint inspectors to check on the service being provided.

The spending of a local authority is also scrutinised through an annual audit. An authority may choose to have the audit carried out by either a 'district auditor' – who is a civil servant appointed by the Secretary of State for the Environment – or by an independent 'approved auditor', nominated by the council. However, the Secretary of State for the Environment must approve the auditor before he is appointed. Most authorities choose a district auditor to carry out the audit.

The authority must make the accounts available for inspection by any elector in the area. An elector is also entitled to attend the audit and question the auditor on any item in the accounts.

After the audit has been made, the auditor sends his report to the Secretary of State and to the authority. The authority must make the report available for any elector to read and any newspaper that wishes to apply for it, and hold a meeting of its full council, as soon as possible after the audit, to discuss the report.

In general terms, a local authority has the power to levy rates, introduce bye-laws, and acquire land by agreement or COMPULSORY PURCHASE, provided that it goes through the procedure for seeking permission. It also has the power to borrow money but every loan has to be sanctioned by the Home Secretary.

If it wants to increase its powers it must promote its own private or local Act of Parliament. It can also object to a local Act being promoted by another local authority or body. To do so, the authority must:
● Give 30 days' notice to members of the council and public that a council meeting has been convened to promote a local Act of Parliament. Only 10 days' notice is needed if it wants to object to a Bill.
● Advertise in the local Press at the same time announcing the meeting and stating the resolution before the council.
● Pass the resolution to promote or oppose the Bill by a two-thirds majority of the whole council.
● Deposit the Bill at Parliament after the first meeting, in accordance with the standing orders of Parliament, or deposit a petition at Parliament objecting to a Bill.
● Hold a second meeting of the full council 14 days' after the Bill has been deposited, and a further 30 days' notice of the second meeting has been given to members of the council and advertised in the local Press in the same way as the first meeting. No second meeting is required if a Bill is being objected to.
● Confirm the resolution of the first meeting by a majority of two-thirds of the whole council at the second meeting. If the second meeting fails to do so, the Bill must be withdrawn. If it is confirmed, the Bill then enters the parliamentary machinery for private Bills where any objections are considered. If the Bill passes its three readings and receives the Royal Assent, it is then an Act of Parliament. *See:* PARLIAMENTARY BILL

The city of Birmingham, for example, set up its Birmingham Municipal Bank with a local Act of Parliament – the Birmingham Corporation Act in 1919. The bank is now owned by Birmingham Metropolitan District Council and managed by a council committee. It has power to provide its services only within the limits of the old City of Birmingham and has 70 branches.

Tyne and Wear County Council received the Royal Assent to its Tyne and Wear Act in 1976 allowing it and its district councils to make rent and interest relief grants to companies providing new jobs in its area and provide financial help with new company premises.

When a council is challenged

A council can be restrained from overstepping its powers by a High Court order known as 'prohibition' or 'certiorari'. It may also be compelled to discharge any of its duties by a High Court order known as 'mandamus'.

If someone decides to challenge the order of a local authority – for example, if he believes a bye-law introduced by the authority is unreasonable, he may object in court on the ground that the authority has acted 'ultra vires', beyond its powers.

Such a case was brought in 1955 when Birmingham Corporation allowed pensioners to travel free on its municipal bus service. A ratepayer objected on the ground that the local authority had overstepped its powers as there was no statutory power and no power in the City's Charter to introduce such a service.

The authority was considered by the High Court to have acted beyond its powers and the scheme stopped.

However, Birmingham and other local authorities in the Midlands promoted their own Act of Parliament, granting powers to provide free transport for certain passengers. That local Act was extended into two 'permissive' Acts of Parliament – the Travel Concessions Act 1964 and the Transport Act 1968 – which now enables all local authorities to provide concessionary fares if they wish to do so.

LOCAL GOVERNMENT IN GREATER LONDON

London's local government system – reorganised in 1965 – is headed by the Greater London Council, with 32 London boroughs and the City of London as a second tier.

The GLC covers an area of 616 square miles and represents a population of over 7 million. The GLC area is divided into electoral areas, known as electoral divisions, each of which elects one councillor. All councillors stand for 4 years and are elected and stand for re-election together. The GLC has over 100 members.

The London boroughs are divided into electoral areas called wards. The borough council is led by a mayor, who is elected annually, and all councillors stand for 4 years, and are elected and stand for re-election together.

The unique City

The City of London is similar to a borough, but is governed by unique rules. For example, the City is the only local authority to retain the title of aldermen for its senior councillors.

It is governed by the Court of Common Council which consists of a lord mayor, 26 aldermen and 156 common councillors.

The City is divided into wards and common councillors are elected annually, not only by the 5,000 residents, but also by the City's 8,000 property owners.

Aldermen are elected for life and make up the Court of Aldermen which elects the lord mayor, who holds office for 1 year only.

The GLC and its boroughs divide or share their services like county and district councils. However, the education service in the 12 boroughs and the City of London which make up 'Inner London' is the re-sponsibility of the Inner London Education Authority. The authority is made up from the GLC councillors representing the Inner London constituencies and a member from each Inner London borough council.

Otherwise, education in Greater London is the responsibility of London borough councils.

Borough councils and the City of London are the only rating authorities for London.

Both the GLC and, through it, the ILEA have to raise their money by asking the borough councils to add their requirements to the rate being levied. The borough councils are responsible for: consumer protection, housing, libraries, art galleries, museums and entertainment, parks, playgrounds and open spaces, planning at a local level, public health, social services and some types of roads.

The GLC is responsible for: art galleries, museums and entertainment, bye-laws, fire services, licensing, overall planning, parks, playgrounds and open spaces.

Services in the City

The services provided by the City of London are the same as those of a London borough. However, there are certain special responsibilities – for example, the markets of Billingsgate, Leadenhall, Smithfields and Spitalfields, the maintenance of its own City of London Police Force – separate from the Metropolitan Police Force and New Scotland Yard which come under the supervision of the Home Secretary – and various open spaces outside London which it owns and maintains – Epping Forest and Coulsdon Commons, for example.

ment to provide information on the authority's make-up and work.

Who may attend council meetings

Any member of the public is entitled to attend meetings of the full council, committees and some sub-committees, provided that a meeting has not agreed to discuss a matter in private. A person is also entitled to inspect minutes of council meetings and committee meetings and any development plans, which are open to inspection at the local authority head office or public library.

Some councils have rules which en-title any person to submit a written question to a member of the council to be answered at a full council meeting. Standing orders may also permit a small deputation to address a council meeting. If you wish to bring a matter to the attention of the council, seek advice from the chief executive whether the council's standing orders include such provisions.

However, if a person wants to complain about his local authority on the ground that it has failed to carry out its duties due to maladministration – which includes malice, unfair discrimination or neglect – he is entitled to complain to the local government OMBUDSMAN.

LODGER
When landlord and occupier share a home

People who live in their landlord's home and who pay for services – such as meals or laundry – as well as lodging, are not protected against EVICTION under the Rent Acts, although they cannot be evicted without a court order. When a fixed period of residence has been agreed, a lodger must leave when it ends, and he can be given notice at any time during such a period. The length of notice required corresponds to the frequency of rental payments – weekly or monthly.

However, lodgers who have exclusive occupation of part of a house – and most can claim this at least for their bedroom – and who do not pay a substantial part of their rent for board are entitled to apply to the local rent assessment committee, sitting as a rent tribunal, to have a fair rent assessed. *See:* RENT REGISTRATION

Short-term security

Although rent tribunals formerly had the authority to grant some limited security of tenure, they lost that power over agreements made on or after November 28, 1980. Lodgers whose agreements were made after that date enjoy no security of tenure except that a landlord must get a court order to evict. The court does, however, have power to suspend the possession order for up to 3 months.

The court will, in suspending possession, order the tenant to pay any arrears of rent owing, unless to do so would be unreasonable or cause exceptional hardship to the tenant.

Contracts made before November 28, 1980, are still within the rent tribunal's power to grant security of tenure.

In those cases, a lodger can ask the tribunal to grant him security of tenure provided he does so before the period of notice given by his landlord has run out. The request must be accompanied by an application for a reasonable rent to be fixed.

The tribunal can then grant successive periods of 6 months' security, although in practice they normally take the view that it is unreasonable to force a landlord to share his house with someone he does not want there. The tribunal would therefore grant the lodger security for a short period in which he can find somewhere else to live.

Lodgers who have exclusive possession of part of a house – giving them the right to exclude the landlord from their area – have complete protection under the Rent Acts, but such agreements are unusual and would not apply, for example, to an HOTEL.

In general, the law considers lodgers to be 'licensees' who are entitled to be on the premises – and cannot be kept out as trespassers – but do not have a tenant's safeguarded right to reside there. *See:* LANDLORD AND TENANT

A lodger may not sub-let his rooms and he must make good any damage he causes to the landlord's property. But it is the landlord's responsibility to carry out repairs and maintenance. Payment for lodgings is by agreement between the two sides and is not subject to any rent controls – unless it qualifies for rent registration.

Tenants who want to take in lodgers should make sure that they are allowed to under their tenancy agreements. A COUNCIL TENANCY, for example, usually forbids taking in lodgers without the council's written consent, unless the lodger is a member of the tenant's family. The presence of a lodger might also affect a tenant's RENT ALLOWANCE or RATES.

Supplementary benefit for lodgers

SUPPLEMENTARY BENEFIT is normally granted to lodgers who qualify for benefit. It includes the full cost of their board and lodging, plus £7.10 a week for personal expenses and an allowance for meals not included in the boarding charge. If the lodger is over pension age, or has received supplementary benefit for 1 year during which he has not been required to register for work, he will receive a higher personal expense allowance of £7.85.

However, if a person is lodging with close relatives, he will receive only the minimum rate – which is the normal rate for a claimant who is not a householder – regardless of how much he is paying.

If it is considered that the charge for board and lodging is unduly high, only as much as is considered reasonable for

the needs of the claimant and the type of accommodation will be allowed. But the full amount must be allowed if the claimant cannot reasonably be expected to move. Even if he is expected to look for cheaper accommodation, the full amount can be allowed for up to 13 weeks to give him time to do so.

A maximum is fixed for each area, but it may be increased by £5.35 a week for long-term claimants who receive the higher personal allowance and by £6 where extra care and attention is provided – for example, for elderly and handicapped people. Where both conditions apply, a claimant may receive both – that is, £11.35.

When benefit is refused

If the full cost of board and lodging is refused, the claimant can go to an appeal tribunal.

If a person receiving supplementary benefit takes in lodgers, one-third of their payments will be treated as his earnings and taken into account to calculate his rate. But, as with any other earnings, part can be disregarded.

LOST PROPERTY

The finder's duty to return his finds

The finder of lost property has a duty to take reasonable steps to trace the owner. Someone who keeps money that he has found is guilty of THEFT.

The correct procedure is to hand the article to the police and let them make inquiries. The police will keep the article on the finder's behalf for 1 month if it is worth less than £30 and for up to 6 months if it is worth more than that. If the owner has not been traced in that time the article is given back to the finder. The finder has shown his honesty and is not guilty of theft if he uses or disposes of the found property. But if its owner appears, he will be entitled to recover it.

A finder is not entitled to a reward unless a reward has been offered. If it has, it must be paid to anyone who knows of it and fulfils the conditions stated in the offer.

If you find a piece of jewellery in a second-hand chest of drawers you have bought, it belongs to the original owner, unless you can prove that when he sold

it to you he intended to transfer ownership of the contents of the drawers.

Property on buses and trains

When you find something on a bus or train, you must hand it to the guard, conductor or driver. The rightful owner is entitled to have his property back – but only if he pays the transport company a fee. After 3 months the company can sell the lost property and it must then give part of the proceeds to the guard, conductor or driver.

Local bye-laws govern the treatment of property found in a TAXI.

If a local council employee – for example, a refuse collector – finds something valuable in the course of his employment, he must hand it to his employer, who should take reasonable measures to trace the owner.

LOTTERIES

Running a fund-raising draw for a club or society

A lottery is a prize draw in which no skill is involved and it is illegal to operate one for private gain. People taking part in a lottery each buy tickets of a fixed price, and amounts of money or a

LADY LUCK CHOOSES
THE WINNERS

A lottery is a prize draw that involves no skill. It must not be operated for private gain.

number of prizes are distributed among winners chosen by lots or by pure chance. A raffle is a form of lottery.

Any sports or social club, charity, local authority or non-profit-making body can operate a lottery providing all the proceeds are used solely for the organising body and providing it meets all the conditions laid down by the Lotteries and Amusements Act 1976.

Rules for lotteries A lottery is legal only if the following rules are applied:

1. No skill is involved; prizes must be awarded by chance alone.

2. No ticket costs more than 25p.

3. The price is printed on each ticket, along with the name and address of the organisers and the date on which the lottery, or draw, is to take place.

4. The amount of money collected by the sale of tickets is not more than £5,000 – more can be raised only if the lottery is registered with the Gaming Board.

5. No more than 25 per cent of the total money raised is used for expenses – the figure is only 15 per cent for registered lotteries collecting more than £5,000.

6. Only half or less of the total amount raised is given away in prizes, and no single prize is worth more than £1,000, but this figure can be increased in lotteries controlled by the Gaming Board.

7. The person organising the lottery is a member of the club or society and is authorised by the committee.

8. Tickets are not sold to anyone under the age of 16.

9. Details of the money raised, the expenses deducted and the way in which the profits are to be spent are sent to the local authority.

Any society or organiser who runs a lottery and breaks any of these regulations can be fined up to £400 or gaoled for up to 2 years in a magistrates' court, or fined an unlimited amount in a crown court.

Planning a lottery A club or society which wishes to run a lottery or a series of lotteries must first write to the local authority to be registered as a lottery operator. The registration fee is £10 and there is a renewal fee of £5 to be paid on January 1 each year.

The local authority can refuse registration only on the grounds that one of the officials or organisers has been convicted of fraud or of an offence under the Lotteries and Amusements Act, or because the club or society is not a non-profit-making body run for the benefit of its members, or is not a charity. A club or society can appeal against refusal to the crown court.

Selling the tickets Tickets for a registered and properly organised lottery can be sold at the club or society's premises or in private houses.

But they cannot be sold in a gaming club, at a bingo hall, from a vending machine, in a licensed betting office, or in an amusement arcade, and they must not be sent through the post.

No club, society or local authority can hold more than 52 lotteries in a year, and at least 7 days must elapse between each lottery.

Local council lotteries All local authorities are permitted under the 1976 Lotteries and Amusements Act to operate local lotteries to raise money, but before they can do so they must register with the Gaming Board.

They cannot run more than 52 lotteries in any one year and many of the same rules apply as those for clubs and societies. Tickets can, however, be sold in street kiosks and in shops.

Local society lotteries Once a club or society has registered with the local authority it can run up to 52 raffles or lotteries a year.

Small lotteries Lotteries or raffles can be run at social events such as sports meetings, fêtes, socials and dances, providing any profits go to the organising body and are not for private gain.

The organisers do not need to be registered with the local authority, providing:
● The lottery is not the main purpose of the event.
● Tickets are sold only at the event.
● No cash prizes are given.
● Not more than £50 is deducted from the proceeds for prizes.
● The result of the lottery is declared during the event. Prizes totalling more than £50 in value can be given only if some of them are donated.

Private lotteries These are legal if they are organised exclusively among a group of people who work together, live on the same premises, or all belong to the same club or society.

Expenses can be deducted only for printing and stationery and the rest of the proceeds must be used up in prizes or for the mutual benefit of the group of people or the society.

Tickets must not go on general sale, must not be sent through the post, and the purpose of the lottery must be advertised on the tickets.

Claiming the prize Anyone taking part in a lawful raffle or lottery who is not given a prize he has rightly won can sue the organisers for it. If a lottery is unlawful, no winner can sue for his prize.

LOWER EARNINGS LIMIT
When national insurance is compulsory

Every working person whose earnings from one employment in any tax year are above a certain level must pay class 1 NATIONAL INSURANCE CONTRIBUTIONS – and so must his employer. If, however, his earnings are below that limit (£27 a week in 1981) – called the lower earnings limit – neither he nor his employer pays class 1 contributions.

The figure changes from year to year. You can check the up-to-date limit by asking for leaflet NI 208 at your local social security office.

Separate employments

When someone works for two or more employers, each employment is treated separately. If no single employment reaches the lower earnings limit, then neither he nor his employer pays class 1 contributions – even if the total from all his jobs is above the lower earnings limit.

If, for example, you employ a part-time cleaner, neither she nor you have to pay class 1 contributions unless you pay her more than the lower earnings limit.

The fact that she earns more by working also for a friend is irrelevant.

LUNCHEON VOUCHER
When tax must be paid

The first 15p of luncheon vouchers provided by an employer for his employees is not taxed. Over that daily limit, however, the employee must be taxed, whatever his earnings.

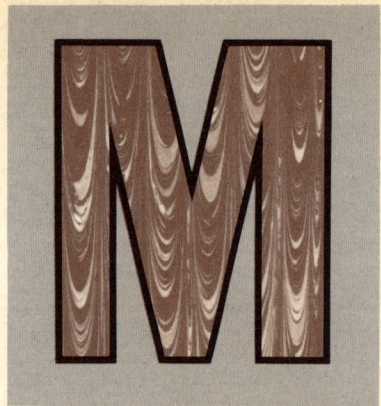

MAGISTRATE

Guardian of the Queen's peace

Since 1327 the sovereign has appointed a number of leading citizens to keep the peace in each area of the country. Such people are known as justices of the peace, or magistrates. Modern magistrates hold their Commission of the Peace for a county or borough.

Usually they are laymen who have been active in their local community – for example, in politics, in voluntary work or in the trade union movement. They receive some training in their spare time and are helped by professional clerks of the court.

In London and some other areas, however, there are salaried magistrates who are experienced lawyers and are known as stipendiary magistrates.

Subject to the maximum punishment allowed for any particular offence, both lay magistrates and stipendiaries can impose prison terms of up to 6 months and fines of up to £1,000, except in cases where Parliament has given them extra powers.

More than 98 per cent of criminal cases are dealt with by the 700 or so magistrates' courts in England and Wales. Even in the other cases, the accused person appears first in a magistrates' court, which commits him to a crown court. It does this if:
● The accused has been found guilty, but the magistrates think the case merits a heavier penalty than they have the power to impose.
● The accused chooses to be tried by a jury or the magistrates think he ought to be tried in the crown court.
● The charge is serious and can only be tried in the crown court, and the magistrates think there is a case for the defendant to answer.

There must be at least two lay magistrates on the bench to try a case. There need be only one, however, to remand someone, on bail or in custody, until the case is heard, or to commit him for trial, on bail or in custody. Also, only one magistrate is needed to sign a warrant for someone's arrest.

Specially chosen magistrates deal with juvenile offenders. *See:* JUVENILE COURT

In addition to criminal cases, magistrates also deal with domestic matters such as adoption, maintenance and affiliation proceedings. Outside London, they administer the licensing laws.

MAIL ORDER

The rules that control buying and selling through the post

Mail order customers are protected partly by law and partly by codes of practice drawn up by advertising agents and publishers.

By law, advertisements or catalogues inviting people to order goods by post must include the supplier's name and operating address – a post office box is not enough.

If money is sent with an order, it must be returned as soon as possible if the order is not accepted. A customer can sue if there is an unreasonable delay.

No CONTRACT exists until the supplier accepts an order. So the customer has no right to demand goods if a supplier chooses to reject his order, and no right to compensation if he then has to pay more to buy the goods elsewhere.

But once goods are sent, there is a binding contract. The customer is entitled to his or her money back if the goods do not correspond with their description. If their quality proves unsuitable for their normal purpose, the customer has the right to demand their replacement, or else a refund. *See also:* DEFECTIVE GOODS

Advertisers' code of practice

In addition to any legal requirements, the Advertising Standards Authority administers a code of practice which should be adhered to by advertising agencies and publishers. This code requires mail order suppliers who ask for any money in advance to:
● Provide samples of their goods at the address shown in an advertisement, so that callers can examine them.
● Refund payment in full if goods are returned undamaged within 7 days of receipt. It is not necessary for the customer to give any reason for this. The customer is entitled to try the goods during that period, unless the supplier has previously made it clear that a trial is not permitted – for example, when any use of the goods would make them unfit for sale to anyone else.
● Send goods within 28 days of receiving an order – or failing that, notify the customer within 28 days, with a reply-paid postcard and the offer of a refund. If the customer prefers to wait for the goods he should be sent progress reports every 14 days.

The Mail Order Traders Association also administer their own code.

The Citizens Advice Bureau should hold copies of the codes of practice approved by the Director General of Fair Trading. A suspected breach of a code may be checked with them and a complaint under the code made to the code administrator.

If an advertiser defaults

Most established newspapers and magazines take part in a scheme that guarantees a mail order customer his

THE EVIDENCE YOU NEED TO CLAIM A REFUND

If a mail order advertiser fails to meet your order and your money is not returned within 28 days, the newspaper or magazine that ran the advertisement will investigate.

If it was a 'display' advertisement – not merely a small ad in a classified column – the publisher should be able to arrange a refund, through a customer-protection scheme, even if the trader's business has gone into liquidation.

But you need proof: a record of the payment, including details of when it was made, to whom and for what goods.

When ordering from an advertisement, keep it in a safe place afterwards with a note of the publication it appeared in and the date of publication. If you are required to clip anything from the advertisement,

make sure you have a note of any important details – particularly the full name and address of the advertiser.

If you pay by cheque, cross it, endorse it 'Account payee only', and fill in all the details on the counterfoil or payment list in your cheque book.

If you send a postal order, cross it, fill in the counterfoil and keep it with your record of the advertisement.

If you have to pay by cash – it is better not to, because there is no way of tracing it later – you should do so only in a special post office envelope for registered mail. Keep the receipt with your record of the advertisement.

After 28 days, if nothing is heard from the supplier, contact the advertisement manager of the newspaper or magazine.

---

money back if an advertiser's business collapses and orders are not met. It applies only to what they call 'display' advertisements – not to small ads in their classified columns.

Publishers can refuse to print advertisements that do not conform to the Advertising Standards Authority code.

If a customer hears nothing from an advertiser within 28 days of sending money, he should notify the advertisement manager of the newspaper or magazine concerned. Refund claims should be lodged within 3 months of the date of the advertisement in a daily or weekly newspaper, or in the case of other publications, within 2 months of placing the order.

When books are sent by post

Leading publishers who supply books or records by post, including the Reader's Digest Association Ltd, are subject to the code of practice of the Mail Order Publishers' Authority which requires that:
● Goods may not be sent unless requested.
● Advertisements must state postage and packing charges or quote an inclusive price.
● Advertisers must supply a clearly displayed and simple summary of the essential points of an offer, for the customer to keep.
● If a customer is invited to undertake a continuing commitment – for example to a book or record club – he or she must

have the right to cancel it at any time or after a stated period which must not exceed 1 year.

When credit is offered

Mail order companies offering delayed payment are bound by the laws covering any CREDIT AGREEMENT. They must state the full cost, including any extra charges, and if there is an INTEREST CHARGE, the true annual rate of interest must be given.

Even a mail order· company must offer its goods for cash as well as on credit terms – 'credit only' selling is illegal.

If you order goods on credit after choosing from a catalogue or samples left at your home by a representative, your right to cancel the agreement during a 'cooling-off' period depends on whether your decision followed sales talk. *See:* DOORSTEP CREDIT

If there is no oral negotiation and your decision is based only on what you read, you have no right to a 'cooling-off' period and cannot cancel.

MAINTENANCE

Providing for your spouse and children

Married partners have a legal obligation to provide for each other and for their children. If one of them does not receive adequate support, or is kept at a

much lower standard of living than the other, he or she can apply to a court for an order for maintenance to be paid, for him or herself or for a child.

The court assesses a level of 'reasonable maintenance', which depends on the needs of the person applying and the ability of the other spouse to pay. For example, a working wife would not get an order against her husband unless he was earning substantially more than she. If a husband is unemployed or disabled, he can obtain a maintenance order against his wife if she is earning good money. But neither partner has a right – without a court order – to a particular share of the other's income. *See:* HOUSEKEEPING MONEY

If any member of a family receives SUPPLEMENTARY BENEFIT, the Supplementary Benefits Commission can apply for a maintenance order against a husband, wife or parent who is not fulfilling his obligations when in a position to do so.

A mistress, or COMMON LAW WIFE, has no legal right to be supported by the man she lives with. But she can claim maintenance for their children under an AFFILIATION ORDER, as can any mother of an illegitimate child.

Children generally have the right to be maintained by their parents until they reach 17, or until they cease full-time education.

Parents do not have the right to be maintained by their children.

Applying for maintenance during a marriage

A husband or wife can obtain a maintenance order from a magistrates' court if the married partner:
● Has failed to provide reasonable maintenance for the applicant or any child of their family.
● Has deserted.
● Has behaved in such a way that the other partner could not be expected to live with him or her.

If it finds the claim justified, the court sets a fixed amount to be paid at regular intervals by the partner who has failed to provide. It can also order him or her to make an additional lump payment of up to £500. Either partner can appeal against the order to the High Court.

The same procedure may be followed when a couple decide to separate amicably. Having agreed between themselves on the amount of maintenance to be paid, they can obtain a magistrates' order, which makes the payment eligible for tax relief and can be used to enforce payment if it is withheld. Consent orders can also be made in divorce proceedings in a county court. Where the parties disagree, the cases can be decided either by the magistrates or by the county court. But if the case is at all complicated, it is better dealt with by the county court.

Applying for maintenance when a marriage breaks down

When a couple decide to end their marriage by DIVORCE, NULLITY or by SEPARATION, either partner can apply for a maintenance order to the county court where the hearing is to be held.

When one of them intends to apply he should say so in the petition for divorce or separation, or, if he is being sued for divorce, in his answer. The prayer of the divorce petition – obtainable from the court office – contains a section dealing with maintenance requirements. If maintenance is not requested at that stage, greater legal costs may be incurred.

Formal application for maintenance must be made to the court as soon as possible after it has granted decree nisi of divorce or nullity or a decree of judicial separation. Failure to act promptly can prejudice the case: the partner being sued could claim that the delay showed the other was in no real need, or that he had been lulled into believing that there would be no application.

It is a good idea to submit all applications dealing with financial problems at the same time, as the court will usually insist on hearing them together. For example, a wife can file separate applications for maintenance for herself and her children, for ownership of the matrimonial home and for a share of the family's possessions and all will be heard at the same time. *See also:* MATRIMONIAL PROPERTY

The applications must be accompanied by an affidavit stating the capital, income and expenses of the person applying and an estimate of the other partner's financial position.

The other partner must file an affidavit in reply, with details of his or her finances, within 14 days.

If husband and wife agree on the amount of maintenance and how to divide their property, they should still obtain a court order to enforce payment – if necessary – and to obtain tax relief. However, before reaching agreement each should make quite sure that the other is not concealing any information – orders made by consent can only be subsequently changed if it can be proved that they were based on false information, and this may be difficult.

It is advisable to engage a solicitor to help to make the applications and to give advice at the court hearing. LEGAL AID is available for maintenance applications and hearings – even if there was no legal aid for the divorce.

Neither partner can apply for any of the orders if he or she has remarried, except for the children. But once a notice of application has been lodged, the case can be heard even if the applicant has married again.

How the court decides on financial support

Maintenance applications are heard by the registrar of the county court in his private rooms, or chambers. Only the husband and wife and their lawyers attend. The registrar reads the affidavits, examines any documentary evidence – such as bank statements – and cross-examines the husband and wife, either of whom may call expert witnesses – accountants or valuers, for example – to support their claims.

In making the orders, the court seeks to obtain for the husband, wife and children a financial position as close as possible to that which they would have enjoyed if the marriage had continued and if the husband and wife had fulfilled their financial obligations to each other.

To do so, it takes into account all the circumstances of the case:
● The property, income and earning capacity of both partners, and any that they are likely to have in the foreseeable future – an inheritance, for example.
● The financial needs and obligations of both partners, now and in the future.
● The family's standard of living before the marriage broke down.
● The age of the husband and wife and how long the marriage lasted – if the person claiming is young and likely to remarry, the award might be smaller, although the courts have said that possible remarriage should not reduce the order as the wife is entitled to her share of the assets.
● If the husband or wife has any physical or mental disability – and is therefore likely to need greater support.

MAINTENANCE PENDING SUIT

If the divorce or separation case is likely to be delayed or protracted – usually, when one partner contests the divorce or disputes the amount of maintenance – either partner can ask the court for a temporary maintenance order. Such an order – known as maintenance pending suit – is intended to provide for the dependent spouse and their children until the marriage is legally terminated and permanent financial orders can be given.

Often, a husband and wife agree how much maintenance should be paid during this period, but they should still seek a court order – known as a 'consent order' – to enforce payment if necessary and to be eligible for tax relief on the maintenance.

If they do not agree, the partner claiming support must file a notice in the county court office. It is served on the other partner within 4 days. He or she then has 14 days in which to file an AFFIDAVIT – a written statement of evidence – giving details of his or her income, capital and expenses.

The application is heard by the registrar of the county court, who listens to evidence from both partners and may cross-examine them. If there is disagreement on matters of fact – the husband claims, for example that he earns only £4,000 a year, while the wife alleges that he has additional bonuses of £2,000 and a company car – the registrar or the husband or wife may demand to see documentary evidence, such as pay-slips and bank accounts. In general, though, finances are not examined in great detail.

The registrar then makes an order for maintenance pending suit, to be paid weekly or monthly until the divorce or separation is finalised. The order is valid only until decree absolute – when a permanent maintenance order is normally granted – but it remains in force for children until varied or cancelled.

'

THE WIFE WHO WOULD NOT LEAVE HER PARENTS

Even if there is no moral blame, a woman's conduct can reduce her claim to maintenance.

When Charles and Sonia W married in 1970, he had not found a house to her liking. She stayed with her parents.

Later that year, after a child was born, Charles bought a house with Sonia's agreement – but she still refused to move in. In their first year of marriage they spent only a 3 week holiday together.

After a second child was born, Sonia sought a court order against Charles, alleging wilful neglect to maintain the family. The case was dismissed.

Sonia then went to live with Charles, but stayed only 16 days. In the following year she spent a week with him.

Charles eventually was granted a divorce on the basis of 5 years' separation. He was ordered to pay maintenance of only one-eighth of their joint income, because the judge held that Sonia's conduct justified a substantial reduction in provision for her.

An uncontrollable personality defect stopped her from 'emerging from the parental home into full married life', the judge said. Because of that, she had deserted the marriage from the start.

Sonia appealed, saying that her conduct had not been 'gross', and so the judge should not have taken it into account. The Court of Appeal had to decide whether 'gross' conduct could be found if there was no moral blame.

DECISION

The appeal judges held that the word 'gross' need not imply moral blame. No conduct could have been more gross than Sonia's failure to set up any married life at all. Her appeal was dismissed.

THE INVESTOR WHO LIVED BY BORROWING

A husband's rate of spending – not his taxed income – decides how much maintenance he can afford to pay.

When Mrs J divorced her husband in 1953, his income for tax purposes was only about £60 a year. Yet he spent more than £1,000 a year. The money came from bank overdrafts and business loans, secured by his investments in property.

Mrs J, who had custody of their two children, was first awarded maintenance of £2 a week. On appeal it was raised to £5 10s free of tax. Mr J in turn appealed. The Court of Appeal had to decide whether the amount was rightly based on current expenditure rather than on income.

DECISION

The judges held that a consistent standard of living was the only guide in making provision for a wife. If Mr J was able to raise money for his personal spending, his wife was entitled to a share of it. His appeal was dismissed.

'

● Contributions by the husband and wife to the welfare of the family – both by providing money and by looking after the home.
● Any benefits that either of them will lose the chance of acquiring because of the divorce, such as a widow's pension.
● The conduct of both partners, when one has behaved particularly badly towards the other.

ADULTERY alone will not normally affect a maintenance or lump sum award, nor will cruelty or brutality, unless it can be shown that the conduct of either husband or wife was so serious that it would be unjust to make any award.

When either partner claims that bad conduct by the other should affect the size of the award, or when there is a complicated financial dispute between them, the registrar transfers the case to a High Court, where it is heard by a judge in chambers. The cost of such a hearing is considerably higher.

When children are involved

The court takes into account:
● The child's financial needs.
● Any financial resources – such as a trust fund – he or she may have.
● If the child has any physical or mental disability.
● How he or she is being educated and how the parents want the child to be educated.
● The family's standard of living before the marriage broke down.

How much maintenance is awarded

Although the courts try to protect the living standards of everyone affected by the break-up of a marriage, there is rarely enough money to achieve that – as two households cost much more to run than one – and the husband, wife and their children usually have to manage on less. In some cases – if the husband is unemployed, for example – there may not even be enough money for an order to be made against him, and his ex-wife and children will have to apply for supplementary benefit.

Generally, the wife – who is usually the partner who requires maintenance – receives one-third of the family's possessions and one-third of its pre-tax income, whether or not she had made a financial contribution towards them.

For example, a wife who is looking after the children could be given the whole of the family home – even if it had been bought by the husband out of his own earnings and was his main capital asset – but would then probably be given a reduced maintenance order that allows for her having a rent-free home.

The 'one-third rule', however, is only a general guide to the courts: any of the factors that they must take into account can affect the size of the order. If, for example, the husband is paying a lot of

SECURING THE PERIODICAL PAYMENTS

If the husband or wife is wealthy, the court can order that some of their assets be secured to produce the periodical payments. For example, if the husband owns £100,000 in government bonds, they can be secured against a periodical payments order of £5,000 – meaning that if he fails to pay maintenance, the court will grant his wife the income from the bonds up to the amount of the order. He is not allowed to sell, mortgage or even give away the bonds without court permission. Assets secured under such an order simply cannot be disposed of – even if the owner goes bankrupt.

Another advantage of a secured order is that its payments continue – unlike ordinary periodical payments – even after the death of the owner of the assets.

WHEN A PERIODICAL PAYMENTS ORDER IS MADE

The most common type of maintenance order requires one of the partners to make periodical payments to the other – usually the husband to the wife, for herself and any children – at weekly, monthly or other fixed intervals. It remains in force until either of the partners dies, the recipient remarries, or until the court cancels it.

A husband and wife should try to agree, with the help of their solicitors or other advisers, on the amount of maintenance that is to be paid before going to court – to save both delay and legal costs.

When his earnings are known

If, for example, the husband's only income is his weekly salary of £100 as a bank clerk, he has no fringe benefits, there are no children and the wife earns £20 as a part-time typist, she could safely agree to periodical payments of £25 a week, which would bring her earnings up to more than one-third of the joint income.

However, if a wife is not sure how much her husband earns, or if his takings vary – if he is a shopkeeper or self-employed, for example – she should not agree to an offer without having his accounts examined by an accountant working for her.

Example Take the case of a childless couple, and assume that the husband is working as a senior travel executive while the wife has a full-time post as a hotel receptionist:

Husband's income

Salary	£8,000.00
less	
National insurance	£212.50
Total	£7,787.50
plus	
Company car, say	£750.00
plus	
Own benefit from entertainment allowance, say	£500.00
plus	
Telephone allowance, own benefit	£250.00
Total salary and fringe benefits	£9,287.50

Wife's income

Salary	£2,000.00
less	
National insurance	£160.00
Total	£1,840.00
plus	
Value of free food and lodging, say	£1,500.00
Total	£3,340.00
Total pre-tax income of husband and wife	£9,287.50
	+ £3,340.00
Total	£12,627.50
Divided by three	£4,209.17
less	
Wife's income	£3,340.00
Total	£869.17

The husband would be ordered to pay weekly periodical payments amounting to around £870 per annum.

money for the children's private education, he may be ordered to pay less than one-third of his income to his ex-wife.

A husband can apply for maintenance in the same way as his wife, but he is unlikely to succeed unless his wife is much better off than he.

A maintenance order need not be based on actual earnings, but may take into account the income potential of the husband and wife – for example, if a woman without children is working part-time, the court can assess what she would earn in a full-time job.

Alternatively, if a husband invested his capital at a low interest rate, say 2 per cent – perhaps in order to thwart a claim for maintenance – the court will estimate his income as though the money was earning a realistic rate of 10 per cent. But if it was a reasonable investment – if a farmer bought more land with some spare cash – the court will not usually force him to sell it.

If the husband's real income cannot easily be found out – for example, if he runs a small business with many un-recorded cash transactions, such as a secondhand shop or stall – the court may make an order based on his stan-dard of living. An expensive car and frequent holidays abroad would give the lie to a claim that he earned only £3,000 per annum.

When a maintenance order can be varied

Any party to a maintenance order can apply for it to be changed or even can-celled, when new circumstances arise. A man who loses his job can, for example, ask the court to reduce the payments he has to make; his wife can apply for increased payments if she learns that he is now earning more than at the time of the divorce, or if it is costing her more to feed and clothe the children.

If a wife receiving maintenance sud-denly inherits a fortune, her husband can apply for the order in her favour to be cancelled but he will usually have to go on maintaining the children.

How remarriage affects maintenance

Orders for periodical payments and secured periodical payments come to an end when the person receiving main-tenance remarries. A woman will not lose her maintenance merely by having sexual intercourse with another man after her divorce, unless her lover is supporting her financially.

If a husband continues paying his wife maintenance after she remarries – either because he had not heard of her wedding or because she deceived him about it – he can obtain a court order to recover excess payments.

If the husband remarries, he is still required to maintain his former wife. If he applies to the court to reduce the amount of the payments – because he has a new family to support – the court puts the needs of the divorced wife and her family above those of the new wife, but takes into account any worsening of his financial position.

It also takes into account any finan-cial benefit from remarriage – for example, his former wife may be able to claim increased maintenance if he marries a wealthy woman. It may also ask about the new wife's earnings and take them into account.

The remarriage of either partner does not affect maintenance payments for their children.

MAKING A LUMP-SUM ORDER

When either of the partners has capital, the court can order one to pay a lump sum to the other – instead of or in addition to periodical payments – in order to achieve a fair distribution of the family's property.

As a general rule, the wife will receive about one-third of the family's capital, but the award will take into account any other property she has been given. For example, if the husband has already given her a house worth £30,000 and he is left with only £10,000, the court may charge the house for £10,000, not to be enforced until the house is sold or she remarries.

If the husband has valuable assets that he cannot realise – for example, shares in a private company – he may have to raise a mortgage or loan to pay a lump-sum order. In such circumstances, the periodical payments will be reduced to enable him to meet the interest repayments on the loan. A court will not make an order that will cripple the husband in his business – if he loses his income, the wife will lose her periodical payments.

Only true family assets – those earned either jointly or by the husband while the wife was looking after the home – are divided in this way. An inheritance, gift or pools win will be treated differently, although it will be taken into account.

Another circumstance in which a lump-sum order might be made is if the husband is financially unreliable, or works in a precarious business or profession, and could not be relied on to provide regular periodical payments.

For example, an actor who, though he had earned large sums from films and plays, had failed to maintain his family, was ordered to transfer his half-share of their £150,000 home to his wife and to pay her a lump sum of £24,000 out of the £75,000 he would receive from a film he was to make a few months later. He did not have to pay her periodical payments, but was ordered to maintain their son at the rate of £90 per week.

A wife may be ordered to pay her husband a lump sum.

A lump-sum order is occasionally made in favour of one of the children of the family – if, for example, it is feared that one of the parents would squander their property, or if the child has a special need, such as a spastic child who requires ramps in the house he has moved to.

A lump-sum order can be made only once and cannot be changed afterwards, even if new facts come to light. So, if the two partners try to agree on the size of such an order before they go to court – there to apply for a consent order – they must be fully aware of each other's financial position. The order often contains a provision for payment by instalments.

Enforcing a maintenance order

If a wife thinks her husband might try to delay or shirk maintenance payments, she should ask the registrar to include in the order a requirement that it be registered at a magistrates' court. Before he does so, the registrar may require evidence that the man has been unreliable in the past.

Registration of the order at a magistrates' court requires the husband to make his payments to the court, which then posts them on to the wife. If he is moving to another area, he or the wife can ask the registrar to register the order at his local magistrates' court.

If he fails to pay a registered order,

HOW TO CLAIM TAX RELIEF ON MAINTENANCE

Maintenance payments are eligible for tax relief only if they are made under a court order or other legally binding agreement. Voluntary payments do not qualify for tax relief. Payers not liable for tax do not get any tax relief.

A husband paying maintenance may have an obligation to deduct basic-rate income tax at source and pay his ex-wife only the net amount. For example, if he is ordered to pay £50 a week gross, he deducts tax at the current rate (say 30 per cent) of £15 and pays his wife only £35.

He should deduct basic-rate income tax when
● Maintenance paid under a court order is more than £33 a week for an ex-spouse and £18 a week for each child.
● Maintenance *of any amount* is paid under an agreement other than a court order – for example, a private contract drawn up by solicitors.

The method of obtaining the tax relief differs with whether tax has been deducted or not by the payer. If he deducts tax from the payment, and his income is greater than the payment, he simply pays the net amount to his ex-wife and there is no increase in his own tax liability. He does not have to hand over to the Inland Revenue the tax deducted from the maintenance.

For example, say a man earns £10,000 a year, has tax allowances of £3,000 and the rate of tax is 30 per cent. He would pay tax on £7,000 at 30 per cent – £2,100. Say he is ordered to pay maintenance to his wife of £2,000 a year. He pays her only £1,400 (retaining £600 in tax) but his total tax liability remains £2,000 – he has paid out only £1,400 to satisfy a £2,000 liability.

If he does not deduct tax on the payment he will get an extra tax allowance. Say a man earns £10,000 a year, has tax allowances of £3,000, the rate of tax is 30 per cent and he, by court order, has to pay £1,000 a year in maintenance to his ex-wife. He does not deduct tax at source (being less than £91 a month) and pays the £1,000 to his ex-wife. His tax coding will be altered so that the tax he pays drops from £2,100 to £1,800 – £300, equal to £1,000 at 30 per cent.

If he pays tax above the basic rate, he saves even more tax. For example, a man earns £19,000, has tax allowances of £3,000 and tax is charged on the first £12,000 at 30 per cent and then at 40 per cent on the balance. His tax bill would amount to £5,200. If he was then ordered to pay £1,000 a year maintenance, his tax bill (assuming he paid the £1,000 gross) would drop to £4,800 (equivalent to £1,000 at 40 per cent, his top tax rate).

An ex-wife who receives maintenance (which is not voluntary) is taxed on it and must declare it to the Inland Revenue. If she works, her PAYE code will probably be altered to collect any additional tax due on her maintenance. If tax has been deducted from it, and she is not liable to pay that much, she can get a repayment.

To get this, she should obtain from her husband form R185, showing the amount of maintenance paid and tax deducted, and send it to the Inland Revenue.

If she receives voluntary maintenance she does not usually have to pay tax. She is also not charged CAPITAL TRANSFER TAX or CAPITAL GAINS TAX on court orders for lump-sum payments or any agreed transfer of matrimonial property.

the wife can apply to the magistrates court to enforce it – by attachment of EARNINGS if he is employed, by seizing his property or by sending him to gaol, though this would be a last resort as imprisonment would not produce the money she needs.

She should not delay in seeking enforcement, as the magistrates will not necessarily enforce arrears going back a long way. The High Court and county court will generally enforce arrears for up to 1 year only.

If she did not register the order at the time it was made, she can apply to have it registered later.

If she is left without means because maintenance is withheld by her ex-husband, she can apply for supplementary benefit.

Appealing against an order for maintenance

Within 5 days, either husband or wife can appeal to the county court judge against a registrar's order for maintenance.

Appeals against a judge's order – at either county court or High Court – must be made to the Court of Appeal within 14 days. Legal aid is available for appeals.

Foreign maintenance orders

Maintenance orders made in foreign countries can be enforced in Britain, but only where we have a mutual agreement with the other country for enforcement of orders. Consult a solicitor.

When the payer of maintenance deducts no tax

Under a court order for MAINTENANCE, the payer normally deducts INCOME TAX. But if the order is for no more than £33 a week to an adult, or £18 a week to maintain a child, the whole amount is paid.

If the person making such payments is a taxpayer, he, instead of whoever receives them, can claim tax relief.

As well as getting the benefit of the whole amount of the order, a woman who looks after children and has no other substantial income is unlikely to have to pay tax on it. Her INCOME TAX ALLOWANCES will probably exceed her income.

MALADJUSTED CHILD

When there is a dispute over schooling

If a child's behaviour at school is so disturbed that it interferes with his education, he can be given special schooling.

The decision to send him to a school for the maladjusted is made by the School Psychological Service, after testing by the educational psychologist in consultation with other professionals, and with the parents' consent.

If a head teacher feels he can no longer cope with a particular disturbed child in his school and he gets the doctor's agreement, he can suspend – but never expel – the child for up to 3 months.

The parents can appeal to the school governors against such a decision, or they may seek a second medical opinion to enhance their case.

If the parents still refuse to accept that the child is maladjusted, he or she can return to school for one day, and the head teacher can then suspend him or her again. And so on, indefinitely – until one side gives in.

The parents can ask another school to accept the child and it may do so.

When there is a disagreement between a school and the parents the case is always referred to a case conference, comprising of representatives from the education authority, the local social services department, the educational psychologist and others, such as the teacher or head teacher.

If parents reject the advice of the conference they can appeal to the local education officer, then, if necessary, to their MP and to the Secretary of State for Education.

MALICIOUS PROSECUTION

Claiming damages over a wrongful court action

Anyone cleared of a criminal charge may be able to claim damages, but only if he can prove that the police – or a private person who brought the prosecution – has prosecuted him maliciously.

A person who brings a claim for dam

ages for malicious prosecution has to prove:

1. There was no reasonable cause for bringing the prosecution.

2. The prosecutor acted from motives of malice.

3. The innocent person suffered damage to his reputation, person, freedom or property as a result of the prosecution.

An action for malicious prosecution can be brought only against the person who instigated the prosecution, and not against anyone who gave false evidence to the police. Few actions for malicious prosecution succeed. When they do, damages are assessed on the degree of loss suffered.

MANSLAUGHTER

An unlawful killing that does not amount to murder

Manslaughter is the killing of a person without malice aforethought – which means through:

● Negligence.

● Provocation.

● Recklessly carrying out a lawful act such as driving a car.

● Dangerous or unlawful acts, such as robbery, where no harm or serious harm was intended.

The offence covers a wide range of killings. The maximum penalty, life imprisonment, is normally imposed only for crimes that fall just short of MURDER.

Penalties such as a few years in prison or a fine are more usually imposed where the killing was a result of, say, a negligently caused accident.

Intentional manslaughter

A person charged with murder on the basis of a deliberate intention to kill or a deliberate intention to inflict serious injury, which resulted in death, may be able to have the verdict reduced to manslaughter by reason of provocation.

For example, a father who sees his daughter raped and instantly kills the rapist has killed under extreme provocation, and the crime is manslaughter. If, however, the daughter had gone home and told him of the rape, and as a result, the father then went out, found the rapist and killed him, that would be

"

JOKER SHOT HIS FRIEND DEAD

It is not manslaughter when death is caused by a complete accident, and the accused believes there is no danger.

It was just a practical joke when Terence Lamb pointed a revolver at his best friend and pulled the trigger. There was a bullet in the chamber, but he thought it was not opposite the firing hammer and would not fire. What he did not know was that in closing the revolver the chamber moved round so that in fact the firing hammer became opposite the bullet. The friend fell dead.

Mr Lamb was accused of manslaughter. He denied the charge and said that he had no idea that when he pulled the trigger it would rotate the cylinder and cause a bullet to be fired. He insisted it was a genuine mistake.

An expert witness said in court that it was a natural mistake for someone who did not know how a revolver worked. Mr Lamb was convicted. He appealed.

DECISION

The Court of Appeal quashed the conviction because of misdirection by the judge on the law. Mr Lamb thought that his friend was in no danger and he had no guilty intent.

murder, because the father had time to 'cool off'.

The survivor of a SUICIDE pact is guilty of intentional manslaughter. So are people who plead DIMINISHED RESPONSIBILITY after killing.

Unintentional manslaughter

When someone causes the death of another person through negligence or recklessness, without provocation and intent to kill, he is guilty of unintentional manslaughter.

If a child died of starvation as a result of parental neglect the parent has committed manslaughter. So has a thief who kills someone while trying to escape, or a motorist who drives recklessly and causes a pedestrian to die.

In all such cases the death is more than just an accident. The person responsible has failed in a duty to others in not taking sufficient care or even in disregarding people's safety.

Motor manslaughter is usually prosecuted under causing death by reckless driving.

MANUFACTURERS' LIABILITY

When you can claim compensation from the maker

If you are sold DEFECTIVE GOODS you can claim compensation from the shop for breach of contract. That compensation can include PERSONAL INJURY compensation – for example, if you are scalded when a hot-water bottle bursts.

However, if the hot-water bottle bursts and scalds someone else, he cannot sue the shopkeeper for breach of contract because he made no contract with the shop. His best course is to sue the manufacturer of the hot-water bottle for NEGLIGENCE.

When foreign-manufactured goods are involved

When you are injured by defects in a product made abroad, for example a faulty brake in a foreign car, you still sue the manufacturing company in the normal way if the company has a registered office in this country.

But if it does not, you have to go to the High Court for permission to start an action against the foreign company which will be granted only if the court thinks that in the circumstances it is right to compel the foreign company to come to trial here.

If the foreign manufacturer gave a guarantee, that guarantee may create a contract governed by English law and the courts are more likely then to agree to an action.

Points that have to be proved when a claim is made

For a claim to succeed, it must be shown that the maker had a duty of reasonable care to the person claiming damages and that he failed in his duty by not taking reasonable care. It must also be shown that the damage done, which the manufacturer should have reason-

"

THE SNAIL IN A BOTTLE OF GINGER BEER

A manufacturer must take care to see that a consumer does not suffer injury to health from a product.

A friend treated Mrs M'Alister to a bottle of ginger beer in a cafe in Paisley. It was served from an opaque brown bottle covered with the maker's label and there was a cap on the bottle. Mrs M'Alister drank some. Then her friend poured out the rest of the bottle and 'a snail, which was in a state of decomposition, floated out of the bottle'.

Mrs M'Alister claimed that as a result of the nauseating sight of the snail and the ginger beer which she had already consumed, she suffered shock and gastro-enteritis. She claimed damages from the makers.

DECISION

The House of Lords held that any manufacturer of an article of food or medicine sold in a manner which prevented the distributor or purchaser from seeing or discovering any defect had a legal duty to take reasonable care that the article was free from anything that could cause injury to health. The manufacturer could be liable for negligence and the case was sent back to the Court of Session for proof.

ably foreseen, was caused by his failure to take reasonable care. A pedestrian injured by a car defectively made so that it has inadequate brakes can claim compensation from the manufacturer, for example. A repairer can also be sued for his negligence.

It is no defence for a manufacturer to say that the defect could have been discovered by someone else between the time when the car left his factory and caused harm. He must show that he could reasonably have expected some intermediary to have checked the product and found any defect of the kind that caused the harm.

The law recognises how difficult it might be for the consumer to prove the manufacturer careless. It eases his task by holding that negligence can be inferred from the existence of the defect in the circumstances.

MARRIAGE

Only a recognised ceremony can ensure a couple's rights

The law gives special rights and protection to the partners in a marriage – but only if the marriage is legally valid. Simply living together confers few of those rights. *See:* COHABITATION

In a legally valid marriage, a man and a woman unite as husband and wife, and in many respects they may be treated as one. They accept the duty to live together, behave reasonably towards each other, and support each other. Each has the right to be maintained by the other and to have reasonable sexual relations – to the exclusion of anyone else.

Marriage must be entered into voluntarily, but it cannot be ended merely by agreement. Unlike any other legal contract, it lasts for life unless it is dissolved by a court decree. *See:* DIVORCE

Who can marry

Partners to a valid marriage must be:
● Over the age of 16 – and if under 18 they should have their parents' consent – although if they succeed in marrying without it, the marriage will be valid.
● Not already married.
● Not so closely related that their marriage is forbidden by law.
● Of the opposite sex. Although some other laws (for example, social security) accept sex-change surgery, the courts have ruled that a man cannot marry

THE RELATIVES WHO CANNOT MARRY

A man cannot marry his:
Mother, mother-in-law, aunt, grandmother, step-grandmother, grandmother-in-law, step-mother, adoptive mother, sister, half-sister, daughter, niece, daughter-in-law, step-daughter, grand-daughter, step-grand-daughter, grand-daughter-in-law, adopted daughter.

A woman cannot marry her:
Father, father-in-law, uncle, grandfather, step-grandfather, grandfather-in-law, step-father, adoptive father, brother, half-brother, son, nephew, son-in-law, step-son, grandson, step-grandson, grandson-in-law, adopted son.

THE BRIDE WHO WAS A MALE FOR 25 YEARS

A marriage between people who were born the same sex cannot be legally recognised – even if one has had sex-change surgery.

George Jamieson, born in 1935 and registered as a boy, joined the merchant navy at the age of 16. But at 21 he settled in France and worked as a female impersonator.

In 1960, after surgical operations, the former George arrived in London under the name April Ashley, and dressed and lived as a woman. The name was legally changed by deed poll and April Ashley's status as a female was given official confirmation when she obtained a woman's national insurance card.

Later that year she met Tom Corbett, who was living with his wife and children. He was divorced in 1962 and – aware of the details of Ashley's operations – pressed her to marry him.

In 1963 they went through a ceremony in Gibraltar, but formally parted within 3 months. They had been together for only 14 days after the ceremony.

In 1966 Corbett sought a declaration that the 'marriage' was of no effect because Ashley was a male. Alternatively he petitioned for a decree of nullity because of Ashley's incapacity or wilful refusal to consummate.

Ashley cross-petitioned for nullity on the grounds of Corbett's incapacity or refusal to consummate the marriage. By implication, she was trying to win High Court recognition that she was able to function fully as a woman.

The court, in the first case of its kind, had to decide:
● What factors determine a person's sex.
● What sex April Ashley was for the purpose of marriage.

DECISION

The judge ruled that in marriage law the only test of sex is biological construction, and that biological construction is fixed at birth. It cannot change or be changed.

A term like 'sex change' is appropriate only when a mistake is made immediately after a child's birth, and it is discovered by a medical examination later that the child was wrongly registered.

Corbett was granted a decree of nullity on the ground that he could not have made a valid marriage with another male.

---

another man who has been surgically altered into a woman.
● Married in accordance with certain legal procedures. These vary, depending on whether there is a religious element to the ceremony.

If any of those conditions is not met, apart from parental consent, the arrangement is not a valid marriage. It is legally void, as if it had never taken place.

A marriage can be challenged on other grounds – for example, by showing that one partner's participation was not truly voluntary – but in that case it remains in existence unless it is declared void by a court. *See:* NULLITY

Parental consent

No one can make a legal marriage before reaching the age of 16. Someone who wants to marry at 16 or 17 is required to have the consent of:
● Both parents if they live together.
● The parent with custody after a divorce or judicial separation.
● The surviving parent if one is dead.
● A legal guardian.

● The authority in charge of a child in care.

Someone aged 16–18 who is refused consent can apply for a magistrate's permission, by asking a court clerk to arrange a hearing. There is no right of appeal against a court decision.

Who gives official permission

Although others can perform a marriage ceremony, only two categories of people can give legal approval for a marriage to go ahead:
● Clergy of the Church of England.
● Superintendent registrars, representing the state registry of births, deaths and marriages in each district.

Someone intending to marry – only one of a couple need apply – should arrange an appointment so that details can be taken down on forms held by the clergyman or registrar. Proof of identity or age may be asked for at that stage, or may be left until just before the ceremony.

The fee to give notice of a marriage is £3.50.

The type of approval that a superintendent registrar or an Anglican clergyman may give depends on where and how soon a couple intend to marry. There is normally a waiting time of at least 3 weeks, but in both cases special arrangements can be made sooner.

Arranging a Church of England wedding

Traditional procedure for a Church of England wedding requires its announcement to the public by reading out the couple's names in the parish church of the district where they live so that anyone who knows of a legal obstacle to the marriage can report it to a church officer.

That practice, called 'publishing the banns', must be followed for 3 consecutive Sundays. The couple can marry at any time in the following 3 months. If they do not, the banns must be published again.

Common licence If a couple do not wish banns to be published, they can apply for a licence from the bishop of the diocese in which either of them has lived for at least the past 15 days. It costs £2.75 and allows the couple to marry in a particular church at any time in the following 3 months.

Special licence A couple who cannot meet the 15 day residence qualification but want to marry urgently – for example, because one of them is dying or because of travel arrangements – can apply to the Church of England faculty office in Westminster, London, for a special licence. It can be issued only by the Archbishop of Canterbury and requires sworn statements by the couple, character references, and letters of approval from parents and from the vicar of the church where the couple intend to marry.

The licence fee is £27, and the total cost, including legal fees for the sworn statements, is likely to be more than £50. A special licence is not issued if either of a couple is divorced.

Church law No clergyman is compelled to:
● Solemnise the marriage of any person whose former marriage has been dissolved on any ground and whose former husband or wife is still living.
● Permit the marriage of such a person to be solemnised in the church of which he is the minister.

Except in such circumstances, persons legally qualified to marry are entitled to be married in church if one of them possesses the legal qualification of residence – even if they do not attend church regularly.

A clergyman who refuses to marry a person entitled to be married commits an ecclesiastical offence, but it is doubtful whether he is guilty of any wrong by civil law for so refusing.

Outside the Church of England

Any marriage not performed by a Church of England clergyman requires a certificate from the superintendent registrar of marriages in the district in which it is to take place. A certificate is issued, without charge, after notice of the couple's intention to marry has been displayed at the register office for 3 weeks. The wedding can take place at any time in the following 3 months.

Registrar's licence By issuing a combined 'certificate and licence' – sometimes wrongly called a special licence – a superintendent registrar can allow a couple to marry after waiting only 1 clear weekday. One of them must have lived in the district for the past 15 days, and the other must be living in England or Wales. A certificate and licence cost £13.

Registrar General's licence A Registrar General's licence is equivalent to a Church of England special licence, but for couples who want only a civil ceremony, one of them must be so ill that he or she cannot be moved.

Where and when a couple may wed

Valid marriages can be performed between 8 a.m. and 6 p.m. in a register office or 'registered building' – a term that describes churches and other premises that are certified by the Government as places of worship, and listed by the registrar general for the performance of marriage.

People marrying by the rules of the Society of Friends – commonly called Quakers – or by Jewish law need not marry in a registered building. A valid ceremony can be performed in a private house in their case, at any hour.

Couples who want to go through a wedding ceremony in unusual surroundings – for example, in a favourite

spot out of doors – can do so wherever and whenever they wish. But their marriage has no validity unless they also go through another ceremony which complies with all the normal formalities.

Couples who have a special licence or Registrar General's licence may marry wherever the licence allows – for example, in hospital.

Who must attend

At least two witnesses must attend, and sign the marriage register. They need not know the bride and groom, and there is no minimum age limit, but they must be acceptable to the registrar as 'credible' witnesses. So a young child, or someone who is obviously incapable because of drunkenness or mental disorder, might be rejected.

A registrar, or a minister authorised to register marriage, is the only other person required by law to be present. Clergy of the Church of England are authorised, and some clergy of other faiths may be authorised. In a register office wedding, two registrars must be present.

If the person conducting a wedding ceremony is not authorised to register marriage, a registrar must also attend. Religious custom may call for other people to be present, but that is not a legal requirement.

A registrar charges £6 to conduct a marriage in his office, or £7 for attending a wedding elsewhere.

What must be said in the marriage ceremony

At a civil ceremony in a register office, or in a registered building of any faith, apart from the Church of England, the Society of Friends or the Jewish Faith, the law requires the bride and groom each to make two declarations in the following form.

First they must affirm their freedom to marry by saying: 'I do solemnly declare that I know of no lawful impediment why I (full name) may not be joined in matrimony to (full name).'

They must also say: 'I call upon these persons here present to witness that I (full name) do take thee (full name) to be my lawful wedded wife/husband.'

As soon as the second declaration is completed the couple are legally married. No other wording is required, nor any custom such as the placing of a wedding ring.

Marriage of foreigners

A person who does not normally live in Britain can marry in this country only if the laws of his domicile also allow the marriage.

Exceptions are made however:
● If one party is domiciled in England and the other has an incapacity not recognised in English law – for example, Portugal's prohibition of marriage between cousins.
● If the domicile law does not recognise a divorce that is recognised in English law.

The legal situation of Britons who marry abroad varies according to the country they are in. *See:* FOREIGN MARRIAGE

MARRIAGE CERTIFICATE

Showing proof that you are married

Every married couple is entitled to have a copy of the certificate showing that they are married.

The certificate is a copy of the entry of the wedding in the marriage register of the church or register office in which the marriage took place and it shows the names of the husband and wife, their status – bachelor, spinster, widow, widower or divorced – their occupation and address and those of their parents, the date and place of the wedding, and the names of the witnesses.

If the marriage was by a religious ceremony, the certificate must show the religion under which it was conducted and the name of who officiated.

A marriage certificate issued at the time costs £1.50. It is usually given to the couple when they sign the marriage register books, but may sometimes only be sent to them afterwards by post. The certificate belongs equally to a husband and wife: neither has a special right to keep the 'marriage lines'.

You are not required by law to hold a marriage certificate, but, as it must be produced for certain official purposes – such as applying for a visa to visit certain countries – it is advisable to take the one offered at your wedding. If you decline and need a copy later, you will have to pay £3.50 for it.

How to obtain extra copies

If you lose your marriage certificate or need an extra copy, apply to the register office where you were married,

Copies of fictitious register entries supplied by and reproduced with the approval of the Registrar-General

HOW A MARRIAGE IS REGISTERED BY THE STATE

The official document that certifies a couple have been legally married

The status of the man and woman must be entered on the certificate – for example, bachelor, spinster, widow, widower or divorced

If any notes have been made on the official notice of marriage – for example, if a name has been corrected – they must be entered on the certificate

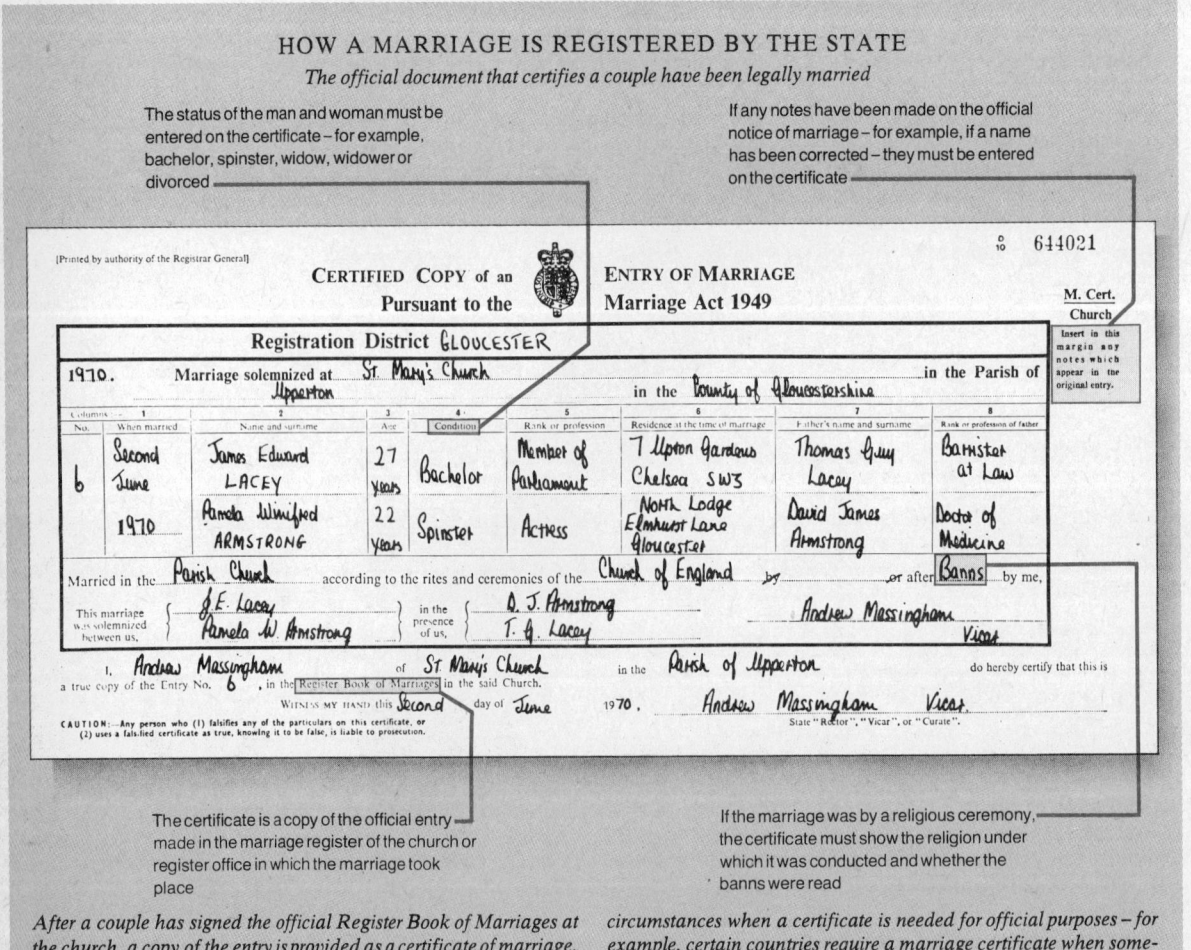

The certificate is a copy of the official entry made in the marriage register of the church or register office in which the marriage took place

If the marriage was by a religious ceremony, the certificate must show the religion under which it was conducted and whether the banns were read

After a couple has signed the official Register Book of Marriages at the church, a copy of the entry is provided as a certificate of marriage. A certificate is not required by law. However, there are certain circumstances when a certificate is needed for official purposes – for example, certain countries require a marriage certificate when someone is applying for a visa to visit the country.

WHEN A MARRIAGE CERTIFICATE MUST BE SHOWN

● A copy of the marriage certificate must be attached to a petition for DIVORCE or judicial SEPARATION.

● If a husband and wife want to share a joint passport, they must send a copy of the marriage certificate.

● A husband and wife may be asked to prove that they are married when applying at a foreign embassy for a visa to travel abroad, or to emigrate.

● A foreigner who married a British citizen and wanted to remain in Britain would have to show his or her marriage certifi-cate to the Home Office in order to obtain the permit.

● When making or changing claims for certain social security benefits, or when applying for a changed rate of national insurance contributions, you may be asked for your marriage certificate.

For example, a widow who remarries has to show her marriage certificate when applying for a new contribution rate. However, someone applying for widow's benefits need show only her husband's death certificate to qualify.

---

or, if you were married at a religious ceremony, to the register office where your marriage was registered – usually the one for the area where your wedding was held.

Alternatively, you can apply to the General Register Office at St Catherine's House, 10, Kingsway, London WC2B 6JP, which keeps records of all marriages in England and Wales going back to July 3, 1837.

The cost of a copy from the local register is £1.50. The General Register Office charges £3.50 for certificates applied for in person and £8 for postal requests.

The only information you need to give is the names of the partners to the marriage, but it helps if you can supply the place and date of the wedding.

How to check if someone is married

If you want to know if someone is or has been married, you are entitled to search the records at the General Register Office or at the local register office where you think the person might have married. There is no charge.

Anyone – not only the parties to a marriage – can obtain a certificate of any entry in the registers for a fee of £3.50.

The registration of a marriage remains unchanged in the register – regardless of whether the parties have died or divorced – and anyone can obtain and keep a copy of the marriage certificate even if the marriage is no longer valid.

However, anyone using such a certificate under false pretences – for exam-ple, a divorced woman who uses a marriage certificate as proof that she is still married – can be prosecuted. *See:* MISREPRESENTATION

MARRIAGE GUIDANCE

When help is available to maintain a relationship

When a marriage is in danger of breaking up either or both partners can voluntarily seek advice from the National Marriage Guidance Council or denominational organisations specialising in the field. Neither party can be made to heed such advice.

If a domestic case reaches the courts, a magistrate may refer it to a probation officer, but neither spouse is obliged to follow his recommendations.

SETTLING A COUPLE'S
DIFFERENCES

Marriage-guidance counsellors are available to advise any couple whose marriage is in danger of breaking up.

All marriage-guidance counsellors maintain complete confidentiality of information they are given. Although they can be ordered to give EVIDENCE in court, they do not voluntarily give such testimony without the consent of both partners.

MARRIED WOMAN

How marriage affects her national insurance obligations

Until April 5, 1977, married women at work could choose whether to pay full or reduced-rate NATIONAL INSURANCE CONTRIBUTIONS. Since then, the only married women who can still pay at a reduced rate are those who:

● Were married before April 6, 1977, and

● Chose before May 11, 1977 to continue at the reduced rate, and

● Since April 5, 1978 have not had two consecutive tax years during which they have not been liable to pay Class 1 contributions, and not been self-employed.

All other married women at work must pay the same contributions as men and single women.

The reduced rate of contribution in 1981–2 was 2.75 per cent of earnings up to £200 a week.

Women who are paying at the reduced rate can elect to pay the full contribution by applying to their local social security office. The full rate becomes payable from the April following their choice. Once you have chosen full liability you cannot change back to the reduced rate.

Women who are resuming work after two complete tax years away from it must pay at the full rate.

Among the benefits you lose by paying the reduced rate are unemployment, sickness and invalidity benefits. A retirement pension may be payable on your husband's contributions but it will be much less than a pension based on your own insurance contributions. *See:* RETIREMENT PENSION

How supplementary benefit is affected

A married woman who is living with her husband cannot normally claim

SOCIAL SECURITY BENEFITS FOR MARRIED WOMEN
Circumstances in which national insurance contributions are required

Benefit	Type of national insurance contributions needed to qualify
Maternity Allowance	Full rate
Unemployment Benefit	Full rate
Sickness Benefit	Full rate
Invalidity Benefit	Full rate
Retirement Pension	Full rate for maximum pension; reduced pension may be paid on husband's contributions
Maternity Grant	Full rate; or may be paid on husband's contributions (non-contributory from 1982)
Death Grant	Full rate; or may be paid on husband's contributions
Widow's Benefit	Husband's contributions
Child's Special Allowance	Full rate; or former husband's contributions
Guardian's Allowance	None
Attendance Allowance	None
Industrial Injuries Benefits	None
Mobility Allowance	None
Non-Contributory Invalidity Pension	None
Child Benefit	None
Family Income Supplement	None
Supplementary Benefit	None

SUPPLEMENTARY BENEFIT in her own right.

A claim for benefit to meet their combined needs must be made by the husband and is normally paid to him.

If the husband fails to support his family, the benefit can be paid to the wife to protect her interests or those of the children.

A wife whose husband is living with her but refuses to support her can also claim supplementary benefit in her own right on grounds of urgent need, but she may have to repay it later if she is in a position to do so.

From November 1983, it will be possible for a wife to claim supplementary benefit instead of the husband provided that she has worked full-time or part-time in the previous 6 months or would have done so but for sickness or unemployment.

MATERNITY

Care and cash benefits for the mother-to-be

Expectant mothers are entitled to a comprehensive range of maternity treatment, care and advice and usually to some financial help from the state. There are extra rights and cash benefits for working women who become pregnant.

Obtaining medical care

Pregnancy tests can be arranged through your family doctor. If the test is positive, the next step is to decide what kind of ante-natal care you want.

Some, but not all, family doctors provide ante-natal care themselves. Those who are specialists in this sort of care are on the Obstetric List published by the local Family Practitioner Committee and available at most post offices. You have the right to consult a doctor on the list purely for maternity care while continuing to use your own doctor for other medical matters.

Many women choose to have their ante-natal check-ups in the outpatients department of the nearest hospital – even if the baby is to be born at home. Your family doctor will arrange the first visit to the hospital.

Time off work

Under the Employment Act 1980 a pregnant employee must be given reasonable paid time off by her employer during working hours to receive ante-natal care advised by a doctor, midwife or health visitor. She must produce at her employer's request a certificate that she is pregnant and an appointment card, except when it is the first appointment during her pregnancy. The amount of pay to which she is entitled is her normal pay as though she had not been absent. If the employer refuses time off, or refuses to pay wages, she can complain to an industrial tribunal within 3 months of the date of her ante-natal appointment.

Your right to decide to have the baby at home

You are entitled to insist on having your baby at home. In practice few women do, and most doctors advise against it, particularly if it is a first child. If you do insist on having the baby at home against your doctor's advice, he may suggest you find another doctor. *See:* DOCTOR AND PATIENT

A midwife is allocated to every home delivery. She visits the mother-to-be before the birth to check that everything is ready and is present at the birth. Your doctor will also try to be present, but it may not be possible.

When the baby is born

Most births, whether at home or in hospital, take place naturally. But if a birth is exceptionally late, or if the mother has been in labour for a long time, the doctor may suggest that birth be induced by the use of drugs. The mother's consent must be obtained.

In difficult births the doctor may suggest using forceps. Again, the mother's permission will be sought.

If a normal birth is not possible, the doctor may decide to deliver the baby by a caesarian section operation, in which he cuts into the abdomen to remove the child.

The mother will be asked to sign a consent form. If she is not fully conscious the operation can proceed without her consent, but an attempt would probably be made, if there was time, to obtain the consent of the next of kin – for example, the husband – although this is not legally essential.

If mother or baby is harmed because of negligence by nursing or medical staff, damages can be claimed in the courts. For example, delays in deciding on the method of delivery that led to brain damage in the baby might amount to negligence.

HOW A WORKING WOMAN'S MATERNITY BENEFITS ARE CALCULATED

A working woman may be entitled to three separate maternity payments – maternity grant, maternity allowance and maternity pay. In the case of a woman earning £50 a week and paying full-rate national insurance contributions the amount, including earnings-related benefit, would total:

Maternity pay at 90% of weekly salary	£45.00
Less flat-rate maternity allowance	£20.65
	£24.35
Less tax (£7.30) and national insurance contributions (£3.37)	£10.67
Net maternity pay per week	£13.68
Maternity pay is paid for 6 weeks – 6×£13.68	£82.08
Plus maternity allowance of £20.65 per week for 18 weeks	£371.70
Plus earnings-related supplement to maternity allowance – 16×£5.50 (1981 only)	£88.00
Plus maternity grant £25.00	£25.00
Total maternity payments	£566.78

After the birth

Mother and baby will receive regular home visits by a HEALTH VISITOR to help and advise on baby care and feeding. There is no obligation to see a health visitor if you do not want her services.

What financial help is available

Most expectant mothers are entitled to a maternity grant – a lump-sum payment – to help with the general expense of having a baby.

The grant, which in 1981 was £25, can be claimed either before or after the birth. If more than one child is born, the mother can claim the maternity grant for each child who lives more than 12 hours. If all the babies were to die within 12 hours, the grant would still be paid for one birth.

In a single birth when the baby is stillborn, the grant is paid only if the pregnancy lasted at least 28 weeks. To qualify for the grant you must have paid a minimum amount of NATIONAL INSURANCE CONTRIBUTIONS.

A married woman can qualify on her own or her husband's contributions. The requirements are:

- Contributions paid on earnings of at least 25 times the lower earnings limit for contributions in any one tax year. Contributions credited during sickness or unemployment do not count.
- In addition, contributions paid or *credited* on earnings of at least 25 times the lower earnings limit during the relevant tax year:

Baby born or due	Relevant tax year
Jan 7, 1979 to Jan 5, 1980	April 6, 1977 to April 5, 1978
Jan 6, 1980 to Jan 3, 1981	April 6, 1978 to April 5, 1979
Jan 4, 1981 to Jan 3 1982	April 6, 1979 to April 5, 1980

A divorced woman can usually claim only on her own contributions. But she can claim on her former husband's contributions if she was still married up to 11 weeks before the baby is due. In such cases the claim must be made before the baby is born.

If she remarries before the baby is born, she can claim on her new husband's contributions. A widow expecting her late husband's child can claim on his contributions.

The maternity grant is to be non-contributory from 1982. Then the payment of the grant will be made by the Child Benefit Centre, near Newcastle upon Tyne, and not by local Department of Health and Social Security Offices. Instead of national insurance contribution conditions having to be met, a 6-month UK residence test will have to be satisfied.

An expectant mother receiving supplementary benefit, or whose husband is receiving it, is entitled to a lump-sum payment to enable her to buy essential items for the baby. The maternity grant of £25 and any savings over £300 are taken into account in deciding how much she needs.

Items that can be provided include baby clothes and nappies, a cot mattress, sheets and blankets, feeding bottles, and a second-hand cot, pram (or carrycot) and baby bath. The payment can be made up to 6 weeks before the baby is due.

A lump-sum payment can also be made for maternity clothing needed at any time while the family is on supplementary benefit.

An expectant mother or young child in a family getting supplementary benefit or a family income supplement is entitled to FREE MILK – a pint a day. Other families with low incomes also qualify.

Special provisions for working women

Pregnant women who have been working may be entitled to other payments as well as the maternity grant, and they have special rights if they want to resume their employment after having the baby.

There are two payments to which they may be entitled – maternity allowance from the state and maternity pay from their employer.

Maternity allowance is a weekly benefit of £20.65 (1981) to make it easier for a pregnant woman to give up work in good time before the baby is born. It is paid for 18 weeks, starting 11 weeks before the baby is due. The allowance may be increased by the addition of an EARNINGS-RELATED SUPPLEMENT or dependency payment.

Maternity allowance is payable if the expectant mother herself has paid a minimum amount of full-rate national insurance contributions. Reduced-rate contributions sometimes paid by married women or widows do not count. The requirements are:

● Contributions paid on earnings of at least 25 times the LOWER EARNINGS LIMIT in any one tax year. Contributions credited during sickness or unemployment do not count.

● Contributions paid or *credited* on earnings of at least 50 times the lower earnings limit in the relevant tax year:

Baby born or due	Relevant tax year
March 25, 1979 to March 22, 1980	April 6, 1977 to April 5, 1978
March 23, 1980 to March 21, 1981	April 6, 1978 to April 5, 1979
March 22, 1981 to March 20, 1982	April 6, 1979 to April 5, 1980

HEALTH CARE DURING PREGNANCY

How the health of a woman and her baby are checked during and after pregnancy

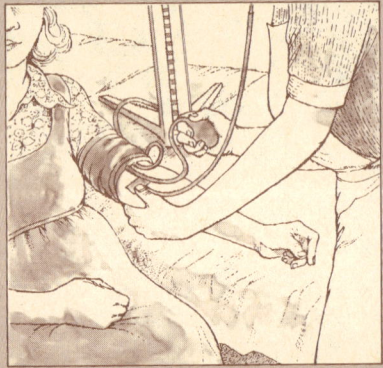

1 When a woman suspects that she might be pregnant, she should visit her doctor and ask to be given a pregnancy test. The doctor will require a urine sample – which she should take with her on her first visit – and may also make an internal examination. If the pregnancy is confirmed and the doctor is not going to give ante-natal care himself, he makes an appointment for the mother-to-be to attend the ante-natal clinic of a local hospital or to see a doctor who specialises in obstetrics. On her first visit to him or to the local hospital, the woman is given a thorough medical examination and all the details of her medical history will be taken in case they might affect the health of her baby.

2 During the first 28 weeks of pregnancy, she attends clinic or a specialist once a month – and more frequently after that time. Regular checks are kept on her health, especially to ensure that her blood pressure does not become too high.

3 She may also decide to attend ante-natal classes at her doctor's surgery or at the hospital ante-natal clinic where she is taught about relaxation and breathing exercises and can obtain information on any aspects of pregnancy and birth.

4 The woman may decide to have her baby at home or in hospital. Most doctors advise a woman having her first baby to do so in hospital. If a woman decides to have her baby at home, a midwife is in attendance throughout the birth.

Even if you do not have contributions or credits on earnings of 50 times the lower limit, you may be able to get a reduced allowance. Special credits may be given to school leavers, students, apprentices, divorced women and widows to enable them to meet the requirements.

Maternity allowance is not payable while you continue to do any paid work, nor if you are getting an equal or higher rate of sickness, unemployment, widow's injury or invalidity benefit or a training allowance.

To claim maternity allowance, complete form BM4 – on which you also claim maternity grant – as soon as possible after the 14th week before the baby is due. If you claim later than the 11th week you may lose benefit.

The allowance is paid by means of a book of orders cashed at a post office.

Maternity pay from your employer

In addition to maternity allowance you can claim 6 weeks' maternity pay from your employer when you leave to have a baby if:
● You have been a full-time employee for at least 2 years, or a part-time employee working more than 8 hours a week for 5 years.

5 After the baby has been born, the parents visit their local registrar of births, marriages and deaths to register their child and receive a certificate of registration. At least one of them must do so within 42 days of the child's birth.

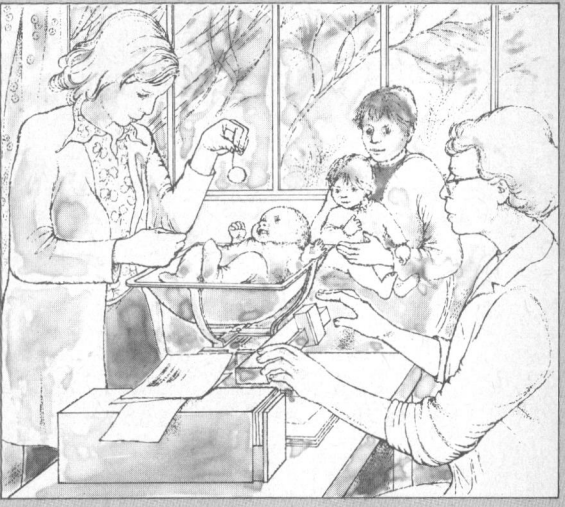

6 The mother will receive regular visits from a health visitor who will give advice on baby care. The mother should also visit the baby clinic to have the child weighed and a check kept on its development – for example, hearing and eyesight.

7 While the progress and health of the new-born baby are kept under close examination, the mother returns to her own doctor between 6 to 8 weeks after the birth of her child. The doctor gives a thorough post-natal examination to make sure the mother's health has not suffered as a result of the birth. If she was working before her pregnancy, she is entitled to return to her job, provided that she has been a full-time employee for at least 2 years and she was employed up to 11 weeks before the baby was due. She must return to work within 29 weeks of the birth and she must have given her employer at least a week's notice of her return. If the mother is ill, she may have the 29 week period extended by up to 4 weeks, provided that she obtains a note from her doctor. There is no legal right to a further extension in any circumstances.

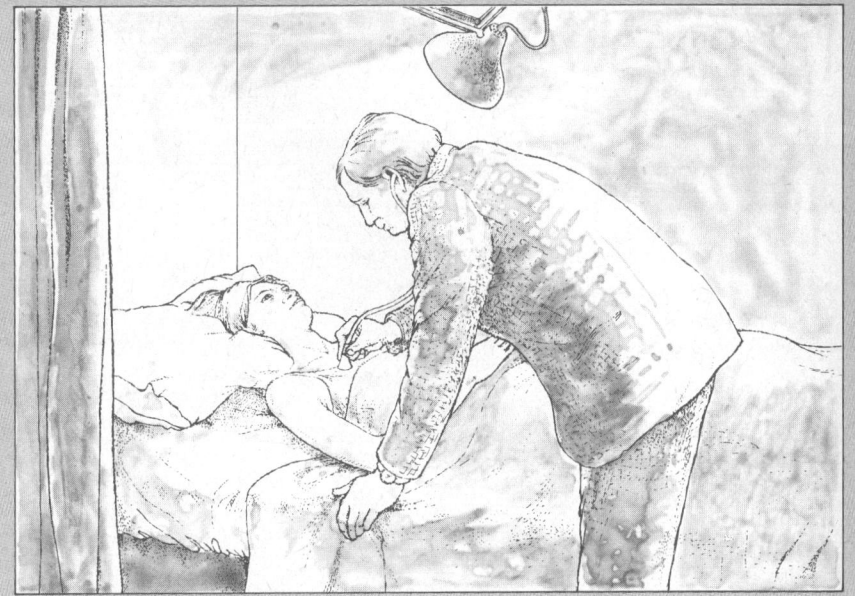

WHEN YOU CAN CLAIM MATERNITY PAY – AND YOUR JOB BACK

Your rights depend on giving proper notice

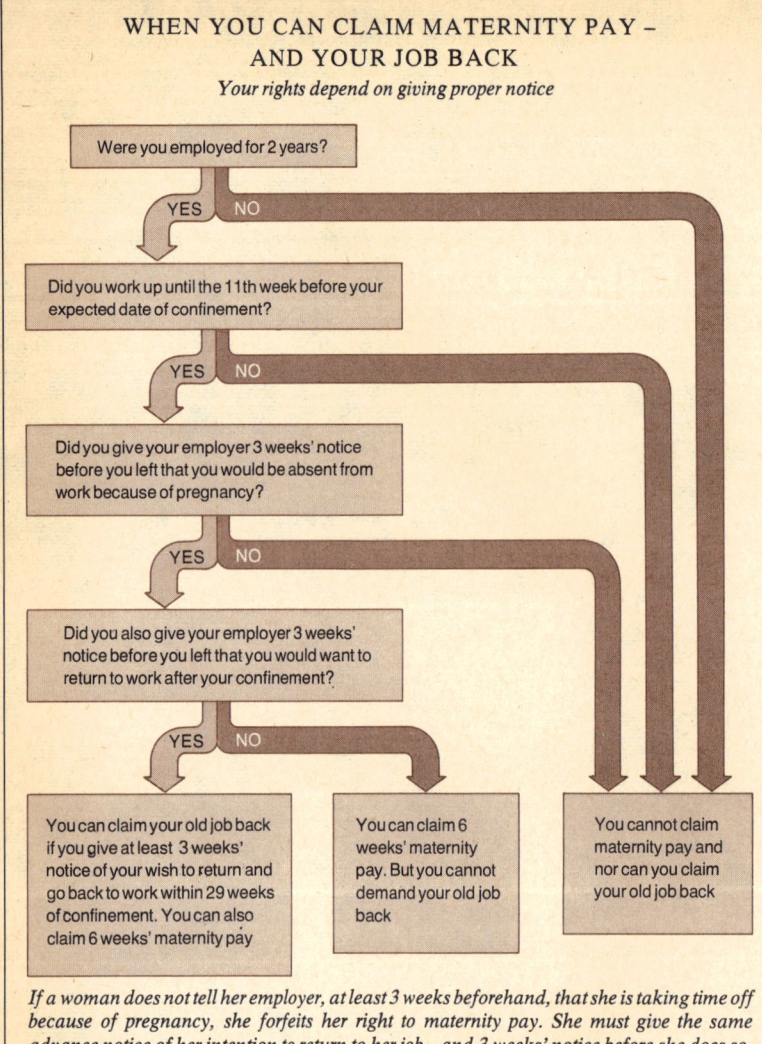

Were you employed for 2 years?

YES / NO

Did you work up until the 11th week before your expected date of confinement?

YES / NO

Did you give your employer 3 weeks' notice before you left that you would be absent from work because of pregnancy?

YES / NO

Did you also give your employer 3 weeks' notice before you left that you would want to return to work after your confinement?

YES / NO

You can claim your old job back if you give at least 3 weeks' notice of your wish to return and go back to work within 29 weeks of confinement. You can also claim 6 weeks' maternity pay

You can claim 6 weeks' maternity pay. But you cannot demand your old job back

You cannot claim maternity pay and nor can you claim your old job back

If a woman does not tell her employer, at least 3 weeks beforehand, that she is taking time off because of pregnancy, she forfeits her right to maternity pay. She must give the same advance notice of her intention to return to her job – and 3 weeks' notice before she does so.

● You continue to be employed until at least the beginning of the 11th week before the baby is due.

You need not actually be at work until the 11th week so long as you are still an employee.

You can work beyond the 11th week if you want without affecting your right to maternity pay.

You must give your employer at least 3 weeks' notice before leaving work. If you have to leave earlier than expected and are unable to give 3 weeks' notice, you must inform your employer as soon as possible. The notice need not be in writing unless the employer insists, though it is advisable to put it in writing so there can be no dispute.

Your employer is entitled to demand a medical certificate showing when the baby is due.

How much maternity pay

You are entitled to 6 weeks' money at the rate of 90 per cent of your usual pay. From that is deducted the flat-rate maternity allowance, which you claim separately from the state.

The amount of the maternity allowance is deducted even if you are not entitled to claim it back from the state – for example, if you have been paying a married woman's reduced-rate national insurance contribution.

Any EARNINGS-RELATED SUPPLEMENT paid in addition to the maternity allowance is not deducted.

Your employer can pay either weekly, or in a lump sum when you leave. He reclaims the money in full from the Department of Employment.

If an employer refused to pay, the pregnant employee could claim maternity pay direct from the Department of Employment.

Maternity pay cannot be claimed by part-time employees, working less than 16 hours a week, or by self-employed women.

Getting your job back

You are entitled to your job back after having a baby if:
● You have been a full-time employee for at least 2 years, or a part-time employee working more than 8 hours a week for 5 years.
● You continue to be employed until the beginning of the 11th week before the baby is due.
● You give your employer at least 3 weeks' notice before leaving work that you intend to return after the baby is born.
● You return to work within 29 weeks of the birth. Your employer is entitled to at least 21 days' notice before you return.

Your employer can ask you not earlier than 49 days after the baby's birth whether you still intend to return. If he does so, you must confirm in writing to him within 14 days that you wish to return (at the latest) 29 weeks after the baby's birth.

The 29 week period can be extended by up to 4 weeks if you are ill and have a doctor's note. You are not allowed a further extension in any circumstances.

The 29 week period can also be extended if there is a strike, holiday or some other interruption beyond your control.

Your employer is entitled to delay your return by up to 4 weeks if he gives you a reason within the 29 week period. He does not have to pay you for those 4 weeks.

Women who are in the police or armed forces are not entitled to reinstatement, nor are those employed in a business of not more than 5 employees where it is not reasonably practicable for the employer to reinstate.

Changing your mind It is advisable always to tell your employer at the outset that you plan to return to work. You have the right to change your mind later without incurring any penalty or forfeiting your maternity pay. You cannot, however, change your mind once the 3 week period has expired.

Alternative work Your employer may offer you a different job on your return if it is not reasonably practicable for him to reinstate you in your old job. The Employment Act 1980 provides that as long as the alternative job is not substantially less favourable than the old one, and is suitable and appropriate for you, you will lose any right to reinstatement or compensation if you unreasonably refuse the employer's offer. Any dispute about what is reasonable may be referred to an industrial tribunal through a claim for UNFAIR DISMISSAL.

Enforcing your rights

If your employer refuses to take you back you can claim compensation for UNFAIR DISMISSAL before an industrial

---

WHEN A MISCARRIAGE PROTECTED HER JOB

A woman employee who becomes pregnant has a wide range of legal protection against dismissal.

Miss B, aged 18, was employed in a bottling factory. Her medical record was not good, and she had a high rate of absenteeism. Between January and March 1976 she had been given oral and written warnings that her attendance must improve or she would be dismissed.

In June 1976 she told her manager that she was pregnant but said she would work normally until the birth. She had a miscarriage and was admitted to hospital on July 18.

Miss B was given notice by her employer when she returned to work on July 27. She took her case to an industrial tribunal.

DECISION

The industrial tribunal held that despite Miss B's poor medical record she had actually been sacked for absences arising from her pregnancy. When her company refused to reinstate her she was awarded compensatory damages.

---

tribunal. However, if his refusal is because of your REDUNDANCY you cannot insist on having your job back. You may, however, be entitled to a redundancy payment.

If you are dismissed

The dismissal of a woman simply because she is pregnant is unfair in law, unless the employer can show that her pregnancy prevents her doing her job.

But if she can do part of the work, the employer must try to find her alternative work.

In rare cases it may be against the law to ask a pregnant woman to do a particular job – exposing her, for example, to high radiation. She can legally be dismissed, however, only if other work cannot be found.

A pregnant woman cannot be dismissed for poor attendance if her absence is caused by her pregnancy.

Part-time employees do not have the same protection as full-time workers and cannot claim unfair dismissal if they are sacked because they are pregnant.

MATRIMONIAL ORDER

How maintenance is obtained without a divorce action

When a marriage is in difficulties but there are no immediate plans for DIVORCE, either the husband or the wife can seek a magistrates' court order for MAINTENANCE from the other.

An order can be sought when there is no intention of petitioning for divorce, or when a separation or desertion has not lasted long enough for divorce proceedings to start.

The court must be shown that the other partner, called the respondent, has defaulted in one of three ways:
● By failing to provide reasonable maintenance for the applicant or for a child of the family.
● By behaving in such a way that the

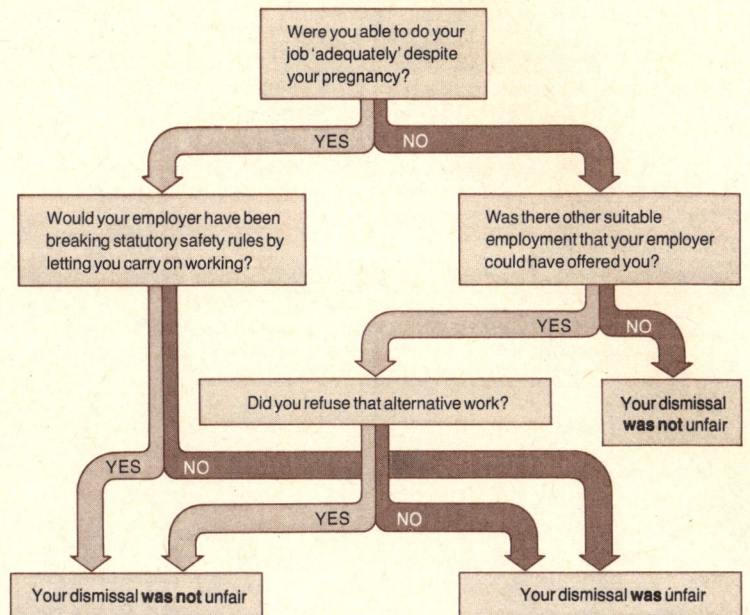

WHEN PREGNANCY COSTS A WOMAN HER JOB
How to tell whether a dismissal is fair

An employer must be able to show that a pregnant woman is no longer able to do her job, and that he has no suitable alternative work available. Otherwise she may be able to persuade an industrial tribunal to award compensation for unfair dismissal.

APPLYING FOR A MATRIMONIAL ORDER

A matrimonial order application involves formal documents similar to those required in divorce proceedings. It is usually advisable to consult a solicitor, and LEGAL AID is available.

However, someone who does not want to see a solicitor is entitled to call at a magistrates' court office. Staff there will explain what is required.

The person against whom an order is sought – called the respondent – receives a copy of the applicant's claim and has the right to contest it.

When a case is not contested

If the respondent does not oppose the application, court proceedings are simple. The applicant still has to appear before a panel of magistrates and give sworn evidence, but only the basic facts need be stated. Hearings are private and cannot be reported.

If the magistrates are satisfied with the facts – they may question the applicant – they will make the order immediately. Any costs involved must usually be paid by the respondent.

When a claim is opposed

If the case is fought, both parties go to court, with witnesses if necessary. Proceedings are formal – although again they are private – and legal representation is most advisable.

In a contested case the applicant has to give full evidence in support of the claim. For example, if it is based on the marriage partner's unreasonable behaviour, the applicant must give details of particular occasions of bad behaviour.

If the applicant also seeks an order for the custody of children, he or she must give detailed evidence of the circumstances in which they are and will be looked after.

The applicant can be questioned by the respondent or his lawyer. Then the applicant can call witnesses, who may also be cross-examined.

After that the respondent presents his evidence. He and his witnesses can be cross-examined in the same way.

When all the evidence is heard, the respondent and the applicant can each make a final speech to the court, either personally or through their lawyers.

Then the magistrates go to another room to confer. In most cases they are ready to give their decision on the order and costs immediately they return. If an order is made, formal copies of the order are supplied later to both parties.

their agreement legally enforceable, which is a condition of qualifying for the INCOME TAX relief that one or both of them might gain. When a couple seek an order to confirm agreed arrangements, there is no need to prove default by either partner. No evidence of their marital difficulties need be given.

It is also possible for one partner to obtain a matrimonial order for maintenance, without having to prove default, if a couple have lived apart by agreement for 3 months and the applicant has been receiving regular voluntary payments. In that case an order can be made for payments to continue at the same level.

Custody of children

When a matrimonial order is applied for – and even if a claim for maintenance is dismissed – the magistrates' court can make orders for the CUSTODY OF CHILDREN of the family.

It can also make a SUPERVISION ORDER, or if necessary commit a child to the care of a local authority. In making any order for the custody or care of a child, it can add a further order prohibiting the child's removal from England and Wales, so that anyone who tries to take it out of the court's area of jurisdiction risks imprisonment.

Grandparents If a child is in the custody of one parent, or its parents are dead, a magistrates' court can grant a grandparent the right of access for visits or outings.

Protecting a battered wife

If either partner in a marriage uses or threatens violence to the other, or to their children, a magistrates' court can make orders:
● Prohibiting violence or threats to the applicant or to a child.
● Requiring the respondent to leave the matrimonial home.
● Prohibiting the respondent from entering the home.
● Requiring the respondent to let the applicant enter and stay in the home.

If the court is satisfied that the respondent has already caused physical injury and is likely to do so again, its order can include a provision for arrest. Then if a police officer has reason to suspect that the respondent is defying the order, he can arrest him at once.

applicant cannot reasonably be expected to live with the respondent.
● By deserting the applicant.

If the court is convinced of any of those facts, it can make an order for payments at regular intervals, or a lump-sum payment, or both. It is not necessary to show which party was to blame for the separation (if any) unless the ground for complaint is desertion.

A lump-sum order, limited to £500, may be made to cover urgent needs – for example, to meet hire-purchase debts, removal costs or living expenses incurred before a periodical payments order takes effect.

In deciding whether to make an order, and if so for what amount, magistrates must assess the earning capacity, property and other financial resources of both partners – not only at the time of the application but also in the foreseeable future. They must consider each partner's financial needs and obligations, and take into account the standard of living they have been used to. They must also assess their contribution to the home – including looking after the home and children.

If children are involved the court has to consider each one's financial resources and needs, and earning capacity, and how they were being educated or trained.

Maintenance of a child is normally ordered only until it reaches 17. If a child stays at school after that, or is taking full-time training for a career, or needs special care because of a disability, an application can be made to continue maintenance.

A matrimonial order lasts as long as a court considers necessary, although either party can apply for reviews, upwards or downwards if circumstances change. In any case an order ceases when either party dies, or if the one receiving maintenance remarries.

When no one need be blamed

Even if a separated couple agree on financial arrangements, it is to their advantage to seek a matrimonial order confirming them. That makes

If a couple are not legally married, a magistrates' court has no power to make orders protecting one of them from violence. A person in that situation has to apply to a county court or the High Court.

MATRIMONIAL PROPERTY

Who owns what in a marriage

Each party to a marriage is entitled to his or her property, whether it was acquired before or after marriage. But a couple can hold property in their joint names if they wish.

When the marriage breaks down, the parties can agree to share out the jointly owned matrimonial property between them according to their needs and the contribution each has made. But if they do not agree, they will have to ask a court to decide on the proper distribution.

When there is no divorce

When the couple are not being divorced or judicially separated – or when they are not seeking a decree of NULLITY – a dispute between them over property can be heard by a registrar of the county court or the Family Division of the High Court.

The procedure, under the Married Women's Property Act 1882, is quick and informal. The applicant files an originating application, setting out what she wants, and the grounds on which she claims to be entitled.

The other party – the respondent – files an AFFIDAVIT putting his side of the case.

The court then decides ownership according to the ordinary rules of law. For example, if the wife claims a motor car and the husband proves that he paid for it and never gave it to his wife, the court will declare that it is his and order the wife to hand it over.

If the court holds that property is jointly owned because each has contributed to the purchase, it can order the couple to sell the property and share the proceeds in proportion to their contribution.

Matrimonial home When the property in dispute is the matrimonial home, the court will declare the parties' shares in the house depending on who paid the deposit and who made the mortgage payments – either directly or indirectly by pooling earnings.

It can order the sale of the home with payment of the proceeds to each in those shares. More often, however, the court will postpone the sale, because one party will still be living there and

FORMER MISTRESS CLAIMS HOUSE

If a man is shown to have acknowledged his former mistress's right to their home he may not be able to regain possession.

Mr Pascoe and Miss Turner lived together as man and wife in a house bought by Pascoe. Subsequently, Mr Pascoe began an affair with another woman but, according to Miss Turner, told her that he would never see her without a roof over her head. Miss Turner said that relying on this statement, she redecorated and carried out improvements and repairs.

Mr Pascoe left her in 1973 and in 1976 sought an order for possession.

DECISION

It was held that the gift of the house was an imperfect gift but that Mr Pascoe had encouraged and agreed to the work on the house. The court found in Miss Turner's favour and ordered the house to be transferred to her.

needs the house for the family. The other party will then have to wait for his share until the children have grown up, or perhaps until the wife remarries.

Wedding presents The ownership of wedding presents depends on who gave them. Presents given by the woman's family or friends generally go to her, and those from the man's side to him unless it can be shown that the donor intended a joint gift.

When the marriage ends in law

Where there is a decree of DIVORCE, judicial SEPARATION or NULLITY, the matrimonial property is dealt with differently. The divorce court which hears the case has much wider powers and can transfer ownership of any sort of property from one to the other without regard to their legal rights, so as to provide for the needs of the whole family.

For example, even if the matrimonial home is in the husband's sole name and he provided all the money to buy it, the court may transfer the house outright to the wife because she needs a home to bring up the children. In such a case, the husband may be given a charge on the house, not to be enforced until it is sold

HOW A WIFE CAN STOP HER HUSBAND SELLING THE FAMILY HOME

Many family homes are owned jointly by the husband and wife, and neither can sell the house or raise money on it without the other's permission. But if the house is in the husband's sole name, he can sell it without his wife's consent.

When the marriage begins to break down, the wife can take legal action to ensure that she keeps a roof over her head, even when she has no claim to ownership.

If the property is registered, she should make an immediate application at the local office of the LAND REGISTRY to have her interest in the property noted on the register. If the property is unregistered, she should apply to the Land Charges Registry (in Plymouth) to register her rights as a Class F land charge. The effect is the same.

When a solicitor working for a prospective buyer inspects the land register, he will see at once that the wife has a right to

occupy the property and the purchaser will not be able to turn her out. To sell the house, the husband will have to persuade the wife to remove the charge or caution – for example, offer her somewhere else to live or offer her a sum of money.

He can ask the local county court to remove the order, but such an application is unlikely to be successful unless the court is satisfied that the wife and children will not be made homeless.

If she is turned out

A wife who has no part-ownership in the family home can ask a county court for help if she is turned out. The court has power to order the husband to allow his wife back into the house and can grant an INJUNCTION ordering the husband not to turn her out again or to molest her. It can even order the husband himself to leave the house.

or the wife remarries.

The court will always try to do justice to both spouses by taking into account their contributions to the family, both financial and by way of caring for the home and family, and also their conduct. *See also:* MAINTENANCE

MEALS ON WHEELS

When hot meals are taken to people who cannot cater for themselves

Most local authorities provide a mobile service to deliver hot meals to elderly or handicapped people who cannot cook for themselves. Some councils run the service themselves, others work in conjunction with the Women's Royal Voluntary Service or other agencies.

The meals, cooked at a central kitchen and delivered in heated containers by vans or private cars, may be available daily or on only 2 or 3 days a week. Cold meals or sandwiches are sometimes provided instead.

Applying for meals

Anyone who is unable to cater for himself or herself – such as the bedridden, housebound, mentally and physically handicapped, frail or confused elderly people – can be provided with meals on wheels if a local service is available.

Ask your doctor, district nurse, health visitor or hospital social worker to apply.

Cost A small charge is made for each meal and that usually has to be paid to the person who delivers the food.

MEDICAL CARD

Everyone's passport to free health treatment

Every person registered for free treatment with a family doctor has a medical card issued by the local family practitioner committee. Anyone who does not have a card may find it difficult to get free Health Service treatment from a doctor, dentist or optician.

How you get a medical card

Every child whose birth is registered is allocated a National Health Service

number by the registrar. The number is on form FP98 handed to the person who registers the birth. It should be taken to the family doctor, who will sign it, and send it to the family practitioner committee for the area. The committee then issues a medical card, which has the child's NHS number on it.

Changing doctors

Anyone who changes doctors should take his or her medical card to the new doctor, who will send it to his local family practitioner committee. They will issue a new medical card.

A new card must also be issued if a person is changing address, but intends to stay with his family doctor. *See:* DOCTOR AND PATIENT

When a card is lost

A free medical card will be issued by the family practitioner committee to anyone who loses his or her medical card.

Tell the committee your full name, address, the name of your doctor and your NHS number if you have it. If you have not kept a note of the number or cannot remember it, there can be a delay of up to 3 months while the committee checks the NHS central register.

A patient without a medical card may be refused free NHS treatment by a doctor, but that is not usual. When a charge is made for treatment, the patient can reclaim the amount from the

YOUR RIGHT TO TREATMENT

In theory, a National Health Service doctor could refuse free treatment to a patient who could not produce his medical card.

family practitioner committee by producing a new medical card or his NHS number and a receipt for the doctor's fee within 14 days of being treated.

Special rules for foreigners

People who arrive in Britain with permission to settle or with a work permit are entitled to receive free NHS treatment even though they do not have a medical card or an NHS number.

They will be asked by the doctor to fill in form FP1. It is sent to the family practitioner committee, which issues them a number.

This procedure can take up to 3 months. In the meantime the visitor can pay the doctor's bill and reclaim the money from the family practitioner committee later when his number is allocated.

Holiday visitors to Britain can get free NHS treatment in an emergency. Britain also has reciprocal arrangements with Common Market countries and some other countries which allow their citizens free NHS treatment.

MEDICAL CERTIFICATE

A doctor's confirmation of a medical condition

General practitioners are required by the terms of service in their contract with the National Health Service to issue certain medical certificates, called Doctor's Statements, free of charge to patients who need them to prove a medical condition.

The principal reasons for which certificates are issued are:

● To confirm pregnancy so that an expectant mother can obtain welfare foods and maternity benefits.
● To state fitness to receive inhalation analgesia for the birth of a child – this is necessary under the Midwives Act.
● To register a stillbirth – necessary under the Births and Deaths Registration Act.
● To register a death – necessary under the Births and Deaths Registration Act.
● To help patients, such as the physically handicapped, to obtain benefits.
● To confirm that a person entitled to any payment out of public funds, such as a pension or supplementary benefit, is mentally incapable of managing his

property, so that payment can be made to someone else – necessary under the Mental Health Act.

● To establish medical unfitness for jury service.

● To enable someone to be registered as an absent voter because of physical incapacity.

Before October 1976 a doctor issued a medical certificate to a patient claiming sickness or industrial injury benefit, but this has now been replaced by a doctor's statement. The statement, which is issued free, records a doctor's advice that the patient should refrain from work, rather than certifying that the patient is suffering from a certain disease and unable to work.

Refusing a patient

If a doctor refuses to issue one of the above certificates when a patient's condition entitles him to it – or if he charges for it – he is in breach of his terms of service and can be reported to the family practitioner committee, who will investigate the matter. The complaint must be in writing and lodged within 8 weeks of the doctor refusing the certificate. *See:* DOCTOR AND PATIENT

Giving false information

A doctor who issues a certificate or sickness statement, although he knows there are no valid grounds for it, commits an offence against the Social Security Act. He is liable to a maximum penalty of £400 and 3 months' imprisonment, as well as disciplinary action by the General Medical Council.

Anyone who gives a doctor false information to obtain a certificate, or knowingly uses a certificate containing false information is liable to the same fine or prison penalty.

Someone who obtains a benefit by knowingly using false information in a certificate can be prosecuted for FRAUD. Maximum penalty: 10 years' imprisonment and an unlimited fine, plus the return of the money obtained.

How to obtain a certificate

If you need a certificate you should go to your doctor and explain why you need it. If you are ill and cannot get to the surgery you can ask the doctor to visit you.

Examination Before issuing a certificate or a sickness statement, a doctor must examine you – either physically or orally. If you refuse to be examined he will not issue the certificate.

Collecting Usually the doctor will give you the certificate when he has examined you. But if there is a delay – perhaps he needs more evidence, or the certificates are not immediately available – he will ask you to collect it later. If you have to send someone else to collect it the person should be known to the doctor or receptionist, or carry a letter of authority from you. The contents of a certificate are confidential and a doctor is entitled to refuse to release it to anyone other than the person for whom he issued it.

If an employer wants proof

Your employer may insist on medical evidence of your illness if you take sick leave. In fact, your employment contract may require you to supply a doctor's certificate after a certain number of days' absence.

Although a doctor's statement of your illness, issued free of charge, is intended solely for Department of Health and Social Security use in granting SICKNESS BENEFIT, some companies expect their employees to let them see such a statement first.

If you pass a doctor's statement to anyone other than a DHSS official, it is your own responsibility to make sure that it is forwarded to the department without delay. If you have any doubt of that, let your employer take a photocopy and send in the form yourself, or ask the doctor for an additional, private certificate.

If you need a private certificate

If you need a certificate for private purposes – rather than to establish your right to a state benefit – your doctor is entitled to charge any fee he chooses.

The amount he charges will depend upon the amount of work he has to do. In 1981 the recommended fee for a sickness certificate was £1.20, but many doctors charge less than this.

Types of certificate Some of the reasons for which a doctor is asked for a private certificate are:

● To confirm sickness – for school or employer, for instance.

● To establish fitness for a particular purpose, such as taking up a new job, playing rugby or other sport at school, or driving a vehicle.

● For vaccination or inoculation.

● For insurance purposes.

Medical report If an employer or insurance company requires more detailed evidence than a certificate and you are asked to have a medical examination, this will usually be paid for by whoever asks for the medical report. But the doctor must have your permission before he can pass on the information.

MEDICAL NEGLIGENCE

When a patient can take action for negligent treatment

A doctor must take all reasonable care in the treatment of a patient. If he fails to do so, and the patient suffers harm as a result, the patient can sue the doctor for negligence.

The standard of care required from a doctor – working privately or for the National Health Service – is that which is accepted as competent medical practice. Therefore, to establish that a doctor has been negligent it is necessary for the patient's solicitor to obtain the opinion of other doctors who treat the same type of complaint to see what they would have done.

If a doctor makes a mistake in the treatment of a patient, it does not automatically follow that he has been negligent. A mere error of judgment may not be negligence.

He will be liable only if the mistake should not, in all the circumstances, have been made. But the law makes no allowance for accidents that happen because of a doctor's inexperience and, except in an emergency, a doctor should not undertake treatment unless he is qualified and competent to do so.

In an emergency, if a more experienced doctor is not available and the patient would suffer if treatment were delayed, a doctor is justified in giving whatever treatment he feels is required. But he must exercise all reasonable care.

When a diagnosis is wrong

If a doctor makes an incorrect diagnosis which results in no treatment, or the wrong treatment, being given, he might be guilty of negligence. For instance, if he failed to notice obvious symptoms, or to carry out tests which are normally conducted when certain symptoms are apparent. But he will not be blamed if he is unable to correctly diagnose a condition that is very rare or difficult to detect.

If a doctor prescribes carelessly

A doctor must ensure that any drugs he prescribes or administers to a patient are correct for the patient's condition, and that the patient is not allergic to them. Some people are allergic to antibiotics such as penicillin, for example, and suffer if they take them.

He will be negligent if he writes out an incorrect prescription, and if the patient is harmed through taking either the wrong drug, or an incorrect dosage, he can sue the doctor.

Side effects A doctor must also warn the patient of any known side-effects. Failure to do so would amount to neg-

ligence. For example, if a drug causes drowsiness, the patient must be told and advised not to drive or engage in any other activity requiring maximum concentration. Or if it is dangerous for the patient to eat or drink certain foods while taking a drug, this must be pointed out.

Certain antidepressant drugs – for example monoamine-oxidase inhibitors (MAOI) – are incompatible with many other drugs and foods such as cheese, yeast and meat extracts, hydrolysed vegetable protein, and alcohol, and to mix them can be fatal.

Injections If the drug is to be injected the doctor must ensure that the correct dosage is used, that the needle is strong enough for the type of injection and not liable to snap, and that he injects into the correct part of the patient's body. For instance, to inject into an artery instead of a vein could be fatal.

German measles Before a woman is inoculated against German measles, a doctor must make sure that she is not pregnant, as the vaccine could damage the foetus.

When a surgeon is negligent

If an operation is not successful the surgeon will be to blame only if it can be shown that he was negligent. If, for instance, a surgeon operates on the wrong patient, or performs the wrong operation, the patient can sue him for negligence. It is the surgeon's duty to satisfy himself that he has the right patient before him, that the details of the operation are correct, and that the patient has been correctly marked out for surgery.

Causing injury It is also negligent for a surgeon to cause a patient's condition to worsen, or to injure him, during the course of an operation, except in the case of an unavoidable accident – such as the patient having a muscle spasm which misdirects the scalpel.

For instance, if a swab, or instrument is left inside a patient after an operation, the surgeon can be sued for negligence, unless the operation had to be abandoned because of a sudden deterioration in the patient's condition. If the degree of urgency is such that there is no

---

THE PATIENT WHO DIED BECAUSE OF A DOCTOR'S INEXPERIENCE

A doctor should not undertake treatment unless he or she is qualified and competent to do so.

If a patient is harmed through the negligence of an inexperienced doctor the patient can sue the doctor. If the doctor is employed in a National Health Service hospital, the area health authority can also be sued.

In 1952 William Jones was taken to the casualty department of a Manchester hospital after being badly burned at work. To relieve the pain he was given nitrous oxide through a mask.

The doctor attending to the burns felt that the mask was in the way, so the anaesthetist, Dr Olive Wilkes, gave Mr Jones an injection of Pentothal.

Dr Wilkes was newly qualified and had no qualifications as an anaesthetist and very little experience of administering anaesthetics.

She failed to appreciate that Mr Jones was already partly anaesthetised by the nitrous oxide and the high dosage of Pentothal, combined with the mode of administration, killed him.

Mr Jones's widow subsequently sued

Dr Wilkes and the hospital for negligence.

DECISION

The judge ruled that Dr Wilkes had been negligent and that her lack of experience was no defence. If she was not competent to act as an anaesthetist she should not have done so.

He also held that the hospital had been negligent in assigning an inexperienced doctor to such a difficult task. So the authority was also liable to pay damages.

The widow was awarded damages totalling £1,433 3s. 3d. (£1,433.16).

THE DOCTOR WHO DID NOT DIAGNOSE THE ONSET OF A RARE CONDITION

If a doctor makes a wrong diagnosis because he fails to observe obvious symptoms or carry out routine tests, he may be guilty of negligence. But he will not be blamed if he is unable to diagnose a condition that is rare or difficult to detect.

In 1953 David Pudney was taken ill on board a ship. He was attended by the ship's doctor who diagnosed mild rheumatism and prescribed aspirin.

Back on dry land, 18 months later, he was diagnosed as suffering from acute arthritis. He was by then severely disabled. He sued the ship's doctor, claiming that he had failed to diagnose his true condition and that because of that failure he had not been correctly treated.

DECISION

After hearing evidence from other doctors who said that from the symptoms

presented by Mr Pudney at the initial examination they would have come to the same conclusion and given the same treatment, the judge held that the ship's doctor had not been negligent. It would have been possible for him to have diagnosed acute arthritis if the appropriate tests had been made, but there was no reason for the doctor to have felt it necessary to do so as the symptoms did not suggest anything so serious and rare as acute arthritis.

> ### THE DOCTOR WHO BROKE A HYPODERMIC NEEDLE IN A PATIENT'S BODY
>
> *It is negligent for a doctor to injure a patient during the course of treatment, except in the case of an unavoidable accident. If the patient has a muscle spasm, for instance, which causes the accident, the doctor will not be held liable.*
>
> In 1935 Mrs Rebecca Gerber was being given an injection by her doctor when the needle snapped and part of it was left in her body.
>
> She sued the doctor, alleging that he had not used a suitable needle, and had
>
> not administered the injection properly.
>
> The doctor claimed that the needle broke because the patient had a sudden muscular spasm and that no amount of skill on his part could have prevented the piece of needle being left behind.
>
> ##### DECISION
>
> The judge decided that the doctor had not been negligent. A doctor could not be held responsible for unforeseen contingencies – the unexpected muscular spasm that caused the needle to break.

time to check that all swabs have been removed, the surgeon is not negligent.

How to sue

Anyone who thinks that he has been harmed as a result of medical negligence should consult a solicitor. If negligence is established the patient can sue the person or authority responsible for the negligence.

Suing a GP A patient can sue his general practitioner for negligence committed by the practitioner himself or anyone in his employ. For instance, if a nurse employed by a GP in his practice, harms a patient, the patient can sue the nurse and the doctor as the nurse's employer.

If a GP practises in partnership with other doctors, each is responsible for the negligence of the other. Therefore, if a negligent doctor is unable to meet a claim against him, the other doctors can be required to pay. But this rarely happens as doctors are invariably insured against medical negligence.

Suing a hospital doctor If a National Health Service hospital doctor is negligent the patient can sue the doctor and the area health authority that employs him. In some cases it is difficult to establish who was negligent as treatment might have been given by more than one doctor and might have involved other hospital employees, such as nurses. But as they are all employed by the health authority, the authority will be liable so long as the patient can prove that someone was negligent, even if he cannot prove whom.

If negligence occurs because the authority fails to provide suitable qualified and experienced staff, or to ensure that equipment is in proper working order, it will be liable for its own default and for that of its staff.

Private treatment If a doctor treats a patient privately in a National Health Service hospital, the health authority is not responsible for any negligence which occurs. The patient can sue only the doctor. But if the hospital allocates staff to look after the private patient, they will be acting in their capacity of hospital employees, and they and the hospital will be liable for any negligence occurring through their fault.

MEDICAL RECORD

The patient's right to complete privacy and confidentiality

Doctors, whether in general practice or in hospitals, must keep records of the illnesses and treatment of their patients. In the National Health Service the records are the property of the Secretary of State for Health and Social Security. In private practice they belong to the doctor. Patients are not entitled to see the records except in the case of a personal injuries action against a doctor, health authority or a third party where details of the medical treatment are relevant.

In these circumstances there are procedures open to the patient whereby the records can be made available. This may involve an application to the High Court under the Administration of Justice Act 1970.

It would almost certainly be neces-

sary to obtain the advice of a solicitor.

Although the records are the property of the Secretary of State, any court action would be taken against the area health authority – as custodians of the records – in the case of hospitals, or the family practitioner committee of the authority, in the case of GPs.

Medical records must not be made available to anyone other than the patient without his consent, and even then only at the discretion of his doctor. In practice, they are disclosed only to other doctors, and perhaps nurses, who are sharing or assuming responsibility for treatment.

Similarly, the disclosure of the results of medical examinations – for insurance companies and prospective employers, for example – can be made only with the agreement of the patient, who will be asked to agree to this in writing.

If a doctor discloses confidential information without a patient's consent, he can be sued or reported to the General Medical Council. *See:* DOCTOR AND PATIENT

Doctors may not break the law or their code of ethics if they disclose a patient's record to police who are seeking someone who may have had to have treatment as a result of being involved in a serious crime.

When a doctor makes a mistake in his records – for example, if he gives incorrect details about treatment – and the patient later receives the wrong treatment or medication because of that

NOT FOR YOUR EYES

Patients are not entitled to see their medical records except in the case of a personal injuries action.

error, the doctor will be liable for his mistake. A doctor may also be liable to defamation proceedings if he makes libellous comments in a patient's records, which are then disclosed to a third party.

MEMBER OF PARLIAMENT

When the voters' choice may be barred from office

Anyone over the age of 21 is entitled to take his seat in the House of Commons when he has been elected to represent a constituency – unless he is disqualified by law.

A candidate's return to Parliament can be challenged only by an election petition. If a voter or defeated candidate believes that a disqualified person has been elected he can lodge a petition within 21 days in the High Court – but he must also pay £1,000 into the court.

The petition is heard publicly by two High Court judges who form an Election Court. The court's judgment is reported to the Speaker of the House who is bound to accept its findings.

Parliament's watchdog committees

One way in which MPs seek to check Government actions is through Select Committees, specialist committees of a few MPs. The powerful Public Accounts Committee, which scrutinises the accounts produced by all Government departments, is long-established; but in 1979 the House of Commons set up 14 new committees, each with about 10 MPs, to examine home affairs, foreign affairs, defence, trade and industry, environment, education and science, health and social services, Treasury and Civil Service, agriculture, energy, employment, transport, Scottish affairs and Welsh affairs.

These committees can take evidence from any member of the public. They have power to demand the attendance of any witness or the production of any document. In practice, they interview (in open session) ministers, senior civil servants, and representatives of organisations or individuals who have views on the subject they are investigating. Their reports can be influential.

WHEN YOU CANNOT BECOME AN MP

You cannot be a member of the House of Commons, even if elected, if you are:
● An alien. Citizens of Ireland and of Commonwealth countries are not aliens.
● Under 21.
● Suffering from a severe MENTAL DISORDER as defined by the Mental Health Act 1959.
● A peer or peeress in your own right, other than a peer of Ireland, unless you disclaim the title.
● Serving a sentence for treason.
● Bankrupt. You remain disqualified for 5 years after your discharge from bankruptcy unless, when being discharged, you are given a certificate by the court stating that the bankruptcy was not attributable to your own fault.
● Convicted of corrupt and illegal practices at elections.

● A minister of the Church of England or the Episcopalian Church of Scotland, or any other Protestant clergyman ordained by a Bishop – except a minister of the disestablished Church of Wales.
● A Roman Catholic priest.
● A minister of the Church of Scotland. Non-conformist ministers and ministers of non-Christian denominations are not disqualified.
● The holder of a public office – such as a judge; civil servant; member of the regular armed forces; full-time member of a police force; member of certain boards and commissions or certain administrative tribunals. A full list of the disqualifications is set out in the House of Commons Disqualification Act 1975.
● Expelled by resolution of the House of Commons.

The duty of a Member of Parliament

It is every MP's duty to represent all his constituents in the House of Commons, at party discussions and to government ministers and their departments – whether or not they voted for him.

If an MP is not a member of the Government he can take any other job he likes, but all MPs must declare all their financial interests to the Speaker. A comprehensive register of those interests is kept in the House of Commons library and is open for public inspection.

An MP is not above the law and can be arrested or prosecuted in the same way as anybody else.

Where to write to your MP

If you want to draw your MP's attention to something or if you want to enlist his help, write to him at the House of Commons. If Parliament is in recess your letter will be forwarded to him.

You may also write to any other MP provided you do not harass him. That would be a breach of PARLIAMENTARY PRIVILEGE. It is a House of Commons convention that MPs always inform the constituent's own MP of any contact that is made.

Seeing your MP at his 'surgery'

Most MPs hold regular consulting sessions in their constituencies.

If you want to see your MP you can ask at his surgery for an appointment – his local party headquarters will give you the address – or you can write to him at the House of Commons.

Lobbying an MP in the Commons

If you wish to see your MP at the House of Commons you can, by custom, lobby him – which means literally to see him in the central lobby of the Houses of Parliament. But you have no legal right to do this. You should write in advance to arrange an appointment, but even without one you can tell the messengers that you wish to talk to him. You will be asked to fill in a green card stating whom you wish to see and why. The messengers will then try to deliver it to the member.

Pressure groups Pressure groups sometimes organise mass lobbies so that their members can meet MPs to make their opinions known on as wide a basis as possible. However, as no procession or demonstration is allowed within a mile of the Houses of Parliament, mass lobbies take place through small groups and individual members meeting their own constituency MPs. Often that means queueing for admission to the House, so anyone intending to lead a mass lobby would be advised – though not obliged – to inform the police so that necessary arrangements for controlling and protecting a crowd can be made. It would also be advisable for him to inform sympathetic MPs so that they can be in the House to accept the lobby.

Petitioning Parliament

The right of any citizen to petition Parliament with a grievance is a fundamental principle that has been exercised since Magna Carta in 1215. In the 17th century, Parliament officially acknowledged that right when the Commons resolved that:

> it is the inherent right of every commoner in England to prepare and present petitions to the House of Commons in the case of grievance, and the House of Commons to receive the same.

There is no special petition form, but certain formal wording must be used. The top copy must be handwritten and every sheet must have the prayer written or printed at the top. There must be no attachments and no words added between the lines.

Delivering a petition A petition can either be sent to the Clerk of the House of Commons or handed in to an MP, who will then pass it on to the office concerned.

Very rarely – perhaps if the petition is a nationwide one – an MP may present it publicly in the House. It would not be debated, but would be referred to the committee for public petitions, and the Government may, after consideration, issue a reply.

How an MP's seat can become vacant

A Member of Parliament cannot legally resign or be made to resign his seat. However, he can be disqualified from sitting in the House if he becomes bankrupt and remains so for 6 months, or if he accepts an office of profit under the Crown.

If an MP wants to give up his seat, therefore, he can apply for the Stewardship of the Chiltern Hundreds or of the Manor of Northstead – both Crown properties. If it is granted to him he is ineligible to sit in the Commons and his seat becomes vacant. His seat also becomes vacant if he dies. When a seat has become vacant a writ for a new election is issued by the Clerk of Parliaments to the returning officer of the constituency concerned. *See:* ELECTION

MENTAL DISORDER
How the law tries to balance welfare and personal freedom

The state has a duty to provide suitable care for anyone who suffers from a mental illness, a psychopathic disorder or a mental handicap.

If treatment or special accommodation is necessary, it must be arranged voluntarily if possible. A mentally disordered person cannot be held compulsorily, except for a short period in a 'place of safety', without medical evidence that detention is required for his or her health or safety, or for the protection of others.

The law defines in broad terms the various types of illness or disability that can lead to a patient's detention. But it does not say what treatments may or may not be given. Those decisions are left to medical judgment.

A patient's loss of liberty by compulsory admission for treatment can be opposed by his or her nearest relative, who can order the patient's discharge at any time.

The medical evidence needed to detain a patient, or to overrule a relative's order to discharge him, is subject to review by an independent tribunal to which the patient or relative can appeal at certain intervals. *See:* MENTAL HEALTH REVIEW TRIBUNAL

More than 90 per cent of the people who are given in-patient treatment in psychiatric hospitals, or in the psychiatric wards of general hospitals, go there voluntarily on the advice of doctors, consultant psychiatrists or social workers. Their admission is called 'informal'.

If compulsion has to be used because a person is unwilling to be admitted, his rights vary according to the type of admission.

Admission for compulsory observation

An admission for compulsory hospital observation lasts for up to 28 days. It is intended to allow time for an exact diagnosis of a patient's disorder.

An observation admission is made on application to a hospital management

---

HOW THE LAW CLASSIFIES MENTAL DISORDER

A mental patient's prospects of being compulsorily detained, or automatically discharged at a certain age, are affected by the legal classification of his or her disorder.

The law does not give a medical definition of mental disorder. It divides the various kinds of handicap or disturbance into four groups, any of which call for treatment or special care:

● *Subnormality* Incomplete mental development that needs or responds to treatment, special care or training.
● *Psychopathic disorder* A persistent disability that causes abnormally aggressive or seriously irresponsible behaviour.
● *Severe subnormality* Incomplete mental development, including subnormal intelligence, that prevents the patient from leading an independent life or protecting himself from serious exploitation.
● *Mental illness* Any disorder serious enough to be defined by doctors as an illness and requiring treatment in the interests of the patient's health or safety, or for the safety of others.

Disabilities in the first two categories, subnormality and psychopathic disorder, are assumed by the law to be minor disorders. For that reason a person who suffers from either or both of them, but no other form of mental illness, cannot be ordered to take hospital treatment if he is over 21. If such a person was compulsorily detained before turning 21, he must be discharged at the age of 25 unless his condition is shown to be a danger to himself or to others. He can, however, be admitted at any age for observation or under a court order.

Disabilities in the last two categories, severe subnormality and mental illness, are classed as major disorders and a patient can be detained at any age – although not necessarily for a long time. The mental illness classification includes disorders that are sometimes quickly cured – for example, conditions that indicate what is commonly called 'nervous breakdown'. Some effects of accidental brain damage are also classified as mental illness.

A patient's classification can change during a stay in hospital, either because the doctor in charge of his case makes a new diagnosis or because a mental health review tribunal disagrees with the diagnosis. Such a change can affect a patient's right to be discharged at the age of 25.

by the patient's nearest relative or by a social worker – a local authority employee authorised to deal with mental disorder.

Application forms are held by doctors, hospitals, area health authorities and local authority social services departments.

An application must be supported by recommendations from two doctors, one of whom must be approved by the health authority as a specialist in psychiatry and one who should have previous experience of the patient – preferably his own doctor. If they do not examine the patient together, their examinations must be no more than 7 days apart. The applicant must have seen the patient within the previous 14 days.

A full diagnosis is not required – the doctors need state only that the patient has a disorder that warrants his detention, in his own interests or for the protection of others.

There is no right of appeal against an observation admission. But if it is not replaced by an admission for long-term treatment within 28 days, it lapses and the patient must be discharged.

Emergency admission

If a person's behaviour is so disturbed that it seems unsafe to wait for two doctors, any relative or an authorised social worker can apply to a hospital management for emergency admission.

It lasts for only 72 hours and requires the recommendation of only one doctor. After the patient has been examined by a hospital psychiatrist, an emergency admission can be replaced by one for 28 days' observation or by a long-term treatment admission.

Treatment during observation

The Mental Health Act places no restriction on the kind of treatment that can be given to a patient during observation.

However, the Department of Health and Social Security advice is to give only what is necessary to ease the symptoms of a disturbed patient or to help in making a precise diagnosis.

A policeman's powers

If a policeman sees someone in a public place who is apparently suffering from mental disorder and needing immediate care or control, it is his duty to take that person to a 'place of safety' – perhaps hospital or social services premises, but sometimes a police station or even a private home may be used.

The person can be held for up to 72 hours while a medical examination and an interview with an authorised social worker are arranged, after which the normal procedures for hospital admission can be used if necessary.

A policeman who uses his 'place of safety' powers in good faith cannot be sued for false arrest or imprisonment, even if an examination produces no medical grounds for detention.

If an authorised social worker has reason to believe that a mentally disordered person is being ill-treated or neglected on private property, he can apply to a magistrate for a warrant allowing a policeman to enter the premises – using whatever force is necessary – and take the person to a 'place of safety'.

The public's role An unrelated member of the public cannot apply for the admission to hospital of a mentally disordered person. If you believe that such a person is in immediate danger or is a danger to others, call the police. If you believe that such a person needs care, or protection from ill-treatment, you should notify your local authority social services department.

When a patient can be held for a year or more

Under an admission for treatment, people suffering from mental illness or severe subnormality can be admitted to hospital compulsorily, and detained initially for up to 1 year in the interests of their own health or safety or for the protection of others.

A person who suffers from a psychopathic disorder or from milder subnormality, can also be admitted for treatment if he or she is under 21.

An admission for treatment can be renewed on the recommendation of the hospital doctor in charge of the case, first for a further year and then for periods of 2 years at a time. The patient

---

WHO REPRESENTS A MENTAL PATIENT'S FAMILY?

One relative has a special right to apply for the treatment of a mentally disordered person, or to order the discharge of a detained mental patient. Normally it is the nearest relative living in Britain – whichever one is highest in the following order:

● Husband or wife.
● Child over 18.
● Father.
● Mother.
● Brother or sister over 18.
● Grandparent.
● Grandchild over 18.
● Uncle or aunt.
● Nephew or niece over 18.

If there are two or more people in the same category, the eldest one is the nearest relative.

A separated husband or wife does not qualify. A cohabitant does, if a couple have lived together for more than 6 months before the hospital admission.

An illegitimate child and its mother can be nearest relatives, but an illegitimate father-child relationship is not recognised. Adoptive and half-blood relationships qualify.

If CHILDREN IN CARE suffer mental disorder, the local authority responsible for them may exercise the rights of a near-est relative. A legal GUARDIAN is deemed to be the nearest relative of a child in his charge; but the guardian of an older patient, placed in guardianship under the Mental Health Act, is not the nearest relative.

How a relative can be replaced

Any relative of a mental patient, or an authorised local authority social worker, can apply for a county court order to replace the nearest relative with another one. That happens when the nearest relative is shown to be acting unreasonably – for example, by objecting to the treatment of an obviously disordered person. A relative who loses his rights in that way can still apply to a tribunal once a year for the patient's discharge.

A nearest relative can also be replaced if someone higher in the order of relationships turns 18, or returns to Britain after living abroad. A person qualifying in that way can choose not to exercise his or her rights, in which case they remain with the present holder.

If a patient has no close relative over 18 in Britain, an authorised social worker or a person with whom the patient has been living can be permitted by court order to exercise the rights of a nearest relative.

HOW A MENTALLY DISORDERED PERSON CAN BE DETAINED

Type of detention	Who can arrange it	Medical recommendation needed	How long it lasts
Place of safety	Policeman	None	Until examination – maximum 72 hours
Emergency observation	Any relative, authorised social worker	1 doctor – patient's own if possible	Up to 72 hours
Restraint of voluntary patient	Doctor in charge of case	Doctor's report	Up to 3 days
Observation	Nearest relative, authorised social worker	2 doctors: 1 acquainted with patient, 1 an approved specialist. Only 1 may be on hospital staff	Up to 28 days
Treatment	Nearest relative, or authorised social worker with nearest relative's consent	2 doctors: 1 acquainted with patient, 1 an approved specialist. Only 1 may be on hospital staff	Up to 1 year, renewable for 1 year, then 2 year periods
Guardianship	Nearest relative, authorised social worker	2 doctors: 1 acquainted with patient, 1 an approved specialist	Up to 1 year, renewable for 1 year, then 2 year periods
Hospital order on criminal offender	Court	2 doctors – at least 1 an approved specialist – who may be called to give evidence in person	Up to 1 year, renewable for 1 year, then 2 year periods
Restriction order on offender's discharge	Court, Home Secretary	None – relies on hospital order evidence as above	If not specified in order until Home Secretary consents to discharge
Transfer from prison	Home Secretary	2 doctors: 1 an approved specialist	If remanded until remand period ends. If serving sentence, until returned to prison or sentence ends

must be informed of a decision to renew his treatment. The original admission and any renewal of detention can be challenged by application to a mental health review tribunal.

Application for admission for treatment is made to a hospital management either by the patient's nearest relative or by a social worker. The applicant must have seen the patient within the previous 14 days.

Relative's consent If a social worker is the applicant, he or she must show that every effort has been made to consult the nearest relative and obtain consent. If the nearest relative objects, the social worker cannot make the application. He or she can, however, apply to a county court for an order appointing someone else as the 'nearest relative', if the refusal is obviously unreasonable.

The application must be supported by two doctors, who have to give an exact diagnosis of the disorder. They must also say why other kinds of care are not suitable and why the patient cannot be admitted voluntarily.

Both doctors must have examined the patient personally, either together or not more than 7 days apart. One, preferably the family doctor, should know the patient's background, and the other – usually a hospital psychiatrist – must be approved by the area health authority as a specialist in the diagnosis or treatment of mental disorder. Neither doctor may have a family relationship with the patient or a financial interest in the patient.

In theory a hospital can refuse an application for admission for treatment, but in practice admissions are arranged in consultation with the hospital management. In nearly every case the patient is already in the hospital's care for observation, or as a voluntary patient or out-patient.

When a prisoner is mentally ill

A court can order hospital detention instead of imprisonment if a person it convicts of a criminal offence is found to be mentally ill, psychopathic or mentally subnormal.

A court must have evidence from two doctors, under the same rules that apply to an admission for treatment. They may be called to give evidence in person.

Under a court order, however, there are no age limits on the admission or detention of a person suffering only from a psychopathic disorder or mild subnormality.

The term of a court order is 1 year, renewable in the same way as an admission for treatment. But if a court decides that the public need special protection, taking into account the seriousness of the crime and the risk of further offending, it may impose a restriction order as well as a hospital order. Then the hospital cannot discharge the patient until the term of restriction expires – or if no term is specified, until the Home Secretary gives his consent.

A patient under a restriction order and his nearest relative do not have the usual right of appeal to a mental health review tribunal. They can only ask the Home Secretary to refer the case to a tribunal, and he is not bound by a tribunal's recommendations.

With the Home Secretary's authority, an offender already serving a sentence in prison or other detention can be transferred to a psychiatric hospital for treatment. So can someone who is in custody on remand. A serving prisoner can be subject to a restriction order until his sentence would have ended, or can be returned to normal imprisonment if the hospital treatment cures his disorder. If there are medical grounds for detaining him after his sentence ends, his case is dealt with under the usual provisions for treatment orders.

People found 'unfit to plead' in a crown court must be committed to hospital under special restrictions. *See also:* INSANITY AS A DEFENCE

How private guardianship is arranged

In some circumstances a mentally disordered person whose condition is not likely to respond to hospital treatment, but who is in need of protection, may be placed in the charge of a GUARDIAN instead of being admitted to hospital. For example, if a severely subnormal adult has always been looked after at home, another relative may be appointed guardian when the parents die or become incapable.

The patient's nearest relative or an authorised social worker can make a guardianship application to the local social services authority. The same medical recommendations are required as for a hospital treatment admission.

The social services authority itself may be nominated as the guardian, or if a private guardian is named, the authority must give its consent on his or her behalf. It remains responsible for arranging regular visits and supervision by a doctor nominated as the patient's medical attendant.

Guardianship applications under the Mental Health Act are seldom made, because health authorities are reluctant to accept the responsibility involved. If possible, they manage such cases on a non-compulsory basis, by social work methods. If not, they prefer to use hospital facilities.

Guardianship is renewable after 1 year by recommendation of the nominated medical attendant. A patient in guardianship has the same rights of tribunal review as a patient detained in hospital. His nearest relative has an absolute right to order discharge from the guardianship order – it cannot be overruled by a medical officer.

Restraining a voluntary patient

Voluntary mental patients are free to leave hospital whenever they please – if their disorder is not serious enough to warrant detention. They may be asked, but cannot be forced, to sign a statement that they are discharging themselves against medical advice. That is to protect the professional reputations of the hospital staff responsible for their treatment.

However, a voluntary patient's admission can be made compulsory if he:
● Refuses treatment that the doctor in charge of the case considers essential to the patient's health or safety, or for the protection of others.
● Insists on discharging himself without taking such treatment.

Detention for treatment can be arranged in the usual way, on the application of the patient's nearest relative or an authorised social worker, with the supporting recommendation of a second doctor from outside the hospital.

To allow a hospital management time to arrange for a treatment application – or simply to give an uncooperative voluntary patient time to reconsider – the law grants the doctor in charge a special holding power. He is entitled to detain a voluntary patient for up to 3 days, using whatever physical restraint he believes necessary, simply by reporting his decision in writing to his management.

The court that can guard a patient's property

A psychiatric patient is not automatically assumed to be incapable of managing property or money, even if he or she is detained under the Mental Health Act.

Many mental disorders have no effect on the sufferer's business sense. On the other hand some disorders, too mild to warrant a patient's admission to hospital, may seriously impair his judgment.

If someone, in or out of hospital, is considered incapable of safeguarding his own financial interests, the Court of Protection can be asked to take responsibility. Application can be made by his doctor, a social worker, a hospital management or by any relative.

The court is administered as an office of the High Court. Judges nominated by the Lord Chancellor consider evidence of the disorder – the applicant must supply a medical certificate from the doctor in charge of treatment – and if they find the patient incapable of managing his affairs they can order any arrangement necessary in his interests or his family's.

A receiver, normally an accountant or a relative, is appointed. He must keep detailed records and obtain the court's permission for all transactions. He is also required to scc that the

HOW THE RULES ALLOW EVEN A VOLUNTARY PATIENT'S MAIL TO BE INTERCEPTED

Mail addressed to any patient in hospital with a mental disorder may be withheld and returned to the sender if the doctor in charge of the case considers that it would interfere with treatment or cause the patient unnecessary distress.

Mail that a patient intends to send out can be confiscated if the person to whom it is addressed has given notice in writing that he or she does not want to receive communications from the patient, or if the doctor in charge considers that it would be:
● Unreasonably offensive.
● Defamatory of someone other than the hospital staff.
● Likely to harm the patient's interests.

A doctor is not entitled to open outward mail unless the patient's disorder is of a kind that makes him likely to send offensive or damaging communications.

But outgoing letters cannot be intercepted in any circumstances if they are addressed to:
● The Minister of Health.
● Any Member of Parliament.
● The Court of Protection.
● The hospital management.
● A mental health review tribunal, at a time when the patient is entitled to apply for a review of his case.
● Anyone else with the power to order the patient's discharge – for example, his nearest relative.

patient is supplied with any pocket money or comforts he needs.

The costs of an application – for example, a solicitor's fees and the charge for a medical certificate – are met out of the patient's funds. So are the receiver's fees and the court itself takes a percentage.

There is no need to see a solicitor: the court is happy to take personal applications.

The Court of Protection's authority includes specific powers to make orders for:
● The control, sale or purchase of property.
● The transfer of property to other people by gift or settlement.
● The continuation of the patient's trade, business or profession under suitable management.
● The payment of the patient's debts – even debts not legally enforceable, if the court considers that he could have been expected to pay them.
● Conducting legal proceedings in the patient's name.
● Exercising any other powers normally belonging to the patient – for example, parental consent to a child's marriage.

People with legal and medical qualifications, called 'Lord Chancellor's visitors', are appointed as an extra safeguard for patients under the jurisdiction of the Court of Protection. At the court's direction they keep watch on a patient's welfare and mental condition, and may examine a patient at any time.

Visiting a mental patient

No relative or other member of the public has an absolute right to visit a psychiatric patient in hospital. However, hospitals should allow visiting at suitable hours for all patients except those whose condition would be made worse, or whose treatment would be interrupted.

Certain authorised visitors must be allowed access to mental patients:
● Independent doctors who are asked to examine patients in support of mental health review tribunal applications.
● Tribunal members.
● Inspectors from the Department of Health and Social Security.
● Lord Chancellor's visitors under the direction of the Court of Protection.

A MENTAL PATIENT'S LIMITED RIGHT TO PROTEST

If a mental patient can show that the proper procedures were not followed in detaining him, or that the authority to detain him has expired, he can seek his discharge by applying to the High Court for a writ of HABEAS CORPUS.

His only other way of pressing for his release is by applying at approved intervals to a mental health review tribunal.

Anyone who ill-treats or neglects mental patients can be prosecuted by the police, but only with the consent of the DIRECTOR OF PUBLIC PROSECUTIONS.

A patient who wants to start civil or criminal proceedings against hospital or nursing home staff, or against anyone else who is acting under the Mental Health Act, can do so only with High Court permission. He must show that the person to be sued or prosecuted acted negligently or maliciously – in other words, he must almost prove his case before starting.

How a compulsory patient can regain his freedom

A compulsory mental patient can be discharged from hospital, or his continued treatment made voluntary, any time the doctor in charge of his case wishes – provided that the patient is not a criminal offender subject to a restriction order. Hospital managements have the same power to discharge a patient from detention, although they are most unlikely to exercise it against the wishes of the doctor in charge.

Discharge on the doctor's own initiative – probably after consulting relatives or social workers about the availability of care outside the hospital – is the most common way of ending detention. But a patient can be legally freed in many other ways.

Lapse of order If an admission for treatment expires, and the doctor in charge has made no formal recommendation to renew it, the patient is automatically at liberty.

Age limit Someone whose disorder is diagnosed as psychopathic or as mild subnormality must be discharged from detention on reaching the age of 25, unless the doctor in charge reports that he or she is likely to be dangerous.

Reclassification Someone detained for treatment for mental illness or severe subnormality, but whose case is reclassified as one of psychopathic disorder or mild subnormality, is automatically discharged if he is 25 or over or if he was originally admitted under the age of 21, unless he is reported to be potentially dangerous.

Tribunal discharge If a mental health review tribunal disagrees with a hospital management's reasons for detaining a patient, it can order his or her discharge.

Tribunal reclassification If a mental health review tribunal disagrees with the diagnosis made by the doctor in charge, it can order reclassification of the patient. If the new classification is one of psychopathic disorder or mild subnormality, and the patient has passed his 25th birthday, he is automatically discharged if not considered dangerous.

Order by relative If a patient's nearest relative gives a hospital management written notice that he intends to exercise his right to discharge the patient, the doctor in charge of the case has 72 hours to report his reasons for opposing the discharge order. If in that time he does not report that the patient is dangerous, the patient is discharged.

Leave of absence If a compulsory patient is allowed leave from a hospital and not recalled after a continuous period of 6 months, his detention automatically lapses. Prolonged leave is used in that way as a form of probationary discharge – if a patient copes with life outside the hospital, he is not recalled. Attendance for outpatient treatment or social worker counselling is often a condition of leave.

Absence without leave A detained patient who leaves hospital without permission can be arrested and taken back by a policeman, a social worker or anyone authorised by the hospital. But if the absconder stays at large long enough – 6 months if he is over 21 and his classification is subnormality or psychopathic disorder, or 28 days in any other case – his detention lapses. If he is found later and his condition still warrants detention, application can be made for a new admission as if he were a new patient.

Expiry of court order If a time limit is

specified in a restriction order against a criminal offender, he can be discharged as soon as the limitation expires or at any time after, depending on the judgment of the doctor in charge of his case.

Home Secretary's order Any patient subject to a restriction order can be discharged at any time on the authority of the Home Secretary. The doctor in charge or the hospital management are entitled to make recommendations to obtain the Home Secretary's consent to a discharge.

Providing care outside hospital

Local authorities have a duty to provide services in the community for the care and after-care of mentally disordered people. Facilities vary from area to area because their development has been uneven, but every local authority social services department provides some help – most often in the field of after-care and social work counselling.

Residential care Hostels provide a bridge towards normal life for patients who are discharged from hospital but are not ready to return immediately to their homes – particularly those whose mental disorder was brought on by their home environment. Some have facilities for carrying on the therapy given in hospital, while others specialise in training and rehabilitation for people who have been in hospital for unusually long periods.

Local authorities that do not provide their own after-care hostels have access to accommodation run by voluntary organisations. The authority pays part of the cost, with the patient making a contribution depending on his means.

Some local authorities run adult fostering or supervised lodging schemes under which ex-patients are boarded privately. They pay an approved rent and continue to receive counselling from a social worker.

Applications for hostel places or lodgings are normally arranged between hospital and local authority social workers when a patient's discharge is being considered by his doctor. The availability of residential after-care may be the deciding factor.

Day care centres Local authorities provide or sponsor centres where former hospital patients can be helped with social or occupational programmes, or where people with an untreatable long-term disorder can be given sheltered employment.

Applications for placement are made through local authority social services departments.

Social work support Apart from the legal duties of authorised social workers – for example, arranging hospital admissions – they and other hospital or local authority social workers offer an advisory service to the mentally disordered and their families.

Most patients are referred by their own doctors or by hospital psychiatrists, but relatives, friends or patients themselves may seek advice by contacting the social services department of their local authority. Emergency cases can be dealt with at any hour.

Voluntary aid More than 100 voluntary organisations provide aid to the mentally disordered through advisory services or by running hostels or homes. Most of them are co-ordinated by the National Association for Mental Health, which is based in London.

Private care and treatment Patients prepared to pay substantial fees may seek private treatment from consultant psychiatrists, and if necessary they can be cared for in private nursing homes. Some nursing homes are approved by the Secretary of State for the detention of compulsory patients.

How the law protects mental patients

It is an offence for any manager, officer or employee of a hospital or nursing home to ill-treat or wilfully neglect a mental patient, and for anyone else to ill-treat or wilfully neglect a mental patient in his guardianship or

---

SOCIAL WELFARE BENEFITS THAT MAY BE AVAILABLE TO PSYCHIATRIC PATIENTS

A psychiatric patient is entitled to social services and national insurance benefits in the same way as the victim of physical disability. The type and amount of benefit paid depends on whether the patient is in hospital or residential care, or is receiving treatment while still in the community.

Hospital and local authority social workers are responsible for seeing that a mental patient is given any benefit or assistance to which he or she is entitled. They can help with administrative procedures.

Provided he has paid enough contributions, someone who is off work because of a mental disorder can claim SICKNESS BENEFIT with a medical certificate issued by whoever is in charge of his treatment. After 28 weeks, if the patient has not been admitted to hospital, that benefit is replaced by an INVALIDITY PENSION.

Dependants of a mental patient may be entitled to SUPPLEMENTARY BENEFIT or FAMILY INCOME SUPPLEMENT. Someone who looks after a mental patient at home may qualify for an INVALID CARE ALLOWANCE.

A patient who has not been able to work, and so make the required national insurance contributions, is entitled to a non-contributory invalidity pension if he is in private care. If he is at home or in a private institution, he may qualify for an ATTENDANCE ALLOWANCE.

A psychiatric patient in hospital receives sickness benefit at the normal rate for 8 weeks, then at a reduced rate because he is maintained free of charge. After 1 year in hospital he receives only £5.45 a week in pocket money, and the balance of his entitlement during the second year is saved for him. It is paid out to help his resettlement if he is discharged to rejoin the community.

Pocket money continues throughout a patient's stay in hospital or residential care, but the resettlement account is not added to after the second year. If a patient is not capable of understanding the use of pocket money, he or she receives personal goods or comforts of a similar value.

If a patient qualifies for a RETIREMENT PENSION, it is paid instead of sickness benefit. The pension is reduced after 8 weeks, again after 1 year and again after 2 years, but the maximum that can be deducted for board and lodging is £21.70 a week. Anything more than that must be given to the patient, if he is capable of managing it, or held in an account for him if he is not.

If an accident at work causes brain damage or a mental disorder, the victim has the same right to INDUSTRIAL INJURY BENEFIT and DISABLEMENT BENEFIT as the victim of physical injury. Victims of crime who suffer brain damage or mental disorder can obtain CRIMINAL INJURIES COMPENSATION.

HOW MENTAL DISORDER AFFECTS A PATIENT'S OTHER RIGHTS

Many of a psychiatric patient's rights are suspended automatically if he or she is detained for treatment. In other cases, the question of a person's legal competence to exercise his rights may have to be argued before a court.

Voting The electoral laws do not prohibit a mentally disordered person from voting. But he or she has to be capable of registering for enrolment – and the law does not allow a voter to give a psychiatric hospital as a home address. Someone who loses his residential qualification through a long stay in hospital also loses his vote.

Driving Any mental disorder for which a person is receiving in-patient treatment disqualifies him from driving a motor vehicle. If the Department of Transport learns that a licence holder is in a hospital for psychiatric treatment, the licence is cancelled, subject to appeal to a magistrate. A licence applicant must disclose that he is receiving in-patient treatment. There is no right of appeal if his own disclosure leads to the licence cancellation or refusal.

Firearms The sale of firearms or ammunition to a mentally disordered person is illegal. The vendor can be punished if the person's condition ought to have been known to him. A licence to own a firearm is cancelled if the holder is receiving in-patient treatment for mental disorder.

Marriage A marriage can be annulled within 3 years on proof that either partner was mentally disordered at the time, provided that the disorder was so bad that the person did not know what he was doing or such as to make him unfit for marriage. *See:* NULLITY

Incurable insanity is no longer a ground for DIVORCE – but hospital admission or the symptoms of the mental disorder could be shown as evidence of separation, desertion or unreasonable behaviour, in proving the breakdown of a marriage.

Wills A will made by a mentally disordered person is valid if it can be shown that he or she was capable of understanding it at the time. Otherwise the rules of INTESTACY apply. A destroyed or muti-lated will, which would normally have no legal force, remains valid if it is shown that a person was mentally disordered when he took the action.

Jury service People liable to detention under the Mental Health Act, or receiving in-patient treatment, are ineligible to serve on a jury.

Civil proceedings If a mental patient is incapable of acting for himself, he is replaced by what is called a 'next friend' (as a plaintiff) or by the authority responsible for his care – as a defendant.

If he is under the jurisdiction of the Court of Protection, that court supervises his representation.

Contracts A contract – for example a hire-purchase agreement – can be voided if it is shown that it was made while a person was mentally disordered and not capable of understanding his obligations, and that the other party ought to have known this. The other parties to any contracts should be notified immediately if someone is admitted to hospital for psychiatric treatment.

care. The maximum penalty is 2 years' imprisonment or an unlimited fine.

Any male manager, officer or employee of a hospital or nursing home commits an offence if he has sexual intercourse with a female mental patient, or on the premises with a woman receiving outpatient treatment for mental disorder. So does any other man who has intercourse with a female mental patient in his guardianship or care under any social services legislation. A charge can be defended if a man had no reason to suspect that the woman was a mental patient. The maximum penalty is 2 years' imprisonment.

Under the Sexual Offences Act, no man may have sexual intercourse with a woman who suffers from severe subnormality. Again it is a defence to prove that he had no reason to suspect her condition. The maximum penalty is 2 years' imprisonment.

It is an offence to forge any document required to deal with a mentally disordered person or his affairs, and to have or use a forged document. It is also an offence to make, have or use something that is intended to deceive people by its resemblance to a required document. The maximum penalty is 2 years' imprisonment or an unlimited fine.

Anyone who deliberately makes a false entry on a required document, or makes use of a statement he knows to be false, commits an offence. The maximum penalty is 2 years' imprisonment or an unlimited fine.

Anyone who induces or helps a mental patient to escape from custody, or to be absent without leave, is guilty of an offence. So is anyone who knowingly shelters such a patient or helps him with the intention of hindering his return. The maximum penalty is 2 years' imprisonment or an unlimited fine.

If someone is authorised under the Mental Health Act to inspect premises or examine a person, it is an offence to refuse him entry or to obstruct him in any other way. It is also an offence to refuse to produce any document that an official is authorised to demand. The maximum penalty is 3 months' imprisonment or a £100 fine.

MENTAL HANDICAP

The services that aim to keep a retarded person in the community

The Mental Health Act classifies incomplete mental development as a MENTAL DISORDER, so a retarded person can be detained if that is necessary for his or her health or safety.

But the law also requires local social service authorities to provide facilities for the care and education of such people without their removal from the community.

The services for which central and local government share responsibility include:

● Prevention or early detection of mental handicap – for example, by immunisation against rubella, by family-planning advice where there is a history of handicap, by ante-natal testing, or by intensive care of certain mothers and some newborn babies.
● Regular re-assessment of a retarded person's capabilities and prospects.
● Family support and practical help by social workers.
● Education by specialised teachers.
● Day care and organised activities.
● Work training and sheltered employment.
● Residential accommodation.
● Medical or nursing care.

When a child is handicapped

Parents who suspect that a young child is not developing normally should

WHEN PARENTS OBJECT TO SPECIAL SCHOOLING

Some parents are unwilling to accept that a child is mentally handicapped. Bitter arguments can arise when a local education authority decides, after reports that a child cannot cope in the normal education system, to arrange for its enrolment in a special class or special school.

A parent who disagrees with special schooling has an immediate right of appeal to the Department of Education, and must be advised of that right by the local education authority. If the parent brings forward medical evidence which conflicts with a school medical officer's opinion, the child is examined by a department doctor or psychiatric consultant.

If local authority officers are convinced that a child needs to live away from its parents, because it needs professional care or because its parents cannot cope with it, they must try to persuade the parents to co-operate. If parents refuse unreasonably, the council can use the compulsory provisions of the Mental Health Act. However, it is more usual for a local authority to support with extra day care. It may alternatively take a child into care. *See:* CHILDREN IN CARE

---

first consult their doctor, who if necessary can arrange for examination and assessment by specialists.

If a serious handicap is confirmed they are offered local authority social work support and counselling to put them in touch with all available services, and to help them to know what to expect as the child grows.

Many local authorities provide special day nursery facilities, or short-term homes where a child can stay for, say, a long weekend to relieve the strain on its parents.

Other practical assistance may range from home nursing to housework help. Local authority social services departments can also arrange an application for a state ATTENDANCE ALLOWANCE if a child over the age of 2 needs constant attention.

Arranging special education

Local education authorities provide special schools for the mentally handicapped, or special classes attached to normal schools. Some schools are run in conjunction with residential homes for the severely subnormal, but nearly all children who are less seriously handicapped go to school from their own homes – often in transport provided by the local council.

When an adult is handicapped

Local authorities provide adult training centres for the mentally handicapped, and continued social work support for them and their families. A local authority must also offer residential facilities, or pay voluntary organisations to provide them.

Most adult training centres are for the more severely handicapped, who after special schooling are still unable to cope with open employment. They offer:
● Continued practical education.
● Art and craft therapy.
● Social training.
● Sheltered employment – with a small independent income – in simple manufacturing, assembly or packaging tasks.

For less severely handicapped people who reach working age, youth employment and disablement resettlement officers try to find suitable work in the community. Social workers continue to check on their welfare.

Local authorities and voluntary organisations run social clubs or activity groups for mentally handicapped adults. In some areas facilities are also offered as part of the further education programme of local education authorities.

MENTAL HEALTH REVIEW TRIBUNAL

A psychiatric patient's court of appeal

Most people over the age of 16 who are compulsorily detained in hospital or placed in guardianship because of MENTAL DISORDER have the right to ask a mental health review tribunal to consider their discharge. This does not apply to short-term detainees or to criminal offenders detained by order of a court.

A patient admitted under a Mental Health Act order must be given a notice of that right, if it applies to him, and the address of the tribunal to which he can apply. So must his nearest relative.

The patient can apply for a hearing once within 6 months of admission or of the patient's 16th birthday, and once during each period for which the order is renewed. He or his nearest relative can also appeal within 28 days if the patient has a minor disorder and is not automatically discharged at the age of 25, or if his case is reclassified from a minor to a major disorder.

Because the nearest relative has a special right to order a patient's discharge, he or she can appeal within 28 days if a discharge order is overruled by the hospital authority.

Different provision is made for patients under 16 who were in official care before being admitted. The authority which had charge of them before admission resumes its responsibility if their condition improves. *See:* CHILD GUIDANCE; CHILDREN IN CARE; MALADJUSTED CHILD

A criminal offender who is detained in hospital instead of prison, or transferred from a prison, can ask for a tribunal hearing and so can his nearest relative – once a year. But if he is also under a restriction order – because of the seriousness of his crime, and the likelihood of further offending – he cannot apply directly to a tribunal.

After a year's detention he can ask the Home Secretary to put his case to a tribunal, but the Home Secretary need not follow its recommendations.

The tribunal's powers

A mental health review tribunal can take evidence on oath. It can order witnesses to appear and to produce documentary evidence. It can inquire not only into a patient's mental state, but also into the conditions in which he will live if he is discharged.

The patient must be discharged if a majority of the tribunal members are satisfied that:
● He is not suffering from mental disorder, or
● His disorder does not require his detention in the interests of his health or safety, or for the protection of other people.

If a tribunal finds that a patient's disorder is wrongly classified, it can direct that the classification be changed. Reclassification from a major to a minor disorder leads to a patient's automatic discharge at the age of 25, if the patient is not likely to act dangerously if released.

How hearings are arranged

Application for a tribunal review must be made on a special form that can be obtained from hospitals, health authorities or the tribunals themselves. A leaflet with the form explains how it should be completed and where it should be sent. Hospital staff are obliged to help a patient with an application if necessary.

The tribunal chairman sends a copy of the application to the authority responsible for detaining the patient – usually a hospital management. Within 3 weeks it must reply with a statement including medical and social details, a diagnosis of the mental disorder and the authority's reasons for being unwilling to discharge the patient.

The applicant is sent a copy of the statement and is entitled to dispute it – but parts of the statement can be withheld from him at the hospital's request.

The patient and his nearest relative must be given at least 7 days' notice of the hearing, which is usually held in private at the hospital or near by. A request for a public hearing can be refused if the tribunal thinks it could be harmful to the patient's health.

If the applicant has asked for a formal hearing – which can also be refused in the patient's interests – everyone concerned attends at the same time, and evidence is taken as if it were a court hearing. But the tribunal can ask anyone, especially the patient, to leave while evidence is being taken. If it is informal, the tribunal gathers evidence in any way it wishes.

Any witness called by an applicant must be heard. A doctor who is called as a witness for the applicant must be allowed access to examine the patient. The tribunal can if it wishes award expenses to any witness except a doctor.

Anyone except another patient in the hospital can be appointed to represent the patient or his nearest relative at the hearing. The patient can still attend – but he or anyone else can be excluded from hearing evidence if the tribunal rules that their presence is undesirable.

In all cases the psychiatrist member of the tribunal must examine the patient, who is also entitled to an interview with the other tribunal members.

What a patient is told

The tribunal's decision is normally given in writing within 7 days to the applicant, to the authority responsible for detaining the patient, and to the patient if he is not the applicant. But the tribunal may decide that it is undesirable for a patient who is not the applicant to receive a formal decision. It can direct that it be conveyed to him in some other way or at some other time.

The tribunal records the reasons for its decision on a document that remains confidential. The parties are not given the reasons when they are notified of the decision. They are told of their right to request the reasons within 3 weeks, but the tribunal can refuse.

There is no direct right of appeal against a tribunal decision, but a patient can apply again to the same tribunal if the order detaining him is renewed. The High Court can quash a tribunal decision if it is shown to be wrong in law, but the procedure is complicated and costly, and should not be undertaken without legal advice.

METRICATION

Changing the system by which measurements are expressed

The use of metric weights and measures has been permitted in Britain since 1864 but the more customary way of expressing quantities has been by the imperial system – that is, pounds and ounces, gallons and pints, and miles, yards, feet and inches.

METRICATION – STILL NOT UNIVERSALLY ADOPTED

Although plans to introduce metrication as the only official measurement system have not yet been implemented, the metric system is the only one taught in many schools. Many consumer goods must be sold only in metric quantities.

Phasing out the old system gradually

It is expected that the use of the imperial system will be gradually phased out, and that eventually there will be a complete change over to metrication. Already that has happened with pre-packed foods, and most are sold in metric quantities.

It is illegal to pack or sell goods that have been designated by the Government in quantities other than those permitted by the Government or to show the quantities in imperial terms only.

It has been permissible to pack instant or soluble coffee in metric quantities since July 1, 1979, but no cut-off date for imperial sizes is known.

Although many industrial goods, such as timber and nails, are sold only in

---

HOW MENTAL HEALTH REVIEW TRIBUNALS ARE FORMED

In each regional health area, three groups of volunteers are approved by the Lord Chancellor to act as mental health review tribunal members. The respective groups are made up of:
● Lawyers.
● Psychiatrists.
● People with experience in social services, senior administration or other public work.

One of the lawyers is appointed perma-

nent chairman. When he receives a valid application for a patient's discharge he chooses at least 1 tribunal member from each of the 3 groups – the president is always a lawyer – and sets the date and place for a hearing.

No tribunal member can hear a case in which he or she has a personal or financial relationship with the patient, or, indeed, any connection with a hospital or home where the patient is detained.

FOODS THAT MUST BE METRIC

Foods which must be packed and sold in metric sizes, include:

● Chocolate bars: 85 g, 100 g, 125 g, 150 g, 200 g, 250 g, 300 g, 400 g, 500 g. No restrictions below 85 g or over 500 g.

● Bread: 400 g and multiples of 400 g. No restrictions up to 300 g.

● Sugar: 125 g, 250 g, 500 g, 750 g, 1 kg, 1.5 kg, 2 kg, 2.5 kg, 3 kg, 4 kg, 5 kg. No restrictions up to 100 g or over 5 kg.

● Biscuits: 100 g, 125 g, 150 g, 200 g, 250 g, 300 g, then multiples of 100 g up to 5 kg. No restrictions up to 85 g or over 5 kg. 175 g is permitted if packed before January 1, 1981.

● Salt: 125 g, 250 g, 500 g, 750 g, 1 kg, 1.5 kg, 2 kg, then multiples of 1 kg up to 10 kg, then 12.5 kg, 25 kg, 50 kg. No restrictions up to 100 g.

● Breakfast cereals in flake form and oat products: 125 g, 250 g, 375 g, 500 g, 750 g, 1 kg, 1.5 kg, 2 kg and multiples of 1 kg. No restrictions up to 50 g or over 10 kg.

● Butter and margarine: 50 g, 125 g, 250 g, 500 g, then multiples of 500 g up to 4 kg, then multiples of 1 kg. No restrictions up to 25 g or over 10 kg.

● Tea – from June 29, 1980: 50 g, 125 g, 250 g, 500 g, 750 g, 1 kg, 1.5 kg, 2 kg, 2.5 kg, 3 kg, 4 kg, 5 kg. No restrictions up to 25 g or over 5 kg.

metric sizes, it is not yet compulsory for them to be so.

All cars manufactured after October 1, 1978, must have speedometers marked in kilometres per hour (km/h) as well as miles per hour (mph).

MILITARY POLICE

Soldiers first and policemen second

Police of the three Armed Services have no greater powers in Britain than any member of the public so far as civilians are concerned, except that they have the power of arrest on Ministry of Defence property.

Courts martial in Britain have no jurisdiction over civilians; anyone detained on Ministry of Defence property has to be handed to the civil police if an offence is suspected.

Overseas, however, civilians employed by the Ministry of Defence and members of servicemen's families can be subject to military law. *See:* ARMED FORCES

Military police have power to direct military traffic on civil roads, but civilian drivers are not bound to heed their directions. The fact that a driver had ignored a warning signal by a military policeman might, however, be considered by the civil police to be a basis for prosecution on a driving charge.

Even if someone is suspected of being a deserter or absentee from the Services, the matter is dealt with by civil police. They must bring him before a magistrates' court as soon as possible. If the court is satisfied he is a member of the Services, it orders him into military custody.

MINIBUS

Using a vehicle to transport members of groups

Anyone who wants to operate a minibus – a vehicle that can carry more than 7 but less than 16 passengers – must have a road service licence. If the vehicle is a public service vehicle a PSV licence is also needed.

The only exceptions are people who drive such vehicles on behalf of educational, social welfare, religious or other community groups. They need only a special permit, which costs £7 and is obtainable from the traffic commissioner of the area in which the vehicle is normally kept, or from the local education or social services authority. Traffic commissioners operate in London, Birmingham, Bristol, Cambridge, Eastbourne, Leeds, Manchester, Newcastle and Nottingham.

A minibus for which such a permit has been granted must not be used for the general public and it must be operated only by the body to whom the permit is issued. Any special conditions imposed must be kept and the vehicle must carry a disc showing that it is permitted to operate as a minibus. The organisation in whose name the minibus is operated can charge fares, but it must not make a profit from doing so.

A minibus driver must be over 21 and hold a full DRIVING LICENCE.

MINICAB

When you are driven in a hired car other than a hackney carriage

Only licensed TAXIS are allowed to ply for hire at cab ranks or in the street. Members of the public, however, can order private taxis, usually known as minicabs, to pick them up at one address and take them to another. This is usually done by telephone, but it can also be done in person at a minicab office.

Every district council in England and Wales has the right, under the Local Government (Miscellaneous Provisions) Act 1976 to operate a licensing scheme for these private hire cars and their drivers, in the same way that hackney carriages are licensed.

The councils have the right to inspect vehicles and to ensure that they are adequately insured for the purpose for which they are being used. They also have the right to refuse to license any vehicle or driver found to be unfit for public hire service.

If a vehicle is licensed, a disc must be displayed on the car.

Most minicab firms have a higher minimum fare for a journey than a taxi, but the rate per mile is cheaper, so it pays to use them on longer journeys. When you order a minicab, always ask the firm to quote you its price for the journey.

How to find out if a car is licensed

If you intend to hire a car, find out whether it is licensed to carry paying passengers. Ask the proprietor of the car service or find out from the information department at the local council if hire cars in its area have to be licensed.

Whether or not a car is licensed, always ask what the fare will be and make sure that the driver knows his way.

MINOR

Protection and restraints on the under-18 s

The law classes anyone under the age of 18 as a minor. A person under that age cannot vote, marry without parental consent or own a house or land. He can, however, make legally binding contracts and be held responsible for civil or criminal wrongs.

Although 18 is the age at which young people gain full legal status in most matters, the law sets minimum ages below that for a wide variety of lesser rights and responsibilities.

Suing a young person

A minor is legally responsible for his actions if he is old enough to be aware of their consequences. A 16 year old who knocks someone down while cycling on the footpath is liable – a 3 year old is not. Usually, however, there is little point in suing a minor for damages when he is unlikely to be able to pay.

Parents can be sued for the wrongdoings of their children only if they share the blame. For example, a father who asks his 11-year-old son to drive the family car can be sued if there is an accident. So can a parent who buys a cycle for his child and then, without giving any instructions, allows him to ride on a busy road, causing a motorist to crash. But if a boy kicks a football through a neighbour's window his parents are not liable.

Can a young person sue?

A child who is a victim of someone else's negligence can sue. He can even sue his parents, so that, for instance, if he is negligently injured while a passenger in his father's car he can obtain compensation from his father's insurance company.

A PARENT'S DUTY WHEN A CHILD FINDS A JOB

Any parent who lets a child under 16 take employment in breach of an education authority bye-law is guilty of an offence. The parent and the employer are liable to a fine of £20.

All regular work by children requires a permit – sometimes called an employment card – from the local education authority. There is no charge.

It is the employer's responsibility to obtain a permit. But some education authorities require a parent to countersign an application form.

Parents should check with an education authority welfare officer before letting a child under 16 take any job.

SARTORIAL SWINDLER WAS TOO YOUNG TO PAY

If a minor obtains goods on credit he cannot be forced to pay for them, even after he has used them, unless they were essential to his immediate needs. But even food or clothes may not be considered essential if it is shown that he already had sufficient of these items.

In 1902 Roy Inman, the son of a wealthy London architect, ordered suits, fancy waistcoats and overcoats worth £145 from a Savile Row tailor while at Cambridge University. He wore them for a year but never paid. The tailor sued in the High Court but the case was dismissed. The tailor appealed.

DECISION
The Appeal Court said that Inman would have to pay for the clothes only if they were necessary to his requirements. His father, however, had given evidence that his son was adequately provided with clothes. The appeal was dismissed.

YOUNG BOXER LOST HIS PRIZE MONEY

A minor is bound by an employment contract if, taken as a whole, it is to his benefit, even if some provisions do not work out in his favour.

On July 12, 1933 Jack Doyle fought Jack Petersen for the heavyweight championship of Britain. Doyle – a minor – had agreed to a purse of £3,000, win, lose or draw. In the second round he was disqualified for hitting below the belt.

Doyle fought under a licence from the British Boxing Board of Control. One of its provisions was that in cases of disqualification boxers were entitled to receive only travelling expenses.

A week after the fight the board suspended Doyle's licence for 6 months and confiscated all but £260 of the £3,000 purse. Doyle sued and won, but the board appealed.

DECISION
The Appeal Court said that while forfeiture of the purse did not benefit Doyle the rules for clean fighting were, as a whole, to his advantage. He could not claim the rest of the money.

In some cases a child can sue when an adult cannot. For example, a woman who consents to sexual intercourse cannot later claim damages for assault and battery. A girl of 12 who is seduced can – the court will not accept her consent as voluntary and effective.

Handling money

Cash transactions made by minors are fully binding. For example a youngster who spends all his pocket-money savings on a new toy and then once outside the shop changes his mind has no more legal right to his money back than anyone else. But there are special laws designed to discourage traders, banks and others from giving credit to minors for non-essentials.

Loans A minor cannot be made to repay money he has borrowed, even if he fools the lender into believing he is over 18. The only exception to that rule is if the minor spends the money on necessary items, such as food and clothing. Money borrowed for such purposes can be recovered by legal action.

Buying on credit If a minor obtains goods on credit he cannot be forced to pay for them, even after he has used them. As with loans, however, he can be made to pay if the goods are essential to his immediate needs. A minor can cancel goods he has ordered without risk of being sued for breach of contract, though once he has paid for the goods he cannot return them and claim his money back.

It is a criminal offence, punishable by 1 year's imprisonment and/or fine of up to £1,000 to send advertising material to a minor inviting him to borrow money, obtain goods or services on credit or encouraging him to send off for further information about credit facilities.

When criminal charges are involved

No child under 10 can be charged with a crime. A child over 10 but under 14 can be charged but it must be proved in court that he knew he was doing wrong. Up to the age of 17 the maximum penalty for a young offender is a £200 fine or a period in a detention centre. At 17, offenders are dealt with in adult courts and can be sent to prison.

Employing young people

There are strict controls on the kind of work young people can do and on the number of hours they can put in. The controls are aimed mainly at under-16s to safeguard their health and welfare, prevent interference in their education and protect them from exploitation.

The general law lays down basic restrictions, but local education authorities can impose bye-laws, so the regulations vary from area to area.

WORKING HOURS FOR UNDER-16s

The law bars most employment for children under 13. Between 13 and 16 light work is allowed, but precise restrictions on the kind of work and on hours vary from area to area. The Inner London Education Authority's bye-laws are typical:

How many hours
School days Work allowed only from 7–8 a.m. or 5–7 p.m. – maximum 2 hours a day.
Saturdays and holidays Not before 7 a.m. or after 7 p.m. – maximum 4 hours a day if under 15, 8 hours aged 15–16.
Sundays 7–10 a.m. only – maximum 2 hours.
Weekly In addition to daily limits children must not work more than 20 hours a week if under 15, or 30 hours aged 15–16.

Type of work
In inner London under-16s cannot be employed in kitchens, billiard halls, slaughterhouses, scrap or refuse businesses, fairgrounds or racecourses. Children may not be employed in the delivery of inflammable materials or in window cleaning except incidentally as part of light housework. The only Sunday work permitted is milk or newspaper delivery.

Paid work for public performance or broadcasting must be licensed. Licences are not issued for children under 14 if the part can be played by an older child. If a child misses school, special arrangements may have to be made before a licence is granted.

Under 13 The general law bars children from almost any employment before their 13th birthday. Local education authorities can, in their bye-laws, allow light farm or garden work, modelling for advertising, or entertainment performances subject to special licensing if the child misses school. A child cannot take part in any public performance involving 'danger to life or limb' until he is 16, though training can start at 13.

Aged 13–16 A child who has passed his 13th birthday can be employed in light work, but until he leaves school the hours are restricted and many types of work are banned under bye-laws.

Aged 16–18 Until a person is 18, working hours are normally limited to 9 a day and 48 a week. Overtime is also restricted, but exemptions are allowed for seasonal work and emergencies.

In industrial employment minors are subject to the same Factories Act controls as apply to women at work, but:
● A factory inspector can forbid the employment of a worker under 18 on a certain job on health grounds.
● A youth under 18 can work night shifts if a continuous production process makes it necessary.

Contracts A minor is bound by an employment contract unless, taken as a whole, the contract is to his disadvantage.

MISREPRESENTATION

When someone makes a false statement to gain some advantage

A misrepresentation is a false statement of fact made to induce someone to enter into a CONTRACT.

Some misrepresentations made by traders about goods or services are criminal offences under the TRADE DESCRIPTIONS Act 1968, and the traders can be prosecuted. In addition, however, anyone who has been misled may also be able to sue the maker of the false statement.

When the misrepresentation is a promise

Sometimes a statement about a sale is treated as a promise – and a promise is a term of the contract. For example, if a shopkeeper says that a jacket he is selling is made of leather, the sale is said to be a sale by description.

Under the Sale of Goods Act 1893 there is an implied condition of the contract that the goods supplied correspond with the description. If the statement about the jacket is treated as a promise, the shopkeeper is in breach of contract if the statement is false. There is no need to show that he knew it was false, or that he was negligent in making the statement.

There is no hard and fast rule for deciding whether a statement is a promise or not. If the person who makes the statement is – or ought to be – knowledgeable, such as a trader describing goods in which he deals, the statement will very likely be taken by the courts to be a promise. But if he has no special expertise and is merely passing on information he has been given by somebody else, the statement will probably be a representation and not a promise.

Statements made in preliminary discussions, some time before the contract is actually made, are also likely to be representations and not promises.

If the statement is a representation

If the statement is a representation, the person who acted on it may have certain rights if it is false – that is, a misrepresentation. He may be able either to get out of the contract by rescinding it, or to claim damages as compensation. But he has no remedy if the false statement was a statement of opinion, if the opinion was genuinely held by the person who made it.

If the statement was a statement of existing fact, the person to whom it was made may be able to rescind any contract he was induced to enter, even if he might have found out the truth if he had been more careful.

If the person to whom the representation was made knows that the statement is untrue, he cannot claim that it induced him to enter into a contract.

If the statement was not a statement of existing fact, but was a statement of intention, the person to whom it was made has no claim if the person who made it fails to do what was stated, unless:
● The maker of the statement had no

intention of doing it at the time he made the statement, or
● The statement was a contractual promise.

When a contract can be rescinded

Anyone who is induced into a contract by a false statement can rescind the contract, and if he paid any money, or transferred any property, he can get it back. If he parted with goods under the contract he can rescind simply by retaking possession of the goods, but if it transpires later that he was not entitled to rescind, he may then be liable to pay damages.

No right to rescind A person loses the right to rescind a contract for misrepresentation if:
● He lets more than a reasonable time pass without rescinding.
● He affirmed the contract after finding out the statement was false.
● He has used all or part of property received under the contract so can no longer return it.
● Someone else has obtained the goods or property that were the subject of the contract.

For example, if a person sells goods as the result of a misrepresentation and, before he rescinds, the buyer sells the goods to someone who knows nothing of the earlier transaction, the original seller cannot rescind and claim the goods back.

When damages can be claimed

Damages can be claimed by someone who has suffered loss because of misrepresentation if:
● The misrepresentation was a term of the contract – that is, a promise, or
● The misrepresentation was fraudulent. That is, that the person who made the statement knew it to be false, or, although he did not actually know it was false, he did not believe it to be true or did not care whether it was true or false, or
● The person who made the representation cannot prove that he believed it

THE SOLICITOR WHO TRICKED ANOTHER INTO BUYING HIS PRACTICE

If a person is induced to enter a contract by a representation, and then discovers that the representation is untrue, he may be able to rescind the contract, even if he had had the opportunity to discover the truth before he entered into the contract.

In 1880, Mr Redgrave, a solicitor, was selling his house and practice to Mr Hurd, also a solicitor. Mr Redgrave told Mr Hurd that the practice brought in at least £300 a year. On looking at the books produced by Mr Redgrave, Mr Hurd pointed out that the income seemed to be only about £200

a year. Mr Redgrave then produced some letters and papers which he said were not entered in the books but which made up the difference. Mr Hurd could have looked at the letters and papers, but trusting Mr Redgrave, did not do so. After he had entered into a contract to buy the practice and house he discovered that the income represented by the extra letters and papers was negligible. He refused to go on with the purchase, and Mr Redgrave sued him in the High Court claiming specific performance of the contract.

The judge ordered Mr Hurd to perform

the contract. Mr Hurd appealed in the Court of Appeal.

DECISION

The Court of Appeal set aside the High Court order and said that Mr Hurd was entitled to rescind the contract because a misrepresentation had been made. Mr Hurd was induced by the statement about the income of the practice to enter into a contract. The fact that he had an opportunity of looking at the letters and papers before the contract was signed did not take away his right to rescind the contract.

THE ART GALLERY THAT SOLD A FAKE CONSTABLE PAINTING

Anyone who is induced into a contract by a false statement can rescind the contract and claim back any money he has paid for goods or property. But he loses the right to rescind if he lets more than a reasonable time elapse before rescinding.

In March 1944 Mr Leaf bought a painting of Salisbury Cathedral for £85 from a

firm of art dealers, who told him it was painted by Constable. Five years later he took it to Christie's to put up for auction. They told him it was not a Constable.

Mr Leaf took the painting back to the dealers from whom he had bought it and asked for his money back. When they refused he sued. The judge refused to order rescission of the contract and Mr

Leaf appealed to the Court of Appeal.

DECISION

The Court of Appeal upheld the county court's decision. Mr Leaf could not get his money back as he had had the painting for 5 years before he tried to rescind the contract, and that was much more than a reasonable time.

BAD OPINION OR BAD FARMING?

A buyer cannot claim misrepresentation if the vendor's statements were only an opinion.

Mr Wilkinson and a partner bought land in New Zealand for £13,260 which the vendor, Mr Bisset, said could support 2,000 sheep. They paid £2,000 in May 1919 and agreed to pay the balance in May

1924 with payments of interest half yearly.

Mr Wilkinson and his partner failed to make the venture profitable, and when they were pressed for payment of interest they alleged that Mr Bisset's statements were misrepresentations which entitled them to rescission of the contract.

A court found in favour of Mr Bisset on the ground that his statement was only an

opinion. The court of appeal reversed the decision and the case went to the Privy Council in London.

DECISION

The Privy Council held that no person had, as both parties were aware, previously raised sheep on the land. Mr Bisset's statement could be only an opinion.

to be true and that he had reasonable grounds to believe it to be true, or

● One party is entitled to rescind the contract but the court thinks it fairer to both parties to order damages to be paid instead of rescission of the contract.

See: DEFECTIVE GOODS

FRAUD

MISSING PERSON

Your right to 'disappear' without trace

Anyone over the age of 17 can go where he or she likes without letting anyone know his or her whereabouts, unless a court has specifically ordered the person to live in a certain place. *See:* BAIL; PROBATION

The police search for missing persons only if they are suspected of a criminal offence, if there are fears for their safety, perhaps because of old age or poor health, if they are a WARD OF COURT, or if they are under 17. They do not help to trace people against whom someone wants to bring a civil action – for instance, against a husband who has deserted his wife and family.

If young people under 17 are traced, they are restored to their families or, if relations with their parents are unsatisfactory, taken before a court as in need of care and protection.

The International Investigation Department of the Salvation Army, 110–112 Middlesex Street, London E1 7HZ, offers a voluntary service to relatives who are anxious to trace a member of the family who is over 17. It leaves cases of missing persons under 17 to the police.

The aim of this service is reconciliation. If a missing wife or husband is traced, counsellors try to reconcile the missing partner with the family, but keep her or his new address secret. They do not disclose an address to enable a deserted partner to take legal proceedings. They will, however, act as a 'post-box' to enable the two parties to correspond if the missing person so wishes.

Private detectives undertake to try to trace missing persons, but their fees and expenses can be high if the case is at all complicated. Often they are also certified BAILIFFS and can serve any court orders that have been obtained.

The fact that a person has chosen to move to an area where he is unknown in no way lessens his legal obligations, for instance, his duty to maintain his family. A court can compel his attendance to hear any claims against him, unless he leaves the country. The litigant, however, generally has to trace the missing person to serve the necessary papers.

MOBILE HOME

People living in caravans have only limited security

Owner occupiers of mobile homes or caravans who rent their pitch have only a limited legal right to remain on the site unless they have signed an agreement with the site owner.

Many people living permanently in mobile homes have bought their caravans from the site owners, as this is one way of obtaining a pitch on the site. As home-owners, they have no security of tenure under the Rent Act, but they cannot be evicted from the site without a county court order, and the court can suspend its enforcement for up to 12 months at a time. The regulations do not apply to holiday caravan letting.

A few people live in rented mobile homes or caravans and they may have security under the Rent Act and may also qualify for RENT REBATE or RENT ALLOWANCE and RATES rebate.

Signing an agreement

Landowners hiring out pitches to caravan or mobile-home dwellers must be licensed by the local authority. Under the Mobile Homes Act 1975, all licensed site owners must offer a written agreement to new occupiers.

That usually permits the caravan owner to remain on the site for at least 5 years, with an option to renew the tenancy for a further 3 years. An initial rent is fixed for the pitch, which cannot be changed more often than once a year.

A caravan owner who signs such an agreement cannot be turned off the site unless he breaks any site regulations written into the agreement. These are usually about repair or maintenance of the caravan, matters of hygiene, undue noise or unreasonable behaviour. The site owner would need a court order before the tenant could be evicted.

There is no legal obligation for a pitch tenant to sign an agreement when one is offered to him, but those who have no written agreements have only legal protection against summary eviction and harassment.

Site charges

Rent is fixed by the site owner or by agreement with the prospective tenant, and it is usually reviewed each year.

There are often substantial connection charges or premiums to be paid by people moving on to a site for the first time.

Leaving a site

A person who has an agreement under the 1975 Act is entitled to sell his mobile home on site, but he must offer it first at a fair market price (less discount) to the owner of the site. If the owner refuses to buy it, the caravan owner can then sell to anyone he likes, but he must pay a commission to the site owner, usually limited to 15 per cent.

If there is no agreement, the caravan owner may have no right to sell his caravan on site, and the landlord could insist that if the caravan is sold it must be removed from the site. This, in effect, seriously reduces its value. On the whole, site owners are unwilling to rent pitches to owners of second-hand mobile homes.

MOBILITY ALLOWANCE

Cash help to enable a disabled person to get out and about

Anyone over 5 who is unable, or almost unable, to walk can apply for a mobility allowance. To qualify he or she must:

● Be under 65.

● Normally live in the UK, be in the UK when claiming and have been present here for a total of 12 months out of the previous 18.

● Be unable, or almost unable, to walk using artificial limbs or other aids and be likely to remain so for at least a year.

● Be in a condition to make use of the allowance – that is, capable of going out of doors and benefiting from increased mobility.

A person who is in a coma or who for medical reasons cannot be moved – or someone so severely mentally handicapped as not to benefit from the allowance – is not eligible.

How to claim the allowance

If you think you are eligible, obtain leaflet NI 211 from your local social security office and complete form MY 1 attached to it. If you cannot sign the form yourself, someone else can sign it for you.

Disabled child If you are the parent of a disabled child who is living with you, you can claim on his behalf. If the child lives elsewhere, the person in whose household he lives or the responsible local authority official, should claim.

What medical evidence is needed If the Department of Health and Social Security does not have enough medical evidence in its own records to grant your claim, it asks the applicant to attend a medical examination – usually near his home. Travelling expenses for the applicant and an escort, if necessary, are paid. If the claimant cannot travel, he is examined at home.

The allowance is awarded for a definite period – usually at least a year – and can extend up to the age of 75. If it is awarded for less than a year, the claimant is normally asked to attend another medical examination before the period ends to decide whether his allowance can continue and for how long.

Making an appeal

If you are refused an allowance you can appeal against the decision to an appeals tribunal. The reason for refusal and details of how and where to appeal will be explained to you in the notification sent to you by the local social security office.

How the allowance is paid

The allowance is paid weekly – in 1981 it was £14.50 a week – and is reviewed, and usually increased, in November of each year. The current rate is always given in leaflet NI 196, which you can get from your local social security office.

Mobility allowance is paid by order book. Each order covers 4 weeks and can be cashed at a post office chosen by the claimant.

How other benefits are affected

If you are receiving any other social security benefits – such as sickness be-

nefit or attendance allowance – you are still entitled to receive a mobility allowance.

You cannot receive a mobility allowance if you are already receiving a vehicle or private car allowance under the National Health Service or the war pensioners' vehicle service. But you can have a mobility allowance instead. If you wish to change, you should get leaflet NI 225 from your local social security office and complete the form.

Income tax The mobility allowance is taxable and will be added to any other income you have for tax purposes.

Hiring a car or buying on hire purchase

If you have a mobility allowance you are exempt from the usual hire-purchase restrictions on minimum deposit and length of time for payment, when you buy a car.

You have similar exemptions if you hire a car on a long-term basis. *See:* MOTABILITY

MONEY BACK

What you can do when goods are defective

A buyer is entitled to get his money back if the goods are defective – provided that he acts in time.

The law regards the goods as sufficiently defective to allow the purchaser to reject them if they are:

● Not as described. For example, someone who buys a handbag or briefcase labelled 'Real leather' and later finds a label saying it is made of plastic can take it back to the shop and get a refund.

● Not of merchantable quality. Goods sold by a shopkeeper must be reasonably fit for the usual purpose for which people buy goods of that kind. For example, a man who finds a big hole in a newly bought shirt can get his money back.

● Not fit for the purpose. For example, if a householder buys a colour TV set after telling the dealer that he lives in a 'fringe' area where reception is difficult, the set must be sensitive enough to get good reception. If not the buyer can return it and get a refund.

Goods can also be rejected if they

REFUNDS WITH A SMILE

Anyone can demand his money back if the goods are defective, not as described, or not fit for their purpose – if he acts in time.

were bought in reliance on a false statement about them by the shopkeeper.

When time is important

Purchases should be examined thoroughly as soon as they have been taken home, for the buyer's right to reject defective goods does not last for long. You must do so within a 'reasonable time'.

What is a reasonable time cannot be laid down in advance. It depends on all the circumstances, including type and quantity of the goods. It is usually based on the time a reasonable buyer would take to examine them to find out if they are satisfactory or not.

Once the goods are found defective, they should not be used. Using goods may imply acceptance and may lose the buyer his right to reject them. Moreover it might lead to dispute over whether the goods were really defective when they were sold or whether they have been damaged by the buyer.

Your right to a cash refund

Anyone entitled to have his money refunded has the right to insist on cash. A credit note can be spent only in the same shop, and once it is accepted the buyer may have lost his right to exchange it for cash.

Goods must be returnable

It is not possible to reject goods if they have been used up. If food has

483

been eaten and it is found defective only when it makes you ill, you cannot legally reject it. There is no longer anything to reject. You do, however, have the right to claim damages to compensate for any loss suffered.

If the goods were completely worthless, the damages will amount to the same thing as getting your money back. If the defective goods caused illness or damage, the damages could be more than the purchase price.

Even if the goods were not worthless and did not cause injury or damage, the buyer would be entitled to the difference between what he had paid and what they were worth.

To claim in all of these circumstances however, might involve you having to take legal action. As a first step, without incurring costs, consult your local trading standards office.

MORTGAGE

The loan that enables a purchaser to buy a home

Most people who want to buy a house or flat need to borrow most of the purchase price by way of a mortgage loan. The loan is made against the security of the property being bought: the deeds are held by the lender until the money has been repaid.

The size of a mortgage depends on the financial standing of the borrower and the sort of home you want to buy.

Most mortgages are obtained from building societies, but you can also get a loan from a life-insurance company, local authority or bank.

You repay the loan, and interest on it, over an agreed period of time – generally 20 or 25 years.

It is sometimes difficult, especially for a first-time home buyer, to get a mortgage, but it may be easier if the home buyer has had money invested with a building society at least 6 months or a year before the mortgage is needed.

Getting advice on a mortgage

Delays in buying a house usually arise from difficulties in arranging a mortgage. If you intend buying a property, seek advice as soon as possible.

If you are an investor, before you start looking at properties to buy, con-

If you do not save with a building society and want a mortgage, you can get advice from several sources.

Estate agent
Many estate agents are also agents for building societies or insurance companies and will advise you which society or company is likely to give you a loan, and how much you are likely to receive. As the agent only receives commission when a property is sold, it is in his interest to see that you get a mortgage. There is no fee for asking an agent's advice. *See:* ESTATE AGENT

Solicitor
A solicitor can give similar information on the availability of finance from the usual sources. He may also be aware of private lenders.

A home buyer should be frank about his financial status when consulting a solicitor. Overstating your income will only delay a mortgage being arranged, because if the figures do not tally when your application is checked – for example, when a building society consults your employer – the application will be referred back to you – or even be rejected.

Mortgage broker
A mortgage broker should know the companies that lend money and the particular properties and type of borrower they favour. He relies on commissions from lenders, and is not entitled to charge you a fee of more than £1 if he does not arrange a loan.

A person does not need formal qualifications to set up in business as a mortgage broker. But all brokers must hold a licence issued by the Office of Fair Trading under the Consumer Credit Act.

tact the manager of your building society branch and find out what is the maximum loan you can expect.

Where to get the money

Different sources of mortgage give loans on different types of property. Interest rates may also differ.

Building society Generally, a building society lends about $2\frac{1}{2}$ times a man's annual income, plus half the wife's annual income, if she is working. A single woman who is working must be treated in the same way as a single man.

The loan may be limited in any case – usually to about £20,000. *See:* SEX DISCRIMINATION

A borrower is expected to be able to raise part of the house price himself – normally from 10 to 30 per cent of the value assessed by the society. That may be less than the price that the owner is asking – so even if you are willing to pay £25,000, for example, you may be lent only a percentage of the assessed value, which might be £20,000.

You may be able to arrange a mortgage of 95 per cent or 100 per cent of the value, if the circumstances are right – for example, if the property is valued at no more than £14,000 and you can show you are able to meet higher monthly repayments of a loan, without undue strain on your budget.

Societies tend not to lend such high

percentage sums on properties that are 50 or more years old.

Local authority A council will sometimes lend as much as 100 per cent of its valuation of a property in its area. The valuation, like that of a building society, may be lower than the selling price of the property. But council mortgages may not always be available. Authorities are given a yearly allocation of money by the Government for mortgages, and demand may exceed supply.

A local authority is more likely to be willing to offer a mortgage on older properties where a building society may not.

A local authority mortgage usually runs over a longer period than a building society loan – often as long as 30 years – but the interest rate may be slightly higher. To apply for a local authority mortgage, write to the treasurer's department at the council offices.

Life-insurance company Anyone who has an endowment assurance policy may be able to arrange a mortgage with his insurance company – paying regular interest and relying on the policy when it matures to repay the capital sum. If an existing policy is not large enough to cover a mortgage, an additional policy can be bought. You may also be able to get a mortgage if you do not have a policy but agree to take one out.

The interest rate for an insurance-linked mortgage is usually slightly higher than for a building society loan, but the company may lend money on higher-priced or older properties, when a building society will not.

Bank Bank mortgages to established customers usually run for 20 years, at a rate of interest lower than a building society's.

A bank may be willing to go beyond the £20,000 mortgage ceiling usually imposed by building societies. It may also agree to help a well-established customer who can raise, say, 80 per cent of the price of a house and wishes to borrow the remaining 20 per cent over a short period – for example, 3 years.

If a customer has an overdraft on his current account, the bank is entitled to hold the deeds of the property even after the loan has been repaid.

A bank may also make a short-term loan to a customer who is selling his home and buying another – and who needs the money for the purchase before he receives the sale money. *See:* BANK LOAN; BRIDGING LOAN

Staff mortgage Some employers arrange private mortgages for certain staff. In the case of banks and insurance companies especially, they are likely to be at a very low rate of interest. If the employee leaves the job, he normally

ADVANTAGES AND DISADVANTAGES TO CONSIDER WHEN CHOOSING A MORTGAGE
Working out what the difference between capital-repayment and endowment loans means to you

The simplest and most common mortgage is the capital-repayment mortgage, where a borrower pays part of the loan and the interest on it at regular monthly intervals over a period of, usually, 20 or 25 years. The payment is known as the subscription and the loan as the principal.

Interest is calculated on the balance of the debt outstanding at the beginning of a building society's financial year. For example, if you originally borrowed £10,000 and at a particular time have paid off £2,000, you will then be paying interest on the remaining £8,000 and not the full £10,000.

At the start of the mortgage, the interest accounts for the majority of the monthly payment and the actual loan is hardly reduced.

For example, if a loan of £16,000 was arranged at 11.75 per cent over 25 years, the first year's payment would be:

Year's total repayments:	£167.20×12	£2,006.40
Interest due on £16,000 loan at 11.75 per cent	$\frac{£16,000×11.75}{100}$	£1,880
Balance of loan paid off		£126.40

In spite of paying £2,006.40 during the year, the debt has been reduced by only £126.40.

In the second year, the payment would be:

Year's total repayments:	£167.20×12	£2,006.40
Interest due on loan of £15,873.60 (£16,000 *minus* £126.40) at 11.75 per cent	$\frac{£15,873.60×11.75}{100}$	£1,865.15
Balance paid off loan		£141.25

If the householder decides to sell after 5 years and pay off his £16,000 mortgage, he will have paid £10,032 to the lender (5×£2,006.40). Nearly all of that will have been interest: the loan outstanding will be £15,200.98.

The repayment mortgage is often the cheapest – but not necessarily the most advantageous when the tax concessions and profits of the other types of mortgage are taken into account. On a first home, the borrower is entitled to tax relief on the interest on his repayment mortgage, but the tax relief declines as the interest is paid off. There is no tax relief on capital repayments.

A householder with a capital-repayment mortgage has to take out a separate mortgage-protection policy to ensure that his dependants are not left to pay off a mortgage should he die.

When the capital is paid off by insurance

In an endowment mortgage, the capital sum is not repaid until the end of the purchase period – or until the property is sold at some earlier time. Instead, the capital is paid off through an endowment INSURANCE POLICY: the house buyer pays the premiums and the monthly interest on the loan.

An endowment mortgage can be arranged with a building society and an agreed insurance company, or can be arranged direct with an insurance company only.

In either case the size of the monthly premium is fixed when the policy is taken out and does not change thereafter. It is calculated on the size of the loan and the borrower's age, occupation and state of health.

The amount of interest payable varies only if the mortgage rate changes. It is based on the full amount of the loan, for the full period of the contract and not – as with a capital-repayment mortgage – on a gradually decreasing loan.

At the end of the term, the insurance company hands over the sum to the building society – or, if it lent the money, to itself.

The advantages of an endowment mortgage are that there is substantial tax relief available on interest and premium payments. Relief on premiums is received by deducting it from your premium payments and not by a deduction in the income tax that you pay. If the borrower dies before the mortgage term ends, the insurance pays off the whole mortgage debt automatically.

Interest charged by the lenders may be higher for an endowment mortgage, because none of the loan is being repaid until the end of the loan period.

A borrower should not take out an endowment mortgage if he intends to move house within 5 years. With a capital-repayment mortgage he can sell his home and pay off the loan and, provided that the property has not lost value, he may have a substantial sum left over to put down on a new property.

The borrower with an endowment policy can sell his home and pay off the loan, but since the loan is the same as when he took out the mortgage, he will have no extra money in his pocket to use as a deposit, apart from any profit he has made on the sale.

'*With profits*' By paying higher premiums, you can take out a 'with profits' endowment policy which will essentially be worth much more than an ordinary policy giving similar insurance cover.

The home buyer's loan is paid off in the same way when the policy matures, but he receives any profits from his invested money as well. If he dies before the policy matures, his wife or family receive any profits accrued.

ARRANGING A SECOND MORTGAGE

After a few years, because of inflation, it is likely that your home will be worth more than you paid for it. That increase in value can often be the basis of a further loan, or 'second mortgage' – if, for example, you want to make improvements or raise capital to start a business. You can arrange a second mortgage with your building society, at the same rate of interest that you pay for your first mortgage.

For example, if you borrowed £5,000 for a £7,000 house 10 years ago and the house is now worth £15,000, £11,000 of the present value may be available as security for a second loan. That is because you have probably paid off around £1,000 of the original loan, leaving a debt of £4,000 to set against the £15,000 new value.

Once you have been given the second loan, the building society will either increase your monthly payments or extend the period of the first mortgage.

If you want to sell your home while you have a loan, you must give the lender notice of the length stated in the deed. Otherwise you will be charged interest for a similar period as part of the redemption money.

To apply for a second mortgage, contact the manager at your building society branch. If the loan is for home improvements, he will be able to advise you on whether you qualify for a local authority grant instead.

Getting an outside loan

A borrower may alternatively obtain a second mortgage from a finance company instead of a building society. In that case you can expect to pay high interest on the loan – in some cases as high as 25 per cent.

If a borrower defaults on payment to a second lender, he can foreclose the mortgage and sell the house – but only if he first pays off the debt to the main lender. If the proceeds of a sale do not cover both debts, the second lender has to sue for debt, or if necessary start proceedings to make the borrower bankrupt.

Before signing a loan agreement with a finance company, ask a solicitor or Citizens Advice Bureau to check it.

home with an option mortgage is available at most building society offices.

A borrower can change from an option mortgage to an ordinary one with tax relief, provided that the option mortgage has been running for at least 4 years.

It is more difficult to change from ordinary to option mortgage. A lender may agree to change to an option mortgage if the borrower's income is substantially reduced – if, for example, he loses his job or retires or has a serious accident or illness.

It is for the lender to decide whether to make the change: his decision is final. Anyone who wants to make a change, must write to the lender within 12 months of the change of circumstances, asking to change to an option mortgage.

You may also change to an option mortgage if you have an ordinary mortgage for a second home – for example, a holiday home – and it later becomes your only home.

Applying for a mortgage

When you apply for a mortgage you have to fill in an application form, which includes questions on your age, family, occupation, income and nationality, and authorises a request for references from your bank and employer. If you are self-employed, the lender will require an accountant's certificate of your earnings, or figures approved by the Inland Revenue.

You will have to pay a survey fee for

---

has to negotiate a new mortgage with another lender.

Private mortgage A house buyer who has an interest in a private trust may find that the trustees will agree to help with a mortgage. However, the trustees will not usually lend more than two-thirds of the value of a property.

Benefiting from the option mortgage scheme

Anyone on a low income, who does not pay enough tax to obtain full advantage from the tax relief on his mortgage repayments, can join the government-sponsored Option Mortgage Scheme.

Instead of claiming tax relief on his mortgage interest, the borrower receives an annual subsidy from the Government which reduces the interest itself.

To qualify for the scheme, the amount of the mortgage must not exceed £25,000. Joint borrowers are also entitled to join the scheme provided that:

● The mortgage does not exceed £25,000.

● Neither of the joint borrowers owns any other property.

● The borrower will be using the option-mortgaged property as his only home.

The subsidy is paid by the Government to the building society or local authority, which in turn reduces the borrower's debt. As the interest rate is less than that of a normal mortgage, the borrower is paying off more of the actual loan at the start of the mortgage than he would with a normal mortgage.

In January 1979, for example, the subsidy was 3.9 per cent less for a capital-repayment mortgage and 3.85 per cent less for an endowment mortgage. Under the scheme, the interest rate of 11.75 per cent for a repayment mortgage became 7.85 per cent, and the rate of 12 per cent for an endowment mortgage became 8.15 per cent.

Before deciding on an option mortgage you should consider whether your financial circumstances may change.

For example, if the size of your family increases, your taxable income may be reduced and an option mortgage will be of more benefit. If your taxable income increases because you are promoted in your job, the option scheme may be of less benefit.

A free booklet entitled *Buying a*

THE WISDOM OF SAVING

First-time buyers may find it easier to raise a mortgage if they have been saving with the building society for, say, 6 months.

the valuation of the property you want to buy, and the lender's legal fees for drawing up the mortgage deed.

The fees are the same for most building societies and are set out in tables in each society's leaflet. Local authority fees are similar.

The fee for the survey of your property is calculated on its value. For example, the survey fee for a building valued at £14,000 will be £31.32. The survey fee for high-value properties – over £35,000, say – is negotiated between the lender and the valuers.

A valuer's report is confidential, the building society does not legally have to show it to you and will not normally do so. If you are buying a house or flat, arrange for a private survey to be made for you by a chartered surveyor.

The report from the valuers will help the lender to decide how big a mortgage can be given on the property and what work you may be required to do before the whole loan is given to you. In some areas, the valuation is substantially less than the asking price for the property.

HOW TAX RELIEF AFFECTS THE COST OF A MORTGAGE

If you borrow money to buy a house that is your main home, and not used for business, you are entitled to basic-rate tax relief on the mortgage interest payments.

Relief is limited to a loan ceiling of £25,000. Interest on any more than that does not qualify.

If repayment is secured by a life-insurance policy, you also gain relief on the premiums paid, at half the basic rate of income tax.
Example: A couple buy a house with a mortgage of £20,000, which is secured by an endowment life-insurance policy. At an interest rate of 10 per cent they owe £2,000 a year, plus an annual insurance premium of, say, £500.

But their saving in income tax – assuming a basic tax rate of 30 per cent – is:

30 per cent of £2,000 interest	£600
plus 15 per cent of £500 premium	£75
Total	£675

So their net outlay is not £2,500 a year, but only £1,825. In the early years, a mortgage linked to life insurance is more expensive than a capital-repayment mortgage. When tax relief is taken into account, however, a capital-repayment mortgage costs more each year. The total cost of each, by the end of the loan term, works out about the same.

That is because what you have to pay in the early years of a capital-repayment mortgage consists mainly of interest. Not much of the capital sum is repaid. Since tax relief is given only on interest, relief is high at that stage.

Gradually, however, as the capital sum you owe is reduced, less of your annual payment is interest, and more of it goes to pay off the loan. So a smaller part qualifies for tax relief.

With an endowment mortgage there is no capital repayment until the loan period ends. So the interest payments – and therefore the amount of tax relief – remain constant.

The automatic discount on the insurance premiums, at half the basic tax rate, is also constant. So your entitlement to tax relief remains high throughout the period of the loan.
Example: A couple have a choice of two mortgage offers – both of £20,000 for 20 years, at 10 per cent interest. One is for capital repayment, the other is linked with endowment insurance.

Assuming that the interest rate does not change, they would be due to pay off the capital-repayment loan at about £2,350 a year. Each year the interest part of that sum reduces, and the capital part increases.

If they take the insurance-linked offer, however, they would pay a fixed annual interest charge of £2,000, plus a fixed insurance premium of, say, £500 a year.

When tax relief is applied – assuming a basic tax rate of 30 per cent – they save less at first by taking the insurance-linked offer. But as the interest reduces on the capital repayment loan, so does the tax benefit.

By the 7th year, the net cost of each type of mortgage is about the same – and from then on, capital repayment becomes more and more expensive.

If you do not expect to stay in the house you are buying for more than, say, 10 years, choose a capital-repayment mortgage. But if you plan to keep the house longer, an insurance-linked mortgage will bring you more tax benefit.

COMPARING TAX RELIEF ON TWO TYPES OF MORTGAGE

EVERY YEAR		YEAR 1		YEAR 7		YEAR 15	
Endowment		**Capital repayment**		**Capital repayment**		**Capital repayment**	
Interest	£2,000	Interest	£2,000	Interest	£1,750	Interest	£1,000
Premium	£500	Capital	£350	Capital	£600	Capital	£1,350
Total gross cost	£2,500	Total gross cost	£2,350	Total gross cost	£2,350	Total gross cost	£2,350
Relief on interest (30% of £2,000)	£600	Relief on interest (30% of £2,000)	£600	Relief on interest (30% of £1,750)	£525	Relief on interest (30% of £1,000)	£300
Relief on premium (15% of £500)	£75						
Total relief	£675						
Net cost	£1,825	Net cost	£1,750	Net cost	£1,825	Net cost	£2,050

BORROWING MORE THAN THE MORTGAGE OFFER

Most building societies will give a mortgage for only 70 per cent of its valuation of a property, leaving the buyer to find the remainder of the purchase price.

A borrower may, however, be able to borrow 90 or 95 per cent of the price by taking out an insurance guarantee policy to cover the additional sum.

The borrower pays a single premium to the insurance company, which covers the lender against any loss that might be sustained as a result of the additional loan.

For example, if a property is valued at £10,000, the borrower may receive an 80 per cent mortgage – £8,000. He may be able to obtain an additional loan of 15 per cent – an extra £1,500. The premium to insure that extra loan would be £56.25.

If the lender decides you are a suitable borrower, you will receive an 'offer of advance', usually on a standard form, giving details of the size of the offer, the rate of interest on the loan and the right to vary the rate of interest at any time and the period of the loan. It also gives the name of the lender's solicitors and any restrictions on the offer – for example, whether you are allowed to sub-let the property.

Accepting an offer

If you agree to the terms, you sign the acceptance form and return it to the lender. But if there are restrictions that you do not agree with, contact the lender's solicitors to see if the detail can be changed before you sign the form. If you are buying a home that is still being built, your solicitor, in consultation with the lender's representative, can make sure that the money is made available at various stages of the work.

If you do not sign the acceptance form within 3 months, the offer lapses.

If you do not wish to accept an offer, it is advisable always to write informing the lender. There is no reason to assume that the lender will not deal with you again because you have turned down his offer. If you simply ignore the offer of advance and allow it to expire without contacting the lender, you may find that it is unlikely the lender will grant you another offer for some time.

After you have accepted the offer, the lender's solicitor will check the ownership of the property and draw up the mortgage deed – the legal document recording the transaction and setting out the size and terms of the loan made in the offer of advance.

Fees for the solicitor's work on the deed depend on the size of the loan advanced. Building societies have a scale of recommended charges, but solicitors are not bound to follow it. A typical fee on a loan of £10,000, however, is about £45.

You can generally choose to make the monthly payments on the loan and the interest charged, either directly to the lender, by standing order from a bank or through the NATIONAL GIRO-BANK system.

Insuring a capital-repayment mortgage

When a borrower arranges an endowment mortgage, it is linked to a life-insurance policy and gives him the security of knowing that, if he dies, the policy will immediately pay off his mortgage debt.

But if you arrange a capital-repayment mortgage you have no such protection unless you specifically arrange a mortgage-protection policy.

A single premium can be paid when the policy is taken out, or premiums can be paid over a period of years. In either case, tax relief reduces the premium bill.

If the insurer dies, the policy produces the lump sum that is needed exactly to pay off the loan so that the deeds of the property, clear of debt, can be handed over to a wife or dependant.

If a borrower sells his home and pays off his mortgage to buy another, the policy could be kept up to protect the second mortgage. A further policy may well be needed, however, if the amount borrowed on the repayment period is different.

If the period of the mortgage is extended because the interest rate rises, you may also have the policy extended.

When your mortgage is paid off at the end of its term, the insurance company's obligation on a mortgage-protection policy normally ends. It does not have anything to pay out either to you or to the lender.

You can, however, take out a mortgage-protection policy with 'survival benefit' by paying a higher premium. A cash sum is paid to you at the end of the policy term, in the same way as any endowment policy.

What happens after a death or marriage breakdown

If a person dies and leaves a mortgaged freehold property in his will as a gift, the recipient of the gift has to take on the mortgage payments if he does not want to sell it.

When the property is leasehold, the mortgage is repaid out of the remaining estate, unless the will directs otherwise or unless there is not enough money to do so. In these cases, the house must be sold.

Marriage breakdown If a marriage breaks down, the mortgage payments still have to be met. To protect her interest in the house, and to ensure that the building society does not try to end the mortgage and take over the property, a deserted wife should write to the lender immediately, explaining what has happened. She should also try to obtain a MAINTENANCE order from a court, and tell the building society that she is doing so.

If the lender is a local council, its housing office may find a wife alternative accommodation.

Insuring a mortgaged home

Building societies insist that your mortgaged home is covered by insurance against fire and other risks – for example, flood or storm. A society usually states, in its mortgage offer, how much insurance must be taken out. In most cases the society takes charge of the insurance premium payments, by paying the insurance company and charging the borrower, either direct or through his account.

The policy usually covers the full reinstatement value of the property, which will alter as building costs rise. Some building societies automatically increase the insurance cover to keep up with building costs.

If your building society does not do so, check with it – say – once a year, to make sure that your cover is up to date.

How changing interest rates may affect you

Interest you pay on your mortgage can be affected by the national economic climate. When the minimum lending rate changes and banks start to pay a higher or lower rate of interest to depositors, the building societies usually change interest rates to investors to attract or keep investments. That change in interest is passed on to those who are borrowing from the society. Rates for local authorities, banks and insurance companies also rise or fall with the national trend.

A rise of as little as 1 per cent in the interest rate can have a substantial effect on a borrower with a capital-repayment mortgage. If he had a loan of £12,000, repayable over 20 years at 11 per cent interest, he would have to pay £125.64 a month. But if the rate went up to 12 per cent, his monthly payment would rise to £133.92 – an increase of £8.28 a month.

The difference over 20 years would be nearly £2,000.

When interest rates rise, a borrower may be able to choose either to pay more each month or to have the length of his mortgage agreement extended and pay at the old rate of interest.

If you have an endowment mortgage, however, you do not have that choice. You must keep to the agreed purchase period and pay higher interest instalments. That is because if you continued

to pay at the previous, lower rate, the additional interest would mount up, the debt would increase and the endowment policy would no longer cover the total debt. An increased interest rate does not alter the insurance premiums.

An insurance company that provides a mortgage as well as the insurance policy may alter its interest rate to keep in step with any change in building society rates, unless the mortgage is at a fixed rate.

In rare cases – usually staff mortgages from banks or insurance companies – the mortgage deed may state that the loan has a fixed rate of interest.

When mortgage payments cannot be met

Anyone who cannot meet his monthly mortgage payments because of a sudden drop in income – for example, through illness, accident or losing a job – should immediately inform the lender in writing.

If the loan is a capital-repayment mortgage, a building society or local authority may allow him to make 'interest only' payments for a short period and suspend payments from the capital loan. The borrower can make up any arrears later on, by paying increased instalments.

An insurance company may also agree to waive premium payments for a time, leaving the borrower to pay only the interest on a loan.

If there is no prospect that the borrower's income will increase, a building society and other lenders may agree to change his mortgage to an option mortgage.

Apart from informing the lender of a drop in income, the borrower should also contact his local social security office. He may be entitled to claim SUPPLEMENTARY BENEFIT to help with the mortgage.

If he is entitled to claim he can receive an allowance for interest payments although not for capital payments. However, as the greater part of the monthly payment at the beginning of a mortgage consists of interest, the allowance can be substantial.

Foreclosing a mortgage

If a borrower continually fails to pay, and if all alternative forms of payment

have failed to solve the problem, the lender can foreclose on the mortgage – cancel it and sell the property. The borrower will receive any surplus left from the sale, after outstanding capital and interest, and the society's expenses in selling the house, have been paid.

If a defaulting borrower refuses to leave after a foreclosure, the lender can obtain possession by a court order.

How the law protects a borrower

Anyone who advertises mortgage facilities must comply with the advertising regulations of the Consumer Credit Act 1974.

For example, it is a criminal offence to publish an advertisement that gives a false and misleading impression of mortgage facilities available, of their true cost or of the true rate of interest. Building societies must, by law, advertise their current rates of interest in their branches.

The maximum penalty for a first offence under the regulations is a fine of £400 in a magistrates' court.

Loans of any size by building societies, local authorities or insurance companies for house improvement or house purchase are exempt from the CONSUMER CREDIT Act.

But loans of less than £5,000 for other purposes from local authorities or insurance companies are subject to the Act. Loans under £5,000 from other sources – for example, a bank or finance company – including those for home improvements or home purchases, are also subject to the Consumer Credit Act.

If a loan comes under the Act, a prospective borrower has a breathing space before agreeing to the terms.

He must first be given a copy of the agreement that he will be asked to sign. He must then be allowed 7 days in which to consider it, after which he can be sent a copy of the formal contract. He then has a further 7 days to consider the terms. At the end of the 7 days, the prospective borrower can be asked to sign and return the formal contract if he wants the loan.

The borrower can pull out at any time before signing. After signing, he is bound to the terms of the contract.

However, if the lender communicates, unasked, with the prospective borrower during the legal breathing

---

WHEN HOUSE VALUES RISE

Borrowers who have a mortgage may be able to obtain a further loan to pay for home improvements or business development.

'I'd like a second mortgage to pay off my first'

space, any loan agreement signed has no legal force.

If the lender does not follow the correct procedure and you refuse to repay the loan, he cannot sue you for the money, or repossess or sell your house or land, without a court order. The court is unlikely to make an order unless the lender can prove there was a genuine, reasonable and honest mistake that caused the breach in procedure. *See:* CONSUMER CREDIT; CONSUMER PROTECTION; CREDIT AGREEMENT

Selling a mortgaged home

A mortgage on your home does not prevent you from selling it. You are legally entitled to pay off the debt whenever you wish. The sale of the property and the redemption of the mortgage are completed at the same time, so that the money from your purchaser can be used, in part, to pay off your mortgage.

Some lenders make a charge if a borrower redeems his mortgage within 5 years of raising it. The fee can be 3 months' interest on the loan remaining at the time of the sale.

You are also entitled to pay off your mortgage more quickly by increasing your payments. But the building society or other lender will want to be sure you can afford the increased payments before agreeing to that.

MOT TEST

Car safety – by order

On their third birthday – 3 years after first registration – vehicles become due for the statutory annual vehicle test, commonly known as the MOT test.

The test covers lighting equipment, steering, including suspension, brakes, tyres and roadwheels, seat belts and general items such as windscreen wipers, washers, exhaust system and horn. The condition of the vehicle structure is examined for any fractures, damage or corrosion which could affect the correct functioning of the braking system or the steering gear.

Tests are conducted by authorised examiners at approved testing stations displaying the triple triangle sign.

If the car passes the test, the examiner signs and issues a test certificate. If the car fails, he issues a notification of refusal, specifying the defects. In all cases, the examiner issues a list showing what has been checked and its condition.

The 1981 fee for a vehicle test is £6.70 for cars or £4 for motor cycles. If the car is left at the testing station to be repaired, only one fee is payable. If it is removed, but within fourteen days taken to the same or another testing station for repair and re-testing, only half the normal fee is payable.

A car can be tested up to 1 month before its current test certificate is due for renewal. The new certificate will run from the expiry date of the old.

Generally, it is illegal to use or permit to be used on a public road any 3-year-old vehicle without a current test certificate. The maximum penalty is a fine up to £100, but without risk of endorsement or disqualification. A police constable can require production of a test certificate on demand or within 5 days at a nominated police station.

It is a defence to a charge of not having an MOT certificate that the driver had made an appointment with a testing station and was in fact on his way directly there at the time he was stopped. If, however, the vehicle is actually defective, the driver can be prosecuted.

A road vehicle licence will not be issued without production of a current test certificate.

Failure to have a current MOT certificate could affect an insured's claim.

MOTABILITY

A government-backed scheme to provide cars for the disabled

Disabled people can exchange their weekly MOBILITY ALLOWANCE for a car, leased to them through Motability, an independent scheme that operates with government support.

The scheme covers all recipients of mobility allowance whether they can drive or not and includes the parents of disabled children.

How to apply Ask for leaflets at your local social security office, or from Motability in London.

If you have an invalid carriage Disabled people still using the government-supplied single-seater invalid carriages can switch to the Motability scheme.

MOTOR CYCLE

A rider must be sure his machine is not dangerous

The rider of a motor cycle is responsible for the safety of his machine when it is on the road. He must see that the tyres are in good condition and that the brakes and lights are in proper working order.

Tyres For motor cycles of 50 cc or less there is no minimum depth of tread, as there is for car tyres, but the tread must be visible for at least three-quarters of the breadth of the tyre around the circumference. Over 50 cc the minimum depth is the same as for car tyres. All motor-cycle tyres are cross-ply.

Brakes There must be two independently operated brakes, one for each wheel or one braking system with two means of operation. No parking brake is required.

Noise The maximum noise level for motor cycles over 125 cc is 90 decibels, and for those under 125 cc it is 80 decibels – compared with 87 decibels for cars. It is an offence to alter a motorcycle's silencer to increase the noise.

Lights Motor cycles without a sidecar need only one front white light, one red rear light and one red reflector. No parking light is needed, but a stop light is compulsory.

Traffic indicators are not compulsory, but if they are fitted they must comply with the same rules as those for cars.

Mirror At least one rear-view mirror is compulsory on machines first used after October 1, 1978.

Speedometer Only motor cycles of more than 100 cc are required to have a speedometer in working order. It must be accurate to within 10 per cent.

Passengers It is an offence for the rider of a motor cycle without a sidecar to carry more than one passenger. The passenger must sit astride a fixed pillion seat, and the cycle must have suitable footrests.

A learner rider of a solo motor cycle cannot carry a passenger unless that passenger holds a current, valid, full licence to ride a motor cycle.

Crash helmets Both the motor cyclist and his pillion rider must wear a CRASH HELMET.

Trailer Solo motor cycles must not be

PENALTIES FOR MOTOR-CYCLING OFFENCES
The charges that affect only motor cyclists and their pillion passengers

	Offence	Maximum penalty	Average penalty imposed by magistrates for first offence
Brakes	Riding or permitting use with defective brakes	£100 and endorsement	£25 and endorsement
Helmet	Riding with no helmet – even as a pillion passenger	£50	£10
Lights	Riding or permitting use with defective lights	£100	£15 parked £20 moving
Mirror	Riding or permitting use of cycle first used after Oct 1, 1978 without rear-view mirror	£100	£10
Noise	Adapting silencer to increase noise level	£100	£10
Passenger	Carrying a pillion passenger without footrests	£100	£15
	Carrying an unqualified pillion passenger when only a provisional-licence holder	£100 and endorsement	£15 and endorsement
Speedometer	Riding or permitting use of motor cycle with no, or defective, speedometer	£100	£10
Trailer	Towing a trailer by solo motor cycle	£100	£20
Tyres	Riding or permitting use with defective tyre	£100 and endorsement	£25 and endorsement for each tyre

used to draw a trailer – except to tow another motor cycle that has broken down.

MOTOR-CYCLE INSURANCE

How the law treats a two-wheeled driver

The use of a motor cycle on a public road is governed by the same insurance laws as apply to a motor car. Whenever it is on the road, the owner must ensure that it is insured at least against the risk of injury to other people, including a pillion passenger.

Type of cover

Four types of cover are available:
● Road Traffic Act – the minimum legal requirement but rarely offered by insurers.
● Third party only – including the risk of damaging other people's property.
● Third party, fire and theft – including loss of, or damage to, the motor cycle by fire or theft.
● Comprehensive – including accidental damage to the motor cycle and the costs of removal to a repairer and re-delivery after repairs.

Compared with the normal motor-car policy, there are several items not normally covered by a motor-cycle policy:
● Personal accident benefits to yourself if you are injured.
● Medical expenses of you or your passenger.
● Loss of, or damage to, personal possessions.

● Claims against your passenger for injury or damage caused by him.
● Legal costs incurred on a charge of manslaughter or causing death by reckless driving.
● Theft of accessories unless stolen with the motor cycle.

Driving other motor cycles

Most policies allow the policyholder to drive other motor cycles that do not belong to him provided he has the owner's permission. The cover is usually for third party risks only – even if your policy is comprehensive.

Your policy will usually allow your motor cycle to be driven only by yourself. Other named drivers may be included but only on payment of an extra premium.

Policies for mopeds usually allow driving by anyone with a valid licence.

The proposal form

The rules for completing a proposal form are the same as in MOTOR INSURANCE, and the questions asked are very similar. There are, however, generally fewer questions – particularly for small machines like mopeds where a proposal may be dispensed with altogether.

The premium

The premium is normally determined by the type of machine, where it is kept, and the age and experience of the driver.

If more than one driver is to be included on the policy the premium is determined by the youngest.

Apart from higher premiums, the young and/or inexperienced driver may have to be responsible for a larger amount of damage to the cycle – the policy excess – if comprehensive cover is arranged.

As with car insurance, an accident and conviction record may result in higher premiums and/or restrictions in policy cover.

MOTOR INSURANCE

Compulsory and voluntary cover for drivers and vehicles

Whenever a motor vehicle is on a public road – whether it is driven, towed, pushed or parked – the owner and the person in charge of it must be insured against the risk of injury to other people.

The law requires every vehicle owner to buy at least that much insurance before the vehicle goes on the road. It holds him responsible for seeing that anyone else who drives it with his permission is also covered.

Any owner with a valid driving licence should be able to obtain the legal minimum cover from a motor insurance company.

Insurers are not bound to provide cover but do not normally refuse. They are entitled, however, to charge more from someone they regard as a high risk, and to impose their own limits on who else can drive a vehicle.

Voluntary cover

Most vehicle owners can buy wider insurance cover on a voluntary basis. What it includes depends on an insurance company's willingness to accept the risk, and the owner's willingness to pay the premium asked.

Charges to cover the same risk will vary between companies, and one company's charges may vary according to its view of the owner's experience and reliability.

Four types of insurance policy are usually available for a private car:
● Road Traffic Act – the minimum laid down by law.
● Third party only.
● Third party, fire and theft.
● Comprehensive – the widest cover under a standard policy.

When you arrange insurance, make sure that you know exactly what is included in a policy.

If a policy document is not available, or its wording is confusing, ask for a leaflet or brochure that summarises the risks covered, and states the main limits or exclusions.

Choosing a policy

If a motorist or his car are considered an unreasonably high risk, an insurance company is entitled to refuse to give him full insurance.

In other cases a driver may be required to take out comprehensive insurance by the person from whom he borrows or hires a car.

Otherwise it is up to a motorist to decide what insurance, beyond the legal minimum, he needs and can afford.

Road Traffic Act only

A policy limited to the requirements of the Road Traffic Act 1972 covers you only for personal injury caused to someone else by your vehicle. Such a policy includes cover for claims by any passengers in your car and it provides payment for emergency hospital charges. Costs incurred with the insurer's consent in dealing with any claim covered by the policy are also included.

A Road Traffic Act only policy does not cover injury to yourself, or damage to other people's property or your own.

For that reason, a motorist should never settle just for Road Traffic Act insurance if he can obtain more extensive cover.

Third party only

A third party policy includes the protection provided by a Road Traffic Act policy, and covers liability for damage to someone else's vehicle or other property. It also provides cover for any legal costs that may be incurred in defending yourself or another permitted driver against a claim for damages after an accident.

The cover includes the costs of any appeal, and the sum insured for that purpose is unlimited.

It is for the insurance company, however, to decide how far an appeal may be taken when it is paying your legal expenses.

A third party policy also covers a motorist for the cost of being legally represented at an inquest, if someone dies in an accident in which he is involved.

If the motorist is subsequently charged with manslaughter or causing death by reckless driving, the policy normally covers his defence costs up to £1,000.

A third party only policyholder is usually insured for driving other cars or motor cycles that do not belong to him, provided that he has the owner's permission and is not hiring the vehicle or buying it under a hire purchase agreement. If he is covered for business use, the policy will cover use of such other vehicles on business.

That extra cover may not be available to a driver under the age of 25, or if he already owns an exceptionally high-powered vehicle. The policy states any such limitations.

Third party, fire and theft

If you take out a third party, fire and theft policy you have third party cover plus insurance against the theft of your own vehicle, any damage to it caused by a thief, and any loss or damage caused by fire.

Damage when someone steals or attempts to steal something in your car – for example, a radio – is covered. Damage to your car in a collision is not, unless it has been stolen.

The amount that insurers will pay on a claim for fire or theft is normally limited to the sale value of the vehicle at the time of the loss, as shown in motor trade sales guides or newspaper advertisements offering similar vehicles.

The amount for which the car is insured is usually the maximum the insurers will pay. However, if that estimated value is lower than the 'book' price, the insurers may decide to pay more than the 'insured' value.

Some insurers charge an extra premium when the vehicle is to be kept in the open, instead of in a locked garage – especially in a big town. Alternatively, they may require you to fit an approved anti-theft device.

If a higher premium or anti-theft lock is required, you will be told so when you are given the quotation. But you should also read your policy carefully to check on anti-theft requirements.

Comprehensive

About two-thirds of all car policies issued in Britain give comprehensive insurance. It is advisable for any car that has a reasonable cash value.

In addition to third party, fire and theft cover, a comprehensive policy insures against collision damage to your own car and various other risks.

It does not matter if the damage to your car is your own fault – or even if you break the law – provided that you are licensed to drive at the time.

Companies offer varying ranges of cover, but a good comprehensive policy would include:

Damage to your car The company pays the cost of moving your car – usually to the nearest competent repairer – the cost of repairs based on an agreed estimate, and the cost of returning the car to you.

If estimated repair costs exceed the market value of the car at the time, the claim is treated as a total loss and you are paid the market value. The damaged vehicle then becomes the property of the insurers, who can dispose of it as scrap or for spare parts.

If the car is less than 12 months old, and the cost of repair is likely to exceed 50 or 60 per cent of its list price when new, the insurers normally agree to replace it with a similar make and model.

You do not have to accept a replacement. If you do not wish to do so, or if the appropriate car is not available, the claim will be dealt with on a normal repair basis. They will pay the full repair costs even if they exceed 60 per cent of the list price.

Claims for broken windscreen or windows, without loss of no-claim discount, may be limited by the insurers to, say, £75 or £50 per claim.

● *Damage excess* When cover for damage to your vehicle is restricted under the policy, with the insurers expecting you to pay the first part of any repair costs, that payment is known as damage excess.

Compulsory damage excess of £25 or £50 is normally required if the insured driver is under 25, or has not held a full United Kingdom driving licence for 12 months.

If the driver has a bad record of accidents or motoring convictions, or his car has proved to be a high insurance risk, he too may be required to pay a damage excess of as much as £100 – or more.

The excess may be required on more than one ground – for example, if the driver is under 25 and his car is considered a high risk. In that case, the two excess figures may be added together.

Even if no excess is required by the insurers, you can volunteer, when taking out the insurance, to pay part of any damage repair costs. A voluntary excess arrangement reduces your premium – but one imposed at the company's insistence does not. The no-claim discount will be affected as if there was no excess.

● *Personal accident benefits* Insurance companies offer many variations of personal injury cover in their comprehensive policies. Some policies restrict injury cover to the policyholder only. Most, however, cover the policyholder and spouse.

Some policies give cover to anyone who is injured while in the vehicle, provided that the driver is someone allowed to drive under the policy. Cover may not always be restricted to people travelling in the insured vehicle: it may apply to any private car in which the insured persons are travelling. Some insurers will not, however, offer personal accident benefit if the policyholder is under 21 or the car is a high-powered type.

Under any personal accident policy, the injury must arise directly from normal use of the car. The cover would not, for example, apply to a child who was accidentally injured by another child while they were playing with something sharp inside the car.

If the policyholder dies because of an

THREE WAYS TO ARRANGE MOTOR INSURANCE

When you need to insure a vehicle, you have a choice of dealing:
● Direct with a company.
● Through an insurance broker.
● Through an insurance agent.

A registered broker should be able to obtain the policy best suited to your needs, at the lowest possible price. You pay no extra for his services.

Dealing direct

Most insurance companies have public offices in main towns and are prepared to take motor insurance proposals.

You may well get the quickest decision that way. But you may not get the best policy or lowest premium available – and unless you have an expert knowledge of motor insurance law, you may be at a disadvantage when it comes to making a claim that is disputed by the company or another party.

There is no reduction in premiums for dealing direct. The company simply saves the commission it would have paid to a broker or agent.

Dealing with a broker

A registered broker can deal on your behalf with most insurance companies. He can offer a wide range of policies with different types of cover, and he can obtain a range of premium quotations for the same type of cover.

A broker usually has special contacts with a few companies. That may be because they pay him a higher commission, but he is just as likely to favour them because he can deal with them more simply.

That may mean that he overlooks a cheaper premium, and so you lose money by dealing through him. But a strong connection between broker and insurer can help you if there is difficulty over a claim later. It is also a major advantage to someone whose accident record makes it hard to get full insurance.

You are entitled to ask a broker for several alternative premium quotations, or for details of any special features of policies offered by various companies. Essentially, however, you are relying on his knowledge and judgment.

At different stages of an insurance transaction a broker acts on behalf of both sides – you and the insurance company. He has a legal duty to provide proper professional services. If he fails through negligence and either side loses by it, he can be sued for damages.

If a broker thinks your proposal is acceptable to a company and you agree to the premium quotation, you normally pay the premium to him immediately. He issues a temporary cover note to show that your insurance is effective immediately – although the company can still reject your proposal – and you are entitled to put your car on the road.

Your payment is acknowledged and your insurance cover is valid even if a broker becomes insolvent before he has passed your premium on to the company. Later, if a broker becomes insolvent while he is holding money intended for you – for example, a refund or a claim settlement – you would have the right to register as a creditor. But insurance companies would normally settle directly with you.

Dealing with an agent

An insurance agent's services may be helpful if you live in a remote area where companies or brokers cannot be contacted.

An agent – typically an accountant, bank officer, solicitor or motor trader – can work in much the same way as a broker, but he does not have access to the same range of contacts and information. Nor does he usually have the same degree of authority to act for either side.

He is still obliged to exercise proper care, however, and can be sued for negligence.

accident, anyone else insured under his personal accident policy can still claim on it.

Sums insured can vary from £1,000 to £6,000 for death, total blindness or permanent disablement, with lesser amounts to compensate for specified injuries such as the loss of a limb or the sight of one eye.

If someone is temporarily disabled – confined to bed or a wheelchair – by an injury, the company may pay a lump sum to provide benefit for a limited period. A typical cover provides £20 a week for up to 26 weeks.

Some companies offer to double the rates of death or injury compensation if an accident victim is wearing an approved seat belt at the time.

An age limit of 70 or 75 is usually set on personal accident benefits.

● *Medical expenses* Cover for the medical expenses of anyone injured in an accident involving the insured car usually provides a lump-sum payment of up to £75 for each injured person. The cover includes dental fees.

Insurers may choose not to offer medical expenses cover for a high-powered car.

● *Personal possessions* Clothing and personal property carried by anyone in the insured car are covered against any loss or damage arising from normal use of the vehicle. The cover is usually limited to £50 or £100 and does not include cash or trade goods.

If you intend to carry a large quantity of property in your car – for example, when going on holiday – arrange separate cover for it. Remember to lock your car if you leave it for more than a few minutes. Payment of theft claims may depend on the circumstances.

Personal effects cover may not be offered for an open sports car, but it is normally given for a vehicle with a movable sunshine roof.

● *Additional cover* Some insurers provide additional benefits, for no extra premium:

1. Fire damage to garage, up to a specified amount – say, £500.

2. Loss of any part of the Road Fund licence fee that cannot otherwise be recovered, if the vehicle is lost or totally destroyed.

3. Additional travel or overnight accommodation costs arising from an accident. The benefit is payable for all those who were in the car.

4. Part of the cost of hiring a car if your own is stolen or is immobilised after an accident. The cover is for a limited period – usually 14 or 28 days – and may exclude the first three days after the theft or accident.

Some companies may be willing to provide wider cover for car-hire costs, but require an extra premium payment or even a separate policy.

Completing the proposal form

Legally, an insurance company does not offer to sell you a policy. You offer to buy one, and your offer is called a proposal.

A proposal does not bind either side to a contract unless it is accepted and you accept the premium charge, but the proposal form is still the most important document in an insurance transaction.

TELLING ABOUT YOUR DRIVING RECORD

The insurance proposal form asks you for details of any accident or other loss connected with the use of any vehicle, in which you have been involved in the previous 3 to 5 years, and any motoring conviction. The same questions apply to any other driver or potential driver whom you name on the form.

Even if an accident or loss was not the subject of an insurance claim – by you or anyone else – mention it on the form.

If you have been involved in an accident within the time stated on the form, you must mention it, whether or not you consider you were to blame. Even if you cannot remember precise details of an accident or other loss, be as accurate as possible.

Apart from accidents and other losses, you must also disclose:

● Any physical disability or illness that is likely to affect the driving ability of anyone named on the proposal form.

● The name of any insurer who has refused insurance, cancelled a policy or required special terms or premiums.

● Whether the car is to be used for business as well as private purposes – and the nature of that business.

If you have previously been insured as a motorist and are entitled to a no-claim discount, mention the fact on the proposal form. *See:* MOTOR INSURANCE PREMIUM

On it you agree to comply with the conditions of a policy from the time your insurance cover starts – although it may be up to 60 days before you receive the policy document.

In completing the proposal form you must also tell the company all that it needs to know in order to decide whether to insure you and, if so, what premium to charge.

The company may ask for more information after receiving your proposal and before reaching its decision. Until then you are likely to be protected by the temporary insurance described in a cover note, but if you are in any doubt, check with the broker or company before you take your car on the road.

Disclosure of facts The proposal form includes a declaration that to the best of your knowledge you have answered all questions truthfully and have not withheld any material fact – that is one

---

SPECIAL COVER FOR AN ALMOST-NEW CAR

Special insurance – called extended warranty – can be taken out to cover the cost of repairs when the manufacturer's normal warranty on a new car expires. Second-hand cars can also be covered, though not if the car is over a certain age or has done a high mileage – 5 years or 50,000 miles are typical limits.

Most extended warranty policies are arranged by the car dealer when the vehicle is bought. The policy normally covers major components such as engine, gearbox, transmission, steering, brakes and electrical equipment up to a specified limit, which decreases as the car gets older.

A typical policy would give 2 years' cover of up to £350 per breakdown, for a premium of £50–70, if the mileage reading does not exceed 31,000, reducing to £140 up to 65,000 miles. The policyholder is usually required to pay the first £10–25 of any claim himself.

An extended-warranty policy usually stipulates regular servicing according to the manufacturer's requirements. Do-it-yourself servicing is not normally permissible but, if it is allowed, invoices for oil, spark plugs and other items must be produced when you claim against your policy.

Some extended-warranty policies include part of the cost of hiring a car while the repair is being carried out.

which might influence the company's decision, such as an earlier driving disqualification.

If a motorist later makes an insurance claim, or a claim is made against him, and the company discovers that he misstated or withheld a material fact in his proposal, it may be entitled to refuse payment.

What you will be asked

When you complete your proposal form you must give all essential details about yourself, the vehicle and anyone else who is expected to use it.

Yourself Give your full name, address, age and occupation. If you have a secondary job, you must mention it – even if you are not specifically asked to do so.

Your vehicle You will be asked for precise details of the vehicle being insured – including your arrangements for garaging the car. You may be asked to estimate the yearly mileage that the vehicle will travel.

Other drivers You may wish your policy to be restricted to covering one or two other people. If so, you need give only their personal details, including driving records.

If, however, your policy is to cover any driver who takes the vehicle on the road with your permission, the matter becomes more complicated – and the premium could be higher.

You should name any person who, to your knowledge, is likely to drive the vehicle. That normally includes any member of your immediate family who holds a driving licence and lives with you. There is no need to name a representative of the motor trade – such as a garage employee taking your car on a test run. But note that your cover does not extend to others, such as car-park attendants, unless you have explicitly given permission.

If a family member is likely to become a qualified driver during the first policy period, normally 12 months, you should include details now.

It is not necessary, however, to mention a relative or friend who might possibly, on an odd occasion, drive your vehicle.

You must always tell the insurance broker or company in advance if a driver not previously named is to use the vehicle regularly. But if only a single journey is involved, and you know the

driver to be mature and experienced, with no record of accidents or convictions, there is normally no need to inform the company.

If you know that a proposed driver has a poor driving record – or if you are in doubt – do not allow him to drive your vehicle. An 'any driver' policy covers only any driver who, if you disclosed all that you knew about him, would have been covered by your insurers for

no extra cost when you took out the policy.

Getting a quotation

As soon as you have completed the proposal form – and sometimes before – the insurance company, broker or agent normally gives you a written quotation of the premium that you will be expected to pay. *See:* MOTOR INSURANCE PREMIUM

WHAT TO LOOK FOR IN MOTOR INSURANCE
How the cover offered by a 'comprehensive' policy can vary

Any comprehensive car insurance policy covers you for third-party risk, and the loss of your car or damage to it through accident, fire or theft.

Other protection and particular combinations of benefits vary according to the company and how much you are prepared to pay in premiums.

Type of cover	Often available	Sometimes available
Medical expenses – each person	£50–100	£150
Personal accident benefit	Whole family	Any passenger
Double benefit if seat belt worn	No	Yes
Right to buy a new car	In first 12 months if over 50% damage	In first 15 months
No-claim discount on premium	Up to 60%	Up to 65%
Discount 'step back' after a claim	3 years	Only 2 years
Windscreen or window replacement without affecting discount	First claim	Every claim
Fire damage to garage		£500
Personal property in car	£50	£100
Driving other vehicles	Private cars	Any car or motor cycle
Loss or damage abroad	Normal UK cover	Free bail bond, plus cover for risk of forfeiture
Loss or damage in transit abroad	Sea only	Sea and air
Legal costs to defend manslaughter charge	£1,000	Unlimited
Car hire after theft	£50	£60
Hotel or fares after accident	£5 each	£10 each
Suspension rebate – when car is off road	25%	50%
Automatic insurance cover if you change cars		14 days
Right of appeal in dispute over claims	Amount of payment	Any dispute

No car policy offers all of those benefits. An owner has to decide which is best suited to his needs and his budget. In doing so, he also has to take into account that insurance companies impose varying 'excess' figures – the amount an owner might have to pay himself before a claim is met. That applies particularly to young drivers, those with a poor driving record or inexperienced drivers of any age.

SPECIAL COVER FOR CARAVANS AND TRAILERS

All policies other than Road Traffic Act automatically give third party cover for a caravan or any other trailer only while it is attached to an insured car or if it becomes detached and causes damage or personal injury while being towed. If no other cover is required there is no need to tell the insurance company that you plan to tow a caravan or trailer.

Most owners, however, wish to insure the caravan itself and its contents against loss or damage and that calls for a separate policy and a further premium. The policy may include loss-of-use cover, including hire of a new caravan or, if it is rented out to holidaymakers, loss of hiring charges.

Comprehensive cover for smaller trailers can usually be arranged as an extension of the basic motor policy on payment of an extra premium.

That quotation does not bind you or the insurer. Once the insurer has considered the information supplied on the proposal form, he may decide that the premium should be higher. If he does so, you are entitled to reject the quotation and try a different insurer.

Normally, if you wish to have temporary cover while your application is being considered you must pay at least part of the suggested premium. If you do not you are unlikely to be given a MOTOR INSURANCE COVER NOTE, which you legally must have before you take the car on the road.

If you or the insurer subsequently withdraw from the contract, you cannot insist on having all your money returned: the insurer will charge you for the time during which you have used the temporary cover and so have been a risk to him. That charge – known as a 'time on risk' payment – is usually a percentage of the premium originally quoted. It costs very much more proportionately than a full year's cover.

Time on risk continues until the insurer, agent or broker receives the cover note back from you.

MOTOR INSURANCE CLAIM

When you have to report damage or injury

As soon as you know you have a reason to make a claim against your MOTOR INSURANCE policy, inform your insurer, broker or agent.

If you deal with a broker or agent you will be given an accident report and claim form. If you deal direct with the company, a form will be sent to you.

You must give full details of the incident, including, if possible, names and addresses of witnesses, victims and anyone else involved; say how the accident happened, give estimates of speed and weather conditions; state whether the police were called and if prosecutions are pending; and add full descriptions of any damage and/or injuries.

It is a condition of all insurance policies that every incident that could give rise to a claim either by or against the policyholder must be reported.

Some accidents that appear trivial at the time can result in sizeable claims – for example, over an injury that does not show up until some time later.

Insurers are reluctant to take over from policyholders who try to handle matters themselves and then find them too complicated. A company can refuse to negotiate or settle the claim at all if the accident report form was not completed at the right time. Someone who drives a car that is owned and insured by his employer must of course report an accident to the employer.

Most companies also make a rule that they will reject a claim if the policyholder admits liability to other people involved in an accident, but the way in which the rule is implemented may depend on the circumstances of the admission.

Completing the form does not automatically mean that you are making a claim, and so risking the loss of your no-claim discount. You can, if you wish, mark the form 'For Information Only', and make it quite clear in a covering letter that you do not wish the insurance company to take any action.

What to do after a motor accident

If you are claiming against your insurance after an accident:
● Contact your insurer or broker as soon as possible after the accident and give brief details of: the location, date and time of the accident; the vehicles involved and the names of the other drivers and, if possible, their insurance companies; whether anyone was injured and, if so, brief details of their names and the extent of their injuries; a description of the extent of the damage to vehicles or property; whether the police attended the accident; details of any witnesses and the present location of your vehicle.
● Report the accident to the police within 24 hours, if there was damage to someone else's property or someone was injured and the police did not attend. Reporting to the police, however, is not necessary if you give your name and address, those of the owner of the vehicle and its registration mark to anyone who at the time of the accident has reason to ask for them.
● Obtain an estimate from a garage for repairs to your vehicle.
● Complete the accident form that your insurers will send to you as soon as you have notified them of the accident. The form includes a request for a sketch map of the accident area, and you may have to re-visit the area to provide details.
● Send any correspondence that you receive from any other parties involved to your insurers. Do not acknowledge such letters, but if you disagree with

WHO PAYS IF THERE IS NO INSURANCE

All motor-insurance companies are members of the Motor Insurers Bureau, whose chief function is to provide an insurance 'safety net' for road victims.

The bureau pays damages for third party personal injuries caused by a motorist who is either not insured adequately or who cannot be traced. It does not pay for damage to vehicles or other property. The bureau pays out only after the motorist has been sued and damages fixed by a court. If the motorist cannot be traced the bureau will consider paying damages if it decides he could have been successfully sued. The bureau itself can be sued if its decision or award in such cases seems unsatisfactory.

HOW ANOTHER DRIVER'S MISTAKE CAN COST YOU MONEY

If your motor insurance company has to pay out anything on your policy, you lose your no-claim discount next time you renew your insurance – even if the payment is made for damage that was not your fault.

To reduce the time and expense it takes to settle claims if the blame has to be apportioned between two drivers in a collision, insurance companies have agreements with each other to accept liability on what they call a 'knock for knock' basis. That means that each company pays for repairs to its own policyholder's vehicle provided they have both issued comprehensive policies. They will then decide whether or not their own client was entirely blameless and adjust his no-claim discount accordingly.

If the same company insures both drivers, and one is clearly to blame for the accident, the other driver can expect the claim not to be recorded against him.

But if two companies are involved, the innocent driver can best save his no-claim discount by producing absolute proof that he did not contribute to the accident.

An insurance company should accept:
● The evidence of independent witnesses to the collision and to what happened before it. Such witnesses must be prepared to be interviewed by an insurance inspector and if necessary to be cross-examined in a court.

Passengers in the motorist's car are not regarded as independent witnesses.
● Unchallenged evidence given in a court prosecution of the other driver. His conviction for a driving offence is not enough in itself: the other driver's failure to take precautions against his bad driving might have contributed to the collision. The unchallenged evidence must make clear that the innocent driver was entirely blameless.

● Proof that the other driver admits liability. An oral apology at the scene of the accident is not enough, even if witnesses heard it, because it does not prove that the allegedly innocent driver was not at least partly to blame.

A written apology entirely excusing the innocent driver is needed.

The innocent driver is, however, unlikely to get a satisfactory admission of liability until his no-claim discount is already threatened. The other driver is likely to be aware that his own policy conditions include a provision that he must not admit liability to another party.

Suing the other driver

If you lose your no-claim bonus as a result of the accident you can recover this item of loss in a successful claim against the other motorist for NEGLIGENCE.

---

anything that has been said in the letters, tell your insurers.
● Advise your insurers immediately if you receive any notice of intended prosecution by the police or any notice to attend a coroner's inquest.
● If you claim for any personal effects being damaged or medical expenses, provide evidence of the expenses incurred or the value of the property that has been damaged when you claim.
● Once your insurers have authorised the repairs to be made to your vehicle, the garage may start work on the vehicle. The bill is sent to your insurers, but you may have to pay any excess due under your policy. The garage asks you to sign a 'satisfaction note' stating that the repairs have been completed satisfactorily. If you then find the repairs are not satisfactory, contact your insurers who will contact the garage.

Claiming against someone else

If you are claiming from another party after an accident:
● Inform your own insurers as soon as possible after the accident and give brief details of what took place.
● Write to the other party involved as soon as possible. Send your letter by recorded delivery and state that you hold him responsible for the accident. Tell him that you will submit your claim in due course. Always mark your correspondence 'without prejudice'.

● If the other party does not respond, send a second letter by recorded delivery reiterating your claim, and suggest that failing to respond could lead to legal action being taken on your part.

Usually, the other party or his insurers will reply. When you receive a reply, send the other party details of your claim and copies of any supporting documents – for example, an estimate for repairs to your vehicle from a garage. In certain cases, his insurers will want to inspect your vehicle before it is repaired.
● Once his insurers have inspected the vehicle, or agreed to the estimate, instruct your garage to go ahead with the repairs. You must pay the bill for repairs in full and seek reimbursement from his insurers. You are not entitled by law to claim a reimbursement of an expense until it has been incurred.
● The other party's insurers will either agree to reimburse you or they may hold you partially or totally to blame for the accident and refuse to pay all of the bill. In that case, it is up to you to continue negotiating with them until you reach what you feel is a fair settlement. Any statement from an independent witness to the accident will help your claim.

If you are unable to reach a settlement, seek advice on how to pursue your claim from a solicitor, an insurance broker or a motoring organisation.

● If your claim involves damages for any personal injury involved, seek advice as soon as possible from a solicitor or motoring organisation on how to claim.

Getting the car repaired

Usually a motorist with comprehensive insurance can ask any garage to carry out repairs, but the insurers may prefer the work to be done by a garage they have approved.

If the damage is substantial, the insurers appoint an engineer to inspect the car, agree the repair costs and authorise the work to begin. For smaller amounts, the motorist can tell the garage to start the work as soon as he has sent an estimate to the insurers and it has been approved.

If the motorist tells the garage to go ahead, he is responsible for paying the bill himself and has to recover the money from his insurers.

On the other hand, when the repairs are authorised directly by the insurance company, the bill will be sent to it by the garage and the motorist can normally collect his car without any payment other than any excess due under his policy.

Betterment payments In some cases the motorist may have to make an extra payment after his car has been repaired if the work done has made the vehicle markedly better than it was before the accident. For example, if it is impossible to match the paint on a damaged area without respraying the whole car the insurers may ask the motorist to pay for part of the cost. In such cases the insurance company still pays the full garage bill and then claims a share from the motorist.

If the car is a write-off

If the insurance company's engineer decides that the car cannot be economically repaired it is 'written off' as a total loss. If the policy includes provision of a replacement car of similar make and value, the insurance company can choose between buying the motorist a car, or having the original car repaired. If the damaged car was less than 12 months old, however, the insured driver can choose.

Most insurers limit the amount to the car's estimated sale value as stated by the motorist when he took out the policy. In times of inflation the estimated value may be considerably below the current market value, but the insurers are within their rights to insist on the lower figure.

Vintage or other very unusual cars may be valued according to a figure agreed between the owner and the insurance company when the policy is taken out and in subsequent years, and this is the amount paid in the event of a total loss.

If the car is being bought on hire purchase, the hire-purchase company has first right to any total-loss payment and the motorist is sent only the balance.

A few policies give the insurance company the right to cancel the policy immediately after a total-loss payment so it can negotiate new terms with a higher premium. That loss of premium is a recoverable item of damage if you are claiming against the other motorist for NEGLIGENCE.

If the car is stolen

Most stolen cars are recovered within a few days so a motorist who is a victim of a car theft cannot expect an immediate total-loss payment under a comprehensive insurance policy. Many insurers are prepared to pay up if the car is not found within 28 days, but the figure varies.

A car theft must be reported to the police to substantiate the claim, as well as to the insurance company. If the car is found after payment has been made it becomes the property of the company.

Damaged cars A stolen car which is found to be damaged after it is recovered can be repaired under both a comprehensive or a third party fire and theft policy – just as if it had been damaged in a collision. The only difference is that the owner does not generally have to pay any accidental damage excess following a theft.

If a comprehensive policy includes an extra benefit allowing a motorist to hire a car when his own is unavailable because of damage, he can claim for hire of the car even if he was to blame for the damage. There are no general rules for such cover, but the motorist is usually entitled to make arrangements immediately, pay the bill later and pass it to the insurance company for reimbursement. It may be up to the motorist to prove that the costs incurred were reasonable and necessary.

MOTOR INSURANCE COVER NOTE

Obtaining temporary cover

An insurance cover note is a temporary certificate of motor insurance. It is issued by the insurance company or agent, usually for 30 days, to cover the period between agreeing to insure a driver and sending him the policy and permanent certificate. If the note is issued by an insurance company, they may send it to the broker to be passed to you. The note sets out the essential points of the insurance cover, such as whether it is comprehensive or third-party, who may drive the vehicle and what it may be used for.

Your insurance technically comes into force only if the cover note is either in your possession or has been put in the post to you. The post office is legally your agent, and once the note is put in a post box, it is considered to have been delivered to you.

It is a criminal offence to use an uninsured vehicle. Never take a vehicle on the road unless you know, with absolute certainty, that you are covered by insurance. Even if the broker tells you that he is putting a cover note in the post, it is

WHEN A COVER NOTE TAKES EFFECT

Once your motor insurance cover note has been put in the post to you, it is legally in your possession, and you are protected by it.

not safe to drive until you are sure that he has done so. He is acting as the insurance company's agent, not yours, and while the cover note is in his possession it has not been delivered to you.

MOTOR INSURANCE POLICY

The document that explains what cover you have

Your insurance policy sets out the details of your cover in formal terms. Although you may not receive it for some time after the cover started, you are bound by its terms and conditions from the start – unless you can show that it is not what you were led to expect.

The policy may appear difficult to understand, but try nevertheless to read it carefully, to ensure that you have the cover you asked for. If you think the document is incorrect, or if you cannot fully understand it, consult the company, or the broker or agent who arranged the insurance.

If there is an error in the policy, the insurer must put it right, no matter how much time passes before you discover it. If anything in the policy is capable of more than one meaning, a court would always interpret it in your favour.

The policy document, usually a booklet, sets out full details of your cover and any conditions or restrictions.

TEMPORARY INSURANCE COVER FOR YOUR CAR

How to make sure it is legal to take a vehicle on the road

Cornhill

Insurance Company Limited

AUTHORISED INSURERS

Head Office: 32 CORNHILL, LONDON, EC3V 3LJ

Cover Note No. ....299053........

Make of Vehicle	C.C.	Year of Make	Present Value	Type of Body No. of Seats	Registration Mark of Vehicle
FORD GRANADA	2.8	1979	7500	SALOON 4	CAP 899T

COVER IS GRANTED in respect of this Motor Vehicle in the terms of the Company's usual form of .... *COMPREHENSIVE* .... policy.
(State whether Comprehensive, Third Party or Third Party, Fire and Theft), subject to the following special terms:–

(if none, state none).
If this Motor Vehicle is a Private Car, cover as required by the law relating to compulsory insurance operates in respect of:–
(a) any private car owned by the Proposer or hired to him under a hire purchase agreement.
(b) any motor car or motor cycle not owned by the Proposer whilst being driven by him.

1. POLICY NO. (if any)   *C 10943X*
2. NAME OF PROPOSER   *J. E. LACEY*
3. EFFECTIVE DATE OF THE COMMENCEMENT OF INSURANCE FOR THE PURPOSES OF THE RELEVANT LAW.   *12.00* HOURS *31.1.* 19 *80*
4. DATE OF EXPIRY. The same time on the twenty-eighth day after the date of commencement.
5. PERSONS OR CLASSES OF PERSONS ENTITLED TO DRIVE:
    (a)   The Proposer.
    (b)   Any person in the Proposer's employ driving with his permission.
    (c)   Any person driving with the Proposer's permission.
    Provided that the person driving holds a licence to drive the vehicle or has held and is not disqualified for holding or obtaining such a licence.
6. LIMITATIONS AS TO USE:
    (i)   For social, domestic and pleasure purposes.
    (ii)   By the Proposer in person for his business or profession.
    (iii)   For the Proposer's business or profession.

CERTIFICATE OF MOTOR INSURANCE

I hereby certify that this covering note satisfies the requirements of the relevant Law applicable in Great Britain, Northern Ireland, the Isle of Man, the Island of Guernsey, the Island of Jersey and the Island of Alderney.

CORNHILL INSURANCE COMPANY LIMITED
AUTHORISED INSURERS

Delivered to Proposer this
31 day of *JANUARY* 19 *80*

Countersigned ....

General Manager
CM 928/8/9
9-74

NOTE: For full details of the insurance cover reference should be made to the Policy.

Although the driver is covering possible loss to himself, third-party cover is included

The hour can be as vital as the date if the driver is stopped by the police and asked to produce evidence of insurance. It is an offence for the agent to backdate the note

A policy for social, domestic and pleasure use of the car can be held to be not valid if the driver uses the car for business or accepts any payment that includes an element of profit, however small, from a passenger

The purpose of a cover note is to cover the driver while the policy is being prepared by the insurance company. A driver is taking a considerable risk if he takes someone's word that a note has been posted to him and drives his car on the road before he has received the note and checked the period for which it is valid.

The restrictions

The details include a list of certain general restrictions on your cover:

● *Who can drive* If your cover is restricted to use of the vehicle by certain drivers, they are usually referred to as 'those named in the certificate of insurance'. Despite any such restriction, however, a comprehensively insured vehicle is normally covered against damage while it is in the hands of a motor tradesman for maintenance or repair. A car park attendant would not normally be covered.

● *Limit on use* Your policy may state that the cover is limited to social, domestic or pleasure use of the car. In that case it cannot be used in the course of work or business – but simply driving to or from work is normally considered as a domestic use. Most policies exclude use of the car for racing or rallying.

● *Outside liabilities* The policy excludes any risk that has not been agreed in advance by the insurer. For example, if you have an accident under a comprehensive policy, you are covered for injury and vehicle damage. But if the accident prevents you from delivering business goods, and you lose money, you cannot claim on your policy for that loss unless such a claim is specifically provided for. That would usually require a separate policy.

● *Nuclear risk* The policy will exclude all losses arising from any atomic source, such as a nuclear power station. That is because such losses, by law, are the responsibility of the user of atomic material.

● *War risk* A loss arising from war between nations is not normally covered.

● *Losses abroad* Losses arising from riot, civil commotion or earthquake, are normally excluded, except for third party liability.

If you expect to take your vehicle to an area where such risks might arise, you can try to arrange additional insurance to cover personal injury or damage to your own vehicle and other property. In any case, you are likely to need special insurance to meet the requirements of a foreign country. *See also:* MOTORING ABROAD

The conditions

The following are the conditions normally set out in the policy document:

● *Making a claim* You must notify the insurer of any possible claim by or against you, as quickly as possible. You must also, when necessary, co-operate fully with your insurer in reaching settlement of any dispute with a third party.

● *Cancelling a policy* The company sets out the terms on which, if it chooses, it can cancel your policy before it expires.

That is likely to happen only if the company finds that it has taken an unexpected risk, or suspects that it has been defrauded but cannot prove it.

The cancellation clause sets out how the policy may be cancelled, and what proportion of your year's premium would be returned. It usually includes your right to cancel the arrangement – for example, if you decide to sell your car and no longer need insurance.

Rules may vary according to whether it is the insurer or you cancelling. If the insurer cancels, he will repay an amount in proportion to the unexpired period of the policy. For example, if your year's policy has run 5 months, you may be repaid 7/12ths of the year's premium.

But if you cancel the insurance, you are likely to be charged the 'short-period' rate, which is high. The insurer may repay only 40 per cent of a year's premium even though the policy has been in force for only 5 months.

If it has been in force for, say, 6 months, the repayment may drop to 30 per cent of the year's premium.

If your policy has been in force for more than a year before you cancel, your insurer may be prepared to make a pro rata repayment of premium. He is not, however, obliged to do so.

If any claim has been met on the policy – to you or to someone else – the insurer will not repay any of the premium.

● *Dual insurance* A loss connected with your car may sometimes be covered by more than one insurance policy. For example, if something is stolen from the vehicle, the theft may be covered by both your motor insurance and a household policy.

If that happens, you are entitled to claim on both policies, but remember that a 'motor' claim will affect your no-claim discount. Normally they divide the liability between them.

● *Care of the vehicle* You are required to maintain your car in an efficient and roadworthy condition. A motorist who

---

PROOF THAT YOU ARE MEETING THE ROAD TRAFFIC ACT REQUIREMENTS

Once your insurance contract is completed, you are sent your policy and a certificate of insurance which shows that you are complying with the minimum requirements of the Road Traffic Act.

The certificate is a vital document: you must always produce it at the request of the police – for example, if you are involved in an accident in which someone is injured. It must also be produced to the vehicle licensing authority when you renew your Road Fund licence.

The certificate mentions your name, your insurance policy number, the period for which you are insured, who may drive

on your insurance and whether you can drive other vehicles on the same insurance.

It also says for what specific purposes the vehicle can be used under the insurance – for example, for domestic and pleasure purposes but not for business use.

Some certificates give the registration number of the vehicle. Most, however, do not specify the vehicle insured, but use some 'blanket' form of wording such as: 'Any motor car, the property of the policyholder or lent or hired to him under a hire purchase agreement and registered in his name.' Lent, in that sense, means commercially leased.

If a particular vehicle is specified on the certificate, you will need a new certificate each time you change your car. If the 'blanket' wording is used, you do not need a new certificate – but must give the insurer full details of any new vehicle, immediately you buy it.

The certificate may not give all the details of your cover or its limitations. For example, your policy may exclude anyone under 25 from driving your car, but there is no provision for any such restriction to appear on a certificate of insurance.

It is your policy, not your certificate that spells out your insurance rights.

blatantly fails to repair a defect, and who is then involved in an accident caused by the defect, could find that his insurer rejects any claim.

For example, if after the accident the insurer's inspecting engineer finds that the insured vehicle has one tyre in a condition that does not comply with the law, the fact may be overlooked. But if 3 or 4 tyres are in an illegal condition, the insurer could well reject liability. *See also:* MOTOR VEHICLE

You must also take reasonable steps to protect yourself from loss by theft. For example, if you leave your ignition key in an unlocked car, and the vehicle or its contents are then stolen, you may be considered not to have taken reasonable steps and may find that your insurer refuses to pay compensation.

● *Policy endorsements* The standard wording of a policy can be changed by the insurer's adding a clause, known as an endorsement. That can be done either when the policy is first issued, or at any time afterwards, if you agree.

An endorsement may restrict your cover or may increase it – for example, it may provide additional insurance covering personal effects for a small extra premium.

Some policies are issued with a full list of possible endorsements and a key to show which, if any, apply to your particular insurance. Other policies have endorsements stuck inside the main document. Make sure you know which endorsements affect your cover.

When there is a dispute

If a motorist is not happy with a decision by his insurance company – for instance over the amount they are prepared to pay on a claim – the policy document may provide for ARBITRATION. But only the policyholder has this means of settlement, not a third party who may have a claim against the policyholder.

MOTOR INSURANCE PREMIUM

How the insurer decides how much you should pay

The way in which insurance premiums are decided can vary greatly from one company to another.

Specially low premiums may be charged for a particular class of car, or for a driver in a particular occupation, or for the employees of a particular company – even on their private cars.

Specially high premiums are charged for certain types of car or driver, and for anything else that the insurer considers an extra accident risk.

If your premium is subject to an extra charge – known as a 'loading' – you are entitled to know, at the quotation or renewal stage, how much extra you are being asked to pay over and above the basic premium, and why.

If you agree to pay a higher premium, you are entitled later to ask the insurer to reconsider – either when the policy is due to be renewed, or if there is a change in the circumstances that led him to impose the extra charge.

The following are the main factors that an insurer takes into account when working out your premium:

● *The vehicle* All modern cars are given an insurance group rating, set by either the Motor Conference, for insurance companies, or the Lloyd's Motor Underwriters' Association, for Lloyd's underwriters.

There can be variations between the two sets of ratings, but they are mainly similar.

The most important factors that contribute to a rating are the power of the car and the potential cost of repairs. Other considerations include an assessment of the type of driver that a particular kind of car may attract.

● *Where the car is kept* The cost of your insurance also depends partly on where your car is based. Insurers divide the country into areas and grade them according to the local traffic density, accident and theft rates.

A mainly rural area such as Devon and Cornwall has a low rating. Central London has the highest in England. Northern Ireland's is the highest in Britain not only owing to a high accident rate, but also because car accident lawsuits are heard before juries, who sometimes award unusually high damages.

Some companies charge extra to insure a car kept in a major city if it is not kept in a garage.

● *How much you drive* From the use to which you say that the vehicle will be put, your insurer will estimate whether you are likely to have a high or low yearly mileage. It is assumed that the higher the mileage, the greater the exposure to risk of accidents.

Someone who uses his own car for business and travels extensively may not be able to obtain the normal 'private and business use' cover without paying much more.

On the other hand, if you volunteer to be restricted to social, domestic and pleasure use only, some insurers charge a reduced premium.

● *Value of the vehicle* If you are insuring your car comprehensively, the insurer is unlikely to be much influenced by the value of the vehicle unless it is one of the more expensive models – costing, say, more than £8,000.

Repair costs for lower valued cars vary little, so premiums are similar. Specialist and high-value cars are charged extra.

For a third party, fire and theft policy, however, the value of the vehicle is taken more into account because it represents a greater proportion of the total risk.

● *Your job* A motorist's occupation, or the occupation of a named 'other driver', may also mean a higher premium because the company considers that certain occupational classes carry a higher than normal risk of accident. That may be because they have unusually active social lives, or because they frequently have to drive quickly in unfamiliar places. Professional sportsmen and entertainers are typical high-risk categories.

However, insurers have widely varying attitudes to such professions, and if you are in such a job, seek professional advice from a broker when arranging your insurance.

● *Age and experience* If a driver is under the age of 25, he is likely to be charged a higher premium than someone in the older, experienced group.

There are many variations in the treatment of drivers according to age and experience. Some insurers continue charging a higher premium until the driver is 34.

At the other end of the scale, premiums may be reduced for an experienced driver at the age of, say, 51. The more usual qualifying age, however, is 60 or 65.

'Experience,' to an insurer, is a combination of age and the length of time a

WHEN YOU QUALIFY FOR A NO-CLAIM DISCOUNT

A driver whose insurance is not claimed against for a whole year is entitled to a percentage reduction in his premium for the following year – although that individual reduction is likely to be outweighed by regular overall increases in motor insurance premiums.

The discount, generally known as 'no-claim bonus', depends on an absence of any claim on the policy whether by the insured driver or by someone else. It does not matter whether or not he was to blame for the incident that led to the claim. The discount increases in size over a series of claim-free years, to a maximum of 60 or 65 per cent.

If you change your insurer, you are entitled to take your discount with you. You are credited with the same number of claim-free years – but the discount rate is not necessarily the same.

In considering a change of insurance company, a motorist has to take into account the basic premium as well as the no-claim discount rate.

Example: Your company gives a 3rd-year discount of 40 per cent on your premium of £200. You pay £120. Another company offers a better discount – 50 per cent. But if your basic premium is going to be more than £240, you lose money by changing over.

Proving a no-claim record If you change your insurer, and wish to transfer your no-claim discount, you must produce proof of your no-claim record with the previous insurer.

You need to show the new insurer the renewal notice from the previous insurer – which indicates the amount of no-claim discount – or a letter from that insurer confirming that a discount has been allowed, and for how long.

Some insurers allow you a discount that you have earned while driving abroad. Other insurers may offer only a reduced discount for foreign driving, and some may not allow it at all.

Few insurers allow a motor-cyclist who has earned discount to transfer it to another type of vehicle, or allow a discount to a motorist whose accident-free record was achieved in cars he did not insure – for example, someone who drove his company's cars. However, a record of safe driving could be a bargaining point in negotiating the basic premium, if necessary.

Nor can the discount normally be transferred from one driver to another. No-claim discount is earned by a motorist rather than his vehicle, and someone else using the vehicle may not be as reliable as the original policyholder.

An exception is when one policy is issued to cover two or more cars, and the policyholder is the main user of only one of them.

If any other vehicle covered by the policy is mainly used by someone else – for example, the policyholder's son or daughter – and the insurers are aware of this, that person can usually take out his or her own insurance and benefit by the vehicle's no-claim record.

If a claim is still outstanding when the policy is due for renewal, the no-claim discount will be lost or reduced, though if the matter is subsequently settled without the insurance company having to make a payment the discount will be reinstated.

Some insurers allow the policyholder to repay a claim made in the previous year if it proves to be less than the no-claim discount that would otherwise be lost.

---

driver has held a full United Kingdom licence. Provided that you are over 25 and have held such a licence for 12 consecutive months, you will not normally be charged an extra premium on the ground of inexperience.

If, however, you cannot meet those requirements, you will probably be charged a higher premium. If you take out comprehensive cover, you may also have to accept a damage excess.

Some insurers do not impose the excess on a driver who has held a foreign licence for more than 2 years.

When considering a foreign driver's application for insurance, an insurer takes into account three factors: Whether he has a sufficient grasp of the English language, whether he is familiar with British traffic conditions – including the need to drive on the left – and how much driving he has done outside Britain.

There is no formal English language test, either written or oral, the insurer, broker or agent must assess the applicant's grasp of the language as best he can – by, for example, the way in which the proposal form is completed.

A foreign driver who has been per-manently living and driving in Britain for 3 years or more should normally have no difficulty in obtaining insurance, without special restrictions.

● *Accidents and convictions* In most instances insurers will ignore a single accident that is disclosed on a proposal form – whether or not the driver seeking insurance was to blame. But a driver with a record of two or more accidents may be asked to pay a higher premium.

Many insurers are more interested in the circumstances of an accident, rather than the cost of the resulting damage or injury.

A driver who, for example, makes a slight misjudgment of speed or distance and has a crash that results in expensive damage to two vehicles, will not normally be penalised as heavily by his next insurer as will someone who causes an accident by reckless or drunken driving but who is lucky enough to cause relatively slight damage.

Most motoring convictions are considered seriously by insurers. Although minor offences, such as illegal parking or an isolated speeding conviction, are not likely to affect your insurance, a motorist who has more serious convictions – for example, if he has been guilty of reckless driving – is likely to be charged a higher premium.

Someone who has a record of accidents and convictions combined will almost certainly have to pay more for his insurance, and is also likely to be given only restricted cover.

Once a loading has been imposed for convictions or past accident claims, the insurer will not usually alter the terms for at least 2 years – and even then may not remove the loading altogether.

A loading imposed for a very serious driving offence, such as causing death by dangerous driving, may not be removed entirely for 5 years or more. Such a loading is normally decreased in yearly stages, starting after 2 years.

If a motorist filling in a claim form mentions a conviction that is covered by the REHABILITATION of Offenders Act, the insurer must disregard it.

● *Physical disability* A driver who has a physical disability, such as loss of an eye or limb, is not normally required to pay a higher premium because of that disability, unless it has happened so recently that he may not have had time to learn to cope with it.

If the disability is recent, a higher premium may be charged for 2 or 3 years, until the motorist has shown that he is still able to drive safely. However, a disability is generally more likely to result in a restriction on the insurance cover than an increase in premium.

For example, if the insured car has to be specially adapted to allow the disabled person to drive, his policy will almost certainly not allow him third party cover for driving other, non-adapted cars.

If a driver suffers a chronic illness, such as diabetes, heart disease or epilepsy, he is likely to have to pay a higher premium and to accept restrictions on his insurance cover. That is because it is usually uncertain when and where the illness may suddenly affect the motorist.

Paying by instalments

Many insurance companies and brokers allow premiums to be paid by instalments rather than in an annual lump sum, though there is a small surcharge. A typical charge is £3 extra for paying by six instalments. Paying by instalments does not usually affect the insurance, but if it does this fact must be mentioned in the policy. The most likely effect is a condition that a total loss claim is met only if the total premium is paid.

MOTOR RALLY

How to go about organising a car event

Anyone who wants to run a motor rally on public roads in Britain is free to do so provided that:
● No more than 12 vehicles are involved.
● There is no set route to the finishing point.

All other rallies must be authorised and conform to Department of Transport regulations, which are administered by the Royal Automobile Club's motor sport division, and the Royal Scottish Automobile Club.

How to get authorisation

Organisers seeking authorisation for a rally should write to the RAC or RSAC for an application form which is always accompanied by explanatory leaflets and details of fees and insurance charges. The completed application form must reach the RAC at least 2 months before the date of the proposed start.

MOTOR VEHICLE

The driver's responsibility for the safety of his car

Anyone who drives or owns a vehicle, has a legal duty to see that it is safe to be on the road. The steering, brakes and lights must work efficiently, the tyres must have a proper tread and the windscreen wipers must work.

Anyone using or allowing to be used a car that fails to comply with all or any of the safety regulations commits an offence and can be fined a maximum of £100, and after three endorsements on three separate occasions he is likely to be disqualified from driving. Only the most important common items are dealt with here.

Steering It is an offence to drive a vehicle on the road with steering that is inefficient or not properly adjusted. Excessive play on the steering wheel is the most common fault.

A steering wheel that can be turned up to 30 degrees without moving the wheels is unsafe and can lead to prosecution. Of course, excessive play under 30 degrees may still be unsafe.

Tyres All tyres must have a tread pattern at least 1 mm. deep for at least three-quarters of the width of the tyre all the way around its circumference. That is the part of the tyre which normally touches the road. Tyres must be properly inflated.

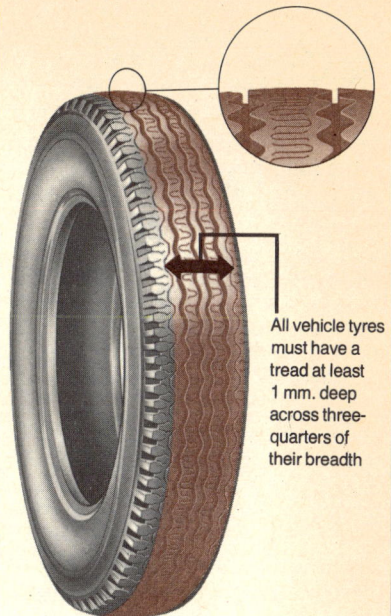

All vehicle tyres must have a tread at least 1 mm. deep across three-quarters of their breadth

The tread pattern on vehicle tyres must cover three-quarters of the breadth all round the circumference and must be at least 1 mm. deep.

Superficial cuts on the walls or on the shoulders of a tyre are not illegal, but a cut more than 25 mm. deep is. Tyres are legally considered defective if the ply or cord is showing through the wall of the tyre or if there are bulges or lumps in it.

It is an offence to put one radial and one cross-ply tyre on the same axle.

Number-plates Every vehicle must have number-plates, with the vehicle's registration number displayed, at the front and the rear. It is an offence to drive without them, or to drive when the plates are so covered by mud or dirt that they are impossible to read.

A PARKED CAR WITH FAULTY TYRES

It is an offence to own a car with faulty tyres, even if it is not being driven.

Graham Mitchell parked his Triumph car in Moordale Avenue, Bracknell, Berkshire, in 1972. The front and rear tyres on the near side were defective.

A policeman questioned Mr Mitchell who said that he knew the tyres were defective, but that he had been ill and had no intention to use the car. He was summoned, but magistrates dismissed the case on the grounds that Mr Mitchell did not intend to use the car. The police appealed.

VERDICT
The Divisional Court ruled that the car was capable of being used, and so an offence had been committed. They sent the case back to the magistrates with a direction to convict.

Front number-plates can be black on a white background or white on black, but all rear number-plates must be black on yellow. They must be clearly visible from 75 ft in daylight. The rear number-plate must be illuminated at night and must be visible from 60 ft. The maximum penalty is £20 and £50 for a second offence.

Speedometer Most vehicles first registered since 1937 must be fitted with a working speedometer. The only exceptions are slow-moving vehicles such as trucks moving at less than 10 mph and motor-cycles of less than 100 cc.

It is an offence to drive a vehicle if the speedometer is not accurate within a margin of 10 per cent at speeds over 10 mph.

Mirrors Most cars built after 1978 must have at least two rear-view mirrors one of which must be on the offside exterior. On cars first used since April 1, 1969, they must have protective edges to prevent injury in an accident.

Goods vehicles and large passenger vehicles must be fitted with two mirrors so that both sides of the vehicle can be seen as well as the rear.

Windscreen wipers An automatic windscreen wiper must be fitted to every vehicle unless the driver can see clearly to the front without looking through the windscreen, either by opening it or looking over it. Washers that can clean the area swept by the wipers are compulsory.

Horn Only works trucks and pedestrian-controlled vehicles do not need to be fitted with a horn that can give an easily heard warning of approach.

Gongs, sirens, two-tone horns and bells are banned from all vehicles ex-

---

DRIVER WHOSE HANDBRAKE WOULD NOT WORK

Even though he is not an authorised examiner, a police officer can bring a case against the owner of a defective vehicle.

Driver Thomas Richardson was stopped by PC Peter Clay in Leeds in 1972. The officer found that with the handbrake full on he was able to push Mr Richardson's vehicle along the road.

Mr Richardson argued before the magistrates that there was no case be-

cause PC Clay was not an authorised examiner. The magistrates dismissed the case and the police appealed.

VERDICT

The Divisional Court said that there was only one issue before the magistrates: Was the handbrake defective? This had been proved. The case was sent back to the magistrates with a direction to convict.

---

cept police or fire service vehicles, ambulances and vehicles used by salvage corps.

All vehicles first used since August 1973 must have a horn that gives a uniform, continuous sound and it must not be strident.

A motorist must not sound a horn while his vehicle is stationary, except in traffic, and not at all between 11.30 p.m. and 7 a.m. in areas where there is a 30 mph speed limit.

Brakes Every driver must be sure that the brakes on his vehicle can stop the vehicle in a reasonable distance in the most adverse conditions. The handbrake and the brakes on each of the four wheels must all be effective.

The Highway Code says that the shortest stopping distance of the average family car, including thinking distance, on a dry road with good brakes is: 75 ft at 30 mph; 175 ft at 50 mph; 315 ft at 70 mph.

Lights a vehicle must have

A driver must be able to see a safe distance ahead at night and his car must be easily visible to others. To ensure

this, the law requires that all vehicles carry white lights at the front (there is no provision in the Regulations for yellow headlamps) and red lights at the rear. New cars used after April 1, 1981, must have high-intensity rear foglamps.

The lights must be positioned to show the width of the vehicle and used in a way that does not dazzle or confuse others.

Lights and reflectors should be kept clean and must always be in good working order – you can be stopped and reported for breaking lighting regulations even during daytime.

When lights must be on The lights on a motor vehicle must be switched on during the hours of darkness – that is from half-an-hour after sunset to half-an-hour before sunrise. Outside built-up areas, where street lamps are more than 200 yds apart, full or dipped headlamps must be used, and it is an offence to drive only on sidelights. Full or dipped headlamps must also be used in poor visibility, such as in fog or heavy sleet, even if it is daytime.

When a motor vehicle is parked in a road the sidelights must be left on except when the vehicle is in a road with a speed limit of 30 mph or less, off a main bus route and in the light of a street lamp. Unlit vehicles must be parked:

● At least 15 yards away from a junction.

● Close and parallel to the kerb.

● Facing in the direction of the traffic flow.

Trailers and vehicles with projecting loads must not be left without lights on a road at night.

Front lights There must be two white lights on either side of the front of the vehicle. They must be at the same height from the ground and not more

---

THE DISC BRAKE THAT WAS WORN

It is an offence if any part of the braking system does not work.

A car owned by British Airports Authority was involved in an accident in 1975. It was later examined by police who found that the front near disc brake had worn down to the metal and the pad was about to break up.

The Authority was charged with using a car in which not every part of the brak-

ing system was in good and working order. Magistrates dismissed the case because although the pads were worn they were serviceable. The police appealed.

VERDICT

The Divisional Court held that the regulations referred to every part of the braking system, so the magistrates did not have to consider the overall efficiency. The Authority was convicted.

than 500 mm from the outermost side of the vehicle.

It is an offence to drive a car night or day with only one working white light at the front. Front lights must by law have a dipped beam and a main beam which can be switched on or off on both lamps simultaneously. Sidelights do not need to dip.

Rear lights Two matching red lights must be fitted to the rear of all motor vehicles. They must be the same height from the ground and not more than 400 mm from the outermost edge of the vehicle.

Rear lamps must be wired so that if one fails the other continues to operate.

Two red reflectors must also be fitted, one each side of the vehicle. If an unlit rear lamp also acts as a reflector, then it will qualify within the law as a reflector, whether it is lit or unlit.

Illegal lights It is an offence for any car to show a red light to the front, or to show a white light to the rear – except while reversing.

Stop lamps Cars in use since 1971 must be fitted with two red stop lamps at the rear. These lights must be operated by applying the brakes, show a steady light and be wired so that one will stay alight if the other's bulb fails. Stop lamps must be at the same height on either side of the vehicle, at least 2 ft apart.

Direction indicators It is compulsory for all cars to have direction indicators, either one pair at the side, or one pair at the front and one at the rear, or one rear pair and one pair of shoulder indicators. They must show amber to both front and rear. Pre-1965 cars may still have arm-type indicators which can show white and red to front and rear and be fitted at a height of 17–90 in.

All indicators must work from the same switch and there must be a device inside the car to show when they are operating. If your vehicle has broken down on the road and is causing an obstruction, you may use the indicators as a hazard warning.

Non-obligatory lamps All obligatory lights must be fitted by manufacturers to strict regulations. Some non-obligatory lights can be fitted, but these, too, must meet strict requirements. You can fit reversing lamps and fog or spot lamps. Reversing lamps must not exceed 24 watts, show a white light to the rear and deflect downwards to minimise

dazzle. Not more than two may be carried.

A single spot lamp may be used only in addition to a car's headlights when driving where there is no street lighting. It must be white or yellow and fixed 24–42 in. from the ground.

Silencer An efficient silencer must be fitted to all cars and it must not be altered so that noise is increased. It is an offence to use a car that creates an excessive noise and the driver can be fined up to £100.

Smoke A car must not give off vapour, smoke or sparks which could cause damage to property or injury to a person. The maximum penalty is £100.

Selling a car

If you dispose (by sale or otherwise) of a vehicle of which you are the registered keeper, you should, as seller, immediately complete the relevant part of the vehicle registration document and send it to the DVLC at Swansea. The address is on the form. You should give the rest of the registration document to the buyer, who must also complete the appropriate part of it and send it to the DVLC. If the buyer is a dealer, he has other obligations.

MOTORING ABROAD

Different legal requirement for different countries

Motorists in most countries require three basic sets of documents: a driving licence, car registration papers and evidence of third-party insurance. A motorist visiting another country, however, must find out first how far he is covered by his existing documents and what extra ones he needs for each country he is visiting or passing through.

Ask your travel agent or the tourist information office of the country you intend to visit whether there are any special formalities or requirements you should observe.

Driving licence

A valid full British licence covers driving in most European countries, but some have their own special rules. Check with a motoring organisation or a tourist information office of any country where you will be driving.

A British licence does not cover you in Hungary, Poland, Spain, the Soviet Union or, if you are not driving your own car, Turkey. In those countries you must have an international driving permit, which can be obtained from the motoring organisations.

Car registration papers

You must carry the registration papers of the vehicle you are driving or a photo-copy authenticated by the issuing tax authority, even if the car is not your own.

If it belongs to someone else, you must also have a signed letter from the owner authorising you to drive it outside Britain. If you intend to drive in Yugoslavia, the letter must be certificated by a British motoring organisation. You must also display a valid British excise licence. In most countries you do not have to pay road tax for visits of less than 3 months.

Insuring your car

Your normal MOTOR INSURANCE policy gives you the minimum legally required third-party cover in all EEC countries and in a number of others. To be covered to the extent of your UK policy, if it is more than third party, you require an international motor insurance certificate – a Green Card – which you can obtain from your insurance company for a small additional premium. The Green Card is compulsory in some non-EEC countries.

Special policies are available to cover the cost of bringing you, your passengers and your car home if it breaks down or if you have an accident.

Remember, too, when you arrange the dates of your insurance cover that your return may be delayed by a breakdown, bad weather or industrial action.

Other requirements

In all countries you require a GB plate fixed to the rear of your car. In many you must also carry a red warning triangle to use if you break down.

How to get a permit Any office or roadside service centre of the Automobile Association or the Royal Automobile Club can issue an international driving permit. To obtain a permit, a motorist need simply show his current British licence and supply a passport-size photograph. The procedure takes only about 5 minutes and the permit fee is £1.50.

MOTORWAY DRIVING

The special rules that apply to motorways

Motorways are specially designed dual-carriageway roads for swift-moving traffic, and special rules apply to them. Drivers can be fined and even be disqualified from driving for breaking the regulations that apply specifically to motorways.

People who are not allowed to use a motorway

It is an offence for pedestrians, learner drivers, cyclists or moped riders to use a motorway. Tractors, other agricultural vehicles and some invalid carriages are also banned.

It is an offence for a driver to pick up or to set down a passenger or hitchhiker on any part of a motorway, including slip roads to and from the motorway.

The verges alongside a motorway can be used by drivers only in an emergency, such as a breakdown, an accident or illness.

Any vehicle that has been driven on to a motorway verge must stay there no longer than necessary, whatever the emergency.

Special motorway signals

It is an offence to ignore flashing light signals which operate on motorways in dangerous or unusual conditions such as fog.

In normal conditions the signal panels are blank, but when there are dangerous conditions ahead, amber lights flash and the signal shows a temporary maximum speed that ought not to be exceeded, or indicates that certain lanes are closed ahead. Ignoring these warnings may result in prosecution.

If the signal shows a red, flashing light, drivers must not pass the signal in the lane it controls. When the restriction has been passed, the signal indicates by a lighted, diagonal bar that normal rules apply.

Observing lane discipline

Drivers who wander from lane to lane

‘

DROWSY DRIVER STOPPED TO REST

A motorist who feels sleepy must not park on the verge of a motorway because the situation is not an emergency. He would be expected to have used his common sense and not started or continued his journey in such a condition.

Driver Arthur Bernard began to feel drowsy as he drove towards a motorway. He had reached the slip road before he saw somewhere suitable to park. The next intersection he knew was 10 miles away, so Mr Bernard stopped on the hard shoulder of the slip road.

He was sitting awake at the wheel when police arrived. Mr Bernard explained that he was sleepy, but he was prosecuted.

The magistrate held that he had stopped in an emergency and he dismissed the case. The police appealed.

DECISION

The High Court held that Mr Bernard was fully aware of his condition before reaching the motorway, so there could be no emergency and an offence had been committed.

The penalty for stopping unlawfully on the hard shoulder is a fine of up to £500. This is, however, the only offence on a motorway that is not endorsable.

’

---

or who doggedly remain in an overtaking lane can be prosecuted for driving without reasonable consideration.

On a two-lane carriageway, the left-hand lane must be used, except for overtaking.

This 'keep left' rule also applies to three-lane motorways, but drivers can stay in the middle lane when there are slow-moving vehicles ahead in the left-hand lane and similarly if the middle lane is full of traffic they will soon be overtaking, vehicles are permitted to remain in the third carriageway.

The right-hand lane on a three-lane motorway is barred to vehicles over 3 tonnes – except coaches – and to any vehicle drawing a trailer. It is always an offence for such vehicles to use the right-hand lane, even for overtaking.

Any vehicle that is permitted to use the right-hand lane should do so only if it is reasonable and safe to overtake another vehicle.

Overall speed limit The maximum speed limit on any motorway is 70 mph and a driver who exceeds that speed can be disqualified and ordered to pay a fine of up to £500.

Special penalties for motorway offences

The maximum penalty for breaking motorway regulations is a fine of £500.

A driver who reverses on a motorway, makes a U-turn, or drives in the wrong direction along a carriageway can be fined up to £500 and disqualified from driving.

MUGGING

The offence that has a new name and a long history

No offence of mugging as such is recognised by the law. Many different crimes may be involved.

To use violence while committing a theft is ROBBERY. If the violent attempt fails, a charge of ASSAULT with intent to rob will be made. The maximum penalty in either case is life imprisonment.

If no theft were attempted, charges of causing grievous BODILY HARM or actual bodily harm may be preferred.

The culprit may also be ordered by the court to pay CRIMINAL INJURIES COMPENSATION.

MURDER

The intentional killing of another person

Murder is the unlawful killing of another person 'with malice aforethought'.

This means that the defendant must have intended to kill, or at least to cause grievous BODILY HARM, to someone – whether or not it was the person killed. For instance, if a man deliberately fires a gun at his wife but misses and unintentionally kills his son that is murder, even though he did not intend to kill the son. It is sufficient that he intended to cause grievous bodily harm to his wife.

Without such intention the killing

amounts to the less serious crime of MANSLAUGHTER. In addition, the death must occur within a year and a day of the attack. If a death occurs after this period the charge would probably be one of manslaughter.

A hangman who carries out a death sentence or a soldier who kills in the line of duty is not guilty of murder because the killing in these cases is not unlawful.

Intentional killing may also be in self defence, but the person would have to show that he used violence only as a last resort and that he used no more force than was necessary.

Provocation can also be a defence to a murder charge, but a person who killed in these circumstances would be guilty of intentional manslaughter.

Murder is tried in the crown court. The compulsory sentence is life imprisonment. The average life sentence for murder lasts 15 years. When passing sentence the judge may recommend that a minimum number of years should be served.

Such a recommendation is not binding on the Home Secretary but it will usually be followed.
See: DIMINISHED RESPONSIBILITY
DRUNKENNESS AS A DEFENCE
INSANITY AS A DEFENCE

MUSIC AND DANCING LICENCE

When permission is needed for entertainment

Anyone who wishes to stage a musical or dance entertainment for the public, or for gain, normally needs a licence from the local authority.

A licence is not needed if the entertainment is to be in a private club, or if it is for a private function, such as a wedding reception or a private or company celebration.

If alcohol is to be sold on the premises a separate licence is needed. *See:* LIQUOR OFFENCES

When a licence is required for an entertainment, it cannot be issued until a fire safety certificate for the building where it is to take place has been issued by a fire safety officer.

Most local authorities require 21 days' notice, including notice to the police, before granting an entertainment licence. If, however, the licence is sought for an isolated occasion in a building not normally used for such a purpose, 14 days' notice may be accepted.

If a licence is refused, or if you object to conditions imposed by the local authority, appeal to the local magistrates' court.

NAME, Change of

Making a new identity officially recognised

Anyone can call himself by any name or style he chooses except for a fraudulent reason, and provided that he always gives his official name on official and legal documents.

First names and surnames The first name of people who have not been baptised can be changed at will, without legal formality. The same applies to all surnames. But simply changing names can lead to complications if there is not some sort of official notification of the change.

There are three ways of officially notifying the change:

Advertising The simplest and cheapest way to make an official notification that you are adopting a new name is to advertise in a local newspaper. Keep copies of the advertisement in case you need evidence of the change later, particularly for tradesmen or companies with whom you wish to open an account.

Statutory declaration Someone using a new name who needs to prove legally who he was – for example, if he is left money in a will under his old name – can do so by swearing before a solicitor to the name he has been using and the name he was given at birth.

The solicitor is likely to charge only £2 for acting as witness and 50p for signing each of the attached documents. *See:* AFFIDAVIT

Deed poll The most widely recognised way to change your name is by deed poll. The deed – a written statement of your original name and the one you now wish to use – must be drawn up by a solicitor.

If you register a copy at the Passport Office, a passport will be issued in your new name only. Otherwise both old and new names will normally be given in the passport.

The same deed poll can be used to change the name of other members of the family, though the surname of children under 16 changes automatically with that of their parents.

Adopting a new Christian name

It is more difficult to change a Christian name – one given in baptism – than to change any other first name or a surname.

A Christian name can be changed only in three ways – by Act of Parliament, by a bishop at confirmation or by the addition of a name on adoption.

There is no legal penalty for using a different name in other circumstances but a charge of FORGERY or FRAUD could arise if there was a dishonest reason for doing so.

Marriage and divorce

A married woman can continue to use her maiden name if she wishes. She may use both – in different situations. For instance, she can continue to use professionally the name she has established, while being known by her married name in private life.

If she is divorced she can still use her married name – or any of her married names if she has been divorced more than once – or revert to her maiden name. But a divorced woman who uses her former husband's name must not do so in a way that implies that she is still married to him. If she does, her former husband can seek a court injunction to stop her.

The woman can also be sued for libel or slander if, by representing herself still to be his wife, she implies that a woman he has later married is not his legal wife.

A widow may revert to her maiden name after her husband's death.

A woman who married a peer, a knight or baronet can use the title she gains even if they are later divorced. She loses that right if she remarries.

Living together

A woman who lives with a man to whom she is not married can change her name to his by deed poll or statutory declaration or she may simply start using his name. In rare circumstances she may wish to advertise the change of name in newspapers.

She should in any case write to the national insurance and tax authorities and to anyone else with whom she is likely to have business so that official documents and records can be altered.

> ### THE IMPORTANCE OF A CHILD'S OWN NAME
>
> *The courts have to be convinced that there is good reason before they allow the names of children to be changed.*
>
> Mrs L remarried after being divorced and asked the High Court to allow her to change the name of her two children, aged 4 and 3, to that of her new husband.
>
> DECISION
> The court refused the application on the ground that a name was of great importance to children.
>
> Their father was a responsible parent who was to be involved in the upbringing of his children, even although custody had been granted to the mother.
>
> Despite possible embarrassment to the mother and her new husband, it was in the children's interest to retain their surname.

NATIONAL ASSISTANCE

Supplementary financial help from official sources

In addition to ordinary social security benefits – such as CHILD BENEFIT, for example – people in real financial need can claim SUPPLEMENTARY BENEFIT, formerly called National Assistance.

NATIONAL CONSUMER COUNCIL

The body that pinpoints consumer needs and speaks for the public

The National Consumer Council has a duty to represent the public interest in consumer matters. It carries out research into general needs and problems, and acts as a spokesman on behalf of the public.

The council can make representations to the Government, to local authorities, to industries or to any other organisations whose policies affect consumers. It also prepares Press publicity and issues research reports.

The work of the council has included:
● A report on rural transport.
● A report on advice centres in rural areas.
● A report on council housing.
● Support for the establishment of a national tenants' organisation.
● Support for a bill on Sunday trading.

It is not allowed to take up individual complaints.

Members are appointed by the Secretary of State for Trade after considering nominations by consumer groups and other public organisations. They serve part-time, for fees that cover their attendance at meetings, and are supported by a small full-time staff in London.

Apart from its income from publications, the council is financed by the Government.

NATIONAL GIROBANK

How post offices act as branches of a bank

Since 1968 the Post Office has offered a service – originally called Post Office Giro and now called National Girobank – for the cheap, speedy and convenient transfer of money by people without a bank account. Since 1975, however, the service has been expanded to provide most of the facilities offered by clearing banks.

Customers can have their pay or salary paid in, can pay cash or cheques into their account, pay bills by transfer cheque, or draft, draw cash up to £50 and pay standing orders free of charge. They even save money on postage – as Girobank provides them with free post-paid envelopes to correspond with it.

In addition, Girobank arranges overdrafts, personal loans, bridging loans, deposit accounts, budget accounts, travellers' cheques and foreign currency. Customers are sent a detailed statement each time there is a credit and after every 10 debits.

Advantage and disadvantage

The main advantage of Girobank, other than cheapness, is that post offices are open for longer during the week than banks and are also open on Saturday mornings. There are also more of them, particularly in out-of-the-way places – more than 21,000 post offices compared with about 14,000 branches of clearing banks.

The main disadvantage is that, because it is centralised, its service is less flexible and personal than that of a clearing bank. It is not possible to build up the sort of relationship that many customers of clearing banks have with their bank manager, who can use his personal judgment and discretion in giving help and advice.

Many individuals and businesses find that the best way to suit their needs is to have an account with National Girobank and also one with a clearing bank. Details of National Girobank can be obtained at any post office.

NATIONAL HEALTH SERVICE

When something goes wrong with health care

The National Health Service has detailed and complex procedures governing the conduct of patients' complaints about a doctor, dentist or optician. *See:* DOCTOR AND PATIENT

Similarly, there is framework within which you should proceed if you have a complaint about any aspect of HOSPITAL care.

HEALTH CENTRES, clinics run by general practitioners and the HEALTH VISITOR service are controlled by the area health authority. *See also:* AMBULANCE

General complaints about the running of the health service in a particular area must be made to the area authority, but eventually a complaint can be pursued to the Department of Health and Social Security and the Secretary of State in London.

NATIONAL INSURANCE CONTRIBUTIONS

How society pays for its welfare benefits

Most employees and self-employed people have to pay national insurance contributions; some employees pay them voluntarily so as to qualify for certain benefits: maternity grant, widow's benefit or retirement pensions among others.

The contributions largely finance Britain's system of social security benefits.

When a refund is due

Contributions must be paid on earnings from all jobs. If by doing this you pay more than the prescribed amount of contributions for a year, you may obtain a refund.

Rights to benefit

Your rights to social security benefits depend on the appropriate contribution requirements being met. Failure to satisfy the requirement may reduce or cancel the benefit.

For example, to qualify for SICKNESS BENEFIT you must have paid in any one income tax year, a certain amount – varying according to circumstances – of Class 1 or 2 contributions. In addition, to obtain full benefit you must have paid contributions of at least 50 times the amount payable on a weekly earnings limit; or 50 Class 2 contributions. These must be paid in the income tax year which ended in the calendar year before that in which you claim benefit. If you have less than 50 times the required amount, but at least 25 times, benefit is still payable at a reduced rate.

How you can pay too much – and what to do about it

If, as an employee, you pay Class 1 contributions in more than one job, you may pay more than the set annual maximum as in 1981–2, for example, £821.50.

If you find you have paid too much get form CF28f from any DHSS office, complete and send it to DHSS, Refunds Group, Records Division, Newcastle upon Tyne, NE98 1YX. Enclose evidence of payment of the contributions, for example form P60, or a statement from your employer.

There are, however, two ways to avoid paying too much and having to wait for a refund.

You can:
● Defer payment of contributions for some of your jobs.
● Pay in advance the maximum amount of contributions due for the year.

Deferring payment You can ask to defer payment of national insurance contributions if you have to pay Class 1 contributions in two or more jobs *and* you expect to pay contributions in one of them on earnings of £200 a week or £866.67 a month (1981–2) throughout the tax year concerned. This also applies where you have a number of jobs and you expect to pay contributions on total earnings of £200 a week or more.

To apply for deferment, fill in form CF379, attached to DHSS leaflet NP28 *More than one job?* and send it to DHSS Class 4 Group, Newcastle upon Tyne NE98 1YX with any relevant evidence – for example, pay slips. To take full advantage of deferment, send the form

before April 6. If it is sent after that date, your employer is responsible for refunding to you any contributions you have paid before the DHSS issues a deferment certificate.

The DHSS decides in which of your jobs contributions are to be deferred, and a deferment certificate is sent to the employer. Employers are not given any information about your other jobs.

If you are both employed and self-employed and expect that your total contributions in the tax year are likely to be £10 more than the annual maximum, you can defer paying your Class 2 and 4 contributions until it is possible to work out your exact liability. To apply, complete form CF359, attached to DHSS leaflet NP18 *Class 4 contributions* and send it to DHSS Class 4 Group.

Advance payments You can pay in advance an amount equal to your max-

THE RATES AT WHICH INDIVIDUALS MUST PAY NATIONAL INSURANCE CONTRIBUTIONS

There are four classes of national insurance contribution:
● Class 1. All people aged between 16 and 65 (60 for women) who work for an employer and whose earnings reach the lower earnings limit (£27 a week in 1981–2) pay Class 1 contributions. They are also paid by company directors on schedule E income tax.

Class 1 contributions consist of a combined payment by employee and employer, and the employee's contribution is deducted from his pay before he receives it.

The amount of your contribution depends on your earnings and on whether you are contracted out of the state pension scheme. *See:* RETIREMENT PENSION

In 1981–2, employees who were not contracted out of the scheme had to pay 7.75 per cent of their gross earnings up to a maximum of £200 a week. Their employer on their behalf paid the equivalent of 13.7 per cent of the employee's earnings.

Those who are contracted out have to pay 7.75 per cent of their gross earnings up to £27 a week and 5.25 per cent on the remainder up to earnings of £200 a week. Their employer pays 13.7 per cent and 9.2 per cent over the same earnings range.

Since April 1978 men and women generally pay the same contributions, but some wives and widows who were entitled to pay reduced rates before that date, still have the right to do so.

Any woman entitled to pay the reduced

(2.75 per cent) rate of Class 1 or Class 2 contributions loses that right if she does not work and pay contributions for two complete tax years after April 6, 1978.

If you are an employee, but are outside the Class 1 age range, ask for a certificate of exemption from your local social security office and give it to your employer.
● Class 2. If you are self-employed between 16 and 65 (60 for women) and earning more than the small-earnings limit (£1,475 in 1981–2), you have to pay the flat-rate Class 2 contribution, £3.40 a week in 1981–2.

Women pay at the same rate as men except for those married women and widows who, before May 11, 1977, exercised their option when self-employed not to pay Class 2 contributions and, if they became liable, to pay Class 1 contributions at a reduced rate.

A self-employed person who expects his earnings to be below the small-earnings limit can apply for a certificate of exemption at the local social security office. But it may be better for him not to take that option, as it means losing his right to sickness benefit and retirement pension and deprives his widow of pension, widow's benefit and death grant.

If you are both self-employed and an employee you are liable for Class 1 and Class 2 contributions up to a specified amount (£823.19 in 1981–2).

You must pay Class 2 contributions as

you earn, either by direct debit on your bank or National Girobank account, or by stamping a contribution card obtainable from your local social security office with stamps bought weekly at a post office. Failure to do so can incur a penalty up to £50.
● Class 3. If you are not liable to pay Class 1 or 2 contributions you may choose to pay flat-rate Class 3 contributions to help you to qualify for certain social security benefits – for example, MATERNITY grant, WIDOW'S BENEFITS and DEATH GRANT. The rate in 1981–2 was £3.30 a week. *See also:* CHILD BENEFIT; RETIREMENT PENSION

Anyone considering making Class 3 contributions should ask the local social security office whether he will gain by it.

Class 3 contributions are paid by direct debit on a bank or National Girobank account, by cheque or by stamping a contribution card.
● Class 4. If you are self-employed you may have to pay an earnings-related contribution in addition to your flat-rate Class 2 contribution. It is charged by the Inland Revenue on profits chargeable to income tax under schedule D.

The rate for 1981–2 was 5.75 per cent of profits between £3,150 and £10,000, with a maximum of £393.87 payable on profits of £10,000 or more.

A man over 65 and a woman over 60, and anyone not resident for tax purposes in Britain, does not pay Class 4 contributions.

imum national insurance contribution liability for the year if you pay Class 1 contributions in two or more jobs and you expect to pay more in contributions than the annual maximum.

The amount you will have to pay varies according to how many of your jobs are contracted out.

To make an advance payment, use form CF379 and send it with your payment to DHSS Class 4 Group. All your employers will then be told not to deduct your part of the national insurance contributions from your earnings.

NATIONAL INSURANCE LOCAL TRIBUNAL

How to appeal if your claim for a state benefit is rejected

Anyone who is refused a SOCIAL SECURITY BENEFIT, including INDUSTRIAL INJURY BENEFIT or UNEMPLOYMENT BENEFIT, is entitled to appeal to an independent National Insurance local tribunal. It costs nothing.

Benefit claims are decided in the first instance by insurance officers at social security or unemployment offices. If an insurance officer turns down your claim he must send you as soon as reasonably possible a notice that tells you of your right to appeal within 28 days.

If you decide to do so, obtain a form from the local DHSS office, complete it and return it as soon as possible.

Even if you do not decide to appeal until after the 28 day limit has expired, you should still complete the form, saying why you did not send it earlier. The chairman of the local tribunal normally gives permission for a late appeal if he regards it as a reasonable one. He reaches that decision without your having to attend.

Preparing for a hearing

About 2 or 3 months after you send the form, you receive a batch of papers from the clerk to the tribunal in your area, telling you where and when your appeal is to be heard. If you, or a witness you need, cannot attend, telephone the clerk. An adjournment is granted for any good reason.

The papers sent to you are exactly the same as those which the members of the tribunal see before they hear your appeal. They include the insurance officer's submission to the tribunal, justifying his decision against you.

The insurance officer's submission gives references to relevant laws and regulations, and to previous decisions reached by the SOCIAL SECURITY COMMISSIONERS in similar cases. You are entitled to read anything mentioned in that way before your appeal is heard. If you contact the tribunal clerk he arranges for you to do so.

Appearing at the tribunal

Your hearing is held informally – not in a court but in a room provided by the department.

The chairman, almost always a lawyer, sits at a table flanked by the two other members of the tribunal. One is chosen from a panel representing employers and the self-employed, the other from a panel representing employees – usually trade union nominees.

The clerk selects the members from each panel. If the tribunal is hearing a woman's appeal, the clerk tries to include at least one woman.

You sit at the table opposite the tribunal. There is space beside you for witnesses if necessary, or simply for someone to accompany you if you wish.

You can appoint anyone to speak for you, but if he is a solicitor you are responsible for his fee.

The clerk and the insurance officer who decided your case sit at other tables.

The chairman first puts you at your ease by explaining the proceedings. Then he usually asks you to put your case. You or your witnesses do not take an oath. It is then up to you to prove your case. Be sure you produce all the evidence, such as documents or witnesses, that you need.

The chairman or members may question you. The insurance officer is invited to do the same. He may also make points of his own, and you are entitled to put questions to him.

After all the evidence is heard, you wait in another room. The insurance officer also goes out while the tribunal comes to its decision. The clerk usually comes and tells you the tribunal's decision immediately.

A few days later you are sent full details of the tribunal's findings and reasons. If you are not satisfied you can appeal further to the Social Security Commissioner. But if the decision is unanimous, you need permission from the tribunal chairman or the commissioner.

Expenses If you lose wages or incur travelling expenses by attending your appeal hearing, tell the tribunal clerk as soon as it is over.

NATIONALISED INDUSTRY

When the state owns a business

Many industries and services are controlled by the Government on behalf of the public – but members of the public have no special say in how they are run. Nor does a Member of Parliament, although he may take part in decisions on general policy – for example, when a government wants legal power to take over an industry, or when there is political argument over meeting losses.

The detailed running of any nationalised enterprise is in the hands of chairmen and directors who are appointed by the Government. They are responsible to various government departments, whose ministers have authority over major financial decisions – but no power to interfere in day-to-day commercial operations.

If you have a dispute or complaint involving a nationalised industry, you normally have to take it up as you would with any other commercial enterprise.

NATIONALITY

The relationship of people to the country where they belong

A person holds the nationality of the country to which he or she belongs – usually by birth, but sometimes through parentage or long residence.

Nationality has no exact legal definition in Britain. It generally has the same meaning as CITIZENSHIP, but not always. For example, someone who obtains citizenship of the United Kingdom and colonies may have to renounce his previous citizenship and all his rights in his birthplace – but he does not lose his nationality there. In that sense many people have a dual nationality, while few have the rights of dual citizenship.

For IMMIGRATION control purposes, in deciding who has the unrestricted right to enter and stay in Britain, the significance of nationality is overshadowed by the rules of PATRIALITY. They recognise links with Britain that have nothing to do with nationality.

The concept of nationality is, however, important in international law. Someone who is subject to a DEPORTATION order, or who is refused entry to a country of which he is not a national, can normally be sent only to the country of which he is a national – usually the one that issued his PASSPORT which is bound to accept him.

What to put as your nationality

Asking someone's nationality – for example, in a job application form – can cause confusion and produce the wrong answer. A carefully designed form provides for people to state separately their:
- Country of birth.
- Country of citizenship.
- Country of usual residence.
- Country of present residence.

All four may be different – and all four might give a person a claim to nationality.

Example: A New Zealand-born nurse lives in London during a working holiday. She was brought up in Sydney and carries an Australian passport. Her permanent home is in Fiji, where her parents have taken citizenship. So in various senses she 'belongs' in New Zealand, Australia and Fiji. And if either of her parents was born in Britain she is a United Kingdom patrial: the law says she 'belongs' in this country too, and cannot be deported.

If you are asked to state your nationality, it is advisable to give your country of citizenship. If you are not a UK citizen, but like the nurse have a certificate of patriality, you should state your citizenship and add: 'UK patrial'. If you are not a citizen but have a UK residence permit, that should be stated.

NATURAL JUSTICE

Basic rules that ensure you get a fair hearing

Tribunals, inquiries and many other bodies with powers to make decisions

STALLHOLDER WAS SEEN BUT NOT HEARD

Under the rules of natural justice a person is entitled to a proper chance to put his side of the case.

Mr Hook, a stallholder in Barnsley market, was seen urinating in the market when the public lavatories were closed. A complaint was made to the market manager and a local council sub-committee revoked Mr Hook's licence. The sub-committee, however, decided the case in the presence of the market manager but in Mr Hook's absence. Mr Hook appealed against the decision to the Divisional Court.

DECISION

The sub-committee's decision was quashed on the grounds that it had disregarded the rules of natural justice.

DOCTOR'S EVIDENCE WAS TOO ONE-SIDED

The most basic, underlying rule of natural justice states that there must be no suspicion of bias in the body that comes to a decision in a dispute.

A police inspector was first put on sick leave and then compulsorily retired because of a mental disorder. Both steps were taken on the evidence of Dr Brown, chief medical officer of Kent Police authority.

The inspector opposed his enforced retirement and sought a court order quashing the police authority's decision in his case.

DECISION

The Court of Appeal held that the authority violated the rules of natural justice by appointing Dr Brown as medical referee when he had already made an unfavourable report on the inspector when recommending him for sick leave.

The court quashed the police authority's decision and ordered an unbiased doctor to act as medical referee.

affecting an individual's welfare must abide by certain basic rules of fair play known as natural justice.

The rules are:

1. The members of the deciding body must not appear to be biased. For example, a miner who has to make a claim for industrial injuries benefit should not have his appeal heard by a tribunal which includes an official or representative of the National Coal Board.

If you suspect bias in a body deciding your case, protest to the chairman. He will probably adjourn the hearing so that a differently constituted body can decide the case.

If you discover only after the case is finished that there has been some kind of bias, ask a solicitor to apply to the Divisional Court of the Queen's Bench to have the decision quashed.

2. You must get a fair hearing. Evidence must not be given behind your back and you must be allowed to put your own side of the case in your own way – within reason – in your own time.

If you think this rule of natural justice has been broken the remedy, again, is to ask a solicitor to make an application to the Divisional Court.

NATURALISATION

How an alien can become a British citizen

An alien – someone who is not a citizen of the Commonwealth or the Republic of Ireland – can apply to become a UK citizen by naturalisation. The process can take up to 2 years and will cost £70.

An application form is obtained from the Home Office Nationality Department, Lunar House, Wellesley Road, Croydon CR9 2BY.

The completed form must be signed by the applicant before a solicitor or justice of the peace. References are required from four householders who must be UK citizens born in Britain. They cannot include relatives or the applicant's solicitor or agent.

The form and the references are then sent to the Home Office Nationality Department. If the application is approved, the Home Office sends the applicant an oath of allegiance that must be sworn before a solicitor or JP.

After that, the applicant is asked to

pay the £70 fee and is issued with a certificate of naturalisation.

The Home Secretary can refuse an application and often does so. He does not need to state his reasons and there is no appeal. The granting of naturalisation to a husband does not give citizenship to his wife, but she can register as the wife of a UK citizen.

Who can apply

An applicant must:

1. Have been ordinarily resident in the United Kingdom or have been in Crown service for the 12 months immediately before the application – and ordinarily resident in the United Kingdom or a colony (or other territory administered by the United Kingdom) or in Crown service, for 4 of the 7 years before that.
2. Be of good character.
3. Have enough grasp of English to fulfil his duties as a citizen and mix easily in society.
4. Intend to go on living in the United Kingdom or a colony, or to continue in 'relevant employment'.

NEGLECTED LAND

How to force an owner to clean up untidy land

An owner who neglects his land and allows weeds to grow or rubbish to pile up on it can be ordered by the local council to tidy the site. Anyone can complain to the council about the condition of any land in its area. The council may also act without a complaint being made, for example if one of its officials feels something should be done about an untidy site.

If the owner of untidy land takes no notice of a council order to clear it up he can be prosecuted and fined up to £50. The local council can also clean up the land and claim the cost of the work from the owner.

Often, the owner cannot be found. It is then a decision for the council whether to clear the site at its own expense. Whether it does so will depend on the seriousness of the problem, and the strength of local feeling about it.

If an owner allows what are called 'injurious weeds' to grow unchecked on his land, he can be reported to the Ministry of Agriculture, which can

order him to prevent the weeds from spreading. Injurious weeds are those – such as spear thistle, creeping or field thistle, curled dock, broad-leaved dock or ragwort – which spread quickly and can stifle and kill farmers' crops.

If the owner ignores a Ministry order to prevent such weeds from spreading, he can be prosecuted and fined up to £75 for a first offence and up to £150 for any subsequent offence.

Your right to grow weeds

Apart from injurious weeds, a person can grow any weeds he likes – for example, to attract butterflies to his garden – provided the weeds do not detract from other people's enjoyment of their land.

If weeds from a neighbour's land spread to your land, or if the condition of his land interferes with your enjoyment of your own land, you may be able to take a civil action against him for NUISANCE.

Alternatively, you could complain to the local council and ask it to require the owner to end the nuisance. Whether it would do so would depend upon the seriousness of the problem and how many people were affected by it. The council might not act, for example, if it felt the matter was simply one between you and a neighbour.

The local council has power to remove any ABANDONED VEHICLE from land in its area.

It is an offence to drop LITTER on any open land and anyone who does so can be fined up to £100.

If you know that a piece of neglected land is infested with rats or mice, inform the PEST CONTROL department of the local council.

NEGLIGENCE

Damages can be claimed for injuries caused by carelessness

Anyone who injures another person or damages his property through an act of carelessness can be liable for damages for negligence.

The law expects a person to take reasonable care at whatever he is doing. Motorists are expected to drive with such care that they do not mount the pavement and run down pedestrians. Employers are expected to see that

WHEN YOU ARE SUED FOR NEGLIGENCE

Damages awarded for negligence can be high, but you can take out insurance to protect yourself in the event of a claim.

All motorists have to be insured by law against the risk of negligently injuring other people in accidents.

Employers must insure against injury to workmen caused by negligence. *See:* ACCIDENT AT WORK

Householders face risks, too. A tree could fall on to a roadway, injuring a passer-by. The dog could dash into the road, causing a driver to swerve wrecking his car. Comprehensive policies can cover such claims. *See:* PROPERTY INSURANCE

their goods are stored safely and do not fall down on top of workmen. *See:* EMPLOYER'S LIABILITY

A householder is expected to take care of his property and to see that unrepaired walls or chimney stacks do not crash on to the house next door. *See:* OCCUPIERS' LIABILITY

A dentist is expected to show enough skill not to break a patient's jaw. *See:* MEDICAL NEGLIGENCE

Three points must be proved in any claim for negligence:
● The defendant owed a duty to the plaintiff to take care.
● The defendant was in breach of that duty.
● The breach of duty caused harm to the plaintiff.

When there is a duty of care

Carelessness alone does not leave a person liable for negligence. The plaintiff has to prove that the defendant foresaw that his actions could lead to injuring someone and that he had a responsibility towards the person whom he harmed.

A building contractor, for instance, has a duty to see that no one is harmed on a site he is working. A nursery school has a duty not to let the children run into the road. A man who makes or repairs goods has a duty to see that they do not harm people who use them.

But, in law, a person who watches a blind man walk over a cliff to his death has no duty of care to the man, even though he could foresee the harm.

> ## THE PHOTOGRAPHER WHO WENT TOO CLOSE
>
> *A competitor in a dangerous sporting event has no duty of care towards a spectator sitting where spectators are not allowed.*
>
> Photographer Edmond Wooldridge was sitting on a bench beside the arena at the White City, London, during the 1959 National Horse Show, and he stayed there, despite being warned by a steward.
>
> A horse, Work of Art, ridden by Mr Holladay, swerved wide and galloped towards Mr Wooldridge. He was scared of horses and took fright and fell into the path of the horse. He was knocked down and suffered severe injuries.
>
> Mr Wooldridge sued Mr Hugh Sumner, the owner of the horse. Mr Sumner's rider was found to be negligent because the horse was going too fast and was a risk to anyone sitting on the benches. He appealed.
>
> ### DECISION
>
> The Appeal Court ruled that Mr Sumner's rider was not negligent. Provided that a competition or game was being performed within the rules by a person of adequate skill and competence, the spectator could not expect his safety to be regarded by the competitor. By sitting where spectators were not allowed, Mr Wooldridge had taken a risk.

A motor-cyclist who knocks down a child has a duty of care to the child – but he cannot be sued for negligence by a woman 30 yds away who faints on sight of the accident, and breaks an arm. *See also:* NERVOUS SHOCK

A man who sees a badly injured person at the roadside and does not stop to help cannot be sued for negligence even if the person dies. But a rescuer who is injured trying to save a person from a fire started by the negligence of a workman, can sue the workman.

The law, however, draws no clear lines on where a duty to avoid foreseeable harm begins or ends. New cases in the courts constantly lead to the definition of new areas of duty.

How much care must you take?

In deciding whether a person has failed in his duty to take care, the courts apply an intangible yardstick – did the defendant take the care that would be taken by a reasonable man?

That cannot be defined. It depends always on the circumstances of the case and the attitude of the court hearing it.

The principle applied is: were the actions of the defendant those of a person of reasonable intelligence?

It is no defence to say that a man acted to the best of his ability if that ability falls below the level that the court would expect from its imaginary reasonable man. A person whose reactions are slower than average is not excused from a charge of negligence.

Knowledge that a situation is dangerous increases a defendant's duty to take care. A motorist who regularly uses a hazardous stretch of road is expected to take a higher measure of care than a stranger would.

An employer who engages a welder with one eye has a greater responsibility to the man to see that he wears goggles. A decorator, left alone in a house, who went out leaving the door open could be sued for negligence if the house was burgled.

Failing to use your skills

Anyone who is given a task because he claims to have a particular skill is negligent if he causes injury by failing to use it. A doctor who fails to diagnose a disease cannot claim that he acted to the best of his ability if a doctor of reasonable skill would have diagnosed it.

A girl, however, who has her ears

> ### CAN YOU GET YOUR DAMAGES?
>
> The first question in all cases where you have suffered damage because of someone's behaviour is – should you sue?
>
> In many cases there is no precedent to guide you on whether a claim for negligence will succeed. Ask your solicitor to write first to the other person claiming damages.
>
> If he refuses to accept liability, you and your solicitor must decide if the claim is worth pursuing in the courts.
>
> Try to find out if the other person is insured. If not, he may have no means of paying damages even if they are awarded to you.

pierced by a jeweller cannot claim damages merely because her ears become infected – the jeweller has to show only the skill of a jeweller, not that of a doctor.

When injury could not be foreseen

A person who has failed to take reasonable care is liable for negligence even if the extent of the injury that occurs could not have been foreseen.

A man who strikes another person a gentle blow and causes a fractured skull because the skull is only egg-shell thick, cannot claim as a defence that he had no idea his gentle blow could cause such damage.

When contributory negligence is involved

A person's injuries are sometimes partly caused by his own fault, even when he is the victim of someone else's negligence. In such cases any damages are reduced, usually by the amount of blame attached to the plaintiff.

A moped rider who is not wearing a crash helmet when injured in an accident has contributed negligence, and so has a car passenger hurt when not wearing a safety belt. A motor-cyclist who runs into the back of an unlighted car at night, shares the negligence with the car owner.

In some cases a plaintiff may be entirely to blame for injuries received through another person's negligence. A photographer who goes too near the jumps at a horse show has no claim if he is hit by a horse which falls, even though the rider is careless. A spectator dozing on the boundary at a cricket match cannot complain if he is hit by the ball.

It is no defence, however, for a motorist to put a notice in his car that all passengers travel at their own risk. If his careless driving causes the passenger injury, he is liable for negligence.

NEIGHBOUR

Settling disputes with the people next door

Most disputes with neighbours can be settled tactfully between the people involved, but when an irritation such as noise or fumes is persistent, a householder may be able to sue for NUISANCE.

The nuisance may be caused by excessive bonfire smoke, noisy radios, dangerous boundary walls, damaging tree roots or noisy work at night.

It is no defence for a neighbour to show that the action has been going on for years without complaint or that it was created by a former owner.

The complainant can ask for a court order stopping the nuisance and in some cases can get damages from the same court. *See also:* BOUNDARIES, WALLS AND FENCES

NERVOUS SHOCK

Claiming damages for injuries that are not physical

Anyone who suffers nervous shock as a result of an accident, whether or not he or she was actually involved, can sometimes claim damages for negli-

PRACTICAL JOKE MADE A WIFE ILL

A person who passes on bad news he knows to be untrue and as a result causes someone nervous shock, can be liable for damages.

Thomas Wilkinson went to the races. In the evening, while he was on his way home, a friend, Mr Downton, went to Mr Wilkinson's home and told his wife that her husband had been in an accident and was lying at a pub in Leytonstone with both legs broken.

It was a practical joke, because there was nothing wrong with Mr Wilkinson. But the shock of the news made Mrs Wilkinson very ill. She suffered from vomiting and physical consequences which at one time threatened her reasoning.

DECISION

The appeal judge said Mr Downton should have realised his statement could cause harm, therefore intent was implied. Damages of £100 were awarded against him.

A FATHER WHO HEARD HIS CHILD SCREAM

A parent who suffers nervous shock because of an accident to his child can claim damages even if he did not witness the incident.

Mr Boardman and his 8-year-old son were going on a seaside trip with a friend, Mr Sanderson, but they had to call first at a garage near Newcastle to collect Mrs Sanderson's car.

Mr Boardman agreed to go to the garage office and pay the service bill while Mr Sanderson backed the car on to the forecourt. The boy stayed playing on the forecourt.

As the car was being backed out by Mr Sanderson, it ran over the boy's foot, trapping him. The boy screamed. Mr Boardman who could hear from within the garage office, dashed out to find his son trapped under the car.

The boy was eventually awarded £1,250 damages. His father, who suffered from shock, also claimed damages from Mr Sanderson. He was awarded £75. Mr Sanderson appealed.

DECISION

The award was upheld. The Appeal Court ruled that Mr Sanderson ought to have known that the boy was on the forecourt, and he certainly knew that the father was within earshot. The accident was one which could have been foreseen. Therefore, Mr Sanderson had a duty to the father as well as to the boy.

gence. He must be able to prove that the defendant was careless and that the shock led to real illness.

A pregnant woman, for example, who sees a carelessly driven car crash into a wall near her and who subsequently has a miscarriage, can claim damages. So can a parent who suffers nervous shock after seeing his or her child hurt in an accident.

NEW HOUSE

A 10 year safeguard against bad building and subsidence

If you are buying a new house, or one that is less than 10 years old, inquire whether it is covered by the registration scheme run by the National House-Building Council to protect housebuyers against defects caused by bad building or subsidence.

Almost all new houses are covered by it; only houses built by a registered builder, or under the supervision of an architect or chartered building surveyor, can be registered.

Protection under the scheme

Building societies insist on registration before offering a mortgage on a new house. Even when a house is more than 10 years old and no longer covered, it is of interest to a prospective buyer to know whether it was built to the standards laid down by the scheme.

For up to 2 years after completion, the builder must return and put right, at his own expense, any defects arising from his failure to comply with the council's minimum standards of workmanship and materials. The scheme does not cover normal wear and tear, normal shrinkage cracks, fences, boundary walls and lifts. Electrical moving parts and central-heating boilers are covered for only 1 year.

If the builder fails to carry out the repairs, the house-purchase agreement provides for arbitration and, if necessary, the council honours any arbitrator's award up to £5,000.

Between 3 and 10 years after completion, the buyer is covered against major structural defects up to the limit set out in the agreement. The scheme does not cover less serious defects, but these may still be the builder's responsibility.

Other legal safeguards

Whether the new house is registered does not affect the buyer's right to claim damages through the courts in the normal way. For example, the original buyer can sue the builder or architect for breach of contract, without needing to prove negligence, for up to 6 years from the time of the contract if the house is not up to specification.

Similarly, under general law, anyone, either the original buyer or any later owner or tenant of the house, can sue the builder or architect over any defect that is a threat to the health or safety of the house's occupants and causes injury or financial loss, provided he can show negligence – that is, lack of proper skill or care.

In the case of personal injury the action can be brought within 3 years of the defect being discovered. In the case of financial loss the time limit is 6 years.

The great advantages of the National House-Building Council scheme are that, in some cases, the buyer can obtain redress if the builder or architect goes bankrupt and that he does not have to prove the defect was caused by negligence.

To ensure that you do not lose your right to benefit, tell the builder, or the council, in writing about any defects as soon as they appear.

If you are a second or subsequent buyer of a house still covered by the scheme, you cannot claim later for any defects that the seller should have reported or were visible, on reasonable inspection, at the time of your purchase. Ask your surveyor to note the items and insist that the seller reports them in writing to the builder or council.

When a deposit is returnable

If a builder requires a deposit from a prospective buyer, the buyer should ensure that the receipt he is given makes clear that the money will be returned if the sale falls through.

NEXT OF KIN

How the law distinguishes between relations and spouses

A person's closest blood relatives are his next of kin. They take precedence in any claim to the estate of a single or widowed person who has died intestate.

A strict order of kinship applies in INHERITANCE claims. If a man dies leaving no wife and no will, his next of kin, in order are:

1. Any children, who share everything equally.
2. His parents.
3. Any brothers and sisters, who share everything equally.
4. Any half-brothers.
5. Any aunts or uncles.
6. The grandparents.
7. Any cousins.
See also: INTESTACY

Married people frequently give the name of their spouse as next of kin, on forms such as those signed on entry to hospital. That has no legal meaning since spouses are not blood relatives and therefore not next of kin, but it identifies the person to be contacted in an emergency.

NOISE OFFENCES

Using the law to stop a nuisance caused by noise

A householder can take action through the courts or through his local council to stop someone – a company or an individual – from making a noise that is causing a NUISANCE.

The noise may be from factory works, from lorries or even a neighbour's stereo record player played consistently too loudly. Generally, you should be able to show that the noise causes disturbance such as regular loss of sleep, excessive vibration or even damage to a property.

When the council can act to stop the nuisance

The simplest course of action is to complain to the police who will visit the source of complaint and ask those concerned to stop the nuisance. However, the police cannot usually prosecute and if the problem continues they will advise you to go to the local council and ask it to serve a noise-abatement notice on the offending premises.

Send the complaint and any evidence of the annoyance you can muster to the local environmental health officer, or go and discuss the problem with him.

If the council agrees that the noise is a nuisance and issues an abatement notice, whoever occupies the premises named in the notice will be forbidden from continuing to make the noise or will be restricted to making it only during certain times of the day.

If the noise continues, the council can prosecute the occupant of the premises. Unless it can be shown that the occupant has taken the best practicable steps to reduce the noise he can be fined up to £200 for a first offence and £400 for any subsequent offences, plus up to £50 for every day the noise continues.

When a council considers a noise to be particularly offensive it may take proceedings in the High Court for an INJUNCTION to stop the noise.

Taking action yourself

Whether or not the local council issues a noise-abatement notice, anyone suffering from a noise nuisance can ask the local magistrates' court to issue a summons against the person making the noise.

Get evidence from neighbours and friends who have also experienced the noise and ask your doctor for a confirmatory letter if the noise has caused a health problem – for instance if you have taken sleeping pills.

The magistrates can issue a noise-abatement notice with the same requirements as that issued by a local council. If someone refuses to comply with such a notice, he can be brought back to court and fined up to £200 for a first offence and £400 for any subsequent offences, plus £50 a day for continued noise.

Local regulations Many local authorities have bye-laws that regulate the amount of noise allowed in certain circumstances. Check with your local environmental health officer if you are being annoyed by a noise. It may be possible to prosecute the offender under the bye-laws.

Sources of noise nuisance

All local authorities have special powers to deal with noise from building sites. If building work is causing you annoyance, contact the local council, who can issue an abatement notice and make specific regulations, for example, to use a pile driver only within certain hours.

Music near houses Bye-laws in many areas ban the playing of musical or noisy instruments in a public place within 100 yds of a house or office. The complainant must show that the noise interferes with normal activities or is unreasonable.

Radios and record players It is possible under some bye-laws to prosecute a person who continually plays a radio, stereo or amplifier so loudly as to cause annoyance, and that applies even if the instrument is being played in a public place.

Before the prosecution can be made,

> ## NOISY PLAYGROUND CUT HOTEL TRADE
>
> *Damages can be awarded if noise interferes with a person's trade.*
>
> Mr and Mrs Dunton ran a hotel in Dover next to an open space owned by Dover council.
>
> Children from a nearby housing estate used the open space as a playground. The Duntons found that the noise of the children playing drove away some of their custom. In 1977 they sued the council.
>
> ### DECISION
>
> The court held that the noise was a nuisance and the council was responsible as owner of the land. The Duntons were awarded £200 damages and an injunction was issued banning use of the playground except between 10 a.m. and 6.30 p.m. and then only by children under 12.

the offender must be served with a written notice by the complainant or his representative, saying that the noise is a nuisance and asking him to stop it within 14 days. If the noise continues after that, the court action can go ahead.

Noisy animals Most councils have bye-laws making it an offence to keep noisy animals, such as a dog which barks continually.

Other noises Councils also have other bye-laws aimed at controlling noise from street vendors, letting off of fireworks, or making excessive noise near a hospital or church.

In 1978 the maximum penalty for contravening a bye-law was raised from £20 to £50. Not all councils have amended all their bye-laws to apply the new maximum. You can check with your local council.

Prosecuting for a bye-law offence

Anyone can bring a prosecution under local bye-laws, but it is always best to try to persuade the council to take action. Check what anti-noise bye-laws your local council has before you complain.

Loudspeakers and chimes The Control of Pollution Act 1974 lays down national regulations about the use of loudspeakers and chimes in the streets.

It is an offence to use a loudspeaker or chimes in a public place between the hours of 9 p.m. and 8 a.m. Loudspeakers and chimes can be used on vehicles selling food and drink, but only between noon and 7 p.m. and only if the noise does not cause unreasonable annoyance to local residents.

A short burst on the chimes of an ice-cream van is considered allowable; a long tune is not.

Action can be brought by the local council or any citizen. The maximum penalty is a fine of £200 and £400 on a subsequent conviction, plus £50 a day.

Car horns Anyone who sounds the horn of a motor vehicle at any time while the vehicle is stationary is committing an offence, unless there is danger to another, moving vehicle.

It is also an offence to sound a horn of a moving vehicle between 11.30 p.m. and 7 a.m. without reasonable cause. The maximum penalty for both offences is £100.

Noisy public-house customers A neighbour continually offended by noisy customers leaving a public house at night can oppose the publican's application for a renewal of licence when it next goes before local magistrates.

Rates reduction A householder who fails to get a noise nuisance stopped can apply to his local council for a reduction in the rateable value of his property.

NOTICE

When employment comes to an end

The relationship between an employer and an employee is defined by the EMPLOYMENT CONTRACT, which may be a comprehensive written agreement or simply an oral understanding, the conditions of which are drawn from custom and practice.

If either party wants to end the agreement, he must inform the other by giving notice of his intention. If he does not do so, he is in breach of contract and may be sued.

How notice is given

Notice need not be in writing to be valid unless that is specifically provided for in the employment contract. However, it is in the interests of the party serving notice to do so in a letter and to keep a copy, in case of future dispute. Anyone – employer or employee – who believes he has been given oral notice should immediately ask for written confirmation.

Determining how long the notice period should be

Many employment contracts specify notice arrangements, including the length of the notice period before the employment relationship is finally severed. In addition, minimum notice periods are fixed by law for most types of employee, though not for part-timers, working less than 16 hours a week, and those who perform their duties mainly overseas. *See:* EMPLOYMENT PROTECTION

The minimum statutory notice entitlements cannot be reduced by an employment contract. An employee dismissed after 13 years' service is entitled to 12 weeks' notice, even though his contract says he should get less. On the other hand, if the contract provision is more generous than the legal minimum, the contract applies.

A 'reasonable' notice period

If the contract does not specify a notice period and the length of notice becomes a matter of legal dispute – for example, in a claim for UNFAIR DISMISSAL – courts and tribunals consider not only the statutory minimum

THE LAW ON MINIMUM NOTICE PERIODS

The statutory minimum notice periods for employees other than part-timers and those who work overseas are linked to length of service.

Length of service with employer	Notice period
Fewer than 4 weeks	None
4 weeks – 2 years	1 week
2 years – 12 years	1 week for each complete year of service
More than 12 years	12 weeks

provisions, but also what would be 'reasonable' under the circumstances. The factors they take into account include length of service, the nature and seniority of the job and the notice customarily given to others in equivalent positions.

Thus a monthly paid employee who, by statute, is entitled to only 1 week's notice, may be able to argue successfully that he should receive a 'reasonable' period of 1 month, particularly if his colleagues are awarded that amount of notice.

There is no firm rule to determine what is 'reasonable' notice if there is no contract provision. But the more senior the job, the longer the notice period is likely to be – 6 months or more in the case of highly placed executives.

Dismissal without notice

Some offences by employees – particularly those which endanger the lives of others or involve a grave breach of the employer's trust – are so serious that they call for summary dismissal without notice. However, if the dismissed employee takes his case to a court or an industrial tribunal, the burden is on the employer to prove that dismissal without notice was justified. *See:* DISCIPLINE AT WORK

Giving the reasons for notice

An employee who hands in his notice is not obliged to give his reasons. Neither is an employer who dismisses an employee.

However, dismissed employees – apart from those who have been in the job for fewer than 26 weeks, part-timers and those who normally work abroad – are entitled to demand the reasons for their dismissal in writing.

An employee who wants to know why he has been given notice should write a formal letter to his employer asking for the information, keeping a copy of his request. If the employer has not replied within 14 days, the employee can ask an industrial tribunal to order him to do so. If he still refuses, the employer can be required to pay compensation of 2 weeks' wages to the employee. *See:* DISMISSAL

If no notice is given

If an employee simply walks out of his job without telling anyone, he is in breach of contract and can be sued for damages resulting from his action. In practice, whether or not the employer does sue depends on the nature of the employee's job. If the worker is a labourer who can easily be replaced, the employer is unlikely to pursue him through a court because he would be unable to show much financial loss. However, if the disappearing employee is a valued chief research chemist, the cost to his employer of his departure may be high, and a court could award substantial damages.

Employers who do not want to go to court have two other sanctions they can impose against an employee who leaves without giving notice. They can refuse to supply a REFERENCE – which they are not obliged to give, even if the employee has given notice – and they can withhold any accrued pay due to the employee, up to the amount of damages they could win from him in court. The employee then has to sue to obtain the money, or at least to bargain over the amount.

An employer may break an employment contract by refusing to pay wages or allocate work. If he does so without proper reasons and formal notice, the employee can leave and sue him for WRONGFUL DISMISSAL to obtain payment for what would have been the notice period. He can also claim constructive DISMISSAL.

Payment in lieu of notice

An employee who has been dismissed cannot insist on working out his period of notice if his employer does not want him to. All he is entitled to is any accrued earnings plus his wages for the notice period – payment in lieu of notice. However, if he does not receive his notice pay, and is not guilty of an offence justifying summary dismissal, he can sue his employer for wrongful dismissal to obtain his notice money.

An employee who leaves with payment in lieu of notice is still entitled to claim REDUNDANCY or unfair dismissal, and failure to give notice may be evidence that the dismissal is unfair.

If an employee does not complete his notice period

An employee who is under notice is not obliged to work out his full notice period if, for example, he finds another job. He must, however, tell his employer.

An employee who leaves before his notice is complete forfeits his pay for the rest of the notice period, but not his right to claim unfair dismissal or redundancy.

NOTICE OF INTENDED PROSECUTION

When police must warn a motorist that they may take him to court

Within 14 days of certain alleged motoring offences, unless they warn him at the time, the police must send the driver or the registered owner of the vehicle involved a written notice that they intend to prosecute.

The offences are:
● Reckless, careless or inconsiderate driving.
● Failure to obey a traffic sign or a police direction.
● Leaving a vehicle in a dangerous position.
● Speeding.

There is no need to send a warning if an accident occurs at the time of the offence or immediately after it is committed, provided that the accident is due to the presence on the road of the vehicle involved in the offence.

It is not easy for a driver to have his case dismissed because no written notice of the intended prosecution has been received. The onus is on him to prove that no notice was sent.

If police have evidence that a notice was sent by registered post or recorded delivery to the driver's or owner's last known address, the courts will accept that it was served. That applies even if for some reason the notice was returned as undelivered or never reached the person for whom it was intended.

The courts will also allow a case to proceed if police are unable to serve 14 days' notice because they cannot find the driver's name and address or the name and address of the registered owner.

Deciding whether to proceed

Police do not have to go ahead with a prosecution after they have given notice of intent to a driver or vehicle owner.

'

THE DRIVER WHO WENT PAST RED

Police have no need to send a second notice to the real owner of a vehicle if it has already been sold by the registered owner.

Police saw Mr Harvey Harrison drive his car past a red traffic sign. He was not stopped, but police noticed his registration number. Within 14 days they sent a notice of intended prosecution to the person named by the local taxation office as the registered owner.

The name they were given was incorrect. The car had been sold to a dealer, then sold to the company employing Mr Harrison.

It was a month later before police were able to interview Mr Harrison and serve on him notice of intended prosecution.

Mr Harrison raised the technical defence that he had not received a notice within 14 days, and the magistrates dismissed the case. They said that a second notice should have been issued within 14 days of Mr Harrison being traced. The police appealed.

DECISION

The Appeal Court held that no second notice was required. The police had acted with reasonable diligence and their failure to serve notice on the real driver or owner was not their fault.

The case was therefore sent back to the magistrates.

They do not have to tell that person that there will be no prosecution.

The only time limit imposed upon them is that they must start legal proceedings within 6 months of the alleged offence.

NOTICE TO QUIT

When a landlord wants a tenant to leave

A tenant renting property on a periodic letting – that is, from week to week or month to month – must be given a proper notice to quit before he can be made to give up the premises.

The landlord must serve a notice to quit, giving a clear direction in writing to the tenant to leave the whole of the premises and to deliver up possession. It is essential that the length of the notice period is stated and the day on which the premises are to be vacated must be clear. In the case of residential property, the minimum notice period is 4 weeks.

The period of notice, moreover, must be served so as to expire exactly on the day on which the current period of renting (week, month or quarter, for example) ends.

The notice must also inform the tenant of his rights. *See:* EVICTION

Renting for a fixed period

Some properties are rented for set periods – for example, for 6 months or 2 years – and these end automatically when the time limit is up.

No notice to quit the premises is required in such cases. On the other hand, any notice to quit that is actually served by the landlord before the agreed tenancy period is up is not valid and can be ignored by the tenant.

NUISANCE

How the law protects your right to a quiet life

Anyone who turns up the radio too loud, lights smoking bonfires, revs up a stationary car, switches on electrical tools that spoil television reception or interferes in any other way with another person's reasonable enjoyment of his own property or of a public place where he is entitled to be, is causing a nuisance.

Provided that the nuisance is 'substantial', the law offers a whole range of remedies; it is up to you or your solicitor to find the best one for your particular case.

In law, nuisances are divided into four categories:

● Private nuisances that affect a person in his own home.
● Public nuisances that interfere with people at large.
● Statutory nuisances that have been made criminal offences by Act of Parliament.
● Bye-law nuisances that have been made criminal offences by the local authority for your particular area.

Private nuisances

For someone to damage your home, whether you own it or rent it, or spoil your pleasure in living there, is what lawyers call a TORT. Often, a next-door neighbour is the cause of the nuisance.

His pop group rehearses at his home late at night; the roots of his poplar tree spread under your soil and undermine the foundations of your house; he lights bonfires that blacken washing drying in your garden; or his electrical equipment has no suppressor so you cannot get a clear picture on your television set.

But the source of a nuisance may be farther afield: drivers from a neighbouring factory park their lorries outside your home and disturb you early every morning when they rev up.

The court looks at each case in the light of the circumstances. What is a nuisance in a quiet suburb might not be one in the middle of an industrial estate.

Public nuisances

Conduct that annoys many people or occurs in a public place is an indictable criminal offence and can also be a tort.

As a common-law crime, it covers almost any interference with the public of any consequence, particularly on the highway. It has been applied to eavesdropping, urinating in a public place and running a factory belching out poisonous fumes.

Many offences that are prosecuted under statutes and bye-laws – for example, those involving danger to the public or its health – could still be dealt with as crimes against the common law of public nuisance.

As a tort, public nuisance is similar to private nuisance, except that its application is wider. Only the owner or occupier of a property can bring an action for private nuisance. Even a member of his family, living with him, cannot do so.

Any adult, however, can bring a civil action for public nuisance if he can show that someone has caused him particular harm in a public place.

It is a public nuisance, for example, if an unsafe wall falls on your daughter as she is walking along a footpath; if you have a caravan near a secluded beach and a family from a neighbouring caravan regularly sit near you on the beach

> ## FAULTY WIRING BURNED DOWN NEIGHBOUR'S HOME
>
> *A householder is liable to pay damages for nuisance if a workman he employs fails to take precautions and causes injury to a neighbour.*
>
> Mr Smee had new electrical wiring installed in his house. The work carried out by the contractor he employed was faulty and it later caused a fire that spread next door, destroying Mr Spicer's bungalow. He sued Mr Smee for causing a nuisance.
>
> ### DECISION
>
> Mr Spicer won his case and was awarded damages. The court held that Mr Smee was responsible for the nuisance even though he did not know the work was faulty.
>
> ---
>
> ## OIL DEPOT MADE THE WASHING DIRTY
>
> *Damage to a person's belongings caused by industrial operations can be a nuisance even if the work is carried out properly.*
>
> Oil was distributed from a depot near Mr Halsey's house in Fulham, London. He sued the company for nuisance and claimed that acidy smuts from the depot damaged washing put out to dry and his car parked in front of the house.
>
> He also complained of a nauseating smell, noise at night and nuisance caused by tankers arriving at night.
>
> ### DECISION
>
> The judge visited Mr Halsey's house one night and Mr Halsey won his case. The company was ordered to stop committing the nuisance and ordered to pay £235 damages.

and play a radio at full volume; or if someone regularly parks his car on the road outside your father's home so that you cannot drive into your father's driveway.

Statutory nuisances

Parliament has passed specific laws to deal with various nuisances that affect the public as a whole, particularly in the field of public health. For example, people or companies engaged in trade or industry are guilty of a criminal offence if they cause blocked drains, dust and noxious fumes, or if they fail to comply with the Control of Pollution Act or the Clean Air Act.

Bye-law nuisances

Parliament has delegated to local authorities the power to make certain nuisances criminal offences. These bye-laws vary all over the country but, generally, they deal with such matters as noise, smells from offensive trades, keeping animals and dumping rubbish.

How to deal with a nuisance

First you must decide whether you want simply to end the annoyance, or whether you want also to claim money for the harm it has caused you.

If you want only to stop the nuisance, do not start a private legal action that may cost you a lot of money unless you are sure that neither the police nor your local authority is willing to take action on your behalf.

The bye-laws are open to inspection, free of charge, at your local council offices during normal opening hours. Go through them and see whether there is one that covers the nuisance you are suffering. If it does, report the matter to the council.

The council can either prosecute the offender in a magistrates' court or apply for an INJUNCTION restraining the offender from continuing the nuisance. It also has powers to bring a similar action under common law in cases of public nuisance.

If you think the nuisance may be a statutory one, report it at the council offices, to the environmental health officer, who is responsible for seeing that the statutes are obeyed. He can serve an abatement notice on the offender, requiring him to end the nuisance.

If the offender disobeys, the officer can summon him before the magistrates' court and ask for an order to abate the nuisance. The person responsible can be fined for every day that he fails to do so.

The local authority has powers to do any work necessary to stop the nuisance and recoup the cost from the offender.

Even if the nuisance is not covered by a bye-law or statute, it can still be a public nuisance. Ask your local police constable or at the police station whether action can be taken under common law.

If neither the council nor the police is prepared to take action, you have the right to bring a prosecution yourself under a bye-law or under common law. *See:* PRIVATE PROSECUTION

Instead of bringing a private prosecution, however, you can seek an injunction ordering the person annoying you to stop.

Whether you do so on the basis of private or public nuisance depends on the circumstances: whether you are bringing the action as the owner or occupier of a property or as a member of the general public.

If the person causing a nuisance ignores an injunction, he can be punished for CONTEMPT OF COURT.

Claiming compensation

In addition to, or instead of, seeking an end to the nuisance, you may wish to seek compensation in an action for private or public nuisance.

Then the onus is on you to prove that you have suffered actual damage. If the nuisance has damaged your health, damages would cover medical bills, loss of earnings, and compensation for pain, suffering and inconvenience. If the nuisance has reduced the value of your house, you can claim damages for that loss.

It is no defence for the other person to say that you knew of the nuisance before you moved into the house. However long his conduct was accepted before you arrived, you still have the right to sue.

NULLITY

How legal defects can invalidate a marriage

Nullity is the legal term for something that does not exist. When a marriage is declared to be a nullity, or 'null and void', the process is known as annulment.

It is much rarer than DIVORCE. But the right to annulment remains important to people whose religion forbids divorce, or remarriage after divorce. It also allows a marriage to end quickly, without the 3 year wait normally required before a petition for divorce.

Some so-called marriages are invalid from the start – void – because basic legal requirements were not met when they were performed. Anyone can challenge them at any time, and no court decree is usually needed, although it is better to obtain a court decree to make the legal position clear.

Other marriages are voidable if they are found to be defective later, for other reasons. They can normally be challenged only by one of the partners, and they remain valid until they are annulled by a court decree.

The child of a couple whose marriage was void from the start is ILLEGITIMATE, unless at the time of its conception one or both parties believed that the marriage was valid. The child of a marriage that is voidable is legitimate and stays legitimate even after the decree.

When a marriage is void

A form of marriage is void if:
● Either partner is under the age of 16.
● Either partner is already married.
● The partners were born the same sex – the effect of sex-change surgery is not a ground for nullity, but may be one for divorce.
● The partners are too closely related, breaking the prohibitions in marriage law.
● In a polygamous marriage made legally abroad, either partner is domiciled in England or Wales.
● In a Church of England marriage, banns are not properly published, or a licence or certificate necessary to dispense with banns is not obtained.
● Banns are published in a false name, with the intention of concealment by both partners.

● In a marriage said to be by licence, no proper licence is obtained and both partners know of the irregularity.
● In a marriage authorised by a superintendent registrar's certificate, proper notice is not given and both partners know of the irregularity.
● Some other necessary legal formalities of the ceremony have not been observed. *See:* MARRIAGE

When a marriage is voidable

A marriage can be made void by a court decree of nullity, if:
● Either partner has never been able to have sexual intercourse since the marriage. If the impotent spouse petitions, he or she must have discovered the defect since marriage.
● Either partner has always refused to have sexual intercourse since the marriage, and the other can show that intercourse was proposed with reasonable tact and encouragement, and that the

---

THE BRIDE WHO HAD NEVER BEEN ALONE WITH HER HUSBAND

A marriage by proxy is valid in England if it is legal where it took place – but it is still voidable on other grounds.

Mr Ponticelli, an Italian immigrant, went back to his home village to find a bride. His relatives negotiated with the parents of 18-year-old Miss Giglio, and an engagement was arranged. The couple were never alone together.

Mr Ponticelli returned to England and signed papers, including a power of attorney, so that a marriage could be performed by proxy – with another man representing him at the ceremony.

More than 3 months after the wedding, Mrs Ponticelli arrived in London. Her

husband, who had a room for them in Bedford, where he worked, met her but she refused to greet him – or to board the train for Bedford.

They went to the police and she asked for help in returning to Italy. She was taken to the Italian consulate and then to a convent, where she told the nuns that her relatives had forced her into the marriage.

Without ever spending a night with her husband, she was soon back in Italy. They never saw each other again.

Mr Ponticelli petitioned for nullity on the ground of his wife's refusal to consummate the marriage by sexual intercourse. She agreed that it had not been consummated, but blamed him for that. She also

disputed the validity of the marriage.

The court had to decide whether the marriage had been valid in the first place, and if so, whether there was proof that it was voidable because of later events.

DECISION

The court found that a proxy marriage, with power of attorney, was valid in Italian law. As the marriage took place in Italy, it was therefore valid even though Mr Ponticelli was domiciled in England at the time. It was therefore valid in England.

But under English law, the marriage was voidable because it had not been consummated. Mr Ponticelli was granted his decree of nullity on that ground.

THE PRISONER WHO MARRIED IN TERROR

If someone enters a marriage out of fear – even if the partner's motives are good – the consent is not voluntary.

Dr Szechter, a blind historian in Warsaw, treated his research assistant, Nina, as a daughter. Both of them were opposed to the Communist regime in Poland.

Nina was arrested and held for daily interrogations, with threats that she would be sent to a mental hospital or sentenced to 15 years' imprisonment.

After she had been detained for more than a year, Dr Szechter and his wife obtained a divorce, and he arranged to marry Nina in prison.

The Polish Government then granted him permission to emigrate, and Nina went with him. The former Mrs Szechter also emigrated. In London the old couple reunited, and Nina petitioned for annulment of the prison marriage.

All were domiciled in England, so the court had full power to consider the peti-

tion. It had to decide whether Nina's part in the scheme amounted to a valid consent to marriage.

DECISION

The court ruled that Nina had been under duress – unreasonable pressure – because of fear of what would happen to her otherwise. Her consent to the arrangement was not freely given, so the marriage was voidable. Nina was granted her decree of nullity.

refusal is wilful, definite and without proper excuse. *See:* CONSUMMATION OF MARRIAGE

● Either partner's consent to the marriage was not voluntary, or not validly obtained – for example, because consent was given through fear, or obtained by deception – or because unsoundness of mind, including extreme drunkenness, made either partner incapable of proper consent. But misleading someone into marriage simply by lying about wealth, occupation or social position is not enough to make consent invalid.

● Either partner – even though capable of valid consent – suffered from a MENTAL DISORDER at the time of the marriage such as to make him or her unfit for marriage.

● Either partner had a venereal disease at the time of the marriage and the other was unaware of it.

● The woman was pregnant by another man at the time of the marriage, and the husband was unaware of it.

Annulment on the grounds of non-consummation can be sought at any time while the marriage lasts. But waiting too long can make the petition unfair. Annulment on other grounds can be obtained only if a petition is filed within the first 3 years of marriage.

Procedure in nullity cases is similar to that in divorce, but there is no provision to allow an undefended case to be dealt with simply, without evidence having to be given in court. It is advisable to consult a solicitor, and LEGAL AID is available.

Courts hearing nullity cases have the same powers as divorce courts to make orders for CUSTODY OF CHILDREN and MAINTENANCE.

When a decree would be unfair

A petition for annulment of a voidable marriage – but not of one that was void from the start – can be opposed on the ground that it is unjust to the other partner. The other partner may be able to show that the petitioner led him or her to believe that no attempt would be made to have the marriage annulled. A court convinced of that cannot allow a nullity petition to proceed.

Foreign marriage

Annulment may be difficult if the marriage took place in a country abroad. The court has to consider whether the formalities required in that country were complied with. *See:* FOREIGN MARRIAGE

NUMBER-PLATE

What must be shown – and how to get the one you want

The law lays down strict rules for showing the registration number of a vehicle. *See:* MOTOR VEHICLE

It also makes provision for transferring a sought-after number – for example, one spelling the owner's initials – to another car.

However, you cannot just buy a number-plate, you must buy the vehicle which has the one you want. Then you arrange to switch the number of that vehicle to your car.

BUYING A SPECIAL NUMBER-PLATE FOR THE CAR

You cannot buy just a number-plate; you must also buy the vehicle that goes with it. Then you must wait at least 3 months, unless the vehicle is new.

To make the change, apply to your local vehicle licensing office. You need to fill in a form, and to be able to show that you have owned both vehicles for at least 3 months (unless one of them is new). Both must be registered in your name and also taxed and insured. If either vehicle is more than 3 years old, it needs a roadworthiness test certificate.

If all these conditions can be complied with, fill in an application form. Then make an appointment with the local licensing office for the car bearing the cherished number to be inspected –

to make sure that its details agree with the registration document (log book).

The cherished number is then transferred to your car, and the other vehicle is issued with a new number corresponding with its year of manufacture. Each vehicle is given a new registration document showing its new licence number. The old number on your car disappears from use.

What it costs The fee for transferring a cherished number is £50. You also have to buy the car for which it was issued and provide a new number-plate for it.

If your car is new You do not need to wait 3 months before making the transfer if you want the cherished number for a new car and the other vehicle has been registered in your name for 3 months. In that case, the transfer can be arranged as soon as you get the new car.

NURSERY SCHOOL

Education for children under 5 years old

Schools where children between the ages of 3 and 5 can learn through play and social contact are available in many areas, but local authorities are not required by the Education Act to provide them. They are given the power to provide them if they choose to do so. Since the passing of the Education Act 1980, local authorities cannot close their nursery schools without following the standard procedure for SCHOOL closures.

If there are any local objections to a closure, the Secretary of State for Education and Science decides whether the school should be closed.

Nursery classes attached to a primary school may also be subject to the same procedure when the local authority wants to close all the nursery classes in a school.

Some are run by the local authority and these are free. Others are privately run and parents have to pay fees.

Privately run nursery schools have to register with the local social services department, which lays down regulations about building and teaching, and has the power to supervise them. The regulations vary from area to area.

State-run nursery schools are provided by the education department. They must be held in safe and adequate buildings and have qualified teachers and staff.

When nursery schools are open

Nursery schools are part of the education system and their hours and holidays approximate to those of primary schools.

Many nursery schools take children for only half the day – one group attending in the mornings and another in the afternoon. The children have books, music and play games indoors and outdoors.

Some nursery classes are attached to state schools, sharing the same building, and the children move into the infants department when they reach 5 years of age.

Who can go to nursery school

No more than one in eight children under 5 can attend state nursery schools because there are not enough places to go around.

Many children go to privately run schools and PLAYGROUPS.

State-run nursery schools usually give priority to children with special needs, such as those with language difficulties or other handicaps, children from a ONE-PARENT FAMILY, or children living in deprived conditions.

If there are not enough nursery school places in your area, get together with other parents and write to the education officer to try to persuade the local education authority to open more.

How parents can participate

The legal position of a child in a nursery school is exactly the same as that of an older child in a more senior school, except that, as education is not compulsory under 5 years of age, it is easier to take the child away. The school takes over the parents' authority and responsibility during school hours. It is up to the teachers how far they consult parents about their children.

Using a nursery centre

Experimental nursery centres have been set up jointly by social services departments and local education authorities in some districts. These try to combine the day-care role of the day nursery with the educational aims of the nursery school.

Teachers and nurses work together and advise parents, child-minders and playgroups.

Nursery centres are state-run and priority is usually given to children from deprived or difficult homes or from one-parent families, but the admission rules vary from district to district.

NURSING HOMES

Halfway houses for the sick

Nursing homes are places where people can go for rest, recuperation or nursing care not requiring the degree of medical attention available only in a HOSPITAL.

There are also special maternity nursing homes and mental nursing homes. Others provide day-to-day services such as dental care.

They are run either by charities or by private concerns for profit. They are not part of the National Health Service.

Entering a nursing home is arranged privately, in most cases by the patient's doctor, who can usually recommend a suitable one.

Charges are generally lower than those made for a private bed in a NHS or private hospital.

Homes must be registered

Nursing homes must be registered with the local health authority.

There must be adequate supervision by a resident doctor or qualified nurse and staff must be considered fit for the job by the local health authority.

Some residential rest homes do not provide nursing services. They too must be registered, but with the local authority rather than the health authority.

When a home is negligent

A patient harmed through the negligence of a doctor or nurse in a nursing home can sue that person, and also the owners of the home if the person responsible is employed by them.

Usually doctors who attend patients in private nursing homes are not actually employed there, but are paid fees for their work.

A patient finding that the services provided by a nursing home are not up to the standard he expected can pay only as much of the fee as he feels appropriate to the services he received.

If the nursing home disagrees it can sue him for the amount outstanding.

In more serious circumstances the patient can sue the nursing home for breach of contract.

Help with payments

A person who cannot afford to go into a nursing home might obtain limited help by applying to his local Department of Health and Social Security for SUPPLEMENTARY BENEFIT.

The benefit payable will include an allowance for board and lodging and an additional amount for personal expenses, but will not cover the full fees because supplementary benefit is not allowed to pay for medical treatment. The most that will be paid is what would be considered reasonable for a person living in an old people's home in the area.

Most other income is taken into account when the benefit is assessed.

OATH

Making a binding promise to tell the truth

Anyone who gives evidence in court or takes part in legal proceedings must first make a formal promise to tell the truth. The person can usually choose whether to make the promise in the form of a religious oath or a non-religious affirmation. Both are legally binding and breaking either can result in prosecution for perjury.

Taking an oath in court

The Oaths Act 1978 lays down the usual procedure for taking an oath in court. The person holds a New Testament in his raised hand and says: 'I swear by almighty God that . . .' followed by the words of the oath, which depend on whether it is for evidence given in court, making an affidavit or statutory declaration, or some other legal proceeding.

Members of different religions can follow their own traditions when taking the oath – Roman Catholics, for example, hold the Douai Bible, Jews cover their heads and hold the Pentateuch, Hindus swear on the Vedas and Mohammedans on the Koran.

It is the custom for the Chinese to kneel and break a saucer, saying: 'I tell the truth and the whole truth, if not, as that saucer is broken, may my soul be broken like it.'

If the traditional procedure for taking the oath is inconvenient or impractical the court can insist that the person affirms instead.

Making an affirmation

A person who chooses to make a non-religious affirmation promises to tell the truth by saying: 'I, ——, do solemnly, sincerely and truly declare and affirm . . .' followed by the words of the oath.

How oaths are valid Oaths and affirmations are binding even if a mistake is made in the formal words of procedure. Someone who takes an oath cannot later claim that it was not binding because he does not believe in God.

OBSCENE PUBLICATIONS

Curbs on the portrayal of sex and violence

A publication is obscene if it tends to deprave or corrupt those likely to see it by its depiction of sex or violence. It is a crime to publish such material in any form, including books, magazines, pictures and films and theatre plays. Publication can include lending or giving away as well as selling it. It is a crime to possess obscene material for gain, but not to purchase obscene material or to read it.

There are two ways of enforcing the Obscene Publications Acts:
● The police or anyone else can prosecute either in the magistrates' court or the crown court. The Attorney General's consent is needed.

The accused publisher or bookseller has the right to insist on trial by jury in the crown court.

The maximum penalty for publishing or possessing obscene material is a fine or imprisonment not exceeding 6 months in a magistrates' court and fine and/or imprisonment not exceeding 3 years in a crown court.
● The material can be seized on the authority of a magistrate's warrant. A case will then be brought in the magistrates' court for the books or magazines to be forfeited. Seizure can be carried out only by the police or the Director of Public Prosecutions and not by a private citizen. There is no right to trial by jury in forfeiture cases.

In prosecutions under the Obscene Publications Acts, and in forfeiture cases, the prosecution has to prove that the material is obscene. It is a defence to show that publication is for the public good, in the interests of science, literature, art or learning or other subjects of general concern.

A number of laws are concerned with obscene and indecent material and a publication which escapes under one definition may be prosecuted under the other.

It is an offence to import indecent or obscene works. Customs officers can seize them without a warrant and bring a case in a magistrates' court that they should be forfeited.

It is also an offence to send obscene or indecent material in the post, with a penalty of up to 12 months' imprisonment and an unlimited fine. The defence of public good cannot be used in such cases.

Under the Vagrancy Acts it is an offence to expose to view an obscene or indecent picture in a public place. The maximum penalty is a fine of £100 and 3 months' gaol. Other offences include conspiracy to corrupt public morals, and outraging public decency. These are concerned with anything lewd and disgusting though not obscene.

OBSTRUCTION

The danger of assuming they are wrong

It is an offence to interfere with a policeman who is carrying out his duties. If he were acting within his

OCCUPATIONAL PENSION

WHEN MRS DUNCAN CHOSE THE WRONG PLACE

Disobeying an instruction from the police can be held to be obstructing them.

Mrs Duncan wanted to hold a street meeting in Liverpool. The meeting was entirely lawful, but the police told her she could not hold it at the place she had chosen. She should move about 175 yds away. Mrs Duncan insisted on holding it at the original place and the police prosecuted her for obstructing them in the execution of their duty.

VERDICT

Mrs Duncan was found guilty. The court accepted statements by the police that they had reason to believe that the meeting could have provoked a BREACH OF THE PEACE at the original site and that they had a duty to prevent such a situation.

There was evidence, the court accepted, that Mrs Duncan was not unmindful of the possible breach of the peace when she planned her meeting.

powers in arresting someone, it would be an offence to try to stop him.

The fact that the person arrested was later acquitted would not excuse the behaviour of anyone who had interfered at the time of the arrest.

The policeman must, however, be entitled to do whatever he was doing. If, for example, he says he is taking you to the police station merely because you decline to give him your name and address and you refuse to go, you are not guilty of an offence. He is not entitled to demand your name and address without legal reason, so you have not obstructed him.

Similarly, if the police want to search your home without a search warrant, and you refuse to let them do so, you are not necessarily guilty of obstruction. But they may have a right to enter to execute an arrest warrant or arrest someone who has committed an arrestable offence. In such cases they may also have a right to search.

A motorist who warns another motorist of a speed trap is not guilty of obstructing the police if the other motorist is not exceeding the speed limit. But if the other motorist is speeding, anyone who warns him is guilty of obstruction. The maximum penalty is a month's imprisonment and a £20 fine.

OCCUPATIONAL PENSION

Providing for retirement through your job

The state provides a RETIREMENT PENSION in two parts – a basic flat rate

paid to national insurance contributors and an additional earnings-related pension. The additional pension can, alternatively, be provided by a private, occupational scheme operated by employers and employees.

About half of Britain's working population are members of occupational pension schemes. In some, both employer and employee make contributions. In others, the employer pays it all. Many companies make membership of an occupational pension scheme a condition of employment.

Most schemes pay a pension based either on the final year's salary before retirement or on the average salary over a number of years. A typical scheme pays 1/60th of the salary for each year of membership in the scheme up to a maximum of 40/60ths – a pension amounting to two-thirds of the salary.

An alternative scheme might pay a lower fraction of the salary – say half – but with the addition of a lump sum equal to, perhaps, 1½ times the salary.

Contracting out

When the earnings-related part of the pension is paid by an occupational scheme it is known as the guaranteed minimum pension. That means it is equal to the amount that would be paid by the state, though many pension schemes pay considerably more.

A scheme that undertakes to pay the guaranteed minimum pension and fulfils certain other conditions allows the employer and employee to contract out of that part of the state scheme, with a consequent reduction in their national insurance contributions.

An employer who wants to start a

contracted-out scheme must give 3 months' notice to all employees, who can raise objections either to the employer or direct to the Occupational Pensions Board. If an employee's objection is over-ruled, however, there is nothing he can do about it.

All occupational pension schemes must be approved by the board before they can be contracted out.

When there are tax advantages

Schemes which fulfil certain conditions qualify for income tax advantages:
● The scheme must be established under a trust that cannot be wound up.
● The scheme's only purpose must be to pay pensions or similar benefits at death or on retirement.
● Employees' contributions must not be more than 15 per cent of their pay.
● Employees must not get contributions refunded except in very limited circumstances.

If an employee leaves and cannot transfer his rights to his new employment, his pension is usually 'frozen' until he reaches retirement age.
● Pensions must not be more than two-thirds of basic pay for 1 year out of the last 5 years at work or, alternatively, of average total pay for 3 or more consecutive years out of the last 10 years at work. The pension can, however, be linked to the cost of living index.

If the scheme meets the conditions, no income tax is paid on either employer's or employee's contributions.

If you change jobs

There are special safeguards covering the pension rights of someone who leaves a job in which he was a member of an occupational pension scheme.

The safeguards apply from April 6, 1975 to pension rights for those who, at the time of leaving, are 26 or over and have been contributing to the scheme for 5 years or more.

If the scheme is not contracted out of the state scheme, the pension rights must be preserved by the employer to be paid when the leaver eventually retires. As an alternative the pension rights may be transferred to a new employer's scheme.

If the scheme is contracted out, the rights must either be preserved by the employer or transferred to another contracted-out scheme.

525

An early leaver in a contracted-out scheme who does not meet the age and length of service qualifications for a preserved pension must have his guaranteed minimum pension rights transferred to the state scheme, and his employer has to pay a special premium to the state.

Refund of contributions

Normally, the rules covering the pre-servation and transfer of occupational pension rights prevent repayment of contributions. But refunds can be made in certain circumstances, providing the employee is leaving the job and not just the scheme and providing the rules of the scheme do not forbid refunds.

The main circumstances under which refunds or part refunds can be made are:
● If the period of service covers any period of occupational pension scheme membership prior to April 6, 1975.
● If the employee leaves his job after less than 5 years. But if the scheme is contracted out, only after the guaranteed minimum pension has been transferred to the state scheme by the payment of a special premium.

Refunds of contributions are taxable.

If a scheme is wound up

An employer who wants to end a contracted-out occupational pension scheme must either preserve the employee's pension rights, to be paid on retirement; or transfer them to another scheme; or pay a special premium for the state to take over responsibility for the guaranteed minimum pension.

Providing pensions for widows

Contracted-out schemes must pay at least half the guaranteed minimum pension to the widow of a member.

Under the state scheme, a widow who qualifies for WIDOW'S PENSION or a widowed mother's allowance normally gets all of the additional pension built up by her husband's national insurance contributions on top of her basic flat-rate pension. So, in order that the widow of someone contracted out of the state scheme is not worse off, the state makes up the guaranteed minimum pension to a full pension.

The widow's guaranteed minimum pension must be paid to her and not to anyone else. But any benefit above the guaranteed minimum can, without her permission, be paid to another dependant; be reduced if she is more than 10 years younger than her husband; or not paid at all if the marriage took place after the husband's contracted-out employment ended and within 6 months of his death.

Claiming a pension

Four months before you reach the official state retirement age – 65 for men, 60 for women – the Department of Health and Social Security will ask you to make a claim for your state pension.

At the same time you will be told the amount of guaranteed minimum pension due to you under any contracted-out occupational pension scheme of which you have been a member. You will also be given the name and address of the administrators of the scheme.

Once you have this information, however, the responsibility for claiming the pension – including anything preserved under schemes you left in the past – is yours. Keep all documents relating to former schemes, and let the administrators of the schemes know if you change your address.

Benefits should be claimed when they become due. If you do not claim within 6 years you may lose money.

The Department of Health and Social Security operates an advice service for occupational pension schemes. The address is: Department of Health and Social Security Records Division, Special Section A (101B), Newcastle upon Tyne, NE98 1YU.

How an occupational pension affects unemployment benefit

Many people retire before the normal state retirement age of 65 (men) or 60 (women) with an occupational pension scheme.

By registering as unemployed, they get national insurance contribution credits which in turn helps them keep a full national insurance record and get an eventual full RETIREMENT PENSION. During the first year they register as unemployed, they can also qualify for UNEMPLOYMENT BENEFIT – £20.65 a week during 1981.

The Government has decided that from April 1981 occupational pensions over a certain level will reduce the amount of unemployment benefit pay-able. This level from April 1981 is £35 a week. This means, in effect, that occupational pensions over £35 will reduce any unemployment benefit you may be entitled to on a £1 for £1 basis. So, if your occupational pension is £56 or more a week, you will not be able to get unemployment benefit. This does not stop you continuing to register as unemployed in order to get the national insurance contribution credits.

OCCUPIER'S LIABILITY

A householder must take care that his home is safe for visitors

The occupier of a house, office, shop or any other building, has a duty to take care that his premises, and any ground belonging to the property are safe for visitors. He can be liable for damages for NEGLIGENCE for any injury caused by the premises being faulty.

An occupier can be sued if, for example:
● A person breaks a leg slipping on a piece of soap left on the kitchen floor or a toy abandoned on the stairs; or if a guest is hit on the head by a chunk of falling ceiling.

The occupier's liability extends to people whose permission to be on the premises is only implied, such as:
● The gasman calling to read the meter who is bitten by the pet dog; the window cleaner injured by a falling roof tile.

It is not a defence to warn a visitor of any danger unless the warning is enough to enable the visitor to be reasonably safe. You may tell your guest – even a member of your family – that the shower mixer is faulty and only hot water comes out. If he scalds himself, you are liable.

The safest course to take, apart from maintaining the property in sound condition, is to get insurance cover. *See:* PROPERTY INSURANCE

Claim against a company

A customer or visitor to an office, shop or professional premises can claim against the firm or occupier for any injury received because the premises are faulty.

There is liability, for example, if:
● A dentist's patient slips on the

'

THE HOUSE THAT FELL DOWN

A surveyor is liable for damages if he approves a site for building which later proves unsuitable.

A builder at Bognor Regis applied for planning consent to develop his own land in 1958. Approval was given by the district council subject to the condition that 'all foundations and drains must be examined by the surveyor before being covered up'.

A council building inspector visited the site later and approved the excavations for the foundations.

In 1960 the house was bought by Mrs Sadie Dutton for £4,800. It collapsed. Mrs Dutton sued the builder and council for negligence. The house had been built on a rubbish tip, and Mrs Dutton claimed the ground was insecure. She claimed the cost of repairing the house and the amount by which its value fell.

The builder settled out of court and the case against the council went to appeal.

DECISION

The appeal court held that the council's inspector was responsible for ensuring that the house was built on solid ground, and Mrs Dutton had no duty to have her own survey made. She was awarded £2,240 for the expense of repairing the house and £500 for loss of value.

polished floor of the waiting room; a shopper is injured by falling shelves in a supermarket; a business representative has his fingers jammed in the faulty gate of a lift at an office block.

Finding out whether the builder can be blamed

In some cases, the dangerous condition of the premises may not be the fault of the occupier, but of the original builder of the property or a contractor who has done work there. Any claim in such cases should be against the occupier and the contractor, or even just against the contractor.

Most new houses are sold with a National House Builders' Registration Certificate. This sets out the rights against the builder of the original owner

and any subsequent owner. *See:* NEW HOUSE

Builders whose houses are not registered under the scheme are liable for faults both to the first owner and to any subsequent owner if 'the work is not done in a workmanlike manner, with proper materials and so that the building will be fit for human habitation'.

Any contractor who has worked on premises and left them unsafe is liable for damages for any injuries that result from his incompetence.

An electrician, for example, who dangerously rewires a building is liable if the cleaner is later electrocuted while using the vacuum cleaner. *See:* CONTRACTOR'S LIABILITY

The same responsibility falls on an architect. He has a duty to inspect a site properly, to draw up competent plans and supervise the work. He will be liable for any subsequent injury caused through his failure to exercise proper care in those respects.

When a landlord is liable for injury or damage

Responsibility for repairs to rented property is set out in any covenant covering a tenancy. If a tenant or some other person is injured because the landlord has failed to carry out statutory repairs or has carelessly carried out any construction or maintenance to the building, then the landlord is liable for damages.

A landlord, however, has no liability for defects which he did not cause and which he is not empowered to repair. He has no legal duty to tell the tenant, even if he knows these defects exist, and he has no liability if they cause injury. *See:* LANDLORD AND TENANT

When even a trespasser may have rights

An occupier of premises may have a liability even to a trespasser. This duty exists when an occupier is aware that there may be trespassers on the property, or knows that their presence may be likely. For example, it may be common for walkers to take a short cut through his property because some fences are down.

A court would take into account the trespasser's purpose for being on the

property, the kind of property and the ease of access. It would be unlikely, for example, to hold that the occupier had a liability to a trespasser who was there to rob him.

Even to a trespasser, however, the occupier has a duty to act with 'common humanity' – a duty which has never been defined clearly. *See:* TRESPASS

OFFENSIVE WEAPON
From guns to lethal potatoes

Anything capable of causing injury can be classed as an offensive weapon, but whether it is illegal to possess such an object depends on the circumstances.

Generally, offensive weapons fall into two categories:
● Those obviously designed to cause injury, such as a gun, a knife, a broken bottle, a club or a potato with a razor blade stuck in it. Possession of such objects without a lawful reason is illegal.
● Objects not specifically designed to cause injury, but which could be used for that purpose. Possession is an offence only if it is shown that there was an intention to use the object as a weapon.

For example, a pair of steel-capped boots may be an offensive weapon if worn by a football supporter but not if simply worn for work. And everyday objects like bags of pepper, bicycle chains, spanners and walking sticks can also be offensive weapons in the wrong place.

Offensive weapon cases are normally tried in the magistrates' court where the maximum penalty is 3 months' imprisonment and a £1,000 fine.

In cases heard before a judge and jury in the crown court, the maximum is 2 years' imprisonment and an unlimited fine.

Weapons that are carried for self-defence

Courts will rarely accept self-defence as a reason for possessing an offensive weapon. A youth who takes a knife with him to a confrontation with a rival cannot justify his possession of the weapon on the grounds of self-defence.

'

ANGRY CARPENTER WHO USED HIS HAMMER

Possession of an object which is not specifically designed as a weapon but may be used as one is only an offence if there was an intention to use it aggressively.

Mr Hylton, a carpenter, quarrelled with a fellow passenger, Mr Ohlson, as they tried to squeeze on board a tube train in London in 1975. Hylton, who had his tools with him, hit Ohlson on the head with his hammer. He was charged with, among other things, possessing an offensive weapon – the hammer.

VERDICT

Not guilty. The court ruled that just because the hammer had been used in the attack, there was no evidence that it had originally been carried by Hylton for that purpose.

ARMED TO THE TEETH, BUT ONLY IN SELF-DEFENCE

Courts will rarely accept self-defence as an excuse for possessing an offensive weapon.

Mr Moss was stopped by the police running along a road. He was found to be carrying a length of steel, a bicycle chain, a clock weight and a studded glove. He said he needed them for self-protection as he had previously been chased and threatened. (In fact 16 days later Moss was attacked and had to have hospital treatment.) He was charged with possessing offensive weapons.

VERDICT

Moss was found guilty. The court decided that carrying a weapon in self-defence is only an excuse if there is an imminent threat. It does not justify regularly carrying a weapon.

Flick-knives There are special laws forbidding the manufacture, sale or possession of flick-knives – knives with a concealed blade that springs out. Maximum penalty: 3 months' imprisonment and a £50 fine. These rise to 6 months' and £200 on second or subsequent conviction.

OFFICIAL SECRETS

Preventing the disclosure of classified information

Anyone who comes into possession of information from a government source may be committing a criminal offence under the Official Secrets Acts if he passes it on to an unauthorised person.

The Acts cover only information obtained from central government, not local government. But that includes much more than military or other matters obviously affecting state security.

A civil servant, for example, who discloses what goes on in the Department of Health and Social Security commits an offence under the Official Secrets Acts. A local government official who reveals information about the town's social services department, however, would not be guilty of any secrets offence.

The penalty for passing on or receiving information contrary to the Official Secrets Acts is 2 years' imprisonment and an unlimited fine. *See:* ESPIONAGE; TREASON

People engaged for government work are often asked to sign an Official Secrets Acts declaration. Such a declaration adds no extra legal consequences to the Acts themselves and it is not an offence to refuse to sign. However, it is likely to prejudice the chance of a job offer in some cases.

Access to information

The Official Secrets Acts are only one aspect of government secrecy. Cabinet proceedings, for example, are secret. There is no right of access to government documents. When documents are 30 years old some are made available in the Public Records Office, but the Government decides which to release and the citizen has no rights to see those not released.

In addition, secret rules and guidelines are used in countless day to day matters, such as deciding priority for the installation of telephones, the allocation of council houses and by the police for deciding which speeding motorists are eventually prosecuted.

Individuals have no right to information on such matters. Even an MP has no rights to investigate them and the powers of the OMBUDSMAN are similarly limited.

OFFICIAL SOLICITOR

When someone under a disability needs a legal representative

The Official Solicitor is a lawyer appointed by the Lord Chancellor to act in legal proceedings for people who are unable to look after themselves, such as a MINOR or someone who is mentally handicapped.

If the High Court feels that there should be an independent solicitor to act for one of the parties or to assist the court in, say, an adoption or child custody case, it can refer the case to the Official Solicitor. He then becomes the guardian ad litem – the guardian in law – for the person concerned during the case.

He also has the authority to apply to the court for the release of anyone committed to prison for civil contempt of court, even though the prisoner may not take any action himself.

OFF-LICENCE

Regulations for shops that sell alcohol

Any shop that sells alcohol, as the whole or part of its business, needs an off-licence – a licence stipulating that the drink can only be consumed off the premises.

Off-licences are granted by the licensing committee of the local magistrates and have to be renewed yearly.

The magistrates can make special conditions about opening hours. Otherwise an off-licence allows alcohol to be sold from 8.30 a.m. until the normal evening closing time of the public houses in the same licensing area – usually 10.30 or 11 p.m. On Sundays, both opening and closing hours must be the same as those of the local public houses.

It is illegal to sell alcohol to anyone under 18. The maximum penalty is a £200 fine or loss of licence.

It is also illegal to allow alcohol to be drunk on the premises or even on the highway outside. Maximum penalty for both offences: £25 fine.

OMBUDSMEN

The officials appointed to keep watch on other officials

The job of an ombudsman is to guard members of the public against injustice or unfair treatment by government officials. Although appointed by the Government, he has the same independence from it as a judge.

The ombudsman's role is largely that of watchdog. He cannot punish erring officials or reverse their decisions; he can only expose bad administration and criticise those responsible. But his judgment usually leads to prompt action by the official bodies he criticises. If they fail to make amends, his opinions could be used as a powerful weapon against them in Parliament, in local councils or in Press and broadcasting.

When a complaint is made

When a complaint is made, an ombudsman will listen to both sides in private. He has the same power as the courts to order people to give evidence, and any attempt to obstruct him or his officials can be punished in the same way as CONTEMPT OF COURT.

At the end of his inquiry, the ombudsman gives an opinion on whether there has been bad administration or injustice. He can recommend changes in the system of administration and suggest that the authority concerned

WATCHDOGS THAT HAVE MORE THAN JUST A BARK

Much of the power of the ombudsmen derives from their ability to expose bad administration and to suggest improvements. They may even recommend compensation for the victims.

should recompense a person he considers to have been badly treated. But his decisions cannot be legally enforced.

Three categories of ombudsman

There are three sorts of ombudsman in Britain, each with his own investigating staff:

● The parliamentary ombudsman. Officially known as the Parliamentary Commissioner for Administration, who deals with complaints against central government departments.

● The health ombudsman. Officially known as the Health Service Commissioner, with the job of investigating complaints about the health service. Three such officials may legally be appointed – one each for England, Scotland and Wales – but the parliamentary ombudsman acts as health ombudsman, with three separate staffs, one for each country.

● Local ombudsmen. Officially known as Commissioners for Local Administration. There are three in England – two in London, one in York – one in Wales, one in Scotland and one in Northern Ireland, called the Commissioner for Complaints.

Grounds for complaining

In considering a complaint, an ombudsman has no power to question the law or a government decision. He can look only for evidence of 'maladministration' by public officials. There is no legal definition of 'maladministration' but the following paragraphs give an idea of what can be considered reasonable grounds for complaint.

● Procedure. A hospital was criticised by an ombudsman for admitting a mentally ill person without following the statutory procedure for dealing with MENTAL DISORDER.

A council was reprimanded for taking 7 days to inform a mother that her daughter had been placed in care.

● Rules. Internal department rules must always be followed. In some cases ombudsmen have decided that the rules themselves amount to maladministration and ought to be changed.

● Discrimination. Government and local authority departments are expected to treat everyone in the same way without discrimination for race, sex, religion, social status or anything else. An ombudsman can look at de-

partment files to reassure himself on this point.

● Delay. When delay is caused by inefficiency and not just overwork, a complaint to an ombudsman is justified.

● Concealing facts. Failure to keep people informed of decisions that affect them – for example in planning matters – is considered to be maladministration. Ombudsmen have wide powers to get information, expose any attempts at concealment and publish the facts.

● Misbehaviour. Officials have been reproved for rudeness or inconsiderate behaviour.

● Faulty advice. It is maladministration to give any faulty official advice, either in printed form or in person to a member of the public.

● Inefficiency. Loss of a file or letter, failure to keep an appointment or bad arithmetic on a tax demand, have all earned the ombudsman's censure.

If a department applies the law correctly, however, it cannot be found guilty of maladministration, however unfair or ridiculous the result may appear. But the ombudsman may report to Parliament any injustice caused by a law.

How a complaint is pursued

When an ombudsman receives a complaint which he decides he can consider, he demands the relevant facts or documents from government ministers, councillors or officials involved. In practice these are almost always made available, for behind him the ombudsman has the powers of a judge to demand evidence – including the ultimate sanction of an action for contempt.

The inquiry is not restricted by the Official Secrets Act, and his findings are protected from the laws of libel.

The person who has complained is

HOW THE OMBUDSMAN GOT HIS NAME

The first ombudsman (which is a Swedish word meaning agent or representative) was appointed in 1809 by the Swedish Government. The idea has since been copied by several other countries.

In Britain the ombudsmen do not have such strong powers as in Sweden. The jobs are usually given to lawyers or senior civil or public servants.

HOW THE OMBUDSMEN'S POWERS ARE LIMITED

An ombudsman has no power to question the law or a decision by Government. He is limited to investigating 'maladministration' of laws and governmental decisions.

He has no power to interfere with a nationalised industry, a private body such as a trade union or a professional organisation. He cannot question the findings of a court or tribunal.

When there is some other way

An ombudsman cannot investigate a complaint when the complainant has the right of appeal to some other body or person. You cannot, for example, complain to him that you are being charged too much tax or that you are not getting enough social security benefit, because in both cases you can appeal to an independent tribunal.

That applies also to decisions by local planning committees, because persons affected can appeal to a government minister.

When a policy decision is involved

When a decision is made by a government official – say a planning officer or a tax inspector – and there is no evidence of bad administration, the ombudsman cannot accept a complaint from the person affected. If, for example, you wish to complain about a ruling on supplementary benefits, you can complain only about any administrative failings which may have led to the decision.

There is one exception to that rule – where a decision is so unjust that the om-budsman rules that the decision itself amounts to maladministration.

When legal issues are in dispute

Legal disputes, which would normally come before the courts, can be settled only by the courts, and the ombudsman cannot interfere.

When professional skill is criticised

A decision taken by a person using his professional judgment cannot be questioned by an ombudsman. The health om-budsman, for example, cannot criticise a clinical decision taken by a doctor.

If a doctor decides that a patient should wait for an operation because other cases are more urgent, the ombudsman cannot intervene.

A complaint can be considered only if it is shown that the hospital handled the waiting list in an inefficient manner.

Specific restrictions in each category

In addition to those general limitations on the ombudsmen's powers of inquiry, there are particular restrictions in each of the three categories:

The parliamentary ombudsman cannot deal with:
● Complaints of individual pay or conditions of employment made by any publicly paid employee.
● Government contracts, commercial deals or tenders, or government securities.

● Any matter involving national security or any investigation of crime ordered by the Home Secretary.
● Honours.
● Extradition.
● Any action taken by British officials (except consuls) outside the United Kingdom.
● Matters in the Channel Islands or the Isle of Man.
● Foreign affairs, if the Foreign Secretary rules that the action complained of could affect international relations.

The health ombudsman cannot deal with:
● Pay or conditions in the Health Service.
● Contracts for the supply of drugs.

The local ombudsmen cannot deal with:
● Individual working conditions or dismissal of local government staff.
● Local contracts involving bus services, docks, markets, entertainment, or the running of industrial estates – but they can deal with complaints about the buying and selling of land and the provision of local services such as housing.
● General policy or spending decisions of the local council.
● Police action in the investigation or prevention of crime.
● Internal school matters relating to curriculum, discipline and management – but they can investigate complaints against the general administration of education and the procedures for changing schools or allocating children to certain schools.

---

usually interviewed at his home, where he can have a Member of Parliament, a local councillor, a friend or a lawyer to help him. The procedure is private. At no time does the complainant have to meet the officials against whom he has made his complaint. There is no opportunity for cross-examination as there is in the courts.

Staff at the government department involved are questioned by the ombudsman's investigators, and their files will be scrutinised by the investigators.

The department is given the opportunity to check the facts in any statement to be used in the ombudsman's report; but it cannot comment on any conclusion he draws.

What does it cost?

It costs nothing to complain to an ombudsman. You do not have to pay fees or legal expenses. If you choose to

consult a solicitor before making a complaint, you may be able to do so under a scheme that allows a certain amount of free legal advice. *See:* LEGAL AID

Even if your complaint is not upheld, there are no costs to pay. Any interviews are normally conducted at a place suitable to a complainant – such as his home – so no expense is involved in giving evidence.

In exceptional cases the ombudsman has the power to reimburse expenses.

Making a complaint to the parliamentary ombudsman

The Parliamentary Commissioner for Administration deals with all complaints against government departments and official Crown bodies.

He can investigate any action that has been ordered or carried out by any minister or official of a government de-partment or anyone acting as agent for the department.

Who can complain? Anyone or any organisation – except for a national or local government committee or department, or an organisation wholly or mainly financed by public funds. However, individual members of such bodies can complain if they consider themselves personally to be victims of maladministration.

All complaints must be made within 12 months of the action complained about. The complainant must be resident in the United Kingdom, except that:
● A person from abroad can complain about unfair action against himself when he was in the United Kingdom at some time in the past.

How to complain All complaints to the parliamentary ombudsman must be made in collaboration with a member of

PURSUING A COMPLAINT AGAINST A HOSPITAL

A complaint about poor administration of a National Health Service hospital may be made – by the patient concerned, a relative or someone else with an interest in the case – to the area health authority that is responsible for the running of the hospital.

In almost every case, there is likely to be a clear sequence of events that can provide a useful guide for anyone wishing to take up a case with the ombudsman. Take, for example, the following fictitious case of Mrs Mary Scott who felt that her mother had been denied reasonable care because of maladministration in a local hospital.

1 In order to pursue her complaint against the hospital, Mrs Scott seeks advice from her local Citizens Advice Bureau and her local COMMUNITY HEALTH COUNCIL.

2 She is advised to write first to the local area health authority, setting out her complaint in detail.

3 The health authority conducts its own internal investigation, sending staff to take evidence from all the people involved at the hospital.

4 Mrs Scott receives a reply from the health authority, but she is still not satisfied and wants to take her complaint further.

5 She again visits the community health council, and its representatives help her to write to the Health Service Commissioner – the health ombudsman. (Alternatively, in some cases, the health authority may itself have decided to refer the case to the commissioner.)

6 If the ombudsman considers that the complaint comes within his jurisdiction, members of his staff visit the hospital and begin interviewing all the hospital employees who were involved during Mrs Scott's mother's last illness there.

7 Meanwhile, a member of the ombudsman's staff visits Mrs Scott and takes her evidence.

8 The ombudsman takes note of all the evidence from both sides and then publishes a report, identifying none of the people involved but giving a judgment on whether the hospital should be censured or not.

9 In cases where the complainant wants to gain publicity, he or she is legally free to give details of the case and the ombudsman's judgment to the press. (Although the ombudsman's report is protected against any action for libel, private efforts to gain publicity are not so privileged.)

the House of Commons – though not necessarily through the Member of Parliament who represents the complainant's constituency.

Usually the first step is to give your own MP full details of your complaint and all the circumstances. He is not obliged to pass your case to the ombudsman. He may deal with it successfully himself or he may think the matter should not be pursued.

If that happens and you still want to press your complaint, you must contact another Member of Parliament and ask for his help.

It is possible for you to write directly to the ombudsman at Church House, Great Smith Street, London SW1P 3BW. But the ombudsman will then ask your MP if he would like to have the matter investigated.

Unless the MP – or another member – agrees, the ombudsman has no power to take your complaint any further.

The complaint need not be made directly by the person involved. It can be made on his behalf by an agent, such as a lawyer or accountant, or by an organisation, such as a trade union or the British Legion.

A complaint can be made on behalf of a person who is dead – for instance, by a widow convinced that her late husband had been unfairly dealt with – or on behalf of a person mentally or physically unable to complain himself. That can be done by a member of the person's family or even by a friend such as the next-door neighbour.

When the ombudsman reports When the ombudsman's investigation is complete, he issues a report, setting out his conclusions and any criticism he may have of the department or individuals involved.

His report is sent to the Member of

Parliament who handled the complaint and to the department and any individual named in the complaint. A copy of his report is presented to Parliament and is published officially by the House of Commons.

The ombudsman is barred by law from saying anything more about the case. But the MP or the complainant can pursue it further if they wish, either by taking the matter up with the Minister concerned, raising it in the Commons or by seeking further Press publicity.

The ombudsman's report is protected from any libel action, but subsequent publicity about the complaint is not.

In most cases the department concerned puts the matter right if the ombudsman upholds a complaint. If it refuses to do so, the MP involved may decide to take further action, or the House of Commons Select Committee on the Ombudsman may ask the department why no action has been taken.

Complaining to the health ombudsman

The Health Commissioner and his staff handle complaints of maladministration in hospitals or elsewhere in the Health Service. They examine allegations of injustice or hardship and complaints that the Health Service has failed to provide the service it is supposed to provide, or that the service has failed.

The health ombudsman is concerned with all regional and area health authorities, family practitioner committees, the Health Service Board and its Welsh Committee, hospital boards of governors and the Public Health Laboratory Service Board.

There is no regional authority in Wales. Supervision of the Health Service there is exercised by the Welsh Office, so complaints about that office's work must be made through an MP to the parliamentary ombudsman.

The general policy of the Health Service is directed by the Department of Health and Social Security. So complaints of general policy should similarly be made through an MP to the parliamentary ombudsman.

Who can complain? Anyone can complain to the health ombudsman provided the complaint is made within 12 months of the action complained about.

Friends or relatives can make a complaint involving someone who has died or someone unable to make the complaint himself.

How to complain Complaints should be made first to the area health authority involved, and it should be given a reasonable time to investigate the matter itself. If the result of this is unsatisfactory, write direct to the health ombudsman.

When the ombudsman reports The ombudsman's report is published in the same way as that of the parliamentary ombudsman. The authorities concerned usually react in the same way as government departments to the parliamentary ombudsman's report.

Complaining to a local ombudsman

The five local ombudsmen can investigate complaints against the administrative actions of officers, committees and councils of local authorities and against local police authorities.

They cannot investigate the actions of individual police officers. *See:* POLICE

Nor can they hear complaints about parish or town councils. In such cases allegations of maladministration should be made to the Clerk or Chairman of the Council.

The local ombudsmen are concerned with all county councils, borough and city councils, the London boroughs, the City of London Council and the Greater London Council, police authorities, national park authorities, regional water authorities, and land authorities.

Who can complain? Anyone can complain to the local ombudsman – provided that the complaint had been made to a local councillor within 12 months of the action being complained about. If a councillor refuses to pass on your complaint, you can write directly to your local ombudsman. The addresses are:
● England: 21 Queen Anne's Gate, London SW1H 9BU.
● Wales: Derwen House, Court Road, Bridgend, Mid-Glamorgan CS31 1BM.
● Scotland: 125 Princes Street, Edinburgh EH2 2QU.

When the ombudsman reports One copy of the local ombudsman's report goes to the complainant, one to the local authority and one to any other person named in the complaint.

The local authority must make the report available for public inspection for 3 weeks and must advertise the facts in the local Press – unless the ombudsman rules that the matter should be kept private in the public interest. Reports are also given to local newspapers, but the people involved in the complaint are not named.

Putting matters right When a complaint has been upheld, the local ombudsman recommends what action should be taken – an apology, a change of council procedure or compensation.

The local authority has to consider the report and tell the ombudsman what action it proposes to take. If no action is taken within a reasonable time, the ombudsman issues another report, drawing attention to the matter.

ONE-PARENT FAMILIES

How extra benefits can be claimed

Single parents of either sex, whether divorced, separated, deserted or unmarried, receive an extra £3 a week for the first child in the family who qualifies for CHILD BENEFIT.

They can also claim SUPPLEMENTARY BENEFIT to raise their income to the fixed minimum level, which depends on how many dependent children they have, their housing costs and other commitments. The parent does not need to register for work if the youngest child is under 16.

Before supplementary benefit is paid all other benefits, including any child benefits, are taken into account. A single parent, for example, on supplementary benefit gets no advantage from the extra £3 child benefit paid to a single-parent not on supplementary benefit.

A single parent who has a job may also qualify for FAMILY INCOME SUPPLEMENT. He or she need only work 24 hours a week, instead of the 30 hours required of a married person.

Is maintenance allowed?

Most sources of income, including any MAINTENANCE paid by a husband or the children's father, are taken into account when a single parent applies for supplementary benefit.

If no maintenance is being paid, the Department of Health and Social Security may urge the claiming parent to press for payment. They can approach a husband or a father and invite him to make voluntary payments of maintenance.

If the husband or father refuses to pay, and the claiming parent will not start a court action, the Department of Health and Social Security itself can take legal action to press for maintenance.

If maintenance is paid

All maintenance payments are deducted from any supplementary benefits which are due to a single parent.

When payments are made by a court order, the amount can be paid direct to the social security department – in this way, no deductions are made from the supplementary benefit due.

This gives the claiming single parent an assured, fixed income each week, whether or not the maintenance payment has been made. When benefit ceases because, for example, the claimant has started work, maintenance payment can be paid direct once more.

Earnings limit A single parent can earn up to £4 a week without it affecting supplementary benefit. In addition he or she can keep half of any earnings between £4 and £20 a week, again without this affecting benefit. Expenses, such as fares to work, can be taken off before deciding how earnings affect benefit.

A single parent getting benefit may have it stopped if another person of the opposite sex joins the household. *See:* COHABITATION

How tax is reduced

If a single parent pays INCOME TAX, his or her liability may be reduced by an additional personal allowance – even though the child allowance itself has not been granted since April 1979.

The additional personal allowance – £650 in the 1979–80 tax year – is claimed in advance of an income tax return. Taxable income is reduced by the amount of the allowance.

Organisations that can help

Some local authorities give special support to one-parent families by establishing mutual help groups. A proportion of council day nursery places is usually reserved for the children of working single parents. Some councils, particularly in London, supply lists of registered child minders.

Help is also available from many voluntary organisations. Their work is co-ordinated by the National Council for One-Parent Families, which also runs its own welfare department to deal with employment and legal problems, and can make emergency grants for clothing or fares, or to meet urgent debts.

Gingerbread, a self-help organisation for one-parent families, has a central office in London and local groups throughout Britain. It provides social contacts and support through regular meetings.

OPTICIAN

What to do if your eyes need testing

Free sight-testing is available for everyone under the National Health Service, but most people have to pay something towards the cost of spectacles if they need them.

Make an appointment with an ophthalmic optician – that is one who is qualified to test eyes rather than a dispensing optician who makes glasses on prescription – after making sure that he accepts work under the National Health Service.

WHEN IN DOUBT, ASK AN OPTICIAN FOR A FREE TEST

Ophthalmic opticians who accept work under the National Health Service do not charge for sight testing unless they have to travel to the patient's home.

Sight-testing is free, except for private patients and in special circumstances when a home visit is necessary. Then a travelling fee is charged.

If you need glasses

The optician will tell you if you need glasses. You then have four choices:
● You can have NHS lenses fitted to a NHS subsidised frame.
● You can have NHS lenses fitted to any frame of your choice and pay the full price for the frame.
● You can have lenses and frame of your own choice and pay full price for both of them.
● If you already have a pair of spectacles, you can keep the frame and have the new lenses fitted into them. In this case there will be a charge for the lenses and the fitting.

When glasses are free

A relatively small charge is usually made for NHS lenses fitted in a NHS frame, but some people are entitled to receive spectacles without any charge:
● Children under 16 years of age, or older children still at school; they must produce a certificate to that effect from the head teacher.
● Persons who (or whose husbands) receive supplementary benefit or family income supplement, or who get free milk and vitamins or free prescriptions because of low income. They should tell the optician, who will give them a declaration to sign.

People with low income who do not fall into the above categories are entitled to free glasses or a reduction in NHS charges. They should ask the optician for form F1, fill in details of their financial circumstances and send it to the local social security office. If the charge has already been paid, a refund can be claimed on form F6, obtained from the local social security office. Leaflet M11, from any post office, explains what counts as low income.

How to complain about an optician

Anyone who is dissatisfied about an eye test or spectacles provided under the NHS should complain within 8 weeks to the local family practitioner committee. *See:* DOCTOR AND PATIENT

If the spectacles are unsatisfactory,

ask first for a new test or for the defect to be corrected. If necessary, withhold any payment until your complaint is remedied.

Complaints about the standard of service, such as missed appointments or long delays, should also be made to the family practitioner committee. If injury or loss is suffered, for example, through an accident caused by wrongly prescribed glasses, an action may be possible for NEGLIGENCE.

Private patients who pay for their spectacles cannot complain to the practitioner committee. If they are dissatisfied with the service they should refuse to pay. All frames and lenses supplied privately are sold under the same rules and laws as any other consumer goods. An optician is obliged to refund the money or put the spectacles right at his own expense.

Any complaints about private treatment can be made to the British Optical Association, whose disciplinary committee can expel, suspend or reprimand members.

Complaints about improper behaviour by an optician can be made to the General Optical Council.

OVERCROWDING

When too many people sleep in one home

Every house or flat is subject to a legal limit on the number of people who can live in it. An owner risks prosecution if he allows overcrowding. So does an occupier who continues to live for what ever reason or purpose in an overcrowded home.

The prosecution of a tenant in such circumstances is most unlikely – but he loses the protection of the Rent Act and has no security of tenure.

The law restricts occupancy in any of three ways. A home is overcrowded if:
● Two people of opposite sex and over the age of 10 – other than a couple living as husband and wife – have to sleep in the same room.
● It does not have enough rooms, according to a special scale.
● Its rooms are too small.

A landlord's responsibility

Anyone who lets living quarters on a

HOW TO TELL IF A HOME IS OVERCROWDED

Household crowding is measured according to the total of what are called occupancy units – a figure based on ages, rather than on the actual number of people.

A child under 1 year is not counted; a child from 1 to 10 years counts as half a unit; and each person over 10 years counts as 1 unit.

If two people of opposite sex and over 10 years – apart from a husband and wife – have to sleep in the same room, the law is broken and no other test is needed.

If not, different scales are used:
● To see if the home has enough rooms – not including kitchen and bathroom – for the total of units.
● To see if the rooms have enough floor area for the total of units.

The *lower* unit total from the two scales is the one applied when deciding whether there is overcrowding.

Example: A married couple – 2 units – have a boy aged 5, who counts as ½, and a baby of 6 months, who is not counted.

Their flat has rooms of 100 sq. ft, 85 sq. ft and 55 sq. ft.

On the rooms allowance scale their three rooms are enough for 5 units. But on

Rooms allowance

Number of rooms	1	2	3	4	5	6	7
Total of occupancy units	2	3	5	7½	10	12	14

the room area scale the rooms allow 1½ units, 1 unit and ½ unit respectively – a total of only 3 units.

The family's own unit total is 2½. There

Room area allowance

Room area sq. ft	Occupancy units per room
Under 50	0
50–70	½
70–90	1
90–110	1½
Over 110	2

is no illegal crowding. Even when the baby turns 1 their unit total will rise by only ½, within their flat's unit allowance.

But when the older child turns 10, or if they have another baby and it passes its first birthday they will exceed their allowance. Then they should report the overcrowding and apply for a larger flat.

---

weekly tenancy must inform the tenant, by a notice in the rent book, of the legal limit on occupancy. When a landlord fails to do so he can be fined up to £50, and up to £100 if he continues to fail.

A landlord also commits offences if he:
● Lets premises when he has reason to believe they will be overcrowded.
● Lets premises without finding out the

BOTH OCCUPANT AND LANDLORD CAN BE FINED FOR OVERCROWDING

A tenant who is living in overcrowded conditions can protect himself against prosecution only by reporting the overcrowding to the local authority housing department.

number, age and sex of his tenants, and overcrowding occurs.
● Does not relieve overcrowding – by providing more space, or evicting some or all of the tenants – after a notice from his local authority.
Penalty: £5 fine and £2 a day if the offence continues.

When the tenant has a responsibility

Anyone who lives in overcrowded premises is required to report it to the local authority environmental health department. But if he is a tenant, he should first apply to the local authority housing department for other accommodation. Whether or not another home is found for him, his application means he cannot be prosecuted for occupying overcrowded premises.

The penalty on an occupant is the same as on an owner: £5 fine and £2 a day for as long as the offence continues.

Council housing Someone who wants action taken against a council for allowing overcrowding can launch a private prosecution, but only with the consent of the Attorney General. Apply to the law officers' department of the Royal Courts of Justice, Strand, London WC2 2LL.

OVERLAPPING BENEFITS

How the state avoids paying out twice

A person who theoretically has a claim to more than one state benefit is normally prevented from actually being paid twice by what are known as the overlapping benefits regulations.

If, for example, someone is incapacitated by an accident at work he may qualify for both SICKNESS BENEFIT and INDUSTRIAL INJURY BENEFIT. The overlapping rules allow him to draw only the larger of the two – industrial injury benefit.

In the same way, a man receiving a maintenance allowance while training for a new job cannot get full UNEMPLOYMENT BENEFIT.

Some benefits are not affected by the overlapping benefits rules and can be paid in addition to other state payments.

These are MATERNITY GRANT, DEATH GRANT, ATTENDANCE ALLOWANCE and MOBILITY ALLOWANCE.

Graduated retirement benefit under the existing regulations is not adjusted unless the recipient also gets a Category D RETIREMENT PENSION, a non-contributory INVALIDITY PENSION or an INVALID CARE ALLOWANCE.

PACKAGE TOUR

Paying for travel and accommodation together

A package tour is usually a contract under which you pay an all-in price for travel and accommodation. It is often cheaper than buying travel tickets and booking accommodation separately, but it is unwise to assume this without checking. *See:* TRAVEL AGENT

PAINTINGS

When you buy a painting 'by' a named artist

Auctioneers have three ways of giving the name of an artist said to have produced a particular painting.

For example, a painting of Salisbury Cathedral may be described as being by John Constable, J. Constable, or Constable.

The full name – John Constable – means that the auctioneer is satisfied that the painting is the authentic work of the named artist.

The surname with initials – J. Constable – means that the auctioneer is not absolutely sure that the painting is by the artist named, but that it is a work of the period during which the named artist painted and may be – wholly or partly – his work.

The surname alone – Constable – indicates that the auctioneer is not willing to say that the painting is by the named artist, but that it is a work of the school of the named artist or by one of his followers, or in his style and of uncertain date.

What to do if you are misled

If you buy a painting in the belief that it is by a particular artist, but it proves later not to be genuine, your rights depend on whether the painting is being sold by description under that artist's name.

If it is, it is a term of the contract of sale, under the Sale of Goods Act 1979, that it should correspond with the description. If that term is broken you have the right to reject the painting and get your money back, and claim damages if the value of a genuine painting would have been greater than the price you paid.

Even if you do not reject the painting, you can claim damages to the value of the difference between the values of the true painting and the painting you bought. *See:* DEFECTIVE GOODS

When there is an exemption clause

If you bought the painting at an art gallery – privately and not in the course of a business – your rights are not affected by any exemption clause in the sale details.

If you bought it at an auction, the exemption clause would be invalid unless it was fair and reasonable. *See:* UNFAIR CONTRACT

If the painting was not being sold by description, you might nevertheless be able to claim that the seller tricked you by MISREPRESENTATION.

PARENTAL OBLIGATIONS

The duty of parents towards their children

Parents have a legal obligation to feed, clothe and properly provide for their children according to the family's standard of living. Neglect is a criminal offence.

There is no legal way that a child can compel its parents to obey the law, except that a child over 16 may be able to intervene in proceedings between his parents to ask for a maintenance order. But if the children are being neglected, neighbours or friends can complain to the social services department of the local council. Social workers will visit the family and if they think it necessary, the council might bring proceedings to put the CHILDREN IN CARE.

Maintenance order A mother who is not living with her husband, can bring an application for an order for MAINTENANCE against him if she believes he is failing to provide reasonable maintenance for their children. If she is living with her husband, she can still obtain the order, but it will last for only 6 months if they are still living together.

If a child is ill

Parents must take care of a child when he is ill and ensure that he gets whatever medical treatment is necessary. Failure to call a doctor when one is needed or to ignore his advice, or to refuse to allow a blood transfusion or an operation even on religious grounds, is a criminal offence, like other forms of neglect, punishable by up to 2 years' imprisonment and an unlimited fine.

Liability for a child's actions

Parents are not liable for contracts entered into by their children unless they have accepted liability in writing. Nor are children under 18 normally liable. *See:* MINOR

Children's tort A parent cannot be sued for a child's TORT unless it is proved that the parent was negligent. For instance, if a parent allowed his 16-year-old child to drive the family car and the child knocked down a pedes-

> ## BOY INJURED BY HIS FRIEND'S SHOTGUN
>
> *A parent can be liable for injury caused by a child if the child has not been properly warned of the dangers of his actions.*
>
> A farmer's son, 12-year-old Stuart Edgerley was allowed by his father to buy a shotgun. Mr Edgerley showed his son how to fire the gun, and told him not to use it when other children were with him.
>
> One day in 1957, Stuart was walking through a wood behind another boy, Harold Newton. A third boy ran up from behind and tried to get hold of the gun. The gun was cocked and loaded and it went off, injuring Harold Newton in the heel.
>
> Newton, through his mother, sued Mr Edgerley for negligence.
>
> ### DECISION
>
> Mr Edgerley was found liable and damages were awarded. The court ruled that the father should have given Stuart careful instruction to uncock the gun when walking in single file. Although the accident had been caused by the third boy, the father should have known that boys were likely to lark about.

trian, the parent would be liable – because the child was too young to drive a car legally.

Or, if a parent employed a 16-year-old as a riding instructor in the family riding school and careless supervision caused a pupil to be thrown from a horse, the parent would be liable.

Harming a child A parent has a duty not to harm his child through carelessness, and if he does the child can sue him for compensation. For instance, if a parent carelessly causes his child, who is a passenger in his car, to be injured in an accident, the child can sue the parent and claim damages from the parent's insurance company.

PARENTS' ASSOCIATIONS

Establishing a link between home and school

Parents have no legal right to interfere in the running of a school. But many do form groups and associations to discuss school activities and to organise social and fund-raising events. Their views are often given consideration in formulating school policy.

Ideally such associations are run in co-operation with the staff as parent-teacher associations, but there is no legal obligation on the part of a school to join such a scheme. It is left to individual head teachers to decide whether to support a parents' association and each teacher has the right to refuse to take part.

The National Confederation of Parent-Teacher Associations offers advice on organising parents' groups. It will supply a suggested constitution that will help to avoid conflict with teaching staff and also conform with the Charities Acts. Its address is 43 Stonebridge Road, Northfleet, Gravesend, Kent DA11 9DS.

However informal the association may be, it is advisable to have a formal committee and a proper procedure for business meetings – an agenda, a chairman who can keep to it, a secretary and minutes recording decisions.

If fund-raising is part of the group's activities a treasurer and properly audited accounts will be needed. Association funds should be kept separate from those under the control of the head teacher or you may not have the right to say how the money is spent.

Going it alone

If parents want to form an association at a state school despite lack of co-operation by the staff they may still be able to use the school premises for meetings. Application should be made to the local education authority.

The head can refuse to allow publicity about the group's activities to be distributed in the school, but he or she cannot prevent members handing out leaflets or other material at the school gates.

PARKING

Where and when you can leave your car

No one can leave a vehicle parked indefinitely at the roadside without committing an offence, even where there are no clear restrictions.

In 1812, long before the arrival of the motor car, Lord Ellenborough, the Lord Chief Justice, laid down a classic ruling which still applies: 'Every unauthorised obstruction of a highway to the annoyance of the King's subjects is an indictable offence . . . no one can make a stableyard of the King's highway.' And you cannot make a garage of it today, either.

A person who leaves a car, lorry or van stationary at the kerbside for a long period in an unrestricted area can be summoned for unreasonable use of the road even if the vehicle is not causing an obstruction. There is no definition in law of a 'long period' and magistrates' opinions will vary from court to court.

A barrister was fined for leaving his car for 5 hours on the Thames Embankment in London, but magistrates in Oswestry found it 'not unreasonable' for Mr Colin Evans to park for 1½ hours on a street busy with market-day traffic; and the High Court upheld their decision.

Obstruction is even harder to define. Leaving a vehicle almost anywhere on the public highway can, by the strict letter of the law, constitute an obstruction. You have no more legal right to park your car in the road outside your own home than anyone else has.

In towns and city centres, parking is governed by strict controls with yellow lines, No Parking signs and parking meters all limiting a motorist's right to stop and stay.

In such a restricted area, parking at the roadside is legitimate only for certain loading or unloading and fetching or delivering. It depends on what you are fetching or carrying.

The general police practice is to allow necessary as distinct from convenient loading or unloading. Picking up passengers and luggage without delay would probably be allowed; but it would not usually be considered necessary for you to park your car outside your bank to cash a £10 cheque.

Another factor taken into consideration is time. A van driver might be allowed 20 minutes to unload his goods, but would probably be booked after an hour or more on a yellow line.

When there are yellow lines

A single yellow line painted at the kerbside means all parking is banned

THE DRIVER WHO WENT UP IN A LIFT

It is not a parking offence to pick someone up or set someone down in a restricted area, but they must be ready and waiting.

A solicitor, Mr Clifford-Turner, parked his car in a meter zone outside his Mayfair flat in 1960 while he went to fetch his elderly wife to take her shopping.

Mr Clifford-Turner had only one lung and could not move quickly. He had to wait for a lift and it was 5 minutes before he was back at the car with his wife.

He refused to accept a £2 fixed penalty from a traffic warden and was summoned for parking in a restricted area. He pleaded not guilty and claimed he was picking up a passenger.

The magistrate told him: 'Persons to be picked up means persons who are ready and waiting to be picked up, not persons who might be ready in 5, 10, or 20 minutes.' He found Mr Clifford-Turner guilty and gave him an absolute discharge on payment of £2.10 (two guineas) costs. Mr Clifford-Turner appealed.

DECISION

Lord Chief Justice Parker upheld the conviction. He said it would be impossible to allow going up and down in a lift as part of boarding or alighting.

THE DRIVER WHO LEFT HIS CAR TOO LONG

It can be unreasonable use of the road to leave a car for a long time even where there are no parking restrictions.

A barrister, Mr Peter Solomon, parked his car by the kerb on the Thames Embankment in London and left it there for 5 hours while he was at his chambers.

There were three lanes of traffic in each direction and no hold up in the traffic was caused, but Mr Solomon was reported by the police. In court it was claimed that his use of the road was unnecessary and an obstruction to other road users who might have wanted to park there for a shorter time.

Mr Solomon's use of the road was held to be unreasonable and he was fined £2. He appealed.

DECISION

Lord Chief Justice Lord Goddard upheld the conviction. He said that it was impossible to walk or drive over a stationary car, and if left in the road too long it became an unnecessary obstruction.

except for loading and unloading, fetching or delivering, for at least 8 hours between 7 a.m. and 7 p.m. on the working days of the week.

This can sometimes be extended to Saturday afternoons and Sundays.

Small discs are erected on posts at the roadside, usually at 200 ft intervals, stating the time between which the restriction applies.

The ban covers every part of the roadway, not just the kerbside, and includes the footpath and any verges.

Double yellow lines mean there is a total ban on parking at any time of the night or day. Do not park without checking the time disc. It is an offence to park on a yellow line during a restricted period and, where there are no fixed penalties, a driver who does so can be fined up to £100.

Where you must never park

In addition to areas that are marked, there are other places where the High-way Code says you should not park your car:

● Where it causes danger to other vehicles or pedestrians – for example, near a school entrance or crossing, where it hides a traffic sign, on a footpath, pavement or cycle path, on or near a bus stop, on or near a level crossing.

● Where it obscures another driver's view of the road, for example, within 15 yds of a junction, on a bend, on a brow of a hill, on a humpback bridge, near a zebra crossing.

● Where it leaves too narrow a passage for other vehicles, for example, opposite a traffic island, beside another stationary vehicle, opposite another stationary vehicle on a narrow road.

● Where it interferes with traffic, for example, on flyovers, in tunnels and underpasses, on fast main roads, except in a lay-by, on a single-track road, blocking a vehicle entrance to properties, or where it would prevent the use of properly parked vehicles.

● Where there is an entrance or exit for emergency vehicles, for instance, at hospitals and fire and police stations.

When a car breaks down

A driver is generally not held to be guilty of a parking offence if he is prevented from proceeding by reasons beyond his control. A car left for a long time with a sign 'broken down' may still be booked – and to be acquitted the owner will need evidence that the car really was out of commission.

Running out of petrol probably does not constitute a breakdown, though the point has not been tested in the High Court. The Central Ticket Office in London takes the view that running out of petrol is avoidable. Wardens therefore book anyone who does so and parks in a restricted area.

Parking in a meter zone

In some areas parking is allowed only at kerbside meters and the driver puts coins into the meter for a fixed period of parking. When the time is up he must move his vehicle or incur an excess charge. A driver who does not pay within 7 days can be fined up to £20.

When a driver's time is up he must move his vehicle from the parking bay, and cannot return to the same meter for at least an hour. It is legal to drive out of one parking bay and pull into another across the road. If a driver goes round the block and back into the bay he has just vacated, he can be fined £20.

Payment for use of a parking meter bay must be made when the vehicle is parked. No time is allowed for going to get change. It is an offence to 'feed' a meter, that is to return later and put more coins into the meter to buy more time. The penalty is a fine of up to £20.

When a motorist leaves his car in a parking space for longer than the time he has paid for and the yellow card is showing on the meter, he is liable to an excess charge. If he leaves it there until the red card is showing, he will incur a fixed penalty of £6 and the car can be towed away. He can, however, use up any surplus time shown on the meter when he arrives at the parking space, even without putting in a coin.

When a meter is out of order

It is not an offence to park without paying at a meter which is out of order.

If the meter has a hood over it saying that its use is suspended, anyone parking there is liable to a fixed fine.

Parking elsewhere in a meter zone

Roadside notices warn motorists when they are entering a zone where street parking is restricted to meters only. The hours during which meter parking operates vary and are clearly stated on the signs and at the meters.

It is an offence to park anywhere else in a meter zone, even where there are no yellow lines.

When penalties are fixed

In most areas there is a fixed penalty of £6 for breaking parking regulations. If this penalty is paid within 21 days, there is no conviction against the driver. Failure to pay can lead to a summons and a fine of up to £20.

Towing away parked cars

Cars causing an obstruction or left in contravention of parking restrictions can be removed by the police and kept in a car pound until removal charges and any parking penalties are paid.

This can be very expensive. Charges made by the police for towing away a vehicle are £29 in London and £27 elsewhere. There is also a storage charge of £2 a day.

PARKING NUISANCE

When a parked vehicle can also be a nuisance

A vehicle left on the highway is a nuisance if it is a danger or obstruction to other users of the road. The person in charge of the vehicle is liable for damage resulting from any collision caused by its position.

Any contributory negligence on the part of a driver who has a collision with the parked car is, however, taken into consideration.

It is dangerous to leave an unlighted vehicle at night on a bend, on an unlighted clearway, on the brow of a hill, or parked on the wrong side of the road.

Parking in daytime may also be considered a nuisance in certain circumstances such as fog.

Parking in front of your home

You have a right of access to your own driveway. If a vehicle is parked so as to prevent such access for your car, the driver may be committing no crime, and the police are unlikely to take action. You can, however, sue him for damages.

If on the other hand the motorist was obstructing the highway, he could also be prosecuted.

When a driver regularly obstructs your access in such a way, you could seek an INJUNCTION.

You cannot take any action simply because a private car is regularly parked outside your home, if it is not obstructing your driveway.

The regular parking of commercial vehicles outside your home, even if they do not restrict your access, may constitute a nuisance, however. Although the police are unlikely to take action, you can complain in writing to the owners of the vehicle asking them to stop the practice. If the complaint is ignored you can go to court to seek an injunction – a court order – for them to cease committing the nuisance.

PARLIAMENTARY BILL

How our laws are made by Parliament

Any new law that is passed by Parliament starts in draft form as a parliamentary Bill. It becomes law only when it comes into effect after being made an Act of Parliament by the House of Commons and the House of Lords and receives the Royal Assent.

A Bill may either be 'public' or 'private'. A public Bill is one that is introduced by the Government or by a member of either the House of Commons or the House of Lords, and applies to the whole country.

Parliament considers about 60 public Bills during a session and in many cases is unable to process all of them. If a general election takes place and a new government is formed from another political party, a Bill promoted by the old government will be discontinued, unless the new government is in favour of it. Any public Bill not given the Royal Assent at the end of the year's session of Parliament is automatically dismissed.

A private Bill is introduced by an outside body or individual to alter or increase their powers. For example, a LOCAL AUTHORITY must promote a private Bill if it wants to alter a service or start a new one.

A Bill may be introduced into either House, except that all finance Bills must originate in the House of Commons.

The stages of a public Bill

Once a Bill has been drafted it is presented to the Public Bills Office in Parliament by its sponsor – the minister or individual member in whose name it is being proposed.

The most important Bills usually start in the House of Commons, but some begin their career in the Lords.

In either case, the Bill must pass through a lengthy process in both Houses, consisting of three 'readings', study in detail by a committee and a report stage when the committee reports to the full House. The Bill then receives the Royal Assent and becomes an Act of Parliament.

However, if a Bill is amended in the House of Lords, after it has been through the Commons, it is returned to the Commons so that the amendment can be approved.

If the Commons disagrees with the amendment made in the House of Lords, it alters it and sends the Bill back to the Lords. In most cases, the Lords accept that later decision of the Commons.

If the House of Lords does not accept the decision, the will of the Commons prevails. The House of Lords may refuse to pass a Bill but it becomes law regardless, provided that 1 year has passed since the Bill was sent from the House of Commons to the House of Lords.

The Lords is not entitled to amend any part of a finance Bill.

The stages of a private Bill

Anyone promoting a private Bill must conform to Parliament's standing orders before the Bill can be introduced into either House.

To do so, the promoter must:
● Deposit a petition and a copy of the proposed Bill at the Private Bills Office in the House of Commons and with the Clerk of the Parliaments in the House of

THE STAGES OF A PARLIAMENTARY BILL
How a Bill becomes an Act of Parliament after passing through both Houses

PUBLIC BILL

First reading The Bill is formally introduced to the House when its title is read out and it is ordered to be printed. No discussion takes place.

Second reading Members of the full House debate the general principles of the Bill and vote on whether it should be studied by a committee.

If the House decides it is not in favour of what the Bill intends to do, it votes against the Bill – and the Bill is abandoned at once.

Committee stage The Bill is discussed in detail, clause by clause, and any amendments are made to it. In the Lords, the committee is the full membership of the House. In the Commons, all finance Bills and any Bill of major importance are referred to the Committee of the Whole House for detailed discussion by all members.

Otherwise, a public Bill is discussed by a committee known as a Standing Committee, which must have at least 16 and not more than 50 members, chosen by the Commons Committee of Selection. The membership reflects the political balance of the House, although the chairman of a standing committee does not always belong to the majority party.

When particular members have an interest in a Bill, they are generally selected to sit on the committee – for example, a Bill concerning Scotland will be discussed by a committee consisting of a majority of Scottish members.

It is at the committee stage that the opposition party can voice its objections to a Bill, but any member of the House is entitled to table an amendment at the Public Bills Office. Opponents may make amendments to try to delay a Bill or simply to embarrass the Government. The Government may also decide to amend clauses if outside pressure groups have made representations to the committee.

Report stage The committee reports its suggested amendments back to the full House. The House may decide to accept the amendments or it may decide to make further amendments or refer the Bill to another committee.

Third reading When the amendments are agreed by the House, the Bill receives its third reading. A member of the House of Commons is entitled to make a verbal amendment at that stage, but a member of the House of Lords is not.

After the third reading, the Bill is sent to the other House where it has to pass through the same 6-stage procedure.

PRIVATE BILL

First reading The Bill is formally introduced to the House when its title is read out. The Bill has already been printed. No discussion takes place.

Second reading The full House votes on whether to give the Bill a passage.

This does not mean that it approves the general principle of the Bill; it is simply passing it to a committee on the condition that the promoters prove the necessity of the Bill to that committee.

Committee stage In the House of Commons, if there are no objections to a private Bill, it is passed to a Select Committee on Unopposed Bills, comprising six members of the Commons. In the House of Lords, unopposed Bills are discussed by a committee consisting of as many Lords as the House appoints.

The promoters of the Bill are represented before those committees by a parliamentary agent, usually a solicitor.

An agent may also be engaged by a group opposing a Bill. When acting for the promoters of an unopposed Bill, the agent sets out the Bill's principles before the committee which decides whether it should continue its passage through the House. If the committee agrees it should continue, the members discuss the Bill, clause by clause.

An opposed Bill is sent to a Select Committee on Opposed Bills, comprising four members of the Commons. In the Lords an opposed Bills committee consists of five peers. Both promoter and objector may be represented by counsel, who outlines the purpose of the Bill or the objections to the committee. The committee decides whether the Bill is rejected or allowed to continue its passage through the House. If the Bill is passed, it is then discussed in detail, clause by clause, by the committee.

Report stage The committee reports back to the full House with any amendments it has made. The House decides whether to pass the Bill or send it back for further amendments.

Third reading When the amendments are agreed, or disposed of in some other way, by the House, the Bill receives its third reading.

If it is passed, the Bill is sent to the other House where it has to pass through exactly the same detailed, 6-stage procedure before it can become law.

Royal Assent When a public or a private Bill has received its third reading in the second House, it receives the Royal Assent and becomes an Act of Parliament and is the law.

The Royal Assent is no longer given by the sovereign in person in Parliament – Queen Victoria was the last to do so in 1854. The Speakers in each House now simply inform members that the Royal Assent has been given.

In theory, it is still possible for the Queen to refuse to give her consent to a Bill, but that has not happened since 1707 when Queen Anne vetoed the Scottish Militia Bill.

Lords before November 27 in the session in which it is hoped to obtain a passage for the Bill.

● Give notice of the Bill's proposals to owners, lessees and occupiers of land or property who might be affected by it.

● Advertise in the local Press for the area in which the Bill will be introduced, outlining the Bill.

● Send copies of the Bill to any government department that might be interested.

How private Bills are scrutinised by examiners

The House of Lords and the Speaker of the House of Commons each appoint one examiner to look at all private Bills to ensure that promoters have conformed to standing orders. The examinations begin in December each year and take place in one of the committee rooms of the Houses of Parliament. The examiner gives a Bill's promoter 7 days' notice when his petition is to be examined. Notice of the examination is also given in the daily notices for private business issued by both Houses. Anyone claiming that formalities have not been met may object to the examiners before December 17. If a promoter does not attend the examination of his Bill, his petition falls, and no further progress is made on his Bill.

If the examiner finds that standing orders have been complied with, the Bill is ready for allocation to whichever House is to start debating it.

However, if standing orders have not been complied with, the matter is referred to the House of Commons Standing Orders Committee, who decide whether the Bill is disqualified or whether standing orders may be dispensed with.

If the Bill qualifies, it is allocated to either the House of Lords or Commons in the same way as a public Bill, and it passes through a similar process in both Houses, except that at each stage the petitioners and objectors may state their case.

However, the House where the Bill is started must ratify any alterations made by the second House, whereas the second House is not entitled to restore or even consider any clause that has been struck out in the first House.

When Parliament delegates its powers

To ease the burden of law-making, Parliament can delegate some of its powers by passing Acts that only outline the principles of a law. The Acts simply enable a minister, government department or a local authority to make its own rules and orders – known as

STATUTORY INSTRUMENTS – to carry out that law.

For example, many Acts that cover a service provided by a local authority merely require the authority to make its own plan to carry out that service.

Parliament is able to control the rules and orders made by outside bodies, simply by repealing the Act it has passed. It may also make a provision in the Act that any statutory instruments must be passed by – or at least laid before – both Houses before they can be enforced. The Joint Committee on Statutory Instruments, a committee of both Houses, inspects all statutory instruments.

If the rules have not been approved by Parliament, they may be challenged in a court on the ground that they are 'ultra vires', beyond the powers that the Act of Parliament intended.

PARLIAMENTARY PRIVILEGE

MPs can say what they like in the House

MPs and members of the House of Lords are immune in respect of all statements made during parliamentary proceedings. This is known as parliamentary privilege.

An MP or peer can say what he likes – even if it is a damaging lie – during parliamentary proceedings without risk of being sued for slander or prosecuted for a breach of the Official Secrets Acts.

Parliamentary papers, including reports in *Hansard*, are also privileged and no action for libel can be taken for anything written in them.

The limited privilege of press and broadcasting

Reports, either in newspapers or broadcast, of speeches delivered at debates are also protected, but only provided the reports are without malice and published in good faith.

There is no privilege for anything said or written by MPs or peers which is not in the course of parliamentary proceedings. For example, an MP who says something slanderous in the bar of the House of Commons can be sued.

Breaches of parliamentary privilege are investigated by the Committee of Privileges which is made up of MPs or

---

OBJECTING TO A PRIVATE BILL

Any person or group is entitled to object to a private Bill during its progress through Parliament, provided that he or they can prove that an interest or property will be affected by the proposals contained in the Bill.

There are three stages at which objections may be made:

● When a Bill is being examined to make sure its promoters have complied with standing orders.

● When a Bill has been passed to a committee in the first House.

● When it reaches the committee stage in the second House.

If you do decide to object to a Bill, write to the clerk of the Private Bills Office in either the House of Lords or the House of Commons. You will be given detailed information on how to proceed with your objections.

To be allowed to make representations

against a Bill, an objector must present a petition at the Private Bills Office before January 30 in the House of Commons and February 6 in the House of Lords.

If the Bill's examination has been adjourned until after January 20, present your petition no more than 10 days after the Bill has received its first reading in either House.

If you wish to have professional help in putting your case, write to the secretary of the Society of Parliamentary Agents, 15 Great College Street, London SW1.

The fee for the agent's and counsel's services, which depends on the amount of work involved, may be expensive – for example, promoting an opposed Bill could cost several thousands of pounds.

If your objections fail to stop a Bill in the first House, you are entitled to re-present your objections before a committee of the second House.

peers of all parties. Its report and re-commendation is made to the House which decides what is to be done. *See:* CONTEMPT OF PARLIAMENT

'

THE LETTER THAT TESTED AN MP'S LEGAL IMMUNITY

An MP who writes to a Minister is not taking part in parliamentary proceedings – so he can be sued for what his letter says.

A Member of Parliament, Mr G. R. Strauss, in 1957 alleged a 'public scandal' in the disposal of scrap materials by the London Electricity Board. He made his allegation in a letter to the Paymaster-General, who represented the Minister of Power in the House of Commons.

His letter was referred to the electricity board chairman, who demanded that the statement be withdrawn. When Mr Strauss refused, the board's solicitors threatened to sue for libel.

The MP complained in the Commons that the threat amounted to a breach of parliamentary privilege. Parliament's committee of privileges ruled that Mr Strauss had been engaged in 'a proceeding in Parliament' when he wrote the letter. So the electricity board, in threatening to sue, had breached privilege.

But a committee ruling has no effect unless it is confirmed by a majority of the whole House of Commons. In the debate that followed, supporters of the ruling argued that 'proceedings in Parliament' must include everything said or done by a member in the exercise of his function, as well as in the formal parliamentary business of debating in the chamber.

Opponents of the ruling said that the privilege afforded to MPs was meant to protect only the open, published business of Parliament – not correspondence. An MP could discharge all his responsibilities openly, without claiming further protection.

DECISION

The Commons passed a resolution that Mr Strauss' letter was not part of parliamentary proceedings. So the board – which had dropped its legal threat anyway – had committed no breach of privilege.

'

PAROLE

When a prisoner may be granted conditional release

No prisoner has a right to be freed on parole – which means on his word of honour – but all have a right to be considered for it after a certain length of time in gaol.

The point when a prisoner becomes eligible for parole depends on whether he is serving a fixed term or an indefinite sentence.

Fixed-term prisoners

A prisoner sentenced to a fixed term of more than 18 months can be considered for parole after serving one-third of his sentence, though not before the end of the first 12 months.

Unless they decline the right, prisoners are automatically considered for parole by a local review committee at the prison, which is composed of judges and psychiatrists as members of the Parole Board seconded to the prison. They take into account the prisoner's background, his behaviour in prison, the likely circumstances after release, the offence he committed and whether it is in the public interest to recommend parole.

The committee's recommendation is normally approved by the Home Office, but if the prisoner has committed a serious crime the recommendation will be referred to the Parole Board – a panel of judges, psychiatrists and experts in prison affairs – before a decision is made.

In 1979, out of 10,814 prisoners on fixed sentences, entitled to consideration for parole, 658 declined. Of the 10,156 cases considered, 4,758 (46.8 per cent) were granted parole. A total of 282 prisoners serving life sentences had their cases considered and 76 were granted parole.

Indefinite sentences

Prisoners serving life sentences or young offenders detained indefinitely are also eligible for parole, but the minimum time they must serve before being considered is not specified. It is for the parole board to decide when to consider such a case, though it is rarely less than 7 years.

Even if the board recommends parole in such cases, the Home Office must

consult the Lord Chief Justice and the judge who conducted the original trial before making a decision.

When parole is refused

No reason need be given for refusing parole and a prisoner cannot appeal against the decision, but his case will be reconsidered at regular intervals.

Conditions of parole

A prisoner released on parole is subject to strict conditions. He must remain under the supervision of a probation officer and follow the officer's instructions. He must also 'be of good behaviour and lead an industrious life'.

Parole may be ended and the prisoner recalled to gaol at any time, either by the parole board, the Home Office or by a court if the prisoner is convicted of an indictable offence punishable by imprisonment. Reasons must be given for ending parole and the prisoner can ask to have his case reviewed.

PART EXCHANGE

When trade-in goods are taken instead of money

If goods are accepted as part of the payment for a purchase – for example, when a used car is traded in for a more expensive model – their cash value may have to be paid if the deal goes wrong.

In any such deal, buyer and seller should be in clear agreement over what value is put on trade-in goods.

A buyer's liability

If a buyer has made his purchase and fails to deliver goods that he agreed to trade in, he is liable for their agreed cash value. He can be sued for it.

If trade-in goods have to be returned because they are not the buyer's property, and he has no right to sell them, he can also be sued for their cash value.

But unless the buyer is in business as a trader in the goods, he has no obligation to see that they are in proper order. A private buyer is not liable if goods he trades in are not of suitable condition or quality.

A seller's liability

If the seller is in business as a trader in the goods, he is responsible for their quality. If they are defective, or not fit for their purpose, the buyer is entitled to his money back – and to the return of any goods that were traded in.

If it is impossible to return trade-in goods, the seller who accepted them is liable for their agreed cash value.

When a credit deal is cancelled

If a hire-purchase buyer exercises his right to cancel a CREDIT AGREEMENT, goods traded in as part-payment must be returned within 10 days. They must be in substantially the same condition as when they were accepted, or the dealer can be sued for compensation. If trade-in goods are not returned after 10 days, the agreed cash value must be paid.

PART-TIME WORKER

The legal rights of part-time employees

A part-time worker is defined in law – the Employment Protection (Consolidation) Act 1978 – as someone who normally works for his employer for fewer than 16 hours a week.

The figure of 16 hours is an average that can be calculated over a period of up to 3 months. So someone whose employment is, for example, on a fortnightly basis that requires him to do 30 hours every second week, but nothing in the first week, is still a part-timer.

The Employment Protection (Consolidation) Act makes special provision for part-timers who have worked continuously for the same employer for 5 years. Provided that, during the 5 years, they normally worked for 8 hours or more a week, they are no longer classed as part-timers once the 5 years have elapsed, and they acquire the same legal rights as full-time employees.

A part-timer's legal rights

Part-time workers, like other employees, always have an EMPLOYMENT CONTRACT that may be inferred from custom and practice if it is not in writing. It obliges the employer to pay wages for work done, to provide a safe working place and to ensure that other employees are competent. But part-timers have few other legal rights and are specifically excluded from many of the employment protection rules.

Contracts Part-timers do not have the right to demand written particulars of their employment contracts. If the employer refuses to put details of the job in writing, there is nothing they can do.

Notice Minimum NOTICE periods laid down by law for most categories of worker do not apply to part-timers. However, part-timers are entitled to some form of notice.

If it is not specified in the employment contract, it must be 'reasonable' – that is, normally, at least 1 week for weekly paid employees.

Dismissals Part-timers cannot claim UNFAIR DISMISSAL, no matter how unjust their sacking may be, nor can they claim REDUNDANCY if work is no longer available for them. Unlike most other classes of employee, they cannot insist upon being provided with written reasons for their DISMISSAL.

Maternity A part-timer is not entitled to MATERNITY pay from her employer, nor to reclaim her old job after the child's birth.

Pay Part-timers cannot claim a guaranteed level of pay if they are put on short-time or laid off. *See:* LAY-OFF

They are not entitled to demand an itemised statement of their pay.

Time off Part-timers do not have the right to take time off to undertake public duties, to look for another job if made redundant or to take part in trade union activities.

Additional work

The hours that a part-timer is required to work are stated or implied in his employment contract. If he occasionally works for longer than the contract requires, he remains a part-timer, whether the extra hours are paid at overtime or normal rates.

However, if an employer regularly asks a part-timer to work extra hours, taking the weekly total over 16 hours, it may be argued that he is full-time.

Reducing hours

An employer cannot reduce a full-time employee's hours to reclassify him as a part-timer without the employee's consent. If he does so, the employee can leave and claim unfair dismissal.

However, if the employee does not protest and accepts the change, he may be held to have accepted an alteration in his employment contract.

Paying tax

An employer must deduct income tax from a part-time employee's wages under the PAYE system, as he does for full-time workers. However, many part-timers' wages, with tax allowances taken into account, fall below the tax threshold, so no deduction is made.

If a part-time worker is SELF-EMPLOYED, he is responsible for paying his own tax under Schedule D.

National insurance

Part-time workers are subject to the same national insurance rules as those who work full-time. If a part-timer is an employee, he and his employer must pay Class 1 national insurance contributions, provided that he earns more than the NI lower limit, which in 1981–2 was £27 a week.

A part-time employee who has more than one employer must pay Class 1 contributions for each job in which his earnings exceed the lower limit. So must each employer. He and his employer do not have to pay if he earns below £27 a week in any job. However, if the employee's total payments exceed the NI upper limit – it was set at £821.50 in 1981–2 – the extra payments are refunded.

If he believes his earnings will exceed the upper limit, he can apply for deferment of payment on one or more of his jobs, on form CF379, available at his local social security office. Alternatively, he can pay in advance the entire maximum contribution for the year.

If he does neither, and over the year he pays above the limit, he can apply for a refund on form CF28f after the end of the tax year. Or he can wait until the Department invites him to apply.

Self-employed people working as part-timers pay Class 2 national insurance contributions. However, if their anticipated earnings during the next tax year are below the NI limit – it was £1,475 in 1981–2 – they can apply to the Department of Health and Social Security for a certificate of exception, stating that they do not need to make contributions in that year. The application is made on form CF10, obtainable from any tax or national insurance office. To miss a year's contributions by obtaining an exception may affect the self-employed person's right to SOCIAL

SECURITY BENEFITS, depending upon his contribution record in previous years. The Department can offer advice.

An employee who has a full-time job, but who also works as a self-employed part-timer in his spare time, normally must pay Class 1 and Class 2 contributions. However, he can apply to the Department, using form CF359, to have the Class 2 payments deferred until the end of the tax year, when his exact liability is known.

If his earnings from part-time self-employment are small – less than £1,475 in 1981–2 – he can apply on form CF10 for a certificate of exception from liability for that year. If the earnings are less than £400 in 1980–1 and are unlikely to rise substantially in future years, he can apply to the Department for permanent exception, so that he does not have to complete form CF10 each year. *See:* NATIONAL INSURANCE CONTRIBUTIONS

Unemployment and retirement

If you become unemployed and entitled to UNEMPLOYMENT BENEFIT, you can take part-time employment and at first continue to claim unemployment benefit for those days on which you do not work. If you work on the same days of the week over a period, so that those days are treated as your normal working week, you cease to be entitled to unemployment benefit. That pattern is not regarded as established unless you work part-time on those days for a year.

You can carry on with part-time employment after you have reached retirement age and still draw your RETIREMENT PENSION. Between the ages of 65 and 70 (men) and 60 to 65 (women), your part-time earnings, after deducting allowable expenses, must be less than the amount of earnings-rule limit (£52 a week in 1981).

Retirement pension is taxable, and unemployment benefit is not, and anyone who defers retirement on reaching retirement age is eventually entitled to a higher rate of retirement benefit. In some circumstances, it may be advantageous to continue part-time employment, to forgo the retirement pension, and to claim unemployment benefit.

When you reach 70 – 65 for a woman – you can earn any amount without affecting your pension rights.

PASSPORT

The document you must have to travel abroad

No one needs a passport or any official permission to leave Britain. But other countries may not admit anyone who has no passport – and an airline or shipping company may refuse to issue a ticket.

People may be allowed into Britain without a passport if they can produce some other identity document or if they are refugees, stateless persons or come from a country which does not have a passport system.

Your passport establishes your identity, and calls on foreign governments and people to respect your freedom as a British subject. If a serious problem arises, it proves your right to the help and protection of British diplomatic representatives.

A passport is a state document that remains government property. No citizen is normally refused one, but an application may be declined, or a passport withdrawn, from:

● A child under the age of 18 who wants to leave Britain against the wishes of his parents or guardian.

● Someone for whom an arrest warrant has been issued.

● Someone who is granted bail on a criminal charge.

● Someone who has not repaid the cost of government help to return to Britain.

● In rare cases, a person whose activities cause the Government to rule that granting him a passport is not in the public interest – for example, someone suspected of seeking foreign aid for terrorism in Britain.

The two types of passport that are available

Britain issues a standard passport that is valid worldwide, and a visitor's passport that is simpler and cheaper, but limited in use.

Standard passport A standard British passport costs £11, or £22 if extra pages are required by frequent travellers. It is valid for 10 years, or if issued to a child under the age of 16, for 5 years, renewable for a further 5 years.

Visitor's passport A British visitor's passport is intended only for holiday visits to certain countries that recognise it. It costs £5.50 and is valid for 1 year.

Families On either type of passport, the holder's wife, husband, children under 16 or even the children of relatives can be included at the time of issue, at no extra charge. Someone included in that way can travel only in the company of the passport holder.

Separate standard passports for children over 5 can be issued if requested, but are not issued to younger children except in rare circumstances – for example, when an infant travels with someone who is not a parent or relative. A visitor's passport is not issued separately to children under 8.

How to obtain a passport

Application forms for both types of passport are available at all main post offices, with detailed instructions on how to complete them. With the completed form, countersigned by someone

---

WHERE A SIMPLIFIED PASSPORT IS ACCEPTED

A low-cost British visitor's passport, valid for 1 year, is recognised for holidays of up to 3 months in the following countries:

For up to 3 months

Andorra	Netherlands
Austria	Portugal
Belgium	– including
France	Madeira
– including	Azores
Corsica	San Marino
Gibraltar	Spain
Greece	– including
Italy	Balearic and
– including	Canary Islands
Sicily	Switzerland
Sardinia	Turkey
Elba	West Germany
Liechtenstein	– including
Luxembourg	West Berlin (*but*
Malta	*only if travelling*
Monaco	*by air*)

For not more than 3 months in combination

Denmark	Finland
– including	Iceland
Greenland	Norway
Faroe Islands	Sweden

HELP WHEN IT IS NEEDED

Holders of British passports are entitled to the help of the country's diplomatic missions if they get into difficulties abroad.

of professional standing – for example, a clergyman or doctor – an applicant must supply:
● Proof of British birth or citizenship.
● A marriage certificate or other proof of change of name.
● Two identical, recent photographs taken full-face, without a hat, and measuring no more than $2\frac{1}{2}\times2$ in. or less than $2\times1\frac{1}{2}$ in. The photographs must be verified by the person who countersigns the application.

Waiting time If all the application requirements are met, a visitor's passport is issued immediately at any main post office.

Applications for a standard passport must be posted to the correct regional office as shown on the form. The passport will be posted back to you. You may have to wait up to 4 weeks.

When a woman marries

A woman who marries and already has a passport can choose to:
● Use it until it expires and travel under her maiden name.
● Have the name in it altered for a fee of £2.50.

A woman who has no passport when she marries can:
● Apply for one of her own.
● Apply with her husband for a joint passport.

If a couple intend to go abroad immediately after their wedding, a bride-to-be can apply in advance for a standard passport in her married name. It is

post-dated so that it becomes valid only on their wedding day.

A visitor's passport cannot be issued in a woman's married name until after her wedding.

Special rules for Europe

British passports issued since the beginning of 1973 include a declaration that the holder has the right of abode in the United Kingdom. That entitles a British citizen to seek or take up work in other European Economic Community countries, and to claim a residence permit if he continues in business or employment.

Anyone whose passport was issued before 1973 is entitled to have the declaration of his right of abode added to it. He should send the passport to the Home Office nationality department in London.

Other countries' requirements

The various visas or permits that may be required for admission to other countries are stamped or stapled into a passport. It is a traveller's own responsibility to make sure that he has whatever permission is needed to enter another country. Airlines, shipping companies and major travel agencies can give accurate information.

Some foreign embassies require visa applicants to hand over their passports while applications are checked – a process that can take weeks. For that reason, someone who needs visas for several countries should apply well in advance.

If you lose your passport

The loss of a passport in Britain should be reported to the police. Then apply for a new one in the usual way. If time is short, a restricted passport lasting a year can be issued quickly.

If you lose your passport abroad, report it to the local police then go to the British consul where you can obtain a temporary passport. The £11 replacement fee can be paid when you return home.

If your original passport contained a visa which you require to continue your travels you must go to the consul of the appropriate country to obtain a new visa. That could be a slow process and there is usually no way of speeding things up.

Passport offences Using a false passport or giving false information to obtain a passport are offences carrying a maximum penalty of a £200 fine and 6 months' imprisonment.

PATENT

How to prevent anyone from copying a new invention

Anyone who invents a new device or process can prevent others from copying it by taking out a patent, giving him the sole right for 20 years to manufacture, use or commercially exploit his invention.

No one else – not even someone who genuinely invents the same device independently – can use it if a patent is in force.

Almost anything can be patented so long as it is new and not an obvious development of something else.

However, a patent cannot be obtained for discoveries, scientific theories or mathematical methods. The theory of gravity, if discovered today, could not be patented, though a new machine based on the theory could be.

Literary, musical and artistic works cannot be patented, but they are protected by COPYRIGHT. Nor can you get

> ### NO PATENT FOR WORK ROSTER
>
> *A patent cannot be obtained for a new way of operating an existing production method.*
>
> A steel manufacturer, Quigley Company Inc., applied to patent a 'steel-making process'.
>
> This process used one or more furnaces operating at maximum steel-making heat each day while other furnaces were being relined. Between relining, each furnace was operated at less than maximum steel-producing heat and the steel-producing periods were overlapped with other furnaces.
>
> #### DECISION
> It was held that the company had merely devised a new roster which increased productivity. It was not a new method of manufacture.

APPLYING FOR A PATENT
IN GOOD TIME

If you are developing an idea in a field where there is likely to be competition from rivals, make sure that you apply for a patent as early as possible.

a patent for a particular method of doing business – a new accounting process, for example – nor for new rules for playing a game, computer programmes or for the mere presentation of information, such as a new layout for a form.

Medical treatments for people and animals are not patentable, nor are animal varieties – for example, new breeds of cattle or sheep. New plants and seeds have a different protection under the Plant and Seed Varieties Act 1964.

Applying for a patent

A patent is obtained by filing an application at the Patent Office, 25 Southampton Buildings, London, WC2A 1AY. Special forms must be obtained.

The application must contain a description of the invention, including drawings if necessary.

The claims – the most important part

of the patent – is a precise statement of what the inventor is claiming as his own. The patent will be infringed by anyone who makes something that falls within the claims.

If a claim is badly drawn up, it may be possible for someone else to copy the invention without infringing the patent.

For that reason, applicants should seek advice on drawing up the application from a member of the Institute of Patent Agents, Staple Inn Buildings, London WC1V 7PZ.

The Patent Office may grant a patent immediately or require amendments to be made to the claims, in which case the revised application must be made acceptable within 3½ years from the date it was first filed or the application lapses.

A patent will only be granted if the invention is new. In patent law, an invention is not new if it has been shown in public, or a description of it has been published, before the application is filed. Inventors must, therefore, take care not to publicise their work before filing their application.

However, an invention can be shown to a potential manufacturer without affecting a patent application – provided it is done in confidence. *See:* TRADE SECRET

Cost The patenting process costs £106 – £6 application fee, £50 for a Patent Office search and £50 for the Patent Office examination of the application. These are government fees only. Help from a Patent Agent can cost considerably more. And further government fees of about £1,700 over 20 years are needed to keep the patent in force.

Enforcing patent rights

If a patented invention is used by someone else, the holder of the patent

can seek a court INJUNCTION to restrain the infringement. He can also sue for damages.

PATERNITY

When the father of an illegitimate child denies responsibility

An unmarried mother who wishes to claim maintenance for her child can seek an AFFILIATION ORDER against the man she alleges is the father.

PATRIALITY

The rules that say who has a right to be in Britain

It is a person's patriality, not his citizenship, that gives him or her the right to live in Britain. If you have a passport issued since the Immigration Act came into force on January 1, 1973 it shows, at the top of the first blank page, whether you have the right of abode or are subject to immigration control.

If you have the right of abode you are a patrial; if you are subject to control you are not. There are several ways in which to qualify as a patrial:
● By being a citizen of the United Kingdom or its colonies through birth, adoption, naturalisation or registration in the United Kingdom, the Channel Islands or the Isle of Man. People who acquired citizenship by application to a British high commission or embassy are not included, however.
● By being a citizen and the child or grandchild of a citizen who qualified as a patrial. Although citizenship can be inherited only through the male line, patriality can be conferred by a parent or grandparent of either sex.
● By being a citizen who has been settled in the United Kingdom – that is, allowed to stay without any Home Office restriction – having been a resident for 5 years or more.
● By being a Commonwealth citizen one of whose parents was a citizen of the United Kingdom at the time of the birth.
● By being a Commonwealth citizen and registering as a citizen of the United Kingdom and colonies by virtue of being the wife of a patrial, provided the

A WRANGLE OVER A PATENT HAY RAKE

If the claims in a patent application are not carefully worded they may allow a rival to copy an idea.

Van der Lely patented a hay rake which could be turned into a swathe turner by removing the rear wheels and remounting them parallel with the front wheels.

A similar machine appeared on which the front wheels could be remounted

parallel with the rear wheels. The Van der Lely company took the inventor of the rival machine, Bamfords Ltd, to court alleging an infringement of patent.

DECISION

The court decided that Bamfords had clearly taken Van der Lely's idea. But Van der Lely had patented only the idea of changing round the back wheels, not the front, so there was no infringement.

> ## THE WIFE WHO WOULD NOT JOIN A 21 MONTH QUEUE
>
> *If unreasonable delay by officials abroad forces a patrial immigrant to land in Britain without a patriality certificate, the immigrant cannot be denied the right to enter.*
>
> Maimuna Phansopkar's husband was a UK citizen by registration in Britain. That made him a patrial. So, as an Indian citizen, she became a British patrial when she married him.
>
> In 1975 she applied for a patriality certificate so that she could travel to Britain with her husband. They were told at the British high commission in Bombay that she would have to wait a year and 9 months for an interview.
>
> The couple decided to leave immediately. Mrs Phansopkar arrived in Britain without even an entry certificate.
>
> She was refused entry by an immigration officer.
>
> In appeals to an adjudicator and to the immigration appeals tribunal, the officer's decision was upheld.
>
> The case went to the Court of Appeal, which had to decide whether in the circumstances Mrs Phansopkar was entitled to expect the immigration officer to issue a patriality certificate.
>
> ### DECISION
>
> The court ruled that her patrial right to enter Britain could not be taken away by administrative delay. Because the high commission had been wrong to defer her application, the immigration officer was wrong to refuse her a certificate when she arrived.

marriage took place before 1973.

Anyone who intends to travel to Britain on a passport that was not issued in the United Kingdom or Eire and thinks he qualifies as a patrial should seek a patriality certificate from a British Embassy or high commission. He can apply to an immigration officer on arrival, but risks being refused admission if he cannot establish patriality. Documentary evidence, such as birth certificates, can reduce this risk.

WHEN PATRIALITY CAN BE CLAIMED

Commonwealth citizens can claim patriality in the United Kingdom if either parent was a UK citizen by birth – or if the applicant is a woman married to someone who is a patrial.

Earls Court Road

Patrial rights in the EEC

Patrial British citizens have the right to seek or take up work in other European Community countries. They can claim residence permits if they continue in employment or business.

EEC freedom of movement for employment is not granted to British patrial non-citizens, for example those travelling on Commonwealth passports, although they have the right of abode in Britain.

Patrial immigrants

A patrial has the right to come into Britain whenever he wishes. He cannot be refused entry, provided that he has proof of his patriality – usually a certificate issued in his own country on the basis of documentary evidence supplied there by him.

If an immigrant arrives claiming patriality, but without a certificate or convincing evidence, an immigration officer is entitled to refuse admission. But the Court of Appeal has ruled that if a person is prevented from obtaining a patriality certificate simply because of delay by British representatives abroad, he or she should not be refused the right to enter Britain.

If an immigrant arrives without enough evidence to prove patriality, but qualifies for at least a temporary stay, he can make his claim later to the Home Office immigration department.

PAWNBROKER

Pledging goods as security for a loan

Money can be borrowed from a pawnbroker by leaving goods with him as a 'pledge' – security for the loan – on agreed interest terms. No maximum limit is set on the interest that can be charged, although a county court can reduce any interest rate that, in its view, is excessive. The loan is unlikely to represent the full value of the goods.

Usually the goods must be redeemed – recovered by paying back the loan and interest – within 6 months. The pawnbroker is not entitled to make an extra charge for giving them back.

If goods are not redeemed within the agreed time, the pawnbroker is entitled to make a charge for their safekeeping, or sell them.

A pawnbroker who makes a charge for the safekeeping of goods, after the redemption period has expired, cannot charge at a higher rate than he was charging as interest.

If a pawnbroker decides to sell goods, he must serve written notice on the borrower, ideally by recorded-delivery post.

When the notice has been served, the borrower can ask a county court for more time to pay. If he does not do so –

WHEN A PAWNBROKER MAY REFUSE A PLEDGE

Almost any goods can be pawned, but a pawnbroker is unlikely to accept any perishable goods or anything that would go out of fashion and leave him with an unsaleable security.

PAWNBROKER

HOW PAWNBROKER AGREEMENTS ARE REGULATED

A pawnbroker must be licensed by the Office of Fair Trading, and his credit arrangements are subject to the same controls as other CREDIT AGREEMENTS. His licence might be withdrawn if a pattern of complaints from a number of people is established.

The rules about signing an agreement and supplying copies of it apply in the same way as for other forms of credit, such as hire purchase or bank loans, and a borrower can ask a county court to alter the agreement if he feels that the interest is extortionate. *See:* INTEREST CHARGE

A pawnbroker who takes a pledge without complying with the rules of the Consumer Credit Act can be fined up to £200.

Giving a receipt Anyone who pawns an article must be given a receipt at the time, even if the money is not advanced immediately. If he loses the receipt, he can still recover the goods, by making a formal declaration that they are his, and paying back the loan and interest.

A pawnbroker who refuses to return goods without reasonable cause can be fined up to £200.

Under-age customers It is illegal for a pawnbroker to take a pledge from anyone under the age of 18. If he does so, he can be fined £400 by magistrates or imprisoned for a year, with an unlimited fine, by a crown court.

or if his application is rejected – the pawnbroker is free to sell the goods.

If the pawnbroker makes more money by selling the goods than he is owed, he must hand over the balance to the borrower. If he makes less, he is not entitled to recover the shortfall from the borrower unless he can prove that he exercised all reasonable care to get the true market value.

The pawnbroker is liable for any damage to pledged items. If the item is lost, the owner can sue him.

PAY

Getting the rate for the job

When an employer and an employee enter into an EMPLOYMENT CONTRACT, which may be in writing or simply an oral agreement, the employer takes on a duty to pay contracted wages for the work done.

Normally, the rate and frequency of payment are stipulated in the contract or in a relevant collective agreement. If no mention has been made of money, the employee is entitled to ask a court to order him to be paid *quantum meruit* – the Latin term meaning 'as much as he deserved', or the rate for the job. That can be established by determining how long he worked, the skills involved and the wages paid to other people doing comparable jobs.

GETTING THE RATE FOR THE JOB

The principle of being paid as much as you deserve – in Latin, quantum meruit *– has been recognised in law for centuries, pre-dating by many generations trade union demands for 'the rate for the job'.*

PAY OFFICE

'Do you call this quantum meruit?'

When the employer fails to pay

If an employer fails to pay wages in full and on time, and the employee has carried out his side of the contract, the employee may sue for the money as a DEBT, in a county court if the sum is up to £2,000 or in the High Court if it is more.

He may also be able to claim compensation for UNFAIR DISMISSAL from an INDUSTRIAL TRIBUNAL, if he leaves his job because of his employer's unreasonable conduct in failing to pay.

However, tribunals do not generally award compensation if the employer was merely a day or two late with the wages, and in those circumstances there is little that the employee can do.

If an employer goes bankrupt or into liquidation owing back wages to his employees, the employees become preferential creditors. Their claims, up to a maximum of £800, arising from the 4 months before winding-up proceedings started are given priority over those of ordinary creditors. Any other amounts owed to employees are treated as ordinary debts.

Employees' claims must be submitted to the receiver or liquidator in charge of the employer's affairs. *See:* BANKRUPTCY

How wages are fixed

In Britain, there is no general statutory minimum wage.

Most people's pay is fixed either by direct negotiation with the employer, or through collective bargaining with the assistance of a trade union or professional body. *See:* COLLECTIVE BARGAINING

However, the law does influence pay levels. In some sectors where the trade unions have traditionally been weak – for example, hairdressing – pay rates and holiday entitlements are established through a WAGES COUNCIL and have legal backing.

Companies which undertake work for local or central government bodies are required to accept clauses in their contracts stating that they will not pay their workers less than the general rate for the job, and that their wages will be in line with the general level in their district.

Equal pay laws are intended to ensure that women receive the same pay as men for doing the same work, and that there is no pay differential based on SEX DISCRIMINATION.

Rules on LAY-OFFS give most full-time employees a minimum guaranteed wage if their earnings are substantially reduced because of a temporary cutback or change in their employer's business.

Since the Employment Act 1980 there is now no statutory procedure whereby groups of workers can ask to have their wages increased if they fall below the 'fair' rate paid to other workers in the same type of job.

How wages can be paid by law

The Truck Acts of 1831–1940 prohibit the payment of workmen engaged in manual labour in anything other than cash – for example, by cheque or by direct credit. However, court definitions have varied widely – a television repair man has been held to be a manual labourer while a goods train guard has not.

The Truck Acts do not apply to other categories of employee. An employer can pay them by cheque or direct credit if he wishes, unless their employment contract says otherwise or cash wages are implied by custom and practice.

Under the Payment of Wages Act 1960 and the Truck Acts, anyone can ask to have his wages paid by cheque. However, the employer is not obliged to accept the request, which must be submitted in writing. If he does, either party can cancel the arrangement by giving 4 weeks' written notice.

Payment while you are under notice

An employee who is under NOTICE to leave his job is entitled to normal payment during the notice period. If he does not receive it, he can sue his employer for WRONGFUL DISMISSAL.

If an employee resigns without giving proper notice or part way through the notice period, he is not normally entitled to claim any wages due since his last pay day. However, some lawyers suggest that courts today might not take such a harsh attitude and might award payment for the work actually done, less any damage caused by failure to give notice.

Payment while you are off work

Most full-time employees who have completed a minimum period of service with their employer are entitled to be paid during their holidays, for at least part of the time while off sick, and when they are on maternity leave, or laid-off or on short-time. The service period ranges from 4 weeks for lay-off to 2 years for paid maternity leave.

Obtaining an itemised pay statement

Most employees are entitled, under the Employment Protection (Consolidation) Act 1978, to receive an itemised pay statement from their employer each time they are paid their wages or salaries. Those who are not are part-time workers, people employed by their husband or wife, employees who perform their duties mainly abroad and merchant seamen. *See:* EMPLOYMENT PROTECTION

The statement must show:

Gross pay The total amount earned by the employee during the period covered by the statement, including overtime and bonus payments.

Deductions All deductions – for example, for INCOME TAX, NATIONAL INSURANCE CONTRIBUTIONS, pension contributions and trade union dues – must be itemised, stating what they are and the amount deducted in each category. However, if some deductions are the same each pay day, they can be added together under the heading 'fixed deductions', provided that the employee has previously received written notification of what they are for, the amounts in each case, and the frequency with which they are made.

Net pay The amount the employee receives after all deductions have been made from gross pay.

Payment method Sometimes an employee is paid partly in cash and partly by cheque or credit transfer. In such cases, the methods used, and the amounts paid in each way, must be shown on the statement.

There is no standard form of itemised pay statement, so employers may devise their own, provided that they include the information required by law. If the statement is computer-coded, the code for the figures that must be shown by law must be explained in a key.

If an employer fails to supply an itemised pay statement which meets the legal requirements, the employee can complain to an INDUSTRIAL TRIBUNAL. The tribunal can declare that the statement should be provided, outline the form it should take, and punish the employer by ordering him to pay the employee up to 13 weeks' worth of the deductions from gross pay which he had made but had failed to notify.

So if the employer had failed to tell the employee, in a proper statement, that he was deducting tax and national insurance, he could be required to pay 13 weeks' tax and NI payments as compensation.

PAY AS YOU EARN
The system of deducting tax from wages

All employees have their income tax deducted automatically from their pay by their employer under the system known as Pay As You Earn – PAYE.

Each year, every employee receives a coding notice from the Inland Revenue listing the personal allowances and expenses to which he is entitled and on which he pays no tax. *See:* INCOME TAX ALLOWANCES

The notice also allocates a code number based on those allowances. For example, an employee with allowances of £2,000 gets a code number of 200; if the allowances are £1,200, the code is 120. A letter is added to the code to show allowances:

● L – single person's allowance or wife's earned income allowance.
● H – married man's allowance.
● D – liability to higher-rate tax.
● P – age allowance single person.
● V – age allowance for married couple.
● T – all others: if you don't wish other letters to be used.

Using the code number and tax tables, the employer must deduct the appropriate amount of tax from each person's pay and pass it to the Inland Revenue each month.

Checking your code

Always check your coding notice to see that you are getting all the allowances to which you are entitled. If you think it is wrong, return it to the tax office, pointing out the mistake, otherwise too much tax will be deducted.

Tax refunds

Anyone who stops receiving his wage or salary – whether through losing his job, sickness, being on strike or any other reason – can claim a repayment of tax after 4 weeks without pay on unused personal allowances. Further repayments are payable every subsequent 4 weeks until the earliest of three events:
● The end of the tax year.
● All the tax paid in that year has been refunded.
● Any remaining tax that has not been refunded is needed to pay the tax owed on previous earnings. *See:* INCOME TAX REFUND

Additional income

People with sources of income apart from their wages – for example, working widows and pensioners, or those with more than one job – may have all the tax collected from one source. This will depend on the source of the other income. It would not, for example, be collected from a retirement pension, but it might be from a second job.

A second source of income should be mentioned on your tax return form and the Inland Revenue will also be notified by the employer.

Those with more than one source of income do not normally qualify for rebates.

PEDESTRIAN ACCIDENTS

How a victim of negligent driving can sue

A pedestrian injured because of a motorist's negligence can claim damages in the courts. But the amount he receives may be reduced if he was to some extent to blame for the accident.

The court might consider him guilty of such CONTRIBUTORY NEGLIGENCE if he had been:
● Walking on the road instead of the footpath.
● Walking on the left side of the road instead of facing the oncoming traffic.

....

THE PENALTY FOR IGNORING A
PEDESTRIAN CROSSING

A driver who does not stop to give precedence to a pedestrian on a zebra crossing can be fined up to £100 – and have his licence endorsed.

....

> ### THE WALKER WHO CAUSED A ROAD DEATH
>
> *Someone who steps on to a road without looking and causes a traffic accident can be liable for damages.*
>
> Mr M, one of a theatre crowd going home on a summer night in 1966, was walking on a wide grass verge beside a main road. A scooter rider, Mr B, was driving in the same direction, close to the left side of the road.
>
> M, intending to cross, stepped on to the road. The scooter collided with him and B was thrown off. He died of his injuries.
>
> B's widow sued for damages, alleging that M was negligent in failing to ensure that it was safe to step on to the road. M in his defence claimed that B should not have been driving so close to the verge.
>
> The court had to decide which of the two was responsible for the accident, or whether the blame should be shared.
>
> #### DECISION
>
> The exact distance between the scooter and the verge could not be discovered. But the court held that that did not matter: M's negligence in not looking to his right was the sole cause of the accident. B's widow was awarded damages.

● Stepping off the kerb without looking.
● Crossing at a junction when the lights are in favour of the vehicle involved.
● Using a Pelican PEDESTRIAN CROSSING when the lights are red.

A motorist can sue a negligent pedestrian for damages. Such a case might arise if the pedestrian caused an accident by carelessly stepping into the road.

PEDESTRIAN CROSSING

When a driver must give way

The most common type of pedestrian crossing is the black-and-white striped zebra. Vehicles must give way as soon as a pedestrian is within the limits of the crossing. But they are not obliged to give precedence if the pedestrian is still on the kerb, nor if the vehicle reaches the broken white line immediately in front of the crossing before the pedestrian.

If there is a central reservation halfway across, the parts on each side are treated as separate crossings. A motorist approaching the crossing on one side does not have to give way to a pedestrian already walking on the crossing on the other side.

A pedestrian who joins a zebra crossing other than from the kerb – for example, if he approaches it from a car in the road – still has precedence over vehicles once he has actually reached the striped area.

The pedestrian should not remain on any crossing longer than necessary, and can be fined up to £100 for so doing.

Parking within the zigzag area

It is an offence to park so that any part of a vehicle is within the zigzag area leading up to a zebra crossing. A motorist can also be prosecuted for overtaking a vehicle on the approach to a crossing within the zigzag lines.

He is regarded as having overtaken once any part of his vehicle passes the front of the other vehicle, even if he subsequently drops back again.

The maximum penalty for parking within the zigzag area, failing to give precedence or overtaking at a zebra crossing is a fine of £100, and an endorsement or possible disqualification.

A pelican crossing is controlled by lights that a driver must obey. He must halt at a red light and at the amber when it is first shown, unless he cannot safely do so. At the flashing amber light after the red light he must respect pedestrians already on the crossing.

A driver must not cause his vehicle to stop on the carriageway between the studs of the crossing unless he is obliged to do so by circumstances beyond his control or to avoid an accident.

The maximum penalty for a driver misusing a crossing in any of the above ways is a £100 fine and endorsement.

An illuminated red man signal tells the pedestrian that he should wait on the kerb and a green man that he may use the crossing. At the flashing green man the pedestrian may continue across the carriageway but he should not start to do so. It is not an offence for a pedestrian to ignore the pedestrian signals but he would be held guilty of CONTRIBUTORY NEGLIGENCE in case of an accident. He can, however, be fined up to £100 for loitering on a crossing and is obliged to cross with reasonable despatch.

> ### MOTORIST WHO THOUGHT HE HAD THE RIGHT OF WAY
>
> *Motorists must give way as soon as a pedestrian steps on to the striped crossing.*
>
> Mr Charles Neville, a motorist, was prosecuted for failing to give precedence to a pedestrian. He argued that he had reached the zigzag area before the pedestrian stepped out and, as this is part of the controlled area, he had precedence. Mr Neville was cleared by the magistrates but the police appealed.
>
> #### DECISION
> The appeal court ruled that the zigzag area is only a warning of a crossing ahead. The pedestrian reached the striped area before the vehicle and therefore had precedence. Mr Neville was convicted.
>
> ### POLITE PEDESTRIAN HURT ON A CROSSING
>
> *A motorist is still guilty of failing to give precedence on a zebra crossing even if a pedestrian, out of politeness, allows him to proceed first.*
>
> Two men using a crossing halted halfway over to let a car pass. A second car, driven by Mr Gordon Bedford, followed the first one over the crossing and hit one of the men. Mr Bedford was charged with failing to give precedence. He argued that he thought the pedestrians had waived their precedence.
>
> #### DECISION
> The magistrates cleared Mr Bedford but the prosecution appealed. The appeal court ruled that a belief that a pedestrian has waived his precedence is no defence. Mr Bedford was found guilty.

School crossings do not need to be established on existing zebra or pelican crossings and the motorist is advised by a road sign, sometimes with a flashing light, when these may be in use.

The lollipop man or lady, who must be dressed in the official clothing and display the lollipop sign, has no authority to stop traffic except to facilitate the crossing of roads by children to and from school.

Driving through a lollipop 'stop' signal is an offence. The penalties are a £100 fine and a licence endorsement.

PEDLAR

The laws controlling casual traders

Anyone who goes about on foot offering goods or services for sale on his own behalf is a pedlar. He commits an offence for which he can be fined £25 if he does not obtain a pedlar's certificate from a police station. The fee is £1.25 a year. A pedlar must produce his certificate when asked to do so by a customer or by the police.

Hawkers, tinkers and knife-sharpeners are all pedlars. Salesmen moving from place to place by car are commercial travellers, not pedlars, and do not need a certificate. Those who sell on behalf of a formal body or organisation, such as encyclopaedia salesmen, do not need a licence.

PENSION

Making provision for your retirement

Everyone who pays national insurance contributions is eligible – as are the wives of men who do – for a state RETIREMENT PENSION. In many cases, workers are also part of an OCCUPATIONAL PENSION scheme.

PERFORMING RIGHT

The 'copyright' of plays, songs and music

Song-writers, composers and play-wrights have the right to control and benefit from the public performance of their work.

That right, known as the 'performing right', is similar to COPYRIGHT and lasts for the author's lifetime plus 50 years.

In that time any unauthorised public performance of a song, play or piece of music is an infringement of the performing right.

Putting on a show

If you want to stage a play or an opera in public you must seek permission beforehand.

There is usually a notice inside the front cover of a script or score stating how to get permission.

The British Theatre Association has an information service for its members giving details of the rights and royalties attached to plays, the names and addresses of authors' agents, and useful information on other aspects of staging a performance.

Membership costs £10 a year, and is open to amateur or professional directors and stage managers, drama societies, clubs, schools and universities. The association's address is 9 Fitzroy Square, London W1P 6AE.

When a performance is public

Any performances that are not private or domestic are considered public – including those in private clubs, public houses, hotel lounges and restaurants.

A radio or television set that can be heard or seen in a cafe counts also as a public performance of any music or play that is being broadcast.

But teachers and pupils performing in school are not affected provided the audience is limited to fellow teachers and pupils.

Protecting composers

It is impossible for song-writers and composers to keep track of all public performances of their work, but the Performing Right Society Ltd, known as the PRS, acts on their behalf.

Membership, which is free, is open to composers, lyric writers – and their heirs – and music publishers.

Members assign their performing rights to the society, and the society in turn controls these rights by granting licences to anyone who occupies or owns a place where music is played to the public, either live or on records or tapes.

The society charges royalty fees for

these licences and the royalties are then passed on to the individual members concerned.

Normally these royalties are divided between writers and publishers – two-thirds to the writer and one-third to the publisher. That may be varied by agreement but it is a rule that the writer's share must never be less than half.

The society has more than 40 standard tariffs – mainly for bingo halls, discotheques, cinemas, hotels and restaurants, public houses, village halls, clubs, factories, juke boxes and shops.

If you run any of these and play music to your clients or employees, you should apply for a PRS licence to the society's offices at 29 Berners Street, London W1 4AA.

Records and tapes

Recording companies also have performing rights in their discs and cassettes and can charge a fee if they are played in public.

These charges are collected by the companies' own rights organisation, Phonographic Performance Ltd – PPL.

So wherever music is played in public from a tape or record two licences are needed – one from the PRS and the other from PPL.

The PPL licence can be obtained by writing to its offices at Ganton House, 14 Ganton Street, London W1V 1LB.

Although you need both licences to play taped background music in a cafe, however, only a PRS licence is needed to play background music on the radio or television.

Recording at home

If you make a tape recording of an existing record, even for only private use, legally, you should have a licence from the Mechanical Copyright Protection Society. See: COPYRIGHT

Although you can videotape a live television broadcast free of charge for private use, you cannot videotape a film broadcast on television without infringing copyright.

The maximum penalties for making or selling a pirate film are £50 and 2 months' imprisonment.

If a charge is unfair

If you think you are being overcharged for a licence or that the terms for it are unfair you can appeal to the Performing Right Tribunal – PRT – which will investigate the case.

The PRT was set up in 1957 to resolve disputes between bodies like the PRS and PPL and people needing licences. The tribunal consists of a chairman – a barrister or solicitor – and up to four other members.

A complaint to the tribunal can be made by writing to: The Secretary to the Performing Right Tribunal, Room 105, The Patent Office, 25 Southampton Buildings, London WC2A 1AY.

Where either the PRS or PPL has negotiated a tariff with a representative organisation, such as a restaurant or cafe owners' association, the PRT is unlikely to rule that the rate is unfair – even though an individual cafe owner may think it too much in his case.

PERJURY

The perils of lying in court

Anyone who takes an OATH or makes an affirmation in a court or tribunal must tell the truth. If he does not, and it can be shown that what he said was relevant or important, he can be prosecuted for perjury.

The maximum penalty on conviction in a crown court is 7 years' imprisonment and an unlimited fine.

The prosecution does not have to prove that the accused knew for certain that his evidence was false; it is enough to show simply that he did not believe it to be true.

The only defences are for the accused to prove that he did not believe the evidence was untrue, or that it was entirely irrelevant.

In addition to court and tribunal hearings, perjury can be committed in an AFFIDAVIT – a written statement of evidence. It is also an offence, under the Perjury Act 1911, to give false evidence:
● To obtain a marriage, birth or death certificate.
● To gain admittance to a professional register – for example, by lying about a medical degree.
● In any statutory declaration, such as a formal certificate of ownership.
● In any sworn statement required by law – such as the particulars on an application form for a driving licence.
● In any company accounts.

Anyone helping or persuading someone else to give false evidence is guilty of 'subornation of perjury', for which the penalty is the same as for perjury itself.

Anyone who gives false information to obtain a false marriage, birth or death certificate can be imprisoned for up to 7 years and fined £1,000.

The maximum penalty for perjury in a statutory declaration or affidavit is 2 years' imprisonment and an unlimited fine.

FATHER WHO LIED TO SAVE HIS SONS

Telling lies as a witness under oath almost always carries a prison sentence.

Two sons of John Spencer Davies were charged at Tywyn Magistrates' Court in October 1973 of offences of dishonesty relating to vehicles. They pleaded guilty.

Before sentence was passed, Davies gave false evidence in mitigation saying both boys had been gainfully employed in recent weeks, one earning £25–£28 a week and the other £20–£25. They now showed, he claimed, every prospect of leading a more settled and useful life. The boys were later sent to Borstal by the crown court.

Some months later, under police questioning, Davies admitted that he had lied to the magistrates.

'I only did it to try and help them . . . I told their solicitor they were working and he asked me to go into the witness box,' he told the police.

Davies was tried in June 1974 at Dolgellau Crown Court. He pleaded guilty to perjury and was sent to prison for 12 months. He appealed.

DECISION

The Court of Appeal upheld the sentence. Only in the most exceptional cases, it ruled, was perjury not punishable by a gaol sentence.

The court added: 'Anybody sympathises with a father whose natural instincts are to try to help his sons when they are in trouble – but the right way is not to lie on their behalf.'

PERSONAL ACCIDENT INSURANCE

Providing compensation for death or injury

Financial provision for you if you are injured in an accident – and for your family if you are killed in one – can be provided through a personal accident insurance policy.

The proposal form for this type of insurance includes questions designed to assess the risk involved – about your age, sight, hearing, state of health, drinking habits, and about any circumstances that might make you particularly liable to accidents.

Anyone completing an application form must disclose all material facts and make no deliberately misleading statement. *See:* INSURANCE

The exact wording varies from policy to policy but most relate to 'bodily injury caused by violent accidental, external and visible means, which independently of any other cause, causes death or disablement'.

The injury can include broken bones, sprains, ruptures or almost any kind of physical disablement, but shock alone is not classed as an injury. Medical evidence of the injury must be provided in support of any INSURANCE CLAIM.

The word 'accident' means something unexpected and fortuitous, but it may cover not only such things as train crashes or falls but also injuries sustained while, for example, playing tennis or cricket.

A person deliberately injured by someone else may still be able to claim it as an 'accident' – for example, if he were stabbed while walking home at night. If he had provoked the attack, however, by taunting his assailant, he would not be able to claim.

When you can claim

Different policies may lay down different conditions about how serious the effect of an injury must be before your claim will be allowed.

Common phrases such as 'unable to perform his usual business or occupation' or 'inability to resume his normal calling' mean the company will pay out if the person is unable to carry out a substantial part of his usual working routine.

But if the policy stipulates 'inability to attend to business of any kind', nothing will be paid unless you are completely incapacitated.

When you cannot claim

Most personal accident insurance policies list specific exceptions to the company's liability – for example, accidents while the insured person is engaged in a hazardous pursuit, such as mountaineering, is under the influence of drink or is exposing himself to obvious risk. So if someone is injured while trespassing on a railway line, for example, the company can refuse to pay.

You can arrange cover for any extra risk – for example, if skiing is your hobby – by paying an extra premium.

Most policies exclude death or injury by poisoning, even if it is taken accidentally, or by 'anything inhaled' – which is designed to rule out deaths caused by gas left on in a room by mistake.

How claims are settled

Most personal accident policies provide for a lump sum to be paid for death or injury and weekly payments for a fixed period in the case of disablement.

A typical policy might offer, for example:
- Death after an accident: £2,000.
- Loss of two limbs or two eyes: £2,000.
- Loss of one limb and one eye: £2,000.
- Loss of one limb or one eye: £1,000.
- Permanent disablement: £2,000.
- Temporary disablement: £10 a week for up to 104 weeks.
- Temporary partial disablement: £4 a week for up to 104 weeks.

You can insure for any multiple of these amounts for a corresponding increase in premium.

PERSONAL INJURY

How damages are awarded for losses suffered in an accident

If you have been injured as a result of someone else's NEGLIGENCE, you may be able to recover damages – provided you can prove that he was at fault. It is not advisable either to pursue or to defend an action for damages without engaging a solicitor: claims often fail for lack of expert help.

How damages are assessed

When awarding damages for personal injury, a court seeks to restore the claimant to the financial position he enjoyed before the accident, so far as money can do so. It considers two categories of award: special damages, covering losses and expenses up to the date of the trial, and general damages, compensating for future loss of earnings and happiness, pain and suffering, and future expenses arising out of the accident – such as regular nursing.

Defining special damages

● *Loss of wages* If the claimant was earning a regular salary, he is compensated fully for losing it. He receives an amount equivalent to his total salary for the period involved, after tax and any sick pay from his employer have been deducted.

Such compensation is increased if he can show that his wages would have risen since his injury – for example, if his former workmates had negotiated a pay award. It can also be reduced if it is likely that his employment would have ended through retirement or redundancy.

● *Loss of earnings* If the injured person had no fixed income – if, for example, he was a casual worker, self-employed or a partner in a company – he has to prove how much less he had earned because of the accident.

If he was unable to work at all, he would have to show how much he would normally have earned in that period. If he was a company director, for example, he would demonstrate how its profits were reduced by his absence. Having shown proof, he is compensated for the total sum of what he would have earned after tax.

● *Expenses incurred* The claimant is repaid in full for any nursing, medical or hospital expenses that arose from his accident. He is entitled to have private medical treatment – even if he normally uses only National Health Service facilities – but many accident victims do not take advantage of this right, as they cannot be sure of winning their case for damages, or that the person who injured them is adequately insured.

● *Other expenses* The injured person may also claim the cost of visits to hospital by his or her wife or husband and children, a wife's loss of earnings if she gave up her job and stayed at home to look after her injured husband and a convalescent holiday, if the claimant is ordered by a doctor to take one.

Claims are allowed only for the convalescent's own expenses – unless it was medically necessary for someone to travel with him – and for a standard of accommodation that is no higher than he would normally use.

Defining general damages

● *Future loss of earnings* The award is calculated according to the extent of permanent disability that was suffered, its affect on the claimant's earning power and the number of working years that would have been left to him if the accident had not happened.

The compensation, however, is not equivalent to the total amount of earnings lost, as the court takes into account the advantage of receiving a lump sum immediately rather than regular wage payments over a long period. For example:

George Jones, 40, net salary £2,000 per annum, was left paralysed by a road accident and could not work again.

In theory, the court should have awarded him £50,000 for loss of earnings for the remaining 25 years of his working life. In fact, he received about

£24,000 – 12 years' earnings.

If invested, however, that sum could produce an annual income of about £2,880 – which, after income tax, is the yearly amount that Mr Jones had lost.

The courts rarely award more than 15 years' loss of earnings and do not take account of inflation. The plaintiff must try to protect himself against future inflation by prudent investment.

If an accident victim is only partly disabled, the extent of the injury and its affect on his earning power is assessed. For example, for the loss of a finger, an

LOSS OF EARNINGS – EVEN AFTER DEATH

In giving judgment in a significant appeal case in 1979, the House of Lords ruled that claimants should be compensated for their total loss of earnings, calculated as if their injury had not happened.

Mr Ralph Pickett, a cyclist of Olympic standard, was a coachbuilder employed by British Rail. After 25 years' exposure to asbestos dust in that employment, Mr Pickett found that he had developed a lung disease.

British Rail accepted liability, but contested the amount of damages it should pay.

Between the original trial of the case and the appeal's reaching the House of Lords, Mr Pickett died. British Rail argued then that it should be required to pay damages for loss of earnings only for the year that Mr Pickett had lived after making his claim.

DECISION

The Lords, however, took the view that Mr Pickett's widow was entitled to claim for all the years he would have earned – but for the lung disease which was the subject of the case.

They sent the case back to the original trial court to have the damages calculated on that basis.

orchestral violinist would recover far greater damages than, say, a company director.

● *Future expenses* Allowance is made for future medical costs arising from the accident, including hospital care or private nursing, if required. Other expenses may include having the claimant's home adapted to suit his disability, the cost of a wheelchair, or removal expenses if, for example, he needs to live in a warmer climate.

● *Loss of happiness* The victim is entitled to compensation for losing various

HOW THE COURTS HAVE SETTLED CLAIMS FOR PERSONAL INJURY

There is no fixed award for any loss – no set price for a severed arm, say – and a solicitor can give no more than general guidance in the light of previous awards on how much an injured person may expect to recover in court. A judge may award a lump sum for the general damages without breaking it down into details – though judges usually list the factors they have taken into account in making the award.

● A 9-year-old girl who lost one eye was awarded £5,250.

● A man of 43 was blinded in one eye, but his work was not affected by the accident. He recovered £5,000 in general damages.

● A man of 48 who was totally blinded received £65,000.

● A woman in her 50s suffered partial deafness and was left with a continuous buzzing noise after a syringe broke in her ear. She was awarded £2,750.

● A girl of 20 who was facially disfigured when she was thrown through a

windscreen, but whose looks were repaired by cosmetic surgery, received general damages of £5,000.

● A 10-year-old girl whose eating was permanently affected when she drank caustic soda that was served to her instead of lemonade, scarring her mouth and throat, received £43,000.

● A man of 25 lost the little finger of his left hand, affecting his piano-playing and his golf. He recovered £2,000 in damages.

● A boy of 8 lost the use of his left forearm. He received £13,000 for estimated loss of earnings and £15,000 for other general damages.

● A right-handed man, 37 years old, working as a machine-setter, lost the use of his left wrist. He recovered £24,815.

● A married woman, 42, who lost use of her right hand received £26,300.

● A married mother of 37, earning £26 a week, suffered brain damage during an operation which prevented her working,

doing housework or having sexual intercourse. She received £51,801, of which £5,372 were special damages, £16,429 were for estimated loss of earnings and £30,000 were for pain and suffering.

● A boy of 19 who was left almost totally quadraplegic recovered £134,115.

● A senior hospital registrar, a woman of 41, suffered brain damage from a cardiac arrest while she was under anaesthetic. She would need nursing care for the rest of her life. She received damages of £254,765:
– £8,000 for the costs
– £105,500 for future care
– £14,213 for loss of earnings up to the trial
– £84,000 for loss of future earnings
– £8,000 for loss of pension rights
– £20,000 for the pain, suffering and loss of faculties
– £3,596 for medical and out-of-pocket expenses
– £11,456 interest.

physical pleasures: he may no longer be able to play the piano, go mountaineering, referee a football match or follow other hobbies. If his life expectancy has been reduced by the injury, he is compensated for that loss of expectation of happiness – though, in practice, such damages do not exceed £1,250. But he does recover damages for loss of earnings for any 'lost years' if his life expectancy has been reduced – for example 15 years of working life if his life expectancy is now 50 instead of 70.

● *Loss of faculties* Damages are awarded for the actual loss or impairment of a limb or any of the senses: sight, hearing, touch, taste and smell.

● *Pain and suffering* The injured person is compensated for the discomfort he has endured and may have to live with in the future. Unlike all other awards for damages, this category takes into account the victim's awareness of his condition. If, for example, he had been reduced to the state of a 'human vegetable', damages for pain and suffering would be small, but other damages would reflect the seriousness of his losses and needs.

Deductions from damages

When assessing an award for personal injuries, the courts deduct from the proposed amount one-half of the value of any INDUSTRIAL INJURY BENEFIT, DISABLEMENT BENEFIT or SICKNESS BENEFIT that the claimant is likely to receive in the first 5 years after the accident. They also reduce the amount by whatever he is likely to receive in UNEMPLOYMENT BENEFIT, but do not take into account any RETIREMENT PENSION that he will receive. The award is also not affected by any benefits that the claimant will receive from an insurance policy for which he himself pays all or part of the premium. *See:* PERSONAL ACCIDENT INSURANCE

If the injured person is shown to have been partly responsible for the accident – for example, if he was jay-walking on a busy road when hit by a car – his damages are reduced by the extent to which he was to blame. *See:* CONTRIBUTORY NEGLIGENCE

When damages are taxed

If an injured person invests part or all of his award – by opening a bank deposit account, or buying shares, for example –

> ### HUSBAND WHO THREATENED DIVORCE WITNESSES

Someone who uses threats or persuasion to deter witnesses from giving evidence in court is guilty of perverting the course of justice.

Mr and Mrs Kellett were seeking a divorce. Neighbours made statements to Mrs Margaret Kellett's solicitors to which Mr Alan Kellett objected. He wrote to the neighbours threatening to sue for slander if they did not withdraw their statements. Mr Kellett was charged with perverting the course of justice.

VERDICT

The crown court ruled that although it was not unlawful in itself to threaten to sue for slander, Mr Kellett's intention was to deter the neighbours from giving evidence. He was found guilty.

WHEN TWO NEWSPAPERMEN WENT TO PRISON

Although the reporting of court cases is allowed, it is an offence to publish anything that might interfere with or prejudice a trial.

Crime reporter Charles Windust was at the trial of a couple accused of attempting to murder a child. His reports of the case were published by Charles Tibbits, the editor, in *The Weekly Dispatch*, a newspaper that circulated in Bristol.

The couple in the case were both gaoled in March 1901, and later in the year Tibbits and Windust were accused at Bristol Assizes of attempting to obstruct and pervert the course of justice and con-spiracy to pervert the course of justice. Tibbits and Windust said that there had been no intention to pervert justice and, in any case, the couple had been convicted, so no wrong had been done.

VERDICT

The judge, Lord Alvestone, held that publication of the articles went beyond a fair and bona fide report of the trial and contained statements that were highly detrimental to the prisoners. The articles had established an atmosphere of prejudice at the trial. He found conspiracy proved, too. Both men were gaoled for 6 weeks.

---

he may have to pay tax on the interest. If his interest, when added to his other income, reaches a total that is over the tax-free personal allowance, the excess will be taxed.

PERVERTING THE COURSE OF JUSTICE

The offence of interfering with the processes of the law

Anyone who tries to interfere with the administration of the law risks prosecution for the offence of perverting the course of justice. Most prosecutions under this head arise from attempts to manufacture evidence or to persuade witnesses to alter their evidence.

For example, if a motorist and his passenger concoct a story that leads to the wrong person being suspected of an offence following an accident, both are guilty of perverting the course of justice. So is someone who uses threats or persuasion to deter a witness from giving evidence. In these circumstances the witness may seek police protection.

Many acts that are in contempt of court may also lead to prosecution for perverting the course of justice. A newspaper which prints a story that prejudices a fair trial could face legal proceedings on both counts.

Penalties Perverting the course of justice is a common law offence and therefore a maximum penalty is not laid down.

PEST CONTROL

What to do if you find your house or garden overrun by pests

If your home is plagued by pests, you can seek advice from the Environmental Health Department of the local council.

Generally, the council will tell you how to get rid of creatures such as ants, cockroaches, silver fish or beetles. If rats or mice are the problem, the council

GETTING RID OF UNWANTED RODENTS

Most local councils have experienced rat-catchers or 'rodent operatives' who can quickly rid a home or garden of unwanted pests.

will send an experienced rat catcher to deal with them, but you may in some areas be charged for that service.

If your property becomes infested with bugs or lice the council may have to fumigate it with hydrogen cyanide. This is a dangerous process, and the house will have to be evacuated for 2 or 3 days.

Pests in the garden

A local council is not usually concerned with garden pests other than rats or mice, but it may help you to clear out a wasps' nest.

If bees swarm in your garden try to find a bee-keeper who would be willing to help.

If you find serious pests or diseases, such as colorado beetle or red core disease of strawberry plants, report them immediately to the local office of the Ministry of Agriculture and Fisheries. The address will be listed in the telephone directory or can be obtained from your local council office or police station.

When birds or insects cause nuisance

A local authority has power to take steps to stop any nuisance or annoyance caused by doves, starlings, sparrows or pigeons in a built-up area. It may, for example, put poisonous bait on window ledges in public places.

Neither traps nor poisons that are likely to cause a lingering death are permitted, and precautions must be taken by the users not to harm domestic animals or other wild birds.

If your house is infested with flies or other insects coming from an identifiable source it may be possible for you to sue the owner. *See:* NUISANCE

PETROL STORAGE

Restrictions to avoid hazard

A householder may lawfully keep petrol in the tank of his car or other motor vehicle and he may keep 4 gallons in metal drums of not more than 2 gallons capacity.

For special purposes – such as running lawn mowers or domestic engines – a householder can store up to 60 gallons of petrol without a licence. Any petrol he does keep must be:

● In the open air at least 20 ft from a building, or in a ventilated store well away from any houses.

● In sealed metal cans each holding normally no more than 2 gallons and clearly marked 'Petroleum spirit – Highly Inflammable'.

As near as reasonably practicable, there must be kept fire extinguishers of an appropriate type.

The district council must be informed, and the storage space must be specially constructed if the cans in which the spirit is kept are to exceed 2 gallons in capacity.

A garage must apply to the local council – usually the district surveyor's office – for a licence to store petrol. Very many regulations govern the granting of such a licence.

The maximum fine for breaking any of these storage rules is £20 a day for as long as the offence continues.

PHOTOCOPYING

When you may have to pay a fee

Students, and people who are engaged in private, non-commercial study, are generally allowed to photocopy pages of books and documents – provided that they do not later publish them. *See:* COPYRIGHT

It is never permissible, however, to make any kind of commercial use of such photocopies.

PHYSICAL EDUCATION

When school PE lessons are compulsory

All boys and girls of normal school age must by law attend every class on their timetables unless there is a good excuse. This means that regular physical education and games lessons during school hours are just as compulsory as mathematics or English.

Schools will often accept a parent's note as a temporary excuse for a child's not doing PE or games, but pupils with recurring medical problems must produce a doctor's certificate.

Teachers cannot legally enforce attendance and participation in games or PE outside school hours.

Ensuring adequate facilities

Local education authorities must provide adequate facilities for physical, social and recreational training for everyone receiving primary, secondary or further education in their area. This applies to state or private schools but the facility does not necessarily have to be within the school boundary.

The amount of time allocated to PE is left to individual schools.

When a pupil is injured

Most local authorities have regulations to ensure that qualified staff supervise any potentially dangerous sport. For if a pupil is injured the school can face claims for negligence.

The rules of the sport, approved by its organising body, must be strictly followed. Dangerous play must be penalised at once and the person in charge must take reasonable care and act quickly in an emergency.

If sports facilities are some distance from school premises, the education authority must provide transport and is responsible for the safety of the children while travelling.

The sports arrangements in an INDEPENDENT SCHOOL are laid down usually in the school prospectus and are part of the contract between parent and school. Like state schools, independent schools are liable to negligence claims.

Dressing for games

Head teachers can insist that suitable kit is worn for PE and games. The school could be sued for negligence if, for example, a child was injured because he had been allowed to wear socks instead of plimsolls.

Parents suffering hardship in providing appropriate clothing should put their case to the school or school governors. In such cases, financial help or loan kit may be available. *See:* SCHOOL UNIFORM

PICKETING

When peaceful protest is within the law

When there is a dispute between an employer and his workers or a strike, the workers who are protesting sometimes try to persuade other colleagues to support them or not to work.

ORGANISING A PICKET LINE

Anyone involved in a trade dispute who wants to organise a picket line outside the employer's factory, must ensure that he is acting within the law. To do so, he should:
● Seek advice from his union head office and from a solicitor.
● See the local police and decide the number of pickets they will allow outside the premises and where they should stand so as not to obstruct the highway.
● Ensure that all official pickets wear badges and know exactly how they must behave within the law, and turn away anyone who tries to join the picket who is not an official picket.
● Ensure that the wording on any placards or banners is lawful and not likely to cause a breach of the peace because it is insulting or likely to incite racial hatred.
● Obey any police instruction that is reasonable – for example, if a person is asked to move.
● Ensure that the protest remains peaceful.
● Ensure that workers from other places of work do not join the picket lines.

THE PICKET WHO BROKE A POLICE CORDON

The police can prevent picketing if public order is threatened.

When electricians went on strike at the St Thomas' Hospital building site at Lambeth Palace Road, London, in 1973, non-union labour was employed to do their work.

On March 28, a crowd of 30 to 40 demonstrators, including four official pickets wearing armbands, met outside the site. They intended to approach the coach carrying the replacement workers and try to dissuade them from working during the strike and the driver from carrying them to work.

Fearing that a breach of the peace might be caused, a police superintendent ordered his men to cordon off the path of the coach. He refused to allow even the official pickets to pass through the cordon. When the coach left the site, Peter Roger Kavanagh, a former TGWU official, tried to push through to speak to the driver. When blocked by the police, he punched Constable Hiscock.

Kavanagh was arrested and charged with assault and obstructing the police in the execution of their duty. At the hearing before Lambeth magistrates, Kavanagh claimed in his defence that the police had acted unlawfully in preventing the official pickets – who had a right to peacefully persuade – from approaching the coach. The magistrates found that the police were justified in preventing disorder and Kavanagh was found guilty, fined £10 for assault, £10 for obstruction and made to pay £10 costs. He appealed to the High Court.

DECISION

The High Court upheld the conviction. It ruled that picketing may not impinge on the duty of the police to prevent a breach of the peace.

To do so, they gather outside the factory gates or premises involved and try to persuade others not to enter the premises – known as picketing.

However, there is no general right in law for a person to picket. Alternatively, there are few laws that expressly forbid picketing, but there are many ways in which picketing becomes unlawful.

When a picket breaks the law

If there is a trade dispute between workers and employers, a picket who stands near the premises involved and tries to persuade others not to enter is acting within the law, provided that he outlines his views peacefully.

However, if those entering do not want to listen to him, the picket is acting unlawfully if he continues to argue with a worker and does not allow him to go on his way.

Intimidation   It is a criminal offence for a picket to intimidate or use violence against any person or his family or persistently follow them, hide their work clothes and tools or picket their homes with intent to prevent that person from doing something which he has a legal right to do – for example, going to work.

Anyone convicted of such an offence can be fined up to £20 and be imprisoned for 3 months.

Pickets who use or threaten violence to enter a property are committing an act of criminal TRESPASS and can be prosecuted and gaoled for up to 2 years.
Obstruction   If a picket obstructs a vehicle he may be charged with obstructing the highway. For example, a picket may wave a lorry to a halt at the factory gates so that he can put his points of view to the driver. But it is up to the driver whether he wants to stop to listen to the picket. If the driver decides not to stop, the picket is acting unlawfully if he blocks the driver's way.

A driver must exercise due care when approaching or driving past a picket line, and is liable for NEGLIGENCE if he carelessly knocks down and injures a picket. Similarly, if there are so many pickets outside premises and pedestrians are prevented from walking along the pavement, those pickets are guilty of obstructing the highway. Anyone charged may be fined £50.

If the property is used as a residence and the pickets refuse to leave when asked to do so by the occupier or if they obstruct a bailiff who is serving an eviction order on them, they are guilty of criminal trespass. The penalty for such offences is up to 6 months' imprisonment and a fine of £1,000.

If a person trespasses on a foreign embassy during a political protest, he is a criminal trespasser and may be imprisoned for up to a year. *See:* SIT-IN

If the police decide that a BREACH OF THE PEACE will ensue if picketing continues, they are entitled to order the picketing to stop. A person who refuses to obey the order may be charged with obstructing the police and may be fined up to £200 and 1 month's gaol.

In certain other cases a picket may be arrested for offences concerning PUBLIC ORDER – for example, using ABUSIVE WORDS OR BEHAVIOUR or carrying an OFFENSIVE WEAPON.

Breach of the peace offences carry a maximum penalty of 6 months' imprisonment and a £1,000 fine.

Place of work

An employee can picket only at the entrance to the factory, site or offices at which he works. A mobile worker can picket at the office where he receives his instructions, or is paid, or at the depot from which his vehicle operates. A trade union official can accompany those of his members whom he represents in picketing at their place of work.

A picket is never entitled to stop anyone, even a member of his own union, from crossing a picket line.

Agreement on numbers

The police do not always prosecute for every offence they see when picketing is taking place. Sometimes, they make an informal agreement with pickets that a certain number, usually no more than 6, will be allowed to picket at a particular premises. In that case, the police would agree not to treat that picket as being likely to lead to a breach of the peace, provided the arrangement is honoured.

Furthering a trade dispute

When picketing causes loss to a company and that firm claims damages or an INJUNCTION, a picket usually has a defence that he was acting in furtherance of a trade dispute – for example, taking action that gives practical support.

However, an action that does not give practical support to a dispute – for example, one taken out of spite or to boost the morale of protesters or against a company not directly involved in the dispute – may not be considered to be in furtherance of a trade dispute.

Even if a picket is acting in further-

ance of a dispute, he is liable for damages if he behaves violently or causes an obstruction and someone suffers loss as a result.

Anyone who suffers loss may sue a picket, but the picket's TRADE UNION itself is not liable.

Political dispute If a person organises a picket for political reasons and not as a result of a trade dispute – for example, if he disagrees with his company selling goods to a particular country – he is even more vulnerable to breaking the law.

For example, his employer would be entitled to obtain an injunction ordering the picketing to cease on the ground that it was a NUISANCE. If a picket refused to obey the injunction he would be acting in CONTEMPT OF COURT. The company could also ask for damages for loss of profits from the pickets, but their trade union would not be liable.

Secondary picketing

Employees may contemplate picketing at their own place of work in support of a dispute between another employer and his employees; for example, they may have gone on strike in support of that other dispute, and intend to mount a picket line in support of their strike. Such action is known as secondary picketing.

If such pickets interfere only with contracts of employment, they are legally protected. But if they also interfere with commercial contracts, their activities will be immune from civil proceedings only if:

● Their employer is a supplier to, or customer of, the employer in dispute under a contract to provide goods or services.

● The principal purpose of the picketing is directly to prevent or disrupt the supply of goods or services during the dispute between their employer and the employer in dispute.

● The picketing is likely to achieve that purpose.

There is no immunity for interfering with commercial contracts by indiscriminate picketing at customers and suppliers.

In 1980 the Government issued a code of practice which includes practical guidance on picketing.

Failure to observe the code does not of itself render anyone liable to court

proceedings, but a court can take account of the code whenever it appears relevant to any case.

PLACE OF SAFETY ORDER

Immediate protection for a child who is at risk

When a child is thought to be at risk from his parents, other persons or his own shortcomings, the police may make a place of safety order, sending the child to a place of protection, such as a children's home, hospital, foster home, police station or staying with relatives. Magistrates may also make an order for local authorities to take similar action.

Under the Children and Young Persons Act 1969, anyone under 17 can be removed to a place of safety if there is reasonable cause to believe that:

● His health or proper development is being or is likely to be avoidably impaired or neglected.

● He is being or is likely to be ill-treated or exposed to moral danger.

● He is beyond the control of his parent or guardian.

Police powers

The police can issue a place of safety order to remove a child and keep him in a place of safety for up to 8 days without applying to the magistrates. They need only the approval of an officer of the rank of inspector or above.

If the NSPCC or the local authority decide to take action, they must apply to a magistrate, who will ask an official to swear or affirm that the information given about the child is true. The magistrate may sign an order for a period of up to 28 days.

Parental opposition

Only then can a parent take action to oppose an order. He or she should engage a solicitor to ask for a hearing with a judge in private. If the child is not brought before a court as being in need of care and protection by the time the order expires, he must be released from the place of safety.

The child's parents must be informed of his whereabouts and they can visit him while he is in the place of safety. They cannot remove him even for a short period. *See:* CHILDREN IN CARE

PLANNING BLIGHT

When a local planning decision affects the value of your property

There are three specific circumstances in which compensation can be obtained if a planning decision by a public authority lowers the market value of your property:

● If the house you own and occupy is about to be threatened by a COM-PULSORY PURCHASE order for a road construction scheme that has been delayed you can compel the council to buy it for the full market price – that is, what it would be worth if no development was scheduled. The market price is determined by valuers: one engaged by the person owning the house, one engaged by the local authority. If they fail to agree, the case can be taken to the Lands Tribunal.

● If you have been refused PLANNING PERMISSION for your property which, in its present state, has little value, you can compel the district council to buy it. For example, if you had a small allotment garden on which you were refused permission to build a cottage, you could make the council buy the plot if it became otherwise useless. Although you would be paid only a small amount, you would be relieved of the worry and expense of a useless property.

The value of the plot would be decided by the district council and they would set this according to what the land could be used for. In this case the amount might be only £50.

● If the value of your property has been reduced by noise or fumes from new public works you cannot compel the council to buy it but you can claim compensation.

To be eligible for compensation you must show that the value of the property has been reduced by at least £50, and the works about which you are complaining must have been begun since 1971.

How to get compensation

If you believe the value of your property has been blighted, contact the planning department of your local authority and ask for a 'blight notice'. Complete this form and return it to the planning department, even if another public body is responsible for the reduced value of your property. For example, the Ministry of Defence would be responsible for blight due to a new military airfield, but your form would still be addressed to the planning department.

If you are claiming compensation for reduced value – rather than forcing the council to buy your property – it is advisable to engage a surveyor to assess the change in value and to submit his report with your claim. All reasonable surveyor's charges will be borne by the local authority.

If the local authority accepts your claim and valuation, it will compensate you or buy the property. If it disagrees with your valuation, it will send the district valuer, a government official, to assess the property and prepare an estimate.

If the authority contests your claim, it must serve you with a counter-notice within 2 months. The case then goes before the Lands Tribunal, before which both sides can present their arguments. The tribunal's decision is final. You can challenge it in the courts only if it infringes a point of law.

PLANNING OBJECTION

What you can do to stop a new development

The procedure for objecting to a planning application varies according to whether it is a minor scheme affecting few people, or a major project such as a motorway or the construction of a chemical works.

Opposing a minor scheme

The individual has few legal rights when objecting to minor planning applications – for example, if a neighbour wants to build an extension, or proposals for a new factory threaten to spoil the view. There is no appeal once a planning application has been granted, so objections have to be made before that stage is reached.

Planning authorities are not obliged to inform those affected of any proposed development. If you suspect that planning permission is being sought for a particular scheme you should contact the planning officer at the local district council offices for information. He is not obliged to disclose whether an ap-plication has been received, but usually he will co-operate.

You have a legal right to see the planning register and study the plan accompanying the application. If you were for some reason refused permission to see it, you could apply to the High Court for an order.

You should then write to the district council, stating your objection formally. Your letter will be considered when the planning committee or sub-committee discusses the application. If the matter is raised in sub-committee you have no right to attend. If it is dealt with by the full committee, you normally attend, but not speak.

In certain cases, a planning application may threaten your legal rights – for example, if a neighbour's extension plan affects your RIGHT TO LIGHT.

You should also look at the deeds of your house. There may be a restricting covenant that covers other houses.

Opposing a major project

If the proposed development is a major scheme of national or regional importance, write to the Secretary of State for the Environment asking for a public inquiry. Try to persuade other people to write similar letters.

If a public inquiry is ordered anyone who wishes to speak will be allowed to do so, though if a number of protesters wish to make the same point it is better to appoint one as spokesman at the inquiry, or to instruct a solicitor if enough money is available. Objectors can also employ experts to give evidence. Objectors, however, are not entitled to LEGAL AID.

In some cases objectors may find themselves on the same side as the planning authority – for example, when a planning application has been refused and the developer appeals to the Secretary of State for a public inquiry. Objectors should then contact the planning authority to discuss the best means of making a joint protest.

PLANNING PERMISSION

How a council can control the development of your property

Local authority planning permission is needed for most building or engineering work that changes the outside appearance of a property, and for any 'material change' in its use.

For example, if you turn your house into a business office, or start running a guest house, you must have the consent of your district council.

Minor building alterations or additions, such as the construction of a garage, may not require planning permission. But you should always check with your council, because BUILDING REGULATIONS consent may be required in any case.

Use of land as a CARAVAN site may need not only planning permission, but also a council site licence.

If a development or change of use requires planning permission and you go ahead without it, you can be ordered to stop.

If you ignore the order you can be fined up to £400 – and any building work may have to be pulled down at your expense.

Obtaining permission from your local council

If you intend to alter a building, or change the use of a building or land, explain what you want to do to an officer in your local council planning department.

If your scheme amounts to 'development' under planning law, permission will usually be needed. You will be given an application form, and advice if necessary on how to complete it. Under an Act of Parliament passed in 1980 the local authority may be entitled to charge a fee on the making of an application.

The council may take up to 2 months to decide whether to grant permission. Its decision should be guided by a general development plan for the district, which is prepared by your county coun-

cil and approved by the Department of the Environment.

You are entitled to see a copy of the development plan. It should be available at county council and district council offices.

What you can do if permission is refused

If the council turns down your application, you have 6 months in which to appeal to the Secretary of State for the Environment. You can obtain an appeal form from the Department at 2 Marsham Street, Westminster, London, SW1P 3EB; a further fee will probably be payable. The Secretary of State arranges for an inquiry hearing in your district, with an inspector from his department presiding.

You are given at least 42 days' notice of the hearing. You have the right to put your case – either personally or through a lawyer (at your own expense) – to call witnesses and to cross-examine anyone who gives evidence for the council.

PLANTS AND FLOWERS

How the law links property rights and conservation

A plant is legally a part of the land on which it grows. It belongs to whoever holds the land – although even he is not allowed to pick some species.

Under conservation laws, it is a crime to pick or uproot wild plants – except wild mushrooms, other fungi and algae – without the permission of the land-owner or tenant.

The maximum penalty is a £200 fine for each species involved, although an official prosecution is unlikely unless there is permanent damage to natural plant life.

Under property laws, however, a person who takes someone else's plants or flowers can be sued for TRESPASS, and prosecuted for THEFT.

When picking is completely banned

Some wild flowers, because their species are in danger of extinction, are fully protected by law. No one – not even the owner of the land – may pick,

FLOWERS BELONG TO THE
LAND-HOLDER

Wild plants and flowers are the property of the person who holds the land on which they are growing and cannot be picked without his permission.

uproot or destroy them intentionally without a Nature Conservancy Council licence.

Licences are issued only for research or educational purposes.

Maximum penalty: £500 fine for each species involved in an offence.

Unavoidable destruction of protected plants, as an incidental effect of properly conducted farming or forestry, is not an offence.

Nature reserves In a designated nature reserve, no plant may be picked or uprooted – even if it is not protected in other places. An offender risks the same penalty as if the plant were on the protected list.

National nature reserves are designated by the Nature Conservancy

ADVERTISING ON YOUR LAND

Hoardings, permanent signs and most other advertising displays on private land require local authority consent. Permission is not required, however, for temporary election notices, those advertising local social events and 'for sale' signs.

WHEN PICKING A FLOWER IS THEFT

If plants or flowers are cultivated by the owner or tenant of the land on which they grow, someone who picks them or digs them up without permission can be prosecuted for theft.

If they grow wild, it is not a theft to take them unless they are sold afterwards, or used for some other commercial purpose.

In either case, however, the land holder may be able to sue for trespass and claim damages.

WILD FLOWERS THAT MUST NOT BE PICKED

Because they are in danger of being wiped out, 36 species of wild flower are protected by law:

Adder's-tongue spearwort	Late spider orchid
Alpine catchfly	Limestone woundwort
Alpine gentian	Lizard orchid
Alpine sow-thistle	Military orchid
Alpine woodsia	Monkey orchid
Blue heath	Oblong woodsia
Cheddar pink	Perennial knawel
Diapensia	Red helleborine
Dickie's bladder fern	Rock cinquefoil
	Sea lavender
Downy woundwort	Snowdon lily
Drooping saxifrage	Spiked speedwell
	Spring gentian
Early spider orchid	Starfruit
Fen orchid	Teesdale sandwort
Field eryngo	Tufted saxifrage
Ghost orchid	Water germander
Killarney fern	Wild cotoneaster
Lady's-slipper	Wild gladiolus

Council. A local authority can also set aside land as a nature reserve.

If signs warning of a prohibition on picking plants are prominently displayed, an offender is unlikely to succeed in a plea that he was unaware of the ban.

Breeding a new variety

A grower who develops a new type of plant or flower – for example, a new variety of rose – may be able to claim exclusive rights to sell it.

Claims are tested and registered by the plant variety rights office of the Ministry of Agriculture at White House Lane, Huntingdon Road, Cambridge CB3 0LS. If a plant breeder is granted exclusive rights, anyone else who sells that variety can be sued, and ordered to pay his profits to the breeder.

PLAYGROUND

How safety standards can be checked

The safety of a playground is the responsibility of the local council or education authority that controls it.

Under the Health and Safety at Work Act, which also covers recreation areas, local authorities are required to take reasonable measures to make and keep playgrounds safe.

A local authority can be prosecuted by the government factory inspectorate if it fails in that duty, and does not comply with an inspector's directions to improve safety.

Even without a prosecution, a factory inspector can issue a prohibition notice to whoever controls a playground. That could ban the use of certain equipment, or even close the playground.

An inspector also has the power to seize playground equipment if he thinks there is an immediate danger of injury.

When you see a danger

If you doubt the safety of a public playground, notify the parks department of your local authority. If it is a school playground, notify the headmaster.

If no action is taken and you are convinced that children are in danger, contact the local office of HM Factory Inspectorate, which is listed under F in most local telephone directories.

An inspector will visit the playground

THE PLAYGROUND WITH A DANGEROUS CHUTE

If a child is injured in a playground the local authority can be sued for damages. But it must be proved that the authority neglected its duty to make the playground safe.

A children's recreation ground managed by Stone Parish Council contained a 12 ft chute for children to slide down. In 1934 a small boy had fallen off the platform at the top of the chute and been seriously injured.

The council took note of the accident and built railings around the platform and its groundsmen tried to prevent unaccompanied small children from using it – though there was no notice to warn of any danger.

In May 1950 a 3½-year-old boy went to the playground with another child of 6, with his mother's consent. He climbed to the platform, fell through a gap in the railings and was permanently blinded. His father, Mr Bates, sued the council on the child's behalf.

DECISION

The High Court jury found that the council had been guilty of negligence and awarded damages of £17,500 to the child and £27 to the father for his expenses.

The council appealed against the amount of damages awarded, arguing that since the child had not been in the care and control of a competent person he had been a trespasser – and therefore partly to blame for the accident.

DECISION

The Court of Appeal ruled that since the council admitted all children to the playground, however young and untended they might be, the child could not be a trespasser.

Additionally, the council were aware – from the 1934 accident – of the danger of the chute. They were therefore liable to damages.

However, the court found the damages to be excessive and reduced them to £9,000.

WHEN NOISE FROM A PLAYGROUND DISTURBED A HOTEL

Residents who are disturbed by noise and commotion from a playground can sue the local authority for permitting a nuisance.

When Dover Council built a housing estate behind the privately owned Whitfield Hotel in 1975, it provided a children's playground next to the hotel garden. About 60 children under the age of 12 lived on the estate, and the hotel owner, William Dunton, soon complained to the council of 'a fearful row' from the playground and of children trespassing in his garden. His wife was so bothered by the noise of the playground users that she had to leave the hotel.

Mr Dunton asked the council to close the playground. When it refused, he sued it for NUISANCE and asked for an INJUNCTION to close the site.

DECISION

The High Court ruled that the playground, which was open at all hours and without an age-limit for its users, constituted a nuisance.

It granted an injunction, allowing the playground to open only between 10 a.m. and 6.30 p.m. and to be used only by children under 12.

Mr Dunton was also awarded damages of £200.

and advise the responsible authority of any changes or improvements that are needed, and whether it should close the area in the meantime.

It is unlikely that any more formal action would be necessary. But if the authority were to disregard the inspector's advice, he could issue an improvement notice compelling it to comply, or a prohibition notice forbidding the use of the playground or some of its equipment.

When you can sue

If a child is injured in a playground it may be possible to recover PERSONAL INJURY compensation from the responsible authority – but only if NEGLIGENCE is proved.

The claim would have to establish that the authority failed in its duty to take reasonable care – for example, by neglecting normal inspection and maintenance, or not providing a reasonable degree of supervision.

Noise If noise or other disturbance from a playground has a damaging effect on the lives of residents near by, they may be able to obtain a court INJUNCTION restricting activities in the area – for example, by limiting the hours it is open, or the age of the children who can use it.

PLAYGROUP

Organised play for pre-school children

Parents who cannot or do not want to send their children to a state-run NURSERY SCHOOL may find a place for them at a local playgroup, where they can benefit from contact with other children and learn through play. (The activities do not usually include learning to read or write.)

Playgroups are usually run on a voluntary basis by parents who either take turns to act as playgroup leader, or pay someone to do so. In some cases, playgroups are run by social services departments, voluntary organisations or by individuals for private profit.

Almost all playgroups are part-time, meeting only in the morning, or holding two or three sessions a week. Children can attend as many sessions as their parents wish: there is no compulsory

---

HOW TO FOUND A PLAYGROUP

If you and other parents in your neighbourhood want to start a playgroup, contact the Pre-School Playgroups Association. It will advise you how to get organised and put you in touch with its local representative who will give practical help. You will need:
● A place to meet – which can be anything from someone's front room to a church hall, depending on the size of the group.
● Playleaders – either volunteers or paid.
● Some toys – which can be bought, donated, or borrowed from the local authority.
● Permission from the social services department – which must approve the group's premises and the ratio of adults to children, but does not monitor the group's activities.

Playgroups can cater for any number of infants, though most have between 20 and 30. There must be at least one adult to every 10 children, but he or she does not usually need to be a trained person – although some local authorities insist on playleaders being 'suitably qualified'. The Pre-School Playgroups Association arranges some training courses for parents to help them lead a group.

The playleaders are considered to be in 'loco parentis', entirely responsible for the health and safety of the children at the playgroup.

You and the other group founders must decide among yourselves how much time each parent should devote to the group, whether to hire a trained playleader and what fees to charge.

---

attendance. Playgroups usually break up for school holidays.

How to find a playgroup for your child

If you want to send your child to a playgroup ask the social services department at your local authority if there is one in your area – all such groups must be registered with the department. There may be more than one, in which case ask if they provide different facilities and activities.

As most playgroups are privately organised, you are not entitled to insist that your child be admitted. Usually children are turned away only if the group is full, or if the child is unhappy there, or if the parents refuse to play a role in the group.

If you cannot find a place for your child in a local playgroup, or if no playgroup exists in your area, you can – together with other parents – organise a new one.

POACHING

Hunting game without permission on someone else's land

Anyone who owns land also owns the GAME on it. If you enter someone's land in search of game, you are committing a criminal offence for which you can be prosecuted.

It is not necessary to prove that you shot at game or killed and took any away. Your conduct and the fact that you were equipped to hunt game – for example, by carrying a gun – can be accepted as evidence of your intent.

Even if you shoot a bird over your own land and it falls on your neighbour's land, you are poaching if you trespass on his property to retrieve it.

The occupier of the land, or anyone to whom he has given the right to take game there – or an employee of either of them – can arrest any trespasser hunting game if he refuses to give his name and address.

A policeman can arrest people on reasonable suspicion of poaching and can enter land to make an arrest. He can also stop and search anyone he suspects has been poaching.

Poaching at night

It is a more serious offence to enter land without the owner's permission carrying a gun or net to take or kill game between sunset and sunrise.

It is also poaching to kill any game, or rabbits, on any land, public roads and paths after dark.

When fishing is illegal

Fish are not protected by the same laws as game. Anyone who takes or kills fish in water that is private property, or in which there are private fishing rights, however, is committing a theft. It is no defence to maintain that you did not know the water was private property.

When traps are illegal

A poacher may also be committing other offences if he uses unauthorised traps or snares to capture game, or indeed other birds and animals.

How poaching is punished

Poaching during the day is punishable by a fine of up to £20. Poaching at night, however, is punishable by up to 3 months' imprisonment or a £100 fine. If a night poacher assaults a landowner or his representative, he can be imprisoned for up to 7 years.

Any equipment used in poaching offences, such as guns or snares, is confiscated by the court.

For illegal angling during the day, the maximum penalty is a £20 fine. For other offences the maximum penalty is a £50 fine. The court can also order the confiscation of any fishing tackle used to take fish illegally.

POLICE

The guardians of law and order

The police have a duty to enforce public order and to prevent and detect crime. To do so, they are aided by specific powers granted by law – for example, to arrest a person who is suspected of committing a crime.

But they have no general power to interfere in a citizen's life, and for much

MOTORIST WHO REFUSED TO OBEY A POLICEMAN

A motorist who wilfully obstructs the police in the execution of their duty – say, by refusing to obey a legitimate order – can be prosecuted.

Mr Peter Johnson, a company director, was driving down a one-way street in Birmingham when he found it blocked by an ambulance that had been called to an incident at a public house.

Police asked Mr Johnson to reverse out of the street – a distance of 10–15 yds. Instead he got out of his car and said: 'I'll wait here, thank you.' He was charged with obstructing the police.

In court, Mr Johnson claimed that the police had no authority to instruct him to proceed in the wrong direction down a one-way street because it was both unlawful and dangerous. He was convicted, but appealed.

DECISION

The court ruled that the police were entitled to give whatever instructions were necessary in an emergency.

of the time they rely on the co-operation of members of the public to be as helpful as possible by providing information and answering questions.

Questioning and searching

The police are entitled to stop and question anyone they suspect of having committed a crime or who might be able to provide information about a crime that has been committed. In most cases, there is no obligation to answer or even to give your name and address.

However, if the police suspect a person of committing certain crimes – for example, possessing drugs or carrying an OFFENSIVE WEAPON – they are entitled to demand his name and address. If a person refuses to give his name and address in such instances the police may ARREST him without a warrant.

When dealing with motoring cases the police have further powers to demand names and addresses and to order a motorist to stop or move his vehicle.

In certain circumstances, the police are entitled to stop and SEARCH a person in the street – for example, if they suspect that he is carrying drugs or stolen goods.

A person's home may also be entered in certain circumstances. They are:
● If the police have obtained a search warrant.
● To arrest a person for whom they have an arrest warrant.
● If the police suspect that a person on the premises has committed an arrestable offence.
● To prevent a BREACH OF THE PEACE or injury to someone.

When the police have one of those reasons for entering a property, they are entitled to use reasonable force to do so

THE LAW'S WIDE POWERS OVER THE MOTORIST

Motoring laws have widely extended the powers of the police to stop people and demand information or the production of documents.

The police can demand the name and address of anyone driving a motor vehicle or cycling on a public ROAD, even if no offence is suspected. They can also demand to see a motorist's driving licence, insurance certificate and, where applicable, MOT certificate.

Although the police are entitled to stop a motorist to obtain information, they are not entitled to delay him for longer than he reasonably consents to be delayed unless they make an arrest or have some other authority to hold him up, such as a search warrant.

In an emergency it may be reasonable to refuse to answer a policeman's questions on the spot. A motorist taking his pregnant wife to hospital, for example, can refuse to give his name and address immediately provided he agrees to do so later. But if the motorist has committed an offence – speeding or jumping a red light, say – the policeman can insist on taking his name and address.

Refusing to give information or to produce driving documents is an offence punishable by a fine of up to £50. Someone suspected of dangerous, careless, inconsiderate or reckless driving who refuses to give his name and address can be fined up to £100. It is also an offence to ignore traffic directions given by a policeman in uniform.

The maximum penalty is a £100 fine and a licence endorsement.

When the police can arrest you

Police can arrest any motorist who is suspected of any of these offences:
● Causing death by reckless driving.
● Being unfit to drive through drink or drugs.
● Taking a vehicle without consent or riding in a vehicle knowing it to be stolen.
● Refusing to take a breath-test.
● Failing a breath-test.
● Refusing to give his name and address or failing to produce his driving licence when suspected of reckless or careless driving.
● Driving while disqualified.
● Wilfully obstructing the highway.

POLICE

HOW THE POLICE SERVICE IS ORGANISED

There are about 108,000 policemen and women in England and Wales who are either uniformed officers or plain-clothes police. The uniformed branch maintains a public presence by patrolling streets on foot or in police vehicles, directing traffic or by controlling crowds or demonstrations – for example, attending football matches. The plain-clothes officers are involved in detecting or preventing crime.

There are four types of police force in England and Wales:
● County police force – run by a police authority comprising two-thirds county councillors and one-third magistrates. The authority appoints a chief constable to lead the force, but he is approved by the Home Secretary. There are 31 such forces.
● Combined police force – run by a police authority made up from several county councils. The authority consists of two-thirds councillors and one-third magistrates drawn from the counties involved. The authority appoints a chief constable to lead the force, but he is approved by the Home Secretary. There are 10 such forces.

● Metropolitan Police – under the direct control of the Home Secretary and covering Greater London and parts of Surrey, Hertford and Essex. It is led by a Commissioner of Police, a deputy commissioner and 4 assistant commissioners who are appointed by the Crown after being recommended by the Home Secretary. It has more than 22,000 officers.
● City of London Police – totalling 812 police officers – run by the City's Court of the Common Council which appoints a commissioner, subject to the approval of the Home Secretary.

A chief constable appointed by a police authority must make an annual report to the authority on the state of its police force and make any other reports that his authority asks him to. However, he is also responsible to the Home Secretary who may request him to report on any matter concerning the policing in his area.

The Home Secretary may order an independent inquiry, headed by a judge, into any matter concerning the policing of any part of England and Wales.

handling stolen goods that is punishable by imprisonment.
● He believes there are explosives on the premises which may cause immediate damage or injury.
● He believes immediate action is necessary to look for evidence of terrorism.
● He believes an offence under the Official Secrets Act 1911 has been or is about to be committed.

When you are legally obliged to help the police

The public has no general duty to help the police, provided that a policeman does not specifically ask for assistance. If you see a policeman who is obviously in need of help but does not ask you for it, you may assist him, but you are not guilty of any offence if you do not do so.

However, if he does ask you for help, it is an offence not to do so. For example, if a policeman is being obstructed in making a lawful arrest and you refuse his request for help, you could be fined or imprisoned.

If you have a lawful excuse for not helping – because you were not fit to do so as a result of disability or illness – it would be a defence for not assisting a policeman. But it would not be a defence to claim that your help would have been useless.

if they are refused entry. For example, if there was no way of gaining entry, a policeman would be entitled to break a window to get into a property. If someone tried to stop a policeman from entering he could be charged with OBSTRUCTION.

If the police do not have a search warrant and are not entitled to enter without one, they may not enter your home without your consent. If you do agree to their being in your home, they must leave as soon as you ask them to do so, giving them reasonable time to leave.

When a warrant is issued

If the police have obtained a search warrant from a magistrate, the warrant must state the exact address and premises where a search is authorised. An occupier would be entitled to refuse the police entry to premises not specified – for example, if there is a separately let flat or outbuildings.

The warrant must also specify the law under which the search is authorised and it must give details of any articles it empowers the police to search for or take away. For example, a warrant issued under the Theft Act 1968 empowers the police to search for and take

away any articles they have reason to believe are stolen.

Some warrants can be used only once and then expire; others may be used several times – for example, a warrant issued under the Misuse of Drugs Act 1971 authorises as many searches as the police require to be made within a month of the date of issue. If the police use such a warrant in a public house, they are entitled to search everyone on the premises whether or not there are reasonable grounds for suspecting them of possessing drugs.

Before allowing the police to enter, ask to see the search warrant. If the police refuse to show a search warrant, a person is entitled to refuse them entry. If the warrant does not specify the exact address of the premises or the law under which the search is to be made, entry may also be refused.

Searching without a warrant

In certain cases, a senior police officer – who must be a superintendent or above – is entitled to authorise his officers to search premises. He may do so, for example, if:
● The premises are occupied by someone convicted within the last 5 years of an offence involving dishonesty or

HELPING THE POLICE

The police are entitled to stop and question anyone they suspect of having information about a crime, but there is no legal duty to answer.

563

If you agree to a policeman's request for help or volunteer to help him, and you are injured or your property is damaged, you may be entitled to compensation. *See:* CRIMINAL INJURIES COMPENSATION

There is no general, legal obligation on a person to provide the police with information – although there is always a strong moral obligation to do so.

If a person witnesses an offence and does not inform the police, he is not committing an offence, provided that he does not help the law-breaker to avoid arrest or prosecution. If he does, he may be imprisoned for up to 10 years.

In certain cases, a private citizen is entitled to arrest a person he sees committing a crime. However, he needs to be sure he is acting within the law when doing so. *See:* CITIZEN'S ARREST

COMPLAINING ABOUT THE POLICE

If you are dissatisfied with a police officer's behaviour towards you, complain in person to the duty officer at your local police station or write to the deputy chief constable of the force involved.

Any complaint made against the police must be recorded and investigated. Once you have made your complaint, the chief constable appoints a senior officer to investigate it – in the most serious cases, a senior officer may be appointed from another force.

Giving evidence

The complainant and any witness of the incident are interviewed, and they are asked to sign written statements. They are entitled to have their solicitors present.

The officer in charge reports the facts to the deputy chief constable who, if he has reason to believe that the law may have been broken by the police, must send the evidence collected during the investigation to the Director of Public Prosecutions. If the officer has not already been charged, his department decides whether the matter should be brought before a criminal court.

If it is brought to court, the complainant and witness may be asked to give evidence to the court.

At a disciplinary hearing

If the Director decides not to prosecute the police officer, or if the officer is tried and acquitted, or if the deputy chief constable decides no law has been breached, the deputy chief constable has to decide whether police discipline has been breached. If he decides that it has, he may hold a disciplinary hearing.

The hearing is conducted by the chief constable, and the police officer named in the complaint appears before it. If he admits the breach of discipline, the complainant is not entitled to attend the hearing. In that case, the chief constable decides whether the officer is to be cautioned, fined, reprimanded, have his pay or rank reduced or, in a serious case, be dismissed or be required to resign.

If the police officer denies the charges of a breach of discipline, the complainant is called to give evidence to the hearing. He is entitled to have his questions put to the officer involved, but neither is allowed to be represented by a solicitor.

A report of the case is sent to an independent body before the hearing – the Police Complaints Board, Waterloo Bridge House, Waterloo Road, London SE1 8UT. The Board consists of 18 members who study the reports and make recommendations to the chief constable on what action should be taken.

The board may decide that the hearing should be conducted by a tribunal, and two of its members will be appointed to sit with the chief constable for the hearing. Any punishment is decided by the chief constable of the offender's own force.

If there is to be no hearing

If the chief constable decides that no disciplinary hearing is necessary, he must send the notice of the complaint and his investigating officer's report to the Police Complaints Board, together with his own comments and his reasons for not making a disciplinary charge.

If the board disagrees with the chief constable, it recommends that a hearing is held. The board is ultimately entitled to order a chief constable to hold a hearing if he still refuses.

When police discipline has not been breached but, in the opinion of the chief constable, the complaint has been substantiated, he may send a written apology to the complainant. The complainant is not entitled to see a copy of the investigating officer's report.

If the chief constable decides the complaint has not been substantiated, the Police Complaints Board sends a brief letter to the complainant telling him so.

If you still wish to pursue a complaint after the Director of Public Prosecutions has decided not to prosecute a police officer, apply in a magistrates' court for a private summons. *See:* PRIVATE PROSECUTION

POLITICAL ASYLUM

How a persecuted person can seek refuge in Britain

Certain people who have no right to enter the United Kingdom are sometimes allowed to do so if oppression and persecution in their homeland threatens their lives or their liberty. *See also:* IMMIGRATION

The Home Office decides whether a particular person can stay. Its rules state that the persecution must be because of race, religion, nationality or membership of a political or social group.

It is not enough for a person to be trying to flee his country because he faces criminal charges, objects to doing military service, or simply cannot get a job because of his race. Such a person would be refused political asylum.

The person fleeing must have a real, well-founded fear of persecution, and be unwilling to return to his country.

A person already in Britain who faces DEPORTATION can also claim political asylum for the same reasons. But no one in a foreign country has any automatic right to enter Britain as a political refugee.

How to seek asylum

Many people seeking political asylum do so after they have arrived at a dock or airport in the United Kingdom. Their best course is to tell the immigration officer on duty as soon as they land or to go to a police station.

All applications for asylum are dealt with by the Home Office Immigration and Nationality office at Croydon. Anyone seeking refuge can apply direct, in writing, to this office.

The Home Office finally decides whether or not to grant asylum after getting advice from Britain's diplomatic representative in the applicant's country. It may also ask the advice of the United Nations High Commissioner for Refugees, an international organisation responsible for deciding who may be regarded as a REFUGEE.

A foreign person given permission to stay temporarily in Britain can seek

WHEN AN ALIEN MAY STAY
IN BRITAIN

Only the Home Office has the power to decide whether an alien should be granted political asylum – usually after much investigation through diplomatic channels in the country from which the applicant is fleeing.

confidential advice from the London office of the UNHCR about his chances of being granted asylum before he makes a formal application. The advice is free and is helpful to a person who may have to return to his country, where knowledge of his application for asylum could be damaging to him.

POLITICAL EDUCATION

Teaching schoolchildren to understand their political rights

There is no law about teaching politics in schools. Whether the subject is taught depends upon the discretion of the head teacher.

However, in 1978, HM Inspectorate of Schools recommended that the curriculum for 11–16 year olds, whether in state or private education, should include preparation for responsible participation in politics with discussion of the main political theories and institutions.

If biased views are put forward in a school, the governors and local education authority have the power to ask the school to modify the syllabus or reprimand the teacher.

If you are concerned about the way politics is being taught – or that it is not

being taught – in your child's school, take the matter up with the head teacher and the governors. The school should have a detailed syllabus and programme of work available and should be prepared to discuss it.

POLLUTION

How the law endeavours to maintain a clean environment

Local authorities throughout the United Kingdom are gradually imposing smoke-control zones, where it is an offence to use any fuel not approved in government regulations. Water authorities control the quality of effluents that are permitted to be discharged into estuaries, rivers and water courses. *See:* AIR POLLUTION

POLYGAMY

When a man or woman can have more than one spouse at the same time

A polygamous marriage is one that allows the man or woman to have more than one spouse at the same time – even if he or she does not do so. A monogamous marriage is one that allows only one spouse.

A polygamous marriage cannot take place in Britain. If a man or woman marries again while still married to the first partner, then the offence of BIGAMY has been committed. It makes no difference if the bigamist comes from a country where polygamy is allowed.

When polygamy is recognised

A polygamous marriage is recognised in Britain, however, if it took place in a country where polygamy is legal and if the partner had at the time of the marriage their DOMICILE in a country where the marriage is valid.

For example, if two Muslims domiciled in Saudi Arabia married polygamously in Morocco, the marriage would be recognised in Britain. But if the husband married again in this country, without divorcing his other wife, the second marriage would be bigamous. *See:* FOREIGN MARRIAGE

If a polygamous marriage is recognised in Britain, the husband has the

same duty to maintain all his wives and children as in a monogamous marriage. *See:* MAINTENANCE

Changing a polygamous marriage

A polygamous marriage can be converted into a monogamous one – provided there is only one wife and one husband:
● If the parties agree that the marriage should be monogamous.
● If they change their domicile from a country where polygamy is legal to one which recognises only monogamy – for example, moving from a Muslim country to England.

POOL BETTING

Odds are not fixed, and winnings depend on stakes

A pool bet is one that is not laid at fixed odds – in practice, usually by a number of people whose stakes are redistributed as winnings, after a percentage has been deducted by the organisers.

The best known examples are football pools, but some forms of BINGO and racing tote wagers are also pool bets.

Promoters must be registered by the local council

All pools promoters must be registered by the local authority where they have their principal place of business.

Registration can be refused if the applicant has a criminal record for fraud or dishonesty.

Charity pools promoters must also be registered with the local authority and in addition must have a special licence from the Gaming Board.

The Totalisator Board has special rights to operate pool betting at racecourses. *See:* GAMBLING

PORNOGRAPHY

Controlling the publication of obscene material

It is not an offence for anyone to have or to read pornographic material, but someone who has such material for gain can be prosecuted under the OBSCENE PUBLICATIONS Act.

POST-MORTEM

An examination to establish the cause of death

A post-mortem is a detailed medical examination of a body after death. It is most commonly ordered by a CORONER to establish the cause of death, but in certain circumstances it can be performed at the request of a doctor in pursuit of medical knowledge.

The examination usually involves dissection and tests on blood, tissue or internal organs. It can be carried out by any doctor but is usually performed by a pathologist.

When the coroner orders a post-mortem

Deaths are reported to a coroner for a number of reasons, even if there are no suspicious circumstances – for example,

if the dead person's own doctor is not available or if the cause of death is not immediately apparent. In most cases the cause of death is established with little further inquiry, and permission is given for the funeral to proceed.

However, if a medical examination is needed to establish the cause of death or if medical evidence is needed for an INQUEST, the coroner will order a post-mortem.

The post-mortem is usually carried out with a minimum of delay to avoid deterioration of the body, and the validity of the result.

Objecting to a post-mortem

It is very rare for a coroner's order for a post-mortem to be overruled. The only way in which distressed relatives might prevent it is by applying for a High Court order of certiorari – an order quashing the coroner's decision.

Such an order will be granted only if there is no good reason for the examination – for example, there are no suspicious circumstances and the coroner has no reasonable grounds for believing that death was from a cause unknown.

When a post-mortem is requested in hospital

A doctor can request a post-mortem in the interests of medical research rather than to establish the cause of death.

Such cases usually occur after a death in hospital when doctors want to investigate the nature and extent of a disease.

A post-mortem requested by a doctor rather than a coroner cannot be carried out without the approval of the next of kin.

POST OFFICE

Your rights to an efficient postal service

The Post Office is a state-owned corporation responsible for the postal services and for the National Girobank service.

Responsibility for the telephone and telecommunications services has been transferred from the Post Office to an independent state-owned corporation, British Telecommunications. *See:* TELEPHONES

In some services it has monopoly rights. It also acts as agent for government departments, dealing with such matters as car tax and the payment of welfare benefits.

Using the postal services

The postal services cover four main categories – letters, parcels, newspapers and a special service for articles for the blind.

It is an offence, with a maximum penalty of 12 months' imprisonment or a fine of £100, to send through the post:
● Anything likely to harm anyone handling it during the process of delivery.
● Anything that could damage other post.
● Anything indecent or obscene.

The Post Office can refuse to handle dangerous items – for example, sharp objects or inflammable film – which are not properly wrapped. Overseas post is also subject to customs regulations. *See:* OBSCENE PUBLICATIONS

Letters The Post Office has the exclusive right in Britain to collect, carry and deliver letters, except those sent by

---

' OBJECTING ON RELIGIOUS GROUNDS

Only the High Court can overrule a coroner's order for a post-mortem. Relatives who bring such a case have to prove that a post-mortem examination is unnecessary rather than simply distasteful to them.

In 1969 the relatives of Mr Rainer asked the High Court to overrule a

coroner's order for a post-mortem because it was contrary to the family's religious beliefs.

DECISION
Doctors who had attended the dead man said they could not be sure of the cause of death without a post-mortem. The coroner's order was upheld.

WHEN A COURT WAS ASKED TO BAN A POST-MORTEM

Whatever a person's age, and however ill he has been, the cause of death must be established beyond doubt.

Mr B, aged 81, had been suffering from a serious internal complaint for years before he was admitted to hospital with a burst appendix. He died the same day.

His own general practitioner said then that he would issue a death certificate. Later he changed his mind and refused.

At the inquest that followed, a hospital doctor told the coroner that in view of the sudden deterioration in B's condition, he considered that the cause of death was

unknown. A post-mortem examination was ordered.

Mr R, a friend of B's, applied to the High Court for an order prohibiting the post-mortem because it was contrary to B's religious beliefs. The court had to decide whether a post-mortem was legally essential.

DECISION
The judge ruled that on the evidence of the hospital doctor, the coroner would have had to call for a post-mortem even if B's own doctor had signed a death certificate. R's application was refused. '

means of an employee or a special messenger, those accompanying goods, or news or pictures for a newspaper.

Letters can be sent first or second class according to the amount of postage paid, but neither implies any guaranteed speed of delivery. *See:* FOOTBALL POOL

Any lawful item except perishable goods can be sent by letter post if it comes within certain size limits – a minimum of 100 mm. by 70 mm. and a maximum of 610 mm. by 460 mm. by 460 mm. There is no maximum weight limit, but anything over 750 g. must be sent first class.

When letters are lost

The Post Office is not legally liable for loss, damage or delay to things in the post, unless they are registered. However, under the Code of Practice for Postal Services issued in 1979 in consultation with the Office of Fair Trading, up to £12.50 compensation for loss or damage to the contents of a letter may be offered if it can be shown that a letter was posted, but was lost or damaged in the post. Proof of posting can be obtained at any post office.

Registered post If a letter is sent by registered post (and the special fee paid) up to £600 compensation is pay-

COMPLAINING ABOUT THE
POSTAL SERVICE

Local postal complaints are usually handled by independent advisory committees attached to each head Post Office. Central or national complaints should be taken up with the Post Office Users' National Council.

'Awfully sorry, but your letter of complaint hasn't arrived.'

able for loss or damage to a letter, unless the Post Office shows it was not negligent. The recipient has to sign for the letter, proving delivery. The Post Office will compulsorily register, and charge a fee, if they find a letter or parcel unregistered containing any of the following:

● Uncrossed postal order with payee's name not inserted.
● Cheque or dividend warrant uncrossed and payable to bearer.
● Bearer security.
● Bank or currency note.
● Postage, holiday, trading or National Savings stamps.
● Coupons, vouchers, tokens, coins, jewellery worth £10 or more.

When letters are delivered to the wrong address

If a letter for someone else is delivered to you by mistake you should forward it to the correct person or return it to the Post Office, clearly marked with the reason. You do not have to pay postage for redirecting a letter. It is theft to keep a letter not addressed to you.

Using parcel post

The Post Office does not have a monopoly over parcels delivery as it does over letters. The maximum weight for Post Office parcels is 10 kg.

No postman should ever leave a parcel on a doorstep or in a shed, and the Post Office is liable if it gets stolen.

The Post Office is not legally liable for lost or damaged parcels but may pay compensation under the Code of Practice up to £12.50, unless the parcel is sent registered, or under the Compensation Fee service, where a small payment entitles the sender to up to £200 if loss or damage occurs.

Parcels may also be sent by the Railex services for which there is a charge of £4. This covers parcels not exceeding 450 g. in Great Britain and 60 g. from Northern Ireland. The sender takes the parcel to the Post Office where he completes a form stating where the parcel is to go. It is then taken by Post Office messenger to a station and put on a train. On arrival at its destination it is taken to a Post Office by messenger from where it is collected by the recipient.

WIDE RANGE OF SERVICES

The Post Office, besides being the state-owned corporation responsible for postal services and the National Girobank, also provides facilities for the public to make all sorts of other official payments – for example driving, motor vehicle, television and dog licences.

'May I trouble you for a postage stamp?'

CAR, TV, DOG LICENCES, PREMIUM BONDS, N/SAVINGS, GIRO, O.A. PENSIONS Etc.

Articles for the blind

Braille or talking books and other articles can be posted free so long as no personal message is included. The weight limit is 7 kg.

Articles must state clearly 'for the blind'. They must arrive at the Post Office unwrapped or in an easily removable wrapper.

Rules about payment

Postage must be paid in advance in stamps or by using special franking machines for all postal services unless the recipient contributes to a Freepost or business reply service.

The only letters that are exempt from postage are those addressed to the Queen, either directly or through a member of either House of Parliament.

Attempting to evade postage – for example, by using old stamps or posting letters to different addresses under one cover – is punishable by a maximum of 12 months' gaol or a £100 fine.

All unstamped or not fully stamped letters will be sent second class. Deficits are charged to the receiver at double the total postage or double the deficit.

If the letter is coming from abroad and more than 50 per cent has been paid then the deficit will be charged plus a surcharge. If less than 50 per cent has been paid the letter will be sent surface mail and the amount of the deficit plus a surcharge will be made.

Spoiled stamps The Post Office will refund the cost of stamps spoiled before they are used.

Complaining about the service

If a letter or parcel is lost or damaged, ask a post office for the form *Enquiry about a missing or damaged letter or parcel* and send it when completed to the local head postmaster as soon as possible. If his reply is unsatisfactory, refer it to the postal regional director. Ultimately a dispute on compensation may be referred to an independent complaints panel set up under the Code of Practice.

If your complaint is of delay or some other failure, refer it to the local head postmaster, along with the envelope or cover if available. Grievances can also be raised with the local Post Office Advisory Committee (address in front of the telephone directory), or if a general complaint, with the independent Post Office Users' National Council (Waterloo Bridge House, Waterloo Road, London SE1 8UA, or 2 Park Grove, Cardiff CF1 3BN).

POULTRY KEEPING

When raising chickens can be a nuisance

You do not normally need permission to keep hens or chickens on private property either privately or as a business. In the latter case you may need planning permission for change of use of your property. But it is against the law to keep them under cruel conditions; or in such a way that they annoy neighbours by noise or smell; or if they constitute a health hazard.

Tenants may be restricted in keeping poultry by the terms of their lease. Council tenants, particularly, are unlikely to be allowed to keep poultry without the council's consent, which in most areas is often refused.

ALLOTMENT tenants are generally governed by special rules allowing them to keep hens without permission – but not cockerels, which might cause a nuisance with their crowing. Allotment tenants are not, however, allowed to keep poultry as a business.

MAKING SURE THAT THE
NEIGHBOURS
ARE NOT ANNOYED

It is against the law to keep poultry in such a way that they annoy the neighbours by noise or smell. If a neighbour does believe that the poultry are causing a nuisance, he can complain to the local council who can warn or even prosecute the poultry-keeper.

In some cases the owner of property may be forbidden from keeping poultry by the terms of a restrictive COVENANT imposed on his property by a former owner. If he breaks the terms of such a covenant an owner may have to face court proceedings when an injunction and possibly an order for damages may be made against him.

Stopping a nuisance

If a neighbour's poultry are causing a NUISANCE, or if you consider them to be a health risk, complain to the environmental health officer at the local council offices. He can issue a warning or, if necessary, prosecute the neighbour for a breach of the public health laws.

PREMIUM OFFER

When other goods help sell a product

To promote the sales of his own goods, a manufacturer may offer other goods in exchange for tokens, or at a specially favourable price.

Usually a premium offer is available only by MAIL ORDER. The address to which you write is not necessarily that of the company making the offer – it may

be the office of another company that specialises in sales promotions. But unless a separate company is fully identified, the manufacturer whose goods carry the offer is responsible. If anything goes wrong, your claim is against him.

A British code of sales promotion practice, drawn up on behalf of the advertising industry, lays down rules for companies involved in premium offers.

If an order does not arrive

The code requires enough goods to be available to fill orders within 28 days. Advertisements and other promotional material must state how long the customer should expect to wait. Then if more time is required, the customer should be told so, and given the opportunity to cancel the order.

If stocks run out the manufacturer is obliged under the code to cancel his advertising if possible.

A customer who has sent money is legally entitled to a refund if the goods cannot be supplied. But it has not been established in a court whether a customer has a right to compensation for losing the benefit of the premium offer, or to anything representing the value of coupons or tokens required.

Alternative offers are usually made in such cases. If you are not interested in a second choice, and had to buy extra

A MEANS OF ENCOURAGING
PEOPLE TO BUY

Premium offers are made by manufacturers, usually in exchange for tokens, to promote the sales of their goods. Even when there is no charge for the premium offer, the customer can usually expect to have faulty goods replaced.

'But you wanted the box-top for a premium offer.'

goods – for example, box tops or labels – to qualify for the offer, it is worth writing back to ask for compensation. If it is refused, legal action is unlikely to be worth while – but the Advertising Standards Authority may take up your complaint with the manufacturer.

The code of practice also states that if a manufacturer sends goods and the customer complains that they have not arrived, the company should normally assume that they were lost in transit, and replace them free of charge.

When goods, even free, are unsatisfactory

If premium goods for which you pay any money are faulty, or not of proper quality, your legal rights are the same as if you had bought them at their full price. You are entitled to a replacement or a full refund. *See:* DEFECTIVE GOODS; MONEY BACK

If no payment is required, a customer has no established legal right to claim the replacement of defective goods. The code of practice, however, obliges manufacturers to replace such goods even when there was no charge for them.

PRESCRIPTION

Obtaining drugs cheaply for your illness

The law divides medicines into three categories – those that are obtainable only on a doctor's prescription; those that can be bought from a pharmacist without a prescription; and those that can be bought anywhere. A doctor may, however, prescribe pills that could be bought without a prescription – aspirin or paracetamol, for example – to enable the patient to buy them more cheaply, or to make sure that he knows what the patient is taking.

The details that a prescription must show

When your doctor decides you need medicine, he prescribes the appropriate drug and dosage. If you are a National Health Service patient, the prescription is written on form FP10. It shows the patient's name and address, his age if under 12, the names of the drugs and

the prescribed dosage. At the bottom is the doctor's signature and stamp – without which the prescription is not valid.

Patients who are exempt from charges should complete the form on the back of the prescription. The prescription should be taken to a pharmacist who will make up the drugs as directed and charge those not exempt £1 per drug.

If the pharmacist does not have the drugs in stock he should be able to get them within 24 hours. He is obliged under the terms of his NHS contract to supply the drugs required. If he refuses to serve you during normal shop hours complain to the local family practitioner committee whose address is on your MEDICAL CARD. It can suspend any pharmacist's licence to dispense NHS prescriptions.

Private prescriptions If you are receiving private medical treatment, you cannot be issued with an NHS prescription by your private doctor – even if he also has an NHS practice. Private prescriptions are written on the doctor's own forms, usually his headed notepaper, and entitle you to buy the prescribed drugs from a pharmacist at their full retail price, which, together with his dispensing fee, may amount to several pounds.

There are some treatments – antimalaria drugs, for example – that your doctor cannot provide under the NHS. As your NHS doctor is not allowed to treat you privately, he would have to send you to another doctor to obtain a private prescription.

Where to have your prescription made up

Most chemist's shops employ a registered pharmacist, who must be a member of the Pharmaceutical Society – he will have his qualifications on display. Without a pharmacist, a chemist is not allowed to dispense drugs. If you suspect that an unsupervised and unqualified person is handling prescriptions, report the shop to the local family practitioner committee.

A list of all local pharmacists can be obtained from your doctor, hospital, police station and post office. If you need the prescribed drugs after shops are closed, look in the local newspaper or in the window of a chemist's for a list

showing which pharmacist is on the late-opening rota for that day. If the late-duty chemist has closed and your doctor believes you are in need of urgent medication that he cannot provide from his emergency stock, he would have to send you to hospital for treatment.

When drugs can be given without prescription

Some doctors, particularly in rural areas, dispense their own drugs – saving the patient the need to find a chemist. In such cases, they do not write prescriptions but must levy the £1 charge for each drug.

There is no prescription or charge for medicine given to hospital in-patients. But drugs supplied to out-patients by the hospital pharmacy require both a prescription and charge.

When you are entitled to free prescriptions

Some patients are exempt from prescription charges. All they need to do to have their prescriptions dispensed without charge is to complete the appropriate box on the back of the form.

Those exempt include:
● All children under 16, men aged 65 and over and women aged 60 and over.
● People, and their dependants, receiving supplementary benefit or family income supplement.
● Others on incomes only a little above this level, whether or not in work.
● Expectant mothers and mothers with a child under 1 year old.
● People suffering from certain medical conditions, including the housebound.
● War or Service disablement pensioners (for prescriptions required for their disablement only).

A pharmacist cannot require a patient to prove that he or she is exempt, but the local family practitioner committee checks all prescriptions.

It is an offence to claim exemption falsely, and the maximum penalties are an unlimited fine or 5 years' imprisonment.

Men over the age of 65, women over 60 and children under 16 are entitled to free medicine simply by ticking the box on the back of the prescription.

They do not have to apply for a certificate of exemption or prove their age.

Expectant mothers can receive free drugs by filling in form FW8 – obtainable from a doctor, midwife or health visitor – and sending it to the local family practitioner committee. They send back a certificate, which entitles the woman to exemption until her child is 12 months old.

Mothers with a baby of less than 12 months, who did not apply for exemption while they were pregnant, can do so by filling in form FP91 – obtainable from the post office and social security office – and sending it to the family practitioner committee.

People suffering from one of a list of chronic illnesses – including epilepsy and diabetes – can apply for exemption on form FP91. Your doctor can advise you if you are eligible.

War pensioners and anyone receiving supplementary benefit are issued with an exemption certificate by the Department of Health and Social Security.

People with low incomes, who do not qualify for supplementary benefit or FAMILY INCOME SUPPLEMENT, can apply for exemption by filling in form M11 – obtainable from the post office – and sending it to the local social security office. If they qualify, they are sent a certificate exempting them from prescription charges for 12 months. They may re-apply annually.

How to claim a refund of prescription charges

If you have qualified recently for exemption – if, for example, you are newly pregnant – but have not yet received an exemption certificate, you must pay the prescription fee. You can, however, claim a refund on form FP57, obtainable from the pharmacist, which you must send to the family practitioner committee within 3 months of paying the charge.

Paying prescription charges in advance

Anyone who needs a lot of medicine – for example, someone suffering from a number of ailments at the same time, but who is not exempt from prescription charges, can buy a pre-payment certificate entitling him to medicine without further charge for a limited period. You

can apply for the certificate on form FP95 – obtainable at the post office and social security office. It costs £5.50 for one lasting 4 months and £15 for a year. This is of benefit if you need more than 15 items on prescription in 12 months.

PRESERVATION ORDER

Historic buildings – or even a single tree – can be protected

Every LOCAL AUTHORITY is responsible for protecting the environment in its area and has legal powers to do so.

It can, for example, decide that a particularly attractive spot in its region should be designated a CONSERVATION AREA.

Nobody may change or develop such an area without permission from the district council.

The council can also issue a preservation order on any individual building of special historical or architectural merit, or on a wood or copse – even on a single tree.

Preserving buildings

A preservation order on a building is effective for 6 months while the Department of the Environment decides whether it is justified.

If it is, the building is included in the list of historic buildings scheduled to be preserved.

The owner of such a building will be notified that it has been listed, but once this has happened he will have no right to object. The owner may, however, be able to get a grant from the council to help keep up the property.

Other sources of possible help are the Department of the Environment or organisations such as the Georgian Group or the Society for the Protection of Ancient Buildings.

Anyone wishing to alter, extend or demolish a listed building must first ask the council for permission. If it is refused he can appeal to the Secretary of State for the Environment. But the owner of a listed building is not legally bound to keep it in good repair – he can even let it fall down if he wishes.

The council can, however, issue a repairs notice ordering him to make specific repairs within a given time. If he fails to comply, the council can issue a COMPULSORY PURCHASE order on the property – paying only the value of the building as it stands.

If the Department of the Environment does not uphold a preservation order, the council cannot issue another one on that building for 12 months, and must compensate the owner for any loss

---

HOW TO OBTAIN A PRESERVATION ORDER

If you want to stop someone knocking down or redeveloping one of your favourite buildings, or chopping down trees in your neighbourhood, you can ask your local council's planning department to issue a preservation order protecting them.

The council is not obliged to make the order, and you may stand a better chance of succeeding if you apply as part of a neighbourhood group rather than as an individual.

A petition It might pay, for example, to organise a petition to the council – and the more signatures you get, the more a council should be impressed.

If the council refuses to make a preservation order, you can write to the Department of the Environment stating your case again.

Ultimately it is the duty of the Secretary of State for the Environment to preserve historic buildings, and he can order a

building to be listed without reference to the local authority, if necessary.

Buildings most likely to be preserved are:
- Any that were built before 1700 and survive in something like their original condition.
- Most buildings built between 1700 and 1840.
- Those associated with well-known characters or events – such as the home of a famous writer, or the house where an important invention was made.
- Buildings that represent aspects of social and economic history – such as railway stations, factories, theatres and prisons of different periods – or are outstanding examples of technological innovation, like one of the original prefab houses.
- Buildings that have a special group value, standing perhaps in a handsome terrace or a crescent like Royal Crescent in Bath.

he has suffered – for example, a drop in the building's value as a result of the order.

Appealing against an order

You can appeal within 28 days to the Department of the Environment against a preservation order on your property.

If you do, officials of the Department will examine the property, hear evidence from those involved and either confirm or rescind the order. Their decision is final.

Preserving trees and woods

A district council preservation order on a tree or a wood is different from that on a building: it does not need the approval of the Department of the Environment, and remains in force unless it is withdrawn.

If the order applies to a tree in your garden you can appeal against it to the Department within 28 days and a similar procedure to that involving an order on property will be followed.

Once a tree-preservation order has been made, the tree cannot be felled, lopped or seriously damaged unless:
● It is dead, diseased or dangerous.
● Consent to fell has first been obtained from the local authority on an application made in writing.

If a tree obstructs the view of traffic using a road, the highway authority can order the owner or the occupier of the land on which the tree stands to fell it or cut it back, whether it is a preserved tree or not. No compensation is payable in such a case.

Penalties for damaging preserved trees and buildings

There are heavy penalties for damaging a building or tree that is protected by a preservation order – and for altering it in any way not authorised.

The maximum penalty that can be imposed in a magistrates' court is 3 months' gaol and a fine of £1,000 – or in the case of a tree, twice the tree's value, whichever sum is greater.

In the latter case, the value of the tree is based on evidence given by a valuer, taking into account its position and worth to the community as well as its price as timber.

A particularly serious case may be sent to the CROWN COURT, where an offender can be gaoled for 12 months and fined an unlimited amount.

PRESS COUNCIL

How to make a complaint against a newspaper

The Press Council is an independent body set up by the newspaper industry to deal with complaints about ethical and professional standards in British newspapers and periodicals. Half its members are drawn from the Press and half are laymen.

The council does not make legal judgments – for example in allegations of libel or obscenity; those are dealt with by the courts. Nor does it have powers to make awards or to prevent publication. It investigates complaints of breaches in acceptable standards of journalism and, if it considers there is a case to answer, it will order a hearing and publish its findings. It cannot, however, oblige the offender to publish its findings.

If you have a complaint against an item in a newspaper or magazine write first to the editor. If you are not satisfied with his response, write to the Press Council, enclosing a copy of the item. You must lodge your complaint within 3 months of publication.

The council may ask you to attend a hearing at which you and staff of the newspaper could be required to give evidence.

PRESSURE GROUP

The power of numbers to influence decisions

A number of people acting together are more likely to manage to influence decisions at local or national level than an individual acting alone. You are free to set up any kind of pressure group provided its aims are not criminal or in some other way illegal.

Pressure groups do not have to be registered or abide by any particular rules in their organisation. But their activities, like those of any individual citizen, may be subject to various laws and regulations.

If the group is trying to raise money to fight its cause it must abide by the laws on fund-raising schemes. *See:* CHARITIES; LOTTERY

It is advisable always to consult the police before holding a PROCESSION, DEMONSTRATION or PUBLIC MEETING to make sure there is not likely to be a breach of PUBLIC ORDER.

If the group is campaigning over a local council matter it should approach council officials and councillors, particularly the chairman or deputy chairman of the committee concerned. If it is a central government matter, write to the minister in charge of the department and try to enlist the support of MPs.

PRICE REDUCTION

How the law restricts 'bargain' claims

Any shop or trader who makes misleading or meaningless claims that its or his goods or services are sold for less than their normal price risks prosecution. The maximum penalty is 2 years' imprisonment and an unlimited fine.

It is an offence to state on a label or poster, or in an advertisement, that something is simply worth a higher price, or worth a certain amount more. Even proof that it really is worth more than is being charged is not a defence.

However, a trader is in most cases allowed to advertise his price in comparison with a manufacturer's recommended retail price – sometimes abbreviated to MRP or RRP – provided that the information is correct. Such comparisons are not allowed for beds or mattresses, domestic appliances, carpets and furniture, because manufacturers' price recommendations often bore no relation to anyone's charges.

Quoting a rival's price

A claim that one company's price is lower than another's is illegal unless the rival supplier is identified.

The advertiser must also be able to show that he had good reason to believe that the higher price was the one his rival normally charged, and was still charging when the claim was made.

Quoting an earlier price

A claim that goods or services are being sold for less than the trader's pre-

> ## BARGAIN PRICE THAT STAYED THE SAME
>
> *To prove that a price-reduction claim is false, a prosecution must show that no higher price was charged in any continuous period of 28 days during the previous 6 months.*
>
> On five Sundays in June and July 1969, House of Holland offered a sunchair bed for 45 shillings. Each advertisement said: 'All prices further reduced.'
>
> The weights and measures inspector for the London Borough of Brent prosecuted on the basis of evidence that the same price had been charged for 2 months. Therefore the 'further reduced' claim must be false, he argued. Harrow magistrates agreed, and convicted the company.
>
> On appeal, the High Court had to decide whether the prosecution had brought proof of the offence.
>
> ### DECISION
> The judges observed that although the prosecution had called evidence of the company's pricing for 2 months, the court was told nothing about the preceding 4 months. If a higher price had been charged for any 28-day period then, no offence would have been committed.
>
> The High Court found that no offence had been established, and quashed the conviction.

vious price is permitted only if the goods are being sold on the same premises, or if any other premises are identified in the claim. Unless the trader states otherwise, the earlier price mentioned for goods – but not services – must have been constant for at least 28 days within the preceding 6 months.

Where to complain If you believe that a pricing law has been broken, inform the trading standards office of your local authority.

PRISON

A place of detention for those who offend against the law

England has several types of 'prison', administered by the Home Office's prison department. In addition to ordinary prisons for adult male and female offenders, there are Borstals, to which young offenders under 21 may be sentenced; detention centres, where male offenders under 21 may be sent; and remand centres where prisoners who have not been tried or sentenced – especially those under 21 – may be held.

The kind of prison to which a person is sent depends on his or her age, sex, offence committed and personal circumstances.

A prisoner has no right to choose the prison in which he is detained or to insist that it be near his home. But he or his family can make representations to the prison department if they feel the choice of prison is wrong. If the prison is a long way from his home, he may be allowed a temporary transfer to a local prison to assist visiting.

Restrictions on sentencing

Most courts regard prison as a last resort, to be used only for persistent offenders or those guilty of serious crimes. Before sending a person to prison a court usually asks a PROBATION officer to prepare a social inquiry report, giving details of the defendant's home life, the factors that may have led him to commit the offence and his likely response to a particular sentence.

If the defendant is a woman, or has not been sentenced to prison before, the court will want to be sure that prison is the only answer – or whether probation or a suspended prison sentence would be a suitable alternative.

Safeguards for offenders

A person who has not previously been sentenced to prison is protected by certain rules. A court cannot send him to prison unless:
● He is given the chance to be legally represented. He can apply for legal aid or engage a private solicitor.
● The court feels that no other penalty would be appropriate – usually because of the defendant's previous record, the gravity of the offence or the need to deter other potential offenders. But, whatever the reason, the court must state its reasons.

Offenders under 21 An offender between the ages of 17 and 21 can be sent to prison only if the court thinks that no other penalty would be appropriate.

In addition, to safeguard his welfare and protect him from undesirable surroundings, he must be given a sentence of 6 months or less, or 3 years or more. He cannot be sentenced to a period between 6 months and 3 years, unless he has previously received a 6 month sentence or been to Borstal. In that case the restricted period is reduced to between 6 months and 2 years.

If he is in prison when he is sentenced again for a later offence, there are no restrictions on the sentence.

Offenders under 17 Special rules apply to sentencing people under 17.

HOW A PRISONER IS CLASSIFIED

A person can be detained in prison only if he is committed there by a court. There are six classes of prisoner.
● *Sentenced prisoner* An adult over 21 who has been sentenced to prison for a criminal offence or for not paying a fine or compensation or costs ordered by a court.
● *Young prisoner* A sentenced prisoner under the age of 21.
● *Unconvicted prisoner* Someone who has been remanded in custody during committal proceedings in a magistrates' court or while waiting for trial at a crown court. A magistrates' court can remand such a person in prison for up to 8 days at a time.
● *Convicted, unsentenced prisoner* Someone who has been tried and found guilty by a magistrates' court and is remanded to prison while the court decides on the sentence, or who has been referred by the magistrates' court to the crown court for sentencing. The classification also includes anyone convicted of a crime but not sentenced for it – for instance, because of a MENTAL DISORDER.

An unsentenced prisoner is treated in the same way as a sentenced prisoner, except that he has free access to a lawyer.
● *Unconvicted prisoner* Anyone detained in prison because he is an illegal immigrant, or who is to be the subject of a DEPORTATION order.
● *Civil prisoner* A civil prisoner is a person committed to prison for other than a criminal offence – for example, for CONTEMPT OF COURT or for not paying rates or other debts.

Concurrent and consecutive sentences

If a defendant is found guilty of more than one offence he can receive a separate prison sentence on each count, to run consecutively or concurrently.

Consecutively If sentences run consecutively they run one after the other. For example, if a person has been sentenced to 2 years' imprisonment on each of three charges, to run consecutively, he will serve 6 years in prison.

Concurrently Running concurrently means running together. So if a person receives 2 years' imprisonment on each of three charges to run concurrently, he serves 2 years in prison.

When a person enters prison

When a prisoner arrives at a prison he is searched and all cash and personal belongings to which he is not entitled in prison are taken away from him. He must be given a list of all property taken, and all money must be paid into an account under prison control.

Sentenced and unsentenced prisoners are required to wear prison clothes. They must have a bath, shave and usually have their hair cut.

All other prisoners are entitled to wear their own clothes and to keep certain possessions. They may also pay for specially furnished rooms, when these are available, and have food sent into the prison for them.

They need not work if they prefer not

PRIVILEGES AVAILABLE

Most prisoners are entitled to general privileges – such as receiving books from friends or using the prison library.

GRANTING PRIVILEGES TO PRISONERS

In practice, privileges are granted to most prisoners, but no prisoner has a legal right to them, and they can be withdrawn if he misbehaves.

The usual general privileges include freedom to earn and spend money, use of the prison library, receipt of suitable personal books and periodicals from friends outside, buying and smoking tobacco and having a personal radio.

Prison governors also have the power to grant special privileges – such as having a typewriter or other more personal possessions in a cell, or being allowed to attend lectures or evening classes in prison.

Prisoners who have served at least 3 years of their sentences and who are not in a local prison, may be entitled to the privilege of having such things as mats, flowers or bedspreads in their cells.

Sending and receiving letters

A sentenced or unsentenced prisoner is entitled to write and receive one letter a week. He must be supplied with prison notepaper, envelope and pen. Postage is paid for him.

Where conditions – such as sufficient

staff and accommodation permit – he may be allowed to send and receive more letters each week, but he must pay the postage.

Prison authorities have the right to read all letters to and from all prisoners. Letters that are too long or objectionable – for example, if they deal with a complaint that has not been referred through proper internal channels – can be stopped.

A sentenced or unsentenced prisoner may not, without permission, write to anyone other than his wife – or common law wife – close family, friends known to him at the time he entered prison, and his Member of Parliament. If he wishes to write to anyone else he must seek permission from the prison governor.

Any gift sent to any prisoner will be examined and handed over only if the prisoner is entitled or privileged to receive it. Money is generally sent back, or kept in the prison account.

Stopped letters or gifts

If a letter or gift to a prisoner is stopped, it is returned to the sender. A prisoner's letter that is stopped is returned to him.

---

to. They are entitled to communicate freely with legal advisers, write and receive as many letters as they wish and receive daily visits from family and friends.

How a prisoner must behave

Prisoners, particularly those sentenced and unsentenced, have few rights. Their conduct – but also that of the prison authorities – is subject to prison rules, prison standing orders, and other instructions from the prison department.

Under the Prison Act 1952, prison rules are made public. Standing orders and other instructions are not published.

A prisoner must be aware of the main prison rules, and of the means by which he may complain. He is entitled to receive written information about only 'those provisions of the rules and other matters which it is necessary that he should know'.

Rule 47, for example, deals with many aspects of prison requirements, including 'in any way offending against good order and discipline'.

If a prisoner commits a criminal of-

fence while in prison, it is dealt with by the police and by a further trial. But lesser offences are dealt with under Rule 47.

The governor looks into the case, hears any evidence the prisoner wishes to present and decides whether he is guilty.

Sentence can include loss of privileges and earnings, forfeit of remission for up to 28 days, deprivation of work outside his cell for up to 14 days and solitary confinement for up to 3 days.

When a board of visitors is involved

More serious internal offences are referred to a board of visitors – a body of local citizens, including some magistrates, appointed by the Home Office.

A prisoner has the right to appear before the prison board, but may not be legally represented. The board of visitors has the power to impose more severe penalties than the governor – for example, 180 days' loss of remission, 56 days' stoppage of work outside the cell and greater forfeiture of privileges.

A prisoner has no right of appeal against a decision by the governor or the board of visitors unless it is in breach of NATURAL JUSTICE. He can then get a solicitor to challenge it in the courts.

Deciding where to send a male prisoner

A male prisoner sentenced to 3 or more months in prison is sent to the local prison in the area where he was tried, for assessment. A prisoner sentenced to 5 years or more – 4 years or more for a first offender – or for life, is sent to a special regional assessment centre.

Assessment takes into account his age, offence and his security category – of which there are four:
● Category A – prisoners whose escape would be highly dangerous to the public, the police or the security of the state.
● Category B – prisoners for whom escape must be made very difficult, but for whom the highest security conditions are not necessary.
● Category C – prisoners who cannot be trusted in open conditions, but who do not have the ability or resources to escape.
● Category D – prisoners who can be reasonably trusted to serve their sentences in open conditions – that is, a prison without a secure perimeter fence or wall.

A prisoner has no right of appeal against his security category, but if he thinks it is inappropriate, he or his family can apply to the prison department to have his case reconsidered.

Female prisoners Women are given security categories in the same way as men, and Category A prisoners are kept under high security, but otherwise where possible they are not segregated by age or category.

Accommodation and work

Male and female prisoners are kept in separate prisons. Young prisoners are normally kept separate from older ones.

Accommodation The accommodation provided for a prisoner varies between prisons, but usually he will be required to sleep in a cell shared with one or two other prisoners. His only right to leave the cell is for a period of exercise in the open air of not less than 1 hour each day. However, he will usually be released from the cell during the day for longer periods.

Work A prisoner who is required to work is paid usually about £1 a week.

He is entitled to spend that money on tobacco, sweets and toiletries obtainable from the prison shop.

Sentenced and unsentenced prisoners are usually required to work up to 8 hours a day.

Visiting a prisoner

A sentenced or unsentenced prisoner is entitled to only one visit every 4 weeks, lasting at least half an hour and normally taking place within sight and hearing of a prison officer. He may be visited by his family and friends, but must have permission to see anyone else.

A foreign prisoner may also be visited by a consul.

Extra – or longer – visits may be allowed when circumstances permit, or for special reasons such as a domestic crisis or a legal appeal.

Visitors may give nothing but cigarettes to the prisoner and may not take any notes of the conversation. Personal contact, such as kissing and hugging between husband and wife, is allowed only at the beginning and end of a visit and in the presence of a prison officer.

Visitors to all prisoners must have a visiting order, which the prisoner obtains from the prison governor, through a prison officer.

Writing to an MP

A prisoner is entitled to write to his Member of Parliament at any time without permission from the prison gover-

---

WHEN A PRISONER CAN BE FORCE-FED

Forcible feeding of prisoners is governed by prison regulations, and the law does not make it clear whether forcible feeding is legal.

When a prisoner persists in refusing to eat, the prison medical officer has a duty to satisfy himself that the prisoner's capacity for rational judgment is not impaired by mental or physical illness. If the medical officer is satisfied, he must call in an outside consultant to confirm that opinion.

The prisoner must be told clearly that food will be made available to him, that he will continue to receive medical supervision and advice, and that he will be removed to the prison hospital if necessary but that the consequent and inevitable deterioration in his health may be allowed to continue without medical intervention unless he specifically requests it. He should also be told that no prison rule requires the medical officer to resort to artificial feeding.

Individual medical officers may, however, resort to forcible feeding if they think it right to preserve a prisoner's life in that way. Provided that he reaches his decision on reasonable medical grounds it is unlikely that criminal proceedings would ever be brought against him or that he would be held liable to pay damages for ASSAULT AND BATTERY.

On the other hand, a medical officer who did not forcibly feed a prisoner on hunger strike would not be liable to pay damages if the prisoner died.

WHEN A PRISONER GOES ON HUNGER STRIKE

If a prisoner, who is serving a sentence for a criminal offence, goes on hunger strike and then appeals against his sentence, the fact that he intends to continue his strike and so might die is no ground for reducing the sentence.

The Court of Appeal gave that ruling in 1979 when Robert Relf appealed against his sentence for inciting to racial hatred.

Mr Relf had been on hunger strike before – in 1976 – after being committed to prison for contempt of court for disobeying an injunction under the Race Relations Act ordering him to remove a sign advertising his house 'for sale to an English family'.

In that year the OFFICIAL SOLICITOR, who can act in contempt cases, intervened and asked the Birmingham county court judge to release Mr Relf from prison because the strike was endangering his health. The judge released him, and no further proceedings were taken against him.

The Official Solicitor could not intervene in 1979, however, as he has no power to act on behalf of prisoners serving a fixed term for a criminal offence.

nor. But he may not raise any complaint that has not been made through proper prison channels. He may also be visited by his MP and is entitled to have a conversation with him out of the hearing, but not sight, of a prison officer.

A prisoner's family is entitled to write to his MP on his behalf on any subject, without consulting the prison authorities.

Solitary confinement

Under Rule 43 of the prison rules, a prisoner may ask for solitary confinement if he feels it necessary for his safety. In such cases the prisoner may seek transfer to a prison that has special facilities for Rule 43 prisoners.

Rule 43 may also be used by prison authorities to isolate a prisoner for the maintenance of good order and discipline, even although no individual charge under Rule 47 – 'offending against good order and discipline' – has been brought against him.

When a prisoner is released

A prisoner must be released from prison as soon as his sentence has been completed.

Anyone sentenced to prison for more than 31 days is entitled to have his sentence reduced, or remitted, by one-third, provided that his behaviour has been good.

Parole A prisoner who has served one-third, or 12 months, of his sentence – whichever is the longer – may be released on PAROLE. Prisoners serving life sentences may also be released on

parole, but are subject to recall to prison any time during the rest of their lives – if they become a public risk, say.

Temporary release A prisoner may be granted temporary release from prison, with or without escort, to visit relatives or look for employment, or get married.

Outside employment Prisoners serving long-term sentences may be allowed to work outside the prison for periods of readjustment before their release. They live in the prison or in a prison hostel during those release periods.

On release from prison, a prisoner is entitled to have all his possessions returned to him, clothing provided if he needs it, and to receive his fare home. If he has served a sentence of more than 3 months, he will receive a small discharge grant. Aftercare, such as finding a job or somewhere to stay, is provided by the probation service, and by the National Association for the Care and Resettlement of Offenders.

Supplementary benefit

A person who is in prison cannot claim supplementary benefit. When he is discharged, he may be entitled to benefit until he finds a job. If so, he may also be able to claim a lump-sum payment to clear any arrears of rent, rates or furniture-storage charges that accrued while he was in prison. But payments of this kind are made only if he was in prison for less than a year, is in danger of losing the accommodation or the furniture, and either he is chronically sick, disabled or over pension age or the accommodation is to be occupied by

his wife or children.

If a prisoner's wife is left without support, she must make her own claim for supplementary benefit for herself and any children. She can also ask for help with the cost of visiting him.

If a single parent goes to prison, and the children are looked after by an adult who is entitled to supplementary benefit, their needs can be added to that person's supplementary benefit entitlement.

HOW A PRISONER CAN COMPLAIN

There are several channels open to a prisoner who wishes to make a complaint, and he must use them all before raising the complaint elsewhere.

The issue may be raised direct with the prison governor – or medical officer or chaplain if more appropriate. Alternatively, the prisoner may notify the governor via an officer that he wishes to see a member of the board of visitors or a prison department official on his next visit to the prison. He need not disclose to the officer why he wishes to do so.

If those approaches fail to satisfy the prisoner, he can ask an officer for a form on which to make a formal complaint or 'petition' to be forwarded to the prison department for consideration.

If none of these internal channels is successful, the prisoner is entitled to write to his MP for help. If the prisoner alleges maladministration – for example, in the handling of a request for a transfer – his MP may ask the OMBUDSMAN for an investigation.

As a last resort, the prisoner may write to the European Commission on HUMAN RIGHTS if he alleges that any of his rights have been infringed.

Getting advice from a solicitor

Any prisoner involved in legal proceedings of any kind is entitled to be visited by a solicitor and to apply for legal aid. He may also write to, and conduct interviews with, the solicitor without interference from the prison authorities.

If legal proceedings have not begun, a prisoner can apply to the governor for permission to write to a solicitor about a civil, but not a criminal, matter. His application will be granted unless the matter refers to a complaint against prison authorities which has not been referred to the internal channels.

CLAIMING FOR WRONGFUL IMPRISONMENT

Anyone who is detained in prison and believes the prison authorities have no right to detain him – for example, if he disputes the power of the court that committed him to prison, or if he can show that his sentence has expired – can seek a writ of HABEAS CORPUS to challenge the validity of his detention. A writ can also be obtained on behalf of a prisoner by his relatives, friends or lawyers.

False imprisonment

Anyone who has been wrongfully detained in prison, can take civil action against the prison authorities for FALSE IMPRISONMENT.

Acquittal or royal pardon

If a person who is held in prison on a prison sentence is later retried and acquitted, or is granted a royal pardon, he cannot claim against the prison authorities for wrongful imprisonment. But the Home Office may make a payment to compensate the prisoner for wrongful imprisonment.

Unconvicted prisoner

If an unconvicted prisoner is eventually acquitted at his trial, or convicted but not sentenced to a period of imprisonment, he cannot claim against the authorities for wrongful imprisonment.

PRIVACY

*Is an Englishman's home
still his castle?*

There is no law that specifically protects the ordinary citizen's right to privacy, but several laws protect some aspects of it – particularly when the citizen is in his own home.

For example, if a newspaper reporter bursts into your home demanding an interview or if someone enters to fit listening devices, he is committing a TRESPASS and you can sue.

On the other hand, if a Press photographer, or anyone else, uses a long-range camera from across the street to photograph you through the windows in your own home, you have no legal redress.

Many officials of public authorities have the right to enter your home provided they observe the detailed restrictions laid down by Parliament. *See:* ENTRY, RIGHT OF

Landlords do not have an automatic right to enter their tenants' homes, and the law protects tenants from HARASSMENT by them.

The protection the law of trespass gives to your own home does not extend to a hotel bedroom. If someone hides microphones or cameras in a room a couple is occupying, the couple have no redress, although the hotel might have grounds for legal action.

Intrusions into privacy can sometimes be held to be conduct likely to lead to a BREACH OF THE PEACE. Peeping Toms, for instance, can be prosecuted for that offence.

There is a presumption in law that a houseowner also owns the footpath adjoining his land. So if someone walks up and down the footpath to watch you and your family, he is then committing trespass. He is entitled to use the footpath only for passage.

You can claim damages from him for trespass, and the amount awarded would reflect the inconvenience and interference to which you had been subjected.

The same would apply to Press and television reporters besieging your house, even if they did not actually trespass on your property. In practice, if you called the police, they would probably simply order them to move away.

Dealing with the Press

There is no law to stop the Press publishing details of your private life, provided the details are true. If what they publish is untrue you can sue for LIBEL.

In practice, the Press and broadcasting organisations are deterred from publishing damaging material to some extent because it is no defence for them to say that they honestly believed that what they published was true. They have to be able to prove in court that the material is factually accurate.

If a newspaper obtains private family photographs or diaries, it can be a breach of COPYRIGHT to publish them. Courts can also grant an INJUNCTION to prevent a breach of confidence or to stop someone using your name, without your permission, to promote a commercial product.

Your professional advisers – doctors, lawyers and accountants – have a contractual duty to respect your privacy and not disclose any information about your personal affairs. Employees of banks and bodies like the Inland Revenue are bound by contract not to discuss your affairs with outsiders.

The police also are not allowed to

DUEL BY NEWSPAPER

Confidences shared with a spouse should not be disclosed after divorce, and the publication of divorce proceedings is limited by law.

The Duke and Duchess of Argyll were divorced in 1963. In the same year the duchess published certain statements in the *Sunday Mirror* about the duke's personal conduct and financial affairs.

In 1964 the duchess issued a writ to restrain the duke from publishing information in *The People* about her personal affairs and conduct which she had told him in confidence during their marriage and particulars relating to their divorce proceedings.

DECISION

It was held that there was an implicit obligation of confidence between husband and wife and that was not limited to business matters. Some of the passages the duke intended publishing would be a breach of marital confidence. The wife's adultery did not remove that obligation.

The duchess was entitled to claim an injunction and a party to a divorce was entitled to enforce the Act which prohibits publication of divorce proceedings.

THE EAVESDROPPING TAPE RECORDER

A tape recording is admissible evidence in court provided its accuracy can be proved and the voices properly identified. The evidence taken from it must be relevant to the case and be admissible in all other ways.

On April 27, 1964 the police were called to 161 Tennyson Place, Bradford by Mr Maqsud Ali, the paying guest of Mr Ashiq Hussain. The police found Mr Ashiq's wife dead in the cellar. Both men denied murder, and said it was the work of some enemy of the married couple.

On September 2, the two men went voluntarily to the police station. They were interviewed by a police superintendent in the presence of a race relations liaison officer. They were then left in a room with a hidden microphone connected to a tape recorder. Their conversation was translated and used with other evidence by the prosecution.

At the trial the defence counsel objected to the taped evidence and challenged the method, the effectiveness and accuracy of the translations.

The judge found that there were certain passages common to all the translations which had been made of the recordings which, if accurate, came near to an admission of guilt. He decided that these problems should be left to the jury and that the evidence on the tapes was not so unsatisfactory that it should be withdrawn.

The defendants were convicted and appealed.

DECISION

It was held that a tape recording was no different from eavesdropping. As the defendants had not been in custody, no caution was required. As all the translations had been submitted to cross-examination and the translations had been carefully checked, the trial judge was right in allowing the translations to be used.

Several rules protect the privacy of the citizen – especially when he is in his own home – but there is no general right to privacy in English law.

disclose criminal records to outsiders. If a newspaper publishes the fact that someone was convicted of a criminal offence in his past life, it can in certain circumstances be sued for libel. The fact that the statement is accurate is not a defence if it can be shown that the paper acted out of malice.

Telephone tapping

The Government can authorise the tapping of your telephone. Private detectives or anyone else can also tap it provided they do not enter your property to do so and do not damage telephone equipment or divert electricity.

Your employer

A prospective employer is entitled to ask detailed questions about your personal life, but you have no obligation to answer them. If your employer maintains a personnel file on you, you cannot legally demand to see it.

PRIVATE DETECTIVE

What you can expect of a reputable investigator

A private detective has no greater powers or rights than any other citizen. He can be prosecuted if he breaks the criminal law, or sued in a civil court if any of his actions infringe someone else's legal rights.

No private detective can enter your house without permission, take any-

thing of yours or intercept any correspondence. Nor can one remain on your property if you have ordered him to leave. *See:* TRESPASS

You do not have to give a private investigator any information about yourself or any other person, whatever the purpose of his inquiry and whatever credentials he may produce.

There is no official system of licensing private detectives, or of requiring them to have particular qualifications. The law simply does not recognise them.

Hiring a detective

Someone who wants to conduct a private investigation – for example, to pursue a criminal allegation when the police say they have insufficient grounds to prosecute – usually has no way of knowing whether a particular detective is competent and whether his charges are reasonable.

If the proposed investigation is connected with any legal proceedings, it is usually advisable to discuss it with a lawyer first. He should be able to judge whether it is worth while and whether it involves any legal risks. He may also be able to recommend an investigator.

If a detective is hired through a law firm, the firm takes responsibility for checking and paying his charges. They are passed on to the client.

Someone who wants to deal directly with a private detective is most likely to find a suitable one by contacting the Association of British Investigators, which has a nationwide membership of people who have established their competence in the field and are subject to the association's own discipline.

Its headquarters are at ABI House, 10 Bonner Hill Road, Kingston-upon-Thames, Surrey KT1 3EP.

ABI members are bound to a code of conduct which among other things obliges them to:
● Protect the privacy and confidences of their clients.
● Ensure that a client has 'lawful and moral' reasons to ask for an investigation.
● Conduct investigations 'within the bounds of legality, morality and professional ethics'.

When there is a dispute

A detective is entitled to refuse any work that he cannot or does not want to

carry out. But once he accepts an assignment, and his client agrees to his fees and conditions, the normal laws governing a CONTRACT apply.

A client is entitled to refuse to pay if the agreed work is not done, and either party can sue for money owed – provided that the assignment was lawful.

How to complain The Association of British Investigators can deal with complaints of negligence or failure of duty by its members. ABI discipline is usually effective, because loss of membership could severely damage a detective's livelihood.

However, if you allege serious misconduct by a private detective – whoever he is working for – you should make your complaint to the police.

PRIVATE HEALTH INSURANCE

How an insurance policy can pay for your medical treatment

Patients who want to have their medical treatment privately instead of through the National Health Service can take out an insurance policy to pay for the costs.

There are three basic schemes which are offered by a number of insurance societies.
● An all-in scheme which guarantees payment of any medical bills up to a fixed ceiling, including bills for hospital treatment and nursing.
● A fixed-benefit scheme which will provide a set payment for each day the insured person spends in hospital. The money can be spent in any way you choose.
● Loss-of-earnings scheme which simply compensates for income lost while the sick person is away from work. This scheme is particularly valuable to self-employed people.

Which scheme to choose

Choice of scheme depends on a person's individual needs and how much he can afford to set aside for private medical insurance.

The all-in scheme is the most comprehensive, but it is also likely to be the most expensive.

The fixed-benefit scheme provides cover only while the patient is in hospital – not suitable for a person who needs a long convalescence. The hospital bills are likely to be higher than the cash entitlement.

Loss-of-earnings schemes can be geared to a person's normal income and even increased each year to account for inflation or rising income. Benefits are paid at a fixed rate for a fixed period of time, and are often related to the insured person's age.

What an all-in scheme covers

Do not expect even a comprehensive policy to pay for every single cost you incur in hospital or medical treatment.

No scheme will pay for ordinary, private consultations with a doctor either at his surgery or at your home.

Almost every scheme has a maximum payment. The patient will have to pay for any expense above that figure.

Apart from nursing and treatment in hospital there are many extras to be paid for – X-rays, surgical dressings, anaesthetists, therapy, drugs. Not every scheme will cover all of those. Check when you take out a policy.

What sort of illness is covered

Most insurance schemes cover treatment for the cure or relief of illness or for injuries received in an accident, or dental care which requires hospital treatment.

Treatment of psychiatric illness is usually included, but there is likely to be a time-limit clause, such as a maximum

HOW BENEFITS VARY

Not all private health insurance schemes offer the same range of benefits. Check carefully before you decide to make a proposal.

Private

number of days over which treatment will be paid for. This is because, by its nature, psychiatric treatment is often long term.

A person already suffering from an illness or injury can sometimes insure against the cost of future treatment.

Full details of the complaint, the symptoms and the length of time it has been suffered must be disclosed on the proposal form.

Few schemes cover the cost of pregnancy or childbirth, though it is possible to insure for private treatment for any complications in pregnancy, or when there is some abnormal condition.

It is usually necessary for the woman to insure before she becomes pregnant.

Making a health insurance claim

In most schemes, the cost of treatment is paid direct to the insured person by the company after all bills have been submitted to them.

In the event of a dispute over the bills, it is usual for the company to appoint an independent doctor to arbitrate.

Other forms of financial help available

Other forms of financial help during illness are provided by contributory insurance schemes. The British Hospitals Contributory Schemes Association, 30 Lancaster Gate, London W2 3LT, can provide information on the schemes available, including what they cost and what they provide. Some, for example, help with national health charges for dentures, with home helps and with private specialists.

Self-employed people who wish to insure against loss of earnings during illness also have a choice of policies. Usually it is best to go to an insurance broker for guidance. The amount of the premium depends not only on the sum insured for, but also on the number of weeks or months of illness which it is agreed must elapse before you qualify for payment.

Obtaining help from clubs and societies

Trade unions, employers and other groups sometimes organise sick clubs or

friendly societies that, in return for a small weekly contribution, provide some financial help during sickness. Membership is normally open to only a limited number of people, however, and the scale of operation is usually small.

PRIVATE MEDICINE
How and where a patient can opt out of the National Health Service

No one requiring medical treatment is obliged to use the National Health Service. Instead he can obtain treatment on a private fee-paying basis – often in a National Health Service hospital.

Many doctors, consultants and hospitals accept both private and National Health Service patients. Some treat one or the other, but not both.

However, someone seeking treatment does not have to commit himself at the outset either to private or Health Service medicine. He can decide on a combination of the two.

For example, he may be registered with a general practitioner under the National Health Service, but he can still choose to pay for private consultancy if specialist treatment is required for a particular ailment.

Similarly, a patient registered privately with a family doctor can obtain specialist or hospital treatment under the Health Service.

No single doctor is allowed, however, to offer a patient both types of treatment – private for some purposes, non-private for others.

Hospitals Most, but not all, National Health Service hospitals accept fee-paying patients. In an area where they do not, a patient seeking private treatment would have to enter an exclusively private hospital.

In both cases, it is normally the general practitioner who arranges for the admission.

What it may cost

Outside hospital, it can cost £20 or more for a single consultation with a specialist. A visit from a general practitioner costs a private patient about £5 on average, depending on where he lives.

All prescribed drugs and appliances

are extra, and a private patient is not entitled to the low prescription charges afforded to National Health Service patients.

For a hospital in-patient, treatment can cost several hundred pounds a week just for a bed and basic nursing.

A simple operation – an appendicectomy, for example – adds a further several hundred pounds to the bill, taking into account the fees of the surgeon, anaesthetist and theatre staff, the cost of the drugs and so on.

For prolonged, involved treatment like plastic surgery, the total cost can run into five figures.

However, one of the advantages of private medicine is that the patient can 'shop around' if he considers that he is going to be overcharged.

How to complain about treatment

A private medical patient has the same rights as a National Health Service patient to take action over what he considers to be MEDICAL NEGLIGENCE.

In addition, a private patient may also be entitled to withhold the fees if he has been treated negligently or inadequately. This may result in legal action being taken against him by the doctor or hospital concerned, although doctors who are members of the Royal College of Physicians are not allowed to sue for their fees.

When the complaint is against a private hospital, it is the owners as well as the medical staff who may be liable.

But if the complaint is about treatment in a National Health hospital, the action to be taken depends on who was at fault.

If it was a private consultant or surgeon brought in from outside, it is he who should be sued. If any of the hospital staff were responsible, legal action should be directed against the area health authority.

PRIVATE PROSECUTION

How to start a criminal action against another person

Most prosecutions are brought by the police, but a private individual can start a case himself, if the police decide not to

proceed. That can happen, for example, when someone insists on taking action against a motorist for careless driving or against a neighbour for assault; or when a shopkeeper wants to prosecute a shoplifter for theft.

Private prosecutions are almost always heard in the local magistrates' court. The object is to punish the person accused; the person bringing the action may make no personal gain, although the court might order compensation.

What you must do to start a private prosecution

A person who wants to bring a private prosecution must get permission from the magistrates for the area in which the accused person lives.

Go to the clerk or a court official and tell him what you want. You will eventually be called into the witness box and asked to name the person you want to prosecute and to explain your reasons for doing so.

The complaint must be about an offence in law. There is no need at this stage to prove the case – only to convince the magistrate that there is the basis of a case.

Once the magistrate has agreed that the prosecution can go ahead, a summons will be issued by the court and served on the defendant, not by the person bringing the prosecution.

A clerk at the court will arrange the hearing, and you will be informed of date and time.

If the case is lost

A person who loses a private prosecution because the defendant is found not guilty, can face a claim for damages. The person accused could sue if he can prove that it was a MALICIOUS PROSECUTION.

More serious, however, is the amount of costs the other side may have incurred. The loser may have to pay them – as well as his own.

When a defendant issues a cross-summons

If the defendant in a private prosecution feels that he has a case against the person starting the action he can also issue a summons – called in law a cross-summons.

The outcome in such cases is rarely satisfactory for either side, for if the magistrate is unable to determine the truth between the two versions he is told, he is likely to bind both parties over to keep the peace.

PRIVATE STREET

What it may cost you to live in a private street

A private street is one that is not maintained out of rates or taxes.

People with houses or properties in private streets are called 'frontagers' – meaning that their properties have frontages on, or with access to, the street.

They are responsible jointly for the upkeep of the roadway, but difficulties in organising repairs and getting everyone to pay his share can mean that in practice the road may fall into disrepair.

In those circumstances the householders may ask the local authority to take over or 'adopt' the street.

If the council agrees it then becomes responsible for maintaining the road. But a council will adopt only roads that are up to its standards – which means that the frontagers have first to pay for that work to be done. Alternatively, the council may agree to have the road 'made up' by its own workmen, then ask the householders to meet the cost. Each

---

WHEN YOU ARE DRIVING ALONG A PRIVATE STREET

If a private street is also a public RIGHT OF WAY, anyone who commits an offence while driving along it can be prosecuted in the same way as if he had been on a public road.

The main difficulty is knowing whether the street is a right of way. It is rarely possible to tell without asking someone who lives there – unless the residents have erected a notice stating that the public has no right of way.

When a motorist is driving along a private street that is not a right of way he cannot be prosecuted for a Road Traffic Act offence, but if he is doing so without permission of the owners, he can be sued for TRESPASS.

would be required to pay a share based on the frontage measurement of his property.

When the council decides to adopt a private street

In other circumstances, however, the council may decide itself to adopt the road, having had it made up at the frontagers' expense.

The first a householder may become aware of such a proposal is when he receives a notice of 'provisional apportionment' giving:

● The total estimated cost of making up the whole street.

● The share to be paid by the householder, based on the frontage measurement of his property – or garden – in relation to the street.

At that stage a householder has the right to object to the council's taking over the street, and also to the size of the share of costs he must pay.

If a council rejects a frontager's case, his objection – and any others that may have been made – will be referred to the local magistrates, to whom the objector can put his case again at a court hearing.

Chief grounds for objection

The main grounds on which a householder can object to a private street's being taken over by a local authority are that:

● It is not a 'street' – which is defined as having houses or buildings on at least one side.

● It is unreasonable to have the street made up, having regard to the amount and type of traffic using it.

● The estimated cost of the work is too high, or the standard of work proposed is higher than necessary.

● The council is already legally liable to maintain the street.

● The frontage measurement of the property concerned has been wrongly stated.

A frontager who does want to object to a street adoption proposal should try to persuade his neighbours to join him.

Scope for appeal

There is only one point upon which an objector can appeal, if necessary, to the Secretary of State for the Environment – when the council has included in a householder's apportionment share

THE COST OF 'ADOPTION'

When a council is to adopt a private street, it will require the residents to pay to bring it up to normal road standards.

an element called 'return frontage'. An example is the frontage of a garden that backs on to the street, but does not give access to it.

In such a case a householder can ask the council to reduce the charge on that frontage by, say, 50 per cent.

If the council refuses to agree without good reason, the householder can appeal to the local magistrates on that point.

Working out the final cost

When all objections to provisional apportionment notices have been settled, the council has the street made up and puts in drainage, footpaths and lighting.

It then works out the actual cost of the job and sends 'final apportionment' notices to the frontagers showing how much they must pay.

The final apportionment notices are based on the same proportions of the total costs as those in the provisional apportionment notices, amended to take into account the results of objections and appeals.

Frontagers again have the right to object to their final apportionment, but only on the grounds of some arithmetical or similar simple errors in it. Such objections can be referred to the local magistrates.

Final demand for payment

Final apportionment notices are followed within a few weeks by a demand from the council for payment of the amount due.

There are no grants available to help householders meet the charges for making up a private street, but the council may authorise a loan – usually repayable within 12 months.

Interest is charged at the current general level of interest, plus a small amount to cover administrative costs.

Local authorities have strong powers to enforce payment. In theory, at least, a council can turn a householder out of his home and sell it to raise the money.

If you want to have the street made up

When most of the householders in a private street want to have the road made up they can ask the council to carry out the work, and the council is obliged to do so.

In such a situation a majority is not calculated on the number of frontagers who want the work done, but on the total length of frontages involved.

The cost of the work must be borne by *all* the frontagers, in proportions according to the length of their frontages.

PROBATION

When a court orders a period of guidance instead of prison

Any offender over 17 can, with his consent, be put on probation if the court that finds him guilty thinks fit. Probation is a voluntary order and is used only when the offender could be sent to prison, but needs guidance to help him out of trouble.

When a court orders probation

The aim of probation is rehabilitation of an offender. If a court orders probation, the offender must agree to be supervised by a probation officer for the period of the order – which can be between 1 and 3 years. If he does not consent, the court must impose another sentence.

When an offender agrees to probation

Many of the people placed on probation are first offenders or young people, and a probation officer is required to 'assist, advise and befriend' any person who is placed under his supervision.

Probation orders impose conditions on the offender. The usual conditions are that he shall be of good behaviour and lead an industrious life; that he will tell the probation officer of any change of address or employment; and that he will keep in touch with the probation officer according to his instructions.

Most people on probation are allowed to live in their own homes, but an offender may be required to live in a home or hostel – especially if he is a young person with a disturbed home life.

Some orders require the offender to attend a day training centre for counselling and advice, or to undergo medical or psychiatric treatment.

When a probation order is broken

If someone on probation breaks the terms of his order he can be brought before the magistrates again and sentenced for his original offence.

If the breach is not serious, the magistrates will usually allow the probation order to continue, and may impose a fine of up to £50 or if the offender is under 21 order him to attend a community or attendance centre.

If a person commits another criminal offence while on probation, the court can end his probation and sentence him for both the original and the new offences. The magistrates can send him to prison for up to 6 months – or to a detention centre if he is under 21 – or impose a fine of up to £50.

The fact that he was on probation when he committed the offence will be taken into account and probably increase the severity of the sentence.

A court can end a probation order at any time. But it will usually do so only if the probation officer thinks that probation is no longer necessary. In such cases, when a report has been received from the probation officer, the court will generally agree to cancel the probation order and substitute a conditional discharge.

PROBATIONARY EMPLOYEE

Special rules governing new staff

Probationers have exactly the same rights and duties as other recruits.

The basic rights and obligations are contained in the EMPLOYMENT CONTRACT which a probationer, like any other employee, concludes with his employer. The contract defines wages, and terms and conditions – for example, sick pay arrangements. If it is not in writing, its details may be inferred from a collective agreement, if there is one, from custom and practice, or simply from the stated intention of the parties.

Most recruits, whether on trial or not, do not benefit at first from the rights conferred under the EMPLOYMENT PROTECTION rules, because those require minimum periods of service – for example, 4 weeks to qualify for statutory minimum NOTICE and 52 weeks to be able to claim UNFAIR DISMISSAL.

However, if an employee who is put for a trial period into a new job has until then worked for the same employer in another capacity, that counts as continuous employment, and he carries his acquired rights with him.

Under the job-protection rules, service begins from the day on which the employee starts work, not from the end of any trial period. So an employer cannot use a trial to diminish an employee's rights – for example, by making a trial last for longer than 52 weeks to try to evade the law on unfair dismissal.

The Employment Act 1980 allows small businesses of 20 or fewer employees to impose a trial period of up to 2 years. Those employees cannot claim unfair dismissal until they have been employed for 2 years, as long as the employer told them in writing when they were engaged that they were on trial for that time.

When a trial period ends

An employer can make a trial period as long or as short as he wishes. What law applies when it ends depends in part upon how long it was and in part upon the employment contract. For example, the contract might specifically confer more favourable conditions on the employee than are required by law.

If the trial was for less than 4 weeks, the employer is obliged only to give 'reasonable' notice. In practice, that means that he can dismiss the employee at any time simply by paying him for work done and telling him he is no longer required.

If the trial is for 4 weeks or more, the employer is required to give 1 week's notice of dismissal, unless the employee has been guilty of a serious fault that renders him liable to instant sacking. *See:* DISCIPLINE AT WORK

If the trial is for less than 52 weeks, the employer can dismiss the employee, no matter how good he may have proved himself at his job, without giving any reason – provided that no sex or race discrimination is involved and that the employee is not being dismissed for belonging to a trade union.

In normal cases, after the 52 weeks, the employer may be open to a claim for unfair dismissal unless he can show that the sacking was justified and that he followed the proper dismissal procedures. It may be easier for an employer to justify the dismissal if the employee was a probationer. *See:* UNFAIR DISMISSAL

If, at the end of a trial period, the employer does not confirm the probationer's appointment, but merely allows him to continue work, then his appointment is assumed in law to have been confirmed as permanent and all the normal protections apply to him.

Wages during a trial period are fixed by the employment contract. Unless specifically agreed, they are based upon the 'going rate for the job', which may be defined by custom and practice, by collective agreement or, in some low-paid occupations, by Wage Council order.

Some employers pay probationers below the normal rate, with the promise of a rise as soon as the appointment is confirmed. They are within their rights, provided that they observe any applicable collective agreement or wages order.

If a probationer leaves

If an employee accepts that he is to work for a trial period and leaves before it ends, he cannot claim unpaid wages for the days worked, because he is in breach of contract.

Legally, he is obliged to complete the trial period, or to give the employer the same notice as he was entitled to receive. In theory, his employer can sue him to recover any wages paid to which he was not entitled because of breach of contract. In practice, few employers bother because of the costs involved.

PROCESSION

*Organising a march through
the streets*

If you want to organise a march or procession – perhaps for a political or religious cause – it is best to ask police permission beforehand.

Although individuals have a right to use the highway, the police have a right to regulate the route of processions and to redirect traffic and pedestrians where necessary.

These powers apply to all processions and not just to demonstrations and protest marches. They apply, for example, to Scout marches, student rag processions and religious 'walks'.

Police decisions on processions are final. However, they have no general right to ban a procession altogether, though they can ask for a ban in certain circumstances.

If a chief officer of police believes that a particular procession may cause serious disorder, he can impose whatever directions he thinks necessary to keep the peace.

He can, for example, restrict the use of flags and banners if he thinks their use will provoke disorder. Anyone who wilfully disobeys such directions can be fined up to £500 or imprisoned for 3 months by a magistrates' court.

When police seek a ban

If the chief of police thinks that his forces are inadequate to prevent serious public disorder, he can ask the local authority to seek an order from the Home Secretary banning processions for 3 months. In London, the Commissioner of Police can apply directly to the Home Secretary for an order.

Anyone who defies such an order can be fined up to £500 or imprisoned for 3 months.

Organisers of a procession cannot appeal against police directions or against a banning order by the Home Secretary.

How to apply for permission

Before making any public announcement about a procession, get in touch with your local police headquarters – or, in London, with the A8 Branch at Scotland Yard.

Police will want to know the purpose of the march, its date, time and route, and how many people are likely to take part.

They may suggest an alternative time or route, so that they can provide enough police for the march or keep the marchers away from main traffic thoroughfares.

You would not, for example, be given permission to march down Oxford Street in London on a Saturday afternoon when it is packed with shoppers – but you might be allowed to do so on a Sunday morning.

The police cannot charge a fee for policing a procession, as they do for keeping the peace at, say, a football match within a stadium.

Staging a procession

It is not an offence to stage a procession without police permission, but the police are entitled to arrest marchers for obstructing the highway – a power they would use only if the participants behaved unreasonably in an unapproved procession.

Anyone refusing to move on when ordered to do so can be arrested and charged with obstructing the police.

See also: DEMONSTRATION
OBSTRUCTION
PUBLIC MEETING

PROFESSIONAL NEGLIGENCE

When an expert's professional skill is in question

When you engage a professional – for example, a solicitor, accountant, or doctor – to do something for you, you generally enter into some kind of CONTRACT with him.

If he then fails to perform the task he has undertaken satisfactorily you are entitled to sue him for breach of contract and to recover damages to compensate for any loss you have incurred.

If, however, you have no contract with the professional involved – for example, you have no direct contract with your National Health Service doctor – you cannot sue for breach of contract. Instead you must sue for negligence, and be able to show that he has in some way fallen short of what could reasonably be expected of him.

Even when there is a contract, moreover, it may not specify what degree of skill is to be exercised.

There are in every profession generally accepted standards. If you think that someone working on your behalf has not used the proper degree of skill, try to find another expert in the same field who would be willing to testify that your expert failed in his duty to you.

In medicine, for example, you would have to find one senior doctor willing to give evidence that another should have acted differently and better.

Finding such experts to give evidence on your behalf in a negligence claim is a specialist job for which you should engage a solicitor experienced in handling actions for professional negligence. Seek the advice of your local Citizens Advice Bureau.

When someone else is involved

When the person who is injured or who suffers some other kind of loss did not have a direct contract with the ex-

---

WHEN THE POLICE REFUSED TO BAN A MARCH

Sometimes a local council may ask the police to seek an order banning a march – and the police can refuse.

When the right-wing National Front proposed to march through Lewisham, a London borough with a large immigrant population, Lewisham Council asked the Commissioner for the Metropolitan Police to apply to the Home Secretary for an order banning the procession.

The Commissioner refused, so the council applied to the High Court for an INJUNCTION against the march. But this too was refused, after the court was as-

sured by the Commissioner that his force could control the procession.

The march took place in 1977 amid considerable violence. Some 270 policemen were hurt – 56 of them were taken to hospital – and more than 100 members of the public were injured.

Some months later the National Front planned another march through Hyde, Manchester, and the Chief Constable of Manchester asked Tameside Council to apply for a ban on the march. The council asked the Home Secretary, who ordered the ban and the march was cancelled.

pert responsible, the claim cannot be for breach of contract but for negligence only. He also has in that situation to be able to show that the professional had some special duty of care to third parties as well as to the people to whom he was contracted to do the work.

For example, if a wall falls down and injures a passer-by as a result of the negligence of an architect, the passer-by would usually be able to convince a court that the architect did indeed have a duty to ensure that the wall did not collapse and injure innocent people.

When you might have a claim

Many claims for professional negligence never come to court because the expert involved prefers to settle the claim out of court for an agreed sum rather than risk having his reputation publicly smeared.

In other cases, action is not taken because the client does not realise that he might have a winnable claim. For example, you would be justified in seeking damages for professional negligence if:
● A solicitor loses a case because he was not aware of a legal loophole that he should have known.
● An insurance broker recommends an insurance policy simply because it earns him higher commission when he should have offered one that gave you better terms.
● A doctor should have diagnosed an illness months earlier.
● A bank manager or financial adviser suggests you should buy shares when a more careful market analysis would tell him that they were very risky as an investment.
● An accountant fails to tell you of expenses for which you could have justifiably claimed against your income tax.

When the expert tries to escape liability

A professional can rarely limit his liability legally. For example, when a surveyor agrees to carry out a 'full' survey of a house you are buying and states in his report that he has not examined the property for dry rot or structural conditions, his exemption clause is not valid in law. If he fails to advise you properly and you suffer as a result, you can still sue him for negligence. Only if he restricts what he is going to do at the time he enters into an agreement or contract with you can he fully escape liability later.

PROPERTY INSURANCE

Protecting your home and its contents against damage or loss

Home-owners need two kinds of INSURANCE to protect their property – one to safeguard the premises, including outbuildings, and the other to cover the contents. The two are often combined in a single INSURANCE POLICY, called a 'dwelling and contents' scheme, but they can be taken out separately. However, separate arrangements may complicate the process of making an INSURANCE CLAIM, if the policies are with different insurers.

There is no legal obligation to insure either your home or its contents. But if the property is mortgaged, the building society or other organisation helping with the finance will insist that the building is covered.

Household contents insurance usually covers not only the items in the house and outbuildings, but also third-party claims for damages by accident – for example, if you unwittingly cause an injury to someone else – up to a maximum of £250,000. (Household buildings policies also cover third-party liability.)

For people living in rented accommodation, a contents policy generally provides protection against accidental damage to the landlord's property. Insurers indicate the perils covered under this section and modern practice tends to include all the perils listed under the next two headings, but limits the sum payable to 10 per cent or 20 per cent of the total amount insured on contents.

Basic insurance for any building

All insurance policies for buildings give protection against damage by fire and the related hazards of lightning and explosion. *See:* FIRE INSURANCE

Five other perils can be added to the basic fire cover:
● Civil disturbances – for example, a RIOT or labour dispute.
● Damage by aircraft or items dropped from them, although damage by sonic boom cannot be claimed.
● Storm and floods.
● Leaks from tanks, pipes and other water apparatus – for example, a washing machine.
● Earthquakes.

'Storm' does not include persistent or heavy rain unless accompanied by high winds. 'Storms and floods' do not include damage by frost, subsidence or landslip or damage to fences, gates and hoardings.

Most insurance companies meet the full amount of claims for earthquake, or aircraft damage, but may require the policyholder to pay part of the cost of damage in the other categories – for example, the first £15.

The cover for water leaks does not include the cost of repairing the leak itself except, usually, in the case of pipes burst by frost.

Extra protection for dwellings

Insurance policies for houses and other dwellings include a further series of risks, in addition to those in a basic fire and additional perils policy. However, the precise arrangements vary, so check before taking out a policy.

The extra perils most commonly featured in a dwellings policy are:
● Damage to the building caused by theft or attempted theft.
● Impact by a road vehicle or animal, although the compensation may be limited or excluded if the vehicle or animal belongs to the house-owner or his family.
● Leakage from oil-fired heating apparatus, provided that it is an installation and not, for example, a movable paraffin stove.
● Frost damage, landslip and subsidence when the cost of the damage is more than a certain figure – say £500.
● Accidental breakage of glass in windows and doors, and of sanitary fittings.
● Accidental damage to underground gas, water, oil and sewer pipes, drains and underground electricity and telephone cables.
● Damage caused to the building by the collapse or breakage of radio and television aerials, fittings and masts. The cost of replacing the aerial is often excluded, although most insurance companies will pay if it is brought down by a storm.

Some dwellings policies exclude

PROSECUTION

damage caused by falling trees or branches. Others include that risk, and the collapse of telegraph poles and lighting standards as well.

Safeguarding the contents

Household contents policies cover the items within a home against theft, fire, flooding and the other listed perils included in most dwelling (buildings) policies, with one possible exception. Some insurance companies do not reimburse the cost of damage to household goods caused by the collapse of a radio or TV aerial.

Some articles are subject to restrictions unless you make special arrangements with the insurance company and pay a higher premium. They are works of art, stamp collections, furs, jewellery, and articles of gold, silver and other precious metals. Most policies limit the compensation payable for any one item in those categories to 5 per cent of the total sum insured, and also stipulate that the total value of all items in those categories must not exceed one-third of the overall value of the entire contents of the home. Although some insurers do not include works of art and stamp collections in this latter limitation.

For example, if the contents of your home are insured for £10,000 and include a valuable painting, you will not receive more than 5 per cent of £10,000 – that is, £500 if the painting is stolen. If you have several furs, and some valuable jewellery as well, the most you will get is one-third of £10,000 – that is, £3,333.

There is also a limit – usually £50 or £100 – on the compensation for loose cash in the house.

Items kept in the open – for example, garden furniture – are excluded.

Household contents policies do not cover articles accidentally lost or mislaid, for example, an engagement ring dropped down a sink.

The accidental breakage of mirrors, glass tops and fixed glass in furniture is included in most policies.

Losses outside the home

Household contents – including the clothes you are wearing – are covered against the perils listed in the policy if they are temporarily removed from your home and are in another building – for example, an office, hotel or laundry

or cleaners. They are also protected if they are in a bank or safe deposit, although the insurance company may limit the compensation it pays in all such cases.

To protect valuable items in transit, you should take out ALL-RISKS INSURANCE.

If you work from home

Household contents policies are intended for private dwellings. If you frequently work from home, you should check that a normal contents policy is adequate to suit your needs, in particular if the business involves the use of expensive equipment not usually found in a house or if clients or customers regularly visit the premises. *See:* HOME WORKER

Most insurance companies offer special policies for people whose home and business premises are combined, for example shopkeepers.

Taking in lodgers

If part of a house is let, the insurance company may impose additional restrictions on the owner's dwelling and contents policy. In every case, the insurers must be informed of the letting arrangements. In particular, to claim for theft, the owner may need to show that the thief entered by forcible or violent means.

Which policy to choose?

Insurance companies offer three types of comprehensive dwelling and contents policies.

Indemnity policies An indemnity policy limits compensation to the amount needed to restore buildings or household contents to the state they were in

---

THE MOVING EARTH

Insurance policies that give protection against landslip and subsidence do not automatically cover a third common type of earth movement called 'heave'.

Heave is caused by excessive moisture in the ground, which buckles upwards, but does not shift sideways or downwards, as it does in landslip or subsidence.

Until recently, insurance companies did not accept claims for damage caused by heave. Check your policy to see that it is specifically mentioned.

---

before the damage occurred. The insured person may therefore have to pay part of the cost of rebuilding or replacement, because of previous wear and tear. Indemnity policies are the cheapest of the three.

New-for-old policies Under a new-for-old policy, the insurance company does not make a deduction for wear and tear, but agrees to provide the cost of a new replacement. However, the holder may forfeit part of his compensation if he fails to keep the building in good condition. If a damaged item is capable of being repaired, the company may pay only the repair cost.

Depending on the policy, some items may not be included in the new-for-old arrangement but are covered only by an indemnity scheme. Household linen and clothing are usually excluded. Some companies impose an age limit, and apply the new-for-old rules only to articles that are less than 2, 3 or 5 years old.

All-risks policies An all-risk policy is the most expensive of the three, but covers the widest range of perils, including accidental damage. It incorporates a new-for-old replacement scheme, but holders may have to pay the first £10 or £15 of claims for damage to a building.

Ensuring that the cover is adequate

The sum insured under any dwelling and contents policy should be adequate to cover the full value of the property at risk, or the insurance company may 'average' the claim and pay only a proportion of the cost. *See:* FIRE INSURANCE

Most companies now offer index-linked schemes, in which the value of the building is automatically adjusted according to a housing cost scale prepared by the Royal Institute of Chartered Surveyors, and the value of the contents is tied to the official retail price index. That arrangement takes account of the effects of inflation, and premiums are automatically increased at each renewal date to reflect the rise in the amount of cover.

PROSECUTION

When a suspect is taken to court

Most prosecutions for criminal of-

584

fences are brought by the police. *See:* CRIMINAL PROCEEDINGS

Private individuals can also prosecute for many offences – even when the police have decided not to. *See:* PRIVATE PROSECUTION

PROSTITUTION

Offering sex for money

It is not unlawful for a woman over 16 to accept payment in return for sexual services, nor does a man commit an offence when he pays to have sex. But prostitutes and their protectors can be prosecuted for several offences – though their clients are almost always within the law.

It is an offence to drive a woman into prostitution. To use threats, intimidation or false pretence to procure her to have sexual intercourse can be punished by up to 2 years in gaol and an unlimited fine.

A man who lives off the earnings of a prostitute – even if she is his wife – can be fined up to £1,000 or be sent to prison for up to 6 months. If magistrates decide to send him for trial to a crown court, or if he opts for crown court trial, he can be sentenced to 7 years' imprisonment and be fined an unlimited amount.

A newsagent who allows prostitutes to advertise in his window can face the same charge.

It is an offence to keep a brothel – a place where two or more prostitutes receive clients. If two prostitutes share a flat, for example, they can be charged with keeping a brothel even though their sexual activities are entirely legal. The penalty is 3 months' imprisonment and/or a fine of £100 for a first offence, 6 months and £250 for subsequent convictions.

Although prostitutes can make appointments by telephone or letter – call-girls, for example, do not break the law – they are prosecuted for SOLICITING if they tout for custom in a public place. The penalty is a £50 fine for a first offence, £200 for a second and £200 or 3 months' imprisonment for subsequent convictions.

A homosexual male prostitute who solicits, or a man who seeks customers on behalf of a female prostitute, is guilty

WHEN AIDING AND ABETTING IS ILLEGAL

Anyone who charges for allowing a prostitute to advertise her services can be prosecuted for 'living off her immoral earnings'.

of importuning. They can be fined up to £1,000 and gaoled for 6 months by a magistrates' court, or face an unlimited fine and 2 years' imprisonment in the crown court.

A man who pesters women for prostitution in a public place can be charged with insulting behaviour likely to cause a BREACH OF THE PEACE.

When a prostitute is under age

There are particularly severe penalties for using a child prostitute – even if the client believed the child to be of age:
● Anyone who has sexual intercourse with a girl under 13 – even if she solicited him – or who has homosexual relations with a boy under 16, can be sentenced to life imprisonment.
● Anyone who has intercourse with a girl aged between 13 and 16 can be sentenced to 2 years' imprisonment, unless he had reasonable grounds to believe she was of age, was himself under 24 and had never previously been charged with such an offence.
● Homosexual relations with a boy aged between 16 and 21 are punishable by 5 years' imprisonment if the offender is over 21. If he is younger he can be sentenced to only 2 years' gaol.
● Gross indecency with a child under 14 carries a maximum sentence of 2 years' gaol.
● A parent or guardian who procures or allows a child in his or her care to be-

come a prostitute can be sentenced to 2 years' imprisonment.
● When a child prostitute is found by police, he or she is rarely prosecuted for soliciting but is generally taken into care. *See:* CHILDREN IN CARE

PROVOCATION

A defence against a murder charge

A person accused of MURDER can plead provocation in his defence.

If he can show that he was provoked by the victim beyond a point where a reasonable man would lose his self-control, then the charge against him will be reduced to one of MANSLAUGHTER.

Courts have held that a reasonable man would not be provoked into killing his wife if she *told* him she had committed adultery.

They have also held that he would probably be provoked if he saw his wife committing adultery, but not if he saw his mistress committing adultery.

Provocation is not a defence in less serious charges such as causing grievous BODILY HARM. But it can be pleaded in mitigation of such charges.

Charges involving young people

When a young person is charged with murder, the question of provocation is related to the circumstances when applied to a reasonable person of the same age as the person accused.

PUBLIC HOUSE

A place to drink – under certain conditions

In law, a public house is a private house from which the public can be barred or asked to leave at the discretion of the landlord.

Unlike a HOTEL there is no automatic right to enter a public house, unless it offers accommodation and food to travellers – becoming, therefore, an inn or hotel.

If the only reason for a landlord's refusal to serve a customer is race or sex, he would be guilty of an offence. *See:* LIQUOR OFFENCES
RACIAL DISCRIMINATION
SEX DISCRIMINATION

How opening times are extended

A publican can apply to the licensing magistrates for an extension of opening hours by asking for:
● A special order of exemption, which allows an extension for a special occasion only, such as a General Election day. A regular event like a weekly dance is *not* a special occasion.
● A supper-hour certificate, which allows drinks to be sold for an extra hour if they are being served with meals as an ordinary part of the house's trade, but in a place separate from the bar.
● An extended-hours order, for an extension of the supper-hour certificate until 1 a.m. if there is live music and entertainment with the meal. TV, radio and films are *not* live entertainment.
● A special-hours certificate, by which hours may be extended up to 2 a.m., or 3 a.m. in inner London, if the licensee also has a music and dancing licence.
● A general order of exemption, allowing a permanent alteration of normal opening hours in areas like markets or docks, so that those working unsocial hours can get refreshment.

When children may and may not be in a public house

Any child over the age of 5 can drink beer, wine or even spirits in a public house so long as they are not in a bar and the drink is not bought by the child.

Children under 14 must not enter a bar or anywhere else in a public house where liquor is sold, except to pass through on their way to a restaurant, playroom or lavatory.

A child between 14 and 18 is allowed into a bar but cannot buy or drink liquor there. Children over 16 can, however, buy beer, cider or perry – but not wine – to drink with a meal in a pub restaurant. They cannot drink even shandy at the bar.

The right measure

A public house must serve whisky, gin, rum or vodka in measures of one-sixth, one-fifth or one-quarter of a gill. A gill is a quarter-pint. In England and Wales the usual measure is one-sixth of a gill.

A notice must be displayed saying which measure is being served in the pub, but those regulations do not apply

---

PUBLICAN'S POWER

In law, a public house is a private house from which the public can be barred or where they can be refused service (except on race or sex grounds) entirely at the landlord's discretion.

'Sorry, sir, but I think you've had enough'

---

to any other spirits, including liqueurs.

Most public houses sell draught beer in pints or half-pints. Regulations say it must be served in measures of one-third, one-half or multiples of one-half of a pint.

Glasses or mugs used for draught beer or cider must have the same cap-acity as the drink ordered, except when the glass has an engraved line to show the correct measure, or automatic measuring pumps are installed.

The 'long pull' A barman who gives more than the exact measure – known in the trade as giving the 'long pull' – is also breaking the law and can be fined up to £30.

The licensing of public houses

The licence needed to run a pub is called an 'on-licence'. It allows the licensee or his staff to sell intoxicating liquor to be drunk on the premises or taken away.

Licences that allow the sale of liquor for taking away and drinking elsewhere are called off-licences.

To obtain a licence the publican must apply to the local magistrates' court at the annual brewster sessions, when the magistrates consider applications both for the granting and renewal of liquor licences.

Sometimes there are conditions attached to the granting of a licence – in a holiday town the licence might operate only during the tourist season.

Objecting to a licence

Somebody who is persistently denied

WHEN PUBLIC HOUSES ARE OPEN		
	London	**Outside London**
Monday–Saturday	11 a.m. – 3 p.m. 5.30 p.m. – 11 p.m.	11 a.m. – 3 p.m. 5.30 p.m. – 10.30 p.m.
Sunday, Christmas Day and Good Friday	12 noon – 2 p.m. 7 p.m. – 10.30 p.m.	12 noon – 2 p.m. 7 p.m. – 10.30 p.m.

Opening hours for public houses may vary slightly in different parts of the United Kingdom, but the Licensing Act 1964 lays down the above general rules.

In some parts of Wales, public houses do not open on Sundays.

Outside London, licensing magistrates may extend the evening hours to 11 p.m.

They can also vary the hours so long as the total daily opening time does not exceed 9 hours – or 9½ if the evening has been extended to 11 p.m.

On Sundays an extension to 11 p.m. may also be granted.

These are *maximum* hours of opening: a licensee can open for shorter hours if he

wishes – but may find his licence renewal application opposed by someone who thinks he is not providing a 'reasonable service to the public'.

Drinking-up time An extra 10 minutes is allowed after closing time for customers to finish their drinks – 30 minutes if the drink was supplied to be consumed with a meal on the premises.

No drinks may be bought in that extra time, and any drink unfinished when the time expires must be left.

It is an offence even to take the unfinished drink out of the public house after the drinking-up time. *See:* LIQUOR OFFENCES

service in a public house without good reason or who is in some other way dissatisfied with the way in which it is run can oppose the renewal of its liquor licence.

He can attend the local magistrates' court when the licensee of the public house applies for renewal of the licence at the annual brewster sessions.

Dates of the hearings are advertised in the local Press, or they can be found by telephoning the magistrates' clerk.

When you are objecting to the granting of a licence you do not have to give notice to the applicant, but if you wish to object to the renewal of a licence, you should give the licensee written notice, 7 days before the hearing.

However, if an objector fails to give notice he may still be able to voice his objection, because magistrates can waive the need to give notice.

At the hearing, evidence is given on oath, so an objector may have to go into the witness box. If he can provide the magistrates with evidence that the licensee has failed to give a proper service to the public, the magistrates can refuse to renew the licence. *See also:* LIQUOR OFFENCES

Complaining about drinks

If you think you have been given a short or watered measure of beer or spirits in a public house, complain to the local council's trading standards

---

ON THE SLATE

A customer should never ask a landlord for a drink 'on the slate', meaning that he will pay at some time in the future.

It is illegal to sell liquor in a public house on credit and the licensee – not the customer – can be fined up to £50.

GAMBLING IN A PUBLIC HOUSE

Betting, or passing a betting slip in a public house is illegal, except when there is a room licensed for betting.

Games of skill like darts, billiards or shove ha'penny can be played with no legal restrictions on stakes. But the landlord has a right to limit the stakes.

Other traditional pub games in which there is a chance element such as cribbage or dominoes also come into that category.

Any other games of chance, such as cards or dice, can be played only if the landlord has a permit from the licensing magistrates – and then only for small stakes of perhaps 10p or 20p.

Gaming machines – 'one-armed bandits' – are permitted under certain conditions, and lotteries and sweepstakes are allowed. *See:* GAMBLING

---

or consumer protection department.

After a complaint, an officer from the department usually visits the public house and makes a test purchase without revealing his identity. He measures the drink and – in the case of spirits – may also test the optic measure, from which it was poured, for inaccuracy.

The officer will make at least two or three test purchases perhaps even on different occasions to establish whether there is a pattern of short-measure drinks.

If the officer's tests show that short measure has been given, he will tell the landlord, who may be prosecuted under the Weights and Measures Act for selling spirits or beer in short measure or not in the prescribed quantity. The maximum penalty for a first offence is a £100 fine: for a second offence it is a £250 fine.

Anyone who has made a complaint may be asked to give evidence in court, but he is not obliged to do so.

Beer is classified as food, so if you complain about watered-down beer, any test sample may be examined by the public analyst.

PUBLIC LIABILITY INSURANCE

Insuring against claims from other people

The purpose of a public liability insurance policy is to protect the person insured against liability for the accidental death of or accidental injury to someone other than his employee while at work. It may also include damage to the property of others, including employees. It may be a separate policy or part of another one, for example, a householder's policy.

Instead of using the word 'accidental', some insurers make an exception of 'inevitable' injury or damage.

The policy can be general, covering any kind of accident to anyone other than employers covered by an EMPLOYER'S LIABILITY policy. It can also be limited by a maximum sum that can be claimed in 1 year or in a single accident.

If the accident results in the person insured being sued and the insurance company thinks the claim should be resisted in court, the company pays the legal costs.

PUBLIC LIBRARY

Your right to use a library service

Any person is entitled to join a public library and use its lending facilities provided that he is either a resident, has a place of work or is receiving full-time education in the area. Some authorities, however, impose a minimum age limit.

If you wish to join your local public library, ask at the library's inquiry desk. In most cases, you will be asked to produce some proof of your residence, work or full-time education in the area.

If you are eligible, the library will issue you with a ticket – usually valid for at least 1 to 3 years – which entitles you to borrow from it. Some libraries issue a number of tickets – usually about four – and the borrower hands over one ticket for every book he borrows. He is returned the ticket when he brings the book back.

Some libraries have a rule limiting the proportion of fiction to non-fiction books that may be borrowed. In other cases, libraries make special arrangements for lending books – for example, allowing teachers to take out more than the permitted number of books.

Obeying the library rules

A person who joins a library must abide by its rules concerning the length of borrowing time – usually from 3 to 4 weeks – and, under local bye-laws, pay any fines for not returning a book in time, or for defacing or losing it. A library may also make a small charge if a person wishes to reserve a book.

When a person is on library premises he is subject to any local bye-law in force that concerns libraries. For example, he may be required to keep reasonably quiet in the reading room, or smoking in the library may be prohibited.

USING THE LIBRARY SERVICE

Anyone is entitled to use a library reading room – whether he is a member or not. He must, however, obey all the relevant library bye-laws when he is on the premises.

SILENCE

If a person infringes a bye-law he may be fined, usually not more than £20, in a magistrates' court.

If a person is on holiday, he may be able to borrow a book from the library where he is staying, provided that he produces his home library ticket.

The responsibility of running a library service lies with your county or district council, depending on the area in which you live. A local authority is required by law to provide a comprehensive and efficient library service.

Other library services

Many libraries now lend gramophone records, tapes or pictures either free or for a small charge. They may also provide other facilities – for example, large-type books for readers with poor eyesight, or special sections for children and blind people.

They also provide a range of magazines, daily and local newspapers in reading rooms, information leaflets from government departments and other bodies, and minutes of local council meetings.

If you cannot find a book at your local library, ask the library to obtain it from another library through the 'inter-library loan' service. You will be able to borrow the book, provided that it has not been reserved at another library.

If you are still unable to obtain the book, complain to your local councillor or the chairman of your council's lib-

raries committee. To find the name of your councillor or the committee chairman, ask at your local council offices.

If the book you are unable to obtain is of an educational nature, write to the Secretary of State for Education and Science and tell him that your own library and other branches have been unable to obtain the book for you.

The complaint will be investigated and the Secretary of State may, if necessary, order the local authority to improve its library service as well as supply the book you require.

Protesting about books

If you feel a certain book should not appear on the shelves of a public library you may complain to the Chief Librarian, or County Librarian who can raise the issue with the library committee. If it takes no action, you may start a campaign in the local newspapers or seek the help of your councillors and Member of Parliament.

PUBLIC MEETING

Where and when you may hold a rally

Everyone is entitled to express his views in public and to canvass support for them, provided he does so lawfully. It is an offence, for example, to incite racial hatred or provoke violence in a public speech, or to obstruct the police in exercising their right to maintain PUBLIC ORDER.

Holding a meeting on private premises

If you want to hold a meeting on private land or in a hall, you must first

obtain the consent – preferably in writing – of the owner. Make sure that he knows the purpose of the meeting and its likely size, so that he cannot later withdraw permission by claiming that he was not given all the necessary information.

The owner is entitled to refuse consent without giving a reason, but may not discriminate against you on grounds of race or sex. He may impose conditions – such as restricting the size of the meeting, or the time at which it must end – and demand a fee for the use of his property and a deposit against possible damage by your meeting.

If, for example, you want to hold a meeting in the town hall or public library, you require permission from its lawful owner, the LOCAL AUTHORITY. Like a private landlord, a local authority can impose conditions or refuse permission, except during an election – general or local – when all candidates have a right to use schools and certain other meeting places, upon payment of a reasonable fee.

If the authority refuses permission unreasonably for a non-election meeting – if, for example, it allows the hunt association to use a school hall one week, but turns down a request from an anti-hunt group for the following week – you can try to persuade individual councillors that the decision was unfair and should be reversed. Legally, however, you have no right to appeal.

If you use private property for a meeting without the owner's consent, he can sue you for TRESPASS. Alternatively, if he sees notices of the meeting, he can obtain a court INJUNCTION to prevent you from using his property.

Even when a meeting is to be held on private premises, it is advisable to warn

PUBLIC MEETINGS IN LONDON

Special regulations apply to public meetings in certain parts of London:
● Open-air political meetings of more than 50 people are generally forbidden within 1 mile of the Houses of Parliament, on the north side of the Thames, on days when Parliament is sitting. The ban is designed to allow Members easy access to Parliament and to prevent a mob from approaching it.
● If you want to hold a meeting in Trafal-

gar Square or Hyde Park – except for Speakers' Corner – you need permission from the Department of the Environment. There is no right to appeal. Speakers' Corner is controlled by the Ceremonial Office (Scotland Yard) at Cannon Row.
● You must give the police 48 hours' notice if a loudspeaker is to be used. You may not use a hailer to call people to a meeting, only to announce its place and time.

> ## THE POLICEMEN WHO WERE NOT INVITED
>
> *Police may attend a public meeting on private premises if they suspect that a breach of the peace is likely.*
>
> An inspector and two sergeants of the Glamorgan County Police were refused admission to Caerau Library Hall, where the Communist Party was holding a meeting to protest against the Incitement to Disaffection Bill and to demand the dismissal of the Chief Constable of Glamorgan. They entered nonetheless and sat down in the front row.
>
> Alan Thomas, a speaker at the meeting, asked them to leave, but they refused. He told them they would be
>
> ejected and laid his hand on the inspector's arm. Sergeant Sawkins pushed his hand away and a scuffle ensued. Thomas sued the sergeant for ASSAULT AND BATTERY.
>
> ### DECISION
>
> Sergeant Sawkins was found not guilty.
>
> The magistrates held that the police had a right to attend a meeting where they had reasonable cause to believe that, in their absence, there would be a breach of the peace and seditious speeches would be made.
>
> Thomas appealed to the High Court, but his appeal was turned down.

the police if the audience is to be large. They may wish to regulate traffic around the site, or to police the meeting if there is a possibility of violent clashes. Although the police are not entitled to attend meetings on private premises, they may enter if they reasonably suspect that a BREACH OF THE PEACE is likely to occur.

You have committed no offence if you do not inform the police about such a meeting, but if there is trouble they are more likely to press charges against the participants than if they had been forewarned.

Often, when uninvited, the police attend meetings in plain clothes.

As such, they have the same rights as other members of the public and you can refuse them admission if you so wish.

When a public meeting is held on private land, the organisers have the right to restrict admission to those whom they choose. They can also charge an admission fee and use reasonable force to eject anyone who enters without paying or without their consent. A reasonable number of stewards, issued with badges or armbands, may be used to keep the peace and remove trouble-makers.

Holding a meeting in public

Nobody has the right to hold a public meeting on a highway: the only right you have there is to 'pass and repass'. Nor is there any automatic right to hold meetings in public places such as parks. If you want to stage a meeting there, you need permission of the body that

owns and controls the land – usually the local authority.

Local authorities have power to make BYE-LAWS for the use of their parks. In addition they often have bye-laws regulating public meetings – allowing them only in certain places and under specific conditions – which generally require the organisers of a meeting to give notice both to the town hall and to the police. Find out what bye-laws are in force before organising the meeting.

It is always advisable to discuss a meeting in advance with the officer in charge of the local police station, particularly if it is a mass gathering, even if it is not required by the bye-laws. The police can suggest a change of time or venue for the meeting, with the object of minimising public disturbance.

You do not have to accept their suggestions, but by not doing so you increase the risk that the police will have to disperse the meeting for causing an obstruction. *See:* PROCESSION

Keeping order at meetings

Anyone has the right to heckle at a public meeting, provided he does not seriously disrupt the proceedings. If he does, he can be arrested and charged with trying to break up a lawful public meeting, for which the penalty is 6 months' imprisonment and a fine of up to £1,000.

Alternatively, he can be charged with using words or behaviour likely to cause a breach of the peace.

In public places, the organisers may not use stewards to keep order, but the police are entitled to attend.

PUBLIC ORDER

When an individual disturbs society

Anyone who behaves in a manner which the police consider is likely to cause a BREACH OF THE PEACE can be arrested.

For a first offence it is likely that the court will bind him over – that is ask him to agree to pay a sum of money if he commits a breach of the peace, or certain other offences, during some specified time in the future.

His behaviour does not have to include an act of physical violence. Anyone who uses threatening, abusive or insulting words that are considered likely to cause a breach of the peace can be charged with using ABUSIVE WORDS OR BEHAVIOUR.

If he makes remarks about Christianity that are considered likely to cause a breach of the peace, he may be charged with BLASPHEMY.

A person who threatened to use violence may be charged with assault, even if he does not strike a blow. *See:* ASSAULT AND BATTERY

If he acts recklessly and damages property he could face a charge of CRIMINAL DAMAGE.

Helping someone else to break the law

Anyone who is helping others to carry out a crime or encouraging others to commit a crime, can be arrested.

If he makes an agreement with two or more people to carry out a crime, even though the plan is not executed, he can be charged with CONSPIRACY.

Inciting another person to carry out a crime, whether or not the crime is committed or the other person is influenced by the incitement, is also an offence. *See:* INCITEMENT

Other charges that may be made

A person who does anything to make it more difficult for the police to carry out their duties can be charged with OBSTRUCTION, for example, stopping the police attending a meeting they have a right to attend.

Carrying an OFFENSIVE WEAPON in a public place is also an offence. Any item that is capable of causing injury may be considered an offensive weapon – for example, a spanner or a screwdriver. A steward at a public meeting is not entitled to carry a truncheon.

In many areas local authorities introduce BYE-LAWS to supplement the general law – for example, they may rule that it is to be a criminal offence to act in a disorderly manner in a park, museum or library. *See:* PUBLIC LIBRARY; PUBLIC PARK

Certain NOISE OFFENCES are also controlled by bye-laws, and a person may find he has contravened a bye-law by playing his transistor radio too loud on a public beach.

Controlling the behaviour of a group

Anyone attending a meeting or taking part in a protest march may innocently cause a breach of the peace by his behaviour and find himself arrested.

For example, any group that assembles or demonstrates, in the opinion of the senior police officer present, in a manner that could endanger public peace can be arrested and charged with unlawful assembly.

If a group of people displays any sort of force that could frighten others, even without using actual violence, a charge of causing an AFFRAY may be brought.

Three or more people who assemble with a common purpose and carry out their objective with force or with the threat of using force may be charged with riot.

Members of a procession or a protest march may be arrested for obstructing the highway if the march blocks a public highway or the members are distributing leaflets.

If a procession or demonstration is considered to be interfering with the public's enjoyment of its rights, it may be stopped on the ground that it is a public nuisance. For example, if a sit-in blocks what is usually a public thoroughfare, the protest may be considered a public nuisance.

Special rules for political groups

The activities of political groups are controlled by the Public Order Act 1936. For example, it is a criminal offence to organise or train members of an association so that they can use force to promote a political aim.

The maximum penalty in a magistrates' court is 6 months' imprisonment and a fine of £100, or 2 years' imprisonment and a £500 fine in a crown court.

It is also illegal to wear uniforms that signify an association with a political organisation or the promotion of a political objective.

Someone wearing a Sinn Fein black beret at a Sinn Fein rally in public, for example, could be charged under the Act. The maximum penalty in a magistrates' court is 3 months' imprisonment and/or a £500 fine.

The Prevention of TERRORISM Act in 1976 gave the police and army widespread powers to control public order:

for example, to detain without trial a person suspected of having committed an act of terrorism, or to enter and search private property without a warrant and without notice.

It is also illegal for a person to belong to or to finance any forbidden organisation or to address its meetings. Wearing uniforms or insignia associated with a banned organisation is also illegal.

PUBLIC PARK

Enjoying the fresh air

You have a right to use freely for recreation and open-air exercise any park or recreation ground that is owned and set aside for such purpose by a local authority – even if you do not live in their area.

Charges may be made for the use of some facilities, such as tennis courts or football pitches.

The bye-laws displayed at the park entrance must be observed. They generally regulate opening hours, prohibit the playing of organised games, require dogs to be kept on the lead and ban public meetings or demonstrations. If you do not obey a bye-law, you may be prosecuted and fined up to £20.

A council is entitled at any time to introduce new bye-laws, changing or restricting the use the public is entitled to make of its parks. It must, however, make sure that the new rules have the approval of the Secretary of State.

QUALITY OF GOODS

What a buyer is entitled to expect

Goods sold by a shop, or by anyone who is in business as a dealer, must be of 'merchantable quality'.

That means they must be reasonably fit for the use to which they are commonly put – and if the dealer knows the buyer's particular purpose, they must be reasonably fit for that purpose.

In deciding what is reasonable you have to take into account the description under which goods are sold. The price and other circumstances of the sale may also be relevant.

If you buy goods that turn out not to

....

DESCRIBING THE QUALITY

The description applied to goods by the seller and the price he charges for them help to determine the quality that the buyer has a right to expect.

be of merchantable quality, you may have a claim for:
● A refund of the purchase price.
● A reduction of the price, if the goods are not worth what you paid but you want to keep them.
● Compensation for the cost of repairing faulty goods.

THE CAR THAT WAS 'HARDLY RUN IN'

Goods must be reasonably fit for their common purpose – so a car must be suitable for driving.

When Mr C bought an 8-year-old Jaguar, the dealers told him that at 82,000 miles, a car of that type was 'hardly run in'.

After 3 weeks and a further 2,354 miles, the engine seized and had to be scrapped. C sued the dealers for the cost of a replacement engine.

The previous owner of the Jaguar told Southampton County Court that when he sold it to the dealers, he considered the engine to be clapped out, and not fit for use on a road.

C was awarded damages, but the dealers appealed. The Court of Appeal had to decide whether, at the price – £390 in 1972 – and in all the circumstances, the car was fit for its purpose.

DECISION

The judges ruled that the car's purpose was to be driven, and that it was not reasonably fit for that purpose. The dealers had to pay C's damages and costs.

But you cannot complain later about a defect that was specifically pointed out to you before you bought the goods.

Nor can you complain if you examined the goods before buying them, and should have noticed the defect yourself.

See also: DEFECTIVE GOODS
MONEY BACK
TRADE DESCRIPTION

QUARANTINE

Safety rules for bringing animals into Britain

To prevent the spread of rabies and other diseases, dogs, cats and most mammals must spend 6 months quarantined in special kennels or quarters when they are brought into Britain.

There are special regulations for plants, captive birds, farm livestock and horses.

The rules apply not only to animals brought into the country for the first time, but also to those returning after a visit abroad, however brief. The fact that an animal has been immunised makes no difference.

To bring an animal into Britain you must have a licence – which will not be granted until you have made the quarantine arrangements. The three main steps are:
1. You must book accommodation at a quarantine kennel selected from an official list which can be obtained from the Department of Animal Health, Ministry of Agriculture, Fisheries and Food, Tolworth House, Tolworth, Surbiton, Surrey KT6 7DX.
2. You must employ a carrying agent – usually a representative of the quarantine kennels – to collect the animal on landing as you are not permitted to take it to the kennels yourself.
3. Apply for a licence on form ID1, obtained from the Department of Animal Health, along with the list of quarantine kennels.

On the form you will be asked to state the port of entry. You must choose a port that has facilities for keeping animals for up to 48 hours until they can be taken to the quarantine kennels.

There are such facilities at Dover, Folkestone, Harwich, Hull, Liverpool, London, Tilbury and Newhaven sea-

ENFORCED SEPARATION

A special agent must be engaged to take an animal to quarantine kennels. The animal owner is not allowed to accompany it beyond the port or airport of entry.

ports; Ramsgate and Southampton hoverports; and Birmingham, Edinburgh, Gatwick, Glasgow, Heathrow, Leeds, Manchester and Prestwick airports.

The application form must be returned at least 4 weeks before the journey begins. The Ministry will issue a boarding document to be presented at the despatching point before the animal is allowed on the ship or plane.

Animals travelling by sea must be landed in a crate. Those going by air must travel the whole way in a crate.

Quarantine comfort and cost

The Ministry's approval of the quarantine kennels implies veterinary supervision and minimum standards of sleeping and exercise space according to weight. Animals other than cats and dogs usually spend their quarantine in private zoos. There are special regulations for plants, birds, farm livestock and horses.

The person who brings the animal in must pay the quarantine costs. Charges vary, but a typical bill might be £2 a day for a medium-size dog and £1 a day for a cat. In addition, charges for travel and vaccinations might amount to £50 per animal.

On arrival at the kennels the animal is given an anti-rabies vaccine. For that reason, and to allow it to settle, it is usually recommended that the owner does not visit for 14 days. Rules vary from kennel to kennel.

The penalties for evading quarantine regulations are: an unlimited fine and up to a year's imprisonment.

As a further protection against rabies, the imported animal may also be destroyed.

QUEEN'S PROCTOR

When an independent voice is needed in a divorce case

The Queen's Proctor, an officer of the Crown, independent of the courts and judiciary, is concerned only with divorce cases.

He may, at the invitation of the judge in a divorce case, intervene to argue a novel or difficult point of law.

The Queen's Proctor has, for example, been asked to argue the validity of a foreign marriage or divorce; and to help courts to decide what was wilful refusal to consummate a marriage and whether a marriage by proxy was valid.

When the Queen's Proctor suspects there is something irregular in the proceedings he can intervene uninvited – for example, if he receives information that a decree nisi was unjustly obtained. Anyone can inform the Queen's Proctor at 3 Central Buildings, Matthew Parker Street, London SW1Y 6EE, of any suspected irregularity in a divorce case. Every report is investigated.

When the Queen's Proctor intervenes, his costs may be awarded against one of the parties if the judge considers that the party's conduct made intervention necessary.

QUOTATION

When an estimate for work is binding on both sides

If a quotation for work to be done is given, and a firm price is specified, that price is binding as soon as the quotation is accepted by the customer.

Unless a quotation says that the price may be varied, the contractor cannot charge more even if costs go up before the work is finished.

But if extra work is asked for, or if the work described in the quotation is changed in some way, the price may be adjusted.

That is always the case when an ESTIMATE, giving only the probable cost has been requested.

RACIAL DISCRIMINATION

When it is illegal to treat people unfairly

People who think they have been treated unfairly because of their colour, race or nationality can complain that they are victims of racial discrimination and take legal action.

There are two forms of racial discrimination:
● Direct discrimination – when someone treats a person less favourably than others because of his colour, race or nationality.

An example would be when two people – one black, the other white – apply for a job, and the employer gives the job to the white applicant, although the black person is better qualified.
● Indirect discrimination – when a condition or requirement is applied equally to everyone, regardless of race or colour, but some racial groups find it difficult or impossible to comply with that condition or requirement.

An example would be a ruling that all bus drivers must wear caps: wearing a cap is not vital to the job of driving a bus, but the rule would discriminate against a Sikh wanting the job, because his religion requires him to wear a turban.

How to complain

There are two ways in which victims of racial discrimination can take legal action to seek redress:
● If they feel themselves discriminated against at work, they can complain to an INDUSTRIAL TRIBUNAL.
● In other cases they can take action in a county court.

But before starting legal proceedings either way, they should seek advice from the Commission for Racial Equality at Elliot House, 10–12 Allington Street, London SW1E 5EH.

In addition to giving advice the Commission may be able to provide legal and other assistance if necessary.

It can also provide a questionnaire that can be sent to a person against whom a complaint is being made – say, a landlord or employer. This questionnaire may help decide whether legal action is justified and likely to succeed.

The questionnaire can also be obtained from a local community relations council or Citizens Advice Bureau.

Anyone who is sent a questionnaire is not obliged to complete it, but failure to do so might be taken into account by a court or tribunal if the case is pursued to that extent.

Powers of court and tribunal

Both the county court and an industrial tribunal can award compensation for financial loss or injured feelings, and they can rule that there has been unlawful conduct.

Tribunals can also recommend an offending person or company to stop discriminating – and order more compensation to be paid if they fail to do so.

A county court cannot do so, but it can grant an injunction stopping an offender repeating an act of discrimination. *See also:* RACIAL HATRED

Where you can get legal aid

Anyone deciding to take a case of discrimination to a county court may be eligible for LEGAL AID and advice. Financial help is not available for an industrial tribunal case. However, the Commission for Racial Equality has powers to help in *all* cases.

Unlawful discrimination at work

There are three areas in which it is unlawful for an employer to discriminate against someone applying for a job:
● Methods used to determine who is offered the job.
● Terms of employment.
● Refusing, or deliberately failing, to offer the job.

Similarly, there are three areas in which unlawful discrimination can occur against someone who has a job:
● Terms of employment.
● Opportunities for training, transfer or promotion.
● Circumstances in which an employee is dismissed or treated in a detrimental way.

There are, however, exceptions – for example, an employer can choose people for acting or modelling work on the basis of their race or colour if it is important to ensure authenticity.

A local authority can use only social workers of Asian origin to handle the particular problems of Asian families. Official or factory-sponsored training schemes for people of a racial minority can be started in areas where there are few people of that group already working.

In education, colleges and schools – whether state-supported, 'public' or private – must not discriminate racially by:
● Setting unacceptable terms of entry for students or pupils from particular groups, or by refusing or failing to offer them entry without good reason.
● Refusing certain students and pupils benefits, facilities and services open to others.
● Taking any other action that might have a harmful effect on those students or pupils.

Local education authorities must not discriminate in the travel arrangements they make to enable children to get to school. For example, it is illegal to share

POWERS OF THE COMMISSION FOR RACIAL EQUALITY

The 15 government-appointed members of the Commission for Racial Equality include men and women experienced in politics, business, insurance, trade unionism, education and race relations.

The Commission's main tasks are to:
● Make sure that people of different racial groups are given the same opportunities as everyone else.
● Work towards the eventual elimination of all discrimination.
● Keep a watch on the way the Race Relations Act is working.

● Investigate instances of alleged discrimination.

In the course of an investigation the Commission has powers to oblige a witness to give oral or written evidence, but it can only enforce those powers by obtaining a county court order.

If it is satisfied that discrimination has taken place, the Commission can order the offender to stop discriminating.

If that order is not obeyed, the Commission can ask the county court for an injunction enforcing the order.

children of a racial minority group evenly among schools in an area if that means that some have to travel long distances from home.

Discrimination in housing

In housing, it is illegal to discriminate by:
● Fixing terms on which the premises are offered – for example, asking a higher rent from a coloured person.
● Refusing on the grounds of their race to sell or rent a property to someone who applied first and is ready and able to pay.
● Treating a coloured person less favourably than others in any list of people needing homes.

A local authority allocating homes must not, for example, discriminate against coloured people in the way it awards points in its priority list.

Exceptions to the general rule against discrimination in housing are people renting rooms in their homes and an owner-occupier selling his home without using an estate agent or advertising his wish to sell.

In advertising, it is illegal to indicate an intention to discriminate racially, and anyone who publishes such an advertisement or has it published also breaks the law.

Other fields in which discrimination can be illegal are those involving the sale and supply of goods, services and facilities. The law ensures for everyone the freedom to:
● Enter and use the facilities of any place open to the general public.
● Enter and book rooms in any hotel or guest house that has rooms vacant.
● Use facilities offered by banks, insur-

ance, credit, loan, finance and travel companies and by places of entertainment, refreshment and recreation.
● Use the services offered by any trade or profession.

The licensee of a PUBLIC HOUSE who refuses to serve a black customer because of his colour commits illegal discrimination.

A CLUB or association must not discriminate against people wanting to join unless it has fewer than 25 members or is established for the benefit of a particular group of people.

If the club or association did not stop discriminating, an injunction would then be granted against the club or association restraining repetition of the discriminatory act. This would have the practical effect of compelling the club or association to offer membership to the complainant.

Someone who has been discriminated against can claim compensation for injured feelings and ask for a declaration that the law has been broken.

When discrimination is allowed

It is within the law to offer services and facilities to meet the special needs of a particular racial group.

A local authority could, for example, start a youth club for West Indian youngsters in an area where there was serious unemployment among them.

Clubs and associations whose main object is to benefit a particular group of people for reasons that might be racial, but do not involve colour, are also legal.

In sporting events it is not illegal to choose someone to represent his country or other area because of his nationality – otherwise the Race Relations Act

would have a disastrous effect on international competition.

RACIAL HATRED

The penalties for stirring up racist feelings

It is a criminal offence under the Race Relations Act to use threatening, abusive or insulting words in a public place – or publish or distribute similarly offensive written material – when racial hatred is likely to be stirred up.

The prosecution does not have to prove that any disorder resulted or that the accused intended to incite hatred. A case can be brought, however, only with the Attorney General's consent.

The maximum penalty in a magistrates' court is 6 months' imprisonment and/or a fine of £1,000, and in the crown court 2 years' imprisonment and/or an unlimited fine.

RAFFLE LICENCE

The registration required to run a raffle or lottery

Any social club or charitable organisation is entitled to run a raffle or LOTTERY, provided that it is registered with its local authority as a society entitled to do so.

The law considers that any group of people who join together to form a club, organisation or association constitute a society, even if it has no offices of its own. A society is granted a raffle licence when it registers with its local authority, provided that the lottery or raffle is being run for the benefit of its own members or for charity and not for any profit or private gain.

Once a society is registered, it may run up to 52 lotteries or raffles in a year, provided that it does not contravene the Lotteries and Amusements Act 1976.

If an organiser contravenes the regulations he may be fined a maximum of £400 in a magistrates' court and an unlimited fine or 2 years' imprisonment in a crown court.

Registering a society

If your society wants to run a raffle or lottery, write to the chief executive of your local district council or London borough council if you live in London.

Give the name of your society and the purpose for which it was established, and ask for the society to be registered as a lottery operator.

Your society will have to pay a £10 registration fee to the local authority, who issue an official notification form stating that the society is registered. A society is entitled to renew its registration each year. The renewal fee, payable on January 1 each year, is £5.

A local council only turns down an application if the applicant has ceased to be a proper society or it has contravened the Lotteries and Amusements Act – for example, by running raffles for profit – and is no longer entitled to promote a lottery.

It will also turn down an application if someone connected with the proposed lottery has been convicted of fraud or of contravening the lottery regulations.

If you consider that your society has been turned down unreasonably, appeal against the decision at your local crown court.

What the law requires of a raffle promoter

Anyone who promotes a raffle or lottery and registers his society with the local authority must conform to certain regulations under the Lotteries and Amusements Act concerning the amount of money involved, the distribution of proceeds and the issuing of tickets.

If the turnover of a lottery is more than £5,000 it must be registered with the Gaming Board for Great Britain as well as with the local authority. The Gaming Board headquarters is at Berkshire House, 168–173 High Holborn, London WC1V 7AA.

To register with the Board, a society must pay a registration fee of £100 and a further £15 for every lottery run when the turnover is between £5,000 and £10,000. If the turnover is more than £10,000, a fee of £20 must be paid.

The maximum permitted turnover for a society lottery is £40,000 and no individual prize may cost more than £2,000 in amount or value.

However, if a lottery takes place less than 1 month after the previous lottery it is known as a 'short-term lottery', and

its turnover must not exceed £10,000 and no prize may cost or be valued at more than £1,000.

If a lottery takes place less than 3 months but more than 1 month after the previous lottery, it is known as a 'medium-term lottery' and its turnover must not exceed £20,000 and no prize may cost or be valued at more than £1,500.

The law also requires that:

● The organiser must be a member of the society who is authorised by its committee to run the raffle or lottery.

● The organiser must make a return to the local authority after the lottery, giving the date of the lottery, how much money was raised, how much went on expenses and prizes and the purpose for which the profits were used. If the lottery is registered with the Gaming Board, a similar return must be made to the Board.

● Tickets must be printed with the name and address of the organisation and the date of the raffle. They must all be priced the same and cost no more than 25p.

● Tickets may not be sold on the street, in licensed bingo or gaming clubs, licensed betting offices, amusement or prize bingo arcades or from vending machines. A ticket must not be sold to a person under 16.

● No more than half the proceeds of a raffle totalling up to £5,000 can be used for prizes, and no prize may cost or be valued at more than £1,000.

● Expenses must not be more than 25 per cent of the proceeds – except in the case of a raffle totalling more than £5,000, which is registered with the Gaming Board, when expenses must be no more than 15 per cent.

If a person contravenes the regulations he may be fined a maximum of £400 in a magistrates' court and an unlimited fine or 2 years' imprisonment in a crown court.

When a raffle need not be registered

If a raffle or lottery is run only for people who live or work in the same premises or belong to a society that is not conducted for gaming or betting, it is known as a 'private lottery' and need not be registered with the local authority or Gaming Board.

A FAIR DRAW

The rules governing even small, private lotteries are designed to ensure fairness to all participants and to prevent the organisers from making private gains.

'Get ready to shout 'carve up!'

However, the organisers must:

● Deduct only the cost of stationery and printing of tickets as expenses.

● Spend the rest of the money on prizes or for the purposes of the society.

● Ensure that each ticket costs the same and is printed with the name and address of the organisers.

● Ensure that no tickets are sent through the post.

● Ensure that the raffle or lottery is not advertised.

If the organisers fail to do so, they may be fined a maximum of £400 in a magistrates' court and an unlimited fine or 2 years' imprisonment in a crown court.

Running a small lottery

A 'small' lottery – for example, one run in conjunction with another event such as a fête, bazaar, dance or sports event – is also not required to be registered with a local authority or the Gaming Board.

However, organisers face similar penalties if they do not comply with the special rules involved. They are:

● The raffle must not be the major attraction of the event.

● Proceeds must not be for private gain.

● No more than £50 may be spent on prizes, and money prizes are not allowed.

● The sale of tickets and the draw must take place during the event or entertainment.

RAIL TRAVEL

Rules do not limit a passenger's right to fair treatment

When you travel by train in Britain you have a CONTRACT with British Rail or London Transport. That means that the conditions they lay down for carrying passengers and luggage are legally enforceable.

However, although the railway boards put limits on their liability for compensation for damage, a court may award more. Or it may allow a claim even if railway rules exclude any liability.

When there is an accident

A passenger can claim compensation for injury in an accident only if British Rail or London Transport are to blame – not, for example, if vandals cause a crash. Accidents on railway property, such as stations, are covered by the laws that govern any premises to which the public has lawful access. They must be kept reasonably safe. *See:* OCCUPIER'S LIABILITY

When luggage is lost or damaged

A railway board is liable for loss or damage to luggage if it is caused by an employee's negligence. If the luggage is lost or damaged in the guard's van, the railway management has to prove that it is not to blame. The situation is reversed if the luggage is carried in a passenger compartment – then the passenger must prove the rail staff's negligence. Liability is limited to £100, but even that condition might be held to be unreasonable in a court.

Rail travel abroad

The rights of a passenger who buys a ticket in Britain to a foreign destination are governed by international conventions. If there is an accident, the railway in the country where it happens is liable for compensation. Claims must be made, through British Rail, within 3 months of your becoming aware of any injury or damage. That applies only to foreign travel – in Britain the time limit for starting legal proceedings is 3 years.

If there are no seats

Buying a ticket does not entitle you to a seat. If you have a second-class ticket and all the seats are occupied you are not entitled to sit in a first-class seat, or even to stand in a first-class corridor, without permission from a guard or inspector. Passengers with first-class tickets are not entitled to a refund if second-class passengers are given permission to sit in their carriage.

Reserved seats You are entitled to a seat if you make a reservation. If you find that due to a mistake, someone else with a reservation is sitting in your seat and there is no alternative accommodation, you can claim a refund at the station of departure. The conditions say you are not entitled to any compensation for the inconvenience of having to stand in such cases, but that may be considered unreasonable and a claim for compensation might succeed.

Cancellation and delays

Passengers' legal rights if a train is cancelled or delayed have not been established recently by the courts. Timetables say there is no guarantee that trains will run on time or at all, but someone whose last train is cancelled, at short notice, and has no alternative public transport, might succeed in a claim to the railway management for the cost of an overnight stay or a taxi home.

Strikes A passenger has no right to alternative transport if his train service is suspended because of an industrial dispute. But a season-ticket holder can obtain a partial refund, minus an administration charge, if he claims within 7 days of a stoppage.

Lack of facilities A passenger cannot claim a refund simply because the expected facilities are not provided on his journey – for example, if the heating system does not work, or an advertised buffet car is not available. He has every right, however, to make a complaint.

When a line is to close

Advance public notice must be given in two national newspapers not less than 4 weeks before the formal announcement of a line closure. Six weeks before actual closure, a new notice must be published in two local newspapers for 2 consecutive weeks. It must also be displayed at all stations affected by the closure.

Anybody can raise objections by writing to the local Transport Users' Consultative Committee, whose address is posted at stations. Objections must be lodged within the 6 week period before closure. The committee may decide to hold a public meeting to hear them.

The consent of the Secretary of State for Transport is needed to close a line. That cannot be given until the committee's report has been considered.

When a passenger does not pay

Someone who travels on a train without a ticket, or travels beyond the distance allowed by his ticket, is technically a trespasser. In theory he could be ordered off the train.

In practice, no passenger is put off a train even if he refuses to pay when his offence is detected. His name and address are taken if he refuses to pay or fails to produce a ticket and he is allowed to continue his journey. If he fails to give his true name and address he can be arrested, but he cannot be arrested for travelling without a ticket with intent to avoid payment if he gives his name and address.

Prosecution for fare evasion depends on the railway management's ability to

---

WHEN A TUBE TRAVELLER'S PROTEST BACKFIRED

Failing to pay until forced to do so can be taken as proof that a passenger never intended to pay.

After a London Underground fare increase, Mr Piers Corbyn protested. On 46 occasions he bought the cheapest ticket and used it for longer journeys.

Each time, instead of offering the extra fare at his destination, he gave his name and address on the special form used when a rail passenger is unable to pay. He believed that would make him immune to prosecution. But London Transport charged him with fare evasion.

The court had to decide whether someone who obliged the railway management to pursue him for payment could be regarded as intending to pay.

DECISION
Corbyn was found guilty and fined.

prove that a passenger intended to avoid payment. Someone who does not have time to buy a ticket, or loses his ticket, is unlikely to be prosecuted if he pays readily when asked to during or after his journey.

It is an offence, however, to pass through a ticket barrier without permission.

First-class carriage Someone who rides in a first-class carriage on a second-class ticket can be prosecuted only if he refuses to pay the difference in fares. If he is travelling on a second-class season ticket, he must pay the full first-class fare for his journey.

When other passengers offend

Most railway laws and bye-laws are intended for the safety and comfort of passengers. You are entitled to ask railway staff to enforce them.

It is an offence, punishable by a fine of up to £50, to:
● Board a train while others are trying to get off.
● Smoke in a non-smoking compartment.
● Sing, use a radio or play a musical instrument to the annoyance of other passengers.
● Indulge in drunken, disorderly, indecent, threatening or abusive behaviour.
● Spit in a carriage.
● Deface railway property.

Damaging railway property also carries a £50 bye-law fine – but serious vandalism can be prosecuted as criminal damage, punishable by imprisonment.

When laws and bye-laws overlap, and an offence could be prosecuted in more than one way, the charge carrying the heavier penalty is usually laid.

Endangering safety Any action intended to endanger the safety of passengers or obstruct a train – for example, placing something on a rail or tampering with signals – carries a maximum penalty of life imprisonment. Someone who endangers safety without intending to cause injury or damage – typically, a youth who throws a stone at a train – can be fined up to £200.

Complaining about the railways

Complaints about rail services should be made first to the station manager or to the area or divisional manager. The addresses should be on display at every station, usually near the booking office.

OFFICIAL WATCHDOG

The address of the official complaints body – the Transport Users' Consultative Committee – is posted in every railway station.

'Take a letter to the Transport Users' Consultative Committee'

If those officials do not help, contact the area Transport Users' Consultative Committee, or on matters of national importance, the Central Transport Users' Consultative Committee. The committees are appointed by the Government to deal with issues such as staff rudeness, line closures or requests for trains to make extra stops at stations where there are potential passengers.

RAPE

When forcing a woman to have sex is an offence

Any man who forces a woman – other than his wife – to have sexual intercourse without her freely given consent is guilty of rape and can be gaoled for life. It is rape to use physical strength or intimidation or trickery to make a woman have intercourse.

A man who takes advantage of a woman while she is asleep or drunk can be found guilty of rape. So can a man who pretends to be a doctor and says he is carrying out a medical examination.

Full intercourse does not have to take place for rape to be proved.

Who cannot be charged

A woman cannot be accused of raping a man; and a boy under 14 years of age is presumed to be incapable of intercourse, so he cannot be accused of rape. He can, however, be charged with indecent assault. *See:* INDECENCY

A husband and wife, by marrying, consent to have intercourse with each other. While they remain living as man and wife the man cannot be accused of raping the wife, no matter how much she may have fought off his advances.

A husband can be guilty of rape only if:
● The couple have been divorced and a decree nisi has been obtained.
● The couple have been legally separated and there is an order not to molest the wife.
● The wife has an injunction against her husband ordering him not to molest her.

When someone is raped

Someone who has been raped may or may not feel able to endure a police investigation. But even if not, she should visit her own doctor to ask him or her to check for venereal disease, the possibility of pregnancy or physical damage.

If she does decide to go to the police, she should:
● Go as soon as possible after the rape; the longer she leaves it, the less likely she is to be believed.
● Not wash herself or re-arrange her clothing – that is all part of her evidence. The police may need to keep her clothes, so she should take others.
● Remember the details of the incident and any words exchanged.

A statement will be taken by a police officer. She should read it carefully and correct it if necessary before signing. She can ask to keep a copy.

The police will need the evidence that an internal and external medical examination can provide. She can insist on being examined by a woman doctor and she can demand also to have her own doctor present.

The police may ask her to look at photos of suspects, visit the scene of the crime or assist at an identification parade.

Protecting the victim A woman can ask for her name to be kept secret, at the judge's discretion, to protect her from unpleasant publicity. The defence is also barred from making attempts to besmirch the woman's character by suggesting that she is a woman of low morals.

It is a complete defence for a man

accused of rape to say that he genuinely believed the woman had consented.

RATES

Money paid to the council for the upkeep of local services

Anybody who owns or occupies a property – including council houses – has to pay rates to the local council. Many private and council tenants pay their rates as part of the total rent payment.

The amount payable depends upon the rateable value of the property and the rate in the £ charged by the council.

Assessing rateable value

The rateable value of property is calculated by the local Inland Revenue valuation office. The Inland Revenue should send every occupier a questionnaire periodically asking for information about the property facilities.

From the answers, and other information obtained from a random survey, and measurement of the building, the valuation officer calculates the yearly rent at which the property might be let in current market conditions. That amount is the gross value.

From the gross value, the valuer has to deduct an amount to cover insurance, expenses and repairs that would be needed to maintain the property in a condition to command the rent he has assessed. The amount left after these deductions is called the rateable value.

A list of the rateable values of every property in the area – known as the valuation list – is available for inspection at the local council office.

Fixing the rate in the £

Each local council fixes its own scale of rates by levying a proportion of the rateable value of property in its area – known as the rate in the £.

The rateable value of properties even in the same street can vary greatly, but the rate in the £ is the same for all properties.

How rates are collected

Rates are assessed each financial year (April to March) after the council has estimated its total financial needs.

Rate demand   The council sends each ratepayer a demand note, setting out how much he must pay and showing also how the money is being spent. Rates are officially payable on April 1 each year for the coming year, but they can be paid by two instalments – usually in April and October.

Most councils allow rates to be paid by 10 monthly instalments. If you want to pay monthly you must complete the appropriate form with your rate demand and return it at once. You cannot simply allow the demand date to pass and then ask for time to pay.

When rates are not paid when they become due

If someone does not pay his rates when they are due the council is entitled to apply for a summons to bring him before a magistrates' court. If he decides to pay at this point, he is charged the cost of the summons and if the case is heard, the cost of the hearing, too.

If he still does not pay, or if he cannot offer a valid reason why he should not pay, the council may obtain a distress warrant from the court authorising a bailiff or other responsible official to seize goods to the value of the rates due from his house. He is entitled to hand over the money due (in cash) to the bailiff, but he must also pay the bailiff's fees.

Someone whose goods have been seized in that way has 5 more days in which to pay and recover his property. If he still does not pay, the seized goods will be sold, the rates and costs will be paid from the proceeds and the householder will be entitled to receive any balance of money.

If the BAILIFF cannot gain access to the house, or if there are not enough goods to cover the rates, or if a householder wilfully refuses to pay, the magistrates can impose a prison sentence of up to 3 months.

When you can ask for a rate reduction

There are two ways in which a ratepayer may be able to pay less rates – by a rate reduction or a rate rebate.

A rate reduction means that the rateable value of a property is reduced, and that in turn reduces the amount of rates payable.

If you think that the valuation officer's assessment is too high – because the property could not be let for as much as the figure suggested – you can appeal, even if your neighbour's house has been similarly assessed. Perhaps his house is larger than yours, or he has a garage and you do not.

Often, however, neighbours apply together for a reduction because of changes in the neighbourhood. Perhaps the road has become a main traffic route.

Ask the local valuation officer for a 'Proposal for Alteration of the Valuation List' form. Complete it, saying what you think the assessment should be, and send it back to the valuation officer. The valuation officer's address is listed under Inland Revenue in the local telephone directory.

If the valuation officer refuses to reduce your assessment – or if you do not agree with his suggested amendment – and you do not withdraw your proposal within 14 days, the valuation officer must refer your proposal to the local valuation court which is a special court held usually at the council offices. It has three lay members and a professional clerk. You will be given notice of a hearing, probably about a month later, and you will be invited to attend to state your case.

....

PEACE AND QUIET – OR
PAY LESS

The chances of having your home's rateable value reassessed so that you pay lower rates will be much improved if you make the application in conjunction with as many of your neighbours as possible.

I said we ought to apply for rate re assessment

....

You can, if you wish, engage a valuer, surveyor or solicitor to present your case for you, but that is not essential. The procedure is that you will be allowed to state your case and call any witnesses, and you may be asked questions by the valuation officer or the court.

You will be told in writing of the court's decision, and if you are still not satisfied you can appeal to the Lands Tribunal in London within 28 days. The valuation court will tell you how and where to make this appeal. The decision of the Lands Tribunal is final.

Asking for a rate rebate if you cannot afford to pay

When a householder cannot afford to pay the full amount of the rates due, he may be able to obtain a rate rebate. He must meet the council's means-test requirements, and its decision is based on the applicant's financial responsibilities and also the level of income.

A rebate may also be granted where special facilities have been provided for a disabled person in a house or an institution.

A rate rebate does not affect the rateable value of a property.

If you wish to apply for a rebate you can get an application form from the treasurer's department of your local council. Entitlement to a rebate normally dates from the beginning of the month in which application is made and usually lasts for 6 months. Pensioners' rebates are normally reviewed every 12 months.

When a rate rebate is granted, the occupier must tell the council of any changes in financial, family or housing circumstances that could later affect that entitlement.

If someone is allowed too high a rebate because he fails to give the appropriate information, the council can recover the money – by court action if that is necessary.

If there is a change in the rates during an entitlement period, the council will adjust the rebate automatically.

To renew a rebate, the householder must apply no more than a month before, and not later than a month after, the existing period expires.

When someone asks for a rebate, the council usually asks to see his pay or salary slips for the past 5 weeks, or 2 months.

If he is self-employed, he will be asked to provide an accountant's certificate of earnings.

If he is a pensioner, he will have to show his pension book and any notice of an occupational pension.

Paying rates on empty property

If your house is empty of all furniture and unoccupied for a month or more, tell the council and claim a rate reduction.

When water rates and sewerage have to be paid

Water and sewerage rates are assessed as so much in the £ of your rateable value.

If your property is drained to the normal sewerage system and serviced by the main water supply the local water authority will send you a demand half yearly.

Even if your property is not drained to the sewerage system, nor has it a piped water supply, you will still have to pay a small rate to the water authority to cover their general services.

If the rateable value of your property falls, so do the water authority rates.

RECKLESS DRIVING

Severe penalties for risking others' safety

A driver who takes an unnecessary risk without concern for the possible consequences is guilty of reckless driving. The offence implies knowledge by the driver that he is doing something which can be dangerous to another person, such as overtaking at speed on a blind bend.

The essence of the offence is knowing that life and limb and the safety of others are at risk, and going on regardless. The prosecution must prove that, objectively, the situation was dangerous, that the driver was aware of the situation, and, subjectively, knowing that, he went on.

If a charge of reckless driving is not proved, the court can prefer a charge of careless or inconsiderate driving in its place.

Reckless driving may take many forms. The following situations, if they happened deliberately or recklessly, would constitute reckless driving:
● The driver had been drinking heavily.
● He crossed continuous double white lines.
● He was racing another vehicle.
● He was 'retaliating' as the real or imagined victim of bad driving by somebody else.
● He emerged from a side road, ignoring the road sign, not looking out.
● He struck a pedestrian on a pedestrian crossing.
● He ignored a red traffic light.
● He ignored the road signs at a road junction.
● He fell asleep at the wheel.
● He overtook two or more vehicles at once.
● He was driving much too fast.
● He was involved in a very bad collision, head on, he being on the wrong side of the road.
● He was driving on the wrong side of the road.
● He was involved in two or more accidents within a matter of minutes.

Maximum penalties

A reckless driving charge tried in a magistrates' court carries a maximum penalty of £1,000 fine and imprisonment for 6 months. In a crown court the penalty is an unlimited fine and up to 2 years in prison. NOTICE OF INTENDED PROSECUTION is essential unless the charge is the result of an accident.

Disqualification is at the discretion of the court on a first offence. If a second offence is committed within 3 years, there is an automatic 12 months' disqualification.

RECONCILIATION

Trying to mend a broken marriage

A couple whose marriage has run into serious trouble are encouraged by the divorce laws to try to reconcile their differences – even though proceedings may have started already.

When a solicitor is first consulted about filing a DIVORCE petition, he has a duty to discuss with his client the possibility of a reconciliation. Unless he feels there is absolutely no hope of a reconciliation, the solicitor may advise seeking help from a marriage guidance counsellor, doctor or social worker.

A judge may adjourn the hearing of a divorce case if he considers that there is a chance of saving the marriage.

A husband's or wife's prospects of eventually obtaining a divorce are not jeopardised by attempts at reconciliation – provided that the period, or total number of periods, over which the couple try living together again do not exceed 6 months.

A divorce can be obtained, for example, for DESERTION after 2 years, even though the couple have cohabited in efforts at reconciliation during the separation. The conditions are that they have lived:
● Together for a total of no more than 6 months.
● Apart for a total of 2 years, excluding reconciliation periods. Similar provisions for a reconciliation period of up to 6 months also apply when ADULTERY and unreasonable behaviour are given as reasons for divorce.

REDUNDANCY

When an employee is dismissed because there is no longer work suitable for him

A full-time employee who is made redundant – that is, dismissed because there is no longer work suitable for him – may be entitled to compensation from his employer.

The minimum amount is defined by the Employment Protection (Consolidation) Act 1978, according to a formula that takes into account the employee's age, his length of service, up to a maximum of 20 years, and his basic rate of pay.

A redundant employee should receive his award automatically from his employer when he leaves. But if the employer does not pay – for example, because he does not accept that redundancy was the reason for dismissal – the employee can claim the money through an INDUSTRIAL TRIBUNAL. If the employer fails to pay because he is insolvent, the employee can claim his money from the Department of Employment through his employer's liquidator or official receiver. *See:* BANKRUPTCY

Employees who cannot claim redundancy pay

Some categories of employee are not entitled to a redundancy payment, although they have been made redundant: part-timers; people who have already reached normal retirement age; civil servants and members of the armed forces; registered dock workers; domestic servants who are close relatives of their employers; and people whose duties are mainly performed abroad. *See:* EMPLOYMENT PROTECTION

An employee cannot sign away his right to payment if he is made redundant. The only exception to that rule is if he is on a fixed-term contract of 2 years or more, and a clause waiving payment is included in the contract.

How eligible employees qualify

An employee who is otherwise eligible for a redundancy payment must meet three additional conditions. He must:
● Have worked for his employer continuously for at least 2 years.
● Have been dismissed.
● Be redundant, as defined by law.

If he has refused an offer of suitable alternative work from his employer, he loses his right to an award, although technically he may still be redundant.

How the 2-year service period is calculated

An employee must complete 2 years of CONTINUOUS EMPLOYMENT with his employer before he becomes eligible for a redundancy payment. Service before his 18th birthday does not count towards the total, so he must be at least 20 years old.

Service ends only when the employer's notice of redundancy expires, or, if proper notice is not given, when it would have ended, if it had been served. So an employee who has worked for 103 weeks and is then given 1 week's notice has completed 104 weeks – 2 years.

How the rules define 'dismissed'

An employee is entitled to a redundancy payment only if he has been dismissed or forced out of his job. He does not qualify if he resigns of his own accord – even though he may think redun-

TOLD TO LEAVE

Redundancy payments are available only to an ex-employee who has left his job against his own wishes. If he resigns, he must be able to prove that he did so only because of his employer's unreasonable behaviour.

'Call it redundancy or constructive dismissal – you're fired!'

dancies are in the offing – nor if he ends his job by agreement with his employer. *See:* DISMISSAL

Most dismissals are straightforward, but the employment protection rules recognise two types that are less clearcut – constructive dismissal and the non-renewal of a fixed-term contract.

THE FOREMAN WHO LEFT TOO SOON

An employee who believes that he is to be made redundant and who resigns without waiting to be dismissed may lose his redundancy award.

Mr Shaw was a foreman in the velvets department of a fabric company. His employers told him that the department would eventually be closed, but without specifying a date. Mr Shaw found another job and handed in his notice. Then he claimed a redundancy payment from his former employers.

DECISION
Mr Shaw was not entitled to an award. He had not been dismissed, merely given warning of possible dismissal. However, had a definite date been given for closure of the department, that would have been dismissal.

Dismissals because of redundancy may be further complicated if:
- The employer is asking for volunteers to leave.
- An employee asks to go before his notice period expires.
- A worker involved is facing disciplinary proceedings.
- The employees are on strike.

Constructive dismissal An employer, by his conduct, may effectively bring the employment contract to an end – for example, by refusing to pay wages or to allocate work. In such circumstances, the employee can regard himself as having been dismissed and leave. He does not need to give notice, but he should write to his employer stating that he has not resigned, but has left because the contract has been broken.

An employee who has been constructively dismissed does not forfeit any of the rights he would have had if he had been dismissed normally, including the right to claim redundancy. *See:* UNFAIR DISMISSAL

When a contract is not renewed If an employee has entered a fixed-term contract of 2 years or more which is not renewed when it expires, he may be entitled to a redundancy payment, unless he has signed a clause waiving that right in the contract itself.

Voluntary redundancy An employer planning redundancies sometimes asks for volunteers who will leave. Anyone accepting voluntary redundancy should insist beforehand on a written promise from the employer to pay the redundancy entitlement. Otherwise, if there is a later dispute, a tribunal may hold that the employee resigned, and is therefore not entitled to an award. *See:* UNEMPLOYMENT BENEFIT

Under notice of redundancy An employee who is under notice of redundancy may leave before it expires – for example, to start a new job – without losing his right to a redundancy award. However, he must give written NOTICE of 1 week to his employer and that must be served during his own statutory notice period of between 1 and 12 weeks, depending on length of service.

The statutory notice period may be shorter than that agreed in the employee's contract, but in redundancy claims the statutory period applies.

An employer can try to stop a redundant employee from leaving early by serving a counter-notice demanding that he should stay on until the full notice period has run out. The employer might use a counter-notice if he wants to keep specialist staff until the last moment to maintain his business, or if he hopes to find a suitable alternative job which would avoid the need for a redundancy payment.

The counter-notice must be in writing and must reach the employee before the end of the notice period the employee has given. To reinforce the counter-notice, the employer may threaten in it to withhold redundancy pay and to contest any claim the employee may make.

If the employee ignores the counter-notice, he can still submit a redundancy claim. But the industrial tribunal will examine the reasonableness of the employer's and employee's behaviour and, possibly, the employee's earnings from his new job. It may then decide to reduce the amount of the award.

Misconduct leading to dismissal An employee who commits an offence which is so serious that it justifies instant or summary dismissal – for example, stealing from his employer – may lose all or part of any redundancy award to which he would otherwise have been entitled.

If the summary dismissal takes place before redundancy notice is served, he forfeits all claims. However, if the employer decides to allow the dismissed worker to serve out his notice period, and redundancies are announced during that time, the dismissed employee might succeed in claiming an award.

To avoid that possibility, the employer should state clearly in the original notice that, although the worker could have been sacked on the spot, he is being allowed to work out his notice period.

If an employee commits an offence justifying summary dismissal after a redundancy notice has been served on him, he does not necessarily forfeit his redundancy pay. However, an industrial tribunal will award him only the amount it considers 'just and equitable' – which, depending upon the circumstances, may be nothing. The employee has the right to bring a redundancy claim to the tribunal only if the misconduct occurred during the statutory notice period of between 1 and 12 weeks, depending upon his length of service. If the offence occurred before the beginning of the statutory notice period, but after redundancy notices had been served, the employee will get nothing.

Example John Jones has worked for his employers for 4 years and is therefore entitled to 4 weeks' statutory notice. His employment contract says he is entitled to 8 weeks.

On January 1, he is given 8 weeks notice of redundancy. On January 24, he assaults his supervisor and is dismissed. He cannot claim a redundancy award, because the offence took place outside the 4 weeks' statutory notice period. Had he waited until February 5 before punching the supervisor, he would still probably have been summarily dismissed. But because the offence would have taken place within the statutory 4 weeks, he could have taken a redundancy claim to an industrial tribunal. The tribunal would then have decided how much, if anything, he would get.

Redundancy claims by strikers Someone who is declared redundant while on

---

> ### THE EMPLOYEE WHO GOT THE NOTICE RULES WRONG
>
> *An employee who wants to leave while under notice must inform his employer in writing during the notice period laid down by law. Otherwise, he may be held to have resigned and lose his redundancy award.*
>
> Under the employment protection rules, Mr Lobb was entitled to 2 weeks' notice. On May 11, his employers served notice on him, stating that he was to be dismissed from June 10 – a period of 4½ weeks. Mr Lobb found another job and on May 20 told his employers orally that he wanted to leave early. He then claimed a redundancy payment. His employers argued he was not entitled to one.
>
> **DECISION**
> Mr Lobb was not entitled to a redundancy award. In giving notice, he had made two mistakes. First, he did not do so in writing. Second, he did not do so within the statutory notice period – in his case, the fortnight ending on June 10.

strike may not be entitled to a redundancy award. However, if he goes on strike after he has been served redundancy notice, he is entitled to claim the full redundancy payment. His employer can insist that he must work extra days to make up for those lost as a result of the stoppage.

How the law defines 'redundancy'

Once it has been established that an employee has been dismissed, rather than resigned or left by mutual agreement with his employer, the law assumes that he has been made redundant, unless the dismissal was clearly for disciplinary reasons.

The burden of proof is on the employer to show that the dismissal was not because of redundancy. Otherwise, the worker is entitled to a redundancy payment.

Often, the question of whether an employee was redundant or not can be answered simply by examining whether the employer replaced him. If he did not, the employee was almost certainly redundant. If he did, the employee was probably not redundant, although he may still be entitled to compensation for unfair dismissal.

WHEN THE BOSS TOOK OVER

The owner of a business is not legally an employee. So if he takes on the job of an employee and dismisses him, that employee has not been replaced.

The owner of a grocery shop decided he wanted to work in it himself. He dismissed one of his assistants to make room for himself. The assistant claimed redundancy.

DECISION
The dismissed assistant was redundant. The same work was being done by fewer employees.

When an employee is dismissed and the work he used to do is contracted to someone outside the company – a self-employed person or another company – he is redundant. If his work is taken over by the employer himself, he is also redundant.

There are five sets of circumstances in

THE NUCLEAR WORKER WHO REFUSED A TRANSFER

Mr Claydon worked as a draughtsman for the Atomic Energy Authority at Orford Ness, in Suffolk. In 1971 that establishment was closed and Mr Claydon was told he would be transferred to the Authority's research centre at Aldermaston, Berkshire. He refused to go and claimed a redundancy payment. His employers argued he was not redundant, because his employment contract stated: 'The employers reserve the right to require any member of the staff to work at any of our establishments in G.B. or in posts overseas.'

DECISION
The contract was clear. Mr Claydon had been offered a transfer in accordance with its terms and therefore he had not been made redundant.

WHEN THREE MEN COULD DO THE WORK OF FOUR

Even though the volume of work may remain the same, but reorganisation enables it to be done by fewer people, an employee who is dismissed because there is no longer a job for him is redundant.

Mr Sutton was sacked from his job as a chief accountant. His duties were shared out among his three assistants and he was not replaced. Mr Sutton claimed redundancy. His employers argued he was not redundant, because the amount of work had not changed.

DECISION
Mr Sutton was redundant. Although the work had not changed, fewer people were needed to do it.

THE OLD-FASHIONED BARMAID

In deciding whether an employee dismissed because of business changes is redundant, industrial tribunals consider what he was doing before the changes – and his employer's requirements after them. If the same work remains and the employer still needs someone to do it, the dismissed employee is not redundant.

The management of the Star and Garter public house decided to modernise the premises and to hire young, attractive barmaids. A barmaid who had been employed there for 18 years was dismissed, because it was felt she did not fit in with the pub's new image. She claimed a redundancy payment.

DECISION
The barmaid was not redundant. Her employers needed barmaids and the job she had been doing therefore still existed.

Nowadays she could probably claim UNFAIR DISMISSAL.

which a dismissed employee is, in law, redundant. If:
● All or part of the employer's business closes.
● The employer's business moves.
● The employee's work is reduced.
● The business is sold.
● The employee is laid off or put on short-time.

If all or part of a business closes The closure may be for financial reasons, because of the death of the employer, or as the result of other circumstances – for example, a serious fire. If no work is available for employees, and the employer cannot afford to keep them on, they become redundant.

If part of a business – for example, one factory – is shut down, the employees become redundant if suitable alternative employment cannot be found for them elsewhere in the group.

If the business moves An employee is redundant if his employer moves his business to a new site and does not offer him a job. But the situation may become complicated if the employee is offered a job at the new site and refuses to move.

If that happens, and the employee claims a redundancy award from an industrial tribunal, the tribunal examines the EMPLOYMENT CONTRACT to see if it contains a mobility clause requiring the employee to transfer to a new location at the employer's request. The employee is not entitled to a redundancy payment if he has accepted mobility.

If there is no written requirement, tribunals examine the nature of the job itself, custom and practice in the trade or industry and the employee's previous attitude towards being moved, to see whether those imply that he accepted the principle of mobility.

Some jobs – for example, project engineer or site manager – are clearly mobile. Some industries – for example, construction – require mobility from many of their employees.

THE EMPLOYER WHO ALTERED THE SHIFTS

If an employer changes working hours, but needs the same number of employees to do the same jobs as before, an employee who leaves or is dismissed may not be redundant.

Noreen Johnson was a clerk employed by the Nottinghamshire Combined Police Authority. She and another clerk worked a 5 day week, from 9.30 until 5.30 each day.

The Police Authority changed the hours, requiring the clerks to work two daily shifts, six days a week, in alternate weeks. Noreen refused and was dismissed. She claimed redundancy.

DECISION
Noreen Johnson's redundancy claim was turned down on appeal. Her employers still required her to do the same work as before.

WHEN OVERTIME IS REDUCED

An employer who reduces the opportunities for his employees to work overtime has not made them redundant.

Lesney Products, who make toys, laid off their night shift and reorganised the hours worked by their daytime machine setters, who lost the chance to do extra overtime, worth about £14 a week. Six daytime machine setters refused to accept the change and claimed to have been made redundant.

DECISION
The six were not redundant. They were doing the same work as before. The overtime earnings were not guaranteed in their contracts.

WORKING THE SAME MACHINE–BUT REDUNDANT

If an employer takes over the premises and assets of a business, but changes the purposes for which they are used, any employees he keeps on may not be able to claim service with the previous owner as part of their total service record.

Mr Woodhouse spent 14 years as a machine operative with a Nottingham company making diesel engines. Then his employers decided to transfer to Manchester. They sold their assets in Nottingham, but not the goodwill of the business, which they were continuing.

Mr Woodhouse stayed in Nottingham, working the same machine, but now producing different products for another company. After 6 years, he was made redundant. He said he was entitled to a payment based on 20 years' service. His employers said the amount should be assessed only on 6 years – the length of time he had worked for them.

DECISION
The new owners had not bought the business, only its physical assets. So Mr Woodhouse was entitled only to a payment calculated on 6 years' service. He should have claimed redundancy based on 14 years' service from the previous owners at the time they sold the business.

An employee who accepts one move which is not provided for in his contract does not necessarily weaken his right to refuse a second move and claim redundancy. However, if he accepts several moves, mobility may be held to have become a term of his contract.

If work is reduced or stopped Changes in the organisation of a business – for example, the installation of new machinery or a re-allocation of duties among the staff that allows the work to be done by fewer people – may mean that an employer no longer needs the services or skills of a particular employee. If the employee is dismissed because work is not available, and he is not replaced, he is redundant.

If, after a reorganisation, there is still a need for the sort of work an employee was previously doing, but he is dismissed because his employer feels that the changes have made him unsuitable to do it, he may not be legally redundant, although he might be able to claim unfair dismissal.

An employer may reorganise his business by asking his employees to do the same amount of work, but altering the times at which they are expected to do it. If an employee refuses to accept the change and leaves or is dismissed, he is unlikely to succeed with a redundancy claim. However, if he can show that the employer broke the employment contract by imposing new working hours, he may be entitled to compensation for unfair dismissal.

When the business is sold An employer who sells up his business and dismisses his staff must make redundancy payments to them. However, if he sells the business as a going concern, and the new owner offers the employees the chance to stay in their old jobs, any who reject the offer and leave because of the change cannot claim redundancy. Under such circumstances, service with the old and new employers counts as continuous.

Sometimes, the new owner of the business has bought only the assets and the premises, but not the goodwill, because he does not intend to run it the same way as his predecessor. If that happens, an employee who is dismissed by the new owner immediately after the takeover can claim redundancy from the old owner.

Employees of a business that has been taken over should establish immediately from the new owner whether he bought it as a going concern, and whether their previous service counts as continuous. If it does not, they should claim redundancy payment from their old employer within 6 months.

According to the EMPLOYMENT PROTECTION rules, someone taking over a business, whether as a going concern or not, must, within 13 weeks, amend the written particulars of terms and conditions supplied to staff, or issue new ones. The particulars must state whether service with the old employer counts with the new one. *See:* EMPLOYMENT CONTRACT

If the new owner of a business offers an existing employee a job different from the one he was doing before, the

HOW TO MAKE A REDUNDANCY CLAIM

If you have been dismissed and believe you are entitled to a redundancy payment, you can claim it either through an INDUSTRIAL TRIBUNAL or directly from your former employer.

You must submit your claim within 6 months of leaving the job or it may be ruled to be out of date. If you are also claiming unfair dismissal, the limit is reduced to 3 months.

Obtain form IT1 from a job centre, employment office or unemployment benefit office and send it, when completed, to the Central Office of the Industrial Tribunals, 93 Ebury Bridge Road, London SW1W 8RE. The central office then allocates the case to a local tribunal, which will inform you of the hearing.

If you decide to apply initially to your former employer, rather than to a tribunal, you must do so in a letter, stating clearly that you are seeking compensation for redundancy. Keep a copy. The letter must arrive after you have left the job. If it is sent before that, the claim is not valid.

Provided that your claim to your former employer was submitted within 6 months of your leaving, you can still take the matter to an industrial tribunal if he refuses to pay – even if the tribunal application is not made until the 6 months are over. In such circumstances, tribunals have accepted redundancy cases that were more than 2 years old. However, to make sure you receive a hearing, you should observe the time limit.

---

employee can accept it for a trial period of not less than 4 weeks, unless he asks for it to be shorter, without losing his right to claim redundancy if the job proves unsuitable.

If an employee is laid off If, because of shortage of work, an employee receives less than half his weekly pay in 4 consecutive weeks, or in 6 weeks out of 13, he can declare himself redundant by giving written notice to his employer. However, if the employer does not accept the claim for redundancy, and can show that the employee would have been back working normally within a reasonable period, an industrial tribunal may refuse an award. *See:* LAY-OFF

Statutory redundancy payments are calculated according to a formula, based upon the employee's age and his length of service with his employer, which is applied to his weekly pay – excluding non-contracted overtime and bonuses – at the time he is dismissed. If

weekly earnings are more than a certain amount (£120 in 1980), the sum above that amount is ignored.

In working out length of service, employment before the week in which the employee's 18th birthday falls is disregarded. The maximum length of service that can be taken into account is 20 years. If the employee has been with the employer for longer than that, the most recent 20 years are used for the calculation.

Subject to those conditions, a redundant employee is entitled to:
● Half a week's pay for each year of service completed between the week of his 18th birthday and the eve of his 22nd birthday.
● A week's pay for each year of service completed between his 22nd birthday and the eve of his 41st birthday.
● 1½ weeks' pay for each year of service completed between the 41st birthday and the birthday before the one at

---

WHEN THE NEW JOB MEANT EXTRA TIME TRAVELLING

If the new job is in another place, it may nevertheless be suitable.

A redundant employee of a co-operative society was offered alternative work that added 2 hours a day to his travelling time, and cost him extra money on lunches and fares.

DECISION
The job was suitable alternative employment.

THE JOB OFFERED WAS OF LOWER STATUS

If an employer offers a job which is of lower standing than the old one, it may not be suitable, even if the pay is the same.

Mr Harris was an instructor of apprentices in a joinery business. Because of changes in the organisation, he was offered alternative work as a bench hand, but at the same pay.

DECISION
The alternative job was not suitable. His previous work as an instructor gave him a status not equalled in the post of bench hand.

---

which the employee reaches retirement age. As the normal retirement age is 65 years for men and 60 for women, the formula is generally applied until the 64th birthday for men and the 59th for women.

The maximum award under the scheme was, in 1980, £120 × 20 × 1½ = £3,600. It could be claimed by a male employee who had not reached his 64th birthday or a female worker who had not reached her 59th birthday.

How redundancy awards affect tax and social security

Statutory redundancy awards are tax-free. But if a redundant employee receives extra money – for example, because his employer operates a redundancy scheme which is more generous

---

THE EMPLOYER WHO KNEW A WORKER WOULD REJECT A NEW JOB

Even if a redundant employee says he will not accept a new job, the employer must formally offer one if it is available. Otherwise, he must pay redundancy.

When a small sweet shop was taken over by a large chain, one of the assistants made it clear she would not take a job with the new owners of the business, even if they offered her one. Knowing her

attitude, they did not make an offer. She claimed a redundancy award.

DECISION
The assistant was entitled to her payment. The new owners of the business could not claim she had unreasonably refused an offer of suitable alternative employment when no offer had been made.

than the legal minimum, or because he is compensated for loss of office – which brings his total payment to more than £10,000, he is liable for tax on the

amount above £10,000. *See:* GOLDEN HANDSHAKE

Payment in lieu of NOTICE is also taxable.

Someone who receives a redundancy payment does not lose his right to UNEMPLOYMENT BENEFIT, though he may not be eligible for

DECLARING REDUNDANCIES: STEPS THAT EMPLOYERS MUST FOLLOW

Every employer who intends to dismiss someone as redundant must observe one basic rule – he must warn the employee concerned as far in advance as possible.

The other steps he must follow depend upon whether:
● The employee is legally entitled to a redundancy payment.
● The employer intends to claim part of any redundancy payment back from the state Redundancy Fund.
● The employer recognises an independent TRADE UNION for COLLECTIVE BARGAINING, or has been recommended to do so by the ADVISORY, CONCILIATION AND ARBITRATION SERVICE (ACAS).

Warning the employee Under the Code of Practice implemented under the Industrial Relations Act 1971, all employers must give employees about to be made redundant 'as much warning as practicable' of their dismissal.

The code is not legally binding, but if an employer fails to follow it without good reason – for example, because his business closed suddenly after a fire – a redundant employee may be entitled to claim extra compensation for unfair dismissal.

The rules on advance warning are separate from those on NOTICE, which the employer must also observe. An employer who knows several weeks in advance that his business is to be wound up, but who says nothing to his employees until their notice periods begin, may be held to have broken the code. In that case an employee may be able to claim that the employer acted unreasonably and so claim UNFAIR DISMISSAL.

When a redundancy payment is made

An employer who makes any redundancy payment to a dismissed employee must also supply him with a statement of the amount and an explanation of how it has been calculated. The statement form – RP3 – is obtainable from any employment office. If it is not issued, the employer can be fined up to £20 for a first offence and up to £100 for each subsequent one.

Claiming from the Redundancy Fund An employer who is obliged by law to pay redundancy money can reclaim 41 per cent of it from the Redundancy Fund, which is financed from social security contributions. But if he gives an employee more than the law requires, he cannot obtain a rebate.

If he makes a redundancy payment to an employee who is not entitled to one by law – for example, a part-timer – he cannot normally reclaim any of it from the fund, unless the Department of Employment decides that it would be 'just and equitable' to do so.

To obtain a refund, an employer must:
● Complete form RP1 at his local employment office at least 14 days before the employee's notice period expires. If 10 or more employees are to be made redundant together, the form must be completed at least 21 days before the end of their notice period.
● Claim the money within 6 months of making the redundancy payment from the date on which the employee leaves, by completing form RP2 at the employment office and attaching to it the portion of form RP3 – the redundancy pay statement – signed by the employee. The Department of Employment has discretion to accept late claims.

An employer who believes he is entitled to a higher rebate than that granted from the fund can appeal to an industrial tribunal. The appeal must be lodged within 3 months of the date on which the employer is officially informed of the amount he will receive.

Consulting the union An employer who recognises an independent trade union, or who has been recommended to do so by ACAS, must consult it if he is planning to make any of its members redundant or if he is planning redundancies among non-union members in job categories for which the union is recognised. That rule applies even if the employees concerned are not legally entitled to a redundancy payment – for example, because they have not been in their jobs for long enough.

If fewer than 10 employees are to be dismissed, the consultation must take place 'at the earliest opportunity' – in practice, as soon as the employer is reasonably certain of the need for redundancies.

The employer must give a trade union representative written notice of:
● The reasons for the proposed redundancies.
● The number of employees to be dismissed and their job categories.
● The total number of employees, including those to be dismissed, in those job categories at the affected establishment.

● The way in which employees are to be chosen for redundancy.
● How the dismissals are to be carried out and the period over which they will be spread.

If an employer does not observe the consultation rules, the union – but not individual employees – can report his behaviour to an industrial tribunal. Unless the employer can show that there were 'special circumstances' – for example, bankruptcy – and that he took reasonable steps to follow the procedures, the tribunal can order him to pay extra compensation, called a 'protective award', to each redundant employee.

When fewer than 10 employees are made redundant together, each may receive up to 28 days' pay as a protective award. The maximum amounts are higher for 'mass redundancies' involving 10 or more people.

The protective award is in addition to any redundancy pay to which an employee may be entitled. Individuals may also be able to claim unfair dismissal because their employer had not consulted the union.

Mass redundancies An employer who recognises a trade union and who makes 10 or more people redundant at the same location within 30 days or less must follow special rules on 'mass redundancies' set out in the Employment Protection Act 1975.

If the number of employees involved is between 10 and 99, he must inform the Department of Employment at least 30 days before their dismissals take effect and he must begin consultations with their trade union at the same time.

If more than 100 employees are to be made redundant, the employer must tell the Department of Employment and the unions at least 90 days in advance.

An employer who fails to inform the Department of Employment of a 'mass redundancy' by the appropriate date may be fined up to £400 or lose up to 10 per cent of his rebate from the Redundancy Fund.

If he fails to consult the union, an industrial tribunal may order a protective award to each worker of up to 90 days' pay if there are more than 100 redundancies, or of up to 30 days' pay if between 10 and 99 employees are to be dismissed.

If the employer does not pay the protective award, an individual employee or his union is entitled to complain to an industrial tribunal.

THE EMPLOYER WHOSE OFFER WAS 'TOO LATE'

If an employer's offer of alternative work is delayed and the redundant employee has already found a better job elsewhere, the employee's refusal to stay with the business may not be unreasonable.

Horace Wood worked for a construction company. He was given notice of redundancy, and managed to find another job elsewhere. On his last day with his old employers they offered him suitable alternative work. He refused, because he had already accepted other employment which, he felt, would give him more security.

DECISION

It was reasonable for Mr Wood to refuse the offer of a suitable job in the circumstances.

SUPPLEMENTARY BENEFIT. If an employee receives payment in lieu of notice, he cannot start to qualify for unemployment benefit until the notice period represented by the payment has expired.

If someone accepts a lump sum in addition to his statutory redundancy payment on the termination of his employment, the question of whether he loses unemployment benefit may depend on the wording of the redundancy agreement.

If it specifically provides that part of this sum is payment in lieu of notice then he will not be entitled to benefit until the notice period represented by the payment has expired.

However, if no part of the sum is in consideration of foregoing such notice then the right to unemployment benefit is unaffected, even though the employee waives notice as part of the arrangement.

It does not matter whether payments are called *ex gratia*; the critical issue is whether a specific part of the lump sum is identifiable as consideration for foregoing notice.

Time off during notice of redundancy

Staff who are under notice of redundancy can take a limited amount of unpaid leave to look for a new job or to be re-trained. *See:* TIME OFF WORK

When another job is offered

An employer may avoid having to pay redundancy if he can offer a redundant employee another job. If the employee accepts, he forfeits his award. If he refuses to take the job, he will lose his payment if the employer can show that the job was suitable and that he acted unreasonably by declining.

The job offer must be made before the employee's old employment ends. It is not valid if it is made later.

The job must be with the employer's organisation, an associated company or with the new owners of the business in which the employee works. An employer cannot avoid a redundancy payment by finding a redundant worker employment with another, unrelated business.

[Continued on page 608

HOW REDUNDANCY PAYMENTS ARE CALCULATED

This ready-reckoner shows quickly how much redundancy pay a dismissed worker is entitled to receive by law. First, find the employee's length of service, in complete years, at the top of the table. Then read down that column until you come to the figure opposite his age last birthday, given beside the table on the left. That is the number of weeks' current pay he should get, subject to a maximum (in 1980, £3,600). Only men can claim for service over the age of 59. Service before the age of 18 is disregarded.

Example: Alan Jones joined his employers at the age of 16. He is now 35 and is being made redundant. His current earnings are £150 a week.

If the weekly earnings ceiling is £120, his entitlement is:

Service before 18 (2 years)	Nothing
Service between 18th and 22nd birthdays (4 complete years)	4 × ½ week's pay
Service between 22nd birthday and present (13 complete years)	13 × 1 week's pay
Total	15 weeks

Alan therefore receives £120 × 15 weeks
equals .... £1,800.

Once an employee has reached the birthday – normally, the 64th (men) or 59th (women) – before the one on which he or she attains retirement age, the redundancy award he or she would have been entitled to is reduced by $\frac{1}{12}$ in each succeeding month, so that by the time the next birthday arrives, the employee is not entitled to any redundancy payment.

Example: Mrs Jones is 59 years and 5 months old – 7 months younger than retirement age – when she is made redundant and leaves her job. She was earning £42 per week and had worked for that employer for 7 years. Had she been a year younger, she would have been entitled to a redundancy payment of £42 × 7 years × $1\frac{1}{2}$ = £441. However, because she had reached the birthday before retirement, her award is reduced by $\frac{1}{12}$ for each month she is past that birthday – 5 months. So she actually gets:

$\frac{7}{12}$ of £441 = £257.25

REDUNDANCY OR UNFAIR DISMISSAL?

Under the employment protection rules, redundancy is a 'fair' reason for dismissing someone. An employee who is redundant is not normally entitled to extra compensation – in addition to his redundancy payment – for UNFAIR DISMISSAL.

However, if an employer acts unreasonably in the way he makes an employee redundant, a tribunal may decide the employee was unfairly dismissed and order the employer to pay him more than his redundancy award.

Redundancies in which the employee is forced to leave because of the employer's gross breach of the employment contract are unfair. So are those in which the employer, without good reason, fails to warn an employee of his impending dismissal.

Because the dividing line between unfair dismissal and redundancy is often blurred, many applicants to industrial tribunals submit their claims for 'unfair dismissal or redundancy or both' – leaving the tribunal to decide the most appropriate award in the circumstances. *See:* DISCIPLINE AT WORK

AGE	NUMBER OF YEARS' SERVICE

AGE	2	3	4	5	6	7	8	9	10	11	12	13	14	15	16	17	18	19	20
20†	1	1	1	1	–														
21	1	1½	1½	1½	1½	–													
22	1	1½	2	2	2	2	–												
23	1½	2	2½	3	3	3	3	–											
24	2	2½	3	3½	4	4	4	4	–										
25	2	3	3½	4	4½	5	5	5	5	–									
26	2	3	4	4½	5	5½	6	6	6	6	–								
27	2	3	4	5	5½	6	6½	7	7	7	7	–							
28	2	3	4	5	6	6½	7	7½	8	8	8	8	–						
29	2	3	4	5	6	7	7½	8	8½	9	9	9	9	–					
30	2	3	4	5	6	7	8	8½	9	9½	10	10	10	10	–				
31	2	3	4	5	6	7	8	9	9½	10	10½	11	11	11	11	–			
32	2	3	4	5	6	7	8	9	10	10½	11	11½	12	12	12	12	–		
33	2	3	4	5	6	7	8	9	10	11	11½	12	12½	13	13	13	13	–	
34	2	3	4	5	6	7	8	9	10	11	12	12½	13	13½	14	14	14	14	–
35	2	3	4	5	6	7	8	9	10	11	12	13	13½	14	14½	15	15	15	15
36	2	3	4	5	6	7	8	9	10	11	12	13	14	14½	15	15½	16	16	16
37	2	3	4	5	6	7	8	9	10	11	12	13	14	15	15½	16	16½	17	17
38	2	3	4	5	6	7	8	9	10	11	12	13	14	15	16	16½	17	17½	18
39	2	3	4	5	6	7	8	9	10	11	12	13	14	15	16	17	17½	18	18½
40	2	3	4	5	6	7	8	9	10	11	12	13	14	15	16	17	18	18½	19
41	2	3	4	5	6	7	8	9	10	11	12	13	14	15	16	17	18	19	19½
42	2½	3½	4½	5½	6½	7½	8½	9½	10½	11½	12½	13½	14½	15½	16½	17½	18½	19½	20½
43	3	4	5	6	7	8	9	10	11	12	13	14	15	16	17	18	19	20	21
44	3	4½	5½	6½	7½	8½	9½	10½	11½	12½	13½	14½	15½	16½	17½	18½	19½	20½	21½
45	3	4½	6	7	8	9	10	11	12	13	14	15	16	17	18	19	20	21	22
46	3	4½	6	7½	8½	9½	10½	11½	12½	13½	14½	15½	16½	17½	18½	19½	20½	21½	22½
47	3	4½	6	7½	9	10	11	12	13	14	15	16	17	18	19	20	21	22	23
48	3	4½	6	7½	9	10½	11½	12½	13½	14½	15½	16½	17½	18½	19½	20½	21½	22½	23½
49	3	4½	6	7½	9	10½	12	13	14	15	16	17	18	19	20	21	22	23	24
50	3	4½	6	7½	9	10½	12	13½	14½	15½	16½	17½	18½	19½	20½	21½	22½	23½	24½
51	3	4½	6	7½	9	10½	12	13½	15	16	17	18	19	20	21	22	23	24	25
52	3	4½	6	7½	9	10½	12	13½	15	16½	17½	18½	19½	20½	21½	22½	23½	24½	25½
53	3	4½	6	7½	9	10½	12	13½	15	16½	18	19	20	21	22	23	24	25	26
54	3	4½	6	7½	9	10½	12	13½	15	16½	18	19½	20½	21½	22½	23½	24½	25½	26½
55	3	4½	6	7½	9	10½	12	13½	15	16½	18	19½	21	22	23	24	25	26	27
56	3	4½	6	7½	9	10½	12	13½	15	16½	18	19½	21	22½	23½	24½	25½	26½	27½
57	3	4½	6	7½	9	10½	12	13½	15	16½	18	19½	21	22½	24	25	26	27	28
58	3	4½	6	7½	9	10½	12	13½	15	16½	18	19½	21	22½	24	25½	26½	27½	28½
59*	3	4½	6	7½	9	10½	12	13½	15	16½	18	19½	21	22½	24	25½	27	28	29
60	3	4½	6	7½	9	10½	12	13½	15	16½	18	19½	21	22½	24	25½	27	28½	29½
61	3	4½	6	7½	9	10½	12	13½	15	16½	18	19½	21	22½	24	25½	27	28½	30
62	3	4½	6	7½	9	10½	12	13½	15	16½	18	19½	21	22½	24	25½	27	28½	30
63	3	4½	6	7½	9	10½	12	13½	15	16½	18	19½	21	22½	24	25½	27	28½	30
64*	3	4½	6	7½	9	10½	12	13½	15	16½	18	19½	21	22½	24	25½	27	28½	30

* For women aged between 59 and 60, and men aged between 64 and 65, the cash amount due is to be reduced by $\frac{1}{12}$ for every complete month by which the age exceeds 59 or 64 respectively.

† In some cases, employees whose 20th birthday falls a few days after they become redundant may have the necessary 104 weeks' qualifying service.

The job must start no later than 4 weeks after the end of the present employment.

Making the offer The offer of a new job may be made in writing or orally, but it must be precise. It is not enough for the employer merely to tell a worker 'I'll try to fit you in'. The employee must be told if the terms and conditions of the new job differ from those of the old one.

Trial periods A redundant employee who is offered alternative work can try the new job for at least 4 weeks, provided that the terms and conditions differ from those of the old one. If the terms and conditions are identical, the employee does not qualify for a trial and, if he accepts the job, he loses his right to a redundancy award.

The trial period can be less than 4 weeks only if the employee asks for it to be shorter. It can be longer than 4 weeks if it involves a period of re-training for the new work, but then its length must be agreed in writing.

An employee is not obliged to accept a trial period. He can refuse to try the new job, leave when the old one ends and claim redundancy. However, industrial tribunals are more ready to decide an employee acted unreasonably, and therefore has no right to an award, if he turned down a trial.

If an employee decides to stay in the job once the trial is over, he forfeits his redundancy claim, but does not lose his accumulated service. If he decides to leave, he can claim redundancy at any time during the 6 months from the date on which the trial period ended.

What is a 'suitable alternative'

Under the redundancy rules, alternative work offered by the employer must be 'suitable' for the redundant employee. If it is not, the employee can refuse it without jeopardising his redundancy award.

If the terms of the new job are identical to those of the old one, the job is 'suitable'. But if they differ even slightly, the work may not be suitable.

Industrial tribunals decide each case according to its facts, including the personal circumstances of the employee. They examine not only the nature of the work offered, and the terms and conditions, but also whether it suits the employee's skills, experience, status, temperament and state of health.

When it is 'reasonable' to refuse another job

An employee who is offered alternative work may refuse it, even if it is suitable, without losing his redundancy award, provided that the refusal is not 'unreasonable' in the circumstances.

Generally, industrial tribunals base their decision on what is reasonable or not on the employee's personal situation, rather than on the nature of the alternative work.

REFERENCE

Your right to give an honest opinion of someone's character

If you are asked to give a reference for someone, perhaps a former employee or subordinate, you need fear no legal consequences provided that you tell the truth to the best of your knowledge and belief.

If for some reason you do not want to tell the truth in a reference, it is better not to give one. No one has a right to demand that you do so.

When a reference can lead to an action for damages

The person who is the subject of a bad reference can sue successfully for LIBEL only if he can show that the person giving the reference knew that what he wrote was untrue and wanted to harm the person he was reporting on.

Even if it can be proved that you were wrong in a reference you gave and that you thereby damaged the subject's reputation, he still cannot sue you successfully for libel provided that your opinion was an honest one.

That applies, however, only if you have been asked to give a reference by someone, like a prospective employer, who seems reasonably entitled to ask for one and you seem a reasonably suitable person – for example, a teacher or former employer – to give one.

If a casual acquaintance on a train told you his daughter was about to marry and you volunteered the information that the young man she was marrying had a bad reputation you might be liable for slander. You have no legal or social duty to make a statement like that on a crowded train on such an occasion.

When a reference is too good

Just as you are entitled to tell the truth, the person to whom you are writing the reference is entitled to expect you to tell the truth to the best of your knowledge and belief. If you dismiss an employee for dishonesty but give him a reference saying he is trustworthy, his new employer can sue you for any loss he suffers if the employee steals from him.

A new employer might even succeed in an action for NEGLIGENCE if you said mistakenly that the subject of the reference was trustworthy without bothering to check within your own organisation that this was true. The risk of an action for negligence can be avoided, however, by stating in the reference that you accept no responsibility for its accuracy.

REFUGEE

When a foreigner flees his homeland

Someone with a claim for POLITICAL ASYLUM may be allowed to stay in Britain although he or she does not otherwise qualify for entry under the rules of IMMIGRATION.

Britain is a signatory to a series of United Nations agreements which protect people whose life or freedom in their homeland is threatened because of their race, religion, nationality or politics. The main point of those agreements is that such people must not be forced to return home.

There is no provision, however, to admit people as refugees simply because they cannot make a living in their native land – because of a natural disaster or any other reason.

REFUSE COLLECTION

Local councils have a duty to collect house waste

It is the duty of a district council to collect household waste unless it is left in such an inaccessible place that the cost of collection is unreasonable.

Dustmen can, for example, refuse to collect household rubbish if the dustbin has been left at the back of the house or at some place difficult to reach, and in many areas they can refuse to empty more than one bin.

Councils can insist that the rubbish is left in a proper dustbin or in a regulation dustbin provided by them. They may, for example, insist that it is left in a sack held in a metal holder or that it is placed in plastic bags.

Anything that is too big to go into a dustbin or any other rubbish not in a dustbin can be left by the dustmen. The council refuse department should be asked to make a special collection, and they can charge for it.

Using a council tip

Garden refuse such as grass cuttings or prunings from rose bushes or trees is not household rubbish nor are such things as old mattresses or disused furniture. These should not be left out for the dustmen.

Councils must by law provide dumps where refuse of this sort can be left without charge. The council will tell you which dump is nearest to your home and the hours that it is open to the public. You must arrange to take the rubbish there yourself.

Industrial waste

Dustmen will not collect waste produced in the course of business or industry and council workers can refuse to accept it at the local rubbish dump. Special arrangements should be made with the council to collect industrial waste, and the council can charge for the service.

Roadside refuse tips

County councils, which are responsible for highways, can provide refuse tips and litter bins beside main roads, but they do not have a duty to do so.

It is an offence with a maximum penalty of £100 to leave any LITTER at any open place to which the public has access, such as a street or park.

REHABILITATION

A person's criminal record can sometimes be kept secret

After certain periods of time some convicted criminals and people fined by the courts are allowed to 'wipe the slate clean' under the 1974 Rehabilitation of Offenders Act. It is as if their offence had never been committed.

These ex-offenders have no need to mention their convictions when applying for a job, a mortgage, insurance, or to join a club or trade union.

For example, a thief whose gaol sentence has been spent has no need to tell a prospective employer that he has been in gaol: a motorist fined for driving with excess alcohol need not reveal the offence to an insurance company.

Convictions become spent under the Act at the end of a fixed period from the date of the conviction. A fine, for example, becomes spent after 5 years, a 6 months' prison sentence after 7 years. A sentence of 2½ years or more can never become spent.

When the Act does not apply

There are certain cases when an ex-offender must reveal his criminal record even though, under the provisions of the Act, it has been spent.

1. Spent convictions cannot be con-

HOW LONG IT TAKES FOR A SENTENCE TO BE SPENT
Different time limits based on the severity of the original punishment

Sentence	Rehabilitation period
Prison for over 6 months – 2½ years	10 years*
Prison for up to 6 months	7 years*
Fine	5 years*
Probation	1 year or the length of the order, whichever is the longer
Conditional discharge	
Binding over	
Absolute discharge	6 months
Disqualification	When disqualification ends
Offences in the Services	
Cashiering, discharge with ignominy or dismissal with disgrace	10 years*
Dismissal	7 years*
Detention for disciplinary offence	5 years*
Sentences on children and young people	
Detention for over 6 months – 2½ years (under the Children and Young Persons Act 1933)	5 years
Detention for up to 6 months (under the Children and Young Persons Act 1933)	3 years
Borstal	7 years
Detention centre	3 years
Remand home	1 year after the expiry of the order
Approved school	
Attendance centre	
Care order (under Children and Young Persons Act 1969)	When the order expires (or 12 months after conviction, if longer)
Supervision (under Children and Young Persons Act 1969)	

* *These periods are reduced by half if the offender was under 17 at the time of the conviction.*

SPENT BUT NOT FORGOTTEN

Even when a conviction is spent, it can be presented privately to a court by the prosecutor in any later criminal proceedings against the offender.

---

cealed when applying for a job as a lawyer, doctor, dentist, accountant, nurse, chemist, justices' clerk, prison officer, traffic warden, probation officer, social worker, teacher, or for any position which entails looking after children. In any of these cases an ex-offender must reveal any conviction if he is asked to do so.

2. Spent convictions can be revealed to the court by the prosecution in criminal proceedings, and in applications for custody, care, adoption, wardship or guardianship, but not usually in other court cases.

A witness's past convictions will be revealed only in exceptional circumstances.

3. A conviction can never be spent if the sentence is more than 2½ years, even if the prisoner is released early on parole or is given remission.

When an offender commits a new offence

A conviction that is spent remains spent, even if the offender is convicted later of a new offence.

For example, a man sentenced to 6 months' gaol will have spent the sentence after 7 years. If he is gaoled for another 6 months after his 7 year rehabilitation period is up, his first sentence remains spent and need never be revealed. His second sentence will become spent after a further 7 years, after which that sentence, too, need not be revealed.

A second conviction before the first one is spent will extend the rehabilitation period.

For example, a burglar jailed for 2 years has to wait 10 years before his sentence will be spent. If after only 5 years he gets another 2 year sentence, then neither of his sentences will be spent until 10 years from the date of his second conviction.

When someone is dismissed

It may happen that an employer takes on a new worker and later discovers that the man has a spent conviction. If he then dismisses the ex-offender, the man can claim UNFAIR DISMISSAL and would almost certainly win his case at an INDUSTRIAL TRIBUNAL.

When a conviction is disclosed

A person in an official position who wrongly discloses a spent conviction can be prosecuted and may be fined up to £200.

Anyone who learns of a person's spent conviction from official records by fraud or dishonesty can be gaoled for up to 6 months and fined up to £400.

An ex-offender whose spent conviction is publicly revealed by another person can sue for defamation, but he would have to show that the other person acted maliciously.

REJECTION OF GOODS

If goods sold are unsatisfactory the buyer may be able to claim his MONEY BACK – or refuse to pay, if he has not yet paid.

RELIGION

The freedom to choose your beliefs

The people of Britain are free to follow whichever religion they choose, or no religion at all and the law makes no discrimination against them, provided they do not commit the anti-Christian offence of BLASPHEMY.

But the law does not make special allowances for religious beliefs, either. A person's religious objection to the use of medicine is ignored in deciding whether he is guilty of criminally neglecting a person in his care.

If, for example, a husband refused to give drugs to his wife which might have saved her life, he will be guilty of criminal neglect, whatever his religious beliefs.

The law does make some very limited restrictions because of religion:
● The sovereign must be a member of the Church of England.
● A person who marries a Roman Catholic cannot succeed to the throne.
● Clergy of the Church of England, the Church of Scotland and the Roman Catholic Church cannot become members of the House of Commons.

RELIGIOUS EDUCATION

Some form of religious instruction must be provided at state schools

Every state school must by law hold a daily religious assembly and provide religious instruction for the pupils. The religion is generally Christian.

Parents can insist that their children do not attend any act of worship or receive any religious teaching.

Children cannot opt out of their own accord – exemption can be granted only at the request of the parents. Those who do not go to assembly usually sit in the classroom or library.

The daily assembly

The Education Act 1944 lays down that there must be a single, collective act of worship at all state schools at the start of each day.

No particular religion is defined, but the Act says that in county schools – those entirely provided and maintained by the local authority – the worship must be non-denominational.

Voluntary-aided church schools can hold services in their particular denomination. If a school hall is not large enough to hold all the pupils, separate assemblies can be held.

Teaching religion

The way in which religious education is taught in schools varies from district to district. The syllabus is agreed after talks between teachers, the local education authority and leaders of various local religious factions.

In many cities where there are multi-cultural and multi-racial populations,

HOW RELIGION IS 'TAUGHT'

The method of teaching religion varies greatly. In many areas, it is combined with health and sex education on the syllabus.

broad instruction is given, sometimes with several religions being taught in the same school.

Some school authorities mix religious education with other social studies such as health education, community affairs and sex education, sometimes called moral education. That makes it more difficult for parents to exercise their right to withdraw their children from religious lessons. They still have the right to do so, however, and should discuss the matter with the head teacher.

A group of parents who would like their children to receive education in a religion not taught by the school in their area can ask for facilities for such instruction to be provided. They would, however, have to provide the staff and books at their own expense.

The education authority and school may do their best to meet the parents' request, but they are not bound by law to do so.

Alternatively, parents may be able to persuade the authority to allow their children to attend religious education classes elsewhere.

Can a teacher opt out

No teacher in a state school can be ordered to give religious instruction if he does not wish to.

Nor can a teacher be legally disqualified from an appointment or from possible promotion because of his religious beliefs or lack of them.

Voluntary-aided church schools can insist on religious qualifications when appointing staff.

Days off for religious observances

Children can stay away from school on any days 'exclusively set apart for religious observance' by their religion, whatever religion that is.

For Anglicans this means only Ascension Day, because all other Anglican festivals occur during normal school holidays.

REMAND

When a criminal case is delayed

If there is a delay in dealing with a person at any stage after he or she first appears in court charged with a criminal offence, the defendant stays under the court's control by a process known as remanding. *See:* CRIMINAL PROCEEDINGS

A remand is necessary when:
● A later date is set for the first hearing of evidence.
● The first hearing is adjourned – that is, postponed – beyond the set date because one side or other needs more time to prepare its case or to produce witnesses.

PRIVILEGED PRISONER

When an unconvicted prisoner is held on remand, he is entitled to wear his own clothes, have visitors every day and have meals sent in. He can consult his own lawyer, doctor or dentist – but always at his own expense.

● Magistrates want a defendant to be medically examined.
● Part of the evidence has to be taken before the date fixed for other witnesses to be heard – usually because a witness will be abroad on that date.
● A hearing lasts more than 1 day.
● A hearing is interrupted – for example, by illness.
● After a hearing by magistrates, a defendant who pleads not guilty is committed to the crown court for trial.
● A defendant who pleads guilty in a magistrates' court is committed to the crown court for SENTENCE.
● After a defendant is convicted, the magistrate or judge delays passing sentence – usually because he wants a social worker's or probation officer's report.

Remanding in custody

Most defendants who are remanded are freed on BAIL. Those who are detained in custody – in a special remand centre, in the remand section of a prison, or in a prison hospital – are subject to prison discipline.

But if they have not been convicted, they have rights that are not accorded to other prisoners. They can:
● Receive visitors every day.
● Consult with their lawyers as often as necessary, out of the hearing of prison staff.
● Wear their own clothing and have clothing sent in.
● Have meals sent in.
● Receive books and papers – subject to censorship.
● Send or receive an unlimited number of letters, subject to censorship.
● Be treated – at their own expense – by outside doctors or dentists.

They cannot be made to perform any work, although they may if they wish and receive a prison wage if they do. They cannot be ordered to shave or have a haircut, unless there is a health risk.

REMARRIAGE

When a 'married person' is free to remarry

A previously married man or woman can marry again only if:
1. The previous marriage has been ended by DIVORCE.

2. The previous marriage has been annulled or is automatically void. *See:* NULLITY

3. The previous partner is dead.

A second marriage ceremony while the other spouse is alive and the first marriage still legally binding is bigamous. *See:* BIGAMY

If there has been a divorce, the ex-husband or wife wanting to remarry must wait until the DECREE NISI has been made absolute before a valid ceremony can take place.

A divorced couple can remarry each other, and each is free to marry certain relatives of the other. *See:* MARRIAGE

For example, a man can marry his divorced wife's sister or the divorced wife of his brother. A divorced wife has the same freedom to remarry a relative of her ex-husband.

A woman's remarriage automatically brings to an end any court order for regular payments to her by her ex-husband. But an order for the MAINTENANCE of children is unaffected by remarriage of a parent unless the order is varied or cancelled by a court.

Once someone who is divorced has remarried he or she cannot start any application for financial relief such as maintenance, a lump sum or transfer of property, against the former spouse. But if proceedings have already been started, they can go on, even after that spouse's remarriage.

REMOVAL

When you shift to another home

If you are moving house and have to engage a removal contractor, it is advisable to ask several firms to quote for the job. Prices can vary widely.

Make sure that the quotation you accept is made in writing. It should be for a firm price – not a loose estimate.

Who is liable for damage

Many contractors ask their customers to sign a printed form of agreement before the removal date. It may include a condition relieving the contractor of any liability for loss of or damage to your possessions – even if he or his staff are negligent.

Such a condition is legally effective only if it is fair and reasonable. If the agreement also points out the need for INSURANCE cover, a court might hold that a no-liability clause is reasonable.

If there is no agreement document, the ordinary law makes the contractor liable for loss or damage – but only if he and his staff are negligent. In a dispute, he can avoid liability if he can show that reasonable care was taken.

In either case, you cannot get compensation for accidental loss or damage if the removal company takes reasonable care. So it is always advisable to arrange a special insurance cover.

Special rules apply if you send household effects abroad. *See:* CARRIAGE OF GOODS

Financial help in moving·

If you have to move because of a COMPULSORY PURCHASE, redevelopment or closing order, you are entitled to a disturbance payment from the local authority that makes the order.

As well as the removal bill, the payment may cover incidental expenses – for example, reconnection of electrical equipment or a telephone.

Council tenants Local authorities are also allowed, if they wish, to pay a council tenant's removal costs in a compulsory exchange, or in other cases when a shift is to the council's advantage.

Social security aid Someone who is receiving SUPPLEMENTARY BENEFIT may qualify for a special grant to cover removal costs, provided that social security officials are satisfied that there is good reason for the move. That aid is not available if the beneficiary can afford to pay the cost out of whatever savings he has over £300.

Moving to get a job A family man who is out of work, or about to be made redundant, may qualify for state payment of his removal expenses, and various other benefits, if he finds work in another area. *See:* UNEMPLOYMENT BENEFIT

RENT ALLOWANCE

The help that a private tenant can claim for housing costs

A tenant who rents a house or flat privately, or from any official organisation except a district council, may qual-

ify for council aid in paying the rent. Council tenants can receive similar help in the form of a RENT REBATE.

Rent allowances and rebates are means-tested, but they are not based solely on income or savings. A council's decision on whether an applicant qualifies for assistance, and if so how much, also takes into account:

● The tenant's needs – based mainly on the size of the family and their ages.

● The amount of rent paid.

Councils do not subsidise private rents that they consider excessive. If a tenant is paying too much rent when alternative accommodation is available, or claims assistance in paying rent for accommodation that is larger or more lavish than he needs, a council bases its calculations on a lower rent figure – the one it thinks is reasonable.

If furniture is provided by the landlord, or if the rent entitles the tenant to meals or other services, the value is assessed and deducted from the rent before the tenant's eligibility for an allowance is decided.

Leaflets available from council housing and treasurer's departments explain the method of calculating rent allowances, and show the maximum amount a council can allow. Where rents are unusually high or housing is unusually difficult to find, the Government lets councils pay more.

When a home is sub-let or shared

A person to whom living quarters are genuinely sub-let, by a formal agreement, may be entitled to a rent allowance. If the main tenant is receiving an allowance or rebate, it is reduced.

In a joint tenancy, a council normally treats the tenant with the higher income as the sole tenant, and calculates his entitlement on his share of the rent.

Someone who pays rent as a lodger, or shares a home without a tenancy agreement, cannot qualify for an allowance or rebate. Payments from such a person may reduce the main tenant's own entitlement.

People who live in hostels or hotels cannot claim rent allowances.

When a tenant is on benefit

Social security SUPPLEMENTARY BENEFIT payments include rent assis-

HOW TO APPLY FOR A RENT ALLOWANCE

Any private tenant who has to pay a high rent because of the size of his family, or whose income is low, may qualify for a rent allowance.

Application forms are available from the housing or treasurer's departments of local councils, and from most housing aid agencies or Citizens Advice Bureaux.

Evidence is needed of:
● Income – from an employee's payslips, or an accountant's certificate if the tenant is self-employed.
● Rent – from a weekly rent book, tenancy agreement, receipts or cleared cheques.
● Savings – from bank books or other investment documents. Savings over a certain figure – £1,200 in 1979 – reduce the tenant's entitlement to an allowance.

tance to tenants. For that reason, no one who receives the benefit can be granted a council rent allowance or rebate. Although some people on supplementary benefit might be better off if they received a rent allowance and rate rebate, it is now no longer possible to forgo supplementary benefit and claim rent allowances and rate rebates instead.

How allowances are paid

Tenants who receive rent allowances are sent books of postdated Girobank cheques that can be cashed every 2 weeks. A book lasts for 6 months in the case of an employed person, or 12 months if the tenant is a pensioner.

Application for an allowance must be renewed every 6 or 12 months, depending on how often cheque books are sent. But if a tenant's financial position changes, he must tell the council immediately. Someone who receives an allowance to which he is no longer entitled can be prosecuted for fraud.

When an allowance is refused

The law contains no specific remedies for tenants who wish to challenge a council's refusal to grant an allowance. However, any tenant who believes that he has been wrongfully refused a rent allowance should engage a solicitor to try to obtain a High Court order compelling the council to carry out its legal

duty to grant an allowance. Legal aid may be available, but it may be more practical for a tenant who is aggrieved by the treatment of his application for a rent allowance to complain to the Commissioner for Local Government Administration. *See:* OMBUDSMEN

RENT LIMIT

How the law can hold down private housing rents

If a privately let house or flat has a rateable value of no more than £1,500 in Greater London, or £750 elsewhere, and a tenant's annual rent is at least two-thirds of that figure, an increase in the rent can in most cases be prevented or limited by law.

A local RENT OFFICER can be asked to check the rateable value and set a fair rent for any such home except:
● Council and Crown lettings (unless managed by the Crown Estate Commissioners).
● University or college accommodation for students.
● Holiday lettings.
● Licensed premises.
● Lettings which include the provision of meals or personal services – for example, laundry.
● Premises where the landlord also lives – but if he simply occupies another flat in the same block, the rent can still be scrutinised by the rent officer.

In the last case, although a rent officer cannot fix a fair rent, a rent tribunal can be asked to decide on a reasonable rent. *See:* RENT REGISTRATION

If the rateable value limits are exceeded, the premises are classed as 'luxury' accommodation. There is no rent limit, although the occupier has other rights under LANDLORD AND TENANT legislation.

Tenancies that have continued since July 6, 1957, or before may have been CONTROLLED TENANCIES. These were all converted, on November 28, 1980, into ordinary regulated tenancies, for which the RENT OFFICER can fix a fair rent. The rent under controlled tenancies was approximately twice the 1956 gross rateable value, and this would often work out at less than £2 per week. The landlord cannot now simply increase the rents of these formerly con-

trolled tenancies. To obtain a rent increase the landlord must request the rent officer to fix a fair rent.

When a rise can be prevented

Until the agreed term of a Rent Act tenancy expires, or until someone who stays for automatically renewable periods is given notice to quit, the occupancy is a contractual tenancy.

The rent is fixed either by agreement with the tenant or fair rent registration, in which case it cannot be raised without a new registration. If the house is not let, the landlord can apply to the rent officer for the registered rent to be cancelled – as long as 2 years have elapsed since the rent was last registered.

Even if the tenant exercises his rights to stay after the contractual period ends, he has what is called a statutory tenancy. While that continues, the landlord cannot raise the rent unless he follows strict legal procedures. *See:* EVICTION

WHEN RENT CAN BE RECLAIMED

If a private tenancy comes under the rent limit provisions of the Rent Act, a rent officer may have set a 'fair rent' for the premises.

When the landlord lives on the premises, or provides meals or other personal services such as cleaning, there can be no fair rent figure – but a rent tribunal may have set a 'reasonable rent'.

A tenant can ask at the local rent office whether a fair rent or reasonable rent is registered for his home. If it is less than he has been charged, he has a legal right to reclaim the overpayment.

Excess rent can be recovered up to 2 years later if a fair rent was registered, or up to 6 years later if a reasonable rent was registered.

However, a tenant should not assume that a lower registered rent figure means that he is automatically entitled to a refund. A landlord is entitled to increase a registered rent to take account of an increase in his rates.

A tenant can recover excess rent by making deductions from later payments, or if necessary by taking a county court action for debt. But it is advisable before taking either course to discuss the situation with a RENT OFFICER or a housing aid or advice agency. *See:* RENT REGISTRATION

When a rise is permitted

During a statutory tenancy – after a contractual period has ended – a landlord can legally obtain a rent increase in any of three ways:

● By having a fair rent, or an increased fair rent, registered with the rent officer.

● By serving a formal 'notice of increase', which can be based only on higher rate demands, or on the increased cost of furniture or services.

● By persuading the tenant to enter into a written agreement to pay more.

A new rent agreement is not valid unless it is headed by a statement that the tenant is not obliged to enter into it, and that his security of tenure is not affected if he refuses.

The statement must also tell the tenant of his right to apply for the registration of a fair rent – even after he signs the agreement.

If an agreement fails to comply with those requirements, extra rent obtained by it can be reclaimed for up to 2 years after payment. If a refund is refused, the tenant has a case for civil debt proceedings in a county court.

If a landlord claims extra rent because of increased rates, or increased costs of furniture or services, the notice of increase has to be set out in a certain way. Landlords can copy from a model form available from government stationery offices.

A notice of increase based on higher

RAISING THE RENT

In a statutory tenancy, one of the three ways that a landlord can increase the rent is by issuing a formal notice of increase.

rates or costs can be served even if a fair rent has been registered. But in that case the increase cannot be passed on immediately, but must be phased in over a period of up to 2 years.

The phasing method is complicated, but basically a landlord can pass on one-half of the total increase, or 40p a week – whichever is greater – in any one year. The landlord can pass on the full cost of the increase attributable to payment for services immediately the rent is registered.

Example: Suppose the rent officer awards an increase of 40p per week for the cost of services and 90p a week for the residential element: a total increase of £1.30 per week. The increase is phased in as the increased service charge of 40p a week plus a further 45p a week for the residential element, in the first year: a total of 85p per week. The remainder of the increase (45p) can be claimed in the second year. A total increase of £2.70 a week, with nothing attributable to services, would cost the tenant an increase of £1.35 a week in the first year and £1.35 in the second.

RENT OFFICER

The judge of fair rents

Every local authority has a rent office to administer or explain the Rent Act. Its staff are employed by the authority but are responsible to the Department of the Environment.

Any private tenant or landlord of premises covered by the Act, or the local authority itself, can ask a rent officer to set a fair rent for the premises. His decision is recorded in a public register and it is illegal to charge a higher amount, except for rates. *See:* RENT REGISTRATION

RENT REBATE

Aid for needy council tenants

A council tenant may be entitled to assistance in paying his rent if his family is large or his income is low.

The council calculates an amount, usually fortnightly, to be offset against the rent at the time of payment. In effect the tenant pays a reduced rent.

His legal liability for the whole rent, however, is not reduced. So if a rebate payment is held up – for example, because the council suspects fraud, or simply because of an administrative delay or a clerical error – the tenant must pay the full amount.

Rebates are reviewed every 6 or 12 months. But if a tenant's financial position changes, the council must be told immediately.

How to apply Rent rebate application forms are available from council housing or treasurer's departments, and Citizens Advice Bureaux.

RENT REGISTRATION

How a fair rent is decided and kept on record

Every local rent office must keep a register of fair rents for private tenancies that are protected by the Rent Act, and therefore subject to a RENT LIMIT.

The register must be open to public inspection, so that any landlord or tenant can see whether a fair rent has been fixed for a particular house or flat. Records are kept of rents for furnished lettings since 1974, and other tenancies since 1965.

Either party – although it is usually more in the tenant's interests – is entitled to have a RENT OFFICER assess a fair rent for a tenancy that is covered by the Rent Act but has not been registered before.

A new fair rent can be fixed, normally 2 years after a previous registration. Again either party can apply, but at that stage it is usually more in the landlord's interests to do so. Provided that, at the time he applies, the house is not let, the landlord can apply to the rent officer for the registered rent to be cancelled as long as 2 years have passed since the rent was last registered.

Applying for a fair rent

Fair rent application forms are available from local rent offices and most housing aid or advice agencies. Either party can make an application – or the landlord and tenant can agree to make a joint application.

The local authority itself can arrange for a rent officer to fix a fair rent if it learns of overcharging – usually when a needy tenant applies for a RENT ALLOWANCE.

Application can be made at any time during a tenancy. The fact that a tenant has just signed an agreement does not prevent his seeking a rent officer's ruling if he thinks he is paying too much.

The applicant must state on the form exactly what rent he wants registered. But it does not matter what figure is chosen, provided that it is lower than the present rent if the tenant applies, or higher than the present rent if the landlord applies.

When an application is received the rent officer sends a copy to the other party, who is entitled to put his own point of view. The officer visits the premises and holds an informal discussion involving both parties.

Legal representation is not normally necessary, and LEGAL AID is not available for the application procedure – but it may be possible to get free advice beforehand.

A rent officer's decision may be given immediately or delayed for further consideration, but in either case it must be conveyed in writing. He does not have to explain why he reached a particular figure.

What a rent officer judges

If an application is made for registration of a fair rent, the rent officer must take into account all the factors – except scarcity – that go towards making one home more or less valuable than another. Typically they include:
● Size.
● State of repair.
● Quality of fixed facilities and furniture.
● Age.
● Character.
● Locality.
● Accessibility.
● Availability of transport and other public amenities.

The rent officer must disregard the personal circumstances of both parties – for example, an elderly tenant's difficulties in using stairs, or a landlord's lack of finance to carry out repairs. But the fact that there are many stairs to climb, or that a flat is in poor condition, is taken into account in his assessment.

The officer must also disregard improvements carried out by a tenant – unless he was bound to make them –

and any deterioration of the property caused by a tenant's neglect.

Although it is scarcity more than anything else that causes property values and rents to rise, a rent officer is not allowed to consider that factor.

But in reaching a fair rent figure he takes into account rents for homes of comparable size, nature and locality, and makes allowance for the rising cost of living, and of providing housing and keeping it in good repair.

When a decision is contested

If landlord and tenant apply jointly for a fair rent ruling, the rent officer's decision is final. Otherwise either side has 28 days in which to ask for it to be referred to a rent assessment committee.

An assessment committee has no power to judge points of law – for example, whether a property comes under Rent Act control. It simply follows the same procedure as a rent officer, and comes up with its own fair rent figure.

Assessment committee rents tend to be about 10 per cent higher than those made by rent officers, so it is not generally in a tenant's interests to appeal to an assessment committee unless the officer has obviously made a mistake.

Committee discussions are more formal than a meeting with a rent officer, but legal representation is not normally needed.

There is no provision for review and no right of appeal after an assessment committee has given its decision. However, if a committee or a rent officer seem to have based a fair rent ruling on a point that is wrong in law, a case can be taken to the Divisional Court.

Disputes over whether a home comes under Rent Act jurisdiction can be dealt with by a county court.

Court proceedings on rent issues are likely to require expert legal advice. Legal aid may be available.

How a decision takes effect

The date from which a fair rent can be paid is stated in a rent officer's or assessment committee's decision and must generally be the date when the fair rent is registered by the rent officer or a decision given by the committee.

If the fair rent is lower than the previous rent, and the tenant has made more payments at the old figure by the time

the fair rent is registered, the overpayment must be refunded. The usual method is by deduction from later payments.

But if the fair rent is higher than the previous rent, the landlord cannot start charging it until an existing 'contractual tenancy' has ended. That means the higher rent does not apply until an agreed term of occupancy has expired, or until an indefinite, automatically renewable occupancy is terminated by a notice to quit.

If a higher fair rent is assessed against a tenant who stays on after his contractual tenancy ends, the increase – unless it is very small – may have to be phased in over a period of up to 2 years.

Vacant premises A landlord who intends to carry out work on a property – for example, a conversion from a house to flats – can apply for a fair rent certificate showing what he will be entitled to charge when the work is done. A certificate is issued subject to inspection before the premises are occupied.

Checking the register

When a rent is registered, the public record includes a description of the accommodation and facilities provided, and details of any special obligations on the tenant or landlord.

But anyone who consults a register to see what rent is fixed for his home, or for a comparable home, should treat the information with caution because:
● Registered rents never include rate charges, so tenants often pay more than the registered figure.
● The records take no account of the state of repair, so there may be no real comparison between different homes, or of the same home at different times.

Changing a fair rent

When a fair rent is already registered, it cannot usually be reassessed for 2 years. That applies with a new tenancy or even with a new landlord – so in some cases both sides are bound by a registration that originally concerned neither.

However, the 2 year bar on re-registration does not apply when:
● A landlord and tenant make a joint application.
● There is a major change in the terms of tenancy, the condition of the premises or the provision of furniture or facilities.

When a landlord shares premises

A landlord's occupancy of another flat in the same block does not affect a tenant's Rent Act protection.

But if the landlord lives in the same house as the tenant, only a rent tribunal can assess a 'reasonable rent'. It can make the assessment even where the rent includes substantial payments for personal services, but not where there are substantial payments for board. When food is provided, the contract is outside the jurisdiction of both the rent officer and the tribunal.

A rent tribunal has complete discretion – the guidelines that a rent officer must follow do not apply.

Application, inspection and hearing procedures are similar to those for fair rent registration, and the rents that are fixed can be checked by a new tenant or landlord in the same way.

The major differences are that tribunal registrations:
● Show whether the fixed figure is increased by rate payments.
● Require no 2 year phasing of increases.
● Cannot be made after an agreed letting term ends by expiry or notice to quit.

No new application for a rent to be fixed by a tribunal can be made within 2 years of a previous application. However, a landlord, provided he has no tenant in the house at the time he applies, may ask the tribunal to cancel the previous rent registration, as long as 2 years have passed since the last registration.

CHECKING THE AMENITIES

The rent officer has to disregard an applicant's personal circumstances, but he pays great regard to the property and its environment.

'Take a rest on the next landing'

RENTCHARGE

How a seller obtains income from and keeps control of freehold land

Rentcharge agreements made before 1977, mainly in the Manchester and Bristol areas, give the seller of a freehold the right to impose conditions on the use and upkeep of the property, and to charge the buyer an annual sum. If that is not paid or the other conditions are not met, the seller has the right to take back the property. When the buyer sells the property the obligations are transferred to the new owner.

Rentcharges are like the ground rent arising under a long lease where restrictions may also be imposed. In the Manchester area they are normally called chief-rents.

The chief purposes of pre-1977 agreements were to give the rentcharge owner an income and ensure that the value of neighbouring land was not reduced by the neglect or undesirable use of land that had been sold.

New agreements of that type are now illegal. The only new rentcharge allowed by law is one intended to pay for estate amenities – for example, an annual fee for the care of a communal garden.

The rules covering payment of the rent and action to enforce the restrictions are similar to those for LEASEHOLD LAND.

People who have to pay a rentcharge under a pre-1977 agreement have the right to redeem them by paying cash. The amount is based on a calculation of how much the seller can collect, and how much he would need to invest in government stocks to produce the same income.

Redemption forms are available from the Department of the Environment, 2 Marsham Street, London SW1P 3EB, which also approves the redemption price. Existing rentcharges will automatically come to an end in 2037, and the redemption price will meanwhile reflect that limited life.

REPAIRER

Your right to have a job done properly

If you take something to be repaired, or if a repairman calls to mend something in your home, you are entitled to expect him to use professional care and skill in doing it. He must also use only materials that are fit for the purpose. If he fails in either respect, you can sue him for breach of contract and claim for:
● The defects for which he is responsible.
● The cost of having the defects put right by someone else.
● The loss in value of the goods caused by the defects.
● The cost of any damage done to other property by the defects.
● Compensation for any injury caused.

When he makes a promise

Unless the repairer commits himself to a definite time for completing the repair, the law says only that he must do so within a 'reasonable' time. If you persuade him to give you a definite time, however, he must keep his word or he is in breach of his contract.

That applies also to any other promise he makes about what he will do and what materials he will use. If he misleads you deliberately, either personally, by notices in his shop or in an advertisement, he can be prosecuted under the TRADE DESCRIPTIONS Act.

Repairmen sometimes seek to limit their liability through exemption clauses printed in receipts, quotations or notices on their premises. Usually these have little effect on your rights. *See:* UNFAIR CONTRACT

When leaving goods for repair, ask about the cost if no price list is displayed. Similarly, if you are asking a repairer to call at your home, find out how much he will charge. There may be a high minimum price, however small the repair. If the amount is substantial, ask for a written quotation. *See:* ESTIMATE

If no price has been agreed at the outset, the repairer is entitled to charge a 'reasonable' price. If you do not pay what he asks, he is legally entitled to keep hold of your property until you do. *See:* LIEN

SETTLING, FOR THE TIME BEING

Even when you disagree with a repairer's charge, you must pay if you want your property back. Make sure he knows you disagree.

'Make a note – I'm paying under protest'

Even when you think you are being overcharged, you must pay his price if you want your property back. Tell him, however, that you are paying 'under protest' to keep open your right to dispute the bill.

As soon as you get home, write to the repairer confirming that you paid under protest to get your property back and asking him to refund the amount of the overcharge.

Safe custody

You can sue a repairman for the loss of or damage to any of your property entrusted to him, but, if he can prove that he was not negligent, he is not liable.

For example, if your property is stolen from his premises in spite of normal security precautions, he does not have to pay you compensation – unless it was stolen by one of his employees.

If you leave anything of high value, it is always advisable to arrange your own temporary insurance.

REPATRIATION

Financial help for those who want to leave

Immigrants who want to leave the United Kingdom to make their permanent home elsewhere may be given financial help for travelling expenses under the provisions of the Immigration Act 1973. However, this provision is rarely used. Before the Home Secretary decides to give money for this purpose he must be convinced that the person really wishes to go.

A UK citizen stranded abroad may appeal to the British Embassy or high commission for money to get himself home. He will normally be asked to repay the money and his passport will usually be impounded until he does so.

RESIGNATION

When an employee decides to leave his job

An employee may resign from his job when he chooses, for any reason and no matter how inconvenient his departure may be to his employer. The employer is obliged to accept the resignation, although he is entitled to try to persuade the employee to withdraw it by any legal means – for example, by offering more money.

If the employee has been in the job for 4 weeks or more, and is not a PART-TIME WORKER or someone who customarily works abroad, he must give NOTICE of his intention to leave at least a week before he does so. Longer periods may be laid down in individual contracts. *See:* EMPLOYMENT PROTECTION

NO ARGUMENT

An employer is not entitled to refuse to accept an employee's resignation under any circumstances – although he can try to persuade him to stay in his employment. If the employee insists, however, the employer must let him go without further delay or inconvenience.

'I resign!' 'I accept!'

An employee who resigns may be required to work through his notice period. But if his employer chooses instead to give him payment in lieu of notice, the employee cannot insist upon continuing work.

An employee who fails to observe the notice procedures laid down by law or by his contract may be sued for breach of contract. However, in cases of dispute, his employer is more likely to refuse to supply him with a REFERENCE and may also hold back any wages or holiday pay owed, challenging the employee in his turn to sue.

Notice of resignation does not have to be in writing to be valid unless that is required by the contract. But it is in the employee's interests to write a letter and keep a copy, to prevent confusion.

An employee who resigns cannot claim REDUNDANCY or most types of UNFAIR DISMISSAL. Nor can a woman claim maternity benefits from the employer.

But if an employee leaves because his employer has broken the contract – for example, by failing to pay wages or provide suitable work, or by radically altering the employee's job without his agreement – he or she may claim compensation through an INDUSTRIAL TRIBUNAL.

In such cases, the employee need not observe the notice rules. But he should write his employer a letter, keeping a copy, listing the employer's actions which he regards as breaking the contract. The letter should state clearly that the employee is leaving because of his employer's behaviour and has not resigned. *See also:* RESTRAINT ON EMPLOYMENT

An employee who resigns without having another job to go to may lose unemployment benefit for up to 6 weeks.

RESTAURANT

How the law protects you when you eat out

Anyone who runs a restaurant, café, staff canteen, private club or public house serving meals is bound by the same rules of hygiene and fitness for consumption as a shopkeeper who sells FOOD. The meal, and any drinks served with it, must be of the nature, substance and quality demanded by the customer.

In addition, there are strict laws about displaying prices in eating places that are open to the public at large. There must be an easily read menu that a customer can see before entering. In self-service or take-away restaurants the prices must also be displayed at the place where the customer chooses his food.

In licensed restaurants, it is not necessary to show the full wine list in the same way, but at least an abridged one must be visible.

All prices must include value added tax. If there is a minimum price, a cover charge or a service charge, they must be mentioned at least as prominently as the price of the food. Failure to display prices properly is a criminal offence. The maximum penalty is a fine of £400 in a magistrates' court and of an unlimited amount if convicted by a jury.

Is there enough?

No minimum quantities are laid down by law for portions of food served. If the menu states, however, that, for example, steaks weigh 6 oz. or 8 oz., you are entitled to expect one of that weight. Beer or lager must be sold in the quantity stated, usually a bottle, half a pint or a pint. Any wine served in a container must be served in a sealed bottle or in an open carafe of 25 cl., 50 cl., 75 cl., or 1 litre. If you ask, you must be told which,

---

WHEN YOU HAVE EATEN

You are entitled to refuse to pay for food that is inedible, but if you have eaten part of a meal, you are liable to pay for that.

'Inedible, undrinkable, not what I ordered, obviously inadequate, and may I have the bill, please'

---

either on the wine list, by a notice in the restaurant or by a mark on the carafe. Otherwise, it is an offence. Wine can also be sold by the glass, however, which is an unspecified amount.

Sending back a meal

If you think that what is served is inedible, undrinkable, not what you ordered or obviously inadequate, complain to the manager. Most restaurants try to put the matter right.

If you obtain no satisfaction, however, you are entitled to reject the meal and refuse to pay for it.

If you eat the meal, you can still complain about its quality but you must pay for what you have had. If you do not, the manager can demand your name and address with a view to taking civil action. If you refuse to give it he can detain you and send for the police.

A firm booking for a table creates a contract between you and the restaurant. If the table you booked is not available when you turn up, you can claim for breach of contract. Similarly, if you fail to turn up, the restaurant can sue you for any loss it incurs.

Food poisoning

If you pay for a meal that gives you food poisoning, you can claim compensation from the restaurant under the Sale of Goods Act 1979. If you entertained guests and they were also poisoned, however, they could not claim unless NEGLIGENCE was proved.

If, as a result of your reporting the matter to the local environmental health officer, the restaurant was prosecuted successfully under the Food and Drugs Act 1955, the court can order the restaurant to pay them compensation.

RESTRAINT ON EMPLOYMENT

When your freedom to choose a job is restricted

Everyone has a basic right to take up whatever employment is available to him. But companies are entitled to protect themselves against unfair competition – and some may attempt to do that by putting restrictions on the future employment of their staff.

A company could decide to include a special clause in your EMPLOYMENT

CONTRACT, or ask you to sign a separate covenant, undertaking not to go to a certain rival company, or to do similar work in a certain locality.

Such a condition might apply not only to your next job, but also to any job you take within a specified time after leaving.

Enforcing a restraint

If an employee accepts a condition that restricts his future work, but ignores it after he leaves, his former company could seek a court injunction ordering him not to break the contract, or to cease breaking it. He could be fined or imprisoned for disobeying.

But the courts do not uphold restraints on employment unless they consider them reasonable. It is up to the employer to prove that a restraint is:
● Necessary to protect legitimate business interests – for example, to keep trade secrets.
● Not an unfair limitation of the employee's chances to make his living.
● Not against the public interest – for example, stopping the employee from making a better product or providing a better service than his former employer is willing to offer.

An employee's seniority and business knowledge – especially his access to private information that could be valuable to a competing company – are taken into account in judging whether a restraint is fair.

For example, a court may consider it unreasonable to expect a salesman not to join a competing company for 2 years – but reasonable to put the same ban on a managing director.

A restriction cannot be altered in court. So if an employer finds that his ban on working for rival companies within 100 miles is not acceptable, he cannot settle for a 10 mile limit. If a court holds that the original restraint is unreasonable, no restraint at all can be enforced.

Refusing to sign

Someone who cannot get the job he wants without agreeing to a restraint clause must decide for himself whether the limitation is fair. If he refuses to sign, and the job goes to someone else who does, he has no right to protest.

But someone who is already in employment, and loses his job because he

> ## THE WORK BAN THAT WENT TOO FAR

A restraint that stops an expert from using his skills at all is not in the public interest.

Commercial Plastics Ltd specialised in the manufacture of thin PVC sheeting. About one-fifth of its output was used in making adhesive tape.

When Mr W. W. Vincent joined the company, to co-ordinate its adhesive tape research and development, he signed a 12 month covenant which applied worldwide and to the whole field of thin PVC sheet-ing – not just its use for adhesive tape.

He left after 4 years to join a PVC competitor, Armoride Ltd. Commercial Plastics tried to enforce the covenant by applying for an injunction. The court had to decide whether it was reasonable to prevent him taking a job that did not involve adhesive tape.

DECISION

The court refused an injunction because the covenant prevented Mr Vincent from making normal, legitimate use of his skills and knowledge. Because of that, it must be considered to be against the public interest. The court also held that a worldwide restriction of the type envisaged was legally unenforceable.

The Court of Appeal endorsed the decision. Commercial Plastics' restriction of the whole PVC sheeting field was unnecessary when they needed it only for the production of adhesive tape, the judges held.

> ## THE SALESMAN WHO REFUSED WHEN 86 OTHERS AGREED

When a company can prove that a restraint on future employment is vital – and nearly all its staff agree – sacking a man who refused to sign a restrictive clause is justified.

Mr Irwin, a salesman for an electrical components company, refused to sign a covenant restricting him from operating in competition for 1 year after leaving it.

Ex-employees had already 'poached' some business and the sales force was losing commission earnings. For that reason only 4 of the 90-strong sales force refused to sign.

Mr Irwin was dismissed, but an industrial tribunal ruled that he had been unfairly dismissed. The company appealed.

The appeal body at the time, the Industrial Relations Court, had to decide whether the restraint covenant was necessary and fair, and whether refusal to sign it was sufficient ground for dismissal.

DECISION

The court found that the covenant was fair, and that the potential effect on the company of Mr Irwin's refusal to sign it was so substantial as to justify his dismissal.

> ## THE PLANNER WHO WENT STRAIGHT TO A RIVAL

The more senior the employee, the more likely a court will be to uphold a restraint on his next employment.

Mr Paul Harris, executive director of Littlewoods, was responsible for planning the whole range of the company's mail order catalogues. He resigned and went immediately to work for Littlewood's main rival, Great Universal Stores.

Littlewood's sought a court injunction to stop him taking the new job, on the basis of a covenant he had signed not to join GUS within 12 months of leaving Littlewoods.

The case went to the Court of Appeal, which had to decide whether Littlewoods needed such a covenant and whether it was an unreasonable restriction on Mr Harris.

DECISION

The judges held that the covenant was no more than a reasonable protection of confidential information that Mr Harris, having been in such a senior position, could pass on.

The injunction was granted, therefore, and he was forbidden to work for the rival company's mail order department for at least a year.

refuses to agree to a restraint on future work, is likely to have a case for claiming UNFAIR DISMISSAL.

In those circumstances an industrial tribunal would judge the necessity and fairness of a restraint in much the same way as a court. An offer of a pay increase or bonus for signing would also be taken into account. So would the willingness of fellow employees in similar positions to sign.

If an employee is faced with a condition that is absurdly restrictive, and his job is at stake, he might consider accepting it on the assumption that it could never be upheld in court. But someone who is uncertain about his situation should take legal advice – preferably before signing.

RETAILER'S LIABILITY

The legal obligations of selling to the public

If goods sold are unsatisfactory, the retailer has a legal liability even if he gave no express guarantee about the quality of the goods. Sometimes the buyer can get his MONEY BACK. The retailer cannot claim that a defect was the manufacturer's fault. *See:* DEFECTIVE GOODS

The retailer also has a duty to the buyer and others to take reasonable care that goods will not cause damage or injury. He is not obliged to open sealed packages to examine them, unless that is usually done by retailers. If he fails in his duty he can be sued for NEGLIGENCE.

RETIREMENT PENSION

Benefit paid to people when they reach retirement age and cease work

Anyone who has paid the correct number of national insurance contributions is entitled to a retirement pension from the state when he or she reaches retirement age – that is 65 for a man and 60 for a woman.

If retirement is postponed, a higher rate of pension is paid when the person does retire.

For a retirement pension to be paid to you, you must have retired, or be treated as having retired, from regular employment.

You do not have to give up work completely to be treated as having retired. You can carry on with paid work provided your weekly earnings, after deducting allowable expenses, are less than the amount of the earnings rule limit (£52 a week in 1981). If they exceed that earnings rule limit, you can work only occasionally or for not more than 12 hours a week.

When you reach 70 – 65 for a woman – these rules do not apply and you can earn any amount without affecting your pension rights.

Allowable expenses When you calculate your income for the earnings rule you can deduct reasonable expenses incurred in connection with your work – such as fares, trade union subscriptions, cost of overalls and materials; up to 15p for each meal taken during working hours for which you do not get luncheon vouchers; and reasonable expenses for providing for a member of your household to be looked after because you are at work.

When someone does not want to retire

If neither you nor your employer wishes you to retire at 65 – 60 for a woman – you need not do so. If you do retire and then decide that you want to work again, you can cancel your retirement – but you can cancel only once to gain extra pension under this rule.

You can earn extra pension by deferring or cancelling your retirement for at least 42 days, up to the age of 70 – 65 if you are a woman.

How a pension is worked out

The amount of pension you receive depends upon the national insurance contributions you – or your husband – have paid. A pension may be made up of:
● Flat-rate basic pension.
● Earnings-related additional pension or occupational pension, or both.
● Increase for a wife who is not entitled to a pension herself.
● Increase for any child under 16 – or 19 if in full-time education.
● Graduated pension.

HOW THE EARNINGS RULE AFFECTS A PENSION

If you claim your basic rate pension when you reach 65 – 60 for a woman – but continue to work, your pension will be reduced if you earn more than a given amount – the earnings rule limit. That sum – £52 in 1981 – is increased yearly to keep pace with the rise in earnings generally. Your pension will be reduced by 5p for every 10p in the first £4 you earn over the limit, then by 5p for every 5p until your basic pension is forfeited completely. That reduction does not apply to your earnings-related pension – that is your additional, guaranteed minimum pension or GRADUATED PENSION.

If you are earning more than the earnings rule limit – either as an employee or a self-employed person – you must tell your local social security office. Earnings include wages or salary, overtime, fees, commission, regular tips, bonuses – except Christmas bonuses of up to £10 – and attendance allowances if you are a councillor.

You need not include as earnings meals provided by your employer at your place of work, accommodation provided by your employer in which you have to live as a condition of employment, food or produce provided for your personal needs, or luncheon vouchers up to 15p a day.

In calculating your income you can also deduct reasonable expenses, such as trade union subscriptions, fares, cost of overalls and materials; 15p for each meal taken at work if no luncheon voucher is provided, and reasonable cost of providing for the care of a member of your household because you are at work.

If you are self-employed and make a tax return to the Inland Revenue, your profits for the year will be calculated to a weekly amount and treated as net weekly earnings for the earnings rule. If you do not make a tax return, you may be asked to produce accounts.

If you are a man, your pension is not affected by your wife's earnings unless you are receiving a dependant's increase for her. If you are and her earnings go above her earnings rule limit (£45 in 1981), your dependant's increase will be reduced. If your wife does not live with you, but you are maintaining her and collecting the increase on her behalf, that will not be paid at all if her earnings equal or exceed the amount of that increase.

When you reach 70 – 65 for a woman – your pension will be paid in full regardless of how much you earn.

● Extra pension earned by deferring or cancelling retirement.
● A 25p addition when you reach 80.

The basic pension is provided by the state. The additional pension comes from the state for people who are not contracted out of the state scheme, and from an OCCUPATIONAL PENSION for those who are contracted out.

Basic pension The basic retirement pension – in 1981, £27.15 for a single person, £43.45 for a married couple – is payable to anyone formerly employed or self-employed. To qualify, you must have paid:
● 50 flat-rate national insurance contributions at any time before April 6, 1975, or
● Enough contributions of any class in any tax year since April 6, 1975 for that to be a 'reckonable year'.

To qualify for the maximum basic pension you must have completed the right number of reckonable years in your working life.

A reckonable year is one in which you have paid, or been credited with, contributions on 50 times the weekly

LOWER EARNINGS LIMIT – the amount of weekly earnings below which insurance contributions do not have to be paid (£27 in 1981–2) – or 50 self-employed or voluntary contributions.

Your working life is normally the period from the start of the tax year in which you became 16 to the end of the tax year in which you reach 64 – 59 for a woman. But if you were already paying contributions towards a pension at July 5, 1948, the period of your working life starts from the beginning of the tax year in which you first became insured, or from April 6, 1936, whichever is later.

If you were over 16 at July 5, 1948 but did not start to pay contributions until later, working life counts from April 6, 1948.

If you have paid full contributions during nine-tenths of your working life, you will qualify for a full basic pension.

How to calculate reckonable working years

To qualify for the full basic pension you must have the right number of reckonable years. The following table will help you to make your calculation.

Length of working life	Reckonable years needed
27–30 years	working life minus 3 years
31–40 years	working life minus 4 years
41 years or more	working life minus 5 years

For example, if your working life is 37 years, you deduct 4 years, which means you need 33 years' contributions, paid or credited, to qualify for a basic pension at the full rate.

Reduced pension If you do not have enough reckonable years to qualify for a full basic pension you can get a proportionately reduced pension, provided you have at least a quarter of the reckonable years needed for a full pension.

For example, if your working life is 31 years, you deduct 4 years, which gives 27 years for a full pension. To get any pension at all you need at least 7 years' contributions.

No pension at all If your reckonable years are less than a quarter of the number needed for a full pension, you will not qualify for any pension at all.

A married woman who does not pay full national insurance contributions can get a basic pension on her husband's contributions.

Calculating additional pension

The additional retirement pension is partly earnings related – meaning that the more you earned when you were working, and the more you paid into the pension scheme, the higher your pension will be.

It is paid in addition to the flat-rate basic pension, and you can receive it even if you are not entitled to a basic pension, or are entitled to only a reduced-rate basic pension.

To qualify you must have paid Class 1 national insurance contributions – that is, as an employee. If you are a member of an occupational pension scheme which is contracted out of the additional part of the state scheme, your additional pension – known as your guaranteed minimum pension – is provided by your occupational scheme.

TAX AND COMPULSORY RETIREMENT

A retirement pension is taxable if some other source of income brings you over the tax threshold. Unemployment benefit, however, is not taxable. So a person who is forced to retire at 65 but would prefer to go on working given the chance may well pay less tax by registering himself as unemployed rather than retired.

Rate of pension Your additional pension builds up at the rate of 1/80th – 1¼ per cent – of each year's earnings between a lower level – usually about the amount of the current rate of basic pension – and an upper level of about seven times that amount. You must pay national insurance contributions on the earnings between the two levels for them to count.

For example, if the basic retirement pension in 1980 was £23.30 a week – £1,212 a year – and you earned £4,000 a year, your proportion of additional pension for that year would have been 1/80th of £2,788 – the difference between the pension level and your earnings. If your earnings were £10,000 a year, your proportion of additional pension would have been 1/80th of £7,368 – that is the difference between the lower level of £1,212 and the upper level of £8,580.

Any money you earn above the upper limit cannot count towards additional pension.

The maximum additional pension that can be paid is 25 per cent of earnings in this band. But as the first additional pensions were not paid until April 1979, the full rate will not be paid until April 1998 – that is 20 years × 1¼ per cent = 25 per cent of qualifying earnings as pension.

If you contribute towards additional pension for more than 20 years your pension will be worked out on the 20 years in which your earnings were highest. Pension rights – that is, the amount of qualifying earnings – will be revalued each year to keep pace with any general rise in earnings.

People who retire a few years after the start of the additional pension scheme will receive a proportion of the full rate. For example, if you have paid 3 years' contributions towards additional pension, your pension will be 3¾ per cent – that is, 3 years × 1¼ per cent – of your qualifying earnings.

If a husband and wife are contributors in their own right, they will each receive an additional pension.

If you defer retirement

If you defer or cancel your retirement or are being treated as not being retired because you are earning more than that laid down under the earnings rule, your pension will be increased by 1/7p per £1 for every 6 days of postponement – 7½ per cent increase per year. So if you put off retirement for 5 years, your pension will be increased by 37½ per cent.

A pension for a dependent wife increases in the same way provided she is over pension age.

If you are already retired and decide to cancel your retirement and suspend your pension to get an increased amount, ask for leaflet NI 92 from your local social security office.

If your wife is getting a pension on your contributions, she will have to agree to your cancelling your retirement and sign the wife's consent section. Send the form back to the social security office with your pension book, your wife's pension book, if her pension is on your contributions, or your certificate of earner's non-liability.

You can claim your pension again any time after deferring or cancelling retirement, and even if you are still working it will be paid when you reach 70 – 65 if you are a woman.

Your graduated pension can also be increased by deferring retirement.

Exemption from insurance

When you reach 65 – 60 if a woman – you do not have to pay insurance contributions. If you continue working you will need a 'certificate of age exception' to give to your employer. Your local social security office should send this to you automatically, but if it does not, write and ask for it.

If your employer deducts contributions, ask him for a refund. If the tax year in which the contributions were paid has ended, apply to your local social security office for the refund.

If you are self-employed and continue working you must complete the stamping of your current contributions card, and when you send it to your local social security office tell them you have reached retirement age and ask for a refund.

How to protect your rights

If you cannot work regularly because you have to stay at home to look after someone, your basic pension rights can be protected even though you do not pay national insurance contributions while you are at home. You can claim what is called home responsibilities protection, but to receive a full pension you must have paid full contributions for at least 20 years.

You can also claim pension protection for any tax year in which you:
● Get child benefit for a child under 16.
● Look after someone who is receiving an attendance or constant attendance allowance, for at least 35 hours a week.
● Get supplementary benefit to look after an elderly or sick person at home.

If you qualify, protection can be claimed for every year in which you do not work at all, or do some work but do not pay enough contributions for a reckonable year, or are not being credited with contributions because you are receiving another benefit such as sickness or unemployment benefit.

When your basic pension is being calculated, the number of years for which you claim protection is deducted from the number of reckonable years you need to qualify.

For example, if you need 33 years' contributions to qualify and you have 10 years' home responsibilities protection, you deduct 10 from 33, which leaves you 23 years. If you have worked and paid full contributions for 23 years you will get a full basic pension. If, however, you have worked for less than 20 years, you will qualify for only a reduced rate of pension.

You cannot qualify for protection if you are a married woman or a widow paying lower rate insurance contributions.

How to apply for protection

If you are looking after someone who is getting an attendance or constant attendance allowance you must apply at the end of each tax year, on a form which you can get from the local social security office.

If you are getting supplementary be-

nefit to look after someone at home, or child benefit, there is no need to apply – protection is granted automatically.

If you are a husband whose wife is claiming child benefit, you can have your pension protected if you have the benefit paid to you instead of your wife. To do this your wife must sign a statement telling the social security office that she does not wish to claim.

How to claim your pension

About 4 months before you are due to retire, the Department of Health and Social Security will send you a claim form on which to apply for a pension. If you do not receive it by 3 months before you retire, ask your local social security office to send one.

Deferred pension If you are under 70 – 65 if a woman – and have deferred or cancelled your retirement, you must give notice in writing to the social security office when you wish to give up work and claim your pension. You will be entitled to your pension when you reach that age whether you stop working or not, but you must claim it.

You can apply, on a claim form which you can get from the local social security office, up to 4 months before you reach 70 or 65.

Married women If you are a married woman and want to claim on your husband's contributions you must make a separate application. If you are near to, or over, 60 when your husband claims his pension and you do not receive an application form, ask for one from your local social security office.

You are not entitled to a pension if you are under 60 even though your husband may be over 65 and claiming his. In that case, your husband can claim a dependant's increase for you on his pension, provided you are not earning more than the earnings rule limit (£45 for wives in 1980).

Delaying your claim

If you delay claiming your pension or telling the social security office about your retirement, you may lose money. Unless you have a good reason for the delay you cannot get a pension back-dated more than 3 months before the date on which you give notice of your retirement, or 3 months before the date of your claim if you are over 70 – 65 if a woman.

In other cases, you cannot get a pension back-dated to more than 12 months before the date you notify retirement or claim the pension.

Contesting the amount

When you have made your claim the social security office will notify you how much pension you will receive and how it is made up. If you do not agree with the decision, you can contest it. How and where to do that will be explained in the notice you receive.

How pensions are paid

Retirement pension is usually paid each week through an order book. The orders are payable on the same day each week and you cash them at a post office you have named on your claim form. You cannot normally cash them at any other post office. Each order is valid for 3 months from the date shown on it. If you do not cash it within 3 months you must apply to the social security office for a new one which you must cash within 12 months, or you may lose it altogether.

If you cannot get out to cash your own orders you can arrange for someone else to do this for you. In this case, you sign the back of the pension order, and the person collecting the pension for you signs on the line marked 'agent's signature'.

Losing your book If you lose your pension book tell your post office immediately so that they can prevent the orders being cashed by anyone else. Then tell your local social security office. They will then make out another book and send it to the post office.

Paying into a bank If you prefer to have your pension paid by a 4-weekly or quarterly crossed order which you can then pay into your bank account, ask for leaflet NI 105 at the social security office and complete the application form attached.

Pensions payable to married women

A married woman who has gone out to work can get a basic retirement pension on her own insurance contributions when she reaches 60 and retires from work or is treated as having retired. The rate of pension depends on the number of contributions paid.

If you have not paid enough contributions to qualify for a pension at least equal to the standard rate of a wife's pension from a husband's contributions – or if you do not qualify for any pension in your own right – you can be paid a basic pension on your husband's contributions if you are 60 and your husband is 65 or over and retired or treated as having retired.

Paying contributions If you pay full insurance contributions, you can, when you retire, have your pension paid either on your own or your husband's contributions, whichever is more favourable to you.

You will qualify for home responsibilities protection if you need it, but that may mean that you will collect a reduced pension on your own incomplete contribution record until you can qualify for the married woman's pension on your husband's contributions, if that is larger. Any additional pension you are entitled to will be paid when you are 60 and retire.

If you are still entitled to pay reduced-rate contributions (the phasing out of this choice started in April 1977) or none at all if you are self-employed, you cannot qualify for home responsibilities protection. But you can change to full contributions if you wish – and in that case you can qualify for protection. To do this get leaflet NI 1 from your local social security office and complete the application form attached. You will

....

HOW PENSIONS ARE PAID

Pensions are normally paid through an order book cashable on the same day each week at a post office chosen by the pensioner.

start to pay full contributions from the beginning of the next income tax year.

Once you have changed to full contributions you cannot change back to paying the reduced rate.

Widows If you are a widow, your widow's pension becomes your retirement pension when you reach 60. If you have a reduced-rate widow's pension – or none at all – and you want a full retirement pension, you must pay full national insurance contributions while you are at work. If you are paying reduced-rate contributions and would like to change to full rate, get leaflet NI 51 from your local social security office and complete the application form attached.

If you are widowed after retirement, your basic retirement pension will be brought up to the rate of your late husband's. You can also add any additional pension your husband was getting to your own, up to the maximum amount payable to a single person.

Protecting the pensioner against inflation

Once the basic pension has been awarded it is increased each November in line with the rise in prices.

The additional pension and guaranteed minimum pension are also.

Pension rights – that is qualifying earnings built up before pension age – are revalued to keep pace with the general rise in earnings.

Income tax Retirement pensions, including increases for dependants, and additional and guaranteed minimum pensions, are treated as part of your income for income tax purposes and should be included on any tax returns you have to make.

Providing pensions for overseas residents

Retirement pension can be paid anywhere in the world, but generally only at the rate that was in force when you left the United Kingdom (or retired if you were abroad at the time).

Annual increases of pension (made normally in this country in November) are not paid overseas except in countries with which Britain has reciprocal agreements – that is in all the EEC countries, Austria, Bermuda, the Chan-

nel Islands, Cyprus, Finland, Israel, Jamaica, Malta, Portugal, Spain, Switzerland, Turkey, USA and Yugoslavia.

Pension for the over-80s

People aged 80 or over may be eligible for a special, non-contributory retirement pension. In 1981 it was £16.30 a week for a single person and £26.10 for a married couple.

You can get this pension if you do not get a national insurance retirement pension, or one at less than these rates.

There are two ways to qualify:

● You must be 80 or over and normally live in the United Kingdom. You must also have lived here for at least 10 years in the last 20 years before your 80th birthday, or.

● If a man, you must have been aged 92 or over on July 5, 1975 (a woman must have been 87 or more then) and have lived in the United Kingdom for at least 10 years between July 1948 and July 1970.

If you think you qualify, complete a claim form on leaflet NI 184 and send it to your local Department of Health and Social Security office with your birth certificate, and marriage certificate, if relevant. Do not delay claiming, because a pension cannot normally be backdated for more than 3 months from the date of your claim.

You will be sent a book of orders to cash each week at a post office of your choice.

RIDING SCHOOL

Finding a safe riding school for your child

If your child wants to learn to ride, make sure that the school you send him or her to is licensed by the local authority. The licence is your guarantee that the school is insured against risk of accidents and it makes it more likely that it is run safely and efficiently.

If your child was injured as a result of careless supervision, your claim for damages for NEGLIGENCE would be met by the school's insurance company. If the school was not insured, its owner may well be unable to pay the claim.

In addition, if the horse your child was riding injured a passer-by, you and the school could be sued jointly by the

ENSURING SAFETY FIRST

Make sure that any riding school you use is licensed by the local council – as a safeguard that it is properly and safely run.

injured person. If the school had no funds and was not insured, you would have to meet the entire claim.

RIGHT OF WAY

Where you can go and where you are trespassing

Every square inch of Britain, including the foreshore, has a legal owner – an individual, a commercial concern, a statutory body such as a local authority, or the Crown. Consequently, it is a TRESPASS for you to walk anywhere other than on your own property, unless there is a right of way.

There is such a right on a FOOTPATH, a bridleway, where you can also lead or ride a horse or ride a pedal cycle, on COMMON LAND or on ROADS. In general, the citizen's right is only to 'pass and repass', other than in an area designated for public recreation, such as a park. If he stays, for example, in a short stretch of a public path to watch a sporting event in a neighbouring field, he is trespassing.

If a landowner allows members of the public generally to use a private road or path for 20 years without interruption, it becomes a public right of way, which can be closed only by order of a magistrate or of the Secretary of State for the Environment.

If you buy a house with access across land owned by someone else, your right of way should be recorded in the transfer document or conveyance. Ask your solicitor to check for you.

RIGHT TO LIGHT

The law that protects the view from a window

A window that has had an uninterrupted access to light for more than 20 years may be protected by law so that no one can block out or substantially reduce the light by erecting a building or high fence in front of it.

The glass of a greenhouse could also be protected, with a right to receive sunlight.

It is a right, however, that exists only on older properties. The deeds of many modern homes – on residential estates, for example – include a clause excluding the possibility of any house buyer acquiring rights of light.

'Blocking' the light

An owner of vacant land that is overlooked by the windows of a neighbour's property may wish to protect his right to build there at some future date. He can take steps to stop his neighbour acquiring a right to light by lodging a light obstruction notice in the local land charges register.

The dimensions of a 'notional' building should be entered in the register – which is maintained by the district council – and notice must be served on the owner of the neighbouring property. This notice in the land charges register lasts for a year and effectively 'blocks' the window for that period. The process must be repeated regularly at least once every 20 years to prevent the neighbour acquiring a right to light. If the window has had uninterrupted light for more than 20 years, however, the neighbour will already have acquired rights.

RIOT

Duty of the police to protect property

The criminal charge of riot has largely fallen into disuse. Its legal definition

WHEN THE POLICE MUST PAY

If a private citizen's property is damaged in a riot, he can sue the police for compensation – even if they have not charged anyone with rioting.

still has bearing, however, when people such as private householders or shopkeepers suffer loss through people running wild and destroying their possessions.

People can be charged with riot if they have taken part in an UNLAWFUL ASSEMBLY in which violence has been used.

Even if none has been charged with riot, however, private citizens can sue the police for any loss they suffer as the result of one.

Penalty The maximum penalty for the criminal offence of riot is life imprisonment and an unlimited fine.

ROAD

Using – and maintaining – the public highway

A public road is any highway maintained by a local authority or the Department of Transport. There are three categories – motorways, ordinary roads, major or minor, and bridleways. A public FOOTPATH is for the use of pedestrians only.

Major and minor

Although the way in which roads can be used is limited in the Road Traffic Acts, there are normally no restrictions on the type of vehicle that can use them. They are open to all traffic, vehicular

> ### THE BLIND MAN
> ### WHO TRIPPED
>
> *If an injury results from repairers leaving a hole unprotected or an obstruction unlit, the courts will invariably find the repairers liable for compensation.*
>
> In 1964 the London Electricity Board was excavating the pavement of a street in Woolwich, and to protect one end of the trench it had used a punner – a heavy weight with a long handle.
>
> The weight was on the pavement and the end of the handle was wedged 2 ft up in some railings.
>
> A blind man walking along the road to a bus stop failed to detect the punner handle and tripped over it – even though he was using his white stick correctly.
>
> He injured himself and sued for negligence.
>
> DECISION
>
> The House of Lords held the Electricity Board totally liable, because it was the board's duty to erect a guard that was safe for blind people as well as for those who could see.

and pedestrian, unless otherwise indicated by Department of Transport or police signs.

Pavements running alongside roads are for pedestrians only. It is illegal to park or cycle on them.

Motorway restrictions

A special set of rules applies to motorways. Certain classes of vehicle – indicated on signs at each entrance – are barred from using them.

It is an offence to drive on the hard shoulder of a motorway – which runs the entire length on each side of it – unless you have a breakdown or some other genuine emergency. *See:* MOTORWAY DRIVING

Pedestrians are not permitted anywhere on a motorway, although in practice drivers having to stop in an emergency are allowed to walk along the hard shoulder to the nearest motorway telephone.

Using bridleways

Pedal cycles are the only wheeled vehicles allowed on a bridleway, some of which have survived from being medieval highways.

Even when bridleways cross private land, there is no restriction on those entitled to use them. The owner of the land must allow access. They are open to horse riders and pedestrians, but precedence must always be given by cyclists to anyone on foot.

When a road is private The owner of the land across which there is a private road – that is one that is not open to the public and not maintained by the local council or Department of Transport – has the right to restrict its use in any way.

Who is responsible for repairs

The authority responsible for maintaining motorways and trunk roads – that is, principal main roads carrying through-traffic – is the Department of Transport. Most other public roads must be maintained by the local authority in a reasonable state of repair, safe enough for the traffic and pedestrians expected to use it.

The only exception is when a road is unadopted – usually newly built on a modern housing estate, for example. Until the council agrees or decides eventually to take it over, any repairs must be paid for by the people living on each side of the road. *See:* PRIVATE STREET

If you injure yourself by stumbling over an uneven paving stone in the

---

DAMAGE CLAIMS
MUST SHOW NEGLIGENCE

A local authority that regularly checks pavements is not negligent. If a minor fault appears between inspections and causes injury, no damages will be awarded.

'oops, sorry, sir – hadn't inspected that one yet'

---

dark, you may be entitled to compensation from the highway authority.

Even if a court accepts that a road or pavement was unsafe, the highway authority can still avoid paying compensation if it can show that it has not been negligent. For example, if the authority can show that it inspects its roads and pavements regularly, and that the paving stone had become loosened since the last inspection, it cannot be found guilty of negligence.

The same principles apply if a vehicle is damaged as a consequence of the condition of the road. For example, if a driver damages the back axle by going over a broken piece of road he may be able to sue the highway authority provided:
● It cannot be shown that he himself was careless – for example, because he was driving too fast.
● The authority has been negligent.

If the damage occurs in a private street, the driver would be able to sue only the owners of the buildings in the street.

ROAD TRAFFIC ACCIDENT

*When a motorist must stop
after an accident*

A driver involved in an accident must stop at the scene if:
● Any person apart from himself has been injured.
● Any vehicle other than the one he is driving has been damaged.
● A horse, cow, ass, mule, sheep, pig, dog or goat – but not a cat – has been injured outside his vehicle.
● Any damage has been caused to roadside property.

It is not necessary that the driver was himself involved in the accident. It is sufficient that the accident occurred because of his vehicle's presence – for example, if some other driver swerved, missed him, and hit a tree.

The driver must stay at the scene long enough to enable any other people involved to take his name and address, details of the vehicle's ownership, if it does not belong to him, and the registration mark.

If it is not possible to comply with the law's requirements immediately – for example, when a motorist has hit and damaged an unattended parked car or knocked down a straying farm animal on a lonely road – the driver can simply report the accident to the police as soon as reasonably practicable, but in any case within 24 hours.

After an accident in which someone has been injured the driver must produce his insurance certificate immediately or present proof of his insurance cover within 5 days at any police station of his choice.

Failing to stop

If a motorist who is prosecuted can satisfy the court that he was unaware of the accident, he has not committed an offence by failing to stop.

The courts, however, do not readily accept the defence of ignorance – especially when someone has been injured or a vehicle has been damaged. It does not sound very plausible that a motorist involved in an accident did not see, or hear, or feel anything.

The maximum penalty for failing to stop is a £100 fine, an endorsement and possible disqualification.

Calling the police

There is no obligation to report an accident to the police if names and addresses have been exchanged and insur-ance certificates produced when someone is hurt.

A driver need not wait for the police to arrive, but it is usually in his own interests to do so if he is not to blame for the accident.

Accidents abroad

Compensation for any accident in England and Wales is determined solely by English law. If you are knocked down by a French lorry in London and the driver hurries back to France, you can sue in an English court.

If you are the victim of an accident abroad your rights may be enforceable in an English court if:

● All those involved were English – for example, if you were hurt in an accident while travelling on an English coach and it was caused by the negligence of the English driver.

● The person you wish to claim against visits Britain long enough to be served with a writ or, in the case of a company, if it has an office in this country.

In such cases, however, your rights to compensation depend on a combination of English law and the law of the country where the accident happened. You will normally be entitled to compensation only if the laws of *both* countries provide for it. If compensation for injuries may be substantial you should consider engaging a foreign lawyer to put your case in the courts of the country where the accident happened.

ROAD TRAFFIC OFFENCES

How motoring offenders are punished

Anyone convicted of a road traffic offence may be fined and, in certain cases, disqualified from driving. In the most serious cases – for example, causing death by reckless driving – a driver may be sent to prison.

All motoring offences, except causing death by reckless driving, are heard in a magistrates' court. However, a serious case may be transferred to a crown court after a preliminary hearing.

Certain offences carry an automatic DRIVING DISQUALIFICATION if a person is convicted – for example, driving with excess alcohol. Many offences also carry an automatic endorsement on a driver's licence. If an offence carries an automatic endorsement but no automatic disqualification, the court can decide whether to disqualify a driver.

ROAD TRAFFIC OFFENCES
continued on p. 631

THE PRINCIPAL OFFENCES WITH WHICH MOTORISTS CAN BE CHARGED

How the law can and – more often – does deal with breaches of road traffic law

Offence	Average penalty for first offence	Maximum penalty	Must your licence be endorsed?	Can you be disqualified?
Accident offences				
Failing to stop after an accident	£50 fine, endorsement and possible disqualification	£100 fine	Yes	At the court's discretion
Failing to report an accident within 24 hours	£25 fine and endorsement	£100 fine	Yes	At the court's discretion
Failing to produce certificate of insurance after an accident	£10 fine	£100 fine	Yes	At the court's discretion
Failing to give name and address after an accident	£20 fine	£100 fine	Yes	At the court's discretion
Careless driving offences				
Driving without due care and attention	£50 fine and endorsement	£500 fine	Yes	At the court's discretion
Inconsiderate driving	£50 fine and endorsement	£500 fine	Yes	At the court's discretion

Offence	Average penalty for first offence	Maximum penalty	Must your licence be endorsed?	Can you be disqualified?
Careless driving offences *continued*				
Leaving vehicle without stopping engine or setting handbrake	£10 fine	£100 fine	No	No
Driver not in control of the vehicle	£10 fine	£100 fine	No	No
Reversing vehicle for an unreasonable distance	£10 fine	£100 fine	No	No
Opening vehicle door causing injury or danger	£20 fine	£100 fine	No	No
Driving on a footway	£10 fine	£20 fine	No	No
Driving in a street designated as a play street	£10 fine	£100 fine	Yes	At the court's discretion
Drink and drugs				
Unfit to drive through drink or drugs	£100 fine, endorsement and 12 months' disqualification	£1,000 fine/6 months' gaol	Yes	Yes Minimum 12 months
Driving with alcohol in the blood above the prescribed limit – 80 mg. of alcohol in 100 ml. of blood or 107 mg. of alcohol in 100 ml. of urine	£100 fine, endorsement and 1–3 years' disqualification, depending on the excess amount of alcohol	£1,000 fine/6 months' gaol	Yes	Yes Minimum 12 months
Failing to provide a specimen of blood or urine for a laboratory test	£100 fine, endorsement and 18 months' disqualification	£1,000 fine/6 months' gaol	Yes	Yes Minimum 12 months
In charge of a vehicle while unfit through drink or drugs	£75 fine, endorsement and 6 months' disqualification	£500 fine/3 months' gaol	Yes	At the court's discretion
In charge of a vehicle while having alcohol in the blood above the prescribed limit	£75 fine, endorsement and 6 months' disqualification	£500 fine/3 months' gaol	Yes	At the court's discretion
In charge of a vehicle and failing to provide a specimen of blood or urine for a laboratory test	£75 fine, endorsement and 6 months' disqualification	£500 fine/3 months' gaol	Yes	At the court's discretion
Failing to provide a specimen for initial breath test	£25 fine	£50 fine	No	No
Driving licence offences				
Driving while disqualified	£100 fine and possible suspended prison sentence	£400 fine/3 months' gaol	Yes	At the court's discretion
Driving without a licence when no licence could have been granted	£20 fine and endorsement	£100 fine	Yes	At the court's discretion
Causing or permitting a person to drive without a licence	£20 fine and endorsement	£100 fine	Yes	At the court's discretion
Driving with uncorrected eyesight	£20 fine and endorsement	£100 fine	Yes	At the court's discretion
Refusing to submit to an eyesight test	£20 fine and endorsement	£100 fine	Yes	At the court's discretion
Failing to produce driving licence to police	£20 fine and endorsement	£50 fine	No	No

Continued overleaf

ROAD TRAFFIC OFFENCES *continued*

Offence	Average penalty for first offence	Maximum penalty	Must your licence be endorsed?	Can you be disqualified?
Driving licence offences *continued*				
Obtaining licence while disqualified	£50 fine	£100 fine	No	No
Failing to produce licence to court for endorsement	£20 fine	£100 fine	No	No
Forging licence	£50 fine	£200 fine	No	No
Making false statement to obtain licence	£50 fine	£200 fine	No	No
Failure to sign licence	£5 fine	£50 fine	No	No
Failure to state date of birth or sex when required	£10 fine	£50 fine	No	No
Insurance offences				
Using vehicle uninsured against third-party risks	£60 fine and endorsement	£200 fine	Yes	At the court's discretion
Forging insurance document	£100 fine	£200 fine	No	No
Lighting offences				
When parked	£15 fine	£100 fine	No	No
When moving	£20 fine	£100 fine	No	No
Load offences				
Causing danger by carrying too many passengers	£30 fine	Car: £100 fine Goods vehicle: £400 fine	Yes Yes	At the court's discretion
Causing danger by having an insecure load	£50 fine	Car: £100 fine Goods vehicle: £400 fine	Yes Yes	At the court's discretion
Long and projecting loads	£50 fine	£100 fine	No	No
Exceeding the maximum gross weight or axle weight	£100 fine	£400 fine	No	No
Motor-cycle offences				
Unlawful pillion riding	£15 fine and endorsement	£100 fine	Yes	At the court's discretion
Driving or riding on a motor cycle without protective headgear	£10 fine	£50 fine	No	No
Motorway offences				
Excluded traffic using a motorway	£20 fine and endorsement	£500 fine	Yes	At the court's discretion
Parking on hard shoulder	£20 fine	£500 fine	No	No
Reversing vehicle, making U-turns or driving in the wrong direction on main motorway	£75 fine, endorsement and 3 months' disqualification	£500 fine	Yes	At the court's discretion
Reversing vehicle, making U-turns or driving in the wrong direction on slip roads	£40 fine and endorsement	£500 fine	Yes	At the court's discretion
Vehicles over 3 tons using third lane	£60 fine and endorsement	£500 fine	Yes	At the court's discretion

Offence	Average penalty for first offence	Maximum penalty	Must your licence be endorsed?	Can you be disqualified?
Motorway offences *continued*				
Walking on motorway or slip-road	£25 fine	£500 fine	No	No
Walking on hard shoulder or verge	£15 fine	£500 fine	No	No
Noise offences				
Sounding horn in a built-up area between 11.30 p.m. and 7 a.m.	£10 fine	£100 fine	No	No
Sounding horn when stationary	£10 fine	£100 fine	No	No
Noise caused by faulty silencer	£10 fine	£100 fine	No	No
Use of vehicle or trailer which causes excessive noise	£10 fine	£100 fine	No	No
Parking offences				
Leaving vehicle in a dangerous position	£25 fine and endorsement	£100 fine	Yes	At the court's discretion
Wilful or unnecessary obstruction	£10 fine	£100 fine	No	No
Failing to park on the nearside after dark	£15 fine	£100 fine	No	No
Stopping on a clearway	£15 fine	£100 fine	No	No
Offences against waiting restrictions	£10 fine	£100 fine	No	No
Failure, without reasonable excuse, to make a statutory statement of ownership	£20 fine	£100 fine	No	No
Making a false statement of ownership	£50 fine	£400 fine	No	No
Failure to pay initial parking meter charge	£10 fine	£20 fine	No	No
Exceeding excess period	£10 fine	£50 fine	No	No
Returning to a parking meter bay within one hour	£10 fine	£50 fine	No	No
Parking on a suspended meter	£10 fine	£100 fine	No	No
Improperly parked	£10 fine	£100 fine	No	No
'Feeding' a parking meter by putting in more coins	£20 fine	£50 fine	No	No
Failure to pay excess charge	£10 fine	£20 fine	No	No
Tampering with a meter	£20 fine	£50 fine	No	No
Pedestrian crossing offences				
Breach of zebra regulations by a stationary vehicle	£20 fine and endorsement	£100 fine	Yes	At the court's discretion
Breach of zebra regulations by a moving vehicle	£25 fine and endorsement	£100 fine	Yes	At the court's discretion
Provisional licence offences				
Provisional licence holder not accompanied by a qualified driver	£25 fine and licence endorsed and possible disqualification from driving	£100 fine	Yes	At the court's discretion

Continued overleaf

Offence	Average penalty for first offence	Maximum penalty	Must your licence be endorsed?	Can you be disqualified?
Provisional licence offences *continued*				
Provisional motor cycle-licence holder carrying a passenger who is not qualified	£25 fine and licence endorsed and possible disqualification from driving	£100 fine	Yes	At the court's discretion
Driving without L plates	£15 fine and licence endorsed	£100 fine	Yes	At the court's discretion
Provisional licence holder towing unauthorised trailer	£15 fine and licence endorsed	£100 fine	Yes	At the court's discretion
Reckless driving offences				
Reckless driving	£120 fine, endorsement and 12 months' disqualification	£1,000 fine/6 months' gaol	Yes	Yes
Causing death by reckless driving	Penalty depends on circumstances	5 years' gaol	Yes	Yes
Speed limit offences				
Exceeding speed limit on a motorway	£2 fine for every mile per hour above speed limit and possible disqualification	£500 fine	Yes	At the court's discretion
Exceeding speed limit on other roads	£1.50 fine for every mile per hour above speed limit	£100 fine	Yes	At the court's discretion
Exceeding goods vehicle speed limit	£1.50 fine for every mile per hour above speed limit	£100 fine	Yes	At the court's discretion
Passenger-carrying vehicles limited to 50 mph	£1.50 fine for every mile per hour above speed limit	£100 fine	Yes	At the court's discretion
Traffic directions				
Disobeying a constable directing traffic	£25 fine and endorsement	£100 fine	Yes	At the court's discretion
Disregarding a school crossing patrol sign	£25 fine and endorsement	£100 fine	Yes	At the court's discretion
Disregarding traffic light signals	£25 fine and endorsement	£100 fine	Yes	At the court's discretion
Disregarding a stop sign	£25 fine and endorsement	£100 fine	Yes	At the court's discretion
Disregarding double white lines	£25 fine and endorsement	£100 fine	Yes	At the court's discretion
Disregarding other road signs – for example, 'Give Way' and 'No Entry'	£20 fine	£100 fine	No	No
Vehicle condition offences				
Defective brakes	£25 fine and endorsement	£100 fine	Yes	At the court's discretion
Defective steering	£25 fine and endorsement	£100 fine	Yes	At the court's discretion
Defective tyres	£25 fine and endorsement	£100 fine per tyre	Yes	At the court's discretion
Tyres of different types fitted to the same axle	£25 fine and endorsement	£100 fine	Yes	At the court's discretion

Offence	Average penalty for first offence	Maximum penalty	Must your licence be endorsed?	Can you be disqualified?
Vehicle condition offences *continued*				
Other vehicle parts in dangerous condition	£25 fine and endorsement	£100 fine	Yes	At the court's discretion
Windscreen not maintained so that driver's vision is obscured	£25 fine	£100 fine	No	No
No seat belts or anchorage points	£25 fine	£100 fine	No	No
Unladen weight not marked on goods vehicle	£25 fine	£400 fine	No	No
Vehicle registration offences				
Failure to pay motor vehicle licence duty	Fine of twice the unpaid duty	£50 fine or five times the annual duty	No	No
Registration mark obscured or missing	£10 fine	£20 fine	No	No
Failure to register change of ownership	£20 fine	£50 fine	No	No
Fraudulent use of licence	£50 fine	£200 fine/2 years' gaol	No	No
No MoT certificate	£8 fine – more if over 3 months overdue	£100 fine	No	No

ROAD TRAFFIC OFFENCES
continued from p. 626

If a driver collects more than three endorsements on his licence on three occasions within 3 years, he faces automatic disqualification.

There may, however, be mitigating circumstances that induce the court not to disqualify or to disqualify for less than the statutory 6 months for each endorsable offence.

ROBBERY

When the act of theft involves violence or the threat of it

Robbery is a more serious form of theft, committed only when a thief uses violence to help him to steal or if he

THE PICKPOCKETS WHO NUDGED THEIR VICTIM

Even a small amount of force turns theft into robbery.

Three pickpockets worked as a team. One of them nudged their victim to make him lose his balance, while the other stole his wallet and the third kept a look-out. They were charged, not with theft, but with robbery. They argued that the mere nudging of their victim did not involve sufficient force for them to be guilty of robbery.

DECISION

The Court of Appeal held that nudging was a sufficient act of force to justify a robbery conviction. They were found guilty.

makes a show of violence that makes someone fear that violence will be used. The physical force used may be trivial and no injury need be sustained by the victim.

Robbery cases are tried in the crown court, and the maximum penalty is life imprisonment.

If violence takes place before or after a theft, however, the offence is not robbery. The thief would be charged with the two separate offences of theft and assault.

If a violent attempt to steal failed, the charge would be ASSAULT with intent to rob, for which the maximum penalty – like that for robbery – is life imprisonment.

SALE OF GOODS

When a contract is made between seller and buyer

However informal – for example, putting down 10p and picking up a newspaper at a street stall – the transaction of selling goods involves a contract between the seller and the buyer.

That means that if you buy goods you have rights against the seller if something is wrong with them.

For example, a 6-year-old boy who bought a catapult for sixpence in 1958 was awarded £2,500 damages against the newsagent who sold it to him: the catapult was not fit for use and snapped, and the boy lost an eye. *See:* DEFECTIVE GOODS

Even when nothing is said, a seller in the course of a business – such as a shopkeeper or a dealer – must supply goods that are of merchantable quality and fit for their purpose. In a consumer contract it is not possible to exclude or vary these obligations by an exemption clause. *See:* GOODS, Sale of

SALE OR RETURN

When a shopkeeper can send back his supplies

If goods are delivered to a shopkeeper 'on sale or return', he can sell them if he can find a customer, but if they are not sold he can return them to his supplier.

The shopkeeper is bound to pay only for the goods he sells, or those that he treats as if they were his own property – for example, by leaving them with a pawnbroker in return for a loan.

The legal principles applied are the same as those for sales 'on approval'. *See:* APPROVAL, Goods on

SALES

Buying goods at 'sale' time

Goods sold by a seller in the course of a business must be of merchantable quality and fit for the particular purpose for which the seller knows they are to be used. So your rights if 'sale' goods are defective are exactly the same as if you paid full price. *See:* DEFECTIVE GOODS

The fact that they are 'sale' goods may be relevant, however, in the following ways:

● Merchantable quality. The term 'merchantable quality' means that the goods are as fit for the purpose or purposes for which goods of that kind are commonly bought as it is reasonable to expect in the circumstances.

In deciding what it is reasonable to expect, the price may be relevant. For example, a fur coat with a small bare patch might not be regarded as merchantable if the price is £25,000, but if the same coat is reduced to £25 it might be regarded as merchantable.

Goods sold in 'sales' are sometimes described as 'seconds' or 'rejects'. That might have the effect that they are to be regarded as fit for their usual purposes

despite a defect – if it is reasonable to infer from the description given that there is such a defect.

If a defect is drawn to a buyer's attention before he decides to buy, he cannot later complain about that defect.

● Fitness for purpose. It may be possible for a seller to say that it was unreasonable for the buyer to rely on the seller's skill or judgment about the goods' fitness for a particular purpose if they are sold in a 'sale'.

When a bargain is illusory

Not all goods sold at sale time are reduced. Sometimes shops buy in special lines which they sell at lower prices than their regular stock. That may be because they are of lower quality, but it may simply be that they are someone else's old stock bought in cheaply – and therefore of good value.

If prices are shown as reduced, the law on price marking must be obeyed – even in a sale. *See:* PRICE REDUCTION

Members of the Retail Trading-Standards Association are encouraged to display the Association's statement of sales policy at sale time. This explains why the shop is holding a sale and explains that goods specially purchased for the sale are so described.

SCHOOL

The rights and responsibilities of parents and teachers

The Education Act 1980 states that local education authorities must enable parents to express a preference for a school, and allow them to give their reasons.

Good reasons for a choice are:
● Religious beliefs.
● Wanting to be taught in Welsh.
● Medical reasons supported by a doctor.
● Having an older child at the school.
● Wanting a course provided only at that school.

Local education authorities and voluntary school governors must comply with the preference expressed by the parent unless:
● To comply with it would result in an inefficient use of educational resources or would damage the provision of efficient education.

● It would contravene the local authority's agreement with a voluntary school about how children should be admitted to that school.

● It is a selective school and the child's ability and aptitude would not be suitable.

Nursery schools, special schools and children in need of special education are excluded from these provisions.

Grounds for refusing a place

The Schools Regulations 1959, which are in force until at least 1982, state that a child may not be refused a place at the school of the parent's choice except on reasonable grounds. Although not listed as such in the regulations, reasonable grounds are:

● The school is full. Schools are built to accommodate a fixed number of children – their designated size. Exceeding that number is overcrowding and a good reason for saying 'no vacancies'.

As the falling birthrate affects schools, local authorities may decide to reduce the size of all their schools rather than close some of them.

They must make public the number of places available at each school, and if the reduction is more than one-fifth of the total yearly intake of children, the local authority will have to get approval from the Secretary of State if anyone objects to the change.

Once a reduction is approved, parents cannot claim a place there if this means exceeding the new designated size, even though the school may have originally been built for larger numbers.

● Zoning. Priority can be given to children living in a school's catchment area and places may be reserved for children expected to move in – from a new housing estate, for instance. But if there are still places left, other children cannot be refused entry, just because they live outside the zone.

● The school is not suited to the child's age, ability and aptitude, in the opinion of the local education authority.

This mainly affects children assessed as needing special education, whose parents want an ordinary school for them.

● Distance. The choice involves a tiring journey and a place is available nearer home.

● Changing local education authorities. If you choose a school in another au-

---

IN THE PARENTS' PLACE

'In loco parentis' is a legal phrase explaining the authority of the school and its teachers over their pupils. Literally it means 'in the parents' place'. When you send your child to school, you are surrendering your responsibility as a parent to the school for the duration of school hours.

The courts have held that the school and its teachers must take the same care of their pupils as a careful parent would take of his own children. So parents have the right to expect that the school will protect their children from harm.

To carry out this duty, the school is given the same rights as parents while children are in its care. This means, for instance, that a teacher can cane a pupil in cases where a parent might reasonably have inflicted corporal punishment, even though the parent of that particular child objects strongly to corporal punishment. A parent's individual preference about discipline is irrelevant when the school is acting in a reasonable manner towards the child.

thority's area, your authority has to pay them the cost of the school place.

In the past, local education authorities have sometimes refused to allow this on the grounds of expense. The 1980 Act specifically states that the rules about choice apply equally to parents who want to choose a school in another education authority area.

PUPILS WHO HELP RUN THE SCHOOL

The Taylor Report suggests that pupils should be represented on school boards and should take part as fully as possible in governing their schools.

'Will Pupil Governors kindly refrain from referring to the Head Teacher as 'Old Fishface'.'

How to appeal against a school allocation

You can appeal against the refusal of a place to the authority or – in the case of a voluntary school – to the head teacher and then to the governors. You would need to show that the authority's own rules had not been followed or that your reasons for choosing a particular school had not been given proper consideration.

An important provision of the 1980 Act is that the local education authority and the governors of voluntary schools must set up by 1982 appeals tribunals to hear appeals from parents who are not given a place for their child at the school of their choice. These tribunals will be under the supervision of the Council on Tribunals, and the chairman must not be a member of the education committee or governor of the voluntary school concerned.

Parents and teachers may be members, but not for any case in which they have a personal connection. Elected members of the local education authority (or governors in the case of a voluntary school) must not out-number the other members by more than one, and no employee other than a teacher can be a member of a tribunal.

The decision of the tribunal will be binding on the local authority or the governing body of a voluntary school.

Parents must appeal in writing stating their reasons for doing so, and will have the opportunity of appearing in person, with a friend or someone to help them to put their case. The decision of the tribunal must be notified to the parent in writing, with reasons. These provisions about appeals will not be fully operational until 1982.

If your appeal is rejected, whether or not these new rules apply, you can still write to the Secretary of State and ask him to declare that they are acting unreasonably and oblige them to give your child a place.

You can complain to the local OMBUDSMAN if you suspect maladministration about allocation to a state school. If he accepts your complaint, he will ask the local education authority to take action. If the authority takes no action, appeal to the Secretary of State.

If the Secretary of State does not support you, you must accept an alter-

COMPLAINING ABOUT THE SIZE OF CLASSES

There are no regulations about the size of classes in state schools apart from a general instruction in Schools Regulations that every school should have enough teachers to provide appropriate full-time education.

Schools are built for a fixed number of pupils; but the size of classes depends on the number of teachers the education authority decides to employ, the quota it assigns to each school and how the head teacher decides to deploy them within the school. For instance, small 6th form groups can mean large classes lower down the school.

If you are concerned about class size, start by looking up your area's pupil–teacher ratio in the Department of Education and Science statistics, obtainable from any good reference library. Then compare your local statistics with the national average. In 1980 that was 22.7:1 in English primary schools and 16.6:1 in secondary schools.

These ratios include senior staff who do not teach full-time, so they are not an accurate guide to the size of classes. However, they make a useful basis for comparison.

Next ask the head teacher how many staff your school is allowed. It is the responsibility of the local authority if your school does not get a fair share of teachers. The local authority can employ as many as it likes, provided it can pay for them.

If the deployment of teachers within the school is the problem, ask the governors to take up the matter with the head teacher.

Teachers' unions campaign vigorously for reductions in class size, so local branches may be useful allies in any complaint.

---

native school and hope that your child can change schools later. The alternative is to defy the law by keeping your child at home in the hope of being offered the school you want.

In that case the authority could prosecute you under the SCHOOL ATTENDANCE rules.

If you are unsuccessful in the case, you face fines and imprisonment and your children could be taken into care.

When you can visit a school

Although schools generally encourage co-operation between home and school and welcome parents on many occasions, parents do not have any formal legal rights of access to their child's school. Nor does being a ratepayer provide any right of entry.

Anyone visiting a school is there by permission of the head teacher, who can withdraw that permission at any time, merely by asking him to leave. He is then trespassing and the police may be called to remove him.

Parents do have a right to expect consultation with the teachers about their children's welfare and progress. A government circular – DES 15/77 – states that parents should be told how to arrange a visit to the school and the times at which the head teacher, senior staff members, class or subject teachers, year heads or pastoral tutors are normally available.

If you are not given this information, write to the head teacher and ask for it.

Always write or phone and ask for an appointment if you want to discuss something with the school, otherwise no one may be free to speak to you.

However angry you may feel, try not to lose your temper. You will do your case no good and you can be asked to leave without having the chance to put a perfectly legitimate complaint.

Open days and report meetings

Most schools arrange open days, at which parents can see something of the work being done. Ideally, open days should be kept separate from report meetings, when parents discuss their children's progress with teachers.

If you are not happy about the arrangements for consultation at your children's school, take it up with the head teacher and, if you are still not satisfied, with the school governors.

Access to children while in school

Parents should get the head teacher's permission if they want to contact children in school, although that would probably not be required at break or dinner-hour. It is up to the head teacher to decide whether parents may stay with their children in the classroom.

If a parent goes to school during school hours and wants to take his or her child away, the school has no right to withhold the child, except where parents are separated and there may be some dispute over custody.

In such cases, the school should re-

WHEN A SCHOOL IS TO CLOSE

When a local education authority wants to close a school, make a significant change in its character, or significantly enlarge its premises, it has to follow a procedure laid down in Sections 12–16 of the 1980 Education Act.

A detailed proposal has to be submitted to the Secretary of State for Education and Science, including arrangements that will be made for pupils still at the school.

To give the local community time to comment on any proposal to change a school or to close it altogether, the Department of Education and Science recommends that proposals should be made public 12 months before they are due to be implemented if possible, and that the parents and school governors should be consulted before proposals are formulated. Formal notices about the proposals must always be:

● Published in at least one local newspaper.
● Posted in conspicuous places near the school.
● Posted at or near the school's main entrance.
● Displayed in other ways that the authority thinks appropriate.

Two months are allowed for local people to make their comments.

Any objection must be supported by at least 10 people on the local electoral roll. Objections may also be submitted by governors of any voluntary school affected by the proposals, or by another local education authority concerned. The local authority making the proposal must submit any objections it receives to the Secretary of State.

If no notice of objection is received, the authority can go ahead with the proposals. If there are objections, or if the school concerned is or is to become a voluntary school, the Secretary of State will decide whether or not they should be approved.

These procedures also apply when an authority proposes to reduce the size of the yearly school intake by one-fifth or more, or when a significant change is being made in the school such as a change from single-sex to co-education, or selective to comprehensive intake.

lease a child only to the parent who has custody, unless that parent has given consent. Parents should warn the school if there is a custody problem.

When the curriculum is in dispute

The law intervenes in only two ways to prescribe what must be taught in schools. It:
● Obliges all state schools to provide RELIGIOUS EDUCATION.
● Bars all schools from offering different subjects to boys and girls according to traditional assumptions about the

---

WHEN A SCHOOL CAN BE INSPECTED

There are two kinds of school inspectors: HM inspectors, appointed by the Crown, and local inspectors employed by the local education authority. HM inspectors have a right of access to all schools. They examine what subjects are taught, what methods are used and what standards are reached. Local inspectors have whatever powers the local authority likes to give them.

The 1944 Education Act said schools should be inspected at appropriate intervals, but there is no formal system for them to be regularly examined by a central government agency. Nor is there any compulsion on local education authorities to run their own inspectorate.

Inspectors visit schools to assess their work, not to report on individuals. Occasionally a team of HM inspectors visit a school to make a general inspection, producing a full, confidential report which goes to the staff, governors and local authority.

But they have no legal powers over schools. They can inform and persuade and can draw attention to failings. They cannot insist on changes being made.

Local inspectors have some responsibility for training and promotions, and because schools may need their support to get new equipment or extra staff, they can exert considerable influence on the schools.

Parents have no direct right of access to inspectors. They cannot, for instance, demand an inspection of a school. But if you are concerned about a school, it is worth writing to them. Attention will be paid to your letter, even if you do not see any action.

WHEN PROPERTY IS LOST AT SCHOOL

A local education authority or private school does not have to pay compensation for personal property lost at school. Even if a pupil asks a teacher to look after something, the teacher is not liable for its loss unless it can be shown that he failed to take reasonable care of it.

However, the authority may make an ex-gratia payment, without admitting liability, if you can prove that an expensive, essential item, such as a new coat, was lost at school.

Householders' comprehensive insurance policies with a 'temporary removal' clause may cover loss through fire or theft at school. If your child takes a musical instrument or other expensive equipment to school regularly, it could be worthwhile taking out an 'all risks' policy to cover possible loss.

Make sure that your child's belongings are clearly marked. Every school has a big collection of unclaimed lost property, so if your child loses something, it may be worthwhile asking to go through the lost-property box yourself.

Schools often ask for a contribution towards the cost if a child loses school property, such as textbooks. Most parents feel this is reasonable, but they cannot be forced to pay for accidental loss, such as leaving a book on a bus.

When property is confiscated

A teacher can confiscate any item if he thinks a child should not have it in school. The teacher must take reasonable care of anything confiscated and return it in the same condition as when it was confiscated, although there is no time limit for this restitution. The school could retain illegal property – for example, flick knives.

'proper' role of men and women.

Choice of subjects must be 'genuinely available to all who reveal the relevant interest, ability and determination'.

Complaints about sex discrimination in schools should be made to the Secretary of State for Education and Science in the first place, and not to the Equal Opportunities Commission.

There is otherwise no central control of the school curriculum. Local education authorities have final responsibility for instruction in their schools. They usually delegate the general direction of the curriculum of each school to its governing body, and in practice the head teacher is left with considerable freedom to decide what should be taught. He has, however, to take into account the expectations of parents and employers, the public examination system and the need to act reasonably.

Parents have a legal obligation to see that their children are efficiently and suitably educated. It is assumed that if you send your children to a state school, this duty is fulfilled.

You do not have any obligation or right to satisfy yourself that the school is in fact providing an efficient or suitable education.

Section 76 of the 1944 Education Act states that pupils are to be educated in accordance with the wishes of their parents. But there are two provisos.

The local education authority can claim that to agree would:

● Cause unreasonable public expense.
● Be inefficient. Parents' wishes are often overruled on these grounds.

For example, a parent might want his son to do O-level Latin because the boy hopes to become an archaeologist. The school could refuse on the ground that the cost of providing a teacher for a single pupil would be an inefficient use of resources.

If you are concerned about any aspect of what is taught in school, and if you cannot get satisfaction from the head

---

HOW THE RULES RESTRICT PUNISHMENT

The law allows teachers and authorised prefects to administer punishment to pupils – but with strict safeguards to prevent abuse.

---

teacher, complain to the governors.

Local authorities usually prefer to influence what is taught in schools through their inspectors rather than by direct intervention. You can write to the local inspector at the Education Offices (whose address is listed in the telephone directory), expressing your worries.

Enforcing school discipline

Because head teachers are responsible for discipline in their school, they

EDUCATION: A NATIONAL SERVICE ADMINISTERED LOCALLY
The relationship between central government, local government and the schools system

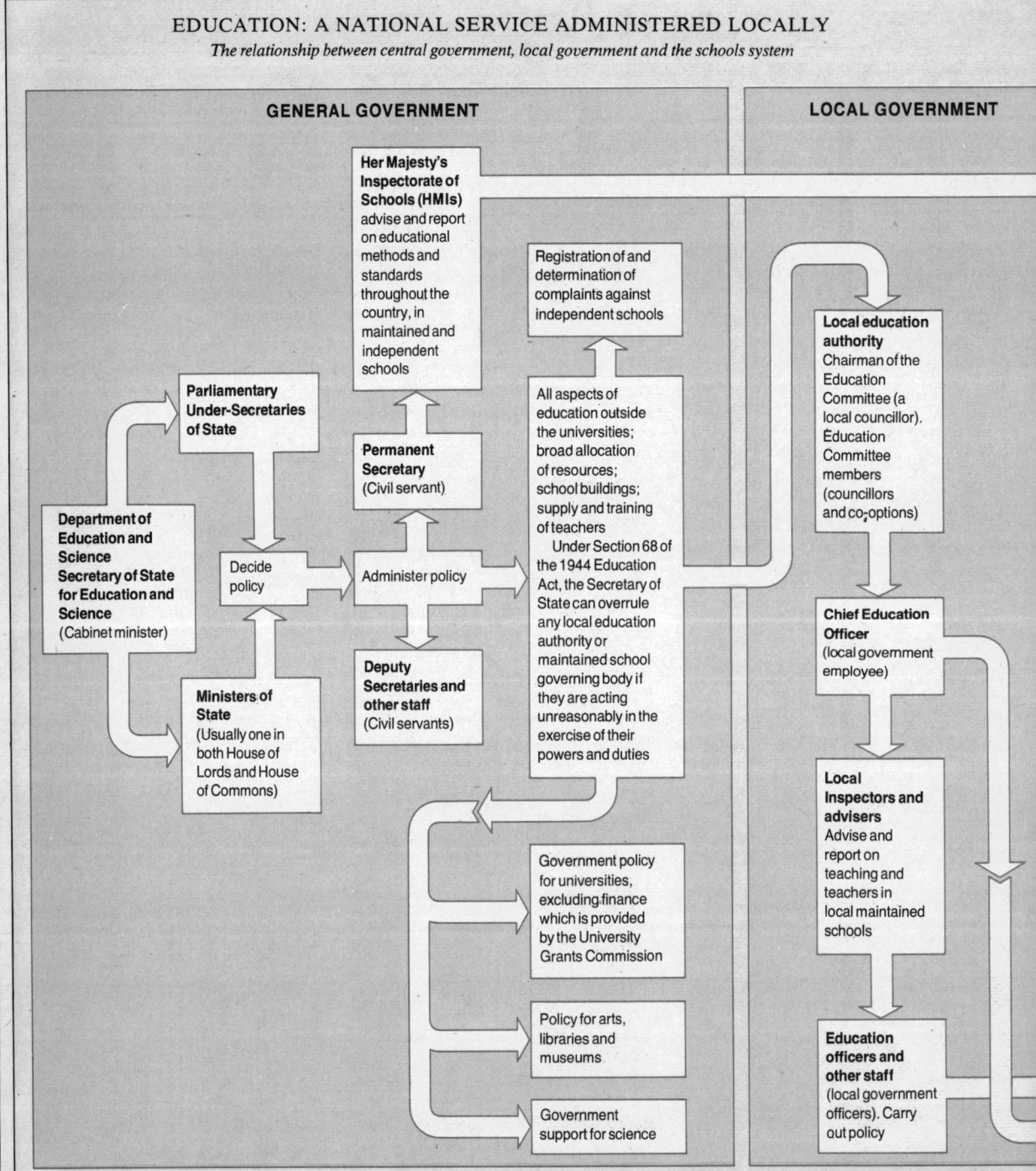

GENERAL GOVERNMENT

Her Majesty's Inspectorate of Schools (HMIs) advise and report on educational methods and standards throughout the country, in maintained and independent schools

Registration of and determination of complaints against independent schools

Parliamentary Under-Secretaries of State

Permanent Secretary (Civil servant)

Department of Education and Science Secretary of State for Education and Science (Cabinet minister)

Decide policy

Administer policy

All aspects of education outside the universities; broad allocation of resources; school buildings; supply and training of teachers

Under Section 68 of the 1944 Education Act, the Secretary of State can overrule any local education authority or maintained school governing body if they are acting unreasonably in the exercise of their powers and duties

Ministers of State (Usually one in both House of Lords and House of Commons)

Deputy Secretaries and other staff (Civil servants)

Government policy for universities, excluding finance which is provided by the University Grants Commission

Policy for arts, libraries and museums

Government support for science

LOCAL GOVERNMENT

Local education authority Chairman of the Education Committee (a local councillor). Education Committee members (councillors and co-options)

Chief Education Officer (local government employee)

Local Inspectors and advisers Advise and report on teaching and teachers in local maintained schools

Education officers and other staff (local government officers). Carry out policy

can enforce whatever reasonable rules they choose. The local authority and the courts will usually support them if they claim that the rules are necessary to maintain discipline and good order.

If you are worried about rules or discipline in your child's school, it is best to get support from other parents and only then to make a joint approach to the head teacher and governors.
Corporal punishment All cases of corporal punishment in school must be re-

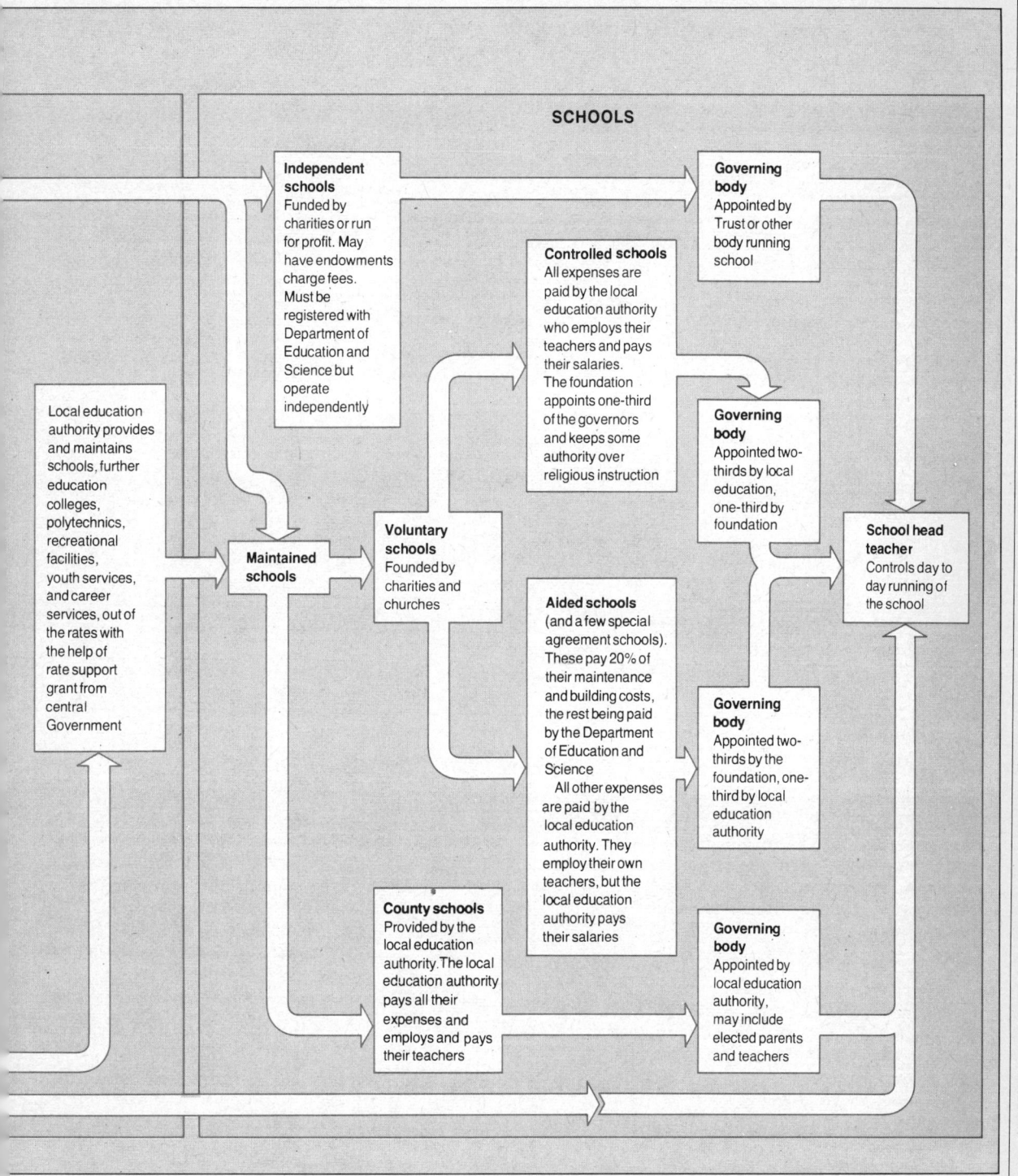

SCHOOLS

WHEN BOARDING SCHOOL EDUCATION IS AVAILABLE

Boarding schools are subject to the same rules as other schools. Local education authorities can run their own boarding schools, use those run by other education authorities or pay for places at independent boarding schools.

If an education authority runs its own boarding schools, or uses boarding schools run by other local authorities, the rules about choice of school apply to them as to ordinary day schools.

If you live too far away from a suitable school for your children to travel there every day, the local education authority must pay for them to board at a suitable school. It must pay the cost of coming home for holidays and returning to school, and may grant fares for visits home during term.

If you want your child to go to an independent boarding school despite the proximity of a local authority school, the local authority may help you with the cost, but it is under no legal obligation to do so. No one can overrule a decision of the authority on this matter, unless you can show that it has acted unfairly towards you in comparison with other families whom they have helped.

Some authorities give a great deal of help; others help only as a last resort. There is no national scale of allowances. Unless your income is very low, or your child is boarding because no other school is available, any grant you get is unlikely to cover the full cost of fees, uniform, fares and other extras.

How to apply

Write to the Chief Education Officer, asking for information about your authority's arrangements for boarding education. Apply as early as possible. The most commonly accepted grounds for applying are:
1. Both parents living abroad. The family must intend to return to this country.
2. Frequent moves. For example, older children are having exam courses disrupted by change of school.
3. Difficult home circumstances. The local authority decides what qualifies.
4. Special aptitudes. For example, children needing specialist training for outstanding musical ability.
5. Religious beliefs. Parents want a denominational education not available in local schools.

Assisted Places

The government's new Assisted Places scheme, for helping children whose parents could not otherwise afford independent SCHOOL FEES, does not cover boarding fees, but the regulations may provide for schools taking part to give help with boarding costs, which will be reimbursed by the Department of Education and Science. It may, therefore, be a way of getting help with the cost of education at independent boarding schools. The scheme should come into effect by autumn 1981.

---

corded in a punishment book kept by the head teacher, who is responsible for its accuracy. The local education authority, governors and inspectors are entitled to look at it.

Local authorities can issue regulations controlling corporal punishment for boys and girls in county schools and some have abolished it altogether – for some age groups at least. But these regulations are not binding on voluntary schools.

Subject to any such regulations, any teacher or authorised prefect can administer reasonable and moderate corporal punishment without risking any accusation of assault.

Teachers claim the legal right to beat children regardless of their parents' wishes. But a parent, objecting to corporal punishment, can tell the head teacher, who may be prepared to substitute some other punishment.

Detention In 1908 Mr Justice Phillimore said that 'it is, I suppose, false imprisonment to keep a child locked up in a classroom or even to order it to stop under penalties in a room for a longer period than the ordinary school time without legal authority'.

Parents normally accept detention as a reasonable punishment as long as they are notified in advance. But if a parent goes to school and asks for his child, or makes it clear that he must not be detained after school, the school must release the child.

Teachers who keep children in are responsible for their safety while in school.

It is not clear who is responsible for a child's safety if his arrangements for getting home are disrupted and parents are not told he is going to be late.

Suspension Schools Regulations say

VISITING THE CLASSROOM

Parents do not have an automatic legal right to visit their child's school. The head teacher can ask them to leave. If they refuse, they are trespassing.

that pupils must not be excluded from school on other than reasonable grounds. Most local authorities allow head teachers – but not other teachers – to suspend children for whatever reason they consider adequate. They must report the suspension to the governors and to the local authority, both of which have normally to confirm the suspension.

There are no national regulations about how long a suspension should last or about providing alternative education. Local authorities may make their own regulations.

If your child is suspended Ask the school for a written statement of the reason for suspension and how long it is to last. Ask for an appointment to discuss it with the head teacher.

If you decide then that you want to appeal, write to the governors asking for your case to be considered, preferably with you in person, whatever the local regulations prescribe.

If your child is at a state school, you may appeal to the Secretary of State for Education and Science if your appeal is rejected by the governors.

Expulsion No child can be expelled without reasonable grounds. Lord Chief Justice Cockburn said in 1865 that although head teachers must have the right to expel pupils whose conduct

THE IMPORTANCE OF THE GOVERNORS

Every state school and some private schools have governors. Some education authorities once grouped schools under one governing body, but under the Education Act 1980, this is no longer allowed. The only exceptions will be for two primary schools, or when the Secretary of State has given special permission – for example, when schools share the same site.

School governing bodies are the link between schools, the community and the local authority. They are the 'guardians and trustees' of the community's interest in schools. So if you have a problem you cannot resolve with the school staff, you can approach the governing body.

Who may be appointed

All governors of county schools are appointed by the local education authorities. Under the 1980 Act, schools must have elected teacher and parent governors. County schools and special schools have two parent governors elected in a secret ballot by the other parents. They must have at least one teacher governor, elected by the staff, two if there are more than 300 pupils.

In voluntary schools, a proportion of the governors are appointed by the foundation, and in future this must include at least one parent of a child at the school. The remainder are appointed by the local education authority, and these must now include an elected parent and one elected teacher governor (two for schools over 300).

Some authorities allow more parent and teacher governors, and also arrange for pupils and non-teaching staff to have elected representatives. Local authorities tend to make their appointments on a political basis, in proportion to party strength on the council.

If you do not know the governors' names and addresses, write to the Clerk to the Governors, X School, c/o Education Offices.

In the case of a private school, write to the chairman of the governors at the school.

What governors can do

The legal powers of governors are set out in the articles of government for each school. These should be available at the education offices, or in the case of voluntary schools at the school itself.

Normally these articles provide that the education authority decides the general educational character of the school; the governors have general oversight of the conduct and curriculum; and the head teacher controls the day-to-day running of the school.

Governors usually have some powers over school finance, the care and use of the school premises, the appointment of the head teacher and other staff, school hours and holidays and the suspension of pupils from school. Voluntary school articles usually also give the governors control over admissions and expulsions or suspensions.

The changes introduced by the 1980 Act will be brought in gradually, and no date has yet been given for making them mandatory on all schools.

---

was damaging the school, this power could not be exercised 'wantonly and capriciously'.

Parents of children at state schools can appeal in writing to the Secretary of State if they think their child's expulsion was unreasonable.

The local authority must provide an alternative school place for a child expelled from any school.

Pupils' rights in school

Because schools are *in loco parentis* (in the parents' place) a school and its teachers have the same rights and duties towards children in their care as parents have out of school.

The school can hardly be *in loco parentis* to pupils who have reached the age of 18, but the school retains the duty to ensure their safety; and pupils who

have chosen to stay on after school-leaving age are presumed to have chosen to obey school discipline.

Establishing a school council

A head teacher has the right to decide whether his school should have a pupils' council, able to raise matters affecting pupils and make representations to him.

If there is a council, the head teacher decides how it should be organised, what it should discuss and what notice should be taken of its recommendations. In any case, the head teacher retains his legal responsibility for what goes on in the school.

When pupils can appoint their own governor

There is some dispute over whether it

is illegal for pupils under 18 to be school governors. Some local education authorities already have elected pupil governors as full members of the governing body, others allow them in as observers without a vote. The new Act does nothing to resolve the question, but the new regulations tacitly accept the existence of pupil governors by referring to their role in disciplinary or financial matters. The government-appointed Taylor Committee recommended in 1977 that pupils should be encouraged to participate in school government to the fullest extent allowed by the law.

Participation in out-of-school activities

Outside school hours, pupils cannot be forced to take part in extra-curricular activities, such as plays, debates or playing in school teams. However, the school can often make it uncomfortable for them to refuse.

While a school cannot forbid pupils to join any organisation, such as the National Union of School Students, many schools impose a ban on any activity within the school to promote or publicise the NUSS and other organisations. But pupils cannot be punished for publicising such organisations away from school premises.

SCHOOL AGE

When attendance at a school is compulsory

Children must start school at the beginning of the term after their 5th birthday. There is no legal obligation for local education authorities to provide a place earlier than that, but many do so.

Compulsory schooling ends at age 16, but not on the pupil's 16th birthday. There are two school-leaving dates in the year. If a pupil's birthday falls on or between September 1 and January 31, he or she can leave at the end of the spring term; if the birthday falls on or between February 1 and August 31, the pupil can leave at the summer half term (the late Spring Bank Holiday).

Pupils over 16

Local authorities must provide education for pupils up to the age of 19, but

WHEN SCHOOLING BECOMES OBLIGATORY

Parents must send a child to school from the start of the term after his fifth birthday. Local authorities are not obliged to find places for younger children.

pupils over 16 do not have an automatic right to a place.

A school can insist on minimum qualifications for the 6th form and can expel a pupil for unsatisfactory behaviour. In such cases the authority is not obliged to provide an alternative place at another of its schools.

Pupils who reach the age of 19 during their last year at school do not have to leave before completing their course.

SCHOOL ATTENDANCE

Parents duty to send children to school every day

Whether state or private, all schools must keep admission and attendance registers, and pupils must be in school by the time the register is called.

They must also be present for the whole day. So it is illegal – though often condoned – to allow even 5-year-olds to attend part-time when they start school.

The courts have ruled that a parent who sends his child to school in circumstances that he knows will cause the child to be refused admission – such as failing to comply with SCHOOL UNIFORM regulations – has not caused the child to attend school.

To check on truants, schools normal-

WHEN BEING LATE MEANS BEING ABSENT

Parents must ensure that their children get to school on time. Otherwise they are liable to prosecution for the children's non-attendance.

Mr Samuel Hinchley of Birmingham was convicted at a magistrates' court in 1961 of failing to have his son, Stephen, attend school regularly. A certificate of non-attendance showed that during a 6 week period of 1960, Stephen was marked absent 29 times and present 27 times. He should have been at school by 9.15 a.m. The attendance register was closed at 9.45 and any pupil arriving after that time was marked as absent.

When Mr Hinchley appealed to the Quarter Sessions, the conviction was quashed on the ground that the certificate of non-attendance might merely have been evidence of unpunctuality rather than of absence. The prosecutor appealed to the Divisional Court.

DECISION

The Divisional Court ruled that absence at the time the register closed was failure to attend school.

---

ly expect a note from parents explaining the reason for any absence.

When a child can stay away

There is a limited number of reasons for which a child may legitimately be absent from school:
● Permission from the school authorities.
● Illness. You do not need a medical certificate but should inform the school about any chronic condition or lengthy illness. If your child refuses to go to school because of genuine school phobia – an irrational terror of school – ask your doctor to write explaining this to the school.
● Infectious disease.
● Cleanliness – for example, when children are excluded from school because of nits or other infestation and are waiting for treatment. *See:* SCHOOL HEALTH SERVICE
● Unavoidable cause. Most schools accept the occasional 'reasonable' cause such as a family party. But, legally, the cause should be something unavoidable and affecting the child – for example, a transport strike or snow-blocked roads. It is not acceptable to keep the child at home because the mother is ill.
● Family holiday. Children may have 2 weeks off school for an annual family holiday.
● Religious observance – for example, on a holy day.
● Transport – for example, when the local authority should provide transport, or lodgings near the school, and fails to do so.
● Entertainment licence – when a child has a licence from the local authority to take part professionally in plays, etc.

Dealing with truancy

Every local authority has a team of education welfare officers, part of whose job is to visit families whose children are not attending school. They usually try at first to persuade the children to return voluntarily.

In addition, the police may decide to look for truants in an area and take them to school. Although legally the children should be taken home to their parents, who are responsible for seeing that they go to school, most parents do not object.

In cases of persistent truancy, a local education authority can have parents of truants prosecuted in a magistrates' court. The maximum penalty is a £200

CATCHING A TRUANT

Legally, a policeman who finds a child playing truant is supposed to escort him home for his parents to deal with.

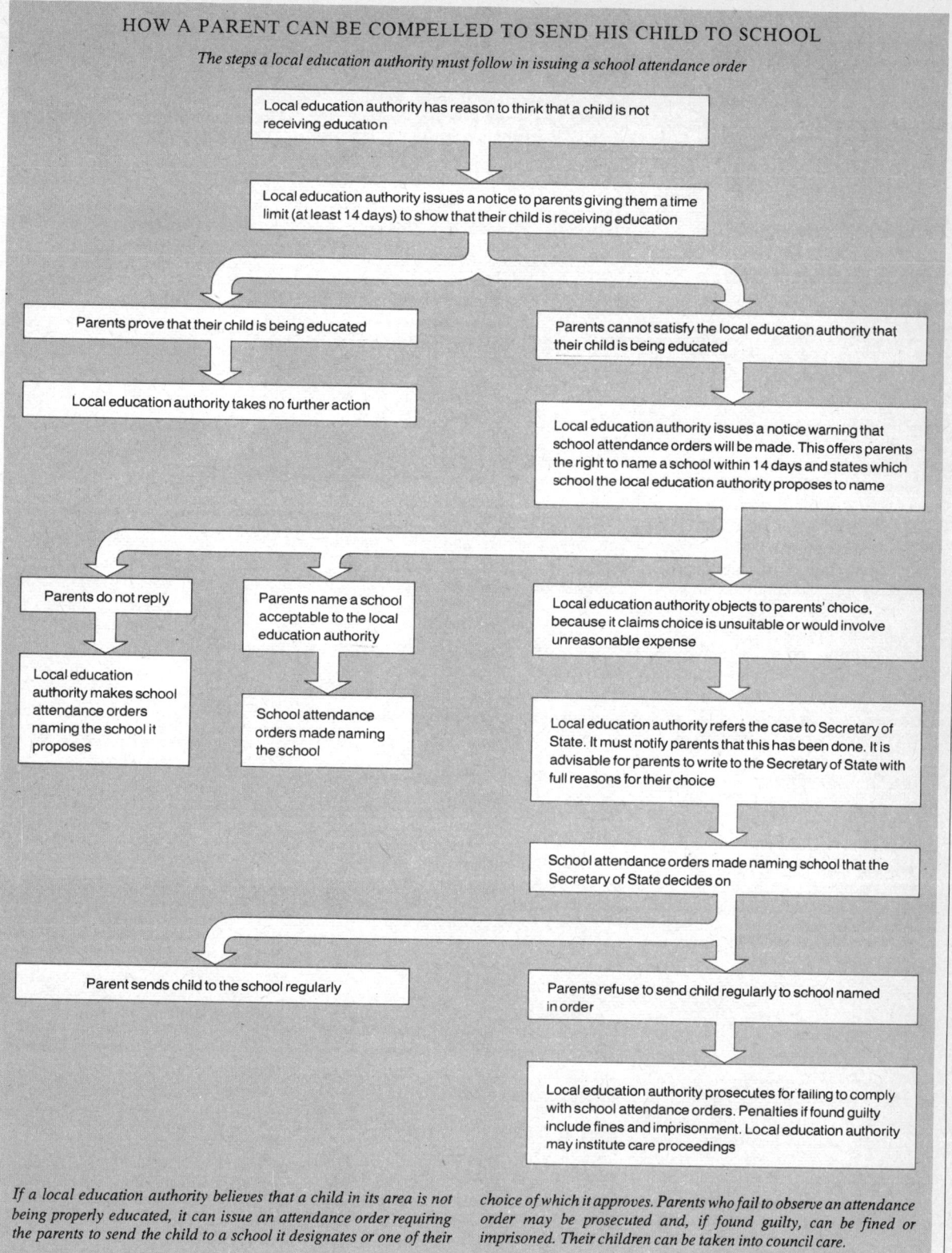

HOW A PARENT CAN BE COMPELLED TO SEND HIS CHILD TO SCHOOL

The steps a local education authority must follow in issuing a school attendance order

Local education authority has reason to think that a child is not receiving education

Local education authority issues a notice to parents giving them a time limit (at least 14 days) to show that their child is receiving education

Parents prove that their child is being educated

Local education authority takes no further action

Parents cannot satisfy the local education authority that their child is being educated

Local education authority issues a notice warning that school attendance orders will be made. This offers parents the right to name a school within 14 days and states which school the local education authority proposes to name

Parents do not reply

Local education authority makes school attendance orders naming the school it proposes

Parents name a school acceptable to the local education authority

School attendance orders made naming the school

Local education authority objects to parents' choice, because it claims choice is unsuitable or would involve unreasonable expense

Local education authority refers the case to Secretary of State. It must notify parents that this has been done. It is advisable for parents to write to the Secretary of State with full reasons for their choice

School attendance orders made naming school that the Secretary of State decides on

Parent sends child to the school regularly

Parents refuse to send child regularly to school named in order

Local education authority prosecutes for failing to comply with school attendance orders. Penalties if found guilty include fines and imprisonment. Local education authority may institute care proceedings

If a local education authority believes that a child in its area is not being properly educated, it can issue an attendance order requiring the parents to send the child to a school it designates or one of their choice of which it approves. Parents who fail to observe an attendance order may be prosecuted and, if found guilty, can be fined or imprisoned. Their children can be taken into council care.

fine with the possibility of a month's imprisonment for third and later offences.

The authority may instead bring care proceedings in a juvenile court if it can also show that the truant needs care and control not provided by his parents. A supervision order or care order may be made, giving responsibility for the child to the local social services department. *See:* CHILDREN IN CARE

When an attendance order is made

Parents who refuse completely to send their children to school may be served with a school attendance order – even if they claim they are educating the children themselves. The test is whether the local authority is satisfied that the education being provided is adequate.

Parents who fail to comply with a school attendance order can be prosecuted. If they are acquitted, the authority can either concede or begin again with a new order, naming another school to which the children should be sent.

If they are convicted, they can be fined; and if they persist, they face increased penalties and imprisonment. The children could be taken into care.

An order stands until the child is 16 unless the authority revokes it. It can be altered if the parents persuade the authority to allow the child to change schools or to be educated at home.

In the past, parents were able to use the Attendance Order procedure to get a better chance of insisting on their choice of school. Sections 10 and 11 of the 1980 Education Act are designed to put an end to this advantage, however.

How the new law works

In future, parents who refuse to send their child to school will have the opportunity to name a school different from the one proposed by the local education authority when it notifies parents that an Attendance Order is to be issued. They will then have the same right of appeal and hearing before an appeal tribunal as other parents contesting a choice of SCHOOL.

If their appeal fails the local education authority will be able to name the school originally proposed in the Attendance Order. The Secretary of State will no longer be involved, unless the parents appeal to him ˙on the general grounds allowed in Section 68 of the 1944 Education Act that the authority is acting unreasonably.

These provisions will be brought into force on July 1, 1982, in time to affect children entering school in the autumn of 1982, when the other provisions about choice will have been implemented.

SCHOOL FEES

When parents must pay for their child's lessons

State education was made free by the 1944 Education Act, which said that 'no fees shall be charged in respect of the education provided in any school'. This includes the use of necessary books, stationery and equipment.

When education budgets are being cut, parents may be asked to make voluntary contributions to help their child's school buy books and equipment it could not otherwise afford.

This is legal as long as the payment of a 'voluntary' contribution is not made a condition of taking part in any curriculum subject.

In any case, parents are usually asked to contribute to the cost of materials for needlework, cookery and other craft subjects. Some children may be discouraged from taking these subjects because their parents cannot afford the cost.

Anybody who thinks that the charges are too high, or that the local authority is not allowing the school enough money for necessary books and materials, should take it up with the school governors and the local authority. *See:* SCHOOL

Local education authorities can decide whether a school should make a charge for extra subjects not on the regular timetable – for example, individual tuition in music or dancing.

Fees at independent schools

The 1980 Education Act made it easier for local education authorities to give grants to parents who want to send their children to independent schools. It is no longer necessary for the Secretary of State to give approval, and local authorities can make what arrangements they choose for giving help towards fees.

These grants, however, are discretionary, and local authorities do not have to provide any help at all, unless there are no suitable places at maintained schools.

The kinds of reasons for which local education authorities are sometimes prepared to pay independent school fees are:
● When parents want a denominational education for their child.
● Where the child would benefit from boarding education.
● When the independent school has special facilities not available elsewhere.

SCHOOL GRANT

When council help is available to parents

Local education authorities must provide free travel to and from school for all children who live beyond walking distance. *See:* SCHOOL TRANSPORT

Since the 1980 Education Act they no longer have to provide free school meals, except to people on supplemen-

---

ASSISTED PLACES SCHEME

The 1980 Education Act set up a scheme, beginning in autumn 1981, to help parents who want their children to go to independent schools but could not otherwise afford the fees. Full regulations about its operation are expected to come into operation during 1981.

The scheme covers tuition and examination fees only, but there may be a provision for schools to give help with other expenses such as boarding costs. The amount of the tuition fee subsidy will depend on the family's 'relevant' income – all income before tax, including any investment income belonging to the children, less an allowance of £600 for each dependant apart from the pupil himself.

In 1981–2, a family with a relevant income of under £4,766 would pay nothing towards the fees. With a relevant income of £11,000 or more, there would be no subsidy.

tary benefit or family income supplement. *See:* SCHOOL MEALS AND MILK

Help in special cases

Local authorities can choose to help schoolchildren in all kinds of ways. It is entirely the responsibility of the local authority to decide what to subsidise and how much to give. But the two most usual grants are:

● Clothing grants. Most local authorities give some grants for school uniform, though seldom covering the full cost.

● Educational maintenance allowances. Local authorities can make grants to children staying on at school after the school-leaving age of 16.

How to apply for a grant

Local authorities have their own means tests for all these grants, and you can find out what these are from the local education office. You can obtain application forms from the school, the education office or the education welfare officer, who may also help you to complete the forms. They may be lengthy and complicated, and will require supporting evidence – from your employer for example.

SCHOOL HEALTH SERVICE

Protecting the health of children at school

The School Health Service became part of the National Health Service in 1974 and is run by the area health authorities. So if you are concerned about any aspect of the health services provided at your school, contact the specialist in community medicine (child health) at the area health authority.

Certain vaccinations – for example against poliomyelitis and German measles – are offered through the school health service, but they are not compulsory. You can have them done by your family doctor if you prefer.

Medical and dental inspections

School medical inspections are not compulsory, and parents can refuse to have their children examined – unless they are being examined for cleanliness or if it is suspected that the child should be receiving SPECIAL EDUCATION.

MEDICAL REASONS FOR KEEPING A CHILD AWAY FROM SCHOOL

When the medical officer can over-ride a parent's wishes and insist on absence

Regulations about exclusion from school on health grounds are made by the area specialist in community medicine (child health). Even if your family doctor thinks a child is fit to attend, the school can exclude him if the medical officer – not the head teacher – issues a notice that the child is to be excluded on health grounds. The child will not be allowed back until the medical officer gives permission.

SCHOOL EXCLUSION PERIODS FOR COMMUNICABLE DISEASES

Disease	Period of exclusion
Chickenpox	6 days from onset of rash
Diphtheria	Until bacteriological examination is clear. Contacts must be similarly excluded
Dysentery	Until bacteriological examination is clear. Brothers and sisters at primary or nursery schools should be excluded until bacteriological examination is clear
Food poisoning	Until bacteriological examination is clear
German measles	4 days from onset of rash
Hepatitis A	7 days from onset of jaundice
Measles	7 days from onset of rash
Meningitis	Until recovery
Mumps	Until swelling has subsided (7 days minimum)
Poliomyelitis	At the discretion of the Medical Officer for Environmental Health. Contacts are dealt with in a similar way
Smallpox	At the discretion of the Medical Officer for Environmental Health. Contacts are dealt with in a similar way
Tuberculosis	At the discretion of the doctor
Typhoid and paratyphoid fever	Until bacteriological examination is clear
Whooping cough	21 days from onset of paroxysmal cough

SCHOOL EXCLUSION PERIODS FOR SKIN INFECTIONS

Infection	Period of exclusion
Impetigo	Until the skin is healed
Pediculosis	Until treatment has been received
Verrucae plantaris (foot warts)	Exclusion unnecessary provided the warts are covered with occlusive plaster
Ringworm of body	Exclusion not normally necessary during treatment, unless evidence of epidemic
Ringworm of feet (athlete's foot)	Exclusion from barefoot activities unnecessary, but treatment always advisable
Ringworm of scalp	Until cured
Scabies	Exclusion unnecessary once adequate treatment begins

The Department of Health and Social Security, however, recommends that:

● All children should have a medical inspection at the beginning of their school career, and at 'appropriate' intervals afterwards.

● Parents should be given the opportunity to attend medical inspections. (It is for the area health authority, and not the school, to make the arrangements.)

● All children should have regular dental inspections.

● If treatment is needed, school health facilities should be available for parents who want to use them instead of their own doctor or dentist.

● If a school or parent is worried about a child, they should be able to ask for a school medical examination.

● Medical and dental records should be kept on all schoolchildren.

It is for the area health authority to decide how to carry out these recommendations, but most follow the general pattern laid down from time to time by the Department of Health and Social Security.

Eyesight and hearing tests

Pupils are normally tested when they start school for sight and hearing defects. The parents of any children who appear to have a problem are offered the chance of a consultation with specialists for full diagnosis.

Parents are not usually expected to be present at the school tests, so ask to be notified if you have a special reason for wishing to be there.

Dealing with infectious diseases

The head teacher is likely to have to report to the area health authority when children are absent with one of the ailments common to children, whether or not these are on the list of notifiable diseases. See: INFECTIOUS DISEASE

Quarantine Children are not expected to stay away from school if they have been in contact with most of the common childhood ailments. Exceptions are contact with diphtheria, polio, smallpox, typhoid and some tropical fevers.

Cleanliness Inspections of hair and feet are carried out regularly by school nurses. Parents are not invited, they have no right to object, but they must be

notified if treatment is needed.

Every local authority must make facilities available for cleansing children who are 'infested with vermin, or in a foul condition'. Children suspected of having nits or other infestation may be compelled to have a special medical examination and can be excluded from school until treated.

If a child is excluded from school because of head-lice and parents have applied for treatment, they cannot be prosecuted for keeping the child at home. But parents who fail to have the child treated can be prosecuted for failing to secure their child's education; and the medical officer can make an order for the child to be cleansed compulsorily.

If a child has been cleansed and gets into a foul condition again, his parents can be prosecuted and fined.

SCHOOL LEAVERS

Joining the social security system

Compulsory schooling ends at age 16, but not on the pupil's 16th birthday. There are two school-leaving dates in the year. If a pupil's birthday falls on or between September 1 and January 31, he or she can leave at the end of the spring term; if the birthday falls on or between February 1 and August 31, the pupil can leave at the summer half term (the late Spring Bank Holiday).

The first day you leave school and are seeking a job, you should register for employment at your local education authority careers office. You are then also credited with NATIONAL INSURANCE CONTRIBUTIONS to help you qualify more quickly for UNEMPLOYMENT BENEFIT, SICKNESS BENEFIT and MATERNITY ALLOWANCE. Everyone over 16 in employment has to pay contributions; if you take up work on leaving school and then become unemployed you will generally qualify for unemployment benefit if you have already paid 26 weekly contributions.

Anyone unemployed who unreasonably refuses to apply for an available vacancy or to accept employment offered to him is liable to be disqualified for unemployment benefit (or not to be credited with contributions) for 6 weeks. That rule applies to school

leavers too.

If the job in question was at a rate of pay less than the normal pay for such a job, or if it were beyond the physical strength of the claimant, it would not be unreasonable to refuse. If you are disqualified, you can appeal to a NATIONAL INSURANCE LOCAL TRIBUNAL.

NHS treatment

If you are under 21, even though you are not at school or in full-time education, you are still entitled to free NHS dental treatment, other than for dentures, by signing a declaration provided by the dentist. If you are receiving supplementary benefit, you are entitled to free prescriptions for medical treatment. Complete the back of the prescription form before going to the chemist. You are also entitled to free NHS glasses simply by signing a declaration provided by the optician.

Although you are working, your income may be low enough to qualify for free glasses, prescriptions and dental treatment. Obtain form M11 from your local social security office.

How parents are affected

The claims of parents for social security benefits may also be affected when their child leaves school. A parent is entitled to CHILD BENEFIT for any child up to the age of 19 as long as he remains at school. If the child ceases this full-time education that entitlement to child benefit lapses. If the parent continues to cash the child benefit order book vouchers she will be required to repay the amount to which she was not entitled.

If at the end of the school year it is uncertain until, for example, examination results are published, whether the child is to continue full-time education, a parent can continue to draw child benefit and would not be required to repay provided that she ceased to receive the benefit as soon as a decision had been made that the child was leaving school.

In the same way a parent receiving industrial injuries benefit, invalidity pension, maternity allowance, sickness benefit or unemployment benefit may also be claiming more money if he has a child for whom child benefit is payable. That extra allowance ceases to be payable for a child over 16 whose full-time education ends. A parent who does not inform the social security office of this and continues to draw the child allowance is also required to repay.

If a single parent taxpayer has an additional personal allowance for having his child living with him or her, this additional income tax allowance is lost if the child ceases to receive full-time education or training for a trade or profession.

Youth opportunities programme

The Government has instructed the Manpower Services Commission to provide opportunities for unemployed school leavers in training courses and work-experience schemes. Those who leave school in 1981 are to be offered such an opportunity by Christmas 1981. An offer will be made immediately to any 16 or 17 year old who has been unemployed for 3 months.

Applications and requests for information should be made to the nearest office of the Manpower Services Commission.

SCHOOL MEALS AND MILK
The minimum service that must be provided

The 1980 Education Act released local authorities from any obligation to provide school milk, although they can continue to do so if they choose, and can make a charge for milk provided at school if they wish.

Providing mid-day meals

Similarly, local education authorities no longer have to provide school meals, except for children whose family receive SUPPLEMENTARY BENEFIT or FAMILY INCOME SUPPLEMENT.

There are no longer any Department of Education and Science regulations about the nutritional content of meals and how much should be charged for them.

Local authorities are free to decide what kind of meals should be provided, what charge should be made for them, and whether there should be any free meals for poorer families in addition to the required free meals for families receiving family income supplement and supplementary benefit.

Schools must, however, provide suitable facilities including accommodation, furniture and supervision for children to eat their own packed lunches. No charge can be made.

A government circular pointed out that although there are no national regulations, pupils receiving free meals should get the same kind of meal as those who are paying for the meal, and that 'so far as is practicable, arrangements for pupils taking free meals are such as will minimise identification and possible embarrassment'.

The head teacher in each school decides how dinner money should be collected: every day, every week or once a term, perhaps. The only rule is that the system must be reasonable. He could not, for example, insist that everyone paid by the term.

SCHOOL RECORDS
Information that may be passed to outsiders

Virtually every school keeps individual records on all its pupils, covering not only educational progress but also personal details about home background and family.

These records can be shown to the police, social workers dealing with the child's family and careers officers without the parents' consent or prior consultation. Parents have no right to sue for breach of confidence; nor do they have a right to see or challenge the records themselves.

If they find out that a record is defamatory, however, they may be able to sue for LIBEL. They would have to prove that the libellous statement had been made maliciously and that it was known by the person making it to be untrue.

Some, but not all, local education authorities allow parents to see the records of their own children.

SCHOOL REPORT
When teachers have a right to express an opinion

All state secondary schools are expected to let parents have periodical

written reports on the progress of their children. State primary schools do not always give written reports.

Private schools can issue reports if and when it is their policy to do so.

A report is a private communication between the head teacher and parents and should not be disclosed to others without the parents' permission. Unlike a SCHOOL RECORD, it should not be shown by the school to outside agencies – such as social workers and careers officers – because it covers only a limited period and would not give a true, overall picture of the pupil.

When teachers are writing reports for parents, they are protected by 'qualified privilege'. That is, they may not be sued for LIBEL as long as it can be shown that statements objected to were not made maliciously and that the teacher honestly believed at the time of writing that they were true.

Parents should always write to the school to ask for correction to a report if they think that a mistake has been made or that it is unfair, in case the report is later used as a basis for reference.

SCHOOL TRANSPORT
Helping children to get to school

Local education authorities must provide free transport for children to and from school if they live more than walking distance away.

For children under 8, that distance is laid down as 2 miles; for children of 8 and over it is 3 miles, measured by the shortest possible route, regardless of whether that route is dangerous for children.

As a result, some children qualify for free travel while others using the same bus stop have to pay because they *live* a few yards nearer the school.

If parents choose a school more than 2 or 3 miles away in preference to one within walking distance, they are not necessarily given free travel. That is at the discretion of the local authority.

Local authorities also have discretion to help any other children with free transport, such as the needy or handicapped.

Children living on the school bus route, who do not qualify for free travel, may be allowed a seat on payment if

> ## THE SHORTEST WAY TO SCHOOL
>
> *The distance between a pupil's home and his school is reckoned by the shortest possible route – even if it is only a cart-track.*
>
> Mr George Hares, a farmer of Cheddar, Somerset, was charged in 1911 with neglecting to send his 13-year-old son, Albert, to school. Under the parish bye-laws, a reasonable excuse for non-attendance would be that there was 'no elementary school . . . within 3 miles, measured according to the nearest road' from the pupil's home.
>
> The father argued that the walk via the nearest road was more than 3 miles. But the court convicted him as the distance was less than 3 miles if Albert used a cart-track through a field. Mr Hares appealed.
>
> ### DECISION
> The Divisional Court dismissed his appeal. It held that 'road' in the bye-law just meant 'a route'.

there are spare places on the bus. The decision lies with the local education authority.

The local education authority is responsible for the safety of children travelling on its school buses or waiting for them at school. Authorities can be sued for negligence if a child is hurt because of inadequate supervision.

SCHOOL UNIFORM

When certain clothes must be worn

If a head teacher decides that school uniform is necessary to maintain discipline in the school, he can refuse to admit children not wearing the prescribed clothing. He may also do so if a child's appearance is contrary to school rules – for example, a boy with long hair.

If a child goes regularly to school, but is sent home each time because he is not wearing the approved uniform, his parents can be prosecuted for failure to send the child to school.

Whether parents are prosecuted depends on the local authorities, some of

WHEN UNIFORM IS COMPULSORY

When a head teacher decides that a uniform is to be worn, neither children nor parents have any right to object. Children who do not comply can be sent home.

which will not prosecute in uniform and appearance cases.

In theory a poor parent, who cannot afford the uniform, can be prosecuted for failing to send his child to school. But local education authorities may make grants towards the cost of school uniform in cases of hardship. *See:* SCHOOL GRANT

SCHOOL VISIT

Safeguarding children on a school outing

There is no legal rule about who pays for school outings. Although visits that are an essential part of the school curriculum ought to be free, it is hard to draw the line between study and enjoyment – for instance between a geography field trip and a climbing holiday.

In practice, schools usually have to ask for a contribution from parents if they offer a full programme of outings and visits. Local authorities or the school can make grants to children who cannot afford to pay. So always ask if help is available if you have difficulty in finding the money.

Ensuring the safety of the children

Local authorities make their own regulations about school trips, such as the

ratio of adults to children, the insurance cover required and financial and medical arrangements. There are no national regulations.

Teachers in charge of state school parties have to conform to the local authority's regulations and would be expected to follow safety codes for adventure pursuits such as canoeing. Teachers at independent schools are not subject to these regulations, but have a general duty of care.

Whatever happens, teachers have to take the same care of pupils as they would do in school – with the standard of care of a reasonable parent according to the age of the child – for the whole time, day and night, that the child is away from home.

On a day outing, the teacher is responsible for the children's safety until they are returned to school and dismissed there in the usual way, unless their parents agree to allow them to go home from some other point. This would depend on the age of the children and the distance involved.

Primary schoolchildren, for example, would certainly not be left to get home on their own from a visit to the zoo; 14-year-olds would be presumed to be able to find their way home from the local museum.

When an indemnity form is offered

Parents are sometimes asked to sign a letter of indemnity for any claims arising from illness, accident or other cause; and schools may refuse to let children go on an outing if their parents do not sign. However, letters of this kind do not legally absolve a teacher or the school from any professional responsibility for the children in their care or from liability for negligence.

Legally, parents cannot in fact sign away their common law rights, especially to proper care and supervision of their child.

Under the Unfair Contract Terms Act 1977, no agreement is valid if it takes away the right to claim compensation for negligence if death or personal injury is caused.

However, it is proper for the school to draw attention to any risks involved in a visit and to get the parents' permission for the child to go.

SEA

Laws that apply to the waters round our coasts

In law, the seas around Britain and the land beneath them are divided into five sectors:
- Internal waters.
- Territorial waters.
- Fishing zones.
- International waters.
- The continental shelf.

Internal waters include rivers, ports and harbours, the sea between the mainland and the Scottish islands and inlets that are less than 24 nautical miles (27.63 land or statute miles) wide – for example, the Thames and Severn estuaries.

The same laws as on the mainland apply in internal waters. No foreign ship has any right to enter our internal waters – nor can British ships enter foreign internal waters – without consent.

Territorial waters extend for 3 nautical miles – 3.45 statute miles – from low-water mark round the coast and islands of Britain. It is a belt that generally follows the contours of the coastline and around any islands except for estuary indentations and other internal waters. Then the 3 miles start from the mouth of the estuary.

Foreign ships have the right to pass through territorial waters provided that they do not threaten Britain's peace or security. That does not give them fishing rights, however.

English and Scottish criminal law apply only in territorial waters. But if an offence is committed on a foreign ship, a prosecution can be made only with the Attorney-General's approval.

Fishing zones stretch 200 nautical (230.30 statute) miles out to sea or up to any other country's limits that have been recognised by Britain. The North Sea, for example, is divided by an imaginary line where British and continental zones meet.

A country has full control over all fishing activity in its own zone. No vessel other than a rowing boat can fish without a licence. Some countries, however, have bilateral agreements to fish in each other's sector.

The skipper of a foreign trawler found fishing without permission in the

FORFEITING THE CATCH

A foreign trawler skipper found fishing within UK territorial waters may forfeit his whole catch and face a large fine.

British zone risks the seizure of the catch and his ship and an unlimited fine.

International waters are the high seas outside the territorial waters of any country. Apart from fishing-zone regulations, they are governed by a combination of international conventions and national laws.

English ships on the high seas, for example, are subject to English law. Criminal law is always applied according to the nationality of the offender – so a United Kingdom citizen who commits a crime on a foreign ship in international waters must be tried under English law.

The continental shelf is the sea-bed off the coast, but forming part of the land mass of the adjoining country. In the case of the North Sea, the shelf links Britain with the European continent and is divided among all the shoreline countries.

Other countries throughout the world claim territorial waters, fishing zones and continental shelves, but the widths of the sectors vary.

Oil and gas rigs

Oil and gas rigs are usually subject to the laws of the country on whose continental shelf they operate. Many North Sea rigs, for example, are governed by Scots law. It is an offence carrying an unlimited fine and/or 1 year's imprisonment for any unauthorised vessel or aircraft to approach within 500 metres of any platform.

Rules of the sea

Anyone who has a vessel other than a rowing boat at sea must comply with the international Safety Of Life At Sea convention, which lays down rules about equipment and handling. Copies can be obtained from the Inter-Governmental Maritime Consultative Organisation, 101 Piccadilly, London W1V 0AE.

Shipping lanes In busy stretches of water, such as the English Channel, vessels may have to stay in set shipping lanes, but otherwise there are no fixed routes that must be followed in international or territorial waters.

Distress calls It is the duty of every vessel to offer assistance to another vessel in distress at sea.

See: BOATING
LIFE-BOAT SERVICE

SEA TRAVEL

When a company can limit liability

A sea-passenger's ticket is likely to show conditions that attempt to exclude or limit the shipping line's liability for accidents to passengers, and for lost or damaged property.

If the traveller is sailing between two British ports, the contract is subject to British law. If the exclusion or limit is unreasonable, it may be invalid. The contract will be invalid if the claim is for death or personal injury caused by negligence. *See:* UNFAIR CONTRACT

Travel between Britain and another country is governed by an international convention that forbids exemption clauses, but sets monetary limits on the liability of shipping lines.

Amounts are related to the price of gold, so their sterling equivalent varies. The approved limits are approximately:

Death or personal injury	£30,000 for each passenger
Lost or damaged cabin baggage	£550 for each passenger
Lost or damaged vehicle, including possessions inside	£2,000 for each vehicle
Other baggage lost or damaged	£800 for each passenger

Those figures are not guarantees of what will be paid. They are ceilings to what might be recoverable in a lawsuit against a shipping company or any of its employees.

They do not apply, however, if injury, loss or damage is deliberate, or caused recklessly with a knowledge of the probable result. Then there is no limit to what a court might award.

Under the international convention, a passenger has only 2 years in which to start legal proceedings. Written notice of a claim must be given immediately if loss or damage is apparent, or otherwise within 15 days of getting off the ship.

SEAMAN

The rights of someone who works aboard ship

A seaman in the Merchant Navy – or one in the Royal Navy, who is classed as a Crown servant – has fewer job-protection rights than most people on land.

He is excluded from the normal rules on TIME OFF WORK, REDUNDANCY and NOTICE and he cannot demand an itemised PAY statement or a written summary of his EMPLOYMENT CONTRACT. *See:* EMPLOYMENT PROTECTION

Merchant seamen are covered by special rules on social security benefits. A seaman who gets paid leave at the

CALLING A CONSUL

A British seaman who has been discharged or stranded abroad may be eligible for social security assistance – provided that he makes his plight known to the nearest British consul within 14 days.

'Where's the nearest British Consul, matey?'

end of a voyage cannot claim UNEMPLOYMENT BENEFIT if he is dismissed during his leave.

When he has a claim

However, if a seaman is left behind or discharged because of sickness or injury or to prevent the spread of infection outside Britain while working aboard ship or travelling under contract to join one, he is entitled to SICKNESS BENEFIT or to an INVALIDITY PENSION provided that he meets the other conditions for a claim.

If he is left behind or discharged for other reasons, he may be entitled to claim social security benefits, provided that he notifies a British consul within 14 days.

SEARCH

When officials may search you or your property

The police have no general power to search a member of the public. They may do so if a person agrees to be searched or when the law allows a search to be made.

For example, if the police make a lawful ARREST they may search a person if they believe he is carrying a weapon or evidence relating to his offence.

The police are entitled by law to stop a person or a vehicle in which he is travelling and make a search if:
● They suspect that he is carrying drugs.
● They suspect that he is carrying firearms – but they may not search if any other weapon is involved.
● They suspect that he has been involved in terrorism.
● They suspect that he is carrying protected game or wild birds or their eggs that have been poached.

In certain areas – for example, London, Manchester and Birmingham – there are local Acts of Parliament entitling the police to stop and search a person or his vehicle if they suspect that he is carrying stolen goods. Otherwise, the police are not entitled to search a person unless they arrest him.

If they do not, the police may ask a magistrate to issue them with a search warrant. To obtain the warrant, the

police must state on oath in writing the reasons why the warrant is required. The magistrate decides whether a warrant will be issued. *See:* POLICE

However, the police are not entitled to obtain a warrant to search a house for murder weapons or for clothing required for forensic examination in a rape case.

If the police search a person without his consent, without giving a reason for the search or without a search warrant, they commit an ASSAULT or battery.

If they enter his home in unlawful circumstances and make a search, they may be sued for TRESPASS.

However, if a person refuses to be searched when the police are entitled to do so, he may be charged with OBSTRUCTION.

When other officials want to make a search

There are certain other officials who are entitled to search people. For example, a Customs officer, a member of the armed forces or a coastguard is entitled to stop and search a person or a vehicle or vessel if he believes that undeclared goods are being carried.

If a person is stopped by a Customs official, he is entitled to ask to be taken before a magistrate or the Chief Customs Officer, who must then decide if there are sufficient grounds for a search.

However, he is not entitled to refuse to be searched. *See:* CUSTOMS DUTY

TRANSPORT POLICE – for example, constables appointed by the British Airports Authority or docks and harbour police – are entitled to search a person who works in the area if they suspect him of theft or carrying stolen goods. They are also entitled to stop and search any vehicle or craft that they suspect of carrying stolen goods.

However, private security forces – for example, security guards at a factory or a store detective – are not entitled to search a person, unless he agrees to be searched.

A security guard at a factory is entitled to search an employee, provided that the employee's contract states that searches may be made.

If an employer orders a security guard to search an employee who has not agreed to such a term in his contract, the employer may be sued for trespass.

If he tries to dismiss an employee who refused to be searched in those circumstances, he would be acting unlawfully. *See:* SECURITY GUARD

SEASONAL WORKER

The rights of someone whose work follows the seasons

A seasonal worker is someone who takes a short-term job which is available only at a certain time of year – for example, as a hop-picker or pea-picker, or as a summer worker in a seaside hotel or restaurant.

Depending upon the nature of his employment, he may be a CASUAL WORKER, a temporary worker or a PART-TIME WORKER.

Some seasonal workers, particularly those with a skilled trade, may work a few hours per week for several employers and be SELF-EMPLOYED. Others, for example fruit-pickers, may work full-time for one employer until the job is done.

Seasonal workers unless they are self-employed, like all other employees, have an EMPLOYMENT CONTRACT, although often it is not put into writing. In such cases, its terms and conditions can be derived from the oral agreement between employer and employee or from custom and practice.

Seasonal workers have few statutory EMPLOYMENT PROTECTION rights because their period of continuous employment is not long enough to acquire them. However, if a seasonal worker is hired full-time for an unspecified period and serves more than 4 weeks, he must give or be given one week's NOTICE before leaving. The notice rules do not apply if there is a fixed-term employment contract for 12 weeks or less.

The rules on HEALTH AND SAFETY AT WORK apply to all workers, including those hired for a season. If a seasonal worker is injured in the course of his job because of negligence by his employer or by a fellow employee, he can sue the employer for damages.

If a seasonal worker is an employee, his employer is obliged to deduct INCOME TAX and NATIONAL INSURANCE CONTRIBUTIONS from his wages, provided that they reach the appropriate lower earnings limits.

SECONDHAND GOODS

Protection even for the buyer of used goods

No one expects secondhand goods to be as good as new, but that does not mean that dealers in secondhand goods are entitled legally to sell worthless junk at high prices.

The Sale of Goods Act 1979 applies to sales of secondhand goods as much as to sales of new goods. So secondhand goods, like new goods, must be of merchantable quality, and must be fit for any particular purpose known to the seller, if the seller sells them in the course of a business. *See:* DEFECTIVE GOODS

'Merchantable quality' means that the goods are as fit for the purpose or purposes for which goods of that kind are commonly bought as it is reasonable to expect in the circumstances. In deciding what it is reasonable to expect, regard must be had to the description

CORROSION IN A SECONDHAND CAR

The seller of secondhand goods has the same legal duty as any other retailer to make sure that what he sells is of merchantable quality.

Mrs Lee bought a secondhand Morris 1100 car for £355. After she bought it she found it needed repairs costing £100. It was potentially dangerous until the repairs were carried out. There was corrosion to the brake pipings and the rear subframe.

The judge in the county court said that as Mrs Lee had driven the car on several occasions before discovering the need for repairs it was of merchantable quality. Mrs Lee appealed to the Court of Appeal.

DECISION

The Court of Appeal said the county court judge was wrong. Even though the danger was only potential, the car was not fit for the purpose of driving on the roads and so was not of merchantable quality when it was sold. Mrs Lee was entitled to damages to compensate her for the cost of repairs.

applied to the goods, and the price may also be relevant.

The fact that goods are sold as secondhand will therefore be taken into account in deciding whether they are merchantable. But even secondhand goods must be fit for use, and a secondhand car, for example, that is not roadworthy because of serious defect will not be of merchantable quality.

SECONDS

When the goods you buy need not be perfect

Goods sold as 'seconds' must nevertheless be of merchantable quality and fit for any particular purpose known to the seller, where the seller is selling the goods in the course of a business.

'Merchantable quality' means that the goods are as fit for the purpose or purposes for which such goods are commonly bought as it is reasonable to expect.

The fact that they are described as 'seconds' means that the goods need not be perfect, but they must still be fit for some purpose. If a specific defect in a particular article is drawn to the buyer's attention before he agrees to buy the goods, he cannot complain about that defect.

In addition, if a buyer examines the goods before he agrees to buy them, he cannot complain about any defect that he ought to have spotted.

If the seller knows the buyer is buying the goods for a particular purpose, the goods must be fit for that purpose. However, the seller can escape liability if he can show that the buyer did not rely on his skill or judgment, or that it was unreasonable for the buyer to rely on the seller's skill or judgment. *See:* DEFECTIVE GOODS

SECURITY GUARD

Company 'police' do not have police powers

Security guards, whether employed at a factory or as escorts, have no more powers than any other private citizen. The fact that they are often called security police does not give them POLICE powers.

An employee who is asked to submit to a search by a security guard as he leaves a factory can refuse unless he has specifically agreed to being searched in his EMPLOYMENT CONTRACT. If he is dismissed for refusing to be searched he can claim for WRONGFUL DISMISSAL.

A security guard who detains an employee who he suspects has stolen something is, in effect, making no more than a CITIZEN'S ARREST. So if his suspicions prove incorrect, he and his employer may be guilty of FALSE IMPRISONMENT.

SELF-EMPLOYED

The rights and duties of those who work for themselves

Anyone who does paid work on his own account as an independent contractor is, in law, self-employed so far as that work is concerned.

Self-employment need not be his only or main source of income. A bus driver who, to supplement his earnings, gives driving lessons or is a part-time mail-order agent is self-employed in those activities, although he remains an employee in his main job.

The relationship between a self-employed person and his customers or clients is governed by a 'contract for

PAYING TAX TWICE A YEAR

Self-employed people do not pay tax weekly or monthly, but twice a year after an assessment by their local inspector of taxes.

services' rather than by the 'contract of service' that exists between employer and employee. Both types of agreement, whether oral or written, are subject to the general law on contracts, but someone who is self-employed has far fewer rights in the course of his work than an EMPLOYED PERSON.

The self-employed are excluded from many of the rules on EMPLOYMENT PROTECTION. If their work ends, they are not entitled to a period of NOTICE unless that is specifically provided for in the contract, and they cannot claim REDUNDANCY or UNFAIR DISMISSAL. Generally, they are not paid while they are sick or on holiday.

Paying national insurance

A man between 16 and 65, or a woman between 16 and 60, who is self-employed and earns more than the LOWER EARNINGS LIMIT must pay Class 2 rate NATIONAL INSURANCE CONTRIBUTIONS.

He or she may also have to pay Class 4 contributions, based on profits or gains chargeable to income tax under Schedule D. The amount charged varies year by year.

Even if a person has a job for which he pays Class 1 contributions, he is still liable for Class 2 and perhaps Class 4 payments on his self-employed income.

Claiming benefits

Although they contribute to national insurance at a higher rate, self-employed people are not entitled to all the benefits of employees. They are not eligible for INDUSTRIAL INJURY BENEFIT, and if their own business ceases they will not have qualified for UNEMPLOYMENT BENEFIT.

Someone who loses a job but has some self-employment cannot draw unemployment benefit unless he proves that his private earnings do not exceed a prescribed maximum and that he is available for full time work. It is no use his claiming that sometimes he has no earnings: his profit is averaged over the period of self-employment.

People whose self-employment is interrupted by illness can claim SICKNESS BENEFIT at the basic rate.

But any sickness beneficiary who takes up self-employment – for example, by helping out in a family business – may lose his benefit if the Department

of Health and Social Security decides that his activity is not consistent with his claim to be unable to work.

A beneficiary who fails to disclose self-employment may have to pay back his benefit – and if his claim included a knowingly false statement, he is liable to a fine of up to £400, or up to 3 months' imprisonment.

Paying tax

Self-employed people do not have their INCOME TAX deducted at source like employed people. Usually they produce a profit and loss account for the inspector of taxes and pay under Schedule D in two half-yearly instalments. Often they also have to pay VALUE ADDED TAX.

There are considerable tax advantages in being self-employed, and it is usually worth employing an accountant to see that you derive full advantage from the regulations. The accountant's fee is allowed against tax.

If you work from your own home you can deduct travelling expenses and subsistence as well as the cost of stationery and at least part of the telephone bill. It is also possible to deduct an amount for the use of part of your house as an office, but if you own your house you risk destroying your exemption from CAPITAL GAINS TAX when you come to sell it.

The inspector of taxes will allow you to deduct part of the cost of heating and lighting the house.

There are special concessions to help you establish your own business. These enable you to set early losses against income of previous years.

There are also allowances to help you to buy any equipment you need for your business, for example, a typewriter or a computer. Office furniture and filing cabinets are also allowable.

If you want to buy a car to run a taxi service or a driving school, you can claim a full capital allowance in the same way. If you want it, however, only as a means of transport in connection with your business, you can write off only 25 per cent a year on a car costing up to £8,000. The method of writing off is slightly different for cars costing more than £8,000. In either case, the inspector may allow you only a proportion of the write off if you are also using the car privately as well.

SENTENCE

*How the courts pass sentence
on offenders*

Criminal courts have a wide range of possible sentences they can impose on convicted offenders – from an ABSOLUTE DISCHARGE or BINDING OVER to a heavy fine or a long term of imprisonment.

In general a court should select the most appropriate sentence to:

● Protect society. Violent criminals and persistent sex offenders are likely always to be imprisoned.

● Reform the offender. Guidance from a probation officer or hospital treatment might help him to change his ways.

● Deter other offenders. Sometimes sentences are increased for crimes which have suddenly become more prevalent – for example, mugging.

Before deciding on a suitable sentence the court will usually take into account the findings of any social inquiry report into the defendant's background and personal circumstances.

The report will try to find out why the defendant committed the offence – there could be a drinking problem, marital trouble or a financial crisis – and suggest how he might respond to various sentences. Such reports are usually prepared by a probation officer.

But if a serious offence is involved, the magistrates or judge are likely to order the preparation of a report before passing sentence.

A court can also defer sentence for up to 6 months. This gives the offender a chance to show whether he is likely to get into trouble again.

Sentences which can be imposed on offenders of various ages are:

● ABSOLUTE DISCHARGE – no punishment imposed. From 10 years old.

● Attendance centre order – attendance for a few hours each week in leisure time. 10–21 years.

● BINDING OVER – offender or sureties can forfeit money if offender misbehaves. From 10 years.

● Borstal – full-time detention aimed at treatment and rehabilitation. 15–21 years.

● CARE order – puts child into care of local authority. Up to 16 years.

● COMMUNITY SERVICE ORDER – unpaid community work. From 17 years.

● CONDITIONAL DISCHARGE – no punishment if offender behaves. From 10 years.

● Criminal bankruptcy – denies offender proceeds of crime. From 17 years.

● Deprivation of property – offender loses property used in commission of crime. From 17 years.

● Detention centre – full-time detention for males aimed at short, sharp lesson. 14–21 years.

● FINE – financial penalty. From 10 years.

● Guardianship order – commits the accused as a mental patient. All ages.

● PRISON – full-time detention. From 17 years.

● PROBATION – supervision by a social worker. From 17 years.

● Restitution order – restores stolen property to its owner. All ages.

● SUSPENDED SENTENCE – threat of prison if offender commits further offence. From 17 years.

SEPARATION

*When a husband and wife decide
to live apart*

If a marriage has broken down, a husband and wife may decide to separate and live apart from one another. To do so, they do not necessarily have to move to separate houses – for example, they may be considered to be living apart if one partner insists on living in only one part of the house and refuses to eat meals with the other partner.

However, such a separation does not mean a marriage has automatically ended, but the husband or wife may be able to seek a MATRIMONIAL ORDER in a magistrates' court for MAINTENANCE or to seek a DIVORCE or a judicial separation in a county court.

If both husband and wife agree to a separation, it is known as a 'consensual separation'. They do not have to apply to a court to settle arrangements about maintenance, CUSTODY OF CHILDREN or the division of possessions. Instead, they may have a formal separation agreement, usually drawn up by their solicitors in the form of a deed, which outlines the details of the agreement.

Such an agreement can be made only if a couple has been separated or is on the point of separating. It may not be made on the ground that a husband and wife may decide to separate in the future.

Once a couple has drawn up a separation agreement, a husband or wife is still entitled to seek a matrimonial order from a magistrates' court. Such an order leaves both parties in no doubt what their legal obligations are.

However, if one of the parties fails to meet a condition of a separation agreement when no matrimonial order is involved – for example, if a husband fails to pay the maintenance agreed – the agreement is treated in law as a CONTRACT and the husband may be sued for breach of that contract.

Any condition in a separation agreement may be altered by a county court or the High Court on the request of one of the parties. However, a magistrates' court is entitled to alter only the amount of maintenance payable. The courts will alter an agreement only if:

● The agreement did not make sufficient financial provision for any child of the family.

● There is a change in the financial circumstances of the parties since the agreement was made.

In most cases, however, a court will not alter an agreement that has been freely entered into by a husband and wife, provided that they have been properly advised by their solicitors.

If a husband or wife wants to end a marriage but the other partner does not, and the husband or wife leaves the other partner – they are guilty of DESERTION.

SEPARATED, BUT NOT APART

A couple who decide to separate do not have to move from their common home. They may simply keep to their own parts of the house.

The other partner is entitled, in that case, to apply for a matrimonial order for maintenance. He or she will not necessarily succeed, however. Need would still have to be proved.

Once a couple separates, whether by agreement or not, the husband and wife have the basis for proving that their marriage has irretrievably broken down so that a divorce may be sought when a separation has lasted for some time (2 years if the partners agree, otherwise 5 years).

Or either party may apply for a judicial separation. This has all the same results as a DIVORCE, except that neither party is free to remarry.

When one spouse has voluntarily paid support to the other for 3 months, the recipient can seek a matrimonial order for MAINTENANCE in the magistrates' court. *See also:* MATRIMONIAL ORDER

Financial help for a wife

A wife who is separated from her husband is entitled to claim SUPPLEMENTARY BENEFIT in the same way as a single woman.

To do so, obtain form SB1 from any post office as soon as possible after the separation, and take it to your local social security office. Benefit is not normally backdated, so a delay could mean that benefit is lost.

Any benefit received includes the needs of any children under 16 or still at school, who are living with the wife.

If the wife is working, part of her earnings may be deducted from her benefit. Any expenses connected with the job, such as fares to work and child-minding fees, are deducted from the weekly wage to arrive at her net earnings. The first £4 of net earnings are ignored. Half of any earnings between £4 and £20 and the whole of any earnings over £20 are deducted from the weekly benefit.

If a separated wife receives benefit because her husband is not maintaining her, the local social security office inquires about her husband's financial situation. If she does not wish to take court action herself, the local social security office may sue the husband. If the maintenance will be more than the benefit being claimed or if the wife intends to work, it is advisable for her to take her own court action.

If a husband is away from home temporarily – for example, because he works abroad – his wife is not entitled to claim benefit as her husband is regarded as being a member of the household.

However, if a wife does not receive the money she usually gets from her husband while he is away, she may be able to claim benefit if she is in urgent need of money.

If a separated couple reunites, or a wife is joined by another man and they live together as man and wife, she is not entitled to claim benefit.

SERVICES

When a customer pays for skill and care

Anyone who charges for services in the course of a trade, business or profession has a duty to provide them with reasonable care and skill. A 'reasonable' standard is that shown by competent people in the same field.

If a customer loses money or is harmed in any other way by negligent or incompetent services, he can sue for damages.

Dissatisfied customers and clients can often get help from trade or professional associations, which try to uphold suitable standards among their members. Some associations have disciplinary powers over their members, and some

---

NOTHING BUT THE TRUTH

It is an offence for someone knowingly and recklessly to advertise dishonestly about any services he is offering the public.

---

have funds out of which compensation is paid in cases of incompetent service.

No one providing a service as part of a trade, business or profession may make a false claim about nature or quality.

For example, it is a TRADE DESCRIPTION offence to claim that a repair service is available at all hours if it is not, or to imply that an after-sales service has the endorsement of a manufacturer unless he has given specific approval. A prosecution must show, however, that such a statement was known to be false, or that it was made recklessly, without caring whether it was true or not.

Maximum penalty: 2 years' imprisonment and an unlimited fine.

SEX DISCRIMINATION

Your right to fair treatment regardless of your sex

Anyone who is treated unfairly at work or when applying for a job because of his or her sex is entitled to demand compensation before an industrial tribunal.

The Sex Discrimination Act 1975 lays down that it is unlawful to discriminate because of a person's sex, in the areas of employment, education, consumer services including housing, and in advertising.

And that Act is complemented by the Equal Pay Act 1970 which states that a woman doing the same job under the same conditions as a man, is entitled to equal pay.

Anybody who wants to bring a claim for equal pay or a complaint about sex discrimination against an employer must do so before an industrial tribunal. Otherwise, a complaint is made to a county court.

How the law defines sex discrimination

There are four types of discrimination defined by the Sex Discrimination Act:

● Direct discrimination. When a person is treated less favourably simply because of his or her sex. For example, if an employer turns down a woman applicant for a job because he wants to employ men only.

● Indirect discrimination. When the same rule is applied to both sexes, but where it has an unequal effect on one sex. For example, if an employer has unjustifiable age limits for a job, which excludes a big proportion of women.

● Discrimination against married people in employment – for example, if an employer offers a job that involves unsocial hours and refuses to employ a person who is married, or he pays removal expenses when a single man's job is transferred but refuses to do so for a married man.

Single people cannot complain if married people are treated more favourably.

Married persons must compare their treatment with that of single persons of the same sex.

● Victimisation. One example is when somebody provides information or brings a complaint under the Sex Discrimination Act and is then subjected to less favourable treatment because of his or her action, provided always that the information or complaint was made in good faith.

Discrimination in employment

It is unlawful for an employer to treat an employee less favourably because of his or her sex or to discriminate between men and women when recruiting new staff.

For example, if an employer has a vacancy in a factory and displays notice of the vacancy only in the part of the factory where men work, he would be discriminating.

If he instructed an employment agency to interview men only for a job, he

---

HOW TO MAKE A COMPLAINT ABOUT SEX DISCRIMINATION OR EQUAL PAY

If you think you have been treated unfairly because of your sex, write to the Equal Opportunities Commission, Overseas House, Quay Street, Manchester, M3 3HN.

The Commission was established under the Sex Discrimination Act 1975 to monitor the workings of that Act and the Equal Pay Act. It will be able to advise you on how to bring your complaint or claim for equal pay. If the case is complicated, the Commission may help you to present it before an industrial tribunal, if it concerns employment, or in a county court, if it concerns education, housing, goods or services.

Employment: Sex discrimination After seeking advice, complain first through the company's grievance procedure and consult your union if you belong to one.

If you are still dissatisfied about the treatment you have received, apply for an INDUSTRIAL TRIBUNAL hearing within 3 months. To do so, fill in an application form IT 1 which can be obtained from your local unemployment benefit office, job centre or Citizens Advice Bureau.

Once you have sent the form it is lodged at the Central Office of Industrial Tribunals and is automatically passed to the Advisory, Conciliation and Arbitration Service – ACAS – who may contact you and your employer to attempt a conciliation.

However, if the complaint is not resolved, it may have to be heard before a tribunal. In order to help a complainant's case, special forms are available from the Equal Opportunities Commission on which questions may be put to the employer about his conduct. The employer is not obliged to reply, but if he does, the complainant may use his replies in evidence before the tribunal.

If your complaint comes before a tribunal, you must prove there has been discrimi-

nation against you. If an employer claims that the job is exempt from the Act, he must prove that to the tribunal. Both parties may be represented by a solicitor, barrister or other expert adviser – for example, a union official.

Once the tribunal has heard the complaint, it may:

● Find the case proved and order the employer to pay compensation for loss of earnings or injury to feelings, up to a maximum of £6,760.

● Find the case proved and order the employer to carry out a course of action. For example, if a woman had complained that she had been passed over for promotion because she was a woman, the tribunal may order the employer to implement that promotion. If he fails to do so, the tribunal may order further compensation for loss of earnings.

● Make an order declaring the rights of both parties.

● Dismiss the complaint.

If the complaint is dismissed, you can appeal to the EMPLOYMENT APPEAL TRIBUNAL, but only on a point of law.

Legal aid is not available for industrial tribunal hearings, but it is if the case goes to appeal. If a person has a low income, he or she may obtain up to £25 of legal advice and assistance from a solicitor for little or no cost. *See:* LEGAL AID

Any complaint to a tribunal must be made within 3 months of the incident complained about. However, in certain cases it will hear a complaint out of time if it considers it reasonable.

Equal pay If you are doing the same or broadly similar work as a person of the opposite sex, or your job has been rated as equivalent under a proper job evaluation scheme, you can claim equal pay by following the same procedure as for a complaint over sex discrimination except for the spe-

cial forms to question employers.

Education If you believe you have been treated unfairly by a college because of your sex, or your children have been treated unfairly by a school, complain first to the head teacher or principal of the establishment involved.

If no action is taken, write to the managers or the governors involved. If you are still dissatisfied, write to the Secretary of State for Education and Science outlining your complaint, and address it to The Permanent Under-Secretary of State, Department of Education and Science, Elizabeth House, York Road, London SE1 7PH, or in Wales to The Secretary for Welsh Education, Welsh Education Office, 31 Cathedral Road, Cardiff CF1 9UJ.

The Secretary will have 2 months in which to take action or inform you of his decision. If he takes no action or you disagree with his decision, write to your local county court asking for a SUMMONS and giving details of the parties involved. You may do so up to 6 months after the incident.

Housing, goods and services Any complaint about goods, services, facilities or housing must be made to a county court within 6 months of the incident by asking for a summons.

Taking court action If you take a case to a county court and lose, you may have to pay the winner's costs.

If the judge finds in favour of you, he may make an injunction or order the person complained of not to commit acts against the law again or he may award damages, depending on the circumstances involved. Either party may appeal against the decision of a county court to the Court of Appeal.

Complaints about advertising being discriminatory should be made to the Equal Opportunities Commission. Individuals cannot take action in advertising cases.

'

WHEN A MARRIED WOMAN DOES NOT NEED HER HUSBAND'S SIGNATURE FOR A HIRE-PURCHASE AGREEMENT

Companies that insist on having a wife's hire-purchase or other credit agreement guaranteed by the husband will be found guilty of sex discrimination, unless they have similar rules for men.

Mrs Quinn, who was a part-time worker, went to buy a three-piece suite from Williams Furniture Store, in Leicester. Before the sale could be completed, she was asked to obtain her husband's signature to guarantee the credit arrangement.

VERDICT

Mrs Quinn won her case of sex discrimination in the Court of Appeal. Lord Denning, Master of the Rolls, said that by insisting, requiring or even suggesting that her husband should sign a guarantee, the company had discriminated against Mrs Quinn.

They would not have asked a married man to obtain his wife's signature, Lord Denning said.

would be discriminating.

The law barring discrimination also covers non-contractual subjects such as company cars and special mortgages, so an employer who provided mortgages for men and not women who did the same job, would be discriminating.

However, a complaint that men were receiving a higher overtime rate than women doing the same job would be brought under the Equal Pay Act, which covers contractual matters and wages.

If an employer has workers contracted to him from an outside company, he must not treat them less favourably because of their sex.

Bodies such as the Manpower Services Commission and Industrial Training Boards must not discriminate on grounds of sex, but can provide special training for one sex only where that sex is in a minority in that kind of work.

Exceptions to the Act

However, there are certain exceptions to the Act. It does not apply to:
● Any company that has five or fewer employees.
● Anyone employed in a private household.
● A person working outside the United Kingdom. However, a person employed on a ship registered at a British port or an aircraft or hovercraft registered in Great Britain and operated by someone who is resident in Great Britain, is covered by the Act, unless he works wholly abroad.
● Any member of the Armed Forces.
● A minister of religion whose doctrine stipulates ministers of one sex only.

The police and the prison services are not exempt from the Act but are entitled to make different regulations about the height, types of uniform and equipment for male and female officers.

Genuine qualifications

In certain other cases, an employer is entitled to stipulate that he wants to employ men or women only. To do so, he must be able to show that the person's sex is a genuine occupational qualification for the job. He would be entitled to do so for:
● A job that requires either a man or a woman as a matter of decency – for example, a public lavatory attendant.
● A job that requires a man or woman for authenticity – for example, acting or modelling.
● A job that entails living on premises occupied by people of one sex where there are no facilities for the opposite sex – for example, a trawler. The employer must be able to show it would be unreasonable to expect separate facilities to be provided.
● A job in a men-only or women-only establishment – for example, a prison – where supervision is required.
● A job that involves looking after an individual's personal welfare, and that can best be done by someone of the same sex as the individual concerned – for example, some social work.
● A job that must be held by a man because of the law restricting the hours that a woman may work – for example, when night work in a factory is required.
● A job requiring frequent visits to a foreign country where the local laws would make it difficult for someone of the other sex to work. In Iran, for example, women are not allowed to drive, so a job requiring some driving in Iran could legitimately stipulate men.
● A job that is one of two for a married couple – for example, a caretaker and housekeeper.

If an employer gives special treatment to a woman who is pregnant, a male colleague is not entitled to claim that he is being discriminated against.

Discrimination in education

Anyone applying to or attending a school, further education college, polytechnic or university must not receive less favourable treatment on the ground of their sex.

A co-educational school is not entitled to refuse an application from parents to send their son there, on the ground that the school has enough boys already. But, a single-sex school or college could because they are exempt from this part of the Act.

Again, if a college is running a sandwich course on mining and is arranging a year in industry for students, it would not be entitled to refuse to make arrangements for a female student on the course, unless it was not making arrangements for its male students.

A school is not entitled to refuse to allow a girl to attend woodwork classes or a boy domestic science classes because of their sex. If a school makes it less favourable to do so – for example, by making a pupil give up a free period or refusing permission to take an O level in that subject – it is discriminating.

However, a complaint about school uniform would be unlikely to be considered as sex discrimination. For example, if a school states that boys must wear ties and blazers and girls must wear skirts and jumpers, a girl could not justifiably complain she is discriminated against because she is not allowed to wear jeans.

Exceptions allowed

There are certain exceptions. For example, if a boys' school allowed a small number of girls from other schools to attend some 6th-form classes, it is entitled to refuse to take any more girls if it thinks it has enough. However, once a school has admitted girls, they must be treated in the same way as boys.

If a single-sex school is becoming co-educational, it is entitled to restrict the number of minority-sex pupils during the transition period. To do so, it must apply for permission to the Secretary of State for Education, if it is a state school, or the EQUAL OPPORTUNITIES Commission if it is a private school.

A co-educational school is permitted to provide boarding facilities for boys or girls only.

Discrimination against the consumer

It is unlawful for anyone providing services or goods to the public to treat a man or a woman less favourably because of his or her sex, regardless of whether the service or goods are paid for or free. Anyone who does so, can be sued for damages in a county court.

For example, if a publican allows his snooker tables to be used only by men, he would be discriminating against women.

If a brewery ran a women-only darts league, it would be discriminating against men. However, a group of private individuals is entitled to run its own single-sex darts league if the members wish, because non-profitmaking voluntary organisations are exempt from that part of the Act.

A bank that required a woman to give details of her husband's occupation when opening an account but did not require a husband to give details of his wife's work, is discriminating.

An organisation that offers its services equally to both sexes, but imposes special conditions that put a large proportion of one sex at a disadvantage, is discriminating.

For example, if a woman who works is seeking credit, she must be assessed for credit-worthiness in her own right. A credit company that requires her husband's signature or a guarantor would be discriminating, unless it made similar conditions for a man. However, if the wife is not working she cannot complain when the company ask for a guarantor, provided that they also ask an unemployed man for one.

When a home is involved

Anyone who lets or sells a house, flat or business premises must not make special conditions for one sex only.

There are certain exceptions, however. Anyone owning and occupying a home may discriminate when selling it, provided they do not advertise the sale.

Anyone who lets part of his home and shares it with the tenant is entitled to discriminate. For example, flatsharers can advertise legally for a man or woman to share. Anyone who wants to share a flat with someone is entitled to stipulate in an advertisement whether a male or female is required.

Discrimination when placing advertisements

If a person places an advertisement in a newspaper offering a job, he must not state whether only a woman or a man may apply, unless the job requires a man or woman as a genuine occupational qualification. For example 'Man wanted for nightshift' may be unlawful. 'Waitress wanted' is not.

If employers send a newspaper an advertisement that they know contravenes the Act or provide false information to a newspaper that contravenes the Act, they may be fined a maximum of £400 in a magistrates' court. Only the Equal Opportunities Commission can prosecute.

Giving lawful preferential treatment

Action that promotes the interests of either men or women is not necessarily discriminating.

For example, in employment, if a trade union has a majority of male shop stewards it is entitled to run a course exclusively for women in order to encourage them to become shop stewards.

WHEN WOMEN ARE RESTRICTED FROM WORKING

If a woman undertakes manual work in a factory – premises in which goods are made, altered, repaired, washed or cleaned – the number of hours that she may work and the type of work that she may do is restricted by the Factories Act 1961 and other statutes.

A woman who does manual work in a factory is not allowed to do night work between 10 p.m. and 5 a.m. The rule does not apply to women in management. If a woman worker breaks the rule and works at night, her employer may be fined up to £50, but she does not commit an offence.

There are certain exceptions when night work may be carried out:
● When night work is necessary because work during the day suffered an interruption that was impossible to foresee.
● If the materials used would deteriorate if they were not used quickly – for example, perishable food in a food-processing plant.
● When work is subject to times of pressure because it is of a seasonal nature – for example, canning fruit and vegetables during summer months.

A woman who works in a factory operating 6 days a week must not work more than 9 hours a day or 48 hours in a week, excluding breaks for meals or rest. If the factory operates a 5 day week she must not work more than 10 hours a day.

The hours that are worked must be between 7 a.m. and 8 p.m. – or 1 p.m. on Saturdays – and during those hours a woman must not work more than 4½ hours

without a break of at least 30 minutes. The period of work may be extended to 5 hours if it contains a 10 minute break.

The number of hours of overtime that a woman doing manual work in a factory may do is also restricted. If a factory operates a 6 day week where the maximum hours that can be worked in a day is 9, a woman must not work more than 11 hours with overtime in a day, including meal breaks. When a factory has a 5 day week, the maximum daily hours are 12. No more than 6 hours' overtime are allowed in a week and 100 hours' overtime in a year.

There are additional restrictions on certain types of work by women – for example, those involving toxic substances such as lead and zinc and underground work in mines. Although the Factories Act forbids the lifting of excessive weights by employees of either sex, women are more likely than men to succeed in a claim for damages if they are injured in carrying a heavy load.

If an employer allowed a woman to work in a factory when he knew she had given birth within 4 weeks, he would be committing an offence and may be fined up to £25.

Any employer is entitled to apply to the Health and Safety Executive if he wants to be exempt from the restrictions.

If you think your employer is not complying with the regulations regarding women employees, contact your local factory inspector. *See:* HEALTH AND SAFETY AT WORK

In that case, a man could not claim he was being discriminated against.

Occupational pensions, retirement age, tax law and social security and citizenship law are not covered by the Act.

There are other circumstances where actions are exempt from the Act. For example, when:
● Voluntary bodies or registered charities seek to provide benefits for one sex.
● Private clubs – for example, golf clubs – seek to restrict the use of their premises to either women or men on certain days. (However, a discotheque where anyone can become a member at the door would not be entitled to discriminate.)
● Insurance companies can charge different premiums and give different benefits if they are based honestly on actuarial data.
● A sportswoman would be at a disadvantage because of her strength or stamina – for example, football or rugby. But a darts or bowls competition would not be exempt.
● Political parties establish single-sex organisations.
● Non-profit-making bodies, such as the Women's Institute, seek to maintain their separate sex identity.

SHAREHOLDER

Rights and duties when liability is limited

Both private and public companies issue shares that confer on their holders certain rights and duties. Usually they include the right to:
● Receive dividends, but only when a dividend is declared by the directors.
● A proportion of the assets remaining on winding up after creditors have been paid.
● Attend general meetings of the company, to speak there and to vote.

In addition to those rights which are usually laid down in a company's memorandum and articles of association, the Companies Acts also confer certain rights:
● To receive a copy of the annual accounts and directors' report.
● To appoint a representative, known as a proxy, to attend general meetings.
● To combine with other shareholders,

owning not less than one-tenth of the company's paid-up capital, to compel the directors to hold an extraordinary general meeting to debate the way the company is being managed.

Shareholders of public companies can sell or give away their shares at any time. The right of shareholders of private companies to dispose of their shares is usually limited by the company's articles.

Responsibilities of shareholders

Individual shareholders are not liable for the debts of the company. Once they have paid in full for their shares, their financial responsibility is at an end.

Any shareholder who controls the general meeting because of the size of his holding must use his controlling powers for the benefit of the shareholders as a whole rather than in his own interest.

Majority shareholders must not act unfairly to minority shareholders. In a small company, which is really an incorporated partnership, any shareholder can apply to have the company wound up if the other shareholders act unfairly towards him.

SHOPS

A shopkeeper can choose the customers he will serve

A shop is not obliged to serve every customer who goes in. The shopkeeper can refuse to serve anyone without giving a reason, subject to discrimination laws. *See:* RACIAL DISCRIMINATION; SEX DISCRIMINATION

The display of an article in a shop window or on a shelf does not commit the shopkeeper to sell it. But if he does sell it, it is a criminal offence to charge more than the price displayed. The maximum penalty is 2 years' imprisonment and an unlimited fine.

Responsible for quality

A shopkeeper is responsible for the quality of the goods he sells. They must be of merchantable quality and, if the shopkeeper knows the purpose for which they are bought, they must be fit for that purpose.

That applies even when the goods have been made by someone else and

when they are obtained by the shopkeeper in a sealed pack, which he cannot or does not open before selling.

If the goods are not of merchantable quality or reasonably fit for their purpose, the customer may be entitled to his MONEY BACK or to damages.

If you drop something

If you carelessly drop something, or knock something over, in a shop, you will be liable for any damage caused by your negligence. But if the accident was not your fault, but caused by an unstable display for example, you are not liable.

If your child causes damage in a shop you are responsible if you are with him – but not if your child goes into a shop on his own.

When it is an offence to serve

Many shops are limited in the hours they can open for business, but some can open and close whenever they like. Shops which are exempt from the regulations include those selling perishable goods such as fish, milk and bread, and tobacco, medicines, newspapers, vehicle accessories, sweets, ice cream and other refreshments. There are special regulations for OFF-LICENCES.

Half-days and Sundays

Shops other than those exempted must close on Sundays and not later than 1 p.m. on one weekday. The local authority can decide which day, or leave it to each individual shop.

It is an offence for a shopkeeper to sell on Sundays anything other than perishable goods and other exempt items, such as medicines and vehicle supplies.

The enforcement of legislation is the responsibility of the local authority. The shopkeeper can be fined up to £50 for the first offence and £200 on any subsequent conviction.

Permissible hours

Shops must close by 6 p.m. between the first Sunday in November and the first Sunday in March, and by 8 p.m. the rest of the year.

But on one day each week they can remain open until 7.30 p.m. in winter and 9 p.m. the rest of the year.

Although a shopkeeper can be prosecuted for breaking the rules on opening, the customer does not commit an offence if he buys outside permitted hours.

SHORT TENANCY

A new form of tenancy with less security

The Housing Act 1980 allows landlords to grant tenancies of residential property for short periods without the tenant acquiring security of tenure. These are called 'shorthold tenancies' and must be for at least 1 year, but not more than 5.

A tenancy already protected under the Rent Act cannot be converted into a shorthold one. A fixed-term tenancy can be so converted.

A tenant, but not a landlord can end a shorthold tenancy, even before a fixed-term tenancy originally granted has expired, provided he serves the appropriate notice to quit:
● 1 month, if the term granted is 2 years or less.
● 3 months, if the term granted is for more than 2 years.

A shorthold tenant cannot assign his tenancy to anyone else, although a court can order its transfer as part of a property settlement on divorce.

Eviction only by order of a court

A landlord can evict a shorthold tenant only by a court order, and the court must order possession if the landlord can show:
● The tenancy was granted for a term of at least 1 year, but not more than 5 years.
● He served a notice on the tenant, before the tenancy began, notifying him that the tenancy was shorthold. (The court has discretion to dispense with this requirement if it thinks it is fair to do so.)
● A fair rent was registered before the tenancy began, or an application to register a fair rent was made not more than 28 days after the tenancy began. (The court also has discretion to dispense with this requirement where it is fair to do so.)
● The landlord has served a notice of proceedings on the tenant and commenced proceedings not later than

3 months after the notice expired. The notice by the landlord must:
● Be in writing.
● Tell the tenant that proceedings may be brought for possession after it expires.
● Inform the tenant of the date when the notice of proceedings expires – which must not be less than 3 months after it was served nor, in the case of a periodic tenancy, before that tenancy could have been brought to an end by a valid notice to quit served on the same day as the notice of proceedings.
● Be served in the 3 months immediately before the shorthold tenancy comes to an end. If the shorthold term has expired or been ended by notice to quit already, the landlord must wait until the 3 months preceding the next or any subsequent anniversary of the ending of the term before serving the notice of proceedings.

If the landlord has served the appropriate notice of proceedings and let it expire without taking court action, he can serve a new notice, provided he does so no sooner than 3 months after the expiry of the last one.

SHOTGUN

The penalties for unauthorised shooting

A shotgun is defined in law as a weapon with a smooth – not rifled – barrel at least 24 in. long. If the barrel is less than 24 in. the gun is classed as a firearm and is subject to stricter control. *See:* GUN

It is an offence to sell, possess or acquire a shotgun without a shotgun certificate from the local police. Unlike firearms, however, there are circumstances where a certificate is not needed. The main exemptions are:
● Visitors to Britain who have spent less than 31 days in the country during the previous year.
● When the shotgun is borrowed, and used on the lender's private property and in his presence.
● People shooting with the approval of the police – for example, members of clubs at authorised practice sessions.

Anyone who sells, possesses or acquires a shotgun without a certificate is liable to a fine of up to £1,000 and

6 months' imprisonment. The magistrates can also order the gun to be confiscated. In a crown court, the maximum penalty is 3 years' imprisonment and an unlimited fine.

If the offence involves a sawn-off shotgun the maximum penalty is 5 years' imprisonment and an unlimited fine in a crown court.

Offences involving shotguns and firearms

Whether or not a person has a certificate, it is an offence to:
1. Have a loaded or unloaded shotgun, weapon or air weapon in a public place without a valid reason. The maximum penalty is 6 months' imprisonment and a £1,000 fine – £400 for an airgun – in a magistrates' court and 5 years' imprisonment and an unlimited fine in a crown court.
2. Trespass with a firearm, shotgun or airgun in a building. The maximum penalty is 5 years' imprisonment and an unlimited fine.
3. Trespass with a firearm, shotgun or airgun on land other than a building. The maximum penalty is 3 months' imprisonment and a £200 fine. The gun can be seized and any existing certificate cancelled.
4. Possess a firearm with intent to endanger life or cause serious injury. The maximum penalty is imprisonment for life.

Imitation firearms

It is also an offence to possess an imitation firearm with intent to resist arrest or commit a serious crime. The maximum penalty is 14 years' imprisonment.

SICKNESS

Your right to be paid when off work through illness

Anyone who has to take time off work through sickness is entitled to be paid a full wage, provided that his EMPLOYMENT CONTRACT does not state otherwise.

Any written particulars of an employment contract must, by law, state the arrangements an employer makes for employees who are sick. For example, the contract may state that an employee is entitled to full pay or half pay while sick, or it may state that sick pay is provided only for a specified period. It may also state that no provisions are made for payment to employees who are sick. Any written particulars of the contract must be sent to an employee within 13 weeks of his starting work.

If an employer simply tells a job applicant what the pay and conditions of the job are and the applicant accepts the job, those conditions are just as legally binding as a written contract.

However, if nothing is said about sick pay and no written contract is provided, an employee is entitled to receive full pay while off sick.

When a person is off work through sickness, he is entitled to claim sickness benefit even if he is receiving full sick pay, although his employment contract may state that sick pay is reduced if an employee who is sick claims benefit.

When a sick employee is sacked

If a sick employee is given NOTICE by his employer when he is off work, he may claim UNFAIR DISMISSAL from an INDUSTRIAL TRIBUNAL, provided that he has been working with the employer for at least 52 weeks.

In that case his employer must prove to the tribunal that the dismissal was 'reasonable'.

For example, it would probably be considered unreasonable if an employer:
● Dismisses a sick employee without consulting him.
● Fails to give a warning that unless the employee is able to return to work by a certain date, he will be dismissed.
● Obtains a medical report on the state of his employee's health and does not allow the employee to obtain his own independent report or does not discuss the report with his employee.
● Fails to offer alternative work if it is available. However, the employer is not expected to create a new job for the employee.

If an employer has one of his key men off sick in a business where penalty clauses for late delivery exist, a tribunal may consider he has acted reasonably if he replaces the sick employee.

The tribunal also takes into account

WHAT TO DO IF YOU FALL SICK

If you have to stop work because you are sick:
● Check your employment contract to see what sick pay you are entitled to and any other conditions involved.
● Obtain a doctor's statement of your incapacity to work – formerly known as a sickness certificate. *See:* MEDICAL CERTIFICATE
● If you are claiming SICKNESS BENEFIT, send it to your local social security office and send a photocopy of the certificate to your employer.
● Keep in touch with your employer, if the illness is prolonged, to show that you regard your employment contract to still be in force and send him photocopies of any sickness certificates regarding your progress.
● If your employer attempts to dismiss you, remind him you can bring an unfair dismissal claim to an industrial tribunal. If your employer tries to claim that your contract has ended through 'frustration', tell him you will claim unfair dismissal and collect any evidence for the tribunal that your contract still exists – for example, if you are still invited to company functions or you are still a member of the company's social club.

the type of illness involved and whether it is a long-term illness and the length of service of an employee who has been dismissed.

Suffering a long-term illness

In certain cases, when an employee is so ill that there is no possibility of his returning to work, an employer is entitled to end the employment contract on the ground that it is impossible for employment to continue – known as a 'frustrated' contract.

As the contract is ended and the employee is neither dismissed nor resigns, he would not be able to claim unfair dismissal or REDUNDANCY.

However, an industrial tribunal considers an employment contract to be frustrated only if:
● The absence from work has been so lengthy and the prospects of a return to work are so poor that it is no longer practical to regard the employment as still existing – for example, a labourer who suffers a severe coronary.
● The injury is particularly serious – for

THE SICK EMPLOYEE WHO WAS SACKED WITHOUT WARNING

An employer acts unreasonably if he sacks an employee who is off work through illness without first consulting him.

Mr Williamson started work as a cold-metal handler in October 1974. In January 1975 he 'slipped a disc' and went off work. In March the following year, Mr Williamson informed his employers that he was on the hospital waiting list but he expected to be able to return to light work soon. In June, Mr Williamson was given notice by his employers.

During the period of notice he met his employers and they arranged for him to see a specialist. The specialist said that Mr Williamson was recovered and fit to return to his old job. Mr Williamson claimed unfair dismissal at a tribunal.

DECISION

The tribunal upheld Mr Williamson's claim. It held that his employers should have consulted with him and discussed his progress and his return to work, before dismissing him.

THE EMPLOYEE WHO WAS UNFIT FOR WORK

If an employee is unfit to undertake his normal job, his employers should offer him alternative work but they are not required to create a special job.

Mr Taylor had worked for the Electricity Board for 38 years. For all but 2 weeks of the last year he had been away from work due to ill health. He was dismissed. Mr Taylor claimed unfair dismissal and

argued his employers should have found him a less strenuous job, especially as he had worked for them for so long.

DECISION

The tribunal held that the dismissal was reasonable. There was no suitable alternative job available and it would not be right to expect the Board to create a special job just for Mr Taylor.

example, a driver who loses his eyesight or a toolmaker who loses a hand.

When work is suspended on health grounds

A worker dealing with certain processes may be suspended from work if it becomes dangerous to his health to continue working – for example, a nuclear power station worker might be sent home if the radiation level became dangerous.

If he is suspended, he is entitled to receive medical suspension pay, provided that he has been working there for at least 4 weeks. He may claim for up to 26 weeks, but he would not be entitled to suspension pay if he refused to accept suitable alternative employment or he was unable to work because he was sick. In that case, he would be entitled to sick pay, provided that his employment contract stated so, and to claim sickness benefit.

Medical suspension pay applies only to those workers who deal with processes involving asbestos, chemicals, dyes containing lead compounds, lead, paint containing lead compounds, pottery dust, radioactive substances, rubber and tin. *See:* EMPLOYMENT PROTECTION

SICKNESS BENEFIT

Financial help when someone is off work through illness

Anyone who is incapable of work because he is sick or disabled, is entitled to claim sickness benefit for up to 28 weeks, provided that he has been paying NATIONAL INSURANCE CONTRIBUTIONS, either as an employed person or as a self-employed person working on his own behalf.

To do so, he must satisfy two conditions. They are:
● His contributions, in any one year since April 1975, must amount to at least 25 times the size of the contribution made by someone on the weekly LOWER EARNINGS LIMIT for the tax year concerned.
● In order to obtain maximum benefit, the contributor must have at least 50 times that amount in the year ending April 5, before the year in which benefit

is claimed. If he is sick and off work for a period, his contributions are credited to him.

For example, if someone claims benefit in 1981, his 50 contributions must have been made between April 6, 1979 and April 5, 1980.

However, if someone becomes ill within 8 weeks of being out of work through a previous illness, his year of contributions is the same as that for his previous illness. For example, if he falls ill in January 1981 after being off work in December 1980 through illness, payment of benefit may be governed by his contributions between April 6, 1978 and April 5, 1979, as it was for his December illness.

If the amount of contributions is less than 50, but not less than 25, the size of benefit is reduced. If there are less than 25 contributions in a year, benefit is not paid.

Anyone paying voluntary contributions instead of the usual employed or self-employed contributions or a woman or widow who pays reduced-rate contributions, is not entitled to claim sickness benefit.

However, anyone who claims benefit may also be entitled to claim an additional EARNINGS-RELATED SUPPLEMENT.

How benefit is paid

The basic rate for sickness benefit is £20.65 a week (1981). However, if someone claims benefit, he may be entitled to claim additional payment for any DEPENDANTS, at a rate of £12.75 a week for a wife or an adult dependant and £1.25 a week for each child.

Sickness benefit is not payable for a single day off work. There must be at least 4 days off due to sickness or unemployment within a period of 6 working days before a claim for benefit may be made.

If someone makes a claim for benefit when he has not previously been off work within 8 weeks of the claim, he does not receive benefit for the first 3 days off – known as 'waiting days'. However, if he has been off work within 8 weeks of a previous claim, benefit is payable for every day off, provided that he is away from work for more than 3 days.

Provided your doctor agrees and you tell your local Department of Health and Social Security office, you can do some 'therapeutic' work to help your recovery. If you do so, you can earn up to £15 a week without your sickness benefit being affected. Certain expenses, for example fares, are not counted in this total.

When someone has been away from work due to illness for 28 weeks and his sickness benefit stops, he may find he is entitled to claim INVALIDITY PENSION.

When a person makes a claim for benefit, he is usually sent a Girocheque by the local social security office about a week to 10 days after his application. The cheque may be cashed at any post office or paid into any bank.

Anyone who is unable to take his cheque to a post office himself is entitled to authorise someone else to cash the cheque for him.

Cheques are valid for 3 months from the date of issue. If a cheque is not cashed within 3 months, apply to the local social security office for a new cheque. However, if a cheque is not

---

HOW TO CLAIM SICKNESS BENEFIT

If you are sick and unable to work, seek advice from your local social security office on what you are entitled to claim and:
● Visit your doctor and ask for a doctor's statement. *See:* MEDICAL CERTIFICATE
● Fill in your name, address and national insurance number on the certificate.
● Complete sections A and C on the back of the certificate, stating your incapacity to work. If the incapacity is due to industrial injury or INDUSTRIAL DISEASE, complete section B on the back of the form.
● Claim for any dependants.

● Send the completed form, signed by your doctor, to your local social security office at once.
● Claim within 6 days of becoming ill or 21 days if it is your first claim for benefit. Otherwise, the benefit may be affected or a person may be disqualified from claiming if the application is late.
● If benefit is refused – for example, because the insurance officer does not consider that your illness makes you incapable of work – appeal as soon as possible to a SOCIAL SECURITY APPEALS tribunal.

cashed after 12 months of issue, the benefit is lost.

If someone is under observation because he has been in contact with or he is suspected of carrying an INFECTIOUS DISEASE, he may be regarded as being incapable of work and entitled to claim sickness benefit. In that case, the local environmental health officer provides evidence of a person's incapacity to work for the purpose of claiming benefit.

When sickness benefit is not paid

Anyone who is claiming sickness benefit should produce a doctor's statement that he is incapable of work. However, benefit is not automatically paid because such a statement has been provided. *See:* INVALIDITY ALLOWANCE

The Department of Health and Social Security employs officers to check on claimants and keeps a record of all sickness claims.

If, for example, an officer finds a man serving behind the counter of his wife's shop when he is supposed to be incapacitated, he may be disqualified from receiving benefit. Similarly, he may be denied benefit if his claims record suggests that he is in the habit of claiming only at holiday times in order to get both benefit and pay.

When a medical examination is required

In certain cases – for example, when a man's sickness record shows a series of minor illnesses – the department may ask him to attend a medical examination by a regional medical officer. If he fails or refuses to attend, he may be disqualified from receiving benefit.

SIT-IN
When a protest turns to trespass

Anyone who refuses to leave premises when ordered to do so by the owner is trespassing. Workers who occupy factories, students who take over administrative buildings at their college and others who stage sit-ins to air their grievances are in law all trespassers.

SKIP
When a permit is needed for a builder's skip

A householder who hires a builder's skip, intending to leave it on the street, must obtain a permit from the local authority. Council permission is not needed if the skip is to be kept on private property.

The local authority is not obliged to give consent for the skip to be left on the highway. But it will usually do so providing it is of an approved size and colour.

The hirer has to comply with whatever conditions the council lays down, on such matters as where the skip is to be parked and how long it may stay there. He may be asked to submit a sketch showing its exact location before a permit is issued.

It is an offence with a fine of up to £100 to deposit a skip on the highway without permission.

It is also illegal not to have the skip adequately lit at night, not to have the owner's name and address clearly displayed and not to remove the skip as soon as practicable.

The law makes the owner of the skip responsible for any infringements, the hirer being treated as the 'owner' when the hiring is for a month or more. But if the leasing company received a summons, say for a lighting offence, it could serve a notice on the prosecution naming the hirer.

Anyone prosecuted is not liable if he can show that despite taking reasonable precautions the offence was the result of someone else's misbehaviour – for example, if warning lights have been stolen or damaged by vandals.

Even when a permit has been issued, however, a uniformed policeman can order a skip to be repositioned or taken away at the owner's or hirer's expense.

SMUGGLING
A smuggled souvenir can be expensive

Anybody who avoids paying CUSTOMS DUTY on goods from abroad is guilty of smuggling. The penalty, however, depends on all the circum-

SOMETHING TO DECLARE

Because the penalties for evading Customs duty are very high, it is always advisable to declare everything – even if you believe that there is no reason to pay duty.

stances and the amount of duty being evaded. If the amount involved was small – or if the Customs officer thinks there could have been a genuine mistake – he is empowered to impose an on-the-spot penalty, extra duty and/or confiscate the goods.

The officer can seize goods and then offer to sell them back as well as imposing a penalty. In more serious cases the offender would be prosecuted. The maximum penalties are a £1,000 fine or a fine three times the value of the smuggled goods – whichever is the greater – and 2 years' imprisonment.

Any vehicle or vessel carrying smuggled goods can be seized and confiscated by a Customs officer. For example, a car with a concealed compartment containing smuggled goods can be forfeited – even if it does not belong to the person trying to smuggle the goods.

If the car is rented, being bought on hire purchase or just borrowed from a friend, it is the responsibility of the legal owner to appeal against the seizure before a court.

SOCIAL SECURITY APPEALS
Action you can take if a claim for benefit is turned down

Everyone has a right of appeal if a claim for a social security benefit is rejected. Appeals over national insurance benefits are made first to the local national insurance tribunal and, if the claimant loses there, he can make a further appeal to the SOCIAL SECURITY COMMISSIONERS. Appeals over SUPPLEMENTARY BENEFIT and FAMILY INCOME SUPPLEMENT are made to supplementary benefit appeal tribunals.

When there is a dispute

Claims for national insurance benefits are decided at local social security department offices by the insurance officer; claims for INDUSTRIAL INJURY BENEFITS are settled by a medical board; and claims for ATTENDANCE ALLOWANCE are decided by the Attendance Allowance Board at Keysign House, 429 Oxford Street, London W1R 2HT.

The insurance officer or the deciding board will inform the claimant in writing whether his claim is successful or not.

If the claim is rejected – or if the award is less than claimed – he will receive a statement giving reasons for the decision and information about how to appeal.

When there is an appeal

All appeals should be made in writing to the local social security office within 28 days of notification that the claim is rejected.

Anyone deciding to appeal after 28 days must write to the clerk of the local national insurance tribunal – his address can be obtained from the social security office – explaining the delay as well as giving grounds for the appeal. The tribunal chairman will decide whether the appeal can go ahead.

A claimant is notified of the time and place of the hearing of an appeal by post. He can either attend or submit written evidence to be heard in his absence.

If the hearing has been fixed for a day on which it is inconvenient to attend, the claimant can ask for the date to be changed.

Included in the notice of hearing will be a statement by the insurance officer setting out the facts of the case and the reasons for his decision. Any Acts or regulations on which he has relied will be listed and so will any decisions by the

Social Security Commissioner which are considered relevant. If the claimant wants to check the Acts or regulations referred to, he should tell the tribunal clerk.

Who pays the costs?

A claimant can have a solicitor to represent him at an appeal, but LEGAL AID cannot be granted. Consultations before the appeal with a solicitor may be possible under the legal aid and advice scheme. Check with the local CITIZENS ADVICE BUREAU.

Travelling expenses and any loss of wages can be claimed by the claimant and by witnesses giving any relevant evidence. The tribunal clerk will provide a claims form.

No claims for expenses can be made by any friend or adviser – such as a trade union official – who accompanies the claimant, but is not a relevant witness.

At the hearing

The hearing is always informal. The claimant will be able to question the insurance officer who made the original decision and any witnesses who are called by him. The claimant may also be questioned by the officer and by any of the three members of the tribunal.

In most cases the clerk will give the claimant a note of the tribunal's decision before he leaves for home. A full statement of the decision with the tribunal's reasons will be sent in the post.

If you lose an appeal

Once a tribunal has rejected an appeal, a further course open to the claimant is to take the case to the social security commissioner. Apply in writing to the local social security office. If the decision was unanimous, you must have leave to appeal from the tribunal chairman or social security commissioner.

There is an ultimate right of appeal to the Court of Appeal – but only on a point of law and with leave from the commissioner or the Court of Appeal.

Injury claims If a claim for industrial injury benefits is rejected on medical grounds, you can appeal to a medical appeal tribunal.

Awards of supplementary benefit and family income supplement are made by Supplementary Benefits officers at local Department of Health and

Social Security offices. Appeals are heard by supplementary benefit appeal tribunals. Notice of appeal to such a tribunal must be given within 28 days of your being told of the decision.

If a claimant does not agree with the supplementary benefit appeal tribunal's decision, he can appeal to the social security commissioner, but only on a point of law and with the leave of the commissioner. There is a further appeal, again by leave of the commissioner, to the Court of Appeal.

SOCIAL SECURITY COMMISSIONERS

Appealing against rejection of a claim for benefits

When a claim for social security benefit has been rejected it is sometimes possible to appeal to the social security commissioners – for example, when:

● An appeal has been turned down by the NATIONAL INSURANCE LOCAL TRIBUNAL.

● The Medical Appeal Tribunal has rejected a claim for INDUSTRIAL INJURY BENEFIT (but such an appeal can be made only on a point of law).

● Someone wishes to appeal against the Attendance Allowance Board's refusal to grant an ATTENDANCE ALLOWANCE.

● Someone wishes to appeal against a decision of a SUPPLEMENTARY BENEFIT Appeals Tribunal (but only on a point of law).

The social security commissioners are lawyers appointed to deal with these appeals. They sit in London, Cardiff and Edinburgh.

To appeal, complete a form obtainable from your local social security office. For an individual, form LT43 is needed. If the appeal is being conducted by an association or trade union, form LT44 is required.

Most cases are decided without a hearing on the evidence supplied on the form – although the commissioner may write asking for further details. He then sends his decision, and his reasons for reaching it, by post. You can ask for a personal hearing, but you cannot insist. When a hearing is granted, it will usually be held in the nearest of the three cities in which the commissioner sits.

The appellant is entitled to reasonable expenses to enable himself and any witnesses to attend. He can be represented by a lawyer, but he cannot claim LEGAL AID.

The commissioner does not announce his decision at the end of the hearing, but, as in a written appeal, sends it in the post. If an appeal fails, the appellant is not liable for any costs.

SOCIAL SECURITY OFFENCES

Penalty for making a false statement to claim benefit

Anyone who is paid social security benefit that he is not entitled to is legally bound to repay it. The only exceptions are cases in which the claimant can show that he took care to see that he was not overpaid, so that the mistake was not his fault. Disputes over liability to repay are treated like any other SOCIAL SECURITY APPEALS.

If the overpayment resulted from a false statement made knowingly by the claimant, he can be prosecuted. The commonest cases are claims by husbands for families they are not supporting and by men who declare they are out of work while earning money doing odd jobs.

If you receive benefit, always read carefully any documents you sign or are shown. Failure to report a change in your circumstances can be as much an offence as a false statement in your original application for benefit.

Social security inspectors have the right to enter premises where anyone is employed and to question both employer and employees.

The maximum penalty for making a false claim knowingly is a fine of £400 and 3 months' imprisonment. The court can also order anyone convicted to pay the Department of Health and Social Security criminal compensation to the amount of the fraud.

The department must bring the prosecution within 12 months of the offence or within 3 months of it coming to light.

The maximum penalty for obstructing an inspector or failing to answer his questions is a £50 fine.

Those who obtain benefit by deliberate DECEPTION are often prosecuted for obtaining property by deception under the Theft Act 1968. The penalty is up to 10 years' imprisonment and an unlimited fine. There is no time limit for Theft Act prosecutions.

SOLICITING

When a prostitute seeks clients in public

Although PROSTITUTION – offering sex for money – is not itself an offence, a prostitute can be arrested if she approaches men in a public place. A policeman can arrest any woman whom he suspects of loitering or soliciting in a public place for immoral purposes.

'Public place' can mean doorways and entrances of any buildings abutting on a street, and a prostitute can be arrested for calling to men while standing at a window or on a balcony. It is not soliciting, however, when she advertises in a shop window, nor can she be prosecuted for displaying her telephone number in a public place.

A man who approaches women for immoral purposes – by kerb-crawling, for example – cannot be arrested for soliciting. At most, he can be charged with behaviour likely to cause a BREACH OF THE PEACE.

Penalties Soliciting offences are tried in the magistrates' court. For a first offence the penalty is a fine of up to £50.

KEEPING PROSTITUTES
OFF THE STREETS

The police can arrest any woman who they suspect is loitering or soliciting for immoral purposes in a public place.

'Dearie' happens to be a plain-clothes officer'

Prostitutes who have been found guilty of soliciting twice or more can be sent to prison for 3 months and be fined £200.

Pimps and male prostitutes A pimp – a man who solicits others on behalf of a prostitute – or a male homosexual prostitute who seeks clients in a public place, is guilty of importuning. He can be fined up to £1,000 and be gaoled for up to 6 months in a magistrates' court, or be sentenced to 2 years' imprisonment and an unlimited fine if he is tried by the crown court.

SOLICITOR

Where to seek professional legal advice

No one can practise as a solicitor who has not passed strict professional examinations and served 'articles', an apprenticeship, to another solicitor for at least 2 years.

After having qualified, a solicitor must wait for at least 3 years before he can practise under his own name. He must also hold a practising certificate, renewable annually, from the Law Society, the solicitors' governing body.

To obtain that certificate, a solicitor must also have taken out insurance against being sued for negligence and must have his accounts audited by an accountant.

Any money held by a solicitor for other people must be put in a special bank account subject to its own rules.

The solicitor's monopoly

The law gives solicitors an exclusive right to charge fees for:
● Drawing up property sale or transfer deeds.
● Obtaining the documents needed to administer a dead person's estate.
● Providing court representation or instructing a BARRISTER to do so.

In a few areas of law, professional advice can be sought elsewhere. An accountant, for example, can charge for consultation about tax law or a debt agency for work in the 'selling' of a debt.

Generally, however, a litigant, unless he is prepared to act for himself, must employ a solicitor to do so.

Anyone seeking help under the LEGAL AID or LEGAL ADVICE schemes is also obliged to go to a solicitor, regardless of the work he wishes done. **Advertising ban** Solicitors cannot advertise or otherwise tout for business. Specialists in particular fields of law can be found on lists kept at local libraries.

There are also the Yellow Pages in the telephone directory to consult for a full list of solicitors in a given area, but it is considered best to act on recommendation if possible.

Paying the bill

A solicitor is entitled to seek payment for all the work he does for a client, including telephone calls and letters, based on the length of time it takes him.

The amount he charges is a matter of agreement between him and his client; £20 to £25 an hour is quite a normal fee, but there is no fixed scale, even for house purchase or court work. A client is always entitled to ask for an estimate and to 'shop around' before giving instructions.

If there is a dispute over a bill, a client should ask for a detailed breakdown of it. If that fails to satisfy him, he should ask the solicitor to provide a remuneration certificate from the Law Society, stating that the bill is 'fair and reasonable'.

When first seeing a solicitor, it is important to let him know whether you are seeking help under the legal aid or legal advice scheme.

If not, and if you want nothing more than his advice, you can ask him to see you under the fixed fee scheme for which the rate, in 1981, was £5 for up to 30 minutes. *See:* LEGAL COSTS

Complaining about a solicitor

A client who considers his solicitor to be guilty of PROFESSIONAL NEGLIGENCE in handling his affairs – and who wishes to take legal action over it – should go to another solicitor.

It is the duty of the original solicitor, if he thinks the client may have a claim against him, to advise the client to instruct someone else.

Complaints about professional conduct other than negligence – for example, if a solicitor has divulged confidential information or misused money deposited with him – should be referred to the Law Society.

The society may decide that the solicitor has a case to answer in which event the matter is heard by the Sol-

icitors' Disciplinary Tribunal. It has the power to impose an unlimited fine on a solicitor or strike him off the official court list, which effectively puts him out of business.

The Law Society also deals with other, less serious complaints – over delay, for example, or lack of information.

Anyone dissatisfied with the outcome of a Law Society investigation can ask for a review of the case from the Lay Observer, a non-lawyer appointed by the Lord Chancellor.

If he agrees with the complainant, he can ask the Council of the Law Society to reconsider the way in which the case has been handled.
See also: LEGAL ADVICE
LEGAL AID

SPARE PARTS

Who is responsible if they do not work

When you buy spare parts for repair work that you are doing yourself, the seller is responsible to you if they do not do what they are supposed to do. *See:* DEFECTIVE GOODS

Similarly, when parts are fitted by a REPAIRER, he is liable to you if they do not suit their purpose.

There is no law, however, that says a manufacturer has to make spare parts or a dealer has to stock them. But in some trades a code of practice covers the point.

In the motor industry, for example, the code lays down that manufacturers should tell customers the minimum period for which spare parts will be available after a model goes out of production.

SPECIAL CONSTABLE

Unpaid volunteers who assist the regular police

Special constables are a voluntary reserve of men and women police constables appointed by chiefs of police authorities for part-time service. They have the same powers – including ARREST – as regular police constables in the police area for which they are appointed or in areas next to it.

They are unpaid, but receive expenses and compensation for loss of pay while serving.

To become a special constable you must be:
● A British subject – born or naturalised – or registered as a citizen of the United Kingdom and Commonwealth.
● Aged over 18 and under 50.
● At least 5 ft 6 in. tall; 5 ft 4 in. if you are a woman.
● In good health and of good character.

You cannot be a special constable if you are a serving member of:
● The armed forces.
● The Territorial Army.
● The fire or ambulance services.
● The medical, nursing or midwifery profession.
● A security organisation or private army.

Anyone with a CRIMINAL RECORD will be rejected by the police.
How to apply If you are eligible and wish to become a special constable, ask your local police station or police headquarters for an application form.

How special constables are trained

Special constables undergo a basic training course at one of the police training centres. In the Metropolitan

ASSISTING THE POLICE

Special constables are recruited to help the police with mainly routine duties – for example, patrolling at football matches and traffic control in busy Saturday afternoon shopping streets.

Police area, for example, training consists of 2 hours a week on a weekday evening over a period of 23 weeks, supplemented by 32 hours' duty on the streets with a regular police officer or an experienced special constable.

If a 'special' does not carry out his training according to the rules he will be asked to leave.

Discipline Special constables are subject to the same discipline as regular police officers and must carry out whatever duties they are allocated.

SPECIAL EDUCATION

Making special provision for the handicapped child

Every handicapped child, however severe his handicap, has the right to an education. Local authorities have a duty to discover which children in their area need special educational treatment and must make provision for them.

Assessment for special education

The law lays down a formal procedure for ascertaining whether a child needs special education. Once a child has reached the age of 2, the local authority, or the parents if they are worried about the child, can insist on a medical examination. Parents must be invited to attend.

If, as a result, it is decided that the child does need special education, the parents must be notified and given details of the doctor's report.

The parents can require the doctor to issue a certificate showing the nature and extent of the child's handicap. If the parents refuse to send their child to a special school the education authority can insist that the doctor issues a certificate.

Parents can appeal to the Secretary of State for Education and Science who can cancel it.

However, that formal procedure has largely been superseded by informal assessment. If a school is concerned about a child, the head teacher completes form SE1. He should also notify the parents and record their views.

The school doctor must complete form SE2, and the parents should be invited to attend a medical examination. Their views should be recorded on the form.

An educational psychologist has then to examine the child and complete form SE3. It is recommended that parents should be invited to attend his examination.

Form SE4, a summary and action sheet, is then completed by a senior educational psychologist or special education adviser. It details the child's disabilities, if any, and recommends whether special education should be provided, and if so what kind.

The disadvantage of that informal procedure, used by about two-thirds of all local authorities, is that although the Department of Education and Science has stated that parents should be consulted and kept informed throughout, they have no legal right to see what is reported on the forms. That makes it difficult for them to challenge decisions taken about their child.

Parents may request copies of the forms and can ask to be present at all tests and case conferences, but there is no obligation on the local authority to comply.

If the parents are not satisfied with the results of the informal procedure they can refuse to send their child to a special school, in which case the authority would carry out a formal assessment. This gives parents a right of appeal to the Secretary of State.

Once a child has been registered at a special school, whether or not he has been formally assessed, he may not be withdrawn without the local authority's consent. Parents can appeal to the Secretary of State if the authority refuses to allow their child to leave.

Special schools

Handicapped children may be educated in special schools, in special units attached to ordinary schools, in hospital schools or at home or by other individual tuition. Wherever the local authority decides to place a child the special education must be free.

The Department of Education and Science makes regulations about staffing, premises, and hours and holidays for special education provided by the local authority.

These regulations also apply to non-maintained special schools run by

charities and voluntary societies. Local education authorities pay the fees of most pupils at those schools but have little say in how they are run.

The regulations do not apply to independent schools providing special education. Local education authorities may pay for handicapped pupils to go to independent, special schools regarded as suitable by the Secretary of State.

Special arrangements can be made for handicapped children taking public examinations. Extra time is usually allowed and candidates may be permitted to use typewriters or to dictate their answers to an amanuensis.

Transport facilities

Transport must be provided if a child lives further than walking distance from his school. Local authorities may provide SCHOOL TRANSPORT for all handicapped children, and most do so for all but the mildly handicapped.

If a child is at boarding school the local education authority must pay the fare to and from school at the beginning and end of term. Local authorities vary widely in their generosity in paying fares for mid-term or weekend visits home, even if the school recommends this.

The authority can also pay for parents to visit the child at school if they are satisfied that without a visit the child's special educational treatment will be impaired, and that the parents cannot afford the cost.

If fares are costing far more than the parents are saving by having the child at boarding school they may be able to get help from charitable organisations. The 'Family Fund' has occasionally helped parents in this kind of difficulty.

When parents have no chance to choose

In practice, parents have very little choice of school because of the shortage of suitable places for handicapped children, although the same principles of choice apply in theory as for ordinary schools. It is often necessary for children to go to boarding school because there is no local day school catering for their type of disability.

Parents have the same right of appeal as parents of non-handicapped children, including appeal to the Secretary of State if they feel their wishes have been unreasonably overruled.

The Education Acts have always allowed handicapped children to be educated in ordinary schools if the local authority felt this was desirable and the handicap was not severe. The law now officially supports this policy unless it would be impracticable, incompatible with the efficiency of the school or would involve unreasonable public expense. This will enable handicapped people as far as possible to take their place in the normal community and not to be isolated from it.

Parents who want their handicapped child to attend an ordinary school need the acceptance and enthusiastic support of the staff, as well as the consent of the local education authority, if integration is to be a success.

SPEED LIMIT

Rules that vary with the road and the vehicle

Traffic on all public roads in Britain is subject to maximum speed limits which vary according to the type of road.

Vehicles other than cars and motor cycles can be governed by lower limits, which again vary according to the type of vehicle.

The normal speed limit on any road can be lowered in an emergency, or because road works are being carried out. The highway authority responsible can make an order at short notice. If new limits are signposted, a driver is bound by them.

Significance of advisory signs If 'advisory' notices suggest a lower speed – for example, in fog or before sharp bends – a driver who exceeds that speed commits no offence provided that he keeps control and causes no danger. However, he may be charged with careless or reckless driving.

Speed limits do not apply to fire brigade, ambulance or police vehicles on emergency calls. But the driver of an emergency vehicle must still exercise proper care for other road users.

How the speed limit varies

On motorways and dual carriageways – where traffic flowing in opposite directions is separated – the normal speed limit is 70 mph. On other roads it is never more than 60 mph, and if the road is 'restricted' the permanent limit is 30 mph unless another limit is signposted.

WHEN A DRIVER IS CAUGHT

The maximum fine for exceeding a speed limit on a public road is £500 for a motorway offence, or £100 on other roads, including dual carriageways that are not designated as motorways.

An offender's licence is endorsed and he can be disqualified from driving – even on a first offence.

A driver who is caught speeding must be warned if the police intend to prosecute him – either at the time or by a notice or a court summons within 14 days.

Notice of intended prosecution can be served on the registered owner of the vehicle. If he was not the driver, he is obliged to supply details of the driver if requested by the police to do so.

What evidence is needed

A driver who is charged with a speeding offence cannot be convicted solely on one policeman's opinion or estimate of his speed. But a second witness, or a speedometer reading if the policeman was following, is enough to substantiate the allegation.

Readings from radar or cable detectors are accepted by the courts. So is evidence of a speed computed by the VASCAR system, even though its operation depends on visual reactions.

Evidence based on electronic detection devices is normally impossible to dispute unless doubt can be cast on the siting, functioning or operation of the equipment.

When a road is restricted

If street lighting is installed at intervals of no more than 200 yds, that indicates what is commonly called a 'built-up area', and in most cases it is automatically a restricted road.

A road may, however, be restricted by highway authority order, provided that signs indicating the beginning and end of speed limits are shown.

If its lamps are more than 200 yds apart, it must also have illuminated or reflecting 'repeater' signs at frequent intervals.

If a road is automatically restricted under the 200 yd rule, it is no defence for a speeding driver to say that a limit sign was obscured, or not seen for some other reason. A driver in doubt in such an area should assume that the limit is 30 mph.

VEHICLES THAT ARE RESTRICTED

Lower speed limits may apply to goods vehicles, vehicles fitted to carry more than 7 passengers, and to any vehicle when it is towing a trailer or caravan.

Type of vehicle	Motorway mph	Other unrestricted road mph
Car with trailer or caravan	40/50	40/50
Goods vehicle under 30 cwt unladen	70	50
Goods vehicle over 30 cwt unladen	70 (up to 3 tons, then 60 mph)	40
Goods vehicle towing trailer (depending on weight ratios)	40/50	30/40/50
Bus or coach	70	50
Other vehicle fitted to carry more than 7 passengers –		
under 30 cwt unladen	70	50
over 30 cwt unladen	70	40
Invalid carriage	–	20
Vehicle without pneumatic tyres	–	20

SPORTING EVENT

When even a boxer can claim for assault

Every sportsman is considered to have consented to risking a certain amount of injury simply by agreeing to take part in the game. But even those who play aggressive sports, such as boxing or rugby, may be able to sue for damages or prosecute for assault if an injury is caused by some action that goes beyond the game's usual hazards.

A fast bowler is not liable to pay damages if the ball rises sharply and breaks the batsman's finger. Such an event is part of the normal risk in cricket. Similarly, a boxer is not liable if he fractures his opponent's jaw during a contest.

But a boxer who after hearing the bell

THE FOLK WHO LIVED IN THE OUTFIELD

Even if a game creates a nuisance, its benefit to the community can outweigh the objections of individual residents.

The village cricket club had played on the same ground for 70 years. Then houses were built in an adjoining field at Lintz, County Durham. Mr and Mrs Miller, who had bought a house on the edge of the ground, complained that balls kept landing in their garden.

The cricket club built a higher fence and offered to pay for any damage. But Mr Miller finally brought an action alleging nuisance and got an injunction to prevent cricket being played at the ground. The case eventually went to the Court of Appeal.

DECISION

The Court of Appeal held that the Millers must have realised when they bought the house that cricket balls would sometimes be hit on to their property. On balance the interests of the villagers in preserving the cricket ground should prevail over the private interest of Mr and Mrs Miller.

The injunction was set aside, but Mr and Mrs Miller were awarded £400 to take account of past and future damages.

FOOTBALLER WHO WAS INJURED BY FOUL

Sportsmen are assumed to accept a certain amount of injury or risk, but they can sue or prosecute if an injury is caused by some action beyond the game's usual hazards.

Frampton Athletic had a local 'derby' soccer match against Stapleton FC in Bristol. When Stapleton was awarded a corner, Derek Shilson, a Frampton defender, tackled a Stapleton striker, Paul Manning, after Manning had parted with the ball.

Mr Shilson was sent off by the referee, and Mr Manning had to have a cartilage operation because of the foul. He could no longer work on roofs as a carpenter and was being paid £5 a week less wages.

He sued Mr Shilson in the High Court for damages for ASSAULT AND BATTERY.

DECISION

Judge Fallon awarded him £2,400 damages and costs.

deliberately injures his opponent – whether by punching, kicking or butting – can be sued or prosecuted. Foul play alone is not the deciding factor, however, particularly if it is a commonplace incident. For example, a late tackle may be against the rules of football but it would not make a player liable for damages even if it resulted in a broken leg.

Any action in the courts arising from an incident during the game depends on the severity of the injury sustained and the circumstances in which it was inflicted.

A player may be able to sue the club or organisers in certain circumstances – for example, if a visiting rugby winger crashes into a wall which he could not have realised was dangerously close to the touchline.

Safety of spectators

The owners of sports grounds and the organisers of sporting events are responsible for the safety of spectators, but not for the normal risks associated with watching the game.

For example, a spectator can sue for damages if he is injured when a crush barrier collapses due to the negligence of the organiser or his staff. But a spectator has no claim if he is hit by a ball while sitting at a cricket match.

Clubs cannot avoid liability, however, simply by putting up notices saying that spectators enter at their own risk.

The owners of a sports ground or club may also be responsible for damage in the surrounding area. If the first tee of a golf course is sited so that balls are repeatedly driven through the window of a nearby house, the club is liable to pay damages for NUISANCE.

SQUATTER

When an empty home is used without consent

Squatting – setting up house in unoccupied premises without the owner's permission – is not a crime unless violence is used or threatened in order to get in, or damage is caused.

In civil law, however, squatting is a TRESPASS and the owner can obtain a court order for possession of the premises. No one else can intervene unless there is OVERCROWDING, or a health risk is alleged. In those cases the local authority can take action.

Getting a squatter out

Unless the owner normally lives, or intends to live, on premises that are taken over by squatters, he should not use violence to enter his property or to evict the squatters. He may legally enter, however, if admission is not resisted or the squatters are absent.

Most landlords rely on the powers of the High Court or a county court, which can grant a possession order once ownership is proved. The procedure usually takes 7 days or less.

Owners have to identify the squatters, but they may proceed if they have made a reasonable attempt to do so. A possession order applies to the premises, so all squatters must go, whether or not they are named.

A possession order entitles an owner to ask a court sheriff or bailiff to carry out the EVICTION, with police help if necessary. Anyone who resists a court officer risks a maximum penalty of 6 months' imprisonment and a £1,000 fine.

WHEN AN OWNER CAN USE FORCE

A squatter who deprives someone of his usual home, or refuses to go when premises are wanted by the owner for use as a home, commits the criminal offence of 'adverse occupancy'. The police can be asked to arrest and prosecute him.

The maximum penalty is 6 months' imprisonment and a £1,000 fine.

A resident owner usually does not need a court order to claim possession in those circumstances. A squatter need only be shown proof of residence – a sworn statement, or a housing authority certificate of allocation.

If he refuses to go it is advisable to call the police. But an owner who wants to take immediate action is entitled to use 'reasonable force' to enter the premises or to evict the squatter.

If excessive or unnecessary force is used, however, he might be open to a charge of assault.

If a squatter is evicted, the owner of the property has a legal responsibility to take care of any possessions that are left behind, until they can be collected.

When a squatter has permission

A local authority that has empty housing – for example, as part of a future redevelopment – may permit squatters to occupy it or may later give permission to an occupation already in force. Occupancy is usually controlled by a system of licensing, and may involve a token rent. It is subject to an agreement that squatters will leave when the premises are needed. They are entitled to 'reasonable' notice – sometimes as little as a week.

Services As occupiers, squatters are entitled to water, gas and electricity supplies. A gas or power board, however, is likely to demand a large deposit before reconnecting the supply.

STAMP DUTY

The tax that must be paid on many legal documents

If a legal document or deed is not properly stamped, it cannot be relied on in any legal action.

The cost of stamping the document at a government stamp office – for example at Bush House, Strand, London WC2, and in many provincial centres – varies according to the type. The amount payable is embossed on the document.

When duty has to be paid on a house purchase

The duty is calculated on the price paid for the property:

Up to £20,000	No stamp duty
£20,001 – £25,000	$\frac{1}{2}$% of whole amount
£25,001 – £30,000	1% of whole amount
£30,001 – £35,000	$1\frac{1}{2}$% of whole amount
Above £35,000	2% of whole amount

Certificate of value

Legally, to qualify for these special low percentages of duty, a house purchase contract must include special wording – 'It is certified that the transaction hereby effected does not form part of a larger transaction or a series of transactions in respect of which the amount or value, or the aggregate amount or value of the consideration exceeds . . .'

That means that putting a false or over-inflated price on fixtures or fittings, so reducing the true price of the house, is illegal.

Duty on a lease

For leases, the duty payable is a percentage of the annual rent:

Length of lease	%
7 years or indefinite	1
Over 7 and under 35 years	2
Over 35 and under 100 years	6
Over 100 years, but not indefinite	12

When a lease is bought outright – on a flat purchase, for example – duty is charged on both the price paid and the rent.

Where freehold or leasehold land is sold or a lease for more than 7 years is made, whether or not any duty is payable, the deed is not properly stamped unless details of the transaction are lodged with the stamp office and a stamp is placed on the deed to show it has been 'Produced'.

Duty on stocks and shares

No duty is payable when you buy government stocks, but you are liable to pay 2 per cent duty on all other transfers.

Duty on gifts

Gifts are stamped on the value of the gift as if that was the price paid. If land is involved, its value must then be agreed with the district valuer and if shares are involved the value must be settled with the Shares Valuation Department of the Inland Revenue.

STANDARD-FORM CONTRACT

When conditions are binding without a signature

The conditions of many types of contract are printed on forms that are standard for all transactions of the same kind.

In some cases there is no provision for signing your agreement to the conditions. You are simply given a form containing them – or they may be incorporated in a ticket or receipt.

Conditions printed on the face of such a document, or referred to there, are legally binding on you if the document is received as part of the transaction and it is one that could reasonably be expected to contain conditions – for example, a railway ticket or a cloakroom receipt.

However, a document that you receive only after the contract is made is not binding on you, unless it can be shown that you knew of the conditions. For example, if you had agreed on previous occasions to the same conditions, you could be bound by them again.

Signing a standard contract

If you sign a standard contract form you are bound by its terms. They can be ignored only if:
● There has been fraud or misrepresen-

tation by the other party or,
● There are terms that a court considers unreasonable. *See:* UNFAIR CONTRACT

Conditions you cannot see

You may be shown, and perhaps asked to sign, a document that does not set out the standard terms of the contract itself. It may refer to terms set out in a notice displayed on the premises, or in another document you have not seen.

Courts regard such terms as binding, even if it is difficult for a customer to read them. But if you have no reasonable opportunity at all to read them, they are invalid.

STEP-PARENTS

Assuming responsibility for someone else's child

A step-parent does not become responsible for his step-child simply because he or she is a step-parent. He or she may acquire rights and responsibilities in the same way as anyone else who, though not a parent, is looking after a child.

A step-parent who assumes responsibility for maintaining a child may be entitled to CHILD BENEFIT. Even after the death of his or her spouse, child benefit can be claimed unless the child's other parent is both alive and contributing to its maintenance.

If the step-parent has custody of a child of compulsory school age, he has the same duties as a parent to see that the child attends school, and is liable to the same penalties for failing to do so. *See:* SCHOOL ATTENDANCE

If a step-parent neglects or ill-treats a child in his custody or care he may be prosecuted for a criminal offence under the Children and Young Persons Act 1933, or the local authority may institute proceedings against him for a care order. *See:* CHILDREN IN CARE

If the step-parent's marriage has broken up, but during the marriage a child was treated as a child of the family, a court may order him to maintain that child. In deciding the amount of such maintenance the court will have regard to whether he had actually assumed responsibility for the child's maintenance, and, if he had, to the extent of that responsibility, and to the length of time

during which he discharged it.

Adopting a step-child

The court may sanction the ADOPTION by the step-parent of the child. Where this is supported by the spouse of the step-parent and the other parent is dead, the court will readily make the order. Where the spouse is divorced and the other parent is alive, the court will have to be satisfied that in all the circumstances adoption is the proper course in the interests of the welfare of the child.

Changing a child's surname

Where a parent has sole parental rights, either because the child is illegitimate or the other parent died without appointing a guardian, the mother can change her child's surname to that of the step-father. If she has custody of the child after a divorce, she cannot change the name without the consent either of her former husband or of the court. *See:* NAME, Change of

Death of a mother

A mother who wishes her new spouse to be responsible for the child after death should appoint him testamentary GUARDIAN in her will. Where no testamentary guardian has been appointed, the court can on the step-parent's application appoint him guardian, if he is in control of the child.

Death of a step-parent

A step-parent who wishes his child to benefit on his death should make provision for the child in his will.

If he dies without leaving a will, a step-child who has not been adopted is not treated as his child in the distribution of his estate. If the step-child can show that he has been unreasonably deprived of adequate maintenance, however, he can apply to the court for an order giving him a share of the estate. *See:* DISINHERITANCE; INTESTACY

When a step-parent is killed in a FATAL ACCIDENT, the child is one of the dependants legally entitled to claim compensation from the person who unlawfully caused the death of his step-parent.

On the death of a child who has not left a will, a step-parent is not entitled to share in the distribution of the estate.

The INCOME TAX ALLOWANCES

which a parent may claim in respect of his child – where the taxpayer brings up the child alone, or through ill-health depends on the child's services – apply also to step-parents.

STERILISATION

Birth control and health safeguard

Sterilisation is the most reliable and permanent means by which men and women can prevent childbirth. Many doctors are prepared to do the operation for only social reasons.

When sterilisation is not medically necessary

Men and women have no right to sterilisation on the National Health Service as a form of birth control, but the operation can usually be obtained privately.

If sterilisation is medically necessary, a patient is entitled to choose whether to have the operation as an NHS patient or a private patient.

The male vasectomy operation is simplest and can be done on an outpatient basis with a local anaesthetic.

Female sterilisation is far more complex and requires a general anaesthetic and a stay in hospital.

When sterilisation is medically necessary

When a woman's body has been seriously damaged by childbirth and she risks injury or death by becoming pregnant again, her doctor may advise sterilisation. Similarly if she suffers from heart disease, he may so advise. The operation cannot be carried out without the woman's express consent. A doctor who did so could be sued for assault, and may have to pay substantial damages.

If your doctor refused your request to be sterilised to prevent a pregnancy that he knew could harm your health or delayed a sterilisation operation that was urgently needed, and you later did suffer damage, you might be able to sue him and the area health authority, if the authority employed him under the National Health Service, for MEDICAL NEGLIGENCE.

'

THE GIRL WHO WAS PRECOCIOUS

A sterilisation may be prevented even when a parent has given consent – by having the child made a ward of court.

In 1975 Mrs D., whose 11-year-old daughter had a congenital disease that made her mentally backward but precocious in her physical development, consulted Dr G. because she was afraid the girl might become pregnant and have an abnormal child.

Dr G. advised that the girl should be sterilised after her mother had agreed, and the operation was arranged for May 6.

The local authority education psychologist who had been caring for the girl for some time did not think, however, that the operation should be carried out. Before the girl went into hospital, the psychologist had her made a ward of court and asked the court to stop the operation.

DECISION

Mrs Justice Heilbron ruled that the operation should not take place, because it would deprive the girl of her basic human right, to reproduce, without her consent, and when there was no medical need for the operation.

The evidence was that Miss D.'s mental condition was improving all the time, and it was held that she should be allowed to make her own choice after she was 18.

If you are considering sterilisation consult your doctor or visit the local family planning clinic. Some health authorities and clinics refuse to allow an operation without the general practitioner's consent. They have a right to do so.

A surgeon can be sued if an operation is badly performed and the patient suffers harm, or if the operation does not work and a pregnancy results.

A parent or guardian can give consent for an operation on a child under 16, but should not do so for sterilisation unless there is some grave medical reason. If a parent does try to have a child sterilised, the courts may prevent this in wardship proceedings.

A child usually cannot give its own consent until it is 18.

If a child were sterilised without a grave medical reason, it could sue the doctor within 3 years of becoming 18 or within 3 years of discovering that the doctor had been negligent.

STOCKBROKER

Seeking advice at your own risk

A stockbroker buys and sells shares according to his client's instructions. He is liable for PROFESSIONAL NEGLIGENCE only if he does not carry out his instructions promptly with the result that the client loses money.

But even if the stockbroker thinks it unwise for a client to make a particular deal, he is not obliged to tell him so.

THE INVESTOR WHO GAMBLED – AND LOST

A stockbroker is not liable for his client's choice of investment and is not obliged to explain the risks.

Mr Briggs, a solicitor, bought nearly £37,000 worth of shares between 1973–5 in GRA Property Trust – a greyhound stadium company – through his broker, Mr Gunner. When Stock Exchange dealings in the shares were suspended, they became virtually worthless. Mr Briggs sued Mr Gunner for damages.

It had been Mr Briggs's idea, not Mr Gunner's, to buy GRA shares. Mr Gunner never warned him of the risks of putting all his cash in one share. However, Mr Gunner did tell Mr Briggs that the assets value was £3 to £5 per share.

What Mr Gunner meant – although he did not say so – was that if GRA ever carried out its development plans, the shares then would be worth £3 to £5 each in the future.

Mr Gunner suggested to the court that if the shares were being sold at 14p each, Mr Briggs could not reasonably have believed that the realisable value was then at least £3 a share.

DECISION

The court held that there was no negligence by Mr Gunner. It dismissed the action and awarded costs against Mr Briggs.

If a client asks for advice about a particular investment the stockbroker can please himself whether he gives it or not. But if he does give advice, it must be honest and to the best of his ability. Even if the advice proves to be wrong, and the client loses money, he will not be able to recover damages from the stockbroker unless he can prove professional negligence.

STOLEN GOODS

A handler is guilty only if he knows goods were stolen

The prosecution must always prove that a person accused of handling stolen goods was aware that the goods had been stolen.

A court may sometimes decide not to convict even when it believes that the accused person suspected that the goods were stolen but turned a blind eye to the fact.

On the other hand, a man who buys a £50 watch for £5 from a stranger in a public house should realise that the goods were probably stolen. He is likely to be convicted unless he can give a satisfactory explanation for the cheapness of the watch.

The maximum penalty for handling stolen goods is 14 years' imprisonment and an unlimited fine. Goods recovered are returned to the owner.

Searching premises Police have powers to SEARCH any premises occupied by a person who has been convicted of handling stolen goods. They may also search premises where they suspect stolen goods are being kept.

STRIKE

Your rights during a dispute at work

A worker who goes on strike is breaking the terms of his EMPLOYMENT CONTRACT. But provided that the strike is in support of a 'trade dispute' – a collective conflict between an employer and his staff or between opposing groups of workers – he is largely immune from claims for civil damages arising from his withdrawal of labour.

However, if strikers commit criminal acts in the course of a dispute – such as damaging property, obstructing the police, or intimidating other workers – they are liable to be prosecuted.

What an employer can do

An employer whose workers strike in support of a trade dispute is entitled to sue them for breach of contract. However, he cannot claim damages for business lost because of the strike and any award he might obtain would be limited to the cost of hiring substitute labour. Claims arising from a trade dispute are rare, because such actions are damaging to long-term industrial relations. In the most recent case, in 1958, the National Coal Board did succeed in obtaining damages from a striker – of £3 18s. 2d.

An employer whose business is affected by a trade dispute can never sue the TRADE UNION that called the strike, and usually has no redress against its officials. Unions are not liable in law for the acts of their officials in taking strike or other industrial action.

Union officials may be liable, however, if:
● They are not acting 'in contemplation or furtherance of a trade dispute'.
● They are taking action which affects businesses not directly involved in the dispute.
● They are using violence or threats of violence.
● They are acting for purely personal reasons but dressing their action up as a genuine trade dispute.

Trade dispute A strike staged for political or purely personal reasons – for example to protest against the policies of the British or a foreign government or in pursuit of a grudge – is not a trade dispute, and those who organise or take part in it are liable in full for any loss.

Secondary action The Employment Act 1980 removes some immunities from trade union officials which were originally conferred on them by the Trade Disputes Act 1906 and later extended by various statutes.

Action can now be taken against union officials if they interfere with the commercial contracts of employers who are neither directly involved in the dispute, nor are the direct suppliers or customers of the employer who is directly involved. Competitors of the employer affected by strike action will, therefore, usually be able to complain if

---

WHEN A STRIKE IS ILLEGAL

Certain groups are not allowed to strike. The only lawful way they may stop work is by giving proper notice of resignation, waiting until it expires and leaving their job. And even this course of action is not available to servicemen.
● Members of the armed forces may not strike. If a soldier stopped work he would, in effect, be disobeying an order and would be disciplined by a military tribunal. Nor may servicemen join a trade union or organise union activities. Someone who was a union member before he joined the forces can remain a member, however, provided he does not take an active part in the union.
● The police are not allowed to strike or to join a trade union. The Police Federation is not a union and is not affiliated to the TUC. It is a criminal offence to 'cause disaffection' among the police, or to induce a policeman to break discipline or withhold his services. The maximum penalty in a crown court is 2 years' imprisonment and an unlimited fine.
● Merchant seamen who disobey an order at sea, or who prevent a ship from sailing by being absent, are committing a criminal offence, for which the maximum penalty is a £100 fine. They are allowed to strike only when their ship is safely moored in a British port and after they have given 2 days' notice of termination of contract.
● It is a criminal offence for post office workers wilfully to delay or detain mail; the maximum penalty for doing so is an unlimited fine and 2 years' imprisonment. A postal worker who fails to deliver or transmit a telephone, telegraph or other message can be fined up to £20. These laws, however, can be enforced only by a police prosecution or by a court injunction taken out by the Attorney-General or by a private individual who is personally affected.

' THE THREAT TO THE CUP FINAL

Only a 'trade dispute' is protected from legal action by an employer

The English FA Cup Final is a great international sporting occasion and pictures of it are transmitted by satellite to countries all over the world. In 1977 South Africa was among the countries scheduled to receive coverage of Liverpool v Manchester United.

The BBC engineers' union threatened, because of South Africa's apartheid policy, that unless the BBC agreed not to transmit pictures to South Africa, the entire transmission would be stopped.

The BBC sought a High Court injunction to require the union's general secretary to desist from calling on the engineers to interrupt the transmission. The injunction was refused, as the judge considered the case to be a trade dispute. The BBC appealed.

DECISION

The Court of Appeal granted an injunction, because the issue was not a trade dispute with the BBC as an employer, but a political gesture directed against the South African Government. The broadcast went ahead as scheduled.

THE POSTAL BOYCOTT THAT COULD NOT BE STOPPED

Only the Attorney-General or a private individual personally affected can seek an injunction to prevent a postal strike.

In 1977 the TUC organised a week of protest against South Africa's apartheid policies. For their part, two Post Office trade unions told their members not to handle mail or other communications to and from South Africa.

The National Association for Freedom asked the Attorney-General to take action to stop the threatened boycott. When he refused, the NAFF leader Mr John Gouriet sought an injunction – first in the High Court which refused it, then in the Court of Appeal – to compel the postal workers to carry out their normal duties.

The Court of Appeal granted the injunction and the postal workers withdrew their threat. The Union of Post Office Workers appealed to the House of Lords.

DECISION

The Lords revoked the injunction, ruling that Mr Gouriet was not personally affected. The court could not question the Attorney-General's reasons for not applying. '

> ## THE FILM-PROCESSING FIRM THAT SACKED ALL ITS STRIKERS
>
> *The law does not interfere where an employer sacks all his strikers during a strike.*
>
> Grunwick, a film-processing company in north London, insisted that its staff work compulsory overtime. In August 1976, when a worker was dismissed for refusing to do so, 137 others came out on strike in sympathy. Grunwick dismissed all 137 strikers. They sued the company for unfair dismissal.
>
> ### DECISION
> The Employment Appeal Tribunal rejected their claim, ruling that as all the strikers had been dismissed during the strike, the law of unfair dismissal did not apply.

the union officials try to take action against them.

Where the union officials are unprotected, the employer can apply to a court for an injunction against the leaders of the strike, ordering them not to induce others to stop work. Failure to obey such an order constitutes CONTEMPT OF COURT, punishable by imprisonment or fine. Union officials could also be sued in these cases for heavy damages which in practice would probably be met from union funds, though in law the union is not liable.

Dismissal An employer is entitled to dismiss all of his workers during a strike. However, if he dismisses only some of the strikers, or if he sacks some or all of them after the strike is over, they may succeed in obtaining compensation for UNFAIR DISMISSAL, on grounds of victimisation or retaliation. If he sacks all his employees, but later re-hires some, the others may succeed in a claim.

Non-striking employees dismissed because it is not profitable to keep them may be entitled to compensation for unfair dismissal, unless the dismissal is reasonable in the circumstances. If the result of the strike is that the employer is in financial difficulties, both strikers and non-strikers may be entitled to REDUNDANCY payments if they are sacked because the employer's business has fallen off. The employer cannot refuse to make redundancy payments by arguing that if the employees had remained at work no redundancies would have been necessary.

When there is a 'lock-out'

Instead of dismissing striking workers, an employer can simply shut down all or part of their place of work, for which he cannot be sued for unfair dismissal. In those circumstances, an employer must, however, give notice of the 'lock-out', otherwise the workers may be entitled to claim wages for the period of notice. The length of notice depends upon each employee's contract.

Wages An employer is not required to pay his workers while they are on strike, nor does he have to pay his share of their national insurance contributions or any other benefits. In practice, some return-to-work agreements contain a clause under which the employer pays the wages he withheld during the strike.

Discipline An employer cannot take disciplinary action – such as demotion – against a striker or strike-leader unless that person consents to the action or his contract specifically authorises it.

If a worker has been wrongfully disciplined for his part in a strike, he is entitled to leave his job and claim UNFAIR DISMISSAL on grounds of victimisation.

What workers may do

Workers are not required by law to give advance notice of a strike, or to have their action recognised by a trade union.

But if notice is given, it should be worded carefully, making clear that the workers are only striking – not terminating their employment – to ensure that their rights to EMPLOYMENT PROTECTION and length-of-service benefits do not suffer. Workers who gave notice of resignation instead of a strike notice would also imperil their claims to redundancy pay and unfair dismissal awards.

Picketing Strikers engaged in a 'trade dispute' may set up pickets in public places. But not on private property.

Pickets may picket outside the employer's premises which are their own place of work, but not outside any other premises of their employer or another company. However, a trade union official is allowed to picket premises which are not his place of work if he is with members of his union, whom he personally represents, at their place of work, and strikers who have been sacked can picket the premises where they used to work. But they must not form an obstruction or disobey a police order to move when the police apprehend a breach of the peace.

As long as the pickets are picketing their own place of work it does not matter that they are not members of the union on strike or that the strike is unofficial.

Pickets may hand out and receive information – on leaflets, for example – about the dispute. They may attempt peacefully to persuade others not to work and to support their cause. But they may not use threats or intimidation, which are criminal offences. *See:* PICKETING

Other action

Strikers may not damage their employer's business in other ways – for example, by encouraging consumers to

OTHER FORMS OF INDUSTRIAL ACTION

Without embarking on an all-out strike, workers can adopt several lawful forms of protest that do not make them liable to dismissal without compensation.

They can, for example, refuse to work overtime – provided they are not obliged to by contract – or apply all contractual working rules literally and pedantically, in order to slow production.

The advantage of such action to the workers is that they are paid in full during their action, whereas they would not receive wages while on strike.

They are, however, considered to have broken their contract of employment if their action substantially disrupts their employer's business – in other words, if it is effective. In such a case, if an employer dismissed all the workers involved in the action while it was in progress, he would probably not be liable for a claim for unfair dismissal.

boycott his products, for which he can sue them for damages.

Sit-ins Strikers who defy a 'lock-out' and persist in attending their normal place of work are not acting unlawfully unless they use or threaten violence to enter – entering in large numbers, for example – by pushing a security guard or by breaking a window. For such offences, they can be fined up to £1,000 and be imprisoned for 6 months.

A company may employ a large number of people, but the fact that they all attempt to enter together is taken in law as evidence that violence is being threatened.

If they enter peacefully, however, and occupy only those parts of the plant where they are normally entitled to be, they cannot be evicted without a court order. *See:* TRESPASS

When the Government can declare a state of emergency

When essential services are disrupted by an industrial dispute, the Government can advise the Queen to declare a 'state of emergency', in which the armed forces and police are called in to ensure the supply and distribution of food, fuel and other essential commodities. Under its EMERGENCY POWERS, the Government cannot abolish the right to strike or introduce conscription, but it can severely restrict the effectiveness of a strike.

How to obtain financial support during a strike

Workers are not usually paid wages while on strike and are not entitled to any state assistance – except to meet the needs of their dependants or in cases of urgent need.

If a strike is 'official' – recognised by a trade union – members of the union may be awarded strike pay, a weekly subsistence allowance smaller than their normal earnings. Payment is at the union's discretion and members have no automatic right to it.

Strikers are not paid unemployment benefit, however justified their cause. Even if an employer has failed to fulfil his obligations – by, for example, not providing adequate lighting or heating, or withholding agreed bonuses – benefit is not usually payable to workers when

MAINTAINING ESSENTIAL
SUPPLIES

If the nation's essential supplies of fuel and food are threatened the Government can advise the Queen to declare a state of emergency, which allows the armed forces to be called in to distribute vital commodities.

work is lost because of a trade dispute.

Workers who are laid off because others have gone on strike are entitled to unemployment benefit only if they can prove that they are not participating in, or directly affected by, the dispute.

For example, a worker who is laid off because he refuses to cross a picket line is considered to be participating in the strike and cannot draw benefit.

Workers who stand to be affected by the issue disputed in the strike – if, for example, the striking union is seeking extra bonuses for all staff, not only its members – cannot claim unemployment benefit.

Anyone disqualified for unemployment benefit because of a trade dispute is not entitled to supplementary benefit for his own needs. He can, however, claim supplementary benefit for his wife and children, if they live with him, and for the whole of his rates and reasonable rent or mortgage interest.

He will get benefit for his dependants only when he has exhausted the current period of his wages – 1 month after going on strike if he is paid monthly, or 1 week if his wages are weekly. And if the last week's wages, together with any other income, are more than twice the family's needs under the normal supplementary benefit rules, the excess is treated as income for the following week.

A means test is applied to a married

striker's savings and other resources – including those of his family. He cannot claim supplementary benefit if he has savings or capital of £2,000 or more.

How the new Supplementary Benefit rules work

From November 1980, new rules began to operate. Supplementary benefit entitlement for a striker's family was reduced by £12 a week, to make unions meet more of the costs of strikes. If a striker actually gets £12 a week from his union, it is not counted again when benefit is being worked out.

Any refunds of PAYE tax, paid because he is not earning, are now fully taken into account. All but £4 of any other earnings he may have are also deducted from the family's benefit entitlement. And all but £4 of his wife's earnings are taken into account, too.

A woman striker cannot claim supplementary benefit for herself, but if she is living with her husband and he is sick, unemployed or a pensioner, he can make a claim. A single or divorced woman who has dependent children can claim supplementary benefit for them while she is on strike.

Under the Social Security (No. 2) Act 1980, unmarried strikers without dependent children, who used to be able to claim payments in cases of urgent need, cannot claim anything to cover the period while they are on strike. The same rule applies against workers who have been laid off because of a strike – unless they can prove that they are not taking part or are not directly affected.

When claiming benefit during or directly after a strike, a claimant must produce proof of his family's income, savings and expenses. He should take with him:

● Some recent payslips for himself and his wife.

● Child benefit, pension, or any allowance books.

● Rent or mortgage payment book.

● Any rates demands or large outstanding bills.

● Bank book or savings statement.

During a strike, the local social security office often cannot cope with the extra claims, and special temporary offices may be set up for the strikers. Their address will be obtainable from the social security office, unemploy-

WHEN TAX IS REPAID

If a strike extends beyond the end of a tax year, or lasts longer than a few weeks, a striker may be entitled to a refund of income tax – as the deductions under PAYE whilst he was working did not take into account a period when he would not be earning.

However, from April 1982 the Government is proposing that tax refunds will be deferred until after the strike is over.

The refund, when due, may be made automatically by the employer under the PAYE system, or repaid direct by the Inland Revenue after the end of the tax year.

If the strike is a short one, he may still be owed some overpaid tax but does not need to make a claim: it is refunded by his employer adjusting his PAYE code when he returns to work.

---

ment benefit office and the trade union involved in the strike.

On resuming work, a striker – whether married or single – is entitled to apply for a loan of supplementary benefit to tide him over until he receives his next pay packet. Payment is subject to a means test. The loan is interest-free and the requirements of the former striker and his family are assessed as though he were normally unemployed. If an advance on earnings is available, it is taken into account. If the benefit payable on loan is less than £3 in any week, no payment is made.

The social security office notifies the employer of the loan and he repays it by making deductions from the worker's wages. The deduction from each week's wages is half the amount by which they exceed the 'protected earnings', which are £8 more than the basic supplementary benefit level for the worker and his family. The protected earnings are calculated by the social security office, which informs the employer.

Such loans are given to provide for the needs of a striker and his family only for the first 15 days after a strike.

If he is still in need after that – if, for example, he is paid only monthly and his employer refuses to give him an advance of wages – he can apply for supplementary benefits because of urgent need, to see him through until he is paid. But he will normally have to pay

that back directly to his local social security office.

STUDENT

How people are helped to gain higher qualifications

Pupils who reach the required academic standard at school, or by taking adult education classes, can usually receive higher education with the aid of a local authority grant.

However, there is no automatic right to a university or polytechnic place – and certainly not to the place of your choice.

The Universities Central Council on Admissions offers qualified candidates up to five choices of university. If you are not accepted by any of those, there are clearing schemes which enable you to apply to other universities which still have vacancies for the coming year.

Teacher-training course applications are dealt with in a similar way by a central register and clearing house. Art and design courses also have a central register. For other courses at polytechnics and colleges, you apply direct to the institution of your choice.

University and college admissions tutors decide whom to accept.

How grants are awarded

A student resident in the United Kingdom for the past 3 years is eligible for a grant if he or she is enrolled for:

● A first-degree course at a university or polytechnic.

● Other courses designated by the Department of Education as being on the same level as a first-degree course – for example, teacher training and other specialised training.

The standard rates of a maintenance grant for 1980–1 are:

● £1,695 for students in London, not living at home.

● £1,430 for students elsewhere, not living at home.

● £1,125 for students living at home.

The tuition fees are also paid.

Additional allowances are payable where the course requires attendance for more than 30 weeks a year, for students over 26 years of age who were previously employed, and in certain other prescribed circumstances.

The fees and compulsory student union subscriptions of all eligible students are paid.

The amount of maintenance grant actually paid to a student is arrived at by deducting from the standard rates a sum to take account of the resources of the student and parents. A grant may be reduced where the student's private income exceeds £265 (apart from vacation earnings and scholarship income).

If a student is under 25 and he has not been self-supporting for 3 years, his parents' gross income for the tax year which ended in the previous April is assessed and deductions for dependants and mortgage, insurance and pension payments are allowed. The parents are

---

THE STUDENT TEACHER WHO LIVED WITH A MAN IN HER ROOM

A college can expel a student who breaks its rules, provided it conforms to the proper procedure.

Miss Ward was a student at a teacher training college in Bradford. One night she was found to have a man in her room at the hall of residence. She admitted that he had, in breach of college rules, been living with her in her room for 2 months.

She was allowed to state her case, in accordance with regulations, before a disciplinary committee consisting of three members each of the governing body, staff and students. The committee recommended expulsion.

When the case came before the Court of Appeal in July 1971, Miss Ward claimed that she should have had a right of appeal to the governing body. She also complained that the director of education had taken part in the deliberations of the committee although not a member.

DECISION

The court dismissed the appeal. It found that under the college regulations Miss Ward had no right to be re-heard by the governing body. The director of education was criticised for taking part in the deliberations, but the court decided the committee was entitled to take his advice.

then expected to make a contribution to the student's upkeep, depending upon the amount of their net income. In 1980–1 parents with a residual income of £5,800 or lower, after allowances had been deducted, would pay nothing.

If parents refuse to disclose their income, a maximum grant of £385 is usually paid to the student. That amount is also the minimum grant paid to any eligible student.

Part-time students Supplementary benefit may be paid to part-time students if they are registered for work and if their studies do not take up more than 21 hours a week.

A student should check whether supplementary benefit is affected before enrolling for a part-time course.

Young students Someone still at school or taking A-levels or a similar full-time course at a technical or further-education college may be paid supplementary benefit in rare cases of hardship – for example, a school pupil over 16 who is an orphan, or a schoolgirl mother.

Vacations Students can claim supplementary benefit during the summer vacation on the same conditions as other unemployed people once they have registered for work. The benefit is not normally paid during the Christmas and Easter vacations unless the student has to pay for his accommodation.

Married students A married student whose grant does not include the normal allowances for dependants – perhaps because his circumstances have changed since the grant was awarded – may be eligible for help under a special hardship allowances scheme. Details can be obtained from: Department of Health and Social Security, Students' Unit, Poulton-le-Fylde, Blackpool FY6 8NW.

Paying national insurance contributions

A student of 16 or over who does any part-time or holiday work should ask the local Careers Office for an insurance number. He becomes liable for Class 1 NATIONAL INSURANCE CONTRIBUTIONS if he earns more than a certain amount in any week (£27 in 1981–2).

If the student is on a sandwich course he is liable for Class 1 contributions during the study periods if his employer continues to pay his wages.

Most social security benefits can be obtained only when certain contribution conditions have been satisfied. Those conditions can be satisfied either by the student having paid contributions or sometimes by him being credited with them.

A student is credited with contributions for each year up to and including the one in which he is 17, and for later years up to and including the first year in which he actually pays contributions.

If a school leaver starts work and then takes up a course of study before he is 21, he is credited with contributions for every year until the end of the course.

However, as well as credited contributions, a student claiming sickness or unemployment benefit must also have actually paid a certain number of contributions in any one tax year.

The special case of married students

If a married student is not 25 years old and has not been self-supporting for 3 years his grant is reduced by the appropriate parental contribution. For other married students, the contribution of his or her spouse is taken into account, but the grant is increased to take account of any dependants.

Obtaining a grant

As soon as a student applies for a place at a university, polytechnic or other college, he or she should ask the local education authority for a grant application form. A delay in applying may mean that the grant is not paid until after the term starts.

Discretionary grants Even if a course is not rated at first-degree level, and a student does not automatically qualify for a grant, local education authorities have the power to make grants at their own discretion.

They decide what courses to support, and how much to pay. Details are available for each local education office.

Joining or refusing to join a student union

At most colleges, membership of the student union is automatic.

Some colleges provide for exemption from student union membership on conscientious objection grounds.

Student unions are represented on advisory or decision-making committees, at some colleges, so that students have a voice in how their institutions are run.

Accepting college discipline on entry

By accepting a place in a college, a student agrees to obey any of its rules and regulations, brought to his notice in its prospectus or other documents.

These explain how he can be disciplined and the power of the college to exclude him for unsatisfactory progress in his studies.

Different colleges have different rules. Normally they give the student the right to appear personally in front of a committee before a serious punishment, such as expulsion or suspension, is imposed on him.

Even though regulations are silent on the point, a college will not be entitled to expel a student on disciplinary grounds without first giving him the opportunity to state his case. However, he cannot insist on having a lawyer to represent him at the hearing.

The college must adhere closely to its own regulations. For example, it may allow a student who fails an examination to sit it again or take an oral exam before he can be excluded from the course.

Most universities have a Visitor – usually the Queen, with the Lord Chancellor acting for her – who has the final say in all disputes over admitting or excluding students, or in disciplining them.

Oxford and Cambridge universities have no Visitor but each college has – although the only students over whom a College Visitor has jurisdiction are Scholars of the college.

In such cases, an aggrieved student must pursue his complaints through the Visitor: he cannot take court action.

If an Oxford or Cambridge student is in dispute with his university or a commoner or exhibitioner is in dispute with his college, or if a student is in dispute with a body that has no Visitor – for example, a college administered by a local education authority – his ultimate appeal is to the High Court.

Hardship at college

Even if a student's grant is inadequate – perhaps because his parents are unable or unwilling to pay their share – he cannot normally obtain SUPPLEMENTARY BENEFIT during term time.

Exceptions are made, however, when a student is a single parent or if he is severely disabled and would, therefore, not normally be expected to register for work.

SUB-CONTRACTOR

When work you ordered is farmed out

If you engage a contractor to do work for you, it is worth making clear whether, under that contract, he is entitled to employ sub-contractors.

If the work depends on his personal skill, such as painting a mural, he is not allowed to do so. If the work involves a more general skill, however, such as painting your house, he can do so unless you both agree a contract stipulating specifically that he cannot.

When a contractor employs a sub-contractor, he is responsible for paying him; you are responsible only to the head contractor for payment. Similarly, it is the contractor, not the sub-contractor, who is responsible to you for the work being carried out properly.

If the sub-contractor damages your property through negligence, however, he bears the responsibility, not necessarily the contractor. It might be much more difficult to recover damages from a self-employed tradesman than from an established firm of contractors.

SUBPOENA

How a witness can be ordered to appear in court

If the evidence of a WITNESS is sought by either side in a court case, the court can instruct him to attend by issuing a SUMMONS. When the case is in the High Court, such a summons is known as a subpoena – Latin for 'under penalty' – because someone who disobeys any type of witness summons can be

RELUCTANT WITNESS

When a witness is reluctant to appear – perhaps because of strong feelings of loyalty – the prosecution may issue a subpoena, compelling attendance.

'Subpoena, sir'

punished for CONTEMPT OF COURT.

A subpoena or any other witness summons must be served on the witness in person – not posted or left in the hands of someone else at the same address. It is not valid unless the witness is given 'conduct money' – any expenses necessary for travel to the court, food or accommodation – paid by whoever applies for the summons.

The application procedure is usually handled by a lawyer, but someone who wants to apply personally is entitled to seek the guidance of court staff.

If a witness is unable to attend because the date of a hearing is unsuitable, he should notify the court office immediately. It may be possible to have the hearing postponed.

A reluctant witness can ask a court to set aside a subpoena, but he will not succeed unless he shows that it is seriously unfair to force him to appear.

In practice, subpoenas are seldom used to force people to give evidence against their will. Such witnesses would be likely to remain unco-operative.

In many cases a subpoena is used to save a witness from embarrassment, when he does not wish to seem too willing to give evidence against someone to whom he owes loyalty. For example, someone who holds office in a club or a union may be unhappy about giving evidence against one of his members – but being called by subpoena enables him to show that he had no choice.

SUB-TENANCY

The position when the landlord is himself a tenant

The main problem facing someone who rents all or part of a house or flat from a sitting tenant is to know whether that tenant is allowed by his own landlord to sub-let. The answer to this question vitally affects the sub-tenant's security of tenure.

Often the sitting tenant offers only a verbal assurance to his sub-tenant that he is within his rights to sub-let, but he may be under a misapprehension or telling a lie.

Ask for a written undertaking not from him, but from his own landlord that the sub-letting is allowed.

If the tenant is unwilling to supply such a written agreement, it may be an indication that he is in breach of his own tenancy in sub-letting. The prospective sub-tenant must then decide whether he wishes to take a chance on moving in without the protection given to a properly authorised sub-tenant. *See:* LANDLORD AND TENANT

If the head landlord does not agree to his being there, a sub-tenant is a trespasser with no rights if he is asked to leave by the head landlord. *See:* TRESPASS

When a sub-tenancy can be lawful

The position of an unauthorised sub-tenant depends on whether the sitting tenant remains on the premises. If so, the sub-tenant is treated as having a resident landlord (if the arrangement was made after August 14, 1974), and he will have no security of tenure, even from a rent tribunal, unless his sub-tenancy was granted before the Housing Act 1980. *See:* EVICTION

The landlord, however, needs a court order if the sub-tenant refuses to leave, and the court may be persuaded to exercise its discretion to suspend the order for up to 3 months.

The sub-tenant has no right to go to a rent officer to have his share of the rent registered, but he can ask a tribunal to fix a 'reasonable' rent.

If the main tenant surrenders his tenancy and leaves the property, however, an authorised sub-tenant becomes the main tenant. Provided that the arrangement to share was made after August 14, 1974, he then has full protection under the Rent Act.

If the arrangement was made before August 14, 1974, the protection given an authorised sub-tenant depends on whether he shared the use of any essential accommodation, other than a bathroom or lavatory, with the landlord. If he did, he has only the protection of the rent tribunal; if he did not, he has full protection under the Rent Act.

When a shorthold tenancy is involved

A sub-tenant of a shorthold tenant has no better security of tenure than the shorthold tenant has, as against the head landlord, even if the sub-tenancy is not itself shorthold. *See:* SHORT TENANCY

When there is overcrowding in a rented home

Tenants and sub-tenants should beware lest the presence of too many people in the same house or flat results in OVERCROWDING.

Not only is overcrowding a criminal offence, by both landlord and occupiers: of more practical significance, it can mean that all the occupiers lose their security of tenure.

A landlord can get a county court order granting him possession of an overcrowded house.

SUICIDE

What happens when someone takes his own life

It is not an offence to commit or attempt suicide but it is a crime to persuade or help someone to kill himself. Anyone who does so can be sentenced to up to 14 years' imprisonment. If a terminally ill patient, for example, asked a doctor for pills to enable him to end his life, the doctor could be prosecuted for aiding and abetting suicide.

Suicide pacts When two people, or a group, agree to help each other commit suicide, but one of them survives, he can be prosecuted for MANSLAUGHTER if it

can be proved that he actually killed the other; otherwise, he can be tried for aiding suicide. He cannot be charged with MURDER unless there is evidence that he intended to survive.

SUMMONS

An order to appear in court

When an alleged criminal offence is not considered serious enough to require a person's ARREST, he or she is ordered by summons to appear in court and answer the charge.

A summons is a document stating the charge and setting out when and where the person must appear. It can be issued only by a magistrate or justices' clerk, after he receives details of the allegation – usually from the police – but the same procedure can be used in a PRIVATE PROSECUTION.

A policeman or court officer delivers the document directly to the accused person if possible. But it can be left with someone else at the accused person's last known address, or sent by post as a registered letter or by recorded delivery.

If someone fails to appear in court after a summons is issued, the case may be adjourned until the magistrate is sure that the summons was received. If there is no doubt of that, the magistrate may:
● Deal with a minor case in the accused person's absence.
● Issue a warrant for his arrest.

However, if someone who is summonsed knows that he cannot appear at the time stated, or that having to appear will cause serious difficulties, he should contact the court immediately and ask for an adjournment – the legal term for postponement of a case. An adjournment can also be granted if he needs more time to prepare his defence, or if witnesses are unable to appear. *See:* CRIMINAL PROCEEDINGS

However, a summons is not confined only to criminal cases – for example, a person may be served with a 'witness summons' in a county court case.

Time limit Details of an allegation – called the 'information' – must be laid before a magistrate within 6 months of the alleged offence. If a summons shows that the information was not laid in time, the case must be dismissed.

SUNDAY TRADING

When a trader may open for business on Sunday

Most shopkeepers and traders are barred by law from opening for business on a Sunday. If a trader is convicted of trading on a Sunday, he may – under the Shops Act 1950 – be fined up to £50 for a first offence and £200 for any subsequent conviction.

There are, however, certain shops exempt from the Act and therefore entitled to trade on a Sunday. These are shops that sell:
● Meals or refreshments, whether for consumption on the premises or not. However, fish-and-chip shops may not open.
● Newly cooked provisions, including cooked or partly cooked tripe.
● Sweets, chocolates, sugar confectionery, ice cream and table waters.
● Fresh fruit and vegetables – but not tinned or bottled – and flowers.
● Fresh milk and cream – but not tinned or dried milk or cream. However, clotted cream may be sold even if it is in a tin.
● Intoxicating liquors.
● Tobacco and smokers' requisites.
● Books and stationery, at bookstalls in certain railway stations, bus stations and airports.
● Newspapers, periodicals and magazines.

BUYING AND SELLING
ON A SUNDAY

Market traders who want to do business on a Sunday must have permission from the local authority.

- Medicines and medical and surgical supplies at a chemist.
- Guide books, post cards and reproductions at art galleries and museums.
- Passport photographs.
- Post office business.
- The business of an undertaker.
- Sports goods at places where sport is played.
- Fodder for horses, mules, ponies and donkeys.
- Motor-cycle or aircraft supplies or accessories – but not motor-car supplies or accessories.

If a shop opens to sell any of those articles, it must not sell an article that is not exempt. If a shopkeeper does so, he is committing an offence. A customer who buys goods that are not exempt does not commit an offence.

There are certain other exceptions. For example, a local authority at a holiday resort may allow shops to open on specified Sundays, if they sell:
- Articles required for bathing or fishing.
- Photographic needs.
- Toys and souvenirs.
- Books, stationery, photographs, reproductions and post cards.
- Food.

However, such a shop must not open on more than 18 Sundays in a year.

Someone who operates a mobile shop is entitled to operate on Sunday, but a stall that is set up each week in the same place is not entitled to do so. However, there are certain special exceptions – for example, stallholders in Petticoat Lane, London are entitled by the local authority to operate on a Sunday.

A shop run by someone of Jewish faith or a denomination that observes Saturday as the sabbath, is entitled to open for business on a Sunday until 2 p.m. However, he must close all day on Saturdays and be registered with the local authority. *See:* SHOPS

SUPERVISION ORDER

When a court decides to keep an eye on a child

If a court is worried about a child's conduct or situation, but does not think the circumstances warrant taking it into care, it may make a supervision order. The parents will usually agree to co-

TAKING A CHILD AWAY FROM HOME

A supervision order is generally made if the child has been before a court for some offence or because he is at risk of harm – perhaps as the victim of domestic disputes between his parents or if he is so out of control as to be in danger.

operate for otherwise the child may be removed from home. *See:* CHILDREN IN CARE

Normally a supervision order is made after a child has been brought before the court for committing an offence, or in care proceedings – for example because the child is at risk, being abused or neglected or in moral danger. In rare instances, however, an order is made as a result of domestic proceedings between his parents.

When an order is made

The aim of a supervision order is to bridge the gap between taking a child from its home and community or leaving it without supervision and guidance.

A supervisor is appointed. If the child is under 13 years of age the supervisor is a local authority social worker, unless the local authority asks a probation officer to be the supervisor because he has been responsible for another member of the child's household.

The duty of the supervisor is to assist, advise and befriend the child and direct its activities.

Intermediate treatment

One possible method of dealing with a child under a supervision order is called intermediate treatment. It seeks to provide an alternative to delinquency by involving him or her in a wide range

of interests and activities with other young people.

Many authorities provide day centres for intermediate treatment that offer programmes, some educational or vocational. The order can also empower the supervisor to send the child to a residential centre for up to 30 days a year.

Other activities include such things as Outward Bound courses on rock climbing and sailing, or instruction in such things as vehicle maintenance or printing. The supervisor discusses alternatives with the child and tries to arrange the best programme for him or her. *See:* YOUNG OFFENDERS

Ending an order

Except when they are made in domestic proceedings, orders may last for up to 3 years – but not beyond a child's 18th birthday, unless the juvenile committed a criminal offence. At any time during the period it is in force, the supervisor, the child or its parents can apply to the court to have the order varied or discharged.

If, for example, the order originally contained a requirement that the child should receive psychiatric treatment, it can be asked to drop it if it no longer seems necessary. Similarly, the parents might be able to put forward good reasons for not requiring the child to go away to a residential centre again.

If the supervisor thinks the child is not responding to treatment, he can apply for the order to be carried out and the child to be taken into care. If, on the other hand, he thinks it has responded so well that treatment is no longer necessary, he can ask the court to discharge the order before it is due to expire.

SUPPLEMENTARY BENEFIT

Money paid to people whose income is less than they need to live on

Anyone who is not in full time employment and whose income is below a certain level is entitled to supplementary benefit. The amount payable depends upon the person's needs and those of his wife and dependent children and upon how much other money he has coming in.

AVAILABLE FOR WORK

Anyone who claims supplementary benefit must sign on for possible work at the local Job Centre – unless he is over pension age or has approved reasons for not doing so.

To qualify you must be over 16 and living in Britain.

If you are under retirement age – 65 for men, 60 for women – benefit is known as supplementary allowance. Over retirement age it is called supplementary pension. In the case of a married couple living together – or an unmarried couple living as man and wife – normally only the man can claim.

If you are in full-time work you cannot normally claim, except in an emergency, however little you earn. But if you have at least one child you may be entitled to FAMILY INCOME SUPPLEMENT.

To show that he is available for work, anyone claiming supplementary allowance is expected to sign on at the local Job Centre as a condition of receiving benefit, unless he has a good reason for not looking for work – such as illness or severe disablement or children to look after. There he is liable to be offered a job and may have his benefit reduced if he refuses it.

Some people are not required to sign on each week and receive their benefit automatically by post.

Single parents, whether men or women, anyone needed at home to look after a severely disabled relative who qualifies for an ATTENDANCE ALLOWANCE, and a woman expecting a baby within 11 weeks, are excused from signing on.

A Supplementary Benefit Officer will decide whether you have to sign on, and if you disagree with his decision you can appeal to an independent appeal tribunal.

Benefit will not be paid in certain circumstances – to full-time students, for example, or to people who persistently refuse jobs that are available to them.

Immigrants Immigrants are entitled to benefit on the same terms as people who were born in Britain. If they are under pensionable age and able to work they are normally required to register for employment.

Benefit covers the needs of the claimant and his wife and children living with him. He cannot claim for a wife or children left behind in his country of origin.

In exceptional cases, benefit can be paid to cover the cost of repatriation if the person concerned has been unable to settle in Britain and wishes to leave, if there will be a saving in public funds, and if there is no other way of finding the money. *See:* IMMIGRATION

Temporary visitors People from EEC and certain other European countries who come to Britain to seek work can claim supplementary benefit – but if they do, they may be asked by the immigration authorities to leave. Normally, a temporary visitor from abroad cannot claim benefit except in an emergency – for example, if his money has been stolen – or to enable him to return home. Benefit can also be paid for a limited period to someone awaiting the result of an immigration appeal.

How income is assessed

Supplementary benefit is intended to bring a claimant's income up to the level of what he needs to live at a modest standard. The resources and requirements of a claimant and his wife and children under 16 or still at school living in the same household, are counted together.

Resources include other social security benefits. Child benefit, family income supplement, weekly maternity allowance and most national insurance benefits are taken into account in full. Mobility allowance, attendance allowance, maternity grant and death grant are ignored.

So are a private pension, sick pay, weekly redundancy payments and students' grants (though in certain cases £2 a week of a grant can be ignored).

Maintenance payments – voluntary or ordered by a court – are counted in full if they are actually received.

Dividends and other income from capital are ignored.

Part-time earnings are taken into account after deducting income tax, national insurance contributions, expenses such as fares to and from work and, in the case of a single parent or working wife, the cost of child minding.

Of the net amount remaining, £4 is ignored for a claimant and £4 for his wife. A single parent has the first £4 of earnings ignored and also half of any earnings between £4 and £20. A child's earnings are ignored entirely. Thus, £8 of the net earnings of an unemployed man and his wife can be ignored – £4 each.

A person in full-time work cannot claim benefit, but a man whose wife is in full-time work can claim if their combined income is low enough.

Voluntary payments by relatives (other than the claimant's husband or wife or the father of her children), friends or charities are ignored if they are for television rental or for items not covered by supplementary benefit – such as holidays or part of a high charge for an old people's home. Before such payments are made, it is advisable to find out whether they will result in a reduction of supplementary benefit.

The first £4 a week of other voluntary payments from the same sources or of most kinds of income from other sources not mentioned above – including war or industrial disablement pensions and war or industrial widows' pensions – is ignored.

If you have savings of up to £2,000 they are ignored completely. But if you have over this amount you are not eligible to claim supplementary benefit at all. Savings include money in the National Savings Bank, a building society, premium bonds, shares or other investments. They also include any property you may own – but *not* your own home.

Calculating requirements

The main rules for calculating how much money a claimant needs each week are laid down in the Supplementary Benefits Act 1976, the Social Security Act 1980 and other regulations.

There are fixed amounts intended to cover normal living expenses, such as food, heat, light, clothing, and small household items such as soap and toilet paper. Rent and allowances for special needs such as heating are added separately. Major household items such as bedding or furniture may also be claimed for separately, in certain circumstances.

There are two sets of rates, basic rates payable to people required to register for work and others under pensionable age who have been drawing supplementary benefit for up to 1 year; and long-term rates, payable to claimants over pensionable age – in the case of a married couple, the man must be over 65 – and younger claimants who are not required to work and who have been on supplementary benefit for 1 year or more continuously. Gaps of up to 13 weeks in the 1 year period are ignored.

The scales of weekly rates in 1981 were:

	Basic	Long term
Married couple	£34.60	£43.45
Single person paying rent or owner occupier	£21.30	£27.15
Anyone living in another person's household, except as a lodger, aged:		
18 or over	£17.05	£21.70
16–17	£13.10	£16.65
11–15	£10.90	–
under 11	£7.30	–

Claimant over 80 If a claimant or his wife is over 80, both get an extra 25p a week benefit.
Blind people Blind or partially blind people are entitled to £1.25 more a week. *See:* BLINDNESS
Lodgers and hospital patients Those rates do not apply to lodgers (except those living with very close relatives), hospital patients and other people provided with board and lodging in residential homes or hostels. They get a small allowance for personal expenses in addition to the board and lodging

charge – but a high board and lodging charge may not be met in full. *See:* HOSPITAL; LODGER
Strikers Special rules apply to strikers, who can normally claim only for their wives and children. *See:* STRIKE
Voluntary unemployed The requirements of people regarded as voluntarily unemployed are normally reduced by either 20 or 40 per cent of the rate for a single person. *See:* UNEMPLOYMENT, Voluntary

How supplementary benefit is calculated

The weekly amount of benefit payable is worked out by taking the requirements of a claimant and his family and deducting their resources. For example, the requirements of a married man with a wife and 2 children aged 4 and 6 living with him are assessed at £49.20 – the £34.60 married couple's allowance, £7.30 for each child – plus rent. If he qualifies for long-term benefit, his requirements are put at £58.05 – that is, £8.85 extra for a married couple – plus rent.

In addition he will receive at least £1.40 a week for extra heating, because there is a child under 5, and he may be entitled to other payments for extra needs such as a special diet.

If he has any income, with the exceptions mentioned on p. 678, it is deducted from the amount of his requirements, and the remainder is paid to him as benefit.

It is seldom possible to say in advance exactly how much a claimant can receive. Each case is considered separately, and the claimant is notified of his weekly entitlement by the local social

security office.

A more detailed calculation is provided on request. If you disagree with the amount awarded to you, you can appeal against the decision by writing to the local social security office.

Allowances for rent or mortgage

The amount added for housing costs usually depends upon how much rent, rates or mortgage the claimant actually pays.
Rent A tenant is normally entitled to receive the full amount of rent and rates he pays – calculated on a weekly basis. But if the rent includes lighting and heating, a deduction is made of the amount included for them.

If that is not known, a fixed amount is deducted – in 1981, £4.35 for heating, £5.70 for heating, lighting, hot water and cooking.

If part of the accommodation is sublet, the money received, minus a small amount for incidental expenses, is deducted from the rent allowance.

If the claimant's household includes anybody other than his wife and dependent children, the rent addition is reduced by £4.60 for each individual or family unit – but only £2.15 is deducted for a person who is under 18 or himself receiving supplementary benefit.
Unreasonable rent If the Supplementary Benefit Officer thinks that the rent for private accommodation is unreasonably high, he will allow only the 'fair rent'. *See:* RENT REGISTRATION

If a fair rent has not been registered, the social security office takes advice from the rent officer or the local authority on what a fair rent would be, and the rent addition is limited to that amount

WHEN BENEFIT CAN BE PAID IN EMERGENCY

In cases of urgent need, when help must be given at once – such as after a flood or fire, or the loss of a pay packet – benefit can be paid to a person who would not normally be eligible.

Urgent-need payments can also be made, in limited circumstances, to other people whose need is too urgent to wait for the normal weekly benefit pay day or who, though not entitled under the normal rules, cannot be left without food or shelter.

Urgent-need payments are made at a reduced rate, and in most cases the claimant has to repay the money unless his normal income is below supplementary benefit level. If the amount involved is £10 or less he is not obliged to repay it.

The Supplementary Benefit Officer decides whether a claimant is entitled to an urgent-need payment and how much it should be. If the claimant disagrees with the amount allowed – or if the claim is refused – he can appeal.

plus rates. But if an application for registration of a fair rent has been made, the full rent is allowed.

The addition for rent can also be restricted on the grounds that the accommodation is unnecessarily large or situated in an unnecessarily expensive area, and it is reasonable to expect the claimant to look for somewhere cheaper. In deciding whether he can reasonably be expected to move, the benefit officer must take account of the age and state of health of the claimant and his wife and children, his job prospects and the effect of a move on the children's education.

If the claimant could afford the rent when he took it on and is doing his best to find cheaper accommodation, the rent is met in full for up to a year, provided that it is not more than the 'fair rent'.

Rent and rate rebates Rent and rate rebates are not awarded to people continuing to draw supplementary benefit. If a rebate has already been awarded it is withdrawn by the local authority after supplementary benefit has been paid for 8 weeks.

Anyone receiving only a small amount of supplementary benefit may be better off by claiming a rent or rate rebate instead. If you think you might benefit in that way, ask your local social security office for advice and a claim form.

Someone else's household Anyone getting supplementary benefit and living in someone else's household, but not as a lodger – for example, a son or daughter of working age, or an elderly relative – receives a fixed rent addition. In 1981 the amount was £2.15 a week.

Mortgage payments The rent addition for an owner-occupier consists of the interest payable on his mortgage – but not the capital – his rates and a fixed allowance for repairs and insurance.

The repairs and insurance allowance was £1.25 a week in 1981.

The same adjustments are made as for a tenant – that is, any money from sub-letting and the share of a non-dependent member of the household are deducted. Mortgage payments are accepted as reasonable unless the property is unnecessarily large or situated in an unnecessarily expensive area. In that case, whether and for how long the mortgage interest and other outgoings

will be met in full is decided in the same way as for a high rent – taking into account whether the claimant could afford it when he took it on and whether it is reasonable to expect him to move.

Capital repayments Supplementary benefit is not allowed for capital repayments on a mortgage. However, any money you receive from a charity or other source, such as sub-letting, for the specific purpose of making the capital repayments will be ignored.

If you cannot raise the money to make these payments, your building society or local authority may be prepared to accept payments of interest only, unless you remain on supplementary benefit for a long period.

Allowances paid for extra needs

If a claimant has extra needs – such as a special diet or extra heating – he can claim additional payments. These can be either extra weekly payments for 'additional requirements' or a lump sum 'single payment'.

Additional requirements These are intended to cover regular extra expenses. The circumstances in which payments can be made are explained in detail in the official *Supplementary Benefit Handbook*. You may be able to borrow it from your local library – otherwise the local social security office should have a copy that you can consult. If you qualify, additional requirements are just as much part of your legal entitlement as the basic benefit rates – they are not discretionary.

The most common additional requirements are:
● Heating. Payments are made in cases of restricted mobility, or illness that requires extra heating, or where the accommodation is centrally heated or is difficult to heat adequately. There are three rates of heating help – £1.40, £3.40 and £5.40 a week (the last for central heating of 5 or more rooms). The appropriate amount depends on the severity of the need. Supplementary pensioners aged 70 or over, and families who have children under 5 and who are living on a supplementary allowance, get the £1.40 a week automatically, if the claimant is a householder. *See:* FUEL BILL
● Special diet. Additions are paid at one of three weekly rates for claimants needing special diets: complaints such

as diabetes and peptic ulcers – £2.80 in 1981; kidney machine patients – £8 in 1981; and any other diet specified by a doctor – £1.20 in 1981.

In rare cases not covered by the £2.80 addition and where the extra cost is much more than £2.80, the full costs of the diet – not just the extra cost – is allowed as an additional requirement.
● Laundry. If the washing is abnormally heavy, for example because of incontinence, or if none of the adults in the household can do the washing because of illness or infirmity, or if the home lacks washing or drying facilities, payment can be made to cover laundry or launderette expenses. The claimant must pay the first 40p of the weekly expense.
● Baths. For a person who needs more than one bath a week for medical reasons, 20p is allowed for each additional bath needed.

Other additions – for needs such as domestic help, heavy wear and tear of clothing caused by disablement, hire-purchase payments and hospital visiting – are based on the actual or estimated cost incurred in the case.

Long-term benefit Long-term benefit includes a certain amount for additional expenses. Anyone receiving this scale must pay the first 50p of any additional expenses, except for heating.

Single payments A single payment is a lump sum paid for an expense which does not occur regularly. The purposes for which single payments can be made are summarised in a leaflet you can get from any social security office – SB16, *Lump-sum payments for special needs.*

Supplementary Benefit Officers also have power to make payments in cases not otherwise provided for in the regulations, if it is the only way to prevent serious damage or serious risk to the health or safety of the claimant or a member of the family.

A single payment will not be made if the need could be met out of the claimant's savings over £300 or, in the case of a 'health or safety' payment, if the claimant has *any* savings.

The most common needs for which single payments are made are:
● Maternity. The payment covers all essential equipment for the baby which the mother does not already possess and cannot buy out of the £25 maternity grant.

● Funerals. If the claimant has to pay for the funeral of a close relative or member of the household, a single payment is made for the balance of the cost that cannot be met from other sources.

● Bed-clothes. A payment is made to bring the stock of bed-clothes up to 3 sheets (or 2 and an eiderdown), 3 blankets, 1 pillow and 2 pillow cases for each bed. These are the quantities considered adequate by the Chief Supplementary Benefit Officer, but more should be allowed if they are needed.

● Furniture. Payments are made for a wide range of items of furniture and household equipment – including such items as a washing machine or a refrigerator where there is a special need.

If the claimant is over pension age or there is an expectant mother, a child under 16 or someone who is chronically sick or disabled in the family, a payment must be made for all items that are needed. Other claimants are entitled to a payment for furniture only if they are moving into an unfurnished or partly furnished home, or have recently done so, and there is a good reason for the move, or if the item needed is a cooker or heater.

● Repairs and redecoration. Payments can be made for house repairs costing up to £225. If the cost is more than that, the interest on money borrowed for the purpose will be added to the weekly benefit payments. A payment can be made for interior decoration – materials only, not labour – if the claimant has lived in his present home for a year or more.

● Travel costs. Payments are made for fares and, where necessary, overnight accommodation if a claimant or a member of the family makes a journey to visit a close relative in hospital, to look for a job or attend a job interview (unless the fares are paid by the Job Centre or the employer), or for other purposes listed in the regulations – the social security office will advise on whether a particular journey is covered.

● Starting work. Payments are made for essential tools or working clothes and for fares to work for up to 2 weeks before the first pay day.

● Clothes. Before November 1980 most lump-sum payments were for clothing. The new regulations are more restrictive but payments can still be made where clothing is needed because of pregnancy, rapid weight loss or gain, heavy wear and tear caused by illness or disablement, admission to hospital, or accidental loss, damage or destruction of clothing – but not for normal wear and tear or clothes that need replacing because the children have grown out of them.

● Rent arrears and fuel debts. Single payments can be made for these purposes only in exceptional cases – usually where money intended for rent or fuel bills has had to be spent on other essential items for which a single payment could have been made, or where benefit payments due in the past have not been claimed. *See:* FUEL BILL

Paying supplementary benefit to a third party

Supplementary benefit – or part of it – can be paid to somebody other than the claimant, either at the claimant's request, or if the Supplementary Benefit Officer thinks it necessary in order to protect the interests of the claimant or his dependants.

If payment is made direct to a landlord for rent arrears, or to the gas or electricity board to prevent the supply being cut off, the social security office usually pays, and deducts from the benefit payable to the claimant, the amount currently due plus an amount towards the arrears. But if this arrangement results in such a large deduction from the weekly benefit that the claimant is left with too little money to meet other living expenses, he should ask the social security office if it can make a single payment to clear all or part of the arrears, on the grounds that this is the only way of preventing serious risk to health or safety.

Paying to a wife If a man neglects his responsibilities to his family, the benefit officer may decide that his benefit should be paid direct to his wife. This depends upon how seriously in need she is considered to be.

How to claim benefit

If you are unemployed, ask for form B1 at the unemployment benefit office and send it or take it to the social security office, where you will be asked for the information and evidence needed to work out the amount of benefit to which you are entitled.

If you are not registered as unemployed you should use the claim form attached to leaflet SB1, which you can get from any post office or social security office.

Fill in your name and address and send the form to your local social security office. An officer from the DHSS will visit you or ask you to call at the local social security office. He will want the information needed to work out your benefit.

If you are urgently in need of money, take the form – together with any benefit books you have, evidence of rent or mortgage payments, and recent wage packets or pay slips – to the social security office. Benefit can then be posted to you on the same day – or the next day. In an emergency it may be possible to hand you a cheque over the counter, but this is seldom done because of the possibility of fraud.

How to appeal against a decision

If you do not agree with a decision made by the Supplementary Benefit Officer about your entitlement to benefit or the amount payable, you can appeal to a supplementary benefit appeal tribunal. The appeal should be in writing and lodged within 28 days of the disputed decision. A later appeal can be heard only if the tribunal chairman agrees.

You can get an appeal form from your local social security office or you can write a letter. You do not have to give full reasons for the appeal if you do not want to. You need say only 'I appeal against the refusal to pay me supplementary benefit' – or whatever you are appealing against. Then send the form or letter to your local social security office.

At the tribunal The appeal tribunal is an independent local body consisting of a chairman, and two other members – one a trade union representative, the other someone, such as a social worker or magistrate, who has knowledge of local conditions and the problems of people living on low incomes.

The hearing is held locally. You do not have to attend, but if you do you can claim your fares from the clerk of the tribunal.

The local Citizens Advice Bureau will

advise on where to get help in preparing and presenting your case or they may themselves be able to help you. Claimants' unions exist in some areas and they offer free help and advice. If you do present the case yourself you should read the Supplementary Benefits Handbook, which explains the law. It may be obtainable from your local library or you can consult a copy at the social security office. But not everything in the Handbook is law, and the tribunal may be able to make a decision in your favour even if it is not in accordance with the policy explained in the Handbook.

You can also ask at the social security office to see the regulations and the guidance issued to benefit officers by the Chief Supplementary Benefit Officer – but remember that his guidance is not binding.

Tribunal hearings are private – the Press and public are not allowed in – and usually informal. Besides the tribunal members, there is an official from the Department of Health and Social Security. He is known as the presenting officer, and puts forward the Supplementary Benefit Officer's view.

Another official from the Department acts as clerk of the tribunal. He organises the hearing but should not intervene in the proceedings unless asked to do so by the chairman.

You can take witnesses to support your case and you – or whoever presents your case – have the right to put questions to the presenting officer and any witnesses called by him. Members of the tribunal and the presenting officer can put questions to you and your witnesses.

If new evidence is produced during the hearing which you need time to consider or rebut, you can ask the tribunal chairman for an adjournment. If this is granted, however, it may mean several weeks' delay before another hearing is arranged.

Decision When the hearing is over, the tribunal considers its decision, which must be sent to you in writing, together with reasons for the decision.

If you disagree with the decision, you may be able to appeal to a SOCIAL SECURITY COMMISSIONER – but only on a point of law. If you do decide to challenge the decision ask the legal department of your local Citizens Advice Bureau to advise you how to do this.

SURETY
Someone who stands security for another's debt

Sometimes, when money is loaned or goods are bought on credit, the seller or creditor will ask the buyer or borrower to provide a surety – somebody who will pay the debt if the borrower does not.

A person may also stand as surety for someone who is on bail while awaiting a court hearing.

Before you agree to stand as surety, even for a relative or close friend, be certain that if the worst happens you can afford to lose the money involved. After all, the creditor would not ask for a surety unless he had some doubts about the borrower's ability to pay, and you cannot cancel your undertaking to reimburse the lender unless the borrower exercises his right to pull out of his agreement.

You can be a surety in three ways:
● As a guarantor, when you undertake to pay if the person borrowing the money does not.
● By giving an indemnity, which is an undertaking that the supplier can approach you directly for payment without recourse to the borrower.
● By depositing money against non-payment of the debt.

Under the CONSUMER CREDIT Act, the style and content of documents to be signed when someone becomes a surety are laid down by law.

If you agree to be a surety, you are entitled to the correct number of copies of the documents (usually two: one signed by you and the other by the lender) and also a copy of the main CREDIT AGREEMENT for which you are standing surety.

Unless you have been supplied with the proper copy agreements, the lender cannot seek to recover any money from you without going to court to get permission.

If the borrower pulls out

If a borrower pulls out legally, under the terms of the Consumer Credit Act, the surety cannot be made to pay anything.

In other circumstances, under that Act, a surety cannot be made to pay more money than the borrower could have been forced to pay. Neither can he

be made to pay in a different way (for example, in goods instead of in cash) or at a different time than would have applied to the borrower.

The surety who has had to pay up is also entitled to recover – through the county court, if necessary – any property or money deposited with the lender as security for the other person's debt.

Those rules apply even if the main credit agreement is found to be unenforceable – if, for example, the lender was unlicensed or he did not comply with rules about supplying documents.

If you stand surety for someone who defaults and you have to pay his creditor, you can sue him for your loss and, if necessary, make him bankrupt.
See: BAIL
BANKRUPTCY

SUSPECTED PERSON
When the police can arrest someone who has not committed an offence

The POLICE do not have to wait for a crime to be committed before they make an arrest. If they suspect someone of loitering with intent to commit an arrestable offence in a public place – if, say, he is trying car-door handles – they can detain and charge him under the Vagrancy Act 1824.

If he is found guilty by magistrates, he can be fined up to £200 or be gaoled for up to 3 months.

The policeman does not have to prove that the suspect was about to commit an offence. A suspected person can be found guilty simply on the grounds that the arresting policeman thought he was acting suspiciously.

SUSPENDED SENTENCE
Giving an offender a last chance

When a court decides to impose a prison sentence of less than 2 years, it can – at its own discretion – give the convicted person one last chance to stay free and mend his ways.

It does so by suspending the sentence for between 1 and 2 years, on condition that he does not commit another offence for which he could be imprisoned in that period.

LAST CHANCE TO MEND HIS WAYS

When a court suspends a sentence, it is giving the convicted person a last chance to mend his ways. If he commits a further offence during the period of suspension, he can be sent to prison for both the first and the later offences.

'okay – off you go, but keep out of trouble'

If he stays out of trouble for the whole of the suspension period, he will not go to prison for the offence.

The conviction, however, remains on his CRIMINAL RECORD and must be disclosed – on insurance forms, for example – for up to 10 years after the end of the period of suspension. *See:* REHABILITATION

One of the main reasons for ordering suspended sentences – which can be passed by both magistrates' and crown courts – is to relieve overcrowding in prisons. They can be imposed on any convicted person – even on someone who has previously served a prison sentence – whenever the court believes that the threat of prison is sufficient to persuade the offender not to break the law again.

The convicted person can appeal against a suspended sentence – if, for example, he feels he was wrongly found guilty – as against any other conviction.

For offenders under 18, a suspended sentence is often accompanied by a SUPERVISION ORDER – a compulsory form of PROBATION.

When another offence is committed

Someone who commits another offence during the period of suspension can be sent to gaol for the duration of the suspended sentence, unless:
● The subsequent offence is not imprisonable – such as speeding.
● For that subsequent offence the court orders an ABSOLUTE DISCHARGE, CONDITIONAL DISCHARGE or PROBATION.
● The court decides it would be 'unjust' to send him to prison.

Wide discretion

Under the last category, courts have wide powers not to activate a suspended sentence. If, for example, a woman given a suspended sentence for assault was later arrested and convicted of shoplifting, the court could activate her prison sentence – even though the second offence, though imprisonable, was only punished by a fine. However, since the second crime was of a different nature from the first and was comparatively trivial, the court may not send her to prison.

Instead of activating a suspended sentence when another offence is committed, a court can fix a new duration for it – so that it starts again on the date of the second conviction, for example. Alternatively, it can activate a sentence for a shorter period than ordered.

SWEEPSTAKE

When running an office sweep is illegal

Any sweepstake, which is a form of LOTTERY, is illegal if it is run for private gain. However, any social club, charitable organisation or group of office workers is entitled to run a sweepstake, provided that it does not contravene the Lotteries and Amusements Act 1976.

In order not to do so, the sweepstake must be run for the benefit of the club or group, and the organisers must:
● Deduct only the cost of stationery and printing of tickets as expenses.
● Spend the rest of the money on prizes or for the purpose of the society or group.
● Ensure that each ticket costs the same and is printed with the name and address of the organisers.
● Ensure that no tickets are sent through the post.
● Ensure that the sweepstake is not advertised.

However, although it is illegal for someone to run an office sweepstake which does not comply with those rules – for example, an office sweep on who will win the Grand National – prosecutions are rare.

The Irish Hospitals Sweepstake, although legal in Eire, is illegal in the UK. A person is not entitled to invite others in the United Kingdom to buy, distribute or advertise tickets for such a lottery. However, prosecutions are also rare if a person buys a ticket.

If a sweepstake is run at social events such as a fête, bazaar, sports event or a dance, it is regarded as a 'small lottery' and is therefore legal, provided that:
● The sweepstake is not the major attraction of the event.
● Proceeds are not for private gain.
● No more than £50 may be spent on prizes and money prizes are not allowed.
● The sale of tickets and the draw of prizes must take place during the event or entertainment.

If a person contravenes the regulations he may be fined a maximum of £400 in a magistrates' court and an unlimited fine or 2 years' imprisonment in a crown court. *See:* RAFFLE LICENCE

TATTOOING

Leaving a permanent colour mark on someone's skin

It is an offence to tattoo a minor – anyone under the age of 18 – even at his or her request. The maximum penalty is a fine of up to £50 for a first conviction and up to £100 for any subsequent offence. The only defence is if the person performing the tattoo had reasonably believed his client to be over 18.

If a minor has to be tattooed for medical reasons – for example, someone suffering from epilepsy or diabetes, or someone with a rare blood group, might be tattooed with identifying information for use in emergency – the operation must be performed by a doctor or by someone directed by him.

In all cases, the person being tattooed must give his permission. If not, the tattooist can be prosecuted for ASSAULT AND BATTERY.

Anyone who is harmed as the result of tattooing – someone, for example, who contracts jaundice because the tattooist failed to keep his equipment clean – can sue the operator for NEGLIGENCE.

TAXI

When a car is licensed to carry passengers

A Hackney carriage, generally known as a taxi, is a vehicle that has been licensed to carry fare-paying passengers and to ply for hire, either by travelling through the streets indicating it is for hire or by standing in a taxi rank waiting for a passenger.

A vehicle that has not been licensed in this way cannot ply for hire. *See:* MINICAB

The licence number of the taxi must be displayed inside the passenger compartment as well as in a prominent position outside the vehicle.

In London, taxis and drivers are licensed by the Metropolitan Police. Elsewhere the licensing authority is the District Council.

In London a driver must, unless he has a good excuse, accept any hiring of up to 6 miles (up to 20 miles from Heathrow Airport) provided that the journey begins and ends within the Metropolitan Police district.

Outside London the licensing authority decides the area, usually that covered by the District Council, within which a driver can be compelled to accept a hiring.

When a driver is entitled to refuse a fare

When a taxi is waiting at a rank the driver must accept the first prospective passenger provided that the destination is within his operating area.

If a destination is outside a driver's operating area, he is entitled to refuse the fare even if his taxi's 'for hire' sign was illuminated and he stopped for the potential customer.

Fares for London taxis are fixed by the Home Office, and local authorities regulate them in other parts of the country. The fares are metered – with the meter in a place where the passenger can see it – and the driver must not charge more than the amount shown.

If there has been a recent fare increase, the new tariff must be displayed in the cab.

If a passenger wants a taxi to take him outside the driver's operating district, he should agree a fare with the driver before starting a journey. If he does not, the fare payable is whatever is shown on the meter (as amended by authorised fare increases).

If a taxi driver accepts a passenger for a journey that begins and ends within his district, even if it is longer than he can be compelled to make, the fare payable is whatever is on the meter. In some places, that fare may be increased by surcharges, depending on the day or time.

A passenger is under no obligation to give a taxi driver a tip.

If you have a complaint or leave something in a taxi

If you are dissatisfied about a taxi driver's behaviour – if you feel you were overcharged, not taken on the most direct route, or you feel the taxi was unroadworthy or dirty, complain to the licensing authority. Give the licence number of the taxi and if possible the driver's number, which should be shown on his badge.

If you think that you have left property in a taxi, claim it from the licensing authority – in London, the Metropolitan Police lost property office.

Private hire vehicles are not subject to the same regulations as licensed vehicles, although in some areas the detailed control of minicabs is the same. *See:* MINICAB

TELEPHONE TAPPING

When your calls may not be private

Police and Home Office officials are allowed to listen in to private telephone conversations, if they are investigating a crime and if the Home Secretary has issued a warrant authorising the eaves-dropping. Evidence recorded during telephone tapping, as it is called, can be used in court.

It is doubtful whether telephone tapping is really legal, but the telephone user has no legal means of redress – even if he can prove that his conversations have been monitored.

The law is not even clear on what offence a private individual – for example, a private detective – commits by listening in to telephone conversations, so long as he uses equipment that does not take power from the telephone line or damage telephone equipment.

It is an offence for Post Office staff to disclose anything they overhear in a telephone conversation. The maximum fine is £100.

TELEPHONES

The state-owned telephone and telecommunications service

The telephone service (formerly run by the Post Office) is now run by a separate state-owned corporation, British Telecommunications (British Telecom). British Telecom also has the exclusive right, subject to government control, to run all telecommunications, that is, all electric, magnetic or similar systems to convey visual or audible signals, or signals which activate machinery or in any way impart any other matter.

Subject to the following exceptions, it is an offence, the maximum penalty for which is an unlimited fine, to break this privilege:
● Activities within a government licence.
● BROADCASTING under licence.
● Purely visual systems.
● Systems contained in one building.
● Systems under one person's control and used for domestic purposes, such as a baby alarm.
● Systems used by businesses for their own purposes and not as a service to others.
● Systems used on licence from British Telecom.

Obtaining a telephone

No one has a legal right to a telephone, but a request for one will normally be met, provided the local ex-change has spare lines. There is also no right to a private line, rather than one which is shared, though the service tries to provide individual lines, particularly if the telephone is for business use.

All users must use the telephone supplied by British Telecom (from the range they stock), but if they have more than one extension, the telephones on the second and other extensions can be purchased privately, provided the equipment is approved.

When a telephone is first installed, a connection charge of £65 (plus VAT) is made to residential users. Residential users who have had a telephone disconnected in the past because of non-payment of bills may be asked for a deposit.

Once the telephone is installed, you can add extra extensions, and equipment such as a telephone-answering machine, provided it is of a type approved for use with the telephone service. You should obtain written authority from British Telecom to use such equipment, and an inspection may be requested. Use of unauthorised equipment may result in the service being disconnected.

How the bill is calculated

Telephone bills are normally calculated every 3 months, and are made up of a quarterly rental for use of the service over the next 3 months, and tariff charges for calls made over the last 3 months. Direct dialled calls are recorded on a meter in the local telephone exchange. Operator-connected calls are recorded separately, and individual details can be obtained from the local Accounts Department.

Non-payment of bills will result in disconnection; and the subscriber has no right to reminders.

When you want to complain

If you get a faulty call or wrong number, call the operator, who will ensure that you do not pay for it. For other faults, telephone the local faults repair service. Faults will be repaired free of charge (unless you are responsible for the damage).

Loss or damage to equipment

Complaints about bills, directory entries or otherwise should be made to the local telephone area office (whose ad-dress and number are in the local telephone directory). If you have a special directory entry, or hire telephone equipment, you are deemed to have a contract with British Telecom under the standard conditions for the service (available from the telephone area office). Otherwise British Telecom is not liable for any loss or damage caused by any breakdown in, or error caused by the service unless you have a contract with them.

However, under the Code of Practice for Telecommunication Services issued in 1979, rebates or compensation may be paid for serious faults or major errors or omissions.

If you are dissatisfied with the response to your complaint by the area office, you can refer it to the regional headquarters, and, if that fails, the matter can be taken to an independent complaints panel set up under the Code of Practice, though a small fee is payable.

Misusing a telephone

It is an offence to use a telephone to send a grossly offensive, indecent, obscene or menacing message, or falsely to send a message to cause annoyance, inconvenience or needless anxiety. The maximum penalty is a £200 fine.

It is a serious offence dishonestly to use a telephone with intent to avoid payment, and the maximum penalty is 2 years' imprisonment and an unlimited fine.

British Telecom has the right to enter any buildings under the terms of the service, and entry cannot be forced. But your telephone can be tapped without your consent for certain purposes. *See:* TELEPHONE TAPPING

TELEVISION LICENCE

When you must buy a licence for a television

Every television receiver in use must be licensed, but it is not necessary to have a separate licence for each set. The licence covers all sets used in one household. A licence holder can use his television at a temporary address when he is away from home. However, if he has two sets and the one at home is being used at the same time he must have a second licence.

Using a television set in rented accommodation

It is the tenant's responsibility to buy a licence for the television set he is using in a rented home, even if the set was provided by his landlord.

If, however, the tenant shares communal facilities with his landlord he is considered part of the landlord's household and the set will be covered by his landlord's licence.

A landlord who installs a television in a holiday flat does not have to buy a licence for it. It is the responsibility of the user to supply the licence. If the user has a licensed set at home, his licence covers his holiday address too.

A hotel proprietor's ordinary licence covers his own private set, those of any domestic staff and those in hotel lounges. Any sets in the hotel bedrooms are covered by the proprietor's licence, provided that the bedrooms are not being used by residents on a permanent basis.

If the hotel room is being used as a permanent residence, the hotel proprietor may take out a 'comprehensive licence'. If he does not do so, the person using the room is responsible for providing a licence. Anyone who is a permanent resident in a hotel should check with the proprietor whether there is a comprehensive licence to cover his television set.

Refunds of licence fees

No refund can be made on television licences except when:
● An unexpired black-and-white licence is exchanged for a colour one. The amount given depends on how long the black-and-white licence has been used.
● A licence has been duplicated. The full amount is refunded.
● A person takes out or renews a television licence and decides he does not need it, provided that he returns the licence within 28 days of issue.

Any refund given amounts to eleven-twelfths of the original licence fee.

The retailer's responsibility

When a retailer sells or hires a set he must advise the National Television Licence Records Office in Bristol of the name and address of his customer. If he does not do so, he may be fined £50 for each offence. If a person is convicted of not having a licence, he may be fined up to £200 in a magistrates' court for a first offence and he will have to pay any licence fee due.

TELEVISION RENTAL

Nothing can take away your right to a set that works

Under a television rental agreement, the set must be reasonably fit for its purpose. Nothing in your agreement can take away your right to a set that works, provided that you are a consumer – that is, if you did not make the agreement in the course of a business.

Sometimes the agreement stipulates that the rental should last for a minimum period. If so, you cannot end the rental until that period elapses or unless the rental company agrees or has itself broken the contract.

The minimum period may be 9 months, 12 months or any other period. But it must not be longer than 18 months. *See:* GOODS RENTAL

TEMPORARY LETTING

Special laws that apply if you rent out your own home

The Rent Act provisions that make it difficult for a landlord to regain possession of rented property do not apply in the case of an owner-occupier who wants to rent his house or flat for a short period – for example, if his work is taking him away from the area for a while.

Someone who wants to grant a temporary tenancy must serve a special notice on the tenant saying that he 'might seek, at a later date, to recover possession of the dwelling on the ground set out in Case 11 of Schedule 15 to the Rent Act 1977 (Recovery where landlord is an owner-occupier)'.

If the notice, served in writing, includes exactly that form of words the landlord will be able to recover possession of the property provided he fulfils three conditions:
● The notice must be served at or before the granting of the tenancy – not afterwards.

● The landlord must be able to show, in court if necessary, one of the following:
1. He needs the property as residence for himself or for any member of his family who lived with him when he last lived there.
2. The original landlord has died, and the house is required as a residence for a member of his family who was living with him at the time of the original landlord's death.
3. The original landlord has died, and the present owner needs vacant possession in order to sell the house.
4. The house is on mortgage, which was taken out before the tenancy was granted, and the mortgagor needs possession because the mortgagee has defaulted on the loan.
5. The house is not suitable for the landlord to live in himself, because of his place of work, and he needs to be able to sell with vacant possession in order to buy another house.
● The landlord has not let the house to a tenant without serving the temporary letting notice on him at any time since December 8, 1965, in the case of unfurnished accommodation, or August 14, 1974, if it was furnished.

Regaining possession

Even if he has fulfilled the conditions the landlord must honour the letting arrangements. If it is a fixed period tenancy he cannot regain possession early. If it is a weekly, monthly or other periodic tenancy he must serve the proper NOTICE TO QUIT.

Like all residential tenants, even temporary tenants are entitled to demand that the landlord obtains a court order before they can be evicted. The difference with a temporary letting, however, is that the court has no discretionary power: it must grant the eviction order if the landlord has fulfilled the conditions. A landlord can recover possession in a similar way if he requires the property to live in after retirement.

TENANTS' ASSOCIATION

Forming a group to fight for tenants' rights

Tenants' associations can help to protect the rights of flatdwellers or householders who have a common landlord.

They can negotiate from a position of collective strength on:

● Rent levels.

● Amenities.

● Repairs and service charges.

● Cleaning and maintenance of common driveways.

● Lifts and staircases.

● Access routes.

In many large blocks of flats landlords make a service charge to the tenants. A tenants' association or an individual tenant has a legal right to challenge the service charge and may:

● Demand to inspect the landlord's service charge accounts.

● Insist that if any work is to be carried out at a cost of more than £500, or £25 multiplied by the number of flats in the building, whichever is the greater, the landlord obtain at least two estimates, at least one of which must be from an independent source.

● Insist that any work falling within the above figures be notified to the residents and the tenants' association, who should be given at least a month to put their views on the matter to the landlord. Unless the work is urgent, it cannot start until these views have been considered by the landlord and discussed with the tenants' association.

To exercise these rights the association must seek recognition, by the landlord in writing or by certificate from a member of the Rent Assessment Committee for the area. Recognition can be withdrawn.

It is illegal for a tenants' association to organise a rent strike or any other form of protest which could lead to individual tenants breaking their agreements. Anyone, including an association, who induces a tenant or conspires with others to induce a tenant to break his contract can be sued for damages in the county court.

TERRORISM

When rights are restricted by the need to combat terrorists

Emergency powers against terrorism – the use of violence for a political purpose – are granted under temporary provisions in force since 1976. They were aimed mainly at combating terrorism in England by pro-IRA extremists,

and the full powers apply only to terrorism relating to Northern Ireland affairs. However, the police can detain anyone suspected of involvement in terrorism by any group.

In the case of Northern Ireland affairs, the Government can prohibit an organisation suspected of terrorism, making it an offence to belong to or support that organisation. An individual suspect, even if he is a United Kingdom citizen, can be deprived of the normal freedom to travel between Northern Ireland and mainland Britain: a non-citizen can be excluded from any part of the United Kingdom.

The police can search premises without a magistrate's authority if they think that the national interest requires urgent action. They can arrest and detain a person for up to 7 days – without laying a charge or taking him to court – if they believe that he:

1. Is concerned in terrorist acts or plans.

2. Is withholding information which could prevent terrorism or help catch a terrorist.

3. Belongs to or supports an organisation banned under the Prevention of Terrorism Act – by 1980 the only organisations banned were the official and provisional Irish Republican Armies and the Irish National Liberation Army.

4. Is under an exclusion order keeping him out of mainland Britain, or if he is a non-citizen, out of the United Kingdom.

5. Has helped or given shelter to someone who is under an exclusion order.

A person suspected of terrorist activities can also be excluded from the country under IMMIGRATION regulations if the Home Secretary considers that his exclusion is 'conducive to the public good'.

There is no right of appeal against an exclusion order. An excluded person who is detained while awaiting removal from the country can ask to be heard by a government-appointed adviser but cannot call witnesses or demand to know the evidence against him.

Special terrorist offences

Involvement in actual or attempted terrorist attacks is dealt with under normal criminal procedure. Other offences that can be prosecuted under the special

provisions are:

1. Belonging to a banned organisation.

2. Raising or receiving money or goods for a banned organisation or encouraging any other support – for example, by arranging meetings.

3. Seeking, lending, giving or receiving money or goods intended for terrorist use.

4. Disobeying an exclusion order.

5. Helping or sheltering someone who is under an exclusion order.

6. Withholding information which could help prevent a terrorist act or catch a terrorist.

The maximum penalty in all cases is 6 months' imprisonment and a £1,000 fine in a magistrates' court, or 5 years' imprisonment and an unlimited fine in a crown court.

THEATRE CENSORSHIP

Freedom for performers within the law

There is no censorship of plays or any other live performance in a theatre. Anyone who presents public performances of obscene plays or ballet can be prosecuted for obscenity, but only with the leave of the Attorney-General. The penalty is a maximum of 3 years' imprisonment and an unlimited fine.

It is an offence to present a play with the intention of stirring up RACIAL HATRED. *See also:* OBSCENE PUBLICATIONS

THEFT

Taking somebody else's property – and meaning to keep it

Theft is dishonestly taking someone else's property. But before anybody can be convicted for stealing it must be shown that he intended to permanently deprive the owner of the property. Someone who takes an umbrella from a public house, say, thinking it is his own is not a thief; he does not mean to be dishonest.

If he takes the umbrella knowing that it does not belong to him but intending to return it next day, he is not a thief; he does not intend to keep it and borrowing is not an offence. Similarly, a youth who borrows a friend's bicycle thinking mistakenly that he has permission is not a thief; he does not mean to take it away from his friend permanently.

Because taking away an article temporarily is not theft, there is a special offence to cover 'joy-riders' who 'borrow' cars. That is the less serious offence of taking and driving away a vehicle without consent. *See:* JOY RIDING; ROAD TRAFFIC OFFENCES

A charge of theft will be heard in a magistrates' court unless the magistrate or the person accused wants it to go before a jury in a crown court. The maximum penalty in a magistrates' court is 6 months' imprisonment and a £1,000 fine.

In a crown court the maximum penalty is 10 years' imprisonment and an unlimited fine.

If someone is convicted of stealing a car, the defendant's driving licence is likely to be endorsed and he may be disqualified.

The offence of stealing by finding

It is an offence to retain somebody else's property. But if an article has been deliberately abandoned no offence is committed by the finder who decides to keep it.

Council dustmen are usually guilty of theft if they take anything from a dustbin because at that stage the contents of the bin are the property of the local authority.

AN 'HONEST' THIEF

A public-house customer who takes someone else's umbrella, meaning to return it, is not a thief in the eyes of the law.

TIED HOME
When accommodation goes with a job

If an employer provides accommodation, the employee's rights when the job ends depend on whether his occupancy amounts to a tenancy.

There is no tenancy with a 'live in' job if occupying particular quarters is essential to the work – for example, as a caretaker or public house manager.

Nor is there a tenancy if the employment contract obliges someone to live in accommodation owned by the employer – provided that the contract condition is genuinely aimed at better performance of the work. For example, a factory engineer who is on call for emergency repairs could be required to live in a company house near by, but he still has no tenancy because his accommodation is part of doing his job.

People in such situations are known as 'licensees' or 'service occupiers'. They have no security of tenure. If their employment ceases, they must leave.

When the tenant has only partial protection

If an employer lets housing to an employee as part of the understanding on which the job is taken – although occupancy is not necessary to do the job properly – it is a 'service tenancy'.

Then the employee has a normal tenant's rights in rent disputes, and even if he loses the job he cannot be put out without a court order.

A service tenancy EVICTION is easier than others, however, because a court can allow it if the employer shows that the accommodation is required for another employee. The new tenant must be specifically identified, and the court has to be convinced that the eviction is not unreasonable or likely to cause undue hardship.

When a tenant has full rights

A service tenancy and its limitations exist only when there is a direct LANDLORD AND TENANT relationship between employer and employee.

If accommodation is arranged with a third party – or even through a partnership, or another company in which the employer has an interest – there is no direct relationship.

The employee then has a normal residential tenancy, with full security of tenure and whatever RENT LIMIT protection might apply to the property.

Special rules for farm workers

If an agriculture or forestry worker is charged for accommodation provided by his employer, he has security of tenure under a special law.

He cannot be evicted without a court order, even if he loses his job, and the only certain grounds on which an order must be made are that a house:
● Was previously the employer's own residence, and he gave notice of requiring it back before the tenancy started.
● Was built for and is now required for the employer's retirement, and he gave notice before the tenancy started.
● Is occupied in breach of OVERCROWDING regulations.

There are additional grounds on which a court may make an eviction order if it sees fit. They deal mainly with the availability of suitable alternative accommodation, and with breaches of the tenancy agreement by the worker.

TIME OFF WORK
When an employee may be absent from his work

An employee is expected to work the hours required by his EMPLOYMENT CONTRACT. His employer is not normally obliged to give him time off unless it is provided for in the contract, nor, if he does, is he obliged to pay any wages.

In practice, most contracts make provisions for unavoidable absence as a result of accident or illness and grant employees a paid HOLIDAY ENTITLEMENT, to be taken at a time agreed with the employer. Agricultural workers and employees in a trade covered by a WAGES COUNCIL have a statutory right to a paid holiday.

Many employers are prepared to give employees additional time off for urgent personal matters – for example, to attend a funeral or a medical examination.

If an employee is absent without permission, however, his employer has the right to discipline him. If his unauthorised absences persist, they may justify DISMISSAL. *See:* DISCIPLINE AT WORK

When an employer must grant time off

In some circumstances, an employer must grant time off, even if it is not provided for in the contract. Most – although not all – full-time employees qualify to claim it, but that right does not extend to part-time workers. *See:* EMPLOYMENT PROTECTION

Public duties Most full-time employees are entitled to time off without pay to serve as a magistrate or as a member of a local authority, tribunal, regional health or water authority or the governing body of a maintained school.

There is no fixed rule on how much time must be granted, but it must be 'reasonable in all the circumstances', taking into account the needs of the business, the effect on it of the employee's absence, the nature of the employee's public duties and time off allowed for other purposes.

Redundancy Full-time employees over the age of 20 – including Crown employees and National Health Service staff, but not merchant seamen or those who work mainly abroad – who are dismissed as redundant and who have been with their employer for 2 years or more are entitled to time off with pay during the NOTICE period to look for a new job or to arrange for, but not to undergo, retraining. *See:* REDUNDANCY

The amount of time they can take depends upon the circumstances, but it must be 'reasonable' – which in practice is often taken to mean 2 full days.

Trade union duties Officers, including shop stewards and branch chairmen, of unions recognised by an employer for COLLECTIVE BARGAINING can take time off with pay to carry out their industrial relations duties and to undergo relevant training.

Members of a recognised union are entitled to time off without pay to participate in union activities – for example, to vote in elections of representatives.

The amount of time officers and members may take is not laid down by law and is usually decided by negotiation. The rules specifically exclude time off 'in contemplation' of a trade dispute – for example, a STRIKE or work-to-rule. *See:* TRADE UNION

Safety duties Safety representatives appointed by recognised trade unions are entitled to time off with pay to perform their duties and to undergo relevant training. *See:* HEALTH AND SAFETY AT WORK

Ante-natal care An employee who is pregnant is entitled to time off with pay to keep an appointment for ante-natal care arranged by a doctor, midwife or health visitor. Except for the first appointment, she must produce a certificate of pregnancy and an appointment card if her employer requests them. *See:* MATERNITY

When an employer refuses time off

If an employer refuses time off to an employee who is entitled to it, the employee can complain to an INDUSTRIAL TRIBUNAL. He must do so within 3 months of the refusal, using form IT1, obtainable from any employment office.

In cases in which the employee is refused time off while under notice of redundancy, the tribunal can order his employer to pay him compensation of up to two-fifths of a week's wages.

In those arising from public, trade union or safety duties, or ante-natal care, the tribunal can award compensation for the loss to the employee and may issue a declaration of the time he or she should have been allowed.

In practice, an employee entitled to time off without pay who was refused permission to take it and who then worked as usual, has not incurred a loss and therefore is unlikely to receive more than a nominal award.

TORT

A loss that can be compensated

Any wrong or injury for which a wrong-doer can be sued for compensation even though it is not a breach of contract, is called a tort.

Torts include injuries to the person or property, libel and fraud, and may often include breach of contract. To prevent a repetition of the harm the victim will claim an INJUNCTION.

TRADE DESCRIPTIONS

The right to be told the truth about what you buy

Anyone in the business of selling goods or providing services is under a legal obligation to avoid making false or misleading statements about them to prospective customers.

Any kind of misleading information or indication – spoken, written or pictorial – constitutes an offence under the Trade Descriptions Act 1968.

The law applies, however, only to statements made in the course of a trade or business, not to private transactions.

The maximum penalty is a £1,000 fine in a magistrates' court, or 2 years' imprisonment and an unlimited fine if there is a trial by jury.

What must be described accurately

Trade descriptions, in relation to goods, cover any information about all the important details of an article – its size and quality, when, how and by whom it was produced, whether it has been tested or approved by any person or authority, and any other history of use or previous ownership.

With services, accommodation and facilities, the Act covers any information about their nature and provision,

HONESTY – THE ONLY
ACCEPTABLE POLICY

A trader must not make any false claims about anything he is selling. If he does so, he can be heavily fined or even be sent to gaol.

'Cures anything – from bunions to bronchitis'

> ### THE JAGUAR WITH ITS CLOCK TURNED BACK
>
> *False reading on the odometers of second-hand cars commonly lead to prosecutions. The dealer must show that he took all reasonable precautions to avoid misleading the buyer.*
>
> An East London firm of second-hand car dealers sold a Jaguar with a recorded mileage of 24,600 miles. It had actually done more than 53,700.
>
> The dealers were convicted under the Trade Descriptions Act at Snaresbrook Crown Court in 1975. They appealed.
>
> In the Court of Appeal, their counsel argued that they should have been ac-quitted because they had supplied the buyer of the car with a guarantee saying, among other things, that the suppliers were not answerable for the mileage shown on the vehicle's odometer.
>
> #### DECISION
>
> The court upheld the conviction. They held that the small print in a document did not effectively disprove the odometer reading. If dealers did not want buyers to take any notice of an odometer, the judges said, they must take positive steps to ensure that buyers realised the reading was meaningless.
>
> ### THE CASE OF THE MISSING NIGHT CLUB
>
> *To avoid conviction for supplying false information about accommodation and other services, a company must show that it tried to establish the facts.*
>
> A large company of tour operators, in their brochure for the 1971 summer season, claimed that among the amenities at a modern hotel in Greece were a private swimming pool, a children's paddling pool and a night club on the beach outside.
>
> Mr and Mrs Brown, from Bury in Lancashire, liked the sound of it and booked a holiday for themselves and their 6-year-old daughter.
>
> When they arrived there, however, they found that the swimming pool was not private and there was neither a paddl-ing pool nor a night club. On their return, they complained to a local inspector of weights and measures, and in due course the tour operators were prosecuted by Manchester Corporation.
>
> The crown court jury found them guilty on three counts of recklessly making false statements about the amenities at the hotel. They were fined a total of £1,000 with costs and ordered to pay £50 compensation to the Browns. An appeal was lodged.
>
> #### DECISION
>
> The Court of Appeal, 'with no hesitation', upheld the conviction and the compensation order. An application for leave to appeal to the House of Lords was refused.

when, how and by whom they are provided, and whether they have been examined or approved by anyone. The location and amenities of any accommodation must be accurately described.

However, there is generally no obligation to say anything, but any information that is given about goods, services or accommodation must be accurate.

Proving an offence

Anyone who thinks he has been misled under the Trade Descriptions Act should complain to the trading standards department of his local council. It is their job to enforce the Act and to prosecute if they think there is a case.

Goods If goods were falsely described by the trader himself, it is not necessary to prove that he knew the description was misleading. The falsity in itself renders him liable, if it is material.

But if the information came from elsewhere – for example, the manufacturers – the trader can successfully plead ignorance provided that he can show that he took every reasonable precaution to discover whether or not the goods conformed to their description.

He would also be acquitted if he could prove that the offence occurred through a genuine mistake or it was someone else's fault or was due to some other reason beyond his control and that he took every reasonable precaution not to make a false statement.

Services In a prosecution brought for misleading information about services, accommodation or facilities, it is necessary to show that the defendant either knew it was misleading or made no effort to find out.

TRADE MARK

How the law protects a brand name or symbol

Many companies and businesses adopt a special name or symbol as a trade mark to identify their goods. A trade mark can be a valuable commercial asset and, because of that, there are laws to prevent one trader using another's trade mark.

The owner of a trade mark has two ways of preventing someone else using it:
● He can register it and take legal action for any infringement.
● He can rely on the general law which prevents anyone from representing his goods or business as being the goods or business of someone else.

Registering a trade mark

To register a trade mark, an application is made to the Trade Marks Registry, 25 Southampton Buildings, Chancery Lane, London, WC2.

Not all trade marks are approved by the registry. A mark must not be so much like an existing mark that it causes confusion.

It is not usually possible to register a surname because that would prevent another trader with that name from using it on his own products. But a surname may be allowed if it is written in a special way – for example, a replica of the trader's signature. It may also be approved if it has already been used as an unregistered name for a number of years and has been identified with a particular product.

A place name cannot be registered if it indicates where the goods originated from. But a place name that obviously has nothing to do with where the goods come from – for example, North Pole could be registered as a trade mark for bananas.

Common words of praise, such as 'splendid', 'superb' or 'perfection', cannot be registered as others may legitimately want to use them to describe their products.

Invented words can be registered – for example, Kodak – but a word that is deliberately mis-spelt may be rejected if it creates a misleading impression of the goods.

The word 'Orlwoola' could not be registered, because it sounds like 'all wool', and would be deceptive if it was used for garments that were not made from 100 per cent wool.

The registry will refuse a mark if its use might be dangerous – for example, if a poisonous disinfectant is given a trade name that makes it sound like a drink.

Similar rules apply to trade marks that include symbols as well as words. So a new oil company could not register the symbol of a shell which resembled that used by the Shell Company.

Trade marks can be registered only for goods and not services, such as banking, insurance or travel agencies, although many do use unregistered symbols and marks.

Even after a trade mark has been registered, the owner must make use of it to keep the registration valid. If the trade mark is not used for 5 years, it can be removed from the register.

It can also be removed if it becomes widely accepted as a descriptive term. For example, 'petrol', 'linoleum' and 'gramophone' were once trade marks but have since become descriptive words.

Any company that has been a supplier to the Queen or a member of the Royal Family for 3 consecutive years is entitled to state that their product is 'by appointment' and use the Royal Arms on the product. To do so, the company must apply to the Lord Chamberlain. If the company stops supplying the Royal Family, the use of the Royal Arms must be withdrawn. Anyone who makes use of the Royal Arms without permission may be fined up to £5 in a magistrates' court.

Trade mark infringements

Anyone who falsely states that a trade mark has been registered may be fined up to £20 in a magistrates' court.

Once a trade mark has been registered, its owner is entitled to sue anyone who uses a similar mark for the same type of goods and he may seek an INJUNCTION to prevent any further infringements.

However, it is not usually an infringement to use someone else's trade mark on goods that are so different that no confusion could reasonably arise.

A trader cannot be sued for using his own name which happens to coincide with a name already registered as a trade mark. But he can be sued if he uses an abbreviation of his name. For example, Ebenezer Smith could not go into business selling crisps under the name of Smith's Crisps. He would have to call them 'Ebenezer Smith's Crisps'.

Unregistered marks

A trade name that is not registered is still protected by the law that prevents anyone representing his goods or business as being the goods or business of someone else. A trader who breaks the law can be sued for what is known as 'passing off'. Passing off may also be committed if goods are packaged or presented in a manner distinctive of another trader.

When a descriptive trade name is used it may be difficult to establish it as being distinctive of one particular person's goods or business. A court will not allow that person to monopolise a description and prevent others using similar names. However, they may be prevented from using the same name.

For example, a company calling itself 'Office Cleaning Services' could not prevent a rival calling itself the 'Office Cleaning Association'.

Public figures, such as a sports or pop star, are also protected from having their names used without permission by a trader who wants to promote a product. Similarly, the titles of films, books, plays or songs, and any characters involved may not usually be used to promote a product without permission.

In most cases, a film or television company owns the COPYRIGHT for their films or shows, and they may sometimes register the names of shows or a cartoon character as a trade mark.

A trader is entitled to use the names of personalities or a title to promote a product, provided that he obtains a licence from the company or personality involved. *See:* BUSINESS NAME

TRADE SECRET

How companies can keep their rivals in the dark

Most businesses possess information, techniques or processes which they wish to keep confidential. The law recognises the value of such trade secrets and helps to preserve the confidentiality of information and know-how.

Trade secrets can include such things as special production methods, recipes for food or drink products, lists of customers, marketing techniques and many other aspects of business which could be of use to a rival.

Many contracts of employment contain a clause – or restrictive covenant – forbidding the employee from using or disclosing his employer's trade secrets. But even if there is no such clause there is an implied obligation on the employee to maintain confidentiality. The obligation ends only when the information ceases to be confidential.

When a worker with access to trade secrets changes jobs

Even if he leaves the job, an employee must not give away trade secrets. It is often difficult, however, to draw a line between his own stock of skills and knowledge and confidential information belonging to his former employer.

For that reason many employment contracts contain a restrictive covenant prohibiting the employee from working for a competitor, or setting up a business in competition with his employer, for a specified time – say a year – after leaving his job.

A former employee can be prevented from breaking a restrictive covenant by a court injunction. But such clauses are void if they are too widely drawn or oppressive, stopping the employee from using his skills altogether.

In businesses such as hairdressing and restaurants employees may build up a valuable relationship with customers. Contracts for such jobs often contain a clause preventing an ex-employee from starting a rival business in the same neighbourhood or 'poaching' clients. Again such clauses are invalid if they are too restrictive.

Licensed secrets

The obligation to respect confidential information is not restricted to employees. For example, a manufacturer may use special production methods not inventive enough to be patented. But they are part of his know-how and may

> ## COMPANY THAT 'BORROWED' AN INVENTOR'S WORK
>
> *An inventor who discloses details of his work to a manufacturer with a view to a joint venture is protected by the law if the negotiations break down.*
>
> In 1962 Mr Seager invented a special type of carpet grip, embodying a device known as a V-tang. He discussed his idea with the Copydex company with a view to marketing the invention, but the negotiations broke down. Some time later Copydex marketed a carpet grip with a V-tang. Mr Seager sought a court injunction against the company.
>
> #### DECISION
>
> The court ruled that Copydex had unconsciously made use of Mr Seager's confidential information. As the company had already begun to market the grip no injunction was granted, but Mr Seager was awarded damages instead.

be licensed to others in return for royalties.

An inventor who is unable to exploit his work through lack of money may ask a manufacturer to consider a joint venture. If the negotiations break down, the manufacturer is not entitled to go ahead on his own. If he does so, he can be stopped by an injunction from using any information given to him in confidence by the inventor.

TRADE UNION

The rights of union members

Every worker has the right to belong to a trade union that accepts him as a member and to take part in its normal activities, as defined by the courts. Provided that the union is 'independent' – recognised by the government-appointed Certification Officer as being free from control or influence, real or potential, by an employer – any employee who belongs to it, or who applies to join, may not be victimised or dismissed by his employer on those grounds.

Anyone who is sacked for joining an independent union or for taking part in its normal activities, or for refusing to join a union that has not been certified as independent, can claim UNFAIR DISMISSAL.

Anyone who is victimised by his employer can apply to an INDUSTRIAL TRIBUNAL for financial compensation if he can show that the employer sought to:
● Prevent or deter him from joining an independent union.
● Prevent or deter him from taking part in that union's normal activities.
● Compel him to join a union that has not been certified as independent.

The rules on victimisation do not apply to job applicants. Someone who is refused employment because he is a union member or because he declines to join a non-independent union has no redress.

Union activities that are allowed

All members of an independent union may take part in its normal activities, whether or not their employer recognises the union as representing some or all of his employees and with or without his permission, provided that they do so outside working hours – before or after work or during meal breaks and rest periods.

THE INFORMATION EMPLOYERS ARE EXPECTED TO GIVE

An ADVISORY, CONCILIATION AND ARBITRATION SERVICE Code of Practice suggests a wide range of information that employers should be prepared to give to union representatives if they need it for collective bargaining. The ACAS list is intended only as a guide – the information needed by the unions may vary according to the size of the company and the nature of its business.

Pay

The structure and principles of payment systems, including the way in which employees are graded.

Employees' earnings and hours worked, analysed by work group, grade, plant, sex, department or company, including the way in which earnings are made up.

Details of fringe benefits and non-wage labour costs.

Conditions of service

Main conditions of service.

Recruitment, redeployment, training and promotion policies and redundancy plans.

Proposed changes in work methods and materials.

Health, safety and welfare matters.

Job evaluation and appraisal systems.

Pension schemes, including benefits, contributions and financial and administrative policy.

Employment

Numbers employed, analysed by grades, departments, location or age.

Overtime and short-time worked.

Employment *continued*

Manning levels and standards.

Proposed organisational or technical changes and manpower plans.

Productivity

Analysis of output.

Schedules and methods of work.

Savings from increased productivity.

Return on capital invested.

Market share of products and the state of the order book.

Financial

Relevant cost structures.

Gross and net profits.

Sources of earnings.

Assets and liabilities.

Allocation of profits.

Details of any government financial assistance being received.

Transfer prices to companies within the same group.

Loans to associated companies and interest charged.

'Normal' activities include recruiting members, collecting subscriptions, distributing union literature and attending meetings off the employer's premises, or on his premises in the members' own time. They do not include activities that cause 'substantial inconvenience' to the business or other staff – for example, by preventing fellow employees from doing their jobs – nor most forms of industrial action. However, an employer may not victimise or dismiss a member of an independent union who takes part in lawful PICKETING during his free time. *See:* STRIKE

When a union is 'recognised'

Members and elected officers of an independent trade union gain additional legal rights if their union is recognised by their employer as representing some or all of his employees. The recognition does not have to be set out formally in writing; it can be implicit in the relationship between the employer and the union – for example, if the two meet regularly to negotiate on matters affecting the workforce.

Once a union has been recognised by an employer, it is entitled to demand:
● Information about his business needed for collective bargaining.
● Advance warning of proposed redundancies.
● Time off work for union representatives, members and union-appointed health and safety representatives to perform their duties and activities.
● Consultation on occupational pension schemes.

Disclosure of information The information an employer is expected to give to a recognised union is listed in *Code of Practice 2: Disclosure of Information to Trade Unions for Collective Bargaining Purposes*, prepared by the ADVISORY, CONCILIATION AND ARBITRATION SERVICE (ACAS).

The code is not legally binding, but an employer who does not follow it in his dealings with a recognised union may be ordered to do so by the CENTRAL ARBITRATION COMMITTEE (CAC) which, in the last resort, has the power to fix the employment terms and conditions of his staff.

The code suggests five broad areas in which information should be provided – pay and related matters, conditions of service, employment within the business, current and planned production and company finances.

However, an employer need give details only if they are required for negotiations which would be 'materially impeded' without them and if disclosure would be good industrial-relations practice.

He is not expected to provide information he, or an associated company, has not got.

He may refuse to give information if to do so would contravene national security, or if it was given to him in confidence, was obtained for legal proceedings or relates to an individual.

He may also refuse to give information if disclosure would cause substantial injury to his business – though not just because it would strengthen the union's bargaining position – or if the cost and effort of getting the information is out of reasonable proportion to its usefulness.

The information need only be given to a union representative authorised to carry out collective bargaining, not to individual members or to those not

VICTIMISED, BUT NOT PROTECTED

If an employer does not recognise a union, and has not given permission for members to take part in its activities during working hours, a member who does so cannot claim compensation if he is victimised.

Leonard Robb was an employee of the Leon Bus Company and a keen member of the Transport & General Workers' Union, which his employers did not officially recognise.

Mr Robb tried strenuously to recruit new members for the union from among his fellow workers. Eventually, his employers transferred him to another job, in which he was isolated from his colleagues. He claimed he had been victimised for his union activities.

DECISION

Mr Robb had been victimised, but he was not entitled to financial compensation because his activities took place in working hours, without permission.

THE MEETING HELD AT THE WRONG TIME

Where a union is unrecognised, even a shop steward has no right to disrupt the employer's business during working hours.

A shop steward of the Amalgamated Union of Engineering Workers took up a member's pay problem with his employers who refused to recognise his authority as shop steward. The steward then called a meeting which resulted in 1 hour's less work. The employers claimed he was not protected from disciplinary action, because they had not given permission.

DECISION

The shop steward was not protected, it was decided.

The Court of Appeal said that there were no grounds for holding that he had implied consent from the management to hold the meeting in working hours. He should have held it during a meal-break or after work.

THE TRADE UNION THAT WAS NOT CONSULTED

Recognition of a trade union need not be in writing, but one meeting is not recognition.

A company had no formal agreement with a trade union representing workers in gold and silver, but it belonged to a trade association which regularly negotiated collective agreements with that union. After some of the company's employees joined the union, the national secretary asked for a meeting to discuss rates of pay, but no agreement was reached. Four employees were then dismissed without consulting the union.

DECISION

The employers did not have to consult the union about redundancy because it was not recognised. Only if the company had regularly negotiated with the union representatives would informal recognition have taken place.

directly involved. It should be set out so that it can be easily understood, but an employer is not obliged to provide copies of the documents from which it is drawn, nor to allow access to his files.

Redundancies An employer who recognises an independent trade union, or who has been recommended to do so by ACAS, must consult it if he is planning to make any of its members redundant or if he is planning redundancies among non-union members in job categories for which the union is recognised. If 10 or more employees are involved, consultations must start at least 30 days before the dismissals take effect, and if 100 or more are to be dismissed the employer must tell the union at least 90 days in advance. *See:* REDUNDANCY

Time off Individual members of a recognised union are entitled to time off, without pay, to take part in union activities during working hours – for example, to attend an urgent meeting or to vote in a union election.

The provisions do not apply to industrial action. But union members are ex-

---

WHEN MEETINGS ARE ALLOWED
IN COMPANY TIME

Employers must allow members of any trade union they have recognised to attend urgent meetings in working time – without reducing their wages.

---

pected to minimise any inconvenience caused by their absence and not to prolong it unnecessarily.

A union member or official whose

---

employer refuses to allow him time off can complain to an industrial tribunal within 3 months of the refusal. The tribunal may order the employer to pay financial compensation. *See:* TIME OFF WORK

Pensions An employer who recognises a trade union must consult it at least 3 months before he contracts out of the state occupational pension scheme. *See:* RETIREMENT PENSION

Dealing with a closed shop

Closed shop, or union membership, agreements require employees to join a particular union as a condition of employment. They need not be set out in writing, but if they are they will not necessarily be upheld if they are not implemented in practice.

An employee who refuses to join an independent union in a business where a closed shop operates cannot claim UNFAIR DISMISSAL if he is sacked because of his refusal, unless he can show that:
● He genuinely objected on grounds of

WHAT TO DO IF YOU ARE VICTIMISED FOR YOUR UNION ACTIVITIES

An employee who is dismissed or otherwise victimised for belonging to or trying to join an independent trade union, or for taking part in its activities can claim compensation by applying to an INDUSTRIAL TRIBUNAL. *If you are dismissed* You can claim UNFAIR DISMISSAL, even though you may not have been in the job for the 12 months normally needed to qualify. *See:* EMPLOYMENT PROTECTION

The onus is on you to prove that your union activity was the cause of dismissal – and not some other reason.

Fill in form IT1, which you can get from any employment office, Job Centre or unemployment office, and send it within 7 days of your dismissal to:

The Secretary of the Tribunals, Central Office of the Industrial Tribunals (England and Wales), 93 Ebury Bridge Road, London SW1W 8RE.

Certificate from the union

You must send with it a certificate from your union, or the one you were planning to join, stating that there are reasonable grounds to believe that the main reason for your dismissal was your union membership or activity.

In answering question 1 on the form – the question you want the tribunal to decide –

state 'whether I was unfairly dismissed' and add: 'I claim interim relief because I was dismissed for an inadmissible reason – namely, because of my trade union activities.'

'Interim relief' is a special procedure intended to lessen the risk of the dismissal developing into a major industrial dispute. Once the application form and union certificate have been received, the tribunal will arrange a preliminary hearing as quickly as possible, subject to the need to give the employer 7 days' notice of the date.

Approaching the employer

The preliminary hearing will not consider all the evidence, but merely enough to decide whether you are likely to win your case at a full hearing later. If the tribunal believes you are likely to win, it will ask your employer if he will give your old job back temporarily until the full hearing takes place. If he refuses, he will be asked if he will re-employ you temporarily in a different job. If he refuses to do that either, the tribunal will order him to continue paying you at the full rate until the case is finally decided. You do not then need to turn up for work, but you will keep your pension and seniority rights for the period.

Once interim relief has been granted, the

claim proceeds as a normal unfair dismissal case. If the full hearing finds you were sacked for union activities, it will award extra compensation in addition to the amount for unfair dismissal.

The extra award will equal your wages – up to a maximum of £120 a week – for between 26 and 52 weeks.

Victimisation short of dismissal If you are victimised – suspended, unfairly selected for dirty or unpopular jobs, subjected to unusually strict supervision or otherwise harassed, but not actually sacked – for your union activities, you can still complain to an industrial tribunal within 3 months, using form IT1.

What the employer must show

At the hearing, the employer must show that his treatment of you, if it was unfair or unreasonable, had nothing to do with your union activities or that he did not intentionally victimise you.

If the victimisation was not intentional, you will not win your claim, even if the effect of the employer's action was discriminatory. If the claim is upheld, the tribunal can order your employer to pay compensation related to your loss of earnings, if any were actually lost, and the seriousness of the victimisation used.

conscience or other deeply held personal conviction to belonging to any trade union or to the particular trade union in question.

● He worked for the employer before the closed shop agreement was made without being required to belong to the trade union.

● Where the closed shop agreement was made after the Employment Act 1980 took effect, the closed shop had not been approved by a secret ballot of employees affected, in which he was entitled to vote. The closed shop must have been approved by 80 per cent of those entitled to vote if the dismissal of the employee who refuses to join the union is to be fair.

A code of practice on closed shop arrangements came into effect in December 1980. It is not legally binding but can be taken into account in court or tribunal proceedings. Copies are obtainable from the Department of Employment.

The normal 52 weeks' service qualification for unfair dismissal complaints does not apply when the employee complains that he is entitled to exemption from a closed shop agreement.

Complaints against the union

An employee who loses his job because he has been expelled from a union, or because the union refuses to accept him as a member, may complain to an INDUSTRIAL TRIBUNAL that he has been unreasonably treated within 6 months of the date of refusal of membership or expulsion from the union. Someone who has failed to obtain a job in a closed shop because he does not belong to the union may also complain to an industrial tribunal. It is for the tribunal to decide whether the trade union acted unreasonably.

The fact that the union obeyed its own rules to the letter does not necessarily mean that it acted reasonably, nor is a breach of those rules necessarily unreasonable – though in the latter case an action for breach of contract might be brought against the union in the county court or the High Court.

If the tribunal finds that the union acted unreasonably it will make a declaration to that effect. If the union does not then admit or readmit the member he can ask for compensation from the union by complaining to the Employ-

ment Appeal Tribunal. Even if he has been given membership he can ask for compensation, but in that case he must go to an industrial tribunal.

Applications for compensation must be made not earlier than 4 weeks and not later than 6 months from the tribunal's declaration. The amount of compensation that may be awarded depends on how much the applicant has lost – up to a maximum of £9,350 in the industrial tribunal and £15,590 in the Employment Appeal Tribunal.

If a trade union is affiliated to the Trades Union Congress, an employee who has lost his job because of expulsion or refusal of membership can appeal to the Independent Review Committee of the TUC as well as, or instead of, bringing legal proceedings in an industrial tribunal. The committee can recommend that the union involved should admit or readmit the employee, but cannot order it to do so.

The union and unfair dismissal

Where an employee is awarded compensation for UNFAIR DISMISSAL against his employer because he has been dismissed in contravention of the closed shop rules, the employer (but not the employee) may ask the tribunal to order that the trade union or other person who put pressure on the employer to sack the employee by organising or threatening industrial action should contribute to the damages – up to 100 per cent at the tribunal's discretion. But the employer cannot evade liability for unfair dismissal by the excuse that he was under pressure of strike action.

How union rules affect members' rights

Every trade union has a rule book that forms the basis of a CONTRACT between itself and individual members. If the union does not follow its own rules, any member can ask a civil court to order it to do so by INJUNCTION.

In cases between unions and individual members, courts tend to interpret any ambiguity in the rule book in favour of the individual. A court can over-ride any union rule that does not comply with NATURAL JUSTICE – for example, by not allowing a member facing disciplinary action time to prepare his case or obtain a fair hearing. A union

rule that states a decision, once reached, cannot be appealed against in the courts is not valid. Neither are rules that provide for automatic loss of membership or prevent a member from leaving – though a condition that arrears of contributions must be paid may be upheld.

Unions are not allowed to discriminate against members or applicants on grounds of sex or race, or because they are nationals of another country in the EUROPEAN COMMUNITIES. Discrimination against members who refuse to contribute to a union's political fund is forbidden, and the members concerned can complain to the Certification Officer who registered the union.

A member who has a complaint or grievance against his union should try to resolve it through the union's own procedures, before taking it to court. Although he is not legally obliged to do so, he has a better chance of obtaining a favourable decision if he can show the court he has exhausted all other steps.

TRADING STAMPS

You can redeem them for cash or goods fit for their purpose

A shop or garage that offers trading stamps must display a notice saying how many stamps you are entitled to receive for the money you spend.

Your right to cash

You have a right to redeem your stamps for cash with the trading stamp company, provided you have stamps with a total face value of at least 25p. Each stamp must have printed on it the amount of cash for which it can be exchanged – for example ·033p. In that case, 31 stamps are worth just over 1p.

Your right to quality goods

Any goods you receive in exchange for the stamps must be of merchantable quality. That means that they must be reasonably fit for the purposes for which such goods are commonly bought.

If they are not of merchantable quality, the trading stamp company will usually exchange them for sound goods, but they are not legally bound to do so. However, you have a legal right to damages, to compensate you for the difference in value between the goods you received and goods in proper condition.

TRADING STANDARDS

Who to tell if a dealer lets you down

Local authorities are responsible for enforcing many consumer protection laws through their trading standards or consumer protection departments.

Trading standards officers are specially trained in the requirements of the Weights and Measures Acts, Trade Descriptions Act, Consumer Safety Act and some parts of the Consumer Credit Act.

Department addresses can be found in the telephone book under the listing for your local council.

Enforcement of the Food and Drugs Act and the food hygiene regulations is the responsibility of environmental health departments, also under the control of local authorities.

TRAFFIC SIGN

Instructions that the road user must obey

Anyone driving or riding a vehicle on the road must obey traffic signs. Failure to do so is not only an offence in itself, but can be the basis for prosecution on more serious driving charges. It can also be an important factor in civil actions for damages.

Signs at junctions

Stop signs at junctions with major roads are used in conjunction with two solid transverse lines marking where the major road begins, reinforced with the word 'stop' painted on the roadway.

Drivers must stop and not pass the line nearest to the major road, or, if the lines are not visible, enter the major road so as to be likely to endanger a vehicle on the major road or make the driver change his speed or swerve to avoid an accident.

A give-way sign indicates that the driver must be ready to let traffic on the major road go first. An octagonal or triangular sign is used in conjunction with two broken transverse lines and a triangle painted on the road. The

broken lines must be crossed in the same way as the solid lines at a stop sign, but the driver need not necessarily stop his vehicle.

Traffic lights

The significance of the sequence of traffic lights is:

Red	Stop and wait behind the stop line.
Red and amber	Stop and wait behind the stop line.
Green	Go if the road is clear.
Amber alone	Do not go beyond the stop line or, if there is no stop line visible, beyond the signal, except when in a vehicle which, when the light first appears, is so close to the line or signals that it cannot safely be stopped.

Flashing red lights on motorways indicate that vehicles in the relevant lane must not go beyond the signal.

At Pelican crossings where only red and amber lights show, motorists must stop on red, but they may drive on when the amber light resumes flashing – provided that any pedestrian already on the crossing is given precedence.

Roadworks and other signs

It is an offence not to stop for a hand-operated 'stop' sign where roadworks are blocking one carriageway. It is not an offence in itself to ignore flags used for the same purpose but a driver could still be charged with careless or reckless driving.

Circular signs with red circles are mostly prohibitive and it is an offence to contravene them. Circular blue signs give a positive instruction and are also compulsory.

Centre line markings

Double continuous white lines require vehicles travelling in either direction to keep to the nearside of the nearest continuous line. Where there is a continuous white line with a broken white line drivers must not cross or straddle a nearside, continuous white line, except for access to premises, or to

pass a vehicle parked, but if the nearer line is broken it may be crossed or straddled if it is safe to do so.

Census signs

Contravention of a traffic direction for the purpose of an approved traffic census is an offence.

Penalties

The maximum fine for a traffic sign offence is £100, but an offender can have his driving licence endorsed only if he ignores:
● A red signal on automatic traffic signs.
● Flashing red lights on motorways.
● Red signals at level crossings and roadworks.
● Double white lines and stop signs.

TRAFFIC WARDEN

The extra 'police' force for parking and traffic control

Traffic wardens are appointed and controlled by the police in their district. They form an auxiliary force, with powers only to direct traffic and enforce parking regulations.

Wardens can issue a fixed-penalty notice, or 'ticket', for a PARKING offence, for leaving a car without lights or for failing to display a valid excise licence.

For offences where there is no fixed penalty procedure – for example, causing unnecessary obstruction – a warden's report can still lead to prosecution.

Wardens cannot order the towing-away of an illegally parked car, but they can 'cause' its removal by reporting it to the police.

When you must obey

A traffic warden can exercise his powers only if he is in uniform.

If he is controlling traffic, or if he signals a driver to move to prevent a road obstruction, any motorist who disobeys his signal commits the same offence as if he ignored the signal of a policeman. The maximum fine is £100.

If you are in charge of a car that is illegally parked, you must give your name and address to a warden if required to do so. But he has no power to

TOO LATE! TOO LATE!

You are entitled to try to dissuade a traffic warden from issuing a parking ticket. But if he has started to write the ticket, he has no power to cancel it.

'Sorry, guv – The moving finger writes, and having writ...'

make you show your driving licence – except to identify yourself if you reclaim a car from a pound.

What you can do if you object to a 'ticket'

A motorist is entitled to try to dissuade a traffic warden from issuing an offence notice. But once a warden has started to write out the 'ticket', there is little point. The warden cannot cancel it.

A motorist who believes he has a good excuse for a parking infringement, or thinks he has been treated too harshly, should write to the prosecution officer at the ticket office address.

If a motorist objects to a fixed-penalty notice and does not pay it within 21 days, either he or the registered owner of the vehicle will receive a 'notice to owner' of the offence. If the owner ignores the notice and fails to pay the penalty or fails to nominate the driver of the vehicle at the time of the offence, he may be prosecuted and fined up to £100, plus court costs.

TRAILERS

What you must think of before you tow another vehicle

The law regards all vehicles towed by a motor vehicle in the same way. It is not concerned whether the vehicle towed is a caravan, a trailer carrying a sailing dinghy, a broken-down car, or a heavy goods trailer; it is concerned only about its dimensions, weight, number of wheels, braking system, lighting and about the speed at which it is travelling.

How big it can be

In general, trailers must not be longer than 7 m. (23 ft), excluding the towing bar, or wider than 2.3 m. (7½ ft). The overall length of the towing vehicle and trailer must not exceed 18 m. (59 ft) unless the vehicle is being towed as a result of a breakdown.

If the trailer is being towed by a rope or chain, the gap between the vehicles must not be more than 4.5 m. (14 ft 9 in.). If the gap is more than 1.5 m. (4 ft 11 in.) you must make sure the rope or chain is clearly visible to other road users.

Generally, the total weight transmitted to the road surface by any two wheels of a trailer must not exceed 9,150 kg. (9 tons), and the combined weight of the towing vehicle and trailer must not exceed 22,360 kg. (22 tons).

How many wheels

Trailers with fewer than four wheels or with four wheels that are close-coupled on either side must not carry passengers. Other vehicles with four or more wheels, however, must carry someone, either on the trailer or on the towing vehicle, to take charge of the trailer, unless:

● It has brakes that work automatically when the trailer overruns the towing vehicle.

● The vehicle being towed has broken down and cannot be steered by its own steering gear.

When it must have brakes

In general, any trailer that weighs more than 102 kg. (2 cwt) unloaded must have an efficient braking system. The technical requirements vary according to the date of manufacture of the vehicle. When you are buying a trailer, make sure, perhaps by consulting a motoring organisation or demanding a guarantee from the dealer, that the brakes meet the requirements for that particular model.

You must never leave a trailer detached from the towing vehicle without either applying the brakes or chaining at least one of its wheels.

How many lights

If the distance between the drawing vehicle and the trailer is more than 5 ft, both must be lit as if they were separate vehicles. As with brakes, the technical requirements for lights vary with the date of manufacture of the trailer. Check that these have been met when you buy the vehicle.

Always make sure that the registration plate, which must be displayed at the rear of the trailer showing the number of the towing vehicle, is properly lit.

Restrictions on speed

The general rule is that no trailer can be towed at more than 40 mph on any road or motorway. There can be higher limits, however, depending on the type of towing vehicle and the type of trailer. Check with a motoring organisation before you take your trailer on the road.

On motorways with three or more lanes you must not use the right-hand lane while towing a trailer, except to pass a vehicle of such exceptional width that it is the only way to do it.

Drivers holding only a provisional licence must not drive a towing vehicle. Before using your car to tow any trailer, ask your insurance company whether your present policy covers you to do so.

TRANSPLANT

When one person's organs are removed to help another

When someone dies in hospital or is dead on arrival there, the local health authority has legal possession of the body. Otherwise the executor of a dead person's estate has legal possession.

Either can authorise a surgeon to remove parts of the body – for example, kidneys – for transplanting into another person, or for research.

The law, however, lays down special rules to govern the removal of any human tissue. Whoever authorises the taking of a dead person's organs has a duty to ensure that he or she when alive never raised an objection to such a practice, and that close relatives also have no objection.

If the dead person expressed a positive wish to donate organs – in a will, by carrying a Department of Health donor card, or orally in the presence of two witnesses – relatives usually have no legal right to be consulted.

Under a separate law governing cornea grafts in eye surgery, however, close relatives can overrule a dead person's wishes.

Once a death is reported to a CORONER, who may want to order a POST-MORTEM examination of the body, nothing can be removed without his permission.

When a donor is alive

Anyone over the age of 18 who is capable of giving a valid consent – not, for example, someone who is mentally subnormal or disordered – can participate as a donor in transplant surgery.

If a proposed donor is under 18, however, the consent of parents or a legal guardian is required.

That consent is legally acceptable only if the operation is in the child's own interests – for example, to save the life of a brother or sister whose death would distress the donor.

When the recipient of a transplant is a child

The consent of parents or a legal guardian must be sought before an organ is transplanted into anyone under the age of 16.

If consent is refused unreasonably, however – for example, when there is an immediate risk of the child's death or permanent disablement – a hospital authority may be justified in ignoring parental opposition.

TRANSPORT POLICE

Where law enforcement is left to specialists

Several official transport authorities have their own police, mainly because of a high risk of theft or vandalism, or a need for specialised skills.

Their powers are similar to those of regular policemen, but normally apply only on the property of the employing authority. Transport police can operate elsewhere, however, if they are follow-

ing up a crime committed on authority property.

They need not be in uniform, but they can be required to produce an identifying document – and must do so if they make an arrest while not in uniform.

The special powers of railway policemen

A British Transport policeman's powers extend to trains as well as stations and goods yards.

Not all offences against railway regulations are arrestable, however. For example, a British Transport policeman cannot arrest someone simply for travelling without the necessary ticket – but if that person refuses to give his name and address, he can be arrested and put in detention.

The special powers of airport policemen

British Airports Authority constables can stop any person, vehicle or aircraft leaving an airport cargo area and inspect any goods being carried. If the vehicle or aircraft is carrying goods not supported by an authorised document they may detain both the goods and the vehicle or aircraft.

They also have the power to make a personal search of anyone working in the airport on suspicion of theft or possession of stolen property.

They do not have the right to search anyone else.

The British Airports Authority is liable for any TORT committed by airport constables in their work.

The special powers of docks and harbour constables

Dock or harbour authorities frequently have their own constables, who operate within the authority's area and are within 1 mile of its limits.

Canal and river constables

The British Canals and Waterways Board and river authorities can if they wish appoint constables to patrol on or along waterways, on the premises of the proprietors and within a $\frac{1}{4}$ mile of them.
See also: SEARCH
SECURITY GUARD
TRAFFIC WARDEN

TRAVEL AGENT

When something goes wrong with the arrangements

When you book a holiday through a travel agent you enter into a contract. Your rights – what you are entitled to under the contract and what happens if things go wrong – depend to some extent on its terms.

Most holiday brochures and booking forms contain conditions to which you agree when you sign the booking form. If a passenger is killed or injured as a result of someone's negligence, the conditions cannot take away the right of compensation. If the travel agent's neg-

> ### HOLIDAY MISERY
>
> *The tour operator must provide the holiday described in his brochure. If he fails he is liable to pay compensation.*
>
> In November 1970 Mr Jackson booked a 4 week package holiday in Ceylon for himself, his wife and his two small children at a cost of £1,200. The brochure described the hotel as having mini golf, a swimming pool, beauty salon, hairdressers, gift shop and an excellent restaurant.
>
> When Mr Jackson booked he had specially asked that the children's room should have a connecting door with the parents' room. This was not provided. The children's room was black with mildew, the toilet and shower were dirty and there was no bath. They complained and were moved, but that was still unsatisfactory. In addition, most of the facilities advertised did not exist. Finally they moved to a better hotel where building work was still going on.
>
> On returning home Mr Jackson sued the tour operators for damages and was awarded £1,100. The tour operators admitted breach of contract but contested the amount of damages. They appealed.
>
> #### DECISION
> The court of appeal confirmed the award. The family had a right to £600, half the cost of the holiday, and £500 for the inconvenience and disappointment.

ligence causes loss or damage, the conditions will protect the agent only if they are fair and reasonable. *See:* UNFAIR CONTRACT

If the travel agent does not provide the holiday described in the brochure he will have broken his contract. The holidaymaker can claim compensation for loss of enjoyment.

Codes of conduct

If a travel agent or tour operator is a member of ABTA, the Association of British Travel Agents, he will be bound by the ABTA codes of conduct – ensuring that:
● Booking conditions are designed to be easily read and understood.
● Booking conditions do not include clauses purporting to exclude the agent's responsibility for misrepresentations, or purporting to exclude a tour operator's responsibility to exercise diligence in making arrangements for his clients, or for consequential loss following from breach of this duty.
● Brochures indicate prominently the circumstances in which clients can be asked to pay surcharges on their holiday costs.
● If a holiday has to be cancelled, clients are offered the choice of an alternative holiday if available or a prompt refund of all money paid.

If the cancellation is for reasons outside the tour operator's control, however, he may keep the amount of his reasonable expenses.
● Retail agents advise clients of the necessary passport, visa and health requirements for the journey.

When you can be surcharged

Once a booking has been made and confirmed, the travel agent can make a surcharge only if the booking conditions allow him to do so. Most booking conditions do contain something like: 'We reserve the right to charge you any increase due to fluctuations in the costs on which our prices are based.'

When you cancel

If the customer cancels a holiday he normally loses any deposit he has paid. In addition, the booking conditions may require him to make an extra payment as a cancellation charge. Most agents require the full purchase price to be paid several weeks in advance. How

much they will refund on late cancellations will often depend on a sliding scale, depending on the length of notice of cancellation, and this can vary from agent to agent.

Arranging insurance

Many travel agents offer insurance cover against cancellations, medical expenses, accidents and loss of luggage. It is always advisable to have insurance cover: make sure always that you disclose any existing medical problem in case the policy excludes cover.

It is also possible to take out insurance against extra expenses incurred due to delays – such as those caused by strikes or bad weather – or cancellation due to delays. Sometimes this is included in the cover offered by the travel agent. You should check when booking.

If an agent becomes bankrupt

If a travel agent or tour operator to whom money has been paid becomes insolvent, holidaymakers on package tours may have special protection in certain circumstances. The Civil Aviation Authority operates a licence system known as ATOL, Air Travel Organisers Licence. Before a licence is issued the financial position of the organiser is checked. Holders of a licence must take out a bond, usually a percentage of their annual turnover.

Members of ABTA also have a bonding system. If a member goes bankrupt they either refund the holidaymaker's money or arrange for the holiday to be taken over by another tour operator. Their address is 55–57 Newman Street, London W1P 4AH.

If the travel agent is not a member of ABTA, the holidaymaker should contact the Air Travel Reserve Fund, 20 Manvers Street, Bath, BA1 1LX.

When you have a claim for compensation abroad

Your rights to certain standards of comfort, efficiency and speed in travel arrangements made with an English company will normally be governed by English law, regardless of the country in which a particular complaint arises.

Travel arrangements made with a foreign company may be governed by English or foreign law. If the company has no office in Britain you may not be

able to enforce your rights in an English court. Some large foreign travel agents and airlines state which country's laws will apply in disputes, and it is often English law that is specified.

TREASON

An alien can be guilty of treason against the British Crown

Treason is an offence for which someone may still be hanged in Britain.

Anyone owing allegiance to the Crown commits treason by:
● Showing his intention to kill the sovereign.
● Taking part in an insurrection against the sovereign's authority.
● Giving aid and comfort to the enemy in time of war.

Allegiance is owed, not only by British subjects, but also by aliens under the protection of the Crown. That means anyone who is voluntarily on British territory and who is neither a diplomat nor a member of an invading or occupying force.

An alien who leaves British territory with a British passport, which he still has at the time he commits a treasonable act, is guilty of treason. That is why William Joyce (Lord Haw-Haw) was guilty of treason when he broadcast propaganda from Germany during the Second World War, although he was a United States citizen.

NO NEED TO BE BRITISH

Even an alien can be convicted of treason against Britain – provided that he is the holder of a British passport.

TREASURE TROVE

*The finder of a valuable object
cannot always claim it*

Any gold, silver, plate, coin, bullion or other valuable objects found hidden in the ground or some secret place is treasure trove.

·It belongs to the Crown unless the original owner can be found.

An article that was not hidden, but could have been merely lost or abandoned, is not treasure trove.

If the original owner cannot be traced, and the article is in or attached to the ground, it rightly belongs to the owner of the land where it was discovered. *See:* LOST PROPERTY

The scope of the law

This law applies in all cases – irrespective of whether the 'find' is a collection of Roman coins or a modern engagement ring.

For example, if the coins are carefully buried, it is most likely that they were deliberately hidden. Coins scattered over a wide area were probably lost or abandoned.

> ### THE COINS THAT HAD TOO LITTLE SILVER
>
> *When a hoard of coins or other valuables has been found, it is for the coroner to decide whether they are indeed treasure trove. That depends on their content and whether they have been hidden or lost.*
>
> In 1975 a farm worker discovered 7,811 3rd-century Roman coins in a field at Coleby in Lincolnshire. The coroner decided that because they had been hidden, not only lost or abandoned, they were treasure trove and therefore belonged to the Crown. The owners of the field challenged this decision in the High Court.
>
> #### DECISION
>
> Because the coins were found to have a low silver content, the judge ruled that they could not be regarded as silver, they were therefore not treasure trove and so they belonged to the owners of the field.

When someone unearths buried treasure

Anyone who finds valuables, such as a bag of gold coins or box of silver plate, either by accident – say, while ploughing – or while searching should tell the police.

They will report the find to the local CORONER, one of whose duties is to decide if it is treasure trove or if it was merely lost.

If he rules that the find is treasure trove, Crown officials may allow the finder to keep the valuables. If they decide to keep them for the Crown, it is usual to pay the finder their value as a reward.

Anyone who does not report a find of treasure trove may be guilty of theft.

When the coroner decides that the discovery is not treasure trove – and in the absence of the original owner – it becomes the property of the owner of the land where it was found, or, if not in the ground, the property of the finder.

Special rules apply to objects that have been washed ashore or have been found in the sea.
See: BEACHCOMBING
WRECK

TREE

When it is illegal to fell a tree

Trees are generally protected by law, but those upon which a tree PRESERVATION ORDER has been placed, are subject to special regulations.

There are, however, severe penalties for anyone who, without authority, 'cuts down, uproots or wilfully destroys' any tree, or 'wilfully damages, tops or lops' it in such a way that he is likely to destroy it.

He can be gaoled for up to 12 months and fined an unlimited amount.

For less serious offences of damaging trees there is a maximum fine of £200, plus £5 a day for as long as the offence is continued.

Obtaining a licence to fell an unwanted tree

A landowner or tenant wishing to fell growing trees on his land must obtain a felling licence from the regional office of the Forestry Commission except when:

● The trees are less than 3 in. in diameter or, in the case of coppice or underwood, not more than 6 in. diameter, or when the object is to improve the growth of other trees, not more than 4 in. diameter.

● They are fruit trees, or trees in orchards, gardens, churchyards or public places.

● The felling does not exceed 825 cu. ft of timber in any calendar quarter and not more than 150 cu. ft is to be sold.

● Hedges are trimmed and laid, or when trees are dangerous or topped or lopped in normal circumstances.

A felling licence may sometimes be issued only on condition that replanting takes place. If a licence is refused, or granted only subject to conditions, the owner can appeal to the Secretary of State for Agriculture, Fisheries and Food.

A felling licence granted after a tree preservation order has been made is still authority enough for the felling. In this situation, however, the Forestry Commission will usually refer any application for a licence to the local authority, which may decide to take it over as an application for consent to fell under the order.

An owner felling trees without a licence can be fined a maximum of £10 or twice the value of the tree.

Control of felling by licence does not apply in inner London boroughs, where tree preservation orders are needed to protect trees.

When tree roots cause damage to neighbouring property

If the roots of a tree damage a neighbouring property owner's land or buildings, he is entitled to claim compensation from the owner of the tree. It is no valid defence for the tree owner to say that his tree was there before the neighbour's damaged property.

The most difficult area of dispute is where the tree is growing on a grass verge outside private property and where the local council refuses to accept that it is the owning occupier of the verge. If you are affected by such a tree, take professional legal advice about suing the council.

When branches overhang the neighbouring garden

If trees in your neighbour's garden overhang your property, you are entitled to cut down the overhanging branches. Any fruit on an overhanging branch belongs to your neighbour, not to you.

If the branches are so high that you cannot reach them, they are still regarded in law as a nuisance to your property. Ask him to arrange to have the offending branch removed at his own expense. If he refuses, you could, if you thought it worthwhile, hire someone to carry out the work and bring an action in the county court to recover the cost.

TRESPASS

What you can do about unwelcome visitors

Trespassing on someone else's land or property is a civil wrong but not a crime. A sign saying 'Trespassers will be prosecuted' has no legal weight. They can be sued for damages, and the owner of the land can forcibly evict a trespasser, but he cannot bring a prosecution.

The essence of trespass is that entry is without the owner's consent. The postman and newspaper boy have implied consent to walk up the front path, but they are trespassing if they go into the greenhouse.

A 'No hawkers, no canvassers' sign at the gate shows they do not have implied permission to come in and they are trespassers if they do so.

Someone may become a trespasser if consent to be on the property is revoked. A policeman has implied consent to come to the door to make inquiries but if he does not have a warrant and refuses a request to leave he becomes a trespasser. So does a tenant who stays on after his tenancy has ended. Sit-in strikes may also be trespassing.

Preventing trespass

Every householder or property owner has a right to take reasonable steps to keep out trespassers, but not to install hidden devices designed to injure those who do trespass. A barbed-wire fence or even broken glass embedded in a wall are reasonable, but not an electric fence carrying sufficient charge to kill anyone who touches it.

A trespasser injured by a guard DOG may or may not be entitled to compensation depending on whether it was reasonable for the owner to keep the dog as protection.

If a trespasser refuses a request to leave, the owner of the property is entitled to use reasonable force to evict him. The amount of force that may legally be used depends on the circumstances.

If a small boy trespasses on a garden to retrieve a ball it is not reasonable to strike him with a spade. But a householder about to be attacked by armed intruders would be justified in firing a shot-gun in their direction.

But even a trespasser has rights. If a property owner injures a trespasser deliberately – rather than accidentally while evicting him – he commits a crime and, in addition, can be sued for damages.

The owner must also avoid reckless disregard for the safety of trespassers known to be on his property. A company that fails to fence off a poison dump knowing that children play there can be sued if a young trespasser comes to harm.

Suing for trespass

If a trespasser is sued the court normally awards whatever it costs to repair

WHEN FORCE MUST BE NO MORE THAN REASONABLE

Householders and property owners have a legal right to keep trespassers out, but they must use only reasonable force to do so.

the damage. It is no defence for a trespasser to claim he did not know he was trespassing. If police or other officials trespass, extra damages may be awarded as a mark of disapproval of the abuse of power.

A trespasser can be sued for trespass even if no damage has been caused and no worthwhile compensation can be expected. Such a case may be brought as a convenient way of settling a dispute over the ownership of land or property.

For example, a householder who believes a neighbour's extension projects on to his property can sue the neighbour for trespass in order to obtain a court ruling on where the boundary lies if the title deeds do not make the line clear.

TRIBUNAL

Dispensing justice without the legal trimmings

A major development in the administration of justice in Britain has been the growth of tribunals and public inquiries for settling disputes without having to go to formal courts of law.

Special tribunals decide claims over a vast range of issues, including unfair dismissal, social security benefits, rents, immigration, mental health, compensation for compulsory purchase and many other matters.

People who appear before tribunals frequently present their own case and have the opportunity to produce witnesses and cross-examine the other side.

Appeals against a tribunal's decision are usually heard by an appeals tribunal. Anyone who thinks a tribunal has acted unfairly or shown bias can ask the High Court to review the case. There are special procedures for such action and a solicitor should be consulted.

Public inquiries When there are disputes over planning decisions, or over the resolution of a public authority to acquire land or property by COMPULSORY PURCHASE, a government department will often open a public inquiry. An inspector is appointed to conduct the inquiry and make a report to the minister. Objectors can put their case in person or appoint a solicitor and they are entitled to see the inspector's report. *See:* PLANNING OBJECTION

The minister's eventual decision can be challenged in the High Court, but only on the grounds that the inquiry went beyond its legal powers or failed to observe the correct procedures. The High Court will not re-examine disputes about the facts. There is usually a time limit – often only 6 weeks – on starting High Court proceedings.

Tribunals' watchdog The Council on Tribunals is appointed by the Lord Chancellor to keep under review the working of most tribunals and important kinds of public inquiry.

The council investigates complaints on general issues concerning the running of such bodies or on specific grievances – for example, that the regulations under which a particular hearing took place were unfair and prevented objectors putting their case. But it does not hear appeals against tribunal or public inquiry decisions.

If you have a complaint about a tribunal or inquiry procedure, write to the Secretary, Council on Tribunals, 6 Spring Gardens, London SWA 2BG. Complaints about inquiries – but not tribunals – can also be made to the OMBUDSMAN.

TRUST

How property can be held by one person for another's benefit

A trust exists when property – such as land or investments – is held by one person or group of persons for the benefit of others.

A trust can be set up to:
● Benefit someone who is incapable of conducting his or her own affairs.
● Protect family assets from extravagance or bankruptcy – for example, so that if a beneficiary becomes bankrupt, the assets of the trust pass to others in the family and not to his creditors.
● Protect land given to a minor. Someone who is under 18 years of age cannot legally own property, but it can be held in trust until he comes of age.
● Keep property for people not yet born – say any grandchildren who might later exist.
● Ensure that an estate is kept intact and not sold to be shared out among the beneficiaries.
● Give a widow the income from a dead

man's estate and then allow his children to sell and share it on her death.
● Benefit people unnamed by the person setting up the trust. He can leave that decision to his trustees – in what is called a discretionary trust.
● Benefit charitable institutions – for example, to provide scholarships at the trustees' discretion to a particular school, or to provide benefits for the poor of a community.
● Control the assets and finances of a club or society.

Many trusts are set up to obtain tax benefits – by reducing liability to pay INCOME TAX and CAPITAL TRANSFER TAX, for example.

How to set up a trust

A trust is best established in a signed, legal document. In the case of land, it must be in writing although this does not apply to other property. Because trust law and tax rules are complex, it is wise to set out your intentions and wishes with the help of a solicitor.

The document should state what the trust is to be called and list the capital assets and incomes to be administered by the trustees. It should then name the beneficiaries or describe them – for example, 'all the children of my sons and daughters'.

You should then set out any conditions – for example:
● How the trust is to be operated.
● Where the assets should be invested.
● How long benefits are to be withheld from the beneficiaries.

You may even lay down a time limit for the trust to remain in existence. Except for charitable trusts, the maximum period is 80 years or 21 years after the death of someone living when the trust first takes effect.

How to choose trustees

Anyone who agrees can be named as a trustee except a minor, and some would be unlikely to be chosen – for example, a person of unsound mind, a person convicted of a serious crime or a bankrupt. They are unpaid unless the trust deed states otherwise.

Any number of trustees can be appointed except in the case of land when the legal limit is four. It is not wise to have too many.

The people chosen should be reliable and businesslike; ideally they should

have a working knowledge of property or be experienced in dealing in stocks and shares. It is helpful if they also know the family background.

If the trust is complicated and is likely to continue for a long time, it may be worthwhile appointing professional trustees or a trust company to operate it. A trust company will not act without being paid. *See:* EXECUTOR

Once the trust has been set up and the trustees appointed, the assets involved must be properly transferred – property by sealed document, and stocks and shares by transfer document – and the trustees must be registered as the owners.

Restricting investment

If the creator of a trust makes no conditions about investments, the trustees are governed by the Trustee Investment Act 1961. That allows them to invest in Defence Bonds, National Savings and bank deposit accounts, but it bars them from investing more than half of a trust's assets in stocks and shares, unit trusts or building societies.

Trustees are liable for losses on improper investments, unless the court is prepared to excuse them.

Trustees who are not familiar with the rules and how to apply them should take advice from a bank, stockbroker or a solicitor.

Any trustee without special powers must take advice on investing.

What are the tax gains of establishing a trust?

Taxation can often be reduced when assets and income are transferred to a trust.

A trust can even be taxed as much as 50 per cent less than an individual.

Payments made to a beneficiary are taxed as personal investment income, and trustees usually deduct the basic rate of tax before handing over the money.

When a parent makes a trust in favour of his or her own unmarried children under 18 years of age, the income from the trust is treated for tax purposes as part of his own income and is taxed accordingly.

Most transfers of assets into or out of a trust will be subject to capital gains tax and capital transfer tax.

UNBORN CHILD

A new-born baby can have rights that pre-date its birth

Until a child is born it is not regarded as a person by the law for most purposes.

Once the child is born and has led an existence independent of its mother, however, its rights can go back to when it was still in the womb.

For example, if someone other than the child's mother caused it damage, through negligence, while it was still in the womb, the child can bring an action for damages. *See:* CHILDREN'S RIGHTS

Similarly, an unborn child named in a WILL can inherit once it is born. It is doubtful whether an unborn child can inherit under an INTESTACY because it was not in existence at the time of the death. *See also:* ABORTION

UNCOLLECTED GOODS

Your goods may be sold if you fail to collect them on time

If you leave goods for repair, valuation or storage, you are responsible for collecting them unless delivery to you has been agreed.

If you do not do so, the repairer, valuer or warehouseman can sell your goods – provided only that he first sends notice to your last-known address by registered post or recorded delivery. It must state:

● That the goods are ready for collection.
● How much is owing.
● That the goods will be sold if not collected by a certain date.

The date given must allow you a reasonable opportunity to collect your goods. If you owe any money for repair or valuation, the date must be 3 months or more from the day the notice is sent.

When the time expires, your goods can be sold by whatever is the best method of sale reasonably available in the circumstances. The proceeds, after deduction of any amount owed for repair, valuation or storage, must be kept and given to you if you claim it later.

UNEMPLOYMENT BENEFIT

How the state helps when a person is out of work

Anyone who is out of work is entitled to claim unemployment benefit, provided that he makes enough NATIONAL INSURANCE CONTRIBUTIONS while he is in work.

If you want to claim, visit the local unemployment benefit office on the first day of unemployment and take a note of your national insurance number or P.45 income tax form, which is given to an employee when he leaves his job.

If you do not go at once you cannot receive unemployment benefit for the days that have elapsed unless you have a good reason for the delay. Always attend even if you have no documents.

The rate of unemployment benefit in 1981 was £20.65 for anyone who paid full rate national insurance contributions. A married man could claim an extra £12.75 for a wife or adult dependant and £1.25 for each child.

A man who does not retire at 65 and a woman who does not retire at 60, but who is entitled to a retirement pension on eventual retirement, is entitled to unemployment benefit when unemployed.

The rate of unemployment benefit for someone in this situation is £26 a week, with an extra £15.60 for his wife.

It is sometimes worth while claiming unemployment benefit in those circumstances as it is not taxable, whereas retirement pension is. Men cease to be eligible at 70 and women at 65.

An EARNINGS-RELATED SUPPLEMENT may also be payable.

How you qualify for unemployment benefit

Anyone seeking unemployment benefit must satisfy two contribution conditions:
● He must have paid, in any single tax year since April 1975, Class 1 national insurance contributions worth 25 times the amount paid by someone on the weekly LOWER EARNINGS LIMIT for that year.
● He must have paid or been credited with Class 1 contributions in the year ending April 5 before the year in which benefit is claimed, that amount to 50 times the contributions paid by someone on the lower earnings limit for that year. Benefit is reduced if the full 50 contributions have not been met. However, if the contributions amount to less than 25 times those paid by someone on the lower earnings limit, benefit is not payable.

For example, if someone is out of work and claims benefit in 1981, his contributions are counted between April 6, 1979 and April 5, 1980.

However, if he is out of work within 8 weeks of a previous period of unemployment, his year of contributions is the same as that for his previous period out of work.

For example, if someone was unemployed in January 1981 having been out of work and claiming benefit at the end of December 1980, payment of benefit may be governed by his contributions in

CLAIMING SUPPLEMENTARY BENEFIT WHEN UNEMPLOYED

Anyone claiming unemployment benefit may also be entitled to receive weekly SUPPLEMENTARY BENEFIT. If you are not entitled to unemployment benefit you may still be able to get supplementary benefit.

However, the amount of supplementary benefit is reduced if the claimant is disqualified from receiving unemployment benefit because, for example, he left his job voluntarily without a good reason, lost it through misconduct or refused to take a suitable job. When the disqualification period – usually 6 weeks – is over, benefit is payable at the full rate.

The usual reduction is 40 per cent of the weekly rate for a single person – in 1981 it was £8.50 a week, or £6.80 for a single person who is not a householder, or £5.25 if he is under 18. But the reduction is only half these amounts if:
● A member of the family – the claimant, his wife or a child – is seriously ill or pregnant.
● There is a child under 5.
● The claimant's last job was part-time or lasted 6 weeks or less.
● His net earnings were below supplementary benefit level.
● The rent or mortgage payments are not allowed in full in calculating his benefit because they are too high.
● Because of circumstances similar to these, the full reduction is not appropriate.

Someone who is not entitled to unemployment benefit because he has not paid enough contributions will have his supplementary benefit reduced in the same way if the Supplementary Benefit Officer considers that he left his job voluntarily and would be disqualified for unemployment benefit for that reason.

Similarly, supplementary benefit is reduced if the insurance officer has not yet decided whether a claimant is disqualified but the Supplementary Benefit Officer has reason to think he may have left his job voluntarily. However, if the insurance officer subsequently decides the claimant is entitled to benefit, arrears are paid.

In certain cases, benefit can be refused or withdrawn altogether – for example, if someone refuses to take a suitable job that is known to be still available to him.

Similarly, in areas where short-term jobs are available – for example, in a seaside town in summer – someone claiming benefit while unemployed, who is under 45 and has no children, can be given 14 days' notice that his benefit will be withdrawn if he remains unemployed without good reason. But this must not be done if the claimant's wife is pregnant or, having regard to all the circumstances, including the state of health of the claimant and his wife, the benefit officer decides that it would be inappropriate to cut off his benefit. If his benefit is cut off, he can apply again after 6 weeks.

If a supplementary benefit claimant has been out of work for a considerable time, he may be given an appointment for an interview with an Unemployment Review Officer. The officer advises and assists anyone who is having difficulty finding a job, and may warn a claimant that his supplementary benefit may be affected if he does not make an effort to find work.

If a person who fails to attend for an interview is sent another appointment within 14 days and again fails to attend, he is treated as not being available for employment and his benefit is withdrawn.

The review officer may suggest that a claimant should attend a 're-establishment course' to help him prepare for a return to work. If he does not go voluntarily, and a benefit officer considers that he is refusing or neglecting to maintain himself or his family, he can be directed to attend – but the direction does not come into effect until he has had an opportunity of appealing against it.

If he does not comply with the direction, he loses his normal entitlement to benefit, though he may still be entitled to urgent-need payments at a reduced rate to avoid serious risk to health.

If a claimant persistently refuses to maintain himself or his family by getting work, he may be prosecuted. Anyone convicted may be imprisoned for up to 3 months and fined up to £400.

Anyone who has his benefit reduced is entitled to appeal to a supplementary benefit appeal tribunal.

the 1978–9 tax year as it was for his claim in December.

When unemployment benefit is payable

Anyone claiming unemployment benefit may do so for up to 312 days – excluding Sundays. After that time, a person is not entitled to claim benefit again until he has worked and paid contributions for 13 weeks. In each week he must have worked at least 16 hours.

Benefit is not paid for the first 3 days of unemployment.

Benefit is then calculated on a daily basis and after a person has registered as being unemployed, he is told to attend the unemployment office on a certain day and at a particular time.

However, benefit is not payable:
● For any period during which you receive wages in lieu of notice. *See:* SOCIAL SECURITY OFFENCES
● For any day on which you are on holiday from work, even if no holiday pay is given by the employer. Holiday or redundancy payments, however, do not affect unemployment benefit.

If someone takes a job as a temporary teacher from September to the end of the academic year, for example, he cannot claim benefit during school holidays, even if he is not paid for holidays.

If someone takes a part-time job he can draw benefit only if his earnings are not more than 75p a day and he is available for full-time work and the job is not his usual main occupation.

If you receive an occupational pension of more than £35 a week (in 1981), your unemployment benefit will be cut by £1 for every £1 you get over this amount.

When you are disqualified from receiving benefit

No benefit is payable if a person places unreasonable restrictions on the nature, hours, rate of pay, locality or other conditions of employment, so that prospects of his getting work are poor.

Reasonableness is determined in the light of a claimant's health, period of unemployment and the nature of his usual occupation.

In certain circumstances, a disqualification from benefit can be imposed for up to 6 weeks at the discretion of the insurance officer, if a person:
● Leaves employment voluntarily and the insurance officer considers his claim for benefit is unjustified.

For example, if a woman works in London but wants to live on the coast

> ## THE MANAGER WHO COULD NOT TRAVEL
>
> *Unemployment benefit will not be paid if you unreasonably restrict your chances of finding a job.*
>
> A man who lived in Epsom gave up his job as a technical manager to a construction company in the City of London on medical advice – because the travelling was too much for him to cope with. When he claimed unemployment benefit he stated that he wanted a job like his old one, but locally.
>
> ### DECISION
> The Commissioner found that there was no reasonable prospect of getting such a job and that he was not entitled to claim benefit.
>
> ## OFF-DUTY CONDUCT THAT COST A GARDENER HIS JOB
>
> *If misconduct while off duty leads to dismissal from a job, a person's entitlement to unemployment benefit may be affected.*
>
> A gardener, aged 30, worked in the parks department of a local authority. While off duty he committed an offence of gross indecency with another man and was later convicted in a magistrates' court. He was also dismissed from his job.
>
> ### DECISION
> The Commissioner held that the misconduct was a valid reason for dismissal as it adversely affected his suitability for his job. It was proper therefore to suspend his unemployment benefit for 1 week.

because she likes swimming, she would not be entitled to claim benefit immediately if she left her London job to move to the coast.

The same would apply if someone left employment for health reasons, but could not supply supporting medical evidence, or if he left because he was dissatisfied with his wages – even though they were the wages that the employer promised when the employee joined in accordance with local rates.

However, there may be just cause for leaving a job if the employer requires a person to do other work than what he is qualified and was originally contracted to perform; if his contract was for day work only and a new transfer to permanent nights is demanded; if the employer refuses to provide safe working conditions.

The 6 week disqualification applies also when someone:
● Is dismissed for misconduct – for example, absenteeism, unpunctuality, refusing to obey reasonable orders or incompetent work.
● Refuses to apply for or to accept suitable employment or if he refuses to accept training facilities offered by the Government.

If a person feels he has been unfairly disqualified from claiming benefit, he is entitled to appeal to a National Insurance appeal tribunal.

UNFAIR CONTRACT

When a condition in a contract is void because it is unfair

A contract condition that takes away a person's legal rights – for example, to compensation for death or injury through negligence – can be challenged in civil proceedings.

The Unfair Contract Terms Act 1977 protects the public. It makes some unfair conditions automatically void even if the contract has been signed.

Conditions that are void

A contract exemption clause is void if it attempts to:
● Exclude one party's right to compensation for death or personal injury caused by the other party's negligence.
● Evade or weaken a dealer's obligation to see that the goods he sells are of suitable quality and fitness.

The second prohibition applies only to sales to consumers – not to trade deals or to goods bought at a trade rate.

Notices A shop sign saying 'No Money Refunded' is illegal unless it goes on to make clear that customers are entitled to refunds for DEFECTIVE GOODS. The maximum penalty is 2 years' imprisonment and an unlimited fine.

A notice saying 'No Goods Ex-

changed', however, is permissible because the only legal obligation is MONEY BACK.

Hire purchase The law applies as much to hire-purchase agreements as to cash sales.

Guarantees Any term in a guarantee or warranty document that attempts to take away the normal rights of a buyer of consumer goods is also automatically void.

When an exemption clause is arguable

Other contract terms controlled by the 1977 law are valid if they are fair and reasonable. If not, they are void.

They are subject to a legal 'reasonableness test', which states that a condition is valid if it was fair and reasonable to include it in the contract at the time it was made, having regard to the circumstances that were known or contemplated then, or should have been.

A court also takes into account a customer's knowledge of the clause – or whether he could reasonably be expected to have known of it – and the relative bargaining strengths of the parties.

In considering whether it is reasonable to place a fixed monetary limit on liability, the law relates the amount of the limit to the financial resources of the contractor, and to how far he could cover himself by insurance.

Contract terms that a court might find valid or void, depending on the reasonableness test, include any that attempt to limit or exclude liability for:
● Property loss or damage through negligence.
● Quality and fitness of goods in business deals.
● Losses caused by breach of contract or misrepresentation.

When circumstances change

A contract term that claims the right to perform the contract in a different way – for example, when a travel operator changes a holiday booking, or a dealer supplies goods of another description – is also subject to the reasonableness test.

Cancellation Clauses that claim the right of the trader to back out in changed circumstances are similarly controlled.

UNFAIR DISMISSAL

How the law protects those who lose their jobs

Most full-time employees who have completed 52 weeks' service with their employer are entitled to apply to an INDUSTRIAL TRIBUNAL for compensation if they are unfairly dismissed. The rules do not apply to part-time workers – normally, those employed for fewer than 16 hours a week – nor to people already over retirement age, merchant seamen and registered dock-workers. *See:* EMPLOYMENT PROTECTION

An employee claiming unfair dismissal must first prove to the tribunal that he was dismissed and did not, for example, resign. If he fails to do so, his claim will automatically be rejected.

Once dismissal has been established, the employer has to give a reason which is a fair one. If he does so – for example, by proving misconduct – the tribunal has to decide whether the employer acted reasonably or unreasonably in treating it as grounds for dismissal and in the way he carried out the dismissal.

Misconduct for example, may not justify dismissal if it is not very serious, or if the employer acted without a proper investigation of the facts.

Was the employee dismissed?

Most dismissals are straightforward – the employee is told, verbally or in writing, that his employment will end and, having served a period of NOTICE or received wages in lieu of notice, he leaves. But some are less clear-cut.

Constructive dismissal An employee who leaves because of a gross breach of his EMPLOYMENT CONTRACT by his employer – for example, refusal to pay agreed wages – is said to have been 'constructively' dismissed. Constructive dismissals are nearly always unfair.

A victim of constructive dismissal does not need to follow the rules on notice. He should, however, write to his employer, keeping a copy of the letter, to make it clear that he is not resigning, but leaving because of the employer's breach of contract.

Leaving while under notice An employee who leaves while under notice – for example, to start a new job – has nevertheless been dismissed and does not forfeit his right to claim unfair dismissal.

Fixed-term contracts Someone who has worked on a fixed-term contract

---

HOW TO CLAIM UNFAIR DISMISSAL

Anyone may pursue a claim for unfair dismissal, provided that he was dismissed and did not resign from his job and he has been working at that job for 52 weeks. When an employer has at no time employed more than 20 employees, the qualifying period is 2 years. If you want to bring a claim:

● Write to your employer as soon as possible after dismissal and ask him to put the reasons for your dismissal in writing. An employer is required by law to reply to such a request within 14 days.

● When you know why you were dismissed, visit your local Job Centre, Citizens Advice Bureau, employment or unemployment office and ask for form IT1.

● Before completing the form, seek advice from the Citizens Advice Bureau, a solicitor or trade union official if you belong to a union, on how to fill in the form. You will have to give your reasons why you feel the dismissal was unfair.

You may also decide that you wish to be represented by a solicitor at the hearing. If you do so, you are not entitled to receive LEGAL AID.

● Send the completed form to the Secretary of the Tribunals, Central Office of the Industrial Tribunals, 93 Ebury Bridge Road, London SW1W 8RE. You must do so within 3 months of dismissal.

Once an employer has agreed that he dismissed his employee, he must show the tribunal that he had fair reason for dismissal and the tribunal will decide whether he acted reasonably. The employer is sent a copy of form IT1. He is invited to reply to the tribunal and give his reasons for the

dismissal on form IT3 – a copy of which is sent to the claimant.

After the application has been made, a conciliation officer from the Advisory, Conciliation and Arbitration Service may contact the claimant and his employer to try to reach a settlement before a hearing. Either may ask an ACAS officer to intervene. Although neither party is required to co-operate with the officer, it is advisable to do so as he may be able to negotiate a suitable compromise.

If an employer and his employee agree to a settlement before a hearing, it is not binding unless it is approved by the conciliation officer. Otherwise, the employee is entitled to change his mind and proceed with a claim for compensation to a tribunal. He is entitled to do so even if he signs an agreement with his employer that states that the agreement is a final settlement. If a claimant wins his case after making such an agreement, the tribunal usually reduces his award by the amount he has already received from his employer.

Such an 'out of court' agreement is binding only if it is set out in writing, signed by both employer and employee and countersigned by a conciliation officer.

● If no settlement is reached and the claim proceeds, you will be notified of the date of the tribunal hearing. Write again to your employer and ask for 'further and better particulars' of the information he gave on form IT3 when he stated why you were dismissed.

● Ask the employer for copies of any documents that may apply to your case – for

example, your personnel file or a copy of the company's disciplinary rules and procedures. If he refuses to supply such information within 14 days, write to the Secretary of the Tribunals and ask for an order to be made to the employer to supply the information required. If he fails to do so, he may be fined up to £100.

● When preparing your case, study your employment contract and the company's disciplinary rules. If the employer has not followed the strict wording of the rules, he is unlikely to have acted 'reasonably' when dismissing you. The employer may argue at the hearing that you have not done all you could to get another job and reduce your loss. Keep a diary of your attempts to find another job and any letters involved and produce those and any other evidence that will help your case at the hearing.

● Ask any colleagues to be witnesses for you at the hearing – for example, there may be a colleague who was in the same situation as you but was not dismissed or a colleague may be able to provide evidence that your employer dismissed you merely because he disliked you.

If a colleague does not want to be a witness, write to the Secretary of the Tribunals and ask for a witness order to be made. However, it is up to you to serve those orders on your colleagues.

Even if a person wins a case, he has to pay all the legal costs and expenses if he was represented by a solicitor. A tribunal awards costs only if it considers one party has acted 'frivolously', 'vexatiously' or 'unreasonably'.

WHEN THE NEW JOB WAS BEYOND HIS CAPABILITIES

An employer who promotes an employee, but then finds him incapable of doing the job, can avoid a claim for unfair dismissal by offering him his old post back or suitable alternative work.

After 8 years as the manager of a depot in which non-food items were stored, Mr Cook was promoted by his employers to manage a food depot. But his performance in the new job was poor.

His employers offered him alternative work managing a non-food depot again.

Mr Cook declined, because his salary would drop and his fares would increase, and he was dismissed. He claimed unfair dismissal.

DECISION

The court held that Mr Cook's dismissal was fair. As Mr Cook's employers had lost confidence in his ability to manage a food depot, it was reasonable for them to offer other work, although on different terms, and to dismiss him when he did not take it.

and is not allowed to renew it has been dismissed. If the contract, or succession of contracts with one employer, ran continuously for 52 weeks, he can claim unfair dismissal. However, an employer is entitled to insert into a fixed-term contract of 1 year or more a clause waiving the employee's right to claim unfair dismissal if he is not kept on when the contract ends.

After maternity leave A woman who is not allowed to resume her old job after childbirth has been unfairly dismissed. *See:* MATERNITY

When there is no dismissal

An employee who resigns of his own free will has not been dismissed. Neither has someone who is suspended with pay from his job. *See:* RESIGNATION

An employee whose job ends because his employer dies has not been dismissed. *See:* EMPLOYER, Death of

If an employee is unable to work for a prolonged period – for example, because of imprisonment – his employment contract may be held to have been 'frustrated' through his failure to fulfil his side of it. Although his job is then at an end, he has not legally been dismissed. *See:* DISMISSAL

The five 'fair' reasons

The employment protection rules recognise five types of reason for dismissal as 'fair':

● Lack of capability or qualifications for doing the job.
● Misconduct by the employee.
● Redundancy.
● When continued employment would lead to a breach of the law.
● Other 'substantial' reasons.

An employee who lacks the skill, aptitude, health or other physical or mental quality needed to do his job can be fairly dismissed on those grounds. But the employer must provide full evidence to the tribunal of his incapability – including relevant documents and the testimony on oath of fellow-workers and managerial staff.

Generally, the longer an employee has been in his job, the more difficult it is for his employer to show he was incapable of doing it.

When the job changes An employee who is not redundant and who is put on to work for which he was not hired under the terms of his employment contract – for example, by switching him from operating one type of machine to another – generally cannot be fairly dismissed for not being able to do it.

But sometimes if the employer has good business reasons for making changes, and he consults fully with his employees before doing so, he can fairly dismiss an employee who unreasonably refuses to agree to the variation of his employment contract.

If the change is the result of promotion which varies the terms of the contract, the employee may succeed in claiming unfair dismissal if he was not given proper help or training or an adequate trial in the new post, or if he was not offered the opportunity to transfer to a more suitable one.

Ill health If an employee is physically or mentally incapable, over a prolonged period, of doing his job, his employer is entitled to consider the employment ended by frustration of contract. If the employee brings an unfair dismissal claim, he must show he would have been fit to resume work within a reasonable time. There is no general rule on what constitutes a 'prolonged' period, but it is often defined by the employment contract or by collective agreement.

Frequent short absences through ill health or persistent failure to observe company rules on reporting sick may be fair grounds for dismissal, but the employer must give the employee ample warning before serving notice. *See:* SICKNESS

Trial periods Employers cannot use a prolonged trial or probationary period to evade a claim for unfair dismissal. Once an employee has been in the job for 52 weeks, he is protected, even though he may still be on trial. *See:* PROBATIONARY EMPLOYEE

However, in highly technical jobs a trial period of more than 52 weeks may be necessary, because the capability of new employees cannot be properly assessed until they have undergone lengthy training.

Tribunals take that into account in deciding whether a dismissal for incapability is fair.

Lack of qualifications An employee who claims, on recruitment, to hold the qualifications essential for the job, but who is discovered later not to possess them, can be fairly dismissed.

DISMISSED – AFTER 5 YEARS AS A PROBATIONER

A probationary employee who is required to pass a test before his appointment becomes permanent and who fails to do so can be fairly dismissed.

Mr Blackman was recruited by the Post Office as a probationary post and telegraph officer in 1968. After 5 years and three attempts, he had still not passed the compulsory aptitude test needed to confirm his appointment as permanent. He was dismissed, but claimed the dismissal was unfair.

DECISION

Mr Blackman lost his claim. Passing the aptitude test was a condition of his employment.

SUBMITTING A CLAIM FOR UNFAIR DISMISSAL
How a dismissed employee brought her case to an industrial tribunal

1 For 6 weeks, Mrs P has been asking her employer at the hairdressers where she has worked for 2 years if she can take a week off, without pay, because her son is due to go into hospital. Her employer says 'no', but Mrs P decides to take the time off.

2 Mrs P hears no more from her employer until she gets a letter saying she has been sacked and containing a week's pay in lieu of notice. Mrs P feels she has been unfairly dismissed. She was not told why she could not take the time, nor that she would be fired.

3 Mrs P decides to take her case to an industrial tribunal. She gets the application form, IT1, from her nearest employment office and, with a friend who is going to speak on her behalf at the hearing, asks her local Citizens Advice Bureau to help them to complete it. She sends the form to the tribunals' central office in London, which allocates the case to a tribunal near where she worked.

4 The local tribunal notifies Mrs P's employer that it is to consider her claim, and he decides to fight. The tribunal then passes the documents to the Advisory, Conciliation and Arbitration Service, which tries to promote a settlement. An ACAS conciliation officer meets Mrs P and her employer separately and together, but his efforts fail.

5 At the tribunal hearing, Mrs P's representative puts her case. Then it is her employer's turn. Proceedings are less formal than in an ordinary court. The three members of the tribunal confer briefly at the end of the hearing and then announce their decision. They decide that Mrs P was unfairly dismissed because her employer did not explain that she would be sacked if she took a week off. But the amount he must pay Mrs P is less than her original claim because she was absent without permission.

An employer may also fairly dismiss an employee who fails to pass a required test or examination, provided that he was told he was expected to do so when he was hired.

However, an employer cannot decide after he has taken on a new recruit that he must obtain a certain qualification and then dismiss him for not earning it, unless he can show that possession of that qualification had become essential to the job.

Misconduct by the employee

Some offences by employees – for example, embezzlement of the employer's funds – are so serious that they justify summary dismissal without notice. Others – for example, lateness or absenteeism – are only fair grounds for dismissal if they are flagrant or persistent, and the employee remains entitled to notice.

In deciding whether a dismissal for misconduct is fair, industrial tribunals consider the gravity of the offence, whether the punishment for it had been previously made clear to the employee – for example, in written particulars of his employment contract – and whether he had been given a chance before dismissal to state his version of events. *See:* DISCIPLINE AT WORK

When an employee is made redundant

REDUNDANCY is a fair reason for dismissal and the employee who loses his job because of it cannot normally claim compensation beyond any redundancy payment to which he is entitled. But his employer must show that the redundancy was genuine. If someone else was appointed to do the same job, or if the redundancy was not dealt with in a

reasonable manner, the dismissed employee may succeed in claiming his dismissal was unfair.

When the law would be broken

An employer may be justified in dismissing someone if to keep him in his job would lead to a breach of the law. A van driver who loses his driving licence might be fairly dismissed for that reason, but the tribunal will consider the surrounding circumstances – including the proportion of his duties occupied by driving and the length of the ban.

Other 'substantial' reasons

There is no general legal definition of 'substantial' reasons justifying dismissal, and tribunals assess each case according to the circumstances. Reasons that have been upheld include:

Incompatibility If an employee causes disharmony among his fellow-workers – for example, by offensive remarks – and continues to do so after warnings, his dismissal may be held to be fair.

Revealing trade secrets An employee who reveals trade secrets to a com-

petitor, or works for one in his free time, can be fairly dismissed.

'Economic necessity' Dismissals on economic grounds – for example, to replace a highly paid employee by someone on a lower salary – have occasionally been held to be fair, but tribunal decisions conflict.

Getting the reasons for dismissal

All employees eligible to bring a claim for unfair dismissal – and some other classes of employee as well – are entitled to ask their employers to state in writing the reasons for which they were dismissed. If an employer fails to provide written reasons within 14 days of being asked to do so, he can be ordered by an industrial tribunal to pay compensation of up to £240.

An employer who has refused to supply written reasons to a dismissed employee is unlikely to be treated sympathetically by a tribunal at any subsequent unfair dismissal hearing. If he refuses to give the reason for dismissal at the hearing itself, he will lose his case.

The employer can give several reasons, but if he does he must also state which was the most important. He cannot cite an offence committed or discovered after notice had been served, although in practice tribunals take such offences into account in fixing compensation. An employee guilty of gross misconduct while under notice will receive a reduced award.

Any employee considering a claim for unfair dismissal should immediately ask his employer to give the reasons for dismissal in writing.

WHEN THE LONGER-SERVING EMPLOYEE WAS REDUNDANT

An employer who makes a long-serving employee redundant, in preference to one with shorter service, must show that he has considered all the factors involved and made his choice in good faith.

Two jobs were to be merged into one and one of the employees occupying them was to be made redundant. The first candidate had been with his employer for only a year, but was already performing many of the functions of the new post.

The other had longer, but interrupted, service and he was made redundant. He claimed unfair dismissal.

DECISION

The dismissal was fair. There was little to choose between the two men, and having considered all the factors, the employers retained the one they believed more capable. They had followed the code of practice on redundancy and had not contravened any local custom.

THE TRAINEE DISPENSER WHO FAILED TO QUALIFY

A potential breach of the law is not always sufficient grounds for dismissal.
The Hearing Aid Council Act 1968 requires people who dispense hearing aids to pass an examination and to register with the Council before they can practise.

Mr Pinney was a trainee dispenser with a hearing-aid company, but he failed the professional examination and could not

register. His employers sacked him because, they argued, the law did not allow them to employ unregistered dispensers. Mr Pinney claimed unfair dismissal.

DECISION

The dismissal was unfair. The employers could have chosen instead to apply for an extension of Mr Pinney's training.

THE EMPLOYEE'S RIGHT TO AN EXPLANATION

THE EMPLOYEE'S RIGHT TO AN EXPLANATION

Every employee who thinks that he has a claim for unfair dismissal is entitled to be given his employer's reasons for sacking him in writing within 14 days.

'And you've 14 days to put your reasons in writing'

Was the employee's dismissal 'reasonable'?

Once an employer has shown that the grounds for a dismissal were fair, the tribunal must decide whether he acted 'reasonably'.

In all dismissals, he will usually lose his case if he has failed to follow the relevant provisions of the employment contract or any applicable collective agreement or established custom and practice. If he fails to pay wages for the notice period – other than in cases of summary dismissal for gross misconduct – he can also be sued in a civil court. *See:* WRONGFUL DISMISSAL

An employer will lose any case in which he unreasonably selected a member of an independent TRADE UNION, or applicant to join one, for dismissal.

In addition, there are general tests that industrial tribunals apply to ascertain whether a dismissal was reasonable and there are special provisions for misconduct and redundancy.

Was suitable alternative work available?

An employer who dismisses someone when suitable alternative work could have been found for him may have acted unreasonably. Conversely, if the employee refuses an offer of suitable work, his unfair dismissal claim is unlikely to succeed. The job does not have to be identical in salary or status – a formerly successful salesman who, as the result of an accident, is no longer able to travel might reasonably be offered office work that pays less, but is also less demanding.

An employee who proves incompatible with his workmates cannot be fairly dismissed if a transfer to another department could have been expected to solve the problem.

Was the employee warned?

An employee facing dismissal is entitled to receive fair warning, preferably in writing, as far in advance as possible and, if the potential reason for his dismissal is within his control – for example, persistently taking time off for trivial ailments – a chance to correct matters.

Has the employer been consistent?

An employer who is inconsistent in his treatment of an employee – for example, praising his work shortly before dismissing him for incompetence – may be held to have acted unreasonably. If

---

MISINFORMED ABOUT HER PROGRESS

An employee who has been warned of possible dismissal for poor work must be given a reasonable opportunity to improve and be kept accurately informed of his or her progress.

Mrs Mughal was employed by the Post Office on a year's probation. She received three written warnings about the poor quality of her work and was told that unless it got better she would be dismissed.

Her supervisor eventually told her that her clerical tasks had come up to standard, but her telephone work still had to improve. Soon afterwards, and with no further warning, she was dismissed by the area sales manager, who did not know about the supervisor's comments. Mrs Mughal claimed unfair dismissal.

DECISION
The dismissal was unfair. It was the employer's duty to keep Mrs Mughal informed and the decision to sack her should only have been taken when all the relevant facts – in this case, the supervisor's opinion – had been assessed.

---

he has not dismissed other employees in similar circumstances, his chances of demonstrating that the dismissal was reasonable are reduced.

Small businesses

The Employment Act 1980 allows the tribunal to take into consideration the size and administrative resources of the employer in deciding whether he acted reasonably.

'Reasonable' treatment of misconduct

The steps an employer is expected to follow in dismissing an employee for misconduct are set out in the ADVISORY, CONCILIATION AND ARBITRATION SERVICE (ACAS) Code of Practice *Disciplinary Practice and Procedures*. It is not legally binding, but an employer who does not observe it will almost certainly lose a claim.

The code urges employers to keep full disciplinary records and to serve unequivocal written warnings. It says

---

DISMISSAL FOR UNION ACTIVITIES

An employee cannot be fairly dismissed for belonging to an independent TRADE UNION or for applying to join one, or for taking part in its activities outside working hours. Union members must not be unfairly selected for redundancy.

Elected officers of an independent union and representatives appointed under the rules on HEALTH AND SAFETY AT WORK are additionally protected

against dismissal for carrying out their duties in working time if the union is recognised by their employer. *See:* TIME OFF WORK

The protection of union members and officers does not apply if they take part in most forms of industrial action, although they cannot be sacked for lawful PICKETING outside working hours. *See:* STRIKE

that all complaints should be thoroughly investigated and that the employee concerned must be allowed to present his side of the case. Companies should also establish an appeals procedure.

'Reasonable' treatment of redundancy

'Reasonable' procedures for handling redundancies are set out in a code of practice originally published under the Industrial Relations Act and available from ACAS. An employer who fails to follow them risks losing an unfair dismissal claim.

There are special rules for redundancies in businesses that recognise an independent trade union. *See:* REDUNDANCY

Selecting employees Employers must act reasonably in choosing who is to be made redundant. If the choice has been discussed and agreed with trade union representatives, the employees selected are unlikely to succeed in claiming unfair dismissal.

If no union is involved, the fairest general rule is 'last in, first out'. An employer who dismisses long-serving employees in preference to newer recruits may be held to have acted unreasonably.

When an employee wins his claim

An employee who wins a claim for unfair dismissal has three choices. He can ask the tribunal for:
● His old job back.
● A new job with his old employer.
● Financial compensation from the employer, up to a maximum, in most cases, of £9,350.

If he chooses his old job, or a new one, the tribunal considers whether it would be practicable to order the employer to take him. If he contributed, by his conduct, to his own dismissal, the tribunal also considers whether an order for reinstatement or re-engagement would be just.

Few employees are reinstated or re-engaged. But if the tribunal makes an order, it will also set out the amount of back-pay that is due to the employee for the time he was out of work and those employment rights – for example, accrued pension – that must be met.

INSURING AGAINST UNFAIR DISMISSAL CLAIMS

Employers can insure themselves against the cost of unfair dismissal awards. The premium is approximately £8 a year for each employee; that provides cover for claims of up to £12,000 for each employee and for legal fees of up to £250,000.

Under the terms of the policy, the employer must give the insurance company 14 days' notice of his intention to dismiss an employee, unless the dismissal is a summary one, without a notice.

Unfair dismissal policies set out procedures that employers must follow in giving notice – for example, the written warnings that must be supplied to employees facing dismissal on disciplinary grounds.

When the employer refuses to take the employee back

The tribunal now has power to force the employer to reinstate the employee. If an employer has been ordered to take an employee back, he may decide that he would prefer to pay the maximum compensation as the price of getting rid of a troublesome employee. In that case, the employee is entitled to a higher additional award, up to a maximum of £6,240 in addition to his basic and compensatory awards.

How the award is calculated by the tribunal

Cash awards for unfair dismissal are made up of two separate sums:
● The basic award, linked to the employee's age and length of service.
● A compensatory award to offset losses incurred as a result of the dismissal.

The total amount may be reduced if the employee contributed by his own conduct to the dismissal.

The basic award

The basic award is calculated according to the same formula as that for redundancy payments. The employee will get:
● $\frac{1}{2}$ × his last normal weekly pay for each complete year of service with the employer between 16 and 21.

● 1 week's pay for each complete year between the ages of 22 and 40.
● $1\frac{1}{2}$ weeks' pay for each complete year in which he was aged 41 or over.

Weekly pay – including normal overtime – is limited to a maximum of £120 and service beyond 20 years is not taken into account, so the most an employee can receive as a basic award is $20 \times 1\frac{1}{2}$ weeks' pay = £3,600. The least he gets is 2 weeks' money.

If the employee has already received a redundancy payment, the amount is deducted from his basic award.

Any compensation awarded under the rules on SEX DISCRIMINATION or RACIAL DISCRIMINATION is also deducted.

The compensatory award

The maximum compensatory award for most unfair dismissals is £5,750. If an employer refuses without good reason to reinstate or re-engage an employee when a tribunal has ordered him to do so, he may be required to pay extra compensation of up to £3,120. If the order concerned an employee unfairly dismissed for trade union activities or for reasons of sex or race, the extra compensation may be increased to a maximum of £6,240. That is known as a higher additional award.

In deciding the amount of a compensatory award, tribunals consider the loss and additional expenses incurred by the employee as the result of his dismissal.

Current wage loss The tribunal takes into account the net earnings – after

WHEN AN AWARD WAS CHANGED

If an unfairly dismissed employee finds another job sooner than a tribunal expected, his award may be reduced.

Mr Vidler won his unfair dismissal claim and received £4,700 because the tribunal thought it unlikely that he would find another job because of his age. But within 2 weeks of the hearing, he had found one and his former employers asked for the award to be reduced.

DECISION
The award was reduced to £3,000.

allowances for tax, national insurance contributions and other deductions – lost by the employee between his dismissal and the tribunal hearing. Any wage increases he would have received during that period had he not been dismissed are considered.

But tax rebates and social security benefits, other than UNEMPLOYMENT BENEFIT, are deducted and normal overtime may be excluded.

Future wage loss If the employee has not already found another job, the tribunal assesses how long it will take him to do so – his future wage loss. It takes into account his age, health, qualifications, experience and the general employment situation in the area, and makes allowance for the likely loss of fringe benefits – for example, a company car or luncheon vouchers.

If the employee has found other work, but at lower pay, his future wage loss is the difference between his net earnings in his old job and those in his new one.

Expenses Any expenses arising from the dismissal may be included in calculating the compensatory award if they represent a significant amount – for example, the cost of travelling or moving to try to find a new job. But minor expenses – stamps and telephone calls – are not taken into account. An employee claiming expenses must produce receipts or other evidence. The legal costs of the employee's claim to the tribunal are not included in the award.

When an employee has not tried to cut his losses

An industrial tribunal can reduce the amount of an unfair dismissal award if it is not convinced that the employee has done all he can to mitigate, or cut, his losses – particularly by trying to find a new job. As evidence of his efforts, the employee should take to the tribunal copies of job application letters and a record of the dates on which he went for interviews or to a job centre.

When an employee's behaviour contributed to his dismissal

If an employee's behaviour contributed to his dismissal – a 'contributory fault' – both his basic and compensatory awards can be reduced or refused al-

together, even though the dismissal was unfair. Contributory faults may range from awkwardness or a reluctance to obey orders to dishonesty or other serious offences.

UNLAWFUL ASSEMBLY

When gathering together can be an offence

It is illegal for three or more people to assemble with intent to do something unlawful and to assemble in a way that makes ordinary, sensible people apprehend, or expect a BREACH OF THE PEACE. *See also:* PUBLIC ORDER

UNMARRIED COUPLE

Limited rights for people who live together

When two people live together without getting married, they have none of the legal rights given by marriage. For example, neither has any legal duty to maintain the other, but the man may have to maintain any child of the relationship. *See:* AFFILIATION ORDER

One may have a claim against the other's property in certain circumstances however.

See: COHABITATION
COMMON LAW WIFE

UNSOLICITED GOODS

When it is a crime to send you a bill

It is a criminal offence for anyone to demand without reasonable cause payment for any goods that he knows to have been sent to you without your asking. Anyone who does so can be fined up to £200.

If he threatens to take legal action, invokes some other method of debt-collecting, or threatens to do so, he can be fined up to £400.

Any document seeking payment for unsolicited goods must state in red in the top left-hand corner:

**THIS IS NOT A DEMAND
FOR PAYMENT
THERE IS NO OBLIGATION TO PAY**

It must also state in red, diagonally across the page:

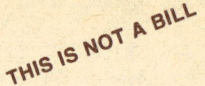

THIS IS NOT A BILL

When you are not obliged to send it back

If you receive goods that you have not ordered, you can:
● Providing that the sender has not tried to collect the goods, keep them for six months, then use or dispose of them as you think fit.
● Write to the sender at any time within five months of receiving the goods, saying that the goods were unsolicited and giving him thirty days to collect them – after which time you can use or dispose of the goods as you think fit.

During the six months, you must not use the goods or damage them deliberately, or you are liable for them. If you damage or mislay them accidentally, however, you are liable.

You must not unreasonably refuse to allow the sender, or his representative, to take back the goods during the six months. If he fails to do so, he loses all right to recover them or to payment for them.

UPPER EARNINGS LIMIT

Calculating national insurance contributions

The maximum weekly, monthly or yearly amount of earnings on which class 1 (employees) national insurance contributions are calculated is known as the upper earnings limit.

It is also the upper level of earnings on which each year's additional RETIREMENT PENSION and EARNINGS-RELATED SUPPLEMENT are calculated.

The upper earnings limit is. about seven times the LOWER EARNINGS LIMIT and it goes up in April each year when the lower level also rises.

The upper earnings limit for 1981–2 was £200 a week; the monthly and annual equivalents were £866.67 and £10,400.

See also: NATIONAL INSURANCE CONTRIBUTIONS

VACCINE DAMAGE

Compensation for people severely disabled by vaccination

Anyone who is severely disabled as a result of being vaccinated may be entitled to receive a tax-free lump sum of £10,000 under the Vaccine Damage Payments Scheme.

To qualify, a claimant must be at least 80 per cent disabled, as defined in the assessment of benefit for people disabled by industrial injury.

The vaccine which caused the disablement must be one which was given against either diphtheria, tetanus, whooping cough, tuberculosis, poliomyelitis, measles, German measles (rubella) or smallpox.

The payment may also be given to a claimant who was not himself vaccinated but who suffered disablement through contact with someone who was – for example, a pregnant woman whose vaccination damaged her unborn child.

Several other conditions must also be met. A claimant must:
● Have been vaccinated in the United Kingdom or Isle of Man no earlier than July 5, 1948. Against smallpox, vaccination must have been given before August 1, 1971. Members of the armed forces or their families are eligible even if the vaccination was given outside the United Kingdom, provided that it was part of the Service's medical facilities.
● Have been vaccinated before his 18th birthday, except against polio or German measles or when the vaccination

was given during an outbreak of any of the prescribed diseases.
● Be at least 2 years old.

No payment is made on behalf of anyone who died before May 9, 1978.
Time limit For a claim to be accepted, it must be made within 6 years from either the date of the vaccination, or the claimant's 2nd birthday, or May 9, 1978, whichever is the latest.

How to claim

A claimant should complete the form attached to the Department of Health and Social Security leaflet HB3, which is obtainable from the Vaccine Damage Payments Unit, DHSS, North Fylde Central Offices, Norcross, Blackpool FY5 3TA.

The completed form should be returned to that address with any supporting evidence that exists. Do not delay in sending the claim because some of the evidence or information required is temporarily unavailable. The Payments Unit will obtain copies of any relevant medical evidence from the doctor or hospital concerned.

The parents or guardian of a claimant under the age of 18 should complete the form. A disabled adult unable to complete it himself can get someone else to do so.

The claimant will be told in writing of the result of his claim. When it is turned down on the grounds that the disablement is not sufficiently severe, or was not due to vaccination, the case can be reviewed, on request, by an independent medical tribunal.

The successful claimant will receive a

single payment of £10,000. If he is under 18 or is unable to manage his own affairs, it will be paid to trustees appointed by the Secretary of State for Social Services. If the disabled person lives with his parents, they can be made the trustees.

VAGRANT

Street beggars can be sent to gaol

People who wander the streets begging, telling fortunes, trading without a licence or sleeping under bridge arches can be gaoled under the Vagrancy Act 1824.

There are three categories of offenders:
● Idle and disorderly. Anyone begging in a public place, trading without a licence or behaving riotously or indecently can be charged with being idle and disorderly. So can street prostitutes. The maximum penalty is 1 month's imprisonment or a £200 fine.
● Rogues and vagabonds. Anyone already convicted of being idle and disorderly can be accused of being a rogue and vagabond. So can a person wandering at large or lodging in a deserted building or the open air, or someone collecting money by falsely pretending that it is for charity.

Anyone pretending to tell a person's fortune by palmistry or some other craft

PENALTY FOR PALMISTRY

Anyone who claims to tell fortunes by palmistry or crystal ball-gazing can be convicted of being a rogue and a vagabond – for which the maximum penalty is a £200 fine and 3 months in gaol.

'Hate to say this but you're a rogue and a vagabond'

can be accused of being a rogue and vagabond. This does not include astrologers writing in general terms in newspapers or magazines.

The maximum penalty for a rogue and vagabond is 3 months' imprisonment and a £200 fine.

● Incorrigible rogues. The most serious charge under the Vagrancy Act is that of being an incorrigible rogue. It includes anyone who has been convicted twice of being a rogue and vagabond and anyone who resists being arrested as a rogue and vagabond.

Anyone who escapes from any place of legal confinement – a prison, remand home or mental home – can be dealt with as an incorrigible rogue. The maximum penalty is 1 year's imprisonment.

People who sing, dance or perform entertainments in the street for money are behaving illegally, but they are not vagrants and are not charged under the Vagrancy Act.

See: BUSKING
SUSPECTED PERSON

VALUE ADDED TAX

*How traders collect revenue
for the Government*

When you buy goods or services and have to pay an extra percentage for value added tax – VAT – your payment is usually just the last in a chain. The tax is chargeable on each business transaction involved in producing and supplying those goods and services.

It is a consumption tax, however, and you as the consumer are normally the only one who loses money. Each trader further back in the chain of manufacture and supply has to pay the tax when he buys, but he generally recovers his cost by charging tax when he sells.

Because a trader sells at a higher price – called 'added value' – he automatically receives more VAT than he pays. He has to account to a Customs and Excise office for his VAT transactions, and pay over the extra amounts he receives. In effect, each trader acts as a collector for part of the tax.

Paying the tax

A trader does not actually have to calculate the amount owing to Customs and Excise from each transaction. His accounts are assessed for VAT every 3 months, simply by charging a percentage on the total of his taxable sales, and reducing that figure by the total of VAT charges that he paid in the same period.

If a trader's quarterly sales are £100,000, for example, he should have invoiced his customers for £115,000 in order to collect VAT at a rate of 15 per cent. He holds the extra £15,000 on behalf of the Government, but pays over only what is left after deducting all the VAT charges on the goods and services that he had to buy for his business.

If his taxable purchases at the 15 per cent rate totalled £40,000, he should have been invoiced by his suppliers for a total of £46,000. His debt to Customs and Excise is the difference between the extra £15,000 that he received and the extra £6,000 that he had to pay. So he hands over £9,000.

It does not matter what else a trader has to spend – staff wages, for example – to create the added value of what he sells. VAT is not a tax on income or profit. Even a business that runs at a loss has to collect VAT if it sells taxable goods or services.

However, if a business pays more VAT to its suppliers than it receives from its customers in the same period, the difference is refunded.

How VAT rates can vary

The Government sets VAT percentage rates in the same way that it fixes income tax rates.

It has the power to introduce different rates for particular goods or services – higher rates for luxuries, for example, or lower rates for second-hand goods.

The Government also decides which goods can be 'zero-rated', so that they attract no VAT, or which traders can be exempted, so that they do not have to account for VAT transactions.

Zero rating If a product or service is zero-rated, the trader selling it does not charge VAT. He may still be registered for VAT, however, which means that although he receives no tax payments on what he sells – called output tax – he can still claim credit for VAT payments to his suppliers – called input tax. So his payments will be refunded.

Exported goods are zero-rated. So are some sold locally – food and books, for example. But the zero rating does not apply until the product is in its final form, which is why VAT is often collected at earlier stages and has to be refunded. For example, the paper, ink, glue and so on that go into a book all incur VAT charges when a printer buys them.

Exemption VAT exemption means that a trader does not have to register and account for his VAT transactions. He is outside the VAT system altogether. A trader whose turnover is less than £13,500 a year does not need to register. Nor do traders whose whole output consists of exempted goods or services. They can, however, register voluntarily.

Some services are automatically exempt – notably health care, education, insurance and finance.

Exemption offers a trader freedom from the need to be involved in VAT administrative and accounting procedures. He is at a disadvantage, however, if his business requires him to pay VAT on purchases. He has no right to reclaim those costs. In fact, he is in the same position as a consumer paying VAT on retail goods – he is at the end of the trading chain for VAT purposes.

Second-hand trading VAT regulations are modified for second-hand trading in cars, motor cycles, caravans, boats, outboard motors, works of art and antiques. The tax is charged only on the dealer's profit margin – not on the full sale price.

If you sell your own car or other personal possessions, you do not charge VAT because the transaction is not part of a business.

Coping with the paperwork

About 2 million trading organisations, professional people and self-employed businessmen are registered for VAT because they sell taxable goods or services and their sales exceed £10,000 a year. Each is allocated a VAT reference number.

Every taxable person or organisation must keep 3 monthly accounts in enough detail to show how much VAT is payable to the Government or refundable from it. They must be available for Customs and Excise inspection at any time. The maximum penalty for failing to keep such accounts is 2 years' imprisonment and a £1,000 fine.

The key to VAT accounting is a special 'tax invoice' which a trader must issue to his customer when he charges VAT. It shows the date, the price, the VAT charge and the supplier's VAT reference number.

If the customer is also registered for VAT, he uses tax invoices as proof of his payments, so that he can offset them against his VAT receipts. But he must not offset the tax paid on any goods or services that are bought for private purposes.

At the end of each 3 month period the trader makes a return of VAT payments and receipts to his local Customs and Excise VAT office. If his receipts are higher, he has 1 further month in which to pay the excess amount to the Government.

Evasion Fraudulent evasion of VAT is a criminal offence.

Maximum penalty 2 years' imprisonment and £1,000 fine or three times the amount of tax involved, whichever is the greater.

Disputes Arguments over the amount of VAT payable to or refundable by the Government, or arguments over registration, rating or exemption, are first referred to the Commissioners of Customs and Excise.

Someone who is dissatisfied with a decision by the Commissioners has a right of appeal to a regional Value Added Tax Appeal Tribunal.

Public complaints If a consumer believes that a trading organisation is overcharging for VAT, or charging the tax when it has no right to, he should complain either to the trading standards or consumer protection department of his local authority or a Customs and Excise office.

VANDALISM

A new word for a very old crime

It is an offence intentionally or recklessly to destroy or damage someone else's property. This crime of CRIMINAL DAMAGE is the one for which vandals are normally prosecuted. They may be guilty of other offences, such as causing a BREACH OF THE PEACE.

When a charge of criminal damage is tried in a crown court the maximum penalty is 10 years' imprisonment and an unlimited fine. Where the amount of

the damage is less than £200, the case must be heard before magistrates. They can impose a maximum penalty of 3 months' imprisonment and a £500 fine.

The culprit may also be ordered by the court to pay CRIMINAL INJURIES COMPENSATION.

VEHICLE EXCISE LICENCE

The disc that shows when road tax is due

The disc on a car windscreen is a vehicle licence receipt showing that the owner has paid excise duty – known as the road-fund tax.

Regulations provide that the licence disc must be displayed on or adjacent to the nearside lower corner of the windscreen so that all particulars are clearly visible by daylight from the nearside of the road.

Licence discs, which also show an expiry date, can be bought for 6 or 12 months, unless the annual rate is £18 or less. Then, only a 12 month licence is available.

If any motor vehicle on a public road – driven, parked, towed or pushed – does not display a current disc, the owner can be fined up to £20. He can also be prosecuted for unlicensed use

....

14 DAYS' GRACE IN PRACTICE

Any car used or parked in a public place must have an up-to-date vehicle excise licence (or trade plates). In practice, however, the police may not prosecute for 14 days after the expiry of the old licence – provided that you applied for renewal before the licence expired.

....

and fined up to £50 or five times the annual rate of duty whichever is the greater, plus any back duty. The maximum fine for fraudulently using a vehicle licence is £200.

In practice, a car can be put on the road without a current disc provided that one has been applied for. A 14 day period of grace is customarily allowed, after a previous licence has expired, in which an owner can apply for renewal.

Licensing a new car

A new car is usually licensed before you take delivery. The dealer makes the application on your behalf, using the same form on which he arranges the car's registration.

If your dealer has not applied for a tax disc, make sure that he gives you an application form.

Licensing a used car

The current licence on a used car is often included as part of the deal when it is sold. But the seller is not obliged to pass on the licence – he can choose to claim a refund instead.

If you buy a used car that has no current tax disc, you must obtain one as soon as possible. Application form V10 is available from post offices and local vehicle licensing offices. Take or send the completed form to a licensing office – or a licensing post office – with:
● The car registration document.
● A certificate of insurance or cover note.
● A current vehicle test certificate if the car is more than 3 years old.
● Your excise duty payment, at the rate shown on the application form.

Renewing a licence

A reminder notice is normally sent about 2 weeks before your licence expires. It works as a simplified application form for renewal.

If the details on it are correct, complete the form and take it with your payment to a post office or local vehicle licensing office. Your new disc is issued immediately.

If the notice details are not up to date, you can still use it for renewal but you will have to take or post it to a local vehicle licensing office – not a post office.

No reminder Licensing renewal is the car owner's responsibility. So if he does not receive a reminder, he must make a full application on form V10, as if he were licensing the car for the first time.

If you lose a disc

If a vehicle licence is lost, stolen or destroyed, whoever is shown as the registered keeper can obtain a duplicate after a check of registration and licensing records. Application forms are available at local vehicle licensing offices. The procedure takes about 3 weeks and costs £2.

Someone who needs a duplicate licence more urgently – for example, because the car is about to be sold – may be issued with a temporary one by his local licensing office if he shows the registration document.

Claiming a refund

If you decide to sell your car without its current licence, or to take your car off the road for a long period, you can surrender the licence disc and claim a refund of unused excise duty.

Application forms are available at local vehicle licensing offices. Leave your disc there, with the completed application, and allow up to 4 weeks for your refund to be posted to you.

Refund periods are counted only in full calendar months, and a month is counted only if the application is made on or before the last day of the preceding month.

Stolen car If a stolen car is not found quickly, the owner is entitled to a refund of unused excise duty. Local vehicle licensing offices have a special form for that purpose.

VENEREAL DISEASE

Treatment is easy to get and strictly confidential

Many hospitals have special clinics for diagnosing and treating sexually transmitted diseases – usually called venereal disease or VD.

Anyone who suspects that he or she might have VD can simply go along to one of these clinics, without any introductory letter from a doctor, and be assured of confidential treatment.

Symptoms of VD After sexual contact with a new partner, any pain when passing urine, a discharge from the penis or vagina, swelling of glands in the groin or a rash in the genital area must lead to a suspicion of VD.

The two principal venereal diseases are gonorrhoea and syphilis. The latter, left untreated, can lead to serious brain or heart damage.

How to find a VD clinic To find a special clinic treating VD, telephone a local hospital, general practitioner, health authority or social services department.

Beside the special clinics, most hospitals have out-patient facilities for diagnosing and treating VD – but a doctor's letter and an appointment are generally required.

Keeping identities secret

Health authorities try to ensure that any information that might lead to a VD patient being identified is kept strictly confidential.

The name of the patient can only be disclosed to a doctor involved in treating the disease or preventing its spread, or to someone working under the doctor's direction in tracing possible contacts.

Someone being treated may be asked for the names of contacts, but the patient is under no obligation to give any information.

VISA

The documentation required to enter a country

Anyone travelling abroad is granted permission to enter most countries by having an entry clearance stamped or fixed in his PASSPORT. That clearance is known as a visa.

In certain cases, a visa states how long a person is permitted to stay in the country.

If someone wants to stay longer than the visa permits, he must visit the country's immigration officials and ask for an extension of stay.

However, there are certain countries where a visitor from the United Kingdom is not required to have a visa. For example, citizens of the EEC countries

EXPLAINING WHERE AND WHY
YOU WANT TO GO

Some countries – for example, the United States – do not allow UK citizens to enter unless they have first applied for and been issued a visa. That is done only after the applicant has satisfied US immigration officials that he does not intend to try to stay permanently.

do not require a visa when visiting other member countries. They are permitted to enter, provided that they produce their identification card or, in the case of a UK citizen, a passport.

Visitors to the United Kingdom from certain foreign countries – for example, East European countries – need an entry clearance authorising an IMMIGRATION official to allow them to enter the country.

If the visitor does not have an entry clearance issued abroad, the officer is entitled to refuse him entry, unless he qualifies for admission under the immigration rules.

However, visitors from other countries such as an EEC country do not need a visa to enter the UK.

If you are planning to travel abroad, check with your travel agent, or the embassy of the country you are visiting, what the visa requirements are. *See:* EMIGRATION

For example, someone travelling to the United States may have to produce evidence that he has a job to return to in the UK before a visa is granted. Other countries may require evidence of a marriage certificate before a visa is granted.

WAGES COUNCILS

Statutory bodies that fix the minimum pay of 3.5 million workers

Wages councils set statutory minimum pay rates, holiday entitlements and other employment conditions for 3.5 million workers in trades in which union organisation is weak – chiefly, most branches of retailing and catering, clothing and textile manufacturing and hairdressing.

The Wages Councils Act 1979 gives them powers to issue, through a central office answerable to the Secretary of State for Employment, Wages Orders that are legally binding on all employers in the trades they cover. Councils can be set up or abolished by order of the Employment Secretary.

Each council is responsible for a particular trade – for example, the Hairdressing Undertakings Wages Council covers women's hairdressers and barbers.

Each consists of equal numbers of employers and union representatives, supplemented by up to three independent members – often lawyers – appointed by the Employment Secretary, who nominates one of the independents as chairman.

What employers must do

Every employer to whom a Wages Order applies must grant his employees at least the pay rates and holidays that the Order lays down. Orders for some trades impose other conditions – for example, the ratio between apprentices and trained staff. An employer who breaks the provisions of an Order may be fined up to £100 for each offence. In addition, if the offence is related to pay, he can be compelled by a court to raise wages to the required level and, if necessary, to backdate the increases for up to 2 years.

Employees who have been underpaid can sue their employer for up to 6 years' wage arrears through a COUNTY COURT or, if the sum involved is more than £2,000, in the High Court.

All employers covered by a Wages Order must display a copy of it where it can be easily read by their employees. Anyone who fails to do so can be fined £100.

How Wages Orders are enforced by Government

Department of Employment Wages Inspectors, organised in 12 regional inspectorates, are responsible for ensuring that Wages Orders are enforced. They can demand to see wage registers to check that employees are not being underpaid and, if necessary, lodge complaints leading to prosecutions.

An employee who believes his employer is not obeying a Wages Order can ask a Wages Inspector, in confidence, to investigate. Any local employment office has the address of the nearest inspectorate.

Wages Inspectors can also advise employers and employees on the contents of an Order, whether it applies to them and what it means.

WAR PENSIONS

The country's debt to its military casualties

A man or woman who is disabled – and the widow of a man who dies – as a result of service in the armed forces is normally entitled to a pension from the state.

In cases of special hardship or need, disablement pensions can be supplemented by one or more of a number of allowances, and widows may be entitled to allowances for their children and to other financial help, if required.

How a claim is made

The war pensions scheme is run by the Department of Health and Social Security, Norcross, Blackpool, FY5 3TA. Claims, complaints and appeals should be addressed to the Controller, Central Office (War Pensions) there.

A disabled serviceman is examined by a medical board before being invalided out. His service pay continues while the board sends a report to the Department for the pension entitlement to be worked out.

There is no time limit on an application. An ex-serviceman, whether or not he has been invalided out, can claim at any time for a disablement that he considers to be a result of his service.

If a man dies during service, the Ministry of Defence provides his widow with the claim forms. If a discharged serviceman dies – and his death is connected with his service – his widow should apply directly to the local Department office.

Assessing a disablement pension

The amount of a disablement pension is based on the degree of the disablement and on the rank held by the applicant.

Disablement below 20 per cent commands a lump-sum payment, but no pension. From 20 per cent, the disability is assessed in steps of 10 per cent up to 100 per cent – but the maximum does not necessarily imply total incapacity.

For example, a 100 per cent pension is paid for the loss of both hands or both legs and for the complete loss of sight or hearing. The loss of an arm brings 90 per cent, a thumb 30 per cent and two fingers 20 per cent.

The rate for such specific disablement is fixed. But when it is more difficult to assess the damage – for example, in cases of facial disfigurement – the pension is worked out individually.

Rank The applicant's rank is also taken into account on a sliding scale. A major-general assessed as 100 per cent disabled received, in 1981, a pension of £50.29 a week; a private received £44.30. The same men on a 20 per cent pension received £10.06 and £8.90 respectively.

When extra help is available

Special allowances are payable to ex-servicemen whose disability has seriously affected their finances.

A man who requires regular personal help, for example, or whose job prospects have suffered, may qualify for one of a number of allowances on top of his pension. They include allowances for:

● Constant attendance, available to pensioners who are 100 per cent disabled, and at least 80 per cent of that disablement is from military service. The length of attendance required – and it can be non-professional help from a relative, for example – determines the amount of the allowance. There is a specially high rate in cases of complete or almost complete incapacitation.

● Exceptionally severe disablement, paid to pensioners with a permanent disablement of exceptional severity.

● Unemployability – a supplement for someone so severely disabled that he is unable to get a job. There is also an extra allowance for a wife and children.

A partially disabled man, unable to take up the work he did before his military service or work of a similar standard, also qualifies for an allowance. But the allowance and pension together must not exceed the 100 per cent rate.

War widows' pensions

A woman is entitled to a war pension if her husband died:

● As the result of service in the 1914–18 war or after September 2, 1939.

● If he was a civilian and his death was the result of a 1939–45 war injury.

● And at the time of his death was receiving a constant attendance allowance for a disability.

Rank There are two levels of war widow's pension – the standard and the lower rate. Their amounts vary with rank.

The standard rate is paid automatically to the widow of an officer above the rank of major. It is also paid to a widow who is aged:

● 40 or more.

● Under 40, but eligible for a child allowance.

● Under 40, but unable to support herself because of prolonged ill-health.

● Under 40, and expecting a baby by her late husband.

The amount of the pension ranged, in 1981, from £8.15 at the lower rate for a private's widow, to £40.40 for the widow of a major-general.

An allowance is payable for a war widow's offspring until the child reaches the age of 16 or leaves school. Help with education and rent may also be available in cases of extreme hardship.

War widows' pensions are not taxable.

How war pensions are paid

Disabled officers and the widows and dependants of officers are normally paid monthly or quarterly in arrears. The Department of Health and Social Security sends them a voucher which has to be presented through a bank.

With other ranks, pensions are paid weekly in advance by books of orders that must be cashed at named post offices on specific days.

If a pensioner does not collect his or her pension for a year, it will probably be cancelled. But payment may be resumed from the date of reapplication if there was a good reason for the failure to collect it.

Appeals Anyone whose application for a war pension is turned down or who is dissatisfied with the amount awarded can appeal to an independent pension appeals tribunal. The relevant appeal form is available from local social security offices.

See also: DISABILITY PENSION

WARD OF COURT

The powers of a court to rule a child's life

Whenever a child or minor under the age of 18 is felt to be in need of the law's protection, there are two possibilities open to the parent, guardian, relative – or any other interested party, such as a local authority.

They can ask a local authority to bring care proceedings in a juvenile court to have the child placed in the care of the authority. Or they can apply in the Family Division of the High Court to have the child made a ward of court.

The court then becomes the legal guardian of the child and can make any orders it feels to be necessary for the care, control and education of the child until he is 18.

What a judge can order

Wardship orders can be made only in the High Court. Although most disputes involving child care are settled in the lower courts, there are some cases in which the special powers of the High Court are felt to be necessary.

For example, a wife who believes that her husband is about to KIDNAP their child and take him abroad can make the child a ward of court.

The judge may then grant an INJUNCTION against the husband empowering all port and airport authorities to prevent his taking the child out of the country.

Similarly, when a young girl runs off with a man, her parents can make her a ward of court to enable a judge to order her to return to her parents.

Anyone who assists her in staying away – for example, by harbouring the runaways – will risk imprisonment for CONTEMPT OF COURT. *See:* ABDUCTION

When a lower court refuses a local authority's request to place a child in its care, the authority can take the case to the High Court and ask a judge for a wardship order.

But when a local authority already has a child in care, the High Court will not interfere – provided that the authority does not act outside its powers or improperly towards the child.

The scope of a wardship order

A High Court judge can make anyone under 18 a ward of court – even a child of foreign birth or citizenship – provided that he is present in England or Wales.

A British subject living abroad can

"

WHEN THE FOSTER PARENTS LOST

When a dispute arises between natural and foster parents over the custody of a child, it may be settled in wardship proceedings.

Jane T, at the age of 3, was taken into care by the local authority because her mother had neglected her. She was boarded out with Mr and Mrs C and lived happily with them for 4 years.

Then, because the mother's circumstances had improved – she was living with a man but was not intending to marry him – the local authority decided to move Jane back to her.

Mr and Mrs C refused to return her. They had come to love Jane as their own child and felt they could give her a much better home than her mother.

They had Jane made a ward of court and asked the judge to order that she stay with them.

DECISION

The High Court judge ruled that he could not interfere with the local authority since it was acting properly within the powers given it by Parliament under a care order.

In any case, he felt the decision to move Jane back to her mother was the right one. Mr and Mrs C were compelled to hand her over.

also be made a ward if the judge considers the High Court the proper place to investigate the case rather than the courts of the child's country of residence.

Cost The procedure in wardship cases is often complicated and costly, but LEGAL AID may be available.

See also: CUSTODY OF CHILDREN
DIVORCE
GUARDIAN
MATRIMONIAL ORDER

WARRANT

The authority to carry out a court order

Certain court orders are automatically issued with a warrant giving the holder the authority to carry them out.

Anyone obstructing him – that is, preventing the warrant-holder from carrying out his task – will usually be in CONTEMPT OF COURT.

He may also be guilty of other offences, such as obstructing the police in the execution of their duty. *See:* OBSTRUCTION

The most common forms of warrant are:

● Arrest warrant – issued by a magistrate allowing the police to arrest a suspect. *See:* ARREST
● Distress warrant – issued by the county court enabling the BAILIFF to seize goods, so that they can be auctioned to pay off a debt. *See:* DISTRESS WARRANT
● Possession warrant – issued by a county court authorising the bailiff to evict a tenant or squatter and take possession of premises. The High Court equivalent is called a Writ of Possession.
● Search warrant – usually issued by a magistrate allowing the police to search named premises. *See:* SEARCH

WARRANTY

When you may have more rights – but never less

Warranty is another name sometimes given to a GUARANTEE, especially in the motor trade.

It can promise any protection or benefit that a manufacturer or trader sees fit – but not at the expense of a customer's rights under general law or under recently enacted consumer protection legislation.

A warranty document must state that the buyer's statutory rights are not affected by its terms.

See also: DEFECTIVE GOODS
UNFAIR CONTRACT

WATER SUPPLY

A right to have water but not to waste it

The water in your taps may be supplied by a regional water authority, or by a commercial water company acting as its agent.

The authority has a legal duty to see that the water it supplies is pure and

TOOTH PROTECTION?

The always-controversial decision whether to add fluoride to a water supply to prevent tooth decay is one for the water authority alone.

wholesome. If you suspect that it is not, complain at once to the authority or to the district council. The council can insist that the authority remedies any defect in the water or the supply system.

The chemical fluoride – believed to prevent dental decay in children – is added to the water in some areas and is a matter for decision by each water authority. The addition of fluoride has been held not to be a breach of an authority's duty to provide pure water.

Anyone objecting, however, can do so by lobbying the local council or water authority or organising opposition in the local community or Press.

Most sources of water are the property of a water authority, but you have a right to the water underneath your own land, unless it connects underground with the authority's supply. In such a case the authority can take action to prevent you or your business from using it.

If your house does not have a piped supply, either because it is new or is supplied from a private source (such as a well), you can require the water authority to connect you to the mains. You would normally be required to pay the connection costs unless a number of houses were being connected together and, over a period of 8 years or less, the income from their combined water rates was enough to cover the costs.

The district council can require you to

connect your house to the mains – for example, when you have a tenant who wants it connected – but you will have to pay only the first £60.

It can also require you to close your well if the water is impure. The council is entitled to carry out inspections.

Paying a water rate

Water rate covers only water for domestic use. Additional charges are made for the use of hoses, sprinklers and swimming pools in all areas.

The water rate is payable half-yearly and usually includes a separate sum for sewerage and for the general services of the water authority. But you need not pay in respect of water unless you are connected to a piped supply.

Paying the penalty for wasting water

It is an offence to waste water, the maximum penalty for which is a fine of £200.

Every householder has a duty to repair any leaks on his property. If he refuses to do so, the water authority can cut off his supply. He will then be required to pay for the re-connection.

Refusal to pay any money owing to the water authority can lead to the disconnection of the supply.

During a drought, excessive or improper use of a sprinkler, for example, is punishable by a fine of £2. But if the Government has made an emergency drought order, a fine of £400 can be imposed.

The water authorities must give notice of their intention to reduce or cut off the supply, but the length of the notice period is not defined exactly in law.

WEIGHTS AND MEASURES

You can insist on getting full weight for your money

Giving short weight is a criminal offence. On first conviction the maximum penalty is 3 months in prison and a fine of £100. This rises to 3 months and £250 for second or subsequent offences.

A magistrates' court can order an offender to pay up to £1,000 compensa-

tion to anyone who has suffered loss or damage arising from the offence.

Weighed or pre-packed

If the goods are weighed in your presence, it is an offence to give you less than you are supposed to receive or less than you should get for the price.

If the goods are pre-packed, each package is marked with its nominal quantity. Any single package may contain less than the stated amount, but the average weight of a group of packages must not be less than the nominal quantity. Not more than a certain proportion of the packages may be underweight.

Where to complain

The Weights and Measures Acts are enforced by weights and measures inspectors – often called trading standards officers – who are employed by local authorities. If you have a complaint about weights and measures, complain to the local trading standards officer.

WELSH LANGUAGE

Preserving a native tongue

English is the general official language in Wales, but Welsh also has equal official status under the Welsh Language Act 1967.

A government department can if it wishes issue any of its forms and documents in Welsh. The Post Office and the Department of Health and Social Sec-

....

DIOGELU'R IAITH

Saesneg yw'r iaith swyddogol gyffredinol yng Nghymru, but Welsh also has equal official status.

LLANLLW...GOCH

....

urity always do so. Other departments use Welsh on a selective basis – for example, in electoral documents, census forms, vehicle licences, birth, marriage and death registrations and some court forms.

Welsh may be spoken or used on a document by anyone involved in any legal proceedings. Courts have a duty to see that any Welsh that is used is translated into English if proper public administration requires it – so that anyone involved knows what is going on.

Teaching Apart from the normal provision of Welsh language classes, each local education authority has the power to decide whether to provide for other school subjects to be taught in Welsh. Students sitting examinations in Welsh may answer the papers in Welsh.

Council work Local councils decide for themselves whether to conduct their proceedings and keep their records in Welsh, and whether their staff should conduct their dealings with the public in Welsh.

Yr Iaith Gymraeg

Saesneg yw'r iaith swyddogol gyffredinol yng Nghymru, ond y mae i'r iaith Gymraeg statws o ddilysrwydd cyfartal â hi yn ôl amodau'r Deddf Yr Iaith Gymraeg 1967.

Mae gan y gwahanol adrannau o'r Llywodraeth hawl, yn ôl eu dymuniad, i gyhoeddi ffurflenni a dogfennau yn Gymraeg. Mae'r Swyddfa'r Post ac Adran Iechyd a Nawdd Cymdeithasol yn gwneud hynny'n barhaus. Mae adrannau eraill yn defnyddio'r Gymraeg mewn modd detholus – er enghraifft, mewn ffurflenni cyfrifiad, trwyddedau modur, a chofrestrau geni, priodi a marwolaeth, ac mewn rhai o ffurflenni'r llysoedd barn.

Mae hawl gan unrhyw un i siarad yn Gymraeg, neu defnyddio'r iaith ar ddogfeu mewn gweithrediadau cyfreithiol. Mae'n ddyletswydd ar y llysoedd i ddarparu cyfleusterau addas i gyfieithu i'r Saesneg, os yw gweinyddiaeth gyhoeddus briodol yn galw am hyn, fel ag y medr pawb sy'n bresennol neu'n gysylltiedig â'r achos wybod beth sy'n mynd ymlaen.

Addysgol

Ar wahân i'r ddarpariaeth reolaidd o ddosbarthiadau yn yr iaith Gymraeg, mae gan bob awdurdod addysg lleol y gallu i benderfynu a ddymunir dysgu pynciau eraill yn yr ysgolion trwy gyfrwng y Gymraeg. Mae gan efrydwyr sy'n eistedd arholiadau yng Nghymru gyfle i ateb y papurau yn Gymraeg.

Gwaith y Cynghorau

Gan yr awdurdodau lleol y mae'r hawl i benderfynu a ddymunent ddwyn ymlaen eu gweithrediadau a chadw eu cofnodion yn Gymraeg; ac yn ogystal os ydynt yn ewyllysio i'w staff ymgyfathrachu â'r cyhoedd yn Gymraeg.

WIDOWED MOTHER'S ALLOWANCE

State provision for the family after the father dies

After receiving WIDOW'S ALLOWANCE for the first 26 weeks of her bereavement, a woman left with at least one child under 19 for whom she receives CHILD BENEFIT, or expecting her late husband's baby, is entitled to widowed mother's allowance, provided her husband paid enough national insurance contributions. If he did not pay enough for her to qualify for the full rate, she may be paid a reduced amount.

In 1981 the widowed mother's allowance was £27.15 a week. In addition, she received an extra £7.50 for each child that qualified for child benefit. That can apply to a child of a previous marriage if that child qualifies for child benefit. She may also be entitled to an additional amount based on her late husband's earnings. The amount is taxable and should be included in her income tax return.

Widowed mother's allowance ceases when the youngest child is no longer eligible for child benefit.

It also ceases if the widow remarries or lives with a man as his wife. If a woman lives with a man without marrying him and later ceases to live with him, she can apply to have her allowance restored.

If the widow is still under 40 when her child last ceases to qualify for child benefit, she receives no more widow's benefit. If she is over 40, instead of the allowance, she receives a WIDOW'S PENSION.

If she chooses to live overseas, she can still claim her own part of the allowance. The increased allowance for her children, however, is only payable for a temporary stay overseas. Inquiries about arrangements abroad should be sent to the Department of Health and Social Security, Overseas Branch, Newcastle upon Tyne, NE98 1YX.

WIDOW'S ALLOWANCE

Financial help during bereavement

For the first 26 weeks after a married man dies, his widow is entitled to a widow's allowance, and possibly an earnings-related addition, provided he paid enough national insurance contributions. If the widow is over 60 she may also be entitled to a graduated pension or an additional pension.

The allowance – £38 a week in 1981 – is paid to widows under 60 and to those who are over 60 whose husbands were not receiving retirement pensions when they died.

Up to another £14 a week could be paid in 1981 only, depending on the husband's earnings. If you are over 60 and are entitled to a graduated pension or an additional retirement pension and the amount comes to more than the earnings-related addition, the difference is added on.

If you have children for whom you receive CHILD BENEFIT, you can get an increase for each one.

The allowance stops if a widow remarries or lives with a man as his wife when not married to him. If they stop living together, she may start receiving the allowance again.

How to claim

When you have registered your husband's death, complete the form on the back of the free DEATH certificate and take or send it to the local office of the Department of Health and Social Security. Post offices supply free stamped and addressed envelopes.

You will be sent form BW1 which you should complete and return at once. If you can, enclose your birth and marriage certificates. If there is any difficulty, do not delay sending the claim form until you have the certificates. You can send them on later.

The allowance is paid by means of a book containing orders that you can cash each week. Each order should be cashed within 3 months. The allowance is taxable and should be included in your income tax return.

WIDOW'S INDUSTRIAL INJURIES PENSION

What you may claim if your spouse dies from an industrial accident or disease

A woman whose husband dies as a result of an accident at work or a recognised industrial disease – of which there are about 50 – can claim a pension under the INDUSTRIAL INJURY BENEFITS scheme. But the claim must be made within 3 months of the death, or she may lose benefit.

Someone receiving an industrial injuries pension cannot obtain a national insurance WIDOW'S PENSION as well.

There are three rates of pension. For the first 26 weeks following the death, the rate is £38 a week, with an earnings-related addition of up to £14 a week on top (in 1981). After the 26 weeks are over, the rate becomes either £27.70 a week or £8.15 a week.

The higher rate is paid if the woman meets any of these conditions:
● If she is entitled to an industrial injuries allowance for a child. *See:* CHILD BENEFIT
● If she is over the age of 40 when this child allowance ends.
● If she is over the age of 50 when her husband dies.
● If she is incapable of supporting herself when her husband dies.
● If she is expecting a child by her late husband.

A woman who does not meet any of those conditions – for example, if she is self-supporting, under 50 and has no children – receives the lower rate.

Remarriage

If a woman receiving an industrial injuries widow's pension remarries, the pension stops, but she will receive a gratuity equal to one year's payments.

If the widow lives with a man as his wife, but without marriage, her pension ceases for that time.

Widowers

A man whose wife dies because of an accident at work or a recognised industrial disease may be entitled to a pension, provided that he is permanently unable to support himself and that his wife was meeting more than half the cost of maintaining him. If he meets both conditions, he will receive a pension at the higher rate of £27.70 a week.

Children

If the surviving spouse has children for whom he or she is entitled to child benefit, and is qualified to claim an industrial injuries benefit, he or she can obtain an allowance of £7.50 a week for each child. The benefit is also payable, in the case of a widow, for a child by her husband born after his death. The allowance is reduced to £1.25 a week on remarriage.

How to claim the benefit

When the death is registered, the widow or widower will receive from the registrar a certificate of application. That must be completed and sent to the local social security office which will then send a second form on which to make the claim for benefit.

WIDOW'S PENSION

Two different ways of helping bereaved women over 40

If a woman is under 40 when her husband dies and has no children, she receives no more widow's benefit after the 26 weeks in which she receives WIDOW'S ALLOWANCE.

If she is over 40, however, or if she is over 40 when she ceases to qualify for WIDOWED MOTHER'S ALLOWANCE, and her husband has paid enough national insurance contributions, she receives one of two benefits:
● An age-related pension payable to widows between the ages of 40 and 49.
● The standard widow's pension paid to women who are over 50 when they become eligible.

In 1981 the age-related pension varied from £8.15 a week at 40 to £25.25 at 49. The pension is pegged to the age at which you become eligible for it; you do not move up the scale with each year that passes. The rates are reviewed each year, however, taking some account of the cost of living. The standard pension during 1981 was £27.15 a week.

All widow's pensions continue until the age of 60 when they become retirement pensions payable at at least the same rate.

It is possible, however, to continue the widow's pension until the age of 65. The advantage in doing this is that there is no earnings rule on widow's pensions as there is on retirement pensions. They are taxable, however, and should be included in your income tax return.

Since April 1979 an additional payment has been made on the basis of the husband's earnings-related pension contributions.

When there is a company pension

An employer who has an approved OCCUPATIONAL PENSION scheme can contract his employees out of the additional part of the state scheme.

When a husband dies, his widow is paid a guaranteed minimum of at least half of what the husband would have been entitled to if he had retired at the time of his death.

This is deducted from the additional pension due to the widow from the state so that she receives:
● Her basic state widow's pension.
● The guaranteed minimum from her husband's private pension scheme.
● Some additional pension from the state.

Widow's pensions are normally paid by means of a book of weekly orders that can be cashed at a post office. You can, however, ask your local office of the Department of Health and Social Security to be paid by crossed orders for 4 or 13 weeks that you pay into your bank. You can also be paid abroad.

Widow's pensions cease if the widow remarries or lives with a man as his wife. If she lives with a man but later leaves him she can apply to have her pension restored.

WIDOW'S TAX

How a widow's pension alters her tax liability

A widow is treated as a single woman for tax purposes and therefore qualifies for the single person's allowance. If she is 65 or over she qualifies for the higher, single person's age allowance. *See:* INCOME TAX ALLOWANCES

In the year she is widowed, she may qualify for:
● A full year's single person's or age allowance from the date of widowhood even though she is only a widow for part of that tax year.
● Widow's bereavement allowance which is equal to the difference between the married and single person's allowances. Again, she gets a full year's allowance even though she may only be a widow for part of that tax year.
● If she has a child to look after she may also get the full additional allowance equal to the difference between the married and single person's allowances (the same amount as the widow's bereavement allowance). She gets this in addition to the single and widow's bereavement allowances.

A widow's pension is taxable income, but on its own is not large enough to be liable for tax as usually it will be less than the single person's allowance. It is only when the pension is combined with some other form of income that this amount will be exceeded and tax will be payable.

If a widow gets a job she should let her inspector of taxes know that she is receiving a pension so that her PAYE deductions can be calculated on her total income. If she does not inform the Inland Revenue about her pension, she may subsequently find herself having to meet a demand for the back taxes. War widows' pensions are not taxable.

WILL

What happens to your possessions after your death

The object of making a will is to state what you want to happen to your possessions after your death, who you want to sort out your affairs and, if necessary, who you want to be the GUARDIAN of your children. You can also express your wishes about such matters as your FUNERAL and burial or cremation.

Anyone over 18 of sound mind can make a will provided that he or she is capable of understanding it.

Few people are eager to contemplate death, but anyone with considerable property may be able to minimise the amount of CAPITAL TRANSFER TAX (death duty) that his heirs have to pay.

HOW TO MAKE A WILL WITHOUT A LAWYER
Taking every precaution to ensure that your intentions are completely clear

Will forms available from most stationers still use the archaic phrase 'Last will and testament'. The 'and testament' has no legal effect and can be sensibly omitted when you are preparing your own simple will

This clause is usually added, even when no will has been made previously. All wills are also revoked automatically when the testator marries or remarries

If you choose a trust company to be executor, use the wording of the appointment clause set out in their brochures so that they can deduct a fee for their services

Give the full name of any beneficiary and state any relationship, so that there can be no doubt about to whom you are referring

Even if the testator tries to specify in detail what should happen to all his property, he should name someone to receive the residue in case anything is overlooked

THIS IS THE LAST WILL of me, THOMAS GUY LACEY, of 7 UPTON GARDENS, LONDON SW3 in the County of LONDON.

I hereby revoke all wills heretofore made by me.

I appoint JAMES EDWARD LACEY of 48 SUNNINGTON ROAD, N18 and RODERICK THOMAS MARTIN of 2a WARREN COURT, NW12 to be executors of this my will

and I direct that all my just Debts and Funeral and Testamentary Expenses shall be paid as soon as conveniently may be after my decease.

I give and bequeath unto my son JAMES EDWARD LACEY the sum of £1,000 tax free

my grandson PIERS GAWAIN LACEY the sum of £500 tax free

my granddaughter EMMA MARY LACEY the sum of £500 tax free

and the residue to my wife JULIET MARY LACEY.

In witness whereof I have hereunto set my hand this eighteenth day of November one thousand nine hundred and seventy seven.

Thomas Guy Lacey

Jane Hickinbottom
27 Homer Row, W1.
Secretary

Signed by the above-named Testator as and for his last will in the presence of us, who at his request, in his presence and in the presence of each other subscribe our names as witnesses

Roger Ponder
42 Flower Way.
Guildford, Surrey.
Journalist.

The witnesses need not see the contents of the will, but they should not be beneficiaries or married to beneficiaries. They are disqualified from inheriting, unless there are at least two other witnesses who were not beneficiaries

If through illness, injury or illiteracy the testator cannot sign his name, his mark is sufficient, with a note by someone else 'The Mark of (the person's full name)'

By stating 'tax free' you make clear that you want the beneficiary to receive the full figure, and for the relevant death duty to be paid out of the rest of the estate

Most men or women can make a will without the help of a lawyer provided their wishes are straightforward. Stationers sell standard forms that make it easy to set the will out properly, but there is no reason why you cannot simply write or type your wishes on an ordinary piece of paper. If your family situation or wishes are at all complicated, however, or if you have involved business arrangements, for example as a member of a partnership, take legal advice about making a will. The solicitor will try to see that there are no ambiguities so that your wishes are not misinterpreted. If, for example, you want to ensure that your children inherit your property if your widow remarries, he can help you to set up a trust in your will that will provide for your widow throughout her life but will eventually hand everything on to the children. If you are wealthy he can also help to keep death duty to the minimum.

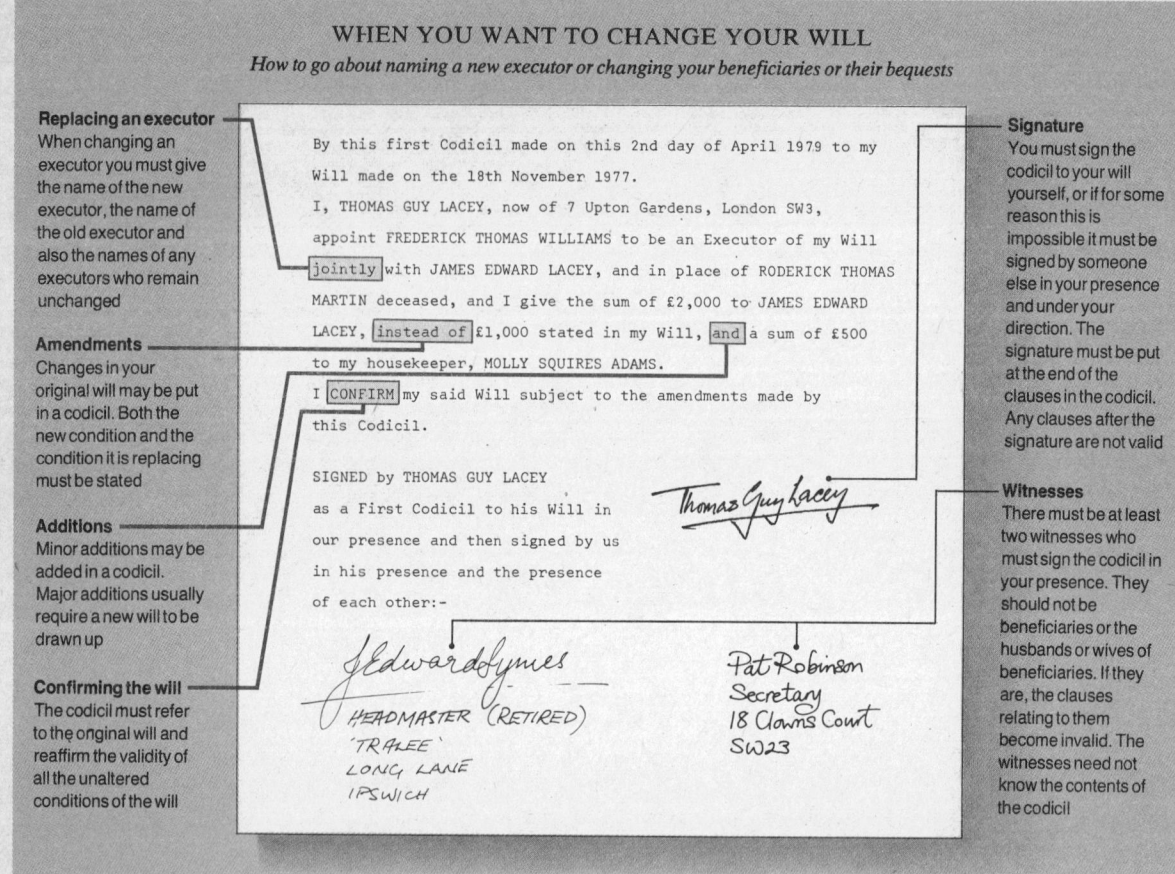

WHEN YOU WANT TO CHANGE YOUR WILL
How to go about naming a new executor or changing your beneficiaries or their bequests

Replacing an executor
When changing an executor you must give the name of the new executor, the name of the old executor and also the names of any executors who remain unchanged

Amendments
Changes in your original will may be put in a codicil. Both the new condition and the condition it is replacing must be stated

Additions
Minor additions may be added in a codicil. Major additions usually require a new will to be drawn up

Confirming the will
The codicil must refer to the original will and reaffirm the validity of all the unaltered conditions of the will

By this first Codicil made on this 2nd day of April 1979 to my Will made on the 18th November 1977.

I, THOMAS GUY LACEY, now of 7 Upton Gardens, London SW3, appoint FREDERICK THOMAS WILLIAMS to be an Executor of my Will jointly with JAMES EDWARD LACEY, and in place of RODERICK THOMAS MARTIN deceased, and I give the sum of £2,000 to JAMES EDWARD LACEY, instead of £1,000 stated in my Will, and a sum of £500 to my housekeeper, MOLLY SQUIRES ADAMS.

I CONFIRM my said Will subject to the amendments made by this Codicil.

SIGNED by THOMAS GUY LACEY
as a First Codicil to his Will in
our presence and then signed by us
in his presence and the presence
of each other:-

Thomas Guy Lacey

J Edward Symes
HEADMASTER (RETIRED)
'TRALEE'
LONG LANE
IPSWICH

Pat Robinson
Secretary
18 Clowns Court
SW23

Signature
You must sign the codicil to your will yourself, or if for some reason this is impossible it must be signed by someone else in your presence and under your direction. The signature must be put at the end of the clauses in the codicil. Any clauses after the signature are not valid

Witnesses
There must be at least two witnesses who must sign the codicil in your presence. They should not be beneficiaries or the husbands or wives of beneficiaries. If they are, the clauses relating to them become invalid. The witnesses need not know the contents of the codicil

Once a will is signed it can be altered only by an amending document that has been signed by the person whose will it is, and his signature must be witnessed. Such a supplement is called a codicil. The witnesses, however, do not need to be the same two people who witnessed the will. If a codicil has not been signed and witnessed properly, the executors of the will have to follow the will's original text.

If a will is not drawn and witnessed correctly, the law treats the estate as though no will had been made. *See:* INTESTACY

Any alterations must be signed by the person making the will, called the testator, and two witnesses. If a mistake is made in the draft it is better to type or write a fair copy before signing.

Later alterations can be made only by codicil or a completely new will.

It is essential that the testator and the witnesses, of which there must be at least two, are all together when the will is signed.

Choosing an executor

The person you choose to wind up your affairs is called the EXECUTOR or, in the case of a woman, executrix. If you are leaving the bulk of your estate to one person, it is often best to make that person the executor. If you know that person is likely to find it a worry, however, it might be better to appoint someone else close to him or her.

If a TRUST is to be set up under the will, you must appoint at least two trustees also. Executors can also be trustees.

If you have young children and wish to appoint a guardian or guardians, write a clause after the one appointing the executor and trustees, if any. All that is needed is a simple sentence saying, for example: 'I appoint . . . of . . . and his wife to be the guardians of my children.'

The guardians can also be executors or trustees.

Deciding what to do

When considering what you want to happen to your possessions, ask:

● What do I own?
● What, including legacies, am I likely to own in the future?
● Who do I want to benefit?
● Who else can claim that I should provide for them?
● What do I want to happen to any gift if the person I name dies before me?

In many cases, all the questions can be answered by a simple will leaving 'my whole estate' to the husband or wife. People making their own wills, however, commonly express their wishes mistakenly by writing something like: 'I leave everything to my wife and, on her death, everything is to be shared among our children.'

Once he has left his whole estate to his wife, a husband has no say in what is to pass to his children. That is for his wife to decide in her will.

To achieve what he wants, he has to

LEAVING YOUR BODY TO SCIENCE

If you want all or part of your body to be used for medical purposes after your death, you can make that request during your lifetime, but there is no guarantee that it will be carried out. Once you are dead, your body does not form part of your property, but belongs to whoever has lawful possession of it – usually, your next-of-kin or a hospital or other medical institution. An undertaker has no rights to it.

The request may be made orally, in the presence of at least two witnesses. However, it is more likely to be observed if you set it out in writing and give copies to the executor of your will, your next-of-kin and your family doctor. The written request may be inserted into your will, but to avoid delay – for example, in transplanting a kidney – you should draw it up as a separate document.

A suitable statement, which you can prepare for yourself, could say:
I (name) ....
of (address) ....
request that after my death my body/the following parts of my body..........................
....
should be used for therapeutic purposes under the Human Tissues Act 1961 or the Anatomy Act 1832, whichever is more suitable.

You must sign and date the statement in the presence of a witness – for example, your doctor or solicitor – who must also sign it and give his address.

Some medical research organisations – for example, the Royal National Institute for the Blind and the Kidney Research Fund – issue bequest cards to potential donors. Surgeons will not normally use a dead person's kidneys unless he is known to have held a donor's card.

Bequeathing a whole body

Bequests of entire bodies for medical research cannot be accepted without the approval of HM Inspector of Anatomy. Once he has agreed, he will issue documents, referred to as statutory forms, which the executor or relatives must complete and return.

You can obtain the forms from the Inspector at the Department of Health and Social Security, 16 Gresse Street, London W1P 1PB and give them, partly completed, to your executor.

What must be done after death

If a dead person has left a request that part of his body should be used for medical purposes, whoever is in charge of the body should contact the family doctor or nearest hospital immediately after the death. No forms need to be completed, but if a CORONER has ordered an inquest or post-mortem, his permission must be obtained before any organs can be removed.

Once the donated organs have been extracted, the body is returned to the executor or relative for burial.

If the entire body has been donated to science, and provided that no inquest or post-mortem examination is necessary, the executor or relative should contact the Inspector of Anatomy and complete the statutory forms. The Inspector may not accept the body if death resulted from a ravaging disease – for example, cancer. He will not accept it if there has been a post-mortem or inquest.

Once the body has been accepted, it will be transferred to a medical school, which must arrange burial or cremation within 2 years.

When relatives can object

Provided that the dead person left a specific request that part of his body should be used for medical purposes, whoever is in legal possession of it can allow organs to be removed, if he is reasonably sure that the donor did not withdraw the request later. The next-of-kin or other relatives have no legal rights to object.

However, if the body is in the charge of a hospital and if the next-of-kin objects immediately after the death to organs being removed, the hospital is unlikely to go ahead.

Donations of an entire body, even if they are made by the dead person in writing, can be over-ruled by a surviving husband or wife or other next-of-kin.

If the dead person has not bequeathed all or part of his body for medical purposes, a doctor or hospital wanting to use it must ensure that the next-of-kin or other relatives have no objections.

---

leave her only a life interest in his estate, which will then pass to his children on her death. Such an arrangement is normally advisable only if the estate is a big one or the wife has adequate money of her own.

It is essential to take professional advice before making anything more than the simplest of wills.

Even when making a straightforward gift you must remember that it is the circumstances at the time of your death rather than at the time of making the will that are important.

For example, a vintage-car enthusiast may decide to leave an old friend his highly prized Lagonda. If it is his only car and he refers to it in his will as 'my car' it is clear what he means at the time of writing.

When he dies, however, he may be running one or more other cars. It is no longer clear what he meant and the gift can be disputed. The testator should be more specific and refer to 'my vintage Lagonda car'.

Similarly, if you wish people to choose mementoes, specify clearly what they can choose from and who shall have first choice, second choice and so on.

Ambiguities in a will mean not only a danger that your wishes may not be carried out correctly, they can also create a great deal of ill-feeling in a family.

If you want to leave money to charity, make sure you write its name and address correctly – many have similar names. It is usually better to get hold of one of their leaflets which contain a draft clause to guide people who leave them money.

This usually contains a phrase limiting your executor's responsibility to obtaining a receipt from an authorised officer of the charity stating it has received the bequest.

Revoking a will

A will is revoked by a later will or codicil – a written declaration signed and witnessed like a will – or simply by the testator, or someone acting on his behalf in his presence, actually destroying it.

In general, marriage also revokes a will, even if the couple were already living together when the will was made. The only exception is if the will states that it was made in contemplation of marriage to the person to whom the testator later was married. Such a clause can, however, make the will conditional on the marriage taking place.

How to dispute a will

Anyone who thinks he has been wrongfully deprived can dispute:

- The genuineness of the signature on the will.
- The testator's ability to understand the implications of the will.
- That the testator was not able to act freely at the time he made the will.
- The way in which the will has been interpreted.
- The fairness of its provisions. *See:* DISINHERITANCE

Whatever the basis of a challenge, legal advice is generally essential.

False signature Anyone who thinks the signature on a will was forged or obtained by a trick should enter a warning, or caveat, at the probate registry so that he is told when an application for probate is lodged and can start an action to set aside the will. As a criminal offence would almost certainly be involved, the matter should also be reported to the police.

Fitness to sign The yardstick of whether a person is mentally qualified to make a will is that he or she must be able to understand:
- The nature and size of the estate.
- The identity of all those who might have a moral claim to benefit under the will.
- What the provisions of the will achieve.

One of the difficulties that can arise is that doctors and nurses are usually unwilling to give a professional opinion on a patient's competence to make a will.

Undue influence A will can be set aside if it is proved that the testator was improperly dominated by someone else when he made it.

Simply influencing him by way of advice, as a solicitor, doctor, priest or close relative might properly do, is not enough to prove undue influence. *See:* GIFT

What did he mean? A beneficiary under a will, or anyone who thinks he should be one, can bring a legal action if he thinks the EXECUTOR is failing to carry out the terms of the will or misinterpreting them.

For example, if there is an ambiguity in the will about how a property should be divided, the executor might read it one way and a beneficiary another.

The beneficiary could seek a court order requiring the executor to accept the beneficiary's interpretation of the testator's intent.

WITNESS

When you give evidence as a witness

Even the most law-abiding person can find himself asked to give evidence, possibly under cross-examination in court, if he witnesses an accident, a fight or a crime.

For example, if someone out walking witnesses an accident in which a cyclist is killed by a car he can be asked to give evidence:
- To the police immediately after the accident.
- To a coroner at the inquest.
- To a magistrates' court if the driver is prosecuted.
- To the High Court if the motorist is sued for negligence by the cyclist's dependants.
- To the solicitors acting for the motorist and the dependants of the dead cyclist.

Making statements

When a witness has been driving or in charge of a motor vehicle he is obliged to give his name and address to a police officer and can eventually be summoned to give evidence. In other cases, a witness is not legally obliged to make a statement to the police; he does not even have to give his name and address. He cannot be prosecuted for obstructing the police by refusing to answer police questions.

Most people, however, do help and make a statement if required.

If the police intend to prosecute someone they usually ask witnesses to make written statements on a standard witness form.

Witnesses may also be approached by lawyers or by insurers acting for one or other parties to a claim. A witness does not have to co-operate in any way. If he does provide a statement, that does not prevent him from giving evidence to the other side as well. The witness is free to speak to anyone he chooses and neither side can claim him as its own witness.

When a witness is subpoenaed

A witness can be ordered to attend court to give evidence. The order is called a SUBPOENA if it is a High Court case or a witness summons if it is a magistrates', county or crown court case. The witness will be given conduct money to enable him to travel to court plus an allowance for food and accommodation, if necessary.

Many witnesses are willing to give evidence, but it may be wise to insist on a witness summons or a subpoena. Many employers insist that a court order be produced before they will release an employee from work to attend court.

If a witness ignores a witness summons or subpoena he can be arrested and brought to court to explain why he disobeyed. He may be fined or even, in exceptional cases, imprisoned. *See:* CONTEMPT OF COURT

If you are asked to attend a court and the date is inconvenient, you can ask the solicitor who issued the summons if he can change it. If he cannot help, apply to the court office. If the clerks cannot re-arrange the date of the hearing, you can as a last resort make a formal application to the court.

Appearing in court as a witness

The dates of some trials are arranged many months in advance. Others, including most High Court cases, are heard at very short notice. The witness may well be given a week's notice that he may be needed and then receive a telegram giving him 24 hours' notice of the hearing.

When you arrive at the court show your summons or subpoena to the usher who will tell you in which court the case is being heard.

Try at once to find the solicitor who requested your attendance to tell him you have arrived.

That person is your reference point and should be able to keep you informed of the progress of the case. If you have any queries, put them to him.

Ask the solicitor for a copy of your own statement so that you can refresh your memory of events that may have happened many months ago.

A witness is not usually allowed in court before he is to give evidence in case he is influenced by what earlier witnesses say. So inevitably you will find yourself waiting in corridors for some time. If you want to go for a coffee or a walk, let the usher or solicitor know, in case you are due to be called.

When you are called to give evidence you will be shown to the witness box, usually in front of the court, and will be asked to swear or affirm. *See:* OATH

You will be taken through your evidence first by the barrister or solicitor representing the party who asked you to attend. Then you are cross-examined by the representative of the opposing side. That lawyer will probably try to weaken your evidence by finding ambiguities in it or suggest you may have been mistaken.

He may even be rude or aggressive to confuse you into contradicting yourself.

Be prepared to spend a long time giving your evidence. Lawyers go through it very slowly to enable the judge to make very full notes.

A witness must not refuse to answer a question if ordered to do so by a judge or magistrate or he will be in contempt of court. If he answers questions untruthfully he commits PERJURY.

After giving your evidence, do not assume you can go home. The subpoena or summons requires you to attend for the duration of the trial. You may be recalled later to give further evidence or to clarify something you said.

Ask whether you can be released. If the lawyers for both parties do not need you any more, the judge will probably agree to let you go.

Send a list of the losses and expenses you incurred by attending court to the solicitor who requested your presence. You may, however, not be able to recover the full amount. Most courts lay down a maximum that can be paid to witnesses. *See also:* EVIDENCE

WORK PERMIT

The system that restricts employment of outsiders

Few people from outside Britain can take up permanent employment in this country unless they qualify:
● For settlement, under the rules of IMMIGRATION.
● For unrestricted entry, under the rules of PATRIALITY.
● For freedom of movement as workers, under the rules of the EUROPEAN COMMUNITIES.

But if some other foreign worker has qualifications for a particular job, and a prospective employer can show that he has been unable to find a British resident suitable for the job, the employer

WHEN A WORK PERMIT IS NOT NEEDED

Work permits are not required for foreign employees in the following categories:
● Doctors and dentists who have been appointed to British posts.
● Ministers, missionaries and members of religious orders, including teachers.
● People appointed to British Government positions – for example, scientists – with Department of Employment approval.
● Staff of overseas governments serving in Britain – for example, trade representatives – or of international organisations of which Britain is a member.
● Private servants of diplomats.
● Representatives of overseas companies that have no branch, subsidiary or other representative in Britain.
● Press and broadcasting representatives.
● Teachers and language assistants under approved exchange schemes.
● Seamen under contract to join ships.
● Airline operational staff.
● Agricultural workers admitted under approved schemes to meet seasonal demands – for example, harvesting.

may succeed in obtaining a Department of Employment work permit.

It is a document that allows an immigrant to enter Britain in order to take up a certain job with a certain employer – not a general permission to work.

The rules for issuing permits differ according to the occupation concerned. Leaflets giving details can be obtained from the Department of Employment's foreign labour section in Ebury Bridge Road, London SW1W 8PY. The department's decision is final and there can be no appeal to a court or appeal tribunal.

Permits are normally granted only for jobs requiring special professional or trade skills. The permit system also covers resident domestic servants – but not AU PAIR visitors.

Generally the worker must have at least 5 years' experience of the work for which he is required, and the employer has to prove that he has tried, by advertising, to find a British resident who meets the requirements.

Work-permit holders are not given unrestricted entry to Britain. Normally their passports are stamped for stays of 12 months at a time, subject to their remaining in the same employment.

A permit holder is not absolutely bound to stay in his first job, but he must have Department of Employment approval to start a new one. Consent is not given unless his new employment would also have qualified him for a permit.

It is not an offence to employ someone who does not have a work permit, but the employee may well not be given permission to stay here.

After 4 years of control, the conditions on a work-permit holder's stay are

lifted. He can take any employment, stay in Britain on a residence permit and qualify eventually for CITIZENSHIP.

Work-permit control is also imposed on employees of foreign companies who are sent to Britain for training, and on professional entertainers and sportsmen under contract to British companies, who are often given short-term work permits. Their permits do not lead to permanent residence.

WORKMEN'S COMPENSATION

Special help for people injured or ill before 1948

Employees who had an accident at work or contracted an industrial disease before July 5, 1948 can qualify for workmen's compensation supplementation.

If the accident happened or the industrial disease was contracted before January 1, 1924, you can get a basic allowance of £2 per week and either a major or lesser incapacity allowance, depending on the degree of your incapacity.

If the accident or disease happened after January 1, 1924, you can get only the major or lesser allowance.

During 1981, the rate of the major allowance was £44.30 a week, and the lesser allowance £16.30

Other allowances payable under the INDUSTRIAL INJURIES scheme, such as constant attendance allowance, exceptionally severe disablement allowance or unemployability supplement, can also be paid with workmen's compensation.

To claim an allowance under the workmen's compensation scheme, write to the Department of Health and Social Security, Workmen's Compensation (Supplementation) Branch, Norcross, Blackpool FY5 3TA and ask for a claim form.

You may need to produce medical evidence or to undergo a medical examination. Any expenses you incur in attending this examination will be refunded. If you do not agree with the decision on your claim you can appeal. You will be told how to do this when you hear whether your claim has been successful or not.

Any benefit awarded will normally be paid by a book of orders to be cashed at a post office of your choice on Wednesdays. Each order must be cashed within 3 months of the date shown on it.

WOUNDING

Serious assault that breaks the skin

Wounding is an assault that breaks the skin and is as serious as the charge of grievous bodily harm. Less serious assault will be charged as actual bodily harm or ASSAULT AND BATTERY. *See also:* BODILY HARM

WRECK

When property found on the beach must be reported to the Receiver of Wrecks

Any object of value, identifiable as belonging to someone, that is washed up on the foreshore or found in territorial waters is 'wreck'. If it is not claimed by the owner it belongs to the Crown, or anyone granted a right to it by the Crown.

Anyone finding any wreck, including fishing tackle or buoys, must give it or report it to the local Receiver of Wrecks – usually a senior Customs officer. Failure to report wreck is an offence for which the maximum fine is £100.

Wreckage or cargo abandoned on the high seas is known as derelict. It belongs to the finder, unless the original owner proves that it was not abandoned, in which case salvage may be payable.

An historic wreck can be protected by the Department of the Environment under the Protection of Wrecks Act 1973, if the wreck is included in the Act by government order. When a wreck is protected it is an offence to tamper with, take or have in your possession any part of the wreck without a licence from the Department of the Environment. An unlimited fine can be imposed on offenders.

WRONGFUL DISMISSAL

When an employer breaks the rules on notice

An employer who dismisses an employee must pay him for any period of NOTICE to which he is entitled, whether he is required to work during that period or not. The only exception is if the employee himself has forfeited his right to notice by misconduct so serious that it justifies instant, or summary, DISMISSAL – for example, by embezzling company funds.

In all other circumstances, if an employer fails to pay wages for all or part of the required notice period, an employee can sue him for breach of the EMPLOYMENT CONTRACT to recover the money he is owed. Such claims, for 'wrongful dismissal', are brought in a county court or, if the amount sought is more than £2,000, in the High Court.

Any employee who is not paid for a notice period to which he is entitled can sue for wrongful dismissal. He does not have to have been with his employer for any specified time. Part-time workers and those on fixed-term contracts can make claims.

Wrongful dismissal cases may be brought up to 6 years from the date on which dismissal took place.

A worker claiming wrongful dismissal may obtain LEGAL AID. If the claim is successful, the court may order the employer to pay the costs.

How damages are assessed

Damages in wrongful dismissal cases are generally limited to the net value of wages unpaid, but the claimant may also seek compensation for the loss, during what should have been the notice period, of fringe benefits – for example, a car or free board and lodging.

Courts expect dismissed employees to do all they can to reduce their losses, in particular by trying to find another job as soon as possible.

If an employee takes new employment during what would have been his notice period, his earnings from it are deducted from his damages.

If he has not found another job, and the court feels he has not made a reasonable effort to do so, it can reduce his damages by the amount it estimates he could have earned.

So anyone bringing a claim for wrongful dismissal should be able to show that the kind of job he is seeking is difficult to get. He should also keep, as evidence of his efforts, a careful record of applications sent, interviews attended and the total time spent job-hunting.

The amount of damages is also reduced by the value of UNEMPLOYMENT BENEFIT received during what should have been the notice period, and by the INCOME TAX and NATIONAL INSURANCE CONTRIBUTIONS the employee would have had to pay. SUPPLEMENTARY BENEFIT and any REDUNDANCY payment are not deducted.

If an employee is seeking unpaid wages for a prolonged period – for example, a year – the court may make an extra deduction from his damages because he is receiving as a lump sum money that would otherwise have been paid over 12 months.

Awards for wrongful dismissal are not taxable unless they exceed £10,000.

Other dismissal claims

Wrongful dismissal cases arise from contract law and are not directly linked to the rules on EMPLOYMENT PROTECTION. An employee who receives damages from a court for wrongful dismissal does not forfeit the rights he may have to apply to an INDUSTRIAL TRIBUNAL for compensation for UNFAIR DISMISSAL, if his employer's behaviour in sacking him was unreasonable, or for REDUNDANCY.

Those rights are not affected even if, in settling the wrongful dismissal claim, the employee signs a declaration provided by his employer stating that the payment is 'in full and final settlement of all claims I may have arising out of the termination of my employment'.

X-RAY

Medical treatment that involves radiation

Anyone who is harmed through exposure to an x-ray, because his doctor did not take the necessary precautions or made a mistake, may sue the doctor for MEDICAL NEGLIGENCE – for example, if a child is harmed due to x-rays given to its mother during pregnancy. *See:* UNBORN CHILD

Because any x-ray involves the use of radiation, stringent safeguards should be made for patients undergoing treatment. For example, protective clothing should be provided to protect certain areas of the body from exposure. Certain parts of the body, such as the head, should not be subjected to an x-ray unless it is absolutely necessary. Simi-

A SPECIALIST ROLE

Most x-rays are taken by a specialist radiographer and are interpreted by a radiologist.

larly, a pregnant woman should be x-rayed only in an emergency, such as a road accident.

Any doctor or dentist may take an x-ray. However, most x-rays are taken by a qualified specialist, known as a radiographer. The results are exposed on film and interpreted by another specialist, known as a radiologist.

There are certain areas outside the National Health Service when x-rays may be given by unqualified staff. For example, someone in prison who has a suspected broken arm may be x-rayed by an unqualified member of the medical staff, or an immigration official may require a person to be x-rayed before he allows him to enter the country.

Although such officials are entitled to do so, anyone who is harmed by an x-ray from such an official, may sue for negligence as he would sue a doctor.

YOUNG OFFENDERS

How the law deals with children who commit an offence

Children under 10 cannot be prosecuted: the law presumes that they cannot be guilty of an offence. Children of that age who do get into trouble, however, can be brought before a juvenile court as being in need of care and control. *See:* CHILDREN IN CARE

A child over 10 and under 17 can be brought before a juvenile court. In the case of a child between 10 and 14 the court must be satisfied that he knew he was doing wrong. Children over 17 usually go before an adult court.

Cautions for first offenders

A child who has admitted his guilt, particularly if he is a first offender, may be given a formal caution by a policeman in the presence of a parent or other adult who has legal control of him. That is a formal dressing-down at the police station instead of going to court. Records of such cautions are kept by the police but they are destroyed when the child is 17, provided that he or she has not meanwhile committed other offences.

The decision whether simply to caution or charge a young offender is usually taken jointly by the police and local authority. In some areas, for example London, the police may often caution first offenders without reference to the local authority, unless the child has been involved with other children with previous convictions.

Children brought before the court

Juvenile court hearings are not open to the public. They are deliberately as informal as possible and police attending do not wear uniform. The hearings themselves must be in a specially chosen room and may not be held where an adult court has been meeting, or is due to meet, within an hour.

The court must consist of not more than three magistrates specially qualified for dealing with juvenile cases. There must be no fewer than two, preferably a man and a woman, but in special circumstances a full-time stipendiary magistrate may sit alone.

Children charged with offences must be given BAIL if they are not brought before the court within 72 hours. The only exceptions are for very serious offences like murder.

The police must notify a child's parents of his attendance at court and the parents are usually expected to come with him, and the court can require them to attend. The police must also notify the local authority and the probation service.

Before deciding how to deal with a child found guilty of an offence, the court may, if appropriate, request a report from his school and a report from the local authority on his home circumstances.

The court may adjourn for up to 4 weeks (3 if bail has not been allowed) for the reports to become available, or to decide how best to deal with the case. When a juvenile is not released on bail he is committed to the care of the local authority.

What decisions the court may reach

A court can order a parent to promise to take proper care and exercise proper control over his child. He might be bound over for up to £50 for up to 3 years. *See:* BINDING OVER

Where an adult could be fined for an offence, the parent of a child under 14 can be fined up to £10. Between 14 and 17, the child himself or his parent can be ordered to pay up to £200.

A compensation order may also be made. A child can be ordered to pay up to £400 compensation for each offence.

A court may not wish to remove a child from home. To prevent his re-offending – particularly when the offence is truancy – it may impose a SUPERVISION ORDER, with the agreement of the child and his parents, or it may place him in the care of the local authority.

A court may also make an order directing the child to participate in certain remedial and preventative activities – called intermediate treatment – which may include a residential programme.

If a court decides it is best to remove the child from home it can commit him to a detention centre for up to 3 months, provided he is medically fit and over 14. In general he will not be sent to a detention centre if he has previously served a detention centre or Borstal sentence.

A child found guilty of an offence for which an adult could be imprisoned may be required to attend an attendance centre. Attendance must not be less than a total of 12 hours, unless he is under 14, or more than a total of 24 hours. He will usually be required to attend on Saturday afternoons.

More serious or persistent offenders between 15 and 21 years old can be sent to a crown court for Borstal sentencing – for between 6 months and up to 2 years.

A child has the same right of appeal to the crown court against conviction as an adult except where there is a conditional discharge. A parent or guardian who is ordered to pay a fine may also appeal to the crown court.

ZEBRA CROSSING

The cross-traffic 'precinct' for pedestrians

Zebra crossings were designed and are recognised in law as a protected area for pedestrians wishing to cross a street.

Under most circumstances drivers must give way to anyone setting foot on a 'zebra'. Unlike pelican crossings, they are not controlled by lights, but they must have flashing amber Belisha beacons. *See:* PEDESTRIAN CROSSING

HOW TO MAKE A COMPLAINT

*The most effective way to obtain redress or compensation
for some damage or injury is to complain systematically and reasonably – with
as much supporting evidence in writing as possible*

A justified complaint, made in the right way, may benefit not only you, but also other people with a similar problem. On the other hand, a complaint taken too far, or pursued in the wrong way, may cost you far more than you originally lost.

So, as well as knowing your rights, you should know how best to secure them.

Complaints about goods and services

The most common sources of complaint are goods and services that fail to live up to their promise – a new washing machine that does not work properly or a restaurant dinner party that is ruined by poor food and service. In such cases, your legal rights are governed by the law of CONTRACT and the rules on sale of GOODS, TRADE DESCRIPTIONS and WEIGHTS AND MEASURES.

Why complain?

Before pressing a complaint, ask yourself why you are complaining and what you hope to achieve by doing so. If your new television fails to work, the answers are clear-cut – you are complaining because the set is not satisfactory and you want it put right.

Other cases are less straightforward. If a waiter or shop assistant is rude to you, you cannot claim redress. Nevertheless, the complaint may still be worth making.

Sometimes, a complaint may stem more from bad temper than from justification. If that is so, you should admit it to yourself – and keep silent.

To whom should I complain?

Once you have decided to press a complaint, the next step is to determine where you should first make it. In shops, hotels, restaurants and offices, the person with whom you have been dealing may not have the authority to put matters right and may even stop your complaint reaching the right quarters.

If you feel your complaint is not receiving proper consideration, ask to see the manager or, in a small business, the owner. But do not aim too high at first in large companies or organisations. Even if you succeed in talking to the managing director of a big department store, he will probably refer you to someone lower in hierarchy, for example, the floor manager, unless the matter is extremely serious.

Some organisations are adept at passing complaints, particularly those made by telephone, from one person to another until the complainant is tired of repeating his story. If that happens, ask for the names of the people to whom you talk and make it clear to them that you will go higher if you do not get satisfaction. In law, an employer is legally responsible for the actions of his employees during the course of their work for him.

Lodging the initial complaint

Many less-serious complaints can be settled on the spot, once you have found the person responsible for dealing with them.

If you decide to complain orally, do so fully, but fairly – and without losing your temper or becoming abusive. If you get angry, the other person may become defensive, or angry himself, and you may weaken your case.

Give the other person a chance to state his views, but leave him in no doubt what you are complaining about and what you expect to be done.

Putting it in writing

If your complaint is serious, or your first attempts to have it settled have failed, make it formally, in writing. Send it by registered or recorded delivery, so that the organisation concerned cannot deny that it has been received. Keep a copy.

Address it to the person in charge of the office, shop or organisation against which you are complaining. But do not aim too high at first: that may delay action.

Your letter should set out, in full, what you consider your complaint to be, including any relevant names and dates, invoice numbers and references to any previous correspondence on the subject. Do not include original documents – for example, bills or contracts – as you may need them later as evidence. If such details matter, send photocopies. (Most large public libraries now have facilities for photocopying, and in many towns, small printing offices also undertake such work.)

State what you expect to be done about your complaint and set a time limit for a reply – say, 14 days. Make it clear that if you have not had a satisfactory response by that date, you will take matters further.

CHECK BEFORE YOU BUY

● *The quality.* Goods approved by the British Standards Institution or the Design Centre carry symbols denoting that they have passed certain tests.

If items are delivered to your home, do not sign a carrier's note saying that they have been received in good condition until you have inspected them thoroughly – or sign 'not examined'.

● *The maker's instructions.* They often define the purpose for which the goods are designed. For example, the instructions accompanying a light electric mower may imply that it is suitable only for trimming well-kept lawns, not for orchard grass.

● *The guarantee.* See how long it lasts and whether it prohibits repairs by anyone other than an authorised agent or dealer, or the use of replacement parts not approved by the maker. But remember that the guarantee cannot limit your normal legal rights. *See:* GUARANTEE

● *The after-sales service offered by the seller or maker.*

● *The true cost and any interest if you are buying by credit or in instalments.*

GET YOUR FACTS STRAIGHT BEFORE TAKING ACTION

Whether your complaint is serious or relatively minor, you stand a better chance of succeeding if you can produce evidence to support the details. So keep all bills, receipts, makers' instructions, guarantees and other relevant documents. When you buy goods by post, keep the newspaper advertisement or promotion brochure.

If you complain by letter, make a copy and file any reply you receive. If you complain in person or by telephone, note the date, the names and job titles of the people you speak to and brief details of what was said. Take a friend as an independent witness to any important interview.

Some complaints about faulty goods or services may justify the cost of obtaining an expert opinion from, for example, a surveyor or a motor engineer.

If your complaint arises from an accident or someone's negligence, get the names and addresses of any witnesses and ask them for written statements. If the police were involved, you can have a copy of their report and any statements they took, for a small fee.

Once you have established the facts, sort them out so that you can present them in a clear, orderly fashion. If you need further details from the person or organisation involved, or from a third party, put your questions to them in writing. However, you can force them to answer only in court.

When there is no response

Once you have submitted a formal, written complaint, you can expect two replies from an efficient organisation:
● An acknowledgment by return of post that your complaint has been received and is being investigated.
● A detailed response to the points that you are raising.

If you receive neither within the time limit you have set, write again, enclosing a copy of the first letter. At that stage, it may help if you send a copy of the second letter to someone higher in the organisation – the area manager, managing director or chief executive, say.

In many cases, you can get his name, or at least the head office address, from a reference book in your local library. The librarian can help you to find what you want.

Some useful books are *Who Owns Whom, Kelly's Manufacturers and Merchants Directory*, the *Retail Directory, Key British Enterprises* and *UK Trade Names*.

Alternatively, call the company and ask the switchboard operator – though without saying why you need to know.

Make sure that the top copy of the second letter, to the person to whom you originally complained, has typed on it 'cc (carbon copy): Mr John Smith, Managing Director', to show you are pursuing the matter seriously.

If you get a reply that does not answer your complaint – particularly common from organisations that use standard, printed, reply letters – write again, pointing out firmly, but politely, that your original point seems to have been ignored.

If the reply answers your complaint but does not offer what seems to you to be adequate redress, consider what to do next. Often, the letter itself will suggest the next stage. For example, if it says 'it is not our policy to make refunds in such circumstances', you may decide to take the matter up with the policy makers – the board of directors.

Getting outside help

Once you have exhausted the immediate possibilities of getting your complaint dealt with by the organisation concerned, you can try to enlist the aid of other interested parties.

One way – if the organisation is a commercial concern – is to write to any trade association of which it is a member. You may find its name on the company's letterhead, or on a sign on their premises. Send a copy of your letter to the company about which you are complaining and keep another for yourself.

If your complaint is one of a number about a member-company, or if it is about something that could bring the whole trade into disrepute, the associa-

REFUSING TO PAY – A POSITIVE FORM OF COMPLAINT

If you buy goods or services that fail to live up to their promise, you can refuse to pay part of the bill by deducting a 'set off' – the legal term for reasonable compensation you have, in effect, awarded yourself for the damage you have suffered.

The onus is then on the seller either to put matters right to your satisfaction or to sue you for the balance.

You will, however, lose the case if the goods or services can be shown to have fulfilled the claims made for them when you agreed to buy.

You may face criminal charges if it can be shown that your refusal to pay was motivated by dishonesty or an attempt to evade liability or to deceive. *See:* THEFT

Even if your action is eventually upheld, the court may adjust the amount you have deducted for yourself.

If you decide to apply the rules of set off – for example, by refusing to pay part of the bill in a restaurant – you should state your reasons clearly to the manager or other responsible person and leave your full name and address. Follow that with a letter explaining what you have done and why, and keep a copy. If the shop or restaurant is part of a group, send another copy to the area manager, managing director or complaints department, if there is one.

What will happen next depends on the organisation and on the amount involved. If the company eventually decides you were in the right, it may make a further refund or replace the goods.

If it believes you are wrong, but the sum you have deducted is small, it may do nothing. If the amount is large, it may sue.

You cannot keep goods that you say are faulty and refuse to pay anything for them. If you do not pay and do not return the goods, the seller can take legal action against you.

Companies have more than one way of getting back at customers who, they believe, have cheated them. The restaurant or shop may refuse to serve you next time – and your gesture may earn you a black mark in the credit records that companies keep and circulate among themselves.

RETAILER OR MANUFACTURER?

If you buy goods that prove to be faulty, you have grounds for complaint – and, in the last resort, legal action – against the shop that sold them to you. They cannot evade their responsibility by referring you to the manufacturer.

If a manufacturer's guarantee came with the goods, you can also claim under the guarantee against the company that made them. But nothing the guarantee says can take away or affect your right to claim against the shop that sold the goods to you.

If the complaint involves services – for example, building work on your house, or repairs to your central-heating boiler – you may be entitled to take it up with both the builder or the engineer and the company that supplied you with the materials or parts.

If you buy goods on credit you also have rights against the credit company. *See:* CONSUMER CREDIT

tion may decide to intervene on your behalf. Some associations will investigate complaints against their members.

You can also use public pressure. If you can find other people with the same complaint – perhaps through a local consumer group – you can send a petition to the company, or write a letter to the local newspaper. But you may need to take legal advice to ensure that what you write does not contravene the law of LIBEL. The newspaper's own legal consultants will certainly advise the editor not to publish anything defamatory.

A public protest – for example, by dissatisfied customers carrying placards – may also be effective. But take police advice and be wary of the law on OBSTRUCTION.

If your complaint involves an offence against the rules on weights and measures – for example, if you believe a public house is watering its drinks or giving short measure – you can call in the local authority trading standards or environmental health department.

If it involves safety or hygiene, inform local consumer groups, the local authority health or safety inspector and, if all else fails, your MP.

Going to law

At any stage in pursuing your com-

plaint you can engage a solicitor, but that is inevitably expensive. Unless the matter is serious, the cost may not be worthwhile. Solicitors generally refuse to take a case if they believe that the client does not understand the full implications or likely cost.

Even if you do your own legal work and present the case yourself, the LEGAL COSTS may be high.

If the amount involved in the claim is £200 or less – a 'small claim' – you will almost certainly have to pay your own costs, win or lose. If the sum involved is more than £200, and you lose, you may be ordered to pay all or part of your opponent's costs in addition to your own.

However, you can ask for a consultation and advice on what you should do next. You may be able to recover part of the solicitor's fee under aid or voluntary advice schemes. *See:* LEGAL AID

A formal solicitor's letter in pursuit of your complaint can help you to obtain redress and costs only a few pounds. But the person to whom you are complaining will almost certainly refer the letter to his own solicitor and begin a cycle of correspondence that could be very expensive.

So if you decide to use a solicitor's

COMPLAINTS ABOUT OFFICIALS

Unless a local government official or an employee of a state body – for example, British Rail – has actually done you physical or financial damage, you cannot claim redress for his actions.

However, if an official is rude or lazy in carrying out his duties, you should register a complaint. Write to his superior.

If your complaint is about an entire official body, write to your elected representative – your councillor, if it is run by the local authority, or your MP, if it is a department of central government.

Faulty administration by a local or central government official or department can be referred to government commissioners called OMBUDSMEN. If the complaint arises from a local authority, you can contact the Ombudsman yourself if your local councillors will not do so for you. But if it involves central government, the matter can be raised only through an MP.

CALLING THE POLICE

Anyone who deliberately harms you or your property is committing a criminal offence and you can call the police for assistance.

But most complaints arise from civil disputes, in which the police have no direct right to intervene. If you and your neighbour argue about his duty to repair his fence and one of you calls a policeman he will do nothing officially – although he might try to arbitrate.

However, if the dispute flares up and becomes abusive or violent, the police can act, because either or both of you will be committing a criminal act – for example, ASSAULT AND BATTERY – or because your conduct threatens a BREACH OF THE PEACE.

If you stand outside someone else's premises arguing your case and refuse to move when asked to do so by a policeman, you may be charged with obstruction. If you refuse to leave private premises when asked to do so by the owner, you may be guilty of TRESPASS.

letter in your campaign, you should be prepared for the matter to end in court.

Arbitration as an alternative

Outside those two areas, as an alternative to going to court, you can ask the local county court office to nominate an independent arbiter to settle your claim. If the amount involved is more than £200, the party against whom you are bringing the claim must agree to accept an arbiter.

Some trade associations – for example, the Radio, Electrical and Television Retailers' Association – operate their own independent schemes. *See:* ARBITRATION

Before deciding whether to pursue your complaint through the courts or to go to arbitration, you should consider the likely cost of each. It may be cheaper, if the amount involved is small, to go to court.

Remember that, once you have accepted an arbiter, his decision is final. There is no appeal and the courts will enforce the decision.

Taking a case to court

Once you have decided to take court action, it is up to you to prove your case – not to your opponent to disprove it.

PETITIONS TO THE QUEEN

Any British subject is entitled, as a last resort, to petition the Queen if he is dissatisfied with the actions or decisions of the government which acts in her name. She does not involve herself in commercial or purely political matters.

A petition to the Queen is delivered free by the Post Office, provided that it is clearly marked as such on the envelope.

```
PETITION

Her Majesty the Queen

Buckingham Palace

London SW1 1AA
```

A reply, stating what action is being taken on the petition, comes from a private secretary or lady-in-waiting.

Petitions do not need to be set out in formal language. However, they should be addressed to 'Her Majesty the Queen' and begin: 'Your Majesty'.

You must satisfy the court that your version of events is factually correct and that the law entitles you to the redress you are seeking.

So do not start court proceedings unless you are very sure that the case can be proved. That means you should have reliable, independent witnesses to support your version of what happened, or at the very least strong circumstantial evidence.

Beware of reluctant witnesses. You can force them to attend court, but they might do your cause more harm than good. Remember, it is not enough to know you are in the right. The judgment will be in your favour only when you prove that you are in the right.

Most court cases proceed slowly. It can take more than a year for a civil case to be heard in the High Court. Only in an emergency, such as when an injunction is sought, can you expect quicker results.

You have therefore to weigh up the worry of having unresolved litigation on your hands against the amount at stake.

If you do decide to go ahead, start proceedings as soon as possible. Courts do not like 'stale' claims – when memories might be unreliable.

Sometimes there is no alternative. If your legal rights are being flouted, going to court may be the only remedy.

Taking county court action

Anyone can start a county court action for damages by writing out the particulars of his or her claim and handing them in at the court office.

Write the name of the court at the top, then give your full name, as plaintiff, and the full name of the defendant, the person or company against whom you are making your claim. Leave a space for the court to fill in the number they will allocate to your case.

Beneath this, write out briefly in numbered paragraphs the time, place and particulars of your complaint. Suppose, for example, you are claiming against a company which supplied you with a new television set which was faulty, caught fire, and damaged some curtains. State when and where you bought the set, and what went wrong. Then put down what you are claiming: the value of the machine and an amount for damages.

You must make your complaint in the court for the district where the company has its head office, or in the same district as the shop from which you bought the machine.

Ask the nearest county court to tell you which covers the area in which you are interested.

When you have taken your particulars of claim to the county court office, you have to complete a request form. This instructs the court to send out a summons to the defendant you have named.

A court fee must be paid with the request form. The minimum is £5. It increases by 10p for every £1 over £50 claimed up to a maximum of £19.

When the action is not defended

The person you are claiming against must file any defence with the court

SIX WAYS TO PROTECT YOUR RIGHTS

If you think your legal rights are being infringed and you want to make it clear to your opponent that you are in the right, you can ask a court to pronounce on the point of law involved.

Such a *declaration*, as it is called, will earn you no compensation, and you might even be heavily out of pocket if the judge decides that the other side should not pay your costs, although that rarely happens.

When you want to stop someone taking a course of action that you believe to be unlawful, you can ask a court for an *injunction* ordering him to stop until the case can be heard fully.

If you want to challenge the actions of official bodies or public authorities, you can apply to the divisional court for what is known as *judicial review*.

That court, which is part of the High Court, can order anyone or any organisation to carry out a public duty; quash a decision of an administrative tribunal or court that the divisional court believes has acted improperly; or prohibit a tribunal or court from hearing a case outside its jurisdiction.

If your land or house has been occupied by squatters or if you are unable to persuade a tenant to give you back your property, you can apply to a court for an *order to recover possession*.

When you are in dispute with someone over a contract – for example, if someone agrees to sell you his house, and then refuses to do so – you can ask a court for an order of *specific performance*, forcing him to keep his part of the bargain.

The courts, however, generally are unwilling to make such an order if they think that it would be enough for you to seek and obtain damages.

An order of specific performance cannot be obtained for a personal contract – for example, a contract of employment. That means that if you agree to work for someone for a fixed period and fail to do so, you cannot be compelled by a court to live up to your side of the contract. You might, however, be ordered to pay damages to the employer.

If you suffer harm as the result of someone else's action or failure to act, you can ask a court to award *damages* – financial compensation – against him. But you must be able to show that he committed a wrong, that you suffered injury, loss or damage as a result and that the harm was foreseeable by the defendant.

But before suing, consider whether your opponent is capable of paying the amount you are seeking. If he is a private individual or a small trader he may not be – and you then have nothing to gain.

THREE CATEGORIES OF COMPENSATION

When someone has suffered injury in an accident, the courts award what are known as *general* damages – representing the value put on the inconvenience, pain, suffering and misery caused by the injury. An example of general damages is the award made to someone who has been made deaf because of another person's negligence.

When someone wins his case but cannot prove any real loss, the compensation is *nominal*. For example, although a land-owner can sue a walker who trespasses on his land, he would be likely to receive only nominal damages as the only damage caused would be some blades of grass.

When a financial loss can be calculated up to the date of trial, *special* damages are awarded. For example, a person who is injured and unable to work will receive compensation for earnings lost before the hearing, in addition to general damages which take into account any future loss.

registrar within 2 weeks of the summons being served. If he fails to do so, the registrar can give judgment for you at once, and you have won your case.

When the action is defended

When a defence has been filed by the defendant, the person you are suing, a copy is sent to you, the plaintiff, and a date is arranged for a pre-trial review, a discussion usually in private between the registrar and both parties about how the action should proceed.

If the defendant fails to appear at the pre-trial review, the registrar may listen to your case in full and settle the issue there and then, giving judgment in your favour if he feels you have proved your case.

He will often, however, give the defendant a further 2 weeks in which to file his defence.

The registrar may order both parties to exchange copies of all the documents relevant to their cases. It is common practice for solicitors acting for each side to exchange photocopies of all documents.

At the pre-trial review, the registrar also fixes a date for a court hearing suitable to both parties.

What happens in court

When the time comes for your case to be heard, both you and the defendant are called before the judge. As you are presenting the case yourself, you may be asked to give the court a brief outline of your claim.

You must then go into the witness box, give evidence on oath and answer any questions put to you by the defendant's lawyer. It is important to take all the relevant documents – such as invoices, bills, contracts or guarantees.

HOW TO ADDRESS THE COURT

A full-time, professional magistrate – called a stipendiary – always sits on his own. He should be called 'Sir'. Lay magistrates sit in threes or twos, and should be called 'Your Worships'.

A county court judge or a circuit judge in a crown court should be addressed as 'Your Honour'.

A High Court judge sitting in a crown court, the High Court or the Court of Appeal, should be addressed as 'Your Lordship' or 'My Lord'.

There are no rules about dress in a court, but it is advisable to wear a sober suit. Outrageous dress could be regarded as CONTEMPT OF COURT, and is in any case not likely to create a good impression.

They may be needed as evidence.

Give your evidence clearly and calmly: do not hurry. The defendant is then asked to put his case, and if he goes into the witness box to give evidence you will be able to ask him any questions you wish.

When the evidence has ended you will be able to sum up your case and emphasise the most important points.

The judge will make his decision usually at once, either dismissing your claim or ordering the defendant to pay you damages.

Getting costs

If you win your action, ask the judge to award you costs against the defendant. Have a list of what you have spent before the case so that you can present the details to the court.

If you lose your action, you may be ordered to pay the defendant's costs – if the sum involved in the action was more than £200.

Any legal cost can be very high, so it is wise before taking up a case to get legal advice about your chances of winning.

A plaintiff who has prepared his own case can charge in his costs for the work he has put in. Any time taken off work can be charged at no more than two-thirds the amount a solicitor would have charged.

If the case was prepared in the evenings or at weekends, the court can allow up to £2 per hour.

The total amount will be decided by the judge, and he is likely to allow only the number of hours a solicitor would have taken to prepare the case. It may have taken a plaintiff 25 hours to get his case ready.

If a solicitor would have taken only 6 hours the judge will allow costs for only that time.

If the total amount of the claim – not the costs – before the court is less than £500, the judge can assess costs as soon as he gives judgment. If it is more, a separate hearing can be held later at which there can be a detailed examination of the costs.

Making an appeal

There is a period, usually 6 weeks, after a court judgment has been made in which either party, winner or loser, can appeal against the decision.

The court office will tell you how to go about an appeal. Take legal advice before you proceed, Court of Appeal applications can be very expensive.

Index

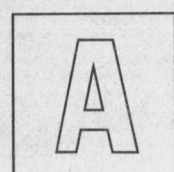

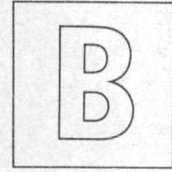

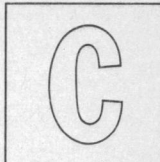

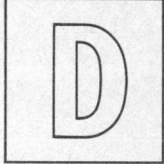

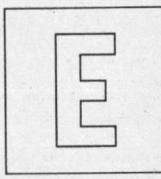

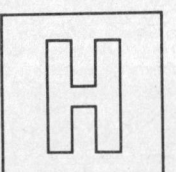

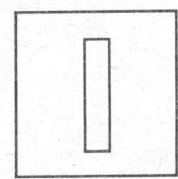

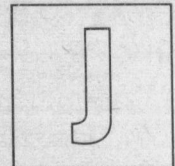

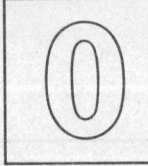

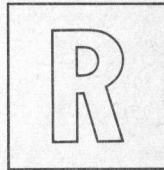

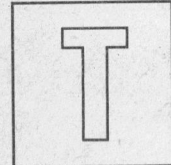